Amnestic Disorders
 Amnestic Disorder Due to a General Medical
  Condition
 Substance-Induced Persisting Amnestic
  Disorder
 Amnestic Disorder NOS
Other Cognitive Disorders
 Cognitive Disorder NOS

Mental Disorders Due to a General Medical Condition Not Elsewhere Classified

 Catatonic Disorder Due to a General Medical
  Condition
 Personality Change Due to a General Medical
  Condition
 Mental Disorder NOS Due to a General Medical
  Condition

Substance-Related Disorders

Alcohol-Related Disorders
 Alcohol Use Disorders
 Alcohol-Induced Disorders
Amphetamine (or Amphetamine-Like)–Related Disorders
 Amphetamine Use Disorders
 Amphetamine-Induced Disorders
Caffeine-Related Disorders
 Caffeine-Induced Disorders
Cannabis-Related Disorders
 Cannabis Use Disorders
 Cannabis-Induced Disorders
Cocaine-Related Disorders
 Cocaine Use Disorders
 Cocaine-Induced Disorders
Hallucinogen-Related Disorders
 Hallucinogen Use Disorders
 Hallucinogen-Induced Disorders
Inhalant-Related Disorders
 Inhalant Use Disorders
 Inhalant-Induced Disorders
Nicotine-Related Disorders
 Nicotine Use Disorder
 Nicotine-Induced Disorder
Opioid-Related Disorders
 Opioid Use Disorders
 Opioid-Induced Disorders

Phencyclidine (or Phencyclidine-Like)–Related Disorders
 Phencyclidine Use Disorders
 Phencyclidine-Induced Disorders
Sedative-, Hypnotic-, or Anxiolytic-Related Disorders
 Sedative, Hypnotic, or Anxiolytic Use
  Disorders
 Sedative-, Hypnotic-, or Anxiolytic-Induced
  Disorders
Other (or Unknown) Substance-Related Disorders
 Other (or Unknown) Substance Use
  Disorders
 Other (or Unknown) Substance-Induced
  Disorders

Schizophrenia and Other Psychotic Disorders

 Schizophrenia
  Paranoid Type
  Disorganized Type
  Catatonic Type
  Undifferentiated Type
  Residual Type
 Schizophreniform Disorder
 Schizoaffective Disorder
 Delusional Disorder
 Brief Psychotic Disorder
 Shared Psychotic Disorder
 Psychotic Disorder Due to a General Medical
  Condition
 Substance-Induced Psychotic Disorder
 Psychotic Disorder NOS

Mood Disorders

Depressive Disorders
 Major Depressive Disorder
 Dysthymic Disorder
 Depressive Disorder NOS
Bipolar Disorders
 Bipolar I Disorder
 Bipolar II Disorder
 Cyclothymic Disorder
 Bipolar Disorder NOS
Other Mood Disorders
 Mood Disorder Due to a General Medical
  Condition
 Substance-Induced Mood Disorder
 Mood Disorder NOS

(Continued on inside back cover)

Abnormal PSYCHOLOGY

second edition

Susan Nolen-Hoeksema

University of Michigan

Boston   Burr Ridge, IL   Dubuque, IA   Madison, WI   New York   San Francisco   St. Louis
Bangkok   Bogotá   Caracas   Lisbon   London   Madrid
Mexico City   Milan   New Delhi   Seoul   Singapore   Sydney   Taipei   Toronto

McGraw-Hill Higher Education

A Division of The **McGraw-Hill** Companies

ABNORMAL PSYCHOLOGY, SECOND EDITION

Published by McGraw-Hill, an imprint of The McGraw-Hill Companies, Inc., 1221 Avenue of the Americas, New York, NY 10020. Copyright © 2001, 1998 by The McGraw-Hill Companies, Inc. All rights reserved. No part of this publication may be reproduced or distributed in any form or by any means, or stored in a database or retrieval system, without the prior written consent of The McGraw-Hill Companies, Inc., including, but not limited to, in any network or other electronic storage or transmission, or broadcast for distance learning.

Some ancillaries, including electronic and print components, may not be available to customers outside the United States.

 This book is printed on recycled, acid-free paper containing 10% postconsumer waste.

2 3 4 5 6 7 8 9 0 QPH/QPH 0 9 8 7 6 5 4 3 2 1

ISBN 0-07-235799-1
ISBN 0-07-118004-4 (ISE)

Vice president and editor-in-chief: *Thalia Dorwick*
Editorial director: *Jane E. Vaicunas*
Executive editor: *Joseph Terry*
Developmental editor: *Mindy De Palma*
Editorial coordinator: *Barbara Santoro*
Marketing manager: *Chris Hall*
Senior project manager: *Gloria G. Schiesl*
Senior media producer: *Sean Crowley*
Production supervisor: *Kara Kudronowicz*
Design manager: *Stuart D. Paterson*
Cover/interior designer: *Jamie O'Neal*
Cover image: *"Shadow of Her Former Self" by Diana Ong/©SuperStock*
Senior photo research coordinator: *Carrie K. Burger*
Photo research: *Toni Michaels*
Supplement coordinator: *Sandra M. Schnee*
Compositor: *GAC–Indianapolis*
Typeface: *10/12 Palatino*
Printer: *Quebecor Printing Book Group/Hawkins, TN*

The credits section for this book begins on page C-1 and is considered an extension of the copyright page.

Library of Congress Cataloging-in-Publication Data

Nolen-Hoeksema, Susan, 1959—
   Abnormal psychology / Susan Nolen-Hoeksema. — 2nd ed.
    p. cm.
   Includes bibliographical references (p.) and index.
   ISBN 0-07-235799-1
   1. Psychology, Pathological.

   RC454 .N64 2001
   616.89—dc21   00-037982
                                     CIP

INTERNATIONAL EDITION ISBN 0-07-118004-4
Copyright © 2001. Exclusive rights by The McGraw-Hill Companies, Inc., for manufacture and export. This book cannot be re-exported from the country to which it is sold by McGraw-Hill. The International Edition is not available in North America.

www.mhhe.com

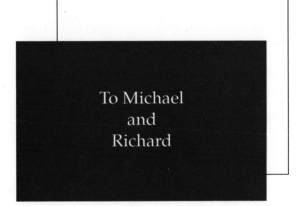

To Michael
and
Richard

CONTENTS IN BRIEF

CONTENTS

Chapter

Dissociative and Somatoform Disorders 370

Chapter

Personality Disorders 402

Chapter

Childhood Disorders 440

Chapter

The Cognitive Disorders: Dementia, Delirium, and Amnesia 652

Chapter

Mental Health, Social Policy, and the Law 678

Although the world is full of suffering, it is full also of the overcoming of it.

—(*Helen Keller*, 1903, p. 1)

When I was doing my clinical training several years ago in Philadelphia, I worked with a man who suffered from paranoid schizophrenia. This man was a clever and successful writer in-between acute episodes of his schizophrenia. When he was psychotic, however, he lived on the streets, huddled on grates, battling with the voices in his mind. One day he told me that the most terrible thing about living on the streets during those times was not the frightening voices he heard, or the awful cold of Philadelphia winter nights, or going without food for days. Instead, it was the way people looked at him as they passed him on the street. Some people looked at him as though he was another piece of garbage littering their pathway. Others didn't see him at all, perhaps because in their eyes, he was not human.

I want students to come away from this book and this course with so much appreciation for the humanity and suffering of people with mental disorders that they will never again look at a person suffering from a disorder with anything but compassion in their eyes. Rather than being frightened or overwhelmed by the behaviors of people with mental disorders, they will understand something about these behaviors and their causes, and the experiences of the people suffering them.

Some of the students reading this book will have suffered mental disorders first-hand. They may already be diagnosed with a disorder. They may be worried that they have a disorder. They may have family members or close friends with a disorder. Whenever I teach abnormal psychology, several students from the class come to talk to me about their own personal experience with mental disorders. Often these students will begin by saying, "I've never told anyone else at school this, but . . ."

I want these students to come away from this book and this course with the power of knowledge. I want them to be empowered, not to suffer in silence, feeling victimized and helpless, but to better understand the sources of their suffering and to make good choices that help them overcome this suffering.

Finally, I want this book to make it easier for instructors to teach abnormal psychology. This course can be difficult to teach because the field is moving so rapidly and because students come to the course with many different perspectives and goals. I have tried to make even the most difficult scientific material easy to understand and interesting to read so that the book is a resource both to the student and to the instructor. I have also tried to pique students' interest and curiosity, not only for the manifestations of the disorders, but for the methods and lives of people who research and treat these disorders. My hope is that instructors who use this book will find that their students learn more about the science of abnormal psychology and have more understanding of the phenomena of mental disorders than with any other book they have ever used.

■ Understanding Brings Compassion and Choices

This section [Extraordinary People] gave a real sense of people with or affected by mental disorders as real people with whom we can empathize and identify. I liked that these did not glorify or dramatize the issues, but brought an experiential component that the text did not always portray

—*Dr. Jill Cermele, Drew University*

How can students understand what it is like to suffer from a mental disorder? They can read the criteria for diagnosing the disorder. But these criteria are often dry lists of symptoms that may be foreign and incomprehensible to the student. In each chapter of this book, I try to bring the symptoms of each disorder alive by describing them in detail and providing many examples. Most importantly, I let people who suffer these symptoms describe them in their own words. In a new feature in this edition, called *Extraordinary People*, I highlight the biographies and autobiographies of people who suffer from mental disorders, which give us a window into the hearts and minds of these extraordinary people. Some of these people have achieved tremendous success despite their mental disorders, such as Nobel prize–winner John Nash, or researcher

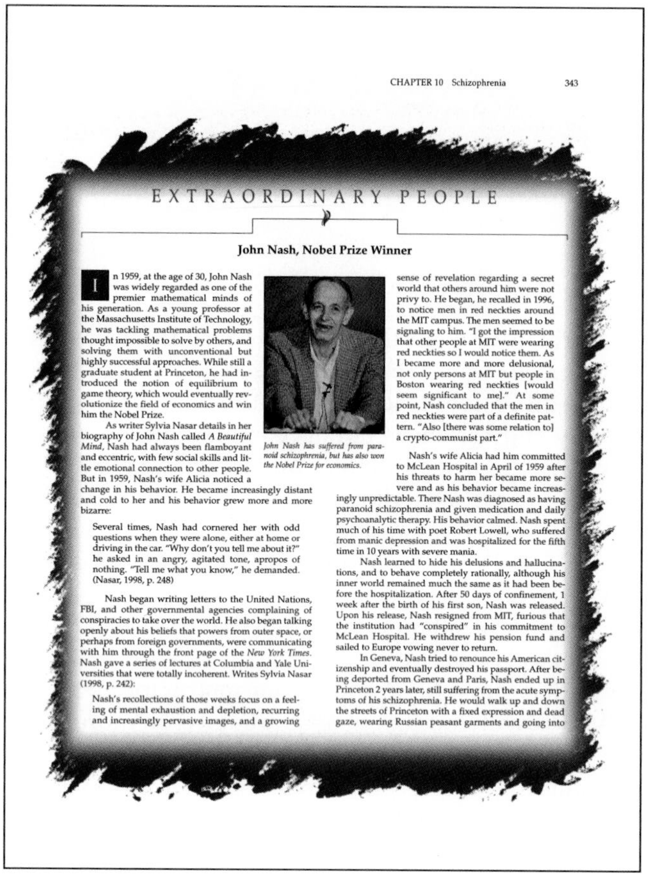

CHAPTER 10 Schizophrenia 343

EXTRAORDINARY PEOPLE

John Nash, Nobel Prize Winner

In 1959, at the age of 30, John Nash was widely regarded as one of the premier mathematical minds of his generation. As a young professor at the Massachusetts Institute of Technology, he was tackling mathematical problems thought impossible to solve by others, and solving them with unconventional but highly successful approaches. While still a graduate student at Princeton, he had introduced the notion of equilibrium to game theory, which would eventually revolutionize the field of economics and win him the Nobel Prize.

As writer Sylvia Nasar details in her biography of John Nash called *A Beautiful Mind*, Nash had always been flamboyant and eccentric, with few social skills and little emotional connection to other people. But in 1959, Nash's wife Alicia noticed a change in his behavior. He became increasingly distant and cold to her and his behavior grew more and more bizarre:

> Several times, Nash had cornered her with odd questions when they were alone, either at home or driving in the car. "Why don't you tell me about it?" he asked in an angry, agitated tone, apropos of nothing. "Tell me what you know," he demanded. (Nasar, 1998, p. 248)

John Nash has suffered from paranoid schizophrenia, but has also won the Nobel Prize for economics.

Nash began writing letters to the United Nations, FBI, and other governmental agencies complaining of conspiracies to take over the world. He also began talking openly about his beliefs that powers from outer space, or perhaps from foreign governments, were communicating with him through the front page of the *New York Times*. Nash gave a series of lectures at Columbia and Yale Universities that were totally incoherent. Writes Sylvia Nasar (1998, p. 242):

> Nash's recollections of those weeks focus on a feeling of mental exhaustion and depletion, recurring and increasingly pervasive images, and a growing sense of revelation regarding a secret world that others around him were not privy to. He began, he recalled in 1996, to notice men in red neckties around the MIT campus. The men seemed to be signaling to him. "I got the impression that other people at MIT were wearing red neckties so I would notice them. As I became more and more delusional, not only persons at MIT but people in Boston wearing red neckties [would seem significant to me]." At some point, Nash concluded that the men in red neckties were part of a definite pattern. "Also [there was some relation to] a crypto-communist part."

Nash's wife Alicia had him committed to McLean Hospital in April of 1959 after his threats to harm her became more severe and as his behavior became increasingly unpredictable. There Nash was diagnosed as having paranoid schizophrenia and given medication and daily psychoanalytic therapy. His behavior calmed. Nash spent much of his time with poet Robert Lowell, who suffered from manic depression and was hospitalized for the fifth time in 10 years with severe mania.

Nash learned to hide his delusions and hallucinations, and to behave completely rationally, although his inner world remained much the same as it had been before the hospitalization. After 50 days of confinement, 1 week after the birth of his first son, Nash was released. Upon his release, Nash resigned from MIT, furious that the institution had "conspired" in his commitment to McLean Hospital. He withdrew his pension fund and sailed to Europe vowing never to return.

In Geneva, Nash tried to renounce his American citizenship and eventually destroyed his passport. After being deported from Geneva and Paris, Nash ended up in Princeton 2 years later, still suffering from the acute symptoms of his schizophrenia. He would walk up and down the streets of Princeton with a fixed expression and dead gaze, wearing Russian peasant garments and going into

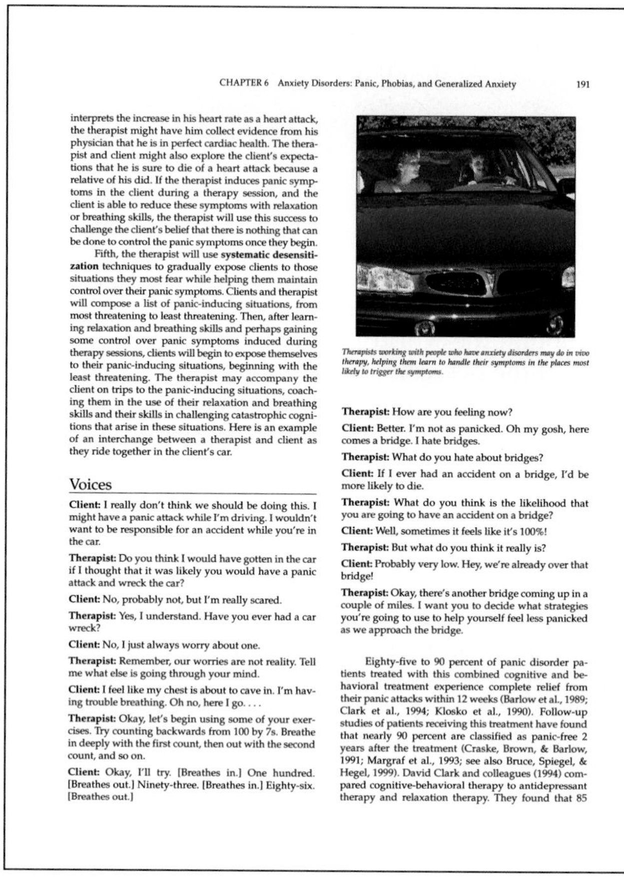

CHAPTER 6 Anxiety Disorders: Panic, Phobias, and Generalized Anxiety 191

interprets the increase in his heart rate as a heart attack, the therapist might have him collect evidence from his physician that he is in perfect cardiac health. The therapist and client might also explore the client's expectations that he is sure to die of a heart attack because a relative of his did. If the therapist induces panic symptoms in the client during a therapy session, and the client is able to reduce these symptoms with relaxation or breathing skills, the therapist will use this success to challenge the client's belief that there is nothing that can be done to control the panic symptoms once they begin.

Fifth, the therapist will use **systematic desensitization** techniques to gradually expose clients to those situations they most fear while helping them maintain control over their panic symptoms. Clients and therapist will compose a list of panic-inducing situations, from most threatening to least threatening. Then, after learning relaxation and breathing skills and perhaps gaining some control over panic symptoms induced during therapy sessions, clients will begin to expose themselves to their panic-inducing situations, beginning with the least threatening. The therapist may accompany the client on trips to the panic-inducing situations, coaching them in the use of their relaxation and breathing skills and their skills in challenging catastrophic cognitions that arise in these situations. Here is an example of an interchange between a therapist and client as they ride together in the client's car.

Therapists working with people who have anxiety disorders may do in vivo therapy, helping them learn to handle their symptoms in the places most likely to trigger the symptoms.

Voices

Client: I really don't think we should be doing this. I might have a panic attack while I'm driving. I wouldn't want to be responsible for an accident while you're in the car.

Therapist: Do you think I would have gotten in the car if I thought that it was likely you would have a panic attack and wreck the car?

Client: No, probably not, but I'm really scared.

Therapist: Yes, I understand. Have you ever had a car wreck?

Client: No, I just always worry about one.

Therapist: Remember, our worries are not reality. Tell me what else is going through your mind.

Client: I feel like my chest is about to cave in. I'm having trouble breathing. Oh no, here I go. . . .

Therapist: Okay, let's begin using some of your exercises. Try counting backwards from 100 by 7s. Breathe in deeply with the first count, then out with the second count, and so on.

Client: Okay, I'll try. [Breathes in.] One hundred. [Breathes out.] Ninety-three. [Breathes in.] Eighty-six. [Breathes out.]

Therapist: How are you feeling now?

Client: Better. I'm not as panicked. Oh my gosh, here comes a bridge. I hate bridges.

Therapist: What do you hate about bridges?

Client: If I ever had an accident on a bridge, I'd be more likely to die.

Therapist: What do you think is the likelihood that you are going to have an accident on a bridge?

Client: Well, sometimes it feels like it's 100%!

Therapist: But what do you think it really is?

Client: Probably very low. Hey, we're already over that bridge!

Therapist: Okay, there's another bridge coming up in a couple of miles. I want you to decide what strategies you're going to use to help yourself feel less panicked as we approach the bridge.

Eighty-five to 90 percent of panic disorder patients treated with this combined cognitive and behavioral treatment experience complete relief from their panic attacks within 12 weeks (Barlow et al., 1989; Clark et al., 1994; Klosko et al., 1990). Follow-up studies of patients receiving this treatment have found that nearly 90 percent are classified as panic-free 2 years after the treatment (Craske, Brown, & Barlow, 1991; Margraf et al., 1993; see also Bruce, Spiegel, & Hegel, 1999). David Clark and colleagues (1994) compared cognitive-behavioral therapy to antidepressant therapy and relaxation therapy. They found that 85

and professor Kay Redfield Jamison. Others have led more ordinary lives, which in itself is a great accomplishment for people suffering serious mental disorders. The stories of these extraordinary people take students far beyond lists of diagnostic criteria and into the subjective experience of a disorder.

In addition, within the text of each chapter is a new feature called *Voices*, which highlights quotes from people with mental disorders. These quotes give students a subjective sense of the symptoms of each disorder, by allowing people who suffer these symptoms to describe their experience of them. The quotes also illustrate key points about a disorder, such as how the disorder affects the functioning of an individual or the individual's family members or friends. My intent with this feature is to help students get inside the experience of people with mental disorders to gain a deeper understanding of the symptoms of the disorder and the impact of the disorder on people's lives.

A third new feature, *Taking Psychology Personally*, addresses the personal questions and concerns students may bring to a course on abnormal psychology, such as concerns about their own mental health and questions of how to get help for themselves or others. In consultation with the major organizations that serve

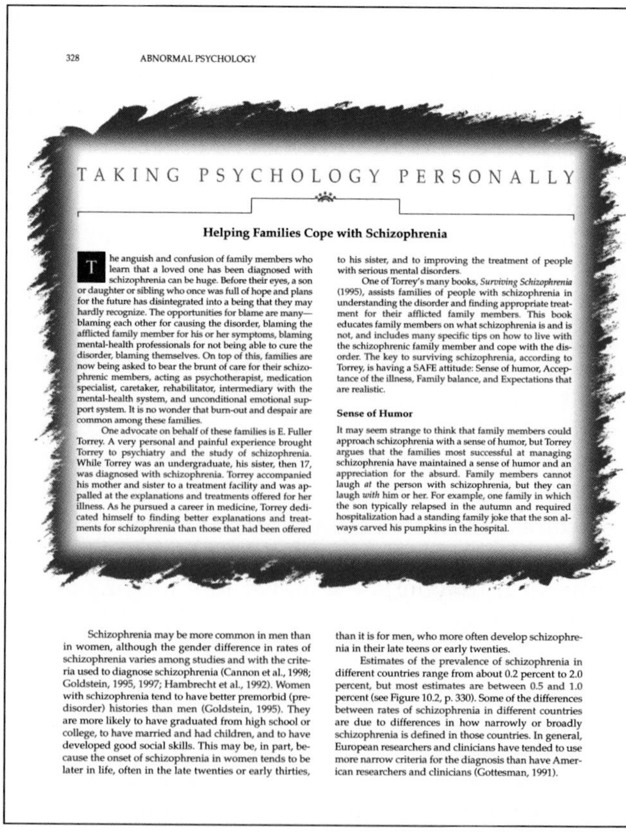

328 ABNORMAL PSYCHOLOGY

TAKING PSYCHOLOGY PERSONALLY

Helping Families Cope with Schizophrenia

The anguish and confusion of family members who learn that a loved one has been diagnosed with schizophrenia can be huge. Before their eyes, a son or daughter or sibling who once was full of hope and plans for the future has disintegrated into a being that they may hardly recognize. The opportunities for blame are many—blaming each other for causing the disorder, blaming the afflicted family member for his or her symptoms, blaming mental-health professionals for not being able to cure the disorder, blaming themselves. On top of this, families are now being asked to bear the brunt of care for their schizophrenic members, acting as psychotherapist, medication specialist, caretaker, rehabilitator, intermediary with the mental-health system, and unconditional emotional support system. It is no wonder that burn-out and despair are common among these families.

One advocate on behalf of these families is E. Fuller Torrey. A very personal and painful experience brought Torrey to psychiatry and the study of schizophrenia. While Torrey was an undergraduate, his sister, then 17, was diagnosed with schizophrenia. Torrey accompanied his mother and sister to a treatment facility and was appalled at the explanations and treatments offered for her illness. As he pursued a career in medicine, Torrey dedicated himself to finding better explanations and treatments for schizophrenia than those that had been offered to his sister, and to improving the treatment of people with serious mental disorders.

One of Torrey's many books, *Surviving Schizophrenia* (1995), assists families of people with schizophrenia in understanding the disorder and finding appropriate treatment for their afflicted family members. This book educates family members on what schizophrenia is and is not, and includes many specific tips on how to live with the schizophrenic family member and cope with the disorder. The key to surviving schizophrenia, according to Torrey, is having a SAFE attitude: Sense of humor, Acceptance of the illness, Family balance, and Expectations that are realistic.

Sense of Humor

It may seem strange to think that family members could approach schizophrenia with a sense of humor, but Torrey argues that the families most successful at managing schizophrenia have maintained a sense of humor and an appreciation for the absurd. Family members cannot laugh *at* the person with schizophrenia, but they can laugh *with* him or her. For example, one family in which the son typically relapsed in the autumn and required hospitalization had a standing family joke that the son always carved his pumpkins in the hospital.

Schizophrenia may be more common in men than in women, although the gender difference in rates of schizophrenia varies among studies and with the criteria used to diagnose schizophrenia (Cannon et al., 1998; Goldstein, 1995, 1997; Hambrecht et al., 1992). Women with schizophrenia tend to have better premorbid (predisorder) histories than men (Goldstein, 1995). They are more likely to have graduated from high school or college, to have married and had children, and to have developed good social skills. This may be, in part, because the onset of schizophrenia in women tends to be later in life, often in the late twenties or early thirties, than it is for men, who more often develop schizophrenia in their late teens or early twenties.

Estimates of the prevalence of schizophrenia in different countries range from about 0.2 percent to 2.0 percent, but most estimates are between 0.5 and 1.0 percent (see Figure 10.2, p. 330). Some of the differences between rates of schizophrenia in different countries are due to differences in how narrowly or broadly schizophrenia is defined in those countries. In general, European researchers and clinicians have tended to use more narrow criteria for the diagnosis than have American researchers and clinicians (Gottesman, 1991).

mental-health consumers (such as the American Psychological Association), I present ideas for how students can think about the meaning of the research they are reading for their own lives and how they can find appropriate help for their concerns. I hope that these sections can be a resource for instructors of abnormal psychology, who are often approached by students for advice on their personal concerns.

■ Challenging Material Doesn't Have to Be Boring

I like the approach of using hypothetical and detailed cases to introduce the issues. Very thorough and balanced with lots of important context for understanding the strengths and limitations of the DSM system.

—*Dr. James Hansell, University of Michigan*

Some students who can appreciate the personal experiences of people with mental disorders have trouble appreciating the science of abnormal psychology. They may find the competing theories and treatments for disorders confusing. They may find the latest scientific discoveries, particularly the biological ones, difficult to understand. This is especially likely if this material is presented in a boring, dry fashion, or in too much or too little detail.

Although the science of abnormal psychology is challenging material, it does not have to be boring or confusing. One of my main goals in this second edition was to present the theories of each disorder, the scientific evidence for these theories, and information about the treatments of each disorder in an engaging and comprehensible way. I listened to instructors' feedback on the first edition and extensively revised sections that either were too difficult, too detailed, or too brief. I surveyed the leaders in research on each disorder for the most important new findings in the field. I updated every chapter with the latest scientific findings. I paid special attention to the material on biological theories and treatments, because this material can be the most challenging to students. I revised this material to make it as accessible as possible to students.

Two new features in this second edition explicitly bring the excitement of the field of abnormal psychology to life for students. *Pushing the Boundaries* focuses on scientific discoveries or treatments that are at the forefront of new knowledge in the field of abnormal psychology, such as rapid transcranial magnetic stimulation (or rTMS). This feature orients students to the new frontiers that researchers believe they can conquer in the early twenty-first century. The feature also gives students a sense of the passion of the researchers who are conquering these frontiers.

The new feature called *Viewpoints* summarizes hot debates in abnormal psychology in an even-handed way, to give students an idea of the major controversies in the field today. Each of the debates featured in *Viewpoints* is also featured in the *Taking Sides* reader that is shrink-wrapped with this second edition of *Abnormal Psychology*. Thus, students can read original articles by key people on both sides of each debate, as well as reading the *Viewpoints* summaries. But these summaries can stand alone without the *Taking Sides* reader to introduce students to the debates, if instructors choose not to assign the reader to their students.

■ Making It Easy to Teach Abnormal Psychology

The author provides the most clearly written and engaging comparison of theories that I have read. Students will appreciate the balanced, unbiased, clear approach that the author provides on this topic.

—*Dr. David Skinner, Valencia Community College*

I love teaching abnormal psychology, but it is not easy. There are many different theories of each disorder, ranging from biological theories to those focusing only on

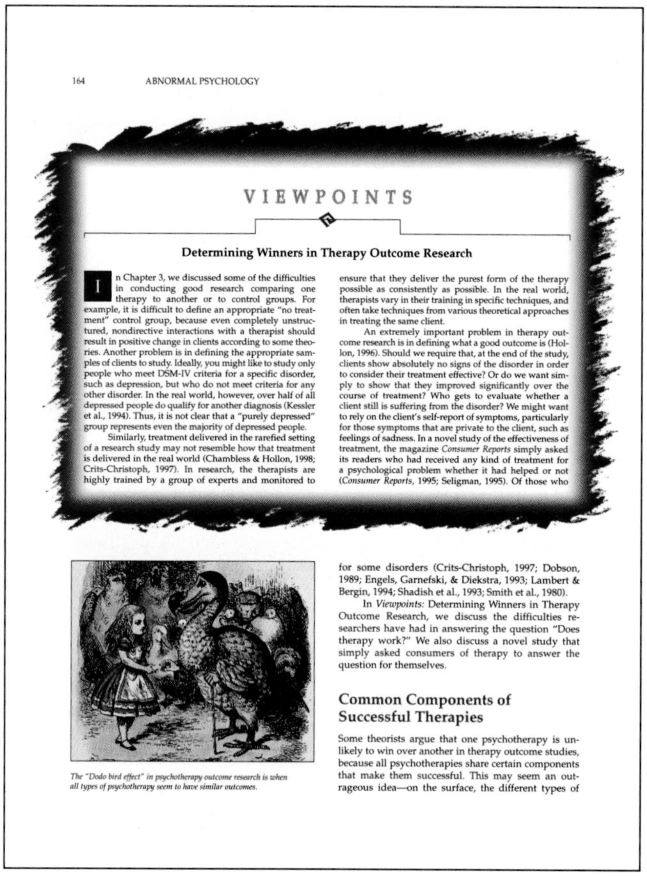

164 ABNORMAL PSYCHOLOGY

VIEWPOINTS

Determining Winners in Therapy Outcome Research

In Chapter 3, we discussed some of the difficulties in conducting good research comparing one therapy to another or to control groups. For example, it is difficult to define an appropriate "no treatment" control group, because even completely unstructured, nondirective interactions with a therapist should result in positive change in clients according to some theories. Another problem is in defining the appropriate samples of clients to study. Ideally, you might like to study only people who meet DSM-IV criteria for a specific disorder, such as depression, but who do not meet criteria for any other disorder. In the real world, however, over half of all depressed people do qualify for another diagnosis (Kessler et al., 1994). Thus, it is not clear that a "purely depressed" group represents even the majority of depressed people.

Similarly, treatment delivered in the rarefied setting of a research study may not resemble how that treatment is delivered in the real world (Chambless & Hollon, 1998; Crits-Christoph, 1997). In research, the therapists are highly trained by a group of experts and monitored to ensure that they deliver the purest form of the therapy possible as consistently as possible. In the real world, therapists vary in their training in specific techniques, and often take techniques from various theoretical approaches in treating the same client.

An extremely important problem in therapy outcome research is in defining what a good outcome is (Hollon, 1996). Should we require that, at the end of the study, clients show absolutely no signs of the disorder in order to consider their treatment effective? Or do we want simply to show that they improved significantly over the course of treatment? Who gets to evaluate whether a client still is suffering from the disorder? We might want to rely on the client's self-report of symptoms, particularly for those symptoms that are private to the client, such as feelings of sadness. In a novel study of the effectiveness of treatment, the magazine *Consumer Reports* simply asked its readers who had received any kind of treatment for a psychological problem whether it had helped or not (*Consumer Reports*, 1995; Seligman, 1995). Of those who

The "Dodo bird effect" in psychotherapy outcome research is when all types of psychotherapy seem to have similar outcomes.

for some disorders (Crits-Christoph, 1997; Dobson, 1989; Engels, Garnefski, & Diekstra, 1993; Lambert & Bergin, 1994; Shadish et al., 1993; Smith et al., 1980).

In *Viewpoints:* Determining Winners in Therapy Outcome Research, we discuss the difficulties researchers have had in answering the question "Does therapy work?" We also discuss a novel study that simply asked consumers of therapy to answer the question for themselves.

Common Components of Successful Therapies

Some theorists argue that one psychotherapy is unlikely to win over another in therapy outcome studies, because all psychotherapies share certain components that make them successful. This may seem an outrageous idea—on the surface, the different types of

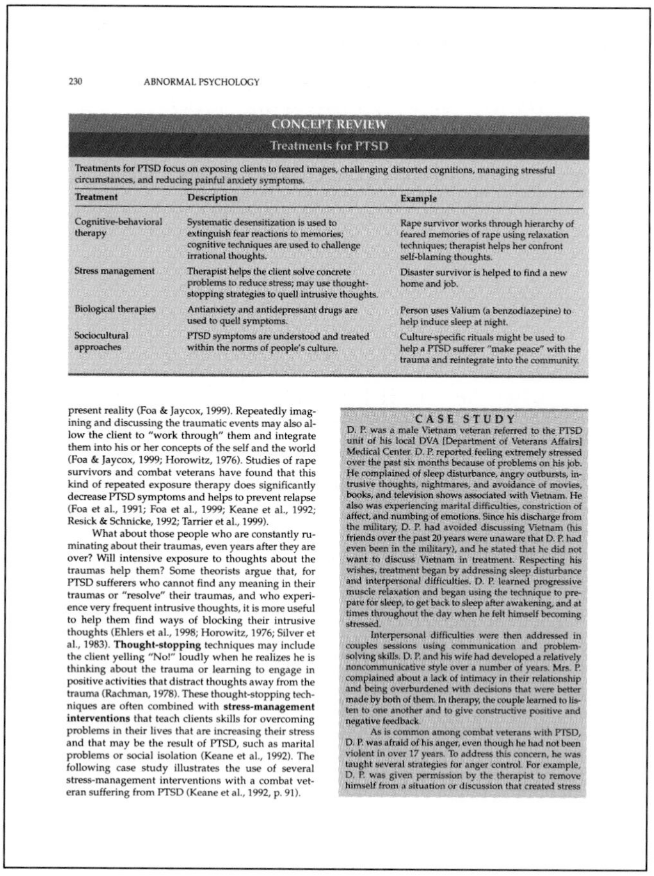

230 ABNORMAL PSYCHOLOGY

CONCEPT REVIEW

Treatments for PTSD

Treatments for PTSD focus on exposing clients to feared images, challenging distorted cognitions, managing stressful circumstances, and reducing painful anxiety symptoms.

Treatment	Description	Example
Cognitive-behavioral therapy	Systematic desensitization is used to extinguish fear reactions to memories; cognitive techniques are used to challenge irrational thoughts.	Rape survivor works through hierarchy of feared memories of rape using relaxation techniques; therapist helps her confront self-blaming thoughts.
Stress management	Therapist helps the client solve concrete problems to reduce stress; may use thought-stopping strategies to quell intrusive thoughts.	Disaster survivor is helped to find a new home and job.
Biological therapies	Antianxiety and antidepressant drugs are used to quell symptoms.	Person uses Valium (a benzodiazepine) to help induce sleep at night.
Sociocultural approaches	PTSD symptoms are understood and treated within the norms of people's culture.	Culture-specific rituals might be used to help a PTSD sufferer "make peace" with the trauma and reintegrate into the community.

present reality (Foa & Jaycox, 1999). Repeatedly imagining and discussing the traumatic events may also allow the client to "work through" them and integrate them into his or her concepts of the self and the world (Foa & Jaycox, 1999; Horowitz, 1976). Studies of rape survivors and combat veterans have found that this kind of repeated exposure therapy does significantly decrease PTSD symptoms and helps to prevent relapse (Foa et al., 1991; Foa et al., 1999; Keane et al., 1992; Resick & Schnicke, 1992; Tarrier et al., 1999).

What about those people who are constantly ruminating about their traumas, even years after they are over? Will intensive exposure to thoughts about the traumas help them? Some theorists argue that, for PTSD sufferers who cannot find any meaning in their traumas or "resolve" their traumas, and who experience very frequent intrusive thoughts, it is more useful to help them find ways of blocking their intrusive thoughts (Ehlers et al., 1998; Horowitz, 1976; Silver et al., 1983). **Thought-stopping** techniques may include the client yelling "No!" loudly when he realizes he is thinking about the trauma or learning to engage in positive activities that distract thoughts away from the trauma (Rachman, 1978). These thought-stopping techniques are often combined with **stress-management interventions** that teach clients skills for overcoming problems in their lives that are increasing their stress and that may be the result of PTSD, such as marital problems or social isolation (Keane et al., 1992). The following case study illustrates the use of several stress-management interventions with a combat veteran suffering from PTSD (Keane et al., 1992, p. 91).

CASE STUDY

D. P. was a male Vietnam veteran referred to the PTSD unit of his local DVA [Department of Veterans Affairs] Medical Center. D. P. reported feeling extremely stressed over the past six months because of problems on his job. He complained of sleep disturbance, angry outbursts, intrusive thoughts, nightmares, and avoidance of movies, books, and television shows associated with Vietnam. He also was experiencing marital difficulties, constriction of affect, and numbing of emotions. Since his discharge from the military, D. P. had avoided discussing Vietnam (his friends over the past 20 years were unaware that D. P. had even been in the military), and he stated that he did not want to discuss Vietnam in treatment. Respecting his wishes, treatment began by addressing sleep disturbance and interpersonal difficulties. D. P. learned progressive muscle relaxation and began using the technique to prepare for sleep, to get back to sleep after awakening, and at times throughout the day when he felt himself becoming stressed.

Interpersonal difficulties were then addressed in couples sessions using communication and problem-solving skills. D. P. and his wife had developed a relatively noncommunicative style over a number of years. Mrs. P. complained about a lack of intimacy in their relationship and being overburdened with decisions that were better made by both of them. In therapy, the couple learned to listen to one another and to give constructive positive and negative feedback.

As is common among combat veterans with PTSD, D. P. was afraid of his anger, even though he had not been violent in over 17 years. To address this concern, he was taught several strategies for anger control. For example, D. P. was given permission by the therapist to remove himself from a situation or discussion that created stress

psychological processes or social context. New treatments for disorders, particularly drug treatments, are introduced almost every day. It is very difficult to keep up with the evidence for and against these theories and new treatments. It is even more difficult to present this material to students so that they can comprehend it.

I have tried to make it as easy as possible for instructors to teach abnormal psychology by using this book. First and foremost, I have tried to write well. Students can understand even the most difficult material if it is presented clearly and in an engaging manner. Second, I have added the features described above to enhance students' appreciation of the personal experiences of people with disorders and the excitement of the field of abnormal psychology.

Third, this book has several pedagogical features that make it easier for students to organize, understand, and remember the material. Two of these features are new to this second edition. *Concept Reviews* summarize the major conceptual points in key sections of a chapter, such as the primary theories of a disorder, or the most commonly used treatments, in a concise table. These tables help to organize critical material in ways that will facilitate students' memories of key concepts. *DSM Tables* present the major symptoms of each disorder, according to the DSM-IV. This allows students to know specifically what symptoms go with

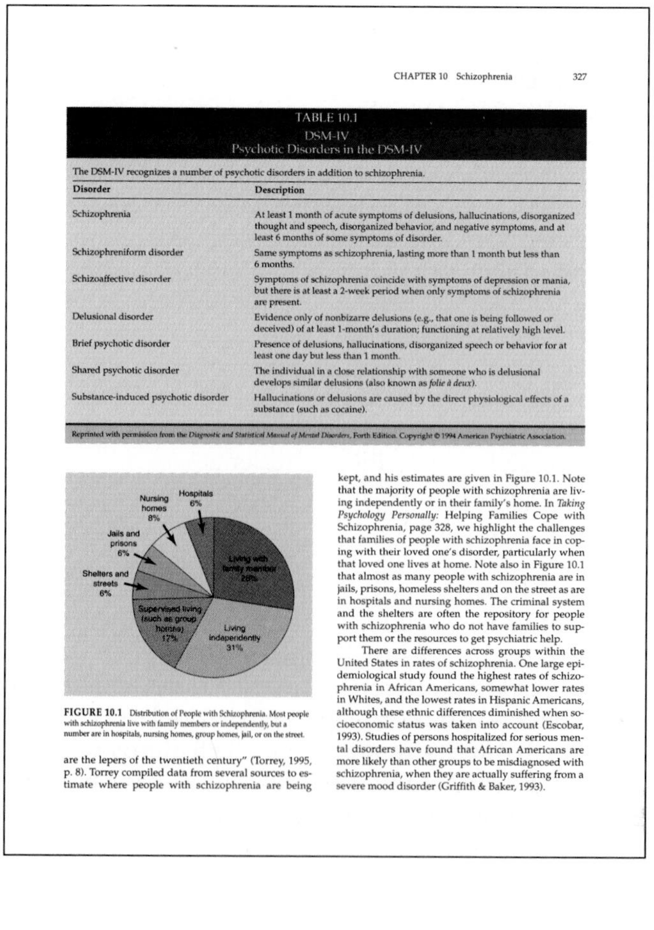

CHAPTER 10 Schizophrenia 327

TABLE 10.1
DSM-IV
Psychotic Disorders in the DSM-IV

The DSM-IV recognizes a number of psychotic disorders in addition to schizophrenia.

Disorder	Description
Schizophrenia	At least 1 month of acute symptoms of delusions, hallucinations, disorganized thought and speech, disorganized behavior, and negative symptoms, and at least 6 months of some symptoms of disorder.
Schizophreniform disorder	Same symptoms as schizophrenia, lasting more than 1 month but less than 6 months.
Schizoaffective disorder	Symptoms of schizophrenia coincide with symptoms of depression or mania, but there is at least a 2-week period when only symptoms of schizophrenia are present.
Delusional disorder	Evidence only of nonbizarre delusions (e.g., that one is being followed or deceived) of at least 1-month's duration; functioning at relatively high level.
Brief psychotic disorder	Presence of delusions, hallucinations, disorganized speech or behavior for at least one day but less than 1 month.
Shared psychotic disorder	The individual in a close relationship with someone who is delusional develops similar delusions (also known as *folie à deux*).
Substance-induced psychotic disorder	Hallucinations or delusions are caused by the direct physiological effects of a substance (such as cocaine).

Reprinted with permission from the *Diagnostic and Statistical Manual of Mental Disorders*, Forth Edition. Copyright © 1994 American Psychiatric Association.

FIGURE 10.1 Distribution of People with Schizophrenia. Most people with schizophrenia live with family members or independently, but a number are in hospitals, nursing homes, group homes, jail, or on the street.

are the lepers of the twentieth century" (Torrey, 1995, p. 8). Torrey compiled data from several sources to estimate where people with schizophrenia are being kept, and his estimates are given in Figure 10.1. Note that the majority of people with schizophrenia are living independently or in their family's home. In *Taking Psychology Personally:* Helping Families Cope with Schizophrenia, page 328, we highlight the challenges that families of people with schizophrenia face in coping with their loved one's disorder, particularly when that loved one lives at home. Note also in Figure 10.1 that almost as many people with schizophrenia are in jails, prisons, homeless shelters and on the street as are in hospitals and nursing homes. The criminal system and the shelters are often the repository for people with schizophrenia who do not have families to support them or the resources to get psychiatric help.

There are differences across groups within the United States in rates of schizophrenia. One large epidemiological study found the highest rates of schizophrenia in African Americans, somewhat lower rates in Whites, and the lowest rates in Hispanic Americans, although these ethnic differences diminished when socioeconomic status was taken into account (Escobar, 1993). Studies of persons hospitalized for serious mental disorders have found that African Americans are more likely than other groups to be misdiagnosed with schizophrenia, when they are actually suffering from a severe mood disorder (Griffith & Baker, 1993).

each disorder. I then elaborate and illustrate each symptom in the main text.

In addition, a number of pedagogical features from the first edition have been retained:

- *Chapter Overviews*. Each chapter begins with a detailed overview of the main points of the chapter.
- *Summing Up Sections*. Each major section within a chapter ends with Summing Up, a bulleted summary of the main points of that section.
- *Case Studies*. Case studies illustrating disorders are systematically presented within each chapter.
- *Bio-Psycho-Social Integrations*. Most chapters end with a Bio-Psycho-Social Integration, which explicitly integrates the various biological, psychological, and social theories and treatments described in the chapter.
- *Chapter Summaries*. The Chapter Summaries at the end of each chapter provide a detailed description of the major points of the chapter in prose form.
- *Key Terms*. The Key Terms for each chapter are listed at the end of the chapter with page numbers referring students to their appearance within the chapter.

Supplements

Finally, the package of ancillaries for this book has undergone major revision and additions to assist the instructor teaching this course.

Clashing Views on Abnormal Psychology: A Taking Sides Custom Reader is a debate-style reader designed to introduce students to controversies in abnormal psychology. Each issue is explored by two articles that represent "Yes" and "No" responses. By requiring students to analyze opposing viewpoints and reach considered judgments, *Clashing Views* actively engages students' critical-thinking skills.

The **Student Study Guide** provides students with a thorough review of the material in the textbook. Each chapter of the study guide includes learning objectives, a list of essential ideas from the chapter in the textbook, a guided review through all of the major sections, a 20-item practice multiple-choice exam with answers, and a practice essay exam with answers.

The **Instructor's Course Planner** includes an overview of each chapter, learning objectives, suggestions and resources for lecture topics, classroom activities, between-class projects, suggestions for video and multimedia that will enhance lectures and discussions, and essay questions that will help students think about material between classes. A special section of the planner includes an Instructor's Manual for the reader, *Clashing*

Views on Abnormal Psychology: A Taking Sides Custom Reader.

The **Test Item File** includes over 2,000 multiple-choice and essay items. Multiple-choice items are classified as factual, conceptual, or applied, and referenced to the appropriate learning objective.

Computerized Test Item Files are available in Micro-Test, a powerful but easy-to-use test-generating program by Chariot Software Group. MicroTest is available for DOS, Windows, and Macintosh. Micro-Test enables you to select questions easily from the Test Item File and print a test and answer key. It also lets you customize questions, headings, and instructions, add or import questions of your own, and print your test in a choice of fonts if your printer supports them.

MindMap CD-ROM is packaged for FREE with each copy of the text, this Student CD-ROM includes video, interactive exercises, chapter quizzes, crossword puzzles, key terms, research questions, an Internet primer to help students learn about psychology research on the Internet, links to the book Web site to enhance student study time, and much more.

Making the Grade—Student CD-ROM is packaged for FREE, this user-friendly CD-ROM gives students an opportunity to test their comprehension for the course material in a manner that is most comfortable and beneficial to them. The CD-ROM opens with a learning style/study skills questionnaire that the students can use to help them identify how they best study. Also included are practice tests that cover topics in the abnormal psychology course, an Internet primer, and a statistics primer.

Psych Online is a supplement designed to help students get the most out of the Internet for psychology research and provides general resource locations. Psychology sites are grouped by topic with a brief explanation of each site. Included in this booklet are a number of general resource sites for students seeking help.

Online Learning Center is the official Web site for the text. It contains chapter outlines, practice quizzes that can be e-mailed to the professor, interactive exercises, PowerPoint lectures, links to relevant psychology sites, Internet primer, career appendix, and a statistics primer.

Faces of Abnormal Psychology Video contains eight short clips suitable for classroom viewing to show students real people who are experiencing a psychological disorder. Schizophrenia, posttraumatic stress disorder, bulimia nervosa, substance abuse, dythymic disorder, personality disorder with dissociative and borderline features, and transvestic fetishism are covered. A guide to the video segments and follow-up questions and activities will be posted to the book Web site.

PageOut—Build your own course Web site in less than an hour. You don't have to be a computer whiz to create a Web site. Especially with an exclusive McGraw-Hill product called PageOut. It requires no prior knowledge of HTML, no long hours of coding, and no design skills on your part. *www.pageout.net*

Presentation Manager CD-ROM is a tool that allows you to build your own media rich presentations. We supply the engine and the images to allow you to assemble customized lectures.

■ Acknowledgments

It takes a large and expert crew to put together a textbook. I have been fortunate to work with people at McGraw-Hill who are not only extremely competent, but a true joy to interact with. I wish to thank each of them for their enthusiasm for this project, the resources they poured into the project, and their good humor—Joseph Terry, Mindy DePalma, Jane Vaicunas, Gloria Schiesl, Barbara Santoro, Jim Rosza, and Christine Hall. A special thanks to Sylvia Shephard, whose expert editing of this book was invaluable. I also thank Toni Michaels for once again bringing her great eye to the art and photo program for the book.

At the University of Michigan, Nicole Thompson and Caitlin Klein put countless hours into library searches, reference checks, and other thankless jobs necessary for a textbook. I thank them for their diligence and enthusiasm.

Many colleagues took time away from their busy schedules to provide me with materials from their own state-of-the-art research programs, or to comment upon sections of the manuscript. Their contributions have helped to ensure that the research presented in this text is the most cutting-edge work available, and that work outside my own area of expertise has been presented accurately and clearly. Thanks to current and previous reviewers:

Ed Abramzon   *California State–Chico*
Gerianne Alexander   *University of New Orleans*
Nancy Andreasen   *University of Iowa*
Adrian Angold   *Duke University*
L. E. Banderet   *Northeastern University*
John Belmont   *University of Kansas Medical Center*
Thomas Borkovec   *Penn State University*
Thomas Bouchard   *University of Minnesota*
Michael Brady   *Delta College*
Joseph Breitenstein   *Luther College*

Jeanne Brooks-Gunn   *Columbia University*
Lawrence Burns   *Grand Valley State University*
Glorisa Canino   *University of Puerto Rico*
Felipe Castro   *Arizona State University*
Salvatore Catanzaro   *Illinois State University*
Jill Cermele   *Drew University*
Shelly Chaiken   *New York University*
Deborah Cook   *University of Colorado–Boulder*
Eric Cooley   *Western Oregon University*
Jerry Cott   *National Institute of Mental Health*
Christopher Davis   *University of Michigan*
Lenore DeFonso   *Indiana Purdue University–Fort Wayne*
Patricia DiBartolo   *Smith College*
Adam Drewnowski   *University of Michigan*
Janice Egeland   *University of Miami School of Medicine*
L. Erlenmeyer-Kimling   *Columbia University*
James Evans   *University of South Carolina*
Christopher Fairburn   *Oxford University*
John Fazio   *Warner Pacific College*
Ellen Frank   *University of Pittsburgh*
Mark Friedman   *Montclair State University*
Judy Garber   *Vanderbilt University*
Paul Garfinkel   *University of Toronto*
C. M. Gibbs   *Midlands Technical College*
Jill Goldstein   *Harvard Medical School*
Norman Gordon   *Eastern Michigan University*
Irving Gottesman   *University of Virginia*
Peter Guarnaccia   *Rutgers University*
Chad Hagans   *University of Florida–Gainsville*
Jim Hansell   *University of Michigan*
Chris Hayward   *Stanford University Department of Psychiatry*
John Helzer   *University of Vermont School of Medicine*
Judith Herman   *Harvard Medical School*
Stephen Hinshaw   *University of California at Berkeley*
Steven Hollon   *Vanderbilt University*
Cooper Holmes   *Arkansas State University*
Jill Hooley   *Harvard University*
Jacqueline Horn   *University of California–Davis*
Captain William Hughes   *Virginia Military Institute*
Gayle Iwamasa   *Ball State University*
Huberta Jackson-Lowman   *Florida A&M University*
Nadine Kaslow   *Emeory University*
Terence Keane   *Boston Veterans Administration Hospital*
Richard Kluft   *Temple University School of Medicine*
Mary Koss   *University of Arizona*

Michael Lambert   *Brigham Young University*

Joe Langer   *LIU–Brooklyn Campus*

Jennifer Langhinrichsen-Rohling   *University of South Alabama*

Chris Layne   *The University of Toledo*

Peter Lewinsohn   *Oregon Research Institute*

Barbara Lex   *McLean Hospital*

Margaret Livingston   *Lousiana Tech University*

Karsten Look   *Columbus State Community College*

Tracy Luchetta   *University of Wisconsin at Green Bay*

Spero Manson   *University of Colorado Health Sciences Center*

Alan Marlatt   *University of Washington*

David Mastofsky   *Boston University*

Andrew Matthews   *MRC Applied Psychology Unit*

Janet Matthews   *Loyola University*

Karen Matthews   *University of Pittsburgh*

Matthew McGue   *University of Minnesota*

Lily McNair   *University of Georgia*

Gary Melton   *Institute for Families in Society at the University of South Carolina*

Jodi Mindell   *St. Joseph's University*

Christine Molnar   *Penn State University*

John Monahan   *University of Virginia*

Diana Morrobel   *Michigan State University*

Edward Mulvey   *University of Pittsburgh*

William Narrow   *National Institute of Mental Health*

Neimeyer   *University of Florida–Gainsville*

Carol Nemeroff   *Arizona State University*

Michael O'Hara   *University of Iowa*

Maribeth Palmer-King   *Broome Community College*

Ronald Palmores   *Texas Woman's University*

Diane Pfahler   *University of California–San Bernadino*

Harrison Pope   *McLean Hospital*

Lynne Rehm   *University of Houston*

Harold Rosenberg   *Bowling Green University*

Anita Rosenfield   *Chaffey Community College*

Norman Rosenthal   *National Institute of Mental Health*

Robert Sapolsky   *Stanford University*

Lisa Scherer   *University of Nebraska–Omaha*

Marc Schuckit   *University of California, San Diego*

Kathleen Blindt Segraves   *Case Western Reserve University*

David Silber   *George Washington University*

David Allen Smith   *Ohio State University*

Gary Smithson   *University of Tennesee*

Ruth Striegel-Moore   *Wesleyan University*

Albert Stunkard   *University of Pennsylvania*

Shelley Taylor   *University of California, Los Angeles*

Lenore Terr   *University of California, San Francisco*

Timothy Trull   *University of Missouri–Columbia*

Michael W. Vasey   *Ohio State University*

Joseph Westermeyer   *University of Minnesota*

Valerie Whiffen   *University of Ottawa*

Fred Whitford   *Montana State University*

Roberta Willim   *Fordham University*

Amy Wolfson   *College of the Holy Cross*

David Wolitski   *New York University*

Janet Wollersheim   *University of Maryland*

Teresa Wozencraft   *Midwestern State University*

Kimberly Yonkers   *University of Texas SW Medical Center*

Audrey Zakriski   *Connecticut College*

Robert Zucker   *University of Michigan*

Once again, my family provided emotional and practical support during the writing of this second edition that truly made it possible. My deep appreciation to Richard Nolen-Hoeksema, Michael Hoeksema, John and Catherine Nolen, and Renze and Marjorie Hoeksema. Thanks also to Judi Larson for her continued willingness to receive and respond perfectly across cyberspace both to my whining and my joys.

Susan Nolen-Hoeksema
Ann Arbor, MI

Susan Nolen-Hoeksema is Professor of Psychology at the University of Michigan. She received her B.A. in psychology from Yale University and her Ph.D. in clinical psychology from the University of Pennsylvania. Her research focuses on emotion regulation, stress and coping, and depression. She is the recipient of an early career award from the American Psychological Association, numerous research grants, and two major teaching awards. Dr. Nolen-Hoeksema has published 8 books and over 40 research articles in the last 14 years. Dr. Nolen-Hoeksema currently directs the Gender and Mental Health Training Program at the University of Michigan, which trains predoctoral and postdoctoral students to do research on the intersection of gender and mental health.

Abnormal

PSYCHOLOGY

Peter Sickles
People Flying

Who, except the gods, can live time through forever without any pain.

—*Aeschylus*

CHAPTER 1

Looking at Abnormality

CHAPTER OVERVIEW

Defining Abnormality

The context for a behavior often determines whether it is considered abnormal. Other criteria that have been used to determine the normality of behaviors are cultural norms for behaviors, how unusual the behaviors are, whether the behaviors cause the person discomfort, the presence of an identifiable illness, and whether the behaviors interfere with the person's functioning and are maladaptive.

Taking Psychology Personally:
When You Wonder If You Are Abnormal

Historical Perspectives on Abnormality

Theories of abnormality across the ages have included biological theories, supernatural theories, and psychological theories. In prehistoric times, supernatural theories of abnormality may have dominated, and a primitive form of brain surgery designed to release demons may have been performed. Some of the most ancient writings about abnormality are from Chinese texts around 2674 B.C. Other prominent writings include the papyri of Egypt and Mesopotamia, the Old Testament, and the works of Greek and Roman philosophers and physicians. In the Middle Ages, many people with mental disorders may have been accused of being witches and killed out of fear. Throughout history, people who acted abnormally have been imprisoned, tortured, or cast out. In the eighteenth and nineteenth centuries, however, several advocates of more gentle treatment of people with mental disorders helped to establish asylums where they could be treated with kindness.

Extraordinary People:
Clifford Beers, *A Mind That Found Itself*

The Emergence of Modern Perspectives

Biological and psychosocial theories of abnormality dominate in mainstream science and practice in abnormal psychology. Some people still bring their own lay and supernatural theories of abnormality into their interactions with therapists, however.

Pushing the Boundaries:
Can Germs Cause Mental Disorders?

Professions Within Abnormal Psychology

The professions in abnormal psychology include psychiatry, clinical psychology, clinical social work, and psychiatric nursing.

Chapter Summary
Key Terms
Critical Thinking Questions

Voices

My illness began slowly, gradually, when I was between the ages of 15 and 17. During that time reality became distant and I began to wander around in a sort of haze, foreshadowing the delusional world that was to come later. I also began to have visual hallucinations in which people changed into different characters, the change indicating to me their moral value. For example, the mother of a good friend always changed into a witch, and I believed this to be indicative of her evil nature. Another type of visual hallucination I had at this time is exemplified by an occurrence during a family trip through Utah: The cliffs along the side of the road took on a human appearance, and I perceived them as women, bedraggled and weeping.

At the time I didn't know what to make of these changes in my perceptions. On the one hand, I thought they came as a gift from God, but on the other hand, I feared that something was dreadfully wrong. However, I didn't tell anyone what was happening; I was afraid of being called insane. I also feared, perhaps incredibly, that someone would take it lightly and tell me nothing was wrong, that I was just having a rough adolescence, which was what I was telling myself.

(Anonymous, 1992, pp. 333–334)

So began the journey of a young woman named Julia into a world and a life that, fortunately, most of us will never have to experience.

The study of abnormal psychology is the study of people like Julia—people who suffer mental, emotional, and often physical pain, as the result of some form of psychological disorder, or **psychopathology.** Sometimes the experiences of people with psychopathology are as bizarre and unusual as Julia's experiences. Sometimes, however, people with psychopathology have experiences that are familiar to many of us, but more extreme, as Jamison (1995b, p. 110) describes:

Voices

From the time I woke up in the morning until the time I went to bed at night, I was unbearably miserable and seemingly incapable of any kind of joy or enthusiasm. Everything—every thought, word, movement—was an effort. Everything that once was sparkling now was flat. I seemed to myself to be dull, boring, inadequate, thick brained, unlit, unresponsive, chill skinned, bloodless, and sparrow drab. I doubted, completely, my ability to do anything well. It seemed as though my mind had slowed down and burned out to the point of being virtually useless. The wretched, convoluted, and pathetically confused mass of gray worked only well enough to torment me with a dreary litany of my inadequacies and shortcomings in character and to taunt me with the total, the desperate hopelessness of it all.

In this book, we explore the lives of people with psychopathology to understand how they think, what they feel, and how they behave. We investigate what is known about the causes and treatments for various types of psychopathology. The purpose of this book is not only to provide you with information, facts and figures, theories and research. It is also to take you into the lives of people with psychopathology and to help you understand their suffering. Some of you may recognize yourself in some of these people, and we hope to give you the knowledge to seek effective treatment.

First, however, we must define what we mean by psychopathology, or more generally, by abnormality. This is often more difficult that it might seem at first glance.

⊙ DEFINING ABNORMALITY

Consider the following behaviors:

1. A man kissing another man.
2. A woman slapping a child.
3. A man driving a nail through his hand.
4. A woman refusing to eat for several days.
5. A man barking like a dog and crawling on the floor on his hands and knees.
6. A woman building a shrine to her dead husband in a corner of her living room and leaving food and gifts for him at the altar.

Do you think these behaviors are abnormal? You may reply, "It depends." In some circumstances, several of these behaviors may seem perfectly normal. In many European cultures, for example, men commonly greet other men with a kiss. In many religious traditions, refusing to eat for a period, or fasting, is a common ritual of cleansing and penitence.

You might expect that some of the other behaviors, such as a driving a nail through one's hand or barking like a dog, are abnormal across all circumstances. Yet, even these behaviors are accepted as normal by some people, and indeed are prescribed for specific situations. In Mexico, some Christians have themselves nailed to crosses at Easter to commemorate the crucifixion of Jesus. Among the Yoruba of Africa, traditional healers act like dogs, barking and crawling

Some behaviors—like one man kissing another man—are considered normal in some cultures but not in others.

on the floor, during healing rituals (Murphy, 1976). In Shinto and Buddhist religions, it is customary to build altars to dead loved ones, to offer them food and gifts, and to speak with them as if they were in the room (Stroebe et al., 1992).

Thus, the **context**, or circumstances surrounding a behavior, influence whether a behavior is viewed as abnormal. Some theorists have gone so far as to argue that cultural or societal norms are the only criterion for labeling a behavior as abnormal (Scheff, 1966). This perspective, known as *cultural relativism*, is discussed further in the next section. A parallel perspective, which might be called gender relativism, argues that behaviors become defined as abnormal if they violate expectations for the behavior of an individual based on his or her gender, also known as *gender roles*. For example, a woman crying in public is not viewed as terribly abnormal in our culture, but a man crying in public is seen as abnormal, because this violates gender roles for men's display of emotions. This gender role account of abnormality is also discussed below.

Other theorists have argued for what might appear, on the surface, to be more objective standards for defining abnormality that do not rely on cultural traditions or gender roles. These include standards focusing on the *unusualness* of the behavior, the *discomfort* of the person exhibiting the behavior, the presence of *mental illness,* and the *maladaptiveness* of the behavior (see *Concept Review:* Criteria for Defining Abnormality). Each of these standards has its advantages and disadvantages.

CONCEPT REVIEW

Criteria for Defining Abnormality

Several different criteria for defining abnormality have been suggested. The maladaptiveness criterion is the one most frequently used today.

Criterion	Definition
Cultural relativism criterion	Norms of a culture set the standard for normal behavior, and abnormality can only be defined in reference to these norms.
Unusualness criterion	Abnormal behaviors are those that are rare or infrequent.
Discomfort criterion	People must suffer as a result of a behavior and wish to be rid of it for it to be called abnormal.
Mental illness criterion	Abnormal behaviors are those that result from mental illness
Maladaptiveness criterion	Behaviors that cause people physical or emotional harm, prevent them from functioning in daily life, and/or indicate that they have lost touch with reality or cannot control their thoughts are abnormal.

Cultural Relativism

A central argument of the **cultural relativism** perspective is that there are no universal standards or rules for labeling a behavior as abnormal. Instead, behaviors can only be abnormal relative to cultural norms (Schur, 1971). Thus, cultural relativists believe that there are different definitions of abnormality across different cultures.

A good example of cultural relativism is bereavement practices. In Western countries, bereaved people are expected to mourn their dead loved ones for a period of time, perhaps a few weeks or months, then to "let go" of the loved one and move on in their lives (Stroebe et al., 1992). People who continue to think about and talk about their dead loved ones a great deal after the specified period of mourning are thought to have "complicated bereavement" and may be encouraged to seek counseling. More often, their family members and friends simply tell them to "get over it." Thus, the norm in these cultures is to break emotional bonds with dead loved ones and people who seem not to have adequately broken those bonds may be labeled as abnormal.

In contrast, many other cultures believe that we cannot and should not break psychological ties with dead loved ones. For example, in Japan, maintaining emotional bonds with deceased loved ones is not only normal, it is prescribed for bereaved people (Yamamoto, 1970). In Egypt, the bereaved are encouraged to dwell profusely on their grief, and other people support them by recounting their own losses and openly expressing their sorrow in emotional outpourings (Wikan, 1991). Even in Western countries, during the romantic age of the nineteenth century, expectations of the bereaved were radically different from current expectations (Rosenblatt, 1983; Stroebe et al., 1992). People's close relationships were at the center of their self-definitions, and the loss of a loved one was a critical defining moment in the survivor's life. "To grieve was to signal the significance of the relationship, and the depth of one's own spirit. Dissolving bonds with the deceased would not only define the relationship as superficial, but would deny as well one's own sense of profundity and self-worth" (Stroebe et al., 1992, p. 1208). People clung to the lost loved one, and wrote about their grief in poetry, diaries, and fiction. The fact that the definitions of normal and abnormal grief can vary not only across culture but across time within a culture strongly suggests that these definitions are bound in larger philosophical and religious traditions rather than in some universal truth.

Opponents of cultural relativism argue that dangers arise when societal norms are allowed to dictate what is normal and abnormal. In particular, psychiatrist Thomas Szasz has noted that, throughout history, societies have labeled individuals and groups abnormal in order to justify controlling or silencing them. Hitler branded Jews abnormal and used this as one justification for the Holocaust. The former Soviet Union branded political dissidents mentally ill and jailed them in mental hospitals.

When the slave trade was active in the United States, slaves who tried to escape their masters could be diagnosed as having *drapetomania*, a sickness that caused them to desire freedom. This provided a justification for capturing them and returning them to their masters (Szasz, 1971). In 1851, Dr. Samuel Cartwright, a prominent physician, published an essay in the prestigious *New Orleans Medical and Surgical Journal* titled "Report on the Diseases and Physical Peculiarities of the Negro Race," in which he argued that

> The cause, in most cases, that induces the Negro to run away from service, is as much a disease of the mind as any other species of mental alienation, and much more curable, as a general rule. With the advantages of proper medical advice, strictly followed, this troublesome practice that

People in some cultures build altars to dead loved ones, leave them food and gifts, and speak to the dead. In other cultures these practices are considered highly abnormal.

many Negroes have of running away, can be almost entirely prevented.

Cartwright also described a disease called *dysaesthesia Aethiopis*, the refusal to work for one's master. To cure this "disease," Cartwright prescribed the following:

> The liver, skin and kidneys should be stimulated to activity, and be made to assist in decarbonising the blood. The best means to stimulate the skin is, first, to have the patient well washed with warm water and soap; then to anoint it all over with oil, and to slap the oil with a broad leather strap; then to put the patient to some hard kind of work in the open air and sunshine, that will compel him to expand his lungs, as chopping wood, splitting rails, or sawing with the cross-cut or whip saw.

According to Cartwright, whipping slaves who refused to work and then forcing them to do hard labor would "revitalize" their lungs and bring them back to their senses. We might like to believe that Cartwright's essay represented the extreme views of just one person, but he was writing on behalf of a prestigious medical association.

In our modern society, labeling of behaviors as normal or abnormal is heavily influenced by **gender role expectations** (Brems & Schlottmann, 1988; Broverman et al., 1970; Hartung & Widiger, 1998). Men who display sadness or anxiety, who choose to stay home to raise their children while their wives work, or who otherwise violate the male gender role are at risk for being labeled as abnormal. Women who are too aggressive, who don't want to have children, or who otherwise violate the female gender role are at risk for being labeled as abnormal. On the other hand, aggression in men, and chronic anxiety or sadness in women, are often dismissed as normal because they do not violate gender-role expectations—we expect these behaviors so we label them as normal.

The cultural relativist perspective obviously raises many difficulties in defining abnormality. Most psychologists these days do not take an extreme relativist view on abnormality, recognizing the dangers of taking society's definitions of what is normal and abnormal as the gold standard. There is increasing sensitivity, however, to the reality that cultural norms and gender-role expectations strongly influence people's feelings and actions.

Unusualness

A second standard or criterion that has been used for designating behaviors as abnormal is **unusualness**. Under this criterion, behaviors that are unusual or rare are considered abnormal, whereas behaviors that are typical or usual are considered normal. Obviously, this criterion has some ties to the relativist criterion—the unusualness of any behavior will depend in part on the norms for that behavior in a culture. For example, the unusualness of a bereaved person wailing in public will depend on whether he or she is in Minneapolis or Cairo.

There are other problems with the unusualness criterion for abnormality. First, although the criterion may seem objective, someone still has to decide how rare a behavior must be in order to call it abnormal. Are behaviors that only 10 percent of the population exhibits abnormal? Or do we want to set a more strict cutoff and say that only behaviors that 1 percent or less of the population exhibits are abnormal? Choosing a cutoff is as subjective as relying on people's personal opinions as to what is abnormal and normal.

The second major problem with the unusualness criterion is that many rare behaviors are positive for the individual and for society, and most people would object to labeling such behaviors as abnormal. For example, we don't label the playing of a piano virtuoso abnormal; we label it gifted. Other people have hobbies or activities that are rare, but are a source of great joy for them and do no harm to others. These people are often referred to as *eccentrics*. Take, for example, Gary Holloway, an environmental planner who works for the city of San Francisco (see Case Study).

One of the few studies of eccentrics estimates that only about 1 in 10,000 people are true eccentrics. This study found that eccentrics certainly have unusual

tastes, but are generally very happy and function well in society (Weeks & James, 1995). Indeed, the rate of serious dysfunction among the eccentrics in this study was lower than the rate among noneccentrics.

CASE STUDY

Gary Holloway's activities certainly are eccentric, but would we call them abnormal?

He is fascinated by Martin Van Buren, the eighth president of the United States. Eighteen years ago, he discovered that Van Buren was the only president not to have a society dedicated to his memory, so he promptly founded the Martin Van Buren Fan Club. "This man did absolutely nothing to further the course of our national destiny," Holloway told us proudly, "yet hundreds of people now follow me in commemorating him."

Holloway has served as the club's president for eighteen consecutive terms, and he has also been the winner for eighteen consecutive years of the Marty, its award for excellence in Van Burenism. Holloway is also a lifelong devotee of St. Francis of Assisi, and frequently dresses in the habit of a Franciscan monk. "It's comfortable, fun to wear, and I like the response I get when I wear it," he explained. "People always offer me a seat on the bus."

Holloway has an obsession with the British Commonwealth and has an encyclopedic knowledge of places such as Tristan da Cunha and Fiji. During the Falklands war he passionately espoused the cause of the islanders, to the point of flying the Falklands flag on the flagpole on his front lawn. After the war he celebrated Britain's victory by renaming his home Falklands House, where he continues to fly its flag. His bedroom at Falklands House still has everything in it that it had when he was a boy. He calls it the Peanuts Room because of his huge collection of stuffed Snoopies and other memorabilia pertaining to the comic strip *Peanuts*. He has slept on the same twin bed there for forty years. He has dozens of toy airplanes, relics of his boyhood and the walls are covered with pennants. "As a monk," he explained, "I'm always doing pennants"—thereby demonstrating the sly sense of humor that many eccentrics possess. (Weeks & James, 1995, pp. 36–37)

Discomfort

Another criterion for abnormality might be the **discomfort** that behaviors or feelings create for the individual experiencing them. Proponents of this view suggest that behaviors should only be considered abnormal if the individual suffers as a result of the behaviors and wishes to be rid of them. This criterion avoids, to some extent, the problems of using societal norms as the criterion for abnormality. If a person's behaviors violate societal norms but do not cause him or her any discomfort, then perhaps the behaviors should not be considered abnormal. This viewpoint contributed to a change in how psychologists and psychiatrists viewed one behavior pattern—homosexuality. Gay men and lesbians argued that their sexual orientation is a natural part of themselves and a characteristic that causes them no discomfort and that they don't wish to alter or eliminate. In addition, despite the stress that gay men and lesbians endure because of prejudice against them, homosexuals are no more likely than heterosexuals to experience serious forms of psychological distress (Herek, 1990). Partially based on these arguments, the American Psychiatric Association removed homosexuality from its list of recognized psychological disorders in 1973 (Spitzer, 1981).

Some therapists object to the subjective discomfort criterion, however, because people are not always aware of problems their behaviors create for themselves or for others. For example, some people who have lost touch with reality wander the streets aimlessly, not eating or taking care of themselves, in danger of starvation or exposure to the elements. These people may not be fully aware that they have severe problems and often do not seek help. If we require that people acknowledge and seek help for their behaviors before we call those behaviors abnormal, some people who could benefit greatly from help might never get it.

Mental Illness Criterion

A fourth way of defining abnormality is as behaviors that result from mental disease or illness. This **mental illness** criterion implies that there is a clear, identifiable physical process that is deviant from "health" and that leads to specific behaviors or symptoms. However, to date, there is no medical test that identifies this process if it does exist. If we give a person's symptoms a diagnosis, this is simply a label for that set of symptoms. For example, when we say someone "has" obsessive compulsive disorder, we can only mean that he or she is exhibiting a set of symptoms, including obsessive thoughts and compulsive behaviors. The term *obsessive-compulsive disorder* does not refer to some

"Do people hate us because we dress this way or do we dress this way because people hate us?"
© Sidney Harris

identifiable physical entity that is found in all people who exhibit these symptoms.

Maladaptiveness

So how do the majority of researchers and clinicians in the mental-health field decide whether a set of behaviors is abnormal? The consensus is that behaviors and feelings that are **maladaptive**—that cause people to *suffer distress* and that *prevent them from functioning in daily life*—are abnormal and should be the focus of research and intervention (Spitzer, 1981). Of course, what is maladaptive and what makes people suffer is in part determined by the norms of society. Psychologists have tried to reserve the label maladaptive for behaviors that have one or more of the following characteristics:

1. They are physically damaging to the individual, such as when a teenager repeatedly cuts herself in an emotional outburst.

2. They cause the individual emotional suffering or harm, such as the emotional pain that people feel when they are depressed.

3. They severely interfere with the individual's ability to function in daily life, as when a person with extreme phobias becomes housebound.

4. They indicate that the individual has lost touch with reality and cannot control his or her behaviors or thoughts, as happens in the disorder called schizophrenia.

Julia's experiences, described at the beginning of this chapter, would be labeled as abnormal by these criteria because they caused her suffering and because she had lost touch with reality. The feelings described by Jamison early in this chapter would also be labeled as abnormal by these criteria because they caused her great suffering and interfered with her ability to function in daily life. The maladaptiveness criteria have attracted the most widespread support among mental-health professionals because they seem to capture what most of us want to mean when we call something abnormal while avoiding some of the problems of using only the cultural relativism, unusualness, discomfort, or illness criteria alone.

Still, the maladaptiveness criteria call for judgments that are subjective—how much emotional suffering or harm must a person be suffering? How much should the behaviors be interfering with functioning? Who determines what is adequate functioning? And the criteria still depend on societal norms. There are many behaviors people engage in that are physically damaging, but are accepted by society, such as smoking cigarettes. There are many beliefs people hold that others may think are "crazy," such as the belief in an afterlife, but that are accepted by society. Throughout this book, as we apply the maladaptiveness criteria to specific types of behavior, we will keep in mind the subjectivity of these criteria and the fuzziness of definitions of abnormality.

Even when the maladaptiveness criteria can be confidently used to identify a certain group of behaviors as abnormal, culture and gender can still influence the expression of those behaviors and how those behaviors are treated (see *Concept Review*: Ways Culture and Gender Affect Maladaptive Behaviors). First, culture and gender influence how likely it is that a given maladaptive behavior will be shown. For example, men are twice as likely as women to suffer problems related to alcohol use. This suggests that something about being male—something about male biology, male personality, or the social pressures put on men—contributes to the development of alcoholism. Second, culture and gender can influence the ways people express distress or lose touch with reality. People who lose touch with reality will often believe that they have divine powers, but whether an individual believes he is Jesus Christ or Buddha depends on his religious background. Third, culture and gender can influence people's willingness to admit to certain types of maladaptive behaviors. People in Eskimo and Tahitian cultures may be reluctant to admit to angry feelings because of strong cultural norms against the expression of anger. However, the Kaluli of New Guinea and the Yanamamo of Brazil value the expression of anger and have elaborate and complex rituals for expressing anger (Jenkins, Kleinman, & Good, 1991). Fourth, culture and gender can

CONCEPT REVIEW
Ways Culture and Gender Affect Maladaptive Behaviors

These are four ways that culture and gender can affect the expression and experience of maladaptive behaviors.

1. Culture and gender influence how likely it is that a maladaptive behavior will be shown.
2. Culture and gender influence the ways people express distress or lose touch with reality.
3. Culture and gender influence people's willingness to admit to maladaptive behaviors.
4. Culture and gender influence the types of treatments people will accept.

influence the types of treatments that are deemed acceptable or helpful for maladaptive behaviors. For example, women may be more willing than men to accept psychological treatments for problems. Throughout this book, we will explore these influences of culture and gender on maladaptive behaviors.

Many students in courses on abnormal psychology come to the course wondering if they are abnormal, because they feel unusual, they are uncomfortable with themselves, or they fear they have inherited a mental illness. *Taking Psychology Personally:* When You Wonder If You Are Abnormal (p. 10) addresses this concern and what you should do when you wonder if you are abnormal.

Summing Up

- Cultural relativism is a perspective on abnormality that argues that the norms of a society must be used to determine the normality of a behavior.
- The unusualness criterion for abnormality suggest that unusual or rare behaviors should be labeled abnormal.
- The discomfort criterion suggests that only behaviors or emotions that an individual finds distressing should be labeled abnormal.
- The mental illness criterion for abnormality suggests that only behaviors resulting from mental illness or disease are abnormal.
- The consensus among professionals in the mental-health field is that behaviors that cause people to suffer distress or that prevent them from functioning in daily life are abnormal. Often these behaviors are referred to as *maladaptive* or *dysfunctional*.

TAKING PSYCHOLOGY PERSONALLY

When You Wonder If You Are Abnormal

Most students reading a book on abnormal psychology will recognize in themselves some behaviors that are labeled as abnormal. In fact, it is often easy to see signs in oneself (or one's close friends or relatives) of almost every type of abnormality discussed in this book! This type of perception is referred to as *medical student's disease.*

Be aware that many of the behaviors discussed in this book occur occasionally, in mild form, in many people. For example, many people between the ages of 18 and 25, even when not under the influence of some drug, have brief "out of body" experiences, in which they feel their "soul" or "self" is floating out of their body. It is even more common for people of all ages to have periods of sad or anxious moods or times when they feel that life is "out of control." For most people, these periods are relatively brief, and these behaviors or feelings do not severely interfere with their ability to function in life.

Yet, if you have been behaving in ways that have been interfering with daily functioning for a long time or that have been causing you or others much suffering, it is a good idea to talk with a professional about these experiences. Your instructor may be willing to speak with you or to provide you with referrals to professionals with whom you may speak. Many colleges offer confidential counseling for students at no cost or minimal cost. Some counties have mental-health associations that provide information on professionals or groups that serve people with specific types of problems; the phone number for your local mental-health association may be in the *Yellow Pages* or available through an operator.

HISTORICAL PERSPECTIVES ON ABNORMALITY

Three types of theories of the causes of mental disorders have competed for dominance across time. The **natural theories** saw mental disorders as similar to physical diseases, caused by the breakdown of some system in the body. The appropriate cure for mental disorders, according to the natural theories, was the restoration of the body to good health. The **supernatural theories** saw mental disorders as the result of divine intervention, curses, demonic possession, and personal sin. To rid the person of the disorder, religious rituals, exorcisms, confessions, and atonement were prescribed. The third type of theory of mental disorder consisted of **psychological** or stress-related **theories,** which saw mental disorders as the result of traumas, such as bereavement, or chronic stress. According to these theories, rest, relaxation, a change of environment, and certain herbal medicines were sometimes helpful to the afflicted person. These different theories influenced how people afflicted with disorders were regarded in the society. Obviously, a person thought to be insane because she was a sinner would be regarded differently from a person thought to be insane because of a medical disorder.

Ancient Theories

References to madness, insanity, or other forms of mental disorder can be found throughout the history of humankind. Our understanding of prehistoric people's conceptions of abnormality is based on inferences from archeological artifacts—fragments of bones, tools, artwork, and so on. But ever since humans developed written language, they have been writing about abnormal behavior, making it clear that humans have always viewed abnormality as something needing special explanation.

Evil Spirits of the Stone Age

Historians speculate that even prehistoric people had a concept of insanity, probably one rooted in supernatural beliefs (Selling, 1940). Demons and ghosts were

Some scholars believe that holes found in ancient skulls are from trephining, a crude form of brain surgery performed on people acting abnormally.

the cause of abnormal behavior. When a person acted oddly, he or she was suspected of being possessed by evil spirits. Curing the behavior meant driving away the evil spirits.

One treatment for abnormality in the Stone Age may have been to drill holes in the skulls of people displaying abnormal behavior to allow the spirits to depart. Archeologists have found skulls dating back to the Stone Age a half-million years ago in which circular sections of the skull have been drilled away (Maher & Maher, 1985). The tool used for this drilling is called a trephine, and thus the operation was called **trephination.** Some historians believe that trephination was prescribed for people who were hallucinating—that is, having bizarre and unreal perceptual experiences—or who were extremely sad or despondent (Selling, 1940). A person who was seeing or hearing things that were not real, or who was chronically sad, might be subjected to this prehistoric form of brain surgery. Presumably, if the person survived this surgery, the evil spirits would have been released and his or her abnormal behavior would have declined. We cannot know with certainty that trephination was used to drive away evil spirits. Some historians suggest that trephination was used primarily to remove blood clots caused by stone weapons during warfare and for other medical purposes (Maher & Maher, 1985).

It is clear, however, that supernatural theories of abnormality have been around for a very long time. The typical treatment for abnormality according to supernatural beliefs was exorcism—driving the evil spirits from the body of the suffering person. Shamans, or healers, would say prayers or incantations, try to talk the spirits out of the body, or make the body an uncomfortable place for the spirits to reside, often

through extreme measures such as starving or beating the person. At other times, the person thought to be possessed by evil spirits would simply be killed.

Ancient China: Balancing Yin and Yang

Some of the earliest written sources on mental disorders are ancient Chinese texts on medicine (Tseng, 1973). *Nei Ching* (Classic of Internal Medicine) was probably written around 2674 B.C. by Huang Ti, the third legendary emperor of China. Chinese medicine was based on the concept of yin and yang; the human body was said to contain a positive force and a negative force that both confront and complement each other. If the two forces are in balance, the individual is healthy. If not, illness, including insanity, can result. For example, *excited insanity* was considered the result of an excessive positive force:

> The person suffering from excited insanity initially feels sad, eating and sleeping less; he then becomes grandiose, feeling that he is very smart and noble, talking and scolding day and night, singing, behaving strangely, seeing strange things, hearing strange voices, believing that he can see the devil or gods, etc. As treatment for such an excited condition withholding food was suggested, since food was considered to be the source of positive force and the patient was thought to be in need of a decrease in such force. (Tseng, 1973, p. 570)

Another theory in ancient Chinese medical philosophy is that human emotions are controlled by

Some of the earliest medical writings on mental disorders come from ancient Chinese texts.

internal organs. When the "vital air" is flowing on one of these organs, an individual experiences a particular emotion. For example, when air flows on the heart, a person feels joy; when on the lungs, sorrow; when on the liver, anger; when on the spleen, worry; and when on the kidney, fear. This theory encourages people to live in an orderly and harmonious way so as to maintain proper movement of vital air.

Although the Chinese perspective on psychological symptoms was largely a natural theory in ancient times, the rise of Taoism and Buddhism during the Chin and T'ang dynasties (A.D. 420 to 618, respectively), led to some religious interpretations of mental disorders. Evil winds and ghosts were blamed for bewitching people, and for their erratic emotional displays, and uncontrolled behavior. Religious theories of abnormality declined in China after this period, however.

Ancient Egypt, Greece, and Rome: Natural Theories Dominate

Other ancient writings on mental disorders are found in the papyri of Egypt and Mesopotamia (Veith, 1965). The oldest of these is a document known as the Kahun Papyrus, after the ancient Egyptian city in which it was found, and dates from about 1900 B.C. This document lists a number of disorders, each followed by a physician's judgment of the cause of the disorder, and the appropriate treatment. Several of the disorders apparently left people with unexplainable aches and pains, sadness or distress, and apathy about life. Some examples are "a woman who loves bed; she does not rise and she does not shake it"; "a woman who is pained in her teeth and jaws; she knows not how to open her mouth"; and "a woman aching in all her limbs with pain in the sockets of her eyes" (Veith, 1965, p. 3).

These disorders were said to occur only in women and were attributed to a "wandering uterus." Apparently, the Egyptians believed that the uterus could become dislodged and wander throughout a woman's body, interfering with her other organs and causing these symptoms. Later the Greeks, holding to the same theory of the anatomy of women, named this disorder hysteria (from the Greek word *hysteria,* which means *uterus*). These days, the term hysteria is used to refer to physiological symptoms that are probably the result of psychological processes. In the Egyptian papyri, the prescribed treatment for this disorder involved the use of strong-smelling substances to drive the uterus back to its proper place. Another and more complete papyrus, the Papyrus Ebers, recommends a combination of physiological interventions and incantations to the gods to assist in the healing process (Veith, 1965). One astounding feature of the Papyrus Ebers is that it provides a detailed description of the

brain, and clearly ascribes mental functioning to the brain. The perspective of the ancient Egyptians on mental disorders was clearly driven by natural theories of these disorders, but they also believed that supernatural powers could intervene in the cure of (and perhaps cause) disorders.

The Old Testament holds several references to madness. In Deuteronomy, which dates from the seventh century B.C., Moses warns his people that if they "will not obey the voice of the Lord your God or be careful to do all his commandments and his statutes . . . the Lord will smite you with madness and blindness and confusion of the mind . . ." (Deuteronomy 28:15, 28). Thus, the Hebrews saw madness as a punishment from God. People stricken with madness were to confess their sins and repent in order to achieve relief. There are several passages in the Old Testament in which people thought to be mad were also attended by physicians, however (e.g., Job 13:4). So the Hebrews believed that physicians could at least comfort, if not cure, people of madness.

Beginning with Homer, the Greeks wrote frequently of people thought to be mad (Veith, 1965). Flute music played an important role in religious rituals, and there are accounts of people hearing and seeing phantom flute players by day and night. The physician Hippocrates (460–377 B.C.) describes a case of a common phobia. A man could not walk alongside a cliff, or pass over a bridge, or jump over even a shallow ditch without feeling unable to control his limbs and having his vision impaired. Another physician, Aretaeus (A.D. 50–130), describes an artisan who appears to have had symptoms of what we now call *agoraphobia* (people with this disorder become housebound because they experience episodes of panic when away from their safe abodes): "If at any time he went away to the market, the bath, or on any other engagement, having laid down his tools, he would first groan, then shrug his shoulders as he went out. But when he had got out of sight of the domestics, or of the work and the place where it was performed, he became completely mad; yet if he returned speedily he recovered his reason again" (cited in Veith, 1965, p. 96). The traditional interpretation of madness throughout much of Greek and Roman history was that it was an affliction from the gods. The afflicted would retreat to temples honoring the god Aesculapius, where priests would hold healing ceremonies. Plato (429–347 B.C.) and Socrates (384–322 B.C.) argued that some forms of madness were divine and could be the source of great literary and prophetic gifts.

For the most part, however, Greek physicians rejected supernatural explanations of mental disorders. Hippocrates, often referred to as the father of medicine, argued that mental disorders were like other

Hippocrates argued that mental disorders were caused by imbalances in the body's essential humors, or elements.

diseases of the body. According to Hippocrates, the body is composed of four basic humors: blood, phlegm, yellow bile, and black bile. All diseases, including mental disorders, were caused by imbalances in the body's essential humors, typically an excess of one of the humors. Based on careful observation of his many patients, including listening to their dreams, Hippocrates classified mental disorders into epilepsy, mania, melancholia, and brain fever. He also recognized hysteria, although he did not view it as a mental disease. Like others, he thought that this was a disorder confined to women and caused by a wandering uterus.

The treatments prescribed by the Greek physicians were intended to restore the balance of the humors. Sometimes these treatments were physiological and intrusive; for example, bleeding a patient was a common practice for disorders thought to result from an excess of blood. Other times, treatments involved rest, relaxation, change of climate or scenery, change of diet, and a temperate life. Some of the nonmedical treatments prescribed by these physicians sound remarkably like prescriptions made by modern psychotherapists. Hippocrates, for example, believed that removing a patient from a difficult family could help to restore mental health.

Plato (429–347 B.C.) took a decidedly psychological view of mental disorders. He argued that madness arises when the rational mind is overcome by impulse, passion, or appetite. Sanity could be restored by a restoration of the rational process through a discussion with the individual designed to induce emotional control (Maher & Maher, 1985). Throughout ancient times, relatives of people considered mad were encouraged to confine the afflicted person to the home. The state claimed no responsibility for insane people; there were no asylums or institutions, other than the religious temples, to house and care for them. The state could, however, take rights away from people declared mad. Relatives could bring suit against those they considered mad, and the state could award the property of the insane person to the relatives. People declared mad could not marry or acquire or dispose of their own property. Poor people who were considered mad were simply left to roam the streets if they were not violent. If they were violent, they were locked away in stocks and chains. The general public greatly feared madness of any form, and people thought to be mad, even if divinely mad, were often shunned or even stoned.

Medieval Views

The Middle Ages (around A.D. 400–1400) are often described as a time of backward thinking, dominated by an obsession with witchcraft and supernatural forces. Yet even within Europe, supernatural theories of mental disorders did not dominate until late in the Middle Ages, between the eleventh and fifteenth centuries. Prior to the eleventh century, witches and witchcraft were accepted as real but considered merely nuisances that were overrated by superstitious people. Physical illness or injury or severe emotional shock were most often seen as the causes of bizarre behaviors. For example, English court records on persons thought to be mentally ill attributed their illnesses to factors such as a "blow received on the head" or explained that symptoms were "induced by fear of his father" or that "he has lost his reason owing to a long and incurable infirmity" (Neugebauer, 1979, p. 481). Laypeople probably did believe in demons and curses as causes of mental disorders, but there is strong evidence that physicians and government officials attributed mental disorders to physical causes or traumas.

Witchcraft

Beginning in the eleventh century, however, the power of the Church was threatened by the breakdown of feudalism, and rebellions caused by the economic and political inequalities of the times. The Church chose to interpret these threats in terms of heresy and satanism. The Inquisition was established originally to rid the earth of religious heretics, but eventually those practicing witchcraft or satanism were also the focus of hunts. The witch hunts continued long after the Reformation and were perhaps at their height during the fifteenth to seventeenth centuries, the period known as the Renaissance (Kroll, 1973).

Some psychiatric historians have argued that persons accused of witchcraft must have been mentally

Some people burned at the stake as witches may have been suffering from mental disorders that caused them to act abnormally.

ill (Veith, 1965; Zilboorg & Henry, 1941). Accused witches sometimes confessed to speaking with the devil, flying on the backs of animals, and other unusual behaviors. Such people may have been experiencing delusions (false beliefs) or hallucinations (unreal perceptual experiences), which are signs of some psychological disorders. Accused witches were also said to have a devil's mark on their bodies, which was often invisible but was insensitive to even the most severe pain. Professional "witch prickers" would poke accused witches all over their bodies to find the devil's mark, and areas of insensitivity were found in some of the accused. Psychiatric historians have interpreted this insensitivity as a sign of hysteria or self-hypnosis.

Yet, many of the confessions of accused witches may have been extracted through brutal torture or under the promise of a stay of execution in exchange for confession (Spanos, 1978). The accused witches' supposed insensitivity to pain indeed could have been real but may have been due to poor nutrition and ill health, common in medieval times, as opposed to any influence of the devil. Professional witch prickers were also known to use techniques to make it falsely appear that a person was insensitive to pain. For example, some witch prickers used collapsible needles attached to hollow shafts. When the needle was pressed against the accused's body, it collapsed into the hollow shaft, making it appear that the needle pierced deeply into the accused's flesh without inducing pain.

Accusations of witchcraft were also used as a means of social punishment or control. For example, in 1581, Johann Klenke was accused of witchcraft by the mayor of his town. This accusation came after Klenke had lent the mayor money and then insisted on having it paid back (Rosen, 1968). In England, during the sixteenth and seventeenth centuries, persons accused of

being witches were typically older women, unmarried and poor, who often begged for food and money, and were considered by their neighbors to be foul mouthed and disgusting. These women sometimes cultivated the myth that they were witches to frighten their neighbors into giving them money. This ploy could backfire, however, if their neighbors attributed some misfortune to a spell cast by the self-acclaimed witch. The woman would be arrested and the neighbor could be rid of her.

Change Comes from Within

Still, there were some people who truly believed they themselves were witches. These people may have been suffering from mental disorders. Indeed, even during the witch hunts, some physicians risked condemnation by the Church and even death by arguing that accused witches were suffering from mental illnesses. In 1563, Johann Weyer published *The Deception of Dreams*, in which he argued that the people accused of being witches were suffering from melancholy (depression) and senility. The Church banned Weyer's writings, however, and he was scorned by many of his peers. Twenty years later, Reginald Scot in his *Discovery of Witchcraft* (1584) supported Weyer's beliefs: "These women are but diseased wretches suffering from melancholy, and their words, actions, reasoning, and gestures show that sickness has affected their brains and impaired their powers of judgment" (Castiglioni, 1946, p. 253). Again, the Church, and this time the State, refuted the arguments and banned Scot's writings.

As is often the case, change came from within. In the sixteenth century, Teresa of Avila, a Spanish nun who was later canonized, explained that the mass hysteria that had broken out among a group of nuns was not the work of the devil but the effect of infirmities or sickness. She argued that these nuns were *comas enfermas,* or "as if sick." She sought out natural causes for the nuns' strange behaviors and concluded that they were due to melancholy, a weak imagination, or drowsiness and sleepiness (Sarbin & Juhasz, 1967).

However, it is also possible that some people who truly believed they were witches were not suffering from mental disorders. The culture in which they lived so completely accepted the existence of witches and witchcraft that these people may simply have used these cultural beliefs to explain their own feelings and behaviors, even when these feelings and behaviors were not components of some type of mental disorder. In addition, most writings of medieval times and Renaissance times, including writings from the witch-hunt period in Salem, Massachusetts, clearly distinguish between people who are mad and people who are witches. This distinction between madness and witchcraft continues to this day in cultures that believe in witchcraft.

Psychic Epidemics

During the Middle Ages, reports of dance frenzies or manias were frequent. A monk, Peter of Herental, described a rash of dance frenzies that broke out over a four-month period in 1374 in Germany:

> Both men and women were abused by the devil to such a degree that they danced in their homes, in the churches and in the streets, holding each other's hands and leaping in the air. While they danced they called out the names of demons, such as Friskes and others, but they were unaware of this nor did they pay attention to modesty even though people watched them. At the end of the dance, they felt such pains in the chest, that if their friends did not tie linen clothes tightly around their waists, they cried out like madmen that they were dying. (Rosen, 1968, pp. 196–197)

Other instances of dance frenzy were reported in 1428 during the feast of Saint Vitus, at Schaffhausen, at which a monk danced himself to death. Again in 1518, a large epidemic of uncontrolled dance frenzy occurred at the chapel of Saint Vitus at Hohlenstein, near Zabern. According to one account, more than 400 people danced during the four-week period the frenzy lasted. Some writers of the time began to call the frenzied dancing *Saint Vitus' dance*.

A similar phenomenon was *tarantism*, which was seen in Italy as early as the fourteenth century but became prominent in the seventeenth century. People would suddenly develop an acute pain, which they attributed to the bite of a tarantula. They would jump around and dance wildly in the streets, tearing at their clothes and beating each other with whips. Some people would dig holes in the earth and roll on the

This picture of "moonstruck" women dancing frenetically in seventeenth-century France illustrates one type of psychic epidemic.

ground; others howled and made obscene gestures. At the time, many people interpreted dance frenzies and tarantism as the results of possession by the devil. The behaviors may have been the remnants of ancient rituals performed by people worshipping the Greek god Dionysus.

Although dance frenzies and similar **psychic epidemics** were observed frequently in the Middle Ages, this phenomenon is not confined to that period in history. Other groups in which dance frenzies or similar behavior patterns were observed later, in the eighteenth century, were religious sects. These included the Shakers, the mystical Russian sects such as the Chlysti, certain Jewish sects, congregations of the early Methodist movement, and the Quakers. During religious services, members of these sects might become so emotionally charged that they would jerk around violently, running, singing, screaming, and dancing. This type of religious service tended to be more popular among people suffering great economic and social deprivation and alienation. The enthusiastic expression of religious fervor can act as a welcome release from the tensions and stresses of simply trying to survive in a hostile world.

Even today, we see episodes of psychic epidemics. On February 8, 1991, a number of students and teachers in a high school in Rhode Island thought they smelled noxious fumes coming from the ventilation system. The first person to detect these fumes, a 14-year-old girl, fell to the floor, crying and saying that her stomach hurt and her eyes stung. Other students and the teacher in that room then began to experience symptoms. They were moved into the hallway with a great deal of commotion. Soon, students and teachers from adjacent rooms, who could clearly see into the hallway, began to experience symptoms. Eventually, 21 people (17 students and 4 teachers) were admitted to the local hospital emergency room. All were hyperventilating, and most complained of dizziness, headache, and nausea. Although some of them initially showed symptoms of mild carbon monoxide intoxication in blood tests, no evidence of toxic gas in the school could be found. The physicians treating the children and teachers concluded that the outbreak was a case of mass hysteria prompted by the fear of chemical warfare during the Persian Gulf War. (Rockney & Lemke, 1992).

Psychic epidemics are no longer viewed as the result of spirit possession or the bite of a tarantula. Rather, psychologists attempt to understand them using research from social psychology about the influence of others on individuals' self-perceptions. The social context can affect even our perceptions of our own body, as we shall see when we discuss people's differing reactions to psychoactive substances, such as marijuana (see Chapter 17) and people's interpretations of physiological arousal in their bodies (see Chapters 6, 11, and 17).

The Growth of Asylums During the Renaissance

As early as the twelfth century, many towns in Europe took some responsibility for housing and caring for people considered mentally ill (Kroll, 1973). Remarkable among these towns was Gheel, in Belgium, where townspeople regularly took into their homes the mentally ill who came to the shrine of Saint Dymphna for cures.

General hospitals began to include special rooms or facilities for people with mental disorders in about the eleventh or twelfth century. In 1326, a *Dollhaus* (madhouse) was constructed as part of the George-hospital at Elbing. In 1375, a *Tollkiste* (mad cell) was mentioned in the municipal records of Hamburg (Kroll, 1973). Unlike the humane treatment people with mental disorders received in places like Gheel, treatment in these early hospitals was far from humane. The mentally ill were little more than inmates, housed against their will, often in extremely harsh conditions. One of the most famous of these hospitals was the Hospital of Saint Mary of Bethlehem, in London, which officially became a mental hospital in 1547. This hospital, nicknamed *Bedlam*, was famous for its deplorable conditions, which were highlighted in Shakespeare's *King Lear*:

> "Bedlam beggers, who, with roaring voices . . . Sometimes with lunatic bans, sometimes with prayers enforce their charity." (*King Lear*, Act II, Scene iii)

Shakespeare is referring to the practice of forcing patients at this hospital to beg in the streets for money. At Bedlam and other mental hospitals established in Europe in the sixteenth, seventeenth, and eighteenth centuries patients were exhibited to the public for a fee. They lived in filth and confinement, often chained to walls or locked in small boxes. The following description of the treatment of patients in La Bicetre Hospital in Paris provides an example of typical care:

> The patients were ordinarily shackled to the walls of their dark, unlighted cells by iron collars which held them flat against the wall and permitted little movement. Ofttimes there were also iron hoops around the waists of the patients and both their hands and feet were chained. Although these chains usually permitted enough movement that the patients could feed themselves out of bowls, they often kept them from being able to lie down at night. Since little was known about dietetics, and the patients were presumed to be

"Bedlam"—the Hospital of St. Mary of Bethlehem—was famous for the chaotic and deplorable conditions in which people with mental disorders were kept.

animals anyway, little attention was paid to whether they were adequately fed or whether the food was good or bad. The cells were furnished only with straw and were never swept or cleaned; the patient remained in the midst of all the accumulated ordure. No one visited the cells except at feeding time, no provision was made for warmth, and even the most elementary gestures of humanity were lacking. (Adapted from Selling, 1940, pp. 54–55)

The laws regarding the confinement of the mentally ill in Europe and the United States were concerned with the protection of the public and the ill person's relatives (Busfield, 1986; Scull, 1993). For example, Dalton's 1618 edition of the *Common Law* states that "It is lawful for the parents, kinsmen or other friends of a man that is mad, or frantic . . . to take him and put him into a house, to bind or chain him, and to beat him with rods, and to do any other forcible act to reclaim him, or to keep him so he shall do no hurt" (Alldderidge, 1979). The first *Act for Regulating Madhouses* in England was not passed until 1774, with the intention of cleaning up the deplorable conditions in hospitals and madhouses and protecting people from being unjustly jailed for insanity. This act provided for the licensing and inspection of madhouses and required that a physician, surgeon, or apothecary sign a certificate before a patient could be admitted. These provisions applied only to paying patients in private madhouses, however, and not to the poor people confined to workhouses for lunatics.

The conditions of asylums in America were not much better. In 1756, Benjamin Franklin helped to establish the Pennsylvania Hospital in Philadelphia, which included some cells or wards for mental patients. In 1773, the Public Hospital in Williamsburg, Virginia, became the first hospital exclusively for the mentally ill. The treatment of patients, although designed to restore health and balance to the mind, included powerful electrical shocks, plunging into ice water or hot water, starvation, and heavy use of restraints (Bennett, 1947).

It is worth noting that these asylums typically were established and run by people who thought that mental disorders were medical illnesses. For example, Benjamin Rush (1745–1813), one of the founders of American psychiatry, believed that abnormal behavior was caused by excessive blood in the brain and thus prescribed bleeding the patient—drawing huge amounts of blood from the body. Thus, although the demonology and witchcraft theories of the Middle Ages have often been decried as leading to brutal treatment of people with mental illnesses, the medical theories of those times and the next couple of centuries did not necessarily lead to much more gentle treatment, largely because these treatments were based on beliefs and understandings about anatomy and physiology that we now know to be incorrect.

Moral Treatment in the Eighteenth Century

Fortunately, the eighteenth and nineteenth centuries saw the growth of a movement toward a more humane treatment of the mentally ill. This new form of treatment was based on the psychological view that people become mad because they are separated from nature and succumb to the stresses imposed by the rapid social changes of the period (Rosen, 1968). This was a heavily psychological theory of mental disorders, which suggested that the appropriate treatment for madness is rest and relaxation in a serene and physically appealing place.

In 1796, Quaker William Tuke (1732–1819) opened a new asylum in England called The Retreat, in direct response to the brutal treatment he saw being delivered to people with mental disorders at other facilities. Tuke's intent was to provide a "mild system of treatment," which he referred to as **moral treatment** (Busfield, 1986; Porter, 1988). This treatment was designed to restore patients' self-restraint by treating them with respect and dignity and encouraging them to exercise self-control.

One of the most militant crusaders for a moral treatment of the insane was Dorothea Dix (1802–1877). A retired schoolteacher living in Boston in 1841, Dix discovered the negligence and brutality that characterized the treatment of poor people with mental disorders, many of whom were simply warehoused in jails, while visiting a jail on a cold Sunday morning to teach a Sunday School class to women inmates.

Following the lesson, Miss Dix focused her attention on conditions in the jail. Prostitutes, drunks, criminals, retarded individuals, and the mentally

Dorothea Dix crusaded for moral treatment of mental patients in the United States.

ill were housed together in unheated, unfurnished, and foul-smelling quarters. Inmates without adequate clothing were huddled and shivering in the chill March New England climate. The conditions offended all the senses. When Dorothea Dix asked why heat was not provided, she was informed that the insane do not feel heat and cold. (Viney & Zorich, 1982, p. 212)

That began Dix's tireless quest to improve the treatment of people with mental disorders. Dix was armed with dogged determinism and considerable political savvy, and went from state to state, speaking to legislators and laypeople, about the conditions in mental hospitals. Dix's lobbying efforts led to the passage of laws and appropriations to fund the clean-up of mental hospitals and the training of mental-health professionals dedicated to the moral treatment of patients. Between 1841 and 1881, she personally helped to establish over 30 mental institutions in the United States, Canada, Newfoundland, and Scotland. Hundreds more public hospitals for the insane were established during this period by others and run according to humanitarian perspectives.

Another leader of the moral treatment of people with abnormality was Philippe Pinel (1745–1826), a French physician, who was put in charge of La Bicêtre, an asylum in Paris for male patients, in 1793. Pinel argued, "To detain maniacs in constant seclusion and to load them with chains; to leave them defenceless, to the brutality of underlings . . . in a word, to rule them with a rod of iron . . . is a system of superintendence, more distinguished for its convenience than for its humanity or success" (Grob, 1994, p. 27). Pinel rejected supernatural theories of abnormality, and believed that many forms of abnormality could be cured by restoring the dignity and tranquility of patients.

Phillipe Pinel, a leader in the moral movement in France, helped to free mental patients from the horrible conditions of the hospitals.

Pinel ordered that patients be released from their chains and allowed walk freely around the asylum. They were provided with clean and sunny rooms, comfortable sleeping quarters, and good food. Nurses and professional therapists were trained to work with the patients, to help them restore their sense of tranquility, and to help them engage in planned social activities. Although many other physicians thought Pinel himself was mad for releasing the patients, his approach was remarkably successful. Many people who had been locked away in darkness for decades became able to control their behavior and re-engage in life. Some improved so much they could be released. Pinel later reformed a mental hospital in Paris for female patients, La Salpetrière, and had remarkable success there as well.

Unfortunately, the moral treatment movement grew too fast. As more asylums were built, and more people went into these asylums, the capacity of the asylums to recruit mental-health professionals, and to maintain a humane and individual approach to each patient, declined (Grob, 1994; Scull, 1993). The physicians, nurses, and other caretakers simply did not have enough time to give each patient the calm and dedicated attention he or she needed. The fantastic successes of the early moral treatment movement gave way to more modest successes, and many outright failures, as patients remained impaired or got even worse. Even some patients who received the best of moral treatment could not benefit from it because their problems were not due to a loss of dignity or tranquility. Because so many patients were being given the moral treatment, the number of patients who failed to benefit from it became larger, and questions about the effectiveness of moral treatment grew louder.

At the same time, the rapid pace of immigration into the United States in the late nineteenth century meant that an increasing percentage of asylum patients were from different cultures, and often were of lower socioeconomic classes. Prejudice against these "foreigners," combined with increasing attention to the failures of moral treatment to cure many patients, led to declines in public support for funding of these institutions. This led to even greater decline in the quality of care given to patients. By the turn of the century, many public hospitals were no better than warehouses, where patients were kept in restraints for long periods of time simply to control their behavior (Grob, 1994; McGovern, 1985; Scull, 1993).

Effective biological treatments were not developed for most major mental disorders until well into the twentieth century. Until these treatments were developed, mental patients who could not afford private care were basically warehoused in large state institutions and not given the psychological and social rehabilitation prescribed by the moral management theories. These institutions were often overcrowded and isolated far from cities or towns. The physical isolation of the mental hospitals contributed to the slow progress in the application of medical advances to the treatment of mental disorders (Deutsch, 1937). *Extraordinary People:* Clifford Beers highlights one man who suffered the conditions of mental hospitals at the turn of the twentieth century, survived them, and was instrumental in changing them.

Summing Up

- There are three types of theories that have influenced the definition and treatment of abnormality over the ages: the natural theories, the psychological theories, and the supernatural theories.

- Stone Age people probably viewed mental disorders as the result of supernatural forces. They may have drilled holes in the skulls of sufferers—a procedure known as trephination—to release the evil forces causing the mental disorders.

- Some of the earliest written references to mental disorders can be found in Chinese medical texts around 2674 B.C. and then in the papyri of Egypt and Mesopotamia, in the Old Testament, and in the writings of Greek and Roman philosophers and physicians. Mental disorders were often described as medical disorders in these ancient writings, although there is also evidence that they were viewed as due to supernatural forces.

- The witch hunts began in the late Middle Ages. Some accused witches may have suffered from mental disorders.

- Psychic epidemics have occurred throughout history. They were formerly explained as due to spirit possession, but are now seen as the result of

EXTRAORDINARY PEOPLE

Clifford Beers: A Mind That Found Itself

Clifford Beers was always an energetic child, moody, with little self-control. Still, he was intelligent and ambitious enough to do well in school and eventually graduated from Yale University. As a teenager, however, Beers' moodiness increased, particularly after his brother Sam began to have severe, convulsive seizures. These seizures were diagnosed as epilepsy (but were probably due to a massive brain tumor discovered upon the brother's death). Clifford Beers developed a morbid fear that he would be overcome with epilepsy. In March 1890, as his brother apparently lay dying in the family home, Beers' moodiness grew to despair, accompanied by deep paranoia. By June, Beers' despair was so great that he became unable to speak. He began contemplating suicide and eventually jumped out a fourth-floor window. He escaped with only broken bones. Beers' obsession with becoming epileptic passed with this incident but was replaced with other paranoid and grandiose beliefs.

Beers was hospitalized, first in a private mental hospital, but later in public mental hospitals when his family ran out of money. His mood alternated between depression and manic excitement. In the early 1900s, there were no drugs that significantly affected manic-depression. Beers endured some of the drugs of the day—strychnine and arsenic tonics. He also was beaten, choked, locked away for long periods in dark, cold cells with no clothes, and put in a straitjacket for up to 21 days. Beers wrote volumes about the hospital conditions. Amazingly, he did not criticize the hospital attendants for cruelty or brutality, but for ignorance and incompetence:

> He realized that because they were poorly supervised and completely untrained, these uninformed, uneducated men, even with the few with good intentions, were easily tempted by the helplessness and unruliness of the patients into gross laziness, neglect, and brutality. Unable to compete for jobs in the outside world, they were trapped together with the patients in a vicious circle of violence. (Dain, 1980, pp. 39–40)

During his hospitalization, Beers wrote hundreds of letters to his family and also to public officials describing the need for better care for the "insane."

Over that three years of hospitalization, Beers' mood swings became less severe, and in 1903 he was declared recovered enough to be released. Beers continued the campaign he had begun in the hospital to change the system of caring for people with mental disorders. He wrote a personal account of his time in the mental hospitals, which was published in 1908 as *A Mind That Found Itself*. This book forever changed how physicians and the lay public viewed mental patients and hospitals. He argued that all mental disorders were medical diseases and should be treated biologically, a view that came to be known as the **mental hygiene movement.** Beers outlined a plan for reforms in the treatment of the mentally ill and for the prevention of mental illness. He advocated public education about mental illness and early treatment for those who were afflicted. One of Beers' supporters was Dr. Adolph Meyer, who was himself revolutionizing the treatment of mental patients by advocating the treatment of the "whole individual," including assisting former mental patients in their reintegration into society. Beers eventually founded the National and International Committees on Mental Hygiene, and became a powerful fund-raiser and lobbyist for the rights of mental patients.

In *A Mind That Found Itself*, Beers explained his motivations and drive to use his experiences to change the lives of others who suffered from psychological disorders:

> When I set out upon a career of reform, I was impelled to do so by motives in part like those which seem to have possessed Don Quixote when he set forth, as Cervantes says, with the intention "of righting every kind of wrong, and exposing himself to peril and danger, from which in the issue he would obtain eternal renown and fame." In likening myself to Cervantes' mad hero my purpose is quite other than to push myself within the charmed circle of the chivalrous. What I wish to do is to make plain that a man abnormally elated may be swayed irresistibly by his best instincts, and that while under the spell of an exaltation, idealistic in degree, he may not only be willing, but eager to assume risks and endure hardships which under normal conditions he would assume reluctantly, if at all. In justice to myself, however, I may remark that my plans for reform have

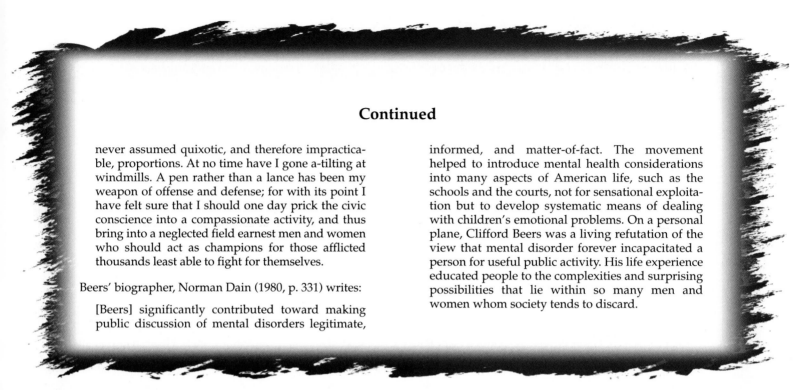

Continued

never assumed quixotic, and therefore impracticable, proportions. At no time have I gone a-tilting at windmills. A pen rather than a lance has been my weapon of offense and defense; for with its point I have felt sure that I should one day prick the civic conscience into a compassionate activity, and thus bring into a neglected field earnest men and women who should act as champions for those afflicted thousands least able to fight for themselves.

Beers' biographer, Norman Dain (1980, p. 331) writes:

[Beers] significantly contributed toward making public discussion of mental disorders legitimate,

informed, and matter-of-fact. The movement helped to introduce mental health considerations into many aspects of American life, such as the schools and the courts, not for sensational exploitation but to develop systematic means of dealing with children's emotional problems. On a personal plane, Clifford Beers was a living refutation of the view that mental disorder forever incapacitated a person for useful public activity. His life experience educated people to the complexities and surprising possibilities that lie within so many men and women whom society tends to discard.

the effects of the social context on people's self-perceptions.

- In the eighteenth and nineteenth centuries, advocates of more gentle treatment of people with mental disorders began to establish asylums for these people.

- The humanitarian movement focused on providing people with mental disorders with clean and safe living conditions and humane treatment.

○ THE EMERGENCE OF MODERN PERSPECTIVES

Although the treatment of people with mental disorders at the turn of the twentieth century had declined somewhat, tremendous advances in the scientific study of disorders were being made in the early twentieth century. These laid the groundwork for the biological, psychological, and social theories of abnormality that now dominate psychology and psychiatry.

The Beginnings of Modern Biological Perspectives

Basic knowledge of the anatomy, physiology, neurology, and chemistry of the body was increasing rapidly in the late nineteenth century. With the advancement

of this basic knowledge came increasing focus on biological causes of abnormality. The German psychiatrist Wilhelm Griesinger (1817–1868) published *The Pathology and Therapy of Psychic Disorders* in 1845, the first systematic argument that all mental disorders could be explained in terms of brain pathology. One of Griesinger's followers, Emil Kraepelin (1856–1926), also published a textbook emphasizing the importance of brain pathology in mental disorders in 1883. More

Emil Kraepelin (1856–1926). Emil Kraepelin developed a classification system for mental disorders that remains very influential today.

PUSHING THE BOUNDARIES

Can Germs Cause Mental Disorders?

Although the discovery that the syphilis infection caused the psychological symptoms of general paresis helped to launch modern biological approaches to mental disorders, germ theories of mental disorders have not been prominent throughout the last century. Instead, biological theories have focused largely on genetics or on the structure or functioning of the brain.

In recent years, however, some scientists have reevaluated the potential role of infectious agents in producing major mental disorders (for a review, see Hooper, 1999). One argument against genetic theories and in favor of germ theories of mental disorders is that these disorders are just too common to have survived natural selection's pressures on genes to maximize fitness. That is, severe mental disorders, such as schizophrenia or severe depression, impair the ability of individuals to reproduce. If individuals do not reproduce, their genes do not proliferate, and the disorders carried by their genes should become rare over time. Major mental disorders are relatively common among humans, in fact, so common that some scientists believe that ordinary germs must play a role in producing them.

There is some evidence for this view. In the early 1990s, a syndrome known as pediatric autoimmune neuropsychiatric disorders associated with streptococcus, or PANDAS, was recognized. A streptococcal infection, if left untreated, can make its way to the brain and attack a region called the basal ganglia, causing clumsiness and arm-flapping movements, along with obsessions, compulsions, and senseless rituals. Susan Swedo, a scientist at the National Institute of Mental Health, noticed the similarities between these effects of untreated streptococcal infection and obsessive-compulsive disorder, or OCD, in children (see Chapter 7). It turns out that some children with OCD get better when they are treated with drugs that rid their bodies of streptococcal infections.

As we discuss in Chapter 10, there is evidence that schizophrenia, a serious mental disorder in which people lose touch with reality, is more common in people whose mothers had measles while pregnant with them, or who lived in geographical regions with high flu rates while pregnant. One way to understand these trends is that something about exposure to the measles or flu virus changed the development of some fetus's brains, contributing to the development of schizophrenia.

Germ theories of mental disorders certainly are not prominent in modern biological perspectives, but they are gaining strength. If a germ theory of any mental disorder can be sufficiently supported, this suggests that preventative efforts could be better directed toward vulnerable populations who have more exposure to disorder-causing germs, thereby reducing their likelihood of developing the disorder.

---

importantly, Kraepelin developed a scheme of classifying symptoms into discrete mental disorders that has stood the test of time and is the basis for our modern classification systems. Having a good classification system gives investigators a common set of labels for disorders, and a set of criteria for distinguishing between one disorder and another. This contributes immensely to the advancement of scientific study of the disorders.

One of the single most important discoveries underpinning modern biological theories of abnormality was the discovery of the cause of **general paresis,** a disease that led to paralysis and insanity, and eventually death. In the mid 1800s, reports that patients with paresis also had a history of syphilis led to the suspicion that syphilis might be a cause of paresis. In 1897, Viennese psychiatrist Richard Krafft-Ebing conducted a daring experiment that would not pass scientific ethics boards today. He injected paretic patients with matter from syphilis sores. None of the patients developed syphilis, and Krafft-Ebing concluded that they must already have been infected with syphilis. The discovery that syphilis was the cause of one form of insanity lent great weight to the idea that biological factors could cause mental disorders.

As we shall discuss in more detail in Chapter 2, modern biological theories of the mental disorders have focused on the role of genetics, structural abnormalities in the brain, and biochemical imbalances. In the *Pushing the Boundaries:* Can Germs Cause Mental Disorders? (p. 21), we describe recent attempts to return to germ theories of mental disorders that harken back to Krafft-Ebing's discovery of the role of syphilis in general paresis.

The Psychoanalytic Perspective

The development of psychoanalytic theory begins with the odd story of Franz Anton Mesmer (1734–1815). Mesmer was an Austrian physician who believed that people had a magnetic fluid in the body and this fluid had to be distributed in a particular pattern in order to maintain health. The distribution of magnetic fluid in one person could be influenced by the magnetic forces of other people, as well as by the alignments of the planets. In 1778, Mesmer opened a clinic in Paris to treat all sorts of diseases by "animal magnetism." The psychological disorders that were the focus of much of Mesmer's treatment were the **hysterical disorders,** in which people lose functioning or feeling in some part of the body for no apparent physiological reason. The patients sat in darkness around a tub containing various chemicals, the affected areas of their bodies prodded by iron rods emerging from the tub. With music playing, Mesmer emerged in an elaborate robe, touching each patient as he passed by, supposedly realigning people's magnetic fluids through his own powerful magnetic force. This process, Mesmer said, cured illness, including psychological disorders.

Mesmer was eventually labeled a charlatan by a scientific review committee that included Benjamin Franklin. Yet, his methods, known as **mesmerism,** continued to fuel debate long after he faded into obscurity. The "cures" Mesmer caused in his psychiatric patients were attributed to the trancelike state that Mesmer seemed to induce in his patients. Later, this state was relabeled *hypnosis.* Under hypnosis, Mesmer's patients appeared very suggestible, and the suggestion that their ailments would disappear seemed enough to make them actually disappear.

The connection between hypnosis and hysteria fascinated several leading scientists of the time, although not all scientists accepted this connection. In particular, Jean Charcot (1825–1893), head of La Salpetrière Hospital in Paris and the leading neurologist of his time, argued that hysteria was caused by degeneration in the brain and had nothing to do with hypnosis. The work of two physicians practicing in the French town of Nancy, Hippolyte-Marie Bernheim (1840–1919) and Ambroise-Auguste Liebault (1823–1904), eventually won Charcot over, however. Bernheim and Liebault argued that hysteria is caused by self-hypnosis. They showed that they could induce the symptoms of hysteria, such as paralysis in an arm or the loss of feeling in a leg, by suggesting these symptoms to patients who were hypnotized. Fortunately, they could also remove these symptoms under hypnosis. Charcot was so impressed by the evidence that hysteria had psychological roots that he became a leading researcher of psychological causes of mental disorders. The experiments of Bernheim and Liebault, and the leadership of Charcot, did a great deal to advance psychological perspectives on abnormality.

One of Charcot's students was Sigmund Freud (1856–1939), a Viennese neurologist. He went to study with Charcot in 1885, and in this work became convinced that much of the mental life of an individual remains hidden from consciousness. This view was further supported by Freud's interactions with Pierre Janet (1858–1947) in Paris, who was investigating multiple personalities—people who appeared to have multiple distinct personalities, each of which operated independently of the others, often not knowing the others existed (Matarazzo, 1985).

When he returned to Vienna, Freud worked with another physician who was interested in hypnosis and the unconscious processes behind psychological problems, Josef Breuer (1842–1925). Breuer had discovered that encouraging patients to talk about their problems while under hypnosis led to a great upswelling and release of emotion, which was eventually called **catharsis.** The patient's discussion of his or her problems under hypnosis was less censored than conscious discussion, allowing the therapist to more easily elicit important psychological material.

Breuer and Freud collaborated on a paper published in 1893 as *On the Psychical Mechanisms of Hysterical Phemonena,* which laid out their discoveries about hypnosis, the unconscious, and the therapeutic value of catharsis. This paper proved to be a foundation stone in the development of **psychoanalysis,** the study of the unconscious. Freud introduced his ideas to America in a series of lectures in 1909 at Clark University, at the invitation of G. Stanley Hall, one of the founders of American psychology.

Freud went on to write dozens of papers and books describing his theory of psychoanalysis, and became the best-known figure in psychiatry and psychology. The impact of Freud's theories on the development of psychology over the next century cannot be underestimated. Freudian ideas influenced not only the professional literature on psychopathology, but are

Anton Mesmer (1734–1815). Anton Mesmer's work on animal magnetism set the stage for the study of hypnosis.

John Watson (1878–1958). Behaviorist John Watson believed that all behavior, including abnormal behavior, was the result of the person's history of rewards and punishments.

used heavily in literary theory, anthropology, and other humanities, and pervade popular notions of psychological processes to this day.

The Roots of Behaviorism

In what seems now like a parallel universe, while psychoanalytic theory was being born, the roots of behaviorism were being planted in Europe and then the United States. Willhelm Wundt (1832–1920) established the first experimental psychology laboratory in 1879 in Leipzig. His work focused on memory and sensation but he and others developed many basic experimental techniques that are the mainstay of behavioral experimentation. In 1896, one of Wundt's students, Lightner Witmer (1867–1956) established the first psychological clinic at the University of Pennsylvania to study the causes and treatment of mental deficiency in children. Witmer thus brought the experimental techniques of the new behaviorism to bear on an important clinical issue—the functioning of children.

Ivan Pavlov (1849–1936), a Russian physiologist, was also developing methods and theories to understand behavior in terms of stimuli and responses, rather than in terms of the internal workings of the unconscious mind. He discovered that dogs could be conditioned to salivate to stimuli other than food if the food was paired with these other stimuli—a process later called *classical conditioning*. Pavlov's discoveries inspired John Watson (1878–1958) to study important human behaviors, such as phobias, in terms of classical conditioning (see Chapter 6). He rejected psychoanalytic and biological theories of abnormal behaviors such as phobias, and explained them entirely on the basis of the individual's history

of conditioning. Watson went so far as to boast that he could train any healthy child to become any kind of adult one wished:

> Give me a dozen healthy infants, well-formed, and my own specified world to bring them up in, and I'll guarantee to take any one at random and train him to be any type of specialist I might select—doctor, lawyer, artist, merchant-chief, and yes, even beggar-man and thief, regardless of his talents, penchants, tendencies, abilities, vocations, and the race of his ancestors. (Watson, 1930, p. 104)

In the meantime, two other psychologists, E. L. Thorndike (1874–1949) and then B. F. Skinner (1904–1990) were studying how the consequences of behaviors shape their likelihood of recurrence. They argued that behaviors that are followed by positive consequences will be more likely to be repeated than behaviors followed by negative consequences. This process came to be known as *operant* or *instrumental conditioning*. This idea may seem simple to us now (which is one sign how much it has influenced thinking over the last century) but the argument that even complex behaviors such as violence against others could be explained by the reinforcement or punishment these behaviors have had in the past was radical at the time.

Behaviorism—the study of the impact of reinforcements and punishments on behavior—has had as profound an impact on psychology and on our common knowledge of psychology as has psychoanalytic theory. We shall see that many types of therapy that are useful in the treatment of various disorders emerge out of behaviorism.

The Cognitive Revolution

In the 1950s, some experimental psychologists began to argue that behaviorism was limited in its explanatory power by its refusal to look at some of the internal thought processes that mediated the relationship between stimulus and response. It wasn't until the 1970s that psychology shifted its focus substantially to the study of **cognitions**—thought processes that influence behavior and emotion. An important player in the cognitive revolution was Albert Bandura, a clinical psychologist trained in behaviorism who had contributed a great deal to the application of behaviorism to psychopathology (see Chapters 2 and 6). Bandura argued that people's beliefs about whether they could execute the behaviors necessary to control important events—which he called **self-efficacy beliefs**—were crucial in determining their well-being. Again, this seems like an obvious notion to us now, but that is only because it took hold of both professional psychology and lay notions of psychology.

Another key figure in the cognitive revolution was Albert Ellis, who argued that people prone to psychological disorders are plagued by irrational negative assumptions about themselves and the world. Ellis developed a therapy for emotional problems based on his theory, called Rational Emotive Therapy. This therapy was controversial because it required therapists to challenge, sometimes quite harshly, their patients' irrational belief systems. It became very popular, however, and moved psychology into the study of the thought processes behind serious emotional problems. Another therapy focused on the irrational thoughts of people with psychological problems was developed by Aaron Beck. Beck's Cognitive Therapy has become one of the widest used therapies for a wide range of disorders (see Chapters 2 and 5).

Integrative Theories

Although the biological and the more psychological theories of abnormality have traditionally been viewed as competing with each other for which one best explains psychological disorders, many clinicians and researchers now believe that theories that integrate biological, psychological, and social perspectives on abnormality will prove most valid and useful. We will highlight these integrated theories throughout each chapter of this book and in special Bio-Psycho-Social Integrations, at the end of each of the following chapters.

What about supernatural theories? Most cultures still have *spiritual healers* of one type or another. As we consider cross-cultural perspectives on psychological disorders, we will note the supernatural theories some cultures hold about abnormality and the healing rituals that emerge from these theories. However, even in cultures in which most healers do not subscribe to supernatural theories of abnormality, laypeople often still believe in the power of supernatural forces to cause or cure their psychological problems. These lay beliefs influence what type of healer a person with a psychological problem might seek out and how he or she might present the psychological problem to a potential therapist. Thus, even though supernatural theories may not be believed by therapists, they arise in the practice of treating people with psychological problems because these clients bring them into discussions with their therapists.

Summing Up

- Modern biological theories and therapies were greatly helped by the development of Kraepelin's classification scheme for mental disorders and the discovery that syphilis causes general paresis, a disease with symptoms including loss of touch with reality.
- The roots of psychoanalytic theory can be found in the work of Mesmer and the suggestion that psychological symptoms could be relieved through hypnosis. Jean Charcot, Sigmund Freud, and Josef Breuer are among the founders of modern psychoanalytic theory, which focuses on the role of the unconscious in psychological symptoms.
- Behavioral approaches to psychopathology began with the development of basic experimental techniques to study the effects of reinforcements and punishments in producing normal, and abnormal behavior.
- Cognitive approaches to abnormality did not emerge until the mid-nineteenth century, when theorists began arguing that the way people think about events in their environment determines their emotional and behavioral responses to those events.

☉ PROFESSIONS WITHIN ABNORMAL PSYCHOLOGY

In our times, there are a number of different professions that are concerned with abnormal or maladaptive behavior. Psychiatry is a branch of medicine that focuses on psychological disorders. Psychiatrists have an M.D. degree and have specialized training in the treatment of psychological problems. Psychiatrists can prescribe medications for the treatment of these problems; some also have been trained to conduct psychotherapies that involve talking with people about their problems. Clinical psychologists typically have a Ph.D. in psychology, with a specialization in psychological problems. Clinical psychologists can conduct psychotherapy, but they do not currently prescribe medications. Many clinical psychologists also conduct research on the causes and appropriate treatments of psychological problems. Marriage and family therapists specialize in helping families, couples, and children overcome problems that are interfering with their well-being. Clinical social workers have a master's degree in social work and often focus on helping people with psychological problems to overcome social conditions contributing to their problems, such as joblessness or homelessness. Psychiatric nurses have a degree in nursing, with a specialization in the treatment of people with severe psychological problems. They often work on inpatient psychiatric wards in hospitals, delivering medical care and certain forms of psychotherapy, such as group therapy to increase patients' contacts with one another.

Dramatic changes are taking place in the field of mental health, due to changes in the funding of mental-health care. Many people in the United States either have no insurance to cover mental-health care, or only limited coverage. The practice of psychiatry has declined in status somewhat over the last two decades, and fewer and fewer students with new M.D.s are pursuing psychiatry (Humphreys, 1996). In contrast, there has been a substantial increase in the number of clinical psychologists, clinical social workers, and marriage and family therapists (Phares, 1992). The increased competition for the mental-health dollar has led to political disagreements between different types of mental health professionals over who has rights to treat what kinds of disorders (Humphreys, 1996).

Each of these professions has its rewards and its limitations. Students who are interested in one or more of these professions often find it helpful to volunteer to be a research assistant in studies of psychological problems or to volunteer to work in a psychiatric clinic or hospital, to learn more about these professions. This type of volunteering can help students determine what type of work within abnormal psychology is most comfortable for them. Some students find tremendous gratification working with people with psychological problems, whereas other students find it more gratifying to conduct research that might answer important questions about psychological problems.

Chapter Summary

- Cultural relativists argue that the norms of a society must be used to determine the normality of a behavior. Others have suggested that unusual behaviors, or behaviors that cause subjective discomfort in a person, should be labeled abnormal. Still others have suggested that only behaviors resulting from mental illness or disease are abnormal. All these criteria have serious limitations, however. Currently, the consensus among professionals in the mental-health field is that behaviors that cause people to suffer distress or that prevent them from functioning in daily life are abnormal. Often these behaviors are referred to as *maladaptive* or *dysfunctional.*

- Historically, theories of abnormality have fallen into one of three categories. Natural or biological theories saw mental disorders as similar to physical diseases, caused by the breakdown of some system of the body. Supernatural theories saw mental disorders as the result of divine intervention, curses, demonic possession, and personal sin. Psychological or stress-related theories saw mental disorders as the results of stress. These three types of theories led to very different types of treatment of people who acted abnormally.

- In prehistoric times, people probably had largely supernatural theories of abnormal behavior, attributing it to demons or ghosts. A treatment for abnormality in the Stone Age may have been to drill holes in the skull to allow demons to depart, a procedure known as trephination.

- Ancient Chinese, Egyptian, and Greek texts suggest they took a natural or biological view of mental disorders, although references to supernatural and psychological theories also can be found.

- During the Middle Ages, mental disorders may have been interpreted as due to witchcraft.

- Throughout history, there have been many examples of psychic epidemics and mass hysterias. Groups of people have shown similar psychological and behavioral symptoms, which usually have been attributed to common stresses or beliefs.

- Even well into the nineteenth and twentieth centuries, people who acted abnormally might be shut away in prisonlike conditions, tortured, starved, and ignored.

- As part of the humanitarian and mental hygiene movements the moral management of mental hospitals became more widespread. Patients in these hospitals were treated with kindness and the best biological treatments available. Effective biological treatments were not available until the mid-twentieth century for most psychological problems, however.

- Modern biological perspectives on mental disorders were advanced by Kraepelin's development of a classification system and the discovery that the syndrome known as general paresis was caused by a syphilis infection.

- The psychoanalytic perspective began with the odd work of Anton Mesmer, but then grew as Jean Charcot, and eventually Sigmund Freud, became interested in the role of the unconscious in producing abnormality.

- Behaviorist views on mental disorders began with the basic work of research such as John Watson and B. F. Skinner, who tried to explain both normal and abnormal behavior in terms of the individual's history of reinforcements and punishments.

- The cognitive revolution was spurred by theorists such as Albert Ellis, Albert Bandura, and Aaron Beck, and focused on the role of thinking processes in abnormality.

- The different professions within abnormal psychology include psychiatrists, psychologists, clinical social workers, and psychiatric nurses.

Key Terms

psychopathology 4	natural theories 10	hysterical disorders 22
context 5	supernatural theories 10	mesmerism 22
cultural relativism 5	psychological theories 10	catharsis 22
gender role expectations 6	trephination 11	psychoanalysis 22
unusualness 7	psychic epidemic 15	behaviorism 23
discomfort 8	moral treatment 17	cognitions 24
mental illness 8	mental hygiene movement 19	self-efficacy beliefs 24
maladaptive 8	general paresis 21	

Critical Thinking Questions

1. Think about people whom you have considered abnormal, unusual, disturbed. What criteria were you using to make this judgment?

2. What are some of the ways the current consensus definitions of abnormality could be misused or exploited?

3. Biological theories and treatments of abnormality were sometimes seen as evil or blasphemous in ancient days. Why might this have happened?

4. What are the modern equivalents of the witch hunts—the singling out of certain groups of people to blame for current societal problems?

5. What are some ways that people considered abnormal in our modern culture are mistreated and ostracized?

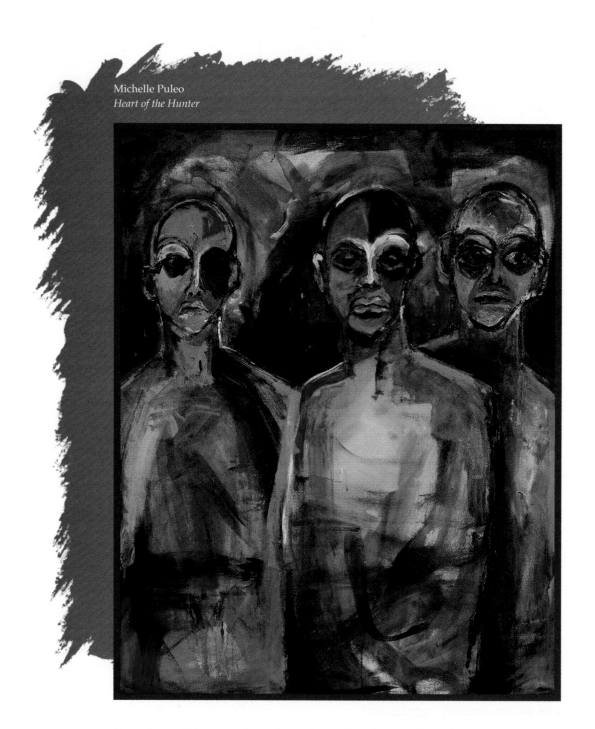

It can be no dishonor to learn from others when they speak good sense.

—*Sophocles, Antigone (442–441 B.C.;*
translated by Elizabeth Wyckoff)

CHAPTER 2

Contemporary Theories of Abnormality

CHAPTER OVERVIEW
Taking Psychology Personally:
How to Learn All These Theories

Biological Approaches
Biological theories suggest that psychological symptoms are due to structural abnormalities in the brain, dysfunctioning of brain neurotransmitter systems, or faulty genes. These three types of biological abnormalities may work independently of each other to create psychological symptoms, or genetic abnormalities may sometimes be the cause of other abnormalities.

Pushing the Boundaries:
rTMS: Mesmer Returns?

Psychological Approaches
Psychodynamic theories of abnormality suggest that psychological symptoms are due to unconscious conflicts. Newer psychodynamic theories focus on concepts of the self that develop from early experiences. Behavioral theories say symptoms result from the reinforcements and punishments people have received for their behaviors. Cognitive theories say that people's ways of interpreting situations determine their emotional and behavioral symptoms. Humanist and existential theories suggest that symptoms arise when people are not allowed to pursue their potential and instead try to conform to others' wishes.

Sociocultural Approaches
Interpersonal theorists focus on the role of interpersonal relationships in shaping normal and abnormal behavior. Family systems theories suggest that psychopathology within individual family members is the result of dysfunctional patterns of interaction within families that encourage and maintain the psychopathology within the individual members. Social structural theorists focus on the influence of structural factors in the environment and culture on individuals' behavior.

Extraordinary People:
Kay Redfield Jamison

Bio-Psycho-Social Integration
Chapter Summary
Key Terms
Critical Thinking Questions

CASE STUDY

Hannah H. is a vibrant, gregarious fifty-two-year-old naturalized American citizen. She was born in Hungary towards the end of World War II. Her parents divorced when she was a baby and she was raised, primarily, by her mother and grandmother, although her mother did remarry when Hannah was eight.

Hannah's mother, Mrs. P., was a prominent woman in the business community in the city where they lived. She had a good bit of money and Hannah went to the best schools and dressed in the best clothes. On the surface, her life seemed serene. However, appearances can be deceiving. Hannah's mother was a difficult, demanding, and judgmental woman. She controlled Hannah's every move, never allowing her an independent thought or movement. She berated her daughter constantly for being fat, stupid, ugly, or selfish. No matter what Hannah tried to do to please her mother, nothing worked.

But this was not the worst of it. Mrs. P. had a serious mental illness in which she had recurrent bouts of suicidal and homicidal feelings. Hannah vividly remembers an incident that occurred when she was about five or six in which her mother was holding her hand as she walked them both into the river near their home, apparently planning to drown them both. Hannah remembers her mother saying, "It's alright, it won't hurt, it will be very peaceful." She remembers crying and struggling, saying, "I don't want to die, mother, please don't." She doesn't remember why her mother stopped, but thinks it was because she remained upset and wouldn't calm down. In those days mental illness carried even more of a stigma than it does today, so Mrs. P.'s family attempted to cover up her illness rather than seek treatment.

When Hannah was ten, her stepfather began to undress and fondle her when no one was around. After about a year of this, Hannah worked up the nerve to tell her mother, who became hysterical and swore she would divorce him. However, after confronting her husband, she became enraged at Hannah and accused her of behaving seductively. She stayed married but saw to it that Hannah was never alone with her stepfather again.

From age ten or eleven on, Hannah suffered from symptoms of panic disorder. These were characterized by difficulty breathing, pain in the chest, and lightheadedness. She was terrified of dying. Gradually these attacks, which lasted from minutes to hours, became more frequent and longer in duration. Despite her suffering with these symptoms for years, she was never taken for treatment.

Hannah married young and bore four children. Her marriage was rocky, to say the least. Following the birth of her last child, she suffered a serious post-partum depression. Her mood gradually worsened, she had difficulty sleeping, and she was horrified to find herself thinking of killing the baby. Hannah was hospitalized and treated with antidepressant medication and psychotherapy. She did well, and gradually stopped taking the medication and attending therapy. (Adapted from Bernheim, 1997, pp. 95–98).

Hannah has far too many reasons to be distressed. She had an abusive and painful childhood. She was in a bad marriage. She had a family history of psychological problems. Which of these factors is the most important in creating Hannah's symptoms?

Your answer to this question depends on your **theoretical approach**, or set of assumptions about the causes of abnormality. If you take a **biological approach** to abnormality, you will suspect that Hannah's symptoms are caused by a biological factor, such as a genetic vulnerability to depression and anxiety, inherited from her mother. If you take a **psychological approach** to abnormality, you will suspect that Hannah's symptoms are rooted in psychological factors, such as her early childhood experiences and her self-concept. If you take a **social approach**, you would look to Hannah's interpersonal relationships and the social environment in which she has lived her life for the sources of her symptoms.

Traditionally, biological, psychological, and sociocultural approaches have been seen as incompatible with one another. People frequently ask, "Is the cause of this disorder biological *or* psychological *or* social?" This is often called the **nature-nurture question**—is the cause of the disorder something in the *nature* or biology of the person, or in the *nurturing* or history of events to which the person was exposed. This question implies that there has to be one cause of a disorder, rather than multiple causes. Indeed, most theories of psychological disorders over history have searched for the one factor—the one gene, the one traumatic experience, the one personality trait—that causes people to develop that disorder.

Many contemporary theorists recognize that there are often many pathways that all lead to the same end, namely the development of a specific disorder (see Figure 2.1). In some cases, it may only take one of these factors to cause a disorder. In most cases, however, it

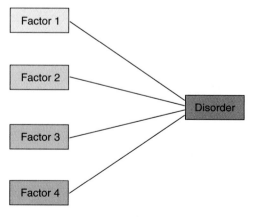

FIGURE 2.1 Many Pathways to Disorder. Several different factors can cause a given disorder.

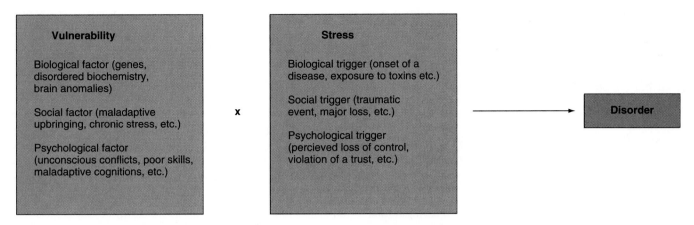

FIGURE 2.2   The Vulnerability-Stress Model of the Development of Disorders. The vulnerability-stress model says that it takes both an existing vulnerability to a disorder and some trigger or stressor to create the disorder.

may take an accumulation of a number of these factors before an individual develops the disorder (Sameroff, 1995). Just one or two of the factors working together may not be enough to create the disorder, but when several of these factors are present in the life of an individual, a threshold is reached, and the disorder will develop.

Biological, psychological and sociocultural approaches are being integrated to develop comprehensive models of the many factors that lead some people to develop a given mental disorder (e.g., Caspi, 1993; Cicchetti & Rogosch, 1996). These integrated models are sometimes referred to as **vulnerability-stress models** (Figure 2.2). According to these models, a person must carry some vulnerability to the disorder in order

to develop it. This vulnerability can be a biological one, such as a genetic predisposition to the disorder. It may also be a psychological or one, such as a personality trait that increases the person's risk to develop the disorder or a history of poor interpersonal relationships. In order for the person to ever develop the disorder, however, he or she has to experience some type of stress or trigger. Again, this trigger can be a biological one, such as illness that changes the person's balance of certain hormones. Or the trigger can be psychological or social one, such as a traumatic event. Only when the vulnerability and the stress come together in the same individual does the full-blown disorder emerge. While Hannah may indeed have a genetic vulnerability to depression and anxiety, she may never have developed serious cases of these problems if she had not been abused in childhood.

Another feature of contemporary theories of abnormality is that they recognize the feedback effects that biological and psychosocial factors have on each other (Caspi et al., in press). **Feedback loops** develop so that changes in one system result in changes in a second system, but then those changes in the second system feedback to change the first system again (see Figure 2.3). For example, a change in a person's biology, such as an increase in the levels of certain brain chemicals, might make the person angry and irritable. The person acts angry and irritable around his friends, and in turn his friends react angrily toward him and begin to avoid him. The rejection of his friends only makes him more angry and irritable, which then causes even greater changes in his brain chemistry.

In this chapter, we describe the general principles of the major biological, psychological, and social theories of abnormality that have dominated the field in its modern history. Treatments or therapies deriving from these theories are explained in Chapter 5.

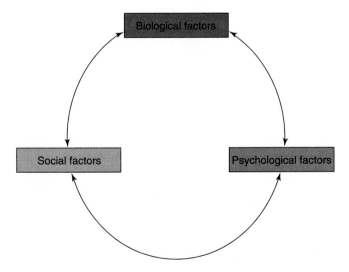

FIGURE 2.3   Feedback Loops between Biological, Social, and Psychological Factors. Some integrative models of psychopathology suggest that biological, social, and psychological factors all affect each other in feedback loops that maintain and enhance psychopathological processes.

☉ BIOLOGICAL APPROACHES

CASE STUDY

On 13 September 1848, Phineas P. Gage, a 25-year-old construction foreman for the Rutland and Burlington Railroad in New England, became the victim of a bizarre accident. In order to lay new rail tracks across Vermont, it was necessary to level the uneven terrain by controlled blasting. Among other tasks, Gage was in charge of the detonations, which involved drilling holes in the stone, partially filling the holes with explosive powder, covering the powder with sand, and using a fuse and a tamping iron to trigger an explosion into the rock. On the fateful day, a momentary distraction let Gage begin tamping directly over the powder before his assistant had had a chance to cover it with sand. The result was a powerful explosion away from the rock and toward Gage. The fine-pointed, 3-cm-thick, 109-cm-long tamping iron was hurled, rocket-like, through his face, skull, brain, and then into the sky. Gage was momentarily stunned but regained full consciousness immediately thereafter. He was able to talk and even walk with the help of his men. The iron landed many yards away.

Phineas Gage not only survived the momentous injury, in itself enough to earn him a place in the annals of medicine, but he survived as a different man, and therein lies the greater significance of this case. Gage had been a responsible, intelligent, and socially well-adapted individual, a favorite with peers and elders. He had made progress and showed promise. The signs of a profound change in personality were already evident during the convalescence under the care of his physician, John Harlow. But as the months passed, it became apparent that the transformation was not only radical but difficult to comprehend. In some respects, Gage was fully recovered. He remained as able-bodied and appeared to be as intelligent as before the accident; he had no impairment of movement or speech; new learning was intact, and neither memory nor intelligence in the conventional sense had been affected. On the other hand, he had become irreverent and capricious. His respect for the social conventions by which he once abided had vanished. His abundant profanity offended those around him. Perhaps most troubling, he had taken leave of his sense of responsibility. He could not be trusted to honor his commitments. His employers had deemed him "the most efficient and capable" man in their "employ" but now they had to dismiss him. In the words of his physician, "the equilibrium or balance, so to speak, between his intellectual faculty and animal propensities" had been destroyed. In the words of his friends and acquaintances, "Gage was no longer Gage." (Damasio et al., 1994, p. 1102)

The story of Phineas Gage is one of the most dramatic examples of the effect of biological factors on psychological functioning. As a result of damage to his brain from the accident, Gage's basic personality seemed to change. He was transformed from a responsible, socially appropriate man to an impulsive, emotional, and socially inappropriate man.

Almost 150 years later, researchers using modern neuroimaging techniques of Gage's preserved skull and a computer simulation of the tamping-iron accident determined the precise location of the damage to Gage's brain (see Figure 2.4). (For a discussion of neuroimaging techniques such as MRI, CT, and PET scanning, see Chapter 4.) Studies of people today who suffer damage to this area of the brain reveal that these people have trouble making rational decisions in personal and social matters and have trouble processing information about emotions. They do not have trouble, however, in tackling the logic of an abstract problem, in performing calculations, or in memory. Thus, like Gage, their basic intellectual functioning remains intact, but their emotional control and judgment in personal and social matters is impaired (Damasio et al., 1994).

Gage's psychological changes were the result of damage to structures in his brain. Structural damage to the brain is one of three causes of abnormality on which biological approaches to abnormality often focus (see *Concept Review*: Biological Theories of Mental Disorders). The other two are biochemical imbalances, and genetic abnormalities. Structural abnormalities, biochemical imbalances and genetic abnormalities can all influence each other. For example, structural abnormalities may be the result of genetic factors, and may cause biochemical imbalances. We explore these three biological causes of abnormality in this section.

Structural Brain Abnormalities

It seems obvious to us today that if areas of the brain responsible for personality and emotional functioning are damaged, this will result in psychological changes. In the days of Phineas Gage and for many

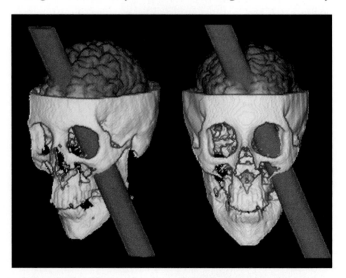

FIGURE 2.4   Phineas Gage's Brain Injury. Modern neuroimaging techniques have helped to identify the precise location of damage to Phineas Gage's brain.

years thereafter, however, this was not a popular perspective. More precisely, it was not popular to believe that a person's character and control over his or her behavior rested, at least in part, in biology, and were not completely the result of will and upbringing.

We now know that people who suffer damage to the brain (often referred to as lesions) or have major abnormalities in the structure of their brains often show problems in psychological functioning. The location of the structural damage influences the specific psychological problems they have. Figure 2.5 (p. 35) shows some of the major areas of the brain. The damage that Phineas Gage suffered was primarily to the frontal area of his cerebrum, one of three concentric layers of the brain. The other two are the limbic system and the central core. Figure 2.6 (p. 36) shows a more

TAKING PSYCHOLOGY PERSONALLY

How to Learn All These Theories

T aking a look at the dozen or more theories presented in this chapter, with all their new terms and jargon, you may be wondering how in the world you'll ever learn them all. A very helpful approach to reading textbook chapters is the PQRST method (Thomas & Robinson, 1982; see also Atkinson et al. 2000).[1] These are the first letters of five steps in reading a chapter—Preview, Question, Read, Self-recitation, Test. Preview and Test apply to the chapter as a whole. Question, Read, Self-recitation apply to each major section of the chapter.

Preview

First, preview the entire chapter to get an idea of the major topics. The Chapter Outline at the beginning of each chapter does this for you, but it's a good idea to skim through the entire chapter, looking for the headings for the main sections and the subsections. Then read the Chapter Summary slowly and carefully. Previewing a chapter will give you a framework for approaching all the details given in the chapter.

Question

As you come to each new section in a chapter, read the heading of that section and the headings of the subsections. Turn the headings into questions that you will try to answer as you read the text of that section, such as "What are the interpersonal theories of abnormality all about?" The overarching question to be asking yourself throughout the chapter is, "What are the main ideas the author is trying to convey in this section?"

Read

Read each section carefully, trying to answer the questions you asked in the previous step. Try also to make connections between the material you are reading and what you already know about psychology, or to situations in your own life. You may want to underline or highlight some of the text, but its is best to mark no more than 10 to 15 percent of the text. Any more than that defeats the purpose of highlighting certain material.

Self-Recitation

When you have finished reading a section, try to recall the main ideas and recite them to yourself. This is a good time to take notes, writing down the main points you

[1] Some textbooks call this the SQ3R method. The S, Q, and three Rs stand for the same five steps but are labeled as Survey, Question, Read, Recite, and Review. PQRST seems to be easier to remember (Atkinson et al., 2000).

Continued

believe are being made in that section. Once you have taken these notes, check them against the text to make sure you remembered them correctly.

Test

Once you have applied Question, Read and Self-recitation to all the sections of the chapter, test yourself on the material. Try to recall the main ideas of the chapter, and then look back at your notes to check your accuracy. Look at the list of key terms at the end of the chapter and see if you could define each term. Try to recall how these key terms relate to one another. Reread the Chapter Summary and see if you can fill in details about each of the topics covered in the summary.

Another good way to learn theories in abnormal psychology is to practice applying each theory to the experiences of individual people. Below we have given you a short case history of a woman named Elaine, who is suffering some distressing psychological symptoms. As you read about Elaine, think about and write down how each of the theories covered in this chapter would conceptualize her problems.

Elaine is a 21-year-old college senior, majoring in computer science. She has always received good grade—that is, until this last quarter. For about 2 months, Elaine has been having trouble concentrating, sleeping, and staying motivated to do her work. She has also been feeling sad and down on herself. These feelings seem to have started over winter break, when Elaine had a huge fight with her parents over what she will do after she graduates in June. Her parents want

her to move back to her hometown on the West Coast and take a job in the local computer software firm. Elaine wants to move to the East Coast to take a job with a large computer firm and live with her best friend.

Elaine's family has always been very close. Elaine always goes home during breaks in the school year and has worked in her hometown every summer. Each member of Elaine's family knows everything about the other members. Elaine has never done anything against her parents' wishes before. Her parents can not understand why she wants to move so far away when she has a good job opportunity near her family. They point out that her father is getting old enough that "he may not be with us for very much longer."

Elaine has been thinking that maybe she is very selfish to want to move to the East Coast. She has also been wondering whether she really wants to make a living in computer science. She is good at it, but she has been having so much trouble lately maintaining her motivation to do her work that she wonders if she really has what it takes to do computer science professionally. Elaine is also beginning to wonder if she will ever have a romantic relationship. She did not have one in college—she did not have time, plus her parents taught her that sex before marriage is a sin, so she decided to avoid relationships so as not to be tempted. Now that she has turned 21 and her college years are almost over, she wonders whether she has missed the opportunity to develop a serious relationship.

detailed labeling of the cross section of the human brain. Some of these brain structures are clearly separated. Others gradually merge into each other, leading to debates about their exact boundaries and the functions they control.

The **cerebrum** is a part of the brain that regulates many of the complex activities that make us human. It is divided into two halves: the left and right hemisphere. The left hemisphere governs the ability to produce language and many complicated logical and

analytic activities, such as mathematical computations. The right hemisphere is involved in spatial perception, pattern recognition, and the processing of emotion. It is important to note that, although certain functions such as language production may be localized in certain areas of the brain, the different structures of the brain are highly interrelated and must work together to produce the complex human behaviors.

The **central core** is a group of structures that regulate some of the most basic functions of the body. One

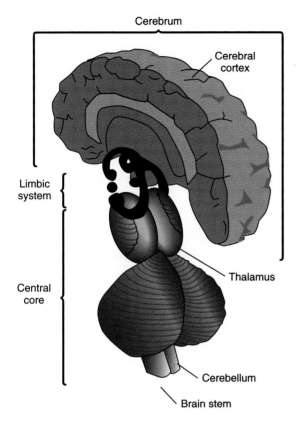

Cerebrum

Cerebral
cortex

Limbic
system

Central
core

Thalamus

Cerebellum

Brain stem

FIGURE 2.5   Three Concentric Layers of the Human Brain. The central core and the limbic system are shown in their entirety, but the left cerebral hemisphere has been removed. The limbic system is concerned with actions that satisfy basic needs and with emotion. The cerebral cortex (an outer layer of cells covering the cerebrum) is the center of higher mental processes, where sensations are registered, voluntary actions initiated, decisions made, and plans formulated.

CONCEPT REVIEW	
Biological Theories of Mental Disorders	
The biological theories of mental disorders can be divided into these three theories.	
Name	**Description**
Structural theories	Abnormalities in the structure of the brain cause mental disorders.
Biochemical theories	Imbalances in the levels of neurotransmitters or hormones, or poor functioning of receptors for neurotransmitters, cause mental disorders.
Genetic theories	Disordered genes lead to mental disorders.

Structural damage to the brain can result from injury, such as from an automobile accident, and from diseases that cause deterioration. In schizophrenia, a severe disorder in which people lose touch with reality, a disease process can cause deterioration in the frontal cerebral cortex of the brain. We will encounter other examples of psychological disorders that appear to be associated with structural abnormalities in the brain.

Often, however, even modern neuroimaging techniques detect no structural abnormalities in the brains of people with psychological disorders, even some severe disorders. Instead, these disorders may be tied to biochemical processes in the brain.

Biochemical Causes of Abnormality

The brain requires a number of chemicals to make it work efficiently and effectively. Chief among these are **neurotransmitters,** biochemicals that act as "messengers" carrying impulses from one neuron to another in the brain and in other parts of the nervous system (see Figure 2.8, p. 38). Each neuron has a cell body and a number of short branches called dendrites. The dendrites and cell body receive impulses from adjacent neurons. The impulse travels down the length of a slender tubelike extension called an axon, and to small swellings at the end of the axon called synaptic terminals. Here the impulse stimulates the release of neurotransmitters through the axon terminal.

The synaptic terminals do not actually touch the adjacent neurons. There is a slight gap between the synaptic terminal and the cell body or dendrite of

component of the central core that can be seen in Figure 2.6 is the **hypothalamus.** The hypothalamus regulates eating, drinking, and sexual behavior. Abnormal behaviors that involve any of these activities may be the result of dysfunction in the hypothalamus. The hypothalamus also influences basic emotions; stimulation of certain areas of the hypothalamus produces sensations of pleasure, whereas stimulation of other areas produces sensations of pain or unpleasantness. The hypothalamus also regulates the body's hormones through the **endocrine system** (Figure 2.7, p. 37)

The third layer of the brain, the **limbic system,** is a collection of structures that are closely interconnected with the hypothalamus and appear to exert additional control over some of the instinctive behaviors regulated by the hypothalamus, such as eating, sexual behavior, and reactions to stressful situations. Monkeys with damage to the limbic system sometimes become chronically aggressive, reacting with rage to the slightest provocation; at other times, they become excessively passive and do not react even to direct threats.

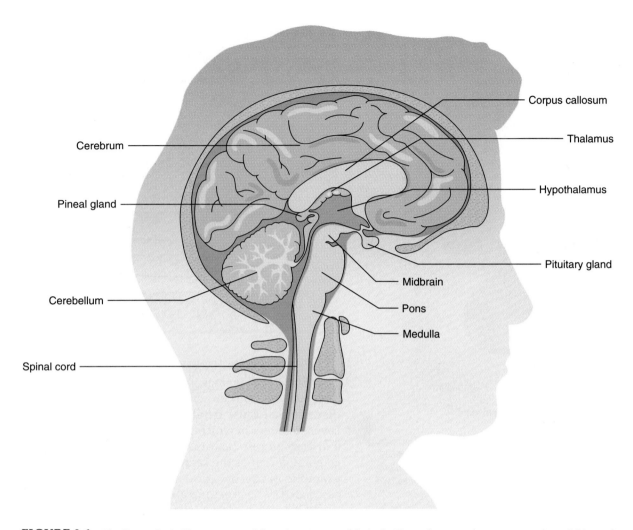

FIGURE 2.6   The Human Brain. These are some of the major structures of the brain. The cerebrum regulates many complex activities, such as speech and analytical thinking. The hypothalamus regulates eating, drinking, sexual desire, and emotions.

adjacent neurons. This gap is called the synaptic gap or **synapse.** Neurotransmitter is released into the synapse. It then binds to special receptors on the membrane of adjacent neurons, something like a key fits into a lock. This stimulates the adjacent neurons to initiate the impulse, which then runs through its dendrites and cell body, down its axon, and causes the release of more neurotransmitter between it and other neurons.

Many of the biochemical theories of psychopathology suggest that too much or too little of certain neurotransmitters in the synapses causes specific types of psychopathology. The amount of a neurotransmitter available in the synapse can be affected by two processes. The process of **reuptake** occurs when the initial neuron releasing the neurotransmitter into the synapse reabsorbs the neurotransmitter, decreasing the amount left in the synapse. Another process, called **degradation,** occurs when the receiving neuron releases an enzyme into the synapse that breaks down the neurotransmitter into other biochemicals. Reup-

take and degradation of neurotransmitters happen naturally. When one or both of these processes malfunction, abnormally high or low levels of neurotransmitter in the synapse result.

Psychological symptoms may also be linked to the number and functioning of the receptors for neurotransmitters on the dendrites. If there are too few receptors or the receptors are not sensitive enough, the neuron will not be able to make adequate use of the neurotransmitter available in the synapse. If there are too many receptors or they are too sensitive, the neuron may be overexposed to the neurotransmitter that is in the synapse.

Scientists have identified more than 100 different neutronsmitters (Valenstein, 1998). Serotonin plays a particularly important role in mental health, regulating emotions and impulses, such as aggression. Norephinephrine (also known as noradrenaline) is a neurotransmitter that is produced mainly by neurons in the brain stem. Two well-known drugs, cocaine and amphetamines, prolong the action of norepinephrine

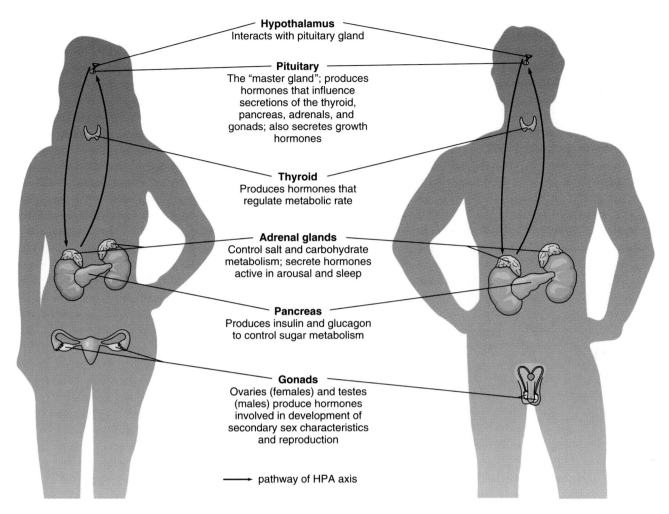

FIGURE 2.7 The Endocrine System. The hypothalamus regulates the endocrine system, which produces most of the major hormones of the body.

From *Psychology*, 1st edition, by E. B. Goldstein, © 1994. Reprinted with permission of Wadsworth, a division of Thomson Learning. Fax 800 730-2215.

by slowing down its reuptake process. Because of the delay in the reuptake, the receiving neurons are activated for a longer period of time, causing the stimulating psychological effects of these drugs. On the other hand, when there is too little norepinephrine in the brain, the person's mood level will be depressed. Another prominent neurotransmitter is gamma-aminobutyric acid, or GABA, one of the major inhibitory transmitters in the nervous system. Certain drugs have a tranquilizing effect because they facilitate the inhibitory activity of GABA.

These are but a handful of the neurotransmitters we discuss in this book. You will find that some neurotransmitters are implicated in a number of different disorders. This is probably because each neurotransmitter plays crucial roles in the functioning of several basic systems in the brain. When the level of that neurotransmitter is off, receptors for that neurotransmitter are not working properly, or there are too few or too many receptors, then several different functions in the brain can go awry.

Other biochemical theories of psychopathology focus on the body's **endocrine system** (refer to Figure 2.7). This system of glands produces many different chemicals called *hormones*, which are released directly into the blood. A hormone acts like a neurotransmitter, carrying messages throughout the system, potentially affecting people's moods, levels of energy, and reactions to stress.

One of the major endocrine glands, the **pituitary,** is partly an outgrowth of the brain and lies just below the hypothalamus (see Figure 2.6). The pituitary gland has been called the "master gland" because it produces the largest number of different hormones and controls the secretion of other endocrine glands. The relationship between the pituitary gland and the hypothalamus illustrates the complex interactions that take place between the endocrine system and the nervous system. In response to stress (fear, anxiety, pain, and so forth) certain neurons on the hypothalamus secrete a substance called corticotropin-release factor (CRF). The pituitary is just below the hypothalamus and CRF is

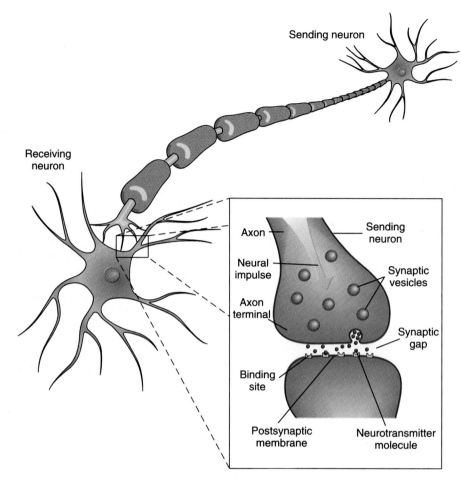

FIGURE 2.8   Neurotransmitters and the Synapse. The neurotransmitter is released into the synaptic gap. There it may bind with receptors on the postsynaptic membrane.

carried to it through a channel-like structure. The CRF stimulates the pituitary to release adrenocorticotrophic hormone (ACTH), which is the body's major stress hormone. ACTH, in turn, is carried by the bloodstream to the adrenal glands and to various other organs of the body, causing the release of some 30 hormones, each of which plays a role in the body's adjustment to emergency situations. As we discuss in Chapters 6 through 9, some theories of anxiety and depression suggest that these disorders result from dysregulation of this hypothalamic-pituitary-adrenal axis (or HPA axis). People who have a dysregulated HPA axis may have abnormal physiological reactions to stress, which make it more difficult for them to cope psychologically with the stress and result in symptoms of anxiety and depression.

The proper working of neurotransmitter and endocrine systems requires a delicate balance, and many forces can upset this balance. One of these is a genetic abnormality, which can affect biochemical systems as well as brain development. The end result can be a psychological disturbance.

Genetic Factors in Abnormality

Behavior genetics, the study of the genetics of personality and abnormality, is a relatively new and fast-growing area of research concerned with two questions: (1) To what extent are behaviors or behavioral tendencies inherited and (2) What are the processes by which genes affect behavior?

Let us begin by reviewing the basics of genetic transmission. At conception, the fertilized embryo has 46 chromosomes, 23 from the female egg and 23 from the male sperm, making up 23 pairs of chromosomes (see Figure 2.9). One of these pairs is referred to as the *sex chromosomes* because it determines the sex of the embryo: The XX combination results in a female embryo, and the XY combination results in a male embryo. The mother of an embryo always contributes an X chromosome; the father can contribute an X or a Y.

Alterations in the structure or number of chromosomes can cause major defects. For example, Down syndrome results when chromosome 21 is present

PUSHING THE BOUNDARIES

rTMS: Mesmer Returns?

Mesmer's theory of animal magnetism held that the body has magnetic fluids that must be properly balanced in order to maintain physical and emotional health (refer to Chapter 1). Mesmer "cured" people of psychological symptoms in elaborate ceremonies in which he used his own "magnetism" to rebalance their magnetic fluids.

Mesmer was rejected as a charlatan. But recent research suggests there may be something to Mesmer's claims about the curative powers of magnetism. Scientists are using powerful magnets such as those used in magnetic resonance imaging (see Chapter 4) to stimulate targeted areas of the brain. The procedure, known as repetitive transcranial magnetic stimulation (rTMS), exposes patients to repeated high-intensity magnetic pulses that are focused on particular brain structures. When treating depressed people, researchers have targeted the left prefrontal cortex, which tends to show abnormally low metabolic activity in some depressed people. Several studies have suggested that depressed patients given rTMS daily for at least a week tend to experience relief from their symptoms (Epstein et al., 1998; Figiel et al., 1998; George et al., 1998). Many of these studies have focused on patients who have not responded to antidepressant medications.

How does rTMS work? Electrical stimulation of neurons can result in long-term changes in neurotransmission across synapses (George, 1998). Neurotranmission can be enhanced or blunted depending on the frequency of the stimulation. By stimulating the left prefrontal cortex of depressed people at particular frequencies, researchers have been able to increase neuronal activity, which in turn, has had an antidepressant effect.

Patients who receive rTMS report few side effects, usually only minor headaches treatable by aspirin. Patients can remain awake, rather than having to be anesthetized as in electroconvulsive therapy (ECT), thereby avoiding possible complications of anesthesia. Thus, there is a great deal of hope that rTMS will be an effective and safe alternative therapy, particularly for people who do not respond to drug therapies and may not be able to tolerate ECT (George, 1998; Kirkcaldie, Pridmore, & Reid, 1997).

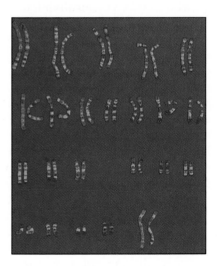

FIGURE 2.9   Human Chromosomes. The normal human has 23 pairs of chromosomes. In this photo, pair 23 is XX, so these are from a female.

in triplicate instead of as the usual pair. Down syndrome is characterized by mental retardation, heart malformations, and facial features such as a flat face, small nose, protruding lips and tongue, and slanted eyes.

Chromosomes are made up of individual genes, which are themselves segments of long molecules of DNA (deoxyribonucleic acid). Genes give coded instructions to cells to perform certain functions, usually to manufacture certain proteins. Genes, like chromosomes, come in pairs. One half of the pair comes from the mother and the other from the father. Abnormalities in genes that make up chromosomes are much more common than are major abnormalities in the structure or number of chromosomes.

Although you may often hear of scientists having discovered "the gene" for a major disorder, most disorders are not the result of single faulty genes but of combinations of altered genes. Each of these altered genes makes only a small contribution to vulnerability for the disorder. But when a critical number of these altered genes comes together, the individual may develop the disorder. This is known as a **polygenic** process—it takes multiple genetic abnormalities coming together in one individual to create a disorder. Most of the genetic models of the major types of mental disorder are also polygenic. There are a number of physiological disorders, such as diabetes, coronary heart disease, epilepsy, and cleft lip and palate, which are the result of such polygenic processes.

People who have disorders caused by polygenic processes often wonder why they have no family history of the disorder and why they are the only ones in their families to inherit the disorder. It may be because none of their relatives accumulated all the different genes necessary for the disorder to develop fully. It just happens that when the people with disorders were conceived, all the genes necessary for the disorders were present in the chromosomes contributed by their mothers and fathers. When their brothers or sisters were conceived, however, different sets of chromosomes were contributed by their mothers and fathers, and these may not have contained all the necessary genes for the disorders, so their siblings did not develop the disorders.

Conversely, many people who have relatives with disorders that are heritable worry that they will inevitably develop the disorders. However, it is the case with most disorders, including psychological disorders, that the odds of an individual inheriting all the genes necessary for a disorder are fairly low, even if a relative who has the disorder is a parent or sibling. For example, the sibling of a person with schizophrenia, which is probably the psychological disorder in which genes play the strongest role, only has about a 9 percent chance of developing schizophrenia at some point in his or her life (see Chapter 10).

Another extremely important characteristic of polygenic disorders is that what is inherited is the **predisposition** to the disorder and not the inevitability of the disorder. Often, this predisposition must interact with other biological or environmental factors for the individual to fully develop the disorder. A good example from the medical field is coronary heart disease. A person can inherit a predisposition to coronary heart disease by inheriting the genes for hypertension, diabetes, or hyperlipidemia (too much fat in the blood). Whether he or she actually develops coronary heart disease depends, however, on a number of environmental and behavioral factors, such as obesity, smoking, exercise, alcohol abuse, hard-driving personality, and living in an industrialized society. The same characteristic may be true of many

psychological disorders. What is inherited is a predisposition to the disorder. Whether an individual ever fully develops the disorder may depend on other biological risks (e.g., malnutrition or negative intrauterine experiences) and other psychosocial risks (e.g., growing up in a dysfunctional family) he or she is exposed to. As we discuss the specific psychological disorders in this textbook, we consider the ways genetic predispositions and other biological or psychosocial factors may interact to increase an individual's risk for the disorder.

First, however, let us consider how we know whether a disorder is heritable. There are three basic types of studies scientists use to determine the heritability of a disorder: family history studies, twin studies, and adoption studies.

Family History Studies

Disorders that are genetically transmitted should, on average, show up more often in the families of people who have the disorder than they do in families of people who do not have the disorder. This is true whether the disorder is caused by a single gene or by a combination of faulty genes. To conduct a **family history study,** scientists first identify people who clearly have the disorder in question; this group is called the **probands.** They also identify a control group of people who clearly do not have the disorder. They then trace the family pedigrees, or family trees, of these two groups of individuals and determine how many of their relatives have the disorder. Researchers are most interested in *first-degree* relatives, because these are the relatives who are most genetically similar to the probands and control subjects (unless they have identical twins, who will be genetically identical to them). Figure 2.10 illustrates the degree of genetic relationship between an individual and various categories of relatives. This figure gives you an idea of why the risk of inheriting the genes for a disorder quickly decreases as the relationship between an individual and the ill relative becomes more distant: It is because the percentage of genes the individual and ill relative have in common decreases greatly with distance.

Although family history studies provide very useful information about the possible genetic transmission of a disorder, they have their problems. The most obvious one is that families share not only genes but also environment. Several members of a family could have a disorder because they share genes or because they share the same environmental stresses. Family history studies cannot tease apart genetic and environmental contributions to a disorder. Researchers often turn to twin studies to do this.

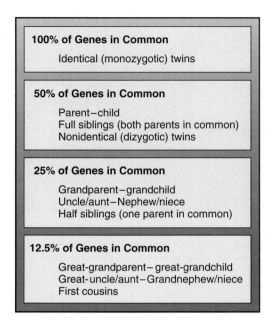

FIGURE 2.10   Degrees of Genetic Relationship. Only monozygotic twins have 100 percent of their genes in common. People with whom you share 50 percent of your genes are your first-degree relatives. People with whom you share 25 percent of your genes are your second-degree relatives. People with whom you share 12.5 percent of your genes are your third-degree relatives.

Twin Studies

Notice in Figure 2.10 that identical or **monozygotic (MZ) twins** share 100 percent of their genes. This is because they came from a single fertilized egg that splits into two identical parts. In contrast, nonidentical or **dizygotic (DZ) twins** share, on average, 50 percent of their genes because they came from two separate eggs fertilized by separate sperm. Researchers have capitalized on this difference between MZ and DZ twins to investigate the contribution of genetics to many disorders through **twin studies.** If a disorder is determined *entirely* by genetics, then when one member of a monozygotic (MZ) twin pair has a disorder, the other member of the pair should always have the disorder. This probability that both twins will have the disorder if one twin has the disorder is called the **concordance rate** for the disorder. So if a disorder is entirely determined by genes, the concordance rate among MZ twins should be 100 percent. The concordance rate for the disorder among dizygotic (DZ) twins will be much lower than 100 percent. The actual concordance rate will depend on the number of faulty genes necessary for the disorder and the dominance of these genes. Even when a disorder is transmitted only partially by genetics, the concordance rate for MZ twins should be considerably higher than the concordance rate for DZ twins, because MZ twins are genetically identical but DZ twins share only about half the same genes.

Let us say that the concordance rate for Disorder X for MZ twins is 48 percent, whereas the concordance rate for DZ twins is 17 percent. These concordance rates tell us two things. First, because the concordance rate for MZ twins is considerably higher than the concordance rate for DZ twins, we have evidence that Disorder X is genetically transmitted. Second, because the concordance rate for MZ twins is well under 100 percent, we have evidence that it takes a combination of a genetic predisposition and other factors (biological or environmental) for an individual to develop Disorder X.

By now, you may be objecting that twin studies do not fully tease apart genetic factors from environmental factors, because MZ twins may have much more similar environments and experiences than do DZ twins. MZ twins typically look alike, whereas DZ twins often do not look alike, and physical appearance can strongly affect other people's reactions to an individual. MZ twins may also be more likely than DZ twins to share talents that influence the opportunities they are given in life. For example, MZ twins may both be athletic or very talented academically or musically, which then affects their treatment by others and their opportunities in life. In contrast, DZ twins much less often share the same talents and thus are less likely to be treated similarly by others. Finally, parents may simply treat MZ twins more similarly than they do DZ twins, for a variety of reasons.

To address these problems, researchers have turned to a third method for studying heritability, the adoption study.

Adoption Studies

An **adoption study** can be carried out in a number of ways. Most commonly, researchers first identify people who have the disorder of interest who were adopted shortly after birth. Then they determine the rates of the disorder in the biological relatives of these adoptees and the adoptive relatives of the adoptees. If a disorder is strongly influenced by genetics, then researchers should see higher rates of the disorder among the biological relatives of the adoptee than among the adoptive relatives. If the disorder is strongly influenced by environment, then they should see higher rates of the disorder among the adoptive relatives than among the biological relatives.

Some of the most interesting studies of the genetics of personality combine the strategies of the adoption study and the twin study. Researchers Thomas Bouchard, David Lykken, Matt McGue, and others at the University of Minnesota identified several dozen pairs of MZ and DZ twins who were reared apart and brought them together at the laboratories to assess their personalities (Bouchard et al., 1990; Lykken et al.,

1993; Tellegen et al., 1988). Some of the twins reared apart had never met each other and had not even known that they had a twin. The personalities and behavioral patterns of the MZ twins reared apart were compared to the personalities of the DZ twins reared apart and to MZ and DZ twins reared in the same households. The results of this study have provided evidence that some aspects of personality and everyday behavior are substantially affected by genetics. Some of the characteristics affected by genetics will not surprise you, nor have they surprised many other scientists. For example, it appears that traits such as shyness or the tendency to become easily upset are between 30 and 50 percent caused by genetics (Bouchard et al., 1990; Newman, Tellegen, & Bouchard, 1998).

Yet, what has rocked the world of behavioral genetics is evidence that even the most mundane of behaviors, which we have thought are shaped by circumstance and rearing, are heavily influenced by genetics, such as the amount of television we watch and what we munch on while we're watching TV (Bouchard, 1994; Hur, Bouchard, & Eckert, 1998). There are startling examples of identical twins reared apart who are amazingly similar, even though they have never met each other. Consider, for example, the "Jim twins" (Holden, 1980). Jim Lewis and Jim Springer were identical twins reunited at the age of 39 after being separated since infancy. Both had married and later divorced women named Linda. Their second wives were both named Betty. Both had sons named James Allan and dogs named Toy. Both chain-smoked Salem cigarettes, worked as sheriffs' deputies, drove Chevrolets, chewed their fingernails, enjoyed stock car racing, had basement workshops, and had built circular white benches around trees in their yards. Genetic researchers do not argue that there are genes for marrying women named Linda or Betty or genes for having basement workshops. However, given similar circumstances, people with identical genes may choose the same activities and have the same likes and dislikes.

You will not be surprised to hear that this work on behavioral genetics has been controversial. Some scientists believe that the behavioral geneticists are underestimating the role of the environment as they overestimate the role of genetics. This work clearly has stimulated a lively and interesting discussion, however, about how deeply and broadly genes affect our behavior.

Thus, adoption studies, twin studies, and family history studies all help to determine whether a characteristic or disorder is influenced by genetics and the degree of this influence. Each type of study has its limitations. Family history and twin studies cannot fully tease apart the impacts of genetics and shared environment. Adoption studies suffer from the fact that it is

Studies of identical twins reared apart have revealed amazing similarities. Jim Lewis and Jim Springer were reared apart but, when reunited, found that they were identical in more than appearance (see text).

difficult to find large numbers of adoptees with the disorder of interest, so the sample sizes in these studies tend to be very small.

Assessing the Biological Theories

Modern biological theories have greatly advanced our understanding of the human mind and the biological influences on behavior. Research on these theories seems to be advancing at a rapid pace, with new discoveries about the role of biology in mental disorders in the news every day. As we discuss in later chapters, these theories have led to new treatments for some disorders that have literally restored the lives of people who suffer the disorders.

The biological theories have their flaws, however. They often seem reductionistic, boiling down the complex human behavior we call psychopathology into the firing of neurons and abnormal genes. Some of these theories ignore the influence of social factors and the environment in shaping the behavior of people who may carry a biological risk for psychopathology. More generally, the biological theories often have trouble explaining why everyone who carries a biological risk for a disorder, such as an unusual level of some hormone or neurotransmitter, does not eventually develop the disorder (Valenstein, 1998).

Although we may think of biological research as "harder science" than the research done to test the psychosocial theories of abnormality, biological research is often at least as messy and nondefinitive as psychosocial research (Valenstein, 1998). Most of the processes thought to cause psychopathology, such as changes in neurotransmitter levels, can only be measured indirectly and quite imprecisely in the brains of live humans (Thase & Howland, 1996). As a result, much of the evidence for the biological theories comes from studies of animals rather than humans. Although animal studies can be informative, it is sometimes difficult to generalize from animals to humans.

Many of the biological theories of psychopathology were developed post hoc, based on accidental discoveries that certain drugs changed behavior in animals or humans. Reasoning backward from the effects of drugs on behavior to a theory of what causes that behavior is a tricky business, particularly since the drugs that are used to alleviate psychopathology have widespread effects on many areas and systems in the brain (Valenstein, 1998).

The biological theories of abnormality have many proponents, however, and seem to have captured the hearts of the general public. Many people find biological theories of psychopathology appealing because they seem to take away any stigma or blame on the individual sufferer for having the disorder. Indeed, many organizations for people with psychological disorders explicitly advocate a biological view of these disorders, emphasizing that people with the disorders need to stop blaming themselves, accept the fact they have a "disease," and obtain the appropriate medical treatment.

Summing Up

- The biological theories of psychopathology hold that psychological symptoms and disorders are caused by structural abnormalities in the brain, disordered biochemistry, or faulty genes.

- Structural abnormalities in the brain can be caused by injury or disease processes. The specific area of the brain damaged will influence the type of psychological symptoms shown.

- Most biochemical theories focus on neurotransmitters, the biochemicals that facilitate transmission of impulses in the brain. Some theories say that psychological symptoms are caused by too little or too much of a particular neurotransmitter in the synapses of the brain. Other theories focus on the number of receptors for neurotransmitters.

- Some people may be genetically predisposed to psychological disorders. Most of these disorders are probably linked not to a single faulty gene but to the accumulation of a group of faulty genes.

- Three methods of determining the heritability of a disorder are family history studies, twin studies, and adoption studies.

☉ PSYCHOLOGICAL APPROACHES

Psychological theories of abnormality vary greatly in the factors and processes they say are involved in the development of abnormal or maladaptive behavior (see *Concept Review*: Psychological Theories of Mental Disorders). Some theories focus on unconscious conflicts and anxiety, some focus on the effects of rewards and punishments in the environment, some focus on thought processes, and some focus on the difficulties humans have in striving to realize their full potentials in a capricious world. There are many more specific psychological theories of abnormality than can be described in this book. We shall discuss the theories that have had the largest and most enduring impacts on how psychologists view abnormality and on the types of psychological therapies that are currently used to treat people with psychological disorders.

CONCEPT REVIEW	
Psychological Theories of Mental Disorders	
Psychological theories of mental disorders tend to focus on the individual—his or her ways of thinking, unconscious conflicts, self-concept, or behavior patterns.	
Name	**Description**
Psychodynamic theories	Unconscious conflicts between primitive desires and the constraints on those desires cause symptoms of mental disorders.
Behavioral theories	Symptoms of mental disorders are due to the reinforcements and punishments for specific behaviors and feelings an individual receives from his or her environment.
Cognitive theories	People's ways of interpreting situations, their assumptions about the world, and their self-concepts can cause negative feelings and behavior.
Humanist and existential theories	Mental disorders arise when people do not pursue their own values and potentials and instead feel they must conform to the demands of others.

Sigmund Freud believed that normal and abnormal behaviors were driven by needs and drives, most of which were unconscious.

Psychodynamic Theories of Abnormality

The **psychodynamic theories** of abnormality suggest that all behavior, thoughts, and emotions, whether normal or abnormal, are influenced to a large extent by unconscious processes. The psychodynamic theories began with Sigmund Freud, and have expanded to include several newer theories that accept many of Freud's basic assumptions about the working of the human mind, but emphasize different processes from those that Freud emphasized.

Freud developed **psychoanalysis**, which refers to (1) a theory of personality and psychopathology, (2) a method of investigating the mind, and (3) a form of treatment for psychopathology (Wolitzky, 1995). As we noted in Chapter 1, Freud was a Viennese neurologist who became interested in unconscious processes while working with Jean Charcot in Paris in the late nineteenth century. He then returned to Vienna and worked with the physician Josef Breuer, most notably on the case of "Anna O." Anna O. had extensive symptoms of hysteria—physical ailments with no apparent physical cause—including paralysis of the legs and right arm, deafness, and disorganized speech. Breuer attempted to hypnotize Anna O., hoping he could cure her symptoms by suggestion. Anna O. began to talk about painful memories from her past that were apparently tied to the development of her hysterical symptoms. She expressed a great deal of distress about these memories, but following the recounting of the memories under hypnosis, many of her symptoms went away. Breuer labeled the release of emotions connected to these memories **catharsis,** and Anna O. labeled the entire process her "talking cure."

Breuer and Freud published papers on their cases together, suggesting that hysteria was the result of traumatic memories that have been repressed from consciousness because they are too painful. **Repression** was defined as the motivated forgetting of a difficult experience, such as being abused as a child, or an unacceptable wish, such as the desire to hurt someone. Repression does not dissolve the emotion associated with the memory or wish, however. Instead, this emotion is "damned-up" and emerges as symptoms.

Freud went on to develop these ideas about dynamic processes within the unconscious into an elaborate and comprehensive theory of human thought and behavior. Freud was a passionate reader of history, archeology, philosophy, and many other fields, and developed theories reaching far beyond psychology and psychiatry. Although a full description of this theory is beyond the scope of this book, we can review the central assumptions of Freudian theory that are most pertinent to abnormal behavior—some of which are summarized in the *Concept Review*: Key Concepts in Freudian Theory.

The Id, Ego, and Superego

Freud believed that the two basic drives that motivate human behavior are the sexual drive, which he referred to as **libido,** and the aggressive drive. The energy from these drives continually seeks to be released, but can be channeled or harnessed by different psychological systems. Most of Freud's writings focused primarily on libido (or libidinal drive) and so our discussion will as well.

Three systems of the human psyche that help to regulate the libido are the id, the ego, and the superego. The **id** is the system from which the libido emerges, and its drives and impulses seek immediate release. The id operates by the **pleasure principle**—the drive to maximize pleasure and to minimize pain, as quickly as possible. A number of reflex actions, such as the infant turning to its mother's breast for milk, are direct expressions of the pleasure principle. When direct action cannot be taken, humans may use fantasies or memories to conjure up the desired object or action. This is known as **primary process thinking** or wish fulfillment. A hungry infant, for example, may imagine its mother's breast when she is not readily available.

As we grow older, we become aware that we cannot always quickly satisfy our impulses without paying a price. We cannot immediately satisfy sexual urges, and cannot carry out aggressive impulses without being punished by society. A part of the id splits off and becomes the **ego,** the force that seeks to gratify our wishes and needs in ways that remain within the rules of society for their appropriate expression. The ego follows the **reality principle**—seeking to satisfy our needs

CONCEPT REVIEW

Key Concepts in Freudian Theory

These are some of the key concepts in Freudian theory.

Name	Description
Repression	Motivated forgetting of memories or desires that cause anxiety.
Catharsis	Release of energy bound up in painful emotions.
Libido	Psychical energy emerging from sexual drive.
Id	Most primitive part of the unconscious that consists of drives and impulses seeking immediate gratification.
Ego	Part of the psyche that channels libido into activities that balance the demands of society and the superego.
Superego	Part of the unconscious that consists of absolute moral standards internalized from one's parents and culture.
Pleasure principle	The principle that desires and wishes should be immediately gratified, without concern for the constraints of society.
Primary process thinking	Thinking oriented toward satisfying primitive urges, perhaps through fantasy.
Reality principle	Realization that primitive urges cannot always be immediately gratified because of the constraints of society.
Secondary process thinking	Rational deliberation about how to satisfy primitive urges within the constraints of society.
Introjection	Incorporating or internalizing the standards or views of others into one's own ways of thinking.
Unconscious	The vast area of the psyche holding desires, memories, and emotions of which we are not aware.
Preconscious	"Way station" between the unconscious and conscious, holding material that is somewhat accessible to consciousness.
Conscious	Aspect of the psyche holding material of which we are aware.
Defense mechanisms	Strategies for transforming unacceptable desires, thoughts, and feelings into a more acceptable form (see Table 2.1, p. 47).
Neurotic paradox	When an individual's defense mechanisms become maladaptive and distressing.
Oedipal complex	Stage of development in which a boy desires his mother and hates his father.
Castration anxiety	Anxiety a little boy feels when he fears his father will castrate him in retaliation for his desire for his mother.
Electra complex	Stage of development in which a girl becomes attracted to her father in hopes he will provide her with a replacement for the penis she lacks.
Penis envy	Female's desire to have a penis.

within the realities of society's rules—rather than the pleasure principle. **Secondary process thinking,** or rational deliberation, rather than primary process thinking, is the ego's primary mode of operation. A preschooler, who may wish to suckle at his mother's breast, but is aware that this is no longer allowed, may satisfy himself with cuddling in his mother's lap.

The **superego** develops from the ego a little later in childhood. It is the storehouse of rules and regula-

tions for the conduct of behavior that are learned from one's parents and from society. These rules and regulations are in the form of absolute moral standards. We **introject,** or internalize, these moral standards because following them makes us feel good and reduces anxiety. The superego is made up of two components, the conscience and the ego ideal. The conscience constantly evaluates whether we are conforming our behavior to our internalized moral standards. The ego

© Sidney Harris

Anna Freud, daughter of Sigmund Freud, was a major contributor to psychodynamic theory and described the basic defense mechanisms people use to control anxiety.

ideal is an image of the person we wish to become, which is formed from images of those people with whom we identified with in our early years, usually our parents.

Most of the dynamics between the id, ego, and superego occur in the **unconscious**—completely out of our awareness. The **preconscious** is a way station or buffer between the unconscious and the **conscious.** Some material (i.e., wishes, needs, or memories) from the unconscious can make its way into the preconscious, but it rarely reaches the conscious level. The ego deflects this material back into the unconscious or changes the material in such a way as to protect the conscious from being fully aware of the unconscious material. This pushing material back into the unconscious is known as repression, as we mentioned earlier. Why must the conscious be protected from unconscious material? In their raw form, unconscious wishes, needs, and memories represent our basic instincts and drives, seeking to be satisfied in the quickest and fullest way possible. Because these unconscious desires are often unacceptable to the individual or society, they cause anxiety if they seep into the conscious, prompting the ego to push the material back into the unconscious.

Freud, and later his daughter Anna Freud, described certain strategies or **defense mechanisms** that the ego uses to disguise or transform unconscious wishes. The particular defense mechanisms a person regularly uses shape his or her behavior and personality. Table 2.1 provides a list and examples of the basic defense mechanisms.

Everyone uses defense mechanisms to one degree or another, because everyone must protect against awareness of unacceptable wishes and conform his or her behavior to societal norms. When our behavior becomes ruled by defense mechanisms when the mechanisms themselves are maladaptive, then the defense

mechanisms can result in abnormal, pathological behavior. Freud called this the **neurotic paradox.** For example, a man whose father physically abused him as a child may develop the tendency to displace his rage— to transfer his feelings to another target—because it was too dangerous to directly express his anger against his father. This displacement may take the form of beating his wife, or getting into frequent fist fights with other men. The displacement behavior is maladaptive in itself, and thus the man is stuck in the neurotic paradox.

Psychosexual Stages

Freud proposed that as they develop, children pass through a series of universal **psychosexual stages** (see *Concept Review*: Psychosexual Stages in Freudian Theory. In each stage, sexual drives are focused on stimulation of certain body areas, and particular psychological issues can arouse anxiety. The id, ego, and superego must negotiate and develop through these stages successfully for the child to develop into a psychologically healthy adult. The responses of caregivers, usually parents, to the child's attempts to satisfy basic needs and wishes can greatly influence whether a given stage is negotiated successfully. If the parents are not appropriately responsive to the child, helping him or her learn acceptable ways of satisfying and controlling drives and impulses, the child can become fixated at a stage, trapped in the concerns and issues of that stage, never successfully moving beyond that stage and through the subsequent stages.

The earliest stage of life, the **oral stage,** lasts for the first 18 months following birth. In the oral stage, libidinal impulses are best satisfied through stimulation of the mouth area, usually through feeding or sucking. At this stage, the child is entirely dependent on care-

TABLE 2.1

Defense Mechanisms

These defense mechanism were described by Sigmund and Anna Freud.

Defense Mechanism	Definition	Example
Regression	Retreating to a behavior of an earlier developmental period to prevent anxiety and satisfy current needs.	A woman abandoned by her lover curls up in a chair, rocking and sucking her fingers.
Denial	Refusal to perceive or accept reality.	A husband whose wife recently died denies she is gone and actively searches for her.
Displacement	Discharging unacceptable feelings against someone or something other than the true target of these feelings.	A woman who is angry at her children kicks the dog.
Rationalization	Inventing an acceptable motive to explain unacceptably motivated behavior.	A soldier who killed innocent civilians may rationalize that he was only following orders.
Intellectualization	Adopting a cold, distanced perspective on a matter that actually creates strong unpleasant feelings.	An emergency room physician who is troubled by seeing young people with severe gunshot sounds every night has discussions with colleagues that focus only on the technical aspects of treatment.
Projection	Attributing one's own unacceptable motives or desires to someone else.	A husband who is sexually attracted to a colleague accuses his wife of cheating on him.
Reaction formation	Adopting a set of attitudes and behaviors that are the opposite of one's true dispositions.	A man who cannot accept his own homosexuality becomes extremely homophobic.
Identification	Adopting the ideas, values, and tendencies of someone in a superior position in order to elevate self-worth.	Prisoners adopt the attitudes of their captors toward other prisoners.
Sublimation	Translating wishes and needs into socially acceptable behavior.	An adolescent with strong aggressive impulses trains to be a boxer.

CONCEPT REVIEW

Psychosexual Stages in Freudian Theory

Freud argued that all children go through these stages of psychosexual development. Fixation at any stage could cause psychological symptoms representing the concerns of that stage.

Stage Name	Age Range	Description
Oral stage	0–18 months	Pleasure centers on the mouth. Concerns are with dependency and reliability of caregivers.
Anal stage	18 months to 3 years	Pleasure centers on the anus. Concerns are with control and order.
Phallic stage	3–6 years	Pleasure centers on genitals. Concerns are with sexual feelings toward parents.
Latency stage	6 years to puberty	Sexual desire diminishes and attention turns to development of talents and skills.
Genital stage	Puberty through adulthood	Concerns are with the maturation of adult sexual interests.

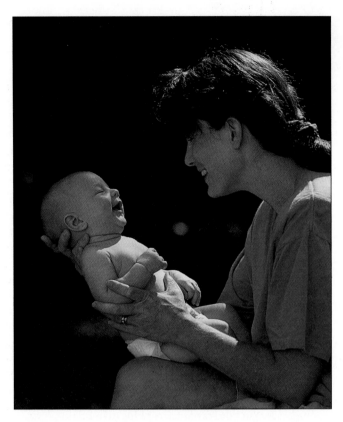

Psychoanalytic theory argues that the nurturance a child receives from his or her early caregivers strongly influences personality development.

givers for gratification, and thus the central issues of this stage are issues of one's dependence and the reliability of others. If the child's caregiver, typically its mother, is not adequately available to the child, he or she can develop deep mistrust and fear of abandonment. Children fixated at the oral stage develop an "oral character"—a personality characterized by excessive dependence on others but mistrust of their love. A number of habits focused on the mouth area—for example, smoking, or excessive drinking and eating—are said to reflect an oral character.

The **anal stage** lasts from about 18 months to 3 years of age. During this phase, the focus of gratification is the anus. The child becomes very interested in toilet activities, particularly the passing and retaining of feces. Parents can cause a child to become fixated at this stage by being too harsh or critical during toilet training. People with an "anal personality" are said to be stubborn, overcontrolling, stingy, and too focused on orderliness and tidiness.

During the **phallic stage,** lasting from about age 3 to 6, the focus of pleasure is the genitals. It is during this stage that one of the most important conflicts of sexual development occurs, and it occurs differently for boys and girls. Freud believed that boys become sexually attracted to their mothers, and hate their

fathers as rivals. Freud labeled this the **Oedipus complex,** after the character in Greek mythology who unknowingly kills his father and marries his mother. Boys fear that their fathers will retaliate against them by castrating them, however. This arouses **castration anxiety,** which is then the motivation for putting aside their desire for their mother and aspiring to become like their father. The successful resolution of the Oedipus complex helps to instill a strong superego in boys because it results in boys identifying with their fathers and their fathers' value systems.

Freud believed that, during the phallic stage, girls recognize that they do not have a penis, and are horrified at this discovery. They also recognize that their mothers do not have a penis and disdain their mothers and all females for this deficit. Girls develop an attraction for their fathers, in hopes that they will provide the penis they lack. He labeled this the **Electra complex,** after the character in Greek mythology who conspires to murder her mother to avenge her father's death. Obviously, girls cannot have castration anxiety, because, according to Freud, they feel they have already been castrated. As a result, girls do not have as strong a motivation as boys to develop a superego. Freud argued that females never do develop superegos as strong as males and this leads to a greater reliance on emotion rather than reason in the lives of women. Freud also thought that much of women's behavior was driven by **penis envy**—the wish to have the male sex organ.

The unsuccessful resolution of the phallic stage can lead to a number of psychological problems in children. If children do not fully identify with their same-sex parent, they may not develop "appropriate" gender roles or a heterosexual orientation. They also may not develop a healthy superego and thus be either too self-aggrandizing or too self-deprecating. If children's sexual attraction to their parents is not responded to with gentle but firm discouragement, they may become overly seductive or sexualized and have a number of problems in romantic relationships.

After the turmoil of the phallic stage, children enter the **latency stage,** during which libidinal drives are quelled somewhat, and their attention turns to the development of skills and interests, and becoming fully socialized into the world in which they live. They play with friends of the same sex and avoid children of the opposite sex—this is when girls hate boys and boys hate girls.

At about the age of 12, children's sexual desires emerge again as they enter puberty, and they enter the **genital stage.** If they have successfully resolved the phallic stage, their sexual interests turn to heterosexual relationships. They begin to pursue romantic alliances, and learn to negotiate the world of dating and early sexual encounters with members of the opposite sex.

Melanie Klein questioned some of the principles of Freudian psychoanalytic theory and helped to develop object relations theory.

Otto Kernberg is one of the leaders of the object relations school.

Newer Psychodynamic Theories

Freud's theories are some of the most intriguing and enduring in psychology, but they had critics even among Freud's followers. Freud viewed behavior and thought as the products of energies that were either contained or released. Where, many people asked, was the person, the self, in Freud's human being? Several of Freud's followers developed new theories, collectively referred to as **psychodynamic theories,** that emphasized the role of the ego as an independent force striving for mastery and competence (e.g., Jacobson, 1964; Mahler, 1968). Others talked explicitly about the concept of a self, and argued that the development of a positive sense of the self is an individual's primary aim (e.g., Kohut, 1984).

Freud downplayed the roles of the environment and interpersonal relationships in the development of personality, and several of his contemporaries believed this was a mistake. Later in this chapter we will review the interpersonal theories, which view social relation-

ships as the driving force of psychological development within individuals. These interpersonal theories grew out of splits between Freud and his followers.

One new school of thought within psychodynamic theory retained significant aspects of Freud's drive theory, but integrated this with discussions of the role of early relationships in the development of self-concept and personality. This school is known as **object relations** theory. According to proponents of this school, such as Melanie Klein, Margaret Mahler, Otto Kernberg, and Heinz Kohut, our early relationships create images or representations of ourselves and others that we carry throughout adulthood and that affect all subsequent relationships we have. There are four fundamental phases in the development of the self-concept (Figure 2.11). In the first phase, known as the *undifferentiated stage*, the newborn infant has only an image of the self and no sense that other people or objects are separate from the self. The infant believes that its caregiver and itself are one and that everything the infant feels or wants the caregiver feels or wants. In the second phase, known as *symbiosis*, the newborn infant still does not distinguish between self and other but does distinguish between good and bad aspects of the self-plus-other image. That is, the child has an image of

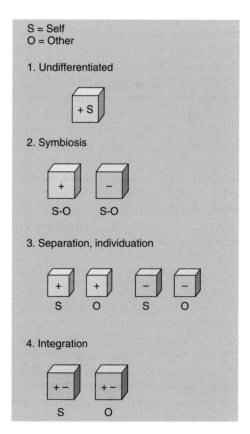

FIGURE 2.11 Stages of Development of Self-Concept According to Object Relations Theory. Object relations theory suggests that infants begin with an undifferentiated sense of self and other and eventually develop an integrated sense of the positive and negative aspects of self and other.

the good self-plus-other and an image of the bad self-plus-other. These images are either all good or all bad. In the third phase, the *separation-individuation phase*, the child begins to differentiate between the self and the other. The child's image of the good self and the bad self are not integrated, however. The child either focuses on the good self or the bad self exclusively. Similarly, the child's image of the good other and the bad other are not integrated, and the child focuses on only the good other or the bad other. A child who is frustrated with a parent may say, "I hate you!" and mean it with all his heart, because he is focusing only on the bad image of the parent at the time. In the fourth stage, the *integration stage*, the child is able to distinguish clearly between the self and the other and is able to integrate the good and bad images of the self and the other into complex representations, allowing a frustrated child to say to a parent, "I am really mad at you, but I still love you."

According to the object relations theorists, many people with psychopathology never fully resolve stages two or three, and are prone to seeing the self and others as all good or all bad. This is known as **splitting,** because the image of the self and other are split into the good image and the bad image, with no appreciation for the mixed qualities of good and bad that are true of all people. Also, a person stuck in stages two or three never fully differentiates between the self and other and expects others to know what they feel and want. As we shall see, this notion of splitting provides an intriguing explanation of the syndrome known as *borderline personality disorder*. People with this disorder tend to view themselves and other people as either all good or all bad and vacillate between these two images, either idealizing themselves and others or hating themselves and others to the point of wanting to hurt themselves or others. People with borderline personality disorder also tend to have trouble accepting the boundaries between themselves and others and, when even slightly rejected by another, feel completely abandoned and empty.

Assessing Psychodynamic Theories

Freud and the psychodynamic theorists who followed him were the first to establish a systematic explanation of abnormal behavior in terms of psychological principles rather than purely biological or supernatural principles. Thus, they were truly the founders of a psychological approach to the study of psychopathology. Moreover, psychodynamic theories are probably the most comprehensive, and for some people the most satisfying, theories of human behavior established to date. They explain both normal and abnormal behavior with similar processes. And they have an "aha!" quality about them that leads us to believe they hold important insights.

Karen Horney was an early critic of Freud's assertions that personality is fixed in childhood and that women suffer from penis envy.

There are many limitations and weaknesses to psychodynamic theories, however. One of the earliest critics of Freud's conceptualization of female development was Karen Horney, who was trained in Berlin by Freud's colleagues, Abraham and Sachs, in the early 1900s. Using research from anthropology, sociology, and her own therapy practice, Horney (1934/67) challenged several assumptions and methods in classical psychoanalysis. These included (1) the emphasis on sexual drives and anatomy in personality, and the exclusion of environmental and cultural influences on personality development; (2) the view that the male is the prototypical human being; and (3) the claim that one could describe a universally applicable psychology of the human based on a small sample.

In particular, Horney felt that Freud and other psychoanalysts had committed a grave error in the collection of observations leading to Freudian theories of female personality: Freud and the other theorists were using the societal ideal of womanhood to describe what they thought was the inherent female character. Horney wrote (1934/67, pp. 182–183):

> This attitude toward women, whatever its basis and however it may be assessed, represents the patriarchal ideal of womanhood, of woman as one whose only longing is to love a man and to be loved by him, to admire him and to serve him, and even to pattern herself after him. Those who maintain this point of view mistakenly infer from external behavior the existence of an innate instinctual disposition thereto, whereas, in reality, the latter cannot be recognized as such, for the reason that biological factors never manifest themselves in pure and undisguised form, but always as modified by tradition and environment.

Horney's reference to "biological factors . . . modified by tradition and environment" illustrates her view that the personality of a man or woman is shaped by the complicated interplay between biological needs and drives and external, environmental demands and experiences.

Another major problem with most psychodynamic theories is that it is difficult or impossible to scientifically test their fundamental assumptions (Erdelyi, 1992; although see Westen, 1998). The processes described by these theories are abstract and difficult to measure. The theories themselves often provide ways of explaining away the results of studies that seem to dispute their fundamental assumptions. Perhaps as a result, there is very little controlled research testing traditional psychodynamic theories and some of the newer theories.

Freud believed that personality was essentially fixed in childhood, with little opportunity for significant change later on, even with therapy. Even many of his early critics believed that human personality continues to grow and change in response to changes in the environment and in personal relationships, and that therapy did offer significant hope for people who wanted to change fundamental aspects of their personalities.

Still, there is no doubt that psychodynamic theories have had a major role in shaping psychology and psychiatry in the last century. The fundamental assumption of traditional psychodynamic theory that unconscious processes drive our behaviors has become a fundamental assumption of laypeople's views of human behaviors. When we find ourselves questioning the "real" motives behind our own or others' behaviors, when we "realize" we are attracted to a certain person because we know our mother would disapprove, when we recall a traumatic event from the past that we believe we have been repressing, we are applying psychodynamic theories.

Behavioral Theories of Abnormality

The motto of the **behavioral theories** is "You are a product of your environment." Thus, behavioral theories reject claims that unconscious conflicts drive human behavior. Instead, behaviorists focus on the influences of reinforcements and punishments in producing behavior.

Like the psychodynamic theorists, behavioral theorists sought to explain both normal and abnormal behavior through the same principles. The principles of behaviorism, however, focus on how behaviors are learned through experiences in the environment. The two core principles or processes of learning according to behaviorism are classical conditioning and operant conditioning. Later, behaviorists acknowledged that learning can occur through modeling and observational learning.

Classical Conditioning

Ivan Pavlov, a Russian physiologist, was conducting experiments on the salivary glands of dogs when he made discoveries that would revolutionize psychological theory. Not surprisingly, his dogs would salivate when Pavlov or an assistant put food in their mouths. Pavlov noticed that, after a while, the dogs would begin to salivate when he or his assistant simply walked into the room. This phenomenon gained the name **classical conditioning.** Pavlov had paired a previously neutral stimulus (himself) with a stimulus that naturally leads to a certain response (the dish of food that leads to salivating), and eventually the neutral stimulus (Pavlov) was able to elicit that response (salivation). He named the stimulus that naturally produced the desired response the **unconditioned stimulus (US)**, and the response created by the unconditioned stimulus was named the **unconditioned response (UR).** So, in Pavlov's experiments, the dish of food was the US and salivation in response to this food was the UR. He named the previously neutral stimulus the **conditioned stimulus (CS)** and the response that it elicited the **conditioned response (CR).** Thus, Pavlov was the CS, and when the dogs salivated in response to seeing him, this salivation became the CR (see *Concept Review*: Stimulus and Response in Classical Conditioning, p. 52).

Classical conditioning has been used to explain people's seemingly irrational responses to a host of neutral stimuli. For example, consider the following case study.

CASE STUDY

A 2-year-old girl named Sarah had undergone major surgery for a congenital defect. The surgery was a success, and Sarah was recovering at home. Her Aunt Jean and Uncle Vern came to visit Sarah about 1 week after she returned home. Sarah had always adored Jean and Vern, but soon after they entered the house, Sarah showed great fear of Vern and began crying hysterically when he tried to console her. Vern and Jean left and came back a few days later. Once again, upon hearing Vern's voice, Sarah began sobbing and ran to her mother's arms in great fear. Vern was heartbroken at Sarah's response and did not understand how she could have suddenly become so fearful of him. After a while, Sarah's mother realized that Vern's voice was extremely similar to the voice of the doctor who had treated Sarah in the hospital. Although this doctor was a kind man, he had had to perform several very painful procedures on Sarah while she was in the hospital. Eventually, Sarah had come to shake and cry simply upon seeing the doctor enter the room and hearing his voice. Sarah had apparently generalized her learned fear of the doctor's voice to Vern's voice because their two voices sounded similar.

CONCEPT REVIEW

Stimulus and Response in Classical Conditioning

Through classical conditioning, Pavlov's dogs came to associate Pavlov with food and thus began to salivate when Pavlov entered the room.

Term	Definition	Example from Pavlov's Experiment
Unconditioned stimulus (US)	Stimulus that naturally produces desired response	Dish of food
Unconditioned response (UR)	Response created by unconditioned stimulus	Salivation
Conditioned stimulus (CS)	Previously neutral stimulus paired with unconditioned stimulus	Pavlov
Conditioned response (CR)	Response elicited by conditioned stimulus	Salivation

Classical conditioning can also explain why heroin addicts sometimes have physiological responses similar to those they have when they take heroin if they simply see a syringe. They have developed a conditioned physiological response to syringes (which have become a conditioned stimulus), because of the frequent pairing of the syringes with the actual physiological action of the drugs.

Operant Conditioning

E. L. Thorndike observed that behaviors that are followed by a reward are strengthened, whereas behaviors that are followed by a punishment are weakened. This simple but important observation, which Thorndike labeled the **law of effect,** led to the development of the principles of **operant conditioning**—the shaping of behaviors by providing rewards for desired behaviors and punishments for undesired behaviors. B. F. Skinner is the psychologist most strongly associated with operant conditioning. He showed that a pigeon will learn to press on a bar if pressing it is associated with the delivery of food, and it will learn to avoid pressing another bar if pressing it is associated with an electric shock. Similarly, a child will learn to make his bed if he receives a hug and kiss from his mother each time he makes the bed, and he will learn to stop hitting his brother if every time he hits his brother he loses 1 hour of television watching.

In operant conditioning, behaviors will be learned most quickly if they are paired with the reward or punishment every time the behavior is emitted. This consistent response is called a **continuous reinforcement schedule.** Behaviors can be learned and maintained, however, on a **partial reinforcement schedule,** in which the reward or punishment occurs only sometimes in response to the behavior. **Extinction**—eliminating a learned behavior—is more difficult when the

behavior was learned through a partial reinforcement schedule than it is when the behavior was learned through a continuous reinforcement schedule. This is because the organism will continue to emit the behavior learned through a partial reinforcement schedule in the absence of the reward, anticipating that the reward will eventually come. A good example is gambling behavior. People who frequently gamble are seldom rewarded, but they continue to gamble in anticipation of that occasional, unpredictable win.

Combinations of classical and operant conditioning can help to explain elaborate responses people develop to avoid situations that arouse fear in them. For example, consider a woman who developed a fear of bridges through classical conditioning: She fell off a

People who gamble may receive rewards on a partial reinforcement schedule, which keeps them gambling even when they encounter long periods with no wins.

bridge into icy waters as a child, and now anytime she nears a bridge, she feels very anxious. This woman has developed elaborate means of getting around her hometown without having to cross any bridges. Avoiding the bridges reduces her anxiety, and thus her avoidant behavior is reinforced. This woman has developed a *conditioned avoidance response* through operant conditioning. As a result, however, she never exposes herself to a bridge and thus never has the opportunity to extinguish her initial fear of bridges. As we shall see, many of the therapeutic techniques developed by behavioral theorists are designed to extinguish conditioned avoidance responses, which can often interfere greatly with a person's ability to function in everyday life.

Modeling and Observational Learning

Skinner and other "pure" behaviorists argued that humans and animals learn behaviors only by directly experiencing the rewards or punishments for these behaviors. In the 1950s, however, psychologist Albert Bandura argued that people could also learn behaviors by watching other people, a view that came to be known as **social learning theory**. First, in **modeling,** people learn new behaviors from imitating the behaviors modeled by important people in their lives, such as their parents. Learning through modeling is more likely to occur when the person modeling the behavior is seen as an authority figure or is perceived to be like oneself. For example, Bandura (1969) argued that children are most likely to imitate the behaviors modeled by their same-sex parent, because this parent is an authority figure and because their same-sex parent seems more similar to them than does their opposite-sex parent.

Observational learning takes place when a person observes the rewards and punishments that another person receives for his or her behavior and then behaves in accord with those rewards and punishments. For example, a child who views her sibling being punished for dropping food on the floor will learn, through observation, the consequences of dropping food on the floor and thus will be less likely to engage in this behavior herself. Some theorists argue that even extreme negative behaviors, such as teenagers going on a shooting rampage, are also due to observational learning. Teenagers see heroes in the media being rewarded for violent behavior and thus learn that behavior. They also are directly rewarded for violent behavior in certain video games.

Assessing Behavioral Theories

The behavioral theorists set the standard for scientifically testing hypotheses about how normal and abnormal behaviors develop. The hypotheses developed from these theories are precise and the studies that have been done to test these hypotheses are rigorously controlled and exact. These studies have provided strong support for behavioral explanations of many types of abnormal behavior, as we shall see in the following chapters (cf. Wolpe, 1997).

The behavioral theories do have limitations, however. Certain types of abnormal behaviors can be created in the laboratory, but is this how they develop in the real world? Laboratory studies are artificial and cannot capture the complexity of environmental experiences that shape people's behavior. In addition, the behavioral theories have been criticized, as have the psychodynamic theories, for not recognizing "free will" in people's behaviors—the active choices they make to defy the external forces upon them.

The movement that eventually overcame behavioral theories of human behavior was the cognitive revolution in psychology. Cognitive psychologists made great strides in understanding the processes of memory, attention, and information processing, and by the late 1960s and early 1970s, much of the theorizing about the causes of abnormal behavior focused on the role of cognitions. The cognitive theorists argued that it is not just rewards, punishments, or even drives that motivate human behavior. Instead, humans actively construct meaning out of their experiences and act in accord with their interpretations of the world.

Cognitive Theories of Abnormality

The motto of the **cognitive theories** of abnormality may be, "You are what you think." These theories argue that **cognitions**—thoughts or beliefs—shape our behaviors and the emotions we experience. Three types of cognitions that have been the focus of several theories of abnormal behavior are causal attributions, control beliefs, and dysfunctional assumptions.

When something happens to us, we ask ourselves why that event happened (Abramson, Metalsky, & Alloy, 1989; Abramson, Seligman, & Teasdale, 1978). The answer to this "why" question is our **causal attribution** for the event. The attributions we make for events can influence our behavior and emotions because they influence the meaning we give to events and our expectations for similar events in the future. For example, if we attribute a friend's rude behavior to temporary or situational factors (he is under a lot of pressure), then we do not evaluate that friend too harshly and we do not expect the friend to act rudely again in the future. However, if we attribute the friend's behavior to personality factors (he is a mean guy), then our evaluations of the friend will be more harsh, and we will expect the friend to act

If we attribute behavior such as rudeness to situational factors, we will react less negatively than if we attribute that behavior to a stable factor such as personality.

rudely again. A personality attribution for the friend's behavior might lead us to avoid the friend or even break up the relationship, whereas a situational attribution would not.

The attributions we make for our own behavior in situations can have a strong effect on our emotions and self-concept. For example, if we act meanly toward another person and attribute this behavior to situational factors (the other person acted mean first), we may feel slightly guilty but we may also feel justified. However, if we attribute this behavior to personality factors (I am a mean person), then we may feel quite guilty and lose self-esteem. Our attributions for our performance in achievement settings can also affect our self-esteem, our emotions, and our willingness to continue striving. Attributing failure on an exam to situational factors (the exam was too hard) will result in less negative emotion than attributing failure on an exam to personality factors (I am not very smart).

A **control theory** focuses on people's expectancies for their abilities to control important events (Bandura, 1977; Rotter, 1954; Seligman, 1975). When people believe they can control an important event, they will behave in ways to control that event. When they do not believe they can control an event, they will not attempt to control it or will easily give up when they have difficulty controlling it. Martin Seligman (1975) argued that repeated experiences with uncontrollable events lead a person to develop **learned helplessness,** the general expectation that future events will be uncontrollable. He described a set of learned helplessness deficits that resulted from this expectation, including lowered self-esteem, lowered persistence and motivation, and the inability to see opportunities for control when they do arise.

In an update of his social learning theory, Albert Bandura (1977) argued that a major contributor to people's sense of well-being, motivation, and persistence

is their sense of *self-efficacy.* Self-efficacy is a person's belief that he or she can successfully execute the behaviors necessary to control desired outcomes. A good example of high self-efficacy is the little train that kept saying, "I think I can! I think I can! I think I can!" People with high self-efficacy expectations for a given situation exert more control over that situation, try harder, are more persistent, and are more successful in that situation than are people with low self-efficacy expectations (Bandura, 1986). High self-efficacy expectations also protect a person against negative emotional reactions to a situation. For example, consider a person whose home was ruined in a flood. If she has high self-efficacy, she will maintain her motivation to rebuild her home, will make better decisions about how to rebuild, and will be less likely to become depressed over the loss of her home than if she has a low sense of self-efficacy.

A different set of cognitive theories of psychopathology suggest that we have broad beliefs about how things work, which can be either positive and helpful to us, or negative and destructive. These broad beliefs are called **global assumptions.** Two of the prominent proponents of this view are Albert Ellis and Aaron Beck. They argued that most negative emotions or maladaptive behaviors are the result of one or more dysfunctional global assumptions that guide a person's life. Some of the most common dysfunctional assumptions are:

1. I should be loved by everyone for everything I do.
2. Things should turn out the way I want them to turn out.
3. I should be terribly upset by dangerous situations.
4. It is better to avoid problems than to face them.
5. I need someone stronger and more powerful than me to rely on.
6. I should be completely competent, intelligent, and achieving in all I do.
7. Once something affects my life, it will affect it forever.
8. I must have perfect self-control.
9. I have no control over my emotions and cannot help feeling certain feelings.

People who hold these beliefs will often react to situations with irrational thoughts and behaviors and negative emotions. For example, someone who believes that she must be completely competent, intelligent, and achieving in all areas in her life will be extremely upset by even minor failures or bad events, such as tearing her blouse or forgetting to return a phone call. If she were to score poorly on an exam, she may have

Calvin and Hobbes   by Bill Watterson

Calvin has a positive cognitive style.
© Bill Watterson, Universal Press Syndicate.

thoughts such as "I am a total failure. I will never amount to anything. I should have gotten a perfect score on that exam." Similarly, someone who believes that things should always turn out the way he wants them to may be unable to respond flexibly to the obstacles and setbacks that inevitably stand in the way of achieving goals in daily life. Rather than finding some way around these obstacles, he may focus on the obstacles, distressed that things are not going his way. Aaron Beck developed an effective and widely used therapy for emotional disorders based on this cognitive theory, which we will explore in Chapter 5. Beck's cognitive therapy helps clients identify and challenge these negative thoughts and dysfunctional belief systems.

Assessing the Cognitive Theories

The cognitive theories may seem most comfortable or familiar to you of all the theories we have discussed thus far. That is probably because they are a product of our times and dominate much of current clinical, personality, and social psychology. The cognitive theories are also attractive because they focus on that distinctly human process of abstract thinking.

Cognitive theorists have worked hard to provide scientific evidence for their explanations of specific disorders, and as we shall see, have been successful in many domains. Particularly in studies of mood disorders and anxiety disorders, and increasingly in studies of sexual disorders and substance use disorders, the cognitive theories have helped to explain how unwanted emotions, thoughts and behaviors develop and are maintained.

The greatest limitation of the cognitive theories has been the difficulty of proving that maladaptive cognitions precede and cause disorders, rather than being the symptoms or consequences of the disorders. For example, it is clear that depressed people think depressing thoughts. But is this a cause of their depression, or a symptom of it? It turns out to be harder than

you might think to answer this question definitively (Coyne & Gotlib, 1983). Even if cognitions can cause changes in mood and behavior, it is clear that changes in mood and behavior can also cause cognition (Bower, 1981). In other words, there are reciprocal effects or feedback loops between cognitions, behaviors, and moods that make it difficult to distinguish what is cause and what is effect.

The cognitive theories have also been criticized for assuming that negative beliefs are always irrational, and for ignoring the negative lives that some people truly lead. People who believe they have little control over their environments, that they are not good at most things, or that no one loves them, may be correct in their beliefs, and not distorting reality. Many cognitive theorists would argue, however, that reality is always in the eye of the beholder to some extent, and that there are more and less adaptive ways of viewing even the most difficult of circumstances.

The Humanistic and Existential Theories of Abnormality

More than any of the other theories of abnormality, the **humanistic and existential theories** focus on what we might call "the person" behind the cognitions, the behaviors, and the unconscious conflicts. These theories are based on the assumption that the human being has an innate capacity for goodness and for living a full life. Pressure from society to conform to certain norms rather than to seek one's most developed self may interfere with the fulfillment of this capacity.

The humanistic theories emerged in the 1950s and 1960s, partially in reaction to the pessimistic and deterministic view of human behavior provided by traditional psychodynamic theory and to the claims of traditional behavioral theory that humans were only products of their environment. The humanistic theorists recognized that we are often not aware of the forces shaping our behavior and that the environment

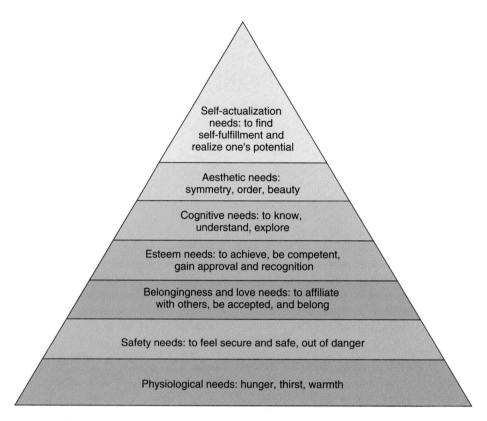

FIGURE 2.12   Abraham Maslow's Hierarchy of Needs. Needs low in the hierarchy must be met before needs higher in the hierarchy are important to motivation.

can play a strong role in our happiness or unhappiness. But they were optimistic that, once people were made aware of these forces and freed to make choices about the direction of their lives, they would naturally make good choices and be happier.

Carl Rogers (1951) developed the most widely known version of humanistic theory. Rogers believed that, without undue pressure from others, individuals naturally move toward personal growth, self-acceptance, and **self-actualization,** which is the fulfillment of their potential for love, creativity, and meaning. We can develop a set of values that are all our own, and an identity that is free from the expectations of others.

Under the stress of pressure from society and family, however, people can develop rigid and distorted perspectives of the self and can lose touch with their own values and needs. This can lead to emotional distress, unhealthy behaviors, and even loss of touch with reality. Rogers developed a form of therapy, called **client-centered therapy,** that is designed to help people realize their genuine selves, to accept themselves entirely, and to begin growing toward self-actualization (see Chapter 5).

Abraham Maslow, another key figure in the development of the humanistic perspective, argued that humans have a hierarchy of needs, and self-

Carl Rogers (1902–1987) is one of the founders of humanistic theory.

actualization can only occur after lower-order needs are satisfied (see Figure 2.12). The most basic needs are physiological needs, such as hunger, while at the highest level of the hierarchy is the need to fulfill one's own personal values and to reach self-actualization. Maslow said that people who were at this highest level of the hierarchy "no longer strive in the ordinary sense, but rather develop. They attempt to grow to perfection and to develop more and more fully in their own style" (Maslow, 1954, p. 211). Maladaptive behavior and general distress can result from a person's inability to fulfill lower-order needs and reach a point of growth instead of striving.

The existential theories of Fritz Perls, Martin Heidegger, and Soren Kierkegaard were based on many of the same beliefs as the humanistic theories. Humans are in control—they have the capacity and the responsibility to direct their lives in meaningful and constructive ways. They also believed that the ultimate goal in human growth is the discovery of one's own values and meaning and living one's life by these values. The existentialists, however, put more emphasis on the difficulties inherent in self-actualization, recognizing that society puts many obstacles in the way of living according to one's own values. *Existential anxiety*, created by the realization of our ultimate death, leads many people to abandon their personal growth and search for meaning. We must overcome this anxiety by choosing to live full and meaningful lives, or our lives will be wasted and corrupted and likely filled with misery and maladaptive behaviors.

Assessing Humanistic and Existential Theories

The humanistic theories struck a positive chord in the 1960s and still have many proponents, especially among self-help groups and peer counseling programs. The optimism and attribution of free will of these theories is a refreshing change from the emphasis on pathology and external forces in other theories. These theories change our focus from what is wrong with people to questions about how we can help people achieve their greatest potential.

The humanistic and existential theories have been criticized, however, for being vague and impossible to test scientifically. And as we discuss in Chapter 5, the humanistic therapies may be helpful and interesting to people who are generally healthy and functioning in society, but it is not clear they can help people with serious psychopathology.

Summing Up

- Psychoanalytic theories of psychopathology focus on unconscious conflicts that cause anxiety in the individual and result in maladaptive behavior.
- The ways people handle their conflicts are defined by the types of defense mechanisms they use. Children can become fixated on certain needs or concerns if their transitions through psychosexual stages are not managed well.
- More recent psychodynamic theories focused less on the role of unconscious impulses and more on the development of the individual's self-concept in the context of interpersonal relationships. They see a greater role for the environment in the shaping of personality and have more hope for change in personality during adulthood than Freud did.
- The behavioral theories of abnormality focus only on the rewards and punishments in the environment that shape and maintain behavior.
- Classical conditioning takes place when a previously neutral stimulus is paired with a stimulus that naturally creates a certain response; eventually the neutral stimulus will also elicit the response.
- Operant conditioning involves rewarding desired behaviors and punishing undesired behaviors.
- People also learn by imitating the behaviors modeled by others and by observing the rewards and punishments others receive for their behaviors.
- Cognitive theories suggest that people's attributions for events, their perceptions of control and self-efficacy, and their beliefs about themselves and the world influence their behaviors and emotions in reaction to situations.
- Humanist and existential theories suggest that all humans strive to fulfill their potential for good and to self-actualize. The inability to fulfill one's potential arises from the pressures of society to conform to others' expectations and values and from existential anxiety.

⊙ SOCIOCULTURAL APPROACHES

The psychological theories we have discussed so far focus primarily on the individual. They attribute problematic psychological symptoms to unconscious conflicts, negative cognitions, existential anxiety, and other factors residing largely within the individual. Although these theories may suggest that the environment played a role in creating these problems, they still consider the individual as the primary unit of analysis.

The sociocultural approaches to abnormality focus more on the larger social structures within which an individual lives (see *Concept Review:* Sociocultural Theories of Mental Disorders, p. 58). These structures can include the individual's marriage or family, and his or her neighborhood, social class, or culture.

Interpersonal Theories of Abnormality

Humans are social beings. The **interpersonal theories** put this fact at the center of their explanations of the

CONCEPT REVIEW

Sociocultural Theories of Mental Disorders

The social theories of mental disorders are concerned with the role of social forces, including interpersonal relationships, family dynamics, and the larger society, in producing psychological symptoms.

Name	Description
Interpersonal theories	Mental disorders are the result of long-standing patterns of negative relationships that have their roots in early experiences with caregivers.
Family systems theories	Families create and maintain mental disorders in individual family members to maintain homeostasis.
Social structural theories	Societies create mental disorders in individuals by putting them under unbearable stress and by sanctioning abnormal behavior.

Erik Erikson and his wife.

development of normal and abnormal behavior more than any of the theories we have discussed so far. Contemporary interpersonal theories grew out of a split between Freud and one of his students, Alfred Adler. Adler disagreed with Freud's singular focus on unconscious processes within the individual as the force behind human behavior, and on Freud's concern with instinctual drives. He argued that the primary motivation of humans was to belong to and participate in social groups. Later, other psychodynamic theorists also split with Freud and emphasized social motives and social forces in shaping humans' behaviors more than sexual drives. These included Erich Fromm, Karen Horney, and Erik Erikson.

Erik Erikson proposed a series of stages of psychosocial development that are not concerned with the gratification of sexual needs, as in Freud's stages, but with the resolving conflicts between issues that are social in nature (see Figure 2.13). In the first year of life, the conflict is between trust and mistrust. In years 2 through 3, the conflict is between autonomy and shame. In years 4 through 5, the conflict is between taking initiative and feeling guilt for that initiative. In years 6 through 11, the child faces conflicts between gaining a sense of industry or mastery and having a sense of inferiority. Ages 12 to 18 are characterized by a search for one's identity versus confusion about one's role in society. During young adulthood, a person faces conflicts between intimacy and isolation. In middle

age, the issue is whether one will be creative and productive or become stagnant. In old age, the individual can develop a sense of integrity or a sense of despair. We never fully resolve all of the conflicts of life, but some people make better resolutions than others, and these people tend to be happier and better adjusted.

Harry Stack Sullivan (1953) developed ideas similar to those of the object relations school about the roles of important others in the development of self-concept, but used very different language from the object relations schools. He noted that children constantly receive feedback from others for their behaviors—criticism for some behaviors and praise for others. The behaviors and aspects of self that are continually criticized become part of the child's self-concept as the *bad-me* and the aspects of self that are praised become part of the self-concept as the *good-me*. The bad-me arouses anxiety, so the child develops ways of averting attention from those aspects of the self. If enough anxiety is aroused by those aspects of self, the child may develop it as the *not-me*, blocking it from consciousness. All of us have aspects of ourselves we wish to deny—our anger, our sexual urges, our competitiveness, perhaps. Even when these not-me aspects are repressed, they still exert influence on our behavior. We may deny we are angry, but everyone else knows we are angry, for example. People with severe psychopathology have images of the self and others that are so painful and conflicted that they engage in self-destructive behavior to avoid these images. For example, a woman whose father secretly abused her as a child may be completely unable to confront these truths about herself and her father, and drink heavily to numb the feelings she has.

The child's self-concept is part of a broader system of **prototypes**—images of the self and others in relation to the self—that are formed from experiences with family members during childhood. Throughout

Stage of life	Psychological crisis	Favorable outcome
I. Infancy	Trust vs. mistrust	Trust and hope
II. Early childhood	Autonomy vs. shame, doubt	Self-control, sense of adequacy
III. Years 3 to 5	Initiative vs. guilt	Purpose and direction, initiative
IV. Years 6 to puberty	Industry vs. inferiority	Competence
V. Adolescence	Identity vs. confusion	Integrated view of self as unique
VI. Early adulthood	Intimacy vs. isolation	Ability to form close relationships
VII. Middle adulthood	Generativity vs. stagnation	Concern for family, society
VIII. Old age	Integrity vs. despair	Fulfillment and satisfaction, willingness to face death

FIGURE 2.13   Erikson's Stages of Psychosocial Development. Erickson proposed eight stages of psychosocial crises that can lead to positive or negative development across the life span.

life, our reactions to others reflect these prototypes. This can lead to irrational and exaggerated reactions. For example, an innocent remark by our boss can lead to extreme anxiety or anger because it activates our prototype of our father, who was constantly critical.

More recently, interpersonal theorists have focused on the "scripts" people develop for their relationships—the set of expectations for how each person in a relationship should behave toward the other. Wives and husbands have implicit scripts for how each other should behave in the marriage, parents and children have implicit scripts for each other's behaviors, and so on. When these expectations are violated, people can become confused, angry, frightened, and relationships can dissolve. Other relationships are conflictual because patterns of communication break down, and the methods partners in the relationship are using to negotiate common goals are not working (Leary, 1957; Wiggins, 1982).

Finally, several theorists have formulated theories of normal and abnormal behavior based on the work of John Bowlby (1969), whose work was influenced by psychodynamic thought but also by ethology—the study of animal behavior. Bowlby argued that early in life we form strong attachments to our caregivers, and the quality of these attachments then determines our expectations for ourselves and our relationships. Children who form secure attachments are confident that their caregivers will be there when they need them. This confidence gives them the courage to explore their environment, returning to their caregivers for comfort and assistance when necessary. As they mature, these children will expect other relationships to be secure, and will seek out and form positive, strong relationships with others. Children who have insecure attachments do not have confidence in their

Children with anxious and insecure attachments to caregivers may develop chronic anxiety as adults.

caregivers because their caregivers have not been consistently trustworthy. They may be anxious and clinging to their caregivers, refusing to leave their side. Or they may be hostile and avoidant of caregivers. In either case, these children will then have negative expectations for future relationships, which will essentially become self-fulfilling prophecies. Children with anxious insecure attachments will become adults who are prone to anxiety, depression, and excessive dependence on others. Children with avoidant insecure

EXTRAORDINARY PEOPLE

Kay Redfield Jamison

In 1995, Dr. Kay Redfield Jamison published another book, which she titled *An Unquiet Mind*. This was not an unusual event in her life or in the field of mood disorders—Jamison had already published two books and dozens of journal articles in her career as a research psychologist and clinician, including a definitive and encyclopedic book describing the causes and treatment of manic-depression, a disorder in which people alternate between periods of depression and periods of manic excitement. What made the publication of *An Unquiet Mind* extraordinary was that it was Jamison's autobiography of her experience with her own manic-depression. In this book, Jamison describes her moods, her psychotic episodes, her suicide attempts, some outrageous things she did while manic, and her resistance to taking medication. It is an intimate look inside the life of a person with severe manic-depression, in all its mystery and tragedy. Seldom does a person in Jamison's position—a professor of psychiatry at Johns Hopkins Medical School, a leading researcher and author in the field of mood disorders, an active clinician who specializes in treating people with mood disorders—reveal that she also suffers from the very disorder she researches and treats.

Such public admissions can have negative consequences. Although many psychiatrists and psychologists have a personal history of mental disorder, they are often reluctant to let it be known, because they fear that it will affect their professional licenses, their privileges to admit patients to the hospital, or their reputations. They are also concerned, as was Jamison, that their revelation of mental illness would have repercussions for their family.

So why did Jamison feel the need to go public with her illness? Jamison's explanation of her decision to reveal her manic-depression indicates her personal triumph over fears of others' opinions, and her dedication to changing cultural attitudes toward mental disorders:

> I have no idea what the long-term effects of discussing such issues so openly will be on my personal and professional life, but whatever the consequences, they are bound to be better than continuing to be silent. I am tired of hiding, tired of misspent and knotted energies, tired of the hypocrisy, and tired of acting as though I have something to hide. One is what one is, and the dishonesty of hiding behind a degree, or a title, or any manner and collection of words, is still exactly that: dishonest. Necessary, perhaps, but dishonest. I continue to have concerns about my decision to be public about my illness, but one of the advantages of having had manic-depressive illness for more than thirty years is that very little seems insurmountably difficult. Much like crossing the Bay Bridge when there is a storm over the Chesapeake, one may be terrified to go forward, but there is no question of going back. I find myself somewhat inevitably taking a certain solace in Robert Lowell's essential question, *Yet why not say what happened?* (Jamison, 1995b, pp. 7–8)

We can only hope that, as the public understands more about mental disorders, fewer people with these disorders will have to fear the consequences of letting it be known that they suffer. Kay Redfield Jamison, through her courageous decision to talk about her manic-depression, and her eloquent and thoughtful writing and speaking on mental disorders, has moved us a bit closer to the fulfillment of that hope.

attachments may become adults who are hostile, isolated, and even violent.

Assessing Interpersonal Theories

The interpersonal theories have recently begun to be put to empirical tests. Some of the hypotheses from these theories about the importance of prototypes or "mental models" of early relationships in shaping adult relationships are being supported (Fonagy et al., 1996; Toth & Cichetti, 1996; van Ijzendoorn & Bakermans-Kranenburg, 1996). In addition, new therapies based on the interpersonal theories are proving helpful in several disorders, as we discuss in Chapter 5. Thus, these theories are promising, but we shall have to wait as more research is done to test their fundamental assumptions.

Family Systems Theories of Abnormality

Most of the theories we have discussed thus far have implicated the family in the development of both normal and abnormal behavior. The **family systems theories** and therapies focus on the family in quite a different manner from the other theories, however (Kaslow & Celano, 1995; Minuchin, 1981; Satir, 1967). These theories see the family as a complex system that works to maintain the status quo, or **homeostasis.** Each family has its own hierarchy and set of rules that govern the behavior of the members and help to maintain homeostasis. The family system can be well-functioning and healthy for its individual members, supporting their growth and accepting their change. Or the family system can be dysfunctional, in essence requiring psychopathology in one or more members in order to maintain homeostasis.

When a member of the family does have a psychological disorder, family systems theorists see it not as a problem within the individual but an indication of a dysfunctional family system. Psychopathology in an individual member reflects pathology or dysfunction in the family unit, according to family systems theory. The particular form that any individual member's psychopathology takes depends on the complex interactions between the family's cohesiveness, adaptability to change and environmental demand, and their communication style. An inflexible family is resistant and isolated from all forces outside the family and does not adapt well to changes within the family, such as a child moving into adolescence. In an enmeshed family, each member is too greatly involved in the lives of the other members, to the point that individuals do not have personal autonomy and can feel controlled. In contrast, a disengaged family is one in which the members pay

Family therapists believe that individuals' problems are rooted in patterns of interaction among family members.

no attention to each other and operate as independent units isolated from other family members. And in pathological triangular relationships, parents avoid dealing with conflicts with each other by always keeping their children involved in their conversations and activities (Kaslow & Celano, 1995).

Some of the research on family systems theories of psychopathology has focused on disorders in the children in the family, particularly eating disorders (e.g., Minuchin, Rosman, & Baker, 1978). This research suggests that young girls who develop eating disorders are often members of enmeshed families. The parents of these girls are overcontrolling and overinvested in their children's success, and in turn the children feel smothered and dependent on their parents. Anorexia nervosa, a disorder in which an individual refuses to eat and becomes emaciated, may be a girl's way of claiming some control over her life. The family system of these girls, rather than working to help her overcome her anorexia, maintains and supports the anorexia. The anorexia becomes a focal point and excuse for the family's enmeshment.

Assessing the Family Systems Theory

As we discuss in Chapter 5, the family systems theories have led to therapeutic approaches that have proven useful for some types of disorders. Family systems therapies may be particularly appropriate in the treatment of children, because children are so much more entwined in their families than adults. Although the details of many family systems theories have not been thoroughly tested in research, it is clear that families can contribute to or help to diminish psychological symptoms in their members suffering from psychological disorders (e.g., Kaslow & Celano, 1995).

Neighborhood Characteristics		**Social Organization**		**Mental Health Outcomes**
Widespread poverty		Lack of common values		Child maltreatment
Prejudice and discrimination		Lack of social control		Juvenile delinquency
Lack of cultural or ethnic ties		Open conflict		Behavioral disorders
High residential turnover				Depression
High child to adult ratio	+	**Psychological Stress**	→	Anxiety
		Insufficient resources		Schizophrenia
		Chronic agitation and fear		Substance abuse
		Subcultural Influences		
		Development of gangs and drug use		

FIGURE 2.14   A Social Structural Model of Mental Health (based on Wandersman & Nation, 1998). Social structural theories focus on the effects of the larger society on individuals' mental health.

Social Structural Theories of Abnormality

Finally, **social structural theories** suggest that we need to look beyond even the family to the larger society to find the causes of psychopathology in individuals (Ensminger, 1995). First, society can create stresses on individuals that increase their risk for psychopathology. These stresses may come in the form of massive reorganization of the society, such as the industrialization of America in the early twentieth century, or the great increases in the presence of people of Hispanic origins in the American west in the last decade. Such societal reorganization changes people's roles and relationships to the society—from factory worker to unemployed person, from member of the majority culture to member of a multicultural society. Societies undergoing significant social change often experience increases in the rates of mental disorders. This is especially true if the change is generally seen as a negative one, as during an economic depression.

Second, some people live in more chronically stressful circumstances than others, and these people appear to be at greater risk for psychopathology (Garbarino, 1995). For example, people living in poverty-stricken, urban neighborhoods experience much more negative mental-health outcomes, especially substance abuse, juvenile delinquency, depression and anxiety (Wandersman & Nation, 1998). Just what makes some neighborhoods toxic is a matter of debate between researchers. One model for the effects of neighborhoods on mental health is given in Figure 2.14. Certain characteristics of neighborhoods seem important, such as high rates of poverty, the frequent experience of prejudice and discrimination due to ethnic minority status, families moving in and out of neighborhoods frequently, lack of cultural or ethnic ties between

People living in chronically stressful environments have higher rates of psychopathology.

neighbors, and high numbers of children relative to the numbers of adults (Coulton et al., 1995; Figueira-McDonough, 1993; Garbarino & Sherman, 1980). These factors contribute to few financial resources for individual families, lack of cohesion and common values in the neighborhood, unwillingness of neighbors to monitor and constrain the behavior of each other's children, and often open conflict between neighbors (Bursik & Grasmick, 1993). In such neighborhoods, subcultures often emerge that offer members a means of coping with the stresses they face but in maladaptive ways, such as through drugs and crime. Other members are chronically agitated and afraid, seeing no way out. All these forces then result in high rates of a number of mental-health problems, from behavioral disorders to depression (Wandersman & Nation, 1998).

Finally, societies may influence the types of psychopathology their members show by having rules, implicit or explicit, about what types of abnormal behavior are acceptable and in what circumstances. Throughout this book we will see that the rates of disorders vary from one culture or ethnic group to another and between males and females. For example, people from "traditional" cultures, such as the Old Order Amish in the United States, appear to have less depression than people from modern cultures (Egeland & Hostetter, 1983). In addition, the particular manifestation of disorders seem to vary from one culture to another. For example, the symptoms of anorexia nervosa, the disorder in which people refuse to eat, appear to be different in Asian cultures and in American culture. Finally, there may be many disorders that are specific to certain cultures.

Assessing the Social Structural Theories

The social structural theories argue we should not only analyze what is going on only in the head of individuals or in their immediate surroundings but also the larger social and cultural forces that may be influencing people's behavior. These theories are often credited for avoiding the "blaming the victim" that can occur with some of the other theories that seem to place responsibility for psychopathology in and with the individual. The theories also raise our consciousness about our responsibility as a society to change the social conditions that put some individual members at risk for psychopathology.

The social structural theories can be criticized, however, for being somewhat vague about the mechanisms leading to psychological disturbance in individuals. Just how is it that social change or stress leads to depression, schizophrenia, and so on? Why does it lead to depression in some people and drug abuse in others? Why do most people exposed to social stress and change develop no psychological disturbance at all? These theories and the studies testing them are becoming more complex as they attempt to answer such questions.

Summing Up

- The interpersonal theories assert that our self-concepts and expectations of others are based on our early attachments and relationships to caregivers.
- Family systems theories suggest that families form cohesive systems that regulate the behavior

of each member in the system. Sometimes these systems support and enhance the well-being of their members and sometimes they do not.

- Social structural theories suggest that society contributes to psychopathology in some members by creating severe stresses for them, then allowing or encouraging them to cope with these stresses with psychological symptoms.

⊙ BIO-PSYCHO-SOCIAL INTEGRATION

Surely, you might be saying to yourself, after decades of research, and with the modern scientific techniques available, we know which of the many theories covered in this chapter is "right" or "correct." Or at least we should know which of these theories best explains specific disorders. Increasingly, however, it is clear that no one of these theories is "right" or "correct" in explaining any psychological disorder. As you read about specific disorders in upcoming chapters, you will see that several theories each seem to explain the disorder to some extent, but seldom does one theory clearly "win" over the other theories.

As noted early in this chapter, many scientists believe that only models that integrate biological, psychological, and social factors can provide comprehensive explanations of psychological disorders. Only integrated models can help us to understand just how a disordered gene or deficiency of a neurotransmitter causes painful emotional symptoms or bizarre thoughts. Only integrated models can explain why many people with disordered genes or deficiencies in neurotransmitters do *not* develop painful emotional symptoms or bizarre thoughts. Similarly, only integrated models can suggest how traumatic experiences or toxic interpersonal relationships can cause changes in the basic biochemistry of the brain, which then cause changes in a person's emotions, thoughts, and behaviors.

Developing and testing integrated bio-psycho-social models are daunting tasks, requiring cooperation among scientists with very different types of training and perspectives on abnormality. Increasingly, however, scientists trained in biology, psychology, and sociology, anthropology, and other fields that study human social systems, are coming together in teams to develop integrated models of specific disorders. One of the most successful efforts has been in the study of aggression and delinquency among youth. As you read about other disorders in this book, think about what kind of experts you would want to get together to formulate a comprehensive, integrated model of each disorder.

Chapter Summary

- Biological theories of psychopathology typically attribute symptoms to structural abnormalities in the brain, disordered biochemistry, or faulty genes. Structural abnormalities in the brain can be caused by faulty genes, by disease, or by injury. The particular area of the brain damaged will influence the symptoms individuals show. Many biological theories attribute psychopathology to imbalances in neurotransmitters or to the functioning of receptors for neurotransmitters. Genetic theories of abnormality usually suggest that it takes an accumulation of faulty genes to cause a psychopathology. Genetic theories are tested with family history studies, twin studies, and adoption studies.

- Psychodynamic theories of psychopathology focus on unconscious conflicts that cause anxiety in the individual and result in maladaptive behavior. These conflicts arise when the libidinal impulses of the id clash with the constraints on behavior imposed by the ego and superego. The ways people handle their conflicts are defined by the types of defense mechanisms they use. How caregivers handle children's transitions through the psychosexual stages determines the concerns or issues the children may become fixated upon.

- More recent psychodynamic theorists focus less on the role of unconscious impulses and more on the development of the individual's self-concept in the context of interpersonal relationships. They see a greater role for the environment in the shaping of personality and have more hope for change in personality during adulthood than Freud did.

- The behaviorist theories of abnormality reject notions of unconscious conflicts and focus only on the rewards and punishments in the environment that shape and maintain behavior. Classi-cal conditioning takes place when a previously neutral stimulus is paired with a stimulus that naturally creates a certain response; eventually, the neutral stimulus will also elicit the response. Operant conditioning involves rewarding desired behaviors and punishing undesired behaviors. People also learn by imitating the behaviors modeled by others and by observing the rewards and punishments others receive for their behaviors.

- Cognitive theories suggest that people's attributions for events, their perceptions of control and self-efficacy, and their global beliefs or assumptions influence the behaviors and emotions they have in reaction to situations.

- Humanist and existential theories suggest that all humans strive to fulfill their potential for good and to self-actualize. The inability to fulfill one's potential arises from the pressures of society to conform to others' expectations and values and from existential anxiety.

- Interpersonal theories suggest that children develop internal models of the self and others through their attachments and relationships with early caregivers. These models then affect their behaviors and later relationships, sometimes in unhealthy ways.

- Family systems theories suggest that psychopathology in individual family members is due to dysfunctional patterns of interaction within families that create and maintain the abnormal behaviors.

- Social structural theories suggest that societies create severe stresses for some people, then subcultures can sanction maladaptive ways of coping with these stresses. Cultures also have implicit and explicit rules for the types of abnormal behavior that are permissible in the society.

Key Terms

theoretical approach 30

biological approach 30

psychological approach 30

social approach 30

nature-nurture question 30

vulnerability-stress models 31

Critical Thinking Questions

1. People are often relieved when they are told that a psychological disorder they are suffering from is due to a "chemical imbalance" in their brains. Why do you think this is so?

2. Could it be true that believing you are doomed by your genes to develop a psychological disorder actually contributes to your developing the disorder? If so, how would this happen?

3. The practice of giving children "time outs" when they misbehave is based on what principles of conditioning?

4. Think back to a recent incident that left you feeling distressed. What were some of your thoughts about that incident that influenced your feelings? Do you think they were rational or irrational?

There's no limit to how complicated things can get, on account of one thing always leading to another.

—E. B. White, Quo Vadimus? (1939)

CHAPTER

3

The Research Endeavor

CHAPTER OVERVIEW
The Scientific Method

Conducting scientific research involves defining a problem, specifying an hypothesis, and operationalizing the dependent and independent variables. Several different methods can be used to test the hypothesis. Once results are obtained, a scientific report can be written.

Taking Psychology Personally:
How to Write a Research Report

Case Studies

Case studies are detailed histories of individuals. They are rich in detail and honor the uniqueness of individuals. They help in generating new ideas and in illuminating rare problems. Case studies suffer from lack of generalizability, vulnerability to bias, and difficulties in replication.

Correlational Studies

Correlational studies examine the relationship between two variables without manipulating them. Correlational studies can involve either continuous variables or group comparisons. Cross-sectional correlational studies examine the relationship between variables at one point in time, and longitudinal correlational studies examine this relationship over time. A correlation coefficient is a statistic used to index the degree and direction of relationship between the variables. Its importance is indicated by its statistical significance. Correlational studies can show that two variables are related, but cannot show that one causes the other.

Experimental Studies

In human laboratory studies, the variables thought to cause psychopathology are controlled. Participants are randomly assigned to the experimental group, which receives a manipulation, or the control group, which does not. The generalizability and ethics of some human laboratory studies are sometimes questioned. In a therapy outcome study, people with psychopathology are given therapy meant to reduce their symptoms, and their outcomes are compared to those of people who received no therapy or an alternative therapy. Although these studies provide an opportunity to help people, they create several methodological and ethical concerns. Animal studies are used to test hypotheses that cannot be tested in humans for ethical reasons or that are better tested in animals than in humans. The generalizability of animal studies to humans has been questioned, as well as the ethics of conducting research on animals.

Cross-Cultural Research

Cross-cultural research examines the similarities and differences in abnormality across cultures. Some special challenges of cross-cultural research include difficulty in accessing populations, in applying theories across cultures, in translating concepts and measures across cultures, in predicting the responses of people in different cultures to being studied, and in demands to define "healthy" and "unhealthy" cultures.

Extraordinary People:
The Old Order Amish of Pennsylvania

Bio-Psycho-Social Integration
Pushing the Boundaries:
A Project for a Scientific Psychopathology

Chapter Summary
Key Terms
Critical Thinking Questions

"Scientists Discover Cause of Schizophrenia"

"New Study Proves Gene Theory of Depression"

"Alcoholism Linked to Social Conditions"

Headlines like these often appear in newspapers, in magazines, and on radio or television news programs. When you see or hear such headlines, you may ask yourself, "How do they know that?" Sometimes the news story provides detailed information on the study that is being reported. More often, the story only briefly describes the study and, instead, presents the results of the study in a simplified, clear-cut, and occasionally misleading manner.

The results of research studies are seldom simple or clear-cut. Within the scientific community, debates can rage for decades over the appropriate interpretation of research results. This type of complication is true in any discipline—from psychology and sociology to physics, chemistry, and biology. Researchers interested in abnormal behavior face some special challenges that make it particularly difficult to find definitive answers.

The greatest challenge is that the phenomena of interest—abnormal behaviors and feelings—are extremely difficult to measure accurately. Researchers must often rely on people's self-reports of their internal states and experiences because they are the only ones who have access to these experiences. We cannot see or hear or feel other people's emotions or thoughts. There are a number of ways in which people's self-reports can be distorted, intentionally or unintentionally, and therefore we must always question the validity of self-reports. Similarly, relying on an observer's assessments of a target person is inherently problematic. The observer's assessments can be biased by his or her gender and cultural stereotypes, idiosyncratic biases, and lack of information.

A second major challenge in psychological research is that people change, often quickly. Someone who is depressed today may not be depressed tomorrow; and someone who does not hear voices this week may begin hearing voices next week. Such changes are often interesting and, indeed, may be the focus of a psychologist's research. However, they complicate the process of measuring and categorizing people's behaviors.

A third challenge is that most forms of abnormality probably have multiple causes. Thus, unless a single study can capture the biological, psychological, and social causes of the abnormality of interest, it cannot fully explain the causes of that abnormality. Unfortunately, a single study can rarely accomplish so much. This means that we are always left with partial answers to

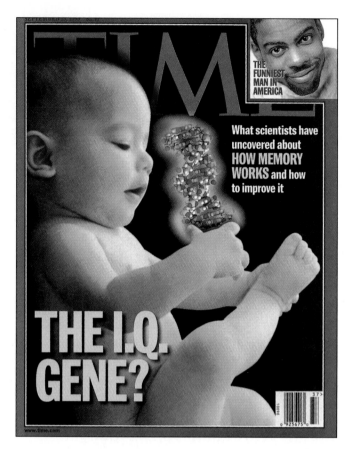

You often see sweeping claims made about the results of research studies made in the popular press.

the question of what causes a certain abnormality and must piece together the partial answers from several studies to get a full picture of that abnormality. A fourth challenge is that we often cannot manipulate or control the variables or phenomena of interest in our research, because doing so would require manipulating humans in ways that would be unethical.

Despite these challenges, tremendous strides have been made in our understanding of many forms of abnormality in the last 40 years or so, thanks to the cleverness and persistence of researchers. Researchers overcome many of the challenges of researching abnormality by using a *multimethod approach*, which means they use a variety of methodologies to research their questions of interest. Each of these methods may have some limitations, but taken together, these different methods can provide convincing evidence for a theory about abnormality.

This chapter discusses the most common methods of testing theories about abnormality, especially psychosocial theories about the causes of abnormality. We will take one simple theory—the theory that stress is a cause of depression—and discuss how different research methods might be used to test this theory. Of course, the research methods we discuss can be used to

	CONCEPT REVIEW	
Primary and Null Hypotheses and Their Application to Stress and Depression		
Term	**Definition**	**Application**
Primary hypothesis	Testable statement of what we expect to happen in our study, based on our theory	People who have recently experienced stress are more likely to be depressed than people who have not.
Null hypothesis	What we would expect to happen in our study if our theory is not correct	People who have recently experienced stress are *not* more likely to be depressed than people who have not.

test many different theories, but by applying all the methods to one theory, we can see how many tools researchers have at their disposal to test a given theory.

⟲ THE SCIENTIFIC METHOD

Any research project involves a basic series of steps. First, a problem must be selected and defined. Then an hypothesis must be formulated. Next, the method for testing the hypothesis must be chosen and implemented. Once the data are collected and analyzed, the researcher draws the appropriate conclusions. Finally, the results are written in a research report.

Underlying this series of steps is the goal of obtaining and evaluating information relevant to a problem in a systematic way—a process often referred to as the **scientific method.** We discuss each of these steps in this chapter. In this section, we discuss how to set up a testable hypothesis and operationalize variables relevant to the hypothesis. In the remaining sections of the book, we discuss different methods for testing hypotheses, and the conclusions one can and cannot draw from these methods. *Taking Psychology Personally: How to Write a Report* (p. 70) describes how to write a report detailing a research project.

Defining the Problem

Throughout this chapter we examine the theory that stress causes depression. Even this simple theory is too broad and abstract to test directly. Thus, we must state an hypothesis based on this theory. An **hypothesis** is a testable statement of what we expect to happen in a research study. To generate a testable hypothesis, we might ask, "What kind of evidence would support the theory that stress causes depression?" Finding that people who had recently experienced stress were more likely to be depressed than people who had not recently experienced stress would support our idea. One hypothesis, then, is that people who have recently

experienced stress are more likely to be depressed than people who have not. This proposition is testable by a number of research methods. If we find support for this hypothesis, we will have support for our theory. Our idea will not be proven correct, however. No one study can do that. However, a series of studies supporting our theory will bolster our confidence in the theory, particularly if these studies have different methodologies.

The alternative to our hypothesis is that people who experience stress are *not* more likely to develop depression than are people who do not experience stress. This is called the **null hypothesis** (see *Concept Review:* Primary and Null Hypotheses and Their Application to Stress and Depression). Results often support the null hypothesis instead of the researcher's primary hypothesis. Does this mean that the underlying idea has been disproved? No. The null hypothesis can be supported for many reasons; most importantly, the study may not be designed well enough to provide support for the primary hypothesis. Researchers will often continue to test their primary hypothesis, using a variety of methodologies. If the null hypothesis is getting much more support than the primary hypothesis, they eventually either modify or drop the primary hypothesis.

Defining and Operationalizing Variables

Other terms that appear in discussions of any study are *variable, dependent variable,* and *independent variable* (see *Concept Review*: Variables, p. 71). A **variable** is a factor or characteristic that can vary within an individual or between individuals. Weight, mood, and attitudes toward one's mother are all factors that can vary over time, so they would be considered variables. Similarly, although height, sex, and ethnicity are not factors that vary for an individual over time; they can vary from one individual to another, so they also would be considered variables. A **dependent variable**

TAKING PSYCHOLOGY PERSONALLY

How to Write a Research Report

Once you have conducted a study testing your hypothesis, how do you write a report on the study? You may have looked at research reports in journals of psychology or psychiatry and wondered about the organization and purpose of the various sections of the reports. Following is an outline and description of the major sections of a report of results of a psychology experiment, according to the style approved by the American Psychological Association.

Title Page

The title page presents the title of your paper, your name and affiliation (your school or the hospital, clinic, foundation, research center, or company you work for), and a running head, or shortened version of your title that will appear in the upper right-hand corner of the remaining pages of your paper. If you are making a presentation of your paper at a conference or your paper has been accepted for publication in a journal, this can be noted near the bottom of the title page.

Abstract

The abstract is a short description of the purpose, design, and results of your study, usually no longer than 200 words. It is presented on a separate page, just after the title page.

Introduction

The introduction to your paper begins on the page immediately following the abstract. In the introduction, you review previous studies and theoretical works relevant to your study and justify the need for your study. This justification might be that previous studies have not addressed your specific hypothesis or research question or that the previous studies that have been conducted were flawed in some way that your study will correct. Make sure that you clearly state your hypothesis at some point in the introduction, so readers will know exactly what your study is intended to test.

is the factor we are trying to predict in our study. In our studies of stress and depression, we will be trying to predict depressive symptoms, so depression is our dependent variable. An **independent variable** is the factor we are using to predict the dependent variable. In our studies, stress will be the independent variable.

Before we examine ways of researching depression and stress, we must define what we mean by these terms. As we will discuss in Chapter 8, depression is a syndrome made up of the following symptoms: sadness, loss of interest in one's usual activities, weight loss or gain, changes in sleep, agitation or slowing down, fatigue and loss of energy, feelings of worthlessness or excessive guilt, problems in concentration or indecisiveness, and suicidal thoughts (APA, 2000). Some researchers define depressed people as those who meet the criteria for one of the depressive disorders. Anyone who has some of these symptoms

of depression but does not meet the criteria for one of the depressive disorders would be considered nondepressed. Other researchers focus on the full range of depressive symptoms, from no symptoms to moderate symptoms to the most severe symptoms. They may divide people up into those who show no depressive symptoms, those who show moderately severe depressive symptoms, and those who show severe depressive symptoms.

Stress is a more difficult term to define, because it has been used in so many ways in research and the popular press. Stressor is used to refer to an *event* that is uncontrollable, is unpredictable, and challenges the limits of people's abilities to cope. *Stress* has been used to refer to people's *emotions and behaviors* in response to stressful events.

Our definition of *depression* or *stress* will influence how we operationalize them. **Operationalization**

Continued

Method

The method section usually has three subsections. The participants subsection provides a detailed description of the participants in your study (their numbers, ages, genders, socioeconomic classes, racial/ethnic distribution) and your methods for recruiting them. The materials subsection provides details of the questionnaires, rating scales, interview questions, tasks, or any other materials you used in your study. The procedures subsection describes how you went about conducting your study. In a questionnaire study, describe where and how participants completed the questionnaires (e.g., as part of a big group or individually in a private room). In an interview study, describe where and how the interviews were conducted and by whom. In an experimental study, describe the details of the manipulations you used and exactly what the participant was made to do over the course of the experiment.

Results

The results section describes the outcome of your study, such as differences between groups on your key variables or correlations between variables, and the results of statistical tests that indicate whether these outcomes were significant (or whether they occurred simply by chance). You might want to present some of your results (e.g., the mean depression scores of your two groups) in a table.

Discussion

In the discussion section, discuss the implications of your findings. Indicate whether your hypothesis was supported by the results of your study and address any alternative explanations for your results. Acknowledge any major weaknesses in your study. Be careful to not draw conclusions from your study that are too generous or extreme. Always remember that no individual study can prove a theory or hypothesis definitively, and there are always questions about the generalizability of any study to the population at large.

References

The formats for referencing some of the most common types of works cited in psychology papers can be found in the *Publication Manual of the American Psychological Association*.

CONCEPT REVIEW
Variables

Term	Definition	Application
Dependent variable	Factor we are trying to predict in our study	Depression
Independent variable	Factor we are using to predict the dependent variable	Stress
Operationalization	Way we measure or manipulate our independent and dependent variables	Questionnaires measuring depression and stress

is the way that we measure or manipulate the variables of interest in a study. If we define depression as symptoms meeting criteria for a depressive disorder, then we will operationalize depression as diagnoses. If we define depression as symptoms along the entire range of severity, then we might operationalize depression as scores on a depression questionnaire.

In operationalizing stress, we must first decide whether we will focus on stressful events or on people's stress reactions to these events. Then we must devise some measure of what we define as stress or some way of manipulating or creating stress so that we can then examine people's reactions to this stress. In this chapter, we describe several operationalizations of stress as we discuss different research methods.

Summing Up

- An hypothesis is a testable statement of what we expect to happen in a research study.

- A null hypothesis is the statement that the outcome of the study will contradict the primary hypothesis of the study. Usually, the null hypothesis is that the factors of interest (such as stress and depression) are unrelated to one another.

- A variable is a factor that can vary within individuals or between individuals.

- A dependent variable is the factor we are trying to predict in a study.

- An independent variable is the factor we are using to predict the dependent variable.

- Operationalization is the way we measure or manipulate the variables of interest.

○ CASE STUDIES

Throughout this book you will see **case studies**—detailed histories of individuals who have suffered some form of psychological disorder. Case studies have been used for centuries as a way of trying to understand the experiences of single individuals and to make more general inferences about the sources of psychopathology.

If we wanted to use a case study to test our idea that stress causes depression, we would focus on one individual, interviewing him or her at length, to discover the links between periods of depression and stressful events in his or her life. We might also interview close friends and family to obtain additional information. Based on the information we gathered, we would create a detailed description of the causes of his or her depressive episodes, with emphasis on the role of stressful events in these episodes.

For example, here is a brief case study of the singer Kurt Cobain of the hit 1990s rock band Nirvana. It was written a week after Cobain committed suicide.

CASE STUDY

Cobain always had a fragile constitution (he was subject to bronchitis, as well as the recurrent stomach pains he claimed drove him to a heroin addiction). The image one gets is that of a frail kid batted between warring parents. "[The divorce] just destroyed his life," Wendy O'Connor tells Michael Azerrad in the Nirvana biography *Come As You Are*. "He changed completely. I think he was ashamed. And he became very inward—he just held everything [in]. . . . I think he's *still* suffering." As a teen, Cobain dabbled in drugs and punk rock and dropped out of school. His father persuaded him to pawn his guitar and take an entrance exam for the navy. But Cobain soon returned for the guitar. "To them, I was wasting my life," he told the *Los Angeles Times*. "To me, I was fighting for it." Cobain didn't speak to his father for 8 years. When Nirvana went to the top of the charts, Don Cobain began keeping a scrapbook. "Everything I know about Kurt," he told Azerrad, "I've read in newspapers and magazines."

The more famous Nirvana became, the more Cobain wanted none of it. . . . Nirvana—with their stringy hair, plaid work shirts, and torn jeans—appealed to a mass of young fans who were tired of false idols like Madonna and Michael Jackson and who'd never had a dangerous rock-and-roll hero to call their own. Unfortunately, the band also appealed to the sort of people Cobain had always hated: poseurs and bandwagoneers, not to mention record-company execs and fashion designers who fell over themselves cashing in on the new sights and sounds. Cobain, who'd grown up as an angry outsider, tried to shake his celebrity. . . .

By 1992, it became clear that Cobain's personal life was as tangled and troubling as his music. The singer married [Courtney] Love in Waikiki—the bride wore a moth-eaten dress once owned by actress Frances Farmer—and the couple embarked on a self-destructive pas de deux widely referred to as a 90s version of *Sid and Nancy*. As Cobain put it, "I was going off with Courtney and we were scoring drugs and we were f—king up against a wall and stuff . . . and causing scenes just to do it. It was fun to be with someone who would stand up all of a sudden and smash a glass on the table." In September 1992, *Vanity Fair* reported that Love had used heroin while she was pregnant with [their daughter] Frances Bean. She and Cobain denied the story (the baby is healthy). But authorities were reportedly concerned enough to force them to surrender custody of Frances to Love's sister, Jamie, for a month, during which time the couple was, in Cobain's words, "totally suicidal." . . .

. . . [T]hose who knew the singer say there was a real fragility buried beneath the noise of his music and his life. . . . If only someone had heard the alarms ringing at that rambling, gray-shingled home near the lake. Long before there was a void in our hearts, there was a void in Kurt Cobain's. (Giles, 1994, pp. 46–47)

Evaluating Case Studies

Case studies are a time-honored method of research for several reasons. No other method captures the uniqueness of the individual as much as a case study. The

In-depth case histories of troubled people like Kurt Cobain may be rich in detail but not generalizable.

nuances of an individual's life and experiences can be detailed, and the individual's own words can be used to describe his or her experiences. Exploring the unique experiences of individuals and honoring their own perspectives on these experiences are important goals for many researchers, and in-depth case studies of individual lives have become more popular in recent years.

Case studies are sometimes the only way to study rare problems, because there simply are not enough people with that problem to study through any other method. For example, much of the research on people with multiple personalities has come from case studies because this form of psychopathology has historically been quite rare.

Case studies can be invaluable in helping to generate new ideas and provide tentative support for those ideas. Most of Freud's theories came from his case studies of people he treated. Freud would listen for hours to his patients' descriptions of their lives, their dreams, and their memories, and would notice themes in these reports that he speculated were related to the psychological symptoms they were suffering. Freud was often quite hesitant in stating his ideas in his reports of his work, encouraging further research to test his ideas. One of the most common uses of case studies today is in drug treatment research to report unusual reactions patients have had to certain drugs. These reports can alert other clinicians to watch for similar reactions in their patients. If enough case reports of these unusual reactions emerge in the literature, then larger-scale research to study the sources of these reactions may be warranted.

Case studies do have their drawbacks, however (see *Concept Review*: Evaluating Case Studies). The first is **generalizability**—the ability to apply what we have learned to other individuals or groups. The conclusions

CONCEPT REVIEW

Evaluating Case Studies

Case studies are rich in detail but difficult to replicate.

Advantages

They are rich in detail

They honor the uniqueness of individual experiences

They allow an individual to provide his or her own perspective.

They can focus on rare problems.

They can help in generating new ideas.

Disadvantages

It is difficult to generalize from them.

Different researchers may obtain different results, creating problems in replication.

Self-reports of participants may be biased.

Researchers' perspectives may be biased.

drawn from the study of an individual may not apply to many other individuals. This is especially true when case studies focus on people whose experiences have been dramatic, but quite unusual. For example, the circumstances leading to Kurt Cobain's death may be very interesting, but may not tell us anything about why other people commit suicide. As we noted in Chapter 2, even some of Freud's contemporaries criticized him for attempting to generate universal theories of human psychological functioning based on the experiences of his patients who were suffering from psychopathology.

Case studies also suffer from a lack of objectivity on the part of both the people telling their stories and the therapists or researchers listening to the story. The people telling their stories might have biased recollections of their pasts and may selectively report events that happen to them in the present. The therapists or researchers listening to the story will filter the story through their beliefs and assumptions about the causes of human behavior and might selectively remember parts of the story that support their beliefs and assumptions and selectively forget parts of the story that do not. Thus, two case studies of the same person, if conducted by two different researchers, may come to very different conclusions about the motivations and key events in that person's life. The researchers bring their own perspectives to the case study, and as a result one case study may not **replicate**—repeat the conclusions—of another. Replication is a key feature of the scientific method. Difficulties in replication are one of the key drawbacks of case studies.

Summing Up

- Case studies are in-depth histories of the experiences of individuals.
- The advantages of case studies are their richness in detail, their attention to the unique experiences of individuals, their ability to focus on rare problems, and in generating new ideas.
- The disadvantages of case studies are their lack of generalizability, their subjectivity, and difficulties in replication.

⊙ CORRELATIONAL STUDIES

Correlational studies examine the relationship between an independent variable and a dependent variable without manipulating either variable. Correlational studies are the most common type of study in psychology and medicine. You will often read about studies of the relationship between television-watching and violence, smoking and heart disease, Internet use and depression, in which researchers have not manipulated any variables, but have examined the naturally occurring relationships between variables.

There are many different kinds of correlational studies (see *Concept Review*: Types of Correlational Studies). The most common type of correlational study done in abnormal psychology is a study of two or more continuous variables. A **continuous variable** is measured along a continuum. For example, on a scale measuring severity of depression, scores might fall along a continuum from 0 (no depression) to 100 (extremely depressed). On a scale measuring number of recent stressors, scores might fall along a continuum from 0 (no stressors) to 20 (20 or more recent stressors). If we measured severity of depression and number of recent stressors in the same group of people and then look at the relationship between these two continuous variables, we would be doing a continuous variable correlational study.

Another type of correlational study is a **group comparison study.** In this type of study, researchers are interested in the relationship between people's membership in a particular group and their scores on some other variable. For example, we might be interested in the relationship between depression and whether or not people have experienced a specific type of stress, such as the loss of a loved one. In this case, the groups of interest are bereaved and nonbereaved people. We would find people who represented these two groups, then measure depression in both groups. This is still a correlational study because we are only observing the relationship between two variables—bereavement and depression—and not manipulating any variable. In this type of study, however, at least one of

CONCEPT REVIEW

Types of Correlation Studies

There are at least four types of correlational studies.

Type	Description	Example
Continuous variable study	Two or more continuous variables are measured and the correlation between them is examined.	Researchers measure how many stressors people have had and the number of depressive symptoms they have, and examine the correlation between these two continuous variables.
Group comparison study	Two or more groups are compared on the variables of interest.	Researchers examine levels of depression in bereaved and nonbereaved people.
Cross-sectional study	Participants in the study are assessed at only one point in time. Can involve either continuous variables or group comparisons.	Either of the above examples would be cross-sectional if participants were assessed only once.
Longitudinal study	Participants in the study are assessed on two or more occasions over time. Can involve either continuous variables or group comparisons.	Either of the above examples would be longitudinal if participants were assessed two or more times over a period of time.

Calvin and Hobbes   **by Bill Watterson**

© Bill Watterson, Universal Press Syndicate.

the variables of interest—group membership—is not a continuous variable.

Both continuous variable studies and group comparison studies can be **cross-sectional**—they observe people at only one point in time, or **longitudinal**—they observe people on two more occasions over time. Longitudinal studies have a major advantage over cross-sectional studies, because they can show that the independent variable precedes and predicts changes in the dependent variable over time. For example, a longitudinal study of stress and depression can show that people who are not depressed at the beginning of the study are much more likely to be depressed later in the study if they have experienced a stressful event in the interim than if they did not.

Measuring the Relationship Between Variables

In most correlational studies, the relationship between the variables of interest is indicated by a correlation coefficient. Let us review what this statistic is, and how to interpret it.

The Correlation Coefficient

A **correlation coefficient** is a statistic used to represent the relationship between variables, and is usually denoted with the symbol r. A correlation coefficient can fall between -1.00 and $+1.00$. A positively valued correlation coefficient indicates that, as values of the independent variable increase, values of the dependent variable increase (see Figure 3.1). For example, a positive correlation between stress and depression would mean that people who report more stressors have higher levels of depression. A negatively valued correlation coefficient indicates that, as values of the independent variable increase, values of the dependent variable decrease (see Figure 3.2). If we were still measuring stressors and depression, this would mean that people who report more stressors actually have lower

levels of depression. This is an unlikely scenario, but there are many instances of negative correlations between variables. For example, people who have more positive social support from others typically have lower levels of depression.

The magnitude of a correlation—the degree to which the variables move in tandem with each other—is indicated by how close the correlation coefficient is to

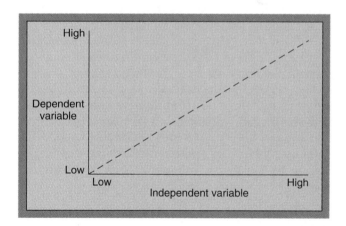

FIGURE 3.1   A Positive Correlation. A positive correlation indicates that, as values of the independent variable increase, values of the dependent variable increase. This graph illustrates a correlation of $+1.00$.

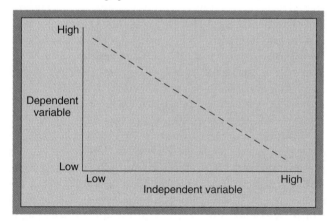

FIGURE 3.2   A Negative Correlation. A negative correlation indicates that, as values of the independent variable increase, values of the dependent variable decrease. This graph illustrates a correlation of -1.00.

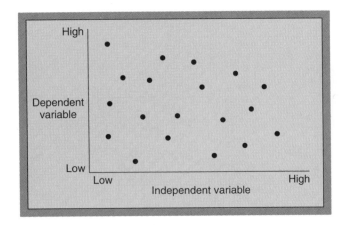

FIGURE 3.3   A Zero Correlation. A zero correlation indicates that there is no relationship between the independent variable and the dependent variable.

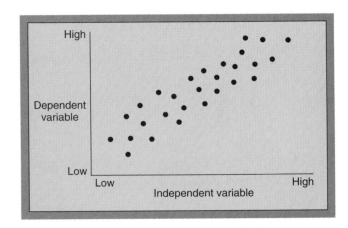

FIGURE 3.4   A Moderate Correlation. A moderate correlation indicates that there is some relationship between the independent and dependent variables, but values of the independent variable are not perfectly predicted by values of the dependent variable.

either −1.00 or +1.00. A correlation of 0 indicates no relationship between the variables (see Figure 3.3). An *r* of −1.00 or +1.00 indicates a perfect relationship between the two variables (as illustrated in Figures 3.1 and 3.2). The value of one variable is perfectly predictable by the value of the other variable, for example, every time people experience stress they become depressed. Seldom do we see perfect correlations in psychological research. Instead, correlations are often in the low-to-moderate range, indicating some relationship between the two variables, but far from a perfect relationship (see Figure 3.4). Many relationships between variables happen by chance and are not meaningful. Scientists evaluate the importance of a correlation coefficient by examining its statistical significance.

Statistical Significance

The **statistical significance** of a result like a correlation coefficient is an index of how likely that result occurred simply by chance. You will often see statements in research studies such as, "The result was statistically significant at $p<.05$." This means that the probability is less than 5 in 100 that the result occurred only by chance. Researchers typically accept results at this level of significance as support of their hypotheses, although the choice of an acceptable significance level is a somewhat arbitrary one.

Whether a correlation coefficient will be statistically significant at the $p<.05$ level is determined by its magnitude and the size of the sample it is based on. Both larger correlations and larger sample sizes increase the likelihood of achieving statistical significance. A correlation of .30 will be significant if it is based on a large sample, say 200 or more, but will not be significant if it is based on a small sample such as 10 or fewer participants. On the other hand, a correlation

of .90 will be statistically significant even if the sample is as small as 30 people.

Correlation versus Causation

One of the most important things to remember about correlations is that they do not tell us anything about causation. That is, even though we may find that an independent and dependent variable are highly correlated with each other, this does not tell us that the independent variable caused the dependent variable. In other words, even if we found a strong correlation between stress and depression, we could not conclude that stress causes depression. All that a correlation coefficient tells us is that there is a relationship between stress and depression. It could be that depression causes stress. Or some other variable may cause both stress and depression. This latter situation is called the **third variable** problem. Often there will be variables not measured in a study that are the real cause of the variables measured in the study. For example, perhaps

A positive correlation between stress and depression could occur because people with difficult temperaments create stress and are prone to depression.

some people with difficult temperaments both generate stressful experiences in their lives by being difficult to live with and are prone to depression. If we only measured stress and depression, we might observe a relationship between them because they do co-occur within the same individuals. But this relationship would actually be due to their common relationship to temperament.

Selecting a Sample

One of the critical choices in a correlational study is the choice of the sample. A **sample** is a group of people taken from our population of interest.

Representativeness

A **representative sample** is highly similar to the population of interest in terms of sex, ethnicity, age, and other important variables. If a sample is not representative—for example, if there are more women or people of color in our sample than in the general population of people of interest—then the sample is said to have bias.

The representativeness of a sample is important to the generalization we want to make from our study. If our sample represents only a small or unusual group of people, then we cannot generalize the results of our study to the larger population. For example, if all of the people in our study are white, middle-class females, we cannot know whether our results generalize to males, people of color, or people in other socioeconomic classes.

Some methods of recruiting subjects into a study create more representative samples than do others. For example, in our study of stress and depression, we could put an advertisement in the local newspaper asking people who had recently experienced stressful experiences to volunteer for our study. This would bias our sample in favor of people who have experienced stress, however, and leave out people who have not. Perhaps many people who have not experienced stress are still depressed. This is important information we need to evaluate our hypothesis that stress causes depression.

An effective way of obtaining a representative sample of a population is to generate a **random sample** of that population. For example, some studies have obtained random samples of the entire U.S. population by randomly dialing phone numbers throughout the country and then recruiting the people who answer the phone into the study. Often, researchers can settle for random samples of smaller populations, such as random samples of particular cities. When a sample is truly random, then the chances are high that it will

be similar to the population of interest in ethnicity, sex, age, and all the other important variables in the study.

Selecting a Comparison Group

In a group comparison study, we are interested in comparing the experiences of one group to another. For example, we may be interested in the depression levels of bereaved and nonbereaved people. We might begin by recruiting our sample of bereaved people, attempting to make this sample as representative as possible of bereaved people in our community.

In selecting the comparison group of nonbereaved people, it is a good idea to match our bereaved group with this comparison group on any variable (other than stress) that we think might influence levels of depression, so that the two groups are alike on these variables. If we do not do this **matching** process, then any differences we found between the two groups on levels of depression could be attributable to variables for which we did not match—the third variable problem again. For example, women are generally more likely to be depressed than men, so if we happened to have more women in our bereaved group than in our comparison group, then higher levels of depression in the bereaved group might be attributable to a third variable—the fact that there are more women in that group—and not to the fact that the group had recently been bereaved. Thus, we need to match our bereaved and comparison groups on all third variables that might influence our dependent variable of depression.

Let us decide to match our two groups on sex, age, race or ethnicity, and socioeconomic status. We can generate the comparison group by consulting the local census records and, for every person in our bereaved group, recruit a person of the same sex, age, race, and socioeconomic status from the local area into our comparison group. Although not a simple task, this is a good way to generate a matched comparison group.

Evaluating Correlational Studies

Correlational studies have provided much important information for abnormal psychology. One of the major advantages of correlational studies is that they focus on situations occurring in the real world, rather than those manipulated in a laboratory (see *Concept Review*: Evaluating Correlational Studies). This gives them relatively good **external validity**—the results of these studies may be generalizable to wider populations of interest and people's actual experiences in life.

Longitudinal correlational studies have several advantages over cross-sectional correlational studies. In

Evaluating Correlational Studies

Correlational studies are a popular method of research but they do have drawbacks.

Advantages

They focus on situations in the real world, rather than in the laboratory, thus have relatively good external validity.

Longitudinal studies can determine whether people change over time as a function of their experiences, thus establishing whether an independent variable precedes and predicts changes in a dependent variable.

Longitudinal studies can examine both short-term and long-term responses to a situation.

Disadvantages

Correlational studies cannot establish whether one variable causes another.

Bad timing can cause researchers to miss key events or people's reactions to them.

Longitudinal studies can be time-consuming and expensive to run.

Ruling out all possible third variables that may account for the observed relationships within a study can be difficult.

these studies, researchers can determine whether there are differences between the groups of interest before the crucial event occurs. If there are no differences before the event but significant differences after the event, then they can have more confidence that it was the event that actually lead to the differences between the groups. Longitudinal designs also allow researchers to follow two groups for long enough to assess both short-term and long-term reactions to the event.

The most significant disadvantage of all correlational studies is that they cannot tease apart what is a cause and what is a consequence. For example, many stressful events depressed people report may be the consequences of their depression rather than the causes. The symptoms of depression can cause stress by impairing interpersonal skills, interfering with concentration on the job, and causing insomnia. The same problem exists for many types of psychopathology: The symptoms of schizophrenia can disrupt social relationships; alcoholism can lead to unemployment; and so on. Some psychological symptoms may even cause physiological changes in people. For example, people who have recently experienced psychological

trauma often develop medical diseases because the traumas reduce the effectiveness of their immune systems, which help to fight disease (Jemmott & Locke, 1984).

Another disadvantage of correlational studies is the potential for bad timing. Stress may indeed cause depression, but if we do not assess these two variables at the right point in time, we may not observe this relationship. For example, in our study of bereavement, we could miss many of the depressed people in our bereaved group if we measured depression either before they developed it, or after they had recovered from it (see Figure 3.5).

Longitudinal studies can be time-consuming and expensive to run. Chapter 10 reports studies in which children at high risk for schizophrenia were studied from their preschool years to their early adult years to determine what characteristics could predict who would develop schizophrenia and who would not (Erlenmyer-Kimling et al., 1991). Some of these studies have been going on for over 25 years and have cost millions of dollars. They are producing extremely valuable data but at a high cost in researchers' time and in research dollars.

Finally, all correlational studies suffer from the third variable problem. Researchers seldom can measure all the possible influences on their subjects' levels of depression or other psychopathologies. Third variable problems are one of the major reasons researchers turn to experimental studies.

Summing Up

- A correlational study examines the relationship between two variables without manipulating either variable.

- A correlation coefficient is an index of the relationship between two variables. It can range from -1.00 to $+1.00$. The magnitude of the correlation indicates how strong the relationship between the variables is. A positive correlation indicates that as values of one variable increase, values of the other variable increase. A negative correlation indicates that as values of one variable increase, values of the other variable decrease.

- A result is said to be statistically significant if it is unlikely to have happened by chance. The convention in psychological research is to accept results for which there is a probability of less than 5 in 100 that they happened by chance.

- A correlational study can show that two variables are related, but cannot show that one variable causes the other. All correlational studies suffer from the third variable problem—the possibility

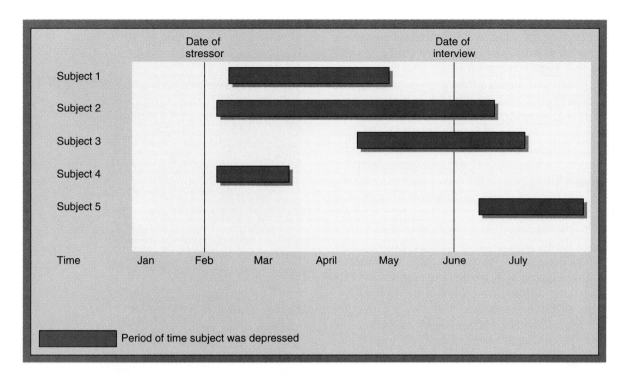

FIGURE 3.5   Timing Problem in Cross-Sectional Design. Here is a case in which the timing of a cross-sectional study was a problem. The stressor occurred in February, and the interview for the study occurred in June. The researchers detected depression in Subjects 2 and 3 because they were depressed in June. They missed the depression experienced by Subjects 1, 4, and 5 because these subjects' periods of depression did not happen to overlap with the time of the interview.

that variables not measured in the study actually account for the relationship between the variables measured in the study.

- Continuous variable studies evaluate the relationship between two variables that vary along a continuum.

- A sample is a subset of a population of interest. A representative sample is similar to the population of interest on all important variables. One way to generate a representative sample is to obtain a random sample.

- Whereas cross-sectional studies assess a sample at one point in time, longitudinal studies assess the same sample at multiple points in time. A prospective longitudinal study assesses a sample that is expected to have some key event in the future both before and after the event, then examines changes in the sample that occurred.

- Group comparison studies evaluate differences between key groups, such as a group that experienced a specific type of stressor and a comparison group that did not experience the stressor, but is matched on all important variables.

- Potential problems in correlational studies include the potential for bad timing and the expense of longitudinal studies.

☉ EXPERIMENTAL STUDIES

The hallmark of **experimental studies** is control. Researchers attempt to control the independent and any potentially problematic third variable before they test their hypotheses. We turn now to a discussion of the various types of experimental studies we could do to test our theory that stress leads to depression. We will examine three in particular. The first, the human laboratory study, has the goal of inducing the conditions that we theorize will lead to our outcome of interest (i.e., increasing stress to cause depression) in people in a controlled setting. The second, the therapy outcome study, also is conducted with humans but has the opposite focus of the first type of study. In a therapy outcome study, the researcher wants to reduce the conditions leading to the outcome of interest so as to reduce that outcome (i.e., decreasing stress to decrease depression). The third, the animal study, attempts to model what happens in humans by manipulating animals in a laboratory.

Human Laboratory Studies

One experimental method for testing our hypothesis that stressors lead to depression is to expose subjects to a stressor in the laboratory and then determine whether it causes an increase in depressed mood—a method known as a **human laboratory study.** Several studies of this type have been done (see Peterson & Seligman, 1984). The stressor that is often used in this study is some type of unsolvable task or puzzle, such as an unsolvable anagram. If we chose this as the type of stress we would induce, then our operationalization would be participants' exposure to unsolvable anagrams. We are manipulating stress, not just measuring it in this study. This gives us the advantage of knowing precisely what type of stress participants are exposed to and when.

This particular type of study is also often called an **analogue study,** because researchers are attempting to create conditions in the laboratory that resemble certain conditions in the real world, but are not exactly like those real conditions. We cannot create in the laboratory many of the types of stress that may cause depression in the real world, such as losing one's home in a hurricane, or continually being assaulted, but we can create analogues—situations that capture some of the key characteristics of these real-world events, such as their uncontrollability and unpredictability.

Internal Validity

We want to ensure that our experiment has **internal validity**—that changes in the dependent variable can be confidently attributed to our manipulation of the independent variable, and not to other factors. Perhaps people who participate in our experiment using anagrams become more depressed over the course of the experiment simply because participating in an experiment is a negative experience, and not because of the unsolvable anagrams. This is basically the same type of third variable problem we encountered in the previous studies. To control third variables, researchers create a **control group** in which participants have all the same experiences as the group of main interest in the study, except that they do not receive the key manipulation—in our case the experience of the unsolvable puzzles. The control group for our study could be made to do puzzles very similar to the unsolvable anagrams the other group works on, but the control group's anagrams could be solvable. Thus, the control group's experience would be identical to that of the other group—the **experimental group**—except that the control group would not receive the stressor of unsolvable anagrams.

If the participants for our experimental group (the one that does the unsolvable anagrams) and for our control group (the one that does the solvable anagrams) differ in important ways before they begin the experiment, then we cannot be sure that our manipulation

Human laboratory studies attempt to create situations analogous to those that affect psychopathology.

was the cause of any changes in our dependent variable. Thus, **random assignment** to the experimental and control groups is a critical step to safeguarding internal validity. This simply means that each individual participant has an equal chance of being in the experimental and the control groups. Often a researcher will use a table of random numbers to assign participants to groups.

Demand Characteristics

Another threat to internal validity is the presence of **demand characteristics**—situations that cause participants to guess the hypothesis of the study and change their behavior as a result. For example, if our measure of depression were too obvious, participants might guess what hypothesis we were testing. To avoid demand characteristics, we could use more subtle measures of depression, such as those illustrated in Figure 3.6, that are embedded in other measures so as to obscure the real purpose of our study. These other

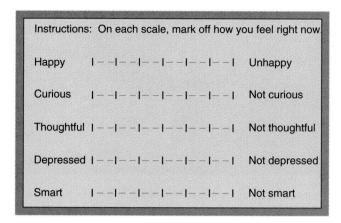

FIGURE 3.6 Scales to Measure Depression, Embedded in Other Scales. The researcher may be interested only in subjects' answers on the scales measuring happiness and depression but may embed these scales in other scales to obscure the purpose of the study.

measures are often called *filler measures.* Researchers also often use *cover stories:* Participants are told a false story to prevent them from guessing the true purpose of the experiment and changing their behavior accordingly.

In order to reduce demand characteristics further, experimenters who actually interact with the participants should be *unaware* of which condition the participants are in, the experimental condition or control condition, so that they do not give off subtle cues as to what they expect the participants to do in the experiment. For example, if experimenters knew that a participant was in the experimental condition, they might suggest to the participant in subtle ways that the anagrams were unsolvable. This obviously would create demands for the participant to behave in ways he or she otherwise might not have if the experimenters had not subtly communicated their expectations.

We have instituted a number of safeguards for internal validity on our study—participants have been randomly selected and assigned, and our experimenters are unaware of the hypothesis of our study and thus to the condition that participants are in. Now the study may be conducted. We find that, as we predicted, participants given the unsolvable anagrams showed greater increases in depressed mood than did participants given the solvable anagrams. What can we conclude about our theory of depression, based on this study? Our experimental controls have helped us rule out third variable explanations, so we can be relatively confident that it was the experience of the uncontrollable stressor that led to the increases in depression in the experimental group. Thus, we can say that we have supported our hypothesis that people exposed to uncontrollable stress will show more depressed mood than will people not exposed to uncontrollable stress.

Evaluating Human Laboratory Studies

As we have already discussed, the primary advantage of human laboratory studies is control. Researchers have more control over third variables, the independent variable, and the dependent variable in these studies than they do in any other type of study they can do with humans (see *Concept Review*: Evaluating Human Laboratory Studies).

Generalizability A primary limitation of human laboratory studies is that we cannot know if our results generalize to what happens outside the laboratory, thus their external validity can be low. Is being exposed to unsolvable anagrams anything like being exposed to major, real-world, uncontrollable stressors, such as the death of a loved one? Clearly there is a difference in the severity of the two types of experiences, but is this the only important difference? Similarly, do the increases in depressed mood in the participants in our study, which were probably small increases, tell us anything about why some people develop extremely severe, debilitating episodes of depression? Experimental analogue studies such as ours have been criticized for the lack of generalizability of their results to the major psychopathology that occurs in everyday life.

Ethical issues Apart from posing the problems of generalizability, human laboratory studies sometimes pose serious ethical issues. Is it ethical to deliberately induce distress, even mild distress, in people? Participants in an experiment can be warned of possible discomfort or distress and told that they can end their participation at any time. Even so, participants rarely stop experiments, even if they are uncomfortable, because of the subtle pressures of the social situation.

CONCEPT REVIEW

Evaluating Human Laboratory Studies

Human laboratory studies provide control but may suffer from problems in generalizability and ethics.

Advantages

The researcher has more control over variables.

Participants can be randomly assigned to groups.

Appropriate control groups can be created to rule out alternative explanations of important findings.

Disadvantages

Results may not generalize to outside the laboratory.

There are possible ethical limitations.

What if a participant, even after being told that the stressful experience he had (e.g., being given an unsolvable anagram) was completely out of his control, believes that he should have been able to control the situation or solve the tasks? It turns out that many participants, especially college students, continue to believe that they should have been able to solve unsolvable tasks or that negative feedback they received in an experiment was a true indication of their abilities, even after being told that they were deceived by the experimenter. The researchers who discovered this phenomenon recommended conducting a *process debriefing* with participants following any potentially upsetting experiments (Ross, Lepper, & Hubbard, 1975). In such debriefings, experimenters slowly draw out the participants' assumptions about the experiments and their performances. They conduct extended conversations with the participants about the purposes and procedures of the experiments, explaining how their behavior was beyond their control and certainly not a reflection of their abilities.

Experimenters must always be aware of the ethical concerns raised by experiments of this sort and take all possible means to limit dangers to participants. All colleges and universities have a human subjects committee that reviews the procedures of studies with humans to ensure that the benefits of the study substantially outweigh any risks to participants, and that the risks to participants have been minimized.

Therapy Outcome Studies

The ethical concerns of human laboratory studies have led some researchers to advocate studies that attempt to *reduce* psychopathology by reducing the factors believed to cause it. Applying this type of study to our theory would mean intervening with depressed participants to reduce stress, which should, in turn, decrease depression, according to our theory. This type of study is called a **therapy outcome study.**

Therapy outcome studies are appealing because they involve helping people while, at the same time, providing information. The goal of therapy outcome studies is to determine the effectiveness of an experimental therapy over no therapy, or compared to other, often established, therapies. We discuss many therapy outcome studies in this book, including some that have compared psychological therapies with drug therapies in the treatment of specific disorders.

Control Groups

Sometimes people get better simply because of the passage of time. Thus, we need to compare the experiences of people who receive our experimental therapy

Therapy outcome studies test hypotheses in the context of providing therapy to people in distress.

with a control group of people who did not receive the therapy to see if our participants' improvement had anything to do with our therapy. Sometimes, researchers use a simple control group of participants who do not receive the experimental therapy but are tracked for the same period of time as were the participants who do receive the therapy. A variation on this simple control group is the **wait list control group.** The participants in this type of group do not receive the therapy when the experimental group does but go onto a wait list to receive the intervention at a later date when the study is completed. Both groups of participants are assessed at the beginning and end of the study, but only the experimental group receives the therapy as part of the study.

Another type of control group is the **placebo control group.** This type of group is used most often in studies of the effectiveness of drugs. The participants in this group have the same interactions with experimenters as do the participants in the experimental group but they take pills that are placebos (inactive substances) rather than the real drug. Usually, both the participants and the experimenters in these studies are unaware what condition the participants are in to prevent demand effects. When this happens, the experiment is known as a **double-blind experiment.**

A placebo control group can also be used to control for the possibility that the simple interaction with the therapist affected the outcome of the participants. This placebo group would interact with a therapist for the same amount of time but receive no therapy. However, some theorists have objected to the idea that interacting with a warm and caring therapist without experiencing any other experimental conditions is a placebo. They suggest that the active ingredient in therapy is receiving unconditional support and encouragement from a warm and caring therapist, not the actual program of therapy (Rogers, 1951). Indeed, psychological placebo interventions have been found to be quite effective with types of problems (Elkin et al., 1989). It seems that a little bit of human caring goes a long way to help people overcome their distress. It also seems it is nearly impossible to construct a true psychological placebo.

Evaluating Therapy Outcome Studies

Although therapy outcome studies might seem the most ethical way of conducting research on people in distress, they carry their own methodological challenges and ethical issues (see *Concept Review*: Evaluating Therapy Outcome Studies). Most psychological therapies involve a package of techniques for responding to people's problems. For example, depressed people in an experimental therapy group might be taught assertiveness skills, social problem-solving skills, and skills at changing self-defeating thinking. Which of these skills was most responsible for alleviating their depression? Even when a therapy works, researchers often cannot know exactly what it is about the therapy that works. This obviously has practical implications, because we need to know what are the effective elements of a therapy in order to bolster those elements and reduce elements that may be useless or even harmful. It also has important theoretical or scientific implications. If we conduct a therapy outcome study to test a particular theory about the cause of a psychopathology, we need to know whether the therapy works for the reasons we theorized. For example, if we are testing our theory that stress causes depression, we will want to know that our intervention reduced depression because it reduced stress and not because it provided the participants with an opportunity to ventilate

When a participant in a therapy outcome study becomes extremely distressed or suicidal, he or she may need to be withdrawn from the study.

their feelings, because it provided them with social support in the form of a therapist, or for some other reason that is not tied to our theory.

Ethical issues There are also ethical problems to using simple control groups, wait list control groups, or placebo control groups in therapy outcome research. Some researchers believe it is unethical to withhold treatment or to provide a treatment they believe is ineffective for people in distress. Many participants assigned to a control group may be in severe distress or in danger of harming themselves or someone else and, therefore, require immediate treatment. In response to this concern, many therapy outcome studies now compare the effectiveness of two or more therapies that are expected to have positive effects. These studies basically are a competition between rival therapies and the theories behind these therapies. Thus, there is some reason to believe that all the participants in such a study will benefit from participation in the study but that the study will yield useful information about the most effective type of therapy for the participants.

Another ethical issue concerns the obligation of the therapist to respond to the needs of the patient. How much can a therapy be modified to respond to a specific participant's needs without compromising the scientific element of the study? Therapists may feel the need to vary the dosage of a drug or deviate from a study's protocol for psychological intervention. If they depart too far from the standard therapy, however, there will be great variation in the therapy that participants in the intervention group receive, which could compromise the results of the study.

Generalizability A related methodological issue has to do with the generalizability of results from therapy outcome studies to the real world. In these studies, the therapeutic intervention is usually delivered to patients in a controlled, high-quality atmosphere by the most competent therapists. The patients are usually screened so they fit a narrow set of criteria for being included in the study, and often only the patients who stick with the therapy to its end are included in the final analyses. In the real world, mental-health services are not always delivered in controlled, high-quality atmospheres by the most competent therapists. Patients are who they are, with their complicated symptom pictures and lives that may not fit neatly into the criteria for an "optimal patient." Patients often leave and return to therapy and may not receive "full trials" of the therapy before they drop out for financial or personal reasons.

Animal Studies

Researchers sometimes try to avoid the ethical issues involved in experimental studies with humans by conducting such studies with animals. Animal research has its own set of ethical issues, which we discuss shortly. However, many researchers feel it is acceptable to subject animals to situations in the laboratory that would not be ethical to impose on humans. **Animal studies** thus provide researchers with even more control over laboratory conditions and third variables than is possible in human laboratory studies.

In a well-known series of animal studies designed to investigate depression (discussed in Chapter 8), Martin Seligman, Bruce Overmier, Steven Maier, and their colleagues subjected mongrel dogs to an uncontrollable stressor in the laboratory (Overmeir & Seligman, 1967; Seligman & Maier, 1967). They did not ask the dogs to do unsolvable anagrams. Instead, they used a stressor over which the researchers could have complete control: a painful electric shock. The experimental group of dogs received a series of uncontrollable shocks. Let us call this *Group E* for *experimental*. In addition, there were two control groups. One control group of dogs received shocks of the same magnitude as the dogs in the experimental group, but they could control the shocks by jumping over a short barrier in their cage. Let us call this *Group J* for *jump*. The dogs in this control group and the dogs in the Group E were yoked—that is, they received exactly the same number and duration of shocks. The only difference between the groups was that the dogs in Group E could not control their shocks, whereas the dogs in control Group J

Animal research on learned helplessness has been generalized to explain why people who have had little control over their lives have difficulty taking advantages of opportunities to exert some control.

could. The second control group of dogs received no shock. Let us call this *Group N* for *none*.

Dogs in Group E initially responded to the shocks by jumping around their cages and protesting loudly. Soon, however, the majority became passive and simply hovered in one part of their cages, whimpering. Later, when the researchers provided the dogs with the opportunity to escape the shock by jumping over a barrier, the dogs did not learn to do this. It seemed that they had an expectation that they could not control the shock, so they were unable to recognize opportunities for control that arose. They seemed to have given up. The researchers labeled this set of behaviors *learned helplessness deficits* and argued that the dogs had learned they were helpless to control their situation.

The dogs in the controllable shock Group J, however, quickly learned how to control the shock and did not develop the learned helplessness deficits shown by the dogs in the uncontrollable shock group. The fact that the two groups of dogs experienced the same amount of shock suggests that lack of control and not the shock alone led to the learned helplessness deficits in the experimental group. The dogs in the control Group N that received no shock also did not develop learned helplessness deficits.

Seligman and colleagues likened the learned helplessness deficits shown by their dogs to the symptoms of depression in humans: apathy, low initiation of behavior, and the inability to see opportunities to improve one's environment (see Seligman, 1975). They

CONCEPT REVIEW

Evaluating Animal Studies

Animal studies allow researchers to investigate some hypotheses they cannot investigate with humans, but raise ethical and generalizability concerns.

Advantages

They allow much more control over experiments.

Many people feel it is acceptable to subject animals to manipulations that most people consider unethical for human subjects.

These studies are especially useful in biological research on new drugs or procedures that might be dangerous.

Disadvantages

Treating animals cruelly is considered unethical by many people.

Results may not generalize to humans.

argued that many human depressions result from people learning they have no control over important outcomes in their lives. This learned helplessness theory of depression seems helpful in explaining the depression and passivity seen in chronically oppressed groups, such as battered wives and some people who grow up in poverty.

A second type of animal study is similar to therapy outcome studies. In studies of the effectiveness of drugs, animals are often given the drugs to determine the effects of the drugs on different bodily systems and behaviors. Sometimes the animals are sacrificed after receiving the drugs so that detailed physiological analyses of the effects of the drugs can be determined. Obviously, such studies could not be done with humans. Animal studies of drugs are particularly useful in the early stages of research, when the possible side effects of the drugs are unknown.

Evaluating Animal Studies

There clearly are problems with animal studies, however (see *Concept Review*: Evaluating Animal Studies). First, some people believe it is no more ethical to conduct painful, dangerous, or fatal experiments with animals than it is to do so with humans. Second, from a scientific vantage point, we must ask whether we can generalize the results of experiments with animals to humans. Are learned helplessness deficits in dogs really analogous to human depression? The debate over the ethical and scientific issues of animal research continues, sometimes leading to violent clashes between

proponents and opponents of animal research. Particularly in the case of research on drug effectiveness, however, animal research is crucial to the advancement of our knowledge of how to help people overcome psychopathology.

Summing Up

- Experimental studies attempt to control all variables affecting the dependent variable.

- In human laboratory studies, the independent variable is manipulated and the effects on people participating in the study are examined. Control groups, in which participants have all the same experiences as the group of main interest in the study, except that they do not receive the key manipulation, are included to control for the effects of being in the experimental situation and the passage of time.

- Demand characteristics are aspects of the experimental situation that cause participants to guess the purpose of the study and change their behavior as a result.

- Disadvantages of human laboratory studies include their lack of generalizability and the ethical issues involved in manipulating people.

- Therapy outcome studies assess the impact of an intervention designed to relieve symptoms. Simple control groups, wait list control groups, and placebo control groups are used to compare the effects of the intervention with other alternatives.

- It can be difficult to determine what aspects of a therapy resulted in changes in participants. Therapy outcome studies also can suffer from lack of generalizability, and assigning people to control groups holds ethical implications.

- Animal studies involve exposing animals to conditions thought to represent the causes of a psychopathology, and then measuring changes in the animals' behavior or physiology. The ethics of exposing animals to conditions that we would not expose humans to can be questioned, as can the generalizability of animal studies.

⊙ CROSS-CULTURAL RESEARCH

Not long ago, most psychological research was conducted with college students, who were mostly White and middle class, and researchers believed that any results they obtained from these samples could be generalized to any other relevant sample. Only anthropologists and a handful of psychologists and psychiatrists assumed that what was true of one ethnic group, culture, or gender was not necessarily true of others.

In the last two decades, however, there has been an explosion of cross-cultural research in abnormal psychology. Researchers are investigating the similarities and differences across culture in the nature, causes, and treatment of psychopathology. Cross-cultural researchers face their own special challenges in addition to the ones common to all research (see *Concept Review*: Evaluating Cross-Cultural Studies; Kleinman & Good, 1985; Rogler, 1999).

First, gaining access to the people one wants to study can be difficult. People who have never participated in research may be wary of cooperating with researchers. In addition, some cultures explicitly shun contact with outsiders. An example is described in the feature on *Extraordinary People*: The Old Order Amish of Pennsylvania. Researcher Janice Egeland spent 20 years gaining the trust of the Amish, and eventually they allowed her to bring in a research team to study major psychopathology in the culture (Egeland & Hostetter, 1983). The result was some of the most exciting research ever published on cross-cultural similarities and differences in manic-depression. Most of us do not have 20 years to gain the trust of the people we want to study and thus will not choose to study populations that are that difficult to access. Nevertheless,

CONCEPT REVIEW

Evaluating Cross-Cultural Studies

Cross-cultural research acknowledges possible differences across cultures but is challenging to conduct.

Advantages

They acknowledge and examine possible differences between cultures.

Disadvantages

Access to some cultures may be difficult.

Concepts and theories can have different meanings or not be applicable in different cultures.

It may be difficult to translate assessment tools across cultures.

There may be cultural or gender differences in people's responses to the social demands of interacting with researchers.

Researchers sometimes label one culture as healthy and another as unhealthy.

most groups of people will take some time to "warm up" to research. Some things researchers can do to facilitate this warming up are to enlist the support of important leaders in the group, provide things that the group needs or wants in exchange for their participation, and learn the customs of the group and adhere to these customs in all interactions with the group.

Second, researchers must be careful in applying theories or concepts that were developed in one culture to another culture (Rogler, 1999). Since the manifestations of disorders can differ across cultures, researchers who insist on narrow definitions of disorders may fail to identify many people suffering from disorders in culturally defined ways. Similarly, theoretical variables can have different meanings or manifestations across cultures. A good example is the variable known as *expressed emotion*. Families high in expressed emotion are highly critical and hostile toward other family members and emotionally overinvolved with each other. Several studies of the majority cultures in America and Europe have shown that people with schizophrenia whose families are high in expressed emotion have higher rates of relapse than do those whose families are low in expressed emotion (Brown, Birley, & Wing, 1972; Vaughn & Leff, 1976). The meaning and manifestation of expressed emotion can differ greatly across cultures, however:

> Criticism within Anglo-American family settings, for example, may focus on allegations of faulty personality traits (e.g., laziness) or psychotic symptom behaviors (e.g., strange ideas). However, in other societies, such as those of Latin America, the same behaviors may not be met with criticism. Among Mexican-descent families, for example, criticism tends to focus on disrespectful or disruptive behaviors that affect the family but not on psychotic symptom behavior and individual personality characteristics. Thus, culture plays a role in creating the content or targets of criticism. Perhaps most importantly, culture is influential in determining *whether* criticism is a prominent part of the familial emotional atmosphere. (Jenkins & Karno, 1992, p. 10)

Thus, today's researchers are more careful to search for culturally specific manifestations of the characteristics of interest in their studies and for the possibility that the characteristics or variables that predict pschopathology in one culture are irrelevant in other cultures.

Third, even if researchers believe they can apply their theories across cultures, they may have difficulty translating their questionnaires or other assessment tools into different languages (Rogler, 1999). A key concept in English may not be precisely translated into another language. Subtle problems can arise because many languages contain variations on pronouns and

EXTRAORDINARY PEOPLE

The Old Order Amish of Pennsylvania

Most tight-knit communities might not want researchers coming in and examining their community members closely, looking for psychopathology. Fortunately, however, one community opened itself to researchers 20 years ago, and from that research has come some of the most interesting and important work on the mood disorders—depression and mania (see Chapter 8)—that has been published in the scientific literature. That community is the Old Order Amish of southeastern Pennsylvania.

The Amish are a religious sect who avoid contact with the "modern" world and live a simple agrarian life much like people lived in the eighteenth century. The Amish use horse and buggy as transportation, most of their homes do not have electricity or telephones, and there is little movement of people into or out of this culture. It is a theocratic society, with the community divided according to church districts, and led by church elders. The Amish are strict pacifists, and avoid involvement with local or national politics or practices. The rules of social behavior among the Amish are very strict, and roles within the community are clearly set. Members who do not comply with community norms are isolated or shunned.

Despite their self-enforced isolation from mainstream American society, the Amish of southeastern Pennsylvania welcomed researcher Janice Egeland and several of her colleagues to conduct some of the most intensive studies of depression and mania ever done (Egeland, 1986, 1994; Egeland & Hostetter, 1983; Pauls, Morton, & Egeland, 1992). These researchers first attempted to ascertain how common depression and mania were among the Amish. They searched the records of local hospitals for Amish people who had been hospitalized for psychological problems. They also interviewed thousands of

members of this community (which in total numbers about 12,000) to discover people with mood disorders who had not yet been hospitalized. They quickly realized that they would have to adjust their definitions of depression and mania to take into account the cultural context of the Amish. As we discuss in more depth in Chapter 8, the manifestations of mood problems, particularly mania, among the Amish were quite different from the manifestations in mainstream culture, due to the strong social norms for behavior among the Amish. This realization alone brought the study of cross-cultural differences in psychiatric disorders into the mainstream psychiatric literature and gave cross-cultural research a legitimacy in that literature it had not had before (Egeland, Hostetter, & Eshleman, 1983).

Egeland and colleagues did not simply describe and count cases of mood disorders among the Amish, however. They took advantage of the fact that the Amish are a closed society, with little movement of individuals in or out, and that the Amish keep extensive genealogical records on their members. In addition, the Amish have essentially only one social class—everyone has the same level of education and similar occupational pursuits, and there is little variation in income. This was a perfect setting for genetic studies of mood disorders. Over the last 20 years, Egeland and colleagues have conducted groundbreaking work that has shaped how we think about the role of heritability in depression and mania (e.g., Ginns et al., 1996, 1998).

Thus, thanks to this closed community that opened itself to research on psychological disorders, and to the tireless work by researcher Janice Egeland and colleagues, we have come a long way in understanding the major mood disorders.

verbs whose usage is determined by the social relationship between the speaker and the person being addressed. For example, in Spanish, the second-person pronoun *usted* connotes respect, establishes an appropriate distance in a social relationship, and is the correct way for a young interviewer to address an older respondent (Rogler, 1989). By contrast, when a young interviewer addresses a young respondent, the relationship is more informal, and the appropriate form of address is *tú*. If an interviewer violates the social norms implicit in a language, he or she can alienate a respondent and impair the quality of the research.

When an interviewer and respondent are of different cultures, miscommunication can happen easily.

Fourth, there may be cultural or gender differences in people's responses to the social demands of interacting with researchers. For example, people of Mexican origin, older people, and people of lower socioeconomic class are more likely to answer "yes" to researchers' questions, regardless of the content, and to attempt to answer questions in socially desirable ways than are Anglo-Americans, younger people, and people of higher socioeconomic class. These differences appear to result from differences among groups in deference to authority figures and concern over presenting a proper appearance (Ross & Mirowsky, 1984). Similarly, it is often said that men are less likely than women to admit to "weaknesses" such as symptoms of distress or problems in coping. If researchers do not take biases into account when designing assessment tools and analyzing data, erroneous conclusions can result.

Fifth, researchers may face pressure to designate one culture as the healthy or normative one, and another culture as the unhealthy or aberrant one. Researchers must constantly guard against such assumptions and must be willing to interpret differences simply as differences, acknowledging that each culture and gender has its healthy and unhealthy characteristics. A good example of a researcher who successfully fought pressure to find one culture deviant and his own culture healthy is psychologist Harold Stevenson. Stevenson studied differences in the educational systems of different countries and the consequences of these differences for children. One stereotype many Americans have of the Japanese educational system is that it drives young

children mercilessly to achieve, creating smart but distressed students. Stevenson's extensive research comparing Japan and the United States found, however, that Japanese children were no more anxious, depressed, or unstable than were American children. However, Japanese children were much more advanced in many educational domains than were American children. When Stevenson first began publishing his findings, they were met with protest and disbelief. He stuck to his findings, using various methodologies to provide additional evidence on differences and similarities between Japan, the United States, and other countries. His basic finding that Japanese children were well-educated and relatively happy has been confirmed many times since (Stevenson, Chen, & Lee, 1993). It has led researchers to search for ways that Japanese culture both motivates children to achieve and supports them emotionally.

Despite the difficulties in conducting cross-cultural research, the need for such research is clear as our understanding of the diversity of human experience of psychopathology becomes greater.

Summing Up

- Cross-cultural research has expanded greatly in recent decades.
- Some special challenges of cross-cultural research include difficulty in accessing populations, in applying theories appropriate in one culture to other cultures, in translating concepts and measures

across cultures, in predicting the responses of people in different cultures to being studied, and in demands to define "healthy" and "unhealthy" cultures.

BIO-PSYCHO-SOCIAL INTEGRATION

Much of the research on abnormality takes an *interactionist* approach: Researchers assume that abnormality is the result of an interaction between characteristics of the person and characteristics of his or her situation. The characteristics of the person that make him or her more vulnerable to abnormality might include biological characteristics, such as genetic predisposition, or psychological characteristics, such as maladaptive styles of thinking about the world. These personal characteristics must interact with characteristics of the situation or environment to actually create the abnormality, however. For example, a woman with a genetic predisposition to schizophrenia may never develop the disorder in its full form if she has a supportive family and never faces major stressors.

Conducting research that reflects this interactionist perspective on abnormality is not easy. Researchers must gather information about people's biological, psychological, and social vulnerabilities and strengths. This may require specialized equipment or expertise. It may also require following subjects longitudinally to observe what happens when people with vulnerabilities face stressors that may trigger episodes of their disorders. Increasingly, researchers are working together in teams to share their expertise in specialized research methods and to share resources that make possible multidisciplinary longitudinal research, as researcher Nancy Andreasen describes in *Pushing the Boundaries*: A Project for a Scientific Psychopathology (p. 90). Researchers are also receiving training in disciplines and methods that are not their primary disciplines. For example, psychologists are learning to use magnetic resonance imaging (MRIs), positron-emission tomography (PET) scans, and other advanced biological methods to investigate abnormality described in the next chapter. If you pursue a career researching abnormality, you may find yourself integrating methods from psychology (which have been the focus of this chapter), sociology, and biology to create the most comprehensive picture of the disorder you are investigating. This may seem a daunting task right now, but this integrationist approach holds the possibility of producing breakthroughs that greatly improve the lives of people vulnerable to psychopathology.

Chapter Summary

- Researchers of abnormal behavior face certain special challenges. First, abnormal behaviors and feelings are difficult to measure objectively because research must rely to a large extent on people's self-reports. Second, people's behaviors and feelings change, often rapidly, complicating assessment. Third, most forms of abnormality probably have multiple causes, and no one study can investigate all possible causes simultaneously. Fourth, ethical concerns limit researchers' abilities to manipulate variables of interest. These challenges require a multimethod approach, in which a variety of methodologies are used to research questions of interest.

- An hypothesis is a statement of what we believe will happen in a study. The primary hypothesis is the one we believe to be true based on our theory. The null hypothesis is the alternative to our primary hypothesis, stating there is no relationship between the independent variable and the dependent variable. The dependent variable is the factor we are trying to predict in our study. The independent variable is the factor we are using to predict the dependent variable.

- In any study, the variables of interest must be operationalized: The researcher must decide how to measure or manipulate the variable. A sample is a group of people taken from our population of interest to participate in our study. The samples for the study must be representative of the population of interest, and the research must be generalizable to the population of interest. A control group is a group of people similar in most ways to our primary group of interest, but who do not experience the variable our theory says causes changes in our dependent variable. Matching our control group to our group of primary interest can help to control third variables, which are variables unrelated to our theory that may still have some effect on our dependent variable.

- Case studies of individuals provide rich and detailed information about their subjects. They

PUSHING THE BOUNDARIES

A Project for a Scientific Psychopathology

The following essay was written by Nancy Andreasen, one of the world's leading researchers on schizophrenia and depression (Andreasen, 1997, pp. 1586–1592). Andreasen lays out her vision of how basic research in psychology and neurology will be integrated in coming decades to provide new insights into major psychological disorders.

Mental illnesses have historically been distinguished from other medical illnesses because they affect the higher cognitive processes that are referred to as "mind." The relationship between mind and brain has been extensively discussed in contemporary philosophy and psychology, without any decisive resolution. One heuristic solution, therefore, is to adopt the position that the mind is the expression of the activity of the brain and that these two are separable for purposes of analysis and discussion but inseparable in actuality. That is, mental phenomena arise from the brain, but mental experience also affects the brain, as is demonstrated by the many examples of environmental influences on brain plasticity. The aberrations of mental illnesses reflect abnormalities in the brain/mind's interaction with its surrounding world; they are diseases of a psyche (or mind) that resides in that region of the soma (or body) that is the brain.

Mind and brain can be studied as they are separate entities, however, and this is reflected in the multiple and separate disciplines that examine them. Each uses a different language and methodology to study the quiddity. The challenge in developing a scientific psychopathology in the 1990s is to use the power of multiple disciplines. The study of mind has been the province of cognitive psychology, which has divided mind into component domains of investigation (such as memory, language, and attention), created theoretical systems to explain the workings of those domains (constructs such as memory encoding versus retrieval), and

designed experimental paradigms to test the hypotheses in humans and animals. The study of brain has been the province of several disciplines. Neuropsychology has used the lesion method to determine localization by observing absence of function after injury, whereas neuroanatomy and neurobiology have mapped neural development and connectivity and studied functionality in animal models. The boundaries between all these disciplines have become increasingly less distinct, however, creating the broad discipline of cognitive neuroscience. The term "cognitive" has definitions that range from broad to narrow; its usage here is broad and refers to all activities of mind, including emotion, perception, and regulation of behavior.

Contemporary psychiatry studies mental illnesses as diseases that manifest as mind and arise from brain. It is the discipline within cognitive neuroscience that integrates information from all these related disciplines in order to develop models that explain the cognitive dysfunctions of psychiatric patients based on knowledge of normal brain/mind function. . . .

Examples of work applying diverse techniques of cognitive neuroscience to the study of depression and schizophrenia indicate that increasingly sophisticated strategies and conceptualizations are emerging as powerful new technologies are being applied. Focal regions have been replaced by circuits and static changes by plasticity and molecular mechanisms. The power of models is enhanced by efforts to design experiments that can be used in nonhuman species, in order to obtain in vivo measures that will illuminate mechanisms. The power of neuroimaging is also permitting in vivo measures of circuits and mechanisms in the human brain. These advances have created an era in which a scientific psychopathology that links mind and brain has become a reality.

also honor the uniqueness of individuals and often allow for individuals to describe their experiences in their own words. They are helpful in generating new ideas and in the study of rare problems. Case studies suffer from problems in generalizability, and the subjectivity of both the person being studied and the person conducting the study.

- Correlational studies examine the relationship between two variables without manipulating the variables. A correlation coefficient is an index of the relationship between two variables. It can range from −1.00 to +1.00. The magnitude of the correlation indicates how strong the relationship between the variables is. A positive correlation indicates that as values of one variable increase, values of the other variable increase. A negative correlation indicates that as values of one variable increase, values of the other variable decrease. A result is said to be statistically significant if it is unlikely to have happened by chance. The convention in psychological research is to accept results for which there is a probability of less than 5 in 100 that they happened by chance. A correlational study can show that two variables are related, but cannot show that one variable causes the other. All correlational studies suffer from the third variable problem—the possibility that variables not measured in the study actually account for the relationship between the variables measured in the study.

- Continuous variable studies evaluate the relationship between two variables that vary along a continuum. A sample is a subset of a population of interest. A representative sample is similar to the population of interest on all important variables. One way to generate a representative sample is to obtain a random sample.

- Whereas cross-sectional studies assess a sample at one point in time, longitudinal studies assess the same sample at multiple points in time. A prospective longitudinal study assesses a sample that is expected to have some key event in the future both before and after the event, then examines changes in the sample that occurred. Group comparison studies evaluate differences between key groups, such as a group that experienced a specific type of stressor and a comparison group that did not experience the stressor, but is matched on all important variables.

- Experimental studies provide more definitive evidence that a given variable causes psycho-

pathology. A human laboratory study has the goal of inducing the conditions that we hypothesize will lead to our outcome of interest (e.g., increasing stress to cause depression) in people in a controlled setting. People are randomly assigned to either the experimental group, which receives a manipulation, or a control group, which does not. Generalizing experimental studies to real-world phenomena is sometimes not possible, however. In addition, manipulating people who are in distress in an experimental study can create ethical problems.

- A special type of experimental study is the therapy outcome study. This type of study allows researchers to test an hypothesis about the causes of a psychopathology while providing a service to subjects. Still, there are several difficult issues researchers face with therapy outcome studies. These include problems in knowing what elements of therapy were effective, questions about the appropriate control groups to use, questions about whether to allow modifications of the therapy to fit individual subjects' needs, and the lack of generalizability of the results of these studies to the real world. In therapy outcome studies, researchers sometimes use wait list control groups, in which control subjects wait to receive the interventions after the studies are completed. Or they may try to construct psychological placebo control groups, in which subjects receive the general support of therapists but none of the elements of the therapy thought to be active. Both of these types of control groups have practical and ethical limitations, however.

- Animal studies allow researchers to manipulate their subjects in ways that are not ethically permissible with human subjects, although many people feel that such animal studies are equally unethical. Animal studies suffer from problems in generalizability to humans, however.

- In doing cross-cultural research, researchers face special challenges. Access to the populations of interest can be difficult. Theories or concepts that make sense in one culture may not be applicable to other cultures. Questionnaires and other assessment tools must be translated accurately. Culture can affect how people respond to the social demands of research. Finally, researchers must be careful not to build into their research assumptions that one culture is the healthy one and another culture is the deviant one.

Key Terms

scientific method 69

hypothesis 69

null hypothesis 69

variable 69

dependent variable 69

independent variable 70

operationalization 70

case study 72

generalizability 73

replicate 73

correlational study 74

continuous variable 74

group comparison study 74

cross-sectional study 75

longitudinal study 75

correlation coefficient 75

statistical significance 76

third variable 76

sample 77

representative sample 77

random sample 77

matching 77

external validity 77

experimental studies 79

human laboratory 80

analogue study 80

internal validity 80

control group 80

experimental group 80

random assignment 80

demand characteristics 80

therapy outcome study 82

wait list control group 82

placebo control group 82

double-blind experiment 82

animal studies 84

Critical Thinking Questions

1. What are some of the motivations people might have for participating in a psychological study that could affect the representativeness of the sample?

2. Under what circumstances do you think it is ethical to deceive the participants in a research study? When it is unethical?

3. Can a researcher from one culture ever truly understand what it is like to be a member of another culture?

Andre Rouillard
Essor

Beauty cannot disguise nor music melt
A pain undiagnosable but felt.

—*Anne Morrow Lindbergh*

The Unicorn and Other Poems, 1935–1955 (1956)

CHAPTER 4

Assessing and Diagnosing Abnormality

CHAPTER OVERVIEW
Gathering Information

Assessment is the process of gathering information about the symptoms people are suffering and the possible causes of these symptoms. Many types of information are gathered during an assessment, including information about current symptoms, recent events and physical condition, drug and alcohol use, personal and family history of psychological disorders, and cognitive functioning. This helps in making a diagnosis. In addition, information about coping styles, social resources, self-concept, and sociocultural background helps in planning treatment.

Assessment Tools

There are many types of assessment tools clinicians use. Any assessment tool should provide valid and reliable information. Neuropsychological tests can help detect neurological problems that may be causing symptoms. Intellectual tests give an indication of cognitive functioning. Structured clinical interviews and symptom questionnaires provide direct information about symptoms. Personality inventories, behavioral observations, self-monitoring, and projective tests can indicate personality styles and behavioral deficits.

Pushing the Boundaries:
Neuroimaging Psychopathology

Taking Psychology Personally:
Is Self-Assessment a Good Idea?

Problems in Assessment

Certain problems complicate the assessment process. Clients may be resistant to providing information. Some clients may be unable to provide information because of cognitive impairment or youth. Children's manifestation of distress can change significantly with age. Cultural biases can impair the accuracy of clinicians' assessments of clients from other cultures.

Diagnosis

The *Diagnostic and Statistical Manual of Mental Disorders* (DSM) is the primary set of rules used for diagnosing psychological disorders in the United States. The first two editions of the DSM had diagnostic criteria that were vague and based on theory. Beginning with the third edition of the DSM in 1980, the diagnostic criteria were revised to be as observable and atheoretical as possible. The current edition, DSM-IV, specifies five axes to be used in making diagnoses. Critics of the DSM have charged that it reflects Western, masculine ideals for a "healthy" person and thus pathologizes normal behaviors of women and people from other cultures. In addition, the subjectivity inherent in psychiatric diagnoses and the stigma attached to these diagnoses raise concerns about application of these diagnoses. Yet having clear criteria for diagnosis is necessary for the progress of research on psychological disorders and for communication among clinicians.

Extraordinary People:
Neil Cargile

Viewpoints:
Cultural and Gender Issues in Diagnosis

Bio-Psycho-Social Integration

Chapter Summary
Key Terms
Critical Thinking Questions

CASE STUDY

It is the year 2023, and Jackson has a problem. For the last several weeks, he has been feeling anxious and agitated most of the time. He cannot concentrate on his work and is so distracted that he has had several accidents. Jackson's thoughts seem to jump from one subject to another.

Jackson goes to see his therapist. The therapist first administers psychological tests to identify all of Jackson's symptoms. Then the therapist administers a series of brain scans and blood tests to determine the causes of these symptoms. The brain scans indicate that Jackson has a deficit in neurotransmitter functioning in the thalamus, combined with abnormal metabolic activity in the prefrontal cortex, suggesting that Jackson is suffering from Bindle's disorder. The blood tests confirm this diagnosis.

The brain scan and blood data suggest the specific type of drug therapy and psychotherapy that will be most useful in treating Jackson's symptoms. The therapist prescribes this drug and begins working with Jackson using the psychotherapy that Jackson needs.

What you have just read is a wishful depiction of what assessment, diagnosis, and treatment planning will be like in the future. **Assessment** is the process of gathering information about people's symptoms and the possible causes of these symptoms. In the future, we may be able to administer psychological and biological tests that pinpoint the nature and causes of people's psychological problems and determine the most appropriate treatment for these problems. Today we have psychological and biological tests that *suggest* the nature and causes of these problems. These tests can provide vital information, although they are seldom foolproof or definitive.

The information gathered in an assessment is used to determine the appropriate diagnosis for a person's problems. A **diagnosis** is a label we attach to a set of symptoms that tend to occur with one another. Most of the chapters of this book address specific diagnoses, such as schizophrenia or depression or eating disorders. Before we discuss these specific diagnoses, however, we must discuss how clinicians and researchers go about assessing what is wrong with a person and making a diagnosis.

In this chapter, we discuss the modern tools of assessment and how they are used to determine the proper diagnosis of psychological symptoms and to understand the nature and causes of psychological problems. Some of these tools are very new, and some have been around for many years. These tools provide information on the individual's personality characteristics, cognitive deficits (such as learning disabilities or problems in maintaining attention), emotional well-being, and biological functioning.

We also consider modern systems of diagnosing psychological problems. There are a number of dangers and problems in applying a psychiatric diagnosis to a person, such as the stigmatizing effects of having a psychiatric diagnosis. We will discuss these dangers. Still, having a standardized system of diagnosis is crucial to communication among mental-health professionals and to good research on psychological problems. We must agree on what we mean when we use a label such as *Bindle's disorder* (which, by the way, is a fictitious disorder), and a standardized diagnostic system provides agreed-upon definitions of disorders.

First, however, we explore the types of information a clinician will want to gather during an assessment. Then we review several methods that can be used to gather this information. Throughout the process of gathering information, the clinician must watch for many pitfalls in the assessment process, and we examine several of these in the next sections.

☉ GATHERING INFORMATION

If Jackson showed up at a therapist's office today, what kind of information would the therapist want to know about Jackson? Let us look at three types of information—symptoms and history, physiological and neurophysiological factors, and sociocultural factors—that will guide the therapist to a diagnosis and will help in formulating a treatment plan.

Symptoms and History

There are a number of types of information about a client's symptoms and history that will be gathered in an assessment (see *Concept Review*: Symptom and History Information to Be Obtained in Assessment). First, the therapist will want to know more about Jackson's *current symptoms*, including their severity and chronicity. Jackson may be able to describe his symptoms in detail and may know exactly when these symptoms began, especially if the onset of the symptoms was associated with a specific event, such as being fired from a job. However, he may only complain of feeling "out of it" or "upset" and may not be able to pinpoint when he first began experiencing these feelings. It may take some gentle prodding by the therapist to determine the exact nature of these symptoms.

The therapist will try to ascertain how much the symptoms are interfering with Jackson's *ability to function* in the different domains in his life (e.g., in his work, his relationships with others, his role as a parent). Jackson will also be asked whether he experiences the symptoms across a wide variety of situations

CONCEPT REVIEW

Symptom and History Information to Be Obtained in Assessment

Assessments are designed to gather a wide range of information.

Type of Information	Types of Questions Asked
Current symptoms	What are the symptoms?
	How severe are they?
	How chronic or acute are they?
	When did they begin?
	How much are they interfering with functioning?
Coping style	Is the client engaging in adaptive or maladaptive coping strategies?
Self-concept and concept of symptoms	Does the client have a strong or weak self-concept?
	What are the client's beliefs about what is wrong?
	What are the client's beliefs about the appropriate treatment?
Recent events	Have any negative or positive events happened lately?
	Are there ongoing stressors in the client's life?
History of psychological disorders	Has the client experienced symptoms similar to the current symptoms at some time in the past?
Family history of psychological disorders	Does the client's family have a history of any psychological disorders or symptoms?

or only in specific types of situations. For example, does he feel anxious only at work or both at work and at home? The criteria for diagnosing most of the major psychological disorders require that the symptoms be severe and pervasive enough that they are interfering with the person's ability to function in daily life. If the symptoms are not that severe and are specific to one situation, then a diagnosis may not be warranted. Information about the pervasiveness and duration of Jackson's symptoms will also help the therapist formulate a plan for treatment that addresses all the areas in which Jackson is having problems.

It is also helpful to know how Jackson tends to *cope* with stressful circumstances, including how he copes with his own symptoms. Does he seek out people whom he trusts to talk about his stresses, or does he retreat to his apartment and drink heavily when stressed? Sometimes the person's ways of coping with his symptoms and stressors create significant problems that must also be addressed in therapy.

The therapist should explore Jackson's *self-concept* and his *concept of his symptoms*. Does Jackson have a strong sense of himself and his ability to overcome his symptoms, or is his self-esteem low and does he feel hopeless and helpless to overcome his symptoms? A client's sense of self-efficacy—ability to overcome the troubles he or she is faced with—is an

important ingredient in therapy (Bandura, 1995). Also, as we discuss more in Chapter 5, how a client conceives of his or her symptoms and problems will affect how he or she reacts to the therapist's interventions. If a client believes his symptoms have biological origins, he may be resistant to psychotherapy. Similarly, if a client believes his symptoms are tied to his relationships to others, he may not want to take pills to get rid of the symptoms.

The therapist will want to know about any *recent events* in Jackson's life. Major negative life events, such as the death of a loved one or a divorce, can be associated with a variety of psychological problems. However, positive changes can also create stress that is associated with psychological symptoms. For example, perhaps Jackson was recently promoted at work and is experiencing his new responsibilities as extremely stressful. Symptoms that arise in response to a specific event are often given a different diagnosis (or in some cases, no diagnosis) from the same ones when they arise with no apparent trigger. For example, a child who becomes depressed after his parents separate might be given a diagnosis of adjustment disorder with depressed mood, whereas a child who gradually becomes more and more depressed for no apparent reason might be given a diagnosis of major depressive disorder. This distinction is made because

*"I was beginning to think of myself as a visionary.
Turned out they were hallucinations."*
© Sidney Harris

symptoms that are triggered by a specific event often have a different prognosis and require different treatment than do symptoms that arise "out of the blue." A child whose symptoms of depression are triggered by a specific event is more likely to recover from these symptoms after a few talks with a supportive counselor than is a child who gradually becomes more and more depressed for no apparent reason. Similarly, if a therapist knows that Jackson's symptoms were triggered by some specific life event, she can address the meanings and consequences of the event in working with Jackson.

Jackson's *past history of psychological problems* is also important in his assessment. This information is especially relevant if Jackson has symptoms that suggest more than one possible diagnosis. For example, imagine that Jackson reports, in addition to the symptoms described earlier, that he believes he has extraordinary powers or talents. He has also heard voices telling him that he has a special mission. These are core symptoms of both schizophrenia and mania, two disorders that require different treatments. Thus, it is crucial to make a **differential diagnosis** to determine which of two or more disorders might be causing Jackson to suffer. One of the best ways to determine whether Jackson is suffering from schizophrenia or from mania is to examine his past history of psychological problems. If Jackson has a clear history of severe mood swings, in which he alternated between elated moods and extremely depressed moods, then the chances are good that his current symptoms are symptoms of mania instead of schizophrenia, and he will respond well to the treatments for mania. If he has no history of mood swings and has responded well in the past to drugs for schizophrenia, then the chances are good that he is currently suffering from schizophrenia. This example also illustrates why it is important that we have a standardized and reliable system of diagnosis. We need to be sure that the diagnoses people such as Jackson received in the past were based on the same criteria we are using to diagnose his

current episode. Otherwise, the information we have on Jackson's past diagnoses will give us no clues as to how to interpret his current symptoms.

Not only is Jackson's personal psychological history critical to making an accurate diagnosis, his *family history of psychological disorders* is also relevant. Again, family history can be extremely helpful when we are unsure of which of two disorders Jackson may have. Some disorders "run true" in a family, meaning that there is a high incidence of that particular disorder in a family but not a high incidence of other disorders in the same family. For example, some families tend to have a high incidence of schizophrenia among their members but not a high incidence of mania. Thus, if Jackson has a strong family history of schizophrenia, the chances are higher that he is suffering from schizophrenia than mania. In contrast, if he has a strong family history of mania, then the chances are that his current symptoms represent mania.

Physiological and Neurophysiological Factors

Jackson's physical and cognitive functioning are key pieces of information to gather in an assessment (see *Concept Review*: Physiological and Neurophysiological Information to Be Obtained in an Assessment). The therapist should ask Jackson to obtain a complete *physical examination* to determine if he is suffering from any medical conditions that can create psychological symptoms. For example, some brain tumors can create the kind of disorientation and agitation that Jackson is reporting. In our story about Jackson at the beginning of this chapter, the therapist pinpointed a specific brain abnormality that was causing Jackson's symptoms. As we discuss in *Pushing the Boundaries*: Neuroimaging Psychopathology (see pp. 105–107), medical technology and our understanding of the underlying neurology of psychological disorders are not yet developed enough for us to pinpoint the biological underpinnings of most disorders. That is, we do not know what the biological causes of most disorders are, and we don't have definitive tests of most of the biological causes we think exist.

What biological tests can sometimes tell us today, however, is whether there is some medical disease that is causing psychological symptoms as side effects. Thyroid disorders can cause people to experience the classic symptoms of depression, but most people who get depressed do not have a thyroid disorder. However, if an individual's depression is caused by a thyroid disorder, we can often simply treat the thyroid disorder and the symptoms of depression will also disappear without any additional antidepressant treatment. Thus, it is important to determine whether a medical disease such as a thyroid disorder might be causing a person's psychological symptoms.

Therapists need to know about any *drugs*—legal or illegal—their clients may be taking. Many drugs can induce distressing psychological symptoms as side effects during drug use or withdrawal from the drug. In such cases, a different diagnosis is given from that given when the symptoms are not the consequence of some drug. Therapists also need to know about any drugs a client is taking to protect against interactions between those drugs and medications the therapist might prescribe for the client's symptoms.

The therapist may need to assess Jackson's *cognitive functioning* and *intellectual abilities*. This information can be crucial to making differential diagnoses. For example, the kinds of symptoms Jackson is showing—disorientation and agitation—can be psychological signs of neurological disorders such as Alzheimer's disorder. Cognitive tests can help to determine the extent of Jackson's disorientation and cognitive deficits. As another example, among the elderly, undetected problems in short-term memory can lead to the symptoms of paranoia. Some older people who cannot remember conversations they had with other people or where they have left items begin to believe that other people are doing things behind their backs. Determining that symptoms of paranoia are due to memory deficits rather than to other causes can have a major impact on the diagnosis and type of treatment the person receives.

It is important for clients to receive a physical examination to determine whether medical problems may be affecting their mental health.

Sociocultural Factors

Finally, Jackson's social environment and cultural background can influence his symptoms and thus need to be assessed (see *Concept Review*: Sociocultural Information to Be Obtained in an Assessment, p. 100). The therapist may want to know about the *social resources* Jackson has available to him—the numbers of friends and family members he has contact with and the quality of his relationships with these people. Social isolation can make it much more difficult for people to overcome psychological problems; on the other hand, friends and family members can also be burdens for the person when these relationships are marked by conflict or create unreasonable demands on the person.

The therapist must obtain information on Jackson's *sociocultural background*. This is an important step for therapists working with a culturally diverse clientele. For immigrant clients, this background includes the specific culture where they were raised, the number of years they have been in this country, the circumstances that brought them to this country (to escape

CONCEPT REVIEW

Sociocultural Information to Be Obtained in an Assessment

An individual's social resources and sociocultural background are relevant in an assessment.

Type of Information	Types of Questions Asked
Social resources	Does the client have a supportive family or friends?
	How supportive are the client's work relationships?
Sociocultural background	In what culture was the client raised?
	How long has the client been in this country?
	Why did the client come to this country?
	What are the client's connections to his or her homeland?
	What is the client's level of acculturation?

Differences between parents and children in levels of acculturation can create family stress.

war or oppression, to seek work), their continuing connections to their homeland, and whether they are currently living with people from their homeland (Dana, 1998; Westermeyer, 1993). As we shall see, immigrants who left their homeland under difficult circumstances and who do not have a strong support system of people from their culture in their new homes are at especially high risk for disorders such as posttraumatic stress disorder (see Chapter 7). It is also useful to know as much as possible about the clients' socioeconomic status and occupation in their homeland—perhaps they were physicians in their homeland and now they are street cleaners—because the contrast between their lives in the homeland and their current lives can be a source of difficulty.

Immigrants and other members of ethnic minority groups differ in their levels of acculturation. **Acculturation** is the extent to which a person identifies with her or his group of origin and its culture or with the mainstream dominant culture (Sue et al., 1998). Some members of ethnic minority groups retain as much of their culture of origin as possible and reject the dominant mainstream culture. They may continue to speak their language of origin and refuse to learn the dominant language. Other members fully identify with the dominant culture and reject their culture of origin. Still others are bicultural—they continue to identify with

their culture of origin and celebrate it but also assimilate as necessary to the dominant culture.

Therapists need to understand their clients' level of acculturation because this can affect how clients talk about and present their problems, the kinds of stresses clients will be exposed to, and clients' responses to interventions therapists might make. We discuss these issues in more depth in Chapter 5 and in later chapters on specific disorders, but let us briefly examine three examples. First, members of some cultures often experience psychological distress in somatic symptoms such as headaches and stomachaches. Knowing that a client remains fully identified with a culture that tends to present psychological symptoms in somatic terms can help a therapist interpret a client's complaints. Second, when members of a family differ in their levels of acculturation, this can cause significant stress for family members. For example, an adolescent who is fully acculturated to the dominant culture may have many conflicts with a parent who remains identified with his or her culture of origin and does not want the adolescent to adopt the mainstream culture. Third, a client who is acculturated to the mainstream American culture will respond differently to certain suggestions a therapist might make, such as to confront an abusive boss, than will a client who remains identified with a culture in which authority figures are never questioned.

Summing Up

- Information concerning clients' symptoms and history is obtained in an assessment. This includes the details of their current symptoms, ability to function, coping strategies, self-concept, recent events, past history of psychological problems, and family history of psychological problems.

- Clients' physiological and neurophysiological functioning are assessed as well. They may be asked to undergo a physical examination to detect medical conditions, questioned about their drug use, and tested for their cognitive functioning and intellectual abilities.

- Clients' sociocultural background—including their social resources and cultural heritage—are important to ascertain in an assessment.

ASSESSMENT TOOLS

How does a clinician gather all this information? There are a number of assessment tools that have been developed to ensure that clinicians gather all the information needed for an accurate assessment.

The Clinical Interview

Much of the information for an assessment is gathered in an initial **interview,** often called an *intake interview,* when the clinician first meets the client. The interview may be an **unstructured interview,** with only a few questions that are open-ended such as "Tell me about yourself." The therapist will listen to the client's answers to the questions and observe how the client answers the questions—does the client hesitate when talking about her marriage, does she avoid questions about her drinking habits, does she look sad when talking about her career—to obtain nonverbal indicators of what is bothering the client.

The clinician may also interview the client's family members for information about the family's history of psychological problems, the client's past history, and the client's current symptoms. Information from family members is especially important if the client is a child, because children cannot always tell us what they are feeling or thinking. In addition, some adults are so impaired that they cannot provide adequate information to the assessor. They may be so depressed or anxious or confused that they cannot properly answer questions. In such cases, an assessor often must rely entirely on family members and friends for information about a client's functioning.

Unstructured interviews have an important place in an assessment. The specific questions asked in an unstructured interview may vary from one assessor to the next, however, making comparisons of the information gathered by different assessors difficult. Increasingly, clinicians and researchers are using what is known as a **structured interview** to gather information about clients. In a structured interview, the clinician

asks the respondent a series of questions about symptoms he or she may be experiencing, or may have experienced in the past. The format of the questions and the entire interview are highly structured and standardized, and the person's answers to each question are scored by the clinician according to concrete criteria (see Table 4.1, p. 102). At the end of the interview, the clinician should have enough information from the respondent to determine whether he or she has symptoms that qualify for a diagnosis of any of the major types of psychological problems. Several such interviews have been developed in recent decades, including the Diagnostic Interview Schedule, or DIS (Robins et al., 1981), and the Structured Clinical Interview for DSM (Spitzer, Williams, Gibbon, & First, 1992). Structured interviews have also been adapted for diagnosing children's problems. Much of the information about a child's symptoms must often come from parents and other sources.

Structured and unstructured interviews can be valuable tools in assessment but they do have limitations. One of the greatest can be **resistance** on the part of the client who is being interviewed. Sometimes the individual being assessed does not want to be assessed or treated. For example, the parents of a teenager may have forced him to see a psychologist because they are worried about recent changes in his behavior. This teenager may be resistant to providing any information to the assessor, however. Because much of the information a clinician needs must come directly from the person being assessed, resistance to providing that information can be a formidable problem. Even when the person is not completely resistant to being assessed, he or she may have a strong interest in the outcome of that assessment and thus may be highly selective in the information provided, may bias his or her presentation of the information, or may even lie to the assessor. Such problems often arise when assessments are being done as part of a legal case, such as when parents are fighting for custody of their children in divorce. Each parent will want to present him- or herself in the best light but may negatively bias his or her reports on the other parent when speaking to psychologists who have been appointed to assess each parent's fitness for custody of the children.

Clinical Tests, Questionnaires, and Inventories

Clinicians have a number of tests that are used to aid in the gathering of information from clients, and we will discuss several of these tests shortly. First, however, let us define two criteria that are used to evaluate the quality of any test: validity and reliability.

TABLE 4.1
Sample Structured Interview

Anxiety Disorders

Panic Disorder	Panic Disorder Criteria					
Have you ever had a panic attack, when you *suddenly* felt frightened, anxious or extremely uncomfortable? **If Yes**: Tell me about it. When does that happen? (Have you ever had one that just seemed to come on out of the blue?) IF PANIC ATTACKS IN EXPECTED SITUATIONS: Did you ever have one of these attacks when you weren't in (EXPECTED SITUATION)?	**A.**	At some time during the disturbance, one or more panic attacks (discrete periods of intense fear or discomfort) have occurred that were (1) unexpected, i.e., did not occur immediately before or on exposure to a situation that almost always causes anxiety, and (2) not triggered by situations in which the person was the focus of others' attention.	? 1 2 3	16
Have you ever had four attacks like that in a 4-week period? **If No**: Did you worry a lot about having another one? (How long did you worry?)	**B.**	Either four attacks, as defined in criterion A, have occurred within a 4-week period, or one or more attacks have been followed by a period of at least a month of persistent fear of having another attack.	? 1 2 3	17
When was the last bad one (EXPECTED OR UNEXPECTED)? Now I am going to ask you about that attack. What was the first thing you noticed? Then what? During the attack . . .	**C.**	At least four of the following symptoms developed during at least one of the attacks:		
. . . were you short of breath? (Have trouble catching your breath?)	1.	shortness of breath (dyspnea) or smothering sensations	? 1 2 3	18
. . . did you feel dizzy, unsteady, or like you might faint?	2.	dizziness, unsteady feelings, or faintness	? 1 2 3	19
. . . did your heart race, pound or skip?	3.	palpitations or accelerated heart rate (tachycardia)	? 1 2 3	20
. . . did you tremble or shake?	4.	trembling or shaking	? 1 2 3	21
. . . did you sweat?	5.	sweating	? 1 2 3	22
. . . did you feel as if you were choking?	6.	choking	? 1 2 3	23
. . . did you have nausea or upset stomach or the feeling that you were going to have diarrhea?	7.	nausea or abdominal distress	? 1 2 3	24
. . . did things around you seem unreal or did you feel detached from things around you or detached from part of your body?	8.	depersonalization or derealization	? 1 2 3	25

Source: Data from Spitzer, Williams, Gibbon, & First, 1992.
? = inadequate information   1 = absent or false   2 = subthreshold   3 = threshold or true

Validity and Reliability

If you administer a test to determine what is wrong with a client, you obviously want assurances that the test is an accurate measure. The accuracy of a test in assessing what it is supposed to measure is called its **validity.** The best way to determine the validity of a test would be to see if the results of the test yielded the same information as some objective and accurate indicator of what the test is supposed to measure. For

CONCEPT REVIEW

Types of Validity

The validity of a test can be evaluated in several different ways.

Face validity	Test *appears* to measure what it is supposed to measure
Content validity	Test assesses all important aspects of a phenomenon
Concurrent validity	Test yields the same results as other measures of the same behavior, thoughts, or feelings
Predictive validity	Test predicts the behavior it is supposed to measure
Construct validity	Test measures what it is supposed to measure and not something else

example, if there were a blood test that definitively proved whether a person had Bindle's disorder, you would want any other test for Bindle's disorder (such as a questionnaire) to yield the same results when administered to the person.

Unfortunately, there are no definitive blood tests, brain scans, or otherwise objective tests for any of the psychological disorders we discuss in this book. There are a number of other ways that the validity of a test can be estimated, however (see *Concept Review*: Types of Validity). A test is said to have **face validity** when, on face value, the items seem to be measuring what the test is intended to measure. For example, a questionnaire for anxiety that includes questions such as "Do you feel jittery much of the time?", "Do you feel like you can't sit still?", and "Do you worry about many things?" has face validity because it seems obvious that it assesses symptoms of anxiety.

Content validity is the extent to which a test assesses all the important aspects of a phenomenon that it purports to measure. For example, if our measure of anxiety included only questions about the physical symptoms of anxiety (nervousness, restlessness, stomach distress, rapid heartbeat) and none of the cognitive symptoms of anxiety (apprehensions about the future, anticipation of negative events), then we might question whether it is a good measure of anxiety.

Concurrent validity is the extent to which a test yields the same results as other measures of the same behavior, thoughts, or feelings. A person's scores on our anxiety questionnaire should bear some relation to information gathered from the client's family members and friends about his or her typical level of anxiety. Information from family members and friends may not be completely accurate or valid, so this is not a definitive standard against which to judge our anxiety questionnaire. However, the notion behind concurrent validity is that any new measure of a variable should yield similar results to established measures of that variable.

A test that has **predictive validity** is good at predicting how a person will think or act or feel in the future. Our anxiety measure has good predictive validity if it correctly predicts which people will behave in anxious ways when confronted with stressors in the future and which people will not be anxious.

Construct validity is the extent to which the test measures what it is supposed to measure and not something else altogether (Cronbach & Meehl, 1955). Consider the construct validity of multiple-choice exams given in courses. These exams are supposed to be measuring a student's knowledge and understanding of what was taught in a course. What they may often be measuring, however, is the student's ability to take multiple-choice examinations—to determine what the instructor is trying to get at with the questions and to recognize any tricks or distractors in the questions. The construct validity of achievement tests and intelligence tests has been questioned, as we discuss later in this chapter (Helms, 1992). Critics have questioned whether these tests really measure what a student knows and how intelligent a student is or just how well the student has been taught to answer the odd types of questions posed on these tests.

The **reliability** of a test is an indicator of the consistency of a test. As with validity, there are several types of reliability (see *Concept Review*: Types of Reliability, p. 104). **Test-retest reliability** is an index of how consistent the results of a test are over time. If a test supposedly measures some enduring characteristic of a person, then the person's scores on that test should be similar when he or she takes the test at two different points in time. So if our anxiety questionnaire is supposed to measure people's general tendencies to be anxious, then their scores on this questionnaire should be similar if they complete the questionnaire once this week and then again next week. On the other hand, if our anxiety questionnaire is a measure of people's current symptoms of anxiety (with questions such as "Do you feel jittery right now?") then we might expect low

CONCEPT REVIEW

Types of Reliability

The reliability or consistency of a test is an important indicator of its value.

Test-retest reliability	Test produces similar results when given at two points in time
Alternate form reliability	Two versions of the same test produce similar results
Internal reliability	Different parts of the same test produce similar results
Interrater or interjudge reliability	Two or more raters or judges who administer and score a test to an individual come to similar conclusions

test-retest reliability on this measure. Typically, measures of general and enduring characteristics should have higher test-retest reliability than measures of momentary or transient characteristics.

When people take the same test a second time, they may remember their answers from the first time and try to repeat these answers to seem consistent. Thus, researchers will often develop two or more forms of a test. When people's answers to these different forms of a test are similar, the tests are said to have **alternate form reliability**. Similarly, a researcher may simply split a test into two or more parts to determine if people's answers to one part of a test are similar to their answers to another part of the test. When there is simi-

larity in people's answers to different parts of the same test, the test is said to have high **internal reliability.**

Finally, many of the tests we examine in this chapter are not self-report questionnaires but interviews or observational measures that require the therapist or researcher to make judgments about the people being assessed. These tests should have high **interrater** or *interjudge* **reliability.** That is, different raters or judges who administer and score the interview or test should come to similar conclusions when they are evaluating the same people.

With that background on how the quality of tests is determined, let us discuss several types of tests used in the assessment process.

Neuropsychological Tests

If some sort of neurological impairment is suspected in a client, the clinician may use paper-and-pencil **neuropsychological tests** that may detect specific cognitive and fine-motor deficits, such as an attentional problem or a tendency to ignore items in one part of the visual field (Gregory, 1999). One frequently used neuropsychological test is the Bender-Gestalt Test (Bender, 1938). This test assesses clients' sensorimotor skills by having them reproduce a set of nine drawings (see Figure 4.1). Clients with brain damage may rotate or change parts of the drawings or be unable to reproduce the drawings. When asked to remember the drawings after a delay, they may show significant memory deficits. The Bender-Gestalt Test appears to be good at differentiating people with brain damage from those without brain damage, but it does not reliably identify the specific type of brain damage a person has (Goldstein & Hersen, 1990).

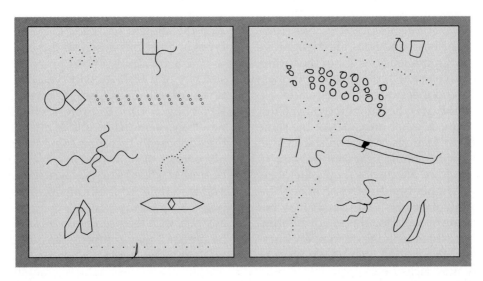

FIGURE 4.1   The Bender-Gestalt Test. On the left are the figures presented to clients. On the right are the figures as copied by a child with a brain tumor that is creating perceptual-motor difficulties.

More extensive batteries of tests have been developed to pinpoint type of brain damage. Two of the most popular batteries are the Halstead-Reitan Test (Reitan & Davidson, 1974) and the Luria-Nebraska Test (Luria, 1973). These batteries contain several tests that provide specific information about an individual's functioning in several skill areas, such as concentration, dexterity, and speed of comprehension. Increasingly, these neuropsychological tests are used in conjunction with brain-imaging techniques—such as those described in *Pushing the Boundaries*: Neuroimaging Psychopathology—to identify specific deficits and possible brain abnormalities.

Intelligence Tests

In clinical practice, **intelligence tests** are used to get a sense of a client's intellectual strengths and weaknesses, particularly when mental retardation or brain damage are suspected (Gregory, 1999). Intelligence tests are also used in school settings to identify children with intellectual difficulties or to place children in

PUSHING THE BOUNDARIES

Neuroimaging Psychopathology

In the case study that began this chapter, Jackson underwent brain scans to determine what disorder he had. There is hope that, in the future, we will have definitive biological tests that determine whether a person has a specific psychological disorder. Unfortunately, we are not yet at that stage.

Still, the biological tests we do have contribute to the assessment procedure. In clinical practice, brain scans are used to determine if a patient has some brain injury or tumor. Blood tests can detect medical problems (such as low blood sugar) that might be contributing to certain psychological symptoms. Researchers use brain scans and blood tests to search for differences in biochemicals or in brain activity or structure between people with a psychological disorder and people with no disorder. Ideally, this research will tell us enough about the biology of psychological disorders that we can develop valid and reliable biological tests for these disorders in the future.

Indeed, both technology and our understanding of the biology of disorders are advancing so rapidly that there will probably be major breakthroughs in biological techniques for assessing and diagnosing psychological disorders in the near future. Thus, let us review the existing technologies and what they can tell us now (Beatty, 1995). We will focus on brain-scanning technology because this technology is providing some of the most exciting new findings in the search for biological underpinnings of psychological disorders.

Computerized tomography (CT) is an enhancement of X-ray procedures. In CT, narrow X-ray beams are passed through the person's head in a single plane from a variety of angles, as shown in Figure 4.2, (p. 106). The amount of radiation absorbed by each beam is measured, and from these measurements a computer program can construct an image that looks like a slice of the brain (see Figure 4.3, p. 107). By taking many different slices of the brain, the computer can reconstruct a three-dimensional image, showing the major structures of the brain. A CT scan can reveal brain injury, tumors, and structural abnormalities (see Figure 4.3). The two major limitations of CT technology are that it exposes patients to X rays, which can be harmful, and it provides only an image of the structure of a brain, rather than an image of the activity in the brain.

Positron-emission tomography (PET) can provide a picture of activity in the brain. PET requires injecting the patient with a harmless radioactive isotope such as fluorodeoxyglucose (FDG). This is a substance that travels through the blood to the brain. The parts of the brain that are active need the glucose in FDG for nutrition, and thus FDG accumulates in active parts of the brain. Subatomic particles in FDG called *positrons* are emitted as the isotope decays. These positrons collide with electrons; both are annihilated and are converted to two photons traveling away from each other in opposite directions (Beatty, 1995). The PET scanner detects these photons and the point at which they are annihilated and constructs an image of the brain showing areas that are most active. PET scans can be used to show differences in the activity levels of specific areas of the brain between

Continued

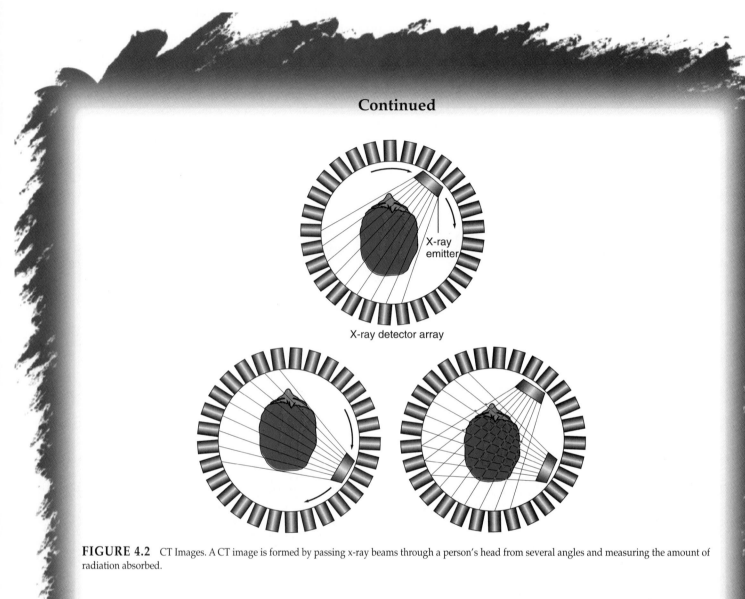

X-ray detector array

FIGURE 4.2 CT Images. A CT image is formed by passing x-ray beams through a person's head from several angles and measuring the amount of radiation absorbed.

people with a psychological disorder and people without a disorder (see Figure 4.4).

Magnetic resonance imaging (MRI) is the newest of the brain-imaging techniques and holds several advantages over both CT and PET technology (Beatty, 1995). It does not require exposing the patient to any form of radiation or injection of radioisotopes. It is safe to use repeatedly in the same patient. It provides much more finely detailed pictures of the anatomy of the brain than do other technologies, and it can image the brain at any angle. It can also provide pictures of the activity and functioning in the brain.

MRI involves creating a magnetic field around the brain of the patient that is so powerful that it causes realignment of hydrogen atoms in the brain. When the magnetic field is turned off and on, the hydrogen atoms change position, causing them to emit magnetic signals. These signals are read by a computer, which reconstructs a three-dimensional image of the brain (Figure 4.5). Researchers are using MRI to study functional and structural brain abnormalities in almost every psychological disorder.

Two other tests that are sometimes used to record brain activity are the **electroencephalogram (EEG)** and **event-related potential (ERP).** EEG is a graph of the electrical activity in the brain, recorded from electrodes placed on the surface of the scalp. Hans Berger, a German psychiatrist, first recorded EEG activity in 1924 (Brazier, 1960). He identified different patterns of EEG activity, which he labeled *alpha, beta, theta,* and *delta* and which differ in frequency and amplitude. These different patterns of activity are correlated with human behavior. In

Continued

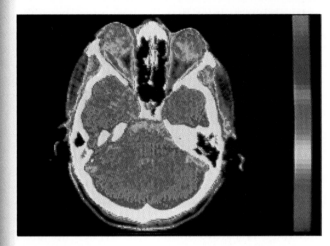

FIGURE 4.3   CT Scan of Human Head. From measures of the amount of radiation absorbed in a CT scan, computers can construct an image of the major structures of the brain.

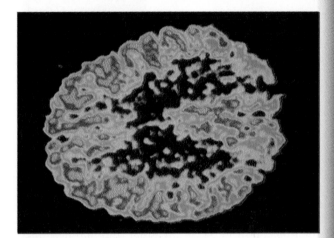

FIGURE 4.4   PET Scan of a Human Brain. PET scans provide a picture of activity in the brain. This scan was taken of a patient with Alzheimer's disease.

normal waking, EEG activity alternates between alpha and beta activity. Theta activity is prominent when we are drowsy, and large delta waves are seen during dreamless sleep. EEGs have been useful in studying people with sleep disorders, who often show abnormalities in EEG activity, and with epilepsy, a disorder in which people experience sudden bursts of electrical activity in the brain.

Event-related potential (ERP) is a component of EEG activity that is elicited by mental events. When a person has a thought or senses something in the environment, there is electrical activity associated with that mental event. By exposing a person to something like the flash of a word on a screen while recording brain activity with an EEG, a researcher can examine the extent and nature of the electrical activity associated with the stimulus. ERP technology is being used to help diagnose attentional difficulties in children suspected of having attention deficit disorder.

In summary, CT, PET, MRI, EEG, and ERP technologies are being used to investigate the structural and functional differences between the brains of people with psychological disorders and those of people without disorders. Sometimes these technologies can also be used to identify gross structural or functional abnormalities such as a brain tumor or severe atrophy (deterioration) in the brain of an individual patient. For the most part, however,

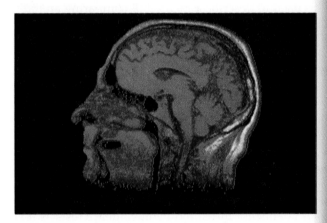

FIGURE 4.5   Magnetic Resonance Image (MRI). An MRI can provide pictures of the structure and activity of the brain.

we cannot yet use these technologies to diagnose specific psychological disorders in individual patients, largely because we do not yet understand the biological underpinnings of these disorders. The future probably holds tremendous advances in the use of these technologies for assessment of psychopathology, though.

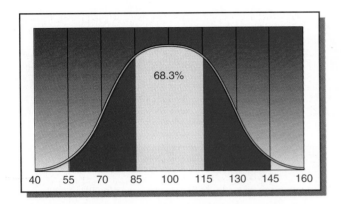

FIGURE 4.6   If the entire population took an IQ test, the scores would fall into a bell-shaped curve around the most frequent score of 100. More than two-thirds of people score between 85 and 115 on IQ tests.

"gifted" classrooms. They are used in occupational settings and the military to evaluate adults' capabilities for certain jobs or types of service. Some examples of these tests are the Wechsler Adult Intelligence Scale–Revised, the Stanford-Binet Intelligence Test, and the Wechsler Intelligence Scale for Children–Third Edition. These tests were designed to measure basic intellectual abilities such as the ability for abstract reasoning, verbal fluency, and spatial memory. The term *IQ* is used to describe a method of comparing an individual's score on an intelligence test with the performance of individuals of the same age group. An IQ score of 100 means that the person performed similarly to the average performance of other people his or her age (see Figure 4.6).

Intelligence tests are controversial in part because there is little consensus as to what is meant by intelligence (Lemann, 1999). The most widely used intelligence tests assess verbal and analytical abilities but do not assess other talents or skills such as artistic and musical ability. Some psychologists argue that success in life is as strongly influenced by social skills and other talents not measured by intelligence tests as it is by verbal and analytical skills (Goleman, 1995; Sternberg, 1988).

Another important criticism of intelligence tests is that they are biased in favor of middle- and upper-class educated European Americans because these people have more familiarity with the kinds of reasoning that are assessed on the intelligence tests (Helms, 1992). In addition, educated European Americans may be more comfortable in taking intelligence tests because testers are often also European Americans, and the testing situation resembles testing situations in their educational experience. In contrast, different cultures within the United States and in other countries may emphasize other forms of reasoning over those assessed on intelligence tests and may not

be comfortable with the testing situations of intelligence tests.

A classic example involves the interpretation of syllogisms, logical problems often used in intelligence tests. A typical syllogism runs like this: All bears in the North are white. My friend saw a bear in the North. What color was that bear? The "right" answer according to intelligence tests is that the bear is white. A subject's ability to infer that the bear must be white is taken as an indication of his or her deductive reasoning skills.

When researchers asked peasant farmers in Central Asia to solve these syllogisms, however, they discovered that this form of reasoning violated a social norm that you never state something you do not know from firsthand experience (Luria, 1976, pp. 108–109):

Voices

[Experimenter]: In the Far North, where there is snow, all bears are white. Novaya Zemlya is in the Far North and there is always snow there. What color are the bears there?

[Respondent]: . . . We always speak only of what we see; we don't talk about what we haven't seen.

[E]: But what do my words imply? [The syllogism is repeated.]

[R]: Well, it's like this: our tsar isn't like yours, and yours isn't like ours. Your words can be answered only by someone who was there, and if a person wasn't there he can't say anything on the basis of your words.

[E]: . . . But on the basis of my words—in the North, where there is always snow, the bears are white, can you gather what kind of bears there are in Novaya Zemlya?

[R]: If a man was 60 or 80 and had seen a white bear and had told about it, he could be believed, but I've never seen one and hence I can't say. That's my last word.

This man may have been interpreted as unintelligent by the rules of the test, but he was only following a social convention of his culture in his answer to the experimenter. Critics of intelligence tests argue that similar cultural clashes happen in more subtle ways whenever persons not of the dominant, educated culture that created intelligence tests are asked to take these tests. A "culture-fair" test would have to include items that are equally applicable to all groups or items that are different for each culture but are psychologically equivalent for the groups being tested. Attempts have been made to develop "culture-fair" tests, but the results have been disappointing. Even if a universal test were created, it would be difficult to make statements about intelligence in different cultures because different nations and cultures vary in the emphasis they place on "intellectual achievement."

So far, we have focused on tests to assess brain abnormalities and cognitive and intellectual functioning. Much of the information that must be gathered in an assessment, however, has to do with the client's emotional, social, and behavioral functioning. Let us turn to tools that help the clinician assess these characteristics.

Symptom Questionnaires

Often when a therapist or researcher wants a quick way to assess what symptoms a person is experiencing, he or she will ask the person to complete a **symptom questionnaire.** These questionnaires may cover a wide variety of symptoms, representing several different disorders. Others focus on the symptoms of specific disorders. One of the most common depression inventories is the Beck Depression Inventory, or BDI (Beck & Beck, 1972). The long form of the BDI has 21 items, each of which describes four levels of a given symptom of depression (see Table 4.2). The respondent is asked to indicate which of the descriptions best fits how he or she has been feeling in the last week. The items are scored to indicate the level of depressive symptoms the person is experiencing. Cutoff scores have been established to indicate moderate and severe levels of depressive symptoms.

Critics of the BDI have argued that it does not clearly differentiate between the clinical syndrome of depression and the general distress that may be related to an anxiety disorder or several other disorders (see Kendall et al., 1987). The BDI also cannot indicate whether the respondent would qualify for a diagnosis of depression. But the BDI is extremely quick and easy to administer and has good test-retest reliability. Hence, it is widely used, especially in research on depression. Clinicians treating depressed people will also use the BDI to keep track of their clients' symptom levels from week to week—that is, as a monitoring tool rather than as a diagnostic tool. A client may be asked to complete the BDI at the beginning of each therapy session; both the client and the therapist then have a concrete indicator of the progress of the client's symptoms.

One of the most commonly used questionnaires for assessing symptoms in children is the Child Behavior Checklist, or CBCL (Achenbach & Edelbrock, 1983). The CBCL presents the parent with a list of over 100 behaviors, thoughts, or feelings that the child may be experiencing and asks the parent to rate how frequently a child shows them. The CBCL can be used to assess specific symptom types (such as aggression and

TABLE 4.2

Items from the Beck Depression Inventory

The Beck Depression Inventory is one of several self-report questionnaires to assess psychological symptoms.

Instructions: Please read each group of statements carefully. Pick out the one statement in each group that best describes the way you have been feeling the past week, including today.

1. I do not feel sad.
   I feel sad.
   I feel sad all the time and I can't snap out of it.
   I am so sad or unhappy that I can't stand it.

2. I am not particularly discouraged about the future.
   I feel discouraged about the future
   I feel I have nothing to look forward to.
   I feel that the future is hopeless and that things cannot improve.

3. I do not feel like a failure.
   I feel I have failed more than the average person.
   As I look back on my life, all I can see is a lot of failures.
   I feel I am a complete failure as a person.

depression) and prosocial or adaptive behavior (such as peer interaction skills). The CBCL has been administered to thousands of healthy children in the general population, so the researcher or clinician can compare an individual child's scores on the CBCL to the scores of children who are functioning well to determine how much the child's functioning is deviating from these norms. The CBCL does well on most indices of validity and reliability.

Personality Inventories

Personality inventories are usually questionnaires that are meant to assess people's typical ways of thinking, feeling, and behaving. These inventories are used as part of an assessment procedure to obtain information on people's well-being, their self-concept, their attitudes and beliefs, their ways of coping, their perceptions of their environment and social resources, and their vulnerabilities. You have probably seen versions of personality inventories in popular magazines, although often these inventories have not undergone much scientific scrutiny, as we discuss in *Taking Psychology Personally*: Is Self-Assessment a Good Idea? (p. 110).

The most widely used personality inventory in professional clinical assessments is the *Minnesota*

TAKING PSYCHOLOGY PERSONALLY

Is Self-Assessment a Good Idea?

Self-help books and magazine articles often feature questionnaires that allow readers to assess their own personal characteristics or weaknesses or the characteristics of their relationships with others. These self-assessment tools typically involve a set of questions that help readers "diagnose" problems and some guidelines as to how to interpret scores on the questionnaires. Are these self-assessment tools a good idea?

In this chapter, we have discussed the problems with the reliability and validity of many assessment tools. The tools that have been described in this chapter are the "best of the bunch"—those most widely used and accepted by professional psychologists and psychiatrists—and yet even these tools have many critics. The self-assessment questionnaires that appear in books and magazines are often not as well-tested or well-conceived as those we discussed in this chapter. In addition, the writers of these questionnaires often make claims about the diagnoses that they produce that are overly conclusive and extreme, such as "If you scored between 10 and 20 on the Relationship Diagnostic Inventory, then your relationship is definitely going to fail. You might as well dump him and find someone else now!"

This does not mean that all self-assessment tools are a bad idea. People often want to deny their problems or are not aware that their symptoms are part of syndromes that can be successfully treated, and self-assessment tools can help people recognize their troubles and seek help. For example, questionnaires that lead people to recognize that they consume much more alcohol than the average person and that withdrawal from the effects of alcohol often interferes with their daily functioning can help these people to moderate their alcohol consumption or seek treatment for alcohol addiction if necessary. Similarly, questionnaires or guidelines that make people aware that the set of symptoms they have been experiencing add up to the syndrome of an anxiety disorder can lead these people into therapy.

One of the most important points to remember about any self-assessment tool is that the information it provides is only suggestive, not conclusive. If you are concerned about the outcome of any self-assessment tool—your score on a questionnaire or how you answered individual questions—it is a good idea to consult with a professional counselor about your concerns to obtain a more thorough and expert assessment of how you are doing.

Multiphasic Personality Inventory (MMPI), which has been translated into over 150 languages and used in over 50 countries (Dana, 1998) (see Figure 4.7). The original MMPI was first published in 1945 and contained 550 items. In 1990, an updated version published under the name MMPI-2 contained 567 items (Butcher, 1990). Both versions of the MMPI present respondents with sentences describing moral and social attitudes, behaviors, psychological states, and physical conditions and ask them to respond either "true," "false," or "can't say" to each sentence. Some examples of items from the MMPI follow:

I would rather win than lose in a game

I am never happier than when alone.

My hardest battles are with myself.

I wish I were not bothered by thoughts about sex.

I am afraid of losing my mind.

When I get bored, I like to stir up some excitement.

People often disappoint me.

The MMPI was developed *empirically*, meaning that a large group of possible items were given to psychologically "healthy" people and people suffering from different psychological problems. Then the items that reliably differentiated among groups of people were included in the inventory. The items on the original MMPI cluster into 10 scales that measure different types of psychological characteristics or problems, such as paranoia, anxiety, and social introversion. An additional four scales have been added to the MMPI-2

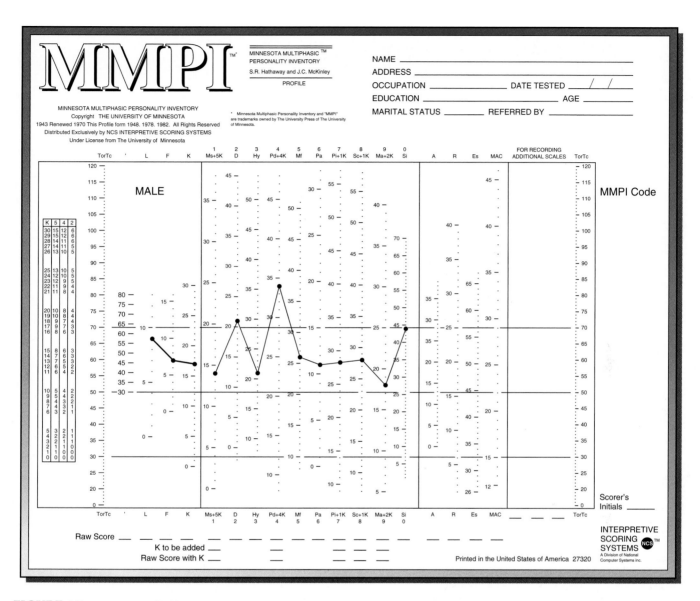

FIGURE 4.7   An MMPI Profile (from MMPI, 1982).

to assess vulnerability to eating disorders, substance abuse, and poor functioning at work. A respondent's scores on each of the scales are compared to scores from the normal population, and a profile of the respondent's personality and psychological problems is derived. There are also four validity scales that determine whether the person tends to respond to the items on the scale in an honest and straightforward manner or tends to distort his or her answers in a way that might invalidate the test (see Table 4.3, p. 112). For example, the Lie scale measures the respondent's tendency to respond to items in a socially desirable way that makes him or her look unusually positive or good.

Because the items on the MMPI were chosen for being those that best differentiated people with specific types of psychological problems from people without psychological problems, the concurrent validity of the

MMPI scales was "built into" the scales in their development. The MMPI may be especially useful as a general screening device for detecting people who are functioning very poorly psychologically. The test-retest reliability of the MMPI has also proven quite high (Parker, Hanson, & Hunsley, 1988).

Many criticisms have been raised about the use of the MMPI in culturally diverse samples, however (Dana, 1998). The norms for the original MMPI—the scores that were considered "healthy" scores—were based on samples of people in the United States that were not representative of people from a wide range of ethnic and racial backgrounds, age groups, and social classes. In response to this problem, the publishers of the MMPI established new norms based on more representative samples of eight communities across the United States. Still, there are concerns that the MMPI

TABLE 4.3

Clinical and Validity Scales of the Original MMPI

The MMPI is one of the most widely used questionnaires to assess people's symptoms and personalities. It also includes scales to assess whether respondents are lying or trying to obfuscate their answers.

Clinical Scales

Scale Number	Scale Name	What It Measures
Scale 1	Hypochondriasis	Excessive somatic concern and physical complaints
Scale 2	Depression	Symptomatic depression
Scale 3	Hysteria	Hysterical personality features and tendency to develop physical symptoms under stress
Scale 4	Psychopathic deviate	Antisocial tendencies
Scale 5	Masculinity-femininity	Sex-role conflict
Scale 6	Paranoia	Suspicious, paranoid thinking
Scale 7	Psychasthenia	Anxiety and obsessive behavior
Scale 8	Schizophrenia	Bizarre thoughts and disordered affect
Scale 9	Hypomania	Behavior found in mania
Scale 0	Social introversion	Social anxiety, withdrawal, overcontrol

Validity Scales

	Scale Name	What It Measures
	Cannot say scale	Total number of unanswered items
	Lie scale	Tendency to present favorable image
	Infrequency scale	Tendency to falsely claim psychological problems
	Defensiveness scale	Tendency to see oneself in unrealistically positive manner

norms do not reflect variations across cultures in terms of what is considered normal or abnormal. In addition, the linguistic accuracy of the translated versions of the MMPI and the comparability of these versions to the English version have been questioned (Dana, 1998).

Projective Tests

A **projective test** is based on the assumption that when people are presented with an ambiguous stimulus, such as an oddly shaped inkblot or a captionless picture, they will interpret the stimulus in line with their current concerns and feelings, their relationships with others, and conflicts or desires of which they may not even be aware. The people are said to project these issues as they describe the "content" of the stimulus, hence the name *projective tests*. Proponents of these tests argue that they are useful in uncovering uncon-

scious issues or motives of a person or when the person is resistant or heavily biasing the information he or she presents to the assessor. Four of the most frequently used projective tests are the Rorschach Inkblot Test, the Thematic Apperception Test (TAT), the Sentence Completion Test, and the Draw-a-Person Test.

The *Rorschach Inkblot Test*, commonly referred to simply as the *Rorschach*, was developed in 1921 by the Swiss psychiatrist Hermann Rorschach. The test consists of 10 cards, each containing a symmetrical "inkblot" in black, gray, and white or in color (see Figure 4.8). The examiner tells the respondent something like "People may see many different things in these inkblot pictures; now tell me what you see, what it makes you think of, what it means to you" (Exner, 1993).

Clinicians are interested in both the content of the clients' responses to the inkblots and the style of their

"Rorschach! What's to become of you?
© Sidney Harris

FIGURE 4.8   Clinicians analyze people's answers to the Rorschach Ink Blot test for particular themes or concerns.

responses. In the content of responses, they will look for particular themes or concerns, such as frequent mentions of aggression or fear of abandonment. Important stylistic features may include the clients' tendency to focus on small details of the inkblot rather than the inkblot as a whole or the clients' hesitations in responding to certain inkblots (Exner, 1993).

The *Thematic Apperception Test (TAT)* consists of a series of pictures. The client is asked to make up a story about what is happening in the pictures (Murray, 1943). Proponents of the TAT argue that the stories clients give reflect their concerns and wishes and their personality traits and motives. As with the Rorschach, clinicians are interested in both the content and style of clients' responses to the TAT cards. Some cards may stimulate more emotional responses than others or no responses at all. These cards are considered to tap the clients' most important issues. The following is a story that a person made up about a picture of a man and young woman (Allison, Blatt, & Zimet, 1968):

Voices

This looks like a nice man and—a sweet girl—They look like this is a happy moment—Looks like he's telling her that he loves her—or something that's tender and sweet. She looks very confident and happy! It looks nice; I like it. Hm! Wait now! Maybe—well—that's right—he looks kind of older—but she looks efficient—and sweet. [Efficient?] Yes [laughs]. Doesn't look particularly efficient at the moment, but I imagine—[puts card away]. [What led up to this?] Well—I think maybe he taught school nearby, and she was a girl in the village—It strikes me as a sort of sweet, old fashioned romance. Maybe she's seen him a long time, and now it has just come to the state where he tells her that he loves her. [What will the outcome be?] I think

they will get married, get some children and be happy—not that they will live happily ever after, not like a fairy tale. They look like ordinary people.

In interpreting the client's story, the clinician might note that it exhibits a romanticized, naive, and childlike quality. The client presents a very conventional scenario but with moral themes and much emotional expression. The clinician might interpret these tendencies as part of the client's basic personality style (Allison, Blatt, & Zimet, 1968).

A third test that is based on the idea that people project their concerns and wishes onto ambiguous stimuli is the *Sentence Completion Test*. Sentence completion tests have been designed for children, adolescents, and adults. The tests provide a "stem," which is the beginning of a sentence, such as "My mother is . . ." or "I wish . . ." The individual is asked to complete the sentence. While more structured than the Rorschach and TAT, sentence completion tests are also interpreted subjectively by the examiner. Clinicians might look for indications of the person's concerns both in what he or she says in response to the sentence stem and in what he or she avoids saying in response to the stem. For example, a clinician might find it interesting that the person seems unable to come up with any response to the stem "Sex is. . . ."

A fourth test is the *Draw-a-Person Test* (Machover, 1949). The client is asked to draw a picture of the self and then to draw a picture of another person of the opposite sex. The clinician examines how the client depicts the self: Does he draw himself as a small figure huddled in the corner of the page or as a large figure filling the page? The drawings of self are thought to reflect the client's self-concept as a strong person or weak person, a smart person or unintelligent person, and so on. The drawing of the other person is thought to reflect the client's attitudes toward the opposite sex and his or her relationships with important members of the opposite sex.

Clinicians from psychodynamic perspectives see projective tests as valuable tools for assessing the underlying conflicts and concerns that clients cannot or will not report directly. Clinicians from other perspectives question the usefulness of these tests. The validity and reliability of all of the projective tests have not proven strong in research (Garb, Florio, & Grove, 1998; Kline, 1993). In addition, because these tests rely so greatly on subjective interpretations by clinicians, they are open to a number of biases.

Behavior Observations and Self-Monitoring

Clinicians will often use **behavioral observation** of clients to assess deficits in their skills or ways of handling situations (Thorpe & Olson, 1997). For example, a clinician might watch a child interact with other children to determine what situations seem to provoke the child to act aggressively. The clinician can then use information from behavior observations to help the client learn new skills, to stop negative habits, and to understand and change the way he or she reacts to certain situations. A couple seeking marital therapy might be asked to discuss with each other a topic on which they disagree. The therapist would observe this interaction, noting the specific ways that the couple handles conflict. For example, one member of the couple may lapse into statements that blame the other member for problems in their marriage, escalating conflict to a boiling point.

The advantages of direct behavioral observations are that they do not rely on the clients' reporting and interpretation of their behaviors. Instead the clinician sees just how skilled the client is or is not in handling important situations. One disadvantage is that different observers may draw different conclusions about an individual's skills. That is, direct behavioral observations may have low interrater reliability, especially when no standard means of making the observations is established. In addition, any individual rater may have difficulty catching everything that is happening in a situation, particularly when he or she is observing two or more people interacting.

In addition, it can be time-consuming and sometimes impossible for a clinician to observe a client's behaviors in key situations. If direct observation is not possible, the clinician may require client **self-monitoring**—that is, ask the client to keep track of the

By observing children's or adults' behavior directly, a clinician can obtain information about their strengths and weaknesses in various settings.

number of times per day he or she engages in a specific behavior (e.g., smoking a cigarette) and the conditions under which this behavior happens. Here is an example (adapted from Thorpe & Olson, 1997, p. 149):

> Steve, a binge drinker, was asked to self-monitor his drinking behavior for two weeks, noting the situational context of urges to drink and his associated thoughts and feelings. These data revealed that Steve's drinking was completely confined to bar situations, where he drank in the company of friends. Gaining relief from stress was a recurring theme.

Self-monitoring is open to biases in what the client notices about his or her behavior and is willing to report. However, the client can gain valuable insight into the triggers of unwanted behaviors through self-monitoring, which can lead to changing these behaviors.

Summing Up

- Paper-and-pencil neuropsychological tests can help to identify specific cognitive deficits that may be tied to brain damage.

- Intelligence tests can indicate a client's general level of intellectual functioning in verbal and analytic tasks.

- Structured interviews provide a standardized way to assess in an interview format people's symptoms.

- Symptom questionnaires allow for mass screening of large numbers of people to determine self-reported symptoms.

- Personality inventories assess stable personality characteristics.

- Projective tests are used to uncover unconscious conflicts and concerns but are open to interpretive biases.

- Behavioral observation and self-monitoring can help detect behavioral deficits and the environmental triggers for symptoms.

☉ PROBLEMS IN ASSESSMENT

We have already mentioned some of the problems that arise in gaining in accurate assessment of clients' problems. These include the client's inability or resistance in providing information to the assessor and the weaknesses of tests assessors use to gain information. In this section, we highlight special challenges that arise in the assessment of certain groups of clients—children and people from cultures different from the assessor's culture.

Evaluating Children

Consider the following conversation between a mother and her 5-year-old son, Jonathon, who was sent home from preschool for fighting with another child.

Mom:	Jonathon, why did you hit that other boy?
Jonathon:	I dunno. I just did.
Mom:	But I want to understand what happened. Did he do something that made you mad?
Jonathon:	Yeah, I guess.
Mom:	What did he do? Did he hit you?
Jonathon:	Yeah.
Mom:	Why did he hit you?
Jonathon:	I dunno. He just did. Can I go now?
Mom:	I need to know more about what happened.
Jonathon:	[Silence]
Mom:	Can you tell me more about what happened?
Jonathon:	No. He just hit me and I just hit him. Can I go now?

Anyone who has tried to have a conversation with a distressed child about why he or she misbehaved has some sense of how difficult it can be to

Just as youngsters can be resistant to talking with their parents about their concerns, clients can be resistant to talking with therapists about their concerns.

engage a child in a discussion about emotions or behaviors. Even when a child readily engages in such a conversation, his or her understanding of the causes of his or her behaviors or emotions may not be very well-developed.

Children, particularly preschool-aged children, cannot describe their feelings, or the events associated with these feelings as easily as adults can (Achenbach, McConaughy, & Howell, 1987). Young children do not differentiate among different types of emotions, often just saying that they feel "bad," for example (Harter, 1983). When distressed, children may talk about physical aches and pains rather than the emotional pain they are feeling. Or a child might not verbalize that he or she is distressed and only show this distress in nonverbal behavior, such as making a sad face, withdrawing, or behaving aggressively. Children who have behavioral problems, such as excessive distractibility or lack of control over their anger, may not believe that they have problems and thus may deny that anything is wrong when asked (Kazdin, 1991).

These problems with children's self-reporting of emotional and behavioral problems have led clinicians and researchers to rely on other people, usually adults in children's lives, to provide information about children's functioning. Parents are often the first source of information about a child's functioning. A clinician may interview a child's parents when the child is brought for treatment, asking the parents about changes in the child's behavior and corresponding events in the child's life. A researcher studying children's functioning may ask parents to complete questionnaires assessing the children's behavior in a variety of settings.

Because parents typically spend more time with their child than any other person does, they potentially have the most complete information about the child's

Clinicians must often engage parents in assessing young children.

functioning and a sense of how the child's behavior has or has not changed over time. Unfortunately, however, parents are not always accurate in their assessments of their children's functioning. Parents' perceptions of their children's well-being can be influenced by their own symptoms of psychopathology and their expectations for their children's behavior (Forehand et al., 1986; Lambert et al., 1992). Indeed, sometimes parents bring children for assessment and treatment of psychological problems as a way of seeking treatment for themselves.

Parents may also be the source of a child's psychological problems and, as a result, unwilling to acknowledge or seek help for the child's problems. The most extreme example of this is parents who are physically or sexually abusing a child. These parents are unlikely to acknowledge the psychological or physical harm they are causing the child or to seek treatment for that harm. A less extreme example is parents who do not want to believe that some action they have taken, such as filing for a divorce or moving the family across the country, is the cause of the child's emotional or behavioral problems. Again, such parents may be slow in taking a child who is distressed to a mental-health professional or in admitting to the child's problems when asked by a researcher.

Cultural norms for children's behaviors differ, and parents' expectations for their children and their tolerance of "deviant" behavior in children will be affected by these norms. For example, Jamaican parents appear more tolerant than American parents of unusual behaviors in children, including both aggressive behavior and behavior indicating that a child is shy and inhibited. In turn, Jamaican parents have a higher threshold than American parents in terms of the appropriate time to take a child to a therapist (Lambert et al., 1992).

Teachers are another source of information about children's functioning. Teachers and other school personnel (such as guidance counselors or coaches) are often the first to recognize that a child has a problem and to initiate an intervention for the problem (Tuma, 1989). Teachers' assessments of children, however, are often discrepant with the assessments given by other adults, including parents and trained clinicians who rate children's behavior. Such discrepancies may arise because these other adults are providing invalid assessments of the children while the teachers are providing valid assessments. The discrepancies may also arise because children function at different levels in different settings. At home, a child may be well-behaved, quiet, and withdrawn, while at school, the same child may be impulsive, easily angered, and distractible. These differences in a child's actual behavior in different settings might make it seem that either a parent's report of the child's behavior or the teacher's report is invalid, when the truth is that the child simply acts differently depending on the situation.

Evaluating People from Other Cultures

A number of challenges to assessment arise when there are significant cultural differences between the assessor and the person being assessed (Manson, 1997; Westermeyer, 1993). Imagine having to obtain all the information needed to assess what is wrong with someone from a culture very different from your own. The first problem you may run into is that the client does not speak the same language that you do or speaks your language only partially (and you do not speak his or hers at all). There is evidence that symptoms can go both underdiagnosed and overdiagnosed when the client and assessor do not speak the same language (Sue & Sue, 1999). Overdiagnosis often occurs because a client tries to describe his or her symptoms in the assessor's language, but the assessor interprets a client's slow and somewhat confused description of symptoms as indicating more pathology than is really present. Underdiagnosis can occur when the client cannot articulate complex emotions or strange perceptual experiences in the assessor's language and thus does not even try.

One solution is to find an interpreter to translate between the therapist and the client. Interpreters can be invaluable to good communication. However, interpreters who are not trained assessors themselves can misunderstand and mistranslate a therapist's questions and the client's answers, as in the following example (Marcos, 1979, p. 173):

Voices

Clinician to Spanish-speaking patient: "Do you feel sad or blue, do you feel that life is not worthwhile sometimes?"

Interpreter to patient: "The doctor wants to know if you feel sad and if you like your life."

Patient's response: "No, yes, I know that my children need me, I cannot give up, I prefer not to think about it."

Interpreter to clinician: "She says that no, she says that she loves her children and that her children need her."

Translators can be invaluable in helping clients communicate with clinicians, but accurate translation is very difficult.

In this case the interpreter did not accurately reflect the client's answer to the therapist's question, giving the therapist a sense that the client was doing much better than the client reported she was. In addition, different people from the same country can speak different dialects of a language or may have different means of expressing feelings and attitudes. Mistranslation can occur when the interpreter does not speak the particular dialect spoken by the client or comes from a different subculture than the client.

Even when mistranslation is not a problem, some of the very questions that the assessor may ask or that may appear on a test or questionnaire that the client is asked to complete may be so culture-bound that they do not make sense to the client, or they can be interpreted by the client in ways the assessor did not anticipate (Manson, 1997). This can happen on even the most "objective" of tests. For example, several assessment tests ask whether a client ever believes that forces or powers other than himself control his behavior or if he ever hears voices talking in his head. According to Western conceptualizations, these are signs of psychosis. Yet many cultures, such as the Xhosa of South Africa, believe that ancestors live in the same psychic world as living relatives and that ancestors speak to the living and advise them on their behavior (Gillis et al., 1982). Thus, members of this culture might answer "yes" to questions intended to assess psychotic thinking, when they are really reporting on the beliefs of their culture.

Cultural biases can arise when everyone is supposedly speaking the same language but comes from quite different cultural backgrounds. There is evidence that African Americans in the United States are overdiagnosed as suffering from schizophrenia (Snowden & Cheung, 1990). For example, African Americans are more likely than Whites to be misdiagnosed as schizophrenic when their symptoms actually fit the diagnosis of manic depression (Mukherjee et al., 1983). Many investigators believe that cultural differences in the presentation of symptoms play a role (Neighbors, 1984). African Americans may present more intense symptoms than Whites, which are then misunderstood by White assessors as representing more severe psychopathology. Another possibility is that some white assessors are too quick to diagnose severe psychopathology in African Americans because of negative stereotypes of them.

Finally, even when clinicians avoid all these biases, they are still left with the fact that people from other cultures often think about and talk about their psychological symptoms quite differently from members of their own culture. We discuss several examples of cultural differences in the presentation of symptoms throughout this book. One of the most pervasive differences is in whether cultures experience and report psychological distress in emotional symptoms or in somatic (physical) symptoms. European Americans tend to view the body and mind separately, whereas many other cultures do not make sharp distinctions between the experiences of the body and the experiences of the mind (Sue et al., 1998). Following a psychologically distressing event, European Americans tend to report that they feel anxious or sad, but members of many other cultures will report having physical aches and maladies (Kleinman & Kleinman, 1985). To conduct an accurate assessment, clinicians must know about cultural differences in the manifestation of disorders and in the presentation of symptoms and correctly use this information in interpreting the symptoms that their clients report to them. This difference is further complicated by the fact that not every member of a culture will conform to what is known about that culture. That is, within every culture, people differ in their acceptance of cultural norms for behavior.

Summing Up

- It is often difficult to obtain accurate information on children's problems because children are unable to report their thoughts and feelings. Parents and teachers may be relied upon for information about children, but can be biased in their own assessments of children's symptoms and needs.

- When the clinician and client are from different cultures, language difficulties and cultural expectations can make assessment difficult. Interpreters can help in the assessment process but must be well-trained in psychological assessment.

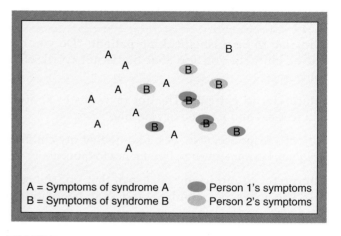

A = Symptoms of syndrome A   ● Person 1's symptoms
B = Symptoms of syndrome B   ● Person 2's symptoms

FIGURE 4.9   Each syndrome is made up of a set of symptoms. Some of the symptoms of one syndrome may overlap with the symptoms of another syndrome. In addition, one person may have a different subset of symptoms within a syndrome than the other person.

☺ DIAGNOSIS

As we stated at the beginning of this chapter, a *diagnosis* is a label we attach to a set of symptoms that tend to occur together. This set of symptoms is referred to as a **syndrome.** In medical models of psychological disorders, a syndrome is thought to be the observable manifestation of an underlying biological disorder. So if you have the symptoms that make up the syndrome we call *schizophrenia*, you are thought also to have a biological disorder we call *schizophrenia*. However, as mentioned repeatedly, there are no definitive biological tests for psychological disorders. Thus, it is impossible to verify whether a given person *has* schizophrenia by giving him or her a biological test for schizophrenia.

Thus, we are left to observe humans and identify what symptoms typically co-occur in them, and then we call those co-occurring symptoms a *syndrome*. Identifying naturally occurring syndromes is no easy task. Typically, several symptoms will make up a syndrome, but there are differences among people in which of these symptoms they experience most strongly. Think about the last time you were in a sad or depressed mood. Did you also feel tired and have trouble sleeping? Do you always feel tired and have trouble sleeping every time you are in a sad or depressed mood or just sometimes? Does everyone you know also experience fatigue and sleeplessness when they are in a sad mood? Or do some of them simply lose their appetite and their ability to concentrate? Thus, syndromes are not lists of symptoms that all people have all of the time if they have any of the symptoms at all. Rather, they are lists of symptoms that tend to co-occur within individuals. There may be overlap between the symptoms of one syndrome and the symptoms of another (see Figure 4.9).

For centuries, humans have tried to organize the confusing array of psychological symptoms into a limited set of syndromes. This set of syndromes and the rules for determining whether an individual's symptoms are part of one of these syndromes are called a classification system. One of the first classification systems for psychological symptoms was proposed by Hippocrates in the fourth century B. C. Hippocrates divided all mental disorders into mania (states of abnormal excitement), melancholia (states of abnormal depression), paranoia, and epilepsy. Modern classification systems divide the world of psychological symptoms into a much larger number of syndromes than did Hippocrates. Let us focus on the classification system most widely used in the United States.

The Diagnostic and Statistical Manual of Mental Disorders (DSM)

For nearly 50 years, the official manual for diagnosing psychological disorders in the United States has been the ***Diagnostic and Statistical Manual of Mental Disorders*** (DSM) of the American Psychiatric Association. The first edition of the DSM was published in 1952. It outlined the diagnostic criteria for all the mental disorders recognized by the psychiatric community at the time. These criteria were somewhat vague descriptions of disorders that were heavily influenced by psychoanalytic theory. For example, the diagnosis of *anxiety neurosis* could have been manifested in a great variety of specific behavioral and emotional symptoms. The key to the diagnosis was whether the clinician inferred that unconscious conflicts were causing the client to experience anxiety. The second edition of the DSM, published in 1968, included some new disorders that had been recognized since the publication of the first edition but was not much different.

Because the descriptions of disorders were so abstract and theoretically based in the DSM-I and DSM-II, the reliability of the diagnoses was low. For example, one study found that four experienced clinicians using the DSM-I to diagnose 153 patients agreed on their diagnoses only 54 percent of the time (Beck et al., 1962). This eventually led psychiatrists and psychologists to call for a radically new system of diagnosing mental disorders that would be more reliable.

The DSM-III, DSM-IIIR, and DSM-IV

In response to the reliability problems with the first and second editions of the DSM, in 1980 the American Psychiatric Association published the third edition of the DSM, known as DSM-III. This third edition was followed by a revised third edition, known as DSM-IIIR, published in 1987, and a fourth edition, known as DSM-IV, published in 1994 and revised in 2000. In these newer editions of the DSM, the developers replaced the vague descriptions of disorders with specific and concrete criteria for each disorder. These criteria are in the form of behaviors people must show or experiences or feelings they must report in order to be given a diagnosis. The developers tried to be as atheoretical and descriptive as possible in listing the criteria for each disorder. Good examples are the diagnostic criteria for panic disorder in the DSM-IV, which are given in Table 4.4. As you can see, a person must have 4 of 13 possible symptoms in order to be given the diagnosis of panic disorder, reflecting the fact that not all the symptoms of panic disorder are going to be present in every individual.

Two other elements distinguished the DSM-III, DSM-IIIR, and DSM-IV from their predecessors. First,

---

TABLE 4.4
DSM-IV Diagnostic Criteria for Panic Disorder

These are the DSM-IV criteria for a diagnosis of panic disorder. They specify core symptoms that must be present and several other symptoms, a certain number of which must be present, for the diagnosis.

A. At some time during the disturbance, one or more panic attacks have occurred that were (1) unexpected, and (2) not triggered by situations in which the person was the focus of another's attention.

B. Either four attacks, as defined in criterion A, have occurred within a 4-week period, or one or more attacks have been followed by a period of at least a month of persistent fear of having another attack.

C. At least four of the following symptoms developed during at least one of the attacks:

1. shortness of breath or smothering sensations
2. dizziness, unsteady feelings, or faintness
3. palpitations or accelerated heart rate
4. trembling or shaking
5. sweating
6. choking
7. nausea or abdominal distress
8. depersonalization or derealization
9. numbness or tingling sensations
10. flushes or chills
11. chest pain or discomfort
12. fear of dying
13. fear of going crazy or doing something uncontrolled

D. During at least some of the attacks, at least four of the C symptoms developed suddenly and increased in intensity within 10 minutes of the beginning of the first C symptom.

E. It cannot be established that an organic factor initiated the disturbance, such as caffeine intoxication.

Reprinted with permission from the *Diagnostic and Statistical Manual of Mental Disorders*, Fourth Edition.
Copyright © 2000 American Psychiatric Association.

EXTRAORDINARY PEOPLE

Neil Cargile

The examples in this chapter of people undergoing assessment for psychopathology have been quite straightforward. It seems obvious that these people are suffering from something, and the goal of the assessment process is to determine what that something is and give it a diagnosis.

The story of Neil Cargile is extraordinary because it highlights the definitions of abnormality behind our assessment procedures and diagnostic classifications. From the information in the story below, it does not appear that Neil Cargile's behavior would qualify for any diagnosis currently listed in the DSM-IV. We will explain why this is so after presenting the story. For now, as you read about Neil Cargile, think about how you would judge Cargile's functioning in the domains we have discussed in this chapter (from Bernheim, 1997, pp. 3–4; based on a story by John Berendt in *The New Yorker* magazine, January 16, 1995):

Neil Cargile is a sixty-five-year-old Nashville millionaire. He is a superb pilot, having been trained in Navy jets, who loves to "push the envelope." He has survived so many emergency landings that he carries the nickname, "Crash Cargile." He began flying as a teenager, in a plane he rebuilt out of surplus parts from the Second World War. As an adult, he built a helicopter pad on the grounds of his mansion. He played football at Vanderbilt College, has driven race cars, sailed yachts, and played polo. A daredevil in business as well as pleasure, he has flown crop-dusters and dredged for gold and diamonds in remote parts of the world. Twice married and twice divorced, the father of three grown children, and decidedly heterosexual, Neil Cargile would be the prototypical "man's man" were it not for one thing: he likes to dress up in women's clothing. He doesn't just dress up in private, either. He often appears at parties and even at restaurants dressed entirely in women's clothes. . . .

Mr. Cargile first wore women's clothing at an out-of-town Halloween party in the mid-1970s when a few women friends talked him into going to the party as Dolly Parton. He won first prize for his costume. Over the next several years he attended

these later editions specify how long a person must show symptoms of the disorder to be given the diagnosis (see Table 4.4, item B). Second, the criteria for most disorders require that symptoms interfere with occupational or social functioning for the person to be diagnosed. This emphasis on symptoms that are long-lasting and severe reflects the consensus among psychiatrists and psychologists that abnormality should be defined in terms of the impact of behaviors on the individual's ability to function and on his or her sense of well-being (see Chapter 1). A good example of how the emphasis on functioning and well-being influence diagnosis in the DSM can be seen in *Extraordinary People*: Neil Cargile.

The DSM-III and its subsequent revisions also include information on how to make a differential diagnosis between a disorder and related disorders and on the course and prevalence of each disorder. The **course** of a disorder is the length of time the disorder typically lasts and the likelihood that the disorder will relapse in the future after the current episode of the disorder has ended.

The **prevalence** of a disorder is the number of people who have the disorder during a specified period of time. **Point prevalence** is the number of people who have the disorder at one given point in time. **Lifetime prevalence** is the number of people who will have the disorder at some time in their lives. So if the point prevalence of anxiety disorders is 8 percent and the lifetime prevalence is 20 percent, this means that 8 percent of people have an anxiety disorder at any given point in time, and 20 percent will develop an anxiety disorder at some time in their lives. Typically, the lifetime prevalence of a disorder is much higher

Continued

several other costume parties in women's clothes—always out of town. Then, gradually, he began to cross-dress at local private parties, beginning subtly, with a kilt along with a jacket and tie, then adding stockings and high heels to the outfit. Finally, he had a party at his house in which guests were required to come dressed as a member of the opposite sex, and shortly thereafter, he appeared at a local costume party in full drag. After that, to the consternation of his friends and family, he began cross-dressing in public in Nashville itself.

Recently, Cargile has taken to calling himself SheNeil when he goes out in women's clothing. Author Berendt asked him if he felt like a different person when he became SheNeil. He replied, "No, I feel like Neil Cargile in a dress."

Cargile seemed to get as much pleasure out of shocking people as in wearing the clothes. He does it, he says, for "fun." Berendt quotes Cargile as saying, "I'm a big showoff. I have a motto: If you aren't doing something different, you aren't doing anything at all. That's the way I've always lived." Still, there were some places Cargile wouldn't go in drag: to church or the local country club. He also attended business meetings dressed in men's clothing, although he sometimes wore pantyhose under his suit and carried a miniskirt and a pair of heels in the car . . . .

Cargile's current girlfriend affectionately indulges his cross-dressing, helping him select outfits and doing his makeup. His daughter bought him a makeup kit one Christmas. His cross-dressing doesn't seem to have altered his social standing in Nashville, nor his capacity to make business deals.

Neil Cargile's cross-dressing is unusual, but it is not diagnosable under the DSM-IV guidelines because the DSM-IV stipulates that it is only when cross-dressing is used to gain sexual stimulation or when it is a manifestation of a wish to become (permanently) the opposite sex that it is diagnosable as a disorder (we will discuss these disorders in Chapter 15).

Even without this knowledge of the technical details of what is diagnosable under DSM-IV, you might have argued that Cargile should not be diagnosed with anything because he clearly is functioning well at work, with his family and friends, and in his community. But to what extent do you think the support others give him for his unusual behavior is influenced by Cargile's wealth? Do you think friends and family, and the Nashville community, would be so accepting of his behavior if he were not a millionaire? Should this matter? Judgments of a person's level of functioning are always subjective and easily influenced by the context or situation.

than the point prevalence because disorders wax and wane, so that a person who is going to have a disorder at some time in his or her life may not be experiencing the disorder at a particular point in time.

Prevalence is often contrasted with the incidence of a disorder. **Incidence** is the number of new cases of a disorder that develop during a specific period of time. The 1-year incidence of a disorder is the number of people who develop the disorder during a 1-year period. Throughout this book, we quote prevalence and incidence statistics for each of the disorders.

Reliability of the DSM

Despite the use of explicit criteria for disorders, the reliability of many of the diagnoses listed in the DSM-III and DSM-IIIR was disappointing. On average, experienced clinicians only agreed on their diagnoses using these manuals about 70 percent of the time (Kirk & Kutchins, 1992). The reliability for some of the diagnoses, particularly the personality disorder diagnoses, was much lower. Low reliability of diagnoses can be caused by many factors. Although the developers of the DSM-III and DSM-IIIR attempted to make the criteria for each disorder explicit, many of these criteria were still vague and required the clinician to make inferences about the client's symptoms or to rely on the client's willingness to report symptoms. For example, most of the symptoms of the mood disorders and anxiety disorders are subjective experiences (sadness, apprehensiveness, hopelessness); only clients can report whether they have these symptoms and how severe they are. To diagnose any of the personality disorders, the clinician must establish that the client has a lifelong history of specific dysfunctional behaviors or ways of relating to the world. Unless the clinician has known the client all his or her life, the clinician must rely on the client and his or her family to provide information about the client's history, and different sources of information can provide very different pictures of the client's functioning.

In an effort to increase the reliability of diagnoses in the DSM-IV, the task force that developed the DSM-IV conducted numerous field trials, in which the criteria for most of the diagnoses to be included in the DSM-IV were tested in clinical and research settings. In a field trial, testing determines if diagnostic criteria can be applied reliably, and if they fit clients' experiences. As a result, the reliability of the DSM-IV diagnoses are higher than the reliability of predecessors, although clearly not perfectly reliable.

The Multiaxial System

Beginning with the third edition of the DSM, the manual has specified five *axes* or dimensions along which a clinician evaluates a client's behavior (see Table 4.5). Only the first two axes list actual disorders and the criteria required for their diagnoses. The other three axes are meant to provide information on physical conditions that might be affecting the person's mental health (Axis III), psychosocial and environmental stressors in the person's life (Axis IV), and the degree of impairment in the person's mental health and functioning (Axis V). Let us take a look at these five axes one by one as defined by the DSM-IV and then apply them to an actual case study.

On Axis I, a clinician lists any major DSM-IV disorders for which the person qualifies, with the exclusion of mental retardation and personality disorders

---

TABLE 4.6
Disorders Listed on Axis I

These disorders, most of which we discuss in this book, represent conditions that typically cause people significant distress or impairment.

Disorders usually first diagnosed in infancy, childhood, or adolescence

- Attention-deficit disorder
- Hyperactivity
- Conduct and oppositional disorder
- Separation anxiety disorder
- Pervasive developmental disorder
- Learning disorders
- Feeding, tic, and elimination disorders

Delirium, dementia, and amnestic or other cognitive disorders

Substance-related disorders

Schizophrenia and other psychotic disorders

Mood disorders

Anxiety disorders

Somatoform disorders

Factitious disorders

Dissociative disorders

Sexual and gender identity disorders

Eating disorders

Sleep disorders

Adjustment disorders

Other conditions that may be a focus of clinical attention

Reprinted with permission from the *Diagnostic and Statistical Manual of Mental Disorders*, Fourth Edition. Copyright © 2000 American Psychiatric Association.

TABLE 4.5
DSM-IV
Axes

The DSM-IV has five axes along which each client should be evaluated.

Axis I	Clinical disorders
Axis II	Personality disorders
	Mental retardation
Axis III	General medical conditions
Axis IV	Psychosocial and environmental problems
Axis V	Global assessment of functioning

Reprinted with permission from the *Diagnostic and Statistical Manual of Mental Disorders*, Fourth Edition. Copyright © 2000 American Psychiatric Association.

(see Table 4.6). The clinician also notes whether these disorders are chronic or acute. Chronic disorders are ones lasting for long periods of time. Acute disorders are ones that have a more recent and abrupt onset of severe symptoms.

On Axis II, the clinician lists mental retardation or any personality disorders for which the person qualifies (see Table 4.7). Mental retardation is listed on Axis II instead of Axis I because it is a lifelong condition, whereas most of the disorders on Axis I tend to wax and wane across the life span. Similarly, a personality disorder is characterized by a chronic and pervasive pattern of dysfunctional behavior that the person has shown since at least adolescence. For example, a person with an antisocial personality disorder has a

TABLE 4.7
Disorders Listed on Axis II

These disorders listed on Axis II typically represent lifelong disorders that pervade every area of the person's life.

Mental retardation

Personality disorders
- Paranoid personality disorder
- Schizoid personality disorder
- Schizotypal personality disorder
- Antisocial personality disorder
- Borderline personality disorder
- Histrionic personality disorder
- Narcissistic personality disorder
- Avoidant personality disorder
- Dependent personality disorder
- Obsessive-compulsive personality disorder

Reprinted with permission from the *Diagnostic and Statistical Manual of Mental Disorders*, Fourth Edition. Copyright © 2000 American Psychiatric Association.

TABLE 4.8
Axis IV Psychosocial and Environmental Problems to Note

These are some of the important problems people might face that should be noted on Axis IV.

Problems with primary support group

Problems related to the social environment

Education problems

Occupational problems

Housing problems

Economic problems

Problems with access to health care services

Problems related to interaction with the legal system and to crime

Reprinted with permission from the *Diagnostic and Statistical Manual of Mental Disorders*, Fourth Edition. Copyright © 2000 American Psychiatric Association.

lifelong pattern of being abusive toward others and violating basic norms of social relationships.

On Axis III, the clinician notes any medical or physical diseases from which the person is suffering. These diseases may or may not be directly related to the psychological disorders from which the person is also suffering. For example, a person may have lung cancer, which has nothing to do with the fact that she also has schizophrenia. However, it is important for the clinician to know about any physical diseases for two reasons. First, these diseases could be related to the person's mental health. For example, a person might be depressed because she has lung cancer. Also, a clinician must guard against any interactions between the treatment the patient may be taking for her physical disease and the treatment the clinician will prescribe for her mental disorder.

On Axis IV, the clinician rates the severity of the psychosocial stressors the client is facing, such as those listed in Table 4.8. Again, these psychosocial stressors may be related to the client's mental disorder, as causes or consequences. Or they may merely be coincidental with the disorder. However, it is important for the clinician to know what types of stressors the client is facing in order to provide a successful treatment plan.

On Axis V, the clinician rates the level at which the client is able to function in daily life on the scale

given in Table 4.9, (p. 124). This helps the clinician quantify and communicate the degree to which the disorder is impairing the client's functioning.

Consider the following case study of a woman who is seeking help for some distressing symptoms. We will see how the clinician incorporates all five of the DSM-IV axes in making a diagnosis.

CASE STUDY

Jonelle is a 35-year-old African American woman who works as a manager of a large bank. She reports at least a dozen incidents in the last 6 weeks in which she has suddenly felt her heart pounding, her pulse racing, and her breathing become rapid and shallow, she has felt faint and dizzy, and she has been sure that she is about to die. These attacks have lasted for several minutes. Jonelle consulted with her physician, who conducted a complete physical checkup and concluded that there was no evidence of cardiac problems or other physical problems that could be causing her symptoms. Jonelle is becoming so afraid of having one of these attacks that it is interfering with her ability to do her job. She is constantly vigilant for signs of an impending attack, and this vigilance is interfering with her concentration and her ability to converse with customers and employees. When she feels an attack may be coming on, she rushes to the rest room or out to her car and remains there, often for over an hour, until she is convinced she will not have an attack. Jonelle reports that the attacks began shortly after her mother died of a heart attack. She and her mother were extremely close, and Jonelle still feels devastated by her loss.

TABLE 4.9

Axis V Global Assessment of Functioning Scale

This is the scale for indicating how well the person is functioning across different domains of his or her life.

Code

100	Superior functioning in a wide range of areas
90	Absent or minimal symptoms; good functioning in all areas
80	If symptoms present, they are transient and expectable reactions to psychosocial stressors; only slight impairment in functioning
70	Some mild symptoms or difficulty in functioning
60	Moderate symptoms and difficulty in functioning
50	Serious symptoms and difficulty in functioning
40	Some impairment in reality testing or communication or major impairment in several domains
30	Considerable delusions and hallucinations or serious impairment in communication and judgment
20	Some danger of hurting self or others or gross impairment in communication
10	Persistent danger of severely hurting self or others

Reprinted with permission from the *Diagnostic and Statistical Manual of Mental Disorders*, Fourth Edition. Copyright © 2000 American Psychiatric Association.

In consulting the five axes, Jonelle's therapist would likely come up with this list:

Axis I: Panic disorder

Axis II: None

Axis III: None

Axis IV: Psychosocial and environmental stressors: recent bereavement

Axis V: Global functioning: 60 (moderate difficulty)

What is particularly interesting is that this case study provides a good example of the importance of Axes III (physical conditions) and IV (psychosocial and environmental stressors). The clinician would certainly want to know if Jonelle had some physical condition that was creating her panic attacks before diagnosing them as a psychological disorder. Similarly, knowing that the panic attacks began to occur shortly after the death of Jonelle's mother from a heart attack gives the clinician a good clue about their possible psychological origins. It is fairly common for people suffering from panic attacks to have lost a close relative or friend to a heart attack or stroke and to then experience symptoms mimicking a heart attack or stroke.

The *Concept Review*: DSM Axes and Assessment outlines how the information gathered in an assessment is reflected in the five axes. Actually, every piece of information in an assessment may be used to make an accurate diagnosis on each of the five axes. However, the *Concept Review*: DSM Axes and Assessment describes the information that is most crucial to making each of the five judgments in the multiaxial system of the DSM.

The Dangers of Diagnosis

In *Viewpoints:* Cultural and Gender Issues in Diagnosis (pp. 126–127) we discuss the possibility of cultural and gender bias in the formulation and application of psychological diagnoses. One influential critic of psychiatry, Thomas Szasz, has argued that there are so many biases inherent in who is labeled as having a mental disorder that the entire system of diagnosis is corrupt and should be abandoned. Szasz (1961) believes that people in power use psychiatric diagnoses to label and dispose of people who do not "fit in." He suggests that mental disorders do not really exist, and that people who seem to be suffering from mental disorders are only suffering from the oppression of a society that does not accept their alternative ways of behaving and looking at the world.

Even psychiatrists and psychologists who do not fully agree with Szasz's perspective on labeling recognize the great dangers of labeling behaviors or people abnormal. The person labeled abnormal is treated differently by society, and this treatment can continue

CONCEPT REVIEW

DSM Axes and Assessment

At the beginning of this chapter, we discussed several types of information gathered during an assessment. This table outlines how each of these pieces of information is reflected across the five axes of diagnosis in the DSM.

Information Reflected on Axis I (clinical disorders):

Current symptoms

Recent events (e.g., diagnosis of Adjustment Disorder requires a recent event in client's life)

Physical condition (symptoms given different diagnosis if caused by general medical disorder than if not)

Drug and alcohol use (may indicate Substance Abuse or Dependence Disorder)

History of psychological disorders (used to make differential diagnosis)

Family history of psychological disorders (used to make differential diagnosis)

Intellectual and cognitive functioning

Information Reflected on Axis II (mental retardation and personality disorders):

Current symptoms

History of psychological disorders

Family history of psychological disorders

Intellectual and cognitive functioning

Coping style (some personality disorders have characteristic coping styles that are indicators of the disorder)

Information Reflected on Axis III (general medical conditions):

Physical condition

Drug and alcohol use

Information Reflected on Axis IV (psychosocial and environmental problems):

Recent events

Social resources

Sociocultural background

Information Reflected on Axis V (global assessment of functioning):

Incorporates all information from an assessment into one global rating

Reprinted with permission from the *Diagnostic and Statistical Manual of Mental Disorders*, Fourth Edition. Copyright © 2000 American Psychiatric Association.

long after the person stops exhibiting behaviors labeled abnormal. This point was made in a classic study of the effects of labeling by psychologist David Rosenhan (1973). He and a group of seven colleagues conducted a study in which they had themselves admitted to 12 different mental hospitals by reporting to hospital staff that they had been hearing voices saying the words "empty," "hollow," and "thud." When they were questioned by hospital personnel, they told the truth about every other aspect of their lives, including the fact that they had never experienced mental-health problems

before. All eight were admitted to the hospital, and all but one with a diagnosis of schizophrenia (see Chapter 10). Once they were admitted to the hospital, the pseudopatients stopped reporting they were hearing voices and behaved as "normally" as they usually did. When asked how they were doing by hospital staff, the pseudopatients said they felt fine and they no longer heard voices. They cooperated in activities. The only thing they did differently from other patients was to write down their observations on notepads occasionally during the day.

VIEWPOINTS

Cultural and Gender Issues in Diagnosis

So how do a disorder and the diagnostic criteria for that disorder become recognized and accepted as part of the DSM system? It happens largely by the consensus of clinicians and researchers in psychiatry and psychology. The diagnostic criteria for the DSM-III, DSM-IIIR, and the new DSM-IV were derived by committees of experts on each of the disorders. These committees conducted comprehensive and systematic reviews of the published literature to determine the evidence for and against the existence of the syndromes being considered for inclusion in the DSM. As noted, the developers of the DSM-IV also conducted field trials to determine the reliability and usefulness of criteria sets in clinical and research settings.

Despite the best efforts of the developers of the DSM to be objective and accurate in their definitions of disorders, these definitions represent a process of consensus-building and compromise among experts with different opinions. The opportunity for political, cultural, and ideological influences on the establishment of the diagnostic criteria for disorders in such a process should be obvious.

One good example of the politicization of the DSM process was the debate over the addition of two personality disorders in the DSM-IIIR. Some members of the committee revising the DSM-IIIR argued for the inclusion of a disorder that they felt was very common and was distinct from all the disorders that were already recognized in the DSM-IIIR. People with this proposed disorder had a lifelong practice of getting themselves into and remaining in situations in which other people used and abused them. The proponents of this disorder suggested that it be labeled masochistic personality disorder. When news of this proposed disorder became public, some psychologists and psychiatrists strongly objected to it (Caplan & Gans, 1991). They argued that it would be used to pathologize women who, because of their lack of power and their social upbringing, found themselves trapped in abusive relationships, such as wife-battering relationships. They demanded a hearing before the committee to discuss the scientific merits of the masochistic personality disorder diagnosis and the social implications of including it as a

disorder in the DSM. What some of the committee members suggested, to address the concerns of the opponents of the masochistic personality disorder diagnosis, was to add yet another disorder, called sadistic personality disorder, that then would pathologize the behavior of the abusers in wife-battering relationships. Soon, however, several people pointed out that one of the political implications of this "solution" was that some wife-batterers could plead "not guilty" by reason of a mental disorder when charged with beating their wives. In the end, the committee could not reach consensus and simply voted on what to do. The masochistic personality disorder was relabeled self-defeating personality disorder, and both it and sadistic personality disorder were included in an appendix of the DSM-IIIR as "Proposed Diagnostic Categories Needing Further Study." The further study of these diagnoses after the publication of the DSM-IIIR did not strongly support the reliability or validity of the diagnoses. Thus, they were dropped altogether from the DSM-IV.

Some critics of the DSM have argued that it reflects only male, Western views of mental health and mental disorders. The model for healthy behavior for Western males is to be assertive and independent. People who appear unassertive and dependent on others—such as women and people from cultures that value interdependence among people—may be labeled as unhealthy. For example, some of the personality disorders, such as the dependent personality disorder, have been said to pathologize behaviors associated with women's sex role, simply because they do not conform to male models of healthy behaviors (Caplan & Gans, 1991; Kaplan, 1983).

We noted in Chapter 1 that different cultures have different ways of conceptualizing mental disorders. There are some disorders defined in one culture that do not seem to occur in other cultures. The developers of the DSM-IV included an appendix that lists many of these culture-specific disorders and brief guidelines for gathering information during the assessment process regarding a client's culture. Table 4.10 describes some of these culture-bound syndromes. The DSM-IV also includes

Continued

TABLE 4.10
Culture-Bound Syndromes

Syndrome	Cultures Where Found	Symptoms
Amok	Malaysia, Laos, Philippines, Polynesia, Papua New Guinea, Puerto Rico	Brooding, followed by an outburst of violent, aggressive, or homicidal behavior
Ataque de nervios	Latin American and Latin Mediterranean cultures	Uncontrollable shouting, attacks of crying, trembling, heat in the chest rising into the head, verbal or physical aggression, sense of out of control
Dhat	India, Sri Lanka, China	Severe anxiety about the discharge of semen, whitish discoloration of the urine, and feelings of weakness and exhaustion
Ghost sickness	Native Americans	Preoccupation with death and the deceased, manifested in dreams and in severe anxiety
Koro	Malaysia, China, Thailand	Episode of sudden and intense anxiety that the penis (or in women, the vulva and nipples) will recede into the body and possibly cause death
Mal de ojo	Mediterranean cultures	Fitful sleep, crying without apparent cause, diarrhea, vomiting, and fever
Shinjing shuairuo	China	Physical and mental fatigue, dizziness, headaches, other pains, concentration difficulties, sleep disturbance, and memory loss
Susto	U.S. Latinos and Mexico Central America, and South America	Appetite disturbances, sleep problems, sadness, lack of motivation, low self-worth, aches and pains; follows a frightening experience
Taijin kyofusho	Japan	Intense fear that one's body displeases, embarrasses, or is offensive to other people

short descriptions of cultural variation in the presentation of the each of the major mental disorders recognized in the manual. For example, it notes differences among cultures in the content of delusions (beliefs out of touch with reality) in schizophrenia. Some critics do not believe it goes nearly far enough in recognizing cultural and gender variation in what is "healthy" and "unhealthy" (see Dana, 1995; Thakker & Ward, 1998). Throughout the remainder of this book, we comment on cultural and gender variations in the experience and prevalence of each of the disorders recognized by the DSM.

Not one of the pseudopatients was ever detected as normal by the hospital staff, although they remained in the hospital for an average of 19 days each. Several of the other patients in the mental hospital detected the pseudopatients' normality, however, making comments such as "You're not crazy, You're a journalist, or a professor [referring to the continual note-taking]. You're checking up on the hospital." (Rosenhan, 1973). When the pseudopatients were discharged, they were given the diagnosis of schizophrenia in remission, meaning that the physicians still believed they had schizophrenia, but the symptoms had subsided for the time being.

Rosenhan concluded that "It is clear that we cannot distinguish the sane from the insane in psychiatric hospitals. The hospital itself imposes a special environment in which the meanings of behavior can be easily misunderstood." He also noted that, if even mental-health professionals cannot distinguish sanity from insanity, the dangers of diagnostic labels are even greater in the hands of nonprofessionals: "Such labels, conferred by mental health professionals, are as influential on the patient as they are on his relatives and friends, and it should not surprise anyone that the diagnosis acts on all of them as a self-fulfilling prophecy. Eventually, the patient himself accepts the diagnosis, with all of its surplus meanings and expectations, and behaves accordingly."

Not surprisingly, Rosenhan's study created a furor in the mental-health community. How could seasoned professionals have made such mistakes—admitting mentally healthy people to a psychiatric hospital on the basis of one symptom (hearing voices), not recognizing the pseudopatients' behavior as normal, allowing them to be discharged carrying a diagnosis that suggests they still had schizophrenia? Even today, Rosenhan's study is held up as a shining example of the abuses of the power—the power to label people as sane or insane, normal or abnormal, good or bad.

The label *abnormal* may be even more dangerous when it is applied to children, as is illustrated by a study of boys in grades 3 through 6 (Harris et al., 1992). Researchers paired boys who were the same age but who were previously unacquainted. In half of the pairs, one of the boys was told that his partner had a behavior problem that made him disruptive. In reality, only some of the boys labeled as having a behavior problem actually had a behavior problem. In the other half of the pairs, the boys were not told anything about each other, although some of the boys actually did have behavior problems. All the pairs worked together on a task while researchers videotaped their interaction. After the interaction, the boys were asked several questions about each other and about their enjoyment of the interaction.

Children who are labeled as abnormal are at particularly high risk for maltreatment by other children.

The boys who had been told that their partners had a behavior problem were less friendly toward their partners during the task, talked with them less often, and were less involved in the interaction with their partners than were the boys who had been told nothing about their partners. In turn, the boys who had been labeled as having a behavior problem enjoyed the interaction less, took less credit for their performance on the task, and said their partners were less friendly toward them than did boys who had not been labeled as having a behavior problem. Most importantly, labeling a boy as having a behavior problem influenced his partner's behaviors toward him and his enjoyment of the task, regardless of whether he actually had a behavior problem. These results show that labeling a child abnormal strongly affects other children's behaviors toward him or her, even when there is no reason for the child to be labeled abnormal.

Should we avoid psychiatric diagnoses altogether? Probably not. Despite the potential dangers of diagnostic systems, they serve vital functions. The primary role of diagnostic systems is to organize the confusing array of psychological systems in an agreed-upon manner. This facilitates communication from one clinician to another and across time. So if Dr. Jones reads in a patient's history that he was diagnosed with schizophrenia according to the DSM-IIIR, she knows what criteria were used to make that diagnosis and can compare the patient's diagnosis then with his symptoms now. Such information can assist Dr. Jones in making an accurate assessment of the patient's current symptoms and in determining what the proper treatment for his symptoms might be. For example, if the patient's current symptoms also suggest schizophrenia and the patient responded to Drug X when he had schizophrenia a few years ago, this suggests that the patient might respond well to Drug X now.

Having a standard diagnostic system also greatly facilitates research on psychological disorders. For example, if a researcher at State University is using the

DSM-IV criteria to identify people with obsessive-compulsive disorder, and a researcher at Private University is using the same criteria for the same purpose, the two researchers will be better able to compare the results of their research than if they were using different criteria to diagnose obsessive-compulsive disorder. This can lead to faster advances in our understanding of the causes of and effective treatment for disorders.

Summing Up

- The *Diagnostic and Statistical Manual of Mental Disorders* (DSM) provides criteria for diagnosing all psychological disorders currently recognized in the United States.

- The first two editions of the DSM provided vague descriptions of disorder based on psychoanalytic theory, and thus the reliability of diagnoses made according to these manuals was low. More recent editions of the DSM contain more specific, observable criteria that are not as strongly based on theory for the diagnosis of disorders.

- Five axes or types of information are specified in determining a DSM diagnosis. On Axis I, clinicians list all significant clinical syndromes. On Axis II, clinicians indicate if the client is suffering from a personality disorder or mental retardation. On Axis III, clinicians list the client's general medical condition. On Axis IV, clinicians list psychosocial and environmental problems the client is facing. On Axis V, clinicians indicate the client's global level of functioning.

- Many critics of the DSM argue that it reflects Western, male perspectives on abnormality, and pathologizes the behavior of women and other cultures. The DSM-IV includes descriptions of culture-bound syndromes—groups of symptoms that appear to occur only in specific cultures.

- Diagnoses can be misapplied for political or social reasons. The negative social implications of having a psychiatric diagnosis can be great. Having a standard diagnostic system helps in treatment and research, however.

☉ BIO-PSYCHO-SOCIAL INTEGRATION

After clinicians administer a battery of assessment tests to a client, they must then integrate the information from these tests to form a coherent picture of the client's strengths and weaknesses. This picture weaves together information on the client's biological functioning (major illnesses, possible genetic vulnerability to psychopathology), psychological functioning (personality, coping skills, intellectual strengths, symptoms), and social functioning (support networks, work relationships, social skills). The clinician comments on ways in which strengths or deficits in one domain are influencing functioning in another domain. For example, the clinician might note that a client with multiple sclerosis is having increasing difficulties performing her job and, as a result, has become anxious about losing her job. To cope with that anxiety, she has begun drinking heavily. This has caused conflict in her marriage, which then has made her even more anxious. The assessment process is thus inherently a process of bio-psycho-social integration of pieces of information about an individual.

The latest edition of the DSM was revised to reflect a more integrated and dynamic view of how biology, psychology, and social factors influence each other. The manual now includes information on cultural differences and similarities for each disorder and biological correlates for each disorder. In addition, the DSM-IV changed the label for an entire set of disorders to enhance an integrated bio-psycho-social view of disorders. The editions prior to DSM-IV included a category called *organic disorders*, which included delirium, dementia, and amnesia. These disorders are still included in the DSM-IV but not under a category labeled *organic disorders*. The developers of the DSM-IV wanted to drop the label *organic disorders* because having one category of disorders labeled as organic implied that these disorders were caused by biological factors but that other disorders listed in the manual under other labels were not.

Thus, both the assessment process and the DSM-IV itself reflect a bio-psycho-social approach to psychopathology. As we shall see as we discuss each of the major disorders recognized by the DSM-IV, this type of approach appears warranted.

Chapter Summary

- Assessment is the process of gathering information about people's symptoms and the causes of the symptoms. Diagnosis is a label we attach to a set of symptoms that tend to co-occur with one another.

- During an assessment, a clinician will want to gather information about an individual's symptoms and history. This will include information about the nature, duration, and severity of their symptoms, their ability to function, coping strategies, self-concept, recent life events, past history of psychological problems, and family history of psychological problems.

- An assessment will also obtain information about physiological and neurophysiological functioning. This includes any medical conditions the client is suffering, any drugs the client is taking, and the client's cognitive and intellectual abilities.

- An assessment should also examine the client's social resources and cultural background.

- The validity and reliability of assessment tools are indices of their quality. Validity is the accuracy of a test in assessing what it is supposed to assess. Five different types of validity are face validity, content validity, concurrent validity, predictive validity, and construct validity. Reliability is the consistency of a test. Types of reliability include test-retest reliability, alternate form reliability, internal reliability, and inter-rater or interjudge reliability.

- Paper-and-pencil neuropsychological tests can assess specific cognitive deficits that may be related to brain damage in patients. Intelligence tests provide a more general measure of verbal and analytical skills.

- To assess emotional and behavioral functioning, clinicians use structured clinical interviews, symptom questionnaires, personality inventories, behavioral observation and self-monitoring, and projective tests. Each of these tests has its advantages and disadvantages.

- During the assessment procedure, many problems and biases can be introduced. Clients may be resistant to being assessed and thus distort the information they provide. Clients may be too impaired by cognitive deficits, distress, or lack of development of verbal skills to provide information. Finally, there are many biases that can arise when the clinician and client are from different cultures.

- A classification system is a set of definitions for syndromes and rules for determining when a person's symptoms are part of each syndrome. The predominant classification system for psychological problems in the United States is the *Diagnostic and Statistical Manual of Mental Disorders* of the American Psychiatric Association. The most recent editions of the DSM have provided specific criteria for diagnosing each of the recognized psychological disorders. The DSM also provides information on the course of disorders and their prevalence. The explicit criteria in the DSM have increased the reliability of diagnoses in the DSM, but there is still room for improvement.

- There are five axes along which clinicians should assess clients, according to the DSM. On Axis I, major clinical syndromes are noted. Axis II contains diagnoses of mental retardation and personality disorders. On Axis III, the clinician notes any medical conditions that clients have. On Axis IV, psychosocial and environmental stressors are noted. On Axis V, clients' general levels of functioning are assessed.

- Critics have charged that the DSM reflects cultural and gender biases in its views of what is psychologically healthy and unhealthy. They also point to many dangers in labeling people with psychiatric disorders, including the danger of stigmatization. Diagnosis is important, however, to communication between clinicians and researchers. Only when a system of definitions of disorders is agreed upon can communication about disorders be improved.

Key Terms

assessment 96	reliability 103	event-related potential (ERP) 106
diagnosis 96	test-retest reliability 103	symptom questionnaire 109
differential diagnosis 98	alternate form reliability 104	personality inventories 109
acculturation 100	internal reliability 104	projective test 112
interview 101	interrater reliability 104	behavioral observation 114
unstructured interview 101	neuropsychological test 104	self-monitoring 114
structured interview 101	intelligence test 105	syndrome 118
resistance 101	computerized tomography (CT) 105	*Diagnostic and Statistical Manual of Mental Disorders* (DSM) 118
validity 102		
face validity 103	positron emission tomography (PET) 105	course 120
content validity 103		prevalence 120
concurrent validity 103	magnetic resonance imaging (MRI) 106	point prevalence 120
predictive validity 103		lifetime prevalence 120
construct validity 103	electroencephalogram (EEG) 106	incidence 121

Critical Thinking Questions

1. Do you think there are some symptoms of psychological disorders that can never be defined by objective, observable criteria but must always rely on people's subjective self-reports?

2. If clinicians feel they get a strong sense of a client's personality and concerns from projective tests, do you think it matters that research has not provided evidence these tests are valid or reliable?

3. How might you frame questions to a parent to get information that is as accurate as possible about a child?

4. What kinds of psychological symptoms might be most vulnerable to misinterpretation due to cultural differences between a therapist and client?

Christian Pierre
Window of Opportunity

The wish for healing has ever been the half of health.

—*Seneca, Hippolytus (first century), 249*

CHAPTER

5

Treatments for Abnormality

Steve and his parents, in the following story, are making use of several kinds of treatment—medication for Steve's symptoms, psychotherapy to help him cope better with his illness, and support groups to help his parents understand and respond effectively to Steve's disorder.

Treatments for mental disorders seek to help people regain positive social, emotional, and occupational functioning.

> ### CASE STUDY
> Steve M. has paranoid schizophrenia. He frequently hears voices berating him and accusing him of having done something wrong. He was convinced that a transmitter had been implanted in his head through which he was receiving these messages. When he takes his medications, the voices are quieted and the paranoid beliefs begin to recede.
>
> But over the last five years, Steve has been hospitalized three times. Each time he had stopped his medication, twice believing himself well and once, just tired of the whole thing. In between hospitalizations, he has spent some time in the day treatment program and some time taking classes at college. He still struggles with determining what is real and what is not, but he has learned through therapy that he can check this out with the people he trusts, principally his stepmother, brother, and father. His self-esteem has been badly shaken, and he no longer has a clear idea what he might reasonably hope to accomplish in his life. Some days, just getting dressed and out of his apartment (which he now shares with two other young men from the day treatment program) is a monumental achievement.
>
> Nonetheless, some gains have been made. Steve has developed a long-term therapy relationship with a psychologist from the clinic whom he sees once a week (in addition to his medication checks with the psychiatrist). Together they confront the very real challenges that his illness and the stigma attached to it pose. He is learning to set short-term goals and to modify his expectations without altogether giving up hope. His parents, through the parent-support group they have joined, are learning to do the same. Steve has learned, through trial and error, that he needs the medication to keep the irrational ideas and the voices at bay. The day treatment program provides practice in socializing and classes in stress management and in independent living. He doesn't feel he really belongs there, but he doesn't feel at home on campus either. His life, though nothing like what he and his family had envisioned for him a decade ago, before his illness struck, holds possibilities for mastery and satisfaction. (Adapted from Bernheim, 1997, pp. 126–130)

Each of the theoretical approaches we discussed in Chapter 2 has led to a treatment approach. Biological approaches to treatment most often involve **medications,** although several other types of biological treatments are discussed in this chapter and throughout this book. The treatment usually prescribed by proponents of psychological and some social approaches to abnormality is **psychotherapy.** There are many forms of psychotherapy, but most involve a therapist (psychiatrist, psychologist, clinical social worker, marriage or family counselor) talking with the person suffering from the disorder (typically called a patient or client) about his or her symptoms and what is contributing to these symptoms. The specific topic of these conversations depends on the therapist's theoretical approach, as described next. Many of the psychotherapies have been adapted for work with couples or families, or with groups of people who share something in common, usually the experience of specific symptoms or disorders.

Both drug therapies and psychotherapy have proven effective in the treatment of many disorders. Drugs and psychotherapy may work on different aspects of a disorder, and they are increasingly used together in an integrated approach to disorders, as we discuss later in this chapter. In *Taking Psychology Personally:* How to Look for a Therapist, we discuss how people go about finding a clinician who will provide them with the kind of treatment they believe they need.

TAKING PSYCHOLOGY PERSONALLY

How to Look for a Therapist

Nationwide studies in the United States suggest that only about 28 percent of people who meet criteria for a mental disorder in a given year seek help for their problem that same time period (Narrow et al., 1993; Regier et al., 1993). Although they may eventually seek out treatment, they typically delay telling a health care professional about their psychological symptoms for several years after these symptoms first appear (Kessler, Olfson, & Berglund, 1998).

Whom do people turn to for mental-health treatment? Of people who do seek treatment, about 40 percent go to a mental-health professional, and 45 percent go to their general practice physician (Narrow et al., 1993; Regier et al., 1993). Religious counselors and clergy make up an important part of the network of care for people with mental disorders (see Figure 5.1). Finally, many people turn to family members, friends, and self-help groups for mental-health care.

Is everyone who seeks mental-health care diagnosable with a mental disorder? Only about half of people seeking care in any given year carry a current diagnosis of a mental disorder (Narrow et al., 1993). Another third of the people seeking care have a history of mental disorders or significant symptoms of a disorder. The remaining people carry no history or current diagnosis, but seek help for symptoms and problems that they feel they cannot cope with alone.

How do you know when you or someone you care about needs a therapist? How do you find a therapist once you decide to seek one? The American Psychological Association has published the following guidelines for evaluating whether you should seek a therapist and for finding a therapist (from *Choosing a Therapist Who Is Right for You,* distributed by the Practice Directorate of the American Psychological Association).

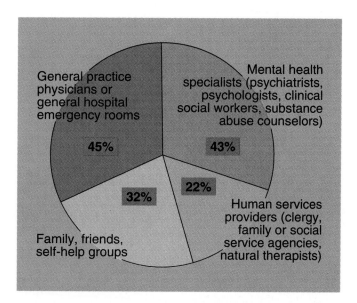

FIGURE 5.1   Sources of Mental Health Care for People with Mental Disorders. People receive mental health care from several sources in addition to mental health specialists.

Continued

Consider Therapy If . . .

- You feel helpless and problems do not seem to get better despite your efforts.
- You feel sad or blue, nervous, or tense for a prolonged period of time.
- You or others notice changes in your mood or behavior or a decrease in your ability to carry out everyday activities.
- You are concerned about the emotional health of a family member or partner.
- You want to look at life and make decisions in a different way.
- You want to find ways of changing your life to feel more satisfied.

How Do You Find a Therapist?

- Talk to friends and family.
- Call your local or state psychological association.
- Contact your community mental-health center.
- Inquire at your church or synagogue.
- Ask your physician or other health professional.
- Consult counseling centers at local colleges and universities.
- Consult your local *Yellow Pages*.

What Should You Consider When Making a Choice?

A therapist and client work together. The right match is important. The following are sample questions that may be useful when considering a particular psychologist:

- Are you a licensed psychologist?
- How many years have you been practicing psychology?
- I've been feeling (anxious, tense, depressed, etc.). I'm having problems (with my job, my marriage, eating, sleeping, etc.). What kind of experience do you have helping people with these types of problems?
- What are your specialty areas? (children, marriage, etc.).
- What might I expect during our sessions?
- What are your fees? (Fees are usually based on a 45-minute to 50-minute session).
- Do you use a sliding-fee scale? Please explain how this works.
- What types of insurance do you accept?
- Do you accept Medicare/Medicaid patients?
- How do you bill for services? Will you bill my insurance company directly or do I bill for reimbursement?

Interview several therapists—by telephone or in person—before making a choice. Following the initial contact, you may want to meet two or three times before you decide to work together. These sessions, called *consultation sessions*, will help you determine if the therapist is right for you.

For further information on choosing a therapist, you can contact the American Psychological Association, Practice Directorate, 1200 Seventeenth Street, N.W., Washington, DC 20036. The telephone number is 202–955–7618.

⊙ BIOLOGICAL TREATMENTS

As we said, most of the biological treatments for abnormality are drug treatments (see *Concept Review: Drug Treatments for Mental Disorders*). These drugs can relieve psychological symptoms by correcting imbalances of neurotransmitters. They may also compensate for structural deficits in the brain or the effects of genetic abnormalities. There are a few other biologi-

cally based therapies that are used for individual disorders. In this chapter, we discuss electroconvulsive therapy and psychosurgery. An alternative treatment based on biological models of psychopathology, herbal medicines, is gaining in popularity, and is discussed in *Pushing the Boundaries:* Herbal Treatments or Phytomedicines (p. 142). Other biological therapies are discussed in chapters on the disorders they are used to treat.

CONCEPT REVIEW

Drug Treatments for Mental Disorders

These are the major types of drugs used to treat several kinds of mental disorders.

Type of Drug	Purpose	Examples
Antipsychotic drugs	Reduce symptoms of psychosis (loss of reality testing, hallucinations, delusions)	Thorazine (a phenothiazine) Haldol (a butyrophenone) Clozaril
Antidepressant drugs	Reduce symptoms of depression (sadness, loss of appetite, sleep disturbances, etc.)	Parnate (an MAO inhibitor) Elavil (a tricyclic) Prozac (a serotonin reuptake inhibitor)
Lithium	Reduce symptoms of mania (agitation, excitement, grandiosity, etc.)	Lithobid Cibalith-S
Antianxiety drugs	Reduce symptoms of anxiety (fearfulness, worry, tension, etc.)	Nembutal (a barbiturate) Valium (a benzodiazepine)

Drug Therapies

You might imagine that most drugs used to treat psychopathology were discovered through a perfectly rational and systematic application of basic science. Some clever scientists did the basic research to discover which systems of the body and brain were responsible for a particular form of psychopathology, and then using their understanding of basic biology, developed a drug that would reverse the bodily processes known to cause the disorder. In truth, most of the drugs now used to treat mental disorders were discovered in roundabout ways, typically by accident.

Antipsychotic Drugs

The beginning of modern drug treatment is generally thought to have begun with the discovery of **chlorpromazine,** a drug now used to treat the symptoms of psychosis (Valenstein, 1998). Psychosis involves the loss of touch with reality, hallucinations (unreal perceptual experiences), and delusions (fantastic, unrealistic beliefs). Chlorpromazine belongs to a group of chemical compounds called **phenothiazines.** While working to produce synthetic dyes in 1883, August Bernthsen, a research chemist in Heidelberg, synthesized phenothiazine, which had a chemical structure very similar to synthetic violet and blue dye products. Later, it was discovered that phenothiazine compounds had a number of biological effects on humans. They could act as antihistamines, and thus were initially thought useful in the treatment of allergies. In the 1940s, researchers in a pharmaceutical company in Paris learned that phenothiazines also resulted in a decrease in muscle tone, the reduction of nausea, and in some cases either sedation

or euphoria. At first these effects were considered unwanted side effects. Some physicians began to use phenothiazines to calm agitated patients, however, and to reduce tremors in patients with Parkinson's disease.

Shortly after World War II, the French surgeon Henri Laborit became interested in using phenothiazines as a presurgery drug to reduce postsurgical shock, a neuroendrocrine response to stress that could sometimes be fatal. Laborit found that administration of a phenothiazine called promethazine created a "euphoric quietude . . . patients are calm and somnolent, with a relaxed and detached expression" (Swazey, 1974, p. 79). Pain was reduced so greatly in some patients that they did not require morphine. Laborit went back to the pharmaceutical company that produced promethazine to ask for a phenothiazine with even greater central nervous system effects. The company suggested he try a compound they had recently synthesized, which was eventually called chlorpromazine.

By the early 1950s, Laborit and a number of other researchers were investigating the effects of chlorpromazine on psychological symptoms. Reports were published that chlorpromazine reduced the hallucinations and delusions of some psychiatric patients. Particularly influential were reports in 1952 by French psychiatrists Jean Delay and Pierre Deniker that chlorpromazine reduced agitation, excitation, confusion and paranoia in patients who were psychotic (Delay, Deniker, & Harl, 1952; Valenstein, 1998). Delay labeled chlorpromazine a **neuroleptic,** implying that this drug depressed the activity of the nervous system. By 1953, Delay and Deniker in France, and other physicians in Switzerland and Great Britain, were reporting that chlorpromazine was having such remarkable effects on psychotic patients that it was transforming psychiatric hospitals.

Soon chlorpromazine was introduced to North American psychiatrists. The American drug company Smith Kline & French began marketing the drug for use in psychiatry in 1954 under the name of Thorazine. At that time, there was little regulation of the prescription drug market, compared to today's standards, so Thorazine was introduced before much research had been done on its effectiveness or side effects. Word spread quickly about remarkable effects of Thorazine on patients with psychotic disorders, however. Within a year of the introduction of Thorazine on the market, over 2 million prescriptions for the drug had been written in the United States. By 1965, chlorpromazine had been the subject of about 10,000 publications worldwide (Valenstein, 1998). By 1970, Smith Kline & French's Thorazine sales totaled over $116 million.

The success of chlorpromazine led other drug companies to develop and patent similar drugs. Some of the more successful phenothiazines that were developed were thioridazine (Mellaril) and trifluoperazine (Stelazine). During the 1950s, researcher Paul Janssen discovered another class of drugs that could reduce psychotic symptoms, **butyrophenone.** The first drug in this class to be marketed was haloperidol (Haldol), in 1957, and it proved at least as effective as chlorpromazine.

Unfortunately, both the phenothiazines and butyrophenone also produce a number of dangerous side effects. These side effects are detailed in Chapter 10, but include severe sedation, visual disturbances, and tardive dyskinesia, a neurological disorder characterized by involuntary movements of the tongue, face, mouth or jaw. Fortunately, new drugs such as clozapine (trade name Clozaril) seem to be effective in treating psychosis without inducing some of the serious side effects of the phenothiazines and butyrophenone (see Chapter 10).

How do these drugs work to reduce psychotic symptoms? The answer to this question is less clear than you might think. Indeed, their use became widespread before researchers had any evidence of how they work (Valenstein, 1998). The leading theories today, however, suggest that these drugs work by reducing levels of the neurotransmitter dopamine, or by influencing receptors for dopamine in the brain.

Antipsychotic drugs—drugs that relieve the symptoms of psychosis—led to a revolution in the treatment and lives of people with psychosis, who had formerly been locked away in mental hospitals and state institutions, perhaps for life, often completely out of touch with reality and sometimes quite difficult to control. Physicians and nurses could do little more than provide for their basic needs and try to keep them from hurting themselves. Within days of receiving antipsychotic drugs, however, a patient might regain control of his or her behavior and grip on reality.

Antidepressant Drugs

The discovery of drugs to treat the symptoms of depression —sadness, low motivation, sleep and appetite disturbances—was just as fortuitous as the discovery of the antipsychotic drugs (Valenstein, 1998). One of the fuels used by the Germans for the V-2 rocket during World War II was hydrazine. When the war ended, drug companies acquired much of the leftover hydrazine, believing that modifications of the chemical could make it useful for medical purposes. In 1951, researchers in the Hoffman-LaRoche pharmaceutical company in New Jersey found that two hydrazine compounds, isoniazid and iproniazid, were effective in treating tuberculosis. One of the "side effects" of these drugs, however, seemed to be euphoria—the tuberculosis patients were dancing with joy in the hospital corridors after treatment with these drugs.

The French psychiatrist Jean Delay, who also played a role in the discovery of chlorpromazine for psychiatric uses, suspected that isoniazid and iproniazid might be useful as **antidepressants**—drugs to treat the symptoms of depression. The initial tests done by him and other physicians, however, proved unsuccessful, probably because they did not allow enough time for the drugs to have any effect. Several years passed before enough research was done to establish that isoniazid and iproniazid truly did have antidepressant effects.

These drugs are part of a class of drugs now called the **monoamine oxidase inhibitors, or MAOIs.** Some trade names of the MAOIs are *Nardil* and *Parnate.* These drugs are currently used in the treatment of depression, with substantial effectiveness. They inhibit the enzyme monoamine oxidase, which results in higher levels of a number of neurotransmitters, such as norepinephrine. Unfortunately, the MAOIs have potentially dangerous side effects, including throbbing headaches, jaundice, a precipitous rise in blood pressure, especially when mixed with certain foods (see Chapter 8). Because of these side effects other drugs are used more often.

Until quite recently, the antidepressants most often used were **tricyclic antidepressants.** In the 1950s, Swiss psychiatrist Roland Kuhn was trying different drugs in an attempt to improve sleep in mental patients. One drug he tried was imipramine, which has a chemical structure similar to a phenothiazine. Imipramine did not induce sleep, but rather energized patients and elevated their mood. Kuhn treated more than 500 psychiatric patients with imipramine over the next three years and reported that imipramine was not simply a stimulant, but a true antidepressant:

> The patients get up in the morning of their own accord, they speak louder and more rapidly, their facial expression becomes more vivacious. They

commence some activity on their own, again seeking contact with other people, they begin to entertain themselves, take part in games, become more cheerful and are once again able to laugh. . . . The patients express themselves as feeling much better, fatigue disappears, the feeling of heaviness in the limbs vanishes, and the sense of oppression in the chest gives way to a feeling of relief. The general inhibition, which led to retardation, subsides. They declare that they are now able to follow other persons' train of thought, and that once more new thoughts occur to them, whereas previously they were continually tortured by the same fixed idea. . . . Instead of being concerned about imagined or real guilt in their past, they become occupied with plans concerning their own future. Actual delusions of guilt, or loss, or hypochondriacal delusions become less evident. The patients declare "I don't think of it anymore" or "the thought doesn't enter my head now." Suicidal tendencies also diminish, become more controllable or disappear altogether. . . . Not infrequently the cure is complete, sufferers and their relatives confirming the fact that they had not been so well for a long time. (Kuhn, 1958, pp. 459–460)

The Geigy pharmaceutical company started marketing imipramine (Tofranil) in 1958. Other tricyclic antidepressants, such as Elavil and Anafranil, were soon introduced by other pharmaceutical companies. By 1980, approximately 10 million prescriptions for antidepressant drugs were being written annually in the United States, and most of these were for tricyclic antidepressants (Valenstein, 1998). Tricyclic antidepressants were quickly favored over MAOIs because they seemed more effective and had fewer dangerous side effects. Tricyclics do have their side effects, however, including sedation, dry mouth, and blurred vision.

The tricyclic antidepressants were thought to work by inhibiting the reuptake of the neurotransmitters norepinephrine, serotonin, and perhaps dopamine, in the brain. Because they have effects on so many neurotransmitter systems, the tricyclic antidepressants are sometimes referred to as "dirty drugs." Researchers thought if they could synthesize drugs that had more specific effects on individual neurotransmitter systems, these drugs could be more effective in treating depression. By the 1980s, the technology for synthesizing drugs that bind to specific neurotransmitter subtypes was advanced enough to make it possible to test many new drugs.

In 1986, the pharmaceutical company Eli Lilly introduced the drug fluoxetine, under the trade name Prozac, as an antidepressant. Prozac is a **selective serotonin reuptake inhibitor** (SSRI), which means that it acts more selectively on serotonin receptors than the tricyclic antidepressants. Some psychiatrists touted Prozac as the "SCUD missile of psychopharmacology," able to zero in on its target with amazing precision (Slater, 1998, p. 10). Other SSRIs were soon introduced by other drug companies, including Zoloft and Paxil. In the 12 months between August 1996 and August 1997, more than 3.5 million prescriptions were written for SSRIs. Lilly's sales of Prozac alone were over $1.8 billion, and Pfizer's sales of Zoloft were almost $1.2 billion. Today, over 30 million people worldwide have taken Prozac, and many more millions have taken one of the other SSRIs (Valenstein, 1998).

Why did the SSRIs become so popular so fast? It is not because they are more effective than the tricyclic antidepressants. Most studies comparing the two classes of drugs find they are equally effective in treating depression (Thase & Howland, 1995). One reason the SSRIs became so popular is that many people can tolerate the side effects of the SSRIs better than the side effects of the tricyclics. Some of the common side effects of the SSRIs are agitation, sexual dysfunction, and gastrointestinal irritation. Another reason for the rapid proliferation of the SSRIs is that they seem useful in the treatment of a number of other psychological problems in addition to depression, including anxiety, poor impulse control, and eating disorders.

Finally, the impact of stories in the media and popular press on the SSRIs cannot be underestimated (see Figure 5.2). These drugs enjoyed unprecedented coverage as "wonder drugs" in their early days, and several popular books have promoted these drugs as the cures

FIGURE 5.2   Magazine Cover Illustrating the Controversy over New Uses of the SSRIs. Our society is debating the wisdom of letting people "change their personalities with a pill."

not only for depression, but also lack of self-confidence, shyness, impulsiveness, and a host of other problems.

Some of the newest antidepressant drugs do not target serotonin or norepinephrine, but an amino acid neurotransmitter known as **substance P.** Substance P is known to be in high concentrations in areas of the brain involved in emotion and pain, such as the amygdala, and was initially studied in 1990 as a way to treat pain. Drugs that serve as receptor antagonists of substance P have proven effective in the treatment of both depression and anxiety in studies conducted by their manufacturers (Kramer et al., 1998).

Lithium and Other Mood Stabilizers

Lithium is a metallic element that is present in the sea, in natural springs, and in animal and plant tissue. It has been used to treat a number of medical disorders, with weak results. In the middle of the nineteenth century, it was widely used to treat rheumatism and gout, and several physicians thought there was a relationship between these disorders and mania—a condition in which people experience agitated, excited, and grandiose ideas. Indeed, mania was often referred to as "brain gout." In 1871, William Hammand, a neurologist at Bellevue Hospital in New York and a former surgeon general of the United States, recommended lithium as a treatment of mania. His recommendation got little attention, however.

The introduction of lithium as a treatment followed a rather unusual path. During World War II, Australian physician John Cade was captured by the Japanese and spent three and a half years in a military prison. He observed the onset of mania in some of his fellow prisoners, and wondered if it was caused by an excessive accumulation of some metabolite that had a toxic effect on the brain (Valenstein, 1998). Cade did not know what the metabolite might be, but he pursued this idea vigorously when he was released after the war. His subjects were guinea pigs. A series of unusual experiments led Cade to discover, quite accidentally, that lithium had a powerful calming effect on the guinea pigs:

> The animals remained fully awake, but after about two hours they became so calm that they lost their "startle-reaction" and frantic righting-reflex when placed on their backs. It was this observation which prompted the trial of lithium salts in that over-excitable state of mania. (Cade, 1949, p. 70–71)

Cade proceeded to experiment on himself to determine the safety of lithium. After being convinced of its safety, he tried a lithium regimen on 19 patients, 10 of whom had frequent bouts of mania. He published his report of the successful treatment of these patients

with lithium in 1949. Unfortunately, however, this was published in an Australian medical journal not widely read outside of Australia, and Cade himself was an unknown psychiatrist working in a small hospital with no research training. Thus, Cade's work went unnoticed for the most part.

It wasn't until a Danish psychiatrist, Mogens Schou, published a series of studies on the effectiveness of lithium in 1970, that lithium was legitimized as a treatment for mania. Schou had come across Cade's report in the early 1950s and had begun experimenting with lithium in a more carefully controlled research procedure. His initial findings had shown lithium to be effective in treating mania. But lithium is a dangerous substance, and can have many severe side effects, even resulting in death. American and European psychiatrists had been reluctant to accept lithium because of its toxicity. Schou's 1970 paper had such convincing evidence of the effectiveness of lithium that psychiatrists were forced to consider using it, especially because there were no effective alternatives in the treatment of mania.

Lithium continues to be widely used in the treatment of mania today. Other drugs, known as the **anticonvulsants,** and **calcium channel blockers,** are also being used in the treatment of mania (see Chapter 8). Fortunately, these newer drugs appear to have fewer side effects than lithium.

Antianxiety Drugs

Anxiety and insomnia are the symptoms for which drugs are most often prescribed. The first group of **antianxiety drugs** were the **barbiturates,** introduced at the beginning of the twentieth century. Barbiturates suppress the central nervous system, decreasing the activity of a variety of types of neurons. Although these drugs are effective for inducing relaxation and sleep, they are quite addictive, and withdrawal from them can cause life-threatening symptoms, such as increased heart rate, delirium, and convulsions.

The other major class of anxiety-reducing drugs, the **benzodiazepines,** was discovered in the 1940s, but were not widely available until the 1960s when drug companies began selling them under names such as Librium, Valium, and Serax. These drugs appear to reduce the symptoms of anxiety without interfering substantially with an individual's ability to function in daily life. The most frequent use of these drugs, accurately referred to as minor tranquilizers, is as sleeping pills. As many as 70 million prescriptions are written each year in the United States for benzodiazepines. Unfortunately, these drugs are also highly addictive, and up to 80 percent of people who take them for 6 weeks or more show withdrawal symptoms, including heart rate acceleration, irritability, and profuse

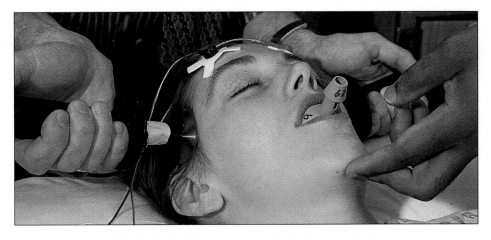

Electroconvulsive therapy has been controversial for much of its history but can be effective for certain disorders.

sweating. The active metabolites of benzodiazepines remain in the body for days, and can create toxic interaction effects with alcohol and other drugs.

Electroconvulsive Therapy

An alternative to drug therapies in the treatment of some disorders is **electroconvulsive therapy,** or **ECT.** ECT was introduced in the early twentieth century, originally as a treatment for schizophrenia. Italian physicians Ugo Cerletti and Lucio Bini decided to experiment with the use of ECT to treat schizophrenia, reasoning that ECT could calm people with schizophrenia much like experiencing an epileptic seizure would calm and sedate people with epilepsy. Eventually, clinicians found that ECT was not effective for schizophrenia, but it was effective for depression.

ECT consists of a series of treatments in which a brain seizure is induced by passing electrical current through the patient's brain. Patients are first anesthetized and given muscle relaxants so that they are not conscious when they have the seizure and so their muscles do not jerk violently during the seizure. Metal electrodes are taped to the head and a current of 70 to 150 volts is passed through one side of the brain for about one-half of a second. Patients typically have a convulsion, which lasts about 1 minute. The full series of treatments consists of 6 to 12 sessions.

In Chapter 8, we discuss the use of ECT in the treatment of depression. Although many mental-health professionals believe that ECT can be useful, it remains a controversial treatment. The idea of passing electrical current through the brain of a person to relieve psychiatric symptoms seems somewhat bizarre. And some critics argue that ECT still results in significant and permanent cognitive damage, even when

done according to modern guidelines (Breggin, 1997). For some seriously depressed people who do not respond to medications, however, ECT may be the only effective alternative.

Psychosurgery

In Chapter 1, we described theories that prehistoric peoples performed crude brain surgery, called trephining, on people with mental disorders in order to release the evil spirits causing the mental disorders. In modern times, brain surgery did not really become a mode of treatment for mental disorders until the early twentieth century. A Portuguese neurologist named Antonio de Egas Moniz introduced a procedure in 1935 in which the frontal lobes of the brain were severed from the lower centers of the brain in people suffering from psychosis. This procedure eventually developed into the procedure known as **prefrontal lobotomies.** Although Moniz won the Nobel Prize for his work, prefrontal lobotomies were eventually criticized as a cruel and ineffective means of treating psychosis (Valenstein, 1986). Patients would often suffer severe and permanent "side effects," including either an inability to control impulses or a loss of the ability to initiate activity, extreme listlessness and loss of emotions, seizures, and sometimes even death.

By the 1950s, the use of **psychosurgery** declined dramatically, especially in countries outside the United States. These days, psychosurgery is used rarely, and only with people with severe disorders that do not respond to other forms of treatment. Modern neurological assessment and surgery techniques make psychosurgery more precise and safe than it formerly was, although it remains highly controversial even among professionals. Neurosurgeons attempt to lesion, or

PUSHING THE BOUNDARIES

Herbal Treatments or Phytomedicines

Y ou have probably heard of St. John's wort (technically known as *Hypericum perforatum*). This little roadside weed became big news in the mid 1990s when the media became aware of studies in Europe suggesting that St. John's wort was an effective treatment for depression. Psychiatrist Harold Bloomfield published the book *Hypericum & Depression,* which reviewed the European studies and concluded that St. John's wort was a reasonable alternative to medications in the treatment of mild or moderate depressions. Since then, sales of St. John's wort, which can be bought without prescription in most pharmacies, have soared, hitting $48 million in the United States in 1997.

American researchers jumped to action to test whether St. John's wort was effective for depression on this side of the ocean. They actually had serious questions about how depression was defined in many of the European studies and differences between the people studied in Europe and those who might seek out St. John's wort in the United States. To date, most studies have supported the conclusion that St. John's wort is effective in the treatment of mild to moderate depression, although it may not be potent enough to relieve more serious depressions (Cott, 1995b; Cott & Fugh-Berman,

1998; Linde et al., 1996). In addition, people tend to experience fewer side effects to St. John's wort than to prescription antidepressant medications, although some people experience gastrointestinal symptoms, fatigue, and increased sensitivity to ultraviolet light (Linde et al., 1996).

What about other "natural" remedies for psychological problems? These have been referred to as phytomedicines, and their use dates back to the beginning of civilization. For example, *Rauwolfia serpentina* was used at least 3,000 years ago by Hindu Ayurvedic healers as a treatment for insanity. In the twentieth century, it was "rediscovered" and chemical analysis of the root extracts of *R. serpentina* led to the discovery of dopamine and its role in Parkinson's disease and schizophrenia.

Phytomedicines are a regular part of modern mainstream medicine in Asia and parts of Western Europe, particularly Germany (Grunwald, 1995). Herbal products account for over $1 billion in sales in the United States annually, with as many as 40 percent of Americans reporting they use herbal products at least occasionally (Astin, 1998; Cott, 1995a). These products are typically sold as foods. They can range from simple and mild products such as chamomile and peppermint to products with potent

---

destroy, minute areas of the brain thought to be involved in a patient's symptoms. One of the greatest remaining problems in psychosurgery, however, is that we do not yet know what areas of the brain are involved in the production of most psychiatric symptoms, and it is likely that many areas of the brain are involved in any given disorder (Valenstein, 1986).

The Social Impact of the Biological Approach to Treatment

The biological therapies have revolutionized the treatment of people with psychological disorders. We entered the twentieth century only able to warehouse

people with severe psychological disturbances. We entered the twenty-first century able to treat many of these people so successfully that they can lead normal lives, thanks to many of the biological therapies that have been developed in recent decades.

Many people find the biological theories appealing because they seem to erase any blame or responsibility that might be put upon the sufferer of a disorder. Indeed, many organizations that advocate for people with mental disorders argue vehemently that mental disorders should be seen as medical diseases, just like diabetes or high blood pressure, and that people who suffer these disorders simply must accept they have a disease and obtain the appropriate medical treatment (see Figure 5.3, p. 144).

Continued

pharmacological activity, such as foxglove, from which digitalis is derived. Two of the most common ailments for which people take herbal products are anxiety and depression (Astin, 1998). People also use herbals to treat chronic pain, chronic fatigue syndrome, addictions, and memory problems.

What is the effectiveness of these products? Only a few of them have been tested in rigorous research. We have already discussed the research on St. John's wort for depression. Two products used to treat anxiety, valerian and kava, have also undergone close scientific scrutiny. Valerian is made from the root of the *Valeriana officinalis,* a common herb native to both Europe and Asia (Cott, 1995b). Valerian appears to be a safe, mild sedative that produces no morning hangover (Balderer & Borbely, 1985; Fugh-Berman & Cott, 1999). Kava is the psychoactive member of the pepper family, widely used in Polynesia, Micronesia, and Melanesia as a ceremonial, tranquilizing beverage, and in Europe and the United States for anxiety and insomnia. Several placebo-controlled studies have shown that kava is a safe herb for short-term relief from stress and anxiety (Fugh-Berman & Cott, 1999; Volz & Keiser, 1997). Although most people who take kava report no side effects, some report mild gastrointestinal complaints or allergic skin reactions. Kava may also interact with benzodiazepines.

Ginkgo biloba is the most widely prescribed phytomedicine in Germany. It is an antioxidant, and some reports suggest it may enhance cognitive functioning in people with Alzheimer's disorder and other memory impairments (Cott, 1995b; Fugh-Berman & Cott, 1999; Kanowksi et al., 1996; LeBars et al., 1997). Germany has approved the use of ginkgo biloba for the treatment of dementia. Although it is rare for humans to experience significant side effects from gingko, it does have anticoagulant effects and in rare cases has been associated with serious bleeding problems, usually in people who are already taking anticoagulant drugs.

Concerns have been raised that many people are using the more potent substances without any supervision from a physician, putting themselves at risk for side effects or interactions with drugs or other substances, when sufficient research on their efficacy and safety has not been done. In addition, even for the products that do seem to be effective, little is known about how they work. Unfortunately, it is unlikely that herbal products will ever be researched to the degree that drugs produced by pharmaceutical companies are researched. Doing sufficient research to have herbal products approved as a drug is extremely expensive in the United States. Meanwhile, botanicals are not patentable and are chemically very complex. The U.S. Congress passed the Dietary Supplement Health and Education Act in 1994 to encourage more research on nutrition and dietary supplements, and increased regulation of this industry.

Thus, although herbal treatments for psychological disorders have been used for centuries, they were largely considered a thing of the past by the mainstream medical community until very recently. Now, in part because the public is asking for more "natural" approaches in medicine, these products are becoming one of the newest tools in the treatment of mental disorders.

Despite their current popularity, the biological therapies are not a panacea. They do not work for everyone. Indeed, as we discuss in the upcoming chapters, significant percentages of people with psychological disorders do not respond to any of the drugs or other biological treatments currently available. With time, new and more effective treatments may be developed that help these people, too.

Most of the biological therapies have significant side effects. Often these side effects are tolerable and people endure them because they are getting relief from their psychological disorder. For some people, however, the side effects are worse than the disorder itself. For others, the side effects can be dangerous and even deadly.

Some critics of biological theories and drug therapies worry that people will turn to the drugs rather than dealing with the difficult issues in their lives that are causing their psychological problems. If people can rid themselves of troubling symptoms by popping a pill, they may never make changes in their lives that could have permanent positive effects on their own psychological health and their relationships with others.

Finally, the widespread use of some drugs, such as the SSRIs and the benzodiazepines, by people who are not suffering from severe depression or anxiety, but who just want a little help getting through the day, has raised many questions about the appropriateness of "changing your personality with a pill." We are

FIGURE 5.3   An advertisement placed by the National Alliance for Research on Schizophrenia and Depression (NARSAD) that appeared in many major newspapers throughout the United States illustrates the pro-biological position many mental health advocacy groups take.

grappling with the ethical and philosophical issues raised by the availability of drugs that offer us the opportunity to be smarter, more confident, less shy, and more energetic. Is this how we want these drugs to be used? Writer Lauren Slater, whose own symptoms of obsessions and compulsions (see Chapter 7) were relieved by Prozac, writes:

Voices

Much has been said about the meanings we make of illness, but what about the meanings we make out of cure? Cure is complex, disorienting, a revisioning of the self, either subtle or stark. Cure is the new, strange planet, pressing in. (Slater 1998, p. 9).

© United Features Syndicate.

No doubt these issues will continue to be debated for many years to come. Biological science is advancing at a rapid pace, presenting us with more alternatives in the treatment of mental disorders, and more questions about how we view the relationship between our body and our mind.

Summing Up

- Anitpsychotic drugs such as phenothiazines and butyrophenone help to reduce symptoms of psychosis.
- Antidepressant drugs, including the monoamine oxidase inhibitors, the tricyclic antidepressants, the selective serotonin reuptake inhibitors, and substance P receptor antagonists help reduce symptoms of depression.
- Lithium is used to treat the symptoms of mania.
- Anticonvulsant drugs and calcium channel blockers also help to treat mania.
- Antianxiety drugs include the barbiturates and the benzodiazepines.
- Electroconvulsive therapy is useful in the treatment of severe depression.
- Psychosurgery is used on rare occasions to help people with severe psychopathology that is not affected by drugs or other treatments.

◔ PSYCHOLOGICAL THERAPIES

Drug treatments can go a long way toward helping people with psychological problems. For many disorders, however, psychotherapy is an effective alternative to drugs (Seligman, 1995). There are many different types of psychotherapy. These are summarized below and in the *Concept Review*: Psychological Treatments for Mental Disorders, page 146. In the remaining chapters of this book, you will see how these therapies are applied to treat specific disorders.

Psychodynamic Therapies

Psychodynamic therapies focus on uncovering and resolving unconscious conflicts that drive psychological symptoms. The goal is to help clients recognize the maladaptive ways they have been trying to cope and the sources of their unconscious conflicts. This insight frees clients from the grip of the past and gives them a sense of agency in making changes in the present (Wolitzky, 1995). Another goal is to help the client integrate aspects of his or her personality that have been split off or denied into a unified sense of self. As Freud stated in 1923:

> It may be laid down that the aim of the treatment is to remove the patient's resistances and to pass his repressions in review and thus to bring about the most far-reaching unification and strengthening of his ego, to enable him to save the mental energy which he is expending on internal conflicts, to make the best of him that his inherited capacities will allow and so to make him as efficient and as capable of enjoyment as possible. The removal of the symptoms of the illness is not specifically aimed at, but is achieved, as it were, as a by-product if the analysis is properly carried through. (Freud, 1923, p. 251)

It is not easy to uncover unconscious conflicts. Freud and others developed the method of **free association,** in which a client is taught to talk about whatever comes to her mind, trying not to censor any thoughts. By "turning off" her censor, a client might find herself talking about subjects or memories that she did not even realize were "on her mind." The therapist notices what themes seem to recur in a client's free associations, just how one thought seems to lead to another thought, and the specific memories that a client recalls. The material that the client is reluctant to talk about when fully awake—that is, the client's **resistance** to certain material—is an especially important clue to the content of the client's most central unconscious conflicts, because the most threatening conflicts are the ones the ego tries hardest to repress. The therapist eventually puts together these pieces of the puzzle

CONCEPT REVIEW

Psychological Treatments for Mental Disorders

These are some of the most commonly used psychologically based therapies used to treat mental disorders.

Type of Therapy	Description
Psychodynamic therapy	Helps clients gain insight into unconscious motives and conflicts, through analysis of free associations, resistances, dreams, and transferences
Humanistic therapy	Helps clients explore their own values and potentials and fulfill their potential more fully by providing a warm and supportive relationship
Behavioral therapy	Helps clients extinguish unwanted behaviors or teach a person new, desired behaviors, such as systematic desensitization or response shaping
Cognitive therapy	Helps clients change maladaptive thought patterns by challenging irrational thoughts and learning new skills

into a suggestion or interpretation of a conflict the client might be facing and voices this interpretation to the client. Sometimes the client accepts this interpretation as a revelation. Other times, the client is resistant to this interpretation. The therapist might interpret this resistance as a good indication that the interpretation identified an important issue in the client's unconscious.

The client's **transference** to the therapist is also a clue to his unconscious conflicts and needs. A transference occurs when the client reacts to the therapist as if the therapist were some important person in his early development, such as his father or mother. For example, a client may find himself reacting with rage or extreme fear when a therapist is just a few minutes late for an appointment, and this might stem from his feelings of having been emotionally abandoned by a parent during childhood. The therapist might point out the ways the client behaves that represent a transference and help the client explore the roots of his behavior in his relationships with significant others.

Here is an example of a therapist noticing and using a transference to identify core issues for a client (adapted from Luborsky, 1984, p. 96):

Voices

Therapist: Each time I notice and comment that you are doing well in your work you get tearful and cry.

Client: [crying] I feel I will be rejected. Father could never stand it. I won a ribbon in a race and he only could say the competition was not too great. Dad did the same restricting with Mother. She even had to limit her vocabulary for him.

Therapist: I see, so you feel you have some well-established old reasons for feeling that way with me.

"Have a couple of dreams, and call me in the morning."
© Sidney Harris

Some psychodynamic therapists also have their clients recount their dreams, and they use this material in analysis of their conflicts. Freud believed that during sleep, the ego loosens its control over the unconscious, and some unconscious material slips out in the form of dreams. These dreams are seldom direct representations of unconscious material, however, because this would be too threatening. Instead, dreams symbolize unconscious material in fascinating and creative ways.

By **working through,** or going over and over, painful memories and difficult issues, clients are able to understand them and weave them into their self-definition in ways that are acceptable and allow them to move forward in their lives. Many therapists believe that **catharsis,** or the expression of emotions connected

Traditional psychodynamic therapy involves listening for a client's unconscious conflicts and concerns.

to memories and conflicts, is also central to the healing processes in psychodynamic therapy. Catharsis unleashes the energy bound in unconscious memories and conflicts, allowing this material to be incorporated into more adaptive self-views.

An important issue in psychodynamic therapy is the **therapeutic alliance.** By being empathic and supportive, and listening nonjudgmentally, the therapist creates a relationship of trust with the client that gives the client the freedom and courage to explore difficult issues. This does not mean that the therapist never confronts the client about issues the client may be avoiding. But the therapist carefully times confrontations and interpretations so that the client can receive and respond to these without undue anxiety. Several studies have shown that the strength of the therapeutic alliance between a therapist and client, even in the early sessions of therapy, is a strong predictor of whether or not the client will benefit from therapy (Luborsky & Crits-Christoph, 1990). Indeed, clients who do not experience their therapists as supportive are prone to quit therapy altogether.

What is the difference between **psychoanalysis** and psychodynamic therapy? Psychoanalysis typically involves three to four sessions per week over a period of many years. The focus of psychoanalysis is primarily on the interpretation of transferences and resistances, and on experiences in the client's past (Wolitzky, 1995). Psychodynamic therapy may also go on for years, but it can be as short term as 12 weeks (Crits-Christoph & Barber, 1991). Transferences and resistances, and the client's relationship with early caregivers, are also the focus of psychodynamic therapy, but the psychodynamic therapist may focus more on current situations in the client's life than the psychoanalyst.

Many people report that the self-exploration of psychodynamic therapy has been valuable to them. The long-term, intensive nature of psychodynamic therapy makes it unaffordable for many people, however. In addition, people suffering from acute problems, such as severe depression or anxiety, often cannot tolerate the lack of structure in traditional psychodynamic therapy and need more immediate relief from their symptoms (Bachrach et al., 1991). Finally, it is unclear whether traditional psychodynamic therapy is effective in the treatment of many mental disorders, largely because the therapy lasts so long that studies have not been conducted to test its effectiveness empirically (Wolitzky, 1995).

For these reasons, modern psychodynamic therapists have developed some shorter-term, more structured versions of psychodynamic therapy (Luborsky, 1984). In these short-term therapies, the therapist and patient contract with each other for a limited number of sessions, usually less than 30, and focus on a limited set of problems the client identifies as causing him or her the most trouble. The few studies conducted on the effectiveness of these short-term therapies suggest they can result in significant improvement in symptoms for many clients (Crits-Christoph, 1992).

Some of these new therapies have incorporated the revisions in psychodynamic thought offered by object relations theorists and other theorists who argued that interpersonal relationships throughout the life span can shape people's behaviors and self-concepts (Anderson & Lambert, 1995). Interpersonal therapies explicitly focus on the people's roles and relationships within their network of relationships with friends, family, and the larger community. We explore interpersonal therapy in the section on sociocultural approaches to therapy later in this chapter.

Humanistic Therapy

The goal of **humanistic therapy,** often referred to as **person-centered therapy,** is to help the client discover his or her potentialities and place in the world and to accomplish self-actualization through self-exploration. Person-centered therapies are unique in the extent to which they emphasize the self-healing capacities of the person (Bohart, 1995). The job of the therapist in person-centered therapy is not to act as an authority or expert who provides healing to the client. Rather, the therapist's job is to provide the optimal conditions for the client to heal him or herself. This therapy rests on the assumption that the natural tendency for humans is toward growth. When obstacles toward growth are removed, then the client will let go of symptoms and move forward in his or her life. Person-centered therapists do not push clients to uncover repressed painful memories or unconscious conflicts. Instead, they believe when clients are supported and empowered to grow and self-actualize, they will eventually face their past when it is necessary for their further development (Bohart, 1995).

The best known of these therapies is Carl Rogers' **client-centered therapy** (CCT). Rogers (1951) identified three essential ingredients to CCT. First, the therapist communicates a genuineness in his role as helper to the client, acting as an authentic, real, living, behaving person rather than as an authority figure. Second, the therapist shows **unconditional positive regard** for the client. Third, the therapist communicates an empathic understanding of the client by making it clear that he understands and accepts the client's underlying feelings and search for self. Through these conditions, the therapist helps the client know that he is fully there with the client, understanding what he or she is experiencing and feeling, and what he or she is trying to bring forth and understand. Rogers believed that this experience of being understood helped clients bring forth their own self-healing powers and have the courage to recognize and pursue their potential.

The main strategy for accomplishing these goals is the use of reflection. **Reflection** is a method of responding in which the therapist expresses her attempt to understand what the client is experiencing and trying to communicate (Bohart, 1995). The therapist does not attempt to interpret the unconscious aspects of the client's experience. Rather the therapist tries to communicate his understanding of the client, and explicitly asks for feedback from the client about this understanding. Here is an example of the difference between a reflection and a psychodynamic interpretation (Bohart, 1995, p. 101):

Voices

Client: "I'm feeling so lost in my career. Every time I seem to be getting close to doing something really creative, which would lead to a promotion, I somehow manage to screw it up. I never feel like I am really using my potential. There is a block there."

Reflection: "It's really frustrating to screw up and kill your chances; and it feels like it's something in you that's making that happen again and again."

A psychodynamic interpretation: "It sounds like every time you get close to success you unconsciously sabotage yourself. Perhaps success means something to you that is troubling or uncomfortable, and you are not aware of what that is."

This interpretation indeed may be true, but the client-centered therapist would view it as inappropriate

because it brings to the client's attention something that is not currently in the client's awareness.

Client-centered therapy has been used to treat people with a wide range of problems, including depression, alcoholism, schizophrenia, anxiety disorders, and personality disorders (Bohart, 1990). An analysis of over 20 studies comparing client-centered and other humanistic therapies to more structured therapies found that the humanistic therapies were generally as effective as the more structured therapies for a variety of disorders (Greenberg, Elliot, & Lietaer, 1994). For example, Borkovec and Mathews (1988) found client-centered therapy to be as effective as behavioral and cognitive therapies (see below) in the treatment of anxiety disorders. Not all studies find client-centered therapy to be an effective treatment, however (Bohart, 1990). Some therapists believe that CCT may be appropriate and sufficient for people who are moderately distressed, but not sufficient for people who are seriously distressed.

Behavior Therapies

Just as behavior theories of psychopathology are radically different from psychodynamic and humanistic theories, **behavior therapies** would seem to be the polar opposite of these other therapies. Whereas psychodynamic therapies focus on uncovering unconscious conflicts and relational issues that developed during childhood and humanistic therapies focus on helping the client discover the inner self, behavior therapies focus only on changing a person's specific behaviors in the present day.

The foundation for behavior therapy is the **behavioral assessment** of the client's problem. The therapist works with the client to identify the specific circumstances that seem to elicit the client's negative behavior or emotional responses: What situations seem to trigger anxiety symptoms? When is the client most likely to begin heavy drinking? What types of interactions with other people make the client feel most distressed? The therapist may ask the client to use some of the techniques of self-monitoring described in Chapter 4 to identify triggers for symptoms. For example, a client who is complaining of frequent attacks of anxiety may be asked to keep a journal in which she notes each time she feels anxious and specifically what is happening in those situations. The therapist may also **role play** situations with the client, with the therapist taking the role of a person to whom the client feels she reacts badly. The therapist would observe the client's behavior in the role play to assess what aspects of that behavior need to change for the client to be effective in interpersonal interactions.

CONCEPT REVIEW

Behavior Techniques

These are some of the methods used in behavior therapy.

Removal of reinforcements	Removes the individual from reinforcing situation or environment
Aversion therapy	Makes situation or stimulus that was once reinforcing no longer reinforcing
Relaxation exercises	Helps the individual voluntarily control physiological manifestations of anxiety
Distraction techniques	Helps the individual temporarily distract from anxiety-producing situations; diverts attention from physiological manifestations of anxiety
Flooding or implosive therapy	Exposes individual to dreaded or feared stimulus while preventing avoidant behavior
Systematic desensitization	Pairs implementation of relaxation techniques with hierarchical exposure to aversive stimulus
Response shaping through operant conditioning	Pairs rewards with desired behaviors
Behavioral contracting	Provides rewards for reaching proximal goals
Modeling and observational learning	Models desired behaviors so that client may learn through observation

Although there are many specific techniques for behavior change (see *Concept Review:* Behavioral Techniques), they can be grouped into two main categories: techniques that extinguish unwanted behaviors and techniques for teaching a person new, desired behaviors. We discuss some examples of each category in this chapter. The application of the other techniques, listed in *Concept Review:* Behavioral Techniques, to specific disorders is discussed in later chapters on those disorders.

Techniques for Extinguishing Unwanted Behaviors

Systematic desensitization therapy is a gradual method for extinguishing anxiety responses to stimuli and the maladaptive behavior that often accompanies this anxiety (Wolpe, 1969). In systematic desensitization, the person first develops a hierarchy of feared stimuli, ranging from stimuli that would cause him only mild anxiety to stimuli that would cause him severe anxiety or panic. A person with a snake phobia might generate the hierarchy in Table 5.1. Then the therapist would help the person proceed through this hierarchy, starting with the least feared stimulus. The person would be instructed to vividly imagine the feared stimulus or even be exposed to the feared stimulus for a short period, while implementing relaxation exercises to control the anxiety he feels. When he gets to the point where he can imagine or experience the first and least feared stimulus without feeling anxious, he moves on to the next most feared stimulus, imagining or experiencing it while implementing relaxation

TABLE 5.1

Hierarchy of Fears for Snake Phobia

This is a hierarchy of feared stimuli for a person with a snake phobia, ranging from the least feared stimulus to the most feared stimulus.

1. Hearing the word *snake*.
2. Imagining a snake in a closed container at a distance
3. Imagining a snake uncontained at a distance
4. Imagining a snake nearby in a closed container
5. Looking at a picture of a snake
6. Viewing a movie or video of a snake
7. Seeing a snake in a container in the same room
8. Seeing a snake uncontained in the same room
9. Watching someone handle a snake
10. Touching a snake
11. Handling a snake
12. Playing with a snake

exercises. This proceeds until he reaches the most feared stimulus on his list and is able to experience this stimulus without feeling extremely anxious. Thus, by the end of systematic desensitization therapy, a person with a snake phobia should be able to pick up and handle a large snake without becoming very anxious.

Calvin and Hobbes

by Bill Watterson

Calvin's attempts at systematic desensitization don't always work.

Often, systematic desensitization therapy is combined with **modeling**—the client might watch a therapist pick up a snake, pet it, and play with it, observing that the therapist is not afraid, is not bitten or choked, and seems to enjoy playing with the snake. Eventually, the client is encouraged to model the therapist's behaviors with and reactions to the snake. In some cases, people undergoing systematic desensitization are asked only to imagine experiencing the feared stimuli. In other cases, they may be asked to experience these stimuli directly, actually touching and holding the snake, for example. This latter method is known as **in vivo exposure,** and generally has stronger results than exposure only in one's imagination (Emmelkamp, 1982).

Another technique for extinguishing unwanted behaviors is **flooding** or **implosive therapy,** which involves exposing clients to feared stimuli or situations to an excessive degree while preventing them from avoiding that situation. An example would be having a person with a deep fear of germs soil her hands with dirt and then not wash her hands for several hours. This may sound relatively benign to you, but for a person with a germ obsession, this would arouse a great deal of anxiety. Over time, however, the anxiety tends to extinguish.

Techniques for Learning Desirable Behaviors

The techniques we have just discussed are designed to extinguish maladaptive responses or behaviors. Often, however, a person wishes to learn a new set of behaviors. A student of B. F. Skinner's named Ogden Lindsley first conceived of using the methods of operant conditioning to create new positive behaviors in people with serious mental disorders. He began working with severely impaired mental patients in the Metropolitan State Hospital just outside Boston, setting up a system whereby they were given rewards for positive, nonpsychotic behavior and rewards were withheld when they exhibited psychotic behavior. This method of shaping the responses of severely impaired people proved extremely successful. Soon, during the 1950s and 1960s, whole wards of state hospitals were being turned over to behavior therapists. In these wards, a **token economy** was often set up in which a patient would receive a small chip or token each time he or she exhibited a desired behavior (e.g., spoke to another person, made his or her bed). These tokens could be exchanged for privileges, such as a walk on the hospital grounds, or desired objects, such as special food. Although this technique may sound simplistic and manipulative, it is credited, along with the introduction of antipsychotic drugs, with helping to cut the populations of inpatient mental hospitals by 67 percent between 1955 and 1980 (Bellack, Morrison, & Meuser, 1992). This type of operant conditioning is frequently used to treat children with severe disorders such as autism.

Response shaping through operant conditioning is also an effective tool in working with children who have behavior problems in the normal range for children. For example, suppose that a child tends to have tantrums in his school class. A behavior therapist might observe that the child initiates these tantrums when it appears he wants, but is not receiving, the teacher's attention. The therapist might prescribe that the teacher put the child in a small empty room for 3 or 4 minutes each time he begins to tantrum—in other words, to give the child a time-out. At the same time, the therapist might train the child to ask the teacher to come and look at his drawing or other accomplishment in an appropriate manner, rather than to tantrum. At first, the child may use these new communication skills poorly, but even a minor attempt at using them instead of tantruming would be rewarded by the teacher's attention. Over time, only completely appropriate communications with the teacher would be rewarded. This is a form of **social skills training,** which has been adapted to help people with a variety of problems in interacting and communicating with others.

Behavior therapies have proven effective for a wide range of emotional problems, especially anxiety, and behavior problems, particularly in children (Thorpe & Olson, 1997). Few therapists use only behavioral strategies, however. Many combine behavioral strategies with cognitive strategies, which we describe in the next section.

Cognitive Therapies

Cognitive therapies focus on challenging people's maladaptive interpretations of events or ways of thinking and replacing them with more adaptive ways of thinking. Cognitive therapists also help clients learn more effective problem-solving techniques to deal with the concrete problems in their lives.

A cognitive therapist might help a woman who feels neglected by her children by challenging her assumptions that her children are ignoring her on purpose.

One of the most widely used forms of cognitive therapy was developed by Aaron Beck (1976). There are many specific techniques in cognitive therapy (see *Concept Review:* Techniques in Cognitive Therapy, p. 152). They can be condensed into three main goals.

The first goal is to assist clients in identifying their irrational and maladaptive thoughts. People often do not recognize the negative thoughts that are swirling in their minds and affecting their emotions and behaviors. Cognitive therapists encourage clients to pay attention to the thoughts that are associated with their moods or with unwanted behaviors, to write these thoughts down, and to bring the thoughts into the therapy session.

The second goal is to teach clients to challenge their irrational or maladaptive thoughts and to consider alternative ways of thinking. Many of the specific techniques listed in the *Concept Review: Techniques in Cognitive Therapy* are designed to challenge clients' irrational thoughts. These techniques tend to be implemented through a Socratic method of asking questions that help clients come to insights about their thoughts on their own. For example, a therapist might ask, "What's the evidence for your perspective or interpretation of this situation?" Sometimes a client will have no evidence for his or her belief about a situation. For example, a man who feels that his wife may be seeing another man may have absolutely no evidence of this and just a nagging fear that it might happen. Other times, a client will have identified pieces of evidence for his or her perspective. For example, suppose an elderly woman believes that her children do not love her anymore. When asked for the evidence for this, she may state that her children do not call her or come to visit her often. In response to this, a therapist might ask the client how often her children do visit or call, to get a sense of the client's expectations.

If the client's children call at least once a week and visit her about once a month, the therapist might ask the second question: "Are there other ways of looking at this evidence or this situation?" Here the therapist is encouraging the client to think of alternative perspectives to her own. The elderly client in our example may answer, "Well, they are very busy, and they have children and lives of their own. Maybe they are calling me as often as they can." Of course, it is not always easy for a client to think of alternative viewpoints to her own. The therapist may have to suggest alternatives, by saying, for example, "What do your children do for a living? Do they have children of their own? How difficult do you think it would be for them to call you or visit you more often?" In her responses to these questions, the client might reveal that she believes that her children should find the time to visit and call her more often, even if they are extremely busy. The therapist might then ask the client once again to consider alternative viewpoints to her own. For example, the therapist might suggest that if the client wants to see her children more often, she call them or visit them rather than waiting for them to call and visit her.

The third question or set of questions the cognitive therapist might ask a client is, "What's the worst that could happen?" and "What could you do if the worst did happen?" The point of these questions is to get the client to face her worst fears about a situation and recognize ways she could cope with even her worst fears. The elderly client in our example may say that her worst fear is that her children truly do not need her or love her as much as they used to. The therapist will then help her explore ways of coping with this if it were true. For example, the client might ask her children if there is anything she needs to change about her behavior to improve their relationship. Or the client might accept that grown children do not need their mothers as much as when they were young and find other sources of gratification in her life.

CONCEPT REVIEW

Techniques in Cognitive Therapy

Cognitive therapists employ many different techniques to challenge clients' thinking.

Label	Description	Example
Challenge idiosyncratic meanings	Explore personal meaning attached to the client's words and ask the client to consider alternatives.	When a client says he will be "devastated" by his spouse leaving, ask just how he would be devastated and ways he could avoid being devastated.
Question the evidence	Systematically examine the evidence for the client's beliefs or assertions.	When a client says she can't live without her spouse, explore how she lived without the spouse before she was married.
Reattribution	Help the client distribute responsibility for events appropriately.	When a client says that her son's failure in school must be her fault, explore other possibilities, such as the quality of the school.
Examine options and alternatives	Help the client generate alternative actions to maladaptive ones.	If a client considers leaving school, explore whether tutoring or going part time to school are good alternatives.
Decatastrophize	Help the client evaluate whether he is overestimating the nature of a situation.	If a client states that failure in a course means he must give up the dream of medical school, question whether this is a necessary conclusion.
Fantasize consequences	Explore fantasies of a feared situation; if unrealistic, the client may recognize this; if realistic, work on effective coping strategies.	Help a client who fantasizes "falling apart" when asking the boss for a raise to role play the situation and develop effective skills for making the request.
Examine advantages and disadvantages	Examine advantages and disadvantages of an issue, to instill a broader perspective.	If a client says she "was just born depressed and will always be that way," explore the advantages and disadvantages of holding that perspective versus other perspectives.
Turn adversity to advantage	Explore ways that difficult situations can be transformed to opportunities.	If a client has just been laid off, explore whether this is an opportunity for him to return to school.
Guided association	Help the client see connections between different thoughts or ideas	Draw the connections between a client's anger at his wife for going on a business trip and his fear of being alone.
Scaling	Ask the client to rate her emotions or thoughts on scales to help gain perspective.	If a client says she was overwhelmed by an emotion, ask her to rate it on a scale from 0 (not at all present) to 100 (I fell down in a faint).
Thought stopping	Provide the client with ways of stopping a cascade of negative thoughts	Teach an anxious client to picture a stop sign or hear a bell when anxious thoughts begin to snowball.
Distraction	Help the client find benign or positive distractions to take attention away from negative thoughts or emotions temporarily.	Have a client count to 200 by 13s when he feels himself becoming anxious.
Labeling of distortions	Provide labels for specific types of distorted thinking to help the client gain more distance and perspective.	Have a client keep a record of the number of times per day she engages in all-or-nothing thinking—seeing things as all bad or all good.

Source: Freeman & Reinecke, 1995.

Behavioral Assignments

An important component of cognitive therapy is the use of **behavioral assignments** to help the client gather evidence concerning his or her beliefs, to test alternative viewpoints about a situation, and to try new methods of coping with different situations. These assignments are presented to the client as ways of testing hypotheses and gathering information that will be useful in therapy regardless of the outcome. The assignments can also involve trying out new skills, such as skills at communicating more effectively, between therapy sessions. Therapists also often use role plays during therapy sessions to elicit the client's reactions to feared situations and to help the client rehearse positive responses to the situation. For example, a therapist might engage our elderly client in a role-play in which the therapist plays the part of one of the client's children and the client rehearses how she might talk with her child about her concerns about their relationship. The following example illustrates how behavioral assignments can provide opportunities both to practice new skills and to gather information about thoughts that contribute to negative emotions:

CASE STUDY

A 29-year-old graduate student was unable to complete her degree because she feared meeting with a professor to discuss an incomplete grade she had received in a course. She was quite convinced that the professor would "scream at her" and had been unable to complete a homework assignment to call the professor's secretary to arrange a meeting. An in vivo task was agreed on in which she called the professor from her therapist's office. Her thoughts and feelings before, during and after the call were carefully examined. As might be expected, the professor was quite glad to hear from his former student and was pleased to accept her final paper. The origins of her beliefs about how others feel toward her were then reviewed and she was able to see that these beliefs were both maladaptive and erroneous. (Freeman & Reinecke, 1995, pp. 203–204)

The incorporation of behavioral strategies into cognitive therapy is one reason that many practitioners call it cognitive-behavioral therapy.

Taking Control

Cognitive therapists attempt to teach clients these skills so that clients can become their own therapists (Beck et al., 1979). Therapists try to get clients to take responsibility and control over their own thoughts and actions, rather than looking to the therapist to tell them what to do, or only reacting to external forces. By learning these strategies and gaining a sense of control over their thinking and emotions, clients not only can overcome current problems, but can handle new problems that arise more effectively.

Do cognitive therapists ever get around to exploring the "deeper" meanings of clients' emotions and irrational thoughts? Most cognitive therapists are not against exploring the origins of clients' negative ways of thinking in their earlier experiences in life. Most believe, however, that clients must first learn how to manage and control these thoughts and the emotions. Once clients have become effective at challenging their irrational thoughts and coping with negative emotions and difficult situations, cognitive therapists may then help them investigate the roots of these patterns.

Cognitive therapy is designed to be short term, on the order of 12 to 20 weeks in duration, with one to two sessions per week (Beck et al., 1979). It has been compared to drug therapies and somewhat to interpersonal therapy in the treatment of depression, anxiety, substance use problems, and eating disorders, and has been shown to be highly effective (Sacco & Beck, 1995). Although the founders of cognitive therapy have argued that it works by changing the content of people's negative beliefs and thoughts, Barber and DeRubeis (1989) have suggested that it works more by changing the process by which people think about situations in their lives. That is, people who undergo cognitive therapy may still have negative thoughts or beliefs in response to situations, but they learn through therapy not to assume these thoughts and beliefs are true, as they once assumed. They are then free to question their thoughts and beliefs and to consider alternative, more positive thoughts and beliefs.

Summing Up

- Psychodynamic therapies focus on uncovering unconscious motives and concerns behind psychopathology through free association and analysis of transferences and dreams.

- Humanistic or client-centered therapy attempts to help clients find their own answers to problems by supporting them and reflecting back these concerns so they can self-reflect and self-actualize.

- Behavioral therapies focus on the reinforcements and punishments people receive for maladaptive behavior, and altering these. Behavioral therapists also help clients learn new behavioral skills.

- Cognitive therapy focuses on the changing maladaptive cognitions behind distressing feelings and behaviors.

The goal of family therapy is to help families develop more healthy ways of interacting so that none of the family members suffers psychopathology.

⟳ SOCIOCULTURAL APPROACHES

Biologically based treatments focus on changing physical systems in the body and psychological treatments focus primarily on changing the ways people think and behave. The sociocultural approaches to treatment we discuss in this section view the individual as a part of a larger system of relationships, influenced by social forces and culture, and believe that this larger system must be addressed in therapy.

The treatments discussed in this section vary greatly in how broadly they reach beyond the individual into the social system in attempting to alleviate the individual's symptoms. Interpersonal therapists work primarily with individuals to help them understand their place in their social system and change their behaviors and roles in that social system. Family systems therapists insist that the whole family needs to be part of therapy because the dynamics that cause and maintain psychopathology rise from the family unit, not from the individual. Group therapies capitalize on the presence of other group members to help individuals learn to cope with their problems more effectively. The community mental-health movement was designed to be a wholistic approach to the treatment of mental disorders that involved the entire community in an individual's treatment. Cultural perspectives on treatment acknowledge the impact of cultural values and norms on people's experiences of mental disorders.

Interpersonal Therapy

As we noted in Chapter 2, **interpersonal therapy,** or **IPT**, emerged out of modern psychodynamic theories of psychopathology, which shifted their focus from the

unconscious conflicts of the individual to the client's pattern of relationships with important people in his or her life (Greenberg & Cheselka, 1995; Klerman et al., 1984; Markowitz & Weissman, 1995). IPT differs from psychodynamic therapies in that the therapist is much more structuring and directive in the therapy, offering interpretations much earlier and focusing on how to change current relationships. In addition, IPT is designed to be a short-term therapy, often lasting only about 12 weeks. The *Concept Review:* Comparisons of Interpersonal Therapy to Traditional Psychodynamic Therapy summarizes some of the key differences between IPT and more traditional psychodynamic therapies.

An example of the application of IPT and some of the differences between an IPT approach and a traditional psychodynamic approach comes in the following case study (adapted from Klerman et al., 1984, pp. 155–182):

CASE STUDY

Mrs. C. was an older woman whose husband died a year earlier after a long and painful illness. Mrs. C. had been extremely dependent on her husband prior to his illness, relying on him to lead their social life and manage all their finances. Over the course of his illness, Mrs. C. became resentful both that her husband was "abandoning her" by becoming incapacitated by his illness at a time they were supposed to be enjoying their retirement and that he was becoming a severe burden on her. Following his death, she still felt a great deal of anger toward him, but also a great deal of guilt for her anger. She came into therapy suffering from unshakable sadness, preoccupation with memories of her husband's death and her guilty feelings, problems in sleeping, and complete social withdrawal.

The IPT therapist began by reassuring Mrs. C. that her feelings were not unusual and telling her that the goal of therapy would be to help her confront all that she has

CONCEPT REVIEW

Comparisons of Interpersonal Therapy to Traditional Psychodynamic Therapy

Although interpersonal therapy has its roots in psychodynamic therapy, it differs in many ways.

Interpersonal Therapy	Traditional Psychodynamic Therapy
Explore what has contributed to this client's depression right now.	Explore why the client became what he or she is.
Determine the client's current stresses.	Determine what the client's childhood was like.
Determine who are the key persons involved in the current stress and what are the current disputes and disappointments.	Determine what is the client's character.
Evaluate whether the client is learning how to cope with the problem.	Evaluate whether the client is cured.
Evaluate what are the client's assets.	Evaluate what are the client's defenses.
Help the client ventilate painful emotions— talk about situations that evoke guilt, shame, resentment.	Find out why this client feels guilty, ashamed, or resentful.
Help the client clarify his or her wishes and have more satisfying relationships with others.	Understand the client's fantasy life and help him or her get insight into the origins of present behavior.

lost and learn to manage her new life better. Much of the therapy then focused on eliciting Mrs. C's feelings about her husband and her loss, helping her to clarify the reasons for these feelings and accept these feelings. At the end of the first session, the therapist said:

"One of the reasons why people sometimes have difficulty starting up again after losing a loved one is because it's been hard to really look the loss straight in the face, and to really think about what it means, and allow yourself to feel the painful feelings. I think one of the things we can do in therapy is to try to look at what's happened with you and your husband, to look at what he meant to you. . . . The other side of trying to look at what's happened with the loss of your husband is for us to look into the ways you can start enjoying life again. And it seems that in fact you've made a start as far as that kind of thing is concerned. However, it also seems that you have a number of long-term attitudes that to some extent you realize aren't realistic, such as the difference between the way things turn out and the way you anticipate them. Also, you have a lot of fears, that somehow people won't like you, that they're avoiding you or perhaps going to exploit you. We will spend some time trying to look at just what makes these things seem so powerful and likely to happen. Also we'll look at ways you can overcome these hesitations." (p. 159)

Like a psychodynamic therapist, the IPT therapist believed that Mrs. C.'s inability to accept the anger she felt against her husband caused her depression. The therapy focused on helping Mrs. C. express her guilt and anger. Unlike a psychodynamic therapist,

who would have focused on the roots of Mrs. C.'s relationship with her husband and feelings about that relationship in her early childhood, the IPT therapist was concerned primarily with Mrs. C.'s recent and current relationships. In addition, the IPT therapist was directive in gently but consistently urging Mrs. C. to increase her social contacts and her activities. The following interchange between the therapist and Mrs. C. illustrates how the therapist focuses on helping Mrs. C. express and clarify her feelings, but stays in the present (p. 172):

Mrs. C.: I like Christmas. I like decorating the house. So . . . I-I just, when my husband isn't there, I still will . . . decorate.

Therapist: It's still hard to think about doing things for yourself.

Mrs. C.: Well, I think that's where the guilt comes in, that he isn't here, you know. I get this pang of guilt, thinking, well, gee, you shouldn't be, you shouldn't be so happy about things.

Therapist: Because if you're enjoying things, that means you can't be thinking about him?

Mrs. C.: I think about him less and less, but I don't . . . suddenly, all of a sudden, when I'm doing something that I'm enjoying, the thought intrudes that, you know, you shouldn't be so happy (chuckles). I'm sure he wouldn't want me to be—sad. . . .

> **Therapist:** But in a way, hanging on to those sad thoughts . . . is a little like hanging on to him?
>
> **Mrs. C.:** Probably.

Because IPT is short term, it has been relatively easy for its proponents to test its effectiveness, and compare that effectiveness to a number of other treatments. IPT has been shown effective in the treatment of depression, anxiety, drug addiction, and eating disorders (Markowitz & Weissman, 1995). In addition, it appears as effective as drug treatments for most of these disorders.

Family Systems Therapy

Family systems theorists believe that an individual's problems are always rooted in interpersonal systems, particularly in the systems we call *families*. According to this viewpoint, you cannot help an individual without treating the entire family system that created and is maintaining the individual's problems. In fact, these theorists argue that the individual may not actually even have a problem but has become the "identified patient" in the family, carrying the responsibility or blame for the dysfunction of the family system.

Two of the most frequently used types of family systems therapy are Virginia Satir's Conjoint Family Therapy (1967) and Salvador Minuchin's Structural Family Therapy (1981). Satir's therapy focuses on the patterns and processes of communication between family members. The therapist identifies and points out dysfunctional communication patterns and teaches family members to communicate better by modeling for them effective communication and by teaching members to be clear and to refrain from inferring meaning.

Minuchin's Structural Family Therapy focuses more on the role each member of the family has come to play in the family system and on changing the structure and dynamics of the relationships among family members. The therapist attempts to "join" with the family, becoming a part of the family so as to exert influence over the processes by which family members interact. By questioning family members about their feelings about one another's behaviors and commenting on the behaviors and feelings of the members, the therapist attempts to bring the family dynamics into the open. What follows is an example of an interchange between Minuchin and a husband and wife with whom he was working (1981, adapted from pp. 35–36):

Voices

Husband: I think when something irritates me, it builds up and I hold it in until some little thing will trigger it, and then I'll be very, very critical and get angry. Then I'll tell her that I just don't understand why it has to be this way. But then I try to be very careful not to be unreasonable or too harsh because when I'm harsh, I feel guilty about it.

Minuchin: So, sometimes the family feels like a trap.

Husband: It's not the family so much; it's just—[indicates wife]

Minuchin [completing husband's gesture]: Your wife?

Husband [looking at wife]: No, not her either. It's just the things she doesn't do versus the things she does in terms of how she spends her time. Sometimes I think her priorities should be changed.

Minuchin: I think you are soft-pedaling.

Wife: About being trapped?

Minuchin: Yes, about being trapped. I think people sometimes get depressed when they are, like your husband, unable to be direct. He's not a straight talker. There's a tremendous amount of indirection in your family, because you are essentially very good people who are very concerned not to hurt one another. And you need to tell white lies a lot. . . .

Wife [to husband]: Am I indirect?

Husband: I don't really know. Sometimes you seem very direct, but I find myself wondering if you are telling me everything about what's bothering you. You know, if you seem upset, I'm not always sure that I know what's bugging you.

Wife: That I can be upset for something like that because it wouldn't upset you?

Husband: Maybe that's part of it.

Wife [smiling, but at the same time her eyes are watering]: Because you always seem to know better than I do what is really upsetting me, what my problem is at the moment.

Minuchin [to husband]: You see what's happening now? She's talking straight, but she's afraid that if she talks straight, you will be hurt, so she begins to cry and she begins to smile. So she's saying, "Don't take my straight talk seriously, because it is just the product of a person who is under stress." And that is the kind of thing you do to each other. So you cannot change too much. Because you don't tell each other in what direction to change.

The goal of the therapist is to challenge and disrupt the current dysfunctional dynamics of the family, so that the family is forced to change these dynamics, ideally toward more adaptive dynamics. Three primary strategies of family therapy are (1) to challenge the family's assumption that "the problem" lies in one member of the family rather than in the family dynamics, (2) to challenge dysfunctional family structures, such as those in which members of the family are overinvolved with each other and do not allow each other sufficient autonomy, and (3) to challenge the family's defensive conception of reality, such as in challenging the belief of two parents that there is nothing wrong with their daughter when she is suffering from a serious eating disorder.

Group Therapy

Most of the psychotherapies we have discussed in this chapter have been applied in **group therapy,** as well as in one-on-one interactions between a therapist and a client. Often, the members of the group will share a common experience, such as a history of sexual abuse, severe problems in social interactions, or the diagnosis of a life-threatening disease. Group therapy offers many potential benefits over individual therapy (see the *Concept Review:* Essential Elements of Group Therapy, p. 158). Irving Yalom (1985), an expert on group therapy, suggests that groups provide individuals with unique opportunities to view their problems from a broader perspective than their own, and to practice new attitudes and skills in a safe environment. Group therapy also is an efficient and cost-effective way for therapists to provide their services to larger numbers of clients. Many studies of group therapies for specific disorders have found these therapies to be effective, as we will discuss when we discuss their application to the specific disorders.

Many group therapy sessions are not led by professional therapists, however. **Self-help groups**—people who come together to deal with a common experience or need—often organize themselves without the help of mental-health professionals. These groups often subscribe to the perspective of Rogers' client-centered therapy that it does not necessarily take a professional to help people in self-exploration—what it really takes is a listening, caring person. In colleges, client-centered approaches are often taught in courses on *peer counseling,* in which students learn to counsel other college students. Client-centered therapy is considered appropriate for such situations because it does not require years of training for the counselor and is based on the premise that the counselor and client are equals.

Self-help groups are extremely popular, with as many as 15 million people in the United States alone attending these groups. One popular type of self-help group is the bereavement support group for people who have recently experienced a loss. The loss of a loved one can be an overwhelming experience, and grief can involve frightening symptoms, such as severe

Group therapy can provide helpful feedback to individual members and make them feel less alone.

problems in concentration, or the sense that the deceased loved one is present. Bereavement support groups provide a safe place for the expression of grief, education on grief, and validation of members' experiences of grief. Support groups can also help to decrease the isolation that many bereaved people feel. Group members may learn new coping strategies as they hear about how others have approached the tasks of mourning. Many people find bereavement support groups helpful, as this 65-year-old man who lost his wife describes (from Nolen-Hoeksema & Larson, 1999, p. 171):

Voices

I've been going to the support group they have once a week, for all the people who lost their loved ones—over a year now. With some other people, we sit around, you know, and everybody tells their problems. You feel then you're not the only one, that some other people are hurting, too.

CONCEPT REVIEW

Essential Elements of Group Therapy

These are some of the crucial elements to successful group therapy according to expert Irving Yalom (1985).

Element	Example
Provides information and advice for members	Bereavement groups help members understand "normal" symptoms of grief.
Provide examples of appropriate conduct	Members of a group focused on anger management learn from each other appropriate ways to express their anger.
Provides a safe place to take risks and accept criticism	An extremely shy group member feels safe enough in the group to speak up and express opinions.
Provides information that other people share the same problem	A person who is ashamed because she is periodically hospitalized for her mental disorder loses some of this shame by getting to know others who face the same problem.
Provides opportunities for growth and personal satisfaction by helping others	A member of Alcoholics Anonymous helps a new member integrate into the group, and gains new self-worth as a result.
Provides opportunities to express feelings and gain self-understanding	A member who has never talked about her rage over having a mental disorder is able to express this and be validated by others.
Provides opportunities to acquire and improve skills	A member who is learning to be assertive practices assertiveness skills with group members before trying them in the real world.

Evaluating the effectiveness of bereavement groups and other self-help groups has not been easy. These groups tend to be fluid, with members coming and going, getting different "dosages" of the group. The effectiveness of one of the most widespread and popular self-help groups, Alcoholics Anonymous, has recently been evaluated and it appears this form of self-help group therapy can be quite effective in the treatment of alcoholism (see Chapter 16).

Community Treatment

The **community mental-health movement** was officially launched in 1963 by President John Kennedy as a "bold new approach" to mental-health care. This movement attempted to provide coordinated mental-health services to people in community-based centers. Patients' rights advocates argued that mental patients could recover more fully or live more satisfying lives if they were integrated into the community, with the support of community-based treatment facilities—a process known as *deinstitutionalization.* Many of these patients would continue to need around-the-clock care, but it could be given in treatment centers based in neighborhoods, rather than in large, impersonal institutions. Let's take a look at some of these community treatment centers.

Community Treatment Centers

Community mental-health centers are intended to provide mental-health care based in the community, often from teams of social workers, therapists, and physicians who coordinate care. **Halfway houses** offer people with long-term mental-health problems the opportunity to live in a structured, supportive environment while they are trying to reestablish a job and ties to family and friends. **Day treatment centers** allow people to obtain treatment all day, as well as occupational and rehabilitative therapies, but to live at home at night. People who have acute problems that require hospitalization may go to inpatient wards of general hospitals or specialized psychiatric hospitals. Sometimes, their first contact with a mental-health professional is in the emergency room of a hospital. Once their acute problems have subsided, however, they often are released back to their community treatment center, rather than remaining for the long term in a psychiatric hospital.

Deinstitutionalization was successful in getting patients out of psychiatric hospitals. The number of patients in large state psychiatric hospitals decreased by 75 percent over the decade after the movement was launched (Kiesler & Sibulkin, 1987). Unfortunately, the resources to care for all the mental patients released from institutions were never adequate. There were not enough halfway houses built or community mental-health centers funded to serve the thousands of men and women who were formerly institutionalized or who would have been if the movement had not happened. Instead, these men and women began living in nursing homes or other types of group homes, where they received little mental-health treatment, or with their families, who were often ill-equipped to handle serious mental illness (Bachrach, 1987). Some of these people began living on the streets.

The mental-health care system in the United States is undergoing another revolution at the turn of the twenty-first century (Torrey, 1997). Mental-health services are expensive, because mental-health problems are sometimes chronic and mental-health treatment can take a long time. Many people are not insured at all, and those who have insurance often find that their mental-health coverage is limited or nonexistent (Seligman, 1995). People with long-term severe mental disorders, such as schizophrenia, often exhaust all sources of funding for their mental-health care and many end up homeless or incarcerated for crimes they committed while not being treated. Although about 60 percent of people with a severe mental illness receive some sort of care, that leaves about 40 percent who receive no care (Narrow et al., 1993; Torrey, 1997). Sometimes people refuse care that might help them. But other times, they fall through the medical safety net because of bureaucratic rules designed to shift the burden of the cost of mental-health care from one agency to another, as in the case of Rebecca J. (Torrey, 1997, pp. 105–106):

CASE STUDY

Because of severe schizoaffective disorder, Rebecca J., age 56, had spent 25 years in a New York State psychiatric hospital. She lived in a group home in the community but required rehospitalization for several weeks approximately once a year when she relapsed despite taking medications. As a result of the reduction in state hospital beds (for people with mental disorders) and attempts by the state to shift readmissions for fiscal reasons, these rehospitalizations increasingly took place on the psychiatric wards of general hospitals that varied widely in quality. In 1994, she was admitted to a new hospital because the general hospital where she usually went was full. The new hospital was inadequately staffed to provide care for patients as sick as Rebecca J. In addition, the psychiatrist was poorly trained and had access to only a small fraction of Rebecca J.'s complex and voluminous past history. During her 6-week hospitalization, Rebecca J. lost 10 pounds because the nursing staff did not help her eat, had virtually all her clothing and personal effects lost or stolen, became toxic from her lithium medication, which was not noticed until she was semicomatose, and was prematurely discharged while she was still so psychotic that she

had to be rehospitalized in another hospital less than 24 hours later. Meanwhile, less than a mile away in the state psychiatric hospital where she had spent many years, a bed sat empty on a ward with nursing staff and a psychiatrist who knew her case well and with her case records readily available in a file cabinet.

As we discuss the research showing the effectiveness of various treatments for specific disorders throughout the remainder of the book, it is important to keep in mind that those treatments can only work if people have access to them. A critical question for society in the twenty-first century is whether we will ensure that the people who could benefit from the treatments we have worked so hard to develop will ever get access to these treatments.

Community Prevention Programs

Obviously, it would be better to prevent people from developing psychopathology in the first place, rather than waiting to treat it once it has developed. This is known as **primary prevention**—stopping the development of disorders before they start. Some primary prevention strategies for reducing drug abuse and delinquency might include changing some of the neighborhood characteristics that seem to contribute to delinquency or drug use. Education is a big part of primary prevention. For example, researchers in the Stanford Heart Disease Program educated townspeople through the local media about how they could reduce their risk of cardiovascular disease (for example, by stopping smoking and reducing fat in their diets). This led to measurable decreases in blood pressure and cholesterol in the townspeople (Maccoby & Altman, 1988).

Secondary prevention is focused on catching disorders in their earliest stages and providing treatment designed to reduce their development. Secondary prevention usually focuses on people at high risk for the disorder. For example, one highly successful study targeted people in low-income minority groups who were suffering from physical ailments (Munoz, 1997; Munoz, Mrazek, & Haggerty, 1996). People in these groups also are at high risk for serious depression. This program provided cognitive-behavioral therapy to people in these groups, teaching them strategies for overcoming or preventing symptoms of depression. It also helped them learn skills for coping more effectively with their physical illnesses, and for dealing with medical professionals. The people who went through this program were less likely to develop serious depression over the year they were followed than a control group of people who did not go through the program. The program participants were also physically healthier at the end of their follow-up year.

Cross-Cultural Issues in Treatment

There are a number of assumptions or values inherent in the psychological therapies we discussed earlier in this chapter that can clash with the values and norms of cultures different from the Western cultures that created those psychotherapies (Sue et al., 1998; Sue & Sue, 1999). First, most psychotherapies are focused on the individual—the individual's unconscious conflicts, dysfunctional ways of thinking, maladaptive behavior patterns, and so on. In contrast, many cultures focus on the group or collective rather than the individual (Markus & Kitayama, 1998). The identity of the individual is not seen apart from the groups to which that individual belongs—his or her family, community, ethnic group. Therapists who fail to recognize this when working with clients from collectivist cultures may make recommendations that are useless or perhaps even harmful, leading to conflicts between clients and important groups in the clients' lives that clients cannot handle.

Second, most psychotherapies value the expression of emotions and disclosure of personal concerns, whereas restraint of emotions and personal concerns is valued in many cultures, such as Japanese culture (Sue & Sue, 1999). Some counselors may see this restraint as a problem and try to encourage clients to become more expressive. Again, however, this can clash badly with the self-concepts of clients and with the expectations that important people have in their lives for their behavior.

Third, in many psychotherapies, clients are expected to take the initiative in communicating their concerns and desires to the therapist, and in generating ideas for what is causing their symptoms and what changes they might want to make. These expectations can clash with cultural norms that require deference to people in authority (Sue & Sue, 1999). A client from a culture in which you only speak when spoken to, and you never challenge an elder or authority figure, may be extremely uncomfortable with a therapist who does not tell the client what is wrong and how to fix it in a very direct manner. In addition, many clients who are in ethnic minority groups may also be in lower socioeconomic groups, whereas their therapists are likely to be in middle- or upper-class socioeconomic groups. This can create tensions due to class differences as well as cultural differences.

Some studies suggest that people from Latino, Asian, and Native American cultures are more comfortable with structured and action-oriented therapies, such as behavior and cognitive-behavior therapies, than with the less structured therapies (see Aponte, Rivers, & Wohl, 1995; Atkinson & Hackett, 1998). The specific form of therapy may not matter so much as the cultural sensitivity the therapist shows the client, whatever therapy is being used (Atkinson & Hackett, 1998). Sue and Zane (1987, pp. 42–43) give the following example of the importance of cultural sensitivity in the interaction between a client and a therapist. First, they describe the problems the client faced, and second, they describe how the therapist (one of the authors) responded to these problems:

CASE STUDY

At the advice of a close friend, Mae C. decided to seek services at a mental health center. She was extremely distraught and tearful as she related her dilemma. An immigrant from Hong Kong several years ago, Mae met and married her husband (also a recent immigrant from Hong Kong). Their marriage was apparently going fairly well until six months ago when her husband succeeded in bringing over his parents from Hong Kong. While not enthusiastic about having her parents-in-law live with her, Mae realized that her husband wanted them and that both she and her husband were obligated to help their parents (her own parents were still in Hong Kong).

After the parents arrived, Mae found that she was expected to serve them. For example, the mother-in-law would expect Mae to cook and serve dinner, to wash all the clothes, and to do other chores. At the same time, she would constantly complain that Mae did not cook the dinner right, that the house was always messy, and that Mae should wash certain clothes separately. The parents-in-law also displaced Mae and her husband from the master bedroom. The guest room was located in the basement, and the parents refused to sleep in the basement because it reminded them of a tomb.

Mae would occasionally complain to her husband about his parents. The husband would excuse his parents' demands by indicating "They are my parents and they're getting old." In general, he avoided any potential conflict; if he took sides, he supported his parents. Although Mae realized that she had an obligation to his parents, the situation was becoming intolerable to her.

I (the therapist) indicated (to Mae) that conflicts with in-laws were very common, especially for Chinese, who are obligated to take care of their parents. I attempted to normalize the problems because she was suffering from a great deal of guilt over her perceived failure to be the perfect daughter-in-law. I also conveyed my belief that in therapy we could try to generate new ideas to resolve the problem—ideas that did not simply involve extreme courses of action such as divorce or total submission to the in-laws (which she believed were the only options).

I discussed Mae during a case conference with other mental health personnel. It is interesting that many suggestions were generated: Teach Mae how to confront her parents-in-law; have her invite the husband for marital counseling so that husband and wife could form a team in negotiation with his parents; conduct extended family therapy so that Mae, her husband, and her in-laws could agree on contractual give-and-take relationships. The staff agreed that working solely with Mae would not change the situation. However, these options entailed extreme response costs. Confronting her in-laws was discrepant with her role of daughter-in-law, and she felt very uncomfortable in asserting herself in the situation. Trying to involve her husband or in-laws in treatment was ill-advised. Her husband did not want to confront his parents. More important, Mae was extremely fearful that her family might find out that she had sought psychotherapy. Her husband as well as her in-laws would be appalled at her disclosure of family problems to a therapist who was an outsider. . . .

How could Mae's case be handled? During the case conference, we discussed the ways that Chinese handle interpersonal family conflicts which are not unusual to see. Chinese often use third-party intermediaries to resolve conflicts. The intermediaries obviously have to be credible and influential with the conflicting parties.

At the next session with Mae, I asked her to list the persons who might act as intermediaries, so that we could discuss the suitability of having someone else intervene. Almost immediately, Mae mentioned her uncle (the older brother of the mother-in-law) whom she described as being quite understanding and sensitive. We discussed what she should say to the uncle. After calling her uncle, who lived about 50 miles from Mae, she reported that he wanted to visit them. The uncle apparently realized the gravity of the situation and offered to help. He came for dinner, and Mae told me that she overheard a discussion between the uncle and Mae's mother-in-law. Essentially, he told her that Mae looked unhappy, that possibly she was working too hard, and that she needed a little more praise for the work that she was doing in taking care of everyone. The mother-in-law expressed surprise over Mae's unhappiness and agreed that Mae was doing a fine job. Without directly confronting each other, the uncle and his younger sister understood the subtle messages each conveyed. Older brother was saying that something was wrong and younger sister acknowledged it. After this interaction, Mae reported that her mother-in-law's criticisms did noticeably diminish and that she had even begun to help Mae with the chores.

If Mae's therapist had not been sensitive to Mae's cultural beliefs about her role as a daughter-in-law and had suggested some of the solutions put forward by his colleagues in the case conference, Mae may have even dropped out of therapy. People from ethnic minority groups in the United States are much more likely than European Americans to drop out of psychosocial therapy (Atkinson & Hackett, 1998). Ethnic minority clients often find the suggestions of therapists strange, unhelpful, and even insulting. Because Mae's therapist was willing to work within the constraints of her cultural beliefs, he and Mae found a solution to her situation that was acceptable to her.

Therapists use play to elicit children's concerns and help children work through these concerns.

In treating children, cultural norms about child-rearing practices and the proper role of doctors can make it difficult to include the family in a child's treatment (Rivers & Morrow, 1995; Tharp, 1991). For example, a study of behavior therapy for children found that Hong Kong Chinese parents were very reluctant to be trained to engage in behavioral techniques, such as responding with praise or ignoring certain behaviors. Such techniques violated the parents' views of appropriate child-rearing practices and their expectations that the therapist should be the person "curing" the child.

However, several clinicians argue that family-based therapies are more appropriate than individual therapy in cultures that are highly family-oriented, including Native American, Hispanic, African American, and Asian American cultures (Tharp, 1991). In the treatment of Latin American children and their families, Vazquez-Nuttal, Avila-Vivas, and Morales-Barreto (1984) argued that the therapist should help the family reinforce the importance of ethnic and family values and explore the conflicts between these values and those of mainstream American culture that could be contributing to the psychological problems a child or family is experiencing. One therapeutic program, the Homebuilders Program, takes the further step of placing the therapist in the home of the troubled child and family, so that therapy is delivered completely in the context of the family and community (Kinney, Haapala, & Booth, 1991). Most of the children in this program are at risk for being placed in foster care because of the severity of their problems or the family's dysfunctions. This program has proven effective for children in many ethnic groups, but African American and Hispanic children and families have seemed to benefit from this approach even more than have European American children and families (Fraser, Pecora, & Haapala, 1991).

Matching Therapist and Client

Must a therapist come from the same culture as the client to fully understand the client? Cultural sensitivity can probably be acquired through training and experience to a large degree (D'Andrea & Daniels, 1995; Sue et al., 1998). In fact, just because a therapist is from the same ethnic or racial group as the client does not mean that therapist and client share the same value system (Sue & Sue, 1990). For example, a fourth-generation Japanese American who has fully adopted American competitive and individualistic values may clash with a recent immigrant from Japan who ascribes to the self-sacrificing, community-oriented values of Japanese culture. These value differences among people of the same ethnic/racial group may explain why studies show that matching the ethnicity, race, or gender of the therapist and client does not necessarily lead to a better outcome for the client (Atkinson & Hackett, 1998).

Several studies have found that African American, American Indian, Asian American, Mexican American, and White clients are more likely to remain in treatment and may benefit more from treatment if they are matched with a therapist of their own ethnicity (see Sue, 1998). There are large individual differences in these preferences, however (Atkinson & Hackett, 1998; Pomales, Claiborn, & LaFromboise, 1986; Sue & Sue, 1999). Although some clients care deeply about having a therapist of the same ethnic group or gender, some only trust a therapist who corresponds to their stereotype of a "doctor," and some have no preferences regarding the ethnicity or gender of their therapist. For clients who wish to be matched with therapists of the same ethnic or gender group, this matching may be necessary for a client to trust the therapist and have faith in the therapy (Sue, 1998). As we discuss shortly, the relationship between a client and therapist, and a client's beliefs about the likely effectiveness of a therapy, contribute strongly to a client's full engagement in the therapy and the effectiveness of the therapy.

Because it is still true that most therapists are White, people from other ethnic groups may have difficulty finding a therapist from their group. The American Psychological Association has published guidelines for mental-health professionals who provide services to culturally diverse populations on competent and ethical treatment. In addition, many training programs for mental-health professionals now emphasize cultural competence (see Atkinson & Hackett, 1998; Sue et al., 1998).

As for gender, there is little evidence that women or men do better in therapy with a therapist of their same gender (Beutler, Crago, & Arizmendi, 1986; Garfield, 1994). In the largest study of the treatment of depression, for example, clients who were matched with a therapist of their gender did not recover more quickly or fully than clients who were matched with a therapist of the other gender (Zlotnick, Elkin, & Shea, 1998). This was true whether the client received cognitive-behavioral therapy, interpersonal therapy, or drug therapy.

Women and men do tend to report that they prefer a therapist of the same gender, however (Simons & Helms, 1976; Garfield, 1994). Again, because the client's comfort with a therapist is an important contributor to a client's seeking therapy and remaining in therapy for an entire course, gender matching may still be important in therapy.

Culturally Specific Therapies

Our review of the relationships between culture and gender and therapy has focused on the forms of therapy most often practiced in modern industrialized cultures, such as psychodynamic, behavioral, and cognitive therapies. Cultural groups, even within modern industrialized countries, often have their own forms of therapy for distressed people, however (Koss-Chioino, 1995). Let us examine two of these.

Several cultures have healing rituals that have been part of their cultural traditions for generations.

Native American Indian healing processes simultaneously focus on the physiology, psychology, and religious practices of the individual (LaFromboise, Trimble, & Mohatt, 1998). "Clients" are encouraged to transcend the self and experience the self as embedded in the community and as an expression of the community. Family and friends are brought together with the individual in traditional ceremonies involving prayers, songs, and dances that emphasize Native American cultural heritage and the reintegration of the individual into the cultural network. These ceremonies may be supplemented by a variety of herbal medicines used for hundreds of years to treat people with physical and psychological symptoms.

Hispanics in the southwestern United States and in Mexico suffering from psychological problems may consult folk healers, known as *curanderos* or *curanderas* (Koss-Chioino, 1995; Martinez, 1993; Rivera, 1988). One survey of urban Hispanic American women in Colorado found that 20 percent had consulted a curandero for treatment (Rivera, 1988). Curanderos use religiously based rituals to overcome the folk illnesses believed to cause psychological and physical problems. These illnesses may be the result of hexes placed on the individual or of soul loss or magical fright. These healing rituals include prayers, use of holy palm, and incantations. Curanderos may also apply healing ointments or oils and prescribe herbal medicines.

Native Americans and Hispanics often seek both folk healers and psychiatric care from mental-health professionals practicing the therapies described earlier in this chapter. Mental-health professionals need to be aware of the practices and beliefs of folk healing when treating clients from these cultural groups and of the possibility that clients will combine these different forms of therapy, following some of the recommendations of both types of healers.

Summing Up

- Interpersonal therapy is a short-term therapy that focuses on clients' current relationships and concerns, but explores the roots of their problems in past relationships.

- Family systems therapists focus on changing maladaptive patterns of behavior within family systems to reduce psychopathology in individual members.

- In group therapy, people who share a problem come together to support each other, learn from each other, and practice new skills. Self-help groups are a form of group therapy that do not involve a mental-health professional.

- The community mental-health movement was aimed at deinstitutionalizing people with mental disorders, and treating them through community mental-health centers, halfway houses, and day treatment centers. The resources for these community treatment centers have never been adequate, however, and many people do not have access to mental-health care.

- Primary prevention programs aim to stop the development of disorders before they start.

- Secondary prevention programs provide treatment to people in the early stages of their disorders in hope of reducing the development of the disorders.

- Values inherent in most psychotherapies that can clash with the values of certain cultures include the focus on the individual, the expression of emotions and disclosure of personal concerns, and the expectation that clients take initiative.

- People from minority groups may be more likely to remain in treatment if matched with a therapist from their own cultural group, but there are large individual differences in these preferences.

- There are a number of culturally specific therapies designed by cultural groups to address psychopathology within the traditions of that culture.

☉ EVALUATING TREATMENTS

In 1952, well-known British psychologist Hans Eysenck stunned the field when he reviewed studies evaluating the effectiveness of psychotherapy and concluded that psychotherapy did not work. People who had received psychotherapy apparently fared no better than people who were untreated or who were placed on a waiting list.

The number and quality of studies evaluating psychotherapies prior to 1952 was limited, however. Not surprisingly, Eysenck's review prompted a great deal of new research. Several reviews of this research over the last four to five decades have concluded that psychotherapy does indeed have positive effects, and is better than no treatment at all or than various placebos (Lambert & Bergin, 1994; Luborsky, Singer, & Luborsky, 1975; Smith, Glass, & Miller, 1980; Wampold et al., 1997). Are some psychotherapies clearly better than others? Some reviews have concluded the answer is "no" (see Wampold et al., 1997). Rosenweig (1936) called this the **Dodo bird verdict**—"Everybody has won and all must have prizes"—quoting from the Dodo bird *in Alice in Wonderland*. Other reviews suggest that some therapies are better than others, at least

VIEWPOINTS

Determining Winners in Therapy Outcome Research

In Chapter 3, we discussed some of the difficulties in conducting good research comparing one therapy to another or to control groups. For example, it is difficult to define an appropriate "no treatment" control group, because even completely unstructured, nondirective interactions with a therapist should result in positive change in clients according to some theories. Another problem is in defining the appropriate samples of clients to study. Ideally, you might like to study only people who meet DSM-IV criteria for a specific disorder, such as depression, but who do not meet criteria for any other disorder. In the real world, however, over half of all depressed people do qualify for another diagnosis (Kessler et al., 1994). Thus, it is not clear that a "purely depressed" group represents even the majority of depressed people.

Similarly, treatment delivered in the rarefied setting of a research study may not resemble how that treatment is delivered in the real world (Chambless & Hollon, 1998; Crits-Christoph, 1997). In research, the therapists are highly trained by a group of experts and monitored to ensure that they deliver the purest form of the therapy possible as consistently as possible. In the real world, therapists vary in their training in specific techniques, and often take techniques from various theoretical approaches in treating the same client.

An extremely important problem in therapy outcome research is in defining what a good outcome is (Hollon, 1996). Should we require that, at the end of the study, clients show absolutely no signs of the disorder in order to consider their treatment effective? Or do we want simply to show that they improved significantly over the course of treatment? Who gets to evaluate whether a client still is suffering from the disorder? We might want to rely on the client's self-report of symptoms, particularly for those symptoms that are private to the client, such as feelings of sadness. In a novel study of the effectiveness of treatment, the magazine *Consumer Reports* simply asked its readers who had received any kind of treatment for a psychological problem whether it had helped or not (*Consumer Reports,* 1995; Seligman, 1995). Of those who

The "Dodo bird effect" in psychotherapy outcome research is when all types of psychotherapy seem to have similar outcomes.

for some disorders (Crits-Christoph, 1997; Dobson, 1989; Engels, Garnefski, & Diekstra, 1993; Lambert & Bergin, 1994; Shadish et al., 1993; Smith et al., 1980).

In *Viewpoints:* Determining Winners in Therapy Outcome Research, we discuss the difficulties researchers have had in answering the question "Does therapy work?" We also discuss a novel study that simply asked consumers of therapy to answer the question for themselves.

Common Components of Successful Therapies

Some theorists argue that one psychotherapy is unlikely to win over another in therapy outcome studies, because all psychotherapies share certain components that make them successful. This may seem an outrageous idea—on the surface, the different types of

Continued

said they were feeling very poor when they began therapy, 54 percent said treatment made things a lot better, and another one-third answered that it made things somewhat better (see Figure 5.4; Seligman, 1995).

Yet, self-reports can be biased by denial, exaggeration, lack of insight, and response biases. We might want to rely on the therapist's report of the client's symptoms, but obviously the therapist can be biased by his or her desire to have had a positive effect on the client. We could conduct structured interviews with the client, but again we are relying mostly on the client's answers to the questions in the interview to evaluate his or her symptoms.

Many of the disagreements between studies of the effectiveness of different treatments for psychological disorders come from differences in how these studies have defined the outcomes they are looking for, the types of clients the studies have recruited, and the implementation of the treatments themselves (see Norcross, 1997). Throughout this book, as we discuss the effectiveness of different treatments for individual disorders, we will keep some of these issues in mind. For better or worse, the competition between proponents of different treatments is getting fiercer, because managed care providers and insurance companies are increasingly turning to research to determine the most effective and cost-efficient means of treatment (Hollon, 1996).

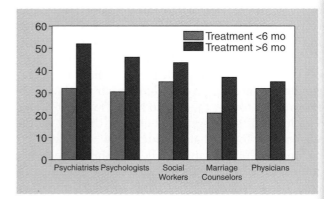

FIGURE 5.4 Percent of People Who Reported that Treatment "Made Things a Lot Better" in a Study by *Consumer Reports* (1995). A novel study by the magazine *Consumer Reports* simply asked people who had received some treatment for psychological symptoms whether it had been helpful or not.

Source: Seligman, 1995, Figure 2, p. 970.

---

therapy described in this chapter may seem radically different. Indeed, proponents of a given approach have often been loud in their opposition to other approaches, decrying these other approaches as useless or even harmful to clients. There is increasing evidence, however, that there are some common components to successful therapies, even when the specific techniques of the therapies differ greatly (see *Concept Review:* Common Components of Successful Therapies).

The first of these is a *positive relationship* with the therapist (Crits-Cristoph et al., 1991). Clients who trust their therapists and believe that the therapists understand them are more willing to reveal important information, engage in homework assignments, and try out new skills or coping techniques that the therapists suggest. In addition, simply having a positive relationship with a caring and understanding human being goes a long way toward helping people overcome distress and change their behaviors.

CONCEPT REVIEW

Common Components of Successful Therapies

All successful therapies may share certain components that contribute to their success.

Component	Result
Positive relationship with therapist	Affirmation and safety to explore difficult issues or make difficult changes
Explanation for symptoms	Insight into symptoms and a a plan for how to alleviate them
Confrontation of negative emotions	Habituation to emotions and/or catharsis

Second, all therapies provide clients with an *explanation or interpretation* of why they are suffering (Garfield, 1992). Simply having a label for painful symptoms and an explanation for those symptoms seems to help many people feel better, much like having a diagnosis for a physical ailment can bring relief. This may suggest that "insight" provides relief. In addition, however, the explanations that therapies provide for symptoms are usually accompanied by a set of recommendations for how to overcome those symptoms. Following these recommendations may provide the main relief from the symptoms.

In any case, it seems clear that a client has to believe the explanation given to him or her for the symptoms in order for the therapy to help (Frank, 1978). For example, studies of cognitive-behavior therapy for depression have found that the extent to which clients believe and accept the rationale behind this therapy is a significant predictor of the effectiveness of the therapy (Fennell & Teasdale, 1987). Clients to whom the rationale behind cognitive therapy makes sense engage more actively in therapy and are less depressed after a course of therapy than are those who don't "buy" the rationale for the therapy from the outset. A major problem in drug therapies is the high dropout rate from these therapies. Often people drop out because they do not experience quick enough relief from the drugs and therefore believe the drugs will not work or because they feel they need to talk about problems to overcome them.

A number of other common components across psychotherapies have been suggested (Beitman, 1992; Frank, 1978; Garfield, 1992; Prochaska, 1995). For example, most therapies encourage clients to confront painful emotions and have techniques for helping them become less sensitive to these emotions. In behavior therapy, systematic desensitization or flooding might be used. In psychodynamic therapy, interpretation of transference and encouraging catharsis might be used. Whatever technique is used, the goal is to help the client stop denying, avoiding, or repressing the painful emotions and become able to accept and experience the emotions without being debilitated by them.

Many theorists have argued for integration of the different psychotherapies, and now psychotherapy and biologically based therapies (Norcross & Goldfried, 1992; Prochaska, 1995; Trierweiler & Stricker, 1998). Although it may be difficult to integrate the theories behind the therapies because these theories disagree too profoundly on the causes of psychopathology, it may be possible to integrate the techniques of the therapies into a group of strategies that are used as the therapist sees fit. Indeed, therapists commonly see themselves as eclectics—using the techniques of different therapies depending on the specific issues needing to be addressed (Norcross, 1997). For example, a psychologist might use behavioral techniques for treating phobias but more psychodynamic techniques for treating people who have chronic moderate anxiety. In addition, team approaches to treatment are becoming increasingly common. A psychologist may provide psychotherapy to clients but a psychiatrist is available to prescribe medications if they are warranted.

A team approach to treatment is especially important for people with chronic mental disorders that can be debilitating, such as schizophrenia. As we discuss in Chapter 10, people with schizophrenia often need drug therapies, psychotherapy that helps them cope with their illnesses, and community-oriented interventions that help them find jobs and housing and reintegrate into society. Unfortunately, many people with chronic disorders do not have access to this kind of team treatment. *Extraordinary People:* The Inside Story on Coping with Schizophrenia highlights a remarkable young woman who has built her own integrated approach to treatment to cope with schizophrenia.

Summing Up

- Some reviews of studies of the effectiveness of psychosocial treatments find they are all equally effective and others suggest that certain treatments are more effective than others in the treatment of specific disorders.

- Methodological and ethical problems make doing good research on the effectiveness of therapy difficult.

- Most therapies involve a positive relationship between a therapist and client, provide an explanation or interpretation to the client, and encourage clients to confront painful emotions.

- Many therapists are eclectic, combining different techniques from various therapeutic approaches.

☯ SPECIAL ISSUES IN TREATING CHILDREN

Every therapy we have described has probably been used at one time or another to treat children and adolescents with psychological disorders. Studies of the effectiveness of psychological, social, and biological therapies generally show that children and adolescents receiving therapy have better outcomes than those receiving no therapy (Weisz et al., 1995). The effectiveness of any specific type of therapy may depend largely on the type of disorder the child or adolescent has.

EXTRAORDINARY PEOPLE

The Inside Story on Coping with Schizophrenia

I t is perhaps easy in reading about the major breakthroughs in biological treatments for serious psychological disorders to believe that the application of these treatments is rather straightforward. All one has to do is to diagnose the disorder accurately, determine the correct dosage of the proper medication, and monitor for side effects.

Unfortunately, it is not that easy. Even people who are going to respond eventually to a medication must often try different types of drugs at different dosage levels before they find one that provides them with relief from symptoms without inducing intolerable side effects. In the meantime, they must try to keep their lives going as well as possible. The following personal account of a young woman with schizophrenia details how complicated, long, and painful a process finding medications that work often is. It also describes how medications and psychotherapy are used together in comprehensive approaches to treatment. This young woman is in school learning to be a pharmacist (Anonymous, 1983, pp. 152–155).

In lectures on antipsychotic drugs I want to tell the faculty and fellow students what it feels like to take these medicines and have to depend on them to function "outside" and what it is like to be titrated as an individual to the proper medication and dosage and the problems involved. I want to talk about schizophrenia and let them know it is not so far removed from them and correct some of the common misconceptions held about people who have schizophrenia.

Let me explain some of the major problems and pressures that schizophrenia has presented to me in getting through pharmacy school.

During my first semester of pharmacy school I was on 2 mg of Haldol (haloperidol) and 2 mg of Cogentin (benztropine, an anticholinergic drug used to reduce such side effects of antipsychotic drugs, such as speech slurring, rigid neck muscles, and fixed gaze) h.s. (at bedtime) as prescribed for me after hospitalization the summer before entry to school. My condition improved psychologically and I seemed to

be in remission until I entered school. I found I could neither read the board nor my notes; everything was blurred no matter where I sat. I called the psychiatrist who had prescribed the drugs and remembered his suggesting that I should take 2 more mg of Cogentin. (It is not clear whether the psychiatrist misunderstood my reason for calling or whether I misunderstood his advice about Cogentin. However, I later learned that Cogentin makes blurred vision worse, not better.) I complied and the next few days I not only had blurry vision, but I could not even see the lines on my notebook paper nor my writing—it was all one blur. In fact, the paper looked colorless. After 2 to 3 days of this, I called the physician back and told him I just could not take this medicine anymore, because I could not read or see with it. I could not even tell if I was taking notes on the lines. This side effect, he said, was as he expected; his recommendation now was to drop down to only 2 mg of Cogentin and switch from Haldol to Stelazine (trifluoperazine) 6 mg every day h.s.

This was a compromise solution because, although I could now read and write, my schizophrenia was not so well-controlled. I wanted to drop out of school 3 weeks into the semester; I was afraid to go outside and felt as though I did not belong in pharmacy school or would not be able to overcome the stresses to be faced there. Fellow students were remarking to me that I seemed to be more impatient, hyperactive, and depressed. I also had problems with what a friend of mine called "the Stelazine stroll"—akathesia (restlessness). I continued to go out of the city once a week to see my psychologist, who helped me with aspects of the pressures I could not face alone or with only the drugs. . . .

In my first semester of my second year . . . I had just restarted Stelazine (after going off it by myself) at 8 mg h.s., an increased dose, and began having what I thought were seizures. In my classes I experienced an aura and then a wave hit me. I felt overstimulated and could hear a lecture but not process the information and take notes. My hand tremor

Continued

was so bad during these episodes that I could not write. My psychologist suggested a consultation with the psychiatrist who had supervised my previous hospitalizations and prescribed the medications.

Although the psychiatrist was hesitant to give me the label for what was happening, I insisted, and he said it was "transient psychotic episodes." The problem with this development was that it began after I had already been taking an increased amount of the medication. Where could we go from here? The psychiatrist recommended titration, increasing the dose of Stelazine. However, it didn't work. He then suggested taking Stelazine along with another antipsychotic drug with more milligram potency (Navane [thiothixene] 5 mg h.s.), but I was still having acute psychotic episodes in my classes. I had taken to sitting in the back of the classroom, although I could not see the board, because I needed to be able to leave the room when this occurred, at the suggestion of the psychiatrist that I not sit there and suffer through it. I had explained away my change in seating to the other students by saying I felt I was going to have a seizure or by joking and saying I had decided I didn't care to see what teachers were writing on the board anymore.

When I got up in the morning, I could predict that the episodes would occur and where—I had a prodrome (a premonitory symptom). There were many frantic long distance calls to my psychologist after these episodes. I had to tell someone who could help me with what was happening to me. I, at this point, felt scared enough that never again would I have a compliance problem. I didn't want to lose all I had worked for in pharmacy school. I noticed the episodes were worse when emotionally volatile material was discussed in classes, such as antipsychotic agents, characteristics of schizophrenia, depression—all problems I had to cope with daily and that remained unresolved for me. . . .

As a consequence of the psychotic episodes and occasionally having to leave the classroom, I missed a lot of notes in my classes. All this work had to be made up. This increased the pressure I was under, which in turn worsened the schizophrenic symptoms and almost forced me into hospitalization. I did

not want to drop out of school or receive too many incomplete grades, which would have been the result of 4 to 8 weeks of hospitalization to get properly titrated on the medication and to decrease disease symptoms. However, most of my instructors had rigid rules about missing exams and taking makeup exams. To reduce the pressure, I told the professor with whom I was doing independent study that for medical reasons I would not be able to finish the paper due in that course. I decided to tell him why and he allowed me the Incomplete grade without requiring a medical letter on file, saving me the possible consequences of having this information on written record. And, most importantly, he did not treat me differently as a result of knowing. This reduced my stress and gave me time to make up work and take my final examinations. It also allowed me to work on my independent study paper during vacation and to do a good job on it while I was finally beginning to get a positive response to the medication.

I enjoyed winter break and finished my independent study project without incident, but as second semester approached I began to fear the room we had classes in, all the people and stimulation, and to fear recurrence of these episodes. What scared me most was the fact that this disease could prevent me from doing something I really wanted to do and needed to do, be psychologically healthy—that is, complete pharmacy school—and the knowledge that schizophrenia does this to many people's lives. I could not accept the fact that intellectually I could be capable of something that I may not at times be capable of emotionally.

When classes started, I still felt overstimulated and again had prodromes of psychotic episodes. I could not process information when people were talking; everything just seemed like noise. I was now on 5 mg of Navane b.i.d. (twice daily) and 2 mg of Cogentin h.s. I got enough courage to sit in front of the class again, but I was very fearful. My psychologist explained that I had begun to associate that classroom with these episodes and that extreme anxiety was causing dissociation reactions in me: I felt I was outside my body; I was watching everything. I wanted an antianxiety agent to get rid

Continued

of these feelings and that constant impending feeling that a psychotic episode would begin. The psychiatrist prescribed 5 mg of Valium (diazepam) in the morning and at bedtime when necessary. I took it only in the morning when I could not restructure my environment and situation to reduce the anxiety. For the first several weeks I was falling asleep in my first class and had double vision because I could not keep my eyes open. Finally, I became tolerant to the sedative effect.

So this is the answer right now for me: a neuroleptic, an antianxiety agent, an anti-Parkinsonian agent, and intense long-term psychotherapy with my psychologist. And I still look around at my fellow students and say to myself, "They do it without medicine, or doctors, or going to a psychiatric ward," but I needed all these things to cope with the pressure and stress of pharmacy school and life.

What I have been trying to express here is the actual reality of what being "individually titrated to an antipsychotic medicine" and having schizophrenia means to someone personally going through it as opposed to how objectively and easily it is expressed in pharmacy classes. My instructors have stated that "antipsychotics alleviate symptoms but do not cure psychoses," but this matter-of-fact statement has very personal meaning for me. It involves internal conflicts and many complicated adjustments—getting to a psychologist outside the city, or if the necessity of hospitalization occurs, getting hospitalized outside the city so fellow students and the pharmacy school will not have access to that information about me. It means never being able to see well because of the side effects of the medication. It also means enormous medical bills and debts. . . .

Finally, I heard a teacher in one class talk about long-term chronic illness such as schizophrenia in a way that suggested the teacher knew something about the disease and had looked beyond the myths. Through this class, I began to understand a little better my own noncompliance with the psychotropic drugs; how unacceptable my illness was not only to me, but would have been to others if they had known my diagnosis. I didn't take the medicine at times because I didn't want the disease, its problems, and its stigma. I wanted to be normal. And even now in the 1980s, in a professional pharmacy school, it would probably shock many people to know a schizophrenic was in their class, would be a pharmacist, and could do a good job. And knowledge of it could cause loss of many friends and acquaintances. So even now I must write this article anonymously. But I want people to know I have schizophrenia, that I need medicine and psychotherapy, and at some times I have required hospitalization. But, I also want them to know that I have been on the dean's list, and have friends, and expect to receive my pharmacy degree from a major university.

When you think about schizophrenia next time, try to remember me; there are more people like me out there trying to overcome a poorly understood disease and doing the best they can with what medicine and psychotherapy have to offer them. And some of them are making it.

Designing and applying effective therapies for children and adolescents are made difficult by problems similar to those that arise in assessing and diagnosing children's and adolescents' disorders (refer to Chapter 4). These include the need to match the therapy to the child's developmental level; the possibility that a therapy, especially a drug therapy, will have long-term negative effects on the child's development; the fact that children are embedded in families, and often the family as well as the child must be treated; and the fact that children and adolescents seldom refer themselves for treatment and thus are often not motivated to engage in treatment.

Matching Psychotherapies to Children's Developmental Levels

As we discussed in Chapter 4, children can have difficulty expressing their feelings and concerns in words, particularly when they are very distressed. Thus, therapists use a variety of methods to elicit information from children about their feelings, such as having children draw pictures or engage in play that might symbolize how they are feeling.

Psychodynamically oriented therapists believe that expressing feelings and concerns through play can

help the child master these feelings and concerns and overcome negative behaviors. Their therapy with a child may consist primarily of helping the child engage in this indirect expression and exploration of feelings and concerns. Other therapists use play or other projective techniques only as tools to assess a child's feelings and concerns.

Can children participate in talking therapies such as cognitive-behavioral therapy? It seems that the answer is "yes," although the conversations between the therapist and child must be at a level that is appropriate for the child's age (Craighead, Meyers, & Craighead, 1985). However, many therapists believe that for children behaviorally oriented therapies are more appropriate than are talking therapies because behavior therapies are not as dependent on children's verbal abilities. Moreover, children may have trouble changing their behaviors only by changing their thinking—it may take repeated practicing of new behaviors and reinforcement for these behaviors for children to learn them. Comparisons of behavioral and nonbehavioral therapies for children have suggested that behavioral therapies produce a larger and more reliable effect, although nonbehavioral therapies do have positive effects on children (Weiss & Weisz, 1995; Weisz et al., 1987).

Effects of Drugs on Children and Adolescents

Drug therapies are becoming increasingly popular in treating children and adolescents with psychological problems (Gadow, 1991). Drugs were initially used to treat only the most severe disorders in children, such as autism, but are now being used to treat disorders such as depression and phobias. The use of drugs in children has been extremely controversial, largely because of fears that drugs will have toxic effects both in the short term and in the long term. Finding a safe dosage of drugs for children is initially tricky, because body size, age, and hormones all affect the metabolism of drugs, and there is more variability in the proper dosage of a drug among children than there is among adults. We do not know the long-term effects of most drugs on children's physical or psychological development because the studies necessary to understand these effects have not been done. Such studies would require administering drugs to thousands of children and following these children (and control groups of children with disorders who do not receive drugs) throughout their development. These studies have not been done partly because of fears about the effects of drugs on children's development and because re-

searchers have only begun to study children's disorders recently (Gadow, 1991).

The Need to Treat the Child's Family

Children are almost always living in some sort of family, whether in the traditional two-parent family, with a single parent or perhaps a grandparent, in a foster-care family, or in some other configuration. Many clinicians believe that children's disorders cannot be effectively treated outside of the context of the family (Kaslow & Racusin, 1990). The family may be the direct cause of a child's disorder, such as in the case when one parent is physically abusive to the child and perhaps to other members of the family. In such cases, treating the child without correcting the cause of the child's problem (i.e., the parental abuse) is ineffective. Indeed, sometimes it is a parent who needs therapy even more than the child. In other cases, the family may not have directly caused the child's problem but may be reinforcing or supporting the child's problem in some way. For example, a child may have trouble controlling aggressive behavior, perhaps because of a biological dysfunction, but the family reinforces the child's aggressivity by allowing her to have what she wants when she threatens to lose control. In such cases, teaching family members how to extinguish the child's aggressive behavior can help the child gain control over that behavior, even if the initial cause of the behavior is biological (Estrada & Pinsof, 1995). Children and their families are sometimes treated with the techniques of family systems therapy, but all the psychotherapies we explored earlier in this chapter have been adapted for application to children and families.

Incorporating the family into a child's treatment creates many difficulties, however. A child may not want his or her family involved in treatment. For example, an adolescent who is depressed because

"Don't you realize, Jason, that when you throw furniture out the window and tie your sister to a tree, you make mommy and daddy very sad?"

© Sidney Harris

her mother is emotionally abusive may not want to confront her mother in therapy and may instead want an exclusive relationship with the caring therapist. The therapist may still choose to meet with the parent, apart from the adolescent, if the therapist believes the parent must be dealt with in order for the adolescent's problems to be overcome. The adolescent must know the therapist is meeting with the parent, however, and must be helped to trust that her relationship with the therapist is not compromised by these meetings with the parent. Family members may themselves not want to join therapy, particularly if they feel they are being blamed for the child's problems. If they do join therapy, they may not be cooperative with the therapist in overcoming the child's and family's problems.

Therapists are sometimes faced with extremely difficult decisions about whether to remove children from their families such as when a therapist believes a family poses a danger to a child. They also must decide when to allow a child to return to a family from which he or she has been removed because of a perceived danger. A therapist's perceptions of the danger a family poses to a child can be influenced by the therapist's biases against the ethnicity or culture of the family or misunderstandings of the parenting practices of that ethnic or cultural group. For example, Gray and Cosgrove (1985) note that spanking is an accepted form of discipline in some ethnic and socioeconomic groups in the United States but can be taken as evidence of child abuse by social workers and therapists who do not believe spanking is appropriate. There may be some parenting practices that are accepted by certain cultures that therapists never want to endorse; but therapists must be careful to take into account the cultural context of a parent's behaviors before passing judgment.

Children Often Do Not Seek Therapy Themselves

Most children and adolescents who enter therapy do not seek it for themselves (Kendall & Morris, 1991). They may be taken by their parents, who are overwhelmed by their children's behavioral or emotional difficulties. Often, troubled children are first identified by school officials, by their pediatricians, by social service agents (e.g., welfare workers), or by the criminal justice system (Tuma, 1989). Children who enter psychotherapy through any of these avenues may enter it reluctantly and thus may not participate wholeheartedly in therapy. Little research has been done on the effects of the relationship between a child and a therapist on the outcome of child psychotherapy, but it is likely that a warm, positive relationship with a therapist is as

important in therapy with children as it is in therapy with adults. Therapists usually must work against a child's initial reluctance to enter therapy in order to establish a good therapeutic relationship.

Unfortunately, most children who could benefit from therapy do not receive any therapy. Treatment facilities specializing in children's problems are unavailable in many parts of the United States and other industrialized countries and nonexistent in other parts of the world. Perhaps 50 percent of psychologically disturbed children receive advice or medications only from their family physicians, who are untrained in the assessment and treatment of psychological disorders (Tuma, 1989). The child welfare system sees many troubled children, often the victims of abuse and neglect. Such children are increasingly placed in long-term foster care rather than given specialized psychological treatment. Many children in the juvenile justice system suffer from psychological disorders, including conduct disorders, depression, and drug addiction, but few receive long-term intensive treatment (Tuma, 1989). There is much room for the expansion of services to psychologically disturbed children.

Summing Up

- Treatments for children must take into account their cognitive skills and developmental levels and adapt to their ability to comprehend and participate in therapy.
- There are reasons to be concerned about the possible toxic effects of drugs on children.
- Often, a child's family must be brought into therapy, but the child or the family may object.
- Most children who enter therapy do not seek it out themselves but are brought by others, raising issues about children's willingness to participate in therapy.

⚘ BIO-PSYCHO-SOCIAL INTEGRATION

Some psychologists and psychiatrists tend to practice only one type of therapy, believing that this type of therapy is effective for all the problems that they treat. Other psychologists and psychiatrists apply different types of therapy for different problems, based on their own clinical experience and research showing what type of therapy works best for a given type of problem. Increasingly, psychologists and psychiatrists are working together and in conjunction with social workers,

"I utilize the best from Freud, the best from Jung and the best from my uncle Marty, a very smart fellow."
© Sidney Harris

psychiatric nurses, and other mental-health professionals in teams that take a comprehensive approach to the treatment of client's problems. For example, a depressed client may receive antidepressant therapy from a psychiatrist, cognitive-behavior therapy from a psychologist, and help in finding a new job and place to live from a social worker.

As we noted earlier, many people do not have access to this kind of integrated care. In the last decade, some psychologists have argued that they should be allowed to prescribe the drugs used to treat medical disorders, so that they can provide the kind of integrated biological and psychological care that some clients need (DeLeon & Wiggins, 1996). Clinical psychologists usually are educated about these drugs, but because they do not have a medical degree, cannot prescribe them. Some argue that they are actually more qualified to know who needs these drugs and how to administer them than general practice physicians, who are often the sources of these drugs for patients. Others argue, however, that psychologists have no business prescribing drugs because they lack comprehensive medical training and because they should focus on the delivery of psychotherapy (Gutierrez & Silk, 1998; Hennessy, 1997). The question of whether psychologists should have "prescription privileges" is one of the most contentious issues in current clinical practice.

Chapter Summary

- A wide variety of biological and psychosocial approaches to the treatment of psychological disorders have been developed in line with different theories of the causes of these disorders. Biological therapies most often involve drugs intended to regulate the functioning of brain neurotransmitters associated with a psychological disorder or to compensate for structural brain abnormalities or the effects of genetics. Antipsychotic medications help reduce unreal perceptual experiences, unreal beliefs, and other symptoms of psychosis. Antidepressant drugs help reduce symptoms of depression. Lithium, anticonvulsants, and calcium channel blockers help reduce mania. Barbiturates and benzodiazepines help reduce anxiety. Electroconvulsive therapy is used to treat severe depression. Psychosurgery is used in rare circumstances.

- Psychological therapies include (1) psychodynamic therapy, which focuses on unconscious conflicts and interpersonal conflicts that lead to maladaptive behaviors and emotions; (2) behavioral therapies, which focus on changing specific maladaptive behaviors and emotions by changing the contingencies for them; (3) cognitive therapies, which focus on changing the way a client thinks about important situations; (4) humanist therapies, which intend to help a client realize his or her potential for self-actualization. All of these therapies can be delivered to individual clients or in a group setting.

- Two types of treatment that focus on the individual's relationships and roles in social systems are interpersonal therapies, which are based on psychodynamic theories, but focus more on current relationships and concerns and family systems therapies, which attempt to break maladaptive patterns of relating between family members.

- The community mental-health movement intended to coordinate community services for people with mental disorders. Patients were deinstitutionalized, and treated in community mental-health centers, day treatment centers, and halfway houses. Because adequate resources were never put into this movement, its goals were never fully realized.

- Prevention programs may focus on preventing disorders before they develop, retarding the development of disorders in their early stages, or reducing the impact of disorders on people's functioning.

- Some clients may wish to work with therapists of the same culture or gender, but it is unclear whether matching therapist and client in terms of culture and gender is necessary for therapy to be effective. It is important for therapists to be sensitive to the influences of culture and gender on a client's attitudes toward therapy and on the acceptability to the client of different types of solutions to problems.

- Doing good research on therapy outcomes is difficult because of methodological and ethical concerns. Some studies comparing different psychotherapies suggest they are equally effec-

tive, whereas others suggest that certain therapies are more effective than others in the treatment of specific disorders. Common components of effective therapy seem to be a good therapist-client relationship and the client's belief that the therapy can be effective.

- Therapy with children has its own set of challenges. First, a therapy must be matched to a child's developmental level for the child to be able to participate fully. Second, therapists must be concerned about the short-term and long-term effects of drugs on children's development. Third, children's families may often need to be brought into therapy. Fourth, children do not tend to seek therapy for themselves and thus are sometimes reluctant to participate.

Key Terms

medication 134

psychotherapy 134

chlorpromazine 137

phenothiazines 137

neuroleptic 137

butyrophenone 138

antipsychotic drugs 138

antidepressant drugs 138

monoamine oxidase inhibitors (MAOIs) 138

tricyclic antidepressants 138

selective serotonin reuptake inhibitors (SSRIs) 139

substance P 140

lithium 140

anticonvulsant drugs 140

calcium channel blockers 140

antianxiety drugs 140

barbiturates 140

benzodiazepines 140

electroconvulsive therapy (ECT) 141

prefrontal lobotomy 141

psychosurgery 141

psychodynamic therapy 145

free association 145

resistance 145

transference 146

working through 146

catharsis 146

therapeutic alliance 147

psychoanalysis 147

humanistic therapy 147

person-centered therapy 147

client-centered therapy (CCT) 148

unconditional positive regard 148

reflection 148

behavior therapy 148

behavioral assessment 148

role play 148

systematic desensitization 149

modeling 150

in vivo exposure 150

flooding 150

implosive therapy 150

token economy 150

response shaping 150

social skills training 150

cognitive therapy 151

behavioral assignments 153

interpersonal therapy (IPT) 154

family systems therapy 156

group therapy 157

self-help groups 157

community mental-health movement 158

community mental-health centers 158

halfway houses 158

day treatment centers 158

primary prevention 159

secondary prevention 159

Dodo bird verdict 163

Critical Thinking Questions

1. What kind of motivation do you think a person would need to have to be willing to undergo systematic desensitization therapy for a phobia?

2. How would you go about adapting cognitive therapy for use with elementary-school children?

3. Is it ethical to force a child or adolescent to receive treatment?

4. Why would clients who develop a warm and trusting relationship with a therapist recover more fully? What would each of the psychological theories discussed in this chapter say are the reasons?

Diana Ong
Birddog

All emotions are pure which gather you and lift you up; that emotion is impure which seizes only one side of your being and so distorts you.

—*Rainer Maria Rilke,* Letters to a Young Poet
(1904, November 4; translated by M. D. Herter)

CHAPTER 6

Anxiety Disorders: Panic, Phobias, and Generalized Anxiety

CHAPTER OVERVIEW

Panic Disorder

People with panic disorder experience sudden bursts of anxiety symptoms, feel out of control, and think they are dying. They may have an overreactive autonomic nervous system that easily goes into a fight-or-flight response. They also may tend to catastrophize their symptoms. Antidepressant and antianxiety drugs can reduce symptoms of panic. Cognitive-behavioral treatments are highly effective for panic disorder.

Extraordinary People:
Albert Ellis, the Phobic Psychologist

Taking Psychology Personally:
Relaxation Exercises

Phobias

People with agoraphobia fear being in places where they might be trapped or unable to get help in an emergency. The emergency they often fear is having a panic attack. The specific phobias focus on animals, elements of the environment (such as water), certain situations (such as flying), and blood, injections, or injuries. Social phobia involves a pervasive fear of scrutiny by others. Psychodynamic theories attribute phobias to the displacement of unconscious conflicts onto symbolic objects. Behavioral theories argue that phobias develop from classical and operant conditioning. Biological theories attribute phobias to genetics. The most effective treatments for phobias are behav-

ioral treatments that expose people to their phobic objects and teach them skills for reducing their anxiety.

Pushing the Boundaries:
Virtual Reality Therapy for Phobias

Generalized Anxiety Disorder

People with generalized anxiety disorder have chronic and pervasive anxiety about most aspects of their lives. Both consciously and unconsciously they are hypervigilant for threat. Cognitive-behavioral therapies have proven most effective for generalized anxiety disorder.

The Sociocultural Approach to the Anxiety Disorders

Sociocultural theorists focus on group differences in anxiety disorders and look to environmental demands and social and cultural norms to explain these differences. Sociocultural perspectives shed some light on the fact that women are more likely than men to have any of the anxiety disorders discussed in this chapter. They also help to explain cross-cultural differences in the manifestation of anxiety.

Bio-Psycho-Social Integration

Chapter Summary
Key Terms
Critical Thinking Questions

We all have our fears. When we were children, we may have been fearful of dogs or strangers. As adults, we may be fearful when we are about to give a speech or when we are walking alone at night down a narrow and deserted street.

Most of us have grown out of our childhood fears, and our adult fears are mild, short term, or reasonable, given the circumstances. People with anxiety disorders live with fears that are neither mild, nor short term, nor reasonable. The fears of people with anxiety disorders are severe and lower the quality of their lives. Their fears are chronic and frequent enough to interfere with their functioning. Finally, their fears are out of proportion to the dangers that they truly face. The following case study illustrates the debilitating fears that one person with an anxiety disorder lived with (adapted from Spitzer, Williams, & Gibbons, 1987, p. 262):

The symptoms of anxiety are emotional, somatic, behavioral, and cognitive.

CASE STUDY

Fredrick is sitting in the waiting room of a cardiologist, hoping that this time, he has found a physician who can do something about his symptoms. Every day for about two years, Fredrick has experienced periods of dizziness, sweating palms, heart palpitations, and ringing of the ears. He has a chronically dry mouth and throat, periods of uncontrollable shaking, and a constant "edgy" and watchful feeling that often interferes with his ability to concentrate.

Because of these symptoms, Fredrick has seen a family practitioner, a neurologist, a neurosurgeon, a chiropractor, and an ear, nose, and throat specialist. He has been placed on a hypoglycemic diet, received physiotherapy for a pinched nerve, and told he might have "an inner ear problem." Nothing has seemed to help, however.

Fredrick has many worries. He constantly worries about the health of his parents. His father, in fact, had a heart attack two years before, but now is feeling well. Fredrick has also worried about whether he is "a good father," whether his wife will ever leave him (there is no indication that she is dissatisfied with the marriage), and whether he is liked by coworkers.

For the past two years, Fredrick has had few social contacts because of his nervous symptoms. Although he has sometimes had to leave work when the symptoms become intolerable, he continues to work for the same company he joined for an apprenticeship following high school graduation.

Fredrick is experiencing four types of symptoms that make up what clinicians refer to as **anxiety** (see Table 6.1). First, he has physiological or *somatic symptoms*, including dizziness, sweating palms, heart palpitations, ringing in his ears, dry mouth and throat, periods of uncontrollable shaking, and a constant "edgy" feeling. Second, he has *emotional symptoms*—primarily a sense of fearfulness and watchfulness. Third, he has *cognitive symptoms*, including unrealistic worries that something bad is happening (that his father is ill) or is about to happen (that his wife will leave him). Finally, he has *behavioral symptoms*—he avoids situations because of his fears.

The physiological and behavioral symptoms listed in Table 6.1 make up what is known as the **fight-or-flight response** (also called the **emergency reaction**). Evolution has prepared our bodies so that we can fight off or flee from threats to our safety, such as hungry lions (in ancient times) or knife-wielding muggers. Quick energy is needed, so the liver releases extra sugar (glucose) to fuel our muscles, and hormones are released that stimulate the conversion of fats and proteins to sugar. The body's metabolism increases to provide energy for physical action. Our heart rate, blood pressure, and breathing rate increase, and our muscles tense. At the same time, certain unessential activities, such as digestion, slow down. Our saliva and mucus dry up, thereby increasing the size of air passages to our lungs. (This is why we get a dry mouth when we are anxious). Our body's natural painkillers, endorphins, are secreted and our surface blood vessels constrict to reduce bleeding in case of injury. Our spleen releases more red blood cells to help carry oxygen.

Most of these physiological changes result from activation of two neuroendocrine systems controlled by the **hypothalamus**: the **sympathetic division of the autonomic nervous system** and the **adrenal-cortical system**. The hypothalamus first activates the sympathetic division of the autonomic nervous system. The sympathetic system acts directly on the smooth muscles and internal organs to produce some of the bodily changes described above—for example, increased heart rate, elevated blood pressure, and dilated pupils. The sympathetic system also stimulates the inner core of the adrenal glands (the adrenal medulla) to release the hormones epinephrine (adrenaline) and norepinephrine into the bloodstream. Epinephrine has the same effect

TABLE 6.1
Symptoms of Anxiety

Somatic	Behavioral	Emotional	Cognitive
Goosebumps emerge	Escape	Sense of dread	Anticipation of harm
Muscles tense	Avoidance	Terror	Exaggerating of danger
Heart rate increases	Aggression	Restlessness	Problems in concentrating
Respiration accelerates	Freezing	Irritability	Hypervigilance
Respiration deepens	Decreased appetitive responding		Worried, ruminative thinking
Spleen contracts	Increased aversive responding		Fear of losing control
Peripheral blood vessels dilate			Fear of dying
Liver releases carbohydrates			Sense of unreality
Bronchioles widen			
Pupils dilate			
Perspiration increases			
Adrenaline is secreted			
Stomach acid is inhibited			
Salivation decreases			
Bladder relaxes			

on the muscles and organs as the sympathetic nervous system does (e.g., it increases heart rate and blood pressure) and thus serves to perpetuate a state of arousal. Norepinephrine, through its action on the pituitary gland, is indirectly responsible for the release of extra sugar from the liver (see Figure 6.1, p. 180).

These events describe only the first function of the hypothalamus: activation of the sympathetic system. The hypothalamus carries out its second function (activation of the adrenal-cortical system) by signaling the pituitary gland, which lies just below it, to secrete adrenocorticotropic hormone (ACTH), the body's "major stress hormone." ACTH stimulates the outer layer of the adrenal glands (the adrenal cortex), resulting in the release of a group of hormones, the major one being **cortisol**. The amount of cortisol in blood or urine samples is often used as a measure of stress. ACTH also signals other endocrine glands to release about 30 other hormones, each of which plays a role in the body's adjustment of emergency situations. Eventually, the hormones signal the hippocampus, a part of the brain that helps to regulate emotions, to turn off this physiological cascade when the threatening stimulus has passed.

The physiological changes of the fight-or-flight response can occur whether we are facing a saber-toothed tiger or a midterm exam. What begins these changes is our perception of threat, whether that perception is realistic and shared by others or not. There are several differences between the adaptive fear response that we have developed through evolution and the maladaptive anxiety that some people suffer:

- In adaptive fear, people's concerns are realistic given the circumstances, but in maladaptive anxiety, their concerns are *unrealistic*. What they are anxious about cannot hurt them or is very unlikely to come about. For example, people having a panic attack may fear they will suddenly keel over and die, although this is highly unlikely.

- In adaptive fear, the amount of fear people experience is in proportion to the real threat they face, but in maladaptive anxiety, the amount of fear experienced is *out of proportion* to the harm the threat could cause. For example, a person with a social phobia may become absolutely panicked over the thought that he could say something that would embarrass him if he were called on in class, and he therefore avoids going to class at all.

- In adaptive fear, people's fear response subsides when the threat ends, but in maladaptive anxiety, people's concern is *persistent* when a threat passes, and they may have a great deal of *anticipatory anxiety* about the future. For example, Fredrick continues to worry about his father's

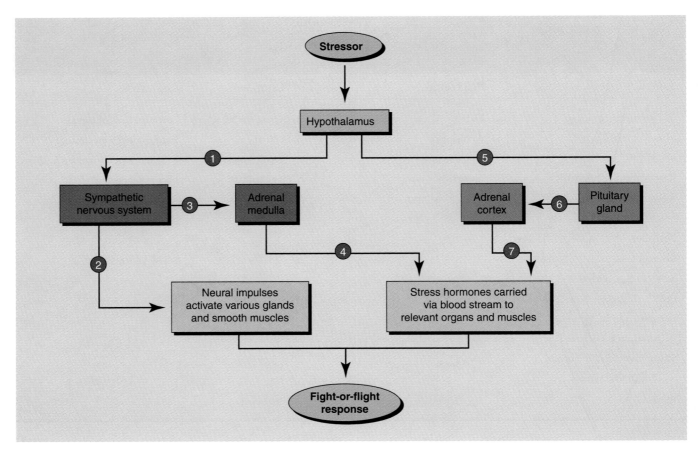

FIGURE 6.1   Fight-or-Flight Response. A stressful situation activates the hypothalamus, which, in turn, controls two neuroendocrine systems: the sympathetic system (shown in red) and the adrenal-cortical system (shown in green). The sympathetic nervous system, responding to neural impulses from the hypothalamus (1), activates various organs and smooth muscles under its control (2). For example, it increases heart rate and dilates the pupils. The sympathetic nervous system also signals the adrenal medulla (3) to release epinephrine and norepinephrine into the bloodstream (4). The adrenal-cortical system is activated when the hypothalamus secretes corticotropin-releasing factor (CRF), a chemical that acts on the pituitary gland lying just below the hypothalamus (5). The pituitary gland, in turn, secretes the hormone ACTH, which is carried via the bloodstream to the adrenal cortex (6), where it stimulates the release of a group of hormones, including cortisol, that regulate blood glucose levels (7). ACTH also signals the other endocrine glands to release some 30 hormones. The combined effect of the various stress hormones carried via the bloodstream plus the neural activity of the sympathetic division of the autonomic nervous system constitute the fight-or-flight response.

health after his heart attack, even though his father now seems healthy, and he worries in anticipation that his wife might become dissatisfied with their marriage.

Anxiety is a prominent feature in many psychological disorders. For example, the majority of people with serious depression also report bouts of anxiety (Kessler et al., 1994; Lewinsohn et al., 1997). People with schizophrenia often feel anxious when they believe they are slipping into a new episode of psychosis. Many people who abuse alcohol and other drugs do so to dampen anxious symptoms.

Freud and many other theorists believed that anxiety was the underlying cause of most forms of psychopathology. He used the term **neurosis** to refer to disorders in which the anxiety aroused by unconscious conflicts could not be quelled or channeled by defense mechanisms. This anxiety could be experienced more

or less directly as conscious symptoms of anxiety. It could also take a number of maladaptive forms, such as depression or hypocondriasis (unrealistic worry about one's health).

The DSM no longer uses the term neurosis. Instead, it classifies disorders in which the predominant symptoms are anxiety as anxiety disorders. Depression, hypocondriasis, and other disorders are classified separately, and it is no longer assumed that anxiety underlies these disorders.

In this chapter and the next, we focus on disorders in which the primary symptoms are anxiety symptoms. We begin with a discussion of panic, which can be a part of many of the anxiety disorders or, when frequent, a disorder in itself. We then discuss agoraphobia, which usually develops in response to a history of panic attacks, and the phobias other than agoraphobia, which are known as simple phobias and social phobias. Finally, we discuss generalized anxiety disorder (GAD), which is characterized not by acute panic attacks but by chronic, diffuse anxiety.

In the next chapter, we discuss posttraumatic stress disorder, which can arise in people who have faced major traumatic events. We also discuss obsessive-compulsive disorder, which is categorized as an anxiety disorder but which has some intriguing features that distinguish it from the other anxiety disorders.

☉ PANIC DISORDER

CASE STUDY

The first time Celia had a panic attack, she was working at McDonald's. It was two days before her 20th birthday. As she was handing a customer a Big Mac, she had the worst experience of her life. The earth seemed to open up beneath her. Her heart began to pound, she felt she was smothering, she broke into a flop sweat, and she was sure she was going to have a heart attack and die. After about twenty minutes of terror, the panic subsided. Trembling, she got in her car, raced home, and barely left the house for the next three months.

Since that time, Celia has had about three attacks a month. She does not know when they are coming. During an attack she feels dread, searing chest pain, smothering and choking, dizziness, and shakiness. She sometimes thinks this is all not real and she is going crazy. She also thinks she is going to die. (Seligman, 1993, p. 61)

Celia is suffering from **panic attacks,** short but intense periods in which she experiences many symptoms of anxiety: heart palpitations, trembling, feeling of choking, dizziness, intense dread, and so on (see Table 6.2). Celia's panic attacks appear to occur in the absence of any environmental triggers; they come "out of the blue." Simply handing a customer a hamburger should not cause such terror. This is one of the baffling characteristics of some panic attacks.

Other people have panic attacks that are triggered by specific situations or events. For example, people with a social phobia may have panic attacks when forced into a social situation. Most commonly, panic attacks are situationally predisposed: The person is more likely to have them in certain situations but does not always have them when in those situations. In all these cases, however, the panic attack is a terrifying experience, causing a person intense fear or discomfort, the physiological symptoms of anxiety, and the feeling of losing control, going crazy, or dying.

As many as 40 percent of young adults have occasional panic attacks, especially during times of intense stress, such as exams week (King, Gullone, & Tonge, 1993). For most of these people, the panic attacks are annoying but isolated events and do not

TABLE 6.2
Symptoms of a Panic Attack

These are the common symptoms of a panic attack. Occasional experiences of these symptoms are common. When 4 or more symptoms occur frequently and interfere with daily living, the individual may be diagnosed with panic disorder.

Heart palpitations

Pounding heartbeat

Numbness or tingling sensations

Chills or hot flashes

Sweating

Trembling or shaking

Sensations of shortness of breath or smothering

Feeling of choking

Chest pain or discomfort

Nausea and upset stomach

Feeling dizzy, unsteady, lightheaded, or faint

Feelings of unreality or being detached from oneself

Fear of losing control or going crazy

Fear of dying

change how they live their lives. When panic attacks become a common occurrence, are usually not provoked by any particular situation, and a person begins to worry about having attacks and changes behaviors as a result of this worry, a diagnosis of **panic disorder** may be given (APA, 2000).

Some people with panic disorder will have many attacks in a short period of time, such as every day for a week, and then go for weeks or months without having another attack, followed by another period in which the attacks come often. Other people will have attacks less frequently but more regularly such as once a week every week for months. In between full-blown panic attacks, they might have more minor bouts of panic.

People who have panic disorder will often fear that they have life-threatening illnesses. Indeed, some people with thyroid disorders, or with a cardiac disorder called mitral valve prolapse, which creates episodes of heart palpitations, can be misdiagnosed as having panic disorder (Schmidt & Telch, 1997). However, even after such illnesses are ruled out, people with panic disorder may continue to believe that they are about to die of a heart attack, a seizure, or some other physical crisis. They may seek medical care frequently, going from physician to physician to find out what is wrong with them. Another common but erroneous belief among people with panic disorder is

Panic attacks are sudden, very frightening onsets of severe anxiety symptoms.

that they are "going crazy" or "losing control." Many people with panic disorder feel ashamed of their disorder and try to hide it from others. If left untreated, they may become demoralized and depressed.

Between 1.5 and 4 percent of people will develop panic disorder at some time in their lives (APA, 2000; Katerndahl & Realini, 1993; Kessler et al., 1994; Regier et al., 1993). Most people who develop panic disorder usually do so sometime between late adolescence and their mid-30s. The disorder tends to be chronic once it begins. One study found that 92 percent of patients with panic disorder continued to experience panic attacks for at

least 1 year, and among those whose symptoms subsided at some time during the year, 41 percent relapsed into panic attacks within the year (Ehlers, 1995).

Panic disorder can be debilitating in its own right. People with panic disorder often also suffer from chronic generalized anxiety, depression, and alcohol abuse (Craske & Barlow, 1993). Those people with panic disorder who are also depressed or abuse alcohol may be at increased risk for suicide attempts (Hornig & Mc-Nally, 1995; McNally, 1994). And about one-third to one-half of people diagnosed with panic disorder develop agoraphobia, as we discuss in the section on phobias.

Biological Theories

Biological theories of panic disorder have been concerned with poor regulation of neurotransmitters in particular parts of the brain and with the role of genetics (see *Concept Review:* Theories of Panic Disorder).

Neurotransmitter Theories

Most of the modern theories of the biology of panic disorder have been the result of the fortuitous discovery by psychiatrist Donald Klein in the 1960s that antidepressant medications reduce panic attacks (Klein, 1964). Because these medications affect levels of the neurotransmitter **norepinephrine,** Klein and others reasoned that norepinephrine may be involved in panic disorder. Over the years, evidence has mounted that norepinephrine may be poorly regulated in people with panic disorder, especially in an area of the brain stem called the **locus ceruleus.** Electrical stimulation of this brain area in monkeys produces paniclike

CONCEPT REVIEW	
Theories of Panic Disorder	

These are the prominent theories of panic disorder.

Theory	Description
Neurotransmitter theories	Poor regulation of norepinephrine, serotonin, and perhaps GABA and CCK in the locus ceruleus and limbic systems causes panic disorder.
Kindling model	Poor regulation in the locus ceruleus causes panic attacks, stimulates and kindles the limbic system, lowering the threshold for stimulation of diffuse and chronic anxiety.
Suffocation false alarm theory	The brains of people with panic disorder are hypersensitive to carbon dioxide and induce the fight-or-flight response with small increases in carbon dioxide.
Genetic theories	Disordered genes put some people at risk for panic disorder.
Cognitive theories	People prone to panic attacks (1) pay very close attention to their bodily sensations, (2) misinterpret these sensations, and (3) engage in snowballing, catastrophizing thinking.

responses, and destruction of this area in monkeys renders them unable to experience fear even in the presence of real threats (Redmond, 1985).

Other research suggests that when people are given drugs that alter the activity of norepinephrine, particularly in the locus ceruleus, this can induce panic attacks (Bourin, Baker, & Bradwejn, 1998; Charney et al., 1992). For example, the drug yohimbine alters norepinephrine, but not other neurotransmitters, in the locus ceruleus. When people with panic disorder take this drug, they typically have a panic attack immediately. Some people with panic disorder also have panic attacks when they take this drug. On the other hand, other drugs that alter norepinephrine activity have been shown to reduce panic attacks in people who suffer from the disorder (Charney et al., 1992; Levy et al., 1996). This, and other evidence, suggests that abnormal activity of norepinephrine, particularly in the locus ceruleus, is involved in human panic attacks.

Other neurotransmitters, particularly serotonin, gamma-aminobutyric acid (GABA), and cholecystokinin (CCK) have been implicated in panic disorders (Bell & Nutt, 1998; Bourin, Baker & Bradwejn, 1998; Gorman, Papp & Coplan, 1995; Stein & Uhde, 1995; Zaleman, 1995). Much recent research has focused on serotonin, following evidence that drugs that alter the functioning of serotonin systems are helpful in reducing panic attacks (Bell & Nutt, 1998). Some theories suggest that panic disorder is due to excessively high levels of serotonin in key areas of the brain; other theories suggest it is due to deficiencies in serotonin levels in the brain (Bell & Nutt, 1998; Bourin, Baker & Bradwejn, 1998). It may be that acute panic attacks have a different association with serotonin than anticipatory anxiety. Animal studies suggest that increases in serotonin in certain areas of the brain stem (specifically the periaqueductal gray) reduce paniclike responses in animals, whereas increases in serotonin in the amygdala increase anxiety, particularly anticipatory anxiety (see Figure 6.2; Graeff et al., 1996).

Some women with panic disorder report increases in anxiety symptoms during their premenstrual periods and the postpartum period (Yonkers & Gurguis, 1995). It may be that the ovarian hormones, particularly progesterone, play a role in vulnerability to panic attacks. Progesterone can affect activity of both serotonin and GABA neurotransmitter systems. Fluctuations in levels of progesterone with the menstrual cycle or in the postpartum period thus might lead to imbalances or dysfunctioning of the serotonin or GABA systems, thereby influencing susceptibility to panic. In addition, increases in progesterone can induce mild chronic hyperventilation. In women prone to panic attacks, this may be enough to tip the balance in their parasympathetic and sympathetic nervous systems and induce full panic attacks.

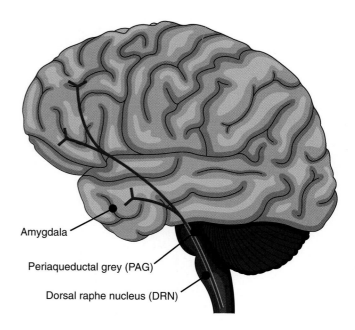

Amygdala

Periaqueductal grey (PAG)

Dorsal raphe nucleus (DRN)

FIGURE 6.2 Increased 5-HT in the periaqueductal gray restrains paniclike responses, whereas in the amygdala it is anxiogenic.
Source: Bell & Nutt, 1998.

Kindling Model

Gorman and colleagues (Gorman, Papp, & Coplan, 1995) have suggested a "kindling" model of panic disorder that draws a link between the anticipatory anxiety that many people with the disorder have chronically, and their experience of panic attacks (see Figure 6.3, p. 184). This link has to do with two parts of the brain, the locus ceruleus and the **limbic system,** which have well-defined pathways between them. They argue that, whereas the locus ceruleus is involved in the production of panic attacks, the limbic system is involved in diffuse, anticipatory anxiety. Poor regulation in the locus ceruleus causes panic attacks, which then stimulate and kindle the limbic system, lowering threshold for stimulation of diffuse and chronic anxiety. This anticipatory anxiety, in turn, may increase the likelihood of dysregulation of the locus ceruleus and thereby a new panic attack.

One thing is clear—people with panic disorders can be induced into a panic attack easily through a number of procedures, such as having them hyperventilate, inhale a small amount of carbon dioxide, ingest caffeine, breathe into a paper bag, or take infusions of sodium lactate, a substance that resembles the lactate produced by our bodies during exercise (e.g., Bourin, Baker, & Bradwejn, 1998; Rapee et al., 1992). In contrast, people without a history of panic attacks may experience some physical discomfort while doing these

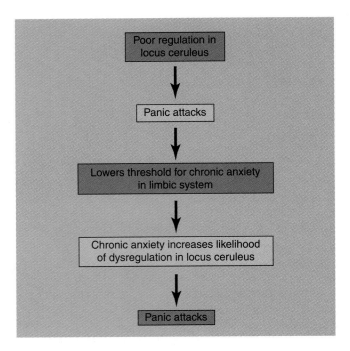

FIGURE 6.3   The Kindling Model of Panic Disorder.

activities but rarely experience a full panic attack (see Figure 6.4). What each of these procedures may have in common is that they initiate the physiological changes of the fight-or-flight response. People who develop panic disorder appear to have a poorly regulated fight-or-flight response, perhaps due to poor regulation of norepinephrine or serotonin in the brain circuits that regulate this response (Gorman et al., 1986; Margraf, 1993). This fight-or-flight response can be initiated without the provocation of a fear stimulus. Once their fight-or-flight response gets going, it operates out of control.

Suffocation False Alarm Theory

Another theory of why people with panic disorder have panic attacks when they hyperventilate, inhale carbon dioxide, or breathe into a paper bag is the **suffocation false alarm theory** (Klein, 1993; see also Papp et al., 1997). Each of these procedures elevates levels of carbon dioxide in the blood and brain. People who develop panic disorder may be hypersensitive to carbon dioxide. When their brains detect even small increases in carbon dioxide, the brain registers "suffocation!!!" and this triggers the autonomic nervous system into a full fight-or-flight response. In contrast, people who are not prone to panic disorders are not as sensitive to carbon dioxide, and therefore small increases in brain levels of carbon dioxide do not trigger a sense of suffocation or the full fight-or-flight response.

Genetic Theories

Finally, panic disorder appears to run in families. One family history study of panic disorder found that nearly one-fourth of the first-degree relatives of patients with panic disorder also had a history of panic disorder, compared to only about 2 percent of people in the general population (Crowe, 1990). Twin studies of panic disorder find a concordance rate of 24 percent in monozygotic twins but 11 percent in dizygotic twins (Kendler, Neale, Kessler, & Heath, 1992, 1993). These studies suggest that a biological vulnerability to panic disorder may be transmitted at least in part through disordered genes.

Family history studies of panic disorder with agoraphobia find that the female relatives of people with this disorder are even more likely than the male relatives to also have the disorder (Crowe, 1990). The male relatives, on the other hand, are more likely to

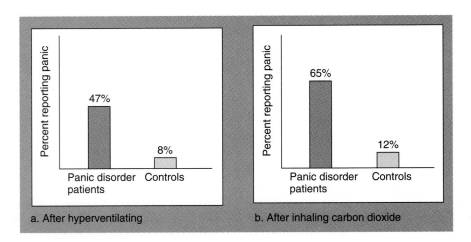

FIGURE 6.4   Panic Attacks of Patients and Controls. People with panic disorder are much more likely than people without panic disorder to have a panic attack when made to hyperventilate or inhale small amounts of carbon dioxide in laboratory experiments.

Source: Rapee et al., 1992.

suffer from alcohol abuse and dependence disorders. This suggests that the genetic vulnerability to panic disorder and agoraphobia is sex-linked. Women may be more likely than men to carry the genetic vulnerability to this disorder. Alternately, women and men may carry an equal genetic vulnerability to some type of disorder, which gets expressed as panic disorder and agoraphobia in women and as alcoholism in men.

Psychological Theories

Although many people who develop panic disorder may have biological vulnerability to this disorder, psychological factors also appear to play a heavy role in determining who will develop the disorder.

The Cognitive Model

The cognitive model of panic disorder argues that people prone to panic attacks tend to (1) pay very close attention to their bodily sensations, (2) misinterpret bodily sensations in a negative way, and (3) engage in snowballing catastrophic thinking (Barlow, 1988; Beck & Emery, 1985; Clark, 1988; Ehlers, 1993). So when a person prone to panic disorder feels a bit dizzy because she stood up too quickly, she might think, "I'm really dizzy. I think I'm going to faint. Maybe I'm having a seizure. Oh God, what's happening!" This kind of thinking increases the subjective sense of anxiety and sympathetic nervous system activity. These feelings then are interpreted catastrophically, and the person is on her way into a full panic attack. In between full panic attacks, the person is hypervigilant for any bodily sensations (Ehlers & Breuer, 1992). She worries about her health generally and about having more panic attacks specifically. This constant arousal makes it more likely that she will have more panic attacks (see *Concept Review:* Theories of Panic Disorder, p. 182).

This belief that bodily symptoms have harmful consequences has been labeled **anxiety sensitivity** (McNally, 1994). Several studies have shown that people high on anxiety sensitivity are more likely to already have panic disorder, to have more frequent panic attacks, or to develop panic attacks over time, compared to people low on anxiety sensitivity (Ehlers, 1995; Maller & Reiss, 1992; Pauli et al., 1997; Zoellner, Craske, & Rapee, 1996).

Evidence for the role of other psychological factors in panic disorder comes from several studies (see McNally, 1994, for a review). In one study, researchers examined the influence of beliefs about the controllability of panic symptoms on the actual experience of panic in the laboratory. Two groups of panic patients were asked to wear breathing masks, which delivered air that was slightly enriched with carbon dioxide.

They were warned that inhaling carbon dioxide could induce a panic attack. One group was told that they could not control the amount of carbon dioxide that came through their masks. The other group was told they could control the amount of carbon dioxide that came through their masks by turning a knob. Actually, neither group had any control over the amount of carbon dioxide they inhaled. Eighty percent of the patients who believed they had no control experienced a panic attack, but only 20 percent of the patients who believed they could control the carbon dioxide had a panic attack. This occurred despite the fact that both groups inhaled the same amount of carbon dioxide. These results strongly suggest that beliefs about the uncontrollability of panic symptoms play a strong role in panic attacks (Sanderson, Rapee, & Barlow, 1989).

In another study, researchers examined whether people with panic disorder could avoid having a panic attack, even after inhaling carbon dioxide, by having a "safe person" nearby. Panic patients exposed to carbon dioxide with their safe person present were much less likely to experience the emotional and physical symptoms of anxiety than were panic patients exposed to carbon dioxide without their safe person present. Indeed, the panic patients who had their safe person with them did not experience significantly more anxiety than a control group of people who were not prone to any type of anxiety disorder. In addition, the panic patients who did not have their safe person nearby when inhaling carbon dioxide reported many more catastrophic cognitions such as "I'm losing control," and "I'm having a heart attack" than did the panic patients who did have their person nearby and than did the control subjects. It seemed that having the safe person nearby reduced the tendency of the panic patients to interpret the bodily changes they were experiencing as dangerous (Carter et al., 1995).

Vulnerability-Stress Model

The biological and cognitive theories of panic disorder have been integrated to create a vulnerability-stress model of this disorder (see Figure 6.5, p. 186; Barlow, 1988): Many people who develop panic disorder seem to have a biological vulnerability to a hypersensitive fight-or-flight response. With just a mild stimulus, these people's hearts begin to race, their breathing begins to become rapid, and their palms begin to sweat. However, they typically will not develop frequent panic attacks or a panic disorder unless they also engage in catastrophizing cognitions about their physiological symptoms. These cognitions will increase the intensity of their initially mild physiological systems to the point of a panic attack. They will also cause them to become hypervigilant for signs of another panic attack, which puts them constantly at a mild-to-moderate

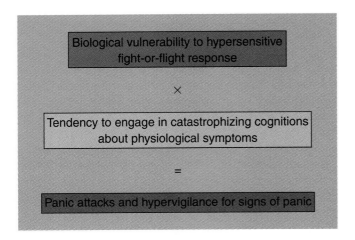

FIGURE 6.5   The Vulnerability-Stress Model of Panic Disorder. The vulnerability-stress model of panic disorder suggests that a biological vulnerability to a hypersensitive fight-or-flight response interacts with the tendency to engage in catastrophizing cognitions to create panic attacks and panic disorder.

level of anxiety. This increases the probability that they will become panicked again, and the cycle continues

Biological Treatments

As we noted earlier, some of the most effective drugs for the treatment of panic and agoraphobia are classified as antidepressant drugs (see *Concept Review*: Drugs Used to Treat Panic Disorder). These include tricyclic antidepressants and the serotonin reuptake inhibitors. In addition, the benzodiazepines, antianxiety drugs, can help some people.

Tricyclic Antidepressants

The **tricyclic antidepressants** such as imipramine can reduce panic attacks in 45 to 70 percent of patients (APA, 1998; Hirschfeld, 1996; Lydiard, Brawman-Mintzer, & Ballenger, 1996; Rapee, 1994). Recall that one of the neurotransmitters that may be involved in panic disorder is norepinephrine. The tricyclic antidepressants are thought to improve the functioning of the norepinephrine system, and this may be why they are effective in treating panic. These drugs also may affect levels of a number of other neurotransmitters, including serotonin, thereby affecting levels of anxiety.

The disadvantages of the tricyclic antidepressants are their side effects and the relapse rate once patients discontinue the drugs. Some of the side effects of the tricyclic antidepressants are due to their effects on the neurotransmitter acetylcholine, and thus are called anticholinergic effects. These include blurred vision, dry mouth, difficulty urinating, constipation, and increased heart rate. Other common side effects include increased sweating, sleep disturbances, hypotension and dizziness, fatigue and weakness, weight gain, and sexual dysfunction (APA, 1998). People with certain cardiac problems may experience significant heart arrhythmias, and overdoses of the tricyclic antidepressants can lead to death. In addition, between 20 and 50 percent of patients relapse into panic attacks when they discontinue the tricyclics (APA, 1998; Telch, 1988).

Serotonin Reuptake Inhibitors

Another class of drugs that is increasingly being used to treat people experiencing situational anxiety or chronic mild anxiety is the **selective serotonin reuptake**

CONCEPT REVIEW		
Drugs Used to Treat Panic Disorder		
Class of Drug	**Mechanism of Action**	**Side Effects and Disadvantages**
Tricyclic antidepressants	Increase levels of norepinephrine and a number of other neurotransmitters	Blurred vision, dry mouth, difficulty urinating, constipation, increased heart rate, sweating, sleep disturbances, hypotension and dizziness, fatigue and weakness, weight gain, and sexual dysfunction
Serotonin reuptake inhibitors	Increase levels of serotonin	Gastrointestinal upset and irritability, initial feelings of agitation, insomnia, drowsiness, tremor, and sexual dysfunction
Benzodiazepines	Suppress the central nervous system and influence functioning in the GABA, norepinephrine, and serotonin neurotransmitter systems	Addictive; interfere with cognitive and motor functioning; withdrawal symptoms, including irritability, tremors, insomnia, anxiety, tingling sensations, and more rarely seizures and paranoia

inhibitors (SSRIs). Some commonly used SSRIs include Paxil, Prozac, and Zoloft. These drugs increase the functional levels of the neurotransmitter serotonin in the brain. Some people can tolerate the side effects of these drugs, which include gastrointestinal upset and irritability, initial feelings of agitation, insomnia, drowsiness, tremor, and sexual dysfunction, better than they can the side effects of the tricyclic antidepressants. The use of these drugs for panic attacks is relatively new, but existing studies suggest that they are effective, with about 80 percent of panic patients experiencing significant reduction in panic attacks after 8 to 12 weeks of taking an SSRI (APA, 1998; Bell & Nutt, 1998). There are some indications, however, that a significant number of people relapse back into panic attacks after discontinuing the SSRIs if they have not also received psychological treatment for their disorder (APA, 1998).

Benzodiazepines

The third class of drugs used to treat panic disorder is the **benzodiazepines,** which suppress the central nervous system and influence functioning in the GABA, norepinephrine, and serotonin neurotransmitter systems. The benzodiazepine most commonly used to treat panic is alprazolam (trade name Xanax). This drug works quickly to reduce panic attacks and general symptoms of anxiety in 60 to 80 percent of persons with panic disorder (APA, 1998; Ballenger et al., 1988; Klosko et al., 1990). Unfortunately, the benzodiazepines have three major disadvantages.

First, they are physically (and psychologically) addictive. People build up a tolerance to these drugs so that they need increasing dosages of the drug to get a positive effect. In turn, when they stop using the drug, they experience difficult withdrawal symptoms, including irritability, tremors, insomnia, anxiety, tingling sensations, and more rarely seizures and paranoia. These withdrawal symptoms can occur even if people are tapered off the drug gradually.

The second major disadvantage of benzodiazepines is that they can interfere with cognitive and motor functioning. People's ability to drive or to avoid accidents is impaired, and their performance on the job, at school, and in the home suffers. These impairments can be especially severe if the benzodiazepines are combined with alcohol.

The third major disadvantage of the benzodiazepines is that about half of the patients begin having panic attacks again shortly after discontinuing treatment with these drugs, and 90 percent of patients eventually relapse into panic disorder after being taken off these drugs (Fyer et al., 1987; Spiegel, 1998). Relapse rates can be greatly diminished, however, if cognitive-behavioral therapies, to be described next, are combined with the benzodiazepines (Otto et al., 1992; Spiegel, 1998; Spiegel et al., 1994).

Cognitive-Behavioral Therapy

Psychological treatments for all the anxiety disorders, including panic disorder, involve getting clients to confront the situations or thoughts that arouse anxiety in them. Confrontation seems to help in two ways: Irrational thoughts about these situations can be challenged and changed, and anxiety reactions to the situations can be extinguished. One of the founders of cognitive-behavioral approaches, Albert Ellis, suffered from severe anxiety symptoms. He developed his rational-emotive therapy as a way of treating himself for his anxiety, as we describe in *Extraordinary People*: Albert Ellis, the Phobic Psychologist.

Cognitive behavioral therapies appear to be highly effective in eliminating panic disorder (APA, 1998; Clark et al., 1999; Klosko et al., 1990; Telch et al., 1993). There are a number of components to these cognitive-behavioral interventions.

First, clients are taught relaxation and breathing exercises such as those described in *Taking Psychology Personally:* Relaxation Exercises (pp. 189–190). These exercises are useful in therapy for anxiety disorders because they give clients some control over their symptoms, which then permits them to engage in the other components of the therapy.

Second, the clinician guides clients in identifying the catastrophizing cognitions they have about changes in bodily sensations. Clients may do this by keeping diaries of the cognitions they have about their bodies on days between therapy sessions, particularly when they begin to feel they are going to panic. Figure 6.6 (p. 190), illustrates the entries in one man's panic thoughts diary. He noted that he had mild symptoms of panic while in his office at work but more severe symptoms while riding the subway home. In both situations, he had thoughts about feeling trapped and suffocating and thought he was going to faint.

Many clients need to experience real panic symptoms in the presence of their therapist before they can begin to identify their catastrophizing cognitions. They are too overwhelmed by their symptoms when they are having them outside the therapy office to pay attention to their thoughts. Thus, the therapist may try to induce panic symptoms in clients during therapy sessions, by having clients exercise to elevate their heart rates or spin to get dizzy or put their heads between their knees and then stand up quickly so they get lightheaded (due to sudden changes in blood pressure). None of these activities is dangerous but all are likely to produce the kind of symptoms that clients catastrophize. As clients are experiencing these symptoms and

EXTRAORDINARY PEOPLE

Albert Ellis, the Phobic Psychologist

Albert Ellis is best known as the psychologist who developed rational-emotive therapy, a form of cognitive therapy in which therapists confront clients with their irrational beliefs in an attempt to change those beliefs (see Chapter 5). What most people don't know about Albert Ellis, however, is that he also suffered from phobias—particularly a phobia of public speaking—that were so severe that they could have prevented his career. Fortunately, Ellis was apparently a born psychologist because he devised methods for treating himself that hadn't been discovered by psychologists at the time, but are now part of many therapists' tool kit:

At 19, Ellis became active in a political group but was hampered by his terror of public speaking. Confronting his worst demons in the first of many "shame-attacking" exercises he would devise, Ellis repeatedly forced himself to speak up in any political context that would permit it. "Without calling it that, I was doing early desensitization on myself," he says. "Instead of just getting good at this, I found I was very good at it. And now you can't keep me away from a public platform."

After mastering his fear of public speaking, Ellis decided to work on the terrors of more private communication. "I was always violently interested in women," he says. "I would see them and flirt and exchange glances, but I always made excuses not to talk to them and was terrified of being rejected.

"Since I lived near The New York Botanical Garden in the Bronx, I decided to attack my fear and shame with an exercise in the park. I vowed that whenever I saw a reasonably attractive woman up to the age of 35, rather than sitting a bench away as I normally would, I would sit next to her with the specific goal of opening a conversation within one minute. I sat next to 130 consecutive women who fit my criteria. Thirty of the women got up and walked away, but about 100 spoke to me—about their knitting, the birds, a book, whatever. I made only one date out of all these contacts—and she stood me up.

According to learning theory and strict behavior therapy, my lack of rewards should have extinguished my efforts to meet women. But I realized that throughout this exercise no one vomited, no one called a cop, and I didn't die. The process of trying new behaviors and understanding what happened in the real world instead of in my imagination led me to overcome my fear of speaking to women." (Warga, 1988, p. 56)

So rational-emotive therapy was born. Ellis later received his doctorate in psychology from Columbia Teacher's College and took training to become a psychoanalyst. He soon rejected psychoanalytic thinking, and by the late 1950s had established the Institute for Rational-Emotive Therapy. Over the subsequent 50 years, he has written many books on this type of therapy, and on sexuality, has treated thousands of clients, and has given thousands of public lectures. He says, "I love my work . . . I like helping people" (Warga, 1988, p. 58).

their catastrophizing cognitions, the therapist helps them "collect" these thoughts.

Third, clients practice using their relaxation and breathing exercises while experiencing panic symptoms in the therapy session. If the panic attacks occur during sessions, the therapist will talk clients through them, coaching them in the use of relaxation and breathing skills, suggesting ways of improving their skills, and noting successes clients have in using these skills to stop the attacks.

Fourth, the therapist will challenge clients' catastrophizing thoughts about their bodily sensations and teach them to challenge their thoughts for themselves, using the cognitive techniques described in Chapter 5. The therapist might help clients reinterpret bodily sensations accurately. For example, the client whose thoughts are illustrated in Figure 6.6 frequently felt he was choking. His therapist might explore whether his choking sensation might be due to the stuffiness of a small office or a subway on a warm summer day. If he

Situation	Symptoms and severity	Thoughts
Office at work	Choking (mild) Dizziness (mild) Heart racing (mild)	Oh, I can't have an attack here. People will see me and I might get fired. I'm suffocating! I'm going to faint.
Riding subway home	Sweating (severe) Choking (severe) Shaking (severe) Heart racing (severe) Dizziness (severe)	I can't stand this! I've got to get out of here. I'm going to choke to death. I'm trapped. I'm going to faint!
At home	Sweating (mild) Heart still racing (moderate) A little faintness	I can't believe I made it home.

FIGURE 6.6   A Panic Thoughts Diary. This man recorded the thoughts he had during panic attacks and then worked on these thoughts in cognitive therapy.

TAKING PSYCHOLOGY PERSONALLY

Relaxation Exercises

Therapists often teach clients with anxiety disorders to use relaxation exercises to quell their anxiety. These exercises can also be used to combat the everyday anxiety and the tension associated with anger that arises in most people's lives. Here are a few exercises that you can use when you feel tense or anxious (taken from Rimm & Masters, 1979; Schafer, 1992).

Six-Second Quieting Response

This is a simple breathing technique that you can use very quickly (it only takes 6 seconds!) and in almost any situation to relax when you feel anxious or angry.

1. Draw a long, deep breath.

2. Hold it for 2 or 3 seconds.

3. Exhale slowly and completely.

4. As you exhale, let your jaw and shoulders drop. Feel relaxation flow into your arms and hands.

Quick Head, Neck, and Shoulder Relaxers

The remainder of the exercises we describe involve tensing or stretching certain muscles. If you have had a signif-icant injury, such as whiplash or an injured back, you should not try these exercises without first consulting your physician or physical therapist.

Some of the muscles that most commonly tense up when we are anxious or angry are the neck and shoulder muscles. A quick way to release some of this tension is to first tighten the neck and shoulder muscles as much as possible, then hold this for 5 to 10 seconds. Then com-pletely release the muscles. Repeat this a number of times, focusing on the contrast between the tension and the relaxation.

You can also release some neck and shoulder ten-sion by gently rotating your shoulders first forward and then backward. You can also gently rotate your head from side to side and from front to back in a circular motion. Then repeat the movements in the opposite direction. Continue this exercise a number of times until you feel more relaxed. Perform this exercise very slowly and gently or you may strain neck muscles.

The muscles on the forehead are also tensed when you are anxious or angry, and your teeth may be clenched. To relax your forehead, lift your eyebrows gently and re-lease lines of tension or fatigue. Then relax your forehead as you use the breathing exercise described. Check to see

Continued

if your teeth are clenched and, if so, relax your jaw while breathing deeply and slowly.

Progressive Muscle Relaxation

Progressive muscle relaxation is a set of techniques for successively tensing and then relaxing voluntary muscles in an orderly sequence until all the muscles are relaxed. Before beginning this exercise, you should get as comfortable as possible, sitting down, with any tight clothing loosened. You might also want to begin by using the Six-Second Quieting Response described to start you down the path to relaxation.

Go through each of the next steps in the order given. Spend 10 seconds tensing each muscle group, and then at least 10 to 15 seconds relaxing. Repeat the 10 seconds of tensing that muscle group, followed by another 10 to 15 seconds relaxing. During the relaxation period, focus on the positive sensations of relaxation and try not to worry about anything else. If you feel that muscle group has relaxed sufficiently, move on to the next one. As you progress through the muscle groups, concentrate hard on tensing only the muscle group you are working on in that step. Try not to let any of the other muscle groups, particularly the ones you have already tensed and relaxed, to be tensed again (the following progression is taken from Rimm & Masters, 1979):

1. *Hands.* Tense your fists, and then relax them. Then extend your fingers as far as possible, and then relax them.

2. *Biceps and triceps.* Tense your biceps, and then relax. Tense your triceps, and then relax

3. *Shoulders.* Pull your shoulders back, and then relax. Push your shoulders forward, and then relax.

4. *Neck.* Slowly roll your head on your neck's axis three or four times in one direction, and then in the opposite direction.

5. *Mouth.* Open your mouth as wide as possible, and then relax. Purse your lips in an exaggerated pout, and then relax.

6. *Tongue.* With your mouth open, extend your tongue as far as possible, and then relax. Next, bring your tongue back into your throat as far as possible, and

then relax. Next, dig your tongue into the roof of your mouth as hard as possible, and then relax. Finally, dig your tongue into the floor of your mouth as hard as possible, and then relax.

7. *Eyes and forehead.* Close your eyes and imagine you are looking at something pleasant far away. Focus your eyes so that you can see and enjoy the distant object. Continue this for about 1 minute.

8. *Breathing.* Take as deep a breath as possible, and then relax.

9. *Back.* With your shoulders resting against a chair, push the trunk of your body forward so as to arch your entire back, and then relax. Do this very slowly, and if you experience any pain, relax immediately and do not repeat this exercise.

10. *Midsection.* Raise your midsection slightly by tensing your buttocks, and then relax. Lower your midsection slightly by digging your buttocks into the seat of your chair, and then relax.

11. *Thighs.* Extend and raise your legs about 6 inches off the floor, trying not to tense your stomach muscles, and then relax. Dig your heels or the back of your feet into the floor, and then relax.

12. *Stomach.* Pull your stomach in as hard as possible, and then relax. Extend your stomach out as much as possible, and then relax.

13. *Calves and feet.* Support your legs, and bend your feet so that your toes are pointed toward your head, and then relax. Next, bend your feet in the opposite direction, and the relax. If your muscles should cramp during this exercise, relax them and shake them loose.

14. *Toes.* With your legs supported and your feet relaxed, dig your toes into the bottom of your shoes, and then relax. Then bend your toes in the opposite direction until they dig into the tops of your shoes, and then relax.

15. *Breathing.* Breathe slowly and deeply for 2 to 3 minutes. Each time you exhale, say the word *calm* to yourself.

interprets the increase in his heart rate as a heart attack, the therapist might have him collect evidence from his physician that he is in perfect cardiac health. The therapist and client might also explore the client's expectations that he is sure to die of a heart attack because a relative of his did. If the therapist induces panic symptoms in the client during a therapy session, and the client is able to reduce these symptoms with relaxation or breathing skills, the therapist will use this success to challenge the client's belief that there is nothing that can be done to control the panic symptoms once they begin.

Fifth, the therapist will use **systematic desensitization** techniques to gradually expose clients to those situations they most fear while helping them maintain control over their panic symptoms. Clients and therapist will compose a list of panic-inducing situations, from most threatening to least threatening. Then, after learning relaxation and breathing skills and perhaps gaining some control over panic symptoms induced during therapy sessions, clients will begin to expose themselves to their panic-inducing situations, beginning with the least threatening. The therapist may accompany the client on trips to the panic-inducing situations, coaching them in the use of their relaxation and breathing skills and their skills in challenging catastrophic cognitions that arise in these situations. Here is an example of an interchange between a therapist and client as they ride together in the client's car.

Voices

Client: I really don't think we should be doing this. I might have a panic attack while I'm driving. I wouldn't want to be responsible for an accident while you're in the car.

Therapist: Do you think I would have gotten in the car if I thought that it was likely you would have a panic attack and wreck the car?

Client: No, probably not, but I'm really scared.

Therapist: Yes, I understand. Have you ever had a car wreck?

Client: No, I just always worry about one.

Therapist: Remember, our worries are not reality. Tell me what else is going through your mind.

Client: I feel like my chest is about to cave in. I'm having trouble breathing. Oh no, here I go. . . .

Therapist: Okay, let's begin using some of your exercises. Try counting backwards from 100 by 7s. Breathe in deeply with the first count, then out with the second count, and so on.

Client: Okay, I'll try. [Breathes in.] One hundred. [Breathes out.] Ninety-three. [Breathes in.] Eighty-six. [Breathes out.]

Therapists working with people who have anxiety disorders may do in vivo therapy, helping them learn to handle their symptoms in the places most likely to trigger the symptoms.

Therapist: How are you feeling now?

Client: Better. I'm not as panicked. Oh my gosh, here comes a bridge. I hate bridges.

Therapist: What do you hate about bridges?

Client: If I ever had an accident on a bridge, I'd be more likely to die.

Therapist: What do you think is the likelihood that you are going to have an accident on a bridge?

Client: Well, sometimes it feels like it's 100%!

Therapist: But what do you think it really is?

Client: Probably very low. Hey, we're already over that bridge!

Therapist: Okay, there's another bridge coming up in a couple of miles. I want you to decide what strategies you're going to use to help yourself feel less panicked as we approach the bridge.

Eighty-five to 90 percent of panic disorder patients treated with this combined cognitive and behavioral treatment experience complete relief from their panic attacks within 12 weeks (Barlow et al., 1989; Clark et al., 1994; Klosko et al., 1990). Follow-up studies of patients receiving this treatment have found that nearly 90 percent are classified as panic-free 2 years after the treatment (Craske, Brown, & Barlow, 1991; Margraf et al., 1993; see also Bruce, Spiegel, & Hegel, 1999). David Clark and colleagues (1994) compared cognitive-behavioral therapy to antidepressant therapy and relaxation therapy. They found that 85 percent of the patients in cognitive-behavioral therapy were classified as panic-free at a follow-up 15 months after the therapy compared to 60 percent of the patients receiving only tricyclic antidepressants and 47 percent of the patients receiving only relaxation therapy. These treatments for panic hold much hope for people suffering from this debilitating condition.

Summing Up

- Panic disorder is characterized by sudden bursts of anxiety symptoms, a sense of loss of control or unreality, and the sense that one is dying.
- Several neurotransmitters, including norepinephrine, serotonin, GABA, and CCK have been implicated in panic disorders.
- The kindling model of panic disorders suggests dysregulation of the locus ceruleus causes panic attacks, and also kindles the limbic system, lowering the threshold for chronic anxiety. This chronic anxiety then increases a person's risk of a new panic attack.
- The suffocation false alarm theory suggests that people with panic attacks are hypersensitive to increases in levels of carbon dioxide in the brain, which sends them into frequent fight-or-flight responses.
- There is some evidence that genetics plays a role in panic disorders.
- The cognitive model suggests that people with panic disorder are hypersensitive to bodily symptoms and tend to catastrophize these symptoms.
- The vulnerability-stress model suggests that people who develop panic disorder are born with a biological predisposition to an overactive fight-or-flight response, but don't develop the disorder unless they also tend to catastrophize their bodily symptoms.
- Tricyclic antidepressants, serotonin reuptake inhibitors, and benzodiazepines can be helpful in reducing symptoms but these symptoms tend to recur once the drugs are discontinued.
- Cognitive-behavioral therapy has proven very useful in reducing and preventing relapse in panic disorder.

↻ PHOBIAS

People can develop phobias of many things. Madonna suffers from brontophobia, the fear of thunder. Michael Jackson has a fear of earthquakes. Johnny Depp has a fear of clowns.

Medical-sounding names have been created for many of these phobias. In this section, we will consider three groups of phobias: agoraphobia, which is a phobia about a wide range of places, often accompanied by panic attacks, specific phobias about objects or situations, and social phobias about social situations in particular (see *Concept Review:* Phobic Disorders).

Agoraphobia

The term *agoraphobia* is from the Greek for "fear of the marketplace." People with **agoraphobia** fear crowded, bustling places, such as the marketplace or, in our times, the shopping mall. They also fear enclosed spaces, such as buses, subways, or elevators. Finally, they fear wide open spaces, such as open fields, particularly if they are alone. In general, people with agoraphobia fear any places where they might have trouble escaping or getting help in an emergency (see Table 6.3). The particular emergency that they fear is often a panic attack. Thus, the person with agoraphobia will think, "If I have a panic attack while I'm in this mall (or on this airplane, or in this movie theater, or on this deserted beach), it will be hard for me to get away quickly or to find help." People with agoraphobia also often fear that they will embarrass themselves if others see their symptoms of panic or their frantic efforts to escape during a panic attack. Actually, other people can rarely tell when a person is having a panic attack.

Agoraphobia can occur in people who do not have panic attacks (Eaton & Keyl, 1990). The vast majority of people with agoraphobia do experience either full-blown panic attacks, more moderate panic attacks, or severe social phobia in which they

TABLE 6.3
Places Avoided by People with Agoraphobia

People with agoraphobia avoid situations in which they would have trouble getting help or would be embarrassed if they had an emergency, such as a panic attack.

Shopping malls	Theaters
Automobiles	Supermarkets
Buses	Stores
Trains	Crowds
Subways	Planes
Tunnels	Elevators
Restaurants	Escalators

Source: Adapted from Barlow & Craske, 1994.

CONCEPT REVIEW

Phobic Disorders

These are the phobic disorders recognized in the DSM-IV.

Phobic Disorder	Description	Example
Agoraphobia	Fear of places where help might not be available in case of an emergency	Person becomes housebound because anyplace other than his apartment arouses extreme anxiety symptoms.
Specific phobias	Fear of specific objects, places or situations:	
Animal type	Specific animals or insects	Person has extreme fear of dogs, cats, or spiders.
Natural environment type	Events or situations in the natural environment	Person has extreme fear of storms, heights, or water.
Situational type	Public transportation, tunnels, bridges, elevators, flying, driving	Person becomes extremely claustrophobic in elevators.
Blood-injection-injury type	Blood, injury, injections	Person panics when viewing a child's scraped knee.
Social phobia	Fear of being judged or embarrassed by others	Person avoids all social situations and becomes a recluse for fear of encountering others' judgment.

experience paniclike symptoms in social situations (Barlow, 1988; McNally, 1994). In most cases, agoraphobia begins within one year after a person begins experiencing frequent anxiety symptoms.

The lives of people with agoraphobia can be terribly disrupted, and even brought to a complete halt. Just think how difficult it would be to carry on daily life if you could not ride in a car, bus, train, or airplane; you could not go into a store; you could not stand being in any kind of crowd. Lia's case illustrates how debilitating agoraphobia can be:

CASE STUDY

Lia was a graduate student who was conducting research on children's styles of learning in the classroom. For her research, Lia needed to travel to local elementary schools and observe children in classrooms for a couple of hours each day. Lia had spent months developing good relationships with the schools, teachers, and children who were participating in her research. Everyone was excited about the potential for Lia's research to improve classroom teaching. It seemed that Lia was on her way toward a promising career as an educational researcher.

The only problem was that Lia could not leave her apartment. Over the last year, she had become terrified at the idea of driving her car, convinced that she would have a fatal car accident. She had tried to ride the public bus instead, but when she got onto the bus, she felt like she was

choking, and she was so dizzy she almost missed her stop. So she began walking everywhere she went. The elementary schools participating in her research were too far away for her to walk to them, however. Moreover, Lia was becoming afraid even when she stepped out of her apartment. When she walked onto her street, it seemed to open into a big chasm. The thought of being confined in a small elementary school classroom for two hours was just intolerable.

Lia was beginning to believe that she was going to have to abandon her research and her degree. She could not see any way to finish her work. Even if she did get her degree, how could she possibly hold a job if she could not even leave her apartment?

Like Lia, people with agoraphobia often get to the point where they will not leave their own homes. Sometimes, they can venture out with a close family member who makes them feel "safe." However, family members and friends often have trouble understanding their anxiety and may not be willing to chaperone them everywhere they go. People with agoraphobia may force themselves to enter situations that frighten them, as Lia had been forcing herself to travel for her research. The persistent and intense anxiety they experience in these situations can be miserable, however, and like Lia, many people just give up and remain confined to their homes. Some agoraphobics turn to

People with agoraphobia fear both crowded places they may not be able to escape, and wide open places where they may not be able to get help, if they should panic.

alcohol and other substances to dampen these anxiety symptoms.

Agoraphobia strikes people in their youth. In one large study, more than 70 percent of people who developed agoraphobia did so before the age of 25, and 50 percent developed the disorder before the age of 15 (Bourden et al., 1988).

Specific Phobias

Agoraphobia is different from many people's conception of a phobia, because people with agoraphobia fear such a wide variety of situations. In contrast, the **specific phobias** conform more to popular conceptions of phobia. Most specific phobias fall into one of four categories, however (APA, 2000): animal type, natural environment type, situational type, and blood-injection-injury type. When people with these phobias encounter their feared objects or situations, their anxiety is immediate and intense, and they may even have full panic attacks. They also become anxious if they believe there is any chance they might encounter their feared objects or situations, and will go to great lengths to avoid the objects or situations. Whoopie Goldberg is one of several movie stars who is afraid of flying in airplanes. She travels from one end of the country to the other in a private bus to avoid flying.

Adults with phobias recognize that their anxieties are illogical and unreasonable. Children may not have this insight, however, and just have the anxiety. As many as one in ten people will have a specific phobia at some time, making it one of the most common disorders (Kessler et al., 1994). Most phobias develop during childhood. Almost 90 percent of people with a specific phobia never seek treatment (Regier et al., 1993).

Animal type phobias are focused on specific animals or insects, such as dogs, cats, snakes, and spiders. A snake phobia appears to be the most common type of animal phobia in the United States (Agras, Sylvester, & Oliveau, 1969). Other animals or insects, such as scorpions, may be more commonly feared in other countries. Many people fear certain animals or insects, such as snakes or spiders, and if they come across one of these they may startle and move away quickly. Most of these people would not be diagnosed with a phobia because they do not live in terror of encountering a snake or spider or organize their lives around avoiding snakes or spiders. People with phobias go to great lengths to avoid the objects of their fears. For example,

Whoopie Goldberg is just one of many celebrities who has suffered from a serious phobia.

One of the most common specific phobias is a snake phobia.

one woman with a severe spider phobia would spray powerful insecticide around the perimeter of her apartment (which was in a pristine, new apartment building) once a week to prevent spiders from coming in. The fumes from this insecticide made her physically ill, and her neighbors complained of the smell. However, this woman was so fearful of encountering a spider that she withstood the fumes and her neighbors' complaints, remaining vigilant for any signs of a spider web in her apartment. She refused to go into older buildings because she believed they were more likely to hold spiders. Since she lived in a city with many old buildings, this meant that she could not go into the homes of many of her friends or into establishments where she might want to do business.

Natural environment type phobias are focused on events or situations in the natural environment, such as storms, heights, or water. As with fears of animals or insects, mild to moderate fears of these natural events or situations are extremely common. Again, however, these fears do not usually cause people much inconvenience or concern in their daily lives and thus would not be considered phobias. It is only when people begin reorganizing their lives to avoid their feared situations or having severe anxiety attacks when confronted with the situations that a diagnosis of phobia is warranted.

Situational type phobias usually involve fear of public transportation, tunnels, bridges, elevators, flying, and driving. Claustrophobia, or fear of enclosed spaces, is a common situational phobia. People with situational phobias believe they might have panic attacks in their phobic situations, and indeed often have had panic attacks when forced into those situations. Unlike people with agoraphobia, people with situational phobias tend to have panic attacks only in the specific situations they fear. Situational phobias often

arise in people between 2 and 7 years of age, but another common period of onset is the mid-20s.

The final type, **blood-injection-injury type phobias,** was first recognized in DSM-IV. People with this type of phobia fear seeing blood or an injury or receiving an injection or experiencing some other invasive medical procedure.

CASE STUDY

When her son José was born, Irene decided to quit her job and become a full-time mother. She had enjoyed José's infancy tremendously. He was a happy baby and had hardly been ill for the first two years of his life. Now that he was a toddler, however, José was beginning to get the usual skinned knees and bumps and bruises that small children do. Irene had always been squeamish about blood, but she thought she could overcome this when it came to caring for her son. The first time José scraped his knee seriously enough for it to bleed, however, Irene became dizzy upon seeing it and fainted. José screamed and cried in terror at seeing his mother faint. Fortunately, a neighbor saw what happened and quickly came over to comfort José and see that Irene was okay. Since then, Irene has fainted three more times upon seeing José injured. She has begun to think that she will not be able to care for José by herself any longer.

Irene's reaction to seeing José's scraped knee illustrates the unusual physiological reaction of people with blood-injection-injury type phobias to their feared objects. Whereas people with one of the other specific phobias typically experience increases in heart rate, blood pressure, and other fight-or-flight physiological changes when confronted with their feared objects or situations, people with blood-injection-injury type of phobia experience significant *drops* in heart rate and blood pressure when confronted with their feared stimuli and are likely to faint. This type of phobia runs more strongly in families than do the other types (Ost, 1992).

Social Phobia

Social phobia is not categorized as a specific phobia because, rather than fearing a specific (often inanimate) object or situation, people with social phobia fear being judged or embarrassing themselves in front of other people. Social phobia also differs from the specific phobias in that it is more likely to create severe disruption in a person's daily life (Kessler et al, 1998). It is easier in most cultures to avoid snakes or spiders than it is to avoid social situations in which you might embarrass yourself. Consider the inner pain that this social phobic suffers and the way that he has organized his life to avoid social situations:

CASE STUDY

Malcolm was a computer expert who worked for a large software firm. One of the things he hated to do most was ride the elevator at the building where he worked when there were other people on it. He felt that everyone was watching him, commenting silently on his ruffled clothes, and noticing every time he moved his body. He held his breath for almost the entire elevator ride, afraid that he might say something or make some sound that would embarrass him. Often, he would walk up the eight flights of stairs to his office rather than take the risk that someone might get on the elevator with him.

Malcolm rarely went anywhere except to work and home. He hated even to go to the grocery store for fear he would run his cart into someone else or say something stupid to a grocery clerk. He found a grocery store and several restaurants that allowed customers to send orders for food over the computer to be delivered to their homes. He liked this service because he could use it to avoid even talking to someone over the phone to place the order.

In the past, Malcolm's job had allowed him to remain quietly in his office all day, without interacting with other people. Recently, however, his company was reorganized and it took on a number of new projects. Malcolm's supervisor said that everyone in Malcolm's group needed to begin to work together more closely to develop these new products. Malcolm was supposed to make a presentation to his group on some software he was developing, but he called in sick the day of the presentation because he could not face it. Malcolm was thinking that he had to change jobs and that perhaps he would go into private consulting so he could work from his home rather than having to work with anyone else.

TABLE 6.4
Lifetime Prevalence of Social Fears in a National Survey

Social Fear	Percent of People Saying They Experienced This Fear in Their Lifetimes
Public speaking	30.2
Talking in front of a small group	15.2
Talking with others	13.7
Using a toilet away from home	6.6
Writing while someone watches	6.4
Eating or drinking in public	2.7
Any social fear	38.6

Source: Kessler, Stein, & Berglund, 1998, p. 614.

Many people get a little nervous when they are speaking in front of a group of people or must join a group of people already engaged in conversation (see Table 6.4). However, people like Malcolm get more than a little nervous. If they find themselves in social situations, they may begin trembling and perspiring, feel confused and dizzy, have heart palpitations, and eventually a full panic attack. Like Malcolm, they are sure that others see their nervousness and judge them as inarticulate, weak, stupid, or "crazy." Malcolm avoided public speaking or having conversations with others for fear of being judged. People with a social phobia may avoid eating or drinking in public, for fear they will make noises when they eat, drop food, or otherwise embarrass themselves. They may avoid writing in public, including signing their name, for fear that others will see their hand tremble. Men with social phobia will often avoid urinating in public bathrooms for fear of embarrassing themselves. People like Malcolm who fear many social situations, from public speaking or attending a party to just having a conversation with another person, are said to have a generalized type of social phobia.

Social phobia is relatively common, with about 8 percent of the U.S. adult population qualifying for the diagnosis in a 12-month period and one in eight people experiencing the disorder at some time in their life (Kessler et al., 1998; Schneier et al., 1992). Social phobia typically begins in the adolescent years, when many people become excessively self-conscious and concerned about others' opinions of them (Blazer et al., 1991). Some people report humiliating experiences that triggered their social phobia. Some children seem excessively shy and fearful of others from a very young age, however, and these children may be more prone to develop social phobia (Biederman, Bolduc-Murphy, & Faraone, 1993). Social phobia is often comorbid with mood disorders, other anxiety disorders, and antisocial personality disorder (Kessler et al., 1998). Once it develops, social phobia tends to be a chronic problem if untreated. Most people with a social phobia do not seek treatment for their symptoms (Kessler et al., 1998).

Psychological Theories of Phobias

The phobias have been the battleground between different psychological approaches to abnormality, and the focus of some of the most revolutionary psychological theories developed in the last century. *Concept Review*: Theories of Phobias summarizes the theories we review in this section.

CONCEPT REVIEW

Theories of Phobias

The psychodynamic, behavioral, and biological theories of phobias take very different approaches to explaining these disorders.

Theory	Description	Example
Psychodynamic theory	Phobias result when unconscious anxiety is displaced onto a neutral object.	Little Hans' development of a horse phobia, which represented his Oedipal fears of his father.
Behavioral theories	1. Classical conditioning leads to fear of the object when it is paired with a naturally frightening event.	1. A child who falls into a river and cannot swim develops a fear of water.
	2. Avoidance of the object reduces anxiety, thus is reinforced through operant conditioning.	2. An agoraphobic learns that by staying in her apartment, panic attacks are less likely, and thus staying in her apartment is reinforced.
	3. Humans are prepared through evolutionary history to develop phobias to objects or situations that were dangerous to our ancient ancestors.	3. Humans develop phobias to spiders and heights more easily than to guns or powerlines.
Biological theories	Genetics contributes to risk for phobias, either directly or by creating certain temperaments that are more prone to phobias.	Children with phobias often have relatives with the same phobia, or tend to be excessively timid or shy.

Psychodynamic Theories of Phobias

Freud's theory of the development of phobias is one of his most well-known. He argued that phobias result when unconscious anxiety is displaced onto a neutral or symbolic object (Freud, 1909). That is, people become phobic of objects not because they have any real fear of the objects, but because they have displaced their anxiety over other issues onto the object. This theory is detailed in a 150-page case history of a little boy named Hans, who had a phobia of horses after seeing a horse fall on the ground and writhe around violently. How did Hans' phobia develop? According to Freud, young boys have a sexual desire for their mother and jealously hate their father, but fear that their fathers will castrate them in retaliation for this desire. As we discussed in Chapter 2, this phenomenon is known as the Oedipus complex. In Freud's interpretation, little Hans found the anxiety created by this conflict so unbearable that he unconsciously displaced this anxiety onto horses, which somehow symbolized his father for him. Freud's evidence for this formulation came from Little Hans' answers to a series of leading questions asked by Freud and by Hans' father. After long conversations about horses and what Hans was "really"

afraid of, Hans reportedly became less fearful of horses because, according to Freud, he had gained insight into the true source of his anxiety.

There is little reason to accept Freud's theory of phobias, either in the case of Hans or in general. Hans never provided any spontaneous or direct evidence that his real concerns were Oedipal concerns instead of fear of horses. In addition, Hans' phobia of horses decreased slowly over time rather than suddenly in response to some insight. Many children have specific fears that simply fade with time with no intervention. In general, psychodynamic therapy for phobias is not highly effective, suggesting that insight into unconscious anxieties is not what is needed in treating phobias.

Behavioral Theories of Phobias

In contrast to the psychodynamic theories, the behavioral theories have been very successful in explaining the onset of at least some phobias. According to these theories, classical conditioning leads to the fear of the phobic object, and operant conditioning helps to maintain that fear. Recall that in classical conditioning a previously neutral object (the conditioned stimulus) is

People with social phobia become highly anxious at the idea that others might observe their behavior.

Classical Conditioning

The first application of these theories to phobias came in a series of studies done 80 years ago by a philosopher turned behaviorist, John Watson, and a graduate student named Rosalie Raynor (1920). Their subject in these studies was an 11-month-old boy named Little Albert. One day, Watson and Raynor placed a white rat in front of Little Albert. As Little Albert playfully reached for the white rat, they banged a metal bar loudly just above his head. Naturally, Little Albert was completely startled, nearly jumped out of his diapers, quickly pulled his hand away from the rat, and then broke down whimpering. This only encouraged Watson and Raynor to continue their study, however. After several more pairings of the white rat with the loud noise from the metal bar, Little Albert would have nothing to do with the creature, in effect developing a fear of the white rat. When presented with it, he would retreat and show distress. Little Albert's fear also generalized to other white furry animals—he would not approach white rabbits either. Although by today's standards, this experiment with Little Albert would raise serious ethical questions, it did lay the groundwork for the behavioral theories of phobias by showing powerfully that a phobia could easily be created through classical conditioning. In the case of Little Albert, the unconditioned stimulus (US) was the loud noise from the banged bar, and the unconditioned response (UR) was his startle response to the loud noise. The conditioned stimulus (CS) was the white rat, and the conditioned response (CR) was the startle and fear response to the white rat (see Figure 6.7).

If Little Albert were subsequently presented with the white rat several times without the bar being banged behind his head, his fear of white rats should have been extinguished, according to what we know about classical conditioning. Most people who develop a phobia, however, will try to avoid being exposed to their feared object. Thus, they avoid the exposure that could extinguish their phobia. In addition, if they are suddenly confronted with their feared object, they will

paired with an object that naturally elicits a reaction (an unconditioned stimulus that elicits an unconditioned response) until the previously neutral object elicits the same reaction (which is now called the conditioned response). So when a tone is paired with an electric shock, the conditioned stimulus is the tone, the electric shock is the unconditioned stimulus, the unconditioned response is anxiety in response to the shock, and the conditioned response is anxiety in response to the tone.

1. Unconditioned stimulus	naturally leads to	Unconditioned response
Banged bar	naturally leads to	Startle
2. Unconditioned stimulus	paired with	Conditioned stimulus
Banged bar	paired with	White rat
3. Conditioned stimulus	then leads to	Conditioned response
White rat	then leads to	Startle

FIGURE 6.7   The Behavioral Account of Little Albert's Phobia. The behavioral account of Little Albert's phobia of the white rat is that the pairing of the banged bar (the US), which naturally leads to a startle response (the UR), and the white rat (the CS) leads eventually to the white rat producing the same startle response (now referred to as the CR).

experience extreme anxiety and run away as quickly as possible. The running away, or avoidance, is reinforced by the subsequent reduction of their anxiety. Thus, through operant conditioning, behaviors that help to maintain the phobia are reinforced.

For example, Malcolm, the social phobic previously described, had developed a wide array of avoidant behaviors to prevent exposing himself to what he feared most: the possibility of scrutiny by others. He would walk up several flights of stairs rather than be trapped in an elevator for a few minutes with another person who might notice something odd about Malcolm's clothes or mannerisms. He paid a great deal of money to have his groceries delivered rather than risk going to a crowded grocery store where he might embarrass himself in front of other people. He was even prepared to quit his job to avoid having to make presentations or work closely with others on projects. These avoidant behaviors created much hardship for Malcolm, but they reduced his anxiety and therefore were greatly reinforced. Also, as a result of this avoidance, Malcolm never had the opportunity to extinguish his anxiety about social situations.

Safety Signal Hypothesis

The behavioral theory also does a good job in explaining why agoraphobia so often develops in people with panic disorder (see Figure 6.8). The fear of panic attacks leads the individual to search for safe people and places that are associated with a low risk of panic attacks. These safe people and places have been referred to as *safety signals*. According to the **safety signal hypothesis** (Seligman & Binik, 1977), people remember vividly the places in which they have had panic attacks, even if the panic attacks have come on by surprise, with no obvious environmental triggers. They associate these places with their symptoms of panic and may begin to feel these symptoms again if they return to these places. By avoiding these places, they reduce their symptoms, and their avoidance behavior is thus highly reinforced. So if a man has a panic attack while sitting in the theater, he may later associate the theater with his panic symptoms and begin to feel anxious whenever he is near the theater. He can reduce his anxiety by avoiding the theater. In addition, other places, such as his own home or perhaps a specific room in his home, may become associated with lowered anxiety levels, and being in these places is thus reinforcing. So through straightforward classical and operant conditioning, the person's behavior becomes shaped in ways that lead to the development of agoraphobia.

The behavioral theory of phobias was one of the most elegant examples of the application of basic learning principles to understanding of a mysterious psychological disorder. Many people with phobias can recount the specific traumatic experiences that triggered their phobias: being bitten by a dog, being trapped in an elevator, nearly drowning in a lake, humiliating themselves while speaking in public. For them, the behavioral accounts of their phobias seem to ring true. In an extension of the behavioral theory, some argued that phobias can develop through observational learning and not just through direct classical conditioning. According to this theory, people can develop phobias by watching someone else experience extreme fear in response to a situation. For example, small children may learn that snakes are to be feared when their parents have severe fright reactions upon seeing snakes (Bandura, 1969; Mineka et al., 1984).

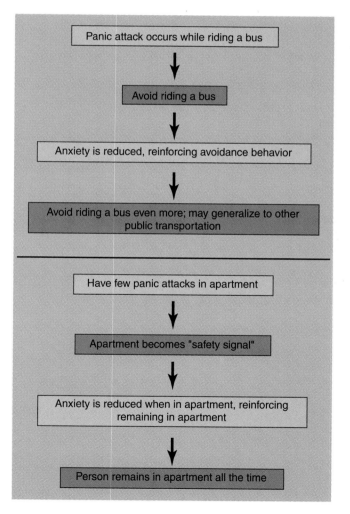

FIGURE 6.8   How Agoraphobic Behaviors Develop in Panic Disorder. Behavioral theories argue that agoraphobic behaviors develop when avoidance of situations in which panic has often occurred and remaining in situations where panic has occurred less often are reinforced by reduction of anxiety.

Prepared Classical Conditioning

Another extension of the behavioral theory of phobias seems to answer an interesting question about phobias: Why do humans develop phobias to some objects or situations and not to others (deSilva, Rachman, & Seligman, 1977; Mineka, 1985; Seligman, 1970)? For example, phobias of spiders, snakes, and heights are common, but phobias of flowers are not. The common characteristic of many phobic objects appears to be that these are things whose avoidance, over evolutionary history, has been advantageous for humans. Our distant ancestors had good reason to be fearful of insects, snakes, heights, loud noises, and strangers. Those who learned quickly to avoid these situations were more likely to survive and bear offspring. Thus, evolution may have selected for rapid conditioning of fear to certain objects or situations. Although these objects or situations are not as likely to cause us harm today, we carry the vestiges of our evolutionary history and are biologically prepared to learn certain associations quickly. This preparedness is known as **prepared classical conditioning.** In contrast, many objects that are more likely to cause us harm in today's world (such as guns and knives) have not been around long enough, evolutionarily speaking, to be selected for rapid conditioning, so phobias of these objects should be relatively difficult to create.

How would you go about proving this idea of prepared classical conditioning? Researchers presented subjects with pictures of objects that theoretically should be evolutionarily selected for conditioning (snakes or spiders) or objects that should not be selected (houses, faces, and flowers) and paired the presentation of these pictures with short but painful electric shocks. The subjects developed anxiety reactions to the pictures of snakes and spiders within one or two pairings with shock, but it took four to five pairings of the pictures of houses, faces, or flowers with shock to create a fear reaction to these pictures. In addition, it was relatively easy to extinguish the subjects' anxiety reactions to houses or faces once the pictures were no longer paired with shock, but the anxiety reactions to spiders and snakes were difficult to extinguish (Hugdahl & Ohman, 1977; Ohman et al., 1976).

Thus, particularly with the addition of principles of observational learning and prepared classical conditioning, the behavioral theory of phobias seems to provide a compelling explanation for this disorder. As we shall see, the behavioral theory has also led to very effective therapies for phobias. The most significant problem with these theories is that many people with phobias can identify no traumatic event in their own lives or in the lives of people they are close to that triggered their phobias. Without conditioned

The theory of prepared classical conditioning says we are evolutionarily prepared to easily develop phobias of things, such as spiders, that have been dangerous to our distant ancestors.

stimuli, it is hard to argue that they developed their phobias through classical conditioning or observational learning.

Biological Theories

Family history studies provide some reason to think that phobias may be transmitted genetically, at least in part. About 30 percent of the first-degree relatives of people with specific phobias have the same phobias or phobias in the same category (Fyer et al., 1990). About 16 percent of the first-degree relatives of people with social phobia have an increased risk of social phobia, compared to 5 percent of the relatives of people without social phobia (Fyer et al, 1993; Kessler et al., 1998).

What may be inherited in some families is a temperament that makes it easier for phobias to be conditioned (Eysenck, 1967; Gray, 1987; Pavlov, 1927). Children who, as toddlers, are behaviorally inhibited—that is, excessively timid and shy—are at higher risk for the development of specific phobias during childhood than those who are not inhibited (Biederman et al, 1990). It may be that some children are born with a general tendency toward anxious reactions but learn their specific fears through their own difficult experiences or by modeling their parents, as illustrated by the case of Jennifer (adapted from Silverman & Ginsburg, 1995, pp. 169–170) on the next page.

In sum, although there is some evidence that genetics may play a role in susceptibility to phobias, the behavioral theories have proven most useful in explaining the development of these disorders. As we shall see in the next section, the behavioral therapies have proven most consistently and powerfully effective in the treatment of phobias, as well.

Treatments for Phobias

A number of different behavioral techniques are used to treat phobias. In addition, some therapists add cognitive techniques, and certain drug therapies, to their treatment regime for people with phobias (see *Concept Review:* Treatments for Phobias).

Behavioral Treatments

The goal of behavioral therapies for phobias is to extinguish fear of the feared object or situation by exposing the phobic person to the object or situation. The vast majority of phobias can be cured with these therapies (Emmelkamp, 1994; Wolpe, 1997). There are three basic forms of therapy in which this is done: *systematic desensitization, modeling,* and *flooding.*

Systematic Desensitization

As we discussed earlier in this chapter, in systematic desensitization clients formulate lists of situations or objects they fear, ranked from most feared to least feared. They learn relaxation techniques that will reduce the symptoms of anxiety they will experience when they are exposed to their feared objects. They

CONCEPT REVIEW

Treatments for Phobias

A number of treatments have proven useful for phobias.

Treatment	Description	Example
Behavioral treatments	Focus on extinguishing fear by exposing the person to the feared object or situation:	
1. Systematic desensitization	1. Gradually exposes the person to a hierarchy of fears while the person practices techniques to reduce the fear response.	Agoraphobic ventures out to least feared situation (such as the local grocery) first, practicing relaxation, and then gradually ventures to more and more fearful situations.
2. Modeling	2. Therapist models behaviors most feared by the client before asking the client to engage in behaviors.	Therapist handles a snake before asking a snake phobic to do so.
3. Flooding	3. Intensively exposes the client to the feared object until anxiety extinguishes.	Person with a fear of heights may look out the window of the 100th floor of a building until her anxiety passes.
Cognitive-behavioral therapy	Helps clients identify and challenge negative, catastrophizing thoughts about feared situations.	Therapist accompanies an agoraphobic to the local grocery, helping him challenge thoughts that he is about to have a panic attack.
Biological treatments	Reduce symptoms of anxiety generally so that they do not arise in the feared situation.	Benzodiazepines, monoamine oxidase inhibitors, serotonin reuptake inhibitors

then begin to expose themselves to the items on their "hierarchy of fears," beginning with the least feared item. For example, a person with a severe dog phobia might have as the first item on his list "seeing a picture of a dog in a magazine." This client might then first visualize a picture of a dog. As the client begins to feel anxious, the therapist will coach him to use his relaxation techniques to quell his anxious feelings. The point is to help the client replace his anxious reaction with the calm that comes with the relaxation techniques. When the client can visualize a picture of a dog without experiencing anxiety, he might move on to actually looking at a picture of a dog in a magazine, again using relaxation techniques to lower his anxiety reaction and replace it with a calm reaction. Gradually, the client and therapist will move through the entire list, until the client is able to pet a big dog without feeling overwhelming anxiety. Eighty to 90 percent of phobias can be cured with this treatment, with little risk of relapse after the therapy (Kazdin & Wilcoxon, 1976).

One of the specific phobias, blood-injection-injury phobia, requires a different approach from the other phobias (Ost & Sterner, 1987). Recall that, unlike people with other specific phobias whose blood pressure and heart rate increase when they confront their phobic objects, people with a blood-injection-injury phobia experience severe decreases in heart rate and blood pressure when confronted with their phobic objects. Sometimes, because less blood is circulating to their heads, they faint. Relaxation techniques would only worsen these people's natural response to their phobic object because such techniques also decrease blood pressure and heart rate. Thus, therapists must take the opposite approach with people with this phobia and teach them to tense the muscles in their arms, legs, and chest until they feel the warmth of their blood rising in their faces. This **applied tension technique** increases blood pressure and heart rate. When a person with a blood-injection-injury phobia learns this technique, she can use it when confronted with her phobic object to counteract her typical biological response and prevent fainting. Then systematic desensitization can be implemented to extinguish her fear of blood, injury, or injections.

Modeling

Modeling techniques are often used in conjunction with systematic desensitization techniques in the treatment of phobias. The therapist models the behaviors most feared by the client before the client attempts them himself. For example, if a therapist is treating a person with a snake phobia, she may perform each of the behaviors on the client's hierarchy of fears before asking the client to perform them: The therapist will stand in the room with the snake before asking the

client to do so, the therapist will touch the snake before the client is asked to do so, the therapist will hold the snake before the client does, and eventually the therapist will allow the snake to crawl around on her before asking the client to attempt this. Through observational learning, the client begins to associate these behaviors with a calm, nonanxious response in the therapist, which reduces the client's own anxiety about engaging in the behaviors. Modeling is as effective as systematic desensitization in reducing phobias (Bandura, 1969; Thorpe & Olson, 1997).

Flooding

The idea behind **flooding** is to intensively expose a client to his or her feared object until anxiety extinguishes. Thus, in a flooding treatment, a person with claustrophobia might lock herself in a closet for several hours, a person with a dog phobia might spend the night in a dog kennel, and a person with social phobia might volunteer to teach a class that meets every day for a semester. The therapist will typically prepare clients with relaxation techniques they can use to reduce their fear during the flooding procedure. Flooding is as effective as systematic desensitization or modeling and often works more quickly. It is more difficult to get clients to agree to this type of therapy, though, because it is frightening to contemplate (Thorpe & Olson, 1997). Some therapists are making use of the latest virtual reality technology to expose their clients to their feared objects, but in a way that clients can tolerate. This new therapy is described in *Pushing the Boundaries:* Virtual Reality Therapy for Phobias.

Cognitive-Behavioral Therapies

Many therapists will combine these behavioral techniques with cognitive techniques that help clients identify and challenge negative, catastrophizing thoughts they are having when they are anxious (Beck & Emery, 1985). For example, when the snake phobic is saying, "I just can't do this, I can't stand this anxiety, I'll never get over this," the therapist might point out the progress the client has already made on his hierarchy of fears and the client's previous statements that the relaxation techniques have been a great help to him. Creating the expectations in clients that they can master their phobias, known as *self-efficacy expectations,* is a potent factor in curing the phobias (Bandura et al., 1977).

In the treatment of social phobia, it is often useful to implement systematic desensitization, modeling, and flooding techniques in a group setting, where all the members, except the therapist, suffer from a social phobia (Heimberg et al., 1995). The group members are an audience for one another, providing exposure to the very situation that each member fears. An individual

PUSHING THE BOUNDARIES

Virtual Reality Therapy for Phobias

Many famous celebrities—Cher, Roseanne, Aretha Franklin, Whoopie Goldberg—have a fear of flying. These folks might benefit from a new form of antiphobia therapy —virtual reality exposure therapy— that capitalizes on new virtual reality technologies. Author Anita Hamilton describes her experience with virtual therapy in this essay (reprinted from Hamilton, 1999, p. 110):

I'm 33,000 ft. up in the sky, and I feel fine. No sweaty palms, no tingling head; I can finally exhale. Along with some 25 million other Americans, I'm usually deathly afraid of airplanes. A bounce here, a FASTEN SEAT BELT light there, and I'm ready to start penning my will on a crumpled cocktail napkin. But I'm sick of being scared. So before boarding my last flight, I took a crash course in virtual-reality exposure therapy—a high-tech technique that is supposed to help people like me overcome our fear of flying.

First developed by psychologist Barbara Rothbaum and computer scientist Larry Hodges to combat fear of heights, VR exposure therapy works on the principle that if you can train people to relax in a simulation of a scary situation, they will relax when confronted with the real thing. I visited the Virtually Better clinic in Atlanta, which charges $150 for a one-hour session. It provides a headset and plane seat that immerse you in a 3-D virtual airplane, complete with vibrations, engine sounds, flight-attendant call bells, and—at touchdown—tire squeals.

O.K., it sounds a little weird, but it can't hurt, right? After all, no matter how scary the high-flying simulation gets, my feet will always be firmly planted on the ground. Before my virtual flight, psychologist Samantha Smith went over a few relaxation techniques: keep breathing, remember that the chance of dying in a plane crash is 1 in 10 million and use special tricks to distract myself from my mind's own in-flight horror movies. So far, so good. In fact, when I glanced over at the dorky plastic seat and headset I was about to don, I could barely suppress a snicker. No way was this setup going to scare me, I thought. I was right. My first reaction, once I got moving, was "Wow! This is fun!" I loved how the picture changed onscreen whenever I moved my head. Swinging to the left, I could peer out a window and see the Atlantic skyline; looking up, I saw overhead bins; straight ahead was my pull-down tray and a row of empty seats. Sure, some essential details were missing—barf bags, crying babies, passengers jabbing me with their elbows—but that was O.K. It would have taken a lot more than that to fool me into thinking I was really flying.

At "takeoff," I heard the familiar rumbling and felt the vibrations that normally start me chanting, "Dear God, please don't let me die." But this time I felt fine. In fact, I never felt the wheels leave the ground, even though I could see we were supposed to be in the air. As we passed through the puffy white clouds, I was so comfortable, I could have taken a nap. I had a sudden craving for a diet Coke, but there wasn't a flight attendant in sight. When the thunderstorms and turbulence came along—the part I secretly hoped would make me scared—the seat simply didn't move violently enough to create that queasy, out-of-control feeling that usually makes me wish I'd packed a parachute.

As I got used to this new world and began talking to the psychologist about my fears, I realized that the simulation was triggering frightening memories without actually making me scared. When I looked at them objectively, my fears seemed to lose their charge. For the first time, I felt safe in a plane. So what if it wasn't real?

Now, back on Delta's B-757 to Newark, just thinking about my session helps me feel at ease. I'm not cured, but I'm definitely calmer.

group member can practice his feared behaviors in front of the other members while the therapist coaches him in the use of relaxation techniques to quell his anxiety. The group can also help the therapist challenge the client's negative, catastrophizing thoughts about his behavior (e.g., "I'm stuttering. I'm being incoherent. My voice is quavering. They probably think I'm stupid."). The group can report to the individual client that he was actually quite coherent in his speech and that his comments seemed intelligent. Through observational learning, the group members' cognitions about incompetence and embarrassment are challenged as they challenge one another. Group-administered cognitive-behavioral therapy has proven effective even for people with generalized social phobia (Foa et al., 1996).

Biological Treatments

Drug therapies have not proven as useful as behavioral therapies for the treatment of specific phobias or social phobia. Some people will use the benzodiazepines to reduce their anxiety when forced to confront their phobic objects. For example, when people with a phobia of flying are forced to take a flight, they might take a high dose of the benzodiazepine Valium to relieve their anxiety. These drugs produce some temporary relief, but the phobia remains. Antidepressants, particularly the monoamine oxidase inhibitors and the selective serotonin reuptake inhibitors, are more effective than placebos in the treatment of social anxiety (Bouwer & Stein, 1998; Liebowitz et al., 1992). Follow-up studies suggest people may soon relapse into social phobia after discontinuing use of the drug, however (Liebowitz et al., 1992). Of course, these drugs also have significant side effects, and the benzodiazepines are addictive. In contrast, the vast majority of people can be cured of phobias with behavioral techniques after only a few hours of treatment (Ost, 1996). For now, it appears that the old advice to "confront your fears" through behavioral therapy is the best advice for people with phobias.

Summing Up

- People with agoraphobia fear a wide variety of situations in which they might have an emergency but not be able to escape or get help. Many people with agoraphobia also suffer from panic disorder.
- The specific phobias include animal type phobias, natural environment type phobias, situational type phobias, and blood-injection-injury type phobias.

- People with social phobia fear social situations in which they might be embarrassed or judged by others.
- Psychodynamic theories of phobias suggest that they represent unconscious anxiety that has been displaced.
- Behavioral theories of phobias suggest that they develop through classical and operant conditioning. Humans may be evolutionarily prepared to develop some types of phobias more easily than others.
- Biological theories of phobias attribute their development to heredity.
- Behavioral treatments for phobias include systematic desensitization, modeling, and flooding.
- Cognitive techniques are sometimes used to help clients identify and challenge negative, catastrophizing thoughts they have when anxious.
- The benzodiazepines and antidepressant drugs can help to quell anxiety symptoms, but people soon relapse into phobias after they are discontinued.

☉ GENERALIZED ANXIETY DISORDER

The phobias, panic, and agoraphobia involve periods of anxiety that are more or less specific to certain situations. In phobias, anxiety is aroused by exposure to phobic stimuli. In agoraphobia and panic, anxiety is aroused by leaving a safe place and going into a place in which one has panicked in the past. Some people are anxious all the time, however, in almost all situations. These people may be diagnosed with a **generalized anxiety disorder** (GAD; see Table 6.5).

People with GAD worry about many things in their lives (Roemer, Monlina, & Borkovec, 1997). They may worry about their performance on the job, about how their relationships are going, about the health of their children or their parents, and about their own health. They also may worry about minor issues, such as whether they will be late for an appointment, whether the hair stylist will cut their hair the right way, whether they will have time to mop the kitchen floor before the dinner guests arrive. The focus of their worries may shift frequently, and they tend to worry about many different things, instead of just focusing on one issue of concern. Their worry is accompanied by many of the physiological symptoms of anxiety, including muscle tension, sleep disturbances, and a chronic sense of restlessness. They report feeling tired much of the time, probably due to their chronic muscle tension and sleep loss.

TABLE 6.5

DSM-IV Symptoms of Generalized Anxiety Disorder

People diagnosed with GAD must show excessive anxiety and worry, difficulty in controlling the worry, and at least three of the other symptoms on this list chronically for at least 6 months.

Excessive anxiety and worry

Difficulty in controlling the worry

Restlessness or feeling keyed-up or on edge

Easily fatigued

Difficulty concentrating, mind goes blank

Irritability

Muscle tension

Sleep disturbance

Source: DSM-IV, APA, 2000.

GAD is relatively common type of anxiety disorder, with about 4 percent of the U.S. population experiencing it in any 6-month period (Blazer, George, & Hughes, 1991; Kessler et al., 1994). Many people with this disorder report they have been anxious all their lives, and the disorder most common first appears in childhood or adolescence. The majority of people with GAD also develop another anxiety disorder, such as phobias or panic disorder, and many experience depression as well (Kendler et al., 1995; Roy-Byrne & Katon, 1997).

Psychological Theories

As we noted earlier, many of the earliest psychological theories saw chronic, generalized anxiety not only as a problem in itself, but the core issue behind many other disorders. Many recent psychological theories, and the biological theories, have come to view generalized anxiety disorder as a distinct disorder that has many differences even from other anxiety disorders (see *Concept Review:* Theories of Generalized Anxiety Disorder, p. 206).

Psychodynamic Theories

Freud (1917) developed the first psychological theory of generalized anxiety. He distinguished between three kinds of anxiety: realistic, neurotic, and moral. **Realistic anxiety** occurs when we face a real danger or threat, such as an oncoming tornado. **Neurotic anxiety** occurs when we are repeatedly prevented from expressing our id impulses. The libidinal energy of those impulses is not allowed release, and it causes anxiety. For example, a person who feels he can never act on his sexual urges may experience neurotic anxiety. **Moral anxiety** occurs when we have been punished for expressing our id impulses, and come to associate those impulses with punishment, causing anxiety. For example, a child who was harshly punished for

Psychodynamic theories of anxiety say that children develop anxiety disorders because they have not been helped by caregivers to develop appropriate ways of dealing with their needs and impulses.

CONCEPT REVIEW

Theories of Generalized Anxiety Disorder

These are the major theories of generalized anxiety disorder.

Theory	Description
Psychodynamic theories	
Freud's theory	GAD results when impulses are feared and cannot be expressed.
Newer psychodynamic theories	Children whose parents are not warm and nurturing develop images of the self as vulnerable and images of others as hostile, which results in chronic anxiety.
Humanistic theory	GAD occurs in children who develop a harsh set of self-standards they feel they must achieve in order to be acceptable.
Existential theory	GAD is due to existential anxiety, a universal fear of the limits and responsibilities of one's existence.
Cognitive theory	Both the conscious and unconscious thoughts of people with GAD are focused on threat, leading to chronic anxiety.
Biological theories	
GABA theory	People with GAD have a deficiency in GABA or GABA receptors, resulting in excessive firing in the limbic system.
Genetic theory	A biological vulnerability to GAD is inherited.

fondling his genitals as a child may, as an adult, have moral anxiety over any sexual impulses. Generalized anxiety occurs when our defense mechanisms can no longer contain either the id impulses or the neurotic or moral anxiety that arises from these impulses. We are anxious all the time because we cannot find healthy ways to express our id impulses and greatly fear the expression of those impulses.

Since more recent psychodynamic theories focus more on the development of self-concept through early close relationships, it is not surprising that these theories have attributed generalized anxiety to poor upbringing that results in fragile and conflicted images of the self and others (Zerbe, 1990). Children whose parents were not sufficiently warm and nurturing, and may have been overly strict or critical, may develop images of the self as vulnerable and images of others as hostile. As adults, their lives are filled with frantic attempts to overcome or hide their vulnerability. But stressors often overwhelm their coping capacities, causing frequent bouts of anxiety.

These psychodynamic formulations have been studied in some empirical research (Eisenberg, 1958; Jenkins, 1968; Luborsky, 1973). Most of these studies are open to multiple interpretations and do not really get at the heart of the causal factors implicated in psychodynamic theories of generalized anxiety disorders.

Humanistic and Existential Theories

Carl Rogers' humanistic explanation of generalized anxiety suggested that children who do not receive unconditional positive regard from significant others become overly critical of themselves and develop **conditions of worth,** a set of harsh self-standards they feel they must meet in order to be acceptable. Throughout their lives, these people then strive to meet these conditions of worth by denying their true selves and remaining constantly vigilant for the approval of others. They typically fail to meet their self-standards, causing them to feel chronically anxious or depressed.

Existential theorists attribute generalized anxiety disorder to **existential anxiety,** a universal human fear of the limits and responsibilities of one's existence (Bugental, 1997; May & Yalom, 1995; Tillich, 1952). Existential anxiety arises when we face the finality of death, or the fact that we may unintentially hurt someone, or the prospect that our life has no meaning. We can avoid existential anxiety by accepting our limits and striving to make our life meaningful. Or we can try to silence that anxiety by avoiding responsibility or by conforming to others' rules. Failing to confront life's existential issues only leaves the anxiety in place, however, and leads us to "inauthentic lives."

Neither the humanistic nor existential theories of generalized anxiety disorder have been extensively researched. Instead, most research attention these days is focused on the cognitive theories of GAD.

Cognitive Theories

Cognitive theories of GAD suggest that cognitions of people with GAD are focused on threat, both at the conscious and nonconscious level (Beck, 1997; Beck & Emery, 1985; Borkovec, 1994; Ellis, 1997; Mathews et al., 1995). At the conscious level, people with GAD have a number of maladaptive assumptions that set them up for anxiety, such as "I must be loved or approved of by everyone," "It's always best to expect the worst," and "I must anticipate and prepare myself at all times for any possible danger" (Beck & Emery, 1985; Ellis, 1997). Many of these assumptions reflect issues of being in control and about losing control. Asking people with GAD to engage in relaxation exercises to reduce their anxiety actually heightens their anxiety (Heide & Borkovec, 1984). It seems that in trying to relax, the GAD sufferers feel they are losing control, which just makes them more tense.

These maladaptive assumptions lead people with GAD to respond to situations with **automatic thoughts** that directly stir up anxiety, cause them to be hypervigilant, and lead them to overreact to situations. For example, when facing an exam, a person with GAD might think, "I don't think I can do this," "I'll fall apart if I fail this test," "My parents will be furious if I don't get good grades."

Although people with GAD are always anticipating some negative event, they do not tend to think through this anticipated event and vividly imagine it happening to them (Borkovec & Hu, 1990). Indeed, they actively avoid images of what they worry about, perhaps as a way of avoiding the negative emotion associated with those images. By avoiding fully processing those images, while still anticipating something bad is going to happen, people with GAD do not allow themselves to consider ways they might cope with an event if it were to happen or to habituate to the negative emotions associated with the image of an event.

The unconscious cognitions of people with GAD may also be focused on detecting possible threats in the environment (Mathews & MacLeod, 1994). One paradigm in which this has been shown is the Stroop color naming task. In this task, participants are presented with words printed in color on a computer screen. The participant's task is to say what color the word is printed in. Some of the words have special significance for a person with chronic anxiety, such as *disease* or *failure,* while other words have no special significance. In general, people are slower in naming the color of words that have special significance to them than nonsignificant words in the Stroop task because they are paying more attention to the content of the significant words than to the color in which the word is printed. One study presented threatening and

Research with monkeys suggests that both genetics and the environment play important roles in infants' development of anxiety disorders.

nonthreatening words to GAD patients and nonpatient controls on the computer screen for only 20 milliseconds, too short a period for the subjects to consciously process the color of the word. The GAD patients were slower in naming the colors of the threatening words than were the nonpatients, but the two groups of subjects did not differ in the time it took them to name the colors of the nonthreatening words. This suggests that people suffering from GAD are always vigilant for signs of impending threat, even at an unconscious level (Mathews & MacLeod, 1994).

Why do some people become vigilant to signs of threat? One theory is that they have a history of experiences in which they have been confronted with stressors or traumas that were uncontrollable and came on without warning—that were completely unpredictable (Mineka & Kelly, 1989; Mineka & Zinbarg, 1998). Animal studies show that animals given unpredictable and uncontrollable shock often show symptoms of chronic fear or anxiety (Mineka, 1985). People who have had unpredictable and uncontrollable life experiences—such as an unpredictably abusive parent—may also develop chronic anxiety. Although these ideas are difficult to test in humans, studies of monkeys have shown that the level of control and predictability in an infant monkey's life is related to the monkey's symptoms of anxiety as an adolescent or adult (Mineka, Gunnar, & Champoux, 1986).

Biological Theories

Recall that the discovery that antidepressant medications reduced panic attacks led to the hypothesis that norepinephrine is involved in panic disorder. Similarly, the discovery in the 1950s that the benzodiazepines provide relief from generalized anxiety has led to theories about the neurotransmitters involved in generalized anxiety. The benzodiazepines increase the activity of **gamma-aminobutyric acid (GABA),** a neurotransmitter that carries inhibitory messages from one neuron to another. When GABA binds to a neuronal receptor, the neuron in inhibited from firing. One theory is that people with generalized anxiety disorder may have a deficiency of GABA or GABA receptors, which results in excessive firing of neurons through many areas of the brain, but particularly in the limbic system, which is involved in emotional, physiological, and behavioral responses to threat (Costa, 1995; Sanders & Shekhar, 1995). As a result of excessive and chronic neuronal activity, the person experiences chronic, diffuse symptoms of anxiety. This theory has been supported in some animal studies. For example, when researchers reduce the capacity of GABA to bind to GABA receptors, they observe heightened anxiety symptoms in animals (Costa, 1985; Mohler, Richards, & Wu, 1981). As yet, definitive evidence that problems in GABA regulation actually cause GAD in humans has not been found (Barondes, 1993).

Is GAD heritable? Here again, the studies produce mixed results. Some studies suggest that there is heritable component to the development of GAD, albeit a modest one (Kendler, Neale, Kessler, & Heath, 1992; Rapee & Barlow, 1993). The results of studies seem to hinge, in part, on how GAD is defined. Over the last decade, our understanding of the phenomenology of GAD has shifted, and so have operationalizations of GAD in studies.

Treatments

Cognitive-behavioral therapies—focusing on helping people with GAD confront those issues they worry most about, challenge their negative, catastrophizing thoughts, and develop coping strategies—have been shown in some studies to be more effective than either benzodiazepine therapy, placebos, or nondirective supportive therapy in the treatment of GAD (Borkovec

& Costello, 1993; Borkovec & Whisman, 1996; Butler et al., 1991; Harvey & Rapee, 1995; Power et al., 1990). One study found that the positive effects of cognitive-behavioral therapies remained in a 1-year follow-up of the GAD clients (Borkovec & Costello, 1993).

In contrast, benzodiazepine drugs (such as Xanax, Librium, Valium, and Serax) produce short-term relief from the symptoms of anxiety for some people (Ballenger, 1995; Barlow, 1998; Solomon & Hart, 1978). Even people who get some short-term relief with the benodiazepines relapse back into GAD when they discontinue the drugs. A relatively new drug, **buspirone** (trade name BuSpar), appears to alleviate the symptoms of generalized anxiety for some people, but has few side effects and is unlikely to lead to physical dependence (Laakmann et al., 1998; Schweizer & Rickels, 1997). Buspirone is not a benzodiazepine, but one of a class of drugs called azaspirones. It appears to reduce anxiety by blocking serotonin receptors.

Summing Up

- Generalized anxiety disorder is characterized by chronic symptoms of anxiety across most situations.
- Freud suggested that GAD develops when people cannot find ways to express their impulses and fear the expression of these impulses. Newer psychodynamic theories suggest that children whose parents are not sufficiently warm and nurturing develop images of the self as vulnerable and images of others as hostile, which results in chronic anxiety.
- Humanistic theories suggest generalized anxiety results in children who develop a harsh set of self-standards they feel they must achieve in order to be acceptable.
- Existential theories attribute generalized anxiety to existential anxiety, a universal fear of the limits and responsibilities of one's existence.
- Cognitive theories suggest that both the conscious and unconscious thoughts of people with GAD are focused on threat.
- Biological theories suggest that people with GAD have a deficiency in GABA or GABA receptors. They may also have a genetic predisposition to generalized anxiety.
- Cognitive-behavioral treatments for people with GAD focus on helping them confront their negative thinking.
- Drug therapies have included the use of benzodiazepines and a newer drug called buspirone.

☉ SOCIOCULTURAL APPROACH TO THE ANXIETY DISORDERS

Sociocultural theorists have drawn attention to the fact that some groups or cultures are more prone than others to many of the anxiety disorders, including panic disorders, phobias, and generalized anxiety disorder. They have tried to understand these differences in light of the environmental demands faced by these groups and cultural norms for behavior. Studies across the world show that people living in countries undergoing rapid societal change, political oppression, and war are much more likely to show anxiety symptoms than those in more stable countries (Compton et al., 1991). In the United States, anxiety disorders are more common among people in disadvantaged minority groups and those in lower educational and socioeconomic groups than they are among Whites and people in higher educational and socioeconomic groups (Manson et al., 1996; Schlenger et al., 1992; Sheikh, 1992). The stressful environment in which disadvantaged people live may create a chronic and pervasive anxiousness that increases their risk for the development of anxiety disorders (Barlow, 1988; Manson et al., 1996).

For example, consider a woman living in poverty who is chronically anxious about the unsafe neighborhood in which she lives. Her chronic apprehensiveness could make it easier for even minor events, such as being trapped briefly in the elevator of her apartment building, to create paniclike symptoms. She would then be likely to associate her panic symptoms with elevators or, perhaps more generally, with enclosed spaces. Claustrophobia might develop.

One of the largest and most robust differences between groups in the anxiety disorders is the gender difference. In the section below, we explore this difference from the sociocultural perspective. Then we discuss differences across cultures in the manifestation of anxiety disorders, which may reflect cultural expectations for what types of symptoms are acceptable.

Gender Differences

Women are more prone than men to all the anxiety disorders we have discussed in this chapter. Compared to men, women have two or three times the rate of panic with agoraphobia, three or four times more specific phobias, one and one-half times more social phobias, and two times more generalized anxiety disorder (Kessler et al., 1995; Yonkers & Gurguis, 1995). Why would women be more likely than men to develop these disorders?

Some sociocultural theories suggest that women have a greater risk of anxiety disorders because of their place in society and the nature of their relationships with others (Chodorow, 1978; Horney, 1934/67; Miller, 1976). Women generally have less power in society than do men, and their status is typically tied to the men they are related to. This causes women to cling to others, play passive and subservient roles in relationships, express a sense of being vulnerable and defenseless, and be hypervigilant to any signs of problems in their relationships. This suppression of their own desires and fearfulness of loss, however, leaves women chronically anxious, as in generalized anxiety disorder. Panic attacks and phobias are simply extreme expressions of these women's ongoing anxiety. Agoraphobia may be another way to express vulnerability and to conform to the passive role. This intriguing and popular theory has not been extensively studied in empirical research.

A different but related perspective is that sex-role socialization and pressures influence how men and women cope with symptoms of distress and thus whether they develop anxiety disorders. First, men may feel it is socially unacceptable to express anxiety, and thus may be more prone to confront their feared situations and thereby extinguish their anxiety (Bruch & Cheek, 1995). Second, men appear more likely than women to seek medical help for anxiety symptoms, especially panic attacks (Yonkers & Gurguis, 1995). Men may view these symptoms as annoying medical problems rather than as signs that there is something wrong in their lives or in their personalities. As a result, men may be more likely than women to receive effective treatment in the early stages of possible anxiety disorders. Not all men who have anxiety symptoms seek appropriate help for them, however. Many men who have panic attacks appear to "self-medicate" by consuming large amounts of alcohol to decrease their panic symptoms, a coping behavior that is more acceptable for men than for women (Chambless et al., 1987; Johannessen et al., 1989). In contrast, because it is more acceptable for women to remain home and to avoid the kinds of situations that agoraphobics avoid, women may be more likely than men to develop agoraphobia as a way of "coping" with their panic attacks.

Women in many cultures face threats in daily life that quite reasonably would lead them to be chronically anxious and more prone to all of the anxiety disorders. In particular, women are more likely than men to be the targets of physical and sexual abuse. Girls and women who have been physically or sexually abused are at increased risk for most anxiety disorders (Burnam et al., 1988). There is a tragic cyclical nature of victimization. Women are more at risk for abuse when they have very low incomes and are newly divorced.

In turn, women who have been abused are more likely to become unemployed, to have reduced income, and to become divorced. Thus, these women suffer a host of circumstances that are difficult to control, may be unpredictable, and thus may contribute to anxiety. Even women who have not yet been victimized may be chronically anxious due to the pervasive threat of violence.

Cross-Cultural Differences

Anxiety may differ across cultures. People in Hispanic cultures report a syndrome known as *ataque de nervios* (attack of the nerves). A typical *ataque de nervios* might include "trembling, heart palpitations, a sense of heat in the chest rising into the head, difficulty moving limbs, loss of consciousness or mind going blank, memory loss, a sensation of needles in parts of the body (paresthesia), chest tightness, difficulty breathing (dyspnea), dizziness, faintness, and spells. Behaviorally, the person begins to shout, swear, and strike out at others. The person then falls to the ground and either experiences convulsive body movements or lies 'as if dead'" (Guarnaccia et al., 1996). When *ataque de nervios* comes "out of the blue," it is often attributed to the stresses of daily living or to spiritual causes. Like panic attacks, *ataque de nervios* is more common among recent trauma victims. A study of Puerto Ricans after the 1985 floods and mudslides in Puerto Rico found that 16 percent of the victims reported experiencing *ataque de nervios.* (Guarnaccia et al., 1993).

In Japan, the term *taijin kyofu-sho* has been used to describe an intense fear of interpersonal relations. *Taijin kyofu-sho* is characterized by shame about and persistent fears of causing others offense, embarrassment, or even harm through one's own personal inadequacies. It is most frequently encountered, at least in treatment settings, among young males. People with this disorder may fear of blushing, emitting body odor,

displaying unsightly body parts, speaking one's thoughts aloud, or irritating others (Chapman, Manuzza, & Fyer, 1995).

Are these just different manifestations of disorders that we call panic attacks or social phobias? Or are they truly culture-bound disorders that don't exactly match onto any disorders in the DSM? The study of people with *ataque de nervios* following the Puerto Rican mudslides found that most of these people could also be diagnosed with anxiety or depressive disorders according to DSM criteria. The authors of this study noted, however, that these people conceptualized their symptoms as *ataque de nervios* and accepting their conceptualization may be more useful and respectful than imposing DSM-IV diagnosis on them.

We are only beginning to understand gender and cross-cultural differences in the anxiety disorders. The sociocultural perspective draws our attention to these differences, as well as differences between other groups, and suggests that we look to factors within the environment, and within interpersonal relationships and culture, for their causes.

Summing Up

- Sociocultural perspectives on anxiety disorders suggest that group differences are tied to environmental pressures and to social and cultural norms.

- Women are more prone than men to panic disorder, phobias, and generalized anxiety disorder. This may be tied to women's role in society and to gender roles.

- The manifestation of anxiety may differ across cultures. As examples, Hispanic cultures have *ataque de nervios* and Japanese culture has *taijin kyofu-sho*, which may represent culturally acceptable forms of panic attacks and social phobia, respectively, or may be true culture-bound syndromes.

☉ BIO-PSYCHO-SOCIAL INTEGRATION

Biology is clearly involved in the experience of anxiety. Evolution has prepared our bodies to respond to threatening situations with physiological changes that make it easier for us to flee from or fight an attacker. For some people, this natural physiological response may be impaired, leading to chronic arousal, to overreactivity, or to poorly regulated arousal. These people may be more prone to severe anxiety reactions to threatening stimuli and to the anxiety disorders.

The syndrome ataque de nervios *may be a culturally specific form of anxiety disorder in Hispanic cultures.*

Psychological and social factors also clearly play a role in anxiety and the anxiety disorders. People differ in what they perceive as threatening, and these differences in perceptions lead to differences in the level of anxiety people fear when faced with potentially threatening situations. These differences in perceptions may be due to upbringing, as in the case of the child who develops a phobia of dogs because her mother modeled a fearful response to dogs or of the child who is chronically anxious and believes he must be perfect because his parents punish him severely if he makes any type of mistake. Differences in perceptions of what is threatening may also be due to specific traumatic experiences that some people have suffered.

Some of the most successful models of the anxiety disorders are vulnerability-stress models. These models stipulate that a person who will develop an anxiety disorder must have an underlying vulnerability to anxiety, in the form of a poorly regulated autonomic nervous system; chronic, mild anxiety or depression; or a genetic predisposition. For the disorder to develop, the person must also have a tendency to catastrophize situations and his or her own emotional reactions to those situations, to think in absolutist, perfectionist ways, and to be hypervigilant for signs of threat. These vulnerability-stress models go far in explaining why some people but not others experience anxiety that is so severe and chronic that it develops into a disorder.

Chapter Summary

- There are four types of symptoms of anxiety: physiological or somatic symptoms, emotional symptoms, cognitive symptoms, and behavioral symptoms.

- A panic attack is a short, intense experience of several of the physiological symptoms of anxiety, plus cognitions that one is going crazy, losing control, or dying. The diagnosis of panic disorder is given when a person has spontaneous panic attacks frequently, begins to worry about having attacks, and changes ways of living as a result of this worry. About one-third to one-half of people diagnosed with panic disorder also develop agoraphobia.

- One biological theory of panic disorder is that these people have overreactive autonomic nervous systems that put them into a full fight-or-flight response with little provocation. This may be the result of imbalances in norepinephrine, serotonin, or in hypersensitivity to feelings of suffocation. There also is some evidence that panic disorder may be transmitted genetically.

- Psychological theories of panic suggest that people who suffer from panic disorder pay very close attention to their bodily sensations, misinterpret bodily sensations in a negative way, and engage in snowballing, catastrophic thinking. This thinking then increases physiological activation, and a full panic attack ensues.

- Antidepressants and benzodiazepines have been effective in reducing panic attacks and agoraphobic behavior, but people tend to relapse into these disorders when they discontinue these drugs.

- An effective cognitive-behavioral therapy has been developed for panic and agoraphobia. Clients are taught relaxation exercises and then learn to identify and challenge their catastrophic styles of thinking, often while having panic attacks induced in the therapy sessions. Systematic desensitization techniques are used to reduce agoraphobic behavior.

- People with agoraphobia fear places from which they might have trouble escaping or where they might have trouble getting help if they should have a panic attack.

- The specific phobias involve fears of specific objects or situations, and most fall into one of four categories: animal type, natural environment type, situational type, and blood-injection-injury type. Social phobia involves fears of being judged or embarrassed.

- Freud argued that phobias symbolize unconscious conflicts and fears that have been displaced onto neutral objects. There has been little support for this theory or for psychoanalytic treatment of phobias.

- Behavioral theories suggest that phobias develop through classical and operant conditioning. The phobic object is a conditioned stimulus that, at some time in the past, was paired with an unconditioned stimulus that elicited fear, leading a person to develop a conditioned response of fear to the phobic object. This fear is maintained because, through operant conditioning, the person has learned that if she avoids the phobic object, her fear is reduced. Phobias can also develop through observational learning. Finally, it appears that through prepared classical conditioning humans develop phobias more readily to objects that our distant ancestors had reason to fear, such as snakes and spiders.

- Behavioral treatments focus on extinguishing fear responses to phobic objects and have proven quite effective. People with blood-injection-injury phobias must also learn to tense up when they confront their phobic objects to prevent the decreases in blood pressure and heart rate they experience. Drug therapies have not proven useful for phobias.

- People with generalized anxiety disorder are chronically anxious in most situations. Psychodynamic theories attribute GAD to the inability to quell neurotic and moral anxiety. Humanistic theories attribute GAD to being compelled to meet conditions of worth in order to feel good about oneself. Existential theories attribute GAD to existential or death anxiety. Cognitive theories argue that people with GAD appear

more vigilant for threatening information, even on an unconscious level.

- Benzodiazepines can produce short-term relief for some people with GAD but have not proven effective in the long-term treatment of GAD. A new drug called buspirone may prove more helpful in treating GAD. Cognitive-behavioral therapies focus on changing the catastrophic thinking styles of people with GAD.

- Sociocultural perspectives on the anxiety disorders focus on differences between groups in the rates and expression of anxiety disorders. Women have higher rates of almost all the anxiety disorders than do men. Sociocultural theorists suggest that women are chronically anxious because they fear separation from others or because they truly are in greater danger of sexual or physical abuse than are men. Another theory is that men are punished for exhibiting signs of anxiety whereas women are not, so men cope with their anxiety through adaptive or maladaptive activities, whereas women go on to develop anxiety disorders. Women may also carry a greater genetic vulnerability to anxiety disorders or may experience dysregulation in the neurotransmitters involved in anxiety with changes in their hormone levels.

- Cultures may differ in their expression of anxiety disorders, or may have distinct types of anxiety disorders not found in other cultures.

Key Terms

anxiety 178
fight-or-flight response 178
emergency reaction 178
hypothalamus 178
sympathetic division of autonomic nervous system 178
adrenal-cortical system 178
cortisol 179
neurosis 180
panic attack 181
panic disorder 181
norepinephrine 182

locus ceruleus 182
limbic system 183
suffocation false alarm theory 184
anxiety sensitivity 185
tricyclic antidepressants 186
selective serotonin reuptake inhibitors (SSRIs) 186
benzodiazepines 187
systematic desensitization 191
agoraphobia 192
specific phobia 194

animal type phobias 194
natural environment type phobias 195
situational type phobias 195
blood-injection-injury type phobias 195
social phobia 195
safety signal hypothesis 199
prepared classical conditioning 200
modeling 202
flooding 202
applied tension technique 202

Critical Thinking Questions

1. What are some of your "safety signals"—situations in which you feel you can relax completely and not be anxious? Why are these situations safety signals for you?

2. If the preparedness theory of phobias is correct, what are some of the objects that are likely to be the focus of phobias among people in the very distant future?

3. Given how common GAD is, it might seem strange that so much less is known about it than is about other anxiety disorders. What are some of the features of GAD that you think might make it more difficulty to study?

Diana Ong
Greg Clowns

As a rule, what is out of sight disturbs men's minds more seriously than what they see.

Julius Caesar, Gallic War *(58–52 B.C.)*

CHAPTER 7

Anxiety Disorders: Posttraumatic Stress Disorder and Obsessive-Compulsive Disorder

CHAPTER OVERVIEW
Posttraumatic Stress Disorder

Posttraumatic stress disorder (PTSD) is a set of symptoms experienced by trauma survivors, including hypervigilance, reexperiencing of the trauma, and emotional numbing. People who have experienced either human-created or natural disasters are at risk for PTSD. Some predictors of people's vulnerability to PTSD are the proximity, duration, and severity of the stressor; the availability of social support; pretrauma distress; and coping strategies. Treatment generally involves exposing people to their fears, challenging cognitions, and helping them manage ongoing problems. Drug therapies may be used to quell distress.

Taking Psychology Personally:
What to Do if You Have Been Sexually Assaulted

Pushing the Boundaries:
Eye Movement Desensitization Therapy

Obsessive-Compulsive Disorder

Obsessive-compulsive disorder (OCD) is classified as an anxiety disorder but has many distinct characteristics. Obsessions are unwanted, intrusive thoughts that the individual feels are uncontrollable. Compulsions are ritualized behaviors that the individual feels forced to engage in. Biological theories attribute obsessive-compulsive disorder to genetics and to dysfunction in areas of the brain regulating primitive impulses. Psychodynamic theories view obsessions and compulsions as symbols of unconscious conflicts. Cognitive-behavioral theories attribute obsessions to absolutist thinking and compulsions to operant conditioning. Treatment for obsessive-compulsive disorder generally involves a combination of drug therapy and cognitive-behavioral therapy.

Extraordinary People:
Sam, a Man with OCD

Bio-Psycho-Social Integration
Chapter Summary
Key Terms
Critical Thinking Questions

215

In this chapter, we consider two additional anxiety disorders—*posttraumatic stress disorder* (PTSD) and *obsessive-compulsive disorder* (OCD). Although both disorders share some similarities with the anxiety disorders discussed in the previous chapter, they both have many features that make them distinct from the other anxiety disorders, and from each other.

Although both panic disorder and generalized anxiety disorder arise in the absence of clear triggers for anxiety symptoms, posttraumatic stress disorder arises following a triggering event. In order to be diagnosed with this disorder, an individual has to have experienced an extremely negative event and to have developed symptoms in response to that event. Over time, some of the symptoms of PTSD resemble those of panic or generalized anxiety disorder—hyperarousal, vigilance, worry. But other symptoms of PTSD suggesting a numbing of the mind and the body—blunted emotions and social withdrawal.

In obsessive-compulsive disorder, triggers for anxiety symptoms are internal—intrusive, unwanted thoughts known as obsessions, and compulsions to engage in ritualized, seemingly nonsensical behaviors. In most respects, however, obsessive-compulsive disorder differs greatly from the other anxiety disorders, and some researchers argue it should not be considered an anxiety disorder.

An extra word of warning is warranted at the beginning of this chapter. Some of the following material on posttraumatic stress disorder may be difficult for some students to take, particularly students who have experienced severe traumas such as a sexual assault. It is important to recognize and respect your own emotional reactions to reading about sufferers of trauma. We hope this material will help all students, including trauma survivors, understand why trauma can have such a lasting impact on psychological health.

☉ POSTTRAUMATIC STRESS DISORDER

Voices

No one except someone who has experienced rape can know the late night, quiet playback and the thousands of stirring memories ready to rear up their ugly heads at the slightest incitement. Even almost a year later, as the "anniversary" draws near, I can feel all of my own original reactions once again full force, and they are something which will not recede in time. Only women who have spent lonely nights such as this one trying to exorcise the ghosts can truly comprehend the insolence and hideousness of rape. And our number is growing, faster all the time (J. Pilgrim, letter quoted by Thom, 1987).

This rape survivor is describing symptoms of **posttraumatic stress disorder (PTSD)**, a syndrome experienced by many people who have survived traumas. A wide range of traumas can induce PTSD, from common events such as car accidents to extraordinary events such as losing one's home in an earthquake. About 20 percent of women and 8 percent of men exposed to trauma will suffer from posttraumatic stress disorder at sometime in their lives (Kessler et al., 1995). The symptoms of PTSD can be mild to moderate, and some people function adequately with these symptoms without ever seeking treatment. For other people, however, the symptoms of PTSD can be immobilizing, causing deterioration in their work, family, and social lives (Putnam, 1996). The diagnosis of PTSD requires that three types of symptoms be present (see Table 7.1).

TABLE 7.1
DSM-IV
Symptoms of Posttraumatic Stress Disorder

Three categories of symptoms characterize PTSD:

Reexperiencing the Event:

Distressing memories of the event

Distressing dreams about the event

Reliving the event by acting or feeling as if the event were recurring

Intense psychological and physiological distress when exposed to situations reminiscent of the event

Emotional Numbing and Detachment:

Avoiding thoughts, feelings, or conversations about the event

Avoiding activities, places, or people associated with the event

Having trouble recalling important aspects of the event

Loss of interest in activities

Feelings of detachment from others

Inability to have loving feelings toward others and a general restriction of feelings

Sense that the future is bleak

Hypervigilance and Chronic Arousal:

Difficulty falling or staying asleep

Irritability or outbursts of anger

Difficulty concentrating

Hypervigilance

Exaggerated startle response

Many Vietnam war veterans have suffered PTSD.

The first set of PTSD symptoms is repeated *re-experiencing of the traumatic event*. PTSD sufferers may experience intrusive images or thoughts, recurring nightmares, or flashbacks in which they relive the event. They will react psychologically and physiologically to stimuli that remind them of the event. One survivor of war atrocities in Bosnia in the 1990s said films of traumas constantly play in his head, and although he tries to look away from them, they continue to intrude on his consciousness (Weine et al., 1995). The rape survivor just quoted vividly remembers her traumatic event to the point of reliving it. Memories of her rape intrude into her consciousness against her will, particularly when she encounters something that reminds her of the event. She also relives her emotional reaction to the event, and since the event she has chronically experienced negative emotions that have not diminished with time.

The second set of symptoms in PTSD involves *emotional numbing and detachment*. People become withdrawn, reporting that they feel numb and detached from others. Especially just after the trauma, they may also feel detached from themselves and their ongoing experiences, with a general sense of unreality, as with Fran, another woman who survived a rape:

> To everyone she knew, she was the picture of mental health. She was able to talk dispassionately about her experience and seemed to be functioning well at her daily routine. However, the feeling of unreality that began at the moment she realized that she was in danger had persisted. She found herself sleeping ten to twelve hours a day, and after some months, her fiancé complained that she seemed emotionally unavailable, short-tempered, and distant. (Bernheim, 1997, p. 34)

The third set of symptoms involves *hypervigilance and chronic arousal*. PTSD sufferers are always on guard for the traumatic event to recur. Sounds or images that remind them of their trauma can instantly create panic and flight. A war veteran, upon hearing a car backfire, may jump into a ditch and begin to have flashbacks to the war, reexperiencing the terror he felt when he was on the front lines.

PTSD sufferers may report "survivor guilt," painful guilt feelings over the fact that they survived or about things that they had to do to survive. For example, one survivor of a flood reported tremendous guilt over not having responded when a neighbor called to him for help (Erikson, 1976). Instead, he chose to save his own family. One Vietnam veteran with PTSD said, "I am a killer. No one can forgive me. I—we—should be shot. There should be a Nuremberg trial for us" (quoted in Langone, 1985). Many Holocaust survivors report guilt for having survived when their families did not or for not having fought more strongly against the Nazis (Krystal, 1968). Even more common, everyday traumas such as traffic accidents can lead to wrenching guilt and searching questions:

CASE STUDY
Walter, a surgeon, had been away on one of his frequent professional trips. On his return, he wanted to relieve Miriam, his wife, from the responsibility of watching over their four-year-old daughter, Rachel, so he planned to spend time with Rachel shopping at a local toy store. En route to the store, Walter asked Rachel which of the two popular toy stores she wanted to visit. Rachel chose the farther store because it had a greater selection of toys. As the two drove on, Walter was reflecting on pressing issues about his work. The car in front stopped short to turn left

without signaling and Walter's car plowed into the rear, crushing the gas tank and bursting into flames. Despite partially crushing his own skull against the windshield, Walter managed to unbuckle, grab his daughter and dash out the passenger side before both cars burned. The driver of the other car escaped but Walter was left with head injuries and several cracked ribs. In the hospital, Walter worked over his responsibility and what he could have done differently. Meanwhile, his wife was agonizing over the brief spat that they had just before the trip and her guilt over how relieved she had felt "to be rid of" the two of them for a time. (adapted from Bernheim, 1997, p. 53)

Children can experience PTSD in much the same way that adults can, but they may have their own particular ways of manifesting PTSD (LaGreca et al., 1996; Lipschitz, Rasmusson, & Southwick, 1998). Children's memories and fears of a traumatic event may generalize to fears of a wide range of stimuli. One 12-year-old girl who was kidnapped along with several of her friends spoke of her feelings several months later (Terr, 1981, p. 18):

Voices

I don't like to turn off the lights. I'm afraid someone would come in and shoot and rob us. When I wake up I turn on the light. . . . I've been in Bakersfield helping my brother. . . . At night in Bakersfield it feels like someone broke in. Nothing is there. I hear footsteps again. I keep going to check. . . . I check where the sound is coming from. . . . I'm very frightened of the kitchen because no one's there at all. I completely avoid it. At home I kept feeling someone was looking in and watching me. I kept the light on. I was afraid they'd come in and kill us all or take us away again.

Children may also show "regressive" behavior, such as bed-wetting, may repeatedly play out the trauma with dolls or other toys, and may express their distress through aches and pains. Children who have been sexually abused may engage in sexual behavior that is inappropriate for their age.

The DSM-IV recognizes another disorder associated with traumas, called **acute stress disorder** (see Table 7.2). Acute stress disorder occurs in response to similar traumas as does PTSD, and has similar symptoms to PTSD. The main difference is that acute stress disorder occurs within 1 month of exposure to the stressor and it is short-lived, not lasting more than 4 weeks. Also, in acute stress disorder, **dissociative symptoms**—symptoms that indicate a detachment from the trauma and from ongoing events—are especially prominent.

TABLE 7.2
DSM-IV
Symptoms of Acute Stress Disorder

Acute stress disorder has symptoms similar to PTSD but occurs within 1 month of a stressor and is less than 4 weeks in duration.

A. While experiencing or after experiencing a traumatic event, the individual has three or more of the following dissociative symptoms:

   1. sense of numbing, detachment, or emotional unresponsiveness

   2. reduced awareness of one's surroundings ("being in a daze")

   3. sense that things are not real

   4. sense that one's body and mind are not connected

   5. inability to recall an important aspect of the trauma

B. Reexperiencing the traumatic event through recurrent images, thoughts, dreams, illusions, flashbacks, or a sense of reliving the experience; distress when exposed to reminders of the trauma

C. Avoidance of stimuli that arouse recollections of the trauma

D. Symptoms of anxiety or increased arousal (such as difficulty sleeping, irritability, poor concentration, hypervigilance, exaggerated startle response, motor restlessness

Source: DSM-IV, APA, 1994.

People may become emotionally unresponsive, finding it impossible to experience pleasure. They may have difficulty concentrating, feel detached from their bodies, experience the world as unreal or dreamlike, and have increasing difficulty recalling details of the trauma. In addition, as in PTSD, the sufferer of acute stress disorder persistently reexperiences the trauma through flashbacks, nightmares, and intrusive thoughts, avoids reminders of the trauma, and is constantly aroused. This is a new diagnosis for the DSM, and little research has been done on it.

The Role of Trauma in PTSD

A wide variety of traumatic events can induce post-traumatic stress disorder. We will focus on four types of events: natural disasters, abuse, combat and war-related traumas, and more common traumatic events such as the loss of a loved one in a car accident,

Natural disasters like floods or earthquakes leave behind people with posttraumatic stress symptoms.

because these are the ones that have been researched most thoroughly.

Disasters

Natural disasters, such as floods, earthquakes, fires, hurricanes, and tornadoes, can trigger a wave of PTSD among the survivors. In 1972, a flood wiped out the community of Buffalo Creek, West Virginia. Shortly after the flood, 60 percent of the 193 survivors of the flood were suffering from PTSD. Fourteen years later, 25 percent still suffered from PTSD (Green et al., 1992). A study of Florida children who lived through Hurricane Andrew in 1992 found that nearly 20 percent were still suffering from PTSD a year after the disaster (La Greca et al., 1996). Another study of children in South Carolina who survived Hurricane Hugo in 1993 found that, 3 years after the hurricane, a third still experienced a sense of detachment and avoided thoughts or feelings associated with the hurricane, one-quarter were irritable and angry, and one-fifth experienced physiological arousal (Garrison et al., 1995).

Abuse

There are unfortunately many kinds of abuse—physical abuse (such as when husbands beat their wives), sexual abuse (as in rape and incest), and emotional abuse (as when parents continually ridicule their children). Each of these forms of abuse can contribute to long-term PTSD.

Studies of rape survivors have found that about 95 percent experience posttraumatic stress symptoms severe enough to qualify for a diagnosis of the disorder in the first 2 weeks following the rape (see Figure 7.1, p. 220). About 50 percent still qualify for the diagnosis 3 months after the rape. As many as 25 percent still suffer from PTSD 4 to 5 years after the rape (Foa & Riggs,

1995; Girelli et al., 1986; Kilpatrick, Veronen, & Resick, 1979; Resnick et al., 1993; Rothbaum et al., 1992).

In the United States alone, over 200,000 cases of verified child sexual abuse and over 380,000 cases of physical abuse are reported each year. Studies of children who were sexually and/or physically assaulted show that they remain at increased risk for PTSD, as well as other anxiety disorders, depression, substance abuse, sexual dysfunction, well into adulthood (Dubner & Motta, 1999; Duncan et al., 1996; Kessler et al., 1997; Saunders et al., 1992). Indeed, over 60 percent of childhood rape survivors develop PTSD at some time in their life (Saunders et al., 1992).

The risk of long-term PTSD can be reduced when a child or an adult who receives compassionate support from family members and friends and professional mental-health care as needed. PTSD and other psychological problems are more likely when abused people try to hide or deny their abuse. *Taking Psychology Personally:* What to Do If You Have Been Sexually

Women who have suffered violence often experience symptoms of posttraumatic stress disorder.

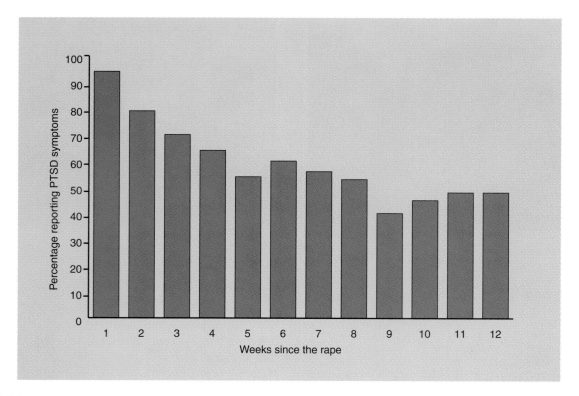

FIGURE 7.1   Posttraumatic Symptoms in Rape. Almost all women show symptoms of posttraumatic stress disorder severe enough to be diagnosed with PTSD in the first or second week following a rape. Over the 3 months following a rape, the percentage of women continuing to show PTSD declines. However, almost 50 percent of women continue to be diagnosed with PTSD 3 months after a rape.

Source: Adapted from Foa & Riggs, 1995.

Assaulted describes what people who have been sexually abused can do to get the help they need.

Combat and War-Related Traumas

Much of what we know about PTSD comes from studies of men and women who have fought in wars and were taken as prisoners of war. There are well-documented cases of "combat fatigue syndrome," "war zone stress," and "shell shock" among soldiers and former prisoners of the two world wars and the Korean War. Follow-up studies of some of these people show chronic posttraumatic stress symptoms for decades after the war (Elder & Clipp, 1989; Sutker, Allain, & Winstead, 1993; Sutker et al., 1991). The Holocaust left in its wake a generation of PTSD sufferers. One study that examined 124 survivors of the Holocaust 40 years later found that almost half were still suffering from posttraumatic stress disorder (Kuch & Cox, 1992). Survivors who had been in concentration camps were three times more likely to have PTSD as were survivors who had not been in concentration camps.

Studies of veterans of the 1991 Persian Gulf War found as many as 13 percent were suffering from PTSD in the year after the war (Sutker et al., 1995; Wolfe et al., 1999). The National Vietnam Veterans Readjustment Study found that nearly half a million Vietnam

Survivors of the Holocaust have been at high risk for PTSD.

TAKING PSYCHOLOGY PERSONALLY

What to Do If You Have Been Sexually Assaulted

Y ou probably don't want to think about how you would cope with being sexually assaulted. But physical and sexual assault happen to a very large segment of the population, particularly among young adults. Sexual assault can be defined as unwanted sexual contact obtained without consent or obtained through the use of force, threat of force, intimidation, or coercion. This includes unwanted sexual contact that occurs after the administration of intoxicants to lower the victim's resistance. Here are some tips on what to do if you have been sexually assaulted from the Sexual Assault Prevention and Awareness Center of the University of Michigan:

1. Believe in yourself. Don't blame yourself, take care of yourself.

2. Tell someone you can trust. Sexual assaults can be terrifying and traumatic. It is an enormous burden to bear alone. Think about who you might trust to tell—maybe a friend, relative, or faculty member. You may also be able to call a 24-hour sexual assault crisis line in your local community—it should be listed in your phone book.

3. Have a medical examination. Even if you don't think you were physically hurt, you may want to be checked for internal injuries, pregnancy, and sexually transmitted diseases as soon as possible. Also, a medical exam within 72 hours is the best time for collecting physical evidence of the rape. Even if you are not sure about pressing charges, it can be reassuring to have the evidence in case you decide to.

4. Report to the police. Choosing whether or not to report the assault is your right. Whether to press charges or not is a decision you do not have to make immediately, but making a criminal report sooner may help if the case is prosecuted. Your local sexual assault counseling center may be able to help you make a third-party report. If you are making an immediate criminal report, do not clean yourself up or touch anything in the area where the assault took place.

5. Seek additional supportive counseling. Regardless of whether you get a medical exam or report the assault, you may need help to deal with the consequences of the assault. Recovering from a sexual assault may take time and professional counseling.

---

veterans still suffered from PTSD 15 years after their military service. Rates of PTSD are highest among Hispanic veterans, next highest among African American veterans, and lowest among European American veterans (see Figure 7.2, p. 222; Schlenger et al., 1992). A separate study of Native American Vietnam veterans found that as many as 70 percent still suffer symptoms of PTSD (Manson et al., 1996).

People from Southeast Asia (Vietnamese, Cambodians, Laotians, and Hmong) have undergone decades of civil war, invasions by other countries, and death at the hands of despots. In the few years that Pol Pot and the Khmer Rouge ruled Cambodia, perhaps one-fourth of Cambodia's 7 million people died. Many others were tortured, starved, and permanently separated

from their families. Hundreds of thousands of Southeast Asians fled to Thailand, Europe, the United States, and Canada. Unfortunately, many of these refugees faced further trauma, being imprisoned in refugee camps for years, often separated from their families (Kinzie & Leung, 1993).

Several studies have now been done to determine the psychological scars left by the extreme traumas these people have suffered. One study found that 10 percent of Vietnamese, Hmong, Laotian, and Cambodian refugees living in California meet the criteria for PTSD, with the greatest percentage of these being Cambodian (Gong-Guy, 1986). These refugees also suffer from a large number of other psychological problems. The need for psychiatric services was moderate

The people of Southeast Asia have been victims of years of war and oppression.

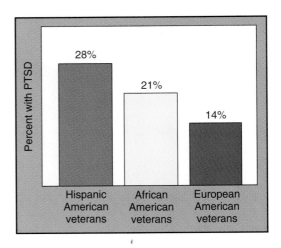

FIGURE 7.2   Rates of PTSD in Vietnam Veterans. A large study of Vietnam veterans found higher rates of PTSD among veterans of color than among White veterans.

Source: Schlenger et al., 1992.

to severe in 31 percent of the Vietnamese, 54 percent of the Hmong, 50 percent of the Laotians, and 48 percent of the Cambodians.

Researchers have assessed the psychological effects of more recent and ongoing wars and conflicts. The wars in the former Yugoslavia have been marked by "ethnic cleansing"—the torture and slaughter of thousands and displacement of millions of former Yugoslavians. This campaign has been one of the most brutal in history, with many atrocities, concentration camps, organized mass rapes, and neighbor murdering neighbor. A study of Bosnian refugees just after they resettled in the United States found that 65 percent suffered from posttraumatic stress disorder (Weine et al., 1995). This woman's story is far too common.

CASE STUDY

A woman in her 40s worked the family farm in a rural village until the day the siege began, when mortar shells turned most of their house to rubble. A few months before, she and her husband had sent their son away to be with relatives in Slovenia. The morning after the shelling, the Chetniks—Serbian nationalist forces—came and ordered everyone to leave their houses at once. Many neighbors and friends were shot dead before the woman's eyes. She and her husband were forced to sign over the title to their house, car, and bank deposits—and watched as the looting began. Looters included neighbors who were their friends. Over the next few days they traveled back from the Muslim ghetto to their land to feed the animals. One day, as she and her husband stood in the garden, the Chetniks captured them. Her husband was taken away with other men. For the next 6 months she did not know if he was dead or alive. She spent days on transport trains with no food or water, where many suffocated to death beside her. On forced marches she had to step over the dead bodies of friends and relatives. Once her group was forced across a bridge that was lined with Chetnik machine gunners randomly shooting to kill and ordering them to throw all valuables over the edge into nets. She

spent weeks in severely deprived conditions in a big tent with many women and children, where constant sobbing could be heard. When she herself could not stop crying she thought that something had broken in her head and that she had gone "crazy." Now she says, "I will never be happy again." When alone, everything comes back to her. But when she is with others or busy doing chores, she can forget. "My soul hurts inside, but I'm able to pull it together." She is able to sleep without nightmares only by using a nightly ritual: "I lie down and go through every step of the house in Bosnia—the stable, everything they took, the rugs, the horses, the doors. I see it all again." (Weine et al., 1995, p. 540).

A follow-up of these refugees 1 year found later that 44 percent still suffered from PTSD, with older refugees more vulnerable to PTSD than younger refugees (Weine et al., 1998). Many refugees from Bosnia and other war-torn countries report having been tortured before they escaped their homeland, and the experience of torture significantly increases the chance that an individual will develop PTSD (Basoglu & Mineka, 1998; Shrestha et al., 1998). Torture survivors who were political activitists appear less prone to develop PTSD than those who were not political activitists (Basoglu et al., 1997). Political activists appeared more psychologically prepared for torture than nonactivists because they expected at some time to be tortured, often had previous experience with torture, and they had a belief system whereby torture was viewed merely as an instrument of repression.

Common Traumatic Events

PTSD can occur following more common events: automobile accidents or other serious accidents; the sudden, unexpected death of a loved one; learning that

The wars in the former Yugoslavia may be creating a whole new group of PTSD sufferers.

one's child has a life-threatening disease; or observing someone else being severely injured or killed. A study of people who attended an emergency room shortly after a motor vehicle accident found that half of them reported intrusive reexperiencing of the accident, hyperarousal, or distress (Ehlers, Mayou, & Bryant, 1998). Over 20 percent suffered symptoms severe enough to meet the diagnostic criteria for PTSD 3 months after the accident, and 17 percent were diagnosed with PTSD 1 year after the accident. Another study found that adults who lost children or spouses in fatal car accidents were still experiencing high levels of anxiety and depression 4 to 7 years after their losses, and those who had lost children were more likely than people in a control group to have divorced (Lehman, Wortman, & Williams, 1987).

As these studies illustrate, PTSD symptoms can last a long time after a trauma. About half the people experiencing a trauma appear to recover from PTSD within 3 months of the trauma, but many others continue to experience symptoms for at least 12 months or much longer (APA, 2000).

Explanations of PTSD Vulnerability

The cause of PTSD seems obvious: trauma. It seems perfectly understandable for PTSD to develop in assault or torture victims, people who have lost a loved one in a car accident, people who have lost their homes in a hurricane, and so on. However, just what is it about traumatic events that can cause long-term, severe psychological impairment in some people? And why do some people develop PTSD in the wake of a trauma whereas others do not? Researchers have identified a number of factors that seem to contribute to PTSD (see *Concept Review:* Contributors to PTSD, p. 224).

Sociocultural Factors

Not surprisingly, the nature of a traumatic event plays an important role in determining people's likelihood of developing PTSD in response to the event. In addition, the response of family members and friends to a trauma survivor is a critical influence on the survivor's vulnerability to PTSD.

Severity, duration, and proximity of trauma   The most potent predictors of people's reactions to trauma are the *severity* and *duration* of the trauma and the *proximity* of the individual to the trauma (Blanchard et al., 1996; Ehlers, Mayou, & Bryant, 1998; Kessler et al., 1995; Putnam, 1996). That is, people who experience more severe and long-lasting traumas, and are directly affected by a traumatic event, are more prone to develop PTSD. For example, war veterans are more likely to experience PTSD if they were on the front lines of the war for an extended period of time or if they were

CONCEPT REVIEW

Contributors to PTSD

A number of sociocultural, psychological, and biological factors may contribute to vulnerability to PTSD.

Contributor	Description	Example
Sociocultural factors		
1. Severity, duration, and proximity of trauma	1. More severe and longer traumas, and traumas directly affecting people, are more likely to lead to PTSD.	1. War veterans who were on the front lines for months at a time are more prone to PTSD.
2. Social support	2. Good social support protects against PTSD.	2. Women whose husbands suicide are less prone to PTSD if they can discuss it with friends.
Psychological factors		
1. Shattering assumptions	1. People whose basic assumptions are shattered are more prone to PTSD.	1. People who believe that bad things happen to others may be more traumatized when they experience a trauma.
2. Preexisting distress	2. People who are already distressed before a trauma are at greater risk for PTSD.	2. People distressed before a natural disaster are more at risk for PTSD after the disaster.
3. Coping styles	3. Use of avoidance, rumination, or dissociation, or inability to make sense of trauma increases risk of PTSD.	3. People who cannot make sense of the loss of a loved one are more prone to PTSD.
Biological factors		
1. Physiological hyperreactivity	1. PTSD sufferers show greater arousal of neurotransmitters, hormones, and brain regions associated with stress response.	1. While imagining combat scenes, combat veterans with PTSD show greater blood flow in areas of the brain involved in emotion and memory.
2. Genetics	2. Vulnerability to PTSD may be influenced by genetic factors.	2. Identical twins show higher concordance for PTSD than fraternal twins.

taken prisoner of war than if they were not (Schlenger et al., 1992; Wolfe et al., 1999). Rape survivors who were violently and repeatedly raped over an extended period are more likely to experience PTSD than are those whose experiences were shorter and less violent (Epstein, Saunders, & Kilpatrick, 1997; Resick, 1993). Victims of natural disasters who lose their homes or loved ones or are themselves injured are more likely to experience PTSD than are those whose lives were less affected by the natural disaster (Nolen-Hoeksema & Morrow, 1991; Norris & Uhl, 1993).

Social support Another predictor of people's vulnerability to PTSD following trauma is the *social support* they have available to them. People who have others who will support them emotionally through recovery from their traumas, allowing them to discuss their feelings and memories of the traumas, recover more quickly than do those who do not (Kendall-Tackett et al., 1993;

King et al., 1999; La Greca et al., 1996; Sutker et al., 1995). For example, women whose husbands have committed suicide show better physical and emotional health and fewer intrusive thoughts about the suicides if they are able to discuss the suicides with supportive friends than if they had not discussed the suicides with others (Pennebaker & O'Heeron, 1984).

Some events may be more difficult to discuss with others and less likely to engender social support from others because of social stigmas against people who experience such events. Examples are the suicides of family members, sexual assault, and the loss of loved ones to AIDS, particularly if the loved ones were homosexual. Some theorists have argued that veterans of the Vietnam War were more likely than veterans from previous wars to experience PTSD because they received less social support from friends and family members upon returning from combat, due to the social controversy over the war (Figley & Leventman, 1980).

In contrast, events that are experienced by whole communities, such as earthquakes, floods, or hurricanes, might engender less PTSD because individuals can talk with many others who have had experiences similar to their own. For example, following the 7.1 earthquake that hit the San Francisco Bay Area in 1989, almost everyone spoke with friends and neighbors about the earthquake every day for the first 2 or 3 weeks after the earthquake (Nolen-Hoeksema & Morrow, 1991). In addition, community leaders mobilized resources to meet people's needs, and there was a spirit of "pitching in" and "supporting each other" that pervaded messages in the media and people's conversations (see also Green et al., 1983; Rachman, 1991).

Differences among ethnic or cultural groups in vulnerability to PTSD may also be linked to differences in the social support available to members of these groups before and after traumas. Groups in which individuals have strong social support networks may be less prone to PTSD than those with weaker networks. For example, Southeast Asian refugees who are able to move into existing communities of people from their homeland when emigrating to a new country are less likely to show PTSD than are those who do not have existing communities in their new home (Beiser, 1988).

Psychological Factors

People facing the same circumstances around a trauma vary greatly in their risk of PTSD. At least three psychological factors have been identified to explain differences between people in response to trauma. First, for some people, a trauma shatters certain basic assumptions about life and the shattering of these assumptions can contribute to long-term psychological distress. Second, some people are already distressed before a trauma occurs and they appear at greater risk for PTSD. Third, certain coping styles seem to increase people's chances of developing PTSD.

Personal assumptions We tend to go through life with a number of assumptions about ourselves and how the world works that help us feel good most of the time, but can be shattered by a trauma (Janoff-Bulman, 1992). The first is the assumption of *personal invulnerability*. Most people believe that bad things happen to other people, and that they are relatively invulnerable to traumas such as severe car accidents, having their homes destroyed in natural disasters, or being kidnapped or raped. When such events do happen, people lose their illusion of invulnerability. Chronically feeling vulnerable, they are hypervigilant for signs of new traumas and may show signs of chronic anxiety (Janoff-Bulman, 1992).

The second basic assumption is the assumption that *the world is meaningful and just* and that *things*

The quality of people's social support following a trauma is an important predictor of their psychological reaction to the trauma.

happen for a good reason (Lerner, 1980). This assumption can be shattered by events that seem senseless, unjust, or perhaps evil, such as the terrorist bombing of a children's day care center or teenagers randomly shooting their classmates.

The third assumption is the assumption that *people who are good, who "play by the rules," do not experience bad things.* Trauma victims often will say that they have lived a good life, have been a good person, and thus they can't understand how the trauma happened to them (Janoff-Bulman & Frieze, 1983). A study of refugees from Bhutan, a region near Nepal, who had been forced from their homes and often tortured, found that many saw their misfortune as a result of past deeds (Shrestha et al., 1998). Although blaming oneself for causing a trauma can help people feel they still have some control over their lives, it can also shatter their view of themselves as good people (Janoff-Bulman & Frieze, 1983).

Lenore Terr (1981, 1983) observed the shattering of these assumptions in the child victims of the 1976 Chowchilla school-bus kidnapping, in which 26 children, 5 to 14 years of age, were kidnapped while riding their school bus and then buried underground in a truck trailer. Twenty-seven hours after their kidnapping, the children were freed when two of the boys were able to dig them out of their prison. When the children were interviewed several months later, some could identify events that they believed "caused" their kidnapping or were "warnings" that the kidnapping would happen. Mary, age 9, said, "That day I stepped in a bad luck square. . . . I think if I hadn't have stepped in that square, it would have happened, but not to me!" Five of the children who were kidnapped blamed

Events that are senseless, such as the shootings of students by fellow students at Columbine High School in 1999, can shatter our basic assumptions about good and evil.

their parents for failing to recognize "signs" that it would happen. Bob, age 14, was one of the boys who dug the children out of the hole. After the kidnapping, he came to believe he was placed on the bus "by chance" in order to help the other children escape. Bob's vision of himself as the hero later led him to engage in quite dangerous behavior. About 18 months after the kidnapping, Bob shot a stranger who was innocently sitting in his car in front of Bob's family's house, to "protect his family from kidnapping."

Distress Another predictor of people's vulnerability to PTSD following a trauma is the level of *distress* they were experiencing *before* the trauma hits. People who are already experiencing increased symptoms of anxiety or depression before encountering a trauma are more likely to develop PTSD following the trauma than are those who were not anxious or depressed before the trauma (Blanchard et al., 1996). For example, a study of the largest natural disaster in U.S. history, Hurricane Andrew, found that children who had already been anxious before the hurricane were more likely to develop posttraumatic stress reactions than those who had not been anxious prior to the hurricane (La Greca, Silverman, & Wasserstein, 1998). War veterans who had psychological problems or poor interpersonal relationships before they entered combat are more likely to develop symptoms of PTSD (Chemtob et al., 1990; King et al., 1999; Orsillo et al., 1996).

As we noted, African American, Hispanic American, and Native American combat veterans from the Vietnam and Persian Gulf Wars appear to have been more vulnerable than White veterans to PTSD (Manson et al., 1996). This may be because they faced discrimination in the United States both before and after the war, increasing their base levels of distress and making it more likely they would respond to the traumas of combat with PTSD.

Coping styles People's styles of *coping* with stressful events and with their own symptoms of distress may also influence their vulnerability to PTSD following a trauma. Several studies have shown that combat veterans who use avoidant coping strategies, such as drinking and self-isolation, are more likely to experience PTSD (Fairbank, Hansen, & Fitterling, 1991; Sutker et al., 1995).

One of the few studies to have gathered data before a trauma happened was conducted around the time of the big 1989 San Francisco earthquake. Fortuitously, researchers had collected information about coping styles and emotional well-being in a group of students shortly before the earthquake. Then, 10 days and again 7 weeks after the earthquake, they assessed depressive symptoms and PTSD symptoms in these same students. They were especially interested in students with ruminative coping styles. People with ruminative coping styles chronically focus on their symptoms of distress and worry about these symptoms without doing anything about them. Students with more ruminative styles of coping were more likely to show symptoms of depression and PTSD both shortly after and 7 weeks after the earthquake than were students with less ruminative coping styles. This was true even after researchers took into account how distressed the students had been before the earthquake and how much stress—property damage, personal injury—they had been exposed to as a result of the earthquake (Nolen-Hoeksema & Morrow, 1991; see also Ehlers et al., 1998).

Another form of coping that may increase the likelihood of PTSD is the use of dissociation (Foa & Hearst-Ikeda, 1996; Spiegel, 1991). As we noted earlier, dissociation involves a range of psychological processes that indicate a detachment from the trauma and from ongoing events. People who dissociate following a trauma may feel they are in another place, or in someone else's body watching the trauma and its aftermath unfold. Studies have shown that people who dissociate shortly after a trauma are at increased risk to develop PTSD (Ehlers, Mayou, & Bryant, 1998; Koopman, Classen, & Spiegel, 1994; Shalev et al., 1996).

Finally, many studies have found that, following a trauma, most people try to *make sense* of the trauma somehow as a way of coping (Lehman, Wortman, & Williams, 1987; Silver, Boon, & Stones, 1983). They try to find some reason or purpose for the trauma or to understand what the trauma means in their lives. Psychodynamic and existential theorists have argued that searching for meaning in a trauma is a healthy process that can lead people to gain a sense of mastery over their traumas and to integrate their traumas into their understandings of themselves (Frankl, 1963; Freud, 1920; Horowitz, 1976). They suggest that people who are able to "make sense" of their traumas are less likely to develop PTSD or other chronic emotional problems and may recover more quickly from their traumas than do people who cannot make sense of their traumas (Bulman & Wortman, 1977; Silver et al., 1983). How do people make sense of traumas? Some people have religious or philosophical beliefs that assist them in making sense. For example, recently bereaved people who are religious often say that God needed their loved ones in Heaven or had a special purpose for taking their loved ones and this seems to help them understand their losses (McIntosh, Silver, & Wortman, 1993; Nolen-Hoeksema & Larson, 1999). Other people say that the deaths of loved ones made them reevaluate their lives and their relationships with others and make positive changes, and this helped them deal with the loss. For example, here are some comments from people who lost a close loved one in recent months (from Nolen-Hoeksema & Larson, 1999):

Voices

Thinking back on it, if I had not done this, look at all I would have missed—all this growth, all this understanding.

I tend to look at it generally as if all the things that happen in my life are a gift, for whatever reason, or however they happen. It doesn't necessarily have to be only pleasant gifts, but everything that happens . . . there's a meaning. I've had a lot of suffering in my life . . . and through that I've learned a great deal. While I wouldn't want to go back and relive that, I'm grateful for that because it makes me who I am. There's a lot of joys and sorrows, but they all enrich life.

I like who I am now because I find at 44 that I really like myself. If I didn't go through a lot of the hardships that I had, I wouldn't be who I am. So in a lot of ways, it's been an OK journey. And if I hadn't had people like that in my life, I wouldn't have a good sense of humor, which is one of the things that helps us get through, right? I feel extremely fortunate lately.

Some people are never able to make sense of their losses or other traumas, and these people are more likely to experience chronic and severe symptoms of PTSD and depression. For example, researchers questioned 77 women who were the survivors of incest, an average 20 years after the incest had ended. They found that 50 percent of the women were still actively searching for meaning in their incest. These women said things such as, "I always ask myself why, over and over, but there is no answer," and "There is no sense to be made. This should not have happened to me or any child" (Silver et al., 1983). The more actively a woman was still searching for meaning in her incest, the more likely she was to be experiencing recurrent and intrusive ruminations about the incest experience, the more distress she was experiencing, and the lower her level of social functioning was. Because those who search for meaning are ruminating about the past, perhaps they are also less able to focus coping efforts on the present and the future. In trying to understand, they may in effect get "stuck" in the past. Finding meaning may be particularly difficult in traumas such as sexual assault or genocide, in which the nature of the event violates basic moral codes and destroys people's basic trust in others (Resick, 1993; Silver et al., 1983).

Biological Factors

In recent years, researchers have been searching for biological factors that determine whether an individual will develop PTSD following a trauma. That search has focused on differences between PTSD sufferers and nonsufferers in the functioning of the biological systems involved in the stress response. Some research also suggests that genetics plays a role in vulnerability to PTSD.

Physiological hyperreactivity Not surprisingly, people with PTSD are more physiologically reactive to situations that remind them of their trauma (Bremner et al., 1999; Keane et al., 1998; Southwick, Yehuda, & Wang, 1998). This activity includes changes in several neuotransmitters and hormones involved in the fight-or-flight response we discussed in Chapter 6. In addition, studies using positron-emission tomography (PET, see Chapter 3) have found some differences between PTSD sufferers and controls in activity levels in parts of the brain involved in the regulation of emotion and the fight-or-flight response (Charney et al., 1994). While imagining combat scenes, combat veterans with PTSD show increased blood flow in the anterior cingulate gyrus and the amygdala—areas of the brain that may play a role in emotion and memory. In contrast, combat veterans without PTSD did not show increases in blood flow in these regions while imagining combat scenes (see Figure 7.3; Rausch et al., 1998; Shin et al., 1997). Some studies also show damage to the hippocampus among PTSD patients (Figure 7.4; Bremner, 1998). The hippocampus is involved in memory. Damage to it may result in some of the memory problems that PTSD sufferers report.

It is not clear whether these neurobiological abnormalities in the PTSD sufferers are a cause or a consequence of their disorder. Deterioration of the hippocampus could be the result of extremely high levels of cortisol at the time of the trauma (Bremner, 1998). Interestingly, however, resting levels of cortisol among PTSD sufferers (when they are not being exposed to reminders of their trauma) tend to be lower than among people without PTSD (Yehuda, 1998). Because cortisol may act to shut down sympathetic nervous system activity after stress, the lower levels of cortisol among PTSD sufferers may result in prolonged activity of the sympathetic nervous system following stress. As a result, they may more easily develop a conditioned fear of stimuli associated with the trauma, and subsequently develop PTSD. We do not currently know, however, whether PTSD sufferers had lower baseline levels of cortisol before they experienced their trauma, or whether cortisol levels are blunted after a trauma in people who develop PTSD (Southwick et al., 1998).

We do know that arousing or emotionally exciting events are remembered more vividly than emotionally neutral events. Pitman has suggested that overstimulation of neurotransmitters such as epinephrine and norepinephrine during traumatic events results in deeply engraved memories for the event (Pitman, 1989). This can then contribute to the intrusive recollections of the event reported by PTSD sufferers.

Genetic factors There is some evidence that a vulnerability to PTSD can be inherited. One study of about 4,000 twins who served in the Vietnam War found that if one twin developed PTSD, the other twin was much more likely also to develop PTSD if he was an identical twin than if he was a fraternal twin (True et al., 1993). On the other hand, the psychosocial factors we have discussed in PTSD may be the primary contributors to

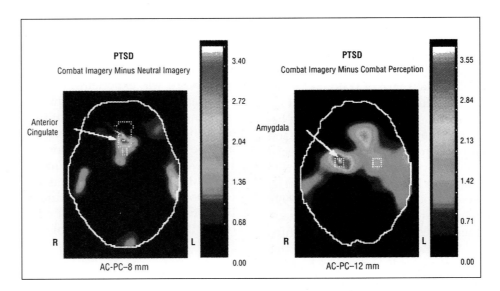

FIGURE 7.3 Combat veterans with PTSD show greater blood flow in the anterior cingulate and amygdala than those without PTSD in studies using positron emission tomography.

Source: Shin et al., 1997.

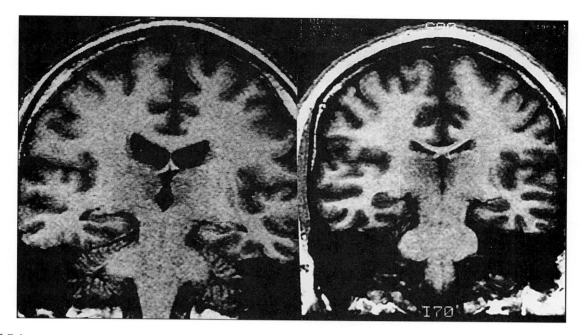

FIGURE 7.4   Studies using magnetic resonance imaging show deterioration in the hippocampus of people with PTSD compared to people without PTSD. Source: Bremner, 1998.

PTSD, and the physiological sensitivity of PTSD sufferers may be another symptom of the disorder, rather than a cause.

Treatments for PTSD

Psychotherapies for PTSD generally have three goals: exposing clients to what they fear in order to extinguish that fear, challenging distorted cognitions that are contributing to symptoms, and helping clients manage their ongoing life problems to reduce the stress in their lives. These goals are addressed in cognitive-behavioral therapy for PTSD and in stress-management therapies. Some people with PTSD also benefit from use of antianxiety and antidepressant medications (see *Concept Review:* Treatments for PTSD, p. 230). After we discuss psychotherapies and drug therapies for PTSD, we address sociocultural perspectives on PTSD and its treatment.

Cognitive-Behavioral Therapy

A major element of cognitive-behavioral therapy for PTSD is **systematic desensitization.** The client identifies those thoughts and situations that create anxiety, ranking them from most anxiety-provoking to least. The therapist then begins to take the client through this hierarchy, using relaxation techniques to quell anxiety. The focus of anxiety in PTSD is the memory of the traumatic event and stimuli that remind the person of the event. It is impossible to return to the actual event that

Psychotherapy for PTSD sufferers focuses on extinguishing fear reactions, challenging distorted cognitions, and helping clients manage stress.

triggered the PTSD in many cases, so imagining the event vividly must replace actual exposure to the event. The combat veteran being treated for PTSD imagines the bloody battles and scenes of killing and death that haunt him; the rape survivor imagines the minute details of the assault. The therapist also watches for distorted thinking patterns, such as survivor guilt, and helps the client challenge these thoughts.

Repeatedly and vividly imagining and describing the feared events in the safety of the therapist's office, the client has an opportunity to habituate to his or her anxiety and to distinguish the memory from

CONCEPT REVIEW

Treatments for PTSD

Treatments for PTSD focus on exposing clients to feared images, challenging distorted cognitions, managing stressful circumstances, and reducing painful anxiety symptoms.

Treatment	Description	Example
Cognitive-behavioral therapy	Systematic desensitization is used to extinguish fear reactions to memories; cognitive techniques are used to challenge irrational thoughts.	Rape survivor works through hierarchy of feared memories of rape using relaxation techniques; therapist helps her confront self-blaming thoughts.
Stress management	Therapist helps the client solve concrete problems to reduce stress; may use thought-stopping strategies to quell intrusive thoughts.	Disaster survivor is helped to find a new home and job.
Biological therapies	Antianxiety and antidepressant drugs are used to quell symptoms.	Person uses Valium (a benzodiazepine) to help induce sleep at night.
Sociocultural approaches	PTSD symptoms are understood and treated within the norms of people's culture.	Culture-specific rituals might be used to help a PTSD sufferer "make peace" with the trauma and reintegrate into the community.

present reality (Foa & Jaycox, 1999). Repeatedly imagining and discussing the traumatic events may also allow the client to "work through" them and integrate them into his or her concepts of the self and the world (Foa & Jaycox, 1999; Horowitz, 1976). Studies of rape survivors and combat veterans have found that this kind of repeated exposure therapy does significantly decrease PTSD symptoms and helps to prevent relapse (Foa et al., 1991; Foa et al., 1999; Keane et al., 1992; Resick & Schnicke, 1992; Tarrier et al., 1999).

What about those people who are constantly ruminating about their traumas, even years after they are over? Will intensive exposure to thoughts about the traumas help them? Some theorists argue that, for PTSD sufferers who cannot find any meaning in their traumas or "resolve" their traumas, and who experience very frequent intrusive thoughts, it is more useful to help them find ways of blocking their intrusive thoughts (Ehlers et al., 1998; Horowitz, 1976; Silver et al., 1983). **Thought-stopping** techniques may include the client yelling "No!" loudly when he realizes he is thinking about the trauma or learning to engage in positive activities that distract thoughts away from the trauma (Rachman, 1978). These thought-stopping techniques are often combined with **stress-management interventions** that teach clients skills for overcoming problems in their lives that are increasing their stress and that may be the result of PTSD, such as marital problems or social isolation (Keane et al., 1992). The following case study illustrates the use of several stress-management interventions with a combat veteran suffering from PTSD (Keane et al., 1992, p. 91).

CASE STUDY

D. P. was a male Vietnam veteran referred to the PTSD unit of his local DVA [Department of Veterans Affairs] Medical Center. D. P. reported feeling extremely stressed over the past six months because of problems on his job. He complained of sleep disturbance, angry outbursts, intrusive thoughts, nightmares, and avoidance of movies, books, and television shows associated with Vietnam. He also was experiencing marital difficulties, constriction of affect, and numbing of emotions. Since his discharge from the military, D. P. had avoided discussing Vietnam (his friends over the past 20 years were unaware that D. P. had even been in the military), and he stated that he did not want to discuss Vietnam in treatment. Respecting his wishes, treatment began by addressing sleep disturbance and interpersonal difficulties. D. P. learned progressive muscle relaxation and began using the technique to prepare for sleep, to get back to sleep after awakening, and at times throughout the day when he felt himself becoming stressed.

Interpersonal difficulties were then addressed in couples sessions using communication and problem-solving skills. D. P. and his wife had developed a relatively noncommunicative style over a number of years. Mrs. P. complained about a lack of intimacy in their relationship and being overburdened with decisions that were better made by both of them. In therapy, the couple learned to listen to one another and to give constructive positive and negative feedback.

As is common among combat veterans with PTSD, D. P. was afraid of his anger, even though he had not been violent in over 17 years. To address this concern, he was taught several strategies for anger control. For example, D. P. was given permission by the therapist to remove himself from a situation or discussion that created stress

PUSHING THE BOUNDARIES

Eye Movement Desensitization Therapy

A relatively new treatment for PTSD is eye movement desensitization and reprocessing, or EMDR (Shapiro, 1995). EMDR treatment focuses on specific traumatic memories. During a session of EMDR, a client attends to the image of the trauma, thoughts about the trauma, and the physical sensations of anxiety aroused by the trauma. At the same time, the therapist quickly moves a finger back and forth in front of the client's eyes to elicit a series of repeated rapid, jerky side-to-side eye movements ("saccades"). During the session, the client provides ratings of his or her anxiety level and how strongly he or she believes negative thoughts pertaining to the trauma.

Several case studies of dramatic improvement in PTSD symptoms after just a few sessions of EMDR have been reported (Shapiro, 1995). The results of the few controlled studies on EMDR have been more modest, but have suggested it may be useful in the treatment of PTSD (Lazrove et al., 1998).

How does EMDR work? It was discovered accidentally, and not derived from some theory of trauma-related disorders. The originator of EMDR, Francine Shapiro (1995), emphasizes the reprocessing of cognitions as essential to the success of EMDR. A few biological theories of the effects of the eye movements have also been suggested (Rothbaum, 1992). To date, it is not clear how EMDR works, but clinicians are quite interested in the technique because of its apparently rapid effects.

---

for him. He was taught to request a time and place to later continue working on that specific problem. This allowed D. P. to work on problem-solving skills while titrating his exposure to aversive, arousing circumstances. Initially, problem solving was conducted only during the session; however, after several weeks, the couple began problem solving at home and reviewed the contracts and solution processes in the following session. As D. P. learned a variety of new skills that enhanced his ability to manage his stress and his interpersonal problems, he became less defensive about Vietnam and began to address those issues more directly in therapy.

Some studies find that these stress-management interventions are helpful both to combat veterans with PTSD and to persons suffering PTSD after rape (Foa et al., 1999; Kilpatrick et al., 1979; Meichenbaum & Jaremko, 1983; Veronen & Kilpatrick, 1983). There is still much work to do, however, before we know just how to treat persons with PTSD. One of the newest and most controversial psychotherapies for PTSD is described in *Pushing the Boundaries: Eye Movement Desensitization Therapy.*

Biological Therapies

Drug therapies, including the benzodiazepines and antidepressant medications, are used by some clinicians to treat PTSD. These drugs can quell certain symptoms of PTSD, especially the sleep problems, nightmares, and irritability. In addition, the serotonin reuptake inhibitors appear to help PTSD sufferers avoid alcohol abuse (Friedman, 1998). This may make it easier for the person with PTSD to face his or her memories and extinguish fears of them. The long-term effectiveness of drug therapies for PTSD has not been established, however (Friedman, 1998; Southwick et al., 1994).

Sociocultural Approaches to Treatment

Treatments for PTSD often must consider the cultural context for this disorder. Some cultural groups have suffered a tremendous number of traumas, and thus are more likely to have high rates of PTSD. The appropriateness of any given treatment for PTSD, however, may depend on the norms and values of that culture. In addition, when whole communities have been the victims of traumas, treatment must often be at a community level, as well as at an individual level.

Cross-cultural issues We mentioned earlier that Southeast Asians may be especially vulnerable to PTSD because of the chronic and severe traumas to which many of them have been exposed. When they do seek treatment for psychological distress, Southeast Asians often present with somatic symptoms such as pain, poor sleeping, and stomachaches, rather than the psychological symptoms of posttraumatic stress disorder. They often do not believe the primary symptoms of PTSD, such as startle reaction, nightmares, reexperiencing the trauma, and irritability, are worth mentioning to a physician, and they steadfastly avoid thinking about or talking about the traumas they experienced (Kinzie & Leung, 1993). Dissociative experiences, such as transient hallucinations or loss of physical functioning for no medical reason, are also common. What follows is a case history of a Cambodian woman with PTSD (adapted from Kinzie & Leung, 1993, p. 292).

CASE STUDY

When originally seen, S. A. was 38 years old. She was a Cambodian refugee brought because she believed she was possessed by her dead mother. During the original evaluation, the patient was so distressed and agitated that no real history could be obtained. A subsequent evaluation showed that she had recently been angry and depressed much of the time and actually felt that her mother had entered her body. This intrusion caused her to become very irritable and angry, and during these episodes, she would lose control.

. . . S. A.'s past history was very disturbing. She was born in a rural area in Cambodia, the third of five children. She worked as a secretary for 1 1/2 years and married at the age of 17. During the Pol Pot regime, she was subjected to 4 years of forced labor. Her father died, and her husband was executed at the time she was in labor with her second child. S. A.'s child died of starvation, and her mother died of disease and starvation. She felt most distressed about the death of her mother, who was the person closest to her and who had helped her with the delivery of her child. In 1979, she left Cambodia and lived in refugee camps for 1 1/2 years before coming to the United States.

. . . At her original presentation, S. A. was extremely agitated and appeared to be in a dissociated state. However, in the second interview, after a week of benzodiazepine treatment, she demonstrated a good fund of knowledge and a good memory for past events. She appeared to be numb and saddened about what she had suffered. Her symptoms included frequent nightmares, intrusive thoughts about the past, startle reaction, irritability, and marked attempts to avoid all memories of the past or any events that would remind her of Cambodia. . . .

Treatment of PTSD in Southeast Asian refugees like S. A. can be especially delicate. They may never have told anyone about the traumas they experienced

Treatments for PTSD must take into account the cultural norms and experiences of people suffering from the disorder.

in their homeland because of strong cultural taboos against discussing these traumas in their families. Thus, therapists must be highly sensitive and supportive in encouraging the refugee to tell his or her own story. The therapist must be careful to avoid any suggestion of interrogating the client as he or she might have been interrogated in the homeland (Kinzie & Leung, 1993). These refugees may need to protect themselves against the agony that memories of their severe traumas arouse and focus more on solving current problems. For example, the therapist treating S. A. might want to ensure that she is getting all the financial support and education available to her to stabilize her income and living situation. Although refugees may be having significant problems in their marital and family relationships due to their PTSD symptoms and the amount of stress their families are facing, they may be reluctant to talk to the therapist about these due to cultural taboos against doing so.

Some cultures have their own treatments for PTSD-like symptoms. For example, some Native American groups have cleansing rituals that absolve combat veterans from their actions during combat and serve to reintegrate veterans into the community and with the values of his or her group. The Navajo have a healing ceremony called the *Enemy Way*, which is explicitly oriented toward returning combat veterans. The ceremony lasts for 7 days and 7 nights. The veteran, his or her family and community members, and a tribal healer actively participate in ritual song designed to return balance and harmony to the individual veteran and the entire community (Manson et al., 1996).

Community-level interventions Often, whole communities are ravaged by a trauma—a tornado might wipe out most businesses in a community or a flood might make most of the homes in a community uninhabitable. Human-made disasters can also ravage whole communities, such as the atrocities committed under "ethnic cleansing" and apartheid. Hundreds of thousands of people in many communities around the world—Kosovo, Bosnia, Rwanda, South Africa, Eritrea—have been forced from their homes, driven out of their countries, tortured, raped, and killed. Mental-health professionals have been on the front lines of these conflicts, attempting to help survivors cope with the traumas they have suffered. Here is the story of one of these helpers, a psychologist in South Africa (from Burnette, 1997).

CASE STUDY

When the civil strife started two years ago, the men of Bhambayi went off to fight and the women were forced to move from their middle-class homes into run-down shacks on barren land. The war, fought by two factions in conflict over apartheid, drastically altered the lives of the people in Bhambayi, a town in KwaZulu-Natal, South Africa. Hundreds of people were killed and the people's homes were destroyed.

Psychologist Craig Higson-Smith, a 27-year-old South African native, became aware of the region's problems while teaching at the University of Natal and founded the KwaZulu-Natal Program for Survivors of Violence. He first brought a team of South African community researchers to help the beleaguered people there in 1992 and their work continues today.

Before the war, most of the families owned their own homes, benefited from two incomes and had gardens where they grew their own vegetables. So, as one of the first priorities, the staff of the KwaZulu-Natal Program for the Survivors of Violence secured a 3,000-square-foot piece of land from the government. While the women toiled, they discussed how the violence had affected their lives and how it felt to lose their husbands and their children.

The garden fulfilled many needs. The 25 women turned the once-barren soil into a flourishing vegetable patch. The garden also became a therapeutic oasis as the women supported each other and spoke with program staff about their experiences, and gained self-esteem from being productive.

"What happened was the same interaction that psychologists think of as group therapy," says Higson-Smith. "But it happened in a different context and was facilitated by a process that we wouldn't have necessarily thought of using."

The program is geared primarily toward communities, although staff conduct some work at the individual, small group and societal levels. With individuals, they conduct traditional psychotherapy to help people cope psychologically in their war-torn environment. At the small group level, they work with families, schools, and churches to restore support systems and foster community empowerment.

And at the societal level, they advocate for government funding for their program, discuss the violence in the region with lawmakers and advocate for conflict-resolution programs in the school curricula.

"The interventions we conduct mean rethinking what we as psychologists understand as our role, particularly in underdeveloped countries," Higson-Smith says. "Our job often includes facilitating, promoting and networking so that the structures [that already exist in the community] can mobilize."

Even the most fragmented communities contain structures, Higson-Smith said. Church groups, stokvels (savings clubs), social clubs and paramilitary units are examples of such networks. His group works with those structures to link people in the communities.

Higson-Smith's team worked with a paramilitary group whose members had become involved in criminal activities, such as stealing and selling drugs. The researchers facilitated discussion among the group members about their problems and helped them come up with concrete strategies they could use to improve their lives, such as getting job training.

At the same time, Higson-Smith and his group were working with nurses at a local clinic, training them in trauma management. The team connected the two groups and now some of the group members are volunteering at the clinic.

Higson-Smith and his staff also have programs designed specifically for the young people whose lives have been ravaged by the war. They recruit youth who have been involved in the conflict to help them resume normal lives and use group discussions to explore topics such as unemployment and coping with anger and grief. They also focus on other issues young people must face, including peer pressure and substance abuse, and explore how those issues relate to the violence they have experienced.

"Political violence is the most salient feature of their lives. Most of the teens there have killed someone, know someone who's been killed or have been forced to leave their homes," Higson-Smith says. "So in the groups we discuss how the violence relates to these other issues they must contend with as adolescents."

The youth groups play games and work on projects aimed at teaching life skills. Last year when the youth group organized a community sports day, they learned to communicate with each other as well as youth from other communities, and take responsibility by seeing the event through to completion.

Higson-Smith and his colleagues also conduct psychodrama, art and music groups that serve as a venue for the youth to express how it felt to live through the conflict. The youth write poems, for example to express their feelings, some of which were published in a book, *On Common Ground* (KwaZulu-Natal Program for Survivors of Violence, 1996).

Higson-Smith says the team's work is difficult yet rewarding. He also emphasizes that he and his colleagues are not the sole cause of healing in these devastated communities. "Before we came, the people here survived, coped, and found joy in their lives," he said.

Summing Up

- People with posttraumatic stress disorder repeatedly reexperience the traumatic event, they avoid situations that might arouse memories of their trauma, and they are hypervigilant and chronically aroused.

- PTSD may be most likely to occur following traumas that shatter people's assumptions that they are invulnerable, that the world is a just place, and that bad things do not happen to good people.

- People who experience severe and long-lasting traumas, who have lower levels of social support, who experience socially stigmatizing traumas, who were already depressed or anxious before trauma, or have maladaptive, ruminative coping styles may be at increased risk for PTSD.

- People who are unable to somehow make sense of a trauma appear more likely to have chronic PTSD symptoms.

- PTSD sufferers show greater physiological reactivity to stressors, and greater activity in areas of the brain involved in emotion and memory, but blunted resting cortisol levels. The meaning of these neurobiological abnormalities is not yet clear.

- The most effective treatment for PTSD involves exposing the person to his or her memories of the trauma, through systematic desensitization and flooding, to extinguish his or her anxiety over these memories.

- Some people cannot tolerate such exposure, however, and may do better with supportive therapy focused on solving current interpersonal difficulties and life problems.

- Benzodiazepines and antidepressant drugs can quell some of the symptoms of PTSD, but these symptoms tend to recur when the drugs are discontinued.

- Clinicians treating people with anxiety disorders must be sensitive to the extraordinary circumstances that may have led to these disorders and to cultural norms for what is appropriate to discuss outside one's immediate family or culture.

☺ OBSESSIVE-COMPULSIVE DISORDER

Obsessions are thoughts, images, ideas, or impulses that are persistent, that the individual feels intrude upon his or her consciousness without control, and that cause significant anxiety or distress. **Compulsions** are repetitive behaviors or mental acts that an individual feels he or she must perform. **Obsessive-compulsive disorder (OCD)** is classified as an anxiety disorder because people with OCD experience anxiety as a result of their obsessional thoughts and when they cannot carry out their compulsive behaviors (see Table 7.3). However, this disorder has quite a different character than the other anxiety disorders we have discussed and may eventually be declassified as an anxiety disorder.

Children can suffer OCD, just as adults can, and this little boy's personal account of OCD illustrates how overwhelming this disorder can be (Rapaport, 1990, pp. 43–48). His name is Zach.

Voices

When I was 6 I started doing all these strange things when I swallowed saliva. When I swallowed saliva I

TABLE 7.3
DSM-IV
Symptoms of
Obsessive-Compulsive Disorder

Obsessive-compulsive disorder is classified as an anxiety disorder but differs from other anxiety disorders in many ways.

The person must show either obsessions or compulsions, which he or she recognizes are excessive or unreasonable.

Obsessions are defined as

1. recurrent and persistent thoughts, impulses, or images that are experienced as intrusive and inappropriate and that cause anxiety or distress

2. thoughts, impulses, or images that are not simply excessive worries about real-life problems

3. thoughts, impulses, or images that the person attempts to ignore or suppress or to neutralize with some other thought or action

4. obsessional thoughts, impulses, or images that the person recognizes are a product of his or her own mind

Compulsions are defined as

1. repetitive behaviors (such as hand washing, ordering, checking) or mental acts (such as praying, counting, repeating words silently) that the person feels driven to perform in response to an obsession or according to rules that must be applied rigidly

2. behaviors or mental acts that are aimed at preventing or reducing distress or preventing some dreaded event or situation; however, these behaviors or mental acts either are not connected in a realistic way with what they are designed to neutralize or prevent or are clearly excessive.

Source: DSM-IV, APA, 2000.

it maybe an hour and a half or sometimes three hours a day.

I had bathroom problems too. I had to take some toilet paper and rip them up a lot of times into teeny pieces that had to be just the right size—only about a millimeter. They had to be torn perfect and then I'd flush them away.

I had to do all kinds of things with my fingers and my mouth. I had to touch all my fingers to my lips a few times if I swallowed saliva. Swallowing was one of the first things. But my elbows were really first. I was afraid of getting my hands dirty. My mind said "Wash them, they're dirty." They *felt* dirty. After I went to the bathroom I had to wash my hands, only mine always felt dirty.

I would forget one thing after another. After I changed one pattern I would completely forget it. I remember one part of one pattern: I had to touch the ends of my thumbs to where the water came out of the faucet. Some other things I don't remember. I couldn't turn off the water with my hands. I was late for school a lot.

You may be thinking that the thoughts and behaviors that Zach describes are "crazy"—that they are so out of touch with reality that they are psychotic. The thoughts and behaviors of people with OCD are not considered psychotic, however, because these people are very aware of how irrational their thoughts and behaviors are. Yet, they cannot seem to control them.

OCD often begins when the person is at a young age; the peak age of onset for males is between 6 and 15 years of age, and for females it is between 20 and 29

had to crouch down and touch the ground. I didn't want to lose any saliva—for a bit I had to sweep the ground with my hand—and later I had to blink my eyes if I swallowed. I was frustrated because I couldn't stop the compulsions. Each time I swallowed I had to do something. For a while I had to touch my shoulders to my chin. I don't know why. I had no reason. I was afraid. It was just so unpleasant if I didn't. If I tried not to do these things, all I got was failure. I had to do it, and no matter how hard I tried, I just *still* had to.

. . . I felt ashamed. I didn't want anyone to know. I wanted it to be just for me to know, no one else.

It wrecked my life. It took away all the time. I couldn't do anything. If you put it all together I did

People with a washing compulsion may wash their hands for hours each day.

years of age (APA, 2000; Rasmussen & Eisen, 1990). It tends to be a chronic disorder if left untreated. Obsessional thoughts are very distressing to people with OCD and engaging in compulsive behaviors can take a great deal of time and even be dangerous (e.g., washing your hands so often that they bleed). As many as 66 percent of people with OCD are also significantly depressed (Edelmann, 1992). Panic attacks, phobias, and substance abuse are also common in OCD.

Somewhere between 1 and 3 percent of people will develop OCD at some time in their lives (Karno & Golding, 1991; Robins et al., 1984). In the United States, Whites show a higher prevalence of OCD than do African Americans or Hispanic Americans (Karno & Golding, 1991). The prevalence of OCD does not seem to differ greatly across countries that have been studied, including the United States, Canada, Mexico, England, Norway, Hong Kong, India, Egypt, Japan, and Korea (Escobar, 1993; Insel, 1984; Kim, 1993). Although some studies have found slightly higher rates of OCD in women than in men, there does not appear to be a large or consistent gender difference in OCD (Edelmann, 1992; Karno & Golding, 1991; Rasmussen & Tsuang, 1984, 1986).

Symptoms of OCD

Zach's obsessions involve dirt and being dirty. The focus of obsessive thoughts seems to be similar across cultures, with the most common type of obsession focusing on dirt and contamination (Akhtar et al., 1975; Insel, 1984; Kim, 1993; Rachman & Hodgson, 1980). Other common obsessions include aggressive impulses (such as to hurt your child), sexual thoughts (such as recurrent pornographic images), impulses to do something against your moral code (such as to shout obscenities in church), and repeated doubts (such as worrying that you have not turned off the stove). Although thoughts of this kind occur to most people occasionally, most of us can "turn off" these thoughts by dismissing or ignoring them (Muris, Merckelbach, & Clavan, 1997). People with OCD cannot turn off these thoughts:

Voices

It's just whatever I try, be it sheer will or mind games or therapy or reassurance from my husband, whether I pray, make pacts with God or try to be a good mother, the thoughts will not go away. (Colas, 1998, pp. 106–107).

People with OCD do not carry out the impulses they have (hurting a baby or shouting obscenities in church), but they are so bothered by the fact that they even have these thoughts that they feel extremely guilty and anxious.

Most people who have severe and persistent obsessions engage in compulsions to try to erase their thoughts and the anxiety the thoughts create. Sometimes an individual's compulsion is tied to his or her specific obsession by some obvious logic. The compulsive behavior becomes so extreme and repetitive, however, that it is irrational. For example, Zach would wash his hands 35 times a day, until they cracked and bled, to rid himself of contamination obsessions. "Checking" compulsions, which are extremely common, are tied to obsessional doubts, as is illustrated in this story (Rapaport, 1990, pp. 21–23):

Voices

I'm driving down the highway doing 55 MPH. I'm on my way to take a final exam. My seat belt is buckled and I'm vigilantly following all the rules of the road. No one is on the highway—not a living soul.

Out of nowhere an obsessive-compulsive disorder (OCD) attack strikes. It's almost magical the way it distorts my perception of reality. While in reality no one is on the road, I'm intruded with the heinous thought that I *might* have hit someone . . . a human being! God knows where such a fantasy comes from. . . .

The pain is a terrible guilt that I have committed an unthinkable, negligent act. At one level, I know this is ridiculous, but there's a terrible pain in my stomach telling me something quite different. . . .

I start ruminating, "Maybe I did hit someone and didn't realize it. . . . Oh, my God! I might have killed somebody! I have to go back and check." Checking is the only way to calm the anxiety. It brings me closer to truth somehow. I can't live with the thought that I actually may have killed someone—I have to check it out. . . .

I've driven 5 miles farther down the road since the attack's onset. I turn the car around and head back to the scene of the mythical mishap. I return to the spot on the road where I "think" it "might" have occurred. Naturally, nothing is there. No police car and no bloodied body. Relieved, I turn around again to get to my exam on time.

Feeling better, I drive for about twenty seconds and then the lingering thoughts and pain start gnawing away again. Only this time they're even more intense. I think, "Maybe I should have pulled *off* the road and checked the side brush where the injured body was thrown and now lies? Maybe I didn't go *far enough* back on the road and the accident occurred a mile farther back."

The pain of my possibly having hurt someone is now so intense that I have no choice—I really see it this way.

I turn the car around a second time and head an extra mile farther down the road to find the corpse. I drive by quickly. Assured that this time I've gone far enough I head back to school to take my exam. But I'm not through yet.

"My God," my attack relentlessly continues, "I didn't get *out* of the car to actually *look* on the side of the road!"

So I turn back a third time. I drive to the part of the highway where I think the accident happened. I park the car on the highway's shoulder. I get out and begin rummaging around the brush.

This man's compulsive checking makes some sense given what he is thinking. However, what he is thinking—that he hit someone on the road without knowing it—is highly improbable. The compulsive checking quells obsessional thoughts briefly, but the obsessional thoughts come back with even more force.

Often, the link between the obsession and compulsion is the result of "magical thinking." For example, many people with OCD feel compelled to repeat a behavior, a ritual, or a thought a certain number of times, as if there were something magical about the specific number of repetitions. Their rituals often become stereotyped and rigid, and they develop obsessions and compulsions about not performing the rituals correctly. For example, one young woman with obsessions about hurting others had a prayer that she felt compelled to say in order to absolve herself from guilt for having had the obsessional thought. Over time, this developed into a ritual of saying the prayer in multiples of six. If she made even one mistake in this series of six prayers, she had to start over again from the beginning and this time say the prayer 12 times. If she made another mistake, she had to start from the beginning and say the prayer 18 times. Some nights this young woman was up all night trying to get her prayer ritual correct before she could go to bed. *Extraordinary People:* Sam, a Man with OCD describes a man

EXTRAORDINARY PEOPLE

Sam, a Man with OCD

The following autobiographical essay was written by a man named Sam, who suffered severe OCD (from Rapaport, 1990, pp. 43–58). Sam was plagued by troubling thoughts about death and had elaborate compulsions designed to erase these thoughts. His obsessions and compulsions occupied much of his day. Nonetheless, Sam was a highly successful businessperson. We do not know how Sam was able to achieve so much despite the liabilities of his OCD. We can get a sense, however, of how much he suffered in silence from this brief glimpse we have into the workings of his mind.

My name is Sam. I am a very successful professional in a very large city, involved with matters of substantial importance and large sums of money, working in a very competitive field. I have a beautiful, loving, understanding wife and three terrific bright children. Times are good. . . .

My secretary doesn't know it and the other senior partners don't know it, but my days are not like the days of the others in my office who also handle multimillion-dollar transactions. They are just doing their job. I have two jobs: my profession and battling obsessions. Come enter my thoughts as I prepare to enter that battle. . . .

I am very careful as I read a book or newspaper or magazine. I never know what terrible things lie on the next page or the next paragraph or the next sentence. I read slowly. I concentrate on the mantra.

Damn! *Death.* There's that awful word. All right, start to offset it. Be careful. Better to go backwards over what you've already read. Try to remember where the words are. You can't go forward anyway, because forward is the future and you don't want to contaminate the future with eyes that have just beheld a word of such terrible consequence. Go back over what you've read. Go to the past. You can't really harm the past (you don't really believe that)—use it to your advantage. Would

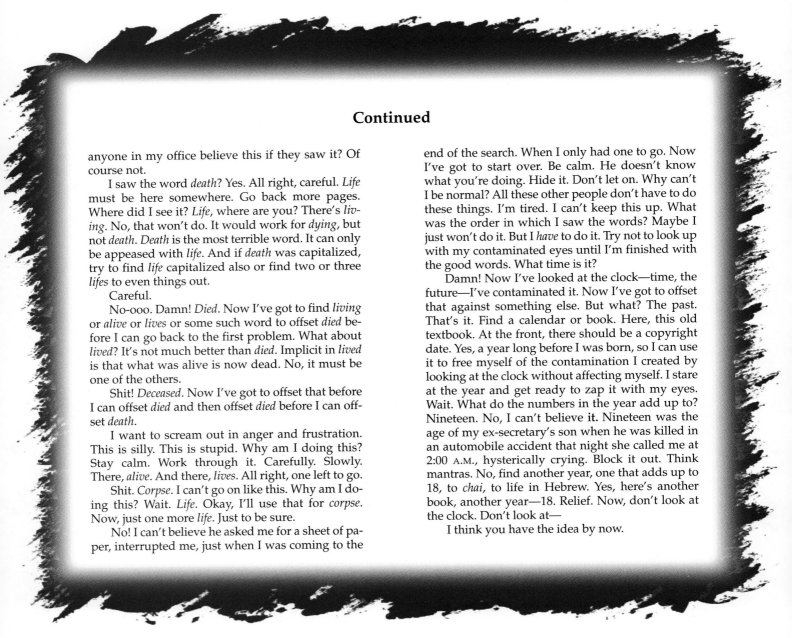

Continued

anyone in my office believe this if they saw it? Of course not.

I saw the word *death*? Yes. All right, careful. *Life* must be here somewhere. Go back more pages. Where did I see it? *Life*, where are you? There's *living*. No, that won't do. It would work for *dying*, but not *death*. *Death* is the most terrible word. It can only be appeased with *life*. And if *death* was capitalized, try to find *life* capitalized also or find two or three *lifes* to even things out.

Careful.

No-ooo. Damn! *Died*. Now I've got to find *living* or *alive* or *lives* or some such word to offset *died* before I can go back to the first problem. What about *lived*? It's not much better than *died*. Implicit in *lived* is that what was alive is now dead. No, it must be one of the others.

Shit! *Deceased*. Now I've got to offset that before I can offset *died* and then offset *died* before I can offset *death*.

I want to scream out in anger and frustration. This is silly. This is stupid. Why am I doing this? Stay calm. Work through it. Carefully. Slowly. There, *alive*. And there, *lives*. All right, one left to go.

Shit. *Corpse*. I can't go on like this. Why am I doing this? Wait. *Life*. Okay, I'll use that for *corpse*. Now, just one more *life*. Just to be sure.

No! I can't believe he asked me for a sheet of paper, interrupted me, just when I was coming to the end of the search. When I only had one to go. Now I've got to start over. Be calm. He doesn't know what you're doing. Hide it. Don't let on. Why can't I be normal? All these other people don't have to do these things. I'm tired. I can't keep this up. What was the order in which I saw the words? Maybe I just won't do it. But I *have* to do it. Try not to look up with my contaminated eyes until I'm finished with the good words. What time is it?

Damn! Now I've looked at the clock—time, the future—I've contaminated it. Now I've got to offset that against something else. But what? The past. That's it. Find a calendar or book. Here, this old textbook. At the front, there should be a copyright date. Yes, a year long before I was born, so I can use it to free myself of the contamination I created by looking at the clock without affecting myself. I stare at the year and get ready to zap it with my eyes. Wait. What do the numbers in the year add up to? Nineteen. No, I can't believe it. Nineteen was the age of my ex-secretary's son when he was killed in an automobile accident that night she called me at 2:00 A.M., hysterically crying. Block it out. Think mantras. No, find another year, one that adds up to 18, to *chai*, to life in Hebrew. Yes, here's another book, another year—18. Relief. Now, don't look at the clock. Don't look at—

I think you have the idea by now.

who had magic rituals for overcoming his obsessions with words related to death.

At times, there is no discernible link between the specific obsession a person has and the specific compulsion that helps to dispel the obsession. Recall that Zach engaged in several behaviors, such as touching the floor or touching his shoulders to his chin, when he had an obsession about losing his saliva. He could not even say how these behaviors were related to his obsession; he just knew he had to engage in them. Thus, although compulsions may often seem purposeful, they are not functional.

In some cases, the family members of people with OCD become accomplices in the disorder, as did the husband of writer Emily Colas, who has written about her OCD (Colas, 1998, pp. 70–72):

Voices

My husband and I generally kept a pile of about twenty garbage bags in one corner of our apartment. Which may seem out of character, for me to let them stay, but it was our trash and I knew nothing bad was in there. It was the communal trash that made me shake. So when it was time to take the bags out to the dumpster, my husband had to follow the whole hygienic procedure. To keep the neighbors' germs out of our place. First the water had to be turned on and left

CONCEPT REVIEW

Theories of OCD

The biological theories of OCD have been dominant in recent years, but psychodynamic and cognitive-behavioral theories have been proposed.

Theory	Description
Biological theory	People with OCD suffer from dysfunction in circuits in the brain regulating primitive impulses, possibly due to deficiencies in serotonin, which cause OCD.
Psychodynamic theory	The obsessions and compulsions of people with OCD represent unconscious wishes or conflicts.
Cognitive-behavioral theory	People with OCD have difficulty turning off intrusive thoughts because of chronic distress, a tendency toward rigid thinking, and the belief they should be able to control their thoughts

that way because if he touched the garbage and then the spigot, the spigot would get contaminated. Next he'd take one bag in his right hand and open the door with his left. Then he'd shut the door behind him and lock it so that no one could get into the house. I guess I could have monitored, but he wanted me upstairs so I couldn't critique him. He'd take the bag down, stand a few feet from the dumpster to be sure not to touch it, and throw the bag in. Then he'd unlock the door, open it, slip his shoes off, come inside, and wash his hands. He used a pump soap so that he could use his clean wrist to pump some in the palm of his hand and not contaminate the dispenser. The water would stay on, and he'd move to the next bag. He went through this procedure twenty times, once for each bag, until they were gone.

Explaining OCD

The biological theories of OCD have dominated research in recent years, and have provided some intriguing hypotheses about the sources of OCD. Psychodynamic and cognitive-behavioral theories of OCD have also been proposed. These theories are summarized in the *Concept Review: Theories of OCD.*

Biological Theories

Some of the most promising research on obsessive compulsive disorder views it as a neurological disorder. Much of this research has focused on a circuit in the brain that is involved in the execution of primitive patterns of behavior, such as aggression, sexuality, and bodily excretion (Baxter et al., 1992, Rapaport, 1990; Swedo et al., 1992). This circuit begins in the orbital region of the frontal cortex, where these impulses arise (see Figure 7.5). These impulses are then carried to a

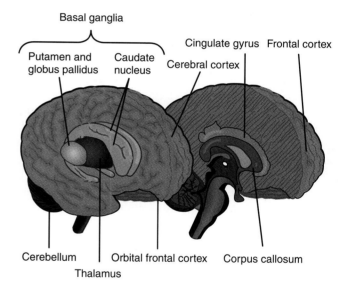

FIGURE 7.5   A three-dimensional view of the human brain (with parts shown as they would look if the overlying cerebral cortex were transparent) clarifies the locations of the orbital frontal cortex and the basal ganglia—areas implicated in obsessive-compulsive disorder. Among the basal ganglia's structures are the caudate nuclei, which filter powerful impulses that arise in the orbital frontal cortex so that only the most powerful ones reach the thalamus. Perhaps the orbital frontal cortex or the caudate nuclei or both are so active in people with obsessive-compulsive disorder that numerous impulses reach the thalamus, generating obsessive thoughts or compulsive actions.

Adapted from Rapoport, 1989, p. 85.

part of the basal ganglia called the **caudate nucleus,** which allows only the strongest of these impulses to carry through to the thalamus. If these impulses reach the thalamus, the person is motivated to think further about and possibly act on these impulses. The action might involve a set of stereotyped behaviors appropriate to the impulse. Once these behaviors are executed, the impulse diminishes. For people with OCD, however, dysfunction in this circuit may result in the inability of the system to turn off these primitive impulses or to turn off the execution of the stereotyped behaviors once they are engaged. For example, most of us when we have the thought that we are dirty will engage in a fairly stereotyped form of cleansing: We wash our hands. People with OCD, however, continue to have the impulse to wash their hands because their brains do not shut off their thoughts about dirt or their behavior when the behavior is no longer necessary. Proponents of this theory have pointed out that many of the obsessions and compulsions of people with OCD have to do with contamination, sex, aggression, and the repetition of patterns of behavior—all issues with which this primitive brain circuit deals.

PET scans of people with OCD show more activity in the areas of the brain involved in this primitive circuit than in people without OCD (Figure 7.6; Baxter et al., 1990; Saxena et al., 1998). In addition, people with OCD often get some relief from their symptoms when they take drugs that better regulate the neurotransmitter serotonin; serotonin plays an important role in the proper functioning of this primitive circuit in the brain (Rapaport, 1991; Saxena et al., 1998). OCD patients who do respond to serotonin-enhancing drugs tend to show more reductions in the rate of activity in these brain areas than do OCD patients who do not respond well to these drugs (Baxter et al., 1992; Swedo et al., 1992). Interestingly, OCD patients who respond to behavior therapies also tend to show decreases in rate of activity in the caudate nucleus and thalamus (see Figure 7.7; Schwartz et al., 1996).

Piecing these studies together, researchers have argued that people with OCD have a fundamental dysfunction in the areas of the brain regulating primitive impulses, perhaps due to a depletion of serotonin in these systems. As a result, primitive impulses about sex, aggression, and cleanliness break through to their consciousness and motivate the execution of stereotyped behaviors much more often than in people without OCD (Rapaport, 1989, 1991; Saxena et al., 1998). Whether these differences in brain functioning are a cause or a consequence of OCD is not clear.

Finally, there is evidence that disordered genes may play a role determining who is vulnerable to OCD (Billett, Richter, & Kennedy, 1998; Samuels & Nestadt, 1997). Most of the studies on the genetics of OCD are family history studies, which show that OCD clearly runs in families. More definitive evidence for a genetic influence on OCD requires large-scale twin and adoption studies.

Psychodynamic Theories

Psychodynamic theorists suggest that the particular obsessions and compulsions of people with OCD are

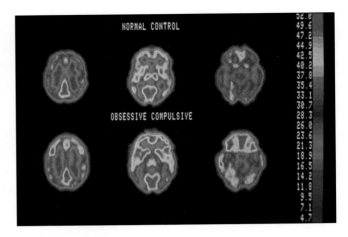

FIGURE 7.6   PET scans of people with OCD show more activity in the frontal cortex, basal ganglia, and thalamus than do PET scans of people without OCD.

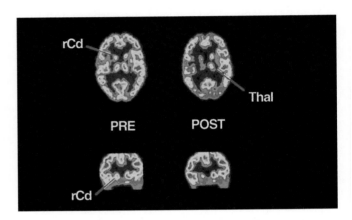

FIGURE 7.7   Studies using positron emission tomography show decreases in metabolic activity in the caudate nucleus and thalamus in OCD patients after they have received behavior therapy.

Source: Schwartz et al., 1996.

symbolic of unconscious conflicts that they are guarding against (Freud, 1909). These conflicts create such anxiety for people that they can only confront them indirectly, by displacing the anxiety created by the conflict onto some other more acceptable thought or behavior. The case of Brenda illustrates how OCD might develop, according to psychodynamic theory.

CASE STUDY

Brenda was about 9 years old when her obsessive thoughts and compulsive behaviors began. She had always been a somewhat emotional child, easily becoming anxious when she had to be away from her family for more than a day or so and becoming quite depressed when she did not do as well in school or in sports as she wanted to. When she was 9, Brenda's parents told her they were going to divorce. She had known that her parents fought a lot, but the announcement of the divorce came as a complete surprise.

It also came as a surprise to Brenda that she began to have "bad thoughts," often having to do with someone being hurt. For example, she would see a knife on the kitchen table, and she would have an image of the knife stabbing her brother. Or she would see one of her classmates playing on a swing set and have the thought, "She's going to fall off and die." Brenda felt very guilty for having these thoughts and she worried greatly about the safety of the people in her thoughts. She would say a prayer when she had these thoughts, asking God for forgiveness and to protect the person who was the target of her thoughts. She often did not feel that the prayers "worked" to absolve her of her guilt, however, and she would say the same prayer again, trying this time to feel more contrite as she said the prayer.

She also began having thoughts about germs and disease. She felt almost sick to her stomach if she touched something she felt was contaminated with germs. She would wash her hands many times per day, with extra-strong soap, until eventually her hands cracked and bled. Having open sores on her hands only made her feel more vulnerable to germs, however, and she would wash that much more to rid herself of the invisible germs. Brenda began avoiding situations that she thought would offer an opportunity for contamination, such as playing outdoors or playing with toys that had been touched by other children. She became more isolated from her peers, more withdrawn, and more clinging to her mother.

According to psychodynamic theory, Brenda's obsessions about others being hurt reflected her anger against her parents for splitting up and her desire to hurt her parents for hurting her. Especially because she was a rather dependent, emotional child, Brenda was terrified of her desire to hurt her parents, on whom she was so dependent. Thus, she unconsciously transformed this desire to hurt her parents into a fear that others would be hurt. Her need to be forgiven for thoughts about others being hurt and her obsession with being contaminated and dirty reflected the terrible guilt Brenda experienced over her desire to hurt her parents.

Psychodynamic theory offers an interesting account of both the development of OCD and the specific content of people's obsessions and compulsions. According to this theory, the reason that so many obsessions and compulsions have to do with contamination, sex, and aggression is that unconscious conflicts have to do with sexual and aggressive impulses. Psychodynamic theory suggests that the way to cure people of their OCD is to help them gain insight into the conflicts their obsessions and compulsions symbolize and better resolve these conflicts. This type of therapy actually helped Brenda. When she recognized her anger against her parents and found appropriate ways of expressing that anger, her obsessions and compulsions subsided. Psychodynamic therapy generally is not considered

effective for the majority of OCD patients, however (Salzman, 1980).

Cognitive-Behavioral Theories

It is clear that most people, including people who do *not* have OCD, occasionally have negative, intrusive thoughts. For example, one study found that 84 percent of normal subjects reported sometimes having repetitive, intrusive thoughts (Rachman & deSilva, 1978). People are more prone to have negative, intrusive thoughts and to engage in rigid, ritualistic behaviors when they are distressed (Clark & Purdon, 1993; Rachman & Hodgson, 1980). For example, many new mothers, exhausted from sleep deprivation and the stresses of caring for a newborn, have thoughts about harming their newborn, even though they are horrified by such thoughts and would never carry them out.

According to the cognitive-behavioral theories of OCD, what differentiates people with OCD from people without the disorder is the ability to turn off these negative, intrusive thoughts (Clark, 1988; Rachman & Hodgson, 1980; Salkovskis et al., 1997). People who do not develop OCD are able to turn off their intrusive thoughts by ignoring or dismissing them, attributing them to their distress, and simply letting them subside with the passage of time. People who develop OCD have trouble turning off their thoughts, for several reasons. First, they may be depressed or generally anxious much of the time, so that even minor negative events are more likely to have intrusive, negative thoughts (Clark & Purdon, 1993). Second, people with OCD may have a tendency toward rigid, moralistic thinking (Rachman, 1993; Salkovskis, 1989). They judge the negative, intrusive thoughts they have as more unacceptable than most people would and become more anxious and guilty over having these thoughts. This anxiety then makes it even harder for them to dismiss the thoughts (Clark & deSilva, 1985). In addition, people who feel more responsible for events that happen in their lives and in the lives of others than other people do will have more trouble dismissing thoughts like "Did I hit someone on the road?" and thus might be more likely to develop OCD. Third, people with OCD appear to believe that they *should* be able to control all thoughts, and have trouble accepting that everyone has horrific thoughts from time to time (Clark & Purdon, 1993; Freeston et al., 1992). They tend to believe that having these thoughts means they are going crazy or they equate having the thoughts with actually engaging in the behaviors (e.g., "If I'm thinking about hurting my child, I'm as guilty as if I actually did hurt my child"). Of course, this just makes them that much more anxious when they have the thoughts, which makes it harder for them to dismiss the thoughts.

How do compulsions develop, according to this theory? They develop largely through operant conditioning. People with anxiety-provoking obsessions discover that if they engage in certain behaviors, their anxiety is reduced. The reduction in anxiety reinforces the behaviors. Each time the obsessions return and they use the behaviors to reduce the obsessions, the behaviors are reinforced. Compulsions are born.

As with the biological theory of OCD, research has supported pieces of the cognitive-behavioral view of OCD, but much more research needs to be done. In particular, because almost all studies investigating the biological and cognitive-behavioral theories of OCD have compared people who already have OCD with those who do not, it is not clear whether the dysfunctions these theories point to are the causes or the consequences of OCD.

Treatment of OCD

Just as biological theories dominate research on OCD, biological therapies have come to dominate the treatment of OCD. Cognitive-behavioral therapies also appear very helpful in treating OCD (see *Concept Review: Treatments for OCD*).

Biological Treatments

Until the 1980s, there were few effective biological treatments for OCD. The antianxiety drugs, the benzodiazepines, were not useful in most cases of OCD, which is one clue that OCD is not like the other anxiety disorders. Then, fortuitously, it was discovered that antidepressant drugs that affect levels of the neurotransmitter serotonin helped to relieve symptoms of OCD in many patients (Abramowitz, 1997; Rapaport, 1989, 1991). These include clomipramine (trade name Anafranil), fluoxetine (trade name Prozac), paroxetine (trade name Paxil), sertraline (trade name Zoloft), and fluvoxamine (trade name Luvox). Controlled studies suggest that 50 to 80 percent of OCD patients experience decreases in their obsessions and compulsions when on these drugs, compared to only 5 percent of patients on placebos (Jenike, 1992; March et al., 1998; Orloff et al., 1994). These drugs may work by inhibiting the reuptake of the neurotransmitter serotonin, increasing the functional levels of serotonin in the brain. Recall that the latest biological theories of OCD suggest that this disorder involves dysfunctioning of areas of the brain rich in serotonin.

These drugs are not the complete answer for people with OCD, however. Even among people who respond to the drug, obsessions and compulsions are only reduced by about 40 or 50 percent, and they tend to relapse if the drugs are discontinued (De-Veaugh-Geiss et al., 1992; Michelson & Marchione, 1991). The drugs have significant side effects, including drowsiness, constipation, and loss of sexual interest, that prevent many people from taking them. And, as writer Emily Colas observes, after living a lifetime with OCD, she needed to learn how to live a normal life once the drugs removed her symptoms:

Voices

You can try really hard not to get better. Use all your strength and will. But when you're on the pill, you get better and there's not a whole lot you can do about it. It takes a little while to kick in, so there are about four or five weeks when you're basically taking medication for the sheer benefit of the side effects. Tired, spacey, constipated. But then it happens. Not dramatically. It comes on slowly, but you can tell. The thoughts and worries become less gripping. I guess I figured that once that began to happen I'd instantly become happy. But the startling realization I made as I was coming to my senses was that life's kind of a drag. There didn't seem to be much to it. And my rituals had been a nice diversion. Without them, I wasn't quite sure what to do with myself. This thought made my head ache. I got anxious, nervous, wondering if I was destined to live

CONCEPT REVIEW		
Treatments for OCD		
Often drug therapies and cognitive-behavioral therapies are combined in the treatment of OCD.		
Treatment	**Description**	**Example**
Biological treatment	Serotonin-enhancing drugs	Paxil, Prozac
Cognitive-behavioral treatments	Expose the client to obsessions until anxiety about obsessions decreases; prevent compulsive behaviors and help the client manage anxiety that is aroused.	Systematic desensitization may be used to help a person with a germ obsession gradually tolerate exposure to "dirty" materials.

this dull and uninteresting life. But because of those damn pills, I wasn't even able to obsess about *that*. (Colas, 1998, p. 138)

Cognitive-Behavioral Treatments

Many clinicians believe that the drugs must be combined with cognitive-behavioral therapies in order to help people recover completely from OCD. The cognitive-behavioral therapies for OCD focus on repeatedly exposing the client to the focus of the obsession and preventing compulsive responses to the anxiety aroused by the obsession (Rachman & Hodgson, 1980; Marks & Swinson, 1992). The repeated exposure to the content of the obsession is thought to habituate the client to obsession so that it does not arouse as much anxiety as it formerly did. Preventing the person from engaging in compulsive behavior allows this habituation to take place. In addition, the person comes to learn that not engaging in the compulsive behavior does not lead to a terrible result.

To implement this repeated exposure and response prevention, the therapist might first model the behavior he wants the client to practice. For example, if the client has an obsession about contamination and a washing compulsion, the therapist might model rubbing dirt on his hands and then not wash his hands during the therapy session. At the next session, the therapist might again rub dirt on his hands but this time encourage the client to get her hands dirty as well. As the client's compulsion to wash her hands grows, the therapist encourages her not to do so but sits with her and uses relaxation techniques to control her anxiety. After several such sessions, the client may be able to sit with dirty hands without feeling anxious and to control her washing compulsion herself.

The client may also be given homework assignments that help to confront her obsession. For example, early in therapy, she might be assigned to simply refrain from cleaning the house every day of the week, as she normally does, and only clean it every 3 days. Later in therapy, she might be assigned to drop a cookie on a dirty kitchen floor, and then pick it up and eat it or drop the kitchen knives on the floor, and then use them to prepare food (Emmelkamp, 1982).

These behavioral therapies have been shown to lead to significant improvement in obsessions and compulsive behavior in 60 to 90 percent of OCD clients (Abramowitz, 1997; Fals-Stewart, Marks, & Schafer, 1993; Marks & Swinson, 1992). Moreover, these improvements are maintained in most clients over periods of up to 6 years (Foa & Kozak, 1993; Marks & Swinson, 1992). Unfortunately, however, this therapy does not tend to eliminate all obsessions and compulsions in OCD patients; in addition, a substantial minority are not helped at all by the therapy. Thus, there remains much work to be done to find a universally and completely effective therapy for OCD. The treatments available now, however, are great improvements over what was available only a few years ago.

Summing Up

- Obsessions are thoughts, images, ideas, or impulses that are persistent, are intrusive, and cause distress, and they commonly focus on contamination, sex, violence, and repeated doubts.

- Compulsions are repetitive behaviors or mental acts that the individual feels he or she must perform to somehow erase his or her obsessions.

- Biological theories of OCD speculate that areas of the brain involved in the execution of primitive patterns of behavior, such as washing rituals, may be impaired in people with OCD. These areas of the brain are rich in the neurotransmitter serotonin, and drugs that regulate serotonin have proven helpful in the treatment of OCD.

- Psychodynamic theories of OCD suggest that the obsessions and compulsions symbolize unconscious conflict or impulses and that the proper therapy for OCD involves uncovering these unconscious thoughts.

- Cognitive-behavioral theories suggest that people with OCD are chronically distressed, think in rigid and moralistic ways, judge negative thoughts as more acceptable than other people do, and feel more responsible for their thoughts and behaviors. This makes them unable to turn off the negative, intrusive thoughts that most people have occasionally.

- Compulsive behaviors develop through operant conditioning; people are reinforced for compulsive behaviors by the fact that they reduce anxiety.

◑ BIO-PSYCHO-SOCIAL INTEGRATION

Posttraumatic stress disorder and obsessive-compulsive disorder both illustrate how inseparable biology and psychology are, but in very different ways. Posttraumatic stress disorder, by definition, is the result of a psychological experience of trauma. Yet, new research is showing just how much traumatic experiences can permanently change an individual's biology. As we discussed in this chapter, people with PTSD show changes in how their brains function and respond to stimuli. Studies of young children who suffered traumas, such as emotional or sexual abuse, show that their brains develop differently from children who have not suffered traumas (Southwick et al., 1998). Thus, a fundamentally psychological experience—trauma—can cause major and permanent biological changes. Those biological changes then may contribute to the lasting symptoms of PTSD.

In contrast, there is increasing evidence that obsessive-compulsive disorder may be fundamentally a biological disorder involving problems in certain circuits in the brain. Yet, one of the most effective treatments for OCD is a psychological treatment—

cognitive-behavioral therapy. How is it that a wholly nonbiological treatment can have such strong effects on a strongly biological disorder? It is because behavior and biology have feedback effects on each other, as we discussed in Chapter 2. Changes in behavior affect biological processes, and changes in biological processes affect behavior.

Thus, although PTSD is initially caused by an external event in the environment, it involves significant biological change that then causes further change in behaviors, thoughts, and emotions. And although OCD may have biological roots in many people, changing behaviors can change the biology of OCD.

Chapter Summary

- Posttraumatic stress disorder occurs after a person experiences a severe trauma. It involves three types of symptoms: first, repeatedly reexperiencing the traumatic event, through intrusive images or thoughts, recurring nightmares, flashbacks, and psychological and physiological reactivity to stimuli that remind the person of the event; second, withdrawal, emotional numbing, and avoidance of anything that might arouse memories of the event; third, hypervigilance and chronic arousal. In addition to having these symptoms, PTSD sufferers report survival guilt.

- Acute stress disorder has similar symptoms to PTSD but occurs within 1 month of a stressor and lasts less than 4 weeks.

- Sociocultural factors appear involved in risk for PTSD. The more severe and long-lasting a trauma and the more involved a person is in the trauma, the more likely he or she is to show PTSD. People who have lower levels of social support, who experience socially stigmatizing traumas are at increased risk for PTSD.

- Psychological factors also play a role in PTSD. People who are already depressed or anxious before a trauma, who have maladaptive coping styles, and who are unable to somehow make sense of a trauma appear more likely to have chronic PTSD symptoms.

- Biological factors involved in vulnerability to PTSD may include physiological hyperreactivity, and a genetic risk.

- The most effective treatment for PTSD involves exposing a person to his or her memories of a

trauma, through systematic desensitization and flooding, to extinguish his or her anxiety over these memories. Some people cannot tolerate such exposure, however, and may do better with supportive therapy focused on solving current interpersonal difficulties and life problems.

- Benzodiazepines and antidepressant drugs can quell some of the symptoms of PTSD, but these symptoms tend to recur when the drugs are discontinued.

- People with obsessive-compulsive disorder experience anxiety when they have obsessions and when they cannot carry out their compulsions. Obsessions are thoughts, images, ideas, or impulses that are persistent, are intrusive, and cause distress. Common obsessions focus on contamination, sex, violence, impulses to do something outside one's moral code, and repeated doubts. Compulsions are repetitive behaviors or mental acts that individuals feel they must perform and that are meant to somehow erase their obsessions. Washing, checking, counting, and stereotyped behavior patterns are common forms of compulsion.

- One theory of OCD speculates that areas of the brain involved in the execution of primitive patterns of behavior, such as washing rituals, may be impaired in people with OCD. These areas of the brain are rich in the neurotransmitter serotonin, and drugs that regulate serotonin have proven helpful in the treatment of OCD.

- Psychodynamic theories of OCD suggest that the obsessions and compulsions symbolize unconscious conflicts or impulses. Psychodynamic therapy, which focuses on helping clients gain insight into these unconscious conflicts or impulses, does not tend to be highly effective with OCD, however.

- Cognitive-behavioral theories suggest that people with OCD are chronically distressed, think in rigid and moralistic ways, judge negative thoughts as more acceptable than other people do, and feel more responsible for their thoughts and behaviors. This makes them unable to turn off the negative, intrusive thoughts that most people have occasionally. Compulsive behaviors develop through operant conditioning; people are reinforced for behaviors by the fact that they reduce anxiety.

- The most effective drug therapies for OCD are the antidepressants known as serotonin reuptake inhibitors.

- Cognitive-behavioral therapies have also proven helpful for OCD. These therapies expose OCD clients to the content of their obsessions while preventing compulsive behavior; the anxiety over the obsessions and the compulsions to do the behaviors are extinguished.

- Unfortunately, neither the drug therapies nor the cognitive-behavioral therapies tend to eliminate the obsessions and compulsions completely. The relapse rate with the drug therapies is high once the drugs are discontinued. Cognitive-behavioral therapies are better at preventing relapse.

Key Terms

posttraumatic stress disorder (PTSD) 216

acute stress disorder 218

dissociative symptoms 218

systematic desensitization 229

thought-stopping 230

stress-management interventions 230

obsessive-compulsive disorder (OCD) 234

obsessions 234

compulsions 234

caudate nucleus 239

Critical Thinking Questions

1. How adaptive do you think it is for people to have an illusion of personal invulnerability?

2. If you have ever experienced a trauma, did you find some meaning in the trauma? If so, how did you do this?

3. Family members and friends of people with OCD often tell them to just stop their obsessions and compulsions, but this seldom helps. If you had a friend with OCD, how might you respond to him or her?

Hyacinth Manning-Carner
Watching from the Steps

How much pain have cost us the evils which have never happened.

—*Thomas Jefferson, Letter to Thomas Jefferson Smith (February 21, 1825)*

CHAPTER

8

Mood Disorders

CHAPTER OVERVIEW
Symptoms, Diagnosis, and Prognosis

People with unipolar depression experience sadness, loss of interest in their usual activities, changes in sleep and activity levels, and thoughts of worthlessness, hopelessness, and suicide. People with bipolar disorder experience both periods of depression and periods of mania, during which their mood is elevated or irritable, and they have great energy and self-esteem. Bipolar disorder is much less common than is unipolar depression.

Biological Theories of Mood Disorders

There clearly is a heritable component to bipolar disorder, but the evidence is less clear for unipolar depression. Biochemical theories suggest that imbalances in certain neurotransmitters or malfunctioning of receptors for these neurotransmitters contribute to mood disorders. Depressed people show disturbances in sleep patterns and on neuroimaging scans. Depressed people show chronic hyperactivity of the system in the body that regulates stress responses.

Psychological Theories of Mood Disorders

Behavioral theories suggest that a lack of positive reinforcements, and the presence of many aversive circumstances, lead to depression. Cognitive theories suggest that depressed people interpret stressful experiences in negative and distorted ways, contributing to their depression. Psychodynamic theories describe depression as anger turned inward on the self.

Taking Psychology Personally:
Dealing with Grief

Sociocultural Perspectives on Mood Disorders

Interpersonal theories of depression attribute it to maladaptive social roles and patterns of relationships. Sociologists have examined the large age, gender, and cross-cultural differences in depression for clues to its origins.

Mood Disorders Treatments

Several drugs are effective in the treatment of depression. Electroconvulsive therapy is also used to treat serious depressions. Lithium, anticonvulsants, antipsychotics, and calcium channel blockers are also used to treat mania. The psychological therapies aim to reverse the processes specific theories say lead to depression. Community-based programs have attempted to educate the public about depression and its treatment, and to intervene with high-risk groups to prevent first onsets of depression.

Pushing the Boundaries:
Can the Serotonin Reuptake Inhibitors Change Your Personality?

Bio-Psycho-Social Integration
Chapter Summary
Key Terms
Critical Thinking Questions

Voices

I was a senior in high school when I had my first attack. At first, everything seemed so easy. I raced about like a crazed weasel, bubbling with plans and enthusiasms, immersed in sports, and staying up all night, night after night, out with friends, reading everything that wasn't nailed down, filling manuscript books with poems and fragments of plays, and making expansive, completely unrealistic plans for my future. The world was filled with pleasure and promise; I felt great. Not just great, I felt *really* great. I felt I could do anything, that no task was too difficult. My mind seemed clear, fabulously focused, and able to make intuitive mathematical leaps that had up to that point entirely eluded me. Indeed, they elude me still. At the time, however, not only did everything make perfect sense, but it all began to fit into a marvelous kind of cosmic relatedness. My sense of enchantment with the laws of the natural world caused me to fizz over, and I found myself buttonholing my friends to tell them how beautiful it all was. They were less than transfixed by my insights into the webbings and beauties of the universe although considerably impressed at how exhausting it was to be around my enthusiastic ramblings: You're talking too fast, Kay. Slow down, Kay. You're wearing me out, Kay. Slow down, Kay. And those times when they didn't actually come out and say it, I still could see it in their eyes: For God's sake, Kay, slow down.

I did, finally, slow down. In fact, I came to a grinding halt. The bottom began to fall out of my life and my mind. My thinking, far from being clearer than a crystal, was tortuous. I would read the same passage over and over again only to realize that I had no memory at all for what I had just read. My mind had turned on me: It mocked me for my vapid enthusiasms; it laughed at all my foolish plans; it no longer found anything interesting or enjoyable or worthwhile. It was incapable of concentrated thought and turned time and again to the subject of death: I was going to die, what difference did anything make? Life's run was only a short and meaningless one; why live? I was totally exhausted and could scarcely pull myself out of bed in the mornings. It took me twice as long to walk anywhere as it ordinarily did, and I wore the same clothes over and over again, as it was otherwise too much of an effort to make a decision about what to put on. I dreaded having to talk with people, avoided my friends whenever possible, and sat in the school library in the early mornings and late afternoons, virtually inert, with a dead heart and a brain as cold as clay.

(Jamison, 1995b, pp. 35–38)

This emotional roller-coaster ride is known as **bipolar disorder** and also *manic depression*. The writer,

Kay Jamison, eloquently describes both poles of this disorder. First, she has **mania**, with great energy and enthusiasm for everything, fizzing over with ideas, talking and thinking so fast that her friends cannot keep up with her. Eventually, though, she crashes into a **depression**. Her energy and enthusiasm are gone, and she is slow to think, to talk, to move. The joy has been drained from her life. Bipolar disorder is one of the two major types of mood disorders. The other type is **unipolar depression**. People with unipolar depression experience only depression and no mania.

☺ SYMPTOMS, DIAGNOSIS, AND PROGNOSIS

The symptoms of unipolar depression and bipolar disorder may, at first glance, seem very familiar. We often talk of feeling depressed when something bad happens. And some people get a "fizzing over" feeling of exuberance and invincibility when things are going really well in their world. People who develop mood disorders, however, experience highs and lows that most of us can only imagine.

Unipolar Depressive Disorder

Voices

From the time I woke up in the morning until the time I went to bed at night, I was unbearably miserable and seemingly incapable of any kind of joy or enthusiasm. Everything—every thought, word, movement—was an effort. Everything that once was sparkling now was flat. I seemed to myself to be dull, boring, inadequate, thick brained, unlit, unresponsive, chill skinned, bloodless, and sparrow drab. I doubted, completely, my ability to do anything well. It seemed as though my mind had slowed down and burned out to the point of being virtually useless. The wretched, convoluted, and pathetically confused mass of gray worked only well enough to torment me with a dreary litany of my inadequacies and shortcomings in character and to taunt me with the total, the desperate hopelessness of it all.

(Jamison, 1995b, p. 110)

Symptoms of Depression

Depression takes over the whole person—emotions, bodily functions, behaviors, and thoughts (see Table 8.1).

Emotional symptoms The most common emotion in depression is *sadness*. This sadness is not the garden-variety type that we all feel sometimes but a deep,

TABLE 8.1
DSM-IV
Symptoms of Depression

Depression includes a variety of emotional, physiological, behavioral and cognitive symptoms.

Emotional Symptoms

Sadness

Depressed mood

Anhedonia (loss of interest or pleasure in usual activities)

Irritability (particularly in children and adolescents)

Physiological and Behavioral Symptoms

Sleep disturbances (hypersomnia or insomnia)

Appetite disturbances

Psychomotor retardation or agitation

Catatonia (unusual behaviors ranging from complete lack of movement to excited agitation)

Fatigue and loss of energy

Cognitive Symptoms

Poor concentration and attention

Indecisiveness

Sense of worthlessness or guilt

Poor self-esteem

Hopelessness

Suicidal thoughts

Delusions and hallucinations with depressing themes

Source: DSM-IV, APA, 2000

When people are depressed, they may be unable to experience joy in any situation.

unrelenting pain. As Kay Jamison wrote, she was "unbearably miserable and seemingly incapable of any kind of joy or enthusiasm." In addition, many people diagnosed with depression report that they have lost interest in everything in life—a symptom referred to as *anhedonia.* Even when they try to do something enjoyable, they may feel no emotional reaction.

Physiological and behavioral symptoms In depression, many bodily functions are disrupted. These *changes in appetite, sleep, and activity levels* can take many forms. Some depressed people lose their appetite, but others find themselves eating more, perhaps even binge eating. Some depressed people want to sleep all day. Others find it difficult to sleep and may experience a particular form of insomnia known as *early morning wakening,* in which they awaken at 3 or 4 A.M. every morning and cannot go back to sleep.

Behaviorally, many depressed people are slowed down, a condition known as *psychomotor retardation.* They walk more slowly, gesture more slowly, and talk more slowly and quietly. They have more accidents because they cannot react to crises as quickly as necessary to avoid them. Many depressed people *lack energy* and report feeling chronically *fatigued.* A subset of depressed people have *psychomotor agitation* instead of retardation. They feel physically agitated, cannot sit still, and may move around or fidget aimlessly.

A few depressed people experience extreme behavioral disturbances referred to as **catatonia.** This is a collection of unusual behaviors that can range from complete lack of movement to excited agitation. One form of catatonia is **catalepsy.** People with this condition seem to be in a trancelike state, and their muscles assume a waxy rigidity, so that they tend to remain in any position in which they are placed. Catatonia can also involve excessive motor activity, such as fidgeting hands, foot tapping, rocking back and forth, and pacing, all without any apparent purpose. People with catatonia may show disturbances in their speech, becoming completely mute or only repeating what others say.

Cognitive symptoms The thoughts of depressed people may be filled with themes of *worthlessness, guilt, hopelessness,* and even *suicide.* They often have trouble concentrating and making decisions. Again, as Kay Jamison described, "It seemed as though my mind had slowed down and burned out to the point of being virtually useless."

In some severe cases, the cognitions of depressed people lose complete touch with reality, and they experience delusions and hallucinations. **Delusions** are beliefs with no basis in reality, and **hallucinations** involve seeing, hearing, or feeling things that are not real. The delusions and hallucinations that depressed people experience usually are depressing and negative in content. For example, people have delusions that they have committed a terrible sin, that they are being punished, or that they have killed or hurt someone. They may have auditory hallucinations in which voices accuse them of having committed an atrocity or instructing them to kill themselves.

Diagnosing depressive disorders Depression takes several forms. The DSM-IV recognizes two categories of unipolar depressive disorders: **major depression** and **dysthymic disorder** (see *Concept Review:* Distinguishing Major Depression and Dysthymic Disorder). In addition to major depression and dysthymic disorder, the DSM-IV recognizes several other subtypes of depression—different forms the disorder can take (see Table 8.2). These subtypes apply both to major depression and to the depressive phase of a bipolar disorder.

Distinguishing major depression and dysthymia The diagnosis of major depression requires that a person experience either depressed mood or loss of interest in usual activities plus at least four other symptoms of depression chronically for at least 2 weeks. In addition, these symptoms have to be severe enough to interfere with the person's ability to function in everyday life.

Dysthymic disorder is a less severe form of depressive disorder than major depression, but it is more

CONCEPT REVIEW

Distinguishing Major Depression and Dysthymic Disorder

Major depression and dysthymic disorder differ in the number of symptoms required and the duration of the disorder.

	Major Depression	Dysthymic Disorder
Number of symptoms	5 or more, including sadness or loss of interest or pleasure	3 or more, including depressed mood
Duration	At least 2 weeks	At least 2 years

TABLE 8.2

DSM-IV
Subtypes of Major Depression (and the Depressive Phase of Bipolar Disorder)

The DSM-IV specifies a number of subtypes of major depression and the depressive phase of bipolar disorder.

Subtype	Characteristic Symptoms
With melancholic features	Inability to experience pleasure, distinct depressed mood, depression regularly worse in morning, early morning awakening, marked psychomotor retardation or agitation, significant anorexia or weight loss, and excessive guilt
With psychotic features	Presence of depressing delusions or hallucinations
With catatonic features	Catatonic behaviors: catalepsy, excessive motor activity, severe disturbances in speech
With atypical features	Positive mood reactions to some events, significant weight gain or increase in appetite, hypersomnia, heavy or laden feelings in arms or legs, long-standing pattern of sensitivity to interpersonal rejection
With postpartum onset	Onset of major depressive episode within 4 weeks of delivery of child
With seasonal onset	History of at least 2 years in which major depressive episodes occur during one season of the year (usually the winter) and remit when that season is over

Source: DSM-IV, APA, 2000.

chronic. To be diagnosed with dysthymic disorder, a person must be experiencing depressed mood plus two other symptoms of depression for at least *2 years*. During these two years, the person must never have been without the symptoms of depression for more than a 2-month period. Said one woman with dysthymic disorder, "It just goes on and on. I never feel really good, I always feel kind of bad, and it seems it's never going to end."

Some unfortunate people experience both major depression and dysthymic disorder. This has been referred to as **double depression**. People with double depression are chronically dysthymic, and then occasionally spike into episodes of major depression. As the major depression passes, however, they return to dysthymia rather than recover to a normal mood. As one might imagine, people with double depression are even more debilitated than are people with major depression or dysthymia. One study that followed people with double depression over about 9 years found that they remained free of symptoms of minor or severe depression only about one-third of that time (Judd et al., 1998). People with double depression also are less likely to respond to treatments.

Over half of the people diagnosed with major depression or dysthymia also have another psychological disorder. The most common disorders to co-occur with depression are substance abuse (e.g., alcohol abuse), anxiety disorders such as panic disorder, and eating disorders (Blazer et al., 1994). Sometimes the depression precedes and perhaps causes the other disorder. Sometimes depression follows and may be the consequence of the other disorder.

Subtypes of depression First, in *depression with melancholic features*, the physiological symptoms of depression are particularly prominent. Second, there is *depression with psychotic features*, in which people experience delusions and hallucinations during a major depressive episode. Third, people with *depression with catatonic features* show the strange behaviors collectively known as catatonia, which we discussed earlier. Fourth, there is *depression with atypical features*. The criteria for this subtype are an odd assortment of symptoms (see Table 8.2).

The fifth subtype is *depression with postpartum onset*. This diagnosis is given to women when the onset of a major depressive episode occurs within four weeks of delivery of a child. More rarely, some women develop mania during the postpartum and are given the diagnosis of *bipolar disorder with postpartum onset*. As many as 30 percent of women experience the *postpartum blues*—emotional lability (unstable and quickly shifting moods), frequent crying, irritability, and fatigue—in the first few weeks after giving birth. For most women, these symptoms are only annoying and

Some women experience serious depressions during the postpartum period, just after they have had a baby.

pass completely within two weeks of the birth. Only about 1 in 10 women experience postpartum depressions serious enough to warrant a diagnosis of a depressive disorder (O'Hara & Swain, 1996).

The final subtype of major depressive disorder is *depression with seasonal pattern*, sometimes referred to as **seasonal affective disorder,** or **SAD.** People with SAD have a history of at least 2 years of experiencing major depressive episodes and fully recovering from them. The symptoms seem to be tied to the number of hours of daylight in a day. People become depressed when the daylight hours are short and recover when the daylight hours are long. In the northern hemisphere, this means people are depressed November through February and not depressed June through August. Some people with this disorder actually develop mild forms of mania or have full manic episodes during the summer months and are diagnosed with *bipolar disorder with seasonal pattern*. In order to be diagnosed with seasonal affective disorder, a person's mood changes cannot be the result of psychosocial events, such as regularly being unemployed during the winter. Rather, the mood changes must seem to come on without reason or cause. Although many of us may feel our mood changes with the seasons, only about 1 percent of the U.S. population experiences a diagnosable seasonal affective disorder (Blazer, Kessler, & Swartz, 1998). This disorder is more common, however, in latitudes where there are fewer hours of daylight in the winter months (Rosen et al., 1990). For example, people in Norway and Sweden are more prone to SAD than are people in Mexico or southern Italy.

Prevalence and Prognosis

Depression is one of the most common psychological problems. At some time in their lives, 17 percent of Americans experience an acute episode of depression, and 6 percent experience more chronic depression (Kessler et al., 1994).

Among adults, 15- to 24-year-olds are most likely to have had a major depressive episode in the past month (see Figure 8.1; Blazer et al., 1994). The lowest rates are among 45- to 54-year-olds, and other studies have found even lower rates in people 55 to 70 years of age, with only about 2 percent diagnosable with a major depression (Newmann, 1989; Zisook & Downs, 1998). The rates of depression do go up among the "old-old," those over 85 years of age (Murrell, Himmelfarb, & Wright, 1983). When they do occur, depressions in older people tend to be quite severe, chronic, and debilitating (Cole & Bellavance, 1997).

Perhaps it is surprising that the rate of depression is so low among older adults. The diagnosis of depression in older adults is complicated (Zisook & Downs, 1998). First, older adults may be less willing than younger adults to report the symptoms of depression, because they grew up in a society less accepting of depression. Second, depressive symptoms in the elderly will often occur in the context of a serious medical illness, which can interfere with making an appropriate diagnosis (Cohen-Cole & Stoudemire, 1987). Third, older people are more likely than younger people to have mild-to-severe cognitive impairment and it is often difficult to distinguish between a depressive disorder and the early stages of a cognitive disorder (Robins & Regier, 1991).

Although these factors may be important, other researchers suggest that the low rate is valid and have offered explanations. The first is quite grim: Depression appears to interfere with physical health and, as a result, people with a history of depression may be more likely to die before they reach old age (Klerman & Weissman, 1989). The second explanation is more hopeful: As people age, they may develop more adaptive coping skills and a psychologically healthier outlook on life, and this may lead them to experience fewer episodes of depression (Elder, Liker, & Jaworski, 1984).

Most studies show that women are about twice as likely as men to experience both mild depressive symptoms and severe depressive disorders (Nolen-Hoeksema, 1990). This gender difference in depression has been found in many different countries, in most ethnic groups, and in all adult age groups (see Figure 8.2). Interestingly, children do not show this gender difference in depression, but around age 14 or 15, girls begin to show dramatic increases in their rates of depression, while boys' rates remain quite stable (Angold, Costello, & Worthman, 1998; Nolen-Hoeksema, 1990; Nolen-Hoeksema & Girgus, 1994). One might think that females are just more willing to admit to depression than males. However, the gender difference in depression is found even in studies that use relatively objective measures of depression that do not rely much on self-reports, such as clinicians' ratings of depression, or the reports of family members or friends. As we discuss the different theories of depression, we highlight how these theories explain this gender difference in depression.

Depression appears to be a long-lasting and recurrent problem for some people. One study of 431 people with major depression followed them an average of 9 years and found that they had moderate-to-severe symptoms of depression 59 percent of the time, and were completely symptom-free only 27 percent of the time (Judd et al., 1998). The picture one gets is of a depressed person spending much of his or her time at least moderately depressed. Then even after the depressed person recovers from one episode of depression, he or she remains at high risk for relapses into new episodes. People with a history of multiple episodes of depression are even more likely to remain depressed for long periods of time. The good news is that once people undergo treatment for their depressions, they tend to recover much more quickly and their risk of relapse is reduced.

The bad news is that the majority of people with depression never seek care, or wait years after their symptoms have begun to seek care (Kessler et al.,

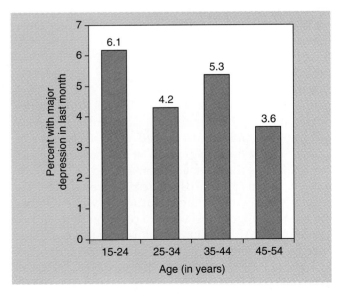

FIGURE 8.1 Age Differences in Depression. Shown are the percentages of people in each age group who were diagnosed with major depression in a 1-month period. Those between 15 and 24 years old have the highest rates of depression and those between 45 and 54 years old have the lowest rates.

Source: Blazer et al., 1994.

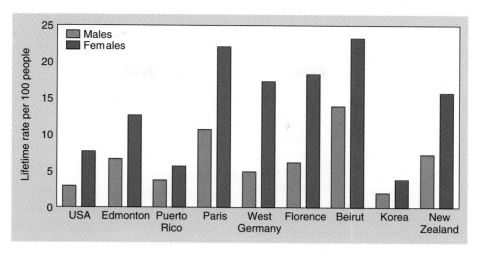

FIGURE 8.2   Gender Differences in Depression Across Cultures. Across many cultures, more women than men are diagnosed with major depression.

Reprinted with permission from M. Weissman and M. Olfson, "Depression in Women: Implications for Health Care Research" in *Science*, 269 (5225): 799–801, 1995. Copyright © 1995 American Association for the Advancement of Science.

1998). Why don't people suffering the terrible symptoms of depression seek treatment? It may be because they do not have the money or insurance to pay for care. But often it is because they feel they should be able to "get over" their symptoms on their own. They believe that the symptoms are just a "phase" they are going through, that they will pass with time and won't affect their lives in the long term.

Depression does sometimes pass without treatment, and without long-term consequences. Some people seem to be left with "scars" from their bouts of depression, however (Lewinsohn et al., 1981). Their ways of thinking, their views of themselves, their social relationships, and their academic and work history, may be changed for the worse by the depression, and may remain impaired for long periods after the symptoms of depression have passed. Even if they do not relapse into additional major depressive episodes, people with previous episodes of major depression tend to have enduring problems in many areas of their lives (Coryell et al., 1993). Their functioning on the job tends to remain impaired even after their depression subsides. They report that they are not interested in sex or do not enjoy sex as much as they used to, and there is chronic conflict and dissatisfaction in their intimate relationships (McCabe & Gotlib, 1993).

Depression in Childhood and Adolescence

Depression is less common among children than among adults. At any point in time, as many as 2.5% of children and 8.3% of adolescents can be diagnosed with major depression, and as many as 1.7% of children and 8.0% of adolescents can be diagnosed with dysthymic disorder (Birmaher et al., 1996; Cicchetti & Toth, 1998; Kovacs & Devlin, 1998 for reviews). Some researchers have argued that depression is

underdiagnosed in children because depressed children don't tend to show adultlike symptoms of depression, but instead "mask" their depression with somatic complaints and acting-out behaviors (for a review see Kovacs & Devlin, 1998). Children under age 8 or 9 clearly do have limitations in their ability to understand and articulate their emotions (Achenbach, McConaughy, & Howell, 1987). Thus, a preschooler is unlikely to report, "Mommy, I feel sad and blue and I don't find anything interesting anymore." Rather, the mother of that child is more likely to notice distress in the child by changes in behavior, sleep patterns, eating patterns, and so on.

Several studies suggest, however, that the notion of masked depression is not valid (see Harrington et al., 1996; Kovacs & Devlin, 1998). When distressed children are directly asked about the symptoms of depression, many can and do report that they are experiencing those symptoms (see Harrington, Rutter, & Fombone, 1996; Kovacs & Beck, 1977; Lewinsohn et al., 1993). Research on the assessment of depressive symptoms in children shows that the adult criteria of depression can be reliably and meaningfully applied to diagnose depression in children and adolescents over the age of about 10 (Rutter, Tizard, & Whitmore, 1970). In addition, the symptoms of depression cluster together in children much the same way they do in adults, suggesting that the syndrome is similar in children and adults (Pearce, 1978). There is substantial continuity from childhood into adulthood in what specific symptoms of depression an individual will show, suggesting that depression does not change its shape much with age (Zeitlin, 1986). Finally, children thought to be showing masked depression through somatic complaints and behavioral disturbances are not at high risk for depression as adults (Champion, Goodall, & Rutter, 1995). Thus, although depressive symptoms in children may need to be inferred by their changes in their behaviors and functioning because children cannot or do not articulate these symptoms, the idea that a wide variety of symptoms not included in the criteria for depression are "really" manifestations of depression has not been strongly supported.

The scars of childhood depression Depression may be most likely to leave psychological and social scars if it occurs initially during childhood, rather than during adulthood (Cole et al., 1998; Girgus & Nolen-Hoeksema, in press). Self-concept is still being developed in childhood and adolescence, much more so than in adulthood. A period of significant depressive symptoms while one's self-concept is undergoing substantial change could have long-lasting effects on the content or structure of self-concept. Similarly, the development of skills and abilities in school is cumulative during childhood and adolescence, thus a bout of depression that interferes with learning could have long-term effects on children's achievement. Finally, children and adolescents are dependent on and connected with other people to a greater extent than adults, so a bout of depression that impairs social skills could have long-term effects on social relationships.

Depression may also increase negative thinking because it brings with it a host of new negative events. Stress generation models suggest that the symptoms of depression—low motivation, fatigue, problems in concentration, low self-esteem, decreases in social interactions and skills—can interfere with youngsters' functioning in all domains of their lives (Hammen, 1991, 1992). Because depression affects so many domains of functioning in a youngster's life, it may lead to increases in many different kinds of stressors. For example, having a depressed child in the family can cause strains on parents that may affect their relationships, perhaps putting a fragile marriage or partnership over the edge and contributing to separation. Or the cost of treatment for a depressed child may cause significant financial strain in a family.

The effects of puberty Girls' rates of depression escalate dramatically in over the course of puberty, but boys' rates do not (see Figure 8.3, Angold, Costello, & Worthman, 1998). The increase in girls' depressions does not seem to be directly tied to the hormonal changes of puberty, however (Angold & Worthman, 1993). Instead, the observable physical changes of adolescence may have more to do with the emotional development of girls and boys than hormonal development because these characteristics affect boys' and girls' self-esteem differently. Girls appear to value the physical changes that accompany puberty much less than do boys. In particular, girls dislike the weight they gain in fat and their loss of the long, lithe look that is idealized in modern fashions. In contrast, boys like the increase in muscle mass and other pubertal changes their bodies undergo (Dornbusch et al., 1984). Body dissatisfaction appears to be more closely related to low self-esteem and depression in girls than in boys (Allgood-Merten, Lewinsohn, & Hops, 1990).

One group of girls who seem especially at risk for depression during puberty is girls who mature much earlier than their peers (Attie & Brooks-Gunn, 1989; Caspi & Moffitt, 1991; Graber et al., 1994; Graber et al., 1997; Hayward et al., 1997; Simmons & Blyth, 1987; although see Angold et al., 1998). Girls whose bodies start changing long before their girlfriends' bodies do have higher rates of depression, anxiety disorders, and eating disorders than do girls who mature later in adolescence (Hayward et al., 1993). Why are early maturing girls at such high risk? First, they have the worst body image of any group of girls, and this may contribute to their vulnerability to depression, anxiety, and eating disorders. Second, these girls seem to become involved in mature dating relationships at a very young age, and they date older boys and become sexually active earlier than do their peers. These relationships may be too difficult for many girls to cope with and may contribute to depression and other problems. Third, because they are becoming sexually mature at a younger age, these girls may be more vulnerable to sexual assault and abuse than are girls who mature later, and as we discuss shortly, sexual abuse contributes to depression (Hayward et al., 1993; Stattin & Magnusson, 1990).

Bipolar Disorder

Voices

There is a particular kind of pain, elation, loneliness, and terror involved in this kind of madness. When you're high it's tremendous. The ideas and feelings are fast and frequent like shooting stars and you follow them until you find better and brighter ones. Shyness goes, the right words and gestures are suddenly there, the power to seduce and captivate others a felt certainty. There are interests found in uninteresting people. Sensuality is pervasive and the desire to seduce and be seduced irresistible. Feelings of ease, intensity, power, well-being, financial omnipotence, and euphoria now pervade one's marrow. But, somewhere, this changes. The fast ideas are far too fast and there are far too many; overwhelming confusion replaces clarity. Memory goes. Humor and absorption on friends' faces are replaced by fear and concern. Everything previously moving with the grain is now against—you are irritable, angry, frightened, uncontrollable, and

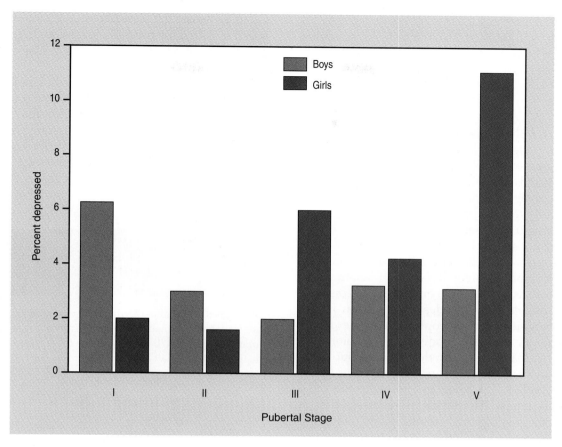

FIGURE 8.3   Percent of Adolescents with DSM-IV Depression Diagnosis by Pubertal Status. Girls show dramatic increases in rates of depressive disorders with pubertal change, whereas boys show no increase, or perhaps a decrease with pubertal change. Pubertal Stage indicates the level of pubertal development, with Level I being prepuberty and Level V meaning puberty is completed (Tanner, 1962).

Source: Angold, Costello, & Worthman (1998), Figure 2, p. 56.

enmeshed totally in the blackest caves of the mind. You never knew those caves were there. It will never end.

(Goodwin & Jamison, 1990, pp. 17–18)

This person is describing an episode of bipolar disorder. When she is manic, she has tremendous energy and vibrancy, her self-esteem is soaring, she is filled with ideas and confidence. Then when she becomes depressed, she is despairing and fearful, she doubts herself and everyone around her, she wishes to die. This alternation between periods of mania and periods of depression is the classic manifestation of bipolar disorder.

Symptoms of Mania

We have already discussed the symptoms of depression in detail, so let us focus on the symptoms of mania (see Table 8.3, p. 256). The moods of people who are manic can be *elated*, but that elation is often mixed with *irritation* and *agitation*. Said one man,

Voices

First and foremost comes a general sense of intense well-being. I know of course that this sense is illusory and transient—Although, however, the restrictions of confinement are apt at times to produce extreme irritation and even paroxysms of anger, the general sense of well-being, the pleasurable and sometimes ecstatic feeling-tone, remains as a sort of permanent background of all experience during a manic period.

(Goodwin & Jamison, 1990, pp. 25–26)

The manic person is filled with a *grandiose self-esteem*, meaning that his view of himself is unrealistically positive and inflated. *Thoughts* and *impulses* race through his mind. At times, these grandiose thoughts are delusional and may be accompanied by grandiose hallucinations. A manic person may *speak rapidly* and *forcefully*, trying to convey the rapid stream of fantastic thoughts he is having. He may become agitated and irritable, particularly with people he perceives as "getting in his way." He may engage in a variety of *impulsive behaviors*, such as ill-advised sexual liaisons or spending sprees. Often he will have *grand plans* and *goals* that he frenetically pursues.

Diagnosis

In order to be diagnosed with mania, an individual must show an elevated, expansive, or irritable mood for at least one week, plus at least three of the other symptoms listed in Table 8.3. As usual, these symptoms must impair the individual's ability to function in order to qualify for the diagnosis.

People who experience manic episodes meeting these criteria are said to have **bipolar I disorder.** Most of these people will eventually fall into a depressive episode. For some people with bipolar I disorder, the depressions are as severe as major depressive episodes, whereas for others, their episodes of depression are relatively mild and infrequent. People with **bipolar II disorder** experience severe episodes of depression that meet the criteria for major depression, but their episodes of mania are milder, and are known as **hypomania** (see Table 8.4). Hypomania involves the same symptoms as mania. The major difference is that in hypomania these symptoms are not severe enough to interfere with daily functioning, and do not involve hallucinations or delusions.

Just as dysthymic disorder is the less severe but more chronic form of depressive disorder, there is a less severe but more chronic form of bipolar disorder known as **cyclothymic disorder.** A person with cyclothymic disorder alternates between episodes of hypomania and moderate depression chronically over at least a 2-year period. During the periods of hypomania, the person may be able to function reasonably well in daily life.

Often, however, the periods of depression significantly interfere with daily functioning, although these periods are not as severe as those qualifying as major depressive episodes.

About 90 percent of people with bipolar disorder have multiple episodes or cycles during their lifetimes (APA, 2000). The length of an individual episode of bipolar disorder varies greatly from one person to the next. Some people are in a manic state for several weeks or months before moving into a depressed state. More rarely, people switch from mania to depression and back within a matter of days. The number of lifetime

---

TABLE 8.3
DSM-IV
Symptoms of Mania

A diagnosis of mania requires that a person show an elevated, expansive, or irritable mood for at least one week, plus at least three of the other symptoms listed here.

Elevated, expansive, or irritable mood

Inflated self-esteem or grandiosity

Decreased need for sleep

More talkative than usual, a pressure to keep talking

Flight of ideas or sense that your thoughts are racing

Distractibility

Increase in activity directed at achieving goals

Excessive involvement in potentially dangerous activities

Source: DSM-IV, APA, 2000.

TABLE 8.4
DSM-IV
Criteria for Bipolar I and Bipolar II Disorders

Bipolar I and II disorders differ in the presence of major depressive episodes, episodes meeting the full criteria for mania, and hypomanic episodes.

Criteria	Bipolar I	Bipolar II
Major depressive episodes	Can occur, but not necessary for diagnosis	Necessary for diagnosis
Episodes meeting full criteria for mania	Necessary for diagnosis	Cannot be present for diagnosis
Includes only hypomanic episodes	Can occur between episodes of severe mania or major depression, but not necessary for diagnosis	Necessary for diagnosis

Source: DSM-IV, APA, 2000.

A number of highly successful people in many walks of life have experienced a mood disorder, including Abraham Lincoln, Winston Churchill, Drew Carey, and Tipper Gore.

episodes also varies tremendously from one person to the next, but a relatively common pattern is for episodes to become more frequent and closer together over time. If a person has four or more cycles of mania and depression within a year, this is known as **rapid cycling bipolar disorder.**

Prevalence and Prognosis

Bipolar disorder is less common than unipolar depression. About 1 or 2 in 100 people will experience at least one episode of bipolar disorder at some time in their lives (Kessler et al., 1994). Men and women seem equally likely to develop the disorder, and there are no consistent differences among ethnic groups in the prevalence of the disorder. Most people who develop bipolar disorder do so in late adolescence or early adulthood (Burke et al., 1990). About half of the people who eventually develop a bipolar disorder experienced their first episode by early adulthood.

Like people with unipolar depression, people with bipolar disorder often face, between their episodes, chronic problems on the job and in their relationships (Coryell et al., 1993; Keck et al., 1998). One study that followed people who had been hospitalized for an episode of bipolar disorder found that over the year following their hospitalization, only about one in four recovered fully from their symptoms and were able to lead a relatively normal life (Keck et al., 1998). The best predictors of recovery were full compliance with medication-taking, and higher social class, which may have afforded people better health care and social support. In addition, people with bipolar disorder often abuse substances (such as alcohol and hard drugs), which also impairs their control over their disorder, their willingness to take medications, and their functioning in life (Goodwin & Ghaemi, 1998; Keck et al., 1998; van Gorp et al., 1998).

Leadership, Creativity, and Bipolar Disorder

Could there possibly be anything good about suffering from bipolar disorder? Some theorists have argued that the symptoms of mania—increased self-esteem, a rush of ideas, the courage to pursue these ideas, high energy, little need for sleep, hypervigilance, decisiveness—can actually benefit people in certain occupations, especially highly intelligent or talented people. In turn, the melancholy of depression is often seen as inspirational for artists. Indeed, some of the most influential people in history have suffered, and perhaps to some extent benefited, from bipolar disorder or depression.

Political leaders including Abraham Lincoln, Alexander Hamilton, Winston Churchill, Napoleon Bonaparte, and Benito Mussolini, and religious leaders including Martin Luther and George Fox (founder of the Society of Friends, or Quakers) have been posthumously diagnosed by psychiatric biographers as having periods of mania, hypomania, or depression (Jamison, 1993). Although during periods of depression these leaders were often incapacitated, during periods of mania and hypomania they accomplished extraordinary feats. While manic they devised brilliant and daring strategies for winning wars and solving domestic problems and had the energy, self-esteem, and persistence to carry out these strategies. The Duke of Marlborough, a great English military commander, was able to put his chronic hypomania to great use:

No one can read the whole mass of the letters which Marlborough either wrote, dictated, or signed personally without being astounded at the mental and physical energy which it attests. . . . After 12 or 14 hours in the saddle on the long reconnaissances often under cannon-fire; after endless inspections of troops in camp and garrison; after ceaseless calculations about food and

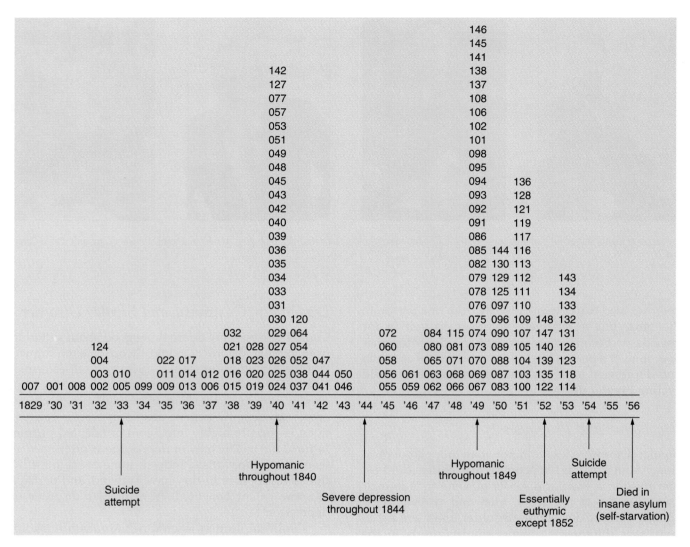

FIGURE 8.4 Robert Schumann's Productivity Reflects His Periods of Depression and Mania. When Robert Schumann was manic, he produced a phenomenal number of musical scores, but when he was depressed, he produced much less.

From *Manic-Depressive Illness* by Frederick K. Goodwin and Kay R. Jamison, copyright © 1990 by Oxford University Press, Inc. Used by permission of Oxford University Press, Inc.

supplies, and all the anxieties of direct command in war, Marlborough would reach his tent and conduct the foreign policy of England, decided the main issues of its Cabinet, and of party politics at home. (Rowse, 1969, pp. 249–250)

Marlborough was an ancestor of Winston Churchill, who was also able to put his cyclothymic temperament to use in his career. However, Churchill's biographer also documented how the grandiosity, scheming, and impulsiveness that are part of mania can be a liability in a leader:

All those who worked with Churchill paid tribute to the enormous fertility of his new ideas, the inexhaustible stream of invention which poured from him, both when he was Home Secretary, and later when he was Prime Minister and director of the war effort. All who worked with him

also agreed that he needed the most severe restraint put upon him, and that many of his ideas, if they had been put into practice, would have been utterly disastrous. (Storr, 1988, pp. 14–15)

Writers, artists, and composers of music have a higher than normal prevalence of mania and depression. For example, a study of 1,005 famous twentieth-century artists, writers, and other professionals found that the artists and writers experienced two to three times the rate of mood disorders, psychosis, and suicide attempts than did comparably successful people in business, science, and public life. The poets in this group were most likely to have been manic (Ludwig, 1992).

Composer Robert Schumann suffered from bipolar disorder, and his productivity closely mirrored his mood state (see Figure 8.4). When he was depressed, he composed relatively little and attempted suicide twice.

When he was manic or hypomanic, he composed musical scores at an astounding rate and apparently thought little of it: "I cannot see that there is anything remarkable about composing a symphony in a month. Handel wrote a complete oratorio in that time" (Robert Schumann, 1850; quoted in Taylor, 1982, p. 285).

Does mania simply enhance (and depression inhibit) productivity in naturally creative people? Or is there some deeper link between creativity and bipolar disorder? This is a difficult question to answer by simply examining how many creative people are also manic. However, one group of researchers found an ingenious way to address this question (Richards et al., 1988). They hypothesized that the genetic abnormalities that cause bipolar disorder are in close proximity to the genetic abnormalities that cause great creativity. According to this hypothesis, the close relatives of patients with bipolar disorder should be more creative, even if they do not have bipolar disorder, than the close relatives of people without bipolar disorder. The participants in this study were patients with bipolar disorder or cyclothymia, their first-degree relatives (siblings, parents, and children), and a control group of people with no psychiatric disorders, and their first-degree relatives. The relatives in both these groups had no history themselves of mood disorders, so any creativity they showed was in the absence of mania or depression.

To measure creativity, the researchers examined the lives of these participants for evidence that they had used their special talents in some original and creative ways. For example, one participant who was rated as extremely creative was an entrepreneur who advanced from a chemist's apprentice to an independent researcher of new products. He then started a major paint manufacturing company, and during the Danish Resistance of World War II, he surreptitiously manufactured and smuggled explosives for the resistance. A participant who was rated as low in creativity had been a bricklayer for 20 years and then inherited a large trust fund and retired to a passive life on a country estate. An advantage of this measure of creativity is that it did not require that a person receive social recognition to be considered creative.

The results of this study suggested that relatives of people with bipolar disorder or cyclothymia were more creative than people with no history of bipolar disorder or cyclothymia or their relatives. The cyclothymics and the normal relatives of people with bipolar disorder had somewhat higher creativity scores than did the patients who had bipolar disorder. This suggests that creativity that is associated with a predisposition toward bipolar disorder is more easily expressed in people who do not suffer from full episodes of mania and depression but may suffer from milder mood swings (Richards et al., 1988).

We should not overemphasize the benefits of bipolar disorder. Although many creative people with bipolar disorder may have been able to learn from their periods of depression and exploit their periods of mania, many also have found the highs and lows of the disorder unbearable and have attempted or completed suicide. As Wurtzel (1995, p. 295) notes,

> While it may be true that a great deal of art finds its inspirational wellspring in sorrow, let's not kid ourselves in how much time each of those people wasted and lost by being mired in misery. So many productive hours slipped by as paralyzing despair took over. This is not to say that we should deny sadness its rightful place among the muses of poetry and of all art forms, but let's stop calling it madness, let's stop pretending that the feeling itself is interesting. Let's call it depression and admit that it is very bleak.

Summing Up

- Depression includes disturbances in emotion (sadness, loss of interest), bodily functions (loss of sleep, appetite, and sexual drive), behaviors (retardation or agitation), and thoughts (worthlessness, guilt, suicidality).

- The two primary categories of unipolar depressive disorders are major depression and dysthymic disorder; in addition, there are several subtypes of major depression.

- Young and middle-aged adults have the highest rates of depression.

- Many people who become depressed remain so for several months or more and have multiple relapses over their lifetime.

- The two major diagnostic categories of bipolar mood disorders are bipolar disorder and cyclothymic disorder.

- Bipolar mood disorders are less common than depressive disorders, but are equally common in men and women.

- The onset of bipolar disorders is most often in late adolescence or early adulthood. Most people with bipolar disorder have multiple episodes.

☺ BIOLOGICAL THEORIES OF MOOD DISORDERS

There are at least four clues that the mood disorders have biological underpinnings (Kraepelin, 1922; Thase & Howland, 1995). First, depression and mania tend to be episodic in nature, as are many physical diseases. Second, many of the symptoms of depression and mania represent disruptions in vital bodily functions, such as sleep, eating, and sexual activity. Third, we have long known that depression and mania run in families, suggesting that they are heritable. Fourth, depression and mania respond to biological treatments, such as drug therapies, and can be induced by certain drugs.

Most of the modern biological theories of the causes of mood disorders focus on genetic abnormalities or dysfunctions in certain neurobiological systems. These two types of theories complement each other: Genetic abnormalities may cause mood disorders by altering a person's neurobiology. In this section, we first review the evidence for a genetic contribution to depression and mania. Second, we review the evidence that neurotransmitters play a role in depression and mania. Third, we examine a variety of neurophysiological abnormalities that have been found in people with mood disorders. Fourth, we explore hypotheses that the neuroendocrine system, which regulates hormones throughout the body, becomes dysregulated in the mood disorders (see *Concept Review:* Biological Theories of Mood Disorders).

✕ The Role of Genetics

Family history studies and twin studies both suggest that the mood disorders can be genetically transmitted.

Family History Studies

Family history studies of people with bipolar disorder find that their first-degree relatives (i.e., parents,

children, and siblings) have rates of both bipolar disorder and depressive disorders at least two to three times higher than the rates in relatives of people without bipolar disorder (see Figure 8.5; Gershon, 1990; Keller & Baker, 1991; MacKinnon, Jamison, & DePaulo, 1997).

One family that appeared to have the "tainted blood" of bipolar disorder was the family of Alfred, Lord Tennyson (see Figure 8.6, p. 262). Alfred experienced recurrent, debilitating depressions and probably hypomanic spells. His father, his grandfather, two of his great-grandfathers, and five of his seven brothers suffered from bouts of what would be diagnosed today as mania, depression, and psychosis. Alfred's brother Edward was confined to an asylum for nearly 60 years before he died from "manic exhaustion." Lionel Tennyson, one of Alfred's two sons, had a mercurial temperament, as did one of his three grandsons (Jamison, 1995a).

Does this mean that if you have a close relative with bipolar disorder you are destined to develop the disorder? No. Most studies find that less than 10 percent (and often less than 5 percent) of the first-degree relatives of people with bipolar disorder go on to develop the disorder themselves (see Figure 8.5; MacKinnon et al, 1997). Thus, the risk is higher for people with a bipolar relative, but still only a minority of them develop the disorder.

The evidence regarding the heritability of unipolar depression is less consistent. Family history studies do find higher rates of unipolar depression in the first-degree relatives of people with unipolar depression than in control groups (Gershon, 1990; Keller & Baker, 1991). Interestingly, relatives of depressed people do *not* tend to have any greater risk for bipolar disorder than do relatives of people with no mood disorder.

CONCEPT REVIEW

Biological Theories of Mood Disorders

A number of biological factors have been implicated in the mood disorders.

Theory	Description
Genetic theory	Disordered genes predispose people to depression or bipolar disorder.
Neurotransmitter theories	Dysregulation of neurotransmitters and their receptors causes depression and mania. The monoamine neurotransmitters—norepinephrine, serotonin and dopamine—have been most researched.
Neurophysiological abnormalities	Altered brain-wave activity during sleep, overactivation in the nondominant side of the brain, atrophy in the cerebral cortex, metabolic activity in the brain may correlate with mood.
Neuroendocrine abnormalities	Depressed people show chronic hyperactivity in the hypothalamic-pituitary-adrenal axis, and slow return to baseline after a stressor, which affects functioning of neurotransmitters.

This suggests that bipolar disorder has a different genetic basis from unipolar depression.

Twin Studies

Twin studies of bipolar disorder have shown that the probability that both twins will develop bipolar disorder, or *concordance rate,* is about 60 percent among monozygotic (identical) twins compared to about 13 percent among dizygotic (nonidentical) twins (Faraone & Tsuang, 1990; MacKinnon et al., 1997; McGuffin & Katz, 1989). Again, twin studies have provided more mixed evidence concerning the heritability of unipolar depression. One large twin studies of depressive disorder focused only on female twins (a total of 1,033 pairs) and found concordance rates for major depression of 48 percent for monozygotic (MZ) twins and 42 percent for dizygotic (DZ) twins (Kendler et al., 1992). Thus, in this study of all female twins, the concordance rate for major depression was not substantially higher for MZ twins than for DZ twins.

Other studies that included both male and female twin pairs have found larger differences between the concordance rates for MZ and DZ twins (McGuffin, Katz, & Rutherford, 1991; Torgersen, 1986). Unfortunately, however, these studies had much smaller numbers of twin pairs than did the study by Kendler and colleagues (1992). For example, McGuffin and colleagues (1991) had 62 pairs of MZ twins and 72 pairs of DZ twins. They found concordance rates for major depression of 53 percent for MZ twins and 28 percent for DZ twins.

Adoption Studies

The largest adoption study of mood disorders to date used Danish adoption records and records of people treated in psychiatric hospitals to identify 71 adults who were adopted at birth and later developed some type of mood disorder (bipolar disorder and unipolar depression were not differentiated in this study). The researchers also identified a control group of 71 adults adopted at birth who had never been treated for any psychiatric disorders. The researchers used psychiatric records to trace the biological and adoptive relatives of these adults to determine how many had been

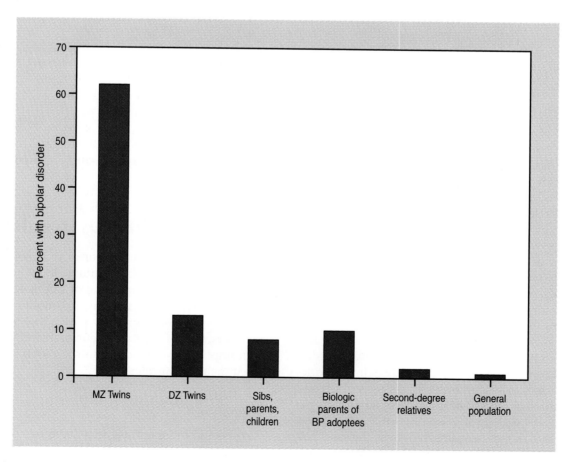

FIGURE 8.5   Risk of Bipolar Disorder in Relatives of People with Bipolar Disorder and in the General Population. The risk of developing bipolar disorder decreases as the genetic similarity between an individual and a relative with bipolar disorder decreases.

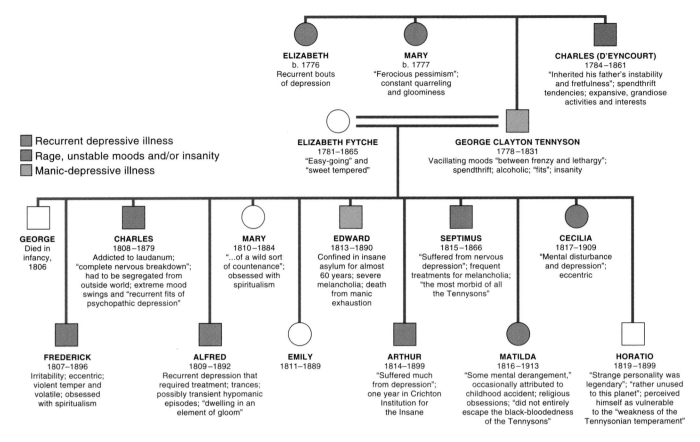

FIGURE 8.6 The "Tainted Blood" of the Tennysons. Alfred, Lord Tennyson, who himself experienced recurrent, debilitating depressions and probably hypomanic spells, attributed his disorder to the "tainted blood" of the Tennysons. His father, his grandfather, two of his great-grandfathers, and five of his seven brothers suffered from insanity, depression, uncontrollable rage, or bipolar disorder. Lionel Tennyson, one of Alfred's two sons, displayed mood swings, as did one of his three grandsons.

Source: From Jamison, 1995a, p. 62–67.

treated for mood disorders. The biological relatives of adoptees with mood disorders had significantly higher rates of mood disorders than did their adoptive relatives or the relatives of adoptees with no mood disorder (see Figure 8.7). In addition, the biological relatives of adoptees with mood disorders had significantly higher rates of attempted or completed suicides than did the relatives in the other three groups (Wender et al., 1986).

Thus, family history studies, twin studies, and adoption studies all suggest that genetic factors play a role in mood disorders, especially in bipolar disorder. So far, researchers have been unable to identify specifically what type of genetic abnormality is involved in mood disorders (MacKinnon et al., 1997). Future advances in the technology of genetic research may reveal the specific genetic abnormalities that predispose some people to mood disorders. It may be the case that there is no single locus on a gene that leads to mood disorders. Many researchers believe that the genetic predisposition to mood disorders is *multifactorial.* That is, a particular configuration of several disordered

genes may be necessary to create a mood disorder (Philibert et al., 1997).

Neurotransmitter Dysregulation

Most of the biochemical theories of mood disorders have focused on neurotransmitters, those biochemicals that facilitate the transmission of impulses across the synapses between one neuron and another. Many different neurotransmitters may play a role in the mood disorders, but the group of neurotransmitters that has been implicated most often in the mood disorders is called the **monoamines.**

Monoamine Theories

The specific monoamines that have been implicated are **norepinephrine**, **serotonin**, and, to a lesser extent, **dopamine.** These neurotransmitters are found in large concentrations in the limbic system, a part of the brain associated with the regulation of sleep, appetite, and

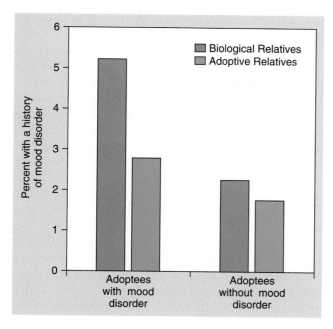

FIGURE 8.7 Mood Disorders in the Biological and Adoptive Relatives of Adoptees with Mood Disorders. Adoptees with mood disorders had higher rates of mood disorders in their biological relatives than their adoptive relatives, but adoptees with no mood disorders had low rates of mood disorders in both their biological and adoptive relations.

Source: Wender et al., 1986.

emotional processes. These neurotransmitters are thought to cause both depression and mania—imbalances in one direction may cause depression and imbalances in the other direction may cause mania.

The early theory of the roles of these neurotransmitters in mood disorders was that depression is caused by a reduction in the amount of norepinephrine or serotonin in the synapses between neurons (Glassman, 1969; Schildkraut, 1965). This depletion could result from numerous mechanisms: decreased synthesis of the neurotransmitter from its precursors, increased degradation of the neurotransmitter by enzymes, or impaired release or reuptake of the neurotransmitter (see Chapter 2 to review these processes). Mania was thought to be caused by an excess of the monoamines or perhaps dysregulation of the levels of these amines, especially dopamine. These theories, taken together, are known as the **monoamine theories** of mood disorders (Schildkraut, 1965; Bunney & Davis, 1965).

More recent studies of the monoamine theories have focused on the number and functioning of receptors for the monoamines on neurons in people suffering from mood disorders. Recall from Chapter 2 that neurotransmitters and their receptors interact like locks and keys. Each neurotransmitter will fit into a particular type of receptor on the neuronal membrane. If there is the wrong number of receptors for a given type of neurotransmitter or the receptors for that neurotransmitter are too sensitive or not sensitive enough,

then the neurons do not efficiently use the neurotransmitter that is available in the synapse.

Several studies suggest that people with major depressive disorder or bipolar disorder may have abnormalities in the number and sensitivity of receptor sites for the monoamine neurotransmitters (e.g., Malone & Mann, 1993; McBride et al., 1994). In major depressive disorder, receptors for serotonin and norepinephrine appear to be too few or insensitive. In bipolar disorder, the picture is less clear, but it is likely that receptors for the monoamines undergo poorly timed changes in sensitivity that are correlated with mood changes (Goodwin & Jamison, 1990).

Other Neurotransmitters

Recent research suggests that excessive changes in levels of the neurotransmitter **glutamate** are involved in bipolar disorder (Dixon & Hokin, 1998). The drugs that relieve depression and mania may work primarily by changing the sensitivity of neuronal receptors for this neurotransmitter (Fava & Rosenbaum, 1995).

Other researchers have focused on **substance P**, a neurotransmitter whose receptors are plentiful in areas of the brain critical for the regulation of emotion and stress responses, particularly the amygdala (Kramer et al., 1998). Experiments with animals showed that drugs that blocked substance P receptors reduced the animals' distress in response to separation from their mother. In turn, an experimental drug that blocks substance P receptors in humans significantly reduced depressive symptoms in people with major depressive disorder. Substance P antagonists appear not to affect norepinephrine or serotonin systems, but rather may have their effect specifically by blocking substance P receptors. This suggests that regulation of substance P is important in depression.

The Kindling-Sensitization Model

One intriguing model, known as the *kindling-sensitization model,* suggests that with each episode of depression or mania, these neurotransmitter systems become more easily dysregulated (Post, 1992; Post & Weiss, 1995). The first episode may take a strong stressor to initiate dysregulation, but subsequent episodes require much more mild stressors (environmental or biological) to cause dysregulation. This model helps to explain why, with each new episode of depression or mania, the cumulative risk of new episodes increases. It also helps to explain why the period between episodes decreases over time in many people with mood disorders.

Most of the neurotransmitter abnormalities found in people with mood disorders are state dependent. That is, these differences are present when the mood disorder is present but tend to disappear when the mood disorder subsides. Thus, all we know now is that certain neurotransmitter abnormalities may be correlated with, but not necessarily causal of, the mood disorders. As the technology for determining the functioning of neurotransmitters systems develops, our understanding of the relationship between neurotransmitters and mood disorders will no doubt increase.

Neurophysiological Abnormalities

A number of neurophysiological abnormalities have been documented in people with mood disorders, although the significance of these abnormalities is not yet clear (Thase & Howland, 1995). One of the most common neurophysiological abnormalities is altered brain-wave activity during sleep. Depressed people have less slow-wave sleep, a type of sleep that helps people feel rested and restored. They go into another form of sleep, rapid eye movement sleep, earlier in the night than do nondepressed people, and they have more of this type of sleep during the night (Figure 8.8). Accompanying these brain-wave changes, which can be seen in an electroencephalogram (EEG), are the subjective sleep disturbances of depressed people: They report having trouble going to sleep or remaining asleep, they wake early in the morning and cannot go back to sleep, and they do not feel rested after they sleep.

EEG recordings in awake depressed people also show some abnormalities. It seems that the nondominant side of these people's brains may be overactivated (Banich et al., 1992). This is interesting because other research on nondepressed people suggests that the nondominant side of the brain (the right side in most people) is particularly active when people are processing information that has a negative emotional tone (Coffey, 1987; Otto, Yeo, & Dougher, 1987). Whether overactivation of the nondominant side of the brain is a cause of depression or simply a symptom of depression is unclear.

Neuroimaging studies using computerized tomography (CT) scans and magnetic resonance imaging (MRI) have found atrophy or deterioration in the cerebral cortex and cerebellum in people with severe unipolar depression or bipolar disorder (Andreasen et al., 1990; Coffey et al., 1993). Positron-emission tomography (PET) scans also show decreased metabolic activity in the frontal area of the cerebral cortex of people with severe depression or bipolar disorder (Figure 8.9; Buchsbaum et al., 1997; Kennedy, Javanmard, & Vaccarino, 1997). An interesting study of one person with rapid-cycling bipolar disorder showed that metabolic activity in the brain was highly correlated with how

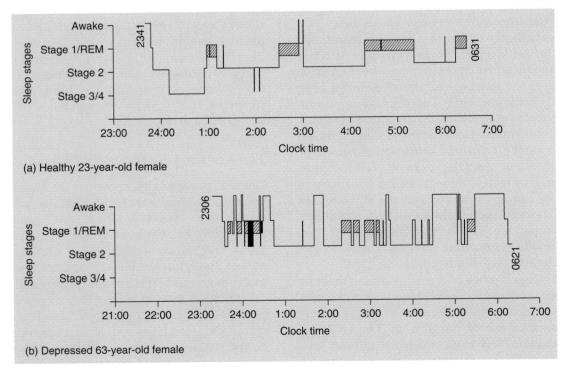

FIGURE 8.8   EEG and Sleep Activity in Normal and Depressed People. (a) The EEG activity of a healthy, 23-year-old female over the course of a night's sleep. (b) the EEG activity of a seriously depressed 63-year-old female over the course of a night. The depressed woman goes into REM sleep much faster than the nondepressed woman and is in and out of REM sleep many more times than the nondepressed woman.

Source: Thase & Howland, 1995, Figure 8.7, p. 236.

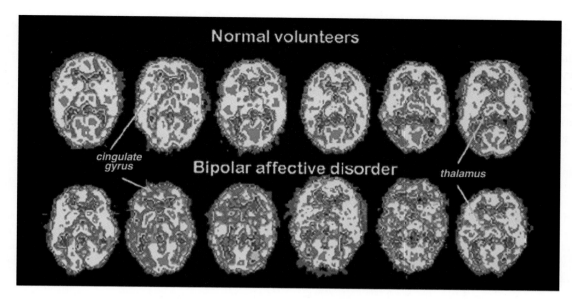

FIGURE 8.9 PET Scans of Bipolar Disorder. PET scans in six control subjects and six patients with bipolar disorder. Note decreases in relative metabolic rate in frontal lobes, cingulate gyrus, and thalamus in bipolar subjects.

Source: Buchsbaum et al., 1997.

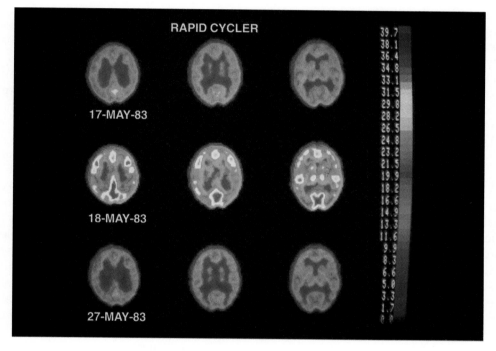

FIGURE 8.10 Changes in Brain Metabolism from Mania to Depression. The relationship between cerebral metabolism and mood is illustrated in these sequential PET scans of a patient with rapid-cycle bipolar disorder. The whole-brain metabolic rate is 36 percent greater on the hypomanic day (middle row of scans) than on the depressed day (upper and lower rows of scans).

Source: Baxter et al., 1985.

depressed or manic this person was: During manic periods, the metabolism rate was 36 percent greater than during depressed periods (see Figure 8.10; Baxter et al., 1985). The meaning of these findings is not yet clear, but suggests that large areas of the brain that control sophisticated thinking processes may be affected in mood disorders.

Hormonal Factors

Hormones have long been thought to play a role in mood disorders, especially depression. The *neuroendocrine system* regulates a number of important hormones that, in turn, affect basic functions such as sleep, appetite, sexual drive, and the ability to experience pleasure. These hormones also help the body respond to environmental stressors. Three key components of the neuroendocrine system—the hypothalamus, pituitary, and adrenal cortex—work together in a feedback system that is richly interconnected with the limbic system and the cerebral cortex (see Figure 8.11). This system is often referred to as the **hypothalamic-pituitary-adrenal axis, or HPA axis.** Normally, when we are confronted with a stressor, the HPA axis becomes more active, increasing levels of hormones like **cortisol,** which help the body to respond to the stressor by making it possible to fight the stressor or flee from it. Once the stressor is gone, the HPA axis returns to homeostasis.

Neuroendocrine Abnormalities

Depressed people tend to show chronic hyperactivity in the HPA axis and an inability for the HPA axis to return to normal functioning following a stressor (Holsboer, 1992; Young & Korszun, 1998). In turn, the excess hormones produced by heightened HPA activity seem to have an inhibiting effect on receptors for the monoamines. One model for the development of depression is that people exposed to chronic stress may develop poorly regulated neuroendocrine systems. Then when they are exposed even to minor stressors later in life, the HPA axis overreacts and does not easily return to homeostasis. This creates change in the functioning of the monoamine neurotransmitters in the brain, and an episode of depression is likely to ensue (Weiss, 1991).

Are Women's Hormonal Cycles a Factor?

Many people have argued over the years that women's greater vulnerability to depression is tied to hormones—specifically, the so-called ovarian hormones, estrogen and progesterone. The main fuel for this idea comes from evidence that women are more prone to depression during the premenstrual period of the menstrual cycle, the postpartum period, and menopause. These are times when levels of estrogen and progesterone change dramatically. There have been raging debates over the evidence that hormones play a role in women's depression (Bebbington, 1998; Nolen-Hoeksema, 1995; Young & Korszun, 1998).

In the 1950s, physician Katherine Dalton labeled the depression, anxiety, and physical discomfort some women report during their premenstrual periods as premenstrual syndrome, and these days everyone knows what PMS is. But does it exist? This turns out to be one of the hottest debates in the depression literature. Theorists who believe that some women develop debilitating symptoms of depression during the premenstrual phase of their cycles argued that this syndrome needed a diagnostic category of its own in

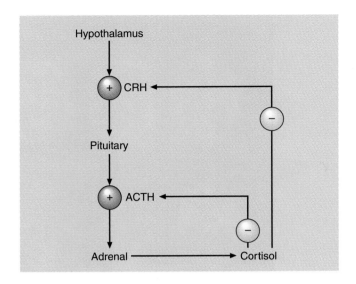

FIGURE 8.11 The Hypothalamic-Pituitary-Adrenal Axis. The hypothalamus synthesizes corticotropin-releasing hormone (CRH). CRH is transported to the pituitary gland, where it stimulates the synthesis and release of adrenocorticotropic hormone (ACTH), which then circulates to the adrenal glands, producing cortisol. Cortisol then inhibits the production of further ACTH and CRH. In normal people, this process prevents too much or too prolonged physiological arousal following a stressor. In major depression, however, people often show abnormal cortisol functioning, suggesting that there is disregulation in this hypothalamic-pituitary-adrenal (HPA) axis.

DSM-IV to facilitate research and treatment. Other theorists argued that PMS is a social myth, used to pathologize women as inherently flawed and crazy (see Tavris, 1992).

So what does the research say about PMS? Old studies suggested that the majority of women are regularly incapacitated by depression, anxiety, and physical discomfort during their premenstrual periods (Reid & Yen, 1981). However, these studies relied on faulty methods. They asked women to complete retrospective questionnaires about their experiences of premenstrual mood changes in the past. It turns out that the information women provide on these questionnaires often bears little resemblance to their actual experiences of mood across the menstrual cycle. For example, in one study, women completed daily mood ratings but did not know that the study was investigating the relationship between mood and the menstrual cycle. At the end of the study, the women were asked to report, retrospectively, on their moods during the different phases of their most recent menstrual cycle. On the retrospective questionnaire, the women reported having experienced significantly more negative symptoms during their premenstrual period than during any other period in their last cycle. However, the daily mood ratings of these same women showed no relationship between cycle phase and moods (Abplanap, Haskett, & Rose, 1979; see also Hardie, 1997; Parlee, 1994; Schnurr et al., 1994).

More recent studies have found that it is possible to identify a small group of women who frequently experience increases in depressive symptoms during the premenstrual phase (Endicott, 1994). These women also tend to have a history of frequent major depressive episodes or anxiety disorders with no connection to the menstrual cycle or of other psychiatric disorders (Yonkers, 1997). This suggests that these women have a general vulnerability to depression or anxiety rather than a specific vulnerability to premenstrual dysphoria (Parry, 1994; Rubinow & Schmidt, 1989). This has led many researchers to argue that depressions during the premenstrual period should not be given a separate diagnosis, such as **premenstrual dysphoric disorder,** but should be considered only exacerbations of major depression or dysthymia. Others argue that we should recognize premenstrual depression separately with its own diagnosis because it is different from depression that has no link with the menstrual cycle and therefore should be studied separately. The DSM-IV dealt with this controversy by putting diagnostic criteria for premenstrual dysphoric disorder in an appendix rather than in the main body of its text with other officially recognized diagnoses.

Even among women who clearly do have PMS, there is little evidence that their symptoms are due to changes in levels of estrogen or progesterone across the menstrual cycle (Young & Korszun, 1998). Many studies have found no differences in levels of estrogen or progesterone between women with PMS and those without PMS. There clearly is something about the menstrual cycle that is worsening mood in women with PMS, but it appears that estrogen or progesterone do not have consistent direct effects on mood.

We noted earlier that about 1 in 10 women experience a severe postpartum depression in the first few months after giving birth. This might seem like strong evidence that hormonal changes play a role in women's depressions, because this is a period of great hormonal change in women's bodies. Yet, studies comparing rates of depression in random samples of postpartum women and matched groups of women who were not postpartum have tended not to find differences in rates of depression between these two groups (O'Hara & Swain, 1996). Even among women who do become seriously depressed during the postpartum, depressions do not seem to be linked to any specific imbalances in hormones (Hendrick, Altshuler, & Suri, 1998; Pedersen et al., 1993). Postpartum depressions are most often linked to severe stress in women's lives, such as financial strain, marital difficulties, lack of social support, and having a fussy baby (Brugha et al., 1998; Hendrick et al., 1998; O'Hara & Swain, 1996). In addition, women who have a past history of depression clearly are at increased risk for postpartum depression (O'Hara et al., 1991). These women may carry a general vulnerability to depression, which is triggered by either the physiological or environmental changes of the postpartum period.

Menopause marks the cessation of menstrual periods, and there is a drastic decrease in circulating ovarian hormones for women at menopause (Young & Korszun, 1998). The belief that women were more prone to depression during menopause was so strong among clinicians that 20 years ago there was a separate diagnostic category in the DSM for this type of depression. Several studies have found, however, that women are no more likely to show depression around the time of menopause than at any other time in their lives (Matthews et al., 1990; Nicol-Smith, 1996). In addition, there are not consistent mood effects of taking estrogen replacement drugs for menopausal women (Young & Korszun, 1998).

In sum, the evidence that women's moods are tied to their hormones is mixed, at best. Some women clearly do experience more depression during the postpartum period, menopause, and other times when their hormone levels change rapidly. The extent to which these experiences of depression account for the generally higher rates of depression among women compared to men is less clear.

Summing Up

- Genetic factors clearly play a role in bipolar disorder, although it is somewhat less clear what role genetics plays in many forms of unipolar depression.

- The neurotransmitter theories suggest that imbalances in levels of norepinephrine or serotonin or dysregulation of receptors for these neurotransmitters contributes to depression, and dysregulation of norepinephrine, serotonin, or dopamine is involved in bipolar disorder.

- Some depressed people have unusual EEG patterns, disrupted sleep patterns, and abnormalities detectable on CT, PET, and MRI scans.

- Depressed people have chronic hyperactivity of the hypothalamic-pituitary-adrenal axis, which helps to regulate the body's response to stress.

⊙ PSYCHOLOGICAL THEORIES OF MOOD DISORDERS

Psychological theories have focused almost exclusively on depression, because the evidence that bipolar disorder is caused by biological factors is strong. However, new episodes of bipolar disorder may be triggered by

CONCEPT REVIEW

Psychological Theories of Mood Disorders

The psychological theories of depression have focused on aspects of the environment, of thinking, and of a person's past.

Theory	Description
Behavioral theories	
Lewinsohn's theory	Depressed people experience a reduction in positive reinforcers and increase in aversive events, which leads to their depression.
Learned helplessness theory	Depressed people lack control, which leads to the belief that they are helpless, which leads to depressive symptoms.
Cognitive theories	
Aaron Beck's theory	Depressed people have a negative cognitive triad of beliefs about the self, the world, and the future, which are maintained by distorted thinking.
Reformulated learned helplessness theory	Depressed people have the tendency to attribute events to internal, stable, and global factors, which contributes to depression.
Psychodynamic theory	Depressed people are unconsciously punishing themselves because they feel abandoned by another person but cannot punish that person; dependency and perfectionism are risk factors for depression.

stressful events or by living in an unsupportive family (Butzlaff & Hooley, 1998; Johnson & Roberts, 1995). This suggests a diathesis-stress model of bipolar disorder, in which the diathesis or vulnerability factor is a biological one, such as a genetic predisposition to the disorder, but stressors, such as the loss of a job, can trigger new episodes.

In this section, however, we focus on depression, and psychological theories that have tried to explain this disorder (see *Concept Review:* Psychological Theories of Mood Disorders).

Behavioral Theories

Depression often arises as a reaction to stressful negative events, such as the breakup of a relationship, the death of a loved one, job loss, or a serious medical illness. Sixty-five percent of people with a nonmelancholic type of depression report a negative life event in the 6 months prior to the onset of their depression (Frank et al., 1994). Depressed people are more likely than nondepressed people to have chronic life stressors, such as financial strain or a bad marriage. People who suffer depression also tend to have a history of traumatic life events in their past, particularly events involving loss (Kessler, Davis, & Kendler, 1997).

Reducing Positive Reinforcers

Peter Lewinsohn's **behavioral theory of depression** suggests that life stress leads to depression because it

Difficulties in close relationships are often tied to depression.

creates a reduction in positive reinforcers in a person's life (Lewinsohn & Gotlib, 1995). The person begins to withdraw, which only results in further reduction in reinforcers, which leads to more withdrawal, and a self-perpetuating chain is created (see Figure 8.12). For example, imagine that a man is having difficulty in his relationship with his wife. Interactions with her are no longer as positively reinforcing as they formerly were, so he stops initiating these interactions as often. This only worsens the communication between him and his wife, however, so the relationship becomes even worse. He withdraws further and becomes depressed about this area of his life. Lewinsohn suggests that such a pattern is especially likely in people with poor social skills, because they are more likely to experience rejection by others and to withdraw in response to this rejection rather than find ways to overcome the rejection (Lewinsohn, 1974). In addition, once a person begins engaging in depressive behaviors, these behaviors are reinforced by the sympathy and attention they engender in others.

Learned Helplessness Theory

Another behavioral theory—the **learned helplessness theory**—suggests that the type of stressful event most likely to lead to depression is an uncontrollable negative event (Seligman, 1975). Such an event, especially if frequent or chronic, can lead people to believe that they are helpless to control important outcomes in their environment. In turn, this belief in helplessness leads people to lose their motivation, to reduce actions that might control the environment, and to be unable to learn how to control situations that are controllable. These deficits, known as **learned helplessness deficit**s, are similar to the symptoms of depression: low motivation, passivity, indecisiveness (Seligman, 1975).

The initial evidence for the learned helplessness theory came from studies with animals, which we described in Chapter 2. Briefly, a group of researchers conducted a series of studies in which dogs were given either controllable shock, uncontrollable shock, or no shock (Overmier & Seligman, 1967; Seligman & Maier, 1967). The dogs in the controllable shock group could turn off the shock by jumping a short barrier, and they quickly learned how to do so (as did the dogs that had previously received no shock). The dogs in the uncontrollable shock group could not turn off or otherwise escape the shock. The dogs in the controllable and uncontrollable shock conditions received the same total amount of shock. However, when the dogs in the uncontrollable shock group were put into a situation in which they could control the shock, they seemed unable to learn how to do so. They would just sit in the box, passive and whimpering, until the shock went off. Even when the experimenter dragged these dogs across the barrier in an attempt to teach them how to turn off the shock, the dogs did not learn the response. The researchers argued that the dogs in the uncontrollable shock group had learned they were helpless to control the shock, and their passivity and inability to learn to control the shock were the result of this learned helplessness.

In turn, the researchers argued that many human depressions are helplessness depressions, resulting when people come to believe they are helpless to control important outcomes in their environment. For

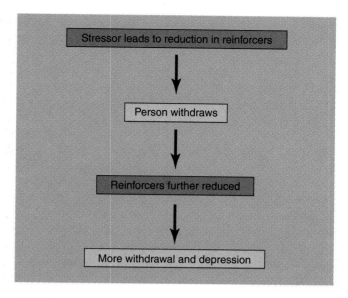

FIGURE 8.12   Lewinsohn's Behavioral Theory of Depression. Lewinsohn's behavioral theory suggests that stressful events lead to reductions in reinforcers. The person withdraws as a result of this reduction, which only leads to further reductions in reinforcers, which leads to more withdrawal and depression, and a self-perpetuating cycle is created.

example, children who lose their mothers may come to believe that important areas of their lives are not under their control. The loss of a mother may not only mean the loss of the person to whom the child is most closely attached. It may also mean years of disruption and instability as the child is moved from one set of relatives to another, if the father is not able to care for the child. Such chronic instability might persuade the child that life truly is uncontrollable, and this may be why childhood bereavement is a predisposing factor for depression. Similarly, women who are frequently battered by their husbands may develop the belief that there is nothing they can do to control their beatings or other parts of their lives, and this may explain the high rates of depression among battered women (Rounsaville, 1978).

Helpless, ruminative coping styles   Research on learned helplessness inspired another line of work on the ways people cope when they are depressed (Nolen-Hoeksema, 1995). Some people, when depressed, focus intently on how they feel—their symptoms of fatigue and poor concentration, their sadness and hopelessness—and can identify many possible causes of these symptoms. They do not attempt to do anything about these causes, however, and instead just continue to engage in **rumination** about their depression. Several studies have shown that people with this more ruminative coping style remain depressed longer than people with a more action-oriented coping style (Nolen-Hoeksema, Larson, & Grayson, 1999; Nolen-Hoeksema, Parker, & Larson, 1994; Nolen-Hoeksema

& Morrow, 1991). Rumination is not just another symptom of depression, although people who are more depressed have more to ruminate about. Depressed people differ in the extent to which they ruminate, and those who ruminate more become more severely depressed over time and remain depressed longer than those who do not.

Women are more likely to ruminate when they are depressed than men are (Nolen-Hoeksema, 1990; Nolen-Hoeksema, Larson, & Grayson, 1999). This may be because women are exposed to more circumstances that make them ruminate—more negative events and circumstances over which they feel they have no control. Regardless of the reasons for this gender difference in rumination, women's tendency to ruminate appears to contribute to the higher rates of depression in women compared to men (Nolen-Hoeksema et al., 1999).

Cognitive Theories

"Good morning, Eeyore," shouted Piglet.
"Good morning, Little Piglet," said Eeyore. "If it *is* a good morning," he said. "Which I doubt," said he. "Not that it matters," he said. (Milne, 1961, p. 54)

Like poor Eeyore, some people have a chronically gloomy way of interpreting the things that happen to them, and they are more prone to depression. Although there are many individual cognitive theories of depression, we focus on the two that have had the most impact: Aaron Beck's cognitive distortion theory and the reformulated learned helplessness theory.

Aaron Beck's Theory

One of the first cognitive theories of depression was developed by psychiatrist Aaron Beck. Beck (1967) argued that depressed people look at the world through a *negative cognitive triad*: They have negative views of themselves, of the world, and of the future. Depressed people then commit many types of errors in thinking, such as jumping to negative conclusions on the basis of little evidence, ignoring good events, focusing only on negative events, and exaggerating negative events that support their negative cognitive triad (see Table 8.5). Depressed people may not be aware that they hold these negative views or that they make these errors in thinking: Often these negative thoughts are so automatic that depressed people do not realize how they are interpreting situations. Beck's theory led to one of the most widely used and successful therapies for depression, cognitive-behavioral therapy. We discuss this therapy in detail in the next chapter.

Students with a pessimistic style of thinking are most distressed when they do poorly on an exam.

Reformulated Learned Helplessness Theory

Another influential cognitive theory of depression, the **reformulated learned helplessness theory**, was proposed to explain how cognitive factors might influence whether a person becomes helpless and depressed following a negative event (Abramson, Seligman, & Teasdale, 1978; Peterson & Seligman, 1984). This theory focuses on people's causal attributions for events. A **causal attribution** is an explanation of why an event happened. According to this theory, people who habitually explain negative events by causes that are internal, stable, and global blame themselves for these negative events, expect negative events to recur in the future, and expect to experience negative events in many areas of their lives. In turn, these expectations lead them to experience long-term learned helplessness deficits plus self-esteem loss in many areas of their lives (see Table 8.6). Take, for example, a student who becomes depressed after failing a psychology exam. The reformulated learned helplessness theory would suspect that she has blamed her failure on internal causes—she didn't study hard enough—rather than external causes—the exam was too hard. Further, she has assumed that the failure was due to stable causes such as a lack of aptitude in psychology, rather than unstable causes like the instructor not allowing enough time, and she can expect to fail again. Finally, she has attributed her failure to a global cause, such as being stupid, as opposed to a specific cause, such as difficulty learning the material for this particular test. This global attribution would lead to failure in other academic areas.

Again, researchers equate learned helplessness deficits with depression and argue that an internal-stable-global attributional style for negative events puts people at risk for depression. Most recently, Abramson, Metalsky, and Alloy (1989) argued that a

TABLE 8.5

Errors or Distortions in Thinking in Depression

The cognitive distortions theory of depression suggests that depressed people commit many errors in thinking.

1. *All-or-nothing thinking.* Seeing things in black-or-white, all-or-nothing terms: "If I don't get an A on this test, I'll be a failure."

2. *Overgeneralization.* Seeing a single negative event as part of a large pattern of negative events: "I messed up this relationship and I'll never have a good relationship."

3. *Mental filter.* Focusing only on the negative aspects of a situation: "I can't believe I missed 5 questions on that test (of 100 questions). What an idiot I am."

4. *Disqualifying the positive.* Rejecting positive experiences by discounting them: "Anyone can run a 4-minute mile. That's nothing."

5. *Jumping to conclusions.* Concluding that something negative will happen or is happening with no evidence: "I haven't heard from my friend for over a week. She's probably angry at me for something."

6. *Emotional reasoning.* Assuming that negative emotions necessarily reflect reality: "I feel dumb so I must be dumb."

7. *Should statements.* Putting constant demands on oneself: "I should be a more upbeat person/better student/better lover."

8. *Labeling.* Overgeneralizing by attaching a negative, global label to a person or situation: "I'm a loser." "This situation is hopeless."

9. *Personalization.* Attributing negative events to the self without reason: "The professor is in a bad mood because she doesn't want to deal with me because I ask such stupid questions."

Source: Data from D. D. Burns, 1980.

TABLE 8.6

Attributional Dimensions Important in Depression

The perceived causes of negative events are as follows:

Internal to the person: "It's my fault I failed the exam."

Stable in time: "The reason I failed the exam will occur over and over again."

Global in effect: "This is going to affect my performance in other classes as well."

particular form of depression, hopelessness depression, develops when people make pessimistic attributions for the most important events in their lives and perceive they have no way of coping with the consequences of these events.

One of the most definitive studies of this theory of depression was a long term study of college students (Alloy, Abramson, & Francis, 1999). These researchers interviewed first-year students at two universities and identified those with pessimistic attributional styles and those with optimistic attributional styles. They then tracked these students for the next 2 1/2 years, interviewing them every 6 weeks. Among the students with no prior history of depression, those with a pessimistic cognitive style were much more likely to develop a first onset of major depression than those with an optimistic attributional style (17% versus 1%). In addition, among those who had a prior history of depression, students with a pessimistic style were more likely to have a relapse of depression than those with an optimistic style (27% versus 6%). Thus, a pessimistic attributional style predicted both first onsets of depression and relapses of depression.

Depressive realism Is it possible that depressed people are not distorted in their negative views of the world but actually are seeing the world realistically for the terrible place that it is? Researchers began investigating this possibility when they stumbled upon a phenomenon that is now referred to as **depressive realism**: When asked to make judgments about how much control they have over situations that are actually uncontrollable, depressed people are quite accurate. In contrast, nondepressed people greatly overestimate the amount of control they have, especially over positive events (Alloy & Abramson, 1979). For example, in one study, depressed and nondepressed people were asked to judge to what degree they could control the onset of a green light by pushing a button on a display panel. In truth, none of the subjects had control over the onset of the light. In conditions in which subjects were rewarded whenever the green light came on, the nondepressed people grossly overestimated their control over the onset of the light. In contrast, the depressed subjects accurately judged that they had no control over the onset of the light.

Subsequently, a long line of research has shown that nondepressed people have a robust illusion that they can control all sorts of situations that truly are out of their control and that they have superior skills compared to most people (Taylor & Brown, 1988). For example, nondepressed people believe they can control games of chance like the lottery, that they are more likely than the average person to succeed in life, that they are more immune to car accidents than other people, and that their social skills are better than most people's. In contrast, depressed people do not seem to hold these illusions of control and superiority. Indeed, depressed people seem amazingly accurate in judging the amount of control they have over situations and their skills at various tasks.

This research on illusion of control calls into question the notion that depression results from unrealistic beliefs that one cannot control one's environment or from negative errors in thinking about oneself and the world. Perhaps it is not accurate and realistic thinking that prevents people from becoming depressed but hope and optimism.

Psychodynamic Theories

Some people seem to find themselves in unhealthy and destructive relationships over and over again. Each time these relationships end, they vow never to get into similar relationships again. However, they do and then find themselves depressed over the problems in the new relationships or when the relationships inevitably end.

Psychodynamic theorists suggest that such patterns of unhealthy relationships stem from people's childhood experiences that prevented them from developing a strong and positive sense of self reasonably independent of others' evaluations (Arieti & Bemporad, 1980; Bibring, 1953; Blatt & Zuroff, 1992; Bowlby, 1980; Freud, 1917). As adults, these people are constantly searching for approval and security in their relationships with others. They are anxious about separation and abandonment and may allow others to take advantage and even abuse them rather than risk losing the relationship by complaining. They are constantly striving to be "perfect" so that they will be loved. Even when they accomplish great things, they do not feel secure or positive about themselves. Eventually, some problem in a close relationship or some failure to achieve perfection occurs, and they plunge into depression.

Psychodynamic theories of depression suggest that children who are anxious about separation and abandonment are at increased risk for depression.

Many modern psychodynamic theorists still rely on the groundbreaking work Freud published in his paper *Mourning and Melancholia* to describe just how depression develops when a person perceives he or she has been abandoned or has failed. Freud pointed out that people who are depressed have many of the symptoms of people who are grieving the death of a loved one: they feel sad, alone, unmotivated, and lethargic. Unlike grieving people, depressed people display severe self-hate and self-blame. Indeed, said Freud, depressed people appear to want to punish themselves, even to the point of killing themselves. Freud argued that depressives are not actually blaming or punishing themselves. Instead, they are blaming or punishing those they perceive have abandoned them. Depressives are so dependent on the approval and love of others that much of their ego or sense of self is made up of their images of these others—what Freud called the "love objects." When they believe others have rejected them, depressives are too frightened to express their rage for this rejection outwardly. Instead, they turn their anger inward on the parts of their own egos that have incorporated the love objects. Their self-blame and punishment is actually blame and punishment of the others who have abandoned them. This is Freud's **introjected hostility** theory of depression.

In *Taking Psychology Personally:* Dealing with Grief, we further explore the differences between grief and depression, and discuss work that has tested some of the traditional concepts of "normal grief." In the

TAKING PSYCHOLOGY PERSONALLY

Dealing with Grief

When my son died, I worried that I was going crazy. I'd go to the store to get milk and bread, and I'd stand there like a fool, and not know why the hell I was in the store. I found out that was normal—the stress and the grieving caused me to be forgetful. And once I found out that it was normal for me to be forgetful, then it was okay. I think it's important for people to know that they are going to do a lot of stupid things, and not know why. And time does heal you. (Mother whose 35-year-old son died of a brain tumor)

At some time in their lives, most people experience the death of someone close to them. Although most bereaved people experience some degree of emotional and physical distress, there are tremendous differences between people in how severe this distress is and how long it lasts.

Many bereavement experts have identified a series of stages in grief (Bowlby, 1980; Glick, Weiss, & Parkes, 1974; Horowitz, 1976; Kubler-Ross, 1969; Shuchter & Zisook, 1993). The first is an initial period of *shock, disbelief, and denial*, which may last from hours to weeks. Bereaved people feel numb and paralyzed, and may not believe that the death is real. They may actively search for the dead loved one, may imagine hearing or seeing the deceased, or may simply yearn and pine for the loved one. As one participant in a long-term study of bereavement conducted by the author and Judith Larson said (Nolen-Hoeksema & Larson, 1999, pp. 4–5):

> The first couple of weeks I had a very strong sense that he was present. If someone asked me a question and I didn't know the answer I would turn around and ask John and realize he wasn't here. Some days I'm numb, some days I think, "God, you really are a bitch, you don't feel anything." (Woman whose 60-year-old husband died of lung cancer 1 month previously)

The second phase begins when people are able to acknowledge the death cognitively and emotionally. This phase of *acute mourning* includes intense feelings of sadness, despair, loneliness, anxiety, and anger. The person may experience the full syndrome of depression, with loss of interest in life, disruptions in sleep and appetite, inability to concentrate or make decisions, a sense of hopelessness and helplessness, and even suicidal wishes.

Eventually, in most people, the acute mourning phase is replaced by a *restitution phase* in which they return to a feeling of well-being and an ability to go on living. They may come to some understanding or acceptance of the loss, and most of the time they are able to be engaged in everyday life in a positive way. Yet, grief can reappear from time to time for years, or throughout one's lifetime (Bornstein et al., 1973; Lehman, Wortman, & Williams, 1987; Parkes, 1971; Zisook, Shuchter, & Lyons, 1987).

Although stage models have been extremely popular among health care professionals and the lay public, research over the last decade or so is strongly suggesting that many of the major assumptions of these models are incorrect (Osterweis et al., 1984; Silver & Wortman, 1980). Many, perhaps most, bereaved people do report the symptoms that stage theories describe—shock, denial, anger, despair, yearning, intrusive thoughts, and eventually a sense of recovery. But there is tremendous variability between people in the order in which these symptoms are experienced, and the duration of specific symptoms.

One major assumption of the traditional grief models is that high levels of depression and distress are inevitable and healthy following a loss, and that failure to experience this distress is pathological (Freud, 1917; Bowlby, 1982). Many studies have reported that feelings of sadness or depressed mood are very common among bereaved people (Bornstein et al., 1973; Faletti et al., 1989; Thompson et al., 1989; Van Zandt, Mou, & Abbott, 1989). Yet, in contrast to what the traditional theories would predict, people who do not experience severe depression following a loss usually do not go on to experience severe distress in the future. Instead, people who are most distressed right after a loss are the ones most likely to be severely distressed in the future.

Continued

The failure of studies to support stage models is important given the influence of these models on interventions with bereaved people. These models form the backbone of education about bereavement for many physicians, nurses, therapists, social workers, members of the clergy, and patients and their families (Silver & Wortman, 1980; Wortman & Silver, 1987). Health care professionals may use models as a yardstick to assess the progress of bereaved people they are serving. Thus, people who are not following these stages might be labeled as pathological and may be intervened with unnecessarily or inappropriately. Lay people who read about the stages of bereavement might also label themselves as "abnormal" because they are not experiencing bereavement as the books "say they should."

One respondent in our study of bereavement put it best:

There's no rules. There's no right way or wrong way to feel. We used to think that you get to a certain point and you're not grieving anymore. What I tell people now is you finally realize you're in a place where you can contain it so that it's manageable. You kind of integrate it into what you're doing every day. But it never really goes away. You don't "get over" a loss. No, you just learn to live with it, but you have to also accept the fact that you're changed as a result of it. (Phyllis, whose 70-year-old mother died of pancreatic cancer)

meantime, though, let us consider the case of Giselle, which illustrates the processes described by the psychodynamic theories of depression.

CASE STUDY

Giselle was raised by two well-meaning but emotionally inhibited parents. The parents had emigrated to the United States from Eastern Europe in the 1970s, fleeing persecution for their anticommunist beliefs. Even after settling in the United States, Giselle's parents remained paranoid about the family's security and constantly told Giselle she had to be "good" or the family would be in danger. Thus, from an early age, Giselle suppressed any childhood willfulness or exuberance. She was not allowed to play with other children; she spent most of her time with the family maid, who had followed them to the United States. Her parents were preoccupied with their uncertain circumstances and also unnecessarily belittled Giselle's childhood concerns. For example, when there was an epidemic of flu at Giselle's school, her mother told her not to worry because only the smart and pretty girls were getting sick. The mother doted on the father when he was in the house, ignoring Giselle. The father paid attention to Giselle only when she was deferential or complimentary.

As an adult, Giselle chose to become a nurse because she felt it would gain her acceptance and love by patients. Giselle married a man who was somewhat solitary and hypercritical. He was prone to periods of depression and always preoccupied with his own concerns. Giselle became the major source of financial support during her marriage, often taking on extra shifts to earn more money. She had done remarkably well in her career because of her hard work and her repeated efforts to please others. She was also the emotional mainstay in her family, being responsible for taking care of the children and for fulfilling the usual responsibilities of running a household. Giselle rarely complained, however. She needed to be certain that everyone liked her and thought well of her and she went to extremes of self-sacrifice to ensure the high regard of others.

After several years, her husband left her, telling her that he did not love her any longer and that she no longer gave him any pleasure in his life. In the first few days after her husband announced he was going to leave, Giselle desperately tried to win back his love by indulging his every whim. Eventually, however, they had a violent confrontation during which he walked out. Later that evening, Giselle emptied her medicine cabinet of all drugs, drove to a secluded area, and ingested the drugs in an effort to kill herself. (Adapted from Bemporad, 1995)

Some research has supported elements of the psychodynamic perspective on depression. For example, depressed people tend to display many of Giselle's personality traits: They are dependent on others, believe that they must be perfect, have poor self-esteem, and are unable to express anger openly (Riley, Trieber, & Woods, 1989; Sacco & Beck, 1995). In addition, many depressed people describe their parents as having characteristics similar to Giselle's parents: They are cold and neglectful, excessively moralistic and demanding of perfection, or requiring of complete devotion and dependency from their children in exchange for their love (Blatt & Zuroff, 1992). Most of these studies are cross-sectional, however, so we do not know whether these characteristics and views are symptoms of the depression or actual causes of the depression. There are a few longitudinal studies that support elements of the psychodynamic theories. For example, one study of middle-aged women found that those who tended to inhibit any expression of anger and who were unassertive in interpersonal interactions were more likely to become depressed over a 3-year period (Bromberger & Matthews, 1996). For the most part, however, psychodynamic theories of depression have not been thoroughly tested.

Summing Up

- The behavioral theories of depression suggest that stress can induce depression by reducing the number of reinforcers available to people.
- The learned helplessness theory of depression says that uncontrollable events can lead people to believe that important outcomes are outside of their control and thus to develop depression.
- The cognitive theories of depression argue that depressed people think in distorted and negative ways, and this leads them to become depressed, particularly in the face of negative events.
- The psychodynamic theories posit that depressed people are overly dependent on the evaluations and approval of others for their self-esteem, as a result of poor nurturing by parents.

SOCIOCULTURAL PERSPECTIVES ON MOOD DISORDERS

The roles we play in our relationships to others and in the larger society are important in determining our vulnerability to depression. Sociocultural approaches analyze social roles and norms to understand why some people are vulnerable to depression whereas others are not, and the impact society can have on how a depressed individual manifests depression.

Interpersonal Theories

Interpersonal theories of depression are concerned with people's close relationships and their roles in those relationships (Klerman et al., 1984). Disturbances in these roles are thought to be the main source of depression. These disturbances may be recent, as when a woman who believes that her marriage has been successful for years suddenly finds that her husband is having an affair. Often, the disturbances are rooted in long-standing patterns of interactions the depressed person typically has with important others.

Drawing from attachment theory (Bowlby, 1982), interpersonal theorists argue that children who do not experience their caregivers as reliable, responsive, and warm develop an insecure attachment to their caregivers that sets the stage for all future relationships (see Chapter 2). These problematic relationship become represented mentally as negative working models of others and of the self in relation to others. These models are essentially operating rules and expectations about the availability of support from others and the implications of others' lack of support for one's self-worth. Children with insecure attachments develop expectations that they must be or do certain things in order to win the approval of others, which have been called **contingencies of self-worth** (Kuiper & Olinger, 1986; Kuiper, Olinger, & MacDonald, 1988). These are "if-then" rules concerning self-worth, such as "I'm nothing if a person I care about doesn't love me." If these contingencies of self-worth sound like the dysfunctional beliefs that Beck and other cognitive theories describe, they are—the interpersonal theorists argue that dysfunctional beliefs are the result of insecure attachments in childhood. As long as an individual meets the contingencies of self-worth set up in his or her working model, then he or she will maintain positive self-esteem and remain nondepressed. Failures to meet these contingencies are inevitable, however, and plunge the person into depression.

A number of influential theories have suggested that women are socialized to base most of their self-concept and self-worth on their relationships with others, and this is what makes them more prone than men to depression. Jack (1991) and Helgeson (1994) both argue that females are more likely than males to silence their own wants and needs in relationships in favor of maintaining a positive emotional tone in the relationships, and to feel too responsible for the quality of the relationship. This leads females to have less power and obtain less benefit from relationships. Some support has been found for this perspective on the gender difference in depression (Baron & Peixoto, 1991; Blatt et al., 1993; Luthar & Blatt, in press).

Although the interpersonal models based on attachment theory are relatively new, considerable evidence supporting them has been found (Armsden et al., 1990; Carnelley, Pietromonaco, & Jaffe, 1994; Hammen et al., 1995). For example, one longitudinal study of college students found that those with an anxious, insecure attachment style had more dysfunctional negative beliefs and subsequently developed lower self-esteem and more depressive symptoms (Roberts, Gotlib, & Kassel, 1996). Most of the research on the interpersonal models of depression has focused on evaluating the therapy that was developed based on this model, which we discuss shortly.

Sociological Perspectives on Mood Disorders

Sociologists have focused on the large age, gender, and cross-cultural differences in rates of depression, and have tried to understand this disorder in light of these differences.

The cohort effect We noted earlier that the rates of depression appear to be lower in people over the age of 65 than in younger people, and presented several explanations of this age difference. There is one further explanation that highlights sociocultural changes over history that may have resulted in more recent generations being at higher risk for depression than people who were born a few generations ago (Klerman & Weissman, 1989). This is called a *cohort effect:* People born in one historical period are at different risk for a disorder than are people born in another historical period. For example, less than 20 percent of people born before 1915 appear to have experienced episodes of major depression at any time in their lives, whereas over 40 percent of people born after 1955 appear to be at risk for major depression at some time in their lives (see Figure 8.13). Proponents of the cohort explanation suggest that more recent generations are more at risk for depression because of the rapid changes in social values that began in the 1960s and the disintegration of the family unit (Klerman & Weissman, 1989). This decrease in social support and in identification with common social values may have put younger generations at higher risk for depression than older generations were. Another possible explanation is that younger generations have higher expectations for themselves than did older generations, but these expectations are too high to be met.

Social status People who have lower status in society generally tend to show more depression. For example, in one large study done in the United States, people of Hispanic origins had a higher prevalence of depression in the previous year than Whites (Figure 8.14, p. 278; Blazer et al., 1994). This may reflect the higher rate of poverty, unemployment, and discrimination that Hispanics suffer compared to Whites. Figure 8.14 also suggests, however, that African Americans have even lower rates of depression than Whites. This may seem puzzling, given the disadvantaged status of African Americans in U.S. society. However, African Americans have high rates of anxiety disorders, suggesting

that the stress of their social status may make them especially prone to anxiety disorders rather than to depression. Other studies have found extremely high rates of depression among Native Americans, especially the young (Manson et al., 1990). Depression among these Native American youth is tied to poverty, hopelessness, and alcoholism.

One of the most compelling social explanations for women's higher rates of depression is that women's lower social status puts them at high risk for physical and sexual abuse, and these experiences often lead to depression. Women are much more likely than men to be the victims of rape, incest, battering, or sexual harassment (Browne, 1993; Fitzgerald, 1993; Koss, 1993). The rates of these types of violence against women are staggering. Most studies of rape estimate that between 14 and 25 percent of women are raped in their lives, most often before the age of 30 (Koss, 1993). One in eight women reports that she has been physically assaulted by their husband in the last year, and 1.8 million women report having been severely assaulted (punched, kicked, choked, threatened with a gun or knife; Straus & Gelles, 1990). Survivors of physical and sexual assault show high rates of major depression, anxiety disorders, and substance abuse. Thus, it seems likely that at least some of the difference between women's and men's rates of depression may be tied to the higher rates of abuse of women than of men and the resulting depression in female abuse survivors (Cutler & Nolen-Hoeksema, 1991).

Cross-cultural studies One cultural group within the United States that has especially low prevalence of unipolar depression is the Old Order Amish of central Pennsylvania. The Amish are a religious community of people who maintain a very simple lifestyle oriented around farming and the church and who reject modern conveniences (such as automobiles, electricity, telephones). Essentially, the Amish live as people did in nineteenth-century rural America. Extensive research on the mood disorders among the Amish has suggested that their prevalence of major depression is only one-tenth of that in mainstream groups in the United States (Egeland et al., 1987). Perhaps the simple agrarian lifestyle of the Amish, with its emphasis on family and community, helps to protect its members against depression.

Similarly, cross-national studies have suggested that the prevalence of major depression is lower among less industrialized and less modern countries than among more industrialized and more modern countries (Cross-National Collaborative Group, 1992). Again, it may be that the fast-paced lifestyles of people in modern industrialized societies, with their lack of stable social support and community values, are toxic

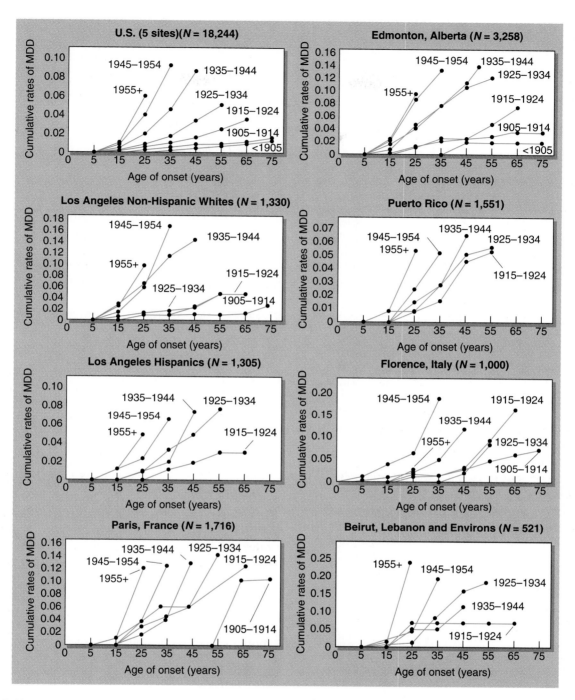

FIGURE 8.13 Rates of Depression in People Born in Different Historical Periods. These graphs show that in many different countries, people born in more recent historical periods have higher rates of depression and an earlier age of first onset of depression than did people born in earlier historical periods.

Source: Cross National Collaborative Group, 1992.

to mental health. In contrast, the community- and family-oriented lifestyles of less modern societies may be beneficial to mental health, despite the physical hardships that many people in these societies face because of their lack of modern conveniences.

Alternately, some researchers have suggested that people in less modern cultures may tend to mani-

fest depression with physical complaints rather than psychological symptoms of depression, such as sadness, loss of motivation, and hopelessness about the future. In China, people facing severe stress often complain of *neurasthenia*, a collection of physical symptoms such as chronic headaches, pain in the joints, nausea, lack of energy, and palpitations:

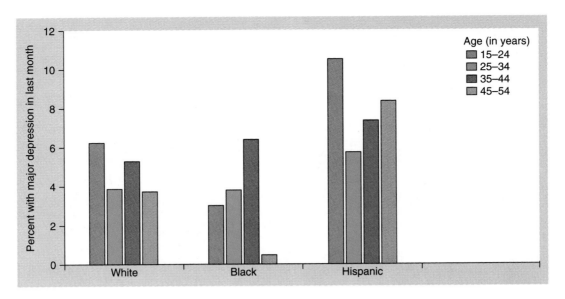

FIGURE 8.14 Ethnic Differences in Major Depression. These are the percentages of people in each age group and by ethnicity diagnosed with major depression in the previous month. Hispanic Americans show the highest rates across all age groups.

Source: Blazer et al., 1994.

CASE STUDY

Lin Hung is a 24-year-old worker in a machine factory who complains of headaches, dizziness, weakness, lack of energy, insomnia, bad dreams, poor memory, and a stiff neck. Pain, weakness, and dizziness, along with bouts of palpitations are his chief symptoms. His symptoms began 6 months ago, and they are gradually worsening. His factory doctors believe he has a heart problem, but repeated electrocardiograms have been normal. He believes he has a serious bodily disorder that is worsened by his work and that interferes with his ability to carry out his job responsibilities.

Until his father retired from the job Lin now occupies, he was a soldier living not far from home. He didn't want to leave the army, but his father was anxious to retire so he could move to a new apartment owned by his factory in another city. Fearing that his son would not be able to stay in the army and thereafter would not find work, Lin's father pressured him to take over his job, a job the younger Lin never liked or wanted for himself. Lin Hung reluctantly agreed but now finds he cannot adjust to the work. He did not want to be a machinist and cries when he recounts that this is what he must be for the rest of his life. Moreover, he is despondent and lonely living so far away from his parents. He has no friends at work and feels lonely living in the dormitory. He has a girlfriend, but he cannot see her regularly anymore, owing to the change in work sites. They wish to marry, but his parents, who have a serious financial problem because of a very low pension, cannot provide the expected furniture, room, or any financial help. The leaders of his work unit are against the marriage because he is too young. They also criticize him for his poor work performance and frequent days missed from work owing to sickness. (Adapted from Kleinman & Kleinman, 1985, pp. 454–455).

Upon questioning Lin Hung, psychiatrists trained in "Western" medicine diagnosed major depressive disorder. Like many Chinese, Lin rejected the psychological diagnosis, believing firmly that he was suffering solely from a physical disorder. A psychological diagnosis would not have garnered any sympathy from Lin's coworkers or family, but a physical diagnosis could provide him with an acceptable reason to leave his job and return to his family.

It is difficult to know whether the apparently low rates of depression in less modern cultures are due to a masking of depression by physical complaints in these cultures. However, in our discussions of many disorders, we will find that some cultures tend to focus on the physical manifestations of disorders, whereas others, such as the dominant U.S. culture, tend to focus on more psychological symptoms of disorders.

Summing Up

- The interpersonal theories of depression suggest that poor attachment relationships early in life can lead children to develop expectations that they must be or do certain things in order to win the approval of others, which puts them at risk for depression.

- More recent generations appear to be at higher risk for depression than earlier generations, perhaps because of historical changes in values and social structures related to depression.

- People of lower social status tend to have higher rates of depression. Women's greater vulnerability to depression may be tied to their lower social status, and the risks of abuse that accompany this social status.

- Less industrialized cultures may have lower rates of depression than more industrialized cultures. Some studies suggest that the manifestation of depression and mania may be different across cultures.

☉ MOOD DISORDERS TREATMENTS

The mood disorders have a tremendous impact on individuals and on society. In the United States alone, between $3 and $6 billion per year is spent on treatment of depression, and over $40 billion per year goes to cover losses in productivity plus health care costs of people with mood disorders (Goleman, 1993; Rost et al., 1998).

In any given year, about 60 percent of people suffering from bipolar disorder and about half of people suffering from major depression will seek out some sort of treatment for their disorder (Regier et al., 1993; Rost et al., 1998). The rest will suffer through their symptoms without any care. People who do seek treatment tend to be more severely impaired by their symptoms than those who do not seek treatment (Angst, 1998). Most often, those people who eventually do seek treatment wait a number of years after their symptoms begin to obtain any help (Kessler et al., 1998).

Fortunately, there are many forms of treatment now available for mood disorders, particularly depression. Most of these types of treatment have been shown to work for the majority of people. Thus, although there are many pathways into a mood disorder, there now are many pathways by which people can overcome or control mood disorders as well.

Biological Treatments for Mood Disorders

Most of the biological treatments for depression and mania are drug treatments (see *Concept Review:* Biological Treatments for Mood Disorders). There are several classes of antidepressant drugs used to treat depression. In addition to being treated with drugs, some depressed people are treated with electroconvulsive therapy, ECT. Lithium is the treatment of choice for mania and bipolar disorder, but anticonvulsants, antipsychotics, and calcium channel blockers are also used. Finally, people with the type of depression known as seasonal affective disorder, or SAD, seem to benefit from a unique type of therapy: exposure to bright lights.

Drug Treatments for Depression

Effective drug treatments for depression have been around since the 1960s. The late twentieth century, however, saw a rapid growth in the number of drugs available for depression and in the use of these drugs by large numbers of people.

Tricyclic antidepressants The **tricyclic antidepressant drugs** help to reduce the symptoms of depression by preventing the reuptake of norepinephrine and serotonin in the synapse or by changing the responsiveness of receptors for these neurotransmitters (Stahl, 1998). These drugs are highly effective: 60 to 85 percent of depressed people can get relief with them from their symptoms of depression (Guze & Gitlin, 1994). Some of the most commonly prescribed tricyclic

---

CONCEPT REVIEW

Biological Treatments for Mood Disorders

Medications, electroconvulsive therapy, and light therapy are useful biological treatments for the mood disorders.

Type of Treatment	Proposed Mechanism of Action
Medications (antidepressants, lithium, anticonvulsants, calcium channel blockers, antipsychotics)	Alter levels of neurotransmitters or sensitivity of receptors for neurotransmitters
Electroconvulsive therapy (ECT)	May increase permeability of blood-brain barrier, cause massive release of neurotransmitters, stimulate hypothalamus, increase sensitivity of serotonin receptors
Light therapy	May "reset" circadian rhythms or increase functioning of serotonin system

antidepressants are imipramine, amitriptylene, and desipramine (see Table 8.7).

Unfortunately, however, the tricyclic antidepressants have a number of side effects. The most common ones are dry mouth, excessive perspiration, blurring of vision, constipation, urinary retention, and sexual dysfunction. Another problem with the tricyclic antidepressants is that they can take 4 to 8 weeks to show an effect (Fava & Rosenbaum, 1995). This is an excruciatingly long time to wait for relief from depression. Finally, the tricyclics can be fatal in overdose, and an overdose is only three to four times the average daily prescription for the drug. Thus, physicians are wary of prescribing these drugs, particularly for depressed persons who might be suicidal.

Monoamine oxidase inhibitors A second class of drugs used to treat depression is the **monoamine oxidase inhibitors (MAOIs;** see Table 8.8). MAO is an enzyme that causes the breakdown of the monoamine neurotransmitters in the synapse (Stahl, 1998). MAO inhibitors decrease the action of MAO and thus result in increases in the levels of the neurotransmitters in the synapse.

The MAOIs are as effective as the tricyclic antidepressants, but physicians are more cautious in prescribing MAOIs in that the side effects of these drugs are potentially more dangerous (Fava & Rosenbaum, 1995). When people taking MAOIs ingest food rich in an amino acid called *tyramine*, they can experience a rise in blood pressure that can be fatal. The foods that can interact with MAOIs include aged or ripened cheeses, red wine, beer, and chocolate. The MAOIs can also interact with several drugs, including antihypertension medications and over-the-counter drugs like antihistamines. Finally, MAOIs can cause liver damage, weight gain, severe lowering of blood pressure, and several of the side effects caused by the tricyclic antidepressants.

Selective serotonin reuptake inhibitors and other second-generation antidepressants The newest class of antidepressant drugs is the **selective serotonin reuptake inhibitors,** or **SSRIs** (Table 8.9). These drugs are similar in structure to the tricyclic antidepressants, but work more directly to affect serotonin than do the tricyclics. These drugs have become extremely popular in the treatment of depression. The SSRIs are not more effective in the treatment of depression than the antidepressants we have already discussed—about the same percentage of people respond to an SSRI as will respond to a tricyclic or MAOI (Thase & Kupfer, 1996). These drugs have several advantages over the other antidepressants, however, that have made them extremely popular (Stahl, 1998). First, many people begin experiencing relief from their depression after a couple of weeks of using these drugs, whereas it often takes 4

TABLE 8.7	
Tricyclic Antidepressants	
A number of tricyclic antidepressants have proven effective in the treatment of mood disorders.	
Generic Name	**Trade Name**
Imipramine	Tofranil
Amitriptyline	Elavil
Doxepin	Adapin
	Sinequan
Trimipramine	Surmontil
Desipramine	Norpramin
	Pertofrane
Nortriptyline	Aventyl
	Pamelor
Protriptyline	Vivactil

TABLE 8.8	
Monoamine Oxidase Inhibitors	
The monoamine oxidase inhibitors are effective treatments for mood disorders, but are not used as often as other drugs.	
Generic Name	**Trade Name**
Isocarboxazid	Marplan
Phenelzine	Nardil
Tranylcypromine	Parnate

weeks or more for the other drugs to show significant effects. Second, the side effects of the selective serotonin reuptake inhibitors tend to be less severe than the side effects of the other antidepressants. Third, these drugs do not tend to be fatal in overdose and thus are safer than the other antidepressants (Nemeroff & Schatzberg, 1998). Fourth, the SSRIs appear to be helpful in a wide range of symptoms in addition to depression, or often associated with depression, such as anxiety symptoms, binge eating, and premenstrual symptoms (Pearlstein et al., 1997; Su et al., 1997). Recent studies also suggest that the SSRIs may be useful in the treatment of the most chronic and persistent types of depression (Keller et al., 1998).

The SSRIs do have their side effects, however (Fisher, Kent, & Bryant, 1995). One of the most common is increased agitation or nervousness. People on

TABLE 8.9

Selective Serotonin Reuptake Inhibitors and other Second-Generation Antidepressants

The selective serotonin reuptake inhibitors and other second-generation antidepressants have become the most widely used medications for mood disorders.

Generic Name	Trade Name
Fluoxetine	Prozac
Sertraline	Zoloft
Paroxetine	Paxil
Venlafaxine	Effexor
Fluvoxamine	Luvox
Nefazodone	Serzone
Buproprion	Wellbutrin
Maprotiline	Ludiomil
Amoxapine	Asendin
Trazodone	Desyrel
Clomipramine	Anafranil
Citalopram	Celexa

SSRIs often report feeling "jittery" or "hyper" and that they cannot sit still. They may have mild tremors and increased perspiration and feel weak. Others may find themselves becoming angry or hostile more often. Nausea and stomach cramps or gas are common side effects, as is a decrease in appetite. Finally, sexual dysfunction and decreased sexual drive are reported by some people on SSRIs. For many people, these side effects diminish after they have taken the drug for a few weeks, so they may be encouraged to stick with the drug even if they are experiencing side effects, in hopes that the side effects will decrease and the positive effects of the drug will begin to be apparent.

In recent years, there have been many books and articles praising the serotonin reuptake inhibitors, not only for their antidepressant effects, but for an ability to change people's basic personalities (e.g., Kramer, 1993). Until recently, these claims have been made only on the basis of clinical observation, and not scientific results. In *Pushing the Boundaries:* Can the Serotonin Reuptake Inhibitors Change Your Personality? (p. 282), we examine the first solid evidence regarding the effects of serotonin reuptake inhibitors on normal personality.

There are a number of other drugs that have been introduced for the treatment of depression in the last decade that share some similarities with the SSRIs or the older antidepressants, but cannot be classified in one of the previous categories (see Table 8.9). These are generally referred to as the "second-generation antidepressants." One of the most widely used is bupropion (trade name Wellbutrin or Zyban). Bupropion affects the norepinephrine and dopamine systems (Stahl, 1998). It may be especially useful in people suffering from psychomotor retardation, anhedonia, hypersomnia, cognitive slowing, inattention and craving (e.g., buproprion can help people stop craving cigarettes). In addition, bupropion appears to overcome the sexual side effects of the SSRIs and thus is sometimes used in conjunction with them. The side effects of bupropion can include agitation, insomnia, nausea, and seizures.

Although there is now a large selection of drug therapies available for the treatment of depression, there are no consistent rules for determining which of the antidepressant drugs to try first with a depressed patient (Nemeroff & Schatzberg, 1998). Many clinicians begin with the serotonin reuptake inhibitors, because their side effects tend to be less significant. Depressed people often must try several different drugs before finding one that will work well for them and has tolerable side effects. When they find the drug that works for them, it is often as if they have regained their lives:

Voices

And then something just kind of changed in me. Over the next few days, I became all right, safe in my own skin. It happened just like that. One morning I woke up, and I really did want to live, really looked forward to greeting the day, imagined errands to run, phone calls to return, and it was not with a feeling of great dread, not with the sense that the first person who stepped on my toe as I walked through the square may well have driven me to suicide. It was as if the miasma of depression had lifted off me, gone smoothly about its business, in the same way that the fog in San Francisco rises as the day wears on.

(Wurtzel, 1995, p. 329)

Electroconvulsive Therapy for Depression

Perhaps the most controversial of the biological treatments for depression is **electroconvulsive therapy,** or *ECT.* ECT was introduced in the early twentieth century, originally as a treatment for schizophrenia. Italian physicians Ugo Cerlettii and Lucio Bini decided to experiment with the use of ECT to treat people with schizophrenia, reasoning that ECT could calm them much like experiencing an epileptic seizure would calm and sedate epileptics. Eventually, clinicians found that ECT was not effective for schizophrenia, but it was effective for depression.

ECT consists of a series of treatments in which a brain seizure is induced by passing electrical current

PUSHING THE BOUNDARIES

Can the Serotonin Reuptake Inhibitors Change Your Personality?

In the United States, over 1 million prescriptions are filled each month for Prozac alone, and annual sales of Prozac top $3 billion. Most of these prescriptions are filled for people who do not meet the diagnostic criteria for depression or any other psychological disorder but want some help in dealing with the stresses they are facing or with moderate levels of distress they are experiencing. They are responding, in part, to testimonials from patients and clinicians that the serotonin reuptake inhibitors can improve people's personalities—making them more self-confident, less shy, and so on (Kramer, 1993). But is this true?

Until recently, we had no way of knowing. Then some clever scientists decided to put the claims that selective serotonin reuptake inhibitors (SSRIs) can change personality in average people to the test (Knutson et al., 1998). They administered Paxil (paroxetine) to 26 healthy volunteers, who were free of depression, for 4 weeks. They chose Paxil because it is a relatively potent and specific inhibitor of serotonin reuptake compared to some of the other SSRIs. They also administered a placebo to another group of healthy volunteers for 4 weeks. Neither the volunteers nor the researchers knew which type of pill an individual volunteer was taking. Personality and social behaviors were assessed in the volunteers 1 week and 4 weeks into the study by having them complete questionnaires and work together with other people on a puzzle task while being observed.

The volunteers who took Paxil became less irritable and hostile toward others, and were more likely to engage in positive social behavior in the puzzle task than volunteers who took the placebo. In addition, the higher the level of Paxil evident in the blood of the volunteers who took the drug, the more their irritability and hostility declined and the more their positive social behavior increased.

These results seem to suggest that Paxil truly did change the healthy volunteers' personalities and social behaviors. It seemed to do so, however, largely by changing their moods. The volunteers who took Paxil showed a significant reduction in negative mood, which fully accounted for the changes in their personalities and social behaviors. This suggests that Paxil may have not had a direct effect on personality and behavior, but an indirect effect by relieving any negative mood the volunteers may have been experiencing.

Quite apart from these scientific findings, we can ask whether it is appropriate for people who are not significantly depressed, anxious, or suffering from any other psychological disorder, to use the serotonin reuptake inhibitors to ease everyday distress. Is this how we, as a society, want these drugs to be used? Is it appropriate for people to be exposed to the potential side effects of these drugs to lift their moods a bit? These social issues, as well as remaining scientific questions about the effects of SSRIs on normal personality, will remain at the center of debates for years to come.

through the patient's brain. Patients are first anesthetized and given muscle relaxants so that they are not conscious when they have the seizure and so that their muscles do not jerk violently during the seizure. Metal electrodes are taped to the head, and a current of 70 to 130 volts is passed through one side of the brain for about one-half of a second. Patients typically go into a convulsion, which lasts about 1 minute. The full ECT treatment consists of 6 to 12 sessions.

ECT is most often given to depressed people who have not responded to drug therapies, and it relieves depression in 50 to 60 percent of these people (Thase & Kupfer, 1996). ECT seems particularly effective in psychotic depression (Coryell, 1998). It is not entirely clear how ECT lifts depression. The seizures may increase the permeability of the blood-brain barrier, allowing the antidepressant medications more fully into the brain. When animals are given ECT, they show an acute release of norepinephrine and dopamine. If this also happens in humans, which is unclear, it may be the mechanism by which depression is decreased. Alternately, ECT may work because it causes a severe stimulation of the hypothalamus, a part of the brain that regulates sleep, eating, sexual drive, and emotion. ECT appears to be especially effective for depressed people suffering from weight loss, loss of sexual drive, and insomnia. The most recent theories about how ECT works suggest that it increases the number and sensitivity of a specific type of receptor for serotonin.

ECT is controversial for several reasons. First, there were reports in the past of ECT being used as a punishment for patients who were unruly, as was depicted in the movie *One Flew Over the Cuckoo's Nest*. Second, ECT can lead to memory loss and difficulties in learning new information. When ECT was first developed, it was administered to both sides of the brain, and the effects on memory and learning were sometimes severe and permanent. These days, ECT is usually delivered only to one side of the brain, usually the right side because it is less involved in learning and memory. As a result, patients undergoing modern ECT do not tend to experience significant or long-term memory or learning difficulties (Swartz, 1995). Because this unilateral administration is sometimes not as effective as bilateral administration, some people are still given bilateral ECT. Third, although ECT can be extremely effective in eliminating the symptoms of depression, the relapse rate among people who have undergone ECT is as high as 85 percent (Swartz, 1995). Fourth, perhaps the strongest reason ECT is controversial is that the idea of having electrical current passed through one's brain is very frightening and seems like a primitive form of treatment.

Still, ECT is sometimes the only form of treatment that works for severely depressed patients. One survey found that about 10 percent of people admitted to the inpatient psychiatric wards of general hospitals in the United States with diagnoses of recurrent major depression received ECT (Olfson et al., 1998). The people most likely to receive ECT were older, White, privately insured, and more affluent. It may be that people of color, and poor people do not have access to ECT in the hospitals in their neighborhoods. In addition, ECT is used more frequently in eastern and midwestern states than in western states. This may be because ECT is regulated more closely, and frowned upon more, in western states such as California. Those people who did receive ECT early in their hospital stay had shorter stays than those who did not, suggesting they recovered more quickly from their depression.

Light Therapy

We noted earlier that seasonal affective disorder, or SAD, is a form of mood disorder in which people become depressed during the winter months when there are the fewest hours of daylight. Their moods then brighten in summer months, when there is more

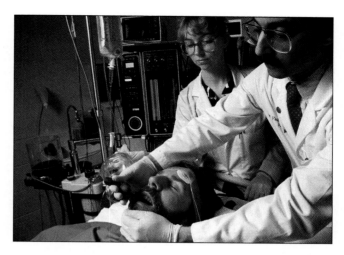

Electroconvulsive therapy is used to treat serious depressions, particularly those that do not respond to drug treatments.

daylight each day. It turns out that people with SAD who are exposed to bright lights for a few hours each day during the winter months often experience complete relief from their depression within a couple of days (Rosenthal, 1993).

Light therapy may help to reduce seasonal affective disorder by resetting depressed people's circadian rhythms. Circadian rhythms are natural cycles of biological activities that occur every 24 hours. The production of several hormones and neurotransmitters varies over the course of the day according to circadian rhythms. These rhythms are regulated by internal clocks but can be affected by environmental stimuli, including light. Depressed people sometimes show disregulation of their circadian rhythms. Light therapy may work by resetting circadian rhythms and thereby normalizing the production of hormones and neurotransmitters (Oren & Rosenthal, 1992; Wehr & Rosenthal, 1989). Another theory is that light therapy works by decreasing levels of the hormone melatonin secreted by the pineal gland. Decreasing melatonin levels can increase levels of norepinephrine and serotonin, thereby reducing the symptoms of depression (Oren & Rosenthal, 1992). Some studies have failed to support the hypothesis that melatonin plays a central role in seasonal affective disorder, however. Finally, recent studies suggest that exposure to bright lights may increase serotonin levels, thereby decreasing depression (Rosenthal, 1995).

Drug Treatments for Bipolar Disorder

There are many fewer drugs available to treat bipolar disorder, because this disorder is understood less well than depression, and because it is more rare. Fortunately, however, recent years have seen an increase in the number of drugs designed to treat bipolar

CONCEPT REVIEW

Drug Treatments for Bipolar Disorder

A number of medications are now available to treat bipolar disorder. Antipsychotic medications are also used in the treatment of bipolar disorder. These medications are discussed in detail in Chapter 10.

Class	Generic Name
Lithium	Lithium carbonate
	Lithium citrate
Anticonvulsants	Carbamazepine
	Valproic acid
	Divalproex sodium
Calcium channel blockers	Verapamil
	Nimodipine

disorder (see *Concept Review:* Drug Treatments for Bipolar Disorder).

Lithium Lithium is the most common treatment for bipolar disorder. Older studies suggested that between 80 and 90 percent of patients experience significant reductions in their symptoms of bipolar disorder under lithium, but more recent studies suggest the response rate is only 30 to 50 percent (Goodwin & Jamison, 1990; Thase & Kupfer, 1996). Lithium seems to stabilize a number of neurotransmitter systems, including serotonin and dopamine systems (Lenox & Manji, 1995). Recent work also suggests that lithium stabilizes levels of the neurotransmitter glutamate (Dixon & Hokin, 1998). Lithium appears to be more effective in reducing the symptoms of mania than the symptoms of depression. People with bipolar disorder are often prescribed lithium to help curb their mania and an antidepressant drug to curb their depression (Frances et al., 1998).

Most people with bipolar disorder take lithium even when they have no symptoms of mania or depression, in order to prevent relapses. Approximately 80 percent of patients maintained on adequate doses of lithium do not relapse into new episodes of bipolar disorder (Keller & Baker, 1991; Maj et al., 1998; Tondo et al., 1997). In contrast, the majority of patients not maintained on lithium experience relapses of their disorder. In addition, a review of 22 studies indicates a six-fold decrease in suicide rates among bipolar patients on lithium compared to bipolar patients not taking lithium (Tondo, Jamison, & Baldessarini, 1997).

Although lithium has literally been a lifesaver for many people with bipolar disorder, it poses some problems. First, there are enormous differences among people in their rates of absorbing lithium, so the proper dosage varies greatly from one person to the

next. Second, the difference between an effective dose of lithium and a toxic dose is small, leaving a very narrow window of therapeutic effectiveness. Thus, people who take lithium must be monitored carefully by physicians who can determine whether the dosage of lithium is adequate to relieve the symptoms of bipolar disorder but not too large to induce toxic side effects.

The side effects of lithium range from annoying to life-threatening. Many patients experience abdominal pain, nausea, vomiting, diarrhea, tremors, and twitches. Says Kay Jamison,

Voices

I found myself beholden to a medication that also caused severe nausea and vomiting many times a month—I often slept on my bathroom floor with a pillow under my head and my warm, woolen St. Andrews gown tucked over me. I have been violently ill more places than I choose to remember, and quite embarrassingly so in public places.

(Jamison, 1995b, p. 93)

People on lithium complain of blurred vision and problems in concentration and attention that interfere with their ability to work. Lithium can cause diabetes and kidney dysfunction, and can contribute to birth defects if taken by pregnant women during the first trimester of their pregnancy.

It is not surprising that many people with bipolar disorder will not take lithium or go on and off of it, against their physicians' advice. In addition to experiencing side effects, many patients complain that they miss the positive symptoms of their mania—the elated moods, flowing ideas, and heightened self-esteem—and feel washed-out on lithium. Especially during periods of calm, they feel they can manage their illness without lithium and that they can detect when a new episode is coming and go back on the medication then. Usually, however, as a new episode of mania becomes more and more severe, their judgment becomes more impaired, and they do not go back on the lithium.

Anticonvulsants, antipsychotics, and calcium channel blockers Sometimes lithium does not overcome mania, and even if it is effective, some people cannot tolerate its side effects. Three other classes of drugs, **anticonvulsant drugs, antipsychotic drugs,** and **calcium channel blockers** are alternatives to lithium for the treatment of mania (see *Concept Review:* Drug Treatments for Bipolar Disorder).

The most commonly prescribed anticonvulsants are carbamazepine (trade name Tegretol) and valproic acid (trade names Depakene and Valproate) or divalproex sodium (trade name Depakote). These drugs can be highly effective in reducing the symptoms of severe and acute mania, although it is not clear they are as effective as lithium in the long-term treatment of bipolar disorder, and thus lithium is still usually used first, before the anticonvulsants are used (Post et al., 1998). The side effects of carbamazepine include blurred vision, fatigue, vertigo, dizziness, rash, nausea, and drowsiness (Goodwin & Jamison, 1990). Valproic acid and divalproex sodium seem to induce many fewer side effects and are now used more often than carbamazepine (Frances et al., 1998). But the anticonvulsants can cause birth defects if women take them while pregnant. The anticonvulsants have effects on a multitude of neurotransmitters, but the mechanism by which anticonvulsants reduce mania is not yet clear (McElroy & Keck, 1996).

The antipsychotic drugs, which are described in more detail in Chapter 10, are also used to quell the symptoms of severe mania (Frances et al., 1998; Post et al., 1998). These drugs reduce functional levels of dopamine and seem especially useful in the treatment of psychotic manic symptoms. They have many neurological side effects, however, the most severe of which is an irreversible condition known as *tardive dyskinesia*. People with tardive dyskinesia have uncontrollable tics and movements of their face and limbs. Newer drugs, such as clozapine and risperidone, do not induce these neurological side effects, and are being investigated for use in bipolar disorder (Post et al., 1998).

Most recently, drugs known as calcium channel blockers, such as verapamil and nimodipine, have been shown to be effective in treating mania in some, but not all, studies (Post et al., 1998). The calcium channel blockers are safe for women to take during pregnancy. They seem to induce fewer side effects than lithium and perhaps the anticonvulsants, but can create dizziness, headache, nausea, and tachycardia. It is not currently known how these drugs work to lower mania.

Combined drug treatment and psychotherapy Studies have shown that combining drug treatment for bipolar disorder with the psychological therapies we discuss below may reduce the rate at which patients stop taking their medications and may lead more patients to achieve full remission of their symptoms, compared to lithium treatment alone (Milkowitz, 1996; Miller, Norman, & Keitner, 1989). Psychotherapy can help people with bipolar disorder understand and accept their need for lithium treatment. It also can help them cope with the impact of the disorder on their lives:

Voices

At this point in my existence, I cannot imagine leading a normal life without both taking lithium and having had the benefits of psychotherapy. Lithium prevents my seductive but disastrous highs, diminishes my depressions, clears out the wool and webbing from my disordered thinking, slows me down, gentles me out, keeps me from ruining my career and relationships, keeps me out of a hospital, alive, and makes psychotherapy possible. But, ineffably, psychotherapy *heals*. It makes some sense of the confusion, reins in the terrifying thoughts and feelings, returns some control and hope and possibility of learning from it all. Pills cannot, do not, ease one back into reality; they only bring one back headlong, careening, and faster than can be endured at times. Psychotherapy is a sanctuary; it is a battleground; it is a place I have been psychotic, neurotic, elated, confused, and despairing beyond belief. But, always, it is where I have believed—or have learned to believe—that I might someday be able to contend with all of this.

(Jamison, 1995b, pp. 88–89)

Psychological Treatments for Depression

Each of the psychological theories of depression discussed earlier has led to a treatment designed to overcome the factors that theory asserts causes depression. Thus, behavioral therapy focuses on changing the depressed person's schedule of reinforcements and punishments, cognitive-behavioral therapy focuses both on changing negative cognitions and maladaptive behaviors, and psychodynamic therapy focuses on uncovering unconscious hostility toward others that is the source of the depressive's self-punishment (see *Concept Review: Psychological Treatments for Depression*, p. 286).

Behavioral Therapy

Behavioral therapy for depression focuses on increasing the number of positive reinforcers and decreasing aversive experiences in an individual's life by helping the depressed person change his or her ways of interacting with the environment and other people (Lewinsohn & Gotlib, 1995). Behavioral therapy is designed to be short term, on the order of about 12 weeks.

The first phase of behavioral therapy involves a *functional analysis* of the connections between specific circumstances and the depressed person's symptoms. When does the depressed person feel the worst? Are there any situations in which he or she feels better? The therapist may visit the home of the depressed client to observe his or her interactions with family members. The client may be asked to fill out questionnaires to assess what events he or she finds pleasant and unpleasant. This analysis helps the therapist pinpoint the behaviors and interaction patterns that need to be the focus of therapy. It also helps the client understand the intimate connections between his or her symptoms and daily activities or interactions. This understanding

CONCEPT REVIEW

Psychological Treatments for Depression

Each of the psychological treatments for depression aims to reverse the processes contributing to depression.

Type of Treatment	Proposed Mechanism of Action
Behavioral therapy	Increase positive reinforcers and decrease aversive events by teaching the person new skills for managing interpersonal situations and the environment and engaging in pleasant activities
Cognitive-behavioral therapy	Challenge distorted thinking and help the person learn more adaptive ways of thinking and new behavioral skills
Psychodynamic therapy	Help the person gain insight to unconscious hostility and fears of abandonment to facilitate change in self-concept and behaviors

challenges the client's belief that he or she is the helpless victim of uncontrollable forces and sets the stage for the therapist's suggestions for changes in behavior.

Once the therapist and client identify the circumstances that precipitate the client's depressive symptoms, a variety of strategies can be used to make the necessary changes in the client's life. These generally fall into three categories (Thorpe & Olson, 1997):

1. *Change aspects of the environment that are related to depressive symptoms.* The depressed person may be encouraged to engage in specific rewarding activities and to avoid depressing activities. For example, a depressed man who typically spent all evening sitting in front of the television being bored and depressed might be encouraged to take a half-hour walk around his neighborhood every evening and to limit his television-watching to 1 hour.

2. *Teach the depressed person skills to change his or her negative circumstances, particularly negative social interactions.* For example, a depressed woman who felt her relationship with her child was "out of control" would be taught parenting skills so that she interacted more effectively and pleasantly with her child.

3. *Teach the client mood-management skills that can be used in unpleasant situations.* It is inevitable that depressed people will find themselves in unpleasant situations some of the time. The therapist may teach the depressed person to use strategies such as relaxation techniques (see Chapter 6) to reduce negative symptoms even while an unpleasant event is happening.

These various strategies must be woven together to meet the specific needs of an individual depressed client. For example, consider the following case (adapted from Yapko, 1997).

CASE STUDY

Mark worked constantly. When he was not actually at work, he was working at home. He had a position of considerable responsibility, and was convinced that if he didn't stay focused on his job, he'd miss something that would result in his being fired or kicked off the career ladder. Mark had not taken a vacation in several years. Although he wanted to continue to get pay raises and promotions, as he has each year, he was also painfully aware that life was passing him by. He felt stressed, depressed, and hopeless about ever having a "normal" life.

Mark clearly felt rewarded for his one-dimensional life with praise, pay raises, promotions, and the absence of mistakes for which he might get punished. Mark's behavior was governed by his work focus. He engaged in no social activities, lived alone, and did not organize his time to include anything but his work.

The behavioral therapist suggested that if he wanted to improve his quality of life, and his outlook on life, he must learn some very specific new behaviors. Mark was encouraged to organize his schedule so that he'd have time for social and recreational opportunities. He learned he needed to actively and deliberately do things that are fun and pleasurable. The therapist practiced with him new ways to meet people and form social relationships (friendships, dating). The therapist also taught him relaxation skills to reduce his stress. Eventually, Mark felt a new sense of control over his life and his depression lifted.

Controlled studies of the effectiveness of behavioral therapy for depression have supported its usefulness, particularly with mildly and moderately depressed people (Lewinsohn & Gotlib, 1995; Teri & Lewinsohn, 1986).

Cognitive-Behavioral Therapy

Cognitive-behavioral therapy represents a blending of cognitive and behavioral theories of depression (Beck

Date	Event	Emotion	Automatic thoughts
April 4	Boss seemed annoyed.	Sad, anxious, worried	Oh, what have I done now? If I keep making him mad, I'm going to get fired.
April 5	Husband didn't want to make love.	Sad	I'm so fat and ugly.
April 7	Boss yelled at another employee.	Anxious	I'm next.
April 9	Husband said he's taking a long business trip next month.	Sad, defeated	He's probably got a mistress somewhere. My marriage is falling apart.
April 10	Neighbor brought over some cookies.	A little happy, mostly sad	She probably thinks I can't cook. I look like such a mess all the time. And my house was a disaster when she came in!

FIGURE 8.15   An Automatic Thoughts Record Used in Cognitive-Behavioral Therapy. In cognitive-behavioral therapy, patients keep records of the negative thoughts that arise when they feel negative emotions. These records are then used in therapy to challenge the patient's depressing thinking.

et al., 1974; Ellis & Harper, 1961; Lewinsohn et al., 1986; Rehm, 1977). There are two general goals in this therapy. First, it aims to change negative, hopeless patterns of thinking described by the cognitive models of depression. Second, it aims to help depressed people solve concrete problems in their lives and develop skills for being more effective in their worlds so that they no longer have the deficits in reinforcers described by behavioral theories of depression.

Like behavioral therapy, cognitive-behavioral therapy is designed to be brief and time-limited. The therapist and client will usually agree on a set of goals that they wish to accomplish in 6 to 12 weeks. These goals focus on specific problems that clients believe are connected to their depression, such as problems in their marriage or dissatisfaction with their job. From the very beginning of therapy, the therapist urges clients to "take charge" of the therapy as much as possible, setting goals and making decisions themselves rather than relying on the therapist to give them all the answers.

Cognitive techniques The first step in cognitive-behavioral therapy is to help clients discover the negative automatic thoughts they habitually have and to understand the link between those thoughts and their depression. Often, the therapist will assign clients the homework of keeping track of times when they feel sad or depressed and writing down on sheets such as the one in Figure 8.15 what is going through their mind at such times. Clients often report that they did not realize the types of thoughts that went through their head when certain types of events would happen. For example, the client whose automatic thought record is given in Figure 8.15 did not realize that she had catastrophic thoughts about losing her job every time her boss was a little cross with her.

The second step in cognitive-behavioral therapy is to help clients challenge their negative thoughts. Depressed people often believe that there is only one way to interpret a situation—their negative way. Therapists will use a series of questions to help clients consider alternative ways of thinking about a situation and the pros and cons of these alternatives, such as "What is the evidence that you are right in the way you are interpreting this situation?" "Are there other ways of looking at this situation?" and "What can you do if the worst-case scenario comes true?" Of course, these questions that a cognitive-behavioral therapist asks don't always move the client toward more positive ways of thinking about the situation. It is important for the therapist also to be flexible in pursuing a line of questions or comments, dropping approaches that are not helpful and trying new approaches to which the client might respond better.

The third step in cognitive-behavioral therapy is to help clients recognize the deeper, basic beliefs or assumptions they might hold that are feeding their depression. These basic beliefs might be ones such as "If I'm not loved by everyone, I'm a failure" or "If I'm not a complete success at everything, my life is worthless." The therapist will help clients question these beliefs and decide if they truly want to live their life according to these beliefs. The case of Susan will illustrate some of the cognitive components of cognitive-behavioral therapy (adapted from Thorpe & Olson, 1997, pp. 225–227):

> Susan was seen for 14 sessions of psychotherapy. She was a young, single, 24-year-old woman. Her goals for therapy were to learn how to overcome chronic feelings of depression and to learn how to deal with temptations to overeat. Susan was unemployed and living with her aunt and uncle in a rural area. She had no means of personal transportation. Hypersensitivity to the reactions of significant others and the belief that they could control her feelings seemed to be central to her low self-concept and feelings of helplessness. Susan described her mother as knowing which "buttons to push." This metaphor was examined and challenged. She was questioned as to how her mother controlled her emotions: Where were these buttons? Did they have a physical reality? Once again, the principle was asserted that it is not the actions of others that cause emotions, but one's cognitions about them. Then the cognitions she had concerning certain looks or critical statements were examined. When her aunt was looking "sickly and silent," Susan believed that it was because she was displeased with her for not helping enough. The evidence for this belief was examined, and there was none. Alternative explanations were explored, such as the aunt might be truly ill, having a bad day, or upset with her spouse. Susan admitted that all explanations were equally plausible. Furthermore, it was noted that in ambiguous social situations, she tended to draw the most negative and personalized conclusions.
>
> Her consistent tendency to evaluate her self-worth in terms of her family's approval was examined. Susan still had fantasies of her family becoming like the "Walton" family (e.g., a "normal" family that was loving and accepting of one another. Instead her own family was distant and argumentative with one another). Susan began to let go of this fantasy and grieved over this loss. Once this had been done, she began to gain a better understanding of how her current cognitive distortions could be related to overconcern with familial approval. As she began to let go of her desire to live up to imagined expectations, she stopped seeing herself as a failure.

Several forms of psychotherapy help clients resolve conflicts in their relationships that are leading to depression.

During the last stage of therapy, Susan's mother visited. This provided a real test of the gains she had made, as it was her mother's criticism that Susan feared the most. At first, she reported feeling easily wounded by her mother's criticism. These examples were used as opportunities to identify and challenge self-defeating thoughts. Soon, Susan was able to see her mother's critical statements as her mother's problem, not her own. She also discovered that as she became better at ignoring her mother's critical remarks and not taking them to heart, her mother began to be more relaxed and open around her, and criticized her less.

Behavioral techniques Cognitive-behavioral therapists also use the behavioral techniques we discussed earlier to train clients in new skills they might need to cope better in their life. Often depressed people are unassertive in making requests of other people or in standing up for their rights and needs. This unassertiveness can be the result of their negative automatic thoughts. For example, a person who often thinks, "I can't ask for what I need because the other person might get mad, and that would be horrible," is not likely to make even reasonable requests of other people. The therapist will first help clients recognize the thoughts behind their actions (or lack of action). Then the therapist may work with clients to devise exercises or homework assignments in which the client practices new skills, such as assertiveness skills, between therapy sessions.

Cognitive-behavioral therapy has proven quite effective in treating depression, including major depression. Several studies have shown that about 60 to 70 percent of depressed people experience full relief from their symptoms with 12 weeks of cognitive therapy (Craighead, Craighead, & Ilardi, 1998; Robinson et al., 1990). Cognitive-behavioral therapy has been successfully adapted for the treatment of depressed children and older persons (Futterman et al., 1995; Gilham et al., 1995; Lewinsohn et al., 1990).

Psychodynamic Therapy

In **psychodynamic therapy,** the therapist will closely observe a depressed client's behavior to analyze the sources of his or her depression, just as a behavioral or cognitive therapist will. The types of behavior the psychodynamic therapist examines, and the therapist's assumptions about potential causes of that behavior, are very different from those that concern the behavioral or cognitive therapist.

The psychodynamic therapist will closely observe the client's *transference* to the therapist—the ways in which the client treats the therapist as though the therapist were someone else, such as a parent—with the assumption that the client's transference represents unconscious conflicts and concerns the client has with important people in his or her life. The therapist will also observe the client's recollections of both recent events and distant events, searching for themes of abandonment, hostility, and disappointment. The therapist may listen to the client's recounting of dreams for further clues as to the unconscious concerns behind the depression. The therapist will acknowledge and interpret the themes he or she observes in the client's behaviors and recollections, to help the client gain insight and accept these unconscious concerns, and move beyond them.

Although it may seem necessary to have insight to fully gain control over one's depression, long-term psychodynamic therapy has not proven very effective in the treatment of depression (Robinson et al., 1990). The nature of depression may make it particularly unsuitable for long-term psychodynamic therapy. Many depressed people are too overcome by symptoms of lethargy, poor attention and concentration, and a sense of hopelessness to participate in this type of therapy. They may not have the energy or motivation to engage in the long process of uncovering and exploring old psychological wounds. They may be so acutely depressed that they need more immediate relief, particularly if they are suicidal.

Sociocultural Approaches to the Treatment of Depression

Interpersonal therapy is a sociocultural approach to treating depression because it views the depressed person's symptoms in the context of his or her relationships and interpersonal roles. The other two sociocultural approaches to depression we discuss are community-based approaches that focus on educating the public and health care professionals about depression in hopes of getting better treatment to depressed people, and intervening with groups at high risk for depression in hopes of preventing first onsets of depression.

Interpersonal Therapy

There are four types of problems that interpersonal therapists will look for in depressed patients (see *Concept Review: Interpersonal Therapy*). First, many depressed patients truly are grieving the loss of loved

CONCEPT REVIEW

Interpersonal Therapy

Interpersonal therapists tend to focus on four types of interpersonal problems as sources of depression.

Type of Problem	Therapeutic Approach
Grief, loss	Help the client accept feelings and evaluate relationship with lost person; help the client invest in new relationships
Interpersonal role disputes	Help the client make decisions about concessions willing to be made and learn better ways of communicating
Role transitions	Help the client develop more realistic perspectives toward roles that are lost and regard new roles in a more positive manner
Interpersonal skills deficits	Review the client's past relationships, helping the client understand these relationships and how they might be affecting current relationships; directly teach the client social skills, such as assertiveness

ones, perhaps not from death but from the breakup of important relationships. Interpersonal therapists help clients face such losses and explore their feelings about the losses. Often clients idealize the people they lost, feeling as if they will never have relationships as good. Therapists help clients reconstruct their relationships with the lost loved ones, recognizing both the good and bad aspects of the relationships and developing more balanced views of the relationships. Therapists also help clients let go of the past relationships and begin to invest in new relationships.

The second type of problem interpersonal therapy focuses on is interpersonal role disputes. Such disputes arise when the people in a relationship do not agree on their roles in the relationship. For example, a husband and wife may disagree on the proper roles each should play in relation to their children. Or a college student and a parent may disagree on the extent to which the student should follow the parent's wishes in choosing a career. Interpersonal therapists first help the clients recognize the disputes and then guide clients in making choices about concessions they are or are not willing to make to the other people in the relationships. Therapists may also need to help clients modify and improve their patterns of communicating with others in relationships. For example, a student who resents his parents' intrusions into his private life may tend to withdraw and sulk rather than directly confront his parents about their intrusions. He would be helped in developing more effective ways of communicating his distress over his parents' intrusions.

The third type of problem addressed in interpersonal therapy is role transitions, such as the transition from college to work or from work to full-time motherhood. Sometimes people become depressed out of grief over the roles they must leave behind. Therapists help clients develop more realistic perspectives toward roles that are lost and help clients regard new roles in more positive manners. If clients feel unsure about their capabilities in new roles, therapists help them develop a sense of mastery in the new roles. Sometimes clients need help in developing new networks of social support within their new roles, to replace the support systems they left behind in old roles.

The fourth type of problem depressed people bring to interpersonal therapy involves deficits in interpersonal skills. Such skill deficits can be the reason that depressed people have inadequate social support networks. Therapists review with clients past relationships, especially important childhood relationships, helping clients understand these relationships and how they might be affecting current relationships. Therapists might also directly teach clients social skills, such as assertiveness.

Interpersonal therapy has been shown to be highly effective in the treatment of depression, with 60 to 80 percent of depressed people recovering during this form of therapy (Craighead et al., 1998; Markowitz & Weissman, 1995). Like cognitive-behavioral therapy, interpersonal therapy has been successfully adapted for treatment of children and older adults with depression. It can be used both in individual therapy and in group therapy settings.

Community Based Interventions: The Depression/Awareness, Recognition, and Treatment Program

We noted at the beginning of this chapter that many people with a mood disorder do not seek any kind of treatment, or wait for years before they seek treatment. When they do seek treatment, many people turn to their general practice physicians and not to mental-health specialists for care, perhaps because of limitations imposed on their access to mental-health professionals by insurance and managed health care companies (Rost et al., 1998). Although general practice physicians are increasingly seeking education in the proper treatment for mood disorders, studies suggest that most people with mood disorders frequently receive inadequate treatment (such as doses of medications that are too low or inappropriate types of psychotherapy) (Hirschfeld et al., 1997).

An innovative program organized by the National Institute of Mental Health (NIMH) of the U.S. federal government is trying to educate the public and health professionals about depression and the available treatments for depression. The Depression/Awareness, Recognition, and Treatment (D/ART) program was established in 1985 as a collaboration between the government and community organizations to benefit the mental health of the American public. D/ART's mission is threefold:

- Increasing the public recognition of the symptoms of depression and expanding knowledge of where to get professional diagnosis and treatment.

- Fostering help-seeking behaviors and more appropriate use of mental-health care systems.

- Providing health and mental-health specialists with up-to-date knowledge about effective treatments for depressive disorders.

The major components of the D/ART program include a public education campaign, a professional training program, and a national worksite program. The public education campaign has included print ads and TV and radio public service announcements, fact

Studies have shown that first onsets of depression in youngsters may be prevented or delayed by a cognitive-behavioral intervention program.

sheets, flyers, and brochures for the public, and a video educational package, all designed to educate the public on depression and to encourage help-seeking. In addition, dozens of local community organizations work in conjunction with the D/ART program to conduct educational activities and media campaigns at a local level.

The professional training program is designed to improve the treatment of depression by general practice physicians as well as mental-health professionals. The program emphasizes reaching practitioners who deal with underserved populations, such as poor people in rural areas. The D/ART program has extended grants and contracts to medical schools and certain professional associations to develop courses on depression and seminars at professional meetings. The program also makes a variety of brochures and pamphlets available to physicians, which they can give to patients or have available in the waiting rooms of their offices.

The national worksite program helps major corporations develop avenues for recognizing and managing depression in the workplace. Human resource managers are educated about depression, and corporate leaders are encouraged to view depression as a medical illness that can reduce productivity and increase employee health costs, but which can be effectively treated.

The D/ART program is an example of the government working with clinicians, scientists, and community leaders to acknowledge and effectively deal with a common mental-health problem. More information about the D/ART program, including order forms for brochures on depression, is available by calling 1-800-421-4211 or on the D/ART Web site (www.nimh.nih.gov/dart/darthome.htm).

Preventing First Onsets of Depression

Given the devastating effects depression can have on people's lives, particularly when it first arises during childhood, an important goal for the future is to prevent depression in vulnerable people before it ever begins. Although there are many small-scale programs conducted by individual schools or community organizations that seek to prevent depression and other mental-health problems, there has been little research on the effectiveness of different kinds of programs.

An ambitious program of research being conducted by psychologists at the University of Pennsylvania is designed to fill that gap (Jaycox et al., 1994; Gillham et al., 1995). The Depression Prevention Project focuses on children in elementary schools in the Philadelphia area. The studies done to date have targeted 10- to 13-year-old children thought to be at risk for future depressions because they either already had mild symptoms of depression or they had parents who often argued with each other. None of these children had yet had a serious depression prior to the beginning of the studies, however.

In the first of this series of studies, children were randomly assigned to a control group or to the experimental group, which we will refer to as the prevention group. The prevention group received therapy designed to help them overcome negative ways of thinking and to learn more effective problem-solving techniques. The children met in small groups with an advanced graduate student in clinical psychology for 2-hour sessions after school. Across a total of 12 sessions, the children learned to identify negative ways of thinking and to challenge their negative thoughts. They practiced being assertive, rather than passive or aggressive, in difficult situations with their peers and in their families.

Happily, the children in the prevention group got some immediate benefit from this intervention: Their levels of depressive symptoms declined over the course of the 12 sessions. The remarkable finding of this study was that the intervention really did seem to reduce risk of future depression in these children (see Figure 8.16). Over the 2 years after the intervention ended, a relatively low percentage of the children who received it developed moderate-to-severe depressive symptoms. In contrast, many of the children in the control group developed moderate-to-severe depressive symptoms. This study gives us hope that many vulnerable children can be spared from the debilitating effects of depressive episodes.

Comparisons of Cognitive-Behavioral, Interpersonal, and Drug Therapies

So which of these many treatments for depression is the best? In the last few decades, several studies have compared cognitive-behavioral therapy, interpersonal therapy, and drug therapies with each other. Perhaps surprisingly, these three therapies, despite their vast differences, appear equally effective for the treatment of most people with depression (see DeRubeis et al., 1999; Hollon et al., 1992; Jacobson & Hollon, 1996). The largest study comparing these therapies was the Collaborative Treatment of Depression Study sponsored by the National Institute of Mental Health (Elkin et al., 1989). In this study, 250 patients with major depressive disorders were randomly assigned to undergo interpersonal therapy, cognitive-behavioral therapy, antidepressant therapy (with imipramine), or pill placebo treatment. After 16 weeks of treatment, the patients in all the groups showed significant reductions in depression. Interpersonal therapy, cognitive therapy, and imipramine appeared to work equally well.

One of the unexpected findings from this study was that the patients in the pill placebo group also tended to improve significantly. Although these patients were not receiving an active drug, they had regular meetings with a psychiatrist who asked them about their symptoms and their lives and gave them advice when asked. The remarkable effectiveness of the placebo treatment suggests that interacting with a warm and caring professional can be quite helpful to a depressed person, even when that professional is not delivering any specific type of therapy. A number of other studies have shown that the relationship between a

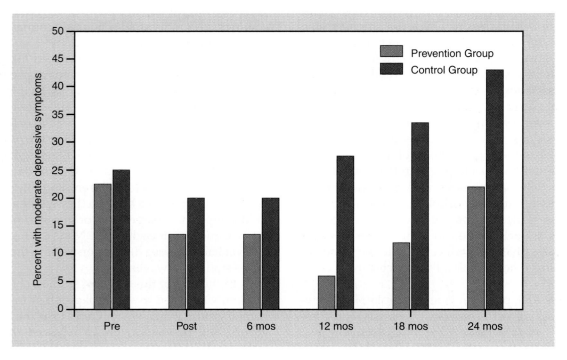

FIGURE 8.16 Results of the Depression Prevention Project. A prevention program that taught children at risk for depression cognitive-behavioral skills reduced their propensity to develop depression over time.

Source: Gillham et al., 1995.

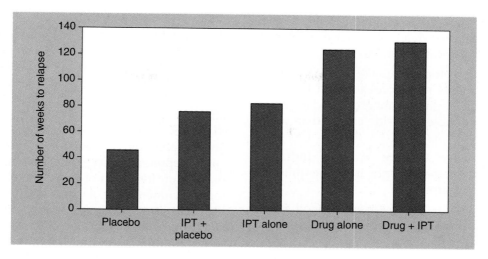

FIGURE 8.17 Effects of Antidepressants and IPT in Preventing Relapse of Depression. Patients maintained on either IPT or antidepressant drugs avoided relapse longer than did patients on placebos.

Source: Frank et al., 1991.

depressed patient and therapist is an important predictor of recovery: Depressed patients who develop a warm and trusting relationship with their therapists recover faster and more fully than those who do not (Burns & Nolen-Hoeksema, 1992; Orlinsky & Howard, 1986).

Although cognitive-behavioral therapy, interpersonal therapy, and the antidepressant drugs all led to substantial relief for the depressed patients in the NIMH study, the drug therapy tended to work faster than the two psychosocial therapies and some (but not all) analyses suggested it was more effective for the severely depressed patients. This finding has not been replicated in other large studies, however (Hollon et al., 1992; Schulberg, Pilkonis, & Houck, 1998). On the other hand, one consistent finding across several studies, including the NIMH study, is that patients who receive cognitive-behavioral therapy or interpersonal therapy were less likely than those who received drug therapy to relapse into new episodes of depression over the 2 years after their treatments had ended (Evans et al., 1992; Hollon et al., 1991; Jacobson & Hollon, 1996; Shea et al., 1992).

The relapse rates in depression are quite high, even among people whose depressions completely disappear in treatment. This has led many psychiatrists and psychologists to argue that people with a history of recurrent depression should be kept on a maintenance dose of therapy even after their depression is relieved (Hirschfeld, 1994). Usually, the maintenance therapy is a drug therapy; many people remain on antidepressant drugs for years after their initial episodes of depression have passed. Studies of interpersonal therapy and cognitive-behavioral therapy show that maintenance doses of these therapies, usually consisting of once-a-month meetings with therapists, can also substantially reduce relapse (Jarrett et al., 1998; Markowitz & Weissman,

1995; Sacco & Beck, 1995). For example, one study compared the effectiveness of maintenance doses of interpersonal therapy and imipramine in preventing relapse in patients with histories of recurrent depressions (see Figure 8.17). Patients receiving interpersonal therapy avoided relapse for significantly longer than did patients receiving pill placebos. Patients receiving imipramine avoided relapse for even longer than the patients on interpersonal therapy. Patients receiving both imipramine and interpersonal therapy went the longest before relapsing to another episode of depression (Frank, 1991; Frank et al., 1990).

The bottom line in the treatment of depression is that there is a choice in treatments. Drug therapies, cognitive behavioral therapy, and interpersonal therapy all seem to be effective for the majority of depressed people. The characteristics of a person's depression—how severe it is, how recurrent it is, what stressors or personal issues are associated with it—probably influence which therapy works best for that individual. In addition, people's beliefs about the causes of their depression and about what type of therapy is most appealing may also influence which therapy is best for them. People who have faith in the type of therapy they are receiving and are willing to go along with their therapist's suggestions recover more fully than do those who are skeptical about the effectiveness of their therapy (Burns & Nolen-Hoeksema, 1991; Frank, 1973; Kazdin, 1986).

Summing Up

- Tricyclic antidepressants are effective in treating depression but have some side effects and can be dangerous in overdose.

- The monoamine oxidase inhibitors also are effective treatments for depression but can interact with certain medications and foods.

- The selective serotonin reuptake inhibitors are effective treatments for depression and have become popular because they are less dangerous and have more tolerable side effects than other drug treatments.

- Electroconvulsive therapy involves inducing seizures in depressed people; it can be quite effective but is controversial.

- Lithium is useful in the treatment of mood disorders but requires careful monitoring to prevent dangerous side effects.

- Anticonvulsants, antipsychotics, and calcium channel blockers can also help to relieve mania.

- Behavioral treatment focuses on increasing positive reinforcers and decreasing aversive events by helping clients change their environments, learn social skills, and learn mood-management skills.

- Cognitive-behavioral treatment combines the techniques of behavioral therapy with techniques to identify and challenge depressive thinking patterns.

- Psychodynamic therapy focuses on uncovering unconscious hostility and fears of abandonment through the interpretation of transference, memories, dreams, and resistance.

- Interpersonal therapy seeks to identify and overcome problems with grief, role transitions, interpersonal role disputes, and deficits in interpersonal skills that contribute to depression.

- Community-based programs such as the D/ART program attempt to educate health care professionals and the lay public about depression in hopes of getting depressed people into more effective therapy.

- Some research suggests that interventions targeting high-risk groups can help to prevent or delay first onsets of depression.

❂ BIO-PSYCHO-SOCIAL INTEGRATION

The mood disorders are phenomena of the whole person. Depression and mania involve changes in every aspect of functioning, including biology, cognitions, personality, social skills, and relationships. Some of these changes may be causes of the depression or mania, and some of them may be consequences of the depression or mania. However, the fact that the mood disorders are phenomena of the whole person illustrates the intricate connections among these different aspects of functioning: biology, cognitions, personality, and social interactions. These areas of functioning are so intertwined that major changes in any one area will almost necessarily provoke changes in other areas. Many recent models of the mood disorders, particularly depression, suggest that most people who become depressed carry some sort of vulnerability to depression for much of their life. This may be a biological vulnerability, such as dysfunctions in neurotransmitters systems, or a psychological vulnerability, such as overdependence on others. It is not until these vulnerabilities intersect with certain stressors that a full-blown depression is triggered, however.

Kendler and colleagues (Kendler, 1998; Kendler & Karkowski-Shuman, 1997) have suggested that, in major depression, genetic factors may influence vulnerability to depression by altering the individual's relationship to the environment, in addition to inducing biological abnormalities that directly cause depression. First, genetic factors may increase the individual's sensitivity to stressors in the environment, making it more likely that he or she will react to a stressor with depression. In their large study of twins, they found statistical evidence that being at genetic risk for depression made twins more prone to depression in the face of negative life events. In twins with a low genetic risk for depression (e.g., a monozygotic twin whose co-twin had no history of depression), the probability of a depressive onset given exposure to a severe life event was 6.2%. In twins with a high genetic risk for depression (a monozygotic twin whose co-twin had a history of depression), the probability of depression given exposure to a severe life event was 14.6%.

Second, genetic factors may influence the probability that individuals will select high- versus low-risk environments for the production of depression. People actively help to create their environments by choosing which other people they will spend time with, where they will live, the type of occupation they will pursue, and so on. In their twin studies, Kendler and colleagues (1993) found, not surprisingly, that co-twins often shared the same life events, such as the death of a family member. This seems mostly likely due to environmental factors, specifically having the same family members. But certain other stressors, including being robbed or assaulted or experiencing a major financial stressor, appeared to be due primarily to genetic factors. That is, similarities in the twins' environments could not account for their common risk of experiencing these events. In addition, these events did not seem to be solely the result of both twins being depressed. Kendler and Karkowski-Shuman (1997) suggest that genetic factors may contribute to broad personality characteristics, such as neuroticism or impulsivity, that then lead both to greater risk for negative life events and greater risk for depression. This intriguing hypothesis requires further research.

Fortunately, the interconnections among these areas of functioning may mean that improving functioning in one area can improve function in other areas. Improving people's biological functioning can improve their cognitive and social functioning and their personality. Improving people's cognitive and social functioning can improve their biological functioning, and so on. Thus, although there may be many pathways into mood disorders (biological, psychological, and social), there may also be many pathways out of the mood disorders, particularly depression.

Chapter Summary

- There are two general categories of mood disorder: unipolar depressive disorders and bipolar disorder. People with a unipolar depressive disorder experience only the symptoms of depression (sad mood, loss of interest, disruption in sleep and appetite, retardation or agitation, loss of energy, worthlessness and guilt, suicidality). People with bipolar disorder experience both depression and mania (elated or agitated mood, grandiosity, little need for sleep, racing thoughts and speech, increase in goals and dangerous behavior).

- Within the unipolar depressive disorders, the two major diagnostic categories are major depressive episode and dysthymic disorder. In addition, there are several subtypes of major depression: with melancholic features, with psychotic features, with catatonic features, with atypical features, with postpartum onset, and with seasonal pattern.

- Depression is one of the most common disorders. There are substantial age, gender, and cross-cultural differences in depression. Bipolar disorder is much less common than the depressive disorders. It tends to be a lifelong problem. The length of individual episodes of bipolar disorder varies dramatically from one person to the next and over the life course as in depression, the expression of mania may depend on cultural norms.

- Genetic factors probably play a role in determining vulnerability to the mood disorders, especially bipolar disorder. Disordered genes may lead to dysfunction in the monoamine neurotransmitter systems. The neurotransmitters norepinephrine, serotonin, and dopamine have been implicated in the mood disorders. In addition, people with mood disorders show a number of neurophysiological abnormalities, such as unusual brain-wave activity during sleep and deterioration of the cerebral cortex and cerebellum, as shown in CT and MRI studies. There is evidence that depressed people have chronic hyperactivity in the hypothalamic-pituitary-adrenal axis, which may make them more susceptible to stress.

- Behavioral theories of depression suggest that people with much stress in their lives may have too low a rate of reinforcement and too high a rate of punishment, which then leads to depression. Stressful events can also lead to learned helplessness—the belief that nothing you do can control your environment—which is linked to depression. Most people who are faced with stressful events do not become depressed, however.

- The cognitive theories of depression argue that the ways people interpret the events in their lives determine whether they become depressed. Some evidence suggests that depressed people are actually quite realistic in their negative views of life, and that nondepressed people are unrealistically optimistic about life.

- Psychodynamic theories of depression suggest that depressed people have chronic patterns of negative relationships and tend to internalize their hostility against others.

- Sociocultural theories attribute depression to the effects of maladaptive social roles, low social status, and changes in the social conditions that different generations face. In addition, there appear to be differences across cultures in how depression is manifested.

- Most of the biological therapies for the mood disorders are drug therapies. Three classes of drugs are commonly used to treat depression:

tricyclic antidepressants, monoamine oxidase inhibitors, and selective serotonin reuptake inhibitors. Each of these is highly effective in treating depression, but each has significant side effects. Electroconvulsive therapy is used to treat severe depressions, particularly those that do not respond to drugs. Lithium is the most effective drug for the treatment of bipolar disorder. It has a number of side effects, including nausea, vomiting, diarrhea, tremors, twitches, kidney dysfunction, and birth defects. Alternatives to lithium include anticonvulsant drugs, antipsychotic drugs and calcium channel blockers.

- Behavioral therapies focus on increasing positive reinforcers and decreasing negative events in depressive lives by building their social skills and teaching them how to engage in pleasant activities and cope with their moods. Cognitive-behavioral therapies focus on helping depressed people develop more adaptive ways of thinking and are very effective in treating depression. Psychodynamic therapies help depressed people uncover unconscious hostility and fears of abandonment.

- Interpersonal therapy helps depressed people identify and change their patterns in relationships and is highly effective in treating depression. Community-based programs have been designed to educate the public about depression and to get high-risk groups into treatment to prevent first onsets of depression.

- Direct comparisons of drug therapies with cognitive-behavioral and interpersonal therapies show that they tend to be equally effective in the treatment of depression. Drug therapies may work more quickly than psychosocial therapies, but the psychosocial therapies appear better than the drug therapies at preventing relapse.

Key Terms

Critical Thinking Questions

1. Given that there are no biological tests that prove a person has depression, how can researchers definitively say that people from other cultures can have depression but manifest it with different symptoms from those present in the researchers' own culture?

2. Some studies suggest that there is less of a gender difference in rates of depression among women and men above the age of 65. How would you explain this?

3. What are some reasons why drug therapies and psychosocial therapies might work equally well in the treatment of depression?

4. If depressed people are more realistic about life, is it possible or ethical to try to change their outlook through psychotherapy?

5. What aspects of bipolar disorder do you think it would be most important to address in psychotherapy?

Bernadita Zegers
Florista

Razors pain you;
Rivers are damp;
Acids stain you;
And drugs cause cramp.
Guns aren't lawful;
Nooses give;
Gas smells awful;
You might as well live.

   Dorothy Parker, The Poetry and Short Stories of Dorothy Parker, *1994, p. 62.*

Suicide

CHAPTER OVERVIEW
Defining and Measuring Suicide

Suicide is the intentional taking of one's own life. Suicidal thoughts and behaviors are on a continuum from those representing a clear intention to die to those representing ambivalence about dying. Suicide is the ninth leading cause of death in the United States, and internationally, at least 160,000 people die by suicide and 2 million other people make suicide attempts each year. Women are more likely than men to attempt suicide, but men are more likely than women to complete suicide. There are substantial cross-cultural and age differences in suicide.

Understanding Suicide

Generally, suicide notes are brief and concrete and leave few clues. Sociocultural approaches to suicide have identified several negative life events or circumstances that increase risk for suicide. The influential theorist Emil Durkheim described several types of suicide that result from individuals' relationships to society. Sometimes suicides occur in groups of people, a phenomenon known as suicide clusters or suicide contagion. Psychodynamic theorists attribute suicide to repressed rage that leads to self-destruction. Several mental disorders increase risk for suicide, including depression, bipolar disorder, substance abuse, schizophrenia, and anxiety disorders. Cognitive-behavioral theorists argue that hopelessness and dichotomous thinking contribute to suicide. Impulsivity is a behavioral characteristic common to people who commit suicide. Finally, biological theories attribute suicidality to genetic vulnerabilities and to low serotonin levels.

Extraordinary People:
A Darkness Visible: A Pulitzer Prize–Winning Author Describes Suicidality

Pushing the Boundaries:
Can Low Cholesterol Lead to Suicide?

Treatment and Prevention

Drug treatments for suicidality most often involve lithium or antidepressant medications to reduce impulsive and violent behavior, depression, and mania. Antipsychotic medications and other medications that treat symptoms of an existing mental disorder may also be used. Psychotherapies for suicide are similar to those used for depression. Dialectical behavior therapy has been specifically designed to address skills deficits and thinking patterns in people who are suicidal. Suicide hot lines and crisis intervention programs provide immediate help to people who are highly suicidal. Community prevention programs aim to educate the public about suicide and encourage suicidal people into treatment. Guns are involved in the majority of suicides and some research suggests restricting access to guns can reduce suicide attempts. Society is debating whether people have a right to choose to suicide.

Taking Psychology Personally:
What to Do If a Friend Is Suicidal

Bio-Psycho-Social Integration

Chapter Summary
Key Terms
Critical Thinking Questions

Voices

Do not grieve for me. My nerves are all shot and for the last year I have been in agony day and night—except when I sleep with sleeping pills—and any peace I have by day is when I am drugged by pills.

I have had a wonderful life but it is over and my nerves get worse and I am afraid they will have to take me away. So please forgive me, all those I love and may God forgive me too, but I cannot bear the agony and it is best for everyone this way. . . .

No one is to blame—I have wonderful friends and they do all they can for me. . . . I've tried very hard all I know for a year and it gets worse inside, so please take comfort in knowing I will not suffer anymore. (Quoted in Curtis, 1998, pp. 384–385)

After penning this suicide note, James Whale, director of such film classics as *The Invisible Man*, *Journey's End*, and the *Frankenstein* films, drowned himself in his swimming pool.

Suicide is both an unusual act and a surprisingly familiar one. We can all name movie stars, political leaders, and other people of prominence who killed themselves. Most of us also have come in personal contact with suicide. Nearly half of all teenagers in the United States say that they know someone who has tried to commit suicide (see Figure 9.1; *New York Times*, October 20, 1999). One in five teenagers admits to attempting or seriously contemplating suicide (NIMH,

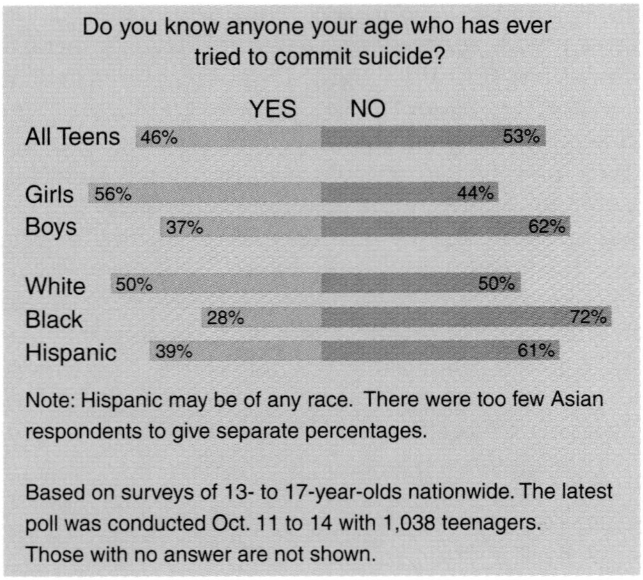

FIGURE 9.1 Teenagers' Experience with Suicide. These are the percentages of teenagers in a national poll who answered "yes" or "no" to the question, "Do you know anyone your age who has ever tried to commit suicide?.

Source: *New York Times*, October 20, 1999, page 1.

2000). Suicide is the ninth leading cause of death in the United States, and third leading cause among people 15 to 24 years of age (NIMH, 2000). More people die from suicide than from homicide.

The impact of suicide on surviving family members and friends can be huge. There is the guilt—over not having prevented the suicide, over things that were said to the person who committed suicide, over things that may have contributed to the suicide. There is the shame and stigma of suicide. And there is the anger at the person who committed suicide.

In this chapter, we try to understand suicide. With the help of biographies and autobiographies, we peer into the minds of people who have attempted or completed suicide to get a glimpse of what they were feeling and thinking. We examine statistics that reveal substantial differences between age groups, genders, and cultural groups in the rates of suicide. We review explanations of why some people commit suicide. Finally, we discuss programs designed to prevent suicide in high-risk groups, and to help survivors of suicide.

◎ DEFINING AND MEASURING SUICIDE

First, however, we need to define **suicide**. This may seem simple—it is the purposeful taking of one's own life. This definition is close to that used by the Centers for Disease Control and Prevention (or CDC), one of the federal agencies in the United States that tracks suicide rates. The CDC says that suicide is "death from injury, poisoning, or suffocation where there is evidence (either explicit or implicit) that the injury was self-inflicted and that the decedent intended to kill himself/herself."

As crisp and clear as this definition seems, there is great variability in the form that suicide takes, and there can be great debate over whether to call particular types of death suicide. We may easily agree that the young man who is despondent and shoots himself in the head has committed suicide. It is harder to agree whether the despondent young man who goes on a drinking binge and then crashes his car into a tree has committed suicide. Is the Indian woman who throws herself on her husband's funeral fire committing suicide? Is the elderly person who refuses life support when dying from a painful disease committing suicide? Is the middle-aged person with severe heart disease who continues to smoke cigarettes, eat fatty foods, and drink excessive alcohol, committing suicide? Clearly, suicidelike behaviors fall on a continuum.

Influential suicide theorist Edwin Shneidman (1963, 1981, 1993) described four different types of people who commit suicide: the death seeker, death initiator, death ignorer, and death darer. **Death seekers**

Mass suicides, such as the suicides of the Heaven's Gate cult may fall into the category of "death ignoring."

clearly and explicitly seek to end their lives. Their intentions to commit suicide may be present for a long period of time, during which they prepare for their death by giving away possessions, writing a will, buying a gun, and so on. More often, their intentions are fleeting, and if they are prevented from committing suicide, they may become ambivalent about their desire to die.

Death initiators also have a clear intention to die, but believe that they are simply hastening an inevitable death. People with serious illnesses who commit suicide often fall into this category. For example, particularly before effective drug treatments for HIV (human immunodeficiency virus) were available, some people infected with HIV committed suicide rather than face the severe illnesses, mental decline, and wasting away that can accompany advanced stages of AIDS (acquired immune deficiency syndrome).

Death ignorers intend to end their lives but do not believe this means the end of their existence. They see their death as the beginning of a new and better life. Mass suicides by members of religious groups, such as the 1997 suicides of 39 members of the Heaven's Gate cult, would fall into this category.

Death darers are ambivalent about dying, and take actions that greatly increase their chances of death,

but do not guarantee they will die. The person who swallows a handful of pills from the medicine cabinet without knowing how lethal they are, then calls a friend, is a death darer. The youngster who randomly loads a gun with one bullet, then points the barrel at his head and pulls the trigger is a death darer. Death darers may often want attention, or to make someone else feel guilty, more than they want to die (Brent et al., 1988).

What about those people who chronically make lifestyle choices that increase their risk for early death, such as the heart patient who continues to smoke cigarettes? Shneidman (1981, 1993) describes acts in which people are indirectly contributing to their own death, perhaps unconsciously, as **subintentional deaths**. Most researchers and theorists, however, reserve the label suicide for deaths that are intentionally caused by the individual.

Suicide Rates

Not surprisingly, it is difficult to obtain accurate suicide rates. The stigma against suicide is a great incentive for labeling a death as anything but a suicide. Sometimes it is absolutely clear that a death was a suicide—a note may be left, the person may have been threatening suicide, a revolver may still be in the victim's hand with powder stains that could only mean a self-inflicted wound. Many deaths are more ambiguous, however, particularly when there were no notes left behind and no clues as to the victim's mental state before the death. Local officials, such as police and coroners, may conspire with family members to label ambiguous deaths as accidents rather than have the family face the questions that come with suicide (Madge & Harvey, 1999). Accurate data on nonlethal suicide attempts are even more difficult to obtain, particularly since over half of people who attempt, but do not complete, suicide never seek professional help and thus may not be detected (Crosby et al., 1999).

As a result, our statistics on the rates of suicide in various groups are probably gross underestimates. Even so, the statistics indicate that suicide is more common than we would like to believe. As we noted earlier, it is the ninth leading cause of death in the United States. More than 31,000 people kill themselves each year in the United States, which averages to nearly 85 people per day or one person every 17 minutes (National Institute of Mental Health [NIMH], 2000). In addition, there are approximately 600,000 nonfatal suicide attempts per year (McIntosh, 1991). As many as 3 percent of the population contemplates suicide at some time in their lives, and between 5 and 16 percent report having had suicidal thoughts at some time (Crosby, Cheltenham, & Sacks, 1999; Statham et al., 1998). Suicide is not just an American phenomenon.

Internationally, at least 160,000 people die by suicide and 2 million other people make suicide attempts each year (McIntosh, 1991).

There are large differences between men and women, age groups, and cultural groups in rates of suicide. We turn to a description of some of these differences.

Gender Differences

We might expect that, since women are more prone to depression than men and depression is often associated with suicide, then rates of suicide in women would be much higher than in men. Indeed, three times more women than men *attempt* suicide. And a study of high school students found that girls were much more likely than boys to have considered or planned a suicide attempt (NIMH, 2000; Lewinsohn et al., 1994). Yet, men and boys are four times more likely than women and girls to complete suicide (Figure 9.2; Kushner, 1995; Moscicki, 1995). This is true across many nations of the world.

The gender difference in rates of completed suicides may be due in part to gender differences in the means of attempting suicide. Men tend to choose more lethal means of suicide than do women (Canetto & Lester, 1995; Crosby et al., 1999). In the United States, men are more likely than women to shoot, stab, or hang themselves. And although guns are still the most common way women commit suicide, women are more likely than men to choose less lethal means, such as drug overdoses. Even if men are often ambivalent about dying, the means they choose to attempt suicide are more likely to be lethal than the means women tend to choose.

Some theorists argue, however, that men tend to be more sure in their intent to die when they attempt suicide than women and this is why they choose more lethal means (Jack, 1992; Linehan, 1973). Men may feel that it is not masculine to be ambivalent about their intent to die or to communicate this intent to others in hopes that they will be prevented. Women, on the other hand, may be more comfortable in using suicide attempts as "cries for help."

Finally, as we discuss later, guns and alcohol play a role in many suicides. Alcohol lowers inhibitions and increases impulsive behavior and guns provide a means for carrying out suicidal thoughts. Men are more likely than women to drink alcohol when they are highly distressed and may have more ready access to guns. This may contribute to men's higher rates of completed suicides compared to women.

Cross-Cultural Differences

Within the United States, there are substantial differences between ethnic/racial groups in rates of suicide (McIntosh, 1991; NIMH, 2000). Whites have higher

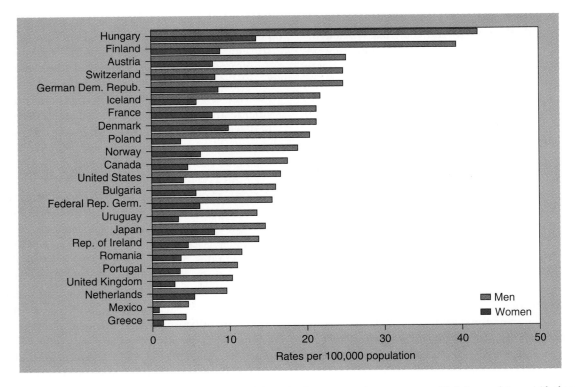

FIGURE 9.2   Gender Differences in Completed Suicides in Several Countries. In most countries, men are more likely to complete a suicide than are women, although women are more likely to attempt suicide than are men.

Source: Moscicki, 1995, p. 25.

One means of suicide among African American males is "suicide by cop."

suicide rates than all other groups, except for Native Americans, where the suicide rate is over twice the national average (Hendin, 1995). Suicide among Native Americans is tied to poverty, lack of education and hope, discrimination, substance abuse, and the easy availability of firearms (Berman & Jobes, 1995).

Several studies have compared rates of suicide among African Americans and White Americans (see Burr, Hartman, & Matteson, 1999). Whites have higher rates of suicide than African Americans (see Figure 9.3), but the rates among African American males have increased greatly in recent decades (NIMH, 2000). Between 1970 and 1985, the suicide rate increased 45 percent for African American males of all ages, and 75 percent for African American teenagers (Crosby et al., 1999). In contrast, the rate among White males between 15 and 24 has risen only 10 percent in the last decade. One means of suicide among African American males is "suicide by cop." A despondent young man will threaten a police officer with what looks like a gun, but is actually a benign object. The young man is shot by officers believing they must defend themselves, the young man is dead, and his family is saved the shame of having a member commit suicide. Many other suicides among African American males are self-inflicted, however.

There are cross-national differences in suicide rates, with higher rates in Hungary, Germany, Austria,

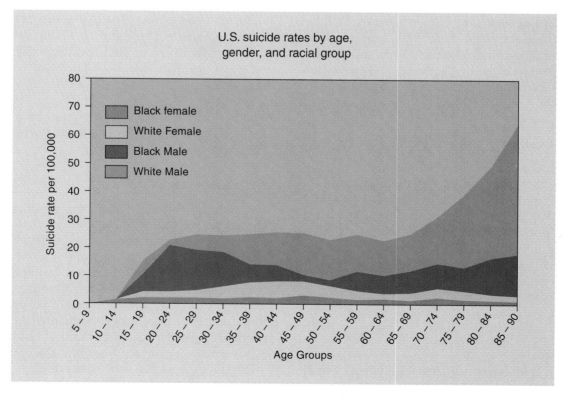

FIGURE 9.3 Whites have higher rates of suicide than African Americans and males have higher rates than females.

Source: National Institute of Mental Health Data: Centers for Disease Control and Prevention, National Center for Health Statistics.

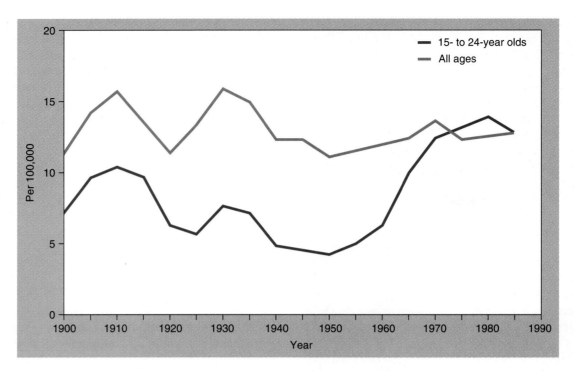

FIGURE 9.4 Increases in Suicide Among Younger Adults Over Recent Decades. In the last several decades, rates of completed suicide have skyrocketed among 15 to 24 year olds, relative to the rates of suicide in the rest of the population.

Source: Diekstra & Garnefski, 1995, p. 48.

Denmark, and Japan, and lower rates in Egypt, Mexico, Greece, and Spain (National Center for Health Statistics [NCHS], 1994; WHO, 1992). The United States, Canada, and England have suicide rates that fall between these two extremes. These differences may have to do with cultural and religious norms against suicide. People who belong to religions that expressly forbid suicide are less likely to attempt suicide (Statham et al., 1998).

Suicide in Children and Adolescents

The overall rate of suicide in the general population has slightly increased over the last 60 years, but the rate among children and adolescents has skyrocketed by nearly 300 percent (see Figure 9.4; Goldman & Beardslee, 1999). Similarly, young adults are more likely than adults of any other age to think about committing suicide (Crosby et al., 1999). This 10-year-old girl had no history of suicide attempts or mental disorder, yet spoke explicitly of her suicidal thoughts (Pfeffer, 1985, p. 80):

Voices

I often think of killing myself. It started when I was almost hit by a car. Now I want to kill myself. I think of stabbing myself with a knife. When Mom yells at me, I think she does not love me. I worry a lot about my family. Mom is always depressed and sometimes she says she will die soon. My brother becomes very angry, often for no reason. He tried to kill himself last year and had to go to the hospital. Mom was in the hospital once also. I worry a lot about my family. I worry that if something happens to them, no one will take care of me. I feel sad about this.

Another child, a 10-year-old boy, describes how anger so often drives suicidal thoughts and actions (Pfeffer, 1985, p. 80):

Voices

I want to hurt myself when I get upset and angry. I bang my head against the wall or punch the wall with my fist. I wish I were dead. I often think about how to kill myself. I think I will go to France to have myself guillotined. It would be quick and painless. Guns are too painful, so is stabbing myself. Once, I put my head into a sink of water and I got scared. My grandmother found me. I told her I was washing my face. Mom was shocked when she heard about this. She began to cry. She worries a lot and always seems sad.

Unfortunately, adults often do not believe children when they voice their suicidal thoughts. Even clinicians formerly thought that young children could not have a concept of suicide and thus were not vulnerable. Now we know that, although suicide is relatively rare in young children, it is not impossible.

As we mentioned, girls are much more likely to attempt suicide, but boys are more likely to complete suicide. The gender ratio for completed suicide is even greater among adolescents and young adults than among older adults: males are five to seven times more likely than females in this age range to commit suicide (NIMH, 2000).

The rate of suicide increases substantially in early adolescence, and as mentioned earlier, suicide is the third leading cause of death among 15- to 24-year-olds. Suicide may become more common in adolescence than in childhood because the rate of several types of psychopathology tied to suicide, including depression, anxiety disorders, and substance abuse, increase in adolescence. Suicide rates may also rise at this age because adolescents are more sophisticated in their thinking than children and can contemplate suicide more clearly. Finally, adolescents may simply have the means to commit suicide (such as access to drugs and guns) more than children.

Warning signs for suicide in adolescents include fatigue, sleep loss, a decline in school performance, social withdrawal, loss of appetite, and changes in sleep patterns (see Table 9.1; Peach & Reddick, 1991; Smith, 1995). Many adolescents contemplating suicide will write letters to friends to say goodbye, and give away possessions. Drug overdoses are the most common means of suicide in adolescents, and an increase in drug and alcohol use are important warning signs for suicide (Diekstra et al., 1995).

Many more adolescents attempt suicide than ever die by suicide. Perhaps as many as 100 teenagers attempt suicide for every 1 who actually kills him or herself (Diekstra et al., 1995). Adolescents may be especially prone to use suicide attempts as a way of getting attention and help for problems. This does not mean that adolescent suicide attempts are unimportant, however. A previous history of a suicide attempt is the single best predictor of future suicide attempts and completions (Lewinsohn et al., 1995). Thus, adolescents who attempt suicide once are at high risk for future attempts, which can be successful.

College Students

The college years are full of pressures and changes. Students may be challenged far beyond any challenges they faced in high school. Academic material is much more difficult and standards are higher. Students who entered college with the expectation that they were going to pursue a particular career, such as medicine, may find that they cannot "make the grades" in necessary

---

TABLE 9.1

Warning Signs for Suicide in Adolescents

These are important warning signs for suicide in adolescence.

Fatigue

Sleep loss, changes in sleep patterns

Decline in school performance

Social withdrawal

Loss of appetite

Giving away possessions

Writing goodbye letters to friends

Increase in drug and alcohol intake

---

classes, such as chemistry and biology. Student athletes who were stars in high school may play second-string, if at all, on their college teams. Student musicians, performers, and artists may despair of pursuing their dreams. And then there are the social and developmental challenges of college—making new friends, dealing with the drug and alcohol culture, coping with being away from home, the changes in values that come with exposure to new ideas.

Those students who enter college already feeling distressed and unsure of themselves may have special difficulty in handling these challenges, and appear at increased risk for suicide (Carson & Johnson, 1985). Some research suggests that students at more prestigious colleges may also be at increased risk for suicide (Seiden, 1969; Stengel, 1974). Whether this is due to the pressures of those colleges, or to the characteristics of students who go to those colleges, is unclear.

Fortunately, suicide among college students is relatively rare, although as many as 20 percent of college students have suicidal thoughts at some time in their college years (Carson & Johnson, 1985). When suicide does occur, it can rock an entire campus, and can devastate the closest friends of the person who died.

Suicide in the Elderly

Although there has been a 50 percent decline in suicide rates among the elderly over the last few decades, the elderly, particularly elderly men, still remain at relatively high risk for suicide. The highest risk of suicide is among White men over the age of 85 (NIMH, 2000). When they attempt suicide, older people are much more likely than younger people to be successful. It seems that most older people who attempt suicide fully intend to die (McIntosh, 1995). In contrast, most young people who attempt suicide are highly ambivalent.

Some older people who commit suicide do so because they cannot tolerate the loss of their spouse or other loved ones. For example, an elderly woman who recently lost her husband to prostate cancer said:

Voices

I think when you live with someone for a long time, that when they go, you should be able to go, too. I think people should be able to go together. I think it's useless for one person of a pair to stick around. I just think that it should be a natural order of things that if you're together with somebody a long time, you should just go with them when they go. It doesn't make any sense. . . . We grew up together, really. All those years and all the things we did. I don't want to do anything by myself. I don't want to be alone. It was great with him. It's sure a big zero without him.

(Nolen-Hoeksema & Larson, 1999)

Suicide rates are highest in the first year after a loss, but remain relatively high for several years after the loss (McIntosh, 1995).

Other elderly persons who commit suicide suffer from debilitating illnesses and wish to escape their pain and suffering. Escape from illness and disabilities may be a particularly strong motive for suicide among men. An older man may have been strong and healthy his entire life, then when stricken with a serious disease in old age, he may become confined to a wheelchair or his bed, or be forced to enter a nursing home. One study of elderly people who committed suicide found that 44 percent had said they could not bear being placed in a nursing home and would rather be dead (Loebel et al., 1991).

Most elderly persons who lose a spouse or become ill do not commit suicide, however. Again, those who enter older age with a history of depression or other psychological problems are at greatest risk for responding to the challenges of old age with suicide (Hendin, 1995).

Summing Up

- Suicide is defined as death from injury, poisoning, or suffocation where there is evidence (either explicit or implicit) that the injury was self-inflicted and that the decedent intended to kill himself or herself.
- Death seekers clearly and explicitly seek to end their lives. Death initiators also have a clear intention to die, but believe that they are simply hastening an inevitable death. Death ignorers intend to end their lives but do not believe this means the end of their existence. Death darers are ambivalent about dying, and take actions that greatly increase their chances of death, but do not guarantee they will die.
- Suicide is the ninth leading cause of death in the United States, and internationally, at least 160,000 people die by suicide and 2 million other people make suicide attempts each year.
- Women are more likely than men to attempt suicide, but men are more likely than women to complete suicide.
- Cross-cultural differences in suicide rates may have to do with religious doctrines, stressors, and cultural norms about suicide.
- Young people are less likely than adults to commit suicide, but suicide rates have been rising dramatically for young people in recent decades. The elderly, particularly elderly men, are at high risk for suicide.

☉ UNDERSTANDING SUICIDE

Our ability to understand the causes of suicide is hampered by many factors. First, although it is a more common event that we would hope, it is still rare enough that it is difficult to study scientifically. Second, in the wake of a suicide, family members and friends may selectively remember certain information about the victim (such as evidence that he or she was depressed) and forget other information. Third, the majority of people who contemplate suicide never actually commit suicide, so it is difficult to determine what causes some people to go through with the act.

Suicide Notes

It would be very helpful if we could get some clues as to the reasons for suicide from the notes left behind by those who commit suicide. Only about one in four people leaves a suicide note, however, and often these notes provide only a glimpse as to their motives (Jamison, 1999). These notes are often brief and vague, and may simply say, "I could not bear it any longer," or "I am tired of living." Many suicide notes are very concrete, with explicit instructions or requests, such as how to handle the body, what to tell others about the suicide, and how to distribute assets. Occasionally, the mental anguish that leads to suicide is expressed more fully in the suicide note (Leenaars, 1988):

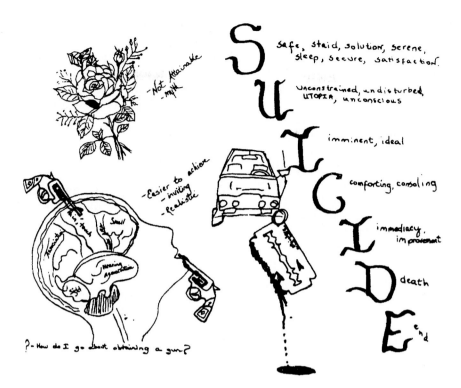

Drawings by a 19-year-old college sophomore.

Voices

I wish I could explain it so someone could understand it. I'm afraid it's something I can't put into words.

There's just this heavy, overwhelming despair—dreading everything. Dreading life. Empty inside, to the point of numbness. It's like there's something already dead inside. My whole being has been pulling back into that void for months. . . .

But there's some core-level spark of life that just isn't there. Despite what's been said about my having "gotten better" lately—the voice in my head that's driving me crazy is louder than ever. It's way beyond being reached by anyone or anything, it seems. I can't bear it anymore. I think there's something psychologically twisted—reversed—that has taken over; that I can't fight anymore. I wish that I could disappear without hurting anyone. I'm sorry.

This writer mentions that family members and friends believe she is "getting better." Suicides often happen when people are not in the deepest depths of depression and despair, but when they seem to be "getting better," having more energy and engagement in life. This energy, however, can simply give them the energy and freedom to commit suicide, as Elizabeth Wurtzel explains in her autobiography *Prozac Nation* (1995, p. 315):

Voices

The suicide attempt startled even me. It seemed to happen out of context, like something that should have taken place months and months ago. It should never have happened within a few days of returning to Cambridge, at a point when, even I had to admit, the fluoxetine (Prozac) was starting to kick in. After all, I was able to get out of bed in the morning, which may not seem like much, but in my life it was up there with Moses parting the Red Sea. Anybody would have thought that these were signs that my mood was on the upswing, and I guess it was. But just as a little bit of knowledge is a dangerous thing, a little bit of energy, in the hands of someone hell-bent on suicide, is a very dangerous thing.

My improved affect did not in any way sway me from the philosophical conviction that life, at its height and depth, basically sucks.

For people with long-term mental disorders, the prospect of sinking once again into despair leads them to take "preventative action"—to kill themselves before it happens again. Virginia Woolf suffered psychotic depressions and manias, and committed suicide when she sensed a new episode coming (Woolf, 1975–1980, pp. 486–487):

Voices

Dearest,

I want to tell you that you have given me complete happiness. No one could have done more than you have done. Please believe that.

But I know that I shall never get over this: and I am wasting your life. It is this madness. Nothing anyone says can persuade me. You can work, and you will be much better without me. You see I can't write this even, which shows I am right. All I want to say is that until this disease came on we were perfectly happy. It was all due to you. No one could have been so good as you have been, from the very first day till now. Everyone knows that.

Most suicide notes are positive in their remarks about remaining family members, expressing love and thanks. Sometimes the note is meant to relieve family members of guilt (Leenaars, 1988):

Voices

Everyone has been so good to me—has tried so hard. I truly wish that I could be different, for the sake of my family. Hurting my family is the worst of it, and that guilt has been wrestling with the part of me that wanted only to disappear.

Thus, suicide notes often only reveal the obvious—that suicide tends to be driven by mental anguish and a sense of futility about going on.

Sociocultural Perspectives on Suicide

Sociocultural theorists have been at the forefront of research and theorizing about suicide. They have identified a number of events, and characteristics of societies, that may contribute to a vulnerability to suicide (see *Concept Review:* Sociocultural Perspectives on Suicide).

Economic Hardship

Stressful life events of a variety of kinds appear to contribute to an increased risk of suicide (Cohen-Sandler et al., 1982; Isometsa et al., 1995; Statham et al., 1998). One type of stressful event consistently linked to increased suicide vulnerability is economic hardship. For example, loss of a job can precipitate suicidal thoughts and attempts (Crosby et al., 1999; Heikkinen et al., 1992). As the farm economy has collapsed in the United States in recent decades, the rate of suicide among farmers has increased considerably (Ragland & Berman, 1990–1991). Men and women who spent their entire lives trying to make a living from land that may

CONCEPT REVIEW
Sociocultural Perspectives on Suicide

Sociocultural theorists have attributed suicide to larger events happening in a culture or to major traumas in an individual's life.

Theory	Description
Economic hardship	People who are chronically impoverished or who recently have lost a job are at increased risk for suicide.
Serious illness	People with serious illnesses are at increased risk for suicide.
Loss and abuse	People who have experienced loss or abuse in the distant or recent past are at increased risk for suicide.
Durkheim's theory	Egoistic suicide is committed by people who feel alienated from others, empty of social contacts, alone in an unsupportive world. Anomic suicide is committed by people who experience severe disorientation because of some large change in their relationships to society. Altruistic suicide is committed by people who believe that taking their own lives will benefit society in some way.
Suicide contagion or clustering	When one member of a group commits suicide, other members are at increased risk for suicide, perhaps because of "contagion" effects, modeling, increased acceptability of suicide, or the impact of the traumatic event on already vulnerable people.

Suicides often happen when people face overwhelming stress and hopelessness.

have been in their families for generations can find their dreams shattered and their farms lost forever.

More chronic economic hardship also contributes to suicidality. One nationwide study found that 8.5% of people living below the poverty level had thought about committing suicide in the previous year, compared to 5.4% of people living above the poverty level (Crosby et al., 1999). The high suicide rate among African American males in recent years may also be tied to perceptions that their economic futures are uncertain at best, and to comparisons of their economic status with the status of the majority culture. One study found that rates of suicide among African American males in the United States were highest in communities where the occupational and income inequalities between African Americans and Whites were the greatest (Burr, Hartman, & Matteson, 1999).

Serious Illness

Many people who commit suicide, especially older people, suffer from serious illnesses that bring them constant pain and debilitation (Lester, 1992). Although people who are seriously ill may always have been at increased risk for suicide, increases in the ability of medical practices to keep people alive long after they have been diagnosed with a serious illness have contributed to the number of seriously ill people wishing they could die. As we discuss shortly, this has led to debates over people's right to die in order to end suffering and pain.

Loss and Abuse

Loss of a loved one through death, divorce, or separation often immediately precedes suicide attempts or completions (Heikkinen et al., 1992). People feel they just cannot go on without the lost relationship, and wish to end their pain. In addition, people who have experienced certain traumas in their childhood, especially loss of a parent or sexual abuse, also appear at increased risk for suicide (Paykel, 1991; Statham et al., 1998). Loss of a parent during childhood may create a lifetime of instability and feelings of abandonment that can contribute to suicidal intentions. Sexual abuse during childhood may shatter people's trust in others and prevent the development of a strong self-concept that can protect against suicide.

Durkheim's Sociological Theory

The sociologist Emil Durkheim (1897) focused not on specific events that precipitate suicide, but on the mindsets that certain societal conditions can create that increase risk for suicide. He proposed that there are three types of suicide, based on his analysis of records of suicide for various countries and across various historical periods. **Egoistic suicide** is committed by people who feel alienated from others, empty of social contacts, alone in an unsupportive world. The schizophrenic patient who kills herself because she is completely isolated from society may be committing egoistic suicide. **Anomic suicide** is committed by people who experience severe disorientation because of some large change in their relationships to society. A man who loses his job after 20 years of service may feel anomie, a complete confusion of his role and worth in society, and may commit anomic suicide. Finally, **altruistic suicide** is committed by people who believe that taking their own lives will benefit society in some way. During the Vietnam War, Buddhist monks burned themselves to death in public suicides to protest the war.

Durkheim's theory suggests that social ties and integration into a society will help to prevent suicide if the society discourages suicide and supports individuals in overcoming negative situations in ways other than suicide. However, if a society supports suicide as an act that benefits the society in some situations, then ties with such a society may actually promote suicide. In the next section, we discuss the special case of suicide clustering and contagion—the spreading of suicide in a social group.

Suicide Contagion

When a well-known member of the society commits suicide, then people who closely identify with that person may see suicide as more acceptable (Hendin, 1995; Stack, 1991). When two or more suicides or attempted suicides are nonrandomly "bunched" in space or time, such as a series of suicide attempts in the same high school or a series of completed suicides in response to the suicide of a celebrity, scientists refer to this as a **suicide cluster** (Joiner, 1999). Suicide clusters appear most likely to occur among people who knew the person who committed suicide. One well-documented example occurred in a high school of about 1,500 students. Two students committed suicide within 4 days. Then, over an 18-day span, 7 other students attempted suicide and an additional 23 reported having suicidal thoughts (Brent et al., 1989). Many of those who attempted suicide or had active suicidal thoughts were friends of each other and of the two students who completed suicide.

Other suicide clusters occur not among close friends, but among people who are linked only by media exposure to the suicide of a stranger, often a celebrity. Some studies have suggested that suicide rates, at least among adolescents, increase after a publicized suicide (Phillips & Carstensen, 1986, 1988; Stack, 1987; although see Kessler et al., 1988). For example, in the week after Marilyn Monroe committed suicide in 1963, the national suicide rate rose 12 percent. More recently, after the suicide of the popular lead singer of the band Nirvana, Kurt Cobain, there were concerns that young people who identified with Cobain and the message in his music would view suicide as an appropriate way of dealing with the social anomie expressed in that music. At least one fan, a 28-year-old man, went home after a candlelight vigil honoring Cobain and killed himself with a shotgun, just as Cobain had.

What is the reason for suicide clustering? Some theorists have labeled this as a **suicide contagion** effect, meaning that people somehow "catch" suicidal intentions and behaviors from those who commit suicide (Phillips et al., 1992; Stack, 1991). Survivors who become suicidal may be modeling the behavior of the friend or admired celebrity who committed suicide. The suicide may also make the idea of suicide more acceptable and thus lower inhibitions for suicidal behavior in survivors. In addition, the local and media attention given to a suicide can be attractive to some people feeling alienated and abandoned. After the murder/suicide rampage of two teenagers at Columbine High School in Littleton, Colorado, some teenagers said that having the media attention given to the shooters would be an attractive way to "go out."

Thomas Joiner (1999) argues that suicide clusters are best understood as the result of several sets of factors coming together in the same time and place. First, people form relationships with others who possess similar qualities or problems—known as *assortative relationships*. People who are at risk for suicide, because of psychopathology, life problems or lack of social support from families, may be more likely to gravitate together. For example, teenagers who are outcasts from the popular groups at their high school may hang out

together, with social alienation as the primary bond between them. Second, severe negative events can be triggers for suicide, as we have discussed, and these negative events often happen to groups of people as well as to individuals. The suicide of a close friend qualifies as a severe negative event, and thus may increase the risk of suicide among others as would any other severe negative event. But when the close friends of the person who committed suicide also carry other risk factors for suicide, then this severe negative event may be especially likely to trigger suicidality in the survivors.

Psychological Theories of Suicide

Psychological theorists have focused on what goes through the mind of the person who commits suicide. Psychodynamic theorists attribute suicide to repressed rage, cognitive-behavioral theorists have identified patterns of thinking that appear to increase risk for suicide, and a great deal of evidence shows that certain mental disorders increase risk for suicide (see *Concept Review: Psychological Theories of Suicide*).

Psychodynamic Theory

Recall that Freud argued that depression is anger turned inward on the self. Instead of expressing anger at people they feel have betrayed or abandoned them, the depressed person expresses that anger at the self, specifically at the part of his or her ego that represents

---

CONCEPT REVIEW

Psychological Theories of Suicide

Psychological theories of suicide focus on the thoughts and motivations of people who attempt suicide.

Theory	Description
Psychodynamic theory	Suicide is the extreme expression of anger at the love object who has abandoned the person.
Mental disorders	Several mental disorders increase risk for suicide, including depression, bipolar disorder, schizophrenia, substance abuse, and anxiety disorders.
Cognitive theories	Hopelessness and dichotomous thinking increase risk for suicide.

the lost person. Sometimes that anger is so great that the depressed person wishes to annihilate that image of the lost person. This means annihilating the self—suicide.

This line of reasoning suggests that suicidal people tend to be filled with rage against others. For example, teenagers who are enraged at their parents but cannot express it may attempt suicide as a means of punishing their parents. As we noted in our discussion of suicide notes, however, anger and rage are not the most common emotions that suicidal people express (Shneidman, 1979). Instead, guilt and emotional despair are more common. A psychodynamic theorist might argue suicidal people don't express anger in suicide notes or otherwise precisely because they cannot express these emotions and are turning the feelings in on themselves. Unfortunately, this argument makes the theory difficult to test.

Near the end of his career, Freud was dissatisfied with his own theory of suicide and believed it a more complex phenomenon than "anger turned inward." Although newer psychodynamic theories of suicide have emerged, most still focus on self-directed anger as the core problem in suicidality (Maltsberger, 1999).

Mental Disorders

Approximately 90 percent of people who commit suicide have probably been suffering from a diagnosable mental disorder (Jamison, 1999; NIMH, 1999). The most common disorder among people who commit suicide is depression (Wulsin, Vaillant, & Wells, 1999). Often, psychiatric diagnoses have not been made before an individual commits suicide. Instead, researchers conduct a *psychological autopsy*—an analysis of the person's moods, thoughts, and behaviors, based on reports of family and friends and the individual's writings—after the suicide has occurred.

One group of researchers was able to conduct a prospective study of people who attempted suicide during a year-long study of 13,673 adults randomly chosen from a community sample. All these adults were interviewed twice, 1 year apart. A structured clinical interview was used to determine whether each adult qualified for the diagnosis of some type of psychological disorder. Over the year between the two interviews, 40 people in the sample attempted suicide. The researchers randomly chose 40 other people from the rest of the sample who had not attempted suicide to make comparisons with the 40 suicide attempters. When the researchers examined the data from the first interview, they found that 53 percent of the suicide attempters had been diagnosed with major depressive disorders, compared to 6 percent of the nonattempters (Petronis et al., 1990).

Similarly, studies of children and adolescents have found that major depression greatly increases the risk for suicide. Kovacs and colleagues (1993) followed 142 children with various depressive disorders into their adolescent years and found that 38 percent had made a suicide attempt by age 17. Weissman and colleagues (1999) followed 73 adolescents who had major depression into their adult years and found that over 50 percent had attempted suicide at some time in their lives, and 22 percent had made multiple attempts.

Several other serious mental disorders also substantially increase risk for suicide. In the longitudinal by Petronis and colleagues (1990), 8 percent of the attempters had been diagnosed with mania at the first interview, compared to 0.6 percent of the nonattempters. As many as half the people with bipolar disorder attempt suicide, and perhaps one in five will complete suicide (Goodwin & Jamison, 1990). It might seem strange that a manic person would attempt suicide, because the symptoms of mania include elation and heightened self-esteem. However, often the predominant feelings of mania are agitation and irritation mixed with despair over having the illness or in contemplating falling into a debilitating depression. Kay Jamison (1995b, pp. 113–114) describes one of her suicide attempts, which occurred when she was in a mixed manic and depressive state, and highly agitated:

Voices

In a rage I pulled the bathroom lamp off the wall and felt the violence go through me but not yet out of me. "For Christ's sake," he said, rushing in—and then stopping very quietly. Jesus, I must be crazy, I can see it in his eyes a dreadful mix of concern, terror, irritation, resignation, and why me, Lord? "Are you hurt?" he asks. Turning my head with its fast-scanning eyes I see in the mirror blood running down my arms. I bang my head over and over against the door. God, make it stop, I can't stand it, I know I'm insane again. He really cares, I think, but within ten minutes he too is screaming, and his eyes have a wild look from contagious madness, from the lightning adrenaline between the two of us. "I can't leave you like this," but I say a few truly awful things and then go for his throat in a more literal way, and he does leave me, provoked beyond endurance and unable to see the devastation and despair inside. I can't convey it and he can't see it; there's nothing to be done. I can't think, I can't calm this murderous cauldron, my grand ideas of an hour ago seem absurd and pathetic, my life is in ruins, and worse still—ruinous; my body is uninhabitable. It is raging and weeping and full of destruction and wild energy gone amok. In the mirror I see a creature I don't know but must live and share my mind with.

I understand why Jekyll killed himself before Hyde had taken over completely. I took a massive overdose of lithium with no regrets.

EXTRAORDINARY PEOPLE

A Darkness Visible: A Pulitzer Prize–Winning Author Describes Suicidality

You may have read some of William Styron's books in your courses on great American literature. This Pulitzer Prize–winning author of such classics as *Sophie's Choice* and *The Confessions of Nat Turner* was at the top of his profession in late October of 1985. Styron was in Paris to receive the Prix Mondial Cino del Duca, given yearly to an artist or scientist whose work reflects certain principles of humanism. This was a high honor and Styron knew he should be feeling full of joy and pride. Instead, as Styron writes (1990, pp. 16–17), "I was feeling in my mind a sensation close to, but indescribably different from, actual pain. . . . For myself, the pain is most closely connected to drowning or suffocation."

In June of that year, Styron had begun drifting into a deep, severe depression that overtook his life. He could not sleep at night or during the day. As each day wore on, his mood became worse and his thinking more clouded. He began to loathe his work and himself. On the day he received the Prix Mondial Cino del Duca, he found himself sitting at a dinner in his honor, unable to speak, to eat, or to respond in any way to his hosts. He reached into his coat pocket and realized he had lost the check for $25,000 that was the cash prize for the del Duca award. He thought it was fitting that this had happened, because he did not believe he deserved the award. Later that night,

on the way back to his hotel, Styron thought of his many friends and heroes who had committed suicide, and realized he would be facing the same decision very soon.

Styron was 60 when depression first cast a shadow over his mind in June of 1985. He had been addicted to alcohol for 20 years, but suddenly that June, his body began to reject alcohol. Even a mouthful of wine made him woozy and dizzy, and he quickly became unable to drink at all. As his alcohol intake stopped, his depression began. At first, it was mild:

> It was not really alarming at first, since the change was subtle, but I did notice that my surroundings took on a different tone at certain times: the shadows of nightfall seemed more somber, my mornings were less buoyant, walks in the woods became less zestful, and there was a moment during my working hours in the late afternoon when a kind of panic and anxiety overtook me, just for a few minutes, accompanied by a visceral queasiness. (1990, p.42)

By December, though, Styron was so deeply mired in his depression that he began taking steps to commit suicide. He consulted his lawyer to ensure that his will and estate were in good order. He destroyed his diary in which he

Another psychological disorder that greatly increases risk of suicide attempts is substance abuse (Statham et al., 1998). Author William Styron discusses the link between his alcoholism, depression, and suicide attempt in *Extraordinary People: A Darkness Visible*. In the prospective study of suicide attempts we have been discussing, 33.0 percent of the attempters were identified as heavy drinkers, compared to 2.5 percent of the nonattempters. When alcoholism co-occurs with depression, the risk of suicide is especially high (Waller, Lyons, & Costantini-Ferrando, 1999). Alcohol lowers people's inhibitions to engage in impulsive acts, even self-destructive ones like suicide attempts. Also, people

with chronic alcohol problems may have a general tendency toward self-destructive acts and may wreck many of their relationships and their careers, making them feel they do not have much reason to live.

Suicide is found among people with all types of psychological disorders. For example, one study found that a history of social phobia (see Chapter 6) was a strong predictor of suicide attempts in women (Statham et al., 1998). Among children and adolescents, antisocial behavior, as well as depression and substance abuse, are strongly associated with suicide attempts and completions (Andrews & Lewinsohn, 1992; Brent et al., 1996; Shaffer et al., 1996; Wannan &

Continued

had written about his despair. He wrote a few words of parting, but tore up all his efforts in disgust.

Late one night, after his wife had gone to bed, Styron sat watching the tape of a movie in his living room. A passage from the Brahms *Alto Rhapsody* was played in the movie. Styron writes:

> This sound, which like all music—indeed, like all pleasure—I had been numbly unresponsive to for months, pierced my heart like a dagger, and in a flood of swift recollection I thought of all the joys the house had known: the children who had rushed through its rooms, the festivals, the love and work, the honestly earned slumber, the voices and the nimble commotion, the perennial tribe of cats and dogs and birds, "laughter and ability and Sighing, / And Frocks and Curls." All this I realized was more than I could ever abandon, even as what I had set out so deliberately to do was more than I could inflict on those memories, and upon those, so close to me, with whom the memories were bound. And just as powerfully I realized I could not commit this desecration on myself. I drew upon some last gleam of sanity to perceive the terrifying dimensions of the mortal predicament I had fallen into. I woke up my wife and soon telephone calls were made. The next day I was admitted to the hospital. (1990, pp. 66–67).

Styron was hospitalized, and after 7 weeks of antidepressant drugs and psychotherapy, overcame his depression.

What was the cause of Styron's depression? Styron speculates that he has always had a propensity to depression and anxiety. His father apparently suffered from depression, although it was never called depression back then. Styron's mother died when he was 13, and he believes this created a psychological vulnerability in him that compounded the genetic vulnerability to depression he may have inherited from his father. Forty years of alcohol abuse may have altered the workings of his neurotransmitters systems, but Styron also believes he used alcohol to dampen his feelings of anxiety and depression all those years.

A few years after he emerged from his depression, Styron wrote *Darkness Visible,* a memoir of his descent into depression and suicide and triumph over it. This book became a national best-seller, but not only because Styron was able to describe with great skill and poetry the deepest horrors of depression and suicidality. *Darkness Visible* also gives hope to those who suffer (p. 84):

> For those who have dwelt on depression's dark wood, and known its inexplicable agony, their return from the abyss is not unlike the ascent of the poet, trudging upward and upward out of hell's black depths and at last emerging into what he saw as "the shining world." There, whoever has been restored to health has almost always been restored to the capacity for serenity and joy, and this may be indemnity enough for having endured the despair beyond despair.

Fombonne, 1998). Between 10 and 15 percent of people with schizophrenia commit suicide (Tsuang, Fleming, & Simpson, 1999). They may kill themselves to end the torment of accusatory hallucinations telling them they are evil or to end the excruciating social isolation they may feel. Most suicide attempts among people with schizophrenia happen not when the people are psychotic but when they are lucid but depressed. The schizophrenics who are most likely to commit suicide are young males who have frequent relapses into psychosis but who had a good educational history and high expectations for themselves before they developed schizophrenia. It seems that these young men cannot face a future that is likely to be so much less

than what they envisioned for themselves (Hendin, 1995; Tsuang, Fleming, & Simpson, 1999).

Cognitive and Behavioral Perspectives

Cognitive theorists have examined the beliefs and attitudes that may contribute to suicide. The cognitive variable that has most consistently predicted suicide is **hopelessness**—the sense that the future is bleak and there is no way of making it more positive (Beck et al., 1985). One group of researchers examined 207 patients who had been hospitalized while contemplating suicide and found that 89 of them expressed utter hopelessness about their futures. Over the next 5 years, 13

Alcohol abuse and dependence is a strong risk factor for suicide.

of these 89 hopeless patients committed suicide, compared to only one patient who had not expressed hopelessness (Beck et al., 1985). In addition, some research suggests that people who attempt or commit suicide tend to be rigid and inflexible in their thinking (Linehan et al., 1987). They engage in **dichotomous thinking**, seeing everything in either/or terms. This rigidity and inflexibility makes it more difficult for them to consider alternative solutions to their situations or to simply "hold out" until the suicidal feelings pass.

The behavioral characteristic that seems best to predict suicide is *impulsivity*. One review concluded that 25 percent of psychiatric patients with a history of impulsive behavior were at high risk for suicide (Roy, 1995). When impulsivity is overlaid on other psychological problems—depression, substance abuse, living in a chronically stressful environment—it can be a potent contributor to suicide. As we discuss in the next section, there also is increasing evidence that impulsivity has biological roots.

Biological Theories of Suicide

Once again, genetics and neurotransmitters have been the focus of biological theories of suicide risk (see *Concept Review:* Biological Theories of Suicide).

Genetics and Suicide

Suicide runs in families. Many studies find that people who attempt or complete suicide often have family members who also attempted or completed suicide (Roy, 1983; Tsuang, 1983). The study of the Old Order Amish mentioned in Chapter 3 found that almost three-quarters of the suicides occurring in this culture

CONCEPT REVIEW	
Biological Theories of Suicide	

Biological theories of suicide focus on genetic and biochemical factors that may increase risk of suicide.

Theory	Description
Genetic theory	Disordered genes increase risk for suicide.
Neurotransmitter theory	Deficiencies in serotonin lead to impulsive, violent, and suicidal behavior.
Low cholesterol theory	Excessively low cholesterol increases risk for suicide, perhaps by affecting serotonin levels.

came from just four large families, all of which had high rates of mood disorders (Egeland & Sussex, 1985).

One extraordinary family that has been plagued by suicide is the Hemingways. Five members of this family, spread across four generations, committed suicide. Acclaimed novelist Ernest Hemingway killed himself with a shotgun after two treatments with electroconvulsive therapy failed to heal his severe depression. His granddaughter Margaux killed herself with an overdose of barbiturates on the thirty-fifth anniversary of her grandfather's suicide. Margaux had suffered from bulimia and alcoholism. She had had a successful modeling career, but after a series of failed movie appearances, her career began to decline. Just before her death, Margaux was reduced to taking parts

The Hemingway family has experienced the suicides of several of its members, including Ernest and Margaux.

in low-budget pictures and making guest appearances at European conventions. She allowed the BBC to tape a therapy session in which she said, "there's so much inside, and . . . sometimes I'm afraid that it's so full that it might kill me" (Masters, 1996).

Although some of this clustering of suicide within families may be due to environmental factors, such as family members modeling each other or sharing common stressors, twin and adoption studies suggest that genetics are involved as well (Roy et al., 1995). One study of suicidal thoughts and attempts among a community sample of 5,995 twins found a concordance rate for serious suicide attempts of 23 percent among the MZ twins and 0 among the DZ twins (Statham et al., 1998). Strong evidence of a genetic component to suicidality remained when the researchers controlled for histories of psychiatric problems in the twins and their families, recent and past negative life events, how close the twins were to each other socially, and personality factors.

Serotonin and Suicide

Many studies have found a link between suicide and low *serotonin* levels (Mann & Arango, 1999). For example, postmortem studies of the brains of people who committed suicide find low levels of serotonin (Gross-Isseroff et al., 1998). Suicide attempters with low serotonin levels are 10 times more likely to make another suicide attempt than those with higher serotonin levels (Roy, 1992). Low serotonin levels are linked with suicidality even among people who are not depressed, suggesting that the connection between serotonin and suicidality is not due entirely to a common connection to depression. Serotonin may generally be linked to impulsive and aggressive behavior (Linnoila & Virkkunen, 1992). Low serotonin levels are most strongly associated with impulsive and violent suicides. Although these pieces of evidence do not prove that low serotonin levels cause suicidal behavior, they suggest that people with low serotonin levels may be at high risk for impulsive and violent behavior that sometimes results in suicide.

In *Pushing the Boundaries:* Can Low Cholesterol Lead to Suicide?, page 316, we describe a controversial new biological theory of suicide that suggests low levels of cholesterol play a role in suicidality.

Summing Up

- Suicide notes suggest that mental anguish and escape from pain are behind many suicides.
- Several negative life events or circumstances increase risk for suicide, including economic hardship, serious illness, loss, and abuse.
- Durkheim distinguished between egoistic suicide, which is committed by people who feel alienated from others, empty of social contacts, alone in an unsupportive world; anomic suicide, which is committed by people who experience severe disorientation because of some large change in their relationships to society; and altruistic suicide, which is committed by people who believe that taking their own lives will benefit society in some way.
- Suicide clusters occur when two or more suicides or attempted suicides are nonrandomly "bunched" in space or time. This phenomenon is sometimes called suicide contagion.
- Psychodynamic theorists attribute suicide to repressed rage that leads to self-destruction.
- Several mental disorders increase risk for suicide, including depression, bipolar disorder, substance abuse, schizophrenia, and anxiety disorders.
- Cognitive-behavioral theorists argue that hopelessness and dichotomous thinking contribute to suicide.
- Impulsivity is a behavioral characteristic common to people who suicide.
- Family history, twin and adoption studies all suggest there is a genetic vulnerability to suicide.
- Many studies have found a link between low serotonin levels and suicide.

PUSHING THE BOUNDARIES

Can Low Cholesterol Lead to Suicide?

For years, we have been encouraged to lower the amount of cholesterol we consume through our diet. Skip the ice cream, red meat, and french fries, and we'll be healthier in every way, right?

Controversial research on a possible link between low cholesterol and suicide suggests this might not be the case. Studies of medical and death statistics show that people with low cholesterol levels, because they were on low-cholesterol diets, taking cholesterol-lowering medications, exercising more, or just naturally had low levels, have higher rates of suicide that people with higher cholesterol levels (Jacobs et al., 1992; Jamison, 1999; Kaplan & Kaufmann, 1993). Initially, researchers thought the link between low cholesterol and suicide may be false, and due to both factors being tied to depression. Depressed people eat less and thus may have lower cholesterol levels, and are more likely to commit suicide. When studies controlled for the impact of depression on suicide rates, however, the link between low cholesterol and suicide remained (Fawcett et al., 1997; Takei et al., 1994).

How could low cholesterol contribute to suicidality? Speculations focus on a possible link between cholesterol and the neurotransmitter serotonin, which in turn is connected to impulsive, violent, and suicidal behavior. Studies of macaque monkeys show that feeding monkeys a low-fat diet leads to increases in physical violence (Kaplan, Muldoon, Manuck, & Mann, 1997). Although this does not definitively prove that there is a pathway from low cholesterol to low serotonin to suicide, it does suggest such a pathway is worth future investigation.

☙ TREATMENT AND PREVENTION

A person who is gravely suicidal needs immediate care. In *Taking Psychology Personally:* What to Do If a Friend Is Suicidal, we discuss useful tips. Sometimes, people require hospitalization to prevent an imminent suicide attempt. They may voluntarily agree to be hospitalized, but if they do not agree, they can be hospitalized involuntarily for a short period of time (usually about 3 days). We discuss the pros and cons of involuntary hospitalization in Chapter 19.

Community-based **crisis intervention** programs are available to help people who are highly suicidal deal in the short term with their feelings, and then refer them for longer care to mental-health specialists. Some crisis intervention is done over the phone, on **suicide hot lines**. Some communities have suicide prevention centers, which may be part of a larger mental-health system, or stand-alone clinics, where suicidal people can walk in off the street and receive immediate care.

Crisis intervention aims to reduce the risk of an imminent suicide attempt by providing the suicidal person someone to talk with and understand their feelings and problems, helping him or her mobilize support from family members and friends, and making a plan to deal with specific problem situations in the short term. The crisis intervention counselor may make a contract with the suicidal person that he or she will not attempt suicide, or at least will re-contact the counselor as soon as suicidal feelings return. The counselor will help the person identify other people he or she can turn to when panicked or overwhelmed. And the counselor will make follow-up appointments with the suicidal person or refer the person to another counselor for long-term treatment.

People who receive longer-term treatment for suicidality typically receive psychotherapies and medications similar to those used to treat mood disorders. Preventative measures are taken with these people in

TAKING PSYCHOLOGY PERSONALLY

What to Do If a Friend Is Suicidal

What should you do if you suspect a friend or family member is suicidal? The National Depressive and Manic-Depressive Association, a patient-run advocacy group, makes the following suggestions in *Suicide and Depressive Illness* (1996):

- Take the person seriously. Although most people who express suicidal thoughts do not go on to attempt suicide, most people who do commit suicide have communicated their suicidal intentions to friends or family members before attempting suicide. Stay calm, but don't ignore the situation.

- Get help. Call the person's therapist, a suicide hotline, 911, or any other source of professional mental-health care.

- Express concern. Tell the person concretely why you think they might be suicidal.

- Pay attention. Listen closely, maintain eye contact, and use body language to indicate that you are attending to everything the person says.

- Ask direct questions about whether the person has a plan for suicide, and if so, what that plan is.

- Acknowledge the person's feelings in a nonjudgmental way.

- Reassure the person that things can be better. Emphasize that suicide is a permanent solution to a temporary problem.

- Don't promise confidentiality. You need the freedom to contact mental-health professionals and tell them precisely what is going on.

- If possible, don't leave the person alone until they are in the hands of professionals.

high-risk groups that have not yet attempted suicide to try to reduce risk of future attempts.

What is most clear from the literature on treatment of suicidal people is that they are woefully undertreated. Most people who are suicidal never seek treatment (Crosby et al., 1999). Even when their families know they are suicidal, they may not be taken for treatment because of denial and fear of the stigma of suicide. Those people who do receive treatment typically receive inadequate care. One study of depressed people on an inpatient psychiatric ward found that less than a third of those with a history of suicide attempts were being adequately treated (Oquendo et al., 1999).

Drug Treatments

The medication most consistently shown to reduce risk of suicide is **lithium**. Tondo, Jamison, & Baldessarini (1997) reviewed 28 published treatment studies that include more than 17,000 people with major depression or bipolar disorder, and found that those *not* treated with lithium were nearly nine times more likely to commit or attempt suicide than those who had been treated with lithium (see also Baldesarrini & Tondo, 1999). Another study concluded that lithium treatment resulted in a 77 percent reduction in the risk of suicide (Nilsson, 1999).

As we noted in Chapter 8, however, many people have difficulty taking lithium, because of its side effects and toxicity. Most recently, studies have focused on the **selective serotonin reuptake inhibitors**, such as Celexa, Prozac, Luvox, Zoloft, and Paxil, in the treatment of suicide risk. Some studies suggest that these drugs can reduce impulsive and violent behaviors in general, and suicidal behaviors specifically (Coccaro & Kavoussi, 1997; Salzman, 1999; Salzman et al., 1995). The evidence supporting the efficacy of the selective serotonin reuptake inhibitors in preventing suicide has been inconsistent, however (Leon et al., 1999).

Antipsychotic medications may be used to treat psychotic symptoms in people with psychotic mood

Psychotherapies for people at high risk for suicide help them to identify times when they are vulnerable and to develop more adaptive coping skills during these times.

disorders or schizophrenia. By reducing psychotic symptoms, the risk of suicidality may also be reduced (Salzman, 1999).

Psychological Treatments

The psychological therapies designed for depression and described in Chapter 8 are most frequently employed in the treatment of suicidality. Psychodynamic therapists would focus more on exploration of unexpressed anger at others, whereas cognitive-behavioral therapists would focus more on the client's hopelessness and dichotomous thinking, and on the environmental triggers for suicidal behavior.

Psychologist Marcia Linehan (1999) has developed a cognitive-behavioral intervention designed specifically to address suicidal behaviors and thoughts, which she calls **dialectical behavior therapy**. This therapy involves a number of techniques aimed at increasing problem-solving skills, interpersonal skills, and skills at managing negative emotions. Studies comparing this therapy to control conditions suggests that it can reduce suicidal thoughts and behaviors, and improve interpersonal skills (Linehan, 1999; Linehan et al., 1991; Shearin & Linehan, 1989).

Therapists will often include spouses, partners, and family members in treatment of suicidal people. Some of the problems behind a suicide attempt may reside in troubled relationships and family environments. Even if this is not the case, family members can play a role in the prevention of future attempts by helping suicidal members recognize when they are

vulnerable and actively seek professional help. Finally, suicidality in one member can devastate a family, and often the entire family is in need of psychological help.

Sociocultural Approaches and Prevention

Suicide hotlines and crisis intervention centers are forms of suicide prevention programs. They provide help to suicidal people in times of most need, hoping to prevent a suicidal act until suicidal feelings have passed.

In addition, many prevention programs aim to educate entire communities about suicide. These programs are often based in schools or colleges. Students are given information about the rates of suicide in their age group, risk factors for suicide, and what to do if they or a friend is suicidal. Unfortunately, studies of the effects of these programs have suggested they may not be very helpful, and indeed could do harm (Garland & Zigler, 1993). One major problem with these programs is that they often simultaneously target the general population of students and students who are at high risk for suicide. The programs may attempt to destigmatize suicide by making it appear quite common and not mentioning that most suicidal people are suffering from a psychological disorder, in hopes that suicidal students will feel more free to seek help. But such messages can backfire among students who are not suicidal, making suicide seem to be an understandable response to stress. In addition, a study of 115 school-based suicide prevention programs found that adolescents who had made prior suicide attempts generally reacted negatively to the programs, saying they were less inclined to seek help after seeing the program than before they saw the program (Garland, Shaffer, & Whittle, 1989).

Recently, researchers have begun tailoring suicide prevention messages to specific populations, particularly high-risk populations, in hopes that the right kind of help will get to the most needy people. David Shaffer and colleagues at Columbia University have designed a program that involves screening adolescents for suicidality, doing a diagnostic interview with the adolescents with the help of a laptop computer, and then interviewing the adolescent to determine the most appropriate referral to a mental-health specialist (Shaffer, personal communication, November, 1999). This program has shown initial success in identifying high-risk youth and getting them into effective treatment.

Guns and Suicide

In the United States, the majority of suicides, particularly those by men, involve guns (Hendin, 1995). Most people who commit suicide by gun do not buy guns expressly to commit suicide. Instead, they use guns that have been in their households for some time. Often, suicide with guns is an impulsive act committed by people under the influence of alcohol: They may be depressed, get drunk, and retrieve family handguns and shoot themselves. Unfortunately, a gunshot to the head is highly likely to end in death, whether or not the person truly intended to commit suicide.

Can we reduce the number of such suicides by restricting people's access to guns? The answer may be yes. Several studies have found that suicide rates decrease when cities or states enact strict antigun legisla-

Some studies have shown that widespread screening of teens by having them complete suicide questionnaires on laptop computers can identify teens at high risk for suicide.

tion that limits people's access to guns (Lambert & Silva, 1998). For example, one study compared two similar metropolitan areas with different degrees of firearms restrictions and found that the urban area with less strict handgun laws had almost six times more suicides involving firearms than the urban area with more strict handgun laws (Sloan et al., 1990). Although people who are intent on committing suicide can find other means to do so if guns are not available, restricting ready access to guns appears to reduce impulsive suicides with guns, particularly among males. In addition, several studies suggest that there is no increase in suicides by means other than guns (e.g., by jumping off buildings or inhaling carbon monoxide) when access to guns is restricted, suggesting that people do not simply substitute different means of committing suicide when guns are not available (Lambert & Silva, 1998). Instead, the lack of availability of guns gives them a "cooling off" period during which suicidal impulses can wane.

Opponents of gun control argue that restricting access to guns only makes people more vulnerable to intruders in their homes or to others wishing to do them harm. One study strongly suggests that this is not the case, however. Researchers examined 398 consecutive deaths by gun in homes of families who owned guns (usually handguns). Of these deaths, only 0.5 percent were intruders shot by families protecting themselves. In contrast, 83 percent of these deaths were suicides of adolescent or adult family members. Another 12 percent were homicides of one adult in the home by another family member, usually in the midst of quarrels. The final 3 percent of deaths were due to accidental gunshots of one of the family members (Kellerman et al., 1992). The mere presence of a firearm in the home appears to be a risk factor for suicide when other risk factors are taken into account, especially when handguns are improperly secured or are kept loaded (Brent et al., 1991). These data strongly suggest that an important preventative measure against suicide is removal of guns from the home.

Is There a Right to Commit Suicide?

Many societies, including the United States, are currently debating whether people have a right to commit suicide. Some people, such as psychiatrist Thomas Szasz and physician Jack Kevorkian, argue that the right to die as one chooses and when one chooses is a fundamental human right that cannot be regulated by the state. Others note that most people who attempt suicide but do not complete it do not later commit suicide, suggesting that they do not truly wish to die (Hendin, 1995). More generally, most people who contemplate suicide, particularly if they are depressed and not suffering from terminal medical illness, are ambivalent about it, and their suicidal wishes pass after relatively short periods of time. This suggests that preventing suicide is appropriate, at least for people who are mentally but not physically ill, because many people who attempt suicide are not making rational or permanent choices.

These debates will only become more heated as the population of the world ages. Currently, suicides by seriously ill people comprise only about 3 percent of all suicides (Hendin, 1995). That number is likely to increase, however, as more people are living to old age and, as a result, suffering serious illnesses that they may want to end through suicide.

Summing Up

- Drug treatments for suicidality most often involve lithium or antidepressant medications to reduce impulsive and violent behavior, and depression and mania. Antipsychotic medications and other medications that treat symptoms of an existing mental disorder may also be used.

- Psychotherapies for suicide are similar to those used for depression. Dialectical behavior therapy has been specifically designed to address skills deficits and thinking patterns in people who are suicidal.

- Suicide hot lines and crisis intervention programs provide immediate help to people who are highly suicidal.

- Community prevention programs aim to educate the public about suicide and encourage suicidal people into treatment.

- Guns are involved in the majority of suicides and some research suggests restricting access to guns can reduce suicide attempts.

- Society is debating whether people have a right to choose to suicide.

☉ BIO-PSYCHO-SOCIAL INTEGRATION

Suicide seems clearly to fit a diathesis-stress model. Several factors seem to determine an individual's vulnerability to suicide. These include a genetic vulnerability to suicide and possibly deficient serotonin levels. They also include early life experiences with loss and abuse, and later life experiences with traumatic events. Hopeless and dichotomous thinking styles, and impulsivity also can lower the threshold for suicidal behavior. And several psychological disorders clearly increase risk for suicide. Many people carry these risk factors, however, and never become suicidal. Something must trigger active suicidal behavior. These triggers also appear to be legion—the suicide of a close friend or relative, a recent traumatic event, a drug or alcohol binge. The difficulty in predicting suicidal behavior is that the specific trigger for one individual may be very different from the trigger for another. This is one reason why psychological treatments for suicidality have focused a great deal on helping people to recognize when suicidal feelings are rising and what their personal triggers are, and to learn more effective ways of coping with mood swings and transient suicidality so that the trigger never gets fully pulled.

Chapter Summary

- Suicide is defined as death from injury, poisoning, or suffocation where there is evidence (either explicit or implicit) that the injury was self-inflicted and that the decedent intended to kill himself or herself. Theorist Edwin Shneidman has described four types of suicide: Death seekers clearly seek to end their lives; death initiators also have a clear intention to die, but believe that they are simply hastening an inevitable death; death ignorers intend to end their lives but do not believe this means the end of their existence; death darers are ambivalent about dying, and take actions that greatly increase their chances of death, but do not guarantee they will die.

- Suicide is the ninth leading cause of death in the United States, and internationally, at least 160,000 people die by suicide every year and 2 million other people make suicide attempts each year. Women are more likely than men to attempt suicide, but men are more likely than women to complete suicide. Cross-cultural differences in suicide rates may have to do with religious doctrines, stressors, and cultural norms about suicide. Young people are less likely than adults to commit suicide, but suicide rates have been rising dramatically for young people in recent decades. The elderly, particularly elderly men, are at high risk for suicide.

- Suicide notes suggest that mental anguish and escape from pain are behind many suicides. Generally, suicide notes are brief and concrete, however, and leave few clues.

- Several negative life events or circumstances increase risk for suicide, including economic hardship, serious illness, loss, and abuse.

- Durkheim distinguished between egoistic suicide, which is committed by people who feel alienated from others, empty of social contacts, alone in an unsupportive world; anomic suicide, which is committed by people who experience severe disorientation because of some large change in their relationships to society; and altruistic suicide, which is committed by people who believe that taking their own lives will benefit society in some way.

- Suicide clusters occur when two or more suicides or attempted suicides are nonrandomly "bunched" in space or time. This phenomenon is sometimes called suicide contagion.

- Psychodynamic theorists attribute suicide to repressed rage that leads to self-destruction. Several mental disorders increase risk for suicide, including depression, bipolar disorder, substance abuse, schizophrenia, and anxiety disorders. Cognitive-behavioral theorists argue that hopelessness and dichotomous thinking contribute to suicide. Impulsivity is a behavioral characteristic common to people who suicide.

- Family history, twin, and adoption studies all suggest there is a genetic vulnerability to suicide.

- Many studies have found a link between low serotonin levels and suicide.

- Drug treatments for suicidality most often involve lithium or antidepressant medications to reduce impulsive and violent behavior, and depression and mania. Antipsychotic medications and other medications that treat symptoms of an existing mental disorder may also be used.

- Psychotherapies for suicide are similar to those used for depression. Dialectical behavior therapy has been specifically designed to address skills deficits and thinking patterns in people who are suicidal.

- Suicide hot lines and crisis intervention programs provide immediate help to people who are highly suicidal.

- Community prevention programs aim to educate the public about suicide and encourage suicidal people into treatment. Guns are involved in the majority of suicides and some research suggests restricting access to guns can reduce suicide attempts. Society is debating whether people have a right to choose to suicide.

Key Terms

suicide 300

death seekers 300

death initiators 301

death ignorers 301

death darers 301

subintentional deaths 301

egoistic suicide 309

anomic suicide 309

altruistic suicide 309

suicide clusters 310

suicide contagion 310

hopelessness 313

dichotomous thinking 314

crisis intervention 316

suicide hot lines 316

lithium 317

selective serotonin reuptake inhibitors 317

dialectical behavior therapy 318

Critical Thinking Questions

1. After reading this chapter, what is your opinion about the controversy over the right to die by suicide?

2. How could suicide prevention programs be designed so that they do not make suicide seem like a common and acceptable means of coping with stress?

3. What might account for the dramatic increases in rates of suicide in children and adolescents in recent decades?

Patricia Schwimmer
My Dog and I Are One

Whom Fortune wishes to destroy she first makes mad.

—*Publilius Syrus,* Moral Sayings *(first century B.C.;
translated by Darius Lyman)*

CHAPTER
10

Schizophrenia

CHAPTER OVERVIEW
Taking Psychology Personally:
Helping Families Cope with Schizophrenia

Symptoms, Diagnosis, and Prognosis

People with schizophrenia have delusions (beliefs with little grounding in reality) and hallucinations (unreal perceptual experiences such as hearing voices) and show grossly disorganized thought, speech, and behavior. They also show absence of motivation, affect, and quality communication. Four types of schizophrenia have been identified: paranoid, disorganized, catatonic, and undifferentiated.

Extraordinary People:
John Nash, Nobel Prize Winner

Biological Theories

There is strong evidence that schizophrenia is transmitted genetically. People with schizophrenia show abnormalities in the prefrontal cortex and ventricles of the brain. A number of prenatal difficulties and obstetrical problems at birth are implicated in the development of schizophrenia, including prenatal hypoxia and exposure to the influenza virus during the second trimester of gestation. Imbalances in the neurotransmitter dopamine are also implicated in schizophrenia.

Psychological Theories

Early psychodynamic theorists suggested that schizophrenia results from overwhelmingly negative experiences in early childhood between a child and his or her primary caregivers. Behavioral theories suggest that symptoms of schizophrenia can develop through operant conditioning. Cognitive theories accept that there is a biological vulnerability to schizophrenia, but see many symptoms as attempts to understand and cope with basic perceptual and attentional problems.

Sociocultural Perspectives

Several sociocultural theories suggest that aspects of family life contribute to schizophrenia. People with schizophrenia tend to live in generally stressful circumstances, but most theorists see this as a consequence rather than a cause of the disorder.

Treatments

Drugs called *neuroleptics* have proven useful in the treatment of schizophrenia. They have significant neurological side effects. New drugs known as *atypical antipsychotics* appear to be effective without inducing as many side effects as previous drugs. Psychosocial therapies focus on teaching communication and living skills and reducing isolation in people with schizophrenia.

Viewpoints:
Is Schizophrenia a Disease?

Bio-Psycho-Social Integration

Chapter Summary

Key Terms

Critical Thinking Questions

Most of us walk around so secure in our perceptions of the world that we would never think to ask whether those perceptions are real or not. We look at a chair, recognize it as an object for sitting in, and use it accordingly. We hear a friend call our name and look for that friend, confident that he or she is somewhere nearby. We have an idea, realize that if others are going to appreciate that idea we have to communicate to them, and articulate the idea clearly enough for them to understand it.

What must it be like to walk around not knowing whether your perceptions map onto reality? You might question whether the things you see before you really exist. You might wonder if the voices you are hearing come from other people or are only in your head. You might believe that the ideas you are having are being broadcast over the television so that others already know what you are thinking. If you are unable to tell the difference between what is real and what is unreal, you are suffering from **psychosis.**

This young woman describes her experience of slipping into psychosis (Sechehaye, 1951, p. 22):

Voices

One day, while I was in the principal's office, suddenly the room became enormous, illuminated by a dreadful electric light that cast false shadows. Everything was exact, smooth, artificial, extremely tense; the chairs and tables seemed models placed here and there. Pupils and teachers were puppets revolving without cause, without objective. I recognized nothing, nobody. It was as though reality, attenuated, had slipped away from all these things and these people. Profound dread overwhelmed me, and as though lost, I looked around desperately for help. I heard people talking, but I did not grasp the meaning of the words. The voices were metallic, without warmth or color. From time to time, a word detached itself from the rest. It repeated itself over and over in my head, absurd, as though cut off by a knife.

Psychosis can take many forms and have many causes. In Chapter 8, we noted that people who suffer mood disorders can become psychotic and have hallucinations and delusions that are horribly depressing or wildly grandiose in content. In addition, the DSM-IV recognizes a number of disorders in which psychosis is the primary feature of the disorder (see Table 10.1).

One of the most common psychotic disorders is **schizophrenia.** Schizophrenia is a truly puzzling disorder. At times, people with schizophrenia may think and communicate clearly, have an accurate view of reality, and function well in daily life. At other times, their thinking and speech are garbled, they lose touch with reality, and they are not able to care for themselves in even the most basic ways.

Schizophrenia exacts heavy costs. There are medical costs: Over 90 percent of people with schizophrenia seek treatment in a mental-health facility or general medicine facility in any given year (Narrow et al., 1993). Studies have estimated that direct medical care alone for people with schizophrenia costs almost $20 billion per year in the United States (Torrey, 1995). Then there are tens of billions of dollars more lost in productivity. Most people who develop schizophrenia do so in the late teenage or early adult years. By then, they have been educated and are ready to assume their place in society, contributing their unique talents. Then the disorder strikes, and often prevents them from making their contributions. Instead, people with schizophrenia may need continual services, including placement in halfway houses and other residential care facilities, rehabilitative therapy, subsidized income, and the help of social workers to obtain needed resources. And they need these services for the rest of their lives, because schizophrenia tends to be a lifelong disorder. As one person said,

Voices

What then does schizophrenia mean to me? It means fatigue and confusion, it means trying to separate every experience into the real and the unreal and not sometimes being aware of where the edges overlap. It means trying to think straight when there is a maze of experiences getting in the way, and when thoughts are continually being sucked out of your head so that you become embarrassed to speak at meetings. It means feeling sometimes that you are inside your head and visualising yourself walking over your brain, or watching another girl wearing your clothes and carrying out actions as you think them. It means knowing that you are continually "watched," that you can never succeed in life because the laws are all against you and knowing that your ultimate destruction is never far away.

(Quoted in Rollin, 1980, p. 162)

Within the United States, approximately 1 to 2 percent of the population will develop schizophrenia at some time in their lives (APA, 2000). This means that over 2 million Americans currently have schizophrenia. Put another way, about 7 people in every 1,000 has schizophrenia; or in a town of 3,000 people, there will be 21 people with schizophrenia (Torrey, 1995). Where are all these people? Unfortunately, schizophrenia is one of the most stigmatized psychological disorders, and we have become experts at hiding away loved ones with this disorder. As E. Fuller Torrey, a schizophrenia expert has said, "People with schizophrenia

TABLE 10.1
DSM-IV
Psychotic Disorders in the DSM-IV

The DSM-IV recognizes a number of psychotic disorders in addition to schizophrenia.

Disorder	Description
Schizophrenia	At least 1 month of acute symptoms of delusions, hallucinations, disorganized thought and speech, disorganized behavior, and negative symptoms, and at least 6 months of some symptoms of disorder.
Schizophreniform disorder	Same symptoms as schizophrenia, lasting more than 1 month but less than 6 months.
Schizoaffective disorder	Symptoms of schizophrenia coincide with symptoms of depression or mania, but there is at least a 2-week period when only symptoms of schizophrenia are present.
Delusional disorder	Evidence only of nonbizarre delusions (e.g., that one is being followed or deceived) of at least 1-month's duration; functioning at relatively high level.
Brief psychotic disorder	Presence of delusions, hallucinations, disorganized speech or behavior for at least one day but less than 1 month.
Shared psychotic disorder	The individual in a close relationship with someone who is delusional develops similar delusions (also known as *folie à deux*).
Substance-induced psychotic disorder	Hallucinations or delusions are caused by the direct physiological effects of a substance (such as cocaine).

Reprinted with permission from the *Diagnostic and Statistical Manual of Mental Disorders*, Fourth Edition. Copyright © 2000 American Psychiatric Association.

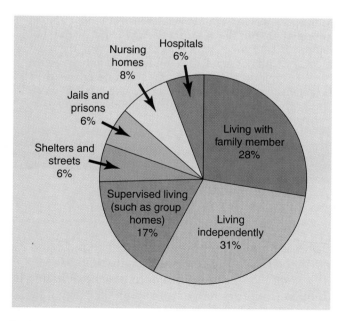

FIGURE 10.1 Distribution of People with Schizophrenia. Most people with schizophrenia live with family members or independently, but a number are in hospitals, nursing homes, group homes, jail, or on the street.

are the lepers of the twentieth century" (Torrey, 1995, p. 8). Torrey compiled data from several sources to estimate where people with schizophrenia are being kept, and his estimates are given in Figure 10.1. Note that the majority of people with schizophrenia are living independently or in their family's home. In *Taking Psychology Personally:* Helping Families Cope with Schizophrenia, page 328, we highlight the challenges that families of people with schizophrenia face in coping with their loved one's disorder, particularly when that loved one lives at home. Note also in Figure 10.1 that almost as many people with schizophrenia are in jails, prisons, homeless shelters and on the street as are in hospitals and nursing homes. The criminal system and the shelters are often the repository for people with schizophrenia who do not have families to support them or the resources to get psychiatric help.

There are differences across groups within the United States in rates of schizophrenia. One large epidemiological study found the highest rates of schizophrenia in African Americans, somewhat lower rates in Whites, and the lowest rates in Hispanic Americans, although these ethnic differences diminished when socioeconomic status was taken into account (Escobar, 1993). Studies of persons hospitalized for serious mental disorders have found that African Americans are more likely than other groups to be misdiagnosed with schizophrenia, when they are actually suffering from a severe mood disorder (Griffith & Baker, 1993).

TAKING PSYCHOLOGY PERSONALLY

Helping Families Cope with Schizophrenia

The anguish and confusion of family members who learn that a loved one has been diagnosed with schizophrenia can be huge. Before their eyes, a son or daughter or sibling who once was full of hope and plans for the future has disintegrated into a being that they may hardly recognize. The opportunities for blame are many—blaming each other for causing the disorder, blaming the afflicted family member for his or her symptoms, blaming mental-health professionals for not being able to cure the disorder, blaming themselves. On top of this, families are now being asked to bear the brunt of care for their schizophrenic members, acting as psychotherapist, medication specialist, caretaker, rehabilitator, intermediary with the mental-health system, and unconditional emotional support system. It is no wonder that burn-out and despair are common among these families.

One advocate on behalf of these families is E. Fuller Torrey. A very personal and painful experience brought Torrey to psychiatry and the study of schizophrenia. While Torrey was an undergraduate, his sister, then 17, was diagnosed with schizophrenia. Torrey accompanied his mother and sister to a treatment facility and was appalled at the explanations and treatments offered for her illness. As he pursued a career in medicine, Torrey dedicated himself to finding better explanations and treatments for schizophrenia than those that had been offered

to his sister, and to improving the treatment of people with serious mental disorders.

One of Torrey's many books, *Surviving Schizophrenia* (1995), assists families of people with schizophrenia in understanding the disorder and finding appropriate treatment for their afflicted family members. This book educates family members on what schizophrenia is and is not, and includes many specific tips on how to live with the schizophrenic family member and cope with the disorder. The key to surviving schizophrenia, according to Torrey, is having a SAFE attitude: Sense of humor, Acceptance of the illness, Family balance, and Expectations that are realistic.

Sense of Humor

It may seem strange to think that family members could approach schizophrenia with a sense of humor, but Torrey argues that the families most successful at managing schizophrenia have maintained a sense of humor and an appreciation for the absurd. Family members cannot laugh *at* the person with schizophrenia, but they can laugh *with* him or her. For example, one family in which the son typically relapsed in the autumn and required hospitalization had a standing family joke that the son always carved his pumpkins in the hospital.

Schizophrenia may be more common in men than in women, although the gender difference in rates of schizophrenia varies among studies and with the criteria used to diagnose schizophrenia (Cannon et al., 1998; Goldstein, 1995, 1997; Hambrecht et al., 1992). Women with schizophrenia tend to have better premorbid (predisorder) histories than men (Goldstein, 1995). They are more likely to have graduated from high school or college, to have married and had children, and to have developed good social skills. This may be, in part, because the onset of schizophrenia in women tends to be later in life, often in the late twenties or early thirties,

than it is for men, who more often develop schizophrenia in their late teens or early twenties.

Estimates of the prevalence of schizophrenia in different countries range from about 0.2 percent to 2.0 percent, but most estimates are between 0.5 and 1.0 percent (see Figure 10.2, p. 330). Some of the differences between rates of schizophrenia in different countries are due to differences in how narrowly or broadly schizophrenia is defined in those countries. In general, European researchers and clinicians have tended to use more narrow criteria for the diagnosis than have American researchers and clinicians (Gottesman, 1991).

Continued

Acceptance of the Disorder

Acceptance of the disorder does not mean giving up, but accepting the reality that the disorder will not go away, is likely to place limitations on the family member, and will need active management by the family. Unfortunately, it is more common for families to be angry at themselves, at the afflicted family member, at God, and so on. This anger can be overtly expressed, or seethe quietly until some trigger causes a family member to explode. Educating family members about the illness and what they can reasonably expect is one of the most important jobs of mental-health professionals because it can be the foundation of acceptance.

Family Balance

Caring for a schizophrenic family member can be overwhelming. Some families put the needs of their schizophrenic members before all the rest. Such families are prone to burn out, and neglected family members can become resentful and hostile. Families must achieve a balance of concern for the schizophrenic member and appreciation for the needs of other family members. This may require caregivers to get away occasionally and to find resources so that they are not providing round-the-clock care and ignoring their own needs.

Expectations That Are Realistic

It can be especially difficult for families to have realistic expectations of their schizophrenic member if that person had a particularly promising future before the illness struck. Pressure can be put on the schizophrenic family member that helps to trigger new episodes of acute symptoms. Lowering expectations can help family members appreciate the schizophrenic member for who he or she is now, rather than focusing on what they wish were true:

> Several relatives mentioned that giving up hope had paradoxically been the turning point for them in coming to terms with their unhappiness. "Once you give up hope," one mother said, "you start to perk up." "Once you realise he'll never be cured you start to relax." These relatives had lowered their expectations and aspirations for the patient, and had found that doing this had been the first step in cutting the problem down to manageable size. (Creer & Wing, 1974, p. 33)

Clearly, family members should not abandon all expectations of the person with schizophrenia. What is important is having realistic expectations. Again, educating the family about the disease is critical to creating such expectations.

Some family members find that becoming politically active on behalf of people with schizophrenia helps them cope. The National Alliance for the Mentally Ill (NAMI) is the largest national organization focusing on serious mental disorders, including schizophrenia. NAMI was created and is run by consumers (people with disorders) and their families to advocate for more research, better health care and access to health care, and public education. Many communities have local chapters of NAMI, which can usually be found in the phone book.

In this chapter, we first consider the symptoms of schizophrenia and the different forms that schizophrenia can take. After reviewing the prognosis of schizophrenia, then we examine its causes. Most theorists view schizophrenia primarily as a biological disorder, but psychological and sociocultural factors can influence how severe this disorder becomes and how often an individual has relapses. Effective biological treatments for schizophrenia have been developed in the last 50 years, as we will learn. These biological treatments are often supplemented by psychological and sociocultural therapies that help the person with schizophrenia cope with the impact of the disorder on his or her life, and we discuss these as well.

☉ SYMPTOMS, DIAGNOSIS, AND PROGNOSIS

Schizophrenia is a complex disorder that can take many forms. Indeed, many researchers and clinicians talk about "the schizophrenias," reflecting their belief that several different types or forms of schizophrenia are

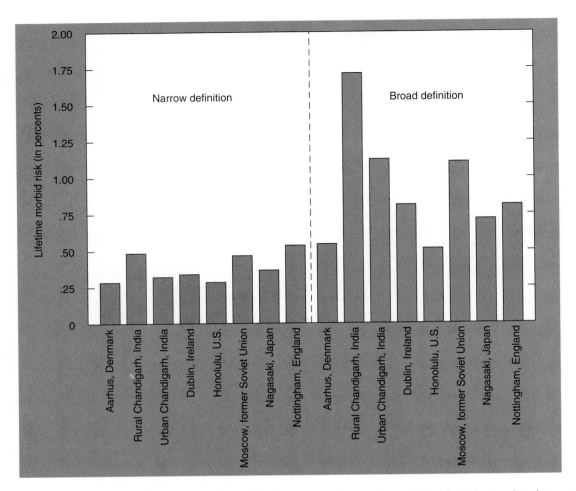

FIGURE 10.2   Prevalence of Schizophrenia in a Cultural Context. This figure shows us the prevalence of schizophrenia in countries using narrow versus broad definitions of the disorder. Despite differences in definitions, the prevalence of schizophrenia is remarkably similar across countries, ranging from about 0.2 to 2.0 percent.

Source: Gottesman, 1991, p. 80.

currently captured by the diagnostic criteria for schizophrenia. There are two categories of symptoms. **Positive symptoms**, also called *Type I symptoms*, are characterized by the presence of unusual perceptions, thoughts, or behaviors. Positive refers to the fact that these symptoms represent very salient experiences. In contrast, **negative symptoms**, or *Type II symptoms*, represent losses or deficits in certain domains. They involve the absence of behaviors rather than the presence of behaviors.

Positive Symptoms

The positive symptoms of schizophrenia include delusions, hallucinations, disorganized thought and speech, and disorganized or catatonic behavior (see *Concept Review:* Positive Symptoms of Schizophrenia). These symptoms can occur in other disorders, particularly in depression and bipolar disorder (see Chapter

8). On the other hand, many people with schizophrenia are also depressed or show tremendous mood swings. This can make the differentiation between schizophrenia and a mood disorder with psychotic features very tricky. If psychotic symptoms occur only during periods of clear depression or mania, then the most appropriate diagnosis is mood disorder with psychotic features. If psychotic symptoms occur substantially in the absence of depression or mania, or the depression or mania do not meet the criteria for a diagnosis of a mood disorder, then the appropriate diagnosis is schizophrenia or schizoaffective disorder (see Table 10.1, p. 332).

Delusions

Delusions are ideas that an individual believes are true but are highly unlikely and often simply impossible. Of course, most people occasionally hold beliefs that are likely to be wrong, such as the belief that they

CONCEPT REVIEW

Positive Symptoms of Schizophrenia

The positive symptoms of schizophrenia represent the presence of unusual perceptions, thoughts, or behaviors.

Symptom	Definition and Example
Delusions	Beliefs with little grounding in reality (e.g., beliefs that you are being persecuted, or that you are the Messiah)
Hallucinations	Unreal perceptual or sensory experiences (e.g., hearing, seeing, and feeling things that are not there)
Disorganized thought and speech	Grossly disorganized patterns of speech (e.g., complete incoherence, linking together words based on sounds instead of meaning)
Disorganized or catatonic behavior	Behavior that is highly unpredictable, bizarre, and/or shows a complete lack of responsiveness to the outside world (e.g., becoming completely motionless for long periods; sudden, untriggered outbursts)

Source: DSM-IV, APA, 2000.

Paranoia is a prominent symptom in some forms of schizophrenia.

will win the lottery. These kinds of *self-deceptions* differ from delusions in at least three ways (Strauss, 1969). First, self-deceptions are not completely implausible, whereas delusions often are. It is possible to win the lottery but it is not possible that your body is dissolving and floating into space. Second, people harboring self-deceptions may think about these beliefs occasionally, but people harboring delusions tend to be preoccupied with them. Delusional people will look for evidence in support of their beliefs, attempt to convince others of these beliefs, and take actions based on them, such as filing lawsuits against the people they believe are trying to control their minds. Third, people holding self-deceptions typically will acknowledge that their beliefs may be wrong, but people holding delusions are often highly resistant to arguments or compelling facts contradicting their delusions. They may view the arguments of others against their beliefs as a conspiracy to silence them and as evidence for the truth of their beliefs.

Common Types of Delusions

Table 10.2 lists some of the most common types of delusions. A **persecutory delusion** is the type of delusion we hear about most often in media depictions of people with schizophrenia and, indeed, is the most common form of delusion. People with persecutory delusions may believe they are being watched or tormented by people they know, such as their professors, or by agencies or persons in authority with whom they have never had direct contact, such as the FBI or a particular congressperson. Another common type of delusion, the **delusion of reference**, in which people believe that random events or comments by others are directed at them, is related to persecutory delusions. People with delusions of reference may believe that the newscaster on the local television news is reporting on their movements, or that the comments of a local politician at a rally are directed at them. Sometimes, delusions of reference are part of a grandiose belief system in which all events are meaningful to the believer. For example, one person with schizophrenia was lying in bed feeling cold and shivering when a small earthquake occurred near his house. He believed that he caused the earthquake with his shivering.

Grandiose delusions are beliefs that one is some special person or being, or holds some special powers. A person may believe that he is a deity incarnated. He may believe he is the most intelligent, insightful, and

TABLE 10.2

Types of Delusions

These are several types of delusions that are often woven together in a complex and frightening system of beliefs.

Delusion	Definition	Example
Persecutory delusions	False belief that one's self or one's loved ones are being persecuted, watched, or conspired against by others	Belief that the CIA, FBI, and local police are conspiring to catch you in a "sting" operation
Delusions of being controlled	Belief that one's thoughts, feelings, or behaviors are being imposed or controlled by some external force	Belief that an alien has taken over your body and is controlling your behaviors
Thought broadcasting	Belief that one's thoughts are being broadcast from one's mind for others to hear	Belief that your thoughts are being transmitted via the Internet against your will
Thought insertion	Belief that another person or object is inserting thoughts into one's head	Belief that your spouse is inserting blasphemous thoughts in your mind through the microwave
Thought withdrawal	Belief that thoughts are being removed from one's head by another person or object	Belief that your roommate is stealing all your thoughts while you sleep
Delusions of guilt or sin	False belief that one has committed a terrible act or is responsible for some terrible event	Belief that you have killed someone
Somatic delusions	False belief that one's appearance or part of one's body is diseased or altered	Belief that your intestines have been replaced by snakes
Grandiose delusions	False belief that one has great power, knowledge, or talent or that one is a famous and powerful person	Belief that you are Martin Luther King Jr. reincarnated

creative person on earth. He may believe he has discovered the cure for a disease. Finally, **delusions of thought control** are beliefs that one's thoughts are being controlled by outside forces, as this person with schizophrenia describes:

Voices

"Suggestions" or "commands" are being transmitted (by a parapsychologist) straight into an unknowing victim's hearing-center, becoming strong impressions on his mind. Those "voices" (which are sometimes accompanied by melodious tones and sounds that either please or irritate the mind) will subliminally change his personality by controlling what kinds of suggestions go into his "subconscious memory" to govern how he feels, or mind-boggle him (trick his mind into believing that they are its own thoughts) during these brainwash and thought-control techniques. Psychotropic medications are given to the victims who can "discern the voices" over other sounds in order to keep them ignorant to the real truth about their dilemma, and to enhance the chemical-reaction in the brain to the stimulation as their souls: (minds): are enslaved by

computers programmed to "think" for them here in George Orwell's America.

Delusional beliefs can be simple and transient, such as when a person with schizophrenia believes the pain she just experienced in her stomach was the result of someone across the room shooting a laser beam at her. Delusional beliefs are often complex and elaborate, however, and the person clings to these beliefs for long periods. The following account illustrates how several types of delusions—grandiose delusions, persecutory delusions, delusions of reference, and delusions of thought control—can co-occur and work together in one person's belief system. Note that, although the following passage is written by a person with schizophrenia about his own experience, he speaks of himself in the third person (Zelt, 1981, pp. 527–531):

Voices

A drama that profoundly transformed David Zelt began at a conference on human psychology. David respected the speakers as scholars and wanted their approval of a paper he had written about telepathy. A week before the conference, David had sent his paper "On the Origins of Telepathy" to one speaker, and the other speakers had all read it. He proposed the novel scientific idea that telepathy could only be optimally studied during the process of birth. . . .

David's paper was viewed as a monumental contribution to the conference and potentially to psychology in general. If scientifically verified, his concept of telepathy, universally present at birth and measurable, might have as much influence as the basic ideas of Darwin and Freud.

Each speaker focused on David. By using allusions and nonverbal communications that included pointing and glancing, each illuminated different aspects of David's contribution. Although his name was never mentioned, the speakers enticed David into feeling that he had accomplished something supernatural in writing the paper. . . .

David was described as having a halo around his head, and the Second Coming was announced as forthcoming. Messianic feelings took hold of him. His mission would be to aid the poor and needy, especially in underdeveloped countries. . . .

David's sensitivity to nonverbal communication was extreme; he was adept at reading people's minds. His perceptual powers were so developed that he could not discriminate between telepathic reception and spoken language by others. He was distracted by others in a way that he had never been before. It was as if the nonverbal behavior of people interacting with him was a kind of code. Facial expressions, gestures, and postures of others often determined what he felt and thought.

Several hundred people at the conference were talking about David. He was the subject of enormous mystery, profound in his silence. Criticism, though, was often expressed by skeptics of the anticipated Second Coming. David felt the intense communication about him as torturous. He wished the talking, nonverbal behavior, and pervasive train of thoughts about him would stop.

David's *grandiose delusions* were that he discovered the source of telepathy, that all the scientists thought highly of him, and that he might be the Messiah. As is often the case, these grandiose delusions were accompanied by *persecutory delusions*—that the scientists were criticizing him out of jealousy. David's delusions of reference were that all the scientists were talking about him, directly and indirectly. David believed that he could read others' minds. Finally, he had *delusions of thought control*, that the scientists were determining what he felt with their facial expressions, gestures, and postures.

Delusions Across Cultures

Although the types of delusions we have discussed probably occur in all cultures, the specific content of delusions can differ across cultures (Tateyama, Asai, Hashimoto, Bartels, & Kasper, 1998). For example, persecutory delusions often focus on intelligence agencies or persons of authority in the person's culture. Urban Whites in the United States might fear that the Central Intelligence Agency is after them; Afro Caribbeans may believe that people are killing them with curses (Westermeyer, 1993). Studies comparing Japanese people with schizophrenia to people in Western Europe with schizophrenia have found that among the Japanese delusions of being slandered by others or delusions that others know something terrible about them are relatively common, perhaps due to the emphasis in Japanese culture on how one is thought of by others. In contrast, among German or Austrian people with schizophrenia, religious delusions of having committed a sin (e.g., "Satan orders me to pray to him; I will be punished") are relatively common, perhaps due to the influence of Christianity in Western Europe (Tateyama et al., 1993).

Some theorists argue that odd or impossible beliefs that are part of a culture's shared belief system cannot be considered delusions when these beliefs are held by individuals in that culture (Fabrega, 1993). For example, if a culture believes that the spirits of dead relatives watch over the living, then individuals in that culture who hold that belief are not considered delusional, although people in other cultures might consider such a belief untrue and impossible. However, even theorists who hold cultural relativist positions on delusions tend to view people who hold extreme manifestations of their culture's shared belief systems as delusional. For example, a person who believed that her dead relatives were tormenting her by causing her heart and lungs to rot would be considered delusional, even if she were part of a culture that holds the belief that dead relatives watch over the living.

Hallucinations and Alterations of the Senses

Have you ever had a strange perceptual experience, such as thinking you saw someone when no one was near, thinking you heard a voice talking to you, or feeling as though your body were floating through air? If so, you are not alone. One study found that 15 percent of mentally healthy college students report sometimes hearing voices, such as the voice of God telling them to do something, their "conscience" giving them advice, or two voices (usually both their own) debating a topic (Chapman, Edell, & Chapman, 1980). Six percent of the students believed they had transmitted thoughts into other people's heads at some time. Most of these students probably would not be diagnosed with schizophrenia because their "hallucinations" were occasional and brief, often occurring when they were tired or stressed or under the influence of alcohol or drugs, and did not impair their daily functioning in any way.

The **hallucinations** and perceptual changes of people with schizophrenia tend to be much more bizarre and troubling than the college students' hallucinations, and are not only precipitated by sleep deprivation, stress, or drugs, as this person describes:

Voices

At one point, I would look at my coworkers and their faces would become distorted. Their teeth looked like fangs ready to devour me. Most of the time I couldn't trust myself to look at anyone for fear of being swallowed. I had no respite from the illness. Even when I tried to sleep, the demons would keep me awake, and at times I would roam the house searching for them. I was being consumed on all sides whether I was awake or asleep. I felt I was being consumed by demons. (Long, 1996)

In the early stages of schizophrenia, alterations of all the senses are especially prominent, as these people describe (from McGhie & Chapman, 1961):

Voices

During the last while back I have noticed that noises all seem to be louder to me than they were before. It's as if someone had turned up the volume. . . . I notice it most with background noises—you know what I mean, noises that are always around but you don't notice them. Now they seem to be just as loud and sometimes louder than the main noises that are going on.

Colours seem to be brighter now, almost as if they are luminous painting. I'm not sure if things are solid until I touch them. The colours of things seem much clearer and yet at the same time there is something missing. The things I look at seem to be flatter as if you were looking just at the surface.

People describe being overwhelmed by a flooding of their senses, as if some natural screening mechanism in their brain is no longer working (McGhie & Chapman, 1961):

Voices

Everything seems to grip my attention although I am not particularly interested in anything. I am speaking to you just now, but I can hear noises going on next door and in the corridor. I find it difficult to shut these

The hallucinations of people with schizoprenia can be very bizzare and frightening.

out, and it makes it more difficult for me to concentrate on what I am saying to you.

For many people, these perceptual changes develop into full-blown hallucinations. An **auditory hallucination** (hearing voices, music, and so on) is the most common hallucination, and even more common in women than in men. Often, people hear voices accusing them of evil deeds or threatening them. The voices may also tell them to harm themselves. People with schizophrenia may talk back to the voices, even as they are also trying to talk to people who are actually in a room with them. The second most common hallucination is the **visual hallucination**, often accompanied by auditory hallucinations. For example, a person may see Satan standing at her bedside telling her she is damned and must die. Hallucinations can involve any sensory modality, however. *Tactile hallucinations* involve the perception that something is happening to the outside of one's body, for example, that bugs are crawling up your back. *Somatic hallucinations* involve the perception that something is happening inside your body, for example, that worms are eating your intestines. These hallucinations are often frightening, even terrifying.

Cross-Cultural Differences

As with delusions, the types of hallucinations people have in different cultures appear similar, but the specific content of hallucinations can be culturally specific. For example, a person from Asia may see the ghosts of ancestors haunting him or her, but this is not a common experience for Europeans (Westermeyer, 1993). And as with delusions, clinicians must interpret hallucinations in a cultural context. For example, a Puerto Rican woman might be diagnosed with schizophrenia by a White American interviewer because she believes she has special powers to anticipate events and because she describes what sounded like hallucinations, such as "I see images of saints, virgins in the house. I also see the image of Jesus Christ, with the crown of thorns and bleeding." Interviewers who know Puerto Rican culture, however, might recognize this woman's beliefs and experiences as consistent with a spiritual group common in Latin America that believes in clairvoyance and religious visions (Guarnaccia et al., 1992, pp. 105–106).

Disorganized Thought and Speech

The disorganized thinking of people with schizophrenia is often referred to as a **formal thought disorder.** One of the most common forms of disorganization in schizophrenia is a tendency to slip from one topic to a seemingly unrelated topic with little coherent transition, often referred to as *loosening of associations* or *derailment.* For example, one person with schizophrenia posted the following "announcement":

Voices

Things that relate, the town of Antelope, Oregon, Jonestown, Charlie Manson, the Hillside Strangler, the Zodiac Killer, Watergate, King's trial in L.A., and many more. In the last 7 years alone, over 23 Starwars scientists committed suicide for no apparent reason. The AIDS coverup, the conference in South America in 87 had over 1,000 doctors claim that insects can transmit it. To be able to read one's thoughts and place thoughts in one's mind without the person knowing it's being done. Realization is a reality of bioelectromagnetic control, which is thought transfer and emotional control, recording individual brain-wave frequencies of thought, sensation, and emotions.

The person who wrote this announcement saw clear connections among the events he listed in the first half of the paragraph and between these events and his concerns about mind reading and bioelectromagnetic control. However, it is hard for us to see these connections.

A person with schizophrenia may answer questions with comments that are barely related to the questions or completely unrelated to the questions. For example, when asked why he is in the hospital, a man with schizophrenia might answer, "Spaghetti looks like worms. I really think it's worms. Gophers dig tunnels but rats build nests." At times, the person's speech is so disorganized as to be totally *incoherent* to the listener, when it is often referred to as **word salad.** They may make up words that mean something to them alone, known as *neologisms.* The person with schizophrenia may make associations between words that are based on the sounds of the words rather than the content, and these are known as *clangs.* For example, in response to the question, "Is that your dog?" a person with schizophrenia might say, "Dog. Dog is Spog. Frog. Leap. Heap, steep, creep, deep, gotta go beep." Or they may *perseverate* on the same word or statement, saying it over and over, again and again.

Men with schizophrenia tend to show more severe deficits in language compared to women with schizophrenia (Goldstein, Seidman, Goodman, Koren, Lee, Weintraub, & Tsuang, 1998). Some researchers have speculated that this is because language is controlled more bilaterally—by both sides of the brain—in women than in men. Thus, the brain abnormalities associated with schizophrenia may not impact women's language and thought as much as men's because women can use both sides of their brains to compensate for problems. In contrast, language is more localized in men, so that when these areas of the brain are affected by schizophrenia, men may not be as able to compensate for these deficits.

Disorganized or Catatonic Behavior

The disorganized behavior of people with schizophrenia is often what leads others to be afraid of them. The person with schizophrenia may display unpredictable and apparently untriggered agitation, suddenly shouting or swearing or pacing rapidly up and down the street. He may engage in socially disapproved behavior, like public masturbation. He is often disheveled and dirty, sometimes wearing few clothes on a cold day or heavy clothes on a very hot day. Short of these more bizarre behaviors, the person with schizophrenia often has trouble organizing his daily routine to ensure that he bathes, dresses properly, and eats regularly. It is as if all his concentration must be used to accomplish even one simple task, like brushing his teeth, and other tasks just do not get done.

In Chapter 8, we discussed **catatonia,** a group of disorganized behaviors that reflect an extreme lack of responsiveness to the outside world. One form of catatonia in schizophrenia is **catatonic excitement,** in which the person becomes wildly agitated for no apparent reason and is difficult to subdue. During a period of catatonic excitement, the individual may articulate a number of delusions or hallucinations, or be largely incoherent. In 1905, Kraepelin gave the following account of a patient showing signs of catatonic excitement (from R. D. Laing, 1971, *The Divided Self*, pp. 29–30).

CASE STUDY

The patient I will show you today has almost to be carried into the rooms, as he walks in a straddling fashion on the outside of his feet. On coming in, he throws off his slippers, sings a hymn loudly, and then cries twice (in English), "My father, my real father!" He is eighteen years old, and a pupil . . . , tall and rather strongly built, but with a pale complexion, on which there is very often a transient flush. The patient sits with his eyes shut, and pays no attention to his surroundings. He does not look up even when he is spoken to, but answers beginning in a low voice, and gradually screaming louder and louder. When asked where he is, he says, "You want to know that too. I tell you who is being measured and is measured and shall be measured. I know all that, and could tell you, but I do not want to." When asked his name, he screams, "What is your name? What does he shut? He shuts his eyes. What does he hear? He does not understand; he understands not. How? Who? Where? When? What does he mean? When I tell him to look he does not look properly. You there, just look. What is it? What is the matter? Attend; he attends not. I say, what is it, then? Why do you give me no answer? Are you getting impudent again? How can you be so impudent? I'm coming! I'll show you! You don't whore for me. You mustn't be smart either; you're an impudent, lousy fellow, such an impudent, lousy fellow I've never met with. Is he beginning again? You understand nothing at all, nothing at all; nothing at all does he understand. If you follow now, he won't follow, will not follow. Are you getting still more impudent? Are you getting impudent still more? How they attend, they do attend," and so on. At the end, he scolds in quite inarticulate sounds.

This patient's catatonic excitement is infused with angry and agitated outbursts that also have the characteristic disorganization of schizophrenic thought.

Attention Deficits

Many researchers have argued that underlying the positive symptoms of schizophrenia—the delusions, hallucinations, disorganized thinking and speech, and disorganized behavior—is a fundamental problem in the deployment and control of basic attentional processes (see Nuechterlein et al., 1992). Much of the research on attentional difficulties in schizophrenia has employed a task called the Continuous Performance Test or CPT (Erlenmeyer-Kimling & Cornblatt, 1987; Nuechterlein et al., 1998). The CPT requires a subject to detect a particular stimulus, such as the letter A, in a series of stimuli presented for very brief periods on a computer screen. The task can be made more difficult by making the stimulus somewhat blurry or embedding the target stimuli in a group of other stimuli rather than presenting each stimulus separately on the screen. Poor performance on the CPT reflects problems in sustaining attention and in detecting a target stimulus when confronted by distracting stimuli (often referred to as detecting the *signal* among the *noise*). Several studies have shown that people with acute symptoms of schizophrenia perform more poorly on the CPT than do normal control subjects or persons with other psychiatric disorders (see Cornblatt et al., 1998 and Nuechterlein et al., 1998 for reviews).

Even more impressive is evidence that people with schizophrenia whose symptoms are in remission continue to show problems in attentional problems on the CPT, and children and siblings of a person with schizophrenia perform more poorly on the CPT than do relatives of normal controls or people with other psychiatric disorders. These children also have more trouble remembering stimuli they have seen if their rehearsal of these stimuli is interrupted by a distraction. In turn, these children who show problems with sustained attention and with detecting signal from noise show more behavioral, social, and emotional problems than do other children (Erlenmeyer-Kimling & Cornblatt, 1992; Erlenmeyer-Kimling, Golden, & Cornblatt, 1989; Erlenmeyer-Kimling et al., 1998). The attentional problems may overwhelm the children's abilities to cope with the everyday stresses of life. The few studies that have followed these children into adulthood have also found they are more prone to develop early symptoms of schizophrenia (Erlenmeyer-Kimling & Cornblatt, 1992; Erlenmeyer-Kimling et al., 1995; see also Cannon, Rosso, Bearden, Sanchez, & Hadley, 1999).

These deficits in attention may contribute to the positive symptoms of schizophrenia by making it nearly impossible for the person with schizophrenia to respond only to relevant or real stimuli. All of us tend to think about more than one thing at a time. While you are reading this book, your thoughts probably also are drifting to other issues, such as what you are going to have for dinner tonight or the content of a conversation you had with a friend this morning. Most of us can differentiate easily between the thoughts that are relevant to our current situations or goals and those that are irrelevant. We can turn off unwanted thoughts, for the most part. For the person with schizophrenia, this ability to differentiate between relevant and irrelevant and between real and unreal may be gone, and every thought and image may seem as relevant and real as the next. For example, as the person with schizophrenia is trying to hold a conversation with a friend, the thoughts she is having about a television show she watched last night might drift in. Unlike the person without schizophrenia, the person with schizophrenia has trouble differentiating signal (thoughts relevant to the current conversation) from noise (thoughts relevant to the television show she watched last night).

People with catatonia will strike strange poses and maintain them for long periods of time without moving.

In the midst of answering her friend's question about how she is feeling, she might begin to relay her thoughts about the television show, without being aware that she has jumped to a new topic irrelevant to the one being discussed with her friend. In short, it would be very difficult for her to maintain a coherent stream of thought or speech if she could not hold her attention on any particular thought or idea for more than a moment in time. As one person put it:

Voices

My thoughts get all jumbled up, I start thinking or talking about something but I never get there. Instead I wander off in the wrong direction and get caught up with all sorts of different things that may be connected with the things I want to say but in a way can't explain. People listening to me get more lost than I do.

(McGhie & Chapman, 1961)

Negative Symptoms

The negative symptoms of schizophrenia, or Type II symptoms, involve losses or deficits in certain domains. Three types of negative symptoms are recognized by DSM-IV as core symptoms of schizophrenia: affective flattening, alogia, and avolition (see *Concept Review:* Negative Symptoms of Schizophrenia).

Affective Flattening

Affective flattening is a severe reduction, or even the complete absence, of affective responses to the environment. This is often referred to as *blunted affect*. The person's face may remain immobile most of the time, no matter what happens, and his or her body language may be unresponsive to what is going on in the environment. One man set fire to his house then sat down to watch TV. When it was called to his attention that his house was on fire, he calmly got up and walked outside (Torrey, 1995). People with blunted affect may speak in a monotone voice without any emotional expression and may not make eye contact with others.

Affective flattening refers to a person's lack of overt expression of emotion. We must be cautious, however, in assuming that people demonstrating affective flattening are actually experiencing no emotion. In one study, people with schizophrenia and people without the disorder were shown emotionally charged films while their facial expressions were observed and their physiological arousal was recorded (Kring &

CONCEPT REVIEW

Negative Symptoms of Schizophrenia

The negative symptoms of schizophrenia represent the absence of usual emotional and behavioral responses.

Symptom	Description	Examples
Affective flattening (or blunted affect)	Severe reduction or complete absence of affective (emotional) responses to the environment	No facial expressions in response to emotionally charged stimuli; no emotional expression in voice
Alogia	Severe reduction or complete absence of speech	Complete mutism for weeks
Avolition	Inability to persist at common, goal-oriented tasks	Inability to get dressed, brush teeth, eat breakfast in morning

Source: DSM-IV, APA, 2000.

Neale, 1996). The people with schizophrenia showed less facial responsiveness to the films than the normal group, but reported experiencing just as much emotion and showed even more physiological arousal. So people with schizophrenia who are showing no emotion may be experiencing intense emotion that they cannot express.

Alogia

Alogia, or poverty of speech, is a reduction in speaking. The person may not initiate speech with others, and when asked direct questions, she may give brief, empty replies. The person's lack of speech presumably reflects a lack of thinking, although it may be caused in part by a lack of motivation to speak.

Avolition

Finally, **avolition** is an inability to persist at common goal-directed activities, including at work, school, or home. The person has great trouble completing tasks and is disorganized and careless, apparently completely unmotivated. She may sit around all day doing almost nothing. She may withdraw and become socially isolated. Again, this behavioral deficit may be due in large part to the stimulus overload and problems in attention in schizophrenia:

Voices

I am not sure of my own movements anymore. It's very hard to describe this but at times I am not sure about even simple actions like sitting down. It's not so much thinking out what to do, it's the doing of it that sticks me. . . . I found recently that I was thinking of myself doing things before I would do them. If I am going to sit down, for example, I have got to think of myself and almost see myself sitting down before I do it. It's the same with other things like washing, eating, and even dressing—things that I have done at one time without even bothering or thinking about at all. . . . All this makes me move much slower now. I take more time to do things because I am always conscious of what I am doing. If I could just stop noticing what I am doing, I would get things done a lot faster.

(McGhie & Chapman, 1961)

The negative symptoms of schizophrenia can be difficult to diagnose reliably. First, they involve the absence of behaviors rather than the presence of behaviors, making them more difficult to detect. Second, they lie on a continuum between normal and abnormal, rather than being clearly bizarre behaviors as are the positive symptoms. Third, they can be caused by a

Avolition—the inability to initiate and maintain activities—is a common symptom in schizophrenia.

host of factors other than schizophrenia, such as depression or social isolation, or may be side effects of medications.

Other Features

There are a number of other symptoms or features of schizophrenia that are not part of the formal diagnostic criteria for the disorder but frequently occur in the disorder. Among these are inappropriate affect, anhedonia, and impaired social skills.

Inappropriate Affect

Instead of showing flattened or blunted affect, the person with schizophrenia may show *inappropriate affect*, laughing at sad things and crying at happy things. This may happen because he or she is thinking about and responding to something other than what is going on in the environment:

Voices

It must look queer to people when I laugh about something that has got nothing to do with what I am talking about, but they don't know what's going on inside and how much of it is running round in my head. You see I might be talking about something quite serious to you and other things come into my head at the same time that are funny and this makes me laugh. If only I could concentrate on the one thing at the one time and I wouldn't look half so silly.

(McGhie & Chapman, 1961)

Inappropriate displays of affect may also occur because the brain processes that match stimuli with the proper emotions and emotional responses to those stimuli are not working properly, so that unhappy stimuli somehow trigger laughter and happy stimuli trigger sadness. Whatever the cause, inappropriate affect is one of the most striking symptoms in schizophrenia. Often the person will switch from one extreme emotional expression to another for no apparent reason.

Anhedonia

We said earlier that many people who display flattened or blunted affect are actually experiencing emotions although they are not showing them. Some people with schizophrenia, however, experience severe *anhedonia*, similar to the anhedonia that characterizes depression (see Chapter 8). They lose the ability to experience emotion, and no matter what happens, they do not feel happy or sad. This emotional void can itself be very aversive. Said Michael Wechsler (1971, p. 17), "I wish I could wake up feeling really bad—it would be better than feeling nothing."

Impaired Social Skills

Not surprisingly, the symptoms of schizophrenia make it difficult to have normal interactions with other people. People with schizophrenia show a wide range of *impaired social skills*, including difficulty in holding conversations, in maintaining relationships, and in holding a job. You may be surprised, however, that the difficulties in social skills in schizophrenia may be due more to the negative symptoms than to the positive symptoms of the disorder. Although the negative symptoms of schizophrenia are less bizarre than the positive symptoms, they are major causes of the problems people with schizophrenia have in functioning in society. People with schizophrenia with many negative symptoms have lower educational attainments and less success in holding jobs, poorer performance on cognitive tasks, and a poorer prognosis do than those with few negative symptoms and predominantly positive symptoms (Andreasen et al., 1990; Eaton et al., 1998). In addition, the negative symptoms are less responsive to medication than are the positive symptoms: The person with schizophrenia may be able to overcome the hallucinations, delusions, and thought disturbances with medication but may not be able to overcome the affective flattening, alogia, and avolition. Thus, he may remain chronically unresponsive, unmotivated, and socially isolated, even when he is not acutely psychotic (Fenton & McGlashan, 1994).

Diagnosis

Schizophrenia has been recognized as a psychological disorder since the early 1800s (Gottesman, 1991).

German psychiatrist Emil Kraepelin is credited with the most comprehensive and accurate description of schizophrenia. In 1883, Kraepelin labeled the disorder *dementia praecox* (precocious dementia) because he believed the disorder resulted from premature deterioration of the brain. He viewed the disorder as progressive, irreversible, and chronic. Kraepelin's definition of this disorder was a narrow one, and resulted in only a small percentage of people receiving this diagnosis.

The other major figure in the early history of schizophrenia research was Eugen Bleuer. Bleuer disagreed with Kraepelin's view that this disorder always developed at an early age, and always led inevitably toward severe deterioration of the brain. Bleuer introduced the label *schizophrenia* for this disorder, from the Greek words *schizein*, meaning "to split," and *phren*, meaning "mind." Bleuer believed that this disorder involved the splitting of usually integrated psychic functions of mental associations, thoughts, and emotions. (Bleuler did not view schizophrenia as the splitting of distinct personalities as in multiple personality disorder nor do modern psychiatrists and psychologists.) Bleuer argued that the primary problem underlying the many different symptoms of schizophrenia was the "breaking of associative threads." Here Bleuer is referring to a breaking of associations between all aspects of thought, language, memory, and problem-solving. He argued that the attentional problems seen in schizophrenia are due to a lack of the necessary links between aspects of the mind, and in turn, the behavioral symptoms of schizophrenia (such as alogia) are similarly due to an inability to maintain a train of thought.

Bleuer's view of schizophrenia was much more broad than Kraepelin's and led to a broader range of people being given this diagnosis. Bleuer's definition of schizophrenia was adopted by clinicians in the United States in the early twentieth century, whereas the Europeans stuck with Kraepelin's narrower definition of schizophrenia. Over the first few decades of the twentieth century, U.S. clinicians further broadened their definition of schizophrenia, so that eventually, anyone experiencing delusions and hallucinations was given the diagnosis (even though delusions and hallucinations can also occur in mood disorders).

Beginning in 1980 with the third edition of the DSM-III, the pendulum began to swing back toward a more narrow definition of schizophrenia in the United States. Now, the DSM-IV states that, in order to be diagnosed with schizophrenia, an individual must show some symptoms of the disorder for at least 6 months. During this 6 months, there must be at least 1 month of acute symptoms, during which two or more of the broad groups of symptoms we have just discussed (delusions, hallucinations, disorganized speech, disorganized or catatonic behavior, negative symptoms) are present and severe enough to impair the individual's social or occupational functioning (see Table 10.3). **Prodromal symptoms** are present before people go into the acute phase of schizophrenia, and **residual symptoms** are present after they come out of the acute phase. During the prodromal and residual phases, people with schizophrenia may express beliefs that are not delusional but are unusual or odd. They may have strange perceptual experiences, such as sensing another person in the room, without reporting full-blown hallucinations. They may speak in a somewhat disorganized and tangential way but remain coherent. Their behavior may be peculiar—for example, it may involve collecting scraps of paper—but not grossly disorganized. The negative symptoms are especially prominent in the prodromal and residual phases of the disorder. The person may be withdrawn and uninterested in others or in work or school. During the prodromal phase, family members and friends may experience the person with schizophrenia as "gradually slipping away."

We have already discussed some of the difficulties in distinguishing schizophrenia from mood disorders with psychotic features. Another differential diagnosis that is difficult to make is between schizophrenia and schizoaffective disorder (see Table 10.4). Schizoaffective disorder is a mix of schizophrenia and mood disorders, with evidence that the schizophrenic symptoms are present even when the mood symptoms are absent. People with schizoaffective disorder simultaneously experience symptoms that meet Criterion A for the diagnosis of schizophrenia (see Table 10.3) and mood symptoms meeting the criteria for a major depressive episode, a manic episode, or an episode of mixed mania/depression. Their mood symptoms must be present for a substantial duration of the time that their schizophrenic symptoms are present. But the main difference between schizoaffective disorder and mood disorders with psychotic features is that in schizoaffective disorder, people experience schizophrenic symptoms, specifically delusions and hallucinations, in the absence of mood symptoms for at least a period of 2 weeks.

If this all sounds a bit confusing to you, it is confusing to mental-health professionals. The diagnosis of schizoaffective disorder is a controversial one because many clinicians believe it is used as a default when the clinician just can't decide whether an individual has schizophrenia or a mood disorder. The reliability of diagnoses of schizoaffective disorder is low, meaning that clinicians don't often agree that an individual warrants this diagnosis.

Within the diagnosis of schizophrenia, there are many subtypes that have been described. In *Type I schizophrenia*, the positive symptoms are much more prominent than the negative symptoms. In *Type II schizophrenia*, the negative symptoms are more prominent than the positive symptoms. As we shall see, this distinction between Type I and Type II schizophrenia is

---

TABLE 10.3
DSM-IV
Diagnostic Criteria for Schizophrenia

The DSM-IV criteria for schizophrenia require the presence of severe symptoms for at least 1 month and the presence of some symptoms for at least 6 months.

A. Core symptoms: two or more of the following present for at least a 1-month period:

  1. delusions

  2. hallucinations

  3. disorganized speech

  4. grossly disorganized or catatonic behavior

  5. negative symptoms

B. Social/occupational functioning: significant impairment in work, academic performance, interpersonal relationships, and/or self-care

C. Duration: continuous signs of the disturbance for at least 6 months; at least 1 month of this period must include symptoms that meet Criterion A above

Reprinted with permission from the *Diagnostic and Statistical Manual of Mental Disorders*, Fourth Edition. Copyright © 2000 American Psychiatric Association.

TABLE 10.4
DSM-IV
Diagnostic Criteria for Schizoaffective Disorder

The major distinction between schizoaffective disorder and schizophrenia is the presence of severe mood symptoms in schizoaffective disorder.

A. An uninterrupted period of illness during which, at some time, there is either a major depressive episode, a manic episode, or a mixed episode concurrent with symptoms that meet Criterion A for schizophrenia.

B. During the same period of illness, there have been delusions or hallucinations for at least 2 weeks in the absence of prominent mood symptoms.

C. Symptoms that meet criteria for a mood episode are present for a substantial portion of the total duration of the active and residual periods of the illness.

Reprinted with permission from the *Diagnostic and Statistical Manual of Mental Disorders*, Fourth Edition. Copyright © 2000 American Psychiatric Association.

---

not part of the official DSM-IV diagnostic framework, but has turned out to be a useful distinction in research on schizophrenia.

TABLE 10.5
DSM-IV
Types of Schizophrenia

The DSM-IV recognizes five subtypes of schizophrenia.

Type	Major Features
Paranoid schizophrenia	Delusions and hallucinations with themes of persecution and grandiosity
Disorganized schizophrenia	Incoherence in cognition, speech, and behavior, and flat or inappropriate affect
Catatonic schizophrenia	Near total unresponsiveness to the environment, and motor, and verbal abnormalities
Undifferentiated schizophrenia	Diagnosis made when a person experiences schizophrenic symptoms but does not meet the criteria for paranoid, disorganized, or catatonic schizophrenia
Residual schizophrenia	History of at least one episode of acute positive symptoms but does not currently have any prominent positive symptoms

The DSM-IV officially divides schizophrenia into five subtypes (see Table 10.5). Three of these types, the paranoid, disorganized, and catatonic types, have specific symptoms that differentiate them from each other. The other two, undifferentiated and residual types, are not characterized by specific differentiating symptoms but by a mix of symptoms that are either acute (in the undifferentiated type) or attenuated (in the residual type).

Paranoid Schizophrenia

The best-known, and most researched, type of schizophrenia is the paranoid type. People with **paranoid schizophrenia** have prominent delusions and hallucinations that involve themes of persecution and grandiosity. They often do not show the grossly disorganized speech or behavior that people with other types of schizophrenia show. They may be lucid and articulate, with elaborate stories of how someone is plotting against them. They may also be able to articulate the deep pain and anguish of believing that they are being persecuted (Torrey, 1995, pp. 53–54):

Anxiety:
like metal on metal in my brain
Paranoia: it is

making me run away, away, away
and back again quickly
to see if I've been caught
Or lied to
Or laughed at
Ha ha ha. The ferris wheel
in Looney Land is not so funny.

People with paranoid schizophrenia are highly resistant to any arguments against their delusions and may become very irritated with anyone who argues with them. They may act arrogant and superior to others or remain aloof and suspicious. The combination of persecutory and grandiose delusions can lead people with this type of schizophrenia to be suicidal or violent toward others.

The prognosis for people with paranoid schizophrenia is actually better than the prognosis for people with other types of schizophrenia, however. They are more likely to be able to live independently and hold down a job, and thus show better cognitive and social functioning (Kendler et al., 1994). The onset of paranoid schizophrenia tends to occur later in life than the onset of other forms of schizophrenia, and episodes of psychosis are often triggered by stress. In general, paranoid schizophrenia is considered a milder, less insidious form of schizophrenia.

Disorganized (Hebephrenic) Schizophrenia

Unlike people with the paranoid type of schizophrenia, people with **disorganized schizophrenia** do not have well-formed delusions or hallucinations. Instead, their thoughts and behaviors are severely disorganized. People with this type of schizophrenia may speak in word salads, completely incoherent to others. They are prone to odd, stereotyped behaviors like frequent grimacing or mannerisms like flapping their hands. They may be so disorganized that they do not bathe or dress or eat if left on their own.

The emotional experiences and expressions of people with disorganized schizophrenia are also quite disturbed. They may not show any emotional reactions to anything, or they may have unusual and inappropriate emotional reactions to events, such as laughing uncontrollably at a funeral. When they talk, they may display emotions that are apparently unrelated to what they are saying or to what is going on in the environment. For example, a young woman with disorganized schizophrenia responded in the following manner when asked about her mother, who was recently hospitalized for a serious illness: "Mama's sick. [Giggle.] Sicky, sicky, sicky. [Giggle.] I flipped off a doctor once, did you know that? Flip. I wanta wear my blue dress tomorrow. Dress mess. [Giggle.]"

This type of schizophrenia tends to have an early onset and a continuous course that is often unresponsive to treatment. People with this type of schizophrenia are among the most disabled by the disorder.

Catatonic Schizophrenia

Catatonic schizophrenia has some of the most distinct features of all the types of schizophrenia. It is very rare, however, and thus has not been well researched. People with catatonic schizophrenia show a variety of motor behaviors and ways of speaking that suggest almost complete unresponsiveness to their environment. (Many of these behaviors were described earlier.) The diagnostic criteria for catatonic type schizophrenia require two of the following symptoms: (a) catatonic stupor (remaining motionless for long periods of time), (b) catatonic excitement (excessive and purposeless motor activity), (c) the maintenance of rigid postures or being completely mute for long periods of time, (d) engaging in odd mannerisms like grimacing or hand flapping, and (e) **echolalia** (senseless repetition of words just spoken by others) or **echopraxia** (repetitive imitation of the movements of another person).

Undifferentiated and Residual Schizophrenia

People with **undifferentiated schizophrenia** have symptoms that meet the criteria for schizophrenia (delusions, hallucinations, disorganized speech, disorganized behavior, negative symptoms) but do not meet the criteria for paranoid, disorganized, or catatonic type schizophrenia. This type of schizophrenia tends to have an onset relatively early in life and to be chronic and difficult to treat.

People with **residual schizophrenia** have had at least one episode of acute positive symptoms of schizophrenia but do not currently have any prominent positive symptoms of schizophrenia. They continue to have signs of the disorder, however, including the negative symptoms and mild versions of the positive symptoms. People may have these residual symptoms chronically for several years.

Prognosis

Schizophrenia is more chronic and debilitating than most other mental disorders. Between 50 and 80 percent of people who are hospitalized for one schizophrenic episode will be rehospitalized for another episode at some time in their lives (Eaton et al., 1992). The life expectancy of people with schizophrenia is as much as 10 years shorter than that of people without schizophrenia (McGlashan, 1988). People with schizophrenia suffer from infectious and circulatory diseases at a higher rate than do people without the disorder, for reasons that are unclear. Importantly, as many as 10 percent of people with schizophrenia commit suicide (Hendin, 1995). The following account of a schizophrenic woman about her suicidal thoughts gives a sense of the pain that many people with schizophrenia live with and wish to end through suicide (Anonymous, 1992, p. 334).

Voices

I had major fantasies of suicide by decapitation and was reading up on the construction of guillotines. I had written several essays on the problem of the complete destruction of myself; I thought my inner being to be a deeply poisonous substance. The problem, as I saw it, was to kill myself, but then to get rid of my essence in such a way that it did not harm creation.

Age and Gender Factors

Contrary to common views of schizophrenia, however, most people with schizophrenia do not show a progressive deterioration in functioning across the life span. Instead, most stabilize within 5 to 10 years of their first episode, and the duration of episodes and the number of rehospitalizations declines as the person grows older (Eaton et al., 1998; Eaton et al., 1992). Studies suggest that between 20 and 30 percent of treated people with schizophrenia recover substantially or completely from their illness within 10 to 20 years of its onset (Breier et al., 1991). One very long-term study that followed people with schizophrenia for an average of 32 years found that 62 percent had completely recovered or showed only minor impairment in functioning at follow-up (Harding, Zubin, & Strauss, 1987). One example of a person whose schizophrenic symptoms gradually diminished with age is John Nash, who is featured in *Extraordinary People: John Nash, Nobel Prize Winner*.

Women who develop schizophrenia have a more favorable course of the disorder than do men who develop schizophrenia (Doering et al., 1998; Hambrecht et al., 1992). Women are hospitalized less often and for briefer periods of time than are men, they show milder negative symptoms between periods of acute positive symptoms, and they have better social adjustment when they are not psychotic (Goldstein, 1995). This may be in part because women tend to develop schizophrenia at a later age than do men, and the later the age of onset of schizophrenia, the more favorable the course of the disorder tends to be (McGlashan, 1988).

Why does the functioning of people with schizophrenia often improve with age? Perhaps it is because they find treatments that help them stabilize or they

EXTRAORDINARY PEOPLE

John Nash, Nobel Prize Winner

In 1959, at the age of 30, John Nash was widely regarded as one of the premier mathematical minds of his generation. As a young professor at the Massachusetts Institute of Technology, he was tackling mathematical problems thought impossible to solve by others, and solving them with unconventional but highly successful approaches. While still a graduate student at Princeton, he had introduced the notion of equilibrium to game theory, which would eventually revolutionize the field of economics and win him the Nobel Prize.

As writer Sylvia Nasar details in her biography of John Nash called *A Beautiful Mind*, Nash had always been flamboyant and eccentric, with few social skills and little emotional connection to other people. But in 1959, Nash's wife Alicia noticed a change in his behavior. He became increasingly distant and cold to her and his behavior grew more and more bizarre:

John Nash has suffered from paranoid schizophrenia, but has also won the Nobel Prize for economics.

> Several times, Nash had cornered her with odd questions when they were alone, either at home or driving in the car. "Why don't you tell me about it?" he asked in an angry, agitated tone, apropos of nothing. "Tell me what you know," he demanded. (Nasar, 1998, p. 248)

Nash began writing letters to the United Nations, FBI, and other governmental agencies complaining of conspiracies to take over the world. He also began talking openly about his beliefs that powers from outer space, or perhaps from foreign governments, were communicating with him through the front page of the *New York Times*. Nash gave a series of lectures at Columbia and Yale Universities that were totally incoherent. Writes Sylvia Nasar (1998, p. 242):

> Nash's recollections of those weeks focus on a feeling of mental exhaustion and depletion, recurring and increasingly pervasive images, and a growing

sense of revelation regarding a secret world that others around him were not privy to. He began, he recalled in 1996, to notice men in red neckties around the MIT campus. The men seemed to be signaling to him. "I got the impression that other people at MIT were wearing red neckties so I would notice them. As I became more and more delusional, not only persons at MIT but people in Boston wearing red neckties [would seem significant to me]." At some point, Nash concluded that the men in red neckties were part of a definite pattern. "Also [there was some relation to] a crypto-communist part."

Nash's wife Alicia had him committed to McLean Hospital in April of 1959 after his threats to harm her became more severe and as his behavior became increasingly unpredictable. There Nash was diagnosed as having paranoid schizophrenia and given medication and daily psychoanalytic therapy. His behavior calmed. Nash spent much of his time with poet Robert Lowell, who suffered from manic depression and was hospitalized for the fifth time in 10 years with severe mania.

Nash learned to hide his delusions and hallucinations, and to behave completely rationally, although his inner world remained much the same as it had been before the hospitalization. After 50 days of confinement, 1 week after the birth of his first son, Nash was released. Upon his release, Nash resigned from MIT, furious that the institution had "conspired" in his commitment to McLean Hospital. He withdrew his pension fund and sailed to Europe vowing never to return.

In Geneva, Nash tried to renounce his American citizenship and eventually destroyed his passport. After being deported from Geneva and Paris, Nash ended up in Princeton 2 years later, still suffering from the acute symptoms of his schizophrenia. He would walk up and down the streets of Princeton with a fixed expression and dead gaze, wearing Russian peasant garments and going into

Continued

restaurants with bare feet. He talked in lofty terms of world peace and made it clear that he was intimately involved in the development of a world government. He wrote endless letters and made many phone calls to friends and eminaries around the world, talking of numerology and world affairs.

Various people—university officials, psychiatrists, friends—began to urge Alicia to have him committed again. This time Alicia could not afford a private hospital, and Nash ended up in Trenton State Hospital. Nash was assigned a serial number as if he was an inmate of a prison and shared a room with 30 or 40 other patients. The nearly 600 patients in Nash's section of Trenton State were cared for by just six psychiatrists. At Trenton State, Nash was given insulin shock therapy, which was a popular treatment for schizophrenia in the early 1960s, but is now discredited. Nonetheless, after 6 weeks, Nash was considered much improved and was moved to another ward of the hospital. There he began to work on a paper on fluid dynamics. After six months of hospitalization, a month after his thirty-third birthday, he was discharged.

During this period of Nash's increased clarity of thinking and hold on reality, Nash was able to obtain funding to continue his research, now focusing on partial differential equations. Nash appeared to be well for some time but then his thinking, his speech, and his behavior began to slip again.

This time, Nash's family found the money to have him committed to a private hospital, the Carrier Clinic. Nash spent 5 months there, receiving medications and psychotherapy, to which he responded well. After discharge, his colleagues again helped him find employment to do his research and over the next few years, he produced a few remarkable papers that were published in leading scientific journals. In between his interludes of rationality, however, were more periods of acute psychosis, and hospitalizations. Eventually, he ended up living with his mother in Roanoke, Virginia:

> On many days, he simply paced round and round the apartment . . . sipping Formosa oolong, whistling Bach. The sleepwalker's gait and fixed, faraway expression gave few hints of the vast and unending dramas unfolding in his mind. "Apparently I am simply passing time visiting my mother," he wrote, "but actually I've been under persecutions which I'm hoping will ease."

His daily rounds extended no farther than the library or the shops at the end of Grandin Road, but in his own mind, he traveled to the remotest reaches of the globe: Cairo, Zebak, Kabul, Bangui, Thebes, Guyana, Mongolia. In these faraway places, he lived in refugee camps, foreign embassies, prisons, bomb shelters. At other times, he felt that he was inhabiting an Inferno, a purgatory, or a polluted heaven ("a decayed rotting house infested by rats and termites and other vermin"). His identities, like the return addresses on his letters, were like the skins of an onion. Underneath each one lurked another: He was C.O.R.P.S.E. (a Palestinian refugee), a great Japanese shogun, C1423, Esau, L'homme d'Or, Chin

and their families learn to recognize the early symptoms of a relapse and seek aggressive treatment before their symptoms become acute. Alternatively, the aging of the brain could somehow reduce the likelihood of new episodes of schizophrenia. It has been speculated that the improvement of people with schizophrenia with age might be related to a reduction of dopamine in the brain with age, excess levels of dopamine have been implicated in schizophrenia (Breier et al., 1991).

Sociocultural Factors

Culture appears to play a strong role in the course of schizophrenia. Schizophrenia tends to have a more benign course in developing countries than in developed countries (Jablensky, 1989; Leff et al., 1992). Cross-national studies conducted in eight countries by the World Health Organization and other studies conducted by individual investigators find that persons who develop schizophrenia in countries such as India, Nigeria, and Colombia are less likely to remain incapacitated by the disorder in the long term than are persons who develop schizophrenia in countries such as Great Britain, Denmark, and the United States (see Figure 10.3, p. 346).

The social environment of the person with schizophrenia in developing countries may facilitate adaptation and recovery better than the social environments of people with schizophrenia in developed countries (Karno & Jenkins, 1993). In developing countries, there

Continued

Hsiang, Job, Jorap Castro, Janos Norses, even, at times, a mouse (Nasar, 1998, pp. 323–324)

After his mother died, Nash returned to Princeton and lived with his wife Alicia, who had long since divorced him. Nonetheless, she felt some responsibility for him and provided him with as much support as she could muster. There Nash finally came to know his son. Nash also slowly reintegrated into the world of mathematics at Princeton.

Over the next several years, in the 1970s and 1980s, Nash's illness gradually seemed to subside, although he was not taking any medications or receiving any other treatment. One of his colleagues, Hale Trotter, said

My impression was of a very gradual sort of improvement. In the early stages he was making up numbers out of names and being worried by what he found. Gradually, that went away. Then it was more mathematical numerology. Playing with formulas and factoring. It wasn't coherent math research, but it had lost its bizarre quality. Later it was real research. (Nasar, 1998, p. 350)

What accounted for the remission of his illness? Some attribute it to Alicia's constant, calm support. Some attribute it to the continued support of his mathematics colleagues. Nash believes he willed himself well, to some extent. Whatever the reason, Nash was one of those lucky people with schizophrenia whose illness seems to diminish, or even subside altogether, with age.

John Nash was awarded the Nobel Prize in economics for his contributions to game theory. He now lives in Princeton with Alicia, and works on his mathematical theories. Nash also helps to care for their son Johnny, who obtained his Ph.D. in mathematics several years ago, and also has developed paranoid schizophrenia. Although Johnny is receiving the newest treatments for schizophrenia, they help only a little, and he is frequently hospitalized.

As Sylvia Nasar (1998, p. 388) concludes:

The extraordinary journey of this American genius, this man who surprises people, continues. The self-deprecating humor suggests greater self-awareness. The straight-from-the-heart talk with friends about sadness, pleasure, and attachment suggests a wider range of emotional experiences. The daily effort to give others their due, and to recognize their right to ask this of him, bespeaks a very different man from the often cold and arrogant youth. And the disjunction of thought and emotion that characterized Nash's personality, not just when he was ill, but even before are much evident today. In deed, if not always in word, Nash has come to a life in which thought and emotion are more closely entwined, where getting and giving are central, and relationships are more symmetrical. He may be less than he was intellectually, he may never achieve another breakthrough, but he has become a great deal more than he ever was—"a very fine person," as Alicia put it once.

---

are broader and closer family networks around the person with schizophrenia, providing more people to care for the person with schizophrenia. This ensures that no one person is solely responsible for the care of the person with schizophrenia, which is risky for both the person with schizophrenia and for the caregiver. Families in some developing countries also score lower on measures of hostility, criticism, and overinvolvement than do families in some developed countries. As we discuss below, this may help lower relapse rates for their schizophrenic family members.

Social factors likely contribute to the gender differences in the course of schizophrenia (Mueser et al., 1990). Deviant behavior may be more socially acceptable in women than in men, so women who develop schizophrenia may experience less loss of social support than do men, which helps them cope better with their disorder. Also women with schizophrenia may have better social skills than do men with schizophrenia. These social skills may help women maintain and make use of their social support networks and reduce stress in their lives, thereby reducing their risk of relapse of symptoms.

Whatever the reasons for variations between cultures and between men and women in the course of schizophrenia, the conventional wisdom that schizophrenia is inevitably a progressive disorder marked by more deterioration with time has been replaced by new evidence that many people with schizophrenia achieve a level of good functioning over time.

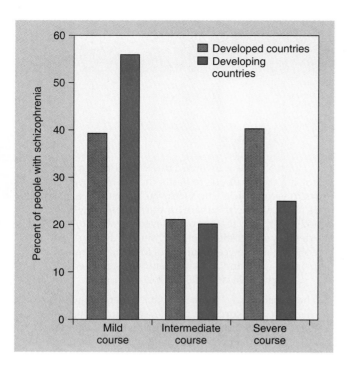

FIGURE 10.3 Cultural Differences in the Course of Schizophrenia. People with schizophrenia in developing countries are more likely to have a mild course of the disorder than are people in developed countries, whereas people in developed countries are more likely to have a severe course of the disorder than are people in developing countries.

Source: Jablensky, 1989, p. 521.

Summing Up

- The positive symptoms of schizophrenia are delusions, hallucinations, disorganized thinking and speech, and disorganized or catatonic behavior. Delusions are beliefs with little grounding in reality. Hallucinations are unreal perceptual experiences, such as hearing voices or having visions of objects that are not really present. The forms of delusions and hallucinations are relatively similar across cultures, but the specific content varies by culture.

- The negative or Type II symptoms are affective flattening, poverty of speech, and loss of motivation.

- Other symptoms of schizophrenia include anhedonia, inappropriate affect, and impaired social skills.

- Prodromal symptoms are more moderate positive and negative symptoms that are present before an individual goes into an acute phase of the illness; residual symptoms are symptoms present after an acute phase.

- The DSM-IV differentiates between schizophrenia and mood disorders with psychotic features

and schizoaffective disorder. Severe mood symptoms are present in both of the latter two disorders. In mood disorders with psychotic features, the mood symptoms occur in the absence of the schizophrenic symptoms at least some of the time, and in schizoaffective disorder, the schizophrenic symptoms occur in the absence of the mood symptoms.

- The DSM-IV further differentiates between paranoid, disorganized (hebephrenic), catatonic, undifferentiated, and residual schizophrenia.

BIOLOGICAL THEORIES OF SCHIZOPHRENIA

Given the similarity across cultures and across time in the symptoms and prevalence of schizophrenia, it is not surprising that biological factors have long been thought to play a strong role in the development of schizophrenia. There are several biological theories of schizophrenia (see *Concept Review:* Biological Theories of Schizophrenia). First, there is good evidence for a genetic transmission of schizophrenia, although genetics do not fully explain who gets this disorder. Second, some people with schizophrenia show structural and functional abnormalities in specific areas of the brain that may contribute to the disorder. Third, many people with schizophrenia have a history of birth complications or prenatal exposure to viruses that may have affected the development of their brains. Fourth, the neurotransmitter theories of schizophrenia hold that excess levels of the neurotransmitter dopamine play a causal role in schizophrenia. New research is also focusing on the neurotransmitters serotonin and glutamate.

Genetic Contributors to Schizophrenia

Family, twin, and adoption studies have all provided evidence that genes are involved in the transmission of schizophrenia. So far, "the gene for schizophrenia" has not been found, and many scientists believe that no single genetic abnormality accounts for this complex disorder (or set of disorders). Some researchers have argued for a polygenic, additive model, in which it takes a certain number and configuration of abnormal genes to create schizophrenia (Gottesman, 1991; Gottesman & Moldin, 1998). Having more disordered genes increases the likelihood of developing schizophrenia, as well as the severity of the disorder. Individuals born with some of these genes but not enough

CONCEPT REVIEW

Biological Theories of Schizophrenia

Biological theories of schizophrenia have attributed the disorder to genetics, structural brain abnormalities, birth complications, prenatal exposure to viruses, and deficits in dopamine and other neurotransmitters.

Theory	Description
Genetic theories	Disordered genes cause schizophrenia, or at least a vulnerability to schizophrenia.
Structural brain abnormalities	Enlarged ventricles may indicate deterioration of a number of brain areas, leading to cognitive and emotional deficits.
	Reduced volume and neuron density in the frontal cortex, temporal and limbic areas cause widespread cognitive and emotional deficits.
Birth complications	Delivery complications, particularly those causing loss of oxygen, could damage the brain.
Prenatal viral exposure	Exposure to viruses during the prenatal period could damage brain.
Neurotransmitter theories	Imbalances in levels or receptors for dopamine cause symptoms; serotonin and glutamate may also play roles.

The Genain quadruplets all have schizophrenia, but the specific forms of schizophrenia differ among the sisters.

to reach the threshold for creating full-blown schizophrenia may still show mild symptoms of schizophrenia, such as oddities in their speech patterns or thought processes, and strange beliefs.

Family Studies

Psychologist Irving Gottesman compiled over 40 studies to determine the lifetime risk for developing schizophrenia for people with different familial relationships to a person with schizophrenia. His conclusions are summarized in Figure 10.4 (p. 348). Children of two parents with schizophrenia and monozygotic (identical) twins of people with schizophrenia, who

share the greatest number of genes with people with schizophrenia, have the greatest risk of developing schizophrenia at some time in their lives. As the genetic similarity to a person with schizophrenia decreases, an individual's risk of developing schizophrenia decreases. Thus, a first-degree relative to a person with schizophrenia, such as a nontwin sibling, who shares about 50 percent of genes with the person with schizophrenia, has about a 9 percent chance of developing schizophrenia. In contrast, a third-degree relative to a person with schizophrenia, such as a first cousin, who shares only about 13 percent of genes with the person with schizophrenia, has only a 2 percent chance of developing schizophrenia. This is not much different from the general population, where the risk is about 1 percent to 2 percent. This relationship between the degree of genetic similarity between an individual and his or her schizophrenic relative and that individual's own risk of developing schizophrenia strongly suggests that genes play a role in the development of the disorder.

According to Figure 10.4, one of the groups at highest risk for developing the disorder is the biological children of schizophrenic parents. Growing up with a parent with schizophrenia and particularly with two parents with the disorder is likely to mean growing up in a stressful atmosphere. When a parent is psychotic, the child may be exposed to illogical thought, mood swings, and chaotic behavior. Even when the parent is not acutely psychotic, the residual negative symptoms of schizophrenia—the flattening of affect, lack of motivation, and disorganization—may impair the parent's child-care skills. Is it possible that the high risk for developing schizophrenia seen in the children of people

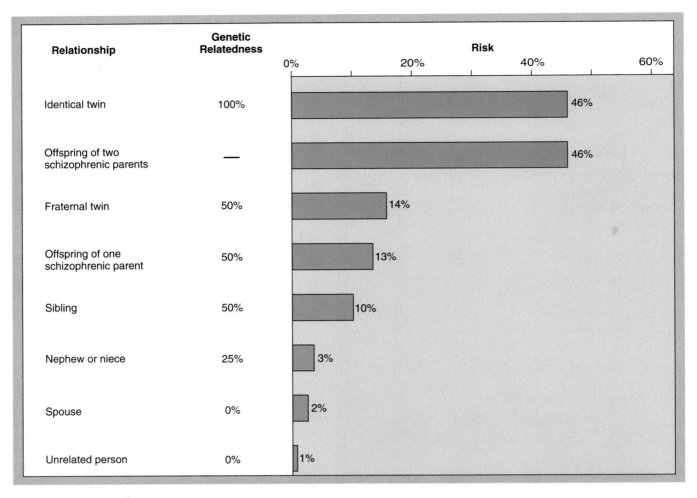

FIGURE 10.4   Risk of Schizophrenia and Genetic Relatedness. This figure shows that one's risk of developing schizophrenia decreases substantially as one's genetic relationship to a person with schizophrenia becomes more distant.

Source: Gottesman, 1991.

with schizophrenia is due, at least in part, to the stress of living with schizophrenic parents? This question has been addressed to some extent in adoption studies.

Adoption Studies

An early and classic adoption study was conducted by Leonard Heston (1966) in the United States and Canada. He interviewed the adult children of 47 women who had been diagnosed with schizophrenia in the Oregon state mental hospitals in the 1930s. All of these children had been placed in orphanages or with nonmaternal relatives within 3 days of their births. He also interviewed a group of 50 adults who had been adopted shortly after birth but whose mothers had no record of mental illness. If living with a parent with schizophrenia contributes significantly to a child's vulnerability to schizophrenia, then the children of people with schizophrenia who were adopted away from their

mothers should have had a lower rate of developing schizophrenia than the 13 percent rate for children who grow up with schizophrenic parents (see Figure 10.4). Heston found, however, that about 17 percent of the adopted-away children of people with schizophrenia developed schizophrenia as adults, a rate even higher than the average rate of 13 percent for children of people with schizophrenia. The rate may be higher for the adopted-away children in the Heston study because the mothers of these children were probably experiencing particularly severe forms of schizophrenia. They had all been hospitalized and deemed unfit to be mothers. In contrast, none of the 50 control group children in the Heston study whose mothers had no mental illness developed schizophrenia as adults.

Other adoption studies have examined the rates of schizophrenia in the biological versus adoptive relatives of adoptees with schizophrenia, and these studies also support a role of genetics in schizophrenia. For example, Kety and colleagues (1994) found that the biological relatives of schizophrenic adoptees were 10 times more likely to have a diagnosis of schizophrenia than the biological relatives of adoptees who did not have schizophrenia. In contrast, the adoptive relatives of schizophrenic adoptees showed no increased risk of schizophrenia.

Twin Studies

Within Figure 10.4, we also see the compiled results of several twin studies of schizophrenia that suggest that the concordance rate for monozygotic twins is 48 percent, while the concordance rate for dizygotic twins is 17 percent. A recent study that assessed all twins born in Finland between 1940 and 1957 used statistical modeling to estimate that 83 percent of the variation in liability to schizophrenia was due to genetic factors (Cannon et al., 1998). Genetic factors may play an even greater role in more severe forms of schizophrenia than mild forms. Gottesman and Shields (1982) found concordance rates for monozygotic twins of between 75 and 91 percent when they restricted their sample to persons with only the most severe forms of schizophrenia. In comparison, the concordance rates for MZ twins with mild forms of schizophrenia ranged from 17 to 33 percent.

The studies we have reviewed thus far make it clear that genetic factors are involved in the transmission of schizophrenia. The type and location of the gene or genes for schizophrenia are currently unknown, however (McGue & Bouchard, 1998). One of the greatest hindrances in the search for the genes for schizophrenia is that schizophrenia is not one disorder manifested in the same way across people but a very heterogeneous group of disorders. Each of the different types of schizophrenia may have its own genetic underpinnings. In addition, there may be forms of schizophrenia that are not genetically transmitted, although they may have another form of biological cause such as those described next. As many as 89 percent of people with schizophrenia have no known family history of schizophrenia (Cromwell & Snyder, 1993; Gottesman & Moldin, 1998). Finally, even when a person carries a genetic risk for schizophrenia, many other biological and environmental factors may influence whether and how he or she manifests the disorder. The classic illustration of this point is found in the Genain quadruplets. These four women, who shared exactly the same genes and grew up in the same family environment, all developed schizophrenia, but the specific symptoms, onset, course, and outcome of the disorder varied substantially among them. Their experiences are evidence that even if we could clone the genes for schizophrenia, we would have a great deal to learn about how

this disorder, or group of disorders, emerges out of a genetic predisposition.

Structural Brain Abnormalities

Clinicians and researchers have long believed that there is something fundamentally different about the brains of people with schizophrenia compared to the brains of people without schizophrenia. It is only in the last 20 years, with the development of technologies such as positron-emission tomography (PET scans), computerized axial tomography (CAT scans), and magnetic resonance imaging (MRI), that scientists have been able to examine in detail the structure and functioning of the brain. The picture of the schizophrenic brain emerging from use of these technologies is not an entirely clear one, again probably because there are many different types of schizophrenia that are often grouped together in studies. However, there is increasing evidence for both major structural and functional deficits in the brains of some people with schizophrenia (Buckley, 1998).

Enlarged Ventricles

The most consistent major structural brain abnormality found in schizophrenia is **enlarged ventricles** (Figure 10.5, p. 350); Andreason et al., 1990; Eyler Zorrilla et al., 1997). The ventricles are fluid-filled spaces in the brain. Enlarged ventricles suggest atrophy or deterioration in other brain tissue. People with schizophrenia with ventricular enlargement also showed reductions in the white matter in the prefrontal areas of the brain and an abnormal connection between the prefrontal cortex and the amygdala and hippocampus. Ventricular enlargement could indicate structural deficits in many other areas of the brain, however. Indeed, the different areas of the brain that can deteriorate to create ventricular enlargement could lead to different manifestations of schizophrenia (Breier et al., 1992).

People with schizophrenia with ventricular enlargement tend to show social, emotional, and behavioral deficits long before they develop the core symptoms of schizophrenia. They also tend to have more severe symptoms than others with schizophrenia and are less responsive to medication, suggesting gross alterations in the functioning of the brain that are difficult to alleviate with treatment.

The gender differences in schizophrenia we discussed earlier may be tied, in part, to gender differences in ventricular size. Some studies find that men with schizophrenia have more severely enlarged ventricles than women with schizophrenia (Nopoulos et al., 1997). This may be because men generally show

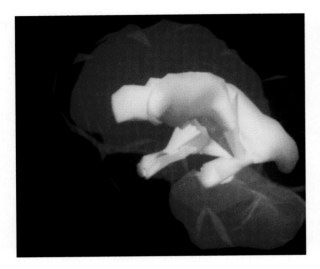
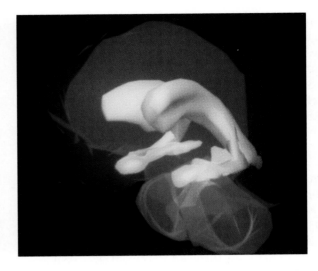

FIGURE 10.5   Enlarged Ventricles in People with Schizophrenia. The left panel shows the enlarged, fluid-filled ventricles (in gray) of a person with schizophrenia compared to a normal person (right panel). This image was taken by Nancy Andreasen.

Source: Gershon & Rieder, 1992, p. 128.

greater loss of tissue volume and increase in ventrical size with age than do women. The normal effects of aging on men's brain may exacerbate the neuroanatomical abnormalities of schizophrenia, causing more severe symptoms, and thus a worse course.

Reduced Volume and Neuron Density in Key Regions

Studies have shown reduced overall volume and lesser density of neurons in a number of areas of the brain in people with schizophrenia, including the frontal cortex, temporal lobe, the basal ganglia, and the limbic area, including the hippocampus and amygdala (Cannon, 1996; Gur et al., 1998; Lawrie & Abukmeil, 1998). The **frontal cortex** of the brain is smaller and shows less activity in some people with schizophrenia than in people without schizophrenia (Figure 10.6; Andreason et al., 1992; Berman et al., 1992; Gur et al., 1998; Sabri et al., 1997). The frontal cortex is the single largest brain region in human beings, constituting nearly 30 percent of the total cortex, and has connections to all other cortical regions as well as to the limbic system, which is involved in emotion and cognition, and the basal ganglia, which is involved in motor movement. The frontal cortex is important in language, emotional expression, planning and producing new ideas, and mediating social interactions. Thus, it seems logical that a person with a frontal cortex that is unusually small or inactive would show a wide range of deficits in cognition, emotion, and social interactions, as people with schizophrenia do. Evidence of this lower level of activity is not found in all people with schizophrenia, however. It is more common in people who exhibit predominantly negative symptoms of schizophrenia (low motivation,

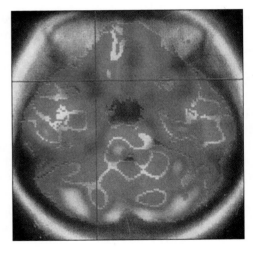

FIGURE 10.6   Lower Activity in the Prefrontal Cortex in Schizophrenia. This neuroimaging scan shows lower levels of activity in the frontal areas of the brain (as indicated in blue) in schizophrenic patients compared to healthy people.

Source: Nancy Andreasen.

poor social interactions, blunted affect) than in people who exhibit predominantly positive symptoms (hallucinations and delusions) or a mixed symptom profile (Andreason et al., 1992; Gur et al., 1998).

Deficits in the temporal and limbic areas of the brain may be particularly important in the development of positive symptoms of schizophrenia (thought disturbances, hallucinations, and delusions). These areas of the brain play important roles in memory, and some theories of the thought disturbances, hallucinations and delusions in schizophrenia suggest that these symptoms may be due to a failure of memory to guide an ongoing stream of thought toward its logically connected conclusion (Cannon, 1996).

Causes of Abnormalities

The neuroanatomical abnormalities in schizophrenia could have a number of causes, including brain injury due to birth injury, head injury, viral infections, deficiencies in nutrition, deficiencies in cognitive stimulation, or genetic abnormalities. Some studies have shown that family members of people with schizophrenia also exhibit several of these neuroanatomical abnormalities, although the evidence is somewhat inconsistent across studies (Cannon, 1996; Sharma et al., 1998). Similarities between family members could be due either to genetic causes or to other biological or environmental factors shared by family members. Some studies of MZ twins who are not both schizophrenic—that is, twins of which one has schizophrenia but the other does not—suggest that the schizophrenic twin tends to show neuroanatomical abnormalities, but the nonschizophrenic twin does not, even though both twins have the identical genetic makeup. (Berman et al., 1992; Cannon, 1996; Suddath et al., 1990). These studies argue against a genetic contribution to family similarities in neuroanatomical abnormalities.

Birth complications Serious prenatal difficulties and obstetrical problems at birth are more frequent in the histories of people with schizophrenia than in those without schizophrenia, and may play a role in the development of their neurological difficulties (Cannon, 1998; Jones & Cannon, 1998). Delivery complications have been found to interact with a familial risk for schizophrenia to predict the degree of enlargement of the ventricles in people with schizophrenia. One study found that the relationship between delivery complications and ventricular enlargement was greater for people with two schizophrenic parents than for people with one schizophrenic parent or no schizophrenic parents (Cannon et al., 1993). One type of obstetrical complication that may be especially important in neurological development is oxygen deprivation during labor and delivery, known as **perinatal hypoxia.** As many as 20 to 30 percent of people with schizophrenia have a history of perinatal hypoxia. A prospective study of 9,236 people born in Philadelphia between 1959 and 1966 found that the odds of an adult diagnosis of schizophrenia increased in direct proportion to the degree of perinatal hypoxia (Cannon, Rosso, Bearden, Sanchez, & Hadley, 1999). The authors of this study suggest that effects of oxygen deprivation must interact with a genetic liability for schizophrenia to result in a person developing this disorder, because the majority of people suffering oxygen deprivation prenatally or at birth do not develop schizophrenia.

Prenatal viral exposure Epidemiological studies have shown high rates of schizophrenia among persons whose mothers were exposed to the influenza virus while pregnant (Cannon, 1996; Jones & Cannon, 1998; Kirch, 1993). For example, persons whose mothers were exposed to the influenza epidemic that swept Helsinki, Finland, in 1957 were significantly more likely to develop schizophrenia than people in control groups, particularly if their mothers were exposed during the second trimester of pregnancy (Mednick et al., 1988, 1998). The second trimester is a crucial period for the development of the central nervous system of the fetus, and disruption in this phase of brain development could cause the major structural deficits found in the brains of some people with schizophrenia. As yet, the specific mechanism by which prenatal exposure to viral infection could lead to schizophrenia or the extent to which prenatal viral exposure contributes to schizophrenia is unknown (Kirch, 1993).

Neurotransmitter Dysregulation: The Role of Dopamine

The neurotransmitter **dopamine** has been thought to play a role in schizophrenia for many years. The original dopamine theory was that schizophrenic symptoms are caused by excess levels of dopamine in the brain, particularly in the frontal lobe and the limbic system. More current theories examine dopamine imbalances and interactions with other neurotransmitters.

The Original Theory: Too Much Dopamine

The original dopamine theory was supported by the following lines of evidence:

1. Drugs that reduce the functional level of dopamine in the brain tend to reduce the symptoms of schizophrenia. These drugs are commonly referred to as **phenothiazines** or **neuroleptics.**

2. Drugs that increase the functional level of dopamine in the brain, such as amphetamines, tend to increase the psychotic symptoms of schizophrenia.

3. Autopsy and PET scan studies showed more neuronal receptors for dopamine and sometimes higher levels of dopamine in some areas of the brains of people with schizophrenia than in the brains of controls (see Figure 10.7, p. 352).

4. Levels of a by-product of dopamine, homovanillic acid (HVA), tend to be higher in the blood and cerebrospinal fluid of people with schizophrenia with more severe symptoms than in those with less severe symptoms.

5. Some people with schizophrenia who take phenothiazines to reduce their psychotic symptoms develop motor movement disorders similar to

those in Parkinson's disease. It is well established that Parkinson's disease is caused by a deficiency of dopamine in the brain. Thus, the movement disorders that people with schizophrenia develop as a result of taking phenothiazines are likely to be caused by these drugs reducing the levels of dopamine in their brains.

Criticisms of the Original Theory

Now, however, research suggests that the original dopamine theory of schizophrenia was too simple (Davis et al., 1991):

1. Many people with schizophrenia do not respond to the phenothiazines, indicating that neurotransmitter systems other than the dopamine system may be involved in their disorders. Even people with schizophrenia who do respond to phenothiazines tend to experience relief only from their positive symptoms (hallucinations and delusions) and not from their negative symptoms. This suggests that simple dopamine depletion does not explain these negative symptoms.

2. Although persons taking the phenothiazines show reductions in dopamine functioning within hours or days of taking the drugs, their symptoms do not abate for several days after that.

3. Although levels of the dopamine by-product HVA tend to be higher in the blood and cerebrospinal fluid of more severely afflicted people with schizophrenia than of those less severely afflicted, comparisons of people with schizophrenia and normal or psychiatric control groups often find no overall differences in HVA levels, suggesting no overall differences in levels of dopamine in the brain. In fact, some studies find *lower* levels of HVA in people with schizophrenia compared to controls.

4. One of the most effective new drugs for schizophrenia, **clozapine**, does not work by blocking the same dopamine receptors that the other neuroleptics block. Instead, clozapine appears to bind to a newly discovered type of dopamine receptor, which has been labeled D4.

Newer Theories: Imbalances and Interactions

Although the original version of the dopamine theory of schizophrenia (that there are generally higher functional levels of dopamine in the brains of people with schizophrenia compared to people without the disorder) is not holding up, it is clear that dopamine is involved in schizophrenia. Let us consider a more complex version of the dopamine theory that can

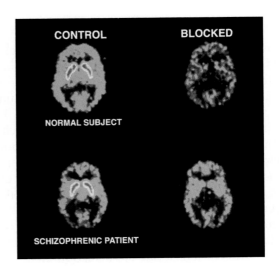

FIGURE 10.7 Greater Dopamine Receptor Activity in Schizophrenia. Schizophrenic people show greater dopamine receptor activity than controls even after taking a drug that blocks these receptors, as indicated by the greater density of blue in the schizophrenic PET scan on the lower right, compared to the control PET scan on the upper right.

Source: Taubes, 1994, p. 1034.

explain both the positive and negative symptoms of schizophrenia (Davis et al., 1991). First, there may be excess dopamine activity in the **mesolimbic system**, a subcortical part of the brain involved in cognition and emotion (see Figure 10.8). The mesolimbic system is rich with the newly discovered receptors for dopamine, known as D4 and D3. High dopamine activity in the mesolimbic system may lead to the positive symptoms of schizophrenia: hallucinations, delusions, and thought disorder. In turn, clozapine may work to reduce the symptoms of schizophrenia by binding to D4 receptors in the mesolimbic system, blocking the action of dopamine in this system. Second, there may be unusually low dopamine activity in the prefrontal area of the brain, which is involved in attention, motivation, and organization of behavior. Low dopamine activity in the prefrontal area may lead to the negative symptoms of schizophrenia: lack of motivation, inability to care for oneself in daily activities, and blunting of affect. This idea fits well with evidence that structural and functional abnormalities in this part of the brain are associated with the negative symptoms, as discussed. This idea also helps to explain why the phenothiazines, which reduce dopamine activity, do not alleviate the negative symptoms of schizophrenia.

This more complex dopamine theory of schizophrenia seems to integrate research and clinical findings that, at first glance, seem to contradict one another. Another theory posits that, while the positive symptoms of schizophrenia are caused by excess dopamine activity in the brain, the negative symptoms are not the result of dopamine imbalances but of structural abnormalities in the frontal lobes of the brain.

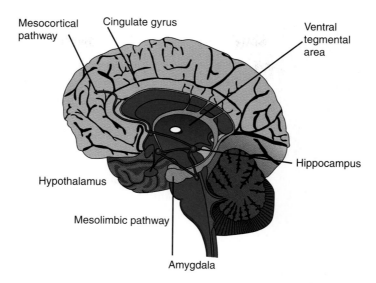

FIGURE 10.8   The Brain and Schizophrenia. The mesocortical pathway begins in the ventral tegmental area and projects to the prefrontal cortex. The mesolimbic pathway also begins in the ventral tegmental area but projects to the hypothalamus, amygdala, hippocampus, and nucleus accumbens.

Finally, other research is suggesting that dopamine is not the only neurotransmitter to play an important role in schizophrenia. Serotonin neurons regulate dopamine neurons in the mesolimbic pathway and some of the newest drugs that treat schizophrenia bind to serotonin receptors (Bondolfieral, 1998). It may be that the intersection between serotonin and dopamine is critical in schizophrenia, not just dopamine alone (Breier, 1995). Other research has found low levels of the neurotransmitter glutamate in people with schizophrenia (Faustman et al., 1999). Glutamate is widespread in the human brain, and deficiencies in this neurotransmitter could contribute to a host of cognitive and emotional symptoms.

Summing Up

- There is strong evidence for a genetic contribution to schizophrenia, although genetics do not fully explain who has the disorder.

- Many people with schizophrenia, particularly those with predominantly negative symptoms, show significant structural and functional abnormalities in the brain, including low frontal activity and ventricular enlargement.

- A number of prenatal difficulties and obstetrical problems at birth are implicated in the development of schizophrenia, including prenatal hypoxia and exposure to the influenza virus during the second trimester of gestation.

- The original dopamine theory of schizophrenia is that the disorder is caused by excessive activity of the dopamine systems in the brain. This theory is

probably too simple, but it seems clear that dopamine does play an important role in schizophrenia, especially in the positive symptoms.

- New research suggests that serotonin and glutamate may also play a role in schizophrenia.

◎ PSYCHOLOGICAL THEORIES OF SCHIZOPHRENIA

Although our view of schizophrenia these days is that it is caused largely by biological factors, there is a history of psychological theories of schizophrenia. Early psychodynamic theorists suggested that schizophrenia results from overwhelmingly negative experiences in early childhood between a child and his or her primary caregivers (usually the mother). Freud (1924) argued that when mothers are extremely harsh and withhold their love from a child, he or she regresses to infantile levels of functioning, and the ego loses its ability to distinguish reality from unreality. Later, psychoanalysts Freida Fromm-Reichmann (1948) and Silvano Arieti (1955) elaborated Freud's theory and more fully described parenting styles in mothers that could cause their children to become schizophrenic. These **schizophrenogenic** *(or schizophrenia-causing)* **mothers** were at the same time overprotective and rejecting of their children. They dominated their child, not letting him or her develop an autonomous sense of self, and simultaneously made the child feel worthless and unlovable.

These theories did not hold up to scientific scrutiny, however. Research comparing the parenting styles of mothers of people with schizophrenia and of

Dr. Freida Fromm-Reichman introduced one of the few psychoanalytic theories of schizophrenia.

mothers of people without the disorder did not confirm this theory. Modern psychodynamic theorists generally see schizophrenia as the result of biological forces that prevent these individuals from developing an integrated sense of self (Kohut & Wolf, 1978).

Behavioral and cognitive theorists have paid limited attention to schizophrenia. Some behaviorists have tried to explain schizophrenic symptoms as having developed through operant conditioning (Ulmann & Krasner, 1975). They suggest that most people learn what stimuli to attend to in the social environment—another person's face, what that person is saying—through experiences in which they attend to these stimuli and are rewarded for doing so. People with schizophrenia did not receive this "basic training" in what social stimuli to attend to, and how to respond to it, because of inadequate parenting, or extremely unusual circumstances. As a result, they attend to irrelevant stimuli in the environment, and do not know the socially acceptable responses to other people.

This behavioral theory of how schizophrenia develops has not been well tested or accepted. But it is clear that behavioral techniques can help people with schizophrenia learn more socially acceptable ways of interacting with others (Belcher, 1988; Braginsky, Braginsky, & Ring, 1969). For example, if family members begin to ignore bizarre comments or behaviors by the person with schizophrenia, and provide reinforcement for socially acceptable behavior, the person with schizophrenia gradually reduces the bizarre behaviors and increases the socially acceptable behaviors.

The few cognitive theorists who have been concerned with schizophrenia acknowledge that the fundamental deficits in perception and attention have biological bases. They then suggest that other symptoms, such as delusions, develop as the schizophrenic person attempts to explain and make sense of these strange perceptions and experiences (Garety, 1991; Maher, 1974; Zimbardo, Andersen & Kabat, 1981). For example, a person who hears strange voices and has tactile hallucinations that something is grabbing his arm may communicate these experiences to family members. The family members may reject these experiences, however, and withdraw. Eventually the person with schizophrenia comes to believe that strange forces are conspiring with his family members against him, and an elaborate paranoid belief system is born.

Most psychologists, however, have taken the view that the fundamental problem in schizophrenia as a biological one. But as we saw earlier, biological factors as we currently understand them cannot explain everything about schizophrenia, such as why one identical twin has the disorder but the other one does not, or why some people are debilitated by the disorder throughout their lives and other people can achieve a high level of functioning. A great deal of research, much of it taking a sociocultural view of schizophrenia, suggests that the environment can interact with a biological vulnerability to schizophrenia to determine whether an individual ever develops the full-blown disorder and how chronic and debilitating the disorder is.

Summing Up

- Early psychodynamic theories viewed schizophrenia as the result of harsh and inconsistent parenting that caused an individual to regress to infantile forms of coping.

- Behavioral theorists view schizophrenic behaviors as the result of operant conditioning.

- Cognitive theorists see some schizophrenic symptoms as attempts to understand perceptual and attentional disturbances.

⟲ SOCIOCULTURAL PERSPECTIVES ON SCHIZOPHRENIA

Sociocultural theorists have focused on the impact of stressful social circumstances on schizophrenia. Although some early theories suggested that stress could cause schizophrenia, most modern sociocultural theories suggest that environmental factors probably do not cause schizophrenia, but can play an important role in determining the course of the disorder. A positive environment, particularly positive family support, may help the person with schizophrenia avoid relapse and function at a high level. A negative environment can trigger new episodes of acute symptoms and make it difficult for an individual to function even when acute symptoms are not present.

Family Interactions and Schizophrenia

The environmental factor most often studied in schizophrenia is families. Families can either support their member with schizophrenia and help him or her function in society despite the disorder, or exacerbate the disorder by creating a climate that undermines the schizophrenic member's ability to cope.

Family Communication Theories

An early family theory of schizophrenia, proposed by Gregory Bateson and colleagues (Bateson et al., 1956), was that parents (particularly mothers) of children who would become schizophrenic put their children in **double binds** by constantly communicating conflicting messages to the children. Such a mother might physically comfort her child when he falls down and is hurt but at the same time be verbally hostile to and critical of the child. Children chronically exposed to such mixed messages supposedly cannot trust their own feelings or their perceptions of the world and thus develop distorted views of themselves, of others, and of the environment, which contribute to schizophrenia. Again, however, empirical research has not supported the specific predictions of this double-bind theory of schizophrenia.

Although the double-bind theory of schizophrenia has not been supported, investigations of the *communication patterns* in families of people with schizophrenia have revealed oddities. Most investigators do not believe that these oddities alone cause schizophrenia in children but that they create a stressful environment that makes it more likely that a child with a biological vulnerability to schizophrenia will develop the full syndrome of schizophrenia or that a person with schizophrenia will have more frequent relapses of psychosis.

Margaret Singer and Lyman Wynne (1965) described **communication deviance** within schizophrenic families as involving vague, indefinite communications; misperceptions and misinterpretations; odd or inappropriate word usage; and fragmented, disrupted, and poorly integrated communication. Controlled comparisons of interactions in families with a person with schizophrenia and in families without a

person with schizophrenia have found significantly higher levels of communication deviance in the families of people with schizophrenia. Some examples of this would be statements such as "But the thing is as I said, there's got . . . you can't drive in the alley," and "It's gonna be up and downwards along the process all the while to go through something like this" (Miklowitz et al., 1991).

Such deviant patterns of communication do not appear to have serious, long-lasting effects on children who do not have family histories of schizophrenia (see Gottesman, 1991). However, among children at risk for schizophrenia because they have family histories of the disorder, those whose families evidenced high levels of communication deviance are more likely to develop schizophrenia than are those whose families have low levels of communication deviance (Goldstein, 1987).

Expressed Emotion

The family interaction style that has received the most attention by researchers of schizophrenia is **expressed emotion**. Families high in expressed emotion are overinvolved with each other, are overprotective of the disturbed family member, and voice self-sacrificing attitudes toward the disturbed family member, while at the same time being critical, hostile, and resentful of the disturbed family member (Brown, Birley, & Wing, 1972; Vaughn & Leff, 1976). Although high expressed-emotion family members do not doubt the legitimacy of their schizophrenic family member's illness, they talk as if they believe the ill family member can exert quite a bit of control over their symptoms. They often have many ideas about what the family member can do to improve their symptoms, as is illustrated in these comments from two high expressed-emotion mothers of people with schizophrenia (Hooley, 1998, p. 636):

> I tell him, "Sit down, you're driving me crazy!" Back and forth, back and forth [pacing]. I say, "Why don't you take some good deep breaths and just relax!"

> She was reading in the hospital. I don't know why she stopped. I've been trying to get her to start again. I said, "Read—even if it's only for 15 minutes, Lori. Try!"

Expressed emotion has been assessed through lengthy interviews with people with schizophrenia and their families, through projective tests, and through direct observation of family interactions. A number of studies have shown that people with schizophrenia whose families are high in expressed emotion are much more likely to suffer relapses of psychosis than are those whose families are low in expressed emotion (e.g., Brown, Birley, & Wing, 1972; Hooley & Hiller, 1998; Kavanagh, 1992; Leff & Vaughn, 1981;

Mintz et al., 1987; Parker & Hadzi-Pavlovic, 1990). An analysis of 27 studies of expressed emotion and schizophrenia showed that 70 percent of patients in high expressed-emotion families relapsed within a follow-up year, compared to 31 percent of patients in low expressed-emotion families (Butzlaff & Hooley, 1998). Being in a high expressed-emotion family may create stresses for the person with schizophrenia that overwhelm his or her ability to cope and that trigger new episodes of psychosis.

The link between high levels of family expressed emotion and higher relapse rates has been replicated in several cultures, including European countries, the United States, Mexico, and India. In Mexico and India, however, families of people with schizophrenia tend to score lower on measures of expressed emotion than do their counterparts in Europe or the United States (see Figure 10.9; Karno et al., 1987; Karno & Jenkins, 1993).

Critics of the literature on expressed emotion argue that the hostility and intrusiveness observed in some families of people with schizophrenia might be the result of the symptoms exhibited by the person with schizophrenia rather than contributors to relapse (Parker, Johnston, & Hayward, 1988). Although families are often forgiving of the positive symptoms of schizophrenia (hallucinations, delusions, thought disturbances) because they view them as uncontrollable,

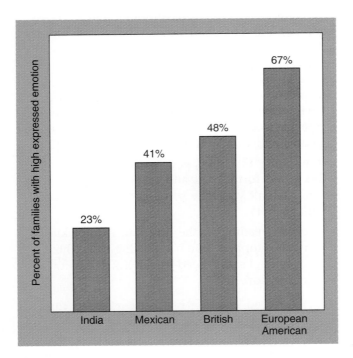

FIGURE 10.9 Cultural Differences in the Prevalence of Expressed Emotion in Families of Schizophrenics. Families of schizophrenics from developing countries tend to show lower levels of expressed emotion than do families of schizophrenics from developed countries. This may be one reason that schizophrenics from developing countries have fewer relapses than do schizophrenics from developed countries.

Source: Karno & Jenkins, 1993.

they can be unforgiving of the negative symptoms (lack of motivation, blunted affect), viewing them as under the control of the person with schizophrenia (Brewin et al., 1991; Hooley et al., 1987; Lopez et al., 1999). People with schizophrenia who have more of these symptoms may elicit more negative expressed emotion from their families and they may be especially prone to relapse. Another alternative explanation for the link between family expressed emotion and relapse in people with schizophrenia comes from evidence that family members who are particularly high on expressed emotion are themselves more likely to have some form of psychopathology (Goldstein et al., 1992). Thus, it may be that people with schizophrenia in these families have high rates of relapse because they have a greater genetic loading for psychopathology, as evidenced by the presence of psychopathology in their family members, rather than because their family members are high in expressed emotion. Perhaps the best evidence that family expressed emotion actually influences relapse in schizophrenic patients is that interventions that reduce family expressed emotion tend to reduce the relapse rate in schizophrenic family members. These studies are reviewed shortly.

Stress and Schizophrenia

Although you may have heard of someone having a "nervous breakdown" following a traumatic event, it is rare for someone to develop full-blown schizophrenia in response to a stressful event. Instead, the term *nervous breakdown* often is used to refer to severe depressions or anxiety disorders that develop following trauma.

Still, it is true that people with schizophrenia are more likely than people without schizophrenia to live in chronically stressful circumstances, such as in impoverished inner-city neighborhoods and in low-status occupations or unemployment (Dohrenwend et al., 1987). Most research supports a **social selection** explanation of this link. According to this explanation, the symptoms of schizophrenia interfere with a person's ability to complete an education and hold a job and thus people with schizophrenia tend to drift downward in social class, compared to their families of origin. One of the classic studies showing the process of social selection in schizophrenia tracked the socioeconomic status of men with schizophrenia and compared it with the status of their brothers and fathers (Goldberg & Morrison, 1963). The men with schizophrenia tended to end up in socioeconomic classes that were well below those of their fathers. For example, if their fathers were in the middle class, the men with schizophrenia were likely to be in the lower classes. In contrast, the healthy brothers of people with schizophrenia tended to end up in socioeconomic classes that were equal to or higher than those of their fathers. More recent data also support the social selection theory (Dohrenwend et al., 1992).

Several studies have shown that people with schizophrenia and other forms of psychosis (such as psychotic bipolar disorder) are more likely to have been born in a large city than in a small town (Kendler et al., 1996; Lewis et al., 1992; Takei et al., 1992, 1995; Torrey, Bowler, & Clark, 1997; van Os et al., 1997). For example, studies in the United States find that people with psychotic disorders are as many as five times more likely to have been born and raised in a large metropolitan area than a rural area. Is it the stress of the city that leads to psychosis? Torrey and Yolken (1998) argue that the link between urban living and psychosis is due not to stress, but to overcrowding, which increases the risk that a pregnant woman or newborn will be exposed to infectious agents. Many studies have shown that the rates of many infectious diseases, including influenza, tuberculosis, respiratory infections, herpes, and measles are higher in crowded urban areas than in less crowded areas. And, as we discussed earlier, there is a link between exposure to infectious disease prenatally or perinatally and schizophrenia.

Stressful circumstances may not cause someone to develop schizophrenia, but they may trigger new episodes in people who are vulnerable to schizophrenia. When researchers looked at the timing of stressful events relative to the onset of new episodes of psychosis, they found higher levels of stress occurring shortly before the onset of a new episode of psychosis as compared to other times in the lives of people with schizophrenia (Norman & Malla, 1993). For example, in one study, researchers followed 30 people with schizophrenia for 1 year, interviewing them every 2 weeks to determine if they had experienced any stressful events and/or any increase in their symptoms. They found that people who experienced relapses of psychosis were more likely than people who did not to experience negative life events in the month before their relapse (Ventura et al., 1989).

It is important not to overstate the link between stressful life events and new episodes of schizophrenia, however. Over half the people in the study who had a relapse of their schizophrenia in the year they were followed had *not* experienced negative life events just before their relapse. In addition, other studies suggest that many of the life events that people with schizophrenia experience in the weeks before they relapse may actually be caused by the prodromal symptoms that occur just before a relapse into psychosis (Dohrenwend et al., 1987). For example, one of the prodromal symptoms of a schizophrenic relapse is social withdrawal; in turn, the negative life events most often preceding a relapse, such as breakup of a relationship or

loss of a job, could be caused partially by the social withdrawal of the person with schizophrenia.

In *Viewpoints*: Is Schizophrenia a Disease (p. 358), we highlight one of the most extreme sociocultural theories of schizophrenia, which suggests it is not a disease or disorder, but a way of living chosen by outcast members of society. Not surprisingly, this is a controversial perspective that has many vocal critics.

Summing Up

- Early theories suggested that families put schizophrenic members in double binds or have deviant patterns of communication.

- Families high in expressed emotion are overinvolved and overprotective, and at the same time critical and resentful. People with schizophrenia who live in families high in expressed emotion may be at increased risk for relapse.

- People with schizophrenia tend to live in highly stressful circumstances. Most theorists see this as a consequence rather than as a cause of schizophrenia.

⊙ TREATMENTS FOR SCHIZOPHRENIA

Comprehensive treatment for people with schizophrenia means providing them with medications to help quell symptoms, therapy to help them cope with the consequences of the disorder, and social services to aid in their reintegration into society and to ensure that they have access to all the resources they need for daily life.

Biological Treatments: Drug Therapy

Over the centuries, many treatments for schizophrenia have been developed, based on the scientific theories of the time. Physicians have performed brain surgery on people with schizophrenia in an attempt to "fix" or eliminate the part of the brain causing their hallucinations or delusions. These patients were sometimes calmer after their surgeries but often also experienced significant cognitive and emotional deficits as a result of the surgery. *Insulin coma therapy* was used in the 1930s to treat schizophrenia. People with schizophrenia would be given massive doses of insulin—the drug used to treat diabetes—until they went into a coma. When they emerged from this coma, however, patients were rarely much better, and the procedure was a

VIEWPOINTS

Is Schizophrenia a Disease?

One radical sociocultural perspective on schizophrenia is that it is not a disease at all, but is a social construction—a label applied to people who are socially unacceptable to justify controlling them and discriminating against them (Modrow, 1995; Sarbin, 1990; Szasz, 1963). This label becomes a self-fulfilling prophecy, so that the individual begins acting in the bizarre ways that are expected of him or her.

Like any worthwhile endeavor, becoming a schizophrenic requires a long period of rigorous training. My training for this unique calling began in earnest when I was six years old. At that time my somewhat befuddled mother took me to the University of Washington to be examined by psychiatrists in order to find out what was wrong with me. These psychiatrists told my mother: "We don't know exactly what is wrong with your son, but whatever it is, it is very serious. We recommend that you have him committed immediately or else he will be completely psychotic within less than a year." My mother did not have me committed since she realized that such a course of action would be extremely damaging to me. But after that ominous prophecy my parents began to view and treat me as if I were either insane or at least in the process of becoming that way. Once, when my mother caught me playing with some vile muck I had mixed up—I was seven at the time—she gravely told me, "They have people put away in mental institutions for doing things like that." Fear was written all over my mother's face as she told me this. . . . The slightest odd behavior on my part was enough to send my parents into paroxysms of apprehension. My parents' apprehensions in turn made me fear that I was going insane. . . . My fate had been sealed not by my genes, but by the attitudes, beliefs and expectations of my parents. . . . I find it extremely difficult to condemn my parents for behaving as if I were going insane when the psychiatric authorities told them that this was an absolute certainty. (Modrow, 1995, pp. 1–2)

In his book *Toxic Psychiatry*, psychiatrist Peter Breggin (1991) argues that many of the symptoms of schizophrenia are actually caused by the antipsychotic medications that are supposed to be treating the disorder. He and other theorists (e.g., Sarbin, 1990) describe the vested interest of pharmaceutical companies, psychiatrists, and mental-health researchers in promoting the idea that schizophrenia is a brain disease. Families are all too ready to believe this because it reduces their self-blame. They argue, however, that the scientific evidence that schizophrenia is a brain disease, or any other kind of medical disease, is weak and inconsistent.

On the other side are the majority of theorists who believe that the scientific evidence that schizophrenia is a valid disorder, and probably has biological causes, is overwhelming (e.g., Gottesman, 1991; Torrey, 1995). Some of these theorists are vehement in their condemnation of the social constructionists for ignoring and misrepresenting the scientific evidence and inflicting blame on families who are anguished over their loved one's schizophrenia (see especially Torrey, 1995). They suggest that, just because current technologies cannot identify the specific pathology that causes schizophrenia, this does not mean such pathology does not exist. Schizophrenia, like many psychiatric disorders, may be more complex in its causes and pathology than many medical disorders such as diabetes or cancer.

At the turn of the twenty-first century, the social constructionists are clearly outnumbered by those who take a medical or biological view of schizophrenia. Every few years, the pendulum swings back a bit, and the social constructionist view again catches the public's attention, often in response to the ubiquitous advertising for psychotropic drugs or when the media claims that "the cause" of schizophrenia has been found.

People with schizophrenia may have trouble caring for their own daily needs, and end up on the streets.

highly dangerous one. *Electroconvulsive therapy,* or *ECT,* was also used to treat schizophrenia for a time, until it was clear that it had little effect on the symptoms of schizophrenia (although it is effective in treating serious depression, as we discussed in Chapters 5 and 8).

Mostly, however, people with schizophrenia were simply warehoused. In 1955, one out of every two people in psychiatric hospitals was diagnosed with schizophrenia (Rosenstein, Milazzo-Sayre, & Manderscheid, 1989). These patients received custodial care—they were bathed, fed, and prevented from hurting themselves physically, often with the use of physical restraints—but few received any treatment that actually reduced their symptoms of schizophrenia.

It wasn't until the 1950s that an effective drug treatment for schizophrenia—chlorpromazine—was introduced, as we discussed in Chapter 5. Since the 1950s, several other antipsychotic drugs have been added to the arsenal of treatments for schizophrenia. Most recently, new types of antipsychotics, called the atypical antipsychotics, hold promise of relieving psychotic symptoms while not inducing as many side effects as the traditional antipsychotics.

Antipsychotic Drugs

As we discussed in Chapter 5, in the early 1950s French researchers Jean Delay and Pierre Deniker found that **chlorpromazine**, one of a class of drugs called the *phenothiazines,* calmed agitation and reduced hallucinations and delusions in patients with schizophrenia. Other phenothiazines that became widely used include trifluoperazine (Stelazine), thioridazine (Mellaril), and fluphenazine (Prolixin) (see Table 10.6, p. 360). As mentioned earlier, they appear to work by blocking the receptors for dopamine known as D1 and D2, thereby reducing the action of dopamine in the brain. For the first time, many people with schizophrenia could control the positive symptoms of schizophrenia (hallucinations, delusions, thought disturbances) by taking this drug prophylactically (i.e., even when they were not experiencing acute symptoms). The need for long-term custodial hospitalization of people with schizophrenia was greatly reduced, so that by 1971, the number of people with schizophrenia who were hospitalized was half of what would have been expected if these drugs had not been available. Other classes of antipsychotic drugs were introduced after the phenothiazines, including the *butyrophenones* (such as Haldol) and the *thioxanthenes* (such as Navane). Collectively, these drugs are known as the *neuroleptics* (see Table 10.6)

Effectiveness and Side Effects

Although the neuroleptic drugs revolutionized the treatment of schizophrenia, they do not work for everyone with the disorder. About 25 percent of people with schizophrenia do not respond to the neuroleptics (Liberman et al., 1994). Even among people who do respond, the neuroleptics are more effective in treating the positive symptoms of schizophrenia than the negative symptoms of schizophrenia: the lack of motivation and interpersonal deficits. Thus, many people with schizophrenia who take these drugs, although not actively psychotic, still are not able to lead normal lives, holding a job and building positive social relationships.

People with schizophrenia typically must take neuroleptic drugs prophalactically—that is, all the time to prevent new episodes of acute symptoms. If the drug is discontinued, about 75 percent of people with schizophrenia relapse within 1 year, compared to 33 percent of people who continue to take their medication (Sampath et al., 1992). Unfortunately, however, these drugs have significant side effects that often cause people to want to discontinue their use. These include grogginess, dry mouth, blurred vision, drooling, sexual dysfunction, visual disturbances, weight gain or loss, constipation, menstrual disturbances in women, and depression. Another common side effect is called **akinesia** and is characterized by slowed motor activity, monotonous speech, and an expressionless face (Blanchard & Neale, 1992). Patients taking the phenothiazines often show symptoms similar to those seen in Parkinson's disease, including stiffness of muscles, freezing of the facial muscles, tremors and spasms in the extremities, and **akathesis**, an agitation that causes them to pace and be unable to sit still. The fact that Parkinson's disease is caused by a lack of dopamine in the brain suggests that these motoric side effects of the phenothiazines result because these drugs reduce functional levels of dopamine in the brain. One of the most serious side effects is a neurological disorder known as **tardive dyskinesia** and involves involuntary movements of the tongue, face, mouth or jaw. People with this disorder may involuntarily smack their lips, make sucking sounds, stick out their tongues, puff their cheeks, or make other bizarre movements, over and over again. Tardive dyskinesia is often irreversible and may occur in over 20 percent of persons with long-term use of the phenothiazines (Morganstern & Glazer, 1993).

The side effects of the neuroleptics can be reduced by reducing dosages, and thus many clinicians maintain people with schizophrenia on the lowest dosage possible that still keeps acute symptoms at bay, known as a *maintenance dose*. Unfortunately, however, maintenance doses are often not enough to restore an individual to full functioning. The negative symptoms of schizophrenia may still be present in strong form, and the individual may experience mild versions of the positive symptoms. This clearly makes it hard for them to function in daily life. Thus, many people with schizophrenia live a revolving-door life of frequent hospitalizations and a marginal life outside the hospital.

Physicians prescribing neuroleptics also have to take cultural differences into consideration. There is some evidence that persons of Asian descent need less neuroleptic medication than do persons of European descent to reach desired blood levels of the drug and to show symptom relief (Lin & Shen, 1991). Asians may also show side effects of neuroleptics at lower dosages. It is currently unclear whether these differences in response are due to biological differences or to differences in diet or some other environmental variable.

TABLE 10.6
Drugs used to Treat Schizophrenia

There are now a number of drugs available for the treatment of schizophrenia.

Class/Generic Name	Trade Name
Phenothiazines:	
Chlorpromazine hydrochloride	Thorazine
Fluphenazine	Prolixin
Thioridazine hydrochloride	Mellaril
Trifluoperazine hydrochloride	Stelazine
Butyrophenones:	
Haloperidol decanoate	Haldol
Dibenzodiazepines:	
Clozapine	Clozaril
Thioxanthenes:	
Chlorprothixene	Taractan
Thiothixene hydrochloride	Navane
Benzisoxazoles:	
Risperidone	Risperdal
Dibenzoxapines:	
Loxapine succinate	Loxitane
Indoles:	
Molindone hydrochloride	Moban
Diphenylbutylpiperidines:	
Pimozide	Orap

Source: Buckley & Meltzer, 1995.

Atypical Antipsychotics

Fortunately, new drugs, referred to as the **atypical antipsychotics**, seem to be even more effective in treating schizophrenia than the neuroleptics, without inducing the same neurological side effects of the neuroleptics. *Clozapine*, mentioned earlier, binds to the D4 dopamine receptor, but it also influences several other neurotransmitters, including serotonin. Clozapine has been effective with many people with schizophrenia who have never responded to the phenothiazines, and it appears to reduce negative as well as positive symptoms of schizophrenia in many patients (Bondolfi et al., 1998;

Buchanan et al., 1998; Wilson & Clausen, 1995). Clozapine does not induce tardive dyskinesia, but it does have some side effects. These can include dizziness, nausea, sedation, seizures, hypersalivation, weight gain, and tachycardia. In addition, in perhaps 1 to 2 percent of people who take this drug, a condition called **agranulocytosis** develops. This is a deficiency of granulocytes, which are substances produced by bone marrow that fight infection. This condition can be fatal, so patients taking clozapine must be carefully monitored for the development of this disease.

Another atypical antipsychotic that has proven effective in the treatment of schizophrenia is **risperidone**. This drug is a serotonin receptor antagonist and a weak blocker of dopamine receptors (Buckley & Meltzer, 1995). Risperidone is as effective as clozapine, and may have a faster onset of action than clozapine (Bondolfi et al., 1998). Risperidone also does not induce tardive dyskinesia, but can cause sedation, hypotension, weight gain, seizures, and problems with concentration.

Despite the potentially serious side effects of the drugs used to treat schizophrenia, many people with schizophrenia and their families regard these drugs as true lifesavers. These drugs have released many people with schizophrenia from lives of psychosis and isolation and have made it possible for them to pursue the everyday activities and goals that most of us take for granted.

Fish Oil for Schizophrenia

One of the most recent and controversial prescriptions for schizophrenia is fish oil, or more precisely, omega-3 polyunsaturated fatty acids, which are found primarily in fish. People with schizophrenia tend to have decreased amounts of the essential fatty acids linolenic acid and arachidonic acid in their red blood cell membranes (Hillbrand, Spitz, & VandenBos, 1997). Even small changes in key polyunsaturated fatty acids can lead to a broad range of neuronal dysfunctions, including receptor binding, neurotransmission, and signal transduction. Thus, deficits of fatty acids could conceivably lead to a wide range of psychological and physical symptoms, such as those seen in schizophrenia. In turn, some preliminary studies suggest that increasing the dietary intake of omega-3 fatty acids, in conjunction with antipsychotic medications, can help to improve the symptoms of schizophrenia (see Mellor, 1995; *Psychopharmacology Update,* December 1998).

So should people with psychiatric disorders eat more fish? Increasing dietary intake of fish oil clearly can have positive effects on cardiovascular functioning, decreasing the risk for heart attacks (Simopoulos, 1998). Thus, even if it does not have a strong effect on psychiatric symptoms, it may have a positive effect on health. Whether dietary supplements of fish oil will prove consistently helpful against the symptoms of schizophrenia or other psychiatric disorders remains to be seen in empirical studies currently ongoing.

Psychological and Sociocultural Treatments for Schizophrenia

With the availability of drugs that control the symptoms of schizophrenia, why would anyone need psychological or social interventions? As this essay illustrates, drugs cannot completely restore the life of a person with schizophrenia:

Voices

A note about becoming "sane": Medicine did not cause sanity; it only made it possible. Sanity came through a minute-by-minute choice of outer reality, which was often without meaning, over inside reality, which was full of meaning. Sanity meant choosing reality that was not real and having faith that someday the choice would be worth the fear involved and that it would someday hold meaning. (Anonymous, 1992, p. 335)

Many individuals who are able to control the acute psychotic symptoms of schizophrenia still experience many of the negative symptoms, particularly problems in motivation and in social interactions. Psychological interventions can help them increase their social skills and reduce their isolation and immobility. These interventions can help people with schizophrenia and their families learn to reduce the stress and conflict in their lives, thereby reducing the risk of relapse into psychosis. Psychological interventions can help people with schizophrenia understand their disorder and the need to remain on their medications and cope more effectively with the side effects of the medications. Finally, because of the severity of their disorder, many people with schizophrenia have trouble finding or holding jobs, finding enough money to feed and shelter themselves, and obtaining necessary medical or psychiatric care. Psychologists, social workers, and other mental-health professionals can assist people with schizophrenia in meeting these basic needs by helping them obtain the resources to meet these needs.

Behavioral, Cognitive, and Social Interventions

Most experts in the treatment of schizophrenia argue for a comprehensive approach that addresses the wide array of behavioral, cognitive, and social deficits in schizophrenia and that is tailored to the specific

TABLE 10.7

Skills Often Needed by People with Schizophrenia

These are some of the skills taught to people with schizophrenia as part of intensive skills-training programs.

Skills for Medication Management

To gain an understanding of how these drugs work, why maintenance drug therapy is used, and the benefits of medication

To learn appropriate procedures in taking medication and how to evaluate responses to medication

To learn the side effects of medications and what can be done to alleviate these effects

To practice ways of getting assistance when problems occur with medication

To desensitize fears of injections and learn benefits of biweekly or monthly injectable medication

Skills for Symptom Management

To learn how to identify personal warning signs and monitor them with the assistance of others

To learn specific techniques for managing warning signs and develop emergency plans

To learn how to recognize persistent symptoms and use techniques for coping with them

To learn about the adverse effects of alcohol and illicit drugs and how to avoid them

Basic Conversational Skills

To learn effective verbal and nonverbal listening techniques

To learn the most likely places to meet people and how to determine whether another is willing to engage in conversation

To learn the techniques that sustain conversations

To learn how to end conversations gracefully

To integrate all skill areas into natural and spontaneous conversations

Source: Liberman and Corrigan, 1993, p. 242.

deficits of each individual with schizophrenia (see Table 10.7; Liberman, 1994). These treatments are given in addition to medication and can increase everyday functioning and reduce risk of relapse significantly (Benton & Schroeder, 1990).

Cognitive interventions can include helping people with schizophrenia recognize demoralizing attitudes they may have toward their illness and then change these attitudes so that they will seek out help when needed and participate in society to the extent that they can. Behavioral interventions, based on social learning theory (see Chapter 5), include the use of operant conditioning and modeling to teach persons with schizophrenia skills such as initiating and maintaining conversations with others, asking for help or information from physicians, and persisting when they are doing some activity such as cooking or cleaning. These interventions may be administered by the family. A therapist would teach a client's family members to ignore schizophrenic symptoms such as bizarre comments, but reinforce socially appropriate behavior by attention and positive emotional responses. In

In the past, psychiatric wards largely left patients to wander about aimlessly, but the introduction of token economies based on behavioral principles increased socially-appropriate activities of patients.

psychiatric hospitals and residential treatment centers, *token economies* are sometimes established, based on principles of operant conditioning. Patients earn tokens, which they can exchange for privileges, such as time watching television or walking on hospital

Individual therapy for people with schizophrenia can help them improve their social relationships and cope with the consequences of their illness.

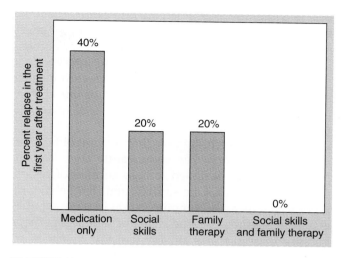

FIGURE 10.10   Effects of Psychosocial Intervention (with Medication) on Relapse Rates. Schizophrenic patients who received either social skills training, family therapy, or both in addition to medication had much lower relapse rates in the first year after treatment than did patients who received only medication.

Source: Hogarty et al., 1986.

grounds, by completing assigned duties (such as making their beds) or even just engaging in appropriate conversations with others.

Social interventions include increasing contact between people with schizophrenia and supportive others, often through self-help support groups. These groups meet together to discuss the impact of the disorder on their lives, the frustrations of trying to make people understand their disorder, their fears of relapse, their experiences with various medications, and other concerns they must live with day to day. Group members can also help each other learn social skills and problem-solving skills, such as those described in Table 10.7, by giving each other feedback on problem areas and by providing a forum in which individual members can role-play new skills.

Family Therapy

We discovered earlier in this chapter that communication deviance and high levels of expressed emotion within the family of a person with schizophrenia can substantially increase the risk and frequency of relapse. This increased risk has led many researchers to examine the effectiveness of family oriented therapies for people with schizophrenia. The successful therapies tend to combine basic education on schizophrenia with training of the family members in coping with the schizophrenic member's inappropriate behaviors and with the impact that the disorder has on their lives (Beels & McFarlane, 1982; Falloon, Brooker, & Graham-Hole, 1992; Halford & Hayes, 1991; Hogarty et al., 1991; McFarlane et al., 1995). In the educational portion of these therapies, families are given information about the biological causes of the disorder, the symptoms of the disorder, and medications and their side effects. The hope is that this information will reduce self-blame in the family members, will increase their tolerance for

the uncontrollable symptoms of the disorder, and will allow them to monitor their schizophrenic member's use of medication and possible side effects. Family members are also taught good listening and communication skills so as to reduce harsh, conflictual interactions with their schizophrenic member. Family members learn problem-solving skills to manage problems in the family (like lack of money) so as to reduce the overall level of stress in the family. They also learn specific behavioral techniques for encouraging appropriate behavior and discouraging inappropriate behavior in their schizophrenic member.

These family oriented interventions, when combined with drug therapy, appear to be more effective than drug therapy alone (Falloon, Brooker, & Graham-Hole, 1992). For example, Hogarty and colleagues (1986, 1991; see also Hogarty et al., 1997a, 1997b) compared the effectiveness of four types of intervention for persons with schizophrenia. The first group received medication only. The other three groups received medication plus one of the following types of psychosocial intervention: social skills training for the person with schizophrenia only; family oriented treatment; or a combination of social skills training for the person with schizophrenia and family oriented treatment for his or her family members. In the first year following these treatments, 40 percent of people with schizophrenia in the medication-only group relapsed, compared to only 20 percent in the first two psychosocial intervention groups and no one in the group that received both individual social skills training and family oriented therapy (see Figure 10.10). In the second year of follow-up, the groups that received family oriented therapy continued to fare better than did those who received medication alone. In this study and others, however, the effects of psychosocial interventions diminished with time if the interventions were not continued. Thus, as with the medications for schizophrenia, psychosocial interventions must be ongoing to continue to reduce the chances of relapse in people with schizophrenia.

Recent research suggests that cultural differences in family interactions can significantly affect the impact of therapies designed to help families of people with schizophrenia. One study found that behavioral therapies to increase communication in these families actually backfired in some Hispanic families, perhaps because these families already had low levels of expressed emotion and found the techniques suggested by therapists to violate their cultural norms for how family members should interact (Telles et al., 1995). For example, some of the most traditional family members in this study expressed great discomfort during exercises that encouraged them to establish eye contact or express negative feelings to authority figures. These were considered disrespectful actions by these family members. This is just another example of how therapists must take into account the culture of clients in designing appropriate interventions for them.

Community Treatment Programs

Many people with schizophrenia do not have families who can care for them. Even those who do have families have such a wide array of needs—for monitoring and adjustment of their medications, occupational training, assistance in getting financial resources (such as social security and Medicaid), social skills training, emotional support, and sometimes basic housing—that comprehensive community-based treatment programs are necessary.

In Chapter 5, we discussed the community mental-health movement, which was initiated by President Kennedy in the 1960s to transfer care of people with serious mental disorders from primarily psychiatric hospitals to comprehensive community-based programs. The idea was that people with schizophrenia and other serious disorders would spend time in the hospital when their symptoms were so severe that hospitalization was necessary. But when discharged from the hospital, they would go to community-based programs that would help them reintegrate in society, maintain their medications, gain needed skills, and function at their highest possible levels. Hundreds of halfway houses, group homes, and therapeutic communities were established for people with serious mental disorders who needed a supportive place to live.

One classic example of this is The Lodge, a residential treatment center for people with schizophrenia established by George Fairweather and colleagues (1969). At the Lodge, mental-health professionals were available for support and assistance, but residents had responsibility for running the household and working with other residents to establish healthy behaviors and discourage inappropriate behaviors. The residents also established their own employment agency to find jobs. Follow-up studies showed that Lodge residents fared much better than people with schizophrenia who were simply discharged from the hospital into the care of their families or less intensive treatment programs (Fairweather et al., 1969). For example, Lodge residents were less likely to be rehospitalized and much more likely to hold jobs than were those in the comparison group, even after the Lodge closed.

Other comprehensive treatment programs provide skills training, vocational rehabilitation, and social support to people with schizophrenia who are living at home. In a model program established in Madison, Wisconsin, mental-health professionals worked with chronically disabled people with schizophrenia

1. to help them gain material resources for food, shelter, clothing, and medical care;
2. to help them gain coping skills to meet the demands of community life, such as using public transportation, preparing simple but nutritious meals, and budgeting money;
3. to motivate them to persevere and remain involved with life even when their lives became stressful;
4. to lessen their dependency on family members; and
5. to educate family and community members about the kind of support they need.

These interventions were provided in the homes or communities of patients for 14 months and then the patients were followed for another 28 months. Their progress was compared to that of another group of patients who received standard hospital treatment for their psychotic symptoms. Both groups were treated with antipsychotic medications (Test & Stein, 1980).

The patients who received the home-based intensive skills interventions were less likely than the control group patients to be hospitalized and more likely to be employed both during the treatment and in the 28 months of follow-up (see Figures 10.11 and 10.12). The home-based intervention group also showed lower levels of emotional distress and psychotic symptoms than did the control group during the intervention. The differences in symptoms between the two groups diminished after the intervention period ended, however. In general, the gains that people in skills-based interventions tend to make decline once the interventions end, suggesting that these interventions need to be ongoing

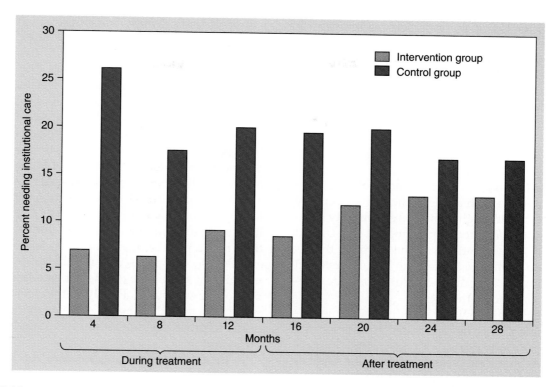

FIGURE 10.11 Effects of Home-Based Treatment on Need for Institutional Care. When schizophrenic patients received intensive home-based skills training and care, they were much less likely to be hospitalized for psychotic symptoms or to need other types of institutional care.

Source: Test & Stein, 1980.

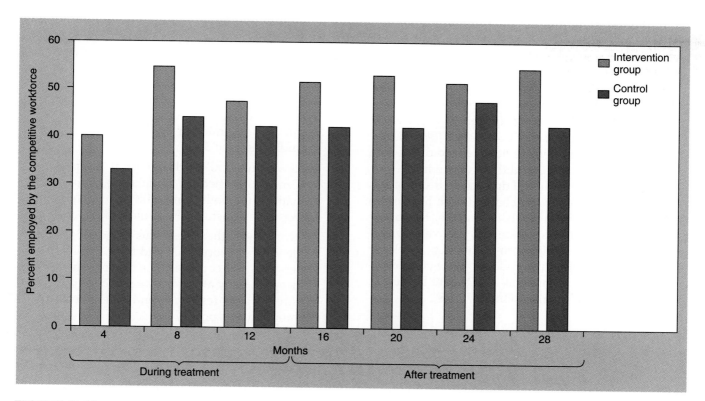

FIGURE 10.12 Effects of Home-Based Treatment on Employment. Home-based skills interventions also increased the number of schizophrenic patients who were able to maintain employment in the competitive workforce.

Source: Test & Stein, 1980.

(Liberman, 1994). However, the benefits of these interventions can be great. A recent study showed that ongoing individually based psychotherapy with people with schizophrenia, designed to teach them skills for coping and to provide both practical and emotional support, greatly reduced relapses into psychosis and increased quality of living (Hogarty et al., 1997a, 1997b). Ongoing psychotherapy is also much more cost-effective than hospitalization (Hogarty et al., 1997b; Weisbrod, Test, & Stein, 1980).

Despite the proven effectiveness of intensive treatment programs such as these, they have been few and far between. Although about 800 community mental-health centers are now operating in the United States, this is only one-third of the number that is needed. Those that do exist tend to be understaffed and underfunded, and thus unable to provide adequate care to the people they serve.

From its beginning, the community mental-health movement was never funded to a level that could support its lofty goals. With the changes in medical insurance in recent years, funding for mental-health care for the seriously mentally ill has been even tighter. Although over $61 billion is spent in mental-health care per year in the United States, much of that money goes not to direct services to people with schizophrenia, but to subsistence programs, such as social security disability income, and to community services for people with less serious mental disorders (Stein, 1993; Torrey, 1997). Much of the financial burden for caring for people with schizophrenia falls to state and local governments, who do not have the necessary financial resources, or to families, who are too often bankrupted by the cost of care.

As a result, nearly half of people with schizophrenia receive little or no care in a given year (Regier et al., 1993; Torrey, 1997; Von Korff et al., 1985). Those who do receive care often are hospitalized only when their symptoms are acute, and then remain in the hospital for inadequate periods of time for their symptoms to stabilize. They may be discharged with little or no follow-up. Some return to their families, but many end up in nursing homes, where they receive only custodial care, or in single-room-occupancy hotels or rooming houses, often in run-down inner-city neighborhoods. Perhaps as many as 300,000 are homeless, and 150,000 end up in prison (Torrey, 1995).

Cross-Cultural Treatments: Traditional Healers

In developing or Third World countries and in parts of industrialized countries, the symptoms of schizophrenia are sometimes treated by folk or religious healers, according to the cultural beliefs about the meaning and causes of these symptoms. Anthropologists and cultural psychiatrists have described four models that traditional healers tend to follow in treating schizophrenic symptoms (Karno & Jenkins, 1993). According to the *structural model*, there are interrelated levels such as the body, emotion, and cognition or the person, society, and culture, and symptoms arise when the integration between these levels is lost. Healing thus involves reintegrating these levels, through change of diet or environment, prescription of herbal medicines, or rituals. The *social support model* holds that symptoms arise from conflictual social relationships and that healing involves mobilizing a patient's kin to support him or her through this crisis and reintegrating the patient into a positive social support network. The *persuasive model* suggests that rituals can transform the meaning of symptoms for the patient, diminishing the pain of the symptoms. Finally, in the *clinical model*, it is simply the faith that the patient puts in the traditional healer to provide a cure for the symptoms that relieves the symptoms.

In developing countries, care for people with schizophrenia is more likely to be carried out by the extended family rather than by a mental-health institution (Karno & Jenkins, 1993). Thus, it may be especially important in these countries that interventions with a person with schizophrenia also include his or her family.

Summing Up

- The phenothiazines were the first drugs to have a significant effect on schizophrenia. They are more effective in treating the positive symptoms than the negative symptoms and a significant percentage of people do not respond to them at all. They can induce a number of serious side effects, including tardive dyskinesia.

- New drugs called the atypical antipsychotics seem more effective in treating schizophrenia than the phenothiazines and have fewer side effects. These include clozapine and risperidone.

- Psychosocial therapies focus on helping the people with schizophrenia and their families to understand and cope with the consequences of the disorder. They also help the person with schizophrenia gain resources and integrate into the community as possible.

- Studies show that providing psychosocial therapy along with medication can significantly reduce the rate of relapse in schizophrenia.

- Community-based comprehensive treatment programs for people with schizophrenia have been underfunded and thus many people with this disorder receive little or no useful treatment.

☉ BIO-PSYCHO-SOCIAL INTEGRATION

There is probably more consensus among mental-health professionals about the biological roots of schizophrenia than of any other psychopathology we discuss in this book. The evidence that the fundamental vulnerability to schizophrenia is a biological one is compelling. Yet there is growing consensus that psychosocial factors contribute to the risk for schizophrenia among people with the biological vulnerability. Theorists are increasingly developing models that integrate the biological and psychosocial contributors to schizophrenia comprehensive explanations of the development of this disorder (Mednick et al., 1998). A person with a biological vulnerability to schizophrenia who is raised in a supportive, low-conflict family with good communication skills and who escapes exposure to major stressors may never develop the full syndrome of schizophrenia. On the other hand, a person who has both a biological vulnerability and grows up in an unsupportive, stressful atmosphere is more likely to develop the full syndrome of the disorder. Psychosocial stress also clearly contributes to new episodes of psychosis in schizophrenic people. Finally, there is widespread consensus among mental-health professionals that the most effective therapies for schizophrenia are those that address both the biological contributors and the psychosocial contributors to the disorder.

Chapter Summary

- The positive (or Type I) symptoms of schizophrenia include delusions (ideas the individual believes are true but are certainly false), hallucinations (unreal perceptual experiences), thought disturbances (incoherence of thought and speech), and grossly disorganized or catatonic behavior. The negative (or Type II) symptoms include affective flattening, alogia (poverty of speech), and avolition (the inability to initiate and persist in goal-directed activities). Prodromal and residual symptoms are mild versions of the positive and negative symptoms that occur before and after episodes of acute symptoms.

- People with the paranoid subtype of schizophrenia have delusions and hallucinations with themes of persecution and grandiosity. This type of schizophrenia tends to begin later in life, and its episodes of psychosis are often triggered by stress. People with this type of schizophrenia have a better prognosis than do people with other types of schizophrenia.

- The disorganized (formerly called *hebephrenic*) subtype of schizophrenia shows especially marked disorganization in thought and behavior and either a flattening of affect or frequent inappropriate affect. People with this subtype of schizophrenia are prone to odd, stereotyped behaviors, and their speech is often incoherent. This type of schizophrenia tends to have an early onset and a continuous course that is often unresponsive to treatment.

- The catatonic subtype of schizophrenia is characterized by motor behaviors and ways of speaking that suggest the person is completely unresponsive to the environment. Symptoms include motoric immobility, excessive and purposeless motor activity, extreme negativism, peculiar movements, and echolalia or echopraxia.

- People with the undifferentiated subtype of schizophrenia have symptoms that meet the criteria for schizophrenia but do not meet the criteria for paranoid, disorganized, or catatonic schizophrenia.

- People with the residual subtype of schizophrenia have had at least one episode of active symptoms but do not currently have prominent positive symptoms of schizophrenia. They continue to have mild positive symptoms and significant negative symptoms.

- Estimates of the prevalence of schizophrenia in different countries range from about 0.2 percent to 2.0 percent, but most estimates are between 0.5 and 1.0 percent. There are some slight ethnic differences in rates of schizophrenia, but these may be due to differences in socioeconomic status. The content of delusions and hallucinations changes somewhat across cultures, but the form of these symptoms remains similar across cultures, and many clinicians and researchers believe schizophrenia can be reliably diagnosed across cultures. Men may be more prone to schizophrenia than are women, and there are some differences in symptoms between genders.

- Biological theories of schizophrenia have focused on genetics, structural abnormalities in the brain, and neurotransmitters. There is clear evidence for a genetic transmission of schizophrenia, although genetics do not fully account for the disorder. People with schizophrenia show lowered functioning in the prefrontal areas of the brain and enlarged ventricles, suggesting atrophy in parts of the brain. Many people with schizophrenia have a history of prenatal difficulties, such as exposure to the influenza virus during the second trimester of gestation, or birth complications, including prenatal hypoxia. Finally, although the original dopamine theory that schizophrenia is the result of too little dopamine is probably too simple, it is clear that dysfunction in the dopamine system is involved in schizophrenia.

- Early psychodynamic theories argued that caregivers who were demanding and excessively harsh toward their children, so-called schizophrenogenic mothers, could cause the children to regress to infantile stages, resulting in schizophrenia. These theories have not been supported.

- Behavioral theories suggest that schizophrenic behaviors are operantly conditioned. Cognitive theories suggest that some schizophrenic symptoms are attempts by the individual to understand and manage perceptual disturbances.

- Several theories have suggested that family communication patterns play a role in schizophrenia. The double-bind theory said that parents put their schizophrenic children in double binds by communicating mutually contradictory demands. The communication deviance theory said that parents create thought disorder in their children by communicating with them

in deviant ways. Expressed emotion theorists argue that some families of people with schizophrenia are simultaneously overprotective and hostile, and that this increases risk of relapse. Only the expressed emotion theories have received empirical support.

- Stressful events probably cannot cause schizophrenia in people who do not have a vulnerability to the disorder, but they may trigger new episodes of psychosis for people with the disorder.

- Drugs known as the phenothiazines were introduced for the treatment of schizophrenia in the 1950s and brought relief to many people with the disorder. The phenothiazines reduce the positive symptoms of schizophrenia but often are not effective with the negative symptoms. These drugs can have major side effects, including tardive dyskinesia, an irreversible neurological disorder characterized by involuntary movements of the tongue, face, mouth, or jaw. New drugs, called the atypical antipsychotics, seem to induce fewer side effects than the phenothiazines and are effective in treating both the positive and the negative symptoms of schizophrenia for many people.

- Psychological and sociocultural therapies for schizophrenia focus on helping people with schizophrenia reduce stress, improve family interactions, learn social skills, and cope with the impact of the disorder on their lives. Comprehensive treatment programs combining drug therapy with an array of psychological and sociocultural therapies have been shown to significantly reduce relapse. These programs tend to be few and underfunded, however.

- People in developing countries tend to show a more positive course of schizophrenia than do people in developed countries, and women tend to have a more positive course than do men.

Key Terms

psychosis 326

schizophrenia 326

positive symptoms 330

negative symptoms 330

delusions 330

persecutory delusion 331

delusion of reference 331

grandiose delusion 331

delusions of thought control 332

hallucinations 334

auditory hallucination 334

visual hallucination 334

Critical Thinking Questions

1. How would you do a study that teased apart the effects of antipsychotic medications on the brains of people with schizophrenia from the effects of the schizophrenia itself?

2. How is it that stress may contribute to relapses in schizophrenia?

3. What would be some of the greatest stresses on the family members of people with schizophrenia?

4. If you were taking antipsychotic medications and they were controlling your delusions and hallucinations but giving you significant symptoms of tardive dyskinesia, do you think you would want to discontinue taking these medications or continue taking them? Why or why not?

5. If a person with schizophrenia says he or she does not want to be medicated and wants to live on the streets, does society have a right or obligation to force him or her to receive treatment?

6. How would you conduct family therapy with the family of a person with schizophrenia so as not to make the family members feel they were being blamed for their loved one's disorder?

Daniel Nevis
Day Dream

The image of myself which I try to create in my own mind in order that I may love myself is very different from the image which I try to create in the minds of others in order that they may love me.

—W. H. Auden, "Hic et Ille," The Dyer's Hand *(1963)*

CHAPTER

11

Dissociative and Somatoform Disorders

CHAPTER OVERVIEW

Dissociative Disorders

People with dissociative identity disorder develop multiple separate personalities. Dissociative identity disorder may develop in people who experience severe traumas, especially during childhood, and who use self-hypnosis to create "alters" to help them cope with these traumas. Treatment for dissociative identity disorder involves discovering the functions of all the personalities and helping the individual to integrate these personalities and find more adaptive ways of coping with stress. People with dissociative fugue move away from home and assume a new identity, with complete amnesia for their previous life. Fugue states may arise following major traumas. People with dissociative amnesia lose their memories for important facts about their lives and personal identities, apparently for psychological reasons. Psychologically based amnesias most frequently occur following traumatic events, such as sexual assaults. Depersonalization experiences involve a sense that one is detached from one's own mental processes or body.

Taking Psychology Personally:
Dissociative Experiences in Everyday Life

Viewpoints:
Is Dissociative Identity Disorder a Valid Diagnosis?

Somatoform Disorders

People with conversion disorder completely lose functioning in some part of their bodies, apparently for psychological reasons. These disorders arise most commonly in response to extreme stress. Psychodynamic treatments involve helping people make the links between their symptoms and traumatic memories. Behavioral treatments focus on relieving people's anxiety about the initiating traumas through desensitization and exposure treatments. People with somatization disorder have histories of multiple physical complaints for which there are no organic causes but for which they have sought a great deal of medical help. People with pain disorder focus their complaints on symptoms of pain. These disorders may represent acceptable ways of expressing distress, especially for people in certain cultures. Cognitive theories of these disorders suggest that they are due to catastrophization of physical symptoms. Treatment for these disorders involves helping people cope more adaptively with the stresses they face. People with hypochondriasis worry chronically that they may be ill, even when they have no physical symptoms and have been thoroughly checked by medical professionals. The causes and treatments for hypochondriasis are similar to those for somatization disorder. People with body dysmorphic disorder are excessively preoccupied with some part of their bodies and go to elaborate means to change that part of their bodies. This disorder may be a form of obsessive-compulsive disorder.

Extraordinary People:
Anna O.

Bio-Psycho-Social Integration
Chapter Summary
Key Terms
Critical Thinking Questions

When we are faced with extremely painful situations or emotions, we often want simply to escape. Some of us may abuse alcohol or binge eat in order to get our minds off our distress. In this chapter, we discuss an extreme form of escape used by some people facing traumatic experiences or intolerable distress. This escape mechanism is known as dissociation. **Dissociation** is a process in which different parts of an individual's identity, memories, or consciousness become split off from one another. The poet Emily Dickinson (1890/1955) describes this process:

> a pain
> so utter
> it swallows substance up
> then covers the Abyss with trance
> so memory can step around, across, upon it
> as one within a swoon goes safely
> where an open eye
> would drop him
> bone by bone.

In this chapter, we focus on extreme forms of dissociation in which people develop multiple separate personalities or completely lose memory for significant portions of their lives. When these dissociative experiences become chronic and defining features of people's lives, they may be diagnosed as a *dissociative disorder*. We also discuss the *somatoform disorders*, in which people appear to develop physiological symptoms that are the result of painful memories or emotions that they are not able to confront. For example, a woman who witnesses her child being killed may lose her vision because she cannot confront her grief and her memory. Many theoreticians believe that dissociative processes are involved in the development of somatoform disorders—that the physical symptoms of a somatofom disorder are due to repression or splitting off of painful memories from one's consciousness.

⟳ DISSOCIATIVE DISORDERS

Most of us have mild dissociative experiences occasionally. Daydreaming is a dissociative experience. When we daydream, we can lose consciousness of where we are and of what is going on around us. Becoming absorbed in a movie is a dissociative experience. Dissociative experiences are especially common when we are sleep deprived and under stress. During exam week or other very stressful times, have you ever felt as if your "soul" is floating outside your body? That is a dissociative experience. We discuss these in

Mild dissociative experiences are common when people are stressed or sleep deprived.

Taking Psychology Personally: Dissociative Experiences in Everyday Life.

Scientific interest in dissociative experiences has waxed and waned over the last few centuries (Ross, 1997). There was a great deal of interest in dissociation in nineteenth-century France and the United States among neurologists and psychologists such as Janet, Charcot, Freud, Jung, and James. French neurologist Pierre Janet viewed dissociation as a process in which systems of ideas are split off from consciousness but accessible through dreams and through hypnosis. One case he investigated was that of a woman named Irene, who had no memory of the fact that her mother had died. Yet, during her sleep, Irene would physically dramatize the events surrounding her mother's death.

After about 1910, interest in dissociative phenomena waned, partly because of the rise of behaviorism and biological approaches within psychology, which rejected the concept of repression and the use of techniques like hypnosis in therapy. Ernest Hilgard (1977, 1986) revitalized interest in dissociation in his experiments on the "hidden observer" phenomenon. He argued that there is an *active mode* to consciousness, which includes our conscious plans and desires and voluntary actions. In its passive *receptive mode*, the conscious registers and stores information in memory without being aware that the information has been processed, as if hidden observers are watching and recording events in people's lives without their being aware.

Hilgard and his associates conducted experimental studies in which participants were hypnotized and given a suggestion that they would feel no pain during a painful procedure but that they would remember the pain when the hypnotist gave them a specific cue. These subjects indeed showed no awareness of pain during the procedure. When cued, they reported memories of the pain in a "matter-of-fact" fashion, as if a "lucid, rational observer" of the event had registered the event for the subject. Other research showed that some anesthetized surgical patients could later recall, under hypnosis, specific pieces of music played during the surgery. Again, it was as if some "hidden observer" were registering the events of the operations even while the patients were completely unconscious under anesthesia (see Kihlstrom & Couture, 1992; Kirsch & Lynn, 1998).

For most people, the active and receptive modes of consciousness weave our experiences together so seamlessly that we do not notice any division between them. People who develop dissociative disorders may have chronic problems integrating their active and their receptive consciousness (Hilgard, 1992; Kihlstrom, 1992). That is, different aspects of consciousness in these people do not communicate with each other in normal ways, but remain split and operate independently of each other.

We begin our discussion of specific dissociative disorders with dissociative identity disorder, formerly known as *multiple personality disorder.* We then move to dissociative fugue, dissociative amnesia, and depersonalization disorder (see *Concept Review:* Key Features of the Dissociative Disorders, p. 375). All these disorders involve frequent experiences in which different aspects of a person's "self" are split off from each other, fragmented, and felt as separate.

TAKING PSYCHOLOGY PERSONALLY

Dissociative Experiences in Everyday Life

You are driving down a familiar road, thinking about a recent conversation with a friend. Suddenly you realize that you've traveled several miles, and don't remember traveling that section of the road. How did you get where you currently are? Obviously, you must have driven there, but you have no memory of passing the usual landmarks.

This kind of dissociative experience is exceedingly common, as researcher Colin Ross (1997) has documented. He asked over 1,000 adults, randomly selected from the community of Winnipeg in Canada, about a number of different dissociative experiences. Table 11.1 (p. 374) presents some of Ross's findings. Missing part of a conversation appears to be the most common dissociative experience, followed by being unsure whether you have actually carried through with something (such as brushing your teeth) or only thought about it. These seem like quite benign experiences. Further down the list are somewhat more bizarre experiences, such as hearing voices in your head, feeling as though your body is not your own, and not recognizing objects or other people as real. As we can see in Table 11.1, even these rather bizarre experiences are reported as happening at least occasionally by a substantial percentage of "normal" people.

Everyday dissociative experiences can be caused by many factors. Fatigue and stress are probably the most common causes. Binge-drinking alcohol or taking other psychoactive drugs can cause many of the memory lapses we see in Table 11.1. Older adults whose short-term memories are fading often forget having done things, and as we discuss in Chapter 18, several cognitive disorders can lead to memory lapses, and even the inability to recognize faces. Most of the time, however, dissociative experiences are transient and do not signal any long-term problems.

Some people do have dissociative experiences frequently enough that they interfere with their functioning. Ross (1997) categorized these people as in the "pathological range" of dissociative experiences. The percentage of people in his sample falling in this range for each of the experiences he studied is given in the right column of Table 11.1 We can see that, whereas occasional dissociative experiences are extremely common, most of the more bizarre dissociative experiences occur infrequently enough that only a small percentage of people are categorized in the pathological range.

So the next time you find yourself wondering how you got to where you are standing, or not remembering dressing in the clothes you are wearing, don't panic. Chances are that it is one of those everyday dissociative experiences we all have.

Continued

TABLE 11.1

Dissociative Experiences in the General Population

These are the percentages of people in random sample of 1,055 adults in Winnipeg, Canada, who acknowledged ever having experienced each item, and who fell into the pathological range for frequency of experiences of the item.

Experience	Percent acknowledging	Percent in pathological range
Missing part of a conversation	83	29
Not sure whether one has done something or only thought about it	73	25
Remembering the past so vividly one seems to be reliving it	60	19
Talking out loud to oneself when alone	56	18
Not sure if remembered event happened or was a dream	55	13
Feeling as though one were two different people	47	12
So involved in fantasy that it seems real	45	11
Driving a car and realizing that one doesn't remember part of the trip	48	8
Finding notes or drawings that one must have done but doesn't remember doing	34	6
Seeing oneself as if looking at another person	29	4
Hearing voices inside one's head	26	7
Other people and objects do not seem real	26	4
Finding unfamiliar things among one's belongings	22	4
Feeling as though one's body is not one's own	23	4
Finding oneself in a place but unaware of how one got there	19	2
Finding oneself dressed in clothes one doesn't remember putting on	15	1
Not recognizing one's reflection in a mirror	14	1

From C.A. Ross, *Dissociative Identity Disorder.* Copyright © 1997 John Wiley & Sons, Inc. Reprinted by permission of John Wiley & Sons, Inc.

The movie Three Faces of Eve *depicted the story of a woman with dissociative identity disorder, who would discover extravagant articles of clothing in her closet that she didn't remember buying.*

CONCEPT REVIEW

Key Features of the Dissociative Disorders

The dissociative disorders represent extreme experiences in which aspects of people's identities become split apart.

Disorder	Key Features
Dissociative identity disorder	There are separate multiple personalities in the same individual. The personalities may be aware of each other or may have amnesia for each other.
Dissociative fugue	The person moves away and assumes a new identity, with amnesia for the previous identity. There is no switching among personalities as in dissociative identity disorder.
Dissociative amnesia	The person loses memory of important personal facts, including personal identity, for no apparent organic cause.
Depersonalization disorder	There are frequent episodes in which the individual feels detached from his or her mental state or body. The person does not develop new identities or have amnesia for these episodes.

Dissociative Identity Disorder

CASE STUDY

Eve White was a quiet, proper, and unassuming woman, a full-time homemaker and devoted mother to a young daughter. She sought help from a psychiatrist for painful headaches that were occurring with increasing frequency. The psychiatrist decided that her headaches were related to arguments she was having with her husband over whether to raise their young daughter in the husband's church (which was Catholic) or in her church (which was Baptist). After undergoing some marital therapy, Mrs. White's marriage improved and her headaches subsided for a year or so. Then, her husband recontacted her therapist, alarmed over changes in his wife's behavior. She had gone to visit a favorite cousin in a town 50 miles away and during the visit had behaved in a much more carefree and reckless manner than she usually did. Mrs. White told her husband over the phone that she was not going to return home, and the two had a terrible fight that ended in an agreement to divorce. When Mrs. White did return home a few days later, however, she said she had no memory of the fight with her husband or, for that matter, of the visit with her cousin. Shortly thereafter, Mrs. White apparently went shopping and bought hundreds of dollars worth of elaborate clothing, which the couple could not afford. When confronted by her husband about her expenditures, Mrs. White claimed to have no memory of buying the clothing.

At the urging of her husband, Mrs. White made an appointment with the therapist whom she had originally consulted about her headaches. In the session, she admitted that her headaches had returned and were much more severe now than before. Eventually, she also tearfully admitted that she had begun to hear a voice other than her own speaking inside her head and that she feared she was going insane. The therapist asked her more questions about the clothes-buying spree, and Mrs. White became more tense and had difficulty getting words out to discuss the incident. Then, as her therapist reported,

> The brooding look in her eyes became almost a stare. Eve seemed momentarily dazed. Suddenly her posture began to change. Her body slowly stiffened until she sat rigidly erect. An alien, inexplicable expression then came over her face. This was suddenly erased into utter blankness. The lines of her countenance seemed to shift in a barely visible, slow, rippling transformation. For a moment there was the impression of something arcane. Closing her eyes, she winced as she put her hands to her temples, pressed hard, and twisted them as if to combat sudden pain. A slight shudder passed over her entire body.
>
> Then the hands lightly dropped. She relaxed easily into an attitude of comfort the physician had never before seen in this patient. A pair of blue eyes popped open. There was a quick reckless smile. In a bright, unfamiliar voice that sparked, the woman said, "Hi, there, Doc!"

Still busy with his own unassimilated surprise, the doctor heard himself say, "How do you feel now?"

"Why just fine—never better! How you doing yourself, Doc?"

Eve looked for a moment straight into his eyes. Her expression was that of one who is just barely able to restrain laughter. Her eyes rolled up and to one side for an instant, then the lids flicked softly before opening wide again. She tossed her head lightly with a little gesture that threw the fine dark hair forward onto her shoulder. A five-year-old might have so reacted to some sudden, unforeseen amusement. In the patient's gesture there was something of pert sauciness, something in which the artless play of a child and a scarcely conscious flirtatiousness mingled. . . .

"She's been having a real rough time. There's no doubt about that," the girl said carelessly. "I feel right sorry for her sometimes. She's such a damn dope though. . . . What she puts up with from that sorry Ralph White—and all her mooning over that little brat . . . ! To hell with it, I say!" . . .

The doctor asked, "Who is 'she'?"

"Why, Eve White, of course. Your long-suffering, saintly, little patient."

"But aren't you Eve White?" he asked.

"That's for laughs," she exclaimed, a ripple of mirth in her tone. . . .

"Why, I'm Eve Black," she said. . . ."I'm me and she's herself," the girl added. "I like to live and she don't. . . .Those dresses—well, I can tell you about them. I got out the other day, and I needed some dresses. I like good clothes. So I just went into town and bought what I wanted. I charged 'em to her husband, too!" She began to laugh softly. "You ought've seen the look on her silly face when he showed her what was in the cupboard!" (Reprinted with permission from C. H. Thigpen and H. M. Cleckley, *The Three Faces of Eve,* Copyright © 1957 McGraw-Hill.)

In later sessions, Eve Black told the psychiatrist of escapades in which she had stayed out all night drinking and then "went back in" in the morning and let Eve White deal with the hangover. At the beginning of therapy, Eve White had no consciousness of Eve Black or of over 20 personalities eventually identified during therapy.

This story of the *Three Faces of Eve* is one of the most detailed and gripping accounts of someone diagnosed with dissociative identity disorder. Eve White eventually recovered from her disorder, "integrating" the aspects of her personality represented by Eve Black and her other personalities into one single entity and living a healthy, normal life.

Dissociative identity disorder (DID), formerly referred to as *multiple personality disorder,* is one of the most controversial and fascinating disorders recognized in clinical psychology and psychiatry. As the

CONCEPT REVIEW
Dissociative Identity Disorder

Dissociative identity disorder, formerly known as multiple personality disorder, is one of the most fascinating dissociative disorders.

Symptoms	Presence of two or more separate personalities or identities in the same individual. These personalities may have different ways of speaking and relating to others, be of different ages and genders, and even have different physiological responses.
Etiology	Alters may be created by people under conditions of extreme stress, often child abuse. Self-hypnosis may be involved. Some evidence it runs in families.
Treatment	Long-term psychotherapy and the use of hypnosis to discover the functions of the personalities and to assist the personalities in "integration." Antidepressants and antianxiety drugs may be used.

name suggests, people with this disorder have more than one distinct identity or personality, and often have more than a dozen personalities (see *Concept Review: Dissociative Identity Disorder*). Each personality has different ways of perceiving and relating to the world, and each personality takes control over the individual's behavior on a regular basis. As was true of Eve White/Black, the alternate personalities, or *alters,* can be extremely different from one another, with distinct facial expressions, speech characteristics, physiological responses, gestures, interpersonal styles, and attitudes (Miller, 1989; Putnam, 1991). They often are different ages and different genders and perform specific functions.

The current estimate of the prevalence of dissociative identity disorder in North America is 1 percent (Ross, 1991). The vast majority of persons diagnosed with this disorder are adult women. It may be that the conditions leading to dissociative identity disorder are more commonly experienced by women than by men (Peterson, 1991). Among children diagnosed with dissociative identity disorder, however, the numbers of females and males appear to be more equal (Dell & Eisenhower, 1990). It may be that boys with dissociative identity disorder are more likely to be taken for treatment than are girls, so as adults, males are less likely to continue to have the disorder than are females (Dell & Eisenhower, 1990). Or girls may be more likely than boys to experience traumas in adolescence that lead to dissociative identity disorder, which continues into adulthood. There are some differences between the characteristics of personalities of male and females with dissociative identity disorder. Males with dissociative identity disorder appear to be more aggressive than females with the disorder. In one study, 29 percent of male dissociative identity patients had been convicted of crimes, compared to 10 percent of female dissociative identity patients (Ross & Norton, 1989). Case reports suggest that females with dissociative identity disorder tend to have more somatic complaints than do males and may engage in more suicidal behavior (Kluft, 1985).

People with dissociative identity disorder often engage in self-mutilative behavior.

Symptoms

The cardinal symptom in dissociative identity disorder is the presence of multiple personalities with distinct qualities. These different personalities are often referred to as alters, and can take many forms and perform many functions. *Child alters*—alters that are young children, who do not age as the individual ages—appear to be the most common type of alter (Ross, Norton & Wozney, 1989). Childhood trauma is often associated with the development of dissociative identity disorder. A child alter may be created during a traumatic experience to become the victim of the trauma, while the "host" personality escapes into the protection of psychological oblivion. Alternately, an alter may be created as a type of big brother or sister to protect the host personality from traumas. When a child alter is "out" or in control of the individual's behavior, the adult will speak and act in a childlike way.

A second type of alter that is very frequent is the *persecutor personality*. These alters inflict pain or punishment on the other personalities by engaging in self-mutilative behaviors such as self-cutting or burning and suicide attempts (Coons & Milstein, 1990; Ross, Norton & Wozney, 1989). A persecutor alter may engage in a dangerous behavior, such as taking an overdose of pills or jumping in front of a truck, and then "go back inside," leaving the host personality to experience the pain. Persecutors may have the belief that they can harm other personalities without harming themselves.

A third type of alter is the protector or *helper personality*. The function of this personality is to offer advice to other personalities or to perform functions the host personality is unable to perform, such as engaging in sexual relations or hiding from abusive parents. Helpers sometimes control the switching from one personality to another or may act as passive observers who can report on the thoughts and intentions of all the other personalities (Ross, 1989).

People with dissociative identity disorder typically have significant periods of amnesia or blank spells. Some personalities may be completely amnesic for the periods when other personalities are in control. Or there may be one-way amnesia between certain personalities in which one personality is aware of what the other is doing, but the second personality is completely amnesic for periods when the first personality is in control. People with dissociative identity disorder may, as with Eve White, suddenly discover unknown objects in their homes, or they may lose objects. People they do not recognize might approach them on the street claiming to know them. They may consistently receive mail or phone calls addressed to someone with a different first or last name.

Self-destructive behavior is very common among people with dissociative identity disorder, and often the reason they seek or are brought for treatment (Ross, 1997). This behavior can include self-inflicted burns or other injuries, wrist slashing, overdoses. About three-quarters of patients with dissociative identity disorder have a history of suicide attempts, and over 90 percent report recurrent suicidal thoughts (Ross, 1997).

Symptoms in children Like adults, children with dissociative identity disorder exhibit a host of behavioral and emotional problems (Putnam, 1991). Their performance in school may be erratic, sometimes very good and sometimes very poor. They are prone to antisocial behavior, such as stealing, fire-setting, and aggression. They may engage in sexual relations and abuse alcohol or illicit drugs at an early age. They tend to show many symptoms of posttraumatic stress disorder (PTSD, see Chapter 7), including hypervigilance, flashbacks to traumas they have endured, traumatic nightmares, and an exaggerated startle response. Their emotions are unstable, alternating among explosive outbursts of anger, deep depression, and severe anxiety. Most children and many adults with dissociative identity disorder report hearing voices inside their heads. Some report being

VIEWPOINTS

Is Dissociative Identity Disorder a Valid Diagnosis?

R esearchers who are skeptical of the recent increase in reported cases of dissociative identity disorder in the United States argue that the disorder is artificially created in suggestible clients by clinicians who reinforce clients for "admitting" to symptoms of dissociative identity disorder and who induce symptoms of the disorder through hypnotic suggestion (see Lilienfeld et al., 1999). Even clinicians who believe dissociative identity disorder exists and is more common that was originally believed acknowledge that some clinicians are too quick to diagnose DID, and can badger clients into believe that they have DID (Ross, 1997).

In a series of laboratory experiences, Nicholas Spanos and colleagues (1985) showed they could create DID symptoms in ordinary college students. In their experiments, the researchers asked participants to role-play Harry or Betty, persons who had been accused of murder and who were undergoing a pretrial psychiatric evaluation. In two conditions of this experiment, the subjects underwent hypnosis and then the experimenter asked them a series of leading questions designed to "uncover" dissociative identity disorder.

In one condition, the experimenter talked with the subject for a while and then said, "I've talked a bit to Harry/Betty but I think perhaps there might be another

Serial killer Kenneth Bianchi tried to claim he had dissociative identity disorder, but experts proved that he did not.

part of Harry/Betty that I haven't talked to, another part that maybe feels somewhat differently from the part that I've talked to. And I would like to communicate with that

aware that their actions or words are being controlled by other personalities. For example, Joe, an 8-year-old boy with dissociative identity disorder, described how "a guy inside of me" called B. J. (for Bad Joey) would make him do "bad things" (Hornstein & Putnam, 1992, p. 1081):

Voices

Well, say B. J. hears someone call me names, then he would strike me to do something, like I'd be running at the other kid, but it wouldn't be my legs, I'd be saying to my legs, "no . . . , stop . . . ," but they'd keep going on their own because that's B. J. doing that. Then my

arm would be going at the other kid, hitting him, and I could see my arm doing that, but I couldn't stop it, and it wouldn't hurt when my hand hit him, not until later when B. J. goes back in and then my arm is my own arm. Then it starts hurting.

Issues in Diagnosis

Dissociative identity disorder was rarely diagnosed before about 1980, but there has been a great increase in the number of reported cases since 1980 (Braun, 1986; Coons, 1986). This is due in part to the fact that dissociative identity disorder was first included as a

Continued

other part. Would you talk to me, Part, by saying, 'I'm here'?" Whatever the subjects' response, the experimenter would say, "Part, are you the same thing as Harry/Betty?" The experimenters called this condition the *Bianchi condition,* because it was modeled after a series of leading questions put to serial killer Kenneth Bianchi in a pretrial psychiatric evaluation, during which he claimed to have dissociative identity disorder.

In the hidden part condition, the experimenter said, "Personality is complex and involves many different ways of thinking and feeling about things. Sometimes part of us thinks about and feels things that other parts of us don't even know about. . . . During hypnosis, it is possible to get behind the mental wall to the blocked off parts of the mind. I am going to put my hand on your shoulder and when I do, I will be in contact with another part of you. I will get behind the wall and will be talking to the part of you that experiences strong feelings and frightening thoughts" (pp. 367–368). In addition, there was a control group of subjects who were not given a hypnotic induction but who were told the same things the subjects in the hidden part condition were told.

The researchers found that most of the participants in the Bianchi and hidden part conditions displayed symptoms of dissociative identity disorder. They claimed to have at least two separate identities, and scored differently on personality tests when they were "in" different personalities. The majority of the participants in the Bianchi condition also assumed different names for their separate parts. In contrast, none of the participants in a control condition showed symptoms of DID. Spanos and colleagues noted that the instructions they used to "induce" dissociative identity disorder were extremely similar to those used in psychiatric evaluations of persons thought to have the disorder (e.g., see Ross, 1989). They argued that the disorder is frequently the creation of the misuse of hypnosis and suggestion by therapists.

Others have argued that the fact that Spanos and colleagues could make participants mimic symptoms of dissociative identity disorder for a short time in a contrived laboratory setting says nothing about the validity of the diagnosis of dissociative identity disorder (Gleaves, 1996; Ross, 1997; Ross, Norton, & Fraser, 1989). The college student participants whom Spanos and others have made mimic DID symptoms do not show all the secondary or accompanying symptoms of DID, such as severe anxiety and depression, and clearly do not have a lifelong history of multiple psychiatric complaints and diagnoses, as is the case in patients diagnosed with DID. In addition, Ross and colleagues (1989) compared DID patients who had been hypnotized by their therapists and DID patients who had never been hypnotized and found no differences in the types of symptoms these two groups of patients displayed, their histories of abuse, or their demographic features (such as age and gender). This suggests that the experience of being hypnotized did not change the features of DID in people diagnosed with the disorder, as we might expect if therapists were inducing symptoms of the disorder by hypnotizing their patients.

---

diagnostic category in the DSM in its third edition, published in 1980. The availability of specific diagnostic criteria for this disorder made it more likely that it would be used as a diagnosis. At the same time, the diagnostic criteria for schizophrenia were made more specific in the 1980 version of the DSM, possibly leading to some cases that would have been diagnosed as schizophrenia being diagnosed with dissociative identity disorder. One final, and important influence on trends in diagnosis was the publication of a series of influential papers by psychiatrists describing persons with dissociative identity disorder whom they had treated (Bliss, 1980; Coons, 1980; Greaves, 1980; Rosenbaum, 1980), which aroused interest in the disorder in the psychi-

atric community. Still, most mental-health professionals are reluctant to give this diagnosis, as we discuss in the *Viewpoints:* Is Dissociative Identity Disorder a Valid Diagnosis?

Most people diagnosed with dissociative identity disorder have already been diagnosed with at least three other disorders (Kluft, 1987). Some of the other disorders diagnosed are secondary to or the result of the dissociative identity disorder. For example, one study of 135 patients with dissociative identity disorder found that 97 percent could also be diagnosed with major depression, 90 percent had an anxiety disorder, most often posttraumatic stress disorder, 65 percent were abusing substances, and 38 percent had an eating disorder (Ellason, Ross, & Fuchs, 1996). In addition, most people with dissociative identity disorder also are diagnosed with a personality disorder (Dell, 1998).

Many of the diagnoses received before the diagnosis of dissociative identity disorder is established may be misdiagnoses of the dissociative symptoms, however. For example, when people with dissociative identity disorder report hearing voices talking inside their heads, they are often misdiagnosed as having schizophrenia (Kluft, 1987). The voices that people with schizophrenia hear, however, often are experienced as coming from outside their heads. In addition, people with schizophrenia will not evidence full-blown alter personalities, even though they may occasionally have the belief that they are someone else. That is, when people with schizophrenia believe they are other people, their entire demeanors will not change in the way that the voices, speech, and physical appearances of people with dissociative identity disorder change when they have switched to other personalities. Conversely, people with dissociative identity disorder will not show schizophrenic symptoms such as flat or inappropriate affect or loose or illogical associations (Ellason et al., 1996).

Cross-cultural considerations There are substantial cross-national differences in rates of diagnosed dissociative identity disorder. This disorder is diagnosed much more frequently in the United States than in Great Britain, Europe, India, or Japan (Ross, 1989; Saxena & Prasad, 1989; Takahashi, 1990). Within the United States, dissociative identity disorder is rarely diagnosed in Latinos (Martinez-Taboas, 1989). Some theorists argue that, instead of dissociative identity disorder, Latinos may experience *ataque de nervios*, a culturally accepted reaction to stress that involves transient periods of loss of consciousness, convulsive movements of a psychological origin, hyperactivity, assaultive behaviors, and impulsive suicidal or homicidal acts (see the discussion of *ataque de nervios* in Chapter 7; Steinberg, 1990). The following case study describes a Hispanic woman believed to experience *ataque de nervios* but later diagnosed with dissociative identity disorder by a non-Hispanic psychiatrist (adapted from Steinberg, 1990, pp. 31–32).

CASE STUDY

Mrs. C., a 40-year-old divorced Hispanic woman, contacted a Hispanic clinic in Connecticut on the suggestion of her previous psychiatrist in Puerto Rico. Over an 18-year period Mrs. C. had made numerous emergency room and follow-up visits to a Puerto Rican psychiatric hospital. Her previous diagnoses included psychotic depression, schizophrenia, posttraumatic stress disorder, schizoaffective disorder, and hysterical personality. A variety of neuroleptics and antidepressants in therapeutic dosages had been prescribed but had provided no relief.

Mrs. C. was the youngest of three daughters born to indigent parents in Puerto Rico and was raised among numerous relatives in an overcrowded setting. Mrs. C. suffered extreme physical and emotional abuse from her mother, including administration of enemas and emetics every other day as punishment "if she was bad." . . . Mrs. C. also recalled being sexually abused by her father and suffered recurrent dreams of this abuse. Married at age 17, she had three children by her first husband, who was physically abusive. After 4 years, Mrs. C. left him and shortly thereafter married another man, whom she described as physically and emotionally abusive. They separated 4 months later. Recently, she moved to Connecticut to be near her grown daughter.

Mrs. C.'s first presentation in Connecticut was with a classic episode of *ataque*. She described an acute onset of distressing auditory and visual hallucinations, . . . stating that the voices were commanding her to harm herself. The initial diagnostic impression at the clinic was of a psychotic depression and she was given a prescription for an antipsychotic drug. Four days later, in a follow-up visit, she had not used the medication, denied having had auditory or visual hallucinations, and was free of any psychotic symptoms. She described rapid mood swings, "out of body experiences," and amnesic episodes which she had experienced since childhood. At this time, Mrs. C. was scheduled for biweekly supportive therapy with a mental health worker. She attended sessions irregularly. Her demeanor, level of functioning, and symptoms fluctuated radically. Several times she spontaneously began acting as though she were a child. Frequently she presented to therapy referring to herself by another name and did not remember previous sessions. During this period, Mrs. C. was brought to the Hispanic clinic by her boyfriend for an emergency consultation due to the acute onset of bizarre behavior. She was childlike and disoriented, suffered auditory and visual hallucinations of suicidal and homicidal nature, and rapidly became restless and agitated. She stated her name was *Rosa*.

At that time the emergency room psychiatrist noted the similarity of her symptoms to the *ataque* and described her presentation: "When she came into the screening area, she took one of the balloons and began to play with it and asked me if I had a doll for her; she also said she was hungry and wanted some cookies and milk." His diagnostic impression was "atypical psychosis." . . . Re-evaluation several hours later revealed a "dramatic change in state." She said she was not Rosa, was not 6 years old, had no interest in playing with a doll, and she did not feel like someone was following her or was telling her to hurt herself. . . .

At this time Mrs. C. began a new course of weekly psychotherapy sessions which she attended fairly regularly. Mrs. C.'s sense of identity, her demeanor, and the content of each session varied significantly. During this treatment, five distinct personalities emerged with different names, ages, memories, and characteristic behaviors. Frequently she would state that she was "unable to remember" what she had discussed in a previous session. Recurrent themes included identity confusion and severe abuse by both parents. Throughout this year she remained off medication. . . .

Latinos may experience ataque de nervios *rather than dissociative identity disorder, as diagnosed in the DSM-IV.*

Some researchers have argued that psychiatrists in the United States are too quick to diagnose dissociative identity disorder, and others argue that psychiatrists in other countries misdiagnose it as some other disorder (Coons et al., 1990; Fahy, 1988).

Theories of Dissociative Identity Disorder

Many theorists who study dissociative identity disorder view it as the result of coping strategies used by persons faced with intolerable trauma, most often childhood sexual and/or physical abuse, from which they are powerless to escape (Bliss, 1986; Kluft, 1987). As Ross (1997, p. 64) describes:

> The little girl being sexually abused by her father at night imagines that the abuse is happening to someone else, as a way to distance herself from the overwhelming emotions she is experiencing. She may float up to the ceiling and watch the abuse in a detached fashion. Now not only is the abuse not happening to her, but she blocks it out of her mind—that other little girl remembers it, not the original self. In this model, DID is an internal divide-and-conquer strategy in which intolerable knowledge and feeling is split up into manageable compartments. These compartments are personified and take on a life of their own.

Most studies find that the majority of people diagnosed with dissociative identity disorder self-report having been the victims of sexual or physical abuse during childhood (Coons, 1994; Dell & Eisenhower, 1990; Hornstein & Putnam, 1992). For example, in a study of 135 persons with dissociative identity disorder, 92 percent reported having been sexually abused and 90 percent reported having been repeatedly physically abused (Ellason et al., 1996; see also Putnam et al., 1986). Similar results have been found in studies in which patients' reports of abuse were corroborated by at least one family member or by emergency room reports (Coons, 1994; Coons & Milstein, 1986). This abuse was most often carried out by parents or other family members and was chronic over an extended period of childhood. Other types of trauma that have been associated with the development of dissociative identity disorder include kidnapping, natural disasters, war, famine, and religious persecution (Ross, 1989).

People who develop dissociative identity disorder tend to be highly suggestible and hypnotizable and may use self-hypnosis to dissociate and escape their traumas (Kihlstrom, Glisky, & Angiulo, 1994). They create the alternate personalities to help them cope with their traumas, much as a child might create imaginary playmates to ease pangs of loneliness. These alternative personalities can provide the safety, security, and nurturing that they are not receiving from their real caregivers. People with dissociative identity disorder become trapped in their own defense mechanisms. Retreating into their alternate personalities or using these personalities to perform frightening functions becomes a chronic way of coping with life.

There is evidence from a few family history studies that dissociative identity disorder may run in some families (Coons, 1984; Dell & Eisenhower, 1990). In addition, one study of twins found evidence that the tendency to dissociate is substantially affected by genetics (Jang et al., 1998). Perhaps the ability and tendency to dissociate as a defense mechanism is, to some extent, biologically determined.

Treatment of Dissociative Identity Disorder

Treatment of dissociative identity disorder can be extremely challenging (Kluft, 1986; Ross, 1997). The goal of treatment is the integration of all the alter personalities into one coherent personality. This is done by identifying the functions or roles of each personality, helping each personality confront and "work through" the traumas that led to the disorder and the concerns each one has or represents, and negotiating with the personalities for fusion into one personality that has learned adaptive styles of coping with stress. Hypnosis is used heavily in the treatment of dissociative identity disorder to contact alters or alternate personalities (Putnam & Lowenstein, 1993). Patients who have been successfully treated report a sense of unity in their personality, no longer report hearing voices, and are consistent in their expression of one personality. In treatment of children with dissociative identity disorder, it is often necessary to work with parents to improve the family life of the children and sometimes to remove the children from abusive homes (Dell & Eisenhower, 1990). Antidepressants and antianxiety drugs are sometimes used as adjuncts to supportive psychotherapy.

Children who are abused may dissociate and even develop alter personalities as a way of dealing with their abuse.

Experts in the treatment of dissociative identity disorder find that treatment is successful in the majority of cases (Kluft, 1987; Ross, 1989), particularly if the treatment is begun in childhood shortly after a child first develops alternate personalities (Peterson, 1991). One of the few studies that has empirically evaluated the treatment of DID found that those patients who were able to integrate their personalities through treatment remained relatively free of symptoms over the subsequent 2 years (Ellason & Ross, 1997). These patients also reported few symptoms of substance abuse and depression, and had been able to reduce their use of antidepressant and antipsychotic medications. In contrast, patients who had not achieved integration during treatment continued to show symptoms of DID and a number of other disorders. This study did not compare the outcome of patients who received therapy to those who did not, and did not compare different types of therapy.

Dissociative Fugue

A person in the midst of a **dissociative fugue** will suddenly pick up and move to a new place, assume a new identity, and have no memory for his previous identity (see *Concept Review: Dissociative Fugue*). He will behave quite normally in his new environment, and it will not seem odd to him that he cannot remember anything from his past. Just as suddenly, he may return to his previous identity and home, resuming his life as if nothing had happened, with no memory for what he did during the fugue. A fugue may last for a matter of days or years, and a person may experience repeated fugue states or a single episode. An extreme and classic case of fugue was that of the Reverend Ansel Bourne, reported by the American philosopher and psychologist William James (1890, Vol. 1, pp. 391–393).

CASE STUDY

The Rev. Ansel Bourne, of Greene, R.I., was brought up to the trade of a carpenter; but, in consequence of a sudden temporary loss of sight and hearing under very peculiar circumstances, he became converted from Atheism to Christianity just before his thirtieth year, and has since that time for the most part lived the life of an itinerant preacher. He has been subject to headaches and temporary fits of depression of spirits during most of his life, and has had a few fits of unconsciousness lasting an hour or less. He also has a region of somewhat diminished cutaneous sensibility on the left thigh. Otherwise his health is good, and his muscular strength and endurance excellent. He is of a firm and self-reliant disposition, a man whose yea is yea and his nay, nay; and his character for uprightness is such in the community that no person who knows him will for a moment admit the possibility of his case not being perfectly genuine.

On January 17, 1887, he drew 551 dollars from a bank in Providence with which to pay for a certain lot of land in Greene, paid certain bills, and got into a Pawtucket horse-car. This is the last incident which he remembers. He did not return home that day, and nothing was heard of him for two months. He was published in the papers as missing, and foul play being suspected, the police sought in vain his whereabouts. On the morning of March 14th, however, at Norristown, Pennsylvania, a man calling himself A. J. Brown, who had rented a small shop six weeks previously, stocked it with stationery, confectionery, fruit, and small articles, and carried on his quiet trade without seeming to anyone unnatural or eccentric, woke up in a fright and called the people of the house to tell him where he was. He said that his name was Ansel Bourne, that he was entirely ignorant of Norristown, and that he knew nothing of shop-keeping, and that the last thing he remembered—it seemed only yesterday—was drawing the money from the bank, etc. in Providence. He would not believe that two months had elapsed. The people of the house thought him insane; and so, at first, did Dr. Louis H. Read, whom they called in to see him. But on telegraphing to Providence, confirmatory messages came, and presently his nephew, Mr. Andrew Harris, arrived upon the scene, made everything straight, and took him home. He was very weak, having lost apparently over twenty pounds of flesh during his escapade, and had such a horror of the idea of the candy-store that he refused to set foot in it again.

The first two weeks of the period remained unaccounted for, as he had no memory, after he had once resumed his normal personality, of any part of the time, and no one who knew him seems to have seen him after he left home. The remarkable part of the change is, of course, the peculiar occupation which the so-called Brown indulged in. Mr. Bourne has never in his life had the slightest contact with trade. "Brown" was described by the neighbors as taciturn, orderly in his habits, and in no way queer. He went to Philadelphia several times, replenished his stock;

cooked for himself in the back shop, where he also slept; went regularly to church; and once at prayer-meeting made what was considered by the hearers as a good address, in the course of which he related an incident which he had witnessed in his natural state of Bourne.

This was all that was known of the case up to June 1890, when I induced Mr. Bourne to submit to hypnotism, so as to see whether, in the hypnotic trance, his "Brown" memory would not come back. It did so with surprising readiness; so much so indeed that it proved quite impossible to make him whilst in the hypnosis remember any of the facts of his normal life. He had heard of Ansel Bourne, but "didn't know as he had ever met the man." When confronted with Mrs. Bourne he said that he had "never seen the woman before," etc. On the other hand, he told of his peregrinations during the lost fortnight, and gave all sorts of details about the Norristown episode. The whole thing was prosaic enough; and the Brown-personality seems to be nothing but a rather shrunken, dejected, and amnesic extract of Mr. Bourne himself. He gives no motive for the wandering except that there was "trouble back there" and "he wanted rest." During the trance he looks old, the corners of his mouth are drawn down, his voice is slow and weak, and he sits screening his eyes and trying vainly to remember what lay before and after the two months of the Brown experience. "I'm all hedged in," he says: "I can't get out at the other end. I don't know what set me down in the Pawtucket horse-car, and I don't know how I ever left that store, or what became of it." His eyes are practically normal, and all his sensibilities (save for tardier response) about the same in hypnosis as in waking. I had hoped by suggestion, etc., to run the two personalities into one, and make the memories continuous, but no artifice would avail to accomplish this, and Mr. Bourne's skill to-day still covers two distinct personal selves.

Some, but not all, persons who experience fugue episodes do so after traumatic events. Many others, such as Rev. Bourne, seem to escape into a fugue state in response to chronic stress in their lives that is within the realm of most people's experience. People are typically depressed before the onset of fugues (Kopelman, 1987). As in dissociative identity disorder, fugue states may be more common in people who are highly hypnotizable. Unlike the person with dissociative identity disorder, however, the person in a fugue state actually leaves the scene of the trauma or stress and leaves his or her former identity behind. Fugue states appear to be more common among people who have previous histories of some type of amnesia, including amnesias due to head injuries (Kopelman, 1987). We do not have an accurate estimate of the prevalence of fugue states, although they appear to be quite rare, and we do not know much about the etiology of fugue states, in part because of their rarity. Clinicians who treat people with this disorder tend to use many of the same techniques used to treat dissociative identity disorder, but again

CONCEPT REVIEW
Dissociative Fugue

Dissociative fugue is a rare form of dissociative disorder.

Symptoms	Person suddenly moves away from home and assumes an entirely new identity, with no memory of the previous identity.
Etiology	Fugue states usually occur in response to some stressor, but because they are extremely rare, little is known about etiology.
Treatment	Psychotherapy to help the person identify the stressors leading to the fugue state and learn better coping skills.

CONCEPT REVIEW
Dissociative Amnesia

Dissociative amnesia is a psychologically-based form of amnesia.

Symptoms	Loss of memory due to psychological rather than physiological causes. The memory loss is usually confined to personal information only.
Etiology	Typically occurs following traumatic events. May involve motivated forgetting of events, to poor storage of information during events due to overarousal, or to avoidance of emotions experienced during an event.
Treatment	Help the individual remember traumatic events and accept them.

because of the rarity of the disorder, we know little about the outcomes of treatment.

Dissociative Amnesia

In both dissociative identity disorder and dissociative fugue states, individuals may have amnesia for the periods of time when their alternate personalities are in control or when they have been in fugue states. Some people have significant periods of amnesia but do not assume new personalities or identities. People who are simply amnesic cannot remember important facts about their lives and their personal identities and are typically aware that there are large gaps in their memory or knowledge of themselves. These people are said to have **dissociative amnesia** (see *Concept Review:* Dissociative Amnesia, p. 383).

Amnesia is considered either organic or psychogenic (see *Concept Review:* Differences Between Psychogenic and Organic Amnesia). **Organic amnesias** are caused by brain injury resulting from disease, drugs, accidents (such as blows to the head), or surgery. Organic amnesia often involves the inability to remember new information, known as **anterograde amnesia. Psychogenic amnesias** arise in the absence of any brain injury or disease and are thought to have psychological causes. Psychogenic amnesias rarely involve anterograde amnesia.

The inability to remember information from the past, known as **retrograde amnesia,** can have both organic and psychogenic causes. For example, persons who have been in serious car accidents can have retrograde amnesia for the few minutes just before the accident. This retrograde amnesia can be due to brain injury resulting from blows to the head during accidents. Or it can be a motivated forgetting of the events leading up to traumatic accidents. Retrograde amnesia for longer periods of time can also occur. When such amnesias are due to organic causes, people usually forget everything about the past, including personal information, such as where they lived and who they knew, and general information, such as who was president and major historical events of the period. They will typically retain memory of their personal identity, however. Thus, although they may not remember their children, they will know their own names. When long-term retrograde amnesias are due to psychological causes, people typically lose their identities and forget personal information but retain memories for general information. The following is a case study of a man with a psychogenic retrograde amnesia (Hilgard, 1986, p. 68).

CASE STUDY

Some years ago a man was found wandering the streets of Eugene, Oregon, not knowing his name or where he had come from. The police, who were baffled by his inability to identify himself, called in Lester Beck . . . , a psychologist they knew to be familiar with hypnosis, to see if he could be of assistance. He found the man eager to cooperate and by means of hypnosis and other methods was able to reconstruct the man's history. . . .

Following domestic difficulties, the man had gone on a drunken spree completely out of keeping with his earlier social behavior, and he had subsequently suffered deep remorse. His amnesia was motivated in the first place by the desire to exclude from memory the mortifying experiences that had gone on during the guilt-producing episode. He succeeded in forgetting all the events before and after this behavior that reminded him of it. Hence the amnesia spread from the critical incident to events before and after it, and he completely lost his sense of personal identity.

Loss of memory due to alcohol intoxication is common, but usually the person only forgets the events occurring during the period he or she was intoxicated. Severe alcoholics can develop a more global retrograde amnesia, known as *Korsakoff's syndrome* (see Chapter 16), in which they cannot remember much personal or general information for a period of several years or decades. However, the type of retrograde amnesia evidenced in the previous case study, which apparently involved only one episode of heavy drinking and the loss of only personal information, typically has psychological causes.

Psychogenic amnesias may be the result of the use of dissociation as a defense against intolerable memories or stressors. They most frequently occur

---

CONCEPT REVIEW

Differences Between Psychogenic and Organic Amnesia

There are several important differences between psychogenic amnesia and organic amnesia.

Psychogenic Amnesia	Organic Amnesia
Caused by psychological factors	Caused by biological factors (such as disease, drugs, and blows to the head)
Seldom involves anterograde amnesia (inability to learn new information learned since onset of amnesia)	Often involves anterograde amnesia
Can involve retrograde amnesia (inability to remember events from the past)	Can involve retrograde amnesia
Retrograde amnesia often only for personal information, not for general information	Retrograde amnesia usually for both personal and general information

People can have amnesia for the events around a traumatic event, like a traffic accident, for both psychological and biological reasons.

following traumatic events, such as wars or sexual assaults. Alternately, amnesia for specific events may occur because individuals were in such a high state of arousal during the events they did not encode and store information during the period of the event and thus were unable to retrieve the information later (Kopelman, 1987). A third explanation for amnesias for specific events is that information about events are stored at the time of the events but are associated with a high state of arousal of painful emotions, and after the events people avoid the emotions and therefore do not gain access to the information associated with the emotions (Bower, 1981). Amnesias for specific periods of time around traumas appear to be fairly common,

Lorena Bobbitt cut off her husband's penis, after years of experiencing his abuse. She claimed to have amnesia for the act of cutting it off.

but generalized retrograde amnesias for people's entire pasts and identities appear very rare.

One complication that arises in diagnosing amnesias is the possibility that amnesias are being faked by people trying to escape punishment for crimes committed during the periods for which they claim to be amnesic. True amnesias can occur in conjunction with the commission of crimes. Many crimes are committed by persons under the influence of alcohol or other drugs, and the drugs can cause blackouts for the periods of intoxication (Kopelman, 1987). Similarly, people who incur head injuries during the commission of crimes—for example, by falling while trying to escape the scene of a crime—can have amnesia for the commission of crimes. Psychogenic amnesias can also occur for the commission of crimes, particularly if the criminals feel extremely guilty about the crimes. For example, a man who beat his wife may feel so guilty for doing so that he develops amnesia for the beating. Amnesia is most often seen in homicide cases, with between 25 and 45 percent of persons arrested for homicide claiming to have amnesia for the killings (Kopelman, 1987). In most of these cases, the victims are closely related to the killers (they are their lovers, spouses, close friends, or family members), the offenses appear to be unpremeditated, and the killers are in states of extreme emotional arousal at the time of the killings. More rarely, the killers appear to have been in psychotic states at the time of the killings. There is no clear-cut way to differentiate true amnesias from feigned ones. Head injuries leading to amnesia may be detectable through neuroimaging of the brain. Some clinicians advocate the use of hypnosis to assist people in remembering events around crimes, if it is suspected that the amnesia is due to psychological causes. However, the possibility that hypnosis will "create" memories through the power of suggestion leads many courts to deny the use of hypnosis in such cases (Kopelman, 1987). In most cases, it can be impossible to determine whether the amnesia is true.

Depersonalization Disorder

The final dissociative disorder is **depersonalization disorder.** People with this disorder have frequent episodes in which they feel detached from their own mental processes or bodies, as if they are outside observers of themselves. Occasional experiences of depersonalization are common, particularly when people are sleep deprived or under the influence of drugs. Depersonalization disorder is diagnosed when episodes of depersonalization are so frequent and distressing that they interfere with individuals' ability to function. We know very little about the causes of this disorder, who is most prone to it, or its prevalence.

Summing Up

- The dissociative disorders include dissociative identity disorder, dissociative fugue, dissociative amnesia, and depersonalization disorder.

- In all these disorders, people's conscious experiences of themselves become fragmented, they may lack awareness of core aspects of their selves, and they may experience amnesia for important events.

- The distinct feature of dissociative identity disorder is the development of multiple separate personalities within the same person. The personalities take turns being in control.

- People with dissociative fugue move away from home and assume entirely new identities, with complete amnesia for their previous identities. They do not switch back and forth between different personalities, however.

- People with dissociative amnesia lose important memories due to psychological causes.

- People with depersonalization disorder have frequent experiences of feeling detached from their mental processes or their bodies.

- These disorders are often, although not always, associated with traumatic experiences.

- Therapists often treat these disorders by helping people explore past experiences and feelings that they have blocked from consciousness and by supporting them as they develop more integrated experiences of self and more adaptive ways of coping with stress.

☉ SOMATOFORM DISORDERS

The **somatoform disorders** are a group of disorders in which people experience significant physical symptoms for which there is no apparent organic cause. Often these symptoms are inconsistent with possible physiological mechanisms, and there is strong reason to believe that psychological factors are involved. People with somatoform disorders do not consciously produce or control the symptoms. Instead, they truly experience the symptoms, and the symptoms only pass when the psychological factors that led to the symptoms are resolved.

Obviously, one of the great difficulties in diagnosing somatoform disorders is the possibility that an individual has a real physical disorder that is simply difficult to detect or diagnose. Many of us have friends or relatives who have complained to their physicians for years about specific physical symptoms that the physicians attributed to "nervousness" or "attention-seeking" but that later were determined to be early symptoms of serious disease. The diagnosis of somatoform disorder is made easier when psychological factors leading to the development of the symptoms can clearly be identified or when physical examination can prove that the symptoms cannot be physiologically possible. For example, when a child is perfectly healthy on weekends but has terrible stomachaches in the morning just before going to school, it is possible that the stomachaches are due to distress over going to school. A more extreme example of a clear somatoform disorder is *pseudocyesis*, or false pregnancy, in which a woman believes she is pregnant, but physical examination and laboratory tests confirm that she is not.

Distinguishing Somatoform from Related Disorders

The somatoform disorders are not the same as **psychosomatic disorders,** which are discussed in Chapter 17. People with psychosomatic disorders have an actual physical illness or defect, such as high blood pressure, that can be documented with medical tests, and that is being worsened by psychological factors. In contrast, a person with a somatoform disorder does not have any illness or defect that can be documented with tests (see *Concept Review:* Distinctions Between Somatoform and Pain Disorders and Related Syndromes). Somatoform disorders are also different from **malingering,** in which people fake a symptom or disorder in order to avoid some unwanted situation, such as military service. Again, the individual with a somatoform disorder subjectively experiences the symptoms, but there is no organic basis for the symptoms. Finally, somatoform disorders are different from **factitious disorders,** in

CONCEPT REVIEW

Distinctions Between Somatoform and Pain Disorders and Related Syndromes

Distinguishing between somatoform disorders and related syndromes can be difficult.

Somatoform and Pain Disorders	Psychosomatic Disorders	Malingering	Factitious Disorder
Subjective experience of many physical symptoms, with no organic cause (pain disorder involves experience of pain only)	Actual physical illness present and psychological factors seem to be contributing to the illness	Deliberate faking of physical symptoms to avoid an unpleasant situation, such as military duty	Deliberate faking of physical illness to gain medical attention

which a person deliberately fakes an illness to gain medical attention. Factitious disorders are also referred to as *Munchhausen's syndrome*.

In recent years, several cases of **factitious disorder by proxy** have come to light. In these tragic cases, parents have faked or even created illnesses in their children in order to gain attention for themselves. They act as devoted and long-suffering protectors of their children, drawing praise for their dedicated nursing. Their children are subjected to unnecessary and often dangerous medical procedures and may actually die from their parents' attempts to make them ill. Seven-year-old Jennifer Bush may be one victim of factitious disorder by proxy:

CASE STUDY

Sitting beside Hillary Clinton at a meeting on Capitol Hill two summers ago, Jennifer Bush cut a heart-breaking figure. The 7-year-old Coral Springs, Florida, girl with big eyes and a perky red bow atop her little Dutch-boy coif seemed the perfect poster child for the Administration's health-care reform plan. Chronically ill almost from birth, Jennifer had already endured nearly 200 hospitalizations and 40 operations, and her $2 million–plus medical bill had exhausted the family's health-insurance benefits. Not surprisingly, Jennifer became a media darling, appearing on the Today show and on the front page of many newspapers.

Now it appears that Jennifer's suffering may have been much worse than was ever reported. Florida officials arrested Jennifer's seemingly devoted mother Kathleen Bush and charged her with aggravated child abuse and fraud. According to authorities, Bush, 38, deliberately caused her daughter's ailments by dosing her with unprescribed drugs, tampering with her medications, and even contaminating her feeding tube with fecal bacteria. As a result, say officials, Jennifer was subjected to dozens of needless operations and invasive procedures. Bush has denied all charges.

Almost as shocking as the charges against Jennifer's mother, however, is the fact that it took more than 4 years

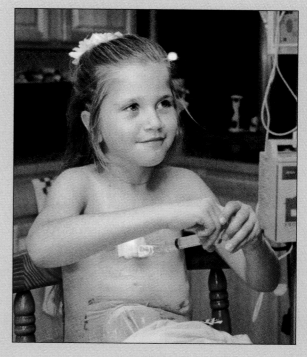

Jennifer Bush has endured hundreds of medical treatments and surgeries in her young life. Her mother is accused of causing Jennifer's illnesses to gain the attention of physicians and the media.

of warnings before state authorities placed the child under protective custody. Nurses at Coral Springs Medical Center began noticing as early as 1991—when Jennifer was just 4—that her condition seemed to worsen whenever her mother visited. . . .

State officials reopened the investigation last April, after receiving an anonymous complaint. According to the arrest affidavit, once her mother was informed of the inquiry, Jennifer's condition improved dramatically. In the preceding 9 months she had been hospitalized seven times for a total of 83 days. In the 9 months afterward she was admitted just once for 4 days. (Toufexis, 1996, p. 70)

Why would it take so long for authorities to intervene in a case like this? Parents with factitious disorder by proxy may be very adept at hiding what they are doing to their children, especially if they have medical backgrounds. Also, authorities must be extremely cautious about accusing a parent of causing harm to his or her children because of the great repercussions of falsely accusing parents, including the destruction of reputations, careers, and family relationships.

The somatoform disorders are grouped in this chapter with dissociative disorders because many theorists believe they have similar causes. Both sets of disorders may result from repression or motivated forgetting of painful memories or emotions. In somatoform disorders, repressed memories or emotions may re-emerge as or be represented by the physical symptoms the person experiences. Or more simply, the physical symptoms may be an acceptable way for an individual to express psychological distress.

There are four distinct types of somatoform disorders: conversion disorder, somatization and pain disorder, hypochondriasis, and body dysmorphic disorder (see *Concept Review:* Somatoform Disorders). Each of these, except body dysmorphic disorder, is characterized by the experience of one or more physical symptoms. Body dysmorphic disorder involves a preoccupation with an imagined defect in one's appearance that is so severe that it interferes with the person's functioning in life.

Conversion Disorder

The most dramatic type of somatoform disorder is **conversion disorder.** People with this disorder lose functioning in some part of their bodies. Some of the most common types of conversion symptoms are paralysis, blindness, mutism, seizures, loss of hearing, severe loss of coordination, and anesthesia in a limb. Conversion disorders typically involve one specific symptom, such as blindness or paralysis, but a person can have repeated episodes of conversion involving different parts of the body. Usually the symptom develops suddenly following an extreme psychological stressor. A common and fascinating feature of conversion disorders is *la belle indifference,* the beautiful indifference—people may be completely unconcerned about the loss of functioning they are experiencing (see *Concept Review:* Conversion Disorder).

Theories of Conversion Disorder

Conversion disorders were formerly referred to as *conversion hysterias,* after the Greek word *hystera,* for womb. Centuries ago, physicians believed that only women developed conversion symptoms and that these symptoms arose when a woman's desires for sexual gratification and children were not fulfilled, causing her womb to dislodge and wander (Veith, 1965). The theory was that the womb would wander into various parts of the body, such as the throat or the leg, causing related symptoms, such as a sensation of choking or paralysis. We know now that conversion symptoms have nothing to do with wandering wombs and that, although they are more common in women than in men, men as well as women can develop these symptoms (Boffeli & Guze, 1992).

Sigmund Freud became fascinated with conversion symptoms early in his career. One particularly

CONCEPT REVIEW

Somatoform Disorders

The somatoform disorders are characterized by physical symptoms or complaints that appear to have psychological causes.

Disorder	Key Features
Conversion disorder	Loss of functioning in some part of the body for psychological rather than physical reasons.
Somatization disorder	History of complaints about physical symptoms, affecting many different areas of the body, for which medical attention has been sought but that appear to have no physical cause.
Pain disorder	History of complaints about pain, for which medical attention has been sought but that appears to have no physical cause.
Hypchondriasis	Chronic worry that one has a physical disease in the absence of evidence that one does; frequently seek medical attention.
Body dysmorphic disorder	Excessive preoccupation with some part of the body the person believes is defective.

CONCEPT REVIEW

Conversion Disorder

Conversion disorder is an extreme form of somatoform disorder.

Symptoms	Loss of functioning in some part of the body due to psychological rather than physiological causes. They may show *la belle indifference*—indifference to the loss of functioning.
Etiology	Often occur after trauma or stress, perhaps because the individual cannot face memories or emotions associated with the trauma.
Treatment	Psychoanalytic therapy focuses on helping the individual expression of emotions or memories associated with the symptoms. Behavioral therapy uses systematic desensitization and other behavioral techniques to reduce anxiety around the initial trauma that caused the symptoms.

dramatic conversion symptom is **glove anesthesia,** in which people lose all feeling in one hand as if they were wearing a glove that wiped out physical sensation. This pattern of feeling loss cannot be physiologically caused, because the nerves do not provide feeling in a glove-like pattern. Freud found that these people tended to regain feeling in their hands when, usually under hypnosis, they recalled painful memories or emotions that had been blocked from consciousness. The study of patients with severe dissociative experiences contributed much to Freud's theory of the structure of the mind and the role of repression in serious psychopathology. Freud and his contemporaries viewed conversion symptoms as results of the transfer of the psychic energy attached to repressed emotions or memories into physical symptoms. The symptoms often symbolized the specific concerns or memories that were being repressed. In *Extraordinary People: Anna O.* (p. 390), we highlight the case of Bertha Pappenheim, also known as Anna O., who suffered conversion symptoms, and whose case greatly influenced the theories of Freud and his contemporaries.

Conversion symptoms were apparently quite common during the two world wars, when soldiers would become paralyzed or blind inexplicably and therefore unable to return to the front (Ironside & Batchelor, 1945). Their symptoms appeared to be real and not faked. Many of the soldiers seemed unconcerned about their paralysis or blindness, showing *la belle indifference*. Sometimes, the physical symptoms the soldiers experienced represented traumas they had witnessed and perhaps were trying to suppress. For example, a soldier who had stabbed a civilian in the throat might lose the ability to talk.

Children can have conversion symptoms as well. Most often, their symptoms mimic those of someone they are close to who has a real illness (Grattan-Smith et al., 1988; Spierings et al., 1990). For example, a child whose cherished grandfather has had a stroke and lost functioning on his right side may become unable to use his right arm.

Conversion disorder is rarely diagnosed in the general population. A review of the medical charts of 220,306 people in Iowa between 9 and 20 years of age found that only 11 people were diagnosed with conversion disorder (Tomasson et al., 1991). Conversion symptoms may be more common among sexual abuse survivors (Anderson, Yasenik, & Ross, 1993). Consider this case of a woman who was raped and later developed both posttraumatic stress disorder (see Chapter 7) and conversion mutism (from Rothbaum & Foa, 1991).

CASE STUDY

At the time she sought treatment, Jane was a 32-year-old divorced black woman living with her 15-year-old son and employed as a lower-level executive. When she was 24, two men entered her home after midnight, held a knife to her throat, and threatened to kill her if she made a sound or struggled. They raped her orally and vaginally in front of her son, who was 7 at the time, and then locked them in the basement before leaving. Several weeks after the rape, Jane's mother, to whom she was very close, died of cancer. Jane felt she had to be "the strong one" in the family and prided herself because she "never broke down."

At the age of 31, during an abusive relationship with a live-in boyfriend, Jane developed conversion mutism. In the midst of attempting to ask her boyfriend to leave her house, she was unable to produce any sound. After several months of treatment with a speech therapist, Jane became able to whisper quietly but did not regain her normal speech. The speech therapist referred Jane to a clinic for the treatment of rape-related PTSD.

The pretreatment interview confirmed that Jane suffered from chronic PTSD as a result of the rape. She presented with fears, panicky reactions, nightmares, flashbacks, and intrusive thoughts about the assault. She reported attempts to avoid thinking about the assault and situations that reminded her of it and feelings of detachment from others. She also complained of sleep problems, exaggerated startle, and hyperalertness. Jane was moderately depressed and quite anxious. During the intake interview, Jane indicated that she had never verbally expressed her feelings about the assault and believed that this constriction underlied her inability to speak.

EXTRAORDINARY PEOPLE

Anna O.

One of the most famous cases of conversion disorder was that of Anna O., a young Viennese woman whose real name was Bertha Pappenheim. She was born in Vienna on February 27, 1859 in a wealthy, orthodox Jewish family. Pappenheim became ill in 1880 at the age of 21, around the time of her father's serious illness and eventual death. Josef Breuer, a colleague of Freud's who treated Pappenheim, wrote about her:

Up to the onset of the disease, the patient showed no sign of nervousness, not even during pubescence. She had a keen, intuitive intellect, and a craving for psychic fodder, which she did not, however, receive after she left school. She was endowed with a sensitiveness for poetry and fantasy, which was, however, controlled by a very strong and critical mind. . . . Her will was energetic, impenetrable, and persevering, sometimes mounting to selfishness; it relinquished its aim only out of kindness and for the sake of others. . . . Her moods always showed a slight tendency to an excess of merriment or sadness, which made her more

Bertha Pappenheim was a patient of Breuer's and Freud's who had several different conversion symptoms.

or less temperamental. . . . With her puritanically-minded family, this girl of overflowing mental vitality led a most monotonous existence. . . .

Upon her father's illness, in rapid succession there seemingly developed a series of new and severe disturbances.

Left-sided occipital pain; convergent strabismus (diplopia), which was markedly aggravated through excitement. She complained that the wall was falling over (obliquus affection). Profound analyzable visual disturbances, paresis of the anterior muscles of the throat, to the extent that the head could finally be moved only if the patient pressed it backward between her raised shoulders and then moved her whole back. Contractures and anesthesia of the right upper extremity, and somewhat later of the right lower extremity. . . .

Breuer treated Pappenheim by asking her to talk about her symptoms under hypnosis, and after 18 months she seemed to be losing her symptoms. Pappenheim dubbed this the "talking cure." After Breuer told Pappenheim he thought she was well and he would not be seeing

People with conversion disorder tend to have high rates of depression, anxiety, alcohol abuse, and antisocial personality disorder (Bofelli & Guze, 1992; Tomasson, Kent, & Coryell, 1991). They may be depressed or anxious over the same traumas or concerns that led to the conversion disorder. The relationship between conversion disorder and antisocial personality disorder and alcohol abuse may arise because the avoidance of negative emotions leads to impulsive, antisocial behavior, to self-medicating through alcohol abuse, and to conversion symptoms.

Distinguishing Conversion Disorders from Physical Disorders

We have emphasized that for a conversion disorder to be diagnosed, it must be shown that there is no physiological cause for the individual's symptoms. Sometimes, a physiological cause of symptoms can be definitively ruled out, as in false pregnancy. Often, however, physiological tests cannot give definitive proof that a person's symptoms cannot have physical causes.

Continued

her again, later that evening he was called back to her house, where he found Pappenheim thrashing around in her bed going through imaginary childbirth. Pappenheim claimed that the baby was Breuer's. He calmed her down by hypnotizing her but soon fled the house and never saw her again. Pappenheim remained ill intermittently for 6 years but by age 30 she recovered. Breuer collaborated with Sigmund Freud in writing about Anna O. in *Studies of Hysteria* (1895) and their descriptions of the "talking cure" launched psychoanalysis as a form of psychotherapy.

Pappenheim did not credit psychoanalysis with her cure, however. She stated, "Psychoanalysis in the hands of the physician is what confession is in the hands of the Catholic priest. It depends on its user and its use, whether it becomes a beneficial tool or a two-edged sword" (Edinger, 1963, p. 12). Apparently, Pappenheim did not think much of Breuer's use of psychoanalysis in her case.

The remainder of Pappenheim's life after psychoanalysis, however, was not spent bashing Breuer or Freud, but serving the poor and afflicted of Vienna. Pappenheim became a social worker and a tireless advocate for the poor and for the Jewish minority in Europe. She was director of the Jewish Orphanage for Girls and founded other welfare organizations to help the poor, homeless, and outcast, and to lift prostitutes out of their hopeless lives. Pappenheim was a strong proponent of emancipation and education for women. She wrote plays on women's rights, and translated Mary Wollstonecraft's book *A Vindication of the Rights of Women* (1792).

Many theorists—psychoanalytic ones and feminist ones—have reinterpreted Breuer's and Freud's case history of Anna O., and many have analyzed Pappenheim's life after psychoanalysis. Was her fight for women's rights a fight against Breuer and Freud? Was her advocacy of the poor and outcasts—which was seen as unusual and inexplicable behavior for a wealthy Viennese socialite—a repudiation of her parents, who were strict and deprived her of opportunities to exercise her own capabilities as a youngster?

Bertha Pappenheim described her own motivations in a prayer she wrote, which was published after her death (Pappenheim, 1936):

> I am grateful that I can dam up
>
> As in a cool mill-pond
>
> Whatever power grows in my mind
>
> Unintentionally and unforced,
>
> Solely for my own pleasure.
>
>
> I thank also for the hour
>
> In which I found the words
>
> For what moves me, so that I could
>
> Move others by them.
>
>
> To feel strength is to live
>
> —to live is to wish to serve.
>
> Allow me to . . .

Over the years, a number of studies have suggested that many people diagnosed with conversion disorder were actually suffering from a physical disorder that diagnostic tests of the times could not identify. For example, one study found that 62.5 percent of people diagnosed with conversion symptoms later were found to have a medical disease, compared to only 5.3 percent of people not diagnosed with conversion symptoms. The most common medical problem found in the conversion group was head injury, which usually occurred about 6 months before the conversion symptoms began. Other common problems were stroke, encephalitis, and brain tumors (See also Fishbain & Goldberg, 1991; Watson & Buranen, 1979).

If diagnostic tests cannot establish a physical cause for puzzling symptoms, then clinicians will try to determine whether the conversion symptoms are consistent with the way the body works. For example, as we noted earlier, glove anesthesia violates what we know about the innervation of the hand, because the anesthesia usually begins abruptly at the wrist and extends throughout the hand. As Figure 11.1 (p. 392)

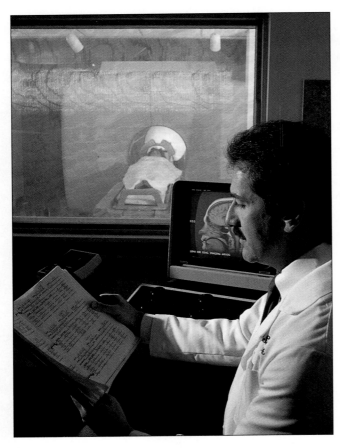

More recent and sophisticated diagnostic techniques may allow physicians to identify physical disorders in people previously diagnosed with a somatoform disorder.

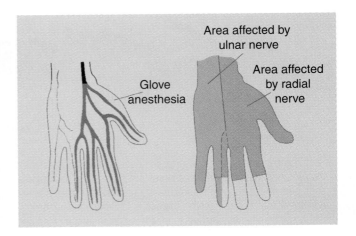

FIGURE 11.1 In the conversion symptom called "glove anesthesia," the entire hand from fingertips to wrist becomes numb. Actual physical damage to the ulnar nerve, in contrast, causes anesthesia in the ring finger and little finger and beyond the wrist partway up the arm; and damage to the radial nerve causes insensitivity only in parts of the ring, middle, and index fingers and the thumb and partway up the arm.

shows, however, the nerves in the hand are distributed in a way that makes this pattern of anesthesia highly unlikely. Similarly, a person with a conversion paralysis from the waist down may not show the deterioration of the muscles in the legs that a person with a physical paralysis typically shows over time. Still, distinguishing conversion disorder from a physical disorder that is simply difficult to diagnose can be tricky.

Treatment of Conversion Disorder

Psychoanalytic treatment for conversion disorder focuses on the expression of painful emotions and memories and insight into the relationship between these and the conversion symptoms (Gavin, 1985). Chronic conversion disorder is more difficult to treat. When symptoms are present for more than a month, the person's history often resembles somatization disorder (discussed next) and is treated as such.

Behavioral treatments focus on relieving the person's anxiety around the initial trauma that caused the conversion symptoms. For example, the treatment of Jane, the woman in the case study, involved both systematic desensitization and in vivo exposure therapy

(refer to Chapter 6). A hierarchy of situations that Jane avoided, mostly situations that reminded her of her rape, was constructed. For the in vivo exposure, Jane was aided in approaching the situations that made her feel anxious, and in progressing up her hierarchy to increasingly more feared situations, while practicing relaxation techniques. During the imagery sessions, Jane recounted the details of the assault first in general terms and later in great detail, including the details of the situation and the details of her physiological and cognitive reactions to the assault. At first, Jane was able to describe the assault in only a whisper, but she cried in full volume. After crying, Jane's speech became increasingly louder, with occasional words uttered in full volume. Eventually, she regained a full-volume voice. Following treatment, Jane's PTSD symptoms also decreased and diminished further over the following year.

People with conversion disorder are difficult to treat because they do not believe there is anything wrong with them psychologically (Krull & Schifferdecker, 1990). If they have *la belle indifference*, they are not even motivated to cooperate with psychological treatment in order to overcome their physical symptoms.

Somatization and Pain Disorder

A person with **somatization disorder** has a long history of complaints about physical symptoms, affecting many different areas of the body, for which medical attention has been sought but that appear to have no physical cause (see *Concept Review:* Somatization and Pain Disorders). The most common types of complaints

CONCEPT REVIEW

Somatization and Pain Disorders

Somatization and pain disorders appear to represent physiological manifestations of psychological concerns or distress.

Symptoms	Somatization disorder involves a long history of multiple physical complaints for which people have sought treatment but for which there is no apparent organic cause. Pain disorder involves only the experience of chronic, unexplainable pain.
Etiology	These disorders run in families, but it is not clear whether this is due to genetics or modeling. Psychodynamic theorists say that the physical symptoms are a more acceptable way to express painful memories and emotions. Cognitive theories say that people focus excessively on physical symptoms and catastrophize the symptoms.
Treatment	Psychoanalytic treatment involves helping people identify feelings and thoughts behind the symptoms and find more adaptive ways of coping. Cognitive treatment helps clients learn to interpret their physical symptoms appropriately and to avoid catastrophizing physical symptoms.

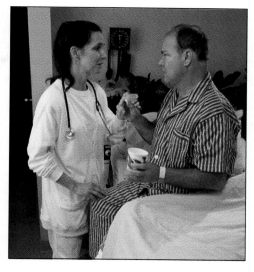

The sympathy and attention of medical professionals can reinforce people with somatoform disorders.

are complaints about chronic pain, including pains in the head, chest, abdomen, and back. People with somatization disorder may also report loss of functioning in some part of the body, as do people with conversion disorder. In somatization disorder, this loss of functioning is just one of a multitude of physical complaints; in conversion disorder, the loss of functioning may be the person's only complaint.

People who complain only of chronic pain may be given the diagnosis of **pain disorder.** Since most of what we know about somatization disorder also applies to pain disorder, these two disorders are discussed together in this section.

To receive a diagnosis of somatization disorder, a person has to complain of pain symptoms in at least four areas of the body, including two gastrointestinal symptoms (such as nausea and diarrhea), a sexual symptom (such as menstrual difficulties or painful intercourse), and an apparent neurological symptom (such as double vision or paralysis) (APA, 2000). A person with somatization disorder will often go from physician to physician, looking for the attention and

sympathy, and for that one test that will prove that they really are sick.

Obviously, it is extremely important that physicians not assume that an individual has a psychological problem just because they cannot identify the cause of the physical complaints. Somatization disorder should only be diagnosed when the person has a clear history of multiple physical complaints for which no organic causes can be found. These complaints are usually presented in vague, dramatic, or exaggerated ways, and the individual may have insisted on medical procedures, even surgeries, that clearly were not necessary. One study of 191 persons in a general medicine outpatient clinic found that about 40 percent who had physical symptoms for which no organic causes could be found met the diagnostic criteria for a somatization disorder, meaning they had long histories of vague and multiple physical complaints with no apparent organic causes (Van Hemert et al., 1993).

As with conversion disorder, people with somatization or pain disorder may be prone to periods of anxiety and depression that they cannot express or cope with adaptively, and they either somatize their distress, or mask the distress in alcohol abuse or antisocial behavior. One large study of people with somatization disorder found that 76 percent had lifetime histories of episodes of major depression (Rief, Hiller, & Margraf, 1998). In addition, people with the disorder frequently have histories of anxiety disorders or drug abuse.

Moderate degrees of somatization are apparently quite common. Very few people tend to meet the diagnostic criteria for somatization disorder. For example, one study found that 4.40 percent of a randomly selected sample of adults had a history of significant somatization, but only 0.03 percent met the criteria for somatization disorder (Escobar et al., 1987). Somatization is much more common in women than in men. Women have more periods of depression and anxiety than do men but are not always comfortable in expressing their distress directly and may instead experience it in physical symptoms.

There also appear to be cultural variations in the prevalence of somatization disorder. Studies in China and Puerto Rico and of different ethnic groups in the United States have found that persons from some Latin American countries and persons of Asian heritage appear more likely to have somatization disorder than do Caucasians (Canino, Rubio-Stipec, & Bravo, 1988; Escobar et al., 1987; Jun-mian, 1987; Shrout et al., 1992; Westermeyer, et al., 1989). Latin and Asian cultures may have higher rates of somatization disorder because of cultural norms of expressing distress in physical complaints rather than admitting to negative emotions.

In the United States, somatization disorder also appears more common in older adults than in middle-aged adults (Grau & Padgett, 1988). The cultural norms with which older adults were raised often prohibited admitting to depression or anxiety, and thus, older adults who are depressed or anxious may be more likely to express their negative emotions in somatic complaints, which are acceptable and expected complaints of old age. Young children also often express their distress in somatic complaints (Garber, Walker, & Zeman, 1991). They may not have the language to express difficult emotions but can say that they feel "bad" or that they have stomachaches or headaches. Ten to 30 percent of children and adolescents report having headaches or abdominal pain on a weekly basis (Fritz, Fritsch, & Hagino, 1997).

Somatization disorder tends to be a long-term problem. In a 2-year study of people with somatization disorder and people with similar physical complaints for which an organic cause could be found, Craig and colleagues (1993) found that the somatizers' symptoms lasted longer than the symptoms of those with medical illnesses. Moreover, changes in the somatizers' symptoms mirrored their emotional well-being: When they were anxious or depressed, they reported more physical complaints than when they were not anxious or depressed.

It can be extremely difficult to differentiate between somatization disorder and organic disorders for which we do not yet have definitive tests. For example, one disorder that is often confused with, or overlaps with, somatization disorder is chronic fatigue syndrome. Chronic fatigue syndrome involves a persistent, debilitating fatigue accompanied by symptoms resembling those of common viral infections (Manu, Lane, & Matthews, 1992). Chronic fatigue syndrome is a real medical syndrome, probably caused by infections and a poorly functioning immune system. It is difficult to diagnose, involves many of the symptoms identified by people diagnosed with somatization disorder. In one study of 100 adults complaining of chronic fatigue syndrome, 15 met the diagnostic criteria of somatization disorder, meaning they had long histories of vague physical complaints involving many parts of their bodies (Manu, Lane, & Matthews, 1989). However, 85 percent had no previous histories of somatic complaints.

Theories of Somatization and Pain Disorder

Family history studies of somatization and pain disorders find that the disorders run in families, primarily among female relatives (Guze, 1993). Anxiety and depression are also common in the female relatives of people with somatization disorder (Garber, Walker & Zeman, 1991). Similarly, 30 percent of patients with pain disorder have family histories of psychological problems, most often pain disorder in the female relatives and alcoholism in the male relatives (Chaturvedi, 1987). The male relatives of persons with somatization disorder also have higher than usual rates of alcoholism and antisocial personality disorder.

It is not clear that the transmission of somatization or pain disorder in families has to do with genetics. One small study of 12 twins with somatization disorder found that none of their cotwins also had somatization disorder, but 9 of the 12 cotwins had some other form of psychological disorder (Torgersen, 1986). The children of parents with somatization or pain disorders may model their parents' tendencies to somatize distress (Craig et al., 1993). Parents who are somatizers also are more likely to neglect their children, and the children may learn that the only way to receive care and attention is to be ill. In general, the children of parents who are somatizers have increased vulnerability to a wide range of psychological problems, to suicide attempts, and to frequent hospitalizations (Livingston, 1993).

A cognitive theory of somatization or pain disorder suggests that persons with these disorders tend to experience bodily sensations more intensely than other people, they pay more attention to physical symptoms than others, and they tend to catastrophize these symptoms (see Table 11.2; Barsky, 1992; Rief, Hiller, & Margraf, 1998). For example, such a person might have a slight case of indigestion but experience it as severe chest pain and interpret the pain as a sure sign of a heart attack. His interpretation of his experience may have a direct influence on his physiological processes, by increasing his heart rate or blood pressure, thereby maintaining and exacerbating his pain. Further, his cognitions will influence the way he presents symptoms to his physician and family. As a result, physicians may prescribe more potent medication

TABLE 11.2
Cognitions of People with Somatization Disorder

These are some statements that people who are somatizers are likely to endorse.

Catastrophizing Interpretations of Bodily Complaints:

A suddenly appearing joint pain can be a sign of a beginning paralysis.

My doctor or I must be capable of finding an explanation for all bodily complaints.

The most serious diseases develop unnoticed and then break out at some time or other.

Bodily complaints are always a sign of disease.

Attention to Autonomic Sensations:

I can sometimes hear my pulse or my heartbeat throbbing in my ear.

When I take a bath I often feel how my heart is beating.

I hate to be too hot or cold.

Bodily Weakness:

I'm not as healthy as most of my friends and acquaintances.

I have to avoid physical exertion in order to save my strength.

I'm physically rather weak and sensitive.

From W. Rief, W. Hiller, and J. Margraf, "Cognitive Aspects of Hypochondriasis and the Somatization Syndrome" in *Journal of Abnormal Psychology,* 107, pp. 587–595. Copyright © 1998 by the American Psychological Association. Reprinted by permission

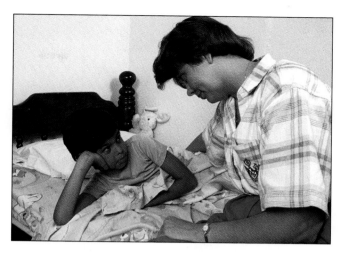

Young children often express psychological distress in somatic complaints.

disorder than either U.S.-born Mexican Americans or Whites. Fifty-two percent of the Central Americans who had fled to the United States to escape war or political unrest had posttraumatic stress disorder and somatization disorder (Cervantes, Salgado de Snyder, & Padilla, 1989). Similarly, a study of Hmong immigrants to the United States, who had fled Cambodia during the Khmer Rouge regime, found 17 percent to have posttraumatic stress disorders characterized by moderate to severe somatizing symptoms (Westermeyer et al., 1989).

Treatment of Somatization and Pain Disorder

Convincing people with somatization or pain disorder that they need psychological treatment is not easy. These are people who have held tightly to the belief that they are physically ill despite dozens of physicians telling them they are not, and hundreds of medical tests that have established no physical illness. If they do agree to psychological treatment, people with these disorders appear to respond well to intervention that teaches them to express negative feelings or memories and to understand the relationship between their emotions and their physical symptoms (Beutler et al., 1988). Psychodynamic therapies focus on providing this insight about the connections between emotions and physical symptoms by helping people recall events and memories that may have triggered the symptoms. Cognitive therapies for these disorders help people learn to interpret their physical symptoms appropriately and to avoid catastrophizing physical symptoms, much as in cognitive treatment of panic symptoms (see Chapter 6 and Turk & Ruby, 1992).

We noted the strong cross-cultural differences in somatization. Some clinicians use the belief systems and cultural traditions of the clients they are treating to motivate the clients to engage in therapy and to help

or order more diagnostic tests, and family members may express more sympathy, excuse the person from responsibilities, and otherwise encourage passive behavior (Turk & Ruby, 1992). Thus, the person's misinterpretation and catastrophizing of his symptoms are reinforced by the physician and family, increasing the likelihood that he will interpret future symptoms in similar ways.

As with conversion disorders, somatization disorder may often be part of a posttraumatic stress disorder experienced by a person who has undergone a severe stressor. People with somatization disorder frequently have histories of physical or sexual abuse (Pribor et al., 1993). Refugees and recent immigrants also have an increased risk of somatization disorder. For example, one study found that immigrants to the United States from Central America and Mexico had higher rates of posttraumatic stress disorder and somatization

Dial 123-SICK and Reach Out to Your Fellow Hypochondriacs.

them overcome their physical complaints. Here is an example of the use of cultural beliefs to treat a Hispanic woman with somatization disorder (adapted from Koss, 1990, p. 22).

CASE STUDY

E was a 45-year-old woman who consulted many doctors for "high fever, vomiting, diarrhea, inability to eat, and rapid weight loss." After numerous negative lab analyses, her doctor told her, "I can't go on with you; go to one of the *espiritistas* or a *curandera*" (traditional healers)." A cousin then took her to a Spiritist center "for medicine." She was given herbal remedies: some baths and a tea of *molinillo* to take in the morning before eating. But the treatment focused mainly on the appearance of the spirit of a close friend who had died a month earlier from cancer. The spirit was looking for help from E who had not gone to help during her friend's illness because of her own family problems. The main thrust of the healers' treatment plan was to help E understand how she had to deal with the feelings of distress related to the stress of a paralyzed husband and caring for two small daughters alone. The spirit's influence on E's body was an object lesson that was aimed at increasing her awareness of how her lifestyle was causing her to neglect the care of her own body and feelings much as she had neglected her dying friend.

The spiritual healer in this case recognized the cause of E's somatic complaints as stress, anger, and guilt and helped her link her physical symptoms with these emotions and find ways to cope more adaptively with the emotions. The context for this intervention,

rather than being cognitive therapy or some other type of psychotherapy used by the dominant non-Hispanic culture, was the cultural belief system concerning the role of spirits in producing physical symptoms.

Hypochondriasis

Somatization disorder and **hypochondriasis** are quite similar and indeed may be variations of the same disorder. The primary distinction in the DSM-IV between the two disorders is that people with somatization disorder actually experience physical symptoms and seek help for them, whereas hypochondriacs worry that they have a serious disease but do not always experience severe physical symptoms (see *Concept Review: Hypochondriasis*). Yet, when they do have any physical complaints, hypochondriacs are more likely to believe they should seek out medical attention immediately, whereas somatizers are more likely to wait and see how the bodily sensations develop (Rief, Hiller, & Margraf, 1998). Hypochondriacs may go through many medical procedures, and float from physician to physician, sure that they have a dread disease. Often their fears focus on a particular organ system. For example, a man may be totally convinced that he has heart disease, even though the most sophisticated medical diagnostic tests have shown no evidence of heart disease.

CONCEPT REVIEW	
Hypochondriasis	

Hypochondriacs worry about being ill but do not always experience physical symptoms.

Symptoms	Chronic worry that one has a serious medical disease despite evidence that one does not; frequent consultations with physicians over this worry.
Etiology	A family history of depression or anxiety is common. These people may suffer from chronic distress and cope with this distress by exaggerating physical symptoms.
Treatment	Same as somatization disorder: Psychoanalytic treatment involves helping people identify feelings and thoughts behind the symptoms and find more adaptive ways of coping. Cognitive treatment helps clients learn to interpret their physical symptoms appropriately and to avoid catastrophizing physical symptoms.

Hypochondriasis is not very common. A study of 1,456 patients in a general medical practice found that only 3 percent met the diagnostic criteria for hypochondriasis (Escobar et al., 1998). There were no gender or ethnicity differences in rates of hypochondriasis.

CASE STUDY

Carlos, a married man of 39, came to the clinic complaining, "I have trouble in my bowels and then it gets me in my head. My bowels just spasm on me, I get constipated, and then my head must get toxic. It seems to poison my system." The patient's complaints dated back 12 years to an attack of "acute indigestion" in which he seemed to bloat up and pains developed in his abdomen and spread in several directions. He traced some of these pathways with his finger as he spoke. Carlos spent a month in bed at this time and then, based on an interpretation of something the doctor said, rested for another 2 months before working again. Words of reassurance from his doctor failed to take effect. He felt "sick, worried, and scared," feeling that he really would never get well again.

For 3 or 4 years after this attack, he took enemas, three a day at first, reducing gradually to one a day. For 8 or 9 years he had taken laxatives and devoted constant attention to his diet. He described variations in residue with enough detail to indicate conscientious watching of his bowel movements. Four months before coming to the clinic he was discharged from his job as a clerk in a paper mill because of too much sick leave and an unwillingness to do anything he considered outside of his duties. Since that time he has lived with his wife's relatives. . . .

Carlos became very dependent upon the woman he married when he was 22 years old. He left most of the decisions to her and showed little interest in sexual relations. His wife was several years older than he and did not seem to mind his totally passive approach to life. His attack of "acute indigestion" followed her death, 5 years after marriage, by 3 months during which he felt lost and hopeless. In time, he moved to a rural area and remarried. His second wife proved less willing to assume major responsibilities for him than the first, and she made sexual demands upon him that he felt unable to meet. He became more and more preoccupied with his gastrointestinal welfare. In the complete absence of community facilities for psychological assistance where he lived, prognosis for recovery from chronic partially disabling hypochondria was deemed poor. (Adapted from Cameron & Rychlak, 1985)

Most studies of hypochondriasis have grouped people with this disorder with people with somatization disorder, in part because people will often qualify for the diagnosis of both disorders. Thus, most of what was said about the causes of somatization disorder also applies to the causes of hypochondriasis. In particular, people with hypochondriasis appear very prone to chronic depression and anxiety and have family histories of these disorders (Barsky, Wyshak, & Klerman, 1992; Escobar et al., 1998). Their fears about

their health often stem from a general distress and inability to cope with that distress in adaptive ways. As is the case with people with somatization disorder, people with hypochondriasis do not appreciate suggestions that their problems are caused by psychological factors and thus tend not to seek psychological treatment. When they do receive psychological treatment, it focuses on helping them understand the association between their symptoms and emotional distress and on helping them find more adaptive ways of coping with their distress.

Body Dysmorphic Disorder

The final disorder we consider in this chapter is **body dysmorphic disorder.** People with this disorder are excessively preoccupied with some part of their bodies that they believe is defective (see *Concept Review:* Body Dysmorphic Disorder). Although there do not appear to be gender differences in the prevalence of this disorder, men and women with body dysmorphic disorder tend to obsess about different parts of their body (Perugi et al., 1997; Phillips & Diaz, 1997). Women seem to be more concerned with their hips and weight, whereas men tend to be preoccupied with a small body build, their genitals, and their hair. People with this disorder will spend hours looking at their "deformed" body parts, perhaps in a mirror, and perform elaborate

---

CONCEPT REVIEW

Body Dysmorphic Disorder

Body dysmorphic disorder differs in several ways from the other somatoform disorders.

Symptoms	Obsessional preoccupation with some parts of their bodies and elaborate attempts to change these body parts.
Etiology	May be a form of obsessive-compulsive disorder. Psychodynamic theorists see it as the result of displaced anxiety.
Treatment	Psychodynamic therapy focuses on gaining insight as to repressed concerns leading to symptoms. Behavioral therapy focuses on exposing the client to feared situations concerning their body, extinguishing anxiety about their body parts, and preventing compulsive responses to those body parts. Serotonin reuptake inhibitors may also quell obsessions and compulsions about body parts.

rituals to try to improve the parts or hide them. For example, they may spend hours styling their hair to hide the defects in their ears or wear heavy makeup to hide their defects. People with this disorder also often seek out plastic surgery to change the offensive body parts (Phillips, 1992). Case studies of some people with this disorder indicate that their perceptions of deformation can be so severe and bizarre as to be considered out of touch with reality (Phillips, 1991). Even if they do not lose touch with reality, people with body dysmorphic disorder tend to have severe impairment in their functioning due to the disorder. For example, a study of 188 people with this disorder found that 98 percent avoided social activities because of their "deformity," 30 percent had become housebound, and about 20 percent had attempted suicide (Phillips & Diaz, 1997).

Body dysmorphic disorder tends to begin in teenage years and be chronic if untreated. The average age of onset of this disorder was 16 years of age, and on average, these people had four or more separate bodily preoccupations. Those who seek treatment wait an average of 6 years from the onset of their concerns before seeking treatment.

Most people worry somewhat about their physical appearance, but people with body dysmorphic disorder worry excessively and go to elaborate means to hide or change their "deformed" body parts.

CASE STUDY

Sydney was a popular 17-year-old who attended a suburban high school near Washington, D.C. During the spring of her senior year, Sydney became preoccupied with her appearance and began to constantly look for her own image in windows and mirrors. In particular, Sydney began to notice that her nose was abnormally shaped. Her friends all told her that she was crazy when she expressed her concern, so she stopped talking about it to them. She began to apply makeup in an attempt to offset what she believed to be the contemptible contour of her nose. She started wearing her hair loose and holding her head down much of the time so that her face was partially obscured and brushing her hair excessively to encourage it to fall forward around her face. Her distress grew, and she repeatedly begged her parents to let her have surgery to correct the shape of her nose, which by now she regarded as hideous. Her pleas turned to volatile arguments when her parents told her that her nose was fine and that they would not agree to surgery. Sydney started finding excuses not to go out with her friends and refused to date because she could not stand the thought of anyone looking at her up close. She stayed home in her room, staring for hours in the mirror. She refused to attend her senior prom or graduation ceremony.

After high school, Sydney got a job as a night security guard, so she could isolate herself as much as possible and not been seen by others. During the next 7 years, she had five surgeries to correct the shape of her nose. Each time, she became even more dissatisfied and obsessed with her appearance. Although everyone who knew Sydney thought she looked fine, she remained obsessed and tormented by her "defect," which now dominated her life.

Although clinicians in Europe have frequently written about body dysmorphic disorder, it has been relatively ignored in the United States (Phillips, Dwight, & McElroy, 1998). The diagnosis was only introduced in the DSM in the 1987 edition. Some researchers suggest that body dysmorphic disorder is not a distinct disorder that deserves its own diagnostic category in the DSM (Hollander et al., 1992). Body dissatisfaction is a feature of many other disorders, including depression, the anxiety disorders, and the eating disorders.

At the same time, people with body dysmorphic disorder also tend to have severe levels of depression or anxiety (Phillips & Diaz, 1997; Rosen & Ramirez, 1998). One anxiety disorder that is relatively common among people with body dysmorphic disorder is obsessive-compulsive disorder (Phillips & Diaz, 1997). Some theorists believe that body dysmorphic disorder may be a form of obsessive-compulsive disorder, in which the person obsesses about some part of her body and engages in compulsive behaviors to change that part of her body (Phillips, 1991).

Psychoanalytically oriented therapy for body dysmorphic disorder focuses on helping clients gain insight into the real concerns behind their obsession with a body part. Behavioral therapies focus on exposing the client to feared situations concerning their body, extinguishing anxiety about their body parts, and preventing compulsive responses to those body parts (Hollander et al., 1992). For example, a client may identify her ears as her deformed body part. The client could develop her hierarchy of things she would fear doing related to her ears, ranging from looking at herself in the mirror with her hair fully covering her ears to going out in public with her hair pulled back and her ears fully exposed. After the client learns relaxation techniques, she would begin to work through the hierarchy, engaging in the feared behaviors beginning with the least feared and using the relaxation techniques to quell anxiety. Eventually, the client would work up to the greatly feared situation of exposing her ears in public. At first, the therapist might contract with the client that she cannot engage in behaviors intended to hide the body part (such as bringing her hair over her ears) for at least 5 minutes after she goes out in public. The eventual goal in therapy would be for the client's concerns about the body part to diminish totally and not affect her behavior or functioning.

Finally, recent studies suggest that serotonin reuptake inhibitors can be effective in some case studies in reducing obsessional thought and compulsive behavior in persons with this disorder (Phillips, Dwight & McElroy, 1998). This fuels theories that body dysmorphic disorder is a form of obsessive-compulsive disorder, because serotonin reuptake inhibitors are effective in treating obsessive-compulsive disorder as well (see Chapter 7).

Summing Up

- Somatoform disorders are a group of disorders in which people experience significant physical symptoms for which there is no apparent organic cause.

- Conversion disorder involves loss of functioning in some part of the body, for no organic reason. Conversion symptoms often occur after trauma or stress, perhaps because the person cannot face memories or emotions associated with the trauma. Treatment for conversion disorder focuses on expression of emotions or memories associated with the symptoms.

- Somatization disorder involves a long history of multiple physical complaints for which people have sought treatment but for which there is no apparent organic cause. Pain disorder involves only the experience of chronic, unexplainable pain. These disorders appear to be common, particularly among women, young children, and the elderly, and among people of Asian or Hispanic heritage.

- Hypochondriasis is a condition in which people worry chronically about having a dread disease, despite evidence that they do not. This disorder appears rare.

- In both somatization and pain disorders, and hypochondriasis, individuals often have a history of anxiety and depression. These disorders

may represent acceptable ways of expressing emotional pain. Cognitive theories of the disorders say that they are due to excessive focus on physical symptoms and the tendency to catastrophize symptoms. Treatment for both disorders involves helping people identify feelings and thoughts behind the symptoms and find more adaptive ways of coping.

- People with body dysmorphic disorder have an obsessional preoccupation with some parts of their bodies and make elaborate attempts to change these body parts. Treatment for body dysmorphic disorder can include psychodynamic therapy to reveal underlying concerns, systematic desensitization therapy to reduce obsessions and compulsions about the body, and serotonin reuptake inhibitors.

BIO-PSYCHO-SOCIAL INTEGRATION

Philosophers and scientists have long debated what is referred to as the *mind-body problem*—Does the mind influence bodily processes? Do changes in the body affect a person's sense of "self"? What are the mechanisms by which the body and mind influence each other?

The dissociative and somatoform disorders are excellent evidence that the mind and body are complexly interwoven. In a person with dissociative identity disorder, different personalities may actually have different physiological characteristics, such as different heart rates or blood pressure, even though they reside in the same body. In conversion disorder, psychological stress causes the person to lose eyesight, hearing, or functioning in some other important physiological system. In somatization and pain disorder, a person under psychological stress experiences physiological symptoms, such as severe headaches.

An underlying theme to these disorders is that it is easier or more acceptable for some people to experience psychological distress through changes in their bodies than to express it more directly as sadness, fear, or anger. We all somatize our distress to some degree—we feel more aches and pains when we are upset about something than when we are happy. People who develop somatoform and perhaps dissociative disorders may somatize their distress to an extreme degree. Their tendency to differentiate between what is going on in their minds and what is going on in their bodies may be low, and they may favor an extreme "bodily" expression of what is going on in their minds.

Chapter Summary

- The dissociative disorders are a fascinating group of disorders in which the individual's identity, memories, or consciousness become separated or dissociated from one another. In dissociative identity disorder, the individual develops two or more separate and distinct personalities that alternate in their control over the individual's behavior. Each personality may be amnesic for the other, or some personalities may be aware of the others. The different personalities appear to serve specific functions, such as protecting the "host" personality against harm or inflicting punishment on the host.

- Persons with dissociative identity disorder often engage in self-destructive and mutilative behaviors. The vast majority of diagnosed cases of dissociative identity disorder are women, and recent cases tend to have histories of childhood sexual and/or physical abuse. The alternate personalities may have been formed during the traumatic experiences as a way of defending against these experiences, particularly among people who are highly hypnotizable. Treatment of dissociative identity disorder has typically involved helping the different personalities integrate into one functional personality.

- Fugue is a disorder in which the person suddenly moves away from home and assumes an entirely new identity, with complete amnesia for the previous identity. Fugue states usually occur in response to some stressor and can disappear suddenly, with the person returning to his or her previous identity. Little is known about the prevalence or causes of fugue states.

- Dissociative or psychogenic amnesia involves loss of memory due to psychological causes. It must be differentiated from organic amnesia, which is caused by brain injury. With organic amnesia, a person may have difficulty remembering new information, a difficulty known as *anterograde amnesia*, but this is rare in psychogenic amnesia. In addition, with organic amnesia, loss of memory for the past (*retrograde amnesia*) is usually complete, whereas with psychogenic amnesia, it is limited to personal information. Psychogenic amnesia typically occurs following traumatic events. It may be due to motivated forgetting of events, to poor storage of information during events due to hyperarousal, or to avoidance of the emotions experienced during events and to the associated memories of events.

- Depersonalization disorder involves frequent episodes in which the individual feels detached from his or her mental processes or body. Transient depersonalization experiences are common, especially under the influence of drugs or sleep deprivation. The causes of depersonalization disorder are unknown.

- The somatoform disorders are a group of disorders in which the individual experiences or fears physical symptoms for which no organic cause can be found. These disorders may result from the dissociation of painful emotions or memories and the re-emergence of these emotions or memories as symptoms, as cries for help, or from the secondary gain people receive for these symptoms.

- One of the most dramatic somatoform disorders is conversion disorder, in which the individual loses all functioning in some part of his or her body, such as the eyes or legs. Conversion symptoms often occur after trauma or stress. People with conversion disorder tend to have high rates of depression, anxiety, alcohol abuse, and antisocial personality disorder. Treatment for the disorder focuses on the expression of emotions or memories associated with the symptoms.

- Somatization disorder involves a long history of multiple physical complaints for which people have sought treatment but of which there is no apparent organic cause. Pain disorder involves only the experience of chronic, unexplainable pain. People with these disorders show high rates of anxiety and depression. The disorders are apparently common and are more common in women, in Asians and Hispanics, and among the elderly and children. Somatization and pain disorders run in families. The cognitive theory of these disorders is that affected people focus excessively on physical symptoms and catastrophize these symptoms. People with these disorders often have experienced recent traumas. Treatment involves understanding of the traumas and helping the person find adaptive ways of coping with distress.

- Hypochondriasis is a disorder in which the individual fears he or she has some disease, despite medical proof to the contrary. Hypochondriasis shares many of the features and causes of somatization disorder and is typically comorbid with somatization disorder.

- The final somatoform disorder is questionably categorized along with the other somatoform disorders. People with body dysmorphic disorder have an obsessional preoccupation with some parts of their bodies, and engage in elaborate behaviors to mask or get rid of these body parts. They are frequently depressed, anxious, and suicidal. This disorder may be a feature of an underlying depression or anxiety disorder or may be a form of obsessive-compulsive disorder. Treatment for the disorder includes psychodynamic therapy to uncover the emotions driving the obsession about the body, systematic desensitization to decrease obsessions and compulsive behaviors focused on the body part, and serotonin reuptake inhibitors to reduce obsessional thought.

Key Terms

dissociation 372

dissociative identity disorder (DID) 376

dissociative fugue 382

dissociative amnesia 384

organic amnesia 384

anterograde amnesia 384

psychogenic amnesia 384

retrograde amnesia 384

depersonalization disorder 386

somatoform disorders 386

psychosomatic disorders 386

malingering 386

factitious disorder 386

factitious disorder by proxy 387

conversion disorder 388

la belle indifference 388

glove anesthesia 389

somatization disorder 392

pain disorder 393

hypochondriasis 396

body dysmorphic disorder 397

Critical Thinking Questions

1. What do the experiments on the "hidden observer" suggest about the plausibility of attempts to influence people through subliminal perception?

2. What might be the relationship between the development of "child alters" by people with dissociative identity disorder and the use of "imaginary playmates" by children who do not go on to develop dissociative identity disorder?

3. In the chapters on anxiety and mood disorders, we discussed the fact that people in certain cultures may express severe anxiety and depression through somatic symptoms rather than through psychological symptoms. How would you differentiate between a somatization disorder and an anxiety or mood disorder manifested through physical complaints?

4. As a clinician, how would you approach someone with a conversion disorder who showed la belle indifference? How could you get him or her to be concerned about the disorder?

5. We mentioned that chronic fatigue syndrome is often misdiagnosed as somatization disorder. Can you think of other "modern disorders" that may be difficult to differentiate from somatization disorder?

Gayle Ray
The Armour

No man can climb out beyond the limitations of his own character.

—*John Morley, "Robespierre," Critical Miscellanies (1871–1908)*

CHAPTER 12

Personality Disorders

CHAPTER OVERVIEW

Defining and Diagnosing Personality Disorders

Personality disorders are long-standing patterns of thought, behavior, and emotions that are maladaptive for the individual or for people around him or her. The DSM-IV organizes personality disorders into three groups based on similarities in symptoms.

Taking Psychology Personally:
Seeing Oneself in the Personality Disorders

The Odd-Eccentric Personality Disorders

People with the odd-eccentric personality disorders—paranoid, schizoid, and schizotypal personality disorders—have odd or eccentric patterns of behavior and thought, including paranoia, extreme social withdrawal or inappropriate social interactions, and magical or illusory thinking. This group of disorders, particularly schizotypal personality disorder, may be linked to schizophrenia genetically and may represent mild variations of schizophrenia.

The Dramatic-Emotional Personality Disorders

The dramatic-emotional personality disorders include four disorders characterized by dramatic, erratic, and emotional behavior and interpersonal relationships: antisocial personality disorder, histrionic personality disorder, borderline personality disorder, and narcissistic personality disorder.

Extraordinary People:
Gary Gilmore

Pushing the Boundaries:
Innovative Therapy for Borderline Personality Disorder

The Anxious-Fearful Personality Disorders

People with anxious-fearful personality disorders—avoidant, dependent, and obsessive-compulsive personality disorders—become extremely concerned about being criticized or abandoned by others and thus have dysfunctional relationships with others.

Alternative Conceptualizations of Personality Disorders

Several alternative conceptualizations of personality disorders have been suggested, based on theories of normal personality. One alternative views personality disorders as extreme versions of five basic personality traits. Another alternative views personality disorders as a cross between two dimensions: dominance versus submission, and nurturance versus cold-heartedness.

Bio-Psycho-Social Integration
Chapter Summary
Key Terms
Critical Thinking Questions

CASE STUDY

Jimmy has been in trouble all his life. As a kid, he skipped school often, and when he was there, he was prone to starting fights with other kids or getting into arguments with teachers. He was suspended several times for stealing. He was finally expelled at the age of 14 for threatening a teacher, and he essentially never went back to school.

Jimmy is now 29 and has been in and out of jail for the last 15 years. Mostly his crimes have involved small-time burglaries or shoplifting, possession of illegal drugs, or driving while intoxicated. He has never kept a job for more than 6 months at a time. He always gets into fights with his bosses or coworkers, whom he usually considers to be stupid. Then he quits or is fired. When his family members ask Jimmy why he gets into so much trouble, he just shrugs and either blames his predicament on someone else or says he cannot control his temper.

Jimmy actually talks to his family members only rarely. He has never gotten along with anyone but his mother and has been physically violent toward several family members. Jimmy's romantic relationships have been few and have largely consisted of meeting a woman, having frequent and somewhat violent sex with her for a few weeks, and then leaving her without a good-bye.

Does Jimmy have a psychological disorder? Some people would say no, that he is just a "rotten kid" who grew into a "rotten adult." Others would say that Jimmy clearly has been troubled most of his life and that his behaviors fit the concept of a personality disorder quite well.

Personality is all the ways we have of acting, thinking, believing, and feeling that make each of us unique and different from every other person. A **personality trait** is a complex pattern of behavior, thought, and feeling that is stable across time and across many situations.

DEFINING AND DIAGNOSING PERSONALITY DISORDERS

A **personality disorder** is a long-standing pattern of behavior, thought, and feeling that is highly maladaptive for the individual or for people around him or her. By definition, a personality disorder must be present continuously from adolescence or early adulthood into adulthood. The personality disorders are highly controversial in modern clinical psychology because of problems theorists see in the current conceptualization of these disorders and their assessment.

The DSM-IV Conceptualization

The DSM-IV calls special attention to personality disorders and treats them as different from the major acute disorders, such as major depression and schizophrenia, by placing the personality disorders on Axis II of the diagnostic system, instead of on Axis I with the acute disorders (see Chapter 4). People with a personality disorder often experience one of the acute disorders, such as major depression or substance abuse, at some time in their lives. Indeed, as we discuss later in this chapter, these acute disorders are often what bring them to the attention of clinicians. People with personality disorders tend not to seek therapy until they experience a bout of major depression or their substance abuse lands them in jail or the hospital because they often do not see the behaviors that comprise their personality disorder as maladaptive. In addition, they often have serious problems relating to other people, and these relationship problems may bring them into therapy.

The DSM-IV groups personality disorders into three clusters (see Table 12.1). *Cluster A* includes three disorders characterized by *odd or eccentric behaviors and thinking*: paranoid personality disorder, schizoid personality disorder, and schizotypal personality disorder. Each of these disorders has some of the features of schizophrenia, but persons with these personality disorders are not psychotic. Their behaviors are simply odd and often inappropriate. For example, they may be chronically suspicious of others, or speak in odd ways that are difficult to understand. *Cluster B* includes four disorders characterized by *dramatic, erratic, and emotional behavior and interpersonal relationships*: antisocial personality disorder, histrionic personality disorder, borderline personality disorder, and narcissistic personality disorder. Persons with these disorders tend to be manipulative, volatile, and uncaring in social relationships and prone to impulsive behaviors. They may behave in wild and exaggerated ways, or even engage in suicidal attempts, in an attempt to gain attention. *Cluster C* includes three disorders characterized by *anxious and fearful emotions and chronic self-doubt*: dependent personality disorder, avoidant personality disorder, and obsessive-compulsive personality disorder. People with these disorders have little self-confidence and difficult relationships with others.

Some of the problems we've just described may sound terribly familiar. Indeed, the personality disorders are some of the easiest to see yourself and your family members in. The criteria for diagnosing personality disorders are more vague than the criteria for many of the other, more acute disorders and thus leave more room for misapplication (Widiger & Costa, 1994). For example, one of the symptoms of dependent

TABLE 12.1
DSM-IV
The DSM-IV Personality Disorders

The DSM-IV groups personality disorders into three clusters.

Cluster A: Odd-Eccentric Personality Disorders

People with these disorders have symptoms similar to those of people with schizophrenia, including inappropriate or flat affect, odd thought and speech patterns, paranoia. People with these disorders maintain their grasp on reality, however.

Cluster B: Dramatic-Emotional Personality Disorders

People with these disorders tend to be manipulative, volatile, and uncaring in social relationships. They are prone to impulsive, sometimes violent behaviors that show little regard for their own safety or the safety or needs of others.

Cluster C: Anxious-Fearful Personality Disorders

People with these disorders are extremely concerned about being criticized or abandoned by others and thus have dysfunctional relationships with others.

Reprinted with permission from the *Diagnostic and Statistical Manual of Mental Disorders*, Fourth Edition. Copyright © 2000 American Psychiatric Association.

personality disorder is "has difficulty expressing disagreement with others because of fear of loss of support or approval." Most of us can probably see signs of this tendency in ourselves or in someone close to us. In *Taking Psychology Personally: Seeing Oneself in the Personality Disorders* (p. 406), we discuss the problems with diagnosing oneself with the personality disorders.

Problems with the DSM Categories

Many theorists have raised objections to the DSM-IV conceptualization and organization of the personality disorders. First, the DSM treats these disorders as categories. That is, each disorder is described as if it represents something qualitatively different from a "normal" personality. Yet there is substantial evidence that several of the disorders recognized by the DSM represent the extreme versions of "normal" personality traits (Livesley et al., 1994). Second, there is a great deal of overlap in the diagnostic criteria for the different personality disorders in the DSM-IV, and the majority of people who are diagnosed with one disorder tend to meet the diagnostic criteria for at least one more personality disorder (Morey, 1988). This suggests that there actually may be smaller numbers of personality disorders that adequately account for the variation in personality disorder symptoms. Third, diagnosing a personality disorder often requires information that is hard for a clinician to obtain, such as accurate information about how an individual treats other people, about how an individual behaves in a wide variety of

situations, or about how stable an individual's behaviors have been since childhood or adolescence.

These problems make it difficult for clinicians to be confident of diagnoses of personality disorders. Indeed, the diagnostic reliability of the personality disorders is extremely low (Livesley et al., 1994). They also make it difficult to do research on personality disorders and there is much less research on the epidemiology, etiology, and treatment of the personality disorders than there is on most of the other disorders described in this book.

Gender Biases in Construction and Application

We will see throughout this chapter that there are differences in the frequency with which men and women are diagnosed with certain personality disorders. One of the greatest controversies in the literature on personality disorders concerns claims that these apparent gender differences in the prevalence of certain personality disorders actually result from gender biases either in the construction of these disorders in the DSM-IV or in clinicians' applications of the diagnostic criteria (Hartung & Widiger, 1998; Widiger, 1998; Widiger & Spitzer, 1991).

First, some theorists have argued that the diagnoses of histrionic, dependent, and borderline personality disorders, which are characterized by flamboyant behavior, emotionality, and dependence on others, are simply extreme versions of negative stereotypes of women's personalities (Kaplan, 1983; Walker, 1994).

TAKING PSYCHOLOGY PERSONALLY

Seeing Oneself in the Personality Disorders

In Chapter 1, we discussed the tendency for students reading an Abnormal Psychology textbook to see signs of many mental disorders in themselves or in the people in their lives. Students may be especially prone to unjustifiably diagnose personality disorders in themselves or in others. Indeed, people are considerably more likely to diagnose themselves on self-report questionnaires as having a personality disorder than are clinicians to diagnose them in the context of psychiatric interviews (Weissman, 1993b). There are at least two possible reasons for this.

Second, people are prone to attribute behaviors to personality traits and to ignore the influence of situations on those behaviors (see Ross & Nisbett, 1991). This tendency is often referred to as the *fundamental attribution error*. A classic study demonstrating how strongly people discount situational influences over dispositional influences was conducted by Jones and Harris (1967). They asked subjects to read essays presumably written by other subjects. The subjects were told that the persons writing the essays were assigned to present a particular viewpoint on the topic of the essay. For example, they were told that a political science student had been assigned to write an essay defending communism in Cuba or that a debate student had been assigned to attack the proposition that marijuana should be legalized. Despite the fact that the subjects were told that the essay writers were assigned to take a particular viewpoint rather than chose a particular viewpoint, the subjects tended to believe that the essay writers actually held the viewpoint they presented in their essays.

If you think you see signs of one or more personality disorders in yourself or someone close to you, stop and ask yourself the following questions:

1. *What are the situational influences that might be driving my behavior or my friend's or relative's behavior?* For example, let us say that you are concerned that your brother has developed an obsessive-compulsive personality disorder since he entered medical school: He is preoccupied with schedules and always has lists of things to do; he has become a workaholic; he has become a perfectionist to the point of not being able to get things done; and he has become even more moralistic than he was in high school. It is true that certain situations can exaggerate the already dysfunctional behaviors of people with obsessive-compulsive personality disorder. However, consider the possibility that your brother's behaviors, particularly the ones that he has developed since entering medical school, are largely driven by the demands of medical school rather than by some enduring personality traits. Medical school is a 24-hour-per-day job, and many students find it necessary to become hyperefficient workaholics in order to get all their work done. Your brother's preoccupation with lists and schedules and his working 20 hours per day are probably behaviors that he shares with many of his medical school classmates, behaviors that are largely the result of the demands of the situation. In addition,

This may lead clinicians to be too quick to see these characteristics in women clients and to apply these diagnoses. It has also been argued that the diagnostic criteria for antisocial, paranoid, and obsessive-compulsive personality disorders, which are characterized by violent, hostile, and controlling behaviors, represent extremes of negative stereotypes of men, and thus clinicians are biased to overapply these diagnoses to men but not to women (Sprock, Blashfield, & Smith, 1990).

Another way that the DSM-IV constructions of personality disorders may be gender biased is in not recognizing that the expressions of symptoms of a disorder may vary between women and men. For example, the diagnostic criteria for antisocial personality disorder emphasize overt signs of callous and cruel antisocial behavior, including committing crimes against property and people. Women with antisocial personality disorder may be less likely than men with

Continued

many medical schools weed out a significant percentage of each new class with grueling examinations. This kind of pressure can cause many people to try to be perfectionists but to become so anxious about the possibility of failing that they cannot do their work.

When you find yourself wondering if you or someone you care about has developed a personality disorder, stop to consider the aspects of the situation that might really be responsible for the behaviors you observe.

2. *Am I selectively remembering behaviors that are signs of a personality disorder and selectively forgetting behaviors that contradict the diagnosis of a personality disorder?* One of the strongest reasons people overestimate the influence of personality traits on the behaviors of themselves and others is that they selectively pay attention to and remember behaviors that are consistent with personality traits and ignore or forget behaviors that are inconsistent with the traits. For example, if you fear that you have a dependent personality disorder, you will probably find it quite easy to remember times in the past when you have had trouble making decisions without much advice from others or have felt uncomfortable and helpless when alone or have been passive in voicing your opinions or needs to others. You will probably forget, however, the many more times when you made decisions with no help from others, actually enjoyed being alone, or spoke up to express your opinions or needs. It can be helpful to try to write down all the times in the recent or distant past when you behaved in ways that contradicted some troubling personality trait you think

you have. Or you might want to ask a trusted friend to help you sort out whether your behaviors are always consistent with some negative personality disposition.

3. *Are the behaviors I am observing part of a long-time pattern of behavior or do they only occur occasionally?* Most of us act in dysfunctional or plainly stupid ways occasionally. Sometimes these actions are obviously driven by the situations in which we find ourselves, but sometimes we act in stupid ways even when there is no apparent situational excuse for our actions. A personality disorder is a pattern of behavior that has existed most of a person's life and that the person demonstrates across a range of situations. Occasional lapses into dysfunctional behavior do not constitute a personality disorder.

4. *Are the behaviors I am observing significantly impairing or causing distress in my life or the lives of other people?* In order to qualify as a personality disorder, a set of behaviors has to cause significant distress or impairment in a person's life. We all have our quirks, our tendencies to act in ways we wish we would not. It can be helpful to examine these behaviors and make attempts to change them if they are not in line with our values or if they get us into occasional trouble. However, most quirks are relatively benign.

As always, if you are quite concerned about whether you or someone you care about has a significant psychological problem, it can be helpful to talk it out with a professional mental-health specialist who is trained to differentiate between psychological disorders and variations in people's behaviors that are not dangerous or unhealthy.

the disorder to engage in such overt antisocial behaviors, because of greater social sanctions against women for doing so. Instead, women with antisocial personality disorder may find more subtle or covert ways of being antisocial, such as acting cruelly toward their children or covertly sabotaging people at work (Rutherford et al., 1995, 1996). As we shall see when we discuss childhood disorders in Chapter 13, this same argument has been made about possible gender differ-

ences in the expression of the childhood form of antisocial personality disorder: conduct disorder.

Similarly, some theorists have argued that the DSM-IV ignores or downplays possible masculine ways of expressing dependent, histrionic, and borderline personality disorders, and this bias contributes to an underdiagnosis of these disorders in men (see Widiger et al., 1995). For example, one of the criteria for histrionic personality disorder is "consistently uses

The ways people exhibit histrionic behavior may depend on gender.

physical appearance to draw attention to the self" (APA, 2000). Although the DSM-IV notes that men may express this characteristic by acting "macho" and bragging about their athletic skills, the wording of the criterion brings to mind everyday behaviors more common among women, such as wearing makeup.

Even if the DSM-IV criteria for personality disorders are not biased in their construction, they may be biased in their application. Clinicians may be too quick to see histrionic, dependent, and borderline personality disorders in women, and perhaps antisocial personality disorder in men. Several studies have shown that, when presented with the description of a person who exhibits many of the symptoms of one of these disorders, say a histrionic personality disorder, clinicians are more likely to give the person the diagnosis if the person is described as a female than if the person is described as a male (see review by Widiger, 1998). It is important to note that these studies did not suggest that the DSM-IV criteria are themselves sex-biased— only that clinicians in seemed to be misapplying the DSM-IV according to gender stereotypes.

In response to these concerns about the gender-biased application of the DSM-IV criteria for personality disorders, Widiger (1998) argues that structured interviews should be used rather than unstructured interviews in assessing personality disorders, to increase the chances that the DSM-IV criteria will be applied systematically and fairly to men and women. Studies

that have used structured interviews tend to show less gender bias in clinicians' applications of the DSM-IV personality disorder criteria than studies that have used unstructured interviews. Importantly, the structured interviews still yield greater numbers of women than men being diagnosed with histrionic, dependent, and borderline personality disorder and more men than women being diagnosed with antisocial personality disorder (e.g., Kessler et al., 1994). This suggests that it is not only clinicians' bias in applying the DSM-IV criteria that leads to gender differences in the apparent prevalence of the disorder.

Other theorists have argued that the DSM-IV criteria should be balanced to include equal numbers of symptoms and diagnoses that are pathological variants of masculine and feminine personality traits (Frances, First, & Pincus, 1995; Kaplan, 1983; Walker, 1994). Indeed, the authors of the DSM-IV did attempt to include more masculine variations of symptoms thought to be more common in women (e.g., masculine forms of dependency) and more feminine versions of stereotypical masculine symptoms (e.g., feminine forms of antisocial behavior). Some theorists argue the DSM-IV did not go far enough, and the next edition of the DSM-IV should strive for even greater balance in pathologizing men and women. However, others argue that just because we could construct a set of diagnostic criteria that yield equal numbers of men and women with each personality disorder, this does

People with paranoid personality disorder are suspicious of everyone and everything.

not mean that these criteria reflect the true structure and distribution of personality disorders in people.

☉ THE ODD-ECCENTRIC PERSONALITY DISORDERS

People with the **odd-eccentric personality disorders** (see *Concept Review*: The Odd-Eccentric Personality Disorders) behave in ways that are similar to people with schizophrenia or paranoid psychotic disorder, but they retain their grasp on reality to a greater degree than do people who are psychotic. That is, they may be paranoid, speak in odd and eccentric ways that make them difficult to understand, have difficulty relating to other people, and may have unusual beliefs or perceptual experiences that fall short of delusions and hallucinations. Many researchers consider this group of personality disorders to be part of the "schizophrenia spectrum." That is, these disorders may be precursors to schizophrenia in some people or milder versions of schizophrenia. As we shall see when we discuss the genetic backgrounds of people with odd-eccentric personality disorders, these disorders often occur in people who have first-degree relatives who have schizophrenia.

Paranoid Personality Disorder

The defining feature of **paranoid personality disorder** is a pervasive and unwarranted mistrust of others. People with this disorder deeply believe that other people are chronically trying to deceive them or to exploit them and are preoccupied with concerns about the loyalty and trustworthiness of others. They are hypervigilant for confirming evidence of their suspicions. They are often penetrating observers of situations, noting details that most other people will miss. For example, they will notice a slight grimace on the face of their boss or an apparently trivial slip of the tongue by their spouse, when these would have gone unnoticed by everyone else. Moreover, paranoid people consider these events highly meaningful and spend a great deal of time trying to decipher these "clues" about other people's true intentions. They are also sensitive to criticism or potential criticism.

Paranoid people misinterpret or overinterpret situations in line with their suspicions. For example, a husband might interpret his wife's cheerfulness one evening as evidence that she is having an affair with a man at work. They are resistant to rational arguments against their suspicions and may take the fact that another person is arguing with them as evidence that this person is part of the conspiracy against them. Some paranoid people become withdrawn from others in an attempt to protect themselves, but others are aggressive and arrogant, sure that their way of looking at the world is right and superior and that the best defense against the conspiring of others is a good offense. Felix, in the following case study, has a paranoid personality disorder:

CASE STUDY

Felix is a 59-year-old construction worker who worries that his coworkers might hurt him. Last week, while he was using a table saw, Felix's hand slipped and his fingers came very close to being cut badly. Felix wonders if someone sabotaged the saw so that somehow the piece of wood he was working with slipped and drew his hand into the saw blade. Since this incident, Felix has observed his coworkers looking at him and whispering to each other. He mentioned his suspicion that the saw had been tampered with to his boss, but the boss told him that was a crazy idea and that Felix obviously had just been careless.

Felix does not have any close friends. Even his brothers and sisters avoid him because he frequently misinterprets things they say as criticisms of him. Felix was married for a few years, but his wife left him when he began to demand that she not see any of her friends or go out without him, because he suspected she was having affairs with other men. Felix lives in a middle-class neighborhood in a small town that has very little crime. Still, he owns three handguns and a shotgun, which are always loaded, in expectation of someone breaking into his house.

Between 0.5 and 4 percent of people in the general population can be diagnosed with paranoid personality disorder (Bernstein, Useda, & Siever, 1995). Among people given treatment for the disorder, males outnumber females three to one (Fabrega, Ulrich, Pilkonis, & Mezzich, 1991). People with paranoid personality disorder appear to be at increased risk for a number of acute psychological problems, including major depression, anxiety disorders, substance abuse, and psychotic episodes (Bernstein, Useda, & Siever, 1995; Fabrega et al., 1991).

Retrospective studies of people with paranoid personality disorder suggest that their prognosis is generally poor, with their symptoms intensifying under stress (Quality Assurance Project, 1990). Not surprisingly, their interpersonal relationships, including intimate relationships, tend to be unstable.

Theories of Paranoid Personality Disorder

Some family history studies suggest that paranoid personality disorder is somewhat more common in the families of people with schizophrenia than in the families of healthy control subjects, suggesting that paranoid personality disorder may be part of the schizophrenic spectrum of disorders (Baron et al., 1985; Kendler, Neale, Kessler, Heath, & Eaves, 1993; Nigg & Goldsmith, 1994). Twin and adoption studies have not been done to tease apart genetic influences and environmental influences on the development of this disorder, however.

Psychoanalytic theorists argue that paranoid personality disorder is the result of a person's need to deny his or her true feelings about others and to project those feelings onto others (Freud, 1911/1958; Shapiro, 1965). For some paranoid persons, their hostility toward others may come from an exaggerated sense of self-worth, whereas for others, it may come from a poor self-concept and the expectation that others will be critical and blame them for any problems (Millon et al., 2000). These attitudes can develop in children whose parents are harsh, critical, and intolerant of any weakness but who also emphasize to their children that they are "special" and "different" from others (Millon et al., 2000; Turkat, 1985). Such parental messages may lead the child to become hypersensitive to evaluations by others and to believe that the world is a hostile place and that he or she is persecuted for being different.

Cognitive theorists see paranoid personality disorder as the result of underlying belief that people are malevolent and deceptive, combined with a lack of self-confidence about being able to defend against others (Beck & Freeman, 1990; Colby, 1981). Thus, the paranoid person must always be vigilant for signs of others' deceit or criticism and must be quick to act against others. Neither the psychoanalytic nor the cognitive theories of the development of paranoid personality disorders have been tested empirically.

Treatment for Paranoid Personality Disorder

People with paranoid personality disorders usually only come into contact with clinicians when they are in crisis. They may seek treatment for severe symptoms of depression or anxiety but often will not feel a need for treatment of their paranoia. In addition, attempts by therapists to challenge their paranoid thinking are likely to be misinterpreted in line with their paranoid belief systems. Obviously, then, it can be quite difficult to treat paranoid personality disorder (Millon et al., 2000).

In order to gain the trust of a person with a paranoid personality disorder, the therapist must be calm, respectful, and extremely straightforward (Siever & Kendler, 1985). The therapist will behave in a highly professional manner at all times, not attempting to engender a warm, personal relationship with the client that might be misinterpreted. The therapist cannot directly confront the client's paranoid thinking but must rely on more indirect means of raising questions in the client's mind about his or her typical way of interpreting situations. Although many therapists do not expect paranoid clients to achieve full insight into their problems, they hope that by developing at least some degree of trust in the therapist, the client can learn to trust others a bit more, and thereby develop somewhat improved interpersonal relationships.

Cognitive therapy with paranoid individuals focuses on increasing their sense of self-efficacy for dealing with difficult situations, thus decreasing their fear and hostility toward others. As an example, consider this interchange between a cognitive therapist and a woman named Ann, who believed that her coworkers were intentionally trying to annoy her and to turn her supervisor against her (Beck & Freeman, 1990, pp. 111–112):

Voices

Therapist: You're reacting as though this is a very dangerous situation. What are the risks you see?

Ann: They'll keep dropping things and making noise to annoy me.

Therapist: Are you sure nothing worse is at risk?

Ann: Yeah.

Therapist: So you don't think there's much chance of them attacking you or anything?

Ann: Nah, they wouldn't do that.

Therapist: If they do keep dropping things and making noises, how bad will that be?

Ann: Like I told you, it's real aggravating. It really bugs me.

Therapist: So it would continue pretty much as it's been going for years now.

Ann: Yeah. It bugs me, but I can take it.

Therapist: And you know that if it keeps happening, at the very least you can keep handling it the way you have been—holding the aggravation in, then taking it out on your husband when you get home. Suppose we could come up with some ways to handle the aggravation even better or to have them get to you less. Is that something you'd be interested in?

Ann: Yeah, that sounds good.

Therapist: Another risk you mentioned earlier is that they might talk to your supervisor and turn her against you. As you see it, how long have they been trying to do this?

Ann: Ever since I've been there.

Therapist: How much luck have they had so far in doing that?

Ann: Not much.

Therapist: Do you see any indications that they're going to have any more success now than they have so far?

Ann: No, I don't guess so.

Therapist: So your gut reaction is as though the situation at work is really dangerous. But when you stop and think it through, you conclude that the worst they're going to do is to be really aggravating, and that even if we don't come up with anything new, you can handle it well enough to get by. Does that sound right?

Ann: [Smiling] Yeah, I guess so.

Therapist: And if we can come up with some ways to handle the stress better or handle them better, there will be even less they can do to you.

In this interchange, the therapist did not directly challenge Ann's beliefs about her coworkers' intentions but did try to reduce the sense of danger Ann felt about her workplace by helping her redefine the situation as aggravating rather than threatening. The therapist also enlisted Ann in an effort to develop new coping skills that might further reduce her aggravation.

Schizoid Personality Disorder

People with **schizoid personality disorder** lack any desire to form interpersonal relationships and are emotionally cold in interactions with others. Others describe them as aloof, reclusive, and detached and they show little emotion in interpersonal interactions. They view relationships with others as unrewarding, messy, and intrusive. Other people experience them as dull, uninteresting, and humorless. The man described next shows several of these symptoms.

CASE STUDY

The patient is a 50-year-old retired police officer who is seeking treatment a few weeks after his dog was run over and died. Since that time he has felt sad, tired, and has had trouble sleeping and concentrating.

The patient lives alone and has for many years had virtually no conversational contacts with other human beings beyond a "Hello" or "How are you?" He prefers to be by himself, finds talk a waste of time, and feels awkward when other people try to initiate a relationship. He occasionally spends some time in a bar but always off by himself and not really following the general conversation. He reads newspapers avidly and is well informed in many areas but takes no particular interest in the people around him. He is employed as a security guard but is known by his fellow workers as a "cold fish" and a "loner." They no longer even notice or tease him, especially since he never seems to notice or care about their teasing anyway.

The patient floats through life without relationships. His only companion is his dog, whom he dearly loves. At Christmas he buys the dog elaborate gifts and gives himself a wrapped bottle of scotch as if it were a gift from the dog. He believes that dogs are more sensitive and loving than people, and he can express toward them a tenderness and emotion not possible in his relationships with people. The loss of his pets are the only events in his life that have caused him sadness. He experienced the death of his parents without emotion and feels no regret at being completely out of contact with the rest of his family. He considers himself different from other people and regards emotionality in others with bewilderment. (Adapted from Spitzer et al., 1981, p. 209)

This man would be diagnosed with schizoid personality disorder because of his long-standing avoidance of relationships with other people and his lack of emotions or emotional understanding. As is often the case with people with personality disorders, he only seeks the help of a clinician when a crisis occurs.

Schizoid personality disorder is quite rare, with about 0.4 to 1.7 percent of adults manifesting the disorder at some time in their lives (Weissman, 1993b). Among schizoid persons seeking clinical treatment, males outnumber females about three to one (Fabrega et al., 1991). Schizoid persons can function in society, particularly in occupations that do not require interpersonal interactions.

Theories of Schizoid Personality Disorder

There is a slightly increased rate of schizoid personality disorder in the relatives of persons with schizophrenia, but the link between the two disorders is not clear (Kendler et al., 1993; Nigg & Goldsmith, 1994). Twin studies of personality traits associated with schizoid personality disorder, such as low sociability and low warmth, strongly suggest that these personality traits may be partially inherited (Tellegen, Lykken, Bouchard, & Wilcox, 1988). This is only indirect evidence for the heritability of schizoid personality disorder, however.

Psychoanalytic theorists suggest that schizoid personality disorder develops out of severely disturbed mother-child relationships, in which the child never learns to give or receive love (Bleuler, 1924; Klein, 1952). These children view relationships and emotions as dangerous and thus remain aloof both from other people and from their own feelings.

Cognitive theorists describe the cognitive styles of schizoid persons as impoverished and unresponsive to cues that produce emotions (Beck & Freeman, 1990). Rather than having a particular set of beliefs that lead them to misinterpret situations in specific ways, schizoid persons simply seem disinterested in life around them and only able to acknowledge intellectually that other people experience situations differently from them. As a result, schizoid persons tend to be lethargic and unexpressive and to have poor social skills.

Treatment for Schizoid Personality Disorder

Both psychoanalytic and cognitive treatments for schizoid personality disorder focus on increasing the person's awareness of his or her own feelings and the person's social skills and social contacts (Beck & Freeman, 1990; Quality Assurance Project, 1990). The therapist may model expression of feelings for the client and will help the client identify and express his or her own feelings. Social skills training, done through role-plays with the therapist and through homework assignments in which the client tries out new social skills with other people, is an important component of cognitive therapies. Some therapists recommend group therapy for people with schizoid personality disorder, so that the group members can model interpersonal relationships and so that the schizoid person can practice new social skills directly with others in the context of group sessions.

Schizotypal Personality Disorder

Like persons with schizoid personality disorder, persons with **schizotypal personality disorder** tend to be socially isolated, have a restricted range of emotions, and be uncomfortable in interpersonal interactions. As children, people who develop schizotypal personality disorder are passive and socially unengaged, and hypersensitive to criticism (Olin et al., 1999). The distinguishing characteristics of schizotypal personality disorder are the oddities in cognition, which generally fall into four categories (Beck & Freeman, 1990). The first is *paranoia or suspiciousness*. Much like people with paranoid personality disorder, people with schizotypal personality disorder perceive other people as deceitful and hostile, and much of their social anxiety emerges from this paranoia. The second category of thought is *ideas of reference*. People with schizotypal personality disorder tend to believe that random events or circumstances are related to them. For example, they may think it is highly significant that a fire

Group therapy can help people with schizoid personality disorder increase their social contacts and social skills.

occurred in a store in which they had shopped only yesterday. The third type of odd cognition is *odd beliefs* and *magical thinking*. For example, they may believe that others know what they are thinking. The fourth category of thought is *illusions* that are just short of hallucinations. For example, they may think they see people in the patterns of wallpaper. In addition to having these oddities of thought, people with schizotypal personality disorder tend to have speech that is tangential, circumstantial, vague, or overelaborate. In interactions with others, they may have inappropriate emotional responses or no emotional responses to what other people say or do. Their behaviors are also odd, sometimes reflecting their odd thoughts. They may be easily distracted or fixate on an object for long periods of time, lost in thought or fantasy. Although the quality of these oddities of thought, speech, and behavior is similar to that in schizophrenia, it is not as severe as in schizophrenia, and people with schizotypal personality disorder maintain basic contact with reality. The woman in the following case study shows many of the oddities of schizotypal personality disorder:

CASE STUDY

The patient is a 32-year-old unmarried, unemployed woman on welfare who complains that she feels "spacey." Her feelings of detachment have gradually become stronger and more uncomfortable. For many hours each day she feels as if she were watching herself move through life, and the world around her seems unreal. She feels especially strange when she looks into a mirror. For many years she has felt able to read people's minds by a "kind of clairvoyance I don't understand." According to her, several people in her family apparently also have this ability. She is preoccupied by the thought that she has

some special mission in life but is not sure what it is; she is not particularly religious. She is very self-conscious in public, often feels that people are paying special attention to her, and sometimes thinks that strangers cross the street to avoid her. She is lonely and isolated and spends much of each day lost in fantasies or watching TV soap operas. She speaks in a vague, abstract, digressive manner, generally just missing the point, but she is never incoherent. She seems shy, suspicious, and afraid she will be criticized. She has no gross loss of contact with reality, such as hallucinations or delusions, and she has never been treated for emotional problems. She has had occasional jobs but drifts away from them because of lack of interest. (Adapted from Spitzer et al., 1981, pp. 95–96)

Between 0.6 and 5.1 percent of people will be diagnosed with schizotypal personality disorder at some time in their lives (Weissman, 1993b). Among people seeking treatment, it is over twice as commonly diagnosed in males as in females (Fabrega et al., 1991). As with the other odd-eccentric personality disorders, people with schizotypal personality disorder are at increased risk for depression and for schizophrenia or isolated psychotic episodes (Siever, Bernstein, & Silverman, 1995).

For a person to be given a diagnosis of schizotypal personality disorder, his or her odd or eccentric thoughts cannot be part of cultural beliefs, such as cultural belief in magic or specific superstitions. Still, some psychologists have argued that people of color are more often diagnosed with schizophreniclike disorders, such as schizotypal personality disorder, than are Whites because White clinicians often misinterpret culturally bound beliefs as evidence of schizotypal thinking (Snowden & Cheung, 1990).

Theories of Schizotypal Personality Disorder

Many more studies of the genetics of schizotypal personality disorder have been conducted than studies of the other odd-eccentric personality disorders. Family history studies, adoption studies, and twin studies all suggest that schizotypal personality disorder is transmitted genetically, at least to some degree (see Nigg & Goldsmith, 1994; Siever et al., 1998). In addition, schizotypal personality disorder is much more common in the first-degree relatives of people with schizophrenia than in the relatives of either psychiatric or healthy control groups (Kendler et al., 1993). Thus, schizotypal personality disorder is often considered a "mild" form of schizophrenia that is transmitted through similar genetic mechanisms as schizophrenia.

Similarly, some of the nongenetic biological factors implicated in schizophrenia are also present in people with schizotypal personality disorder (see Siever et al., 1998; Weston & Siever, 1993). In particular, people with schizotypal personality disorder show problems in the ability to sustain attention on cognitive tasks and deficits in attention similar to those seen in people with schizophrenia (Bergman et al., 1998; Siever et al., 1990). People with schizotypal personality disorder also tend to show low levels of monoamine oxidase, which could increase levels of dopamine in the brain, and higher levels of homovanillic acid, the major metabolite of dopamine (Baron, Perlman, & Levitt, 1980; Siever et al., 1990). Thus, like people with schizophrenia, people with schizotypal personality disorder may have abnormally high levels of dopamine in their brains. Finally, the ventricular regions of the brain of schizotypal patients show enlargement similar to people with schizophrenia.

There is little in the psychoanalytic or cognitive theories about schizotypal personality disorder. Perhaps psychological theories have not paid much attention to this disorder because it is so closely tied to schizophrenia, which appears to have strong biological roots, and because it was not added as a diagnostic category to the DSM until relatively recently.

Treatment for Schizotypal Personality Disorder

Schizotypal personality disorder is most often treated with the same neuroleptic drugs that are used to treat schizophrenia, such as haloperidol and thiothixene (see Siever et al., 1998). As in schizophrenia, these drugs appear to relieve psychoticlike symptoms, including the schizotypal person's ideas of reference, magical thinking, and illusions. Antidepressants are sometimes used to help people with schizotypal personality disorder who are experiencing significant distress.

Although there are few psychological theories of schizotypal personality disorder, psychological therapies have been developed to help these people overcome some of their symptoms. In psychotherapy, it is especially important for therapists to establish good relationships with schizotypal clients because these clients typically have few close relationships and tend to be paranoid (Beck & Freeman, 1990). The next step in therapy is to help schizotypal clients increase social contacts and learn socially appropriate behaviors through social skills training. Group therapy may be especially helpful in increasing clients' social skills. The crucial component of cognitive therapy with schizotypal clients is teaching them to look for objective evidence in the environment for their thoughts and to disregard bizarre thoughts. For example, a client who often thought that he was not real would be taught to identify that thought as bizarre and to discount the thought when it occurred rather than taking it seriously and acting upon it.

Summing Up

- People with the odd-eccentric personality disorders—paranoid, schizoid, and schizotypal personality disorders—have odd thought processes, emotional reactions, and behaviors similar to those of people with schizophrenia, but they retain their grasp on reality.
- People with paranoid personality disorder are chronically suspicious of others but maintain their grasp on reality.
- People with schizoid personality disorder are emotionally cold and distant from others and have great trouble forming interpersonal relationships.
- People with schizotypal personality disorders have a variety of odd beliefs and perceptual experiences but also maintain their grasp on reality.
- These personality disorders, especially schizotypal personality disorder, have been linked to familial histories of schizophrenia and some of the biological abnormalities of schizophrenia.
- People with these disorders tend not to seek treatment, but when they do, therapists pay close attention to their relationships with them and help them learn to reality-test their unusual thinking.
- Antipsychotics may help schizotypal clients reduce their odd thinking.

CONCEPT REVIEW

The Dramatic-Emotional Personality Disorders

People with dramatic-emotional personality disorders tend to have unstable emotions and engage in dramatic and impulsive behavior.

Label	Key Features	Similar Disorders on Axis I
Antisocial personality disorder	Pervasive pattern of criminal, impulsive, callous, or ruthless behavior; disregard for rights of others; no respect for social norms	Conduct disorder (diagnosed in children)
Borderline personality disorder	Rapidly shifting and unstable mood, self-concept, and interpersonal relationships; impulsive behavior; transient dissociative states; self-effacing	Mood disorders
Histrionic personality disorder	Rapidly shifting moods, unstable relationships, and intense need for attention and approval; dramatic, seductive behavior	Somatoform disorders Mood disorders
Narcissistic personality disorder	Grandiose thoughts and feelings of one's own worth; obliviousness to others' needs; exploitative, arrogant demeanor	Cyclothymic disorder

Source: DSM-IV, APA, 2000.

THE DRAMATIC-EMOTIONAL PERSONALITY DISORDERS

People with the **dramatic-emotional personality disorders** tend to engage in behaviors that are dramatic and impulsive and often show little regard for their own safety or the safety of others (see *Concept Review: The Dramatic-Emotional Personality Disorders*). Their behaviors may either harm themselves or others. For example, they may engage in suicidal behaviors or self-damaging acts such as self-cutting. They may also act in hostile, and even violent, ways against others. One of the core features of this group of disorders is a lack of real concern for others. Two of the disorders in this cluster, antisocial personality disorder and borderline personality disorder, have been the focus of a great deal of research, whereas the other two, narcissistic personality disorder and histrionic personality disorder, have not.

Antisocial Personality Disorder

Antisocial personality disorder has been recognized under various names as a serious disorder for over two centuries (Sher & Trull, 1994). Pritchard (1837) used the term *moral insanity* to describe people with little self-control and no concern for the rights of others. Later, in 1891, Koch applied the term *psychopathic* to the same individuals. Subsequent writers in the late nineteenth and early twentieth centuries often applied the term *psychopath* to anyone who had a severely maladaptive personality. Today, the label *psychopath* is not part of the official DSM nomenclature, but it is used loosely to refer to people with antisocial personality disorder.

The key features of antisocial personality disorder are an impairment in the ability to form positive relationships with others and a tendency to engage in behaviors that violate basic social norms and values. People with this disorder are cold and callous, gaining pleasure by competing with and humiliating everyone and anyone. They can be cruel and malicious. People with this disorder commit violent criminal offenses against others, including assault, murder, and rape, much more frequently than people without the disorder (Hart & Hare, 1997). They often insist on being seen as faultless and are dogmatic in their opinions. However, when they need to, people with antisocial personality disorder may act gracious and cheerful, until they get what they want. They then may revert to being brash and arrogant. The terrifying case featured in *Extraordinary People: Gary Gilmore* (p. 416) illustrates these characteristics well.

A prominent characteristic of antisocial personality disorder is poor control of impulses. People with this disorder have a low tolerance of frustration and often act impetuously, with no apparent concern for the consequences of their behavior. They often take

EXTRAORDINARY PEOPLE

Gary Gilmore

People with antisocial personality disorder are prone to aggression toward others. Seldom do their aggressive acts reach the extreme that was reached by Gary Gilmore. Gilmore was eventually sentenced to death for a series of murders. Gilmore became famous because he refused to appeal his death sentence and insisted that it be carried out without delay. He was executed on January 17, 1977, the first person to be executed in the United States since 1966. His life was depicted in *The Executioner's Song* written by Norman Mailer. The following is from a psychologist's evaluation of Gilmore shortly after he was arrested for murder in 1976.

Killer Gary Gilmore had a long history of impulsive behaviors that violated the fundamental rights of others.

The patient grew up in a family that consisted of his father, his mother, and a brother 1 year older than the patient. He indicated that his family was "a typical family, but there wasn't much closeness in it. I was always left to fend for myself and I got in trouble very early."

Though the patient was obviously bright, he received poor grades in school because "I just wasn't interested." He started "sluffing" school at a young age and at least on two different occasions was temporarily suspended for his truancy and for alleged thefts from his schoolmates. At the age of 14 he was sent to a youth correctional center for stealing a car and was at the reform school for 18 months. Almost immediately after being released, he started burglarizing and was in the county jail on three different occasions, the last two for 1 year each time.

When Gilmore was 20 years of age, he was sent to Oregon State Penitentiary for 18 months for burglary and robbery. Following this, he spent 2 years in a city jail for a "long string of traffic offenses including reckless driving and drunk driving. I started drinking before I was 10 years old." In prison, Gilmore gained a reputation for brutality to other inmates and was known as "the enforcer" and "hammerhead." He also was known as a talented artist and tattoo expert. On a number of occasions, he tattooed obscene words on the backs and forearms of ineffectual and disliked inmates: "I thought it was a good way to get back at the snitches. I would tattoo them on their bodies where they could not watch what I was doing. It wasn't until they looked at their tattoos in the mirror that they saw what I had done to them."

After he was released from jail, he committed armed robbery several times within the next month. He was then sent to Oregon State Penitentiary where he stayed for 11 years and then was

chances and seek thrills with no concern for danger. They are easily bored and restless, unable to endure the tedium of routine or to persist at the day-to-day responsibilities of marriage or a job (Millon et al., 2000). As a result, they tend to drift from one relationship to another, and often are in lower-status jobs.

Yet, a pioneer in the study of people with antisocial personalities, Hervey Cleckley, noted that although these people often ended up in prisons or dead, many of them became successful businesspeople and professionals (see Cleckley, 1941). He suggested that the difference between these successful antisocial personalities and those psychopaths who end up in jail is that the successful ones are better able to maintain an outward appearance of being normal, perhaps because they have superior intelligence and can put on a "mask of sanity" and superficial social charm in order to achieve their goals.

Continued

transferred to a federal prison in Illinois, where he stayed for another year and a half.

Gilmore indicated he has used almost all types of illicit drugs including heroin, various types of amphetamines, cocaine, and psychedelics. In more recent years, he quit using drugs, partly because they were not as available in prison, and just smoked marijuana. He drank whenever he had the opportunity in prison but said that since he was released he has mainly been drinking just beer. . . .

He was released from prison in April of 1976 and came to Utah to work with his uncle in a shoe repair shop. This did not turn out well, so he briefly tried painting signs and just before his arrest was insulating houses.

He met a woman on May 13 and the very next day moved in with her. He indicated that this was "probably the first close relationship that I ever had with anyone. I just didn't know how to respond to her for any length of time. I was very insensitive to her. I am more accustomed to violence and fighting. I was thoughtless in the way I treated her. She didn't like me to drink and even offered to quit smoking if I would quit drinking, but I never did quit drinking. Also, her two children bugged me and sometimes I would get angry at them and slap them because they were so noisy. And I always ended up in a fight with some other guy whenever we went to a party."

On July 19, just before midnight, "I pulled up near a gas station. I told the service station guy to give me all of his money. I then took him to the bathroom and told him to kneel down and then I shot him in the head twice. The guy didn't give me any trouble but I just felt like I had to do it."

The very next morning, Gilmore left his car at a service station for minor repairs and walked to a motel.

"I went in and told the guy to give me the money. I told him to lay on the floor and then I shot him. I then walked out and was carrying the cash drawer with me. I took the money and threw the cash drawer in a bush and I tried to push the gun in the bush, too. But as I was pushing it in the bush, it went off and that's how come I was shot in the arm. It seems like things have always gone bad for me. It seems like I've always done dumb things that just caused trouble for me. I remember when I was a boy I would feel like I had to do things like sit on a railroad track until just before the train came and then I would dash off. Or I would put my finger over the end of a BB gun and pull the trigger to see if a BB was really in it. Sometimes I would stick my finger in water and then put my finger in a light socket to see if it would really shock me."

Despite Gilmore's anger at being locked up, he was quite willing to tell me the events of his life and the circumstances that led up to his being charged with the murders. Though he said he was sorry that he killed the two victims, it was without depth of feeling, and he appeared actually to be indifferent. (Spitzer et al., 1983, pp. 66–68)

Unlike many of the extraordinary people we have highlighted in other chapters of this book, Gilmore was not able to overcome his psychological disorder or make contributions to society in spite of it. Rather, Gilmore is extraordinary because his story—his development, his ways of thinking, his behaviors—give us one of the clearest pictures of the life of a person with antisocial personality disorder we have ever had.

Antisocial personality disorder is one of the most common personality disorders, with between 2.3 and 3.3 percent of the population being diagnosed with the disorder at sometime in their lives (Cloninger, Bayon, & Przybeck, 1997; Weissman, 1993b). Men are five times more likely than women to be diagnosed with this disorder; there are no ethnic/racial differences in rates of diagnosis (Cloninger et al., 1997; Fabrega et al., 1991). People with this personality disorder are somewhat more likely than people with the other personality disorders to have low levels of education (Fabrega et al., 1991).

People with antisocial personality disorder are at high risk for substance abuse. One study of persons seeking therapy found that 40 percent of those with antisocial personality disorder also qualified for the diagnosis of substance abuse (Fabrega et al., 1991). Substance use, such as binge drinking, may be just one form of impulsive behavior that is part of antisocial personality disorder. Substance use probably feeds impulsive and antisocial behavior among people with this personality disorder, however. Alcohol and other substances may reduce any inhibitions they do have to control their behavior, making it more likely they will lash out at others violently. People with this disorder are also at somewhat increased risk for suicide attempts (particularly females with the disorder) and for violent death (Perry, 1993).

The tendency to engage in antisocial behaviors is one of the most stable personality characteristics (Loeber & Farrington, 1997; Moffitt, 1993; Perry, 1993). Adults with antisocial personality disorder typically have shown a disregard for societal norms and a tendency for antisocial behavior since childhood, and most would have been diagnosed with conduct disorder as children. For some people with this disorder, however, there is a tendency for antisocial behavior to diminish as they become older adults. This is particularly true of people who were not antisocial as children, and only became antisocial as adolescents or young adults (Moffitt, 1993). This may be due to some kind of psychological or biological maturation process. Or many people with this disorder may simply be jailed or constrained by society in some other way from acting out their antisocial tendencies.

Theories of Antisocial Personality Disorder

There is substantial support for a genetic influence on antisocial behaviors, particularly criminal behaviors (Carey & Goldman, 1997; Robins, 1991). Twin studies find that the concordance rate for such behaviors is near 50 percent in MZ twins, compared to 20 percent or lower in DZ twins (Carey & Goldman, 1997; Rutter et al., 1990). Adoption studies find that the criminal records of adopted sons are more similar to the records of their biological fathers than to those of their adoptive fathers (Cloninger & Gottesman, 1987; Mednick et al., 1987). Family history studies show that family members of people with antisocial personality disorder have increased rates of this disorder, as well as increased rates of alcoholism and criminal activity (Perry, 1993).

One long-standing theory is that aggressiveness, such as that shown by people with antisocial personality disorder, is linked to the hormone testosterone. Although some studies have found that highly aggressive males have higher levels of testosterone than nonaggressive males, the evidence for a role of testosterone in most forms of aggression is weak (Brain & Susman, 1997). Hormones such as testosterone may play a more important role during prenatal development in organizing the fetal brain in ways that promote or inhibit aggressiveness, rather than having a direct influence on behavior in adolescence or adulthood.

As we noted earlier, a prominent characteristic of antisocial personality disorder is a difficulty in inhibiting impulsive behaviors (Morey, 1993; Rutter, 1997; Sher & Trull, 1994). Some researchers argue that poor impulse control is at the heart of antisocial personality disorder (Rutter, 1997). What might be the biological causes of poor impulse control? Many animal studies have shown that impulsive and aggressive behaviors are linked to low levels of **serotonin**, leading to the suggestion that people with antisocial personality

Antisocial tendencies diminish with age, leading some experts to argue that older inmates are probably no threat to society.

disorder may also have low levels of serotonin (Ferris & de Vries, 1997). Several studies of humans also suggest that impulsiveness and aggressiveness are correlated with low levels of serotonin, although the data for humans are more mixed than the data for nonhuman animals (Berman, Kavoussi, & Coccaro, 1997; Moffitt et al., 1998).

Research with children who show antisocial tendencies indicates that a significant percentage, perhaps the majority, have an attention deficit hyperactivity disorder, which involves significant problems with inhibiting impulsive behaviors and with maintaining attention (see Chapter 13). The disruptive behavior of these children leads to frequent punishments and to rejection by peers, teachers, and other adults. These children then become even more disruptive and some become overtly aggressive and antisocial in their behaviors and attitudes. Thus, at least some adults with antisocial personality disorder may have lifelong problems with attentional deficits and hyperactivity, which then contribute to lifelong problems with controlling their behaviors.

People with antisocial personalities also show deficits in verbal skills and the **executive functions** of the brain—the ability to sustain concentration; abstract reasoning and concept formation, formulating goals; anticipating and planning, programming and initiating purposive sequences of behavior, self-monitoring and self-awareness; and shifting from maladaptive patterns of behavior to more adaptive ones (see Henry & Moffitt, 1997). In turn, some, but not all, studies have found differences between antisocial adults (usually prison inmates) and general population in the structure or functioning of the temporal and frontal lobe of the brain (e.g., Blake, Pincus, & Buckner, 1995; Langevin et al., 1988). These deficits in brain functioning and structure could be tied to medical illnesses and exposure to toxins during infancy and childhood, which are both more common among people who develop criminal records than among those who do not (see the discussion in Chapter 13). Or they could be tied to genetic abnormalities. Whatever their causes, low verbal intelligence and deficits in executive functions could contribute to poor impulse control and difficulty in anticipating the consequences of one's actions.

Many studies have suggested that persons with antisocial personality disorder show low levels of arousability, measured by relatively low resting heart rates or skin conductance activity, or more excessive slow-wave electroencephalogram readings (Raine, 1997). One interpretation of these data is that low levels of arousal indicate low levels of fear in response to threatening situations (Raine, 1997). Fearlessness can be put to good use—bomb disposal experts and British paratroopers also show low levels of arousal (McMillan & Rachman, 1987; O'Connor, Hallam, & Rachman, 1985). But fearlessness may also predispose some people to antisocial and violent behaviors that require fearlessness to execute, such as fighting and robbery. In addition, fearless children may not fear punishment, and thus not be deterred from antisocial behavior by the threat of punishment.

A second theory of how low arousability contributes to antisocial personality is that chronically low arousal is an uncomfortable state and leads to stimulation-seeking (Eysenck, 1994). Again, if an individual seeks stimulation through prosocial or neutral acts, such as sky-diving, stimulation-seeking may not lead to antisocial behavior. But some individuals may seek stimulation through antisocial acts that are dangerous or impulsive, such as robbery or picking a fight with others. The direction that stimulation-seeking takes—toward antisocial activities or more neutral activities—may depend largely on the reinforcement individuals receive for their behaviors. Those who are rewarded for antisocial behavior by family and peers may develop antisocial personalities, whereas those who are consistently punished for such behaviors and given alternative, more neutral behaviors may not (Dishion & Patterson, 1997). Intelligence may also influence the direction that stimulation-seeking takes as well (Henry & Moffitt, 1997). Children who are intelligent will experience more rewards from school and thus may be more influenced by the norms of adults and positive peer groups in the choices they make for seeking out stimulation. In contrast, children who are less intelligent may find school punishing and may turn to deviant peer groups for gratification and for stimulating activities.

Much of the empirical research on the social and cognitive factors that contribute to antisocial behavior has been conducted with children. Briefly, children with antisocial tendencies often come from homes in which they have experienced harsh and inconsistent parenting (Dishion & Patterson, 1997). The parents of these children alternate between being neglectful and being hostile and violent toward their children. These children learn ways of thinking about the world that seem to promote antisocial behavior (Crick & Dodge, 1994). They enter social interactions with the assumption that other children will be aggressive toward them, and interpret the actions of their peers in line with this assumption. As a result, they are quick to engage in aggressive behaviors toward others. These social and cognitive factors may be enough, in themselves, to lead to antisocial personalities in some children and adults. Many theorists believe that these social and cognitive factors combine with the biological factors we have been discussing to lead to severe antisocial behavior.

Marital conflict is common in the personality disorders.

Sociocultural Consequences of Antisocial Personality: Domestic Violence

As many as one-third of women will be physically assaulted by a man with whom they are intimate at some time in their lives (Browne & Williams, 1993; Koss, 1990). Over 1 in 10 murders in the United States involve husbands killing their wives. Violence among heterosexual couples starts young—often during dating relationships in the teenage years. Cascardi and O'Leary found that about 27 percent of high school students report they had used aggression in their relationships, and 34 percent reported having experienced violence. Approximately 35 percent of college students have reported at least one instance of violence in a dating relationship, either as the aggressor, victim, or both (Sugarman & Hotaling, 1989).

In the last few decades, there has been a great deal of research on the characteristics of male batterers and battered women (Gelles & Cornell, 1990). Male batterers seem to fall into two groups—those who are violent both within and outside of their close relationships, and those who are violent only with their partners (Dutton, 1988). Men who are violent both within and outside close relationships are more likely to have been severely abused as children, to have witnessed more parental violence, display generally antisocial behavior, have a history of criminal behavior, are "random" in their violence, and have high rates of substance abuse, compared to men who are violent only within their families and men who are not violent (Fagan, Stewart, & Hansen, 1983; Magdol et al., 1997; Saunders, 1992). Men who are violent only within their families tend to have deep concerns about abandonment, especially abandonment by women (Dutton, 1988; Saunders, 1992).

Why do men batter, and why do women stay in battering relationships? Early theories attributed

battering among males to sadistic personality disorders or brain lesions (see Dutton, 1988 for a review). Women who remained in battering relationships were said to suffer from a masochistic personality disorder that caused them to seek out the abuse.

There was little evidence for these views, however, and many theorists have objected in particular to blaming women victims of violence for their situation. These days, biological theories of male batterers tend to be extensions of theories of antisocial personality disorder. Gottman and colleagues (Gottman et al., 1995; Jacobson, Gottman, & Shortt, 1995) have found that male batterers who are particularly violent both toward their partners and toward others tend to have lower heart rates during arguments than less violent men. They argue that this low arousability helps to focus the men's attention in the arguments and increases the impact of their attempts to control and subjugate their partners.

Feminist theories see battering as an extension of the patriarchal society that gives men permission to "own" and subjugate women in any way they wish (Bograd, 1988; Dobash & Dobash, 1979; Russell, 1982). In turn, they point out that many women do not have the means to leave battering relationships, and quite accurately fear that their male partners will severely injure or kill them or their children if they attempt to leave. Social learning theories also examine the reinforcements that men receive for battering, and the constraints women have on leaving battering relationships (Ganley, 1989). Jacobson (1994) has argued for a combined feminist and social learning model of domestic violence which acknowledges the institutionalized oppression of women but examines the individual learning histories of men and women who end up in battering relationships.

Treatments for Antisocial Personality Disorder

People with antisocial personality disorder do not tend to believe they need treatment. They may submit to therapy when forced to because of marital discord, work conflicts, or incarceration. However, they are prone to blaming others for their current situations rather than accepting responsibility for their actions. As a result, many clinicians do not hold much hope for effectively treating persons with this disorder through psychotherapy (Millon et al., 2000).

Lithium has been successfully used to control impulsive/aggressive behaviors in people with antisocial personality disorders (Karper & Krystal, 1997; Sheard et al., 1976). More recently, based on the evidence for low levels of serotonin in some animals prone to impulsive and aggressive behavior, researchers have been suggesting the use of drugs that inhibit the reuptake of serotonin into the synapse, such as fluoxetine (Karper & Krystal, 1997). The efficacy of these drugs in treating antisocial personality disorder is not clear yet.

Borderline Personality Disorder

In the following passage, a clinician describes her introduction to a woman later diagnosed with **borderline personality disorder.**

CASE STUDY

Patty, a 28-year-old woman, looked frail and dissheveled when she entered my office. Her mother had brought her directly from the hospital emergency room, where she had been treated for severe cuts on her forearm. The attending physician had recommended that Patty see me as soon as possible, when he recognized the cuts as self-inflicted wounds. Patty had denied that she had cut herself, but the many scars on both her forearms were clear evidence of her tendency to self-mutilate.

I asked Patty about the wounds and got only silence. After a while, I remarked that sometimes people cut themselves because somehow that relieves tension or pain for them. In response, I got a firestorm.

"You think you're so smart! Just like all the other damn therapists my mother has dragged me to! You don't know anything! Therapists are stupid, ignorant fools who make money off other people's pain! If you had any brains at all, you'd see that this is all her fault!" Patty was pointing toward the waiting room where her mother sat.

I took a deep breath and asked Patty to continue. She did, for the rest of that hour and for several hour-long sessions for the next few weeks. Patty's bitterness was not only directed at her mother, however. She was bitter against her former employer, who let her go after she had missed a great deal of work. She was bitter against the boyfriends with whom she had had mostly brief relationships. She was bitter at the college she had attended for preparing her so badly for the workplace. But most of all, she was bitter at herself. Patty's angry accusations were most often hurled at herself, in phrases such as, "I'm totally ugly and unlovable." and "I'll never be able to cope with everyday life. I'm defective."

I learned that Patty's self-mutilations tended to happen when she was neither angry at others nor angry at herself, but instead when she was feeling nothing. She had periods of absolute emptiness, during which she often felt as though her soul was separated from her body. During these dissociative states, she would cut her forearms with a razor and sit impassively watching the blood flow from her arm.

Even though Patty had made clear what she thought of therapists, including me, at those first few sessions, she kept coming back. In fact, after the first couple of weeks, she began asking for extra sessions, saying she was feeling better than she ever had in therapy, and learning more from me than from any therapist she had ever worked with. I replied that I thought the number of sessions per week we had agreed upon earlier was appropriate and that I did not have room in my schedule to add more sessions per week with her. This was met with an outburst of indignation and accusations that I never really cared about her. Patty stormed out of my office and did not show up for her appointment two days later. Instead, I got a call later that day from the hospital emergency room, informing me that she had cut herself badly again, and that she told the attending physician to call me rather than her mother.

When I saw her next, she held up her bandaged arm and said, "See what you did?" Immediately after that, however, she crumpled into a sobbing mass in the chair, saying over and over again, "I'm sorry!"

Patty's painful symptoms represent some of the benchmarks of borderline personality disorder: out-of-control emotions that cannot be smoothed, a hypersensitivity to abandonment, a tendency to cling too tightly to other people, and a history of hurting oneself.

Instability is a key feature of borderline personality disorder. The *mood* of people with borderline personality disorder is unstable, with bouts of severe depression, anxiety, or anger seeming to arise frequently and often without good reason. The *self-concept* of these people is unstable, with periods of extreme self-doubt and periods of grandiose self-importance. Their *interpersonal relationships* are extremely unstable, and these people can switch from idealizing others to despising them without provocation. Patty also experienced the desperate emptiness that many people with borderline personality disorder describe. This emptiness leads them to cling to new acquaintances or therapists in hopes that they will fill the tremendous void they experience in themselves. They are nearly paranoid about abandonment and misinterpret other people's innocent actions as abandonment or rejection. For example, if a therapist has to cancel an appointment because she is ill, a client with borderline personality disorder might interpret this as a rejection by the therapist and become extremely depressed or angry. Along with the instability of mood, self-concept, and interpersonal relationships comes a tendency toward impulsive self-damaging behaviors, including self-mutilating behaviors and suicidal behavior. Patty's self-mutilating behavior was to cut her arms with razors. Finally, people with borderline personality disorder are prone to transient dissociative states, in which they feel unreal, lose track of time, and may even forget who they are.

The variety of symptoms that make up the criteria for diagnosis of borderline personality disorder reflects, to some extent, the complexity of this disorder. The manifestation of this disorder can be quite different from one person to the next and from one day to the next within any one person. The varied list of symptoms also reflects the difficulty that clinicians have had in agreeing on a conceptualization of this disorder (Gunderson, Zanarini, & Kisiel, 1995). The term *borderline* has been used loosely for many years to refer to people who could not be fit easily into existing diagnoses of emotional disorders or psychotic disorders and who were extremely difficult to treat (Millon et al., 2000). One result of the variety of symptoms listed in the diagnostic criteria for the disorder is that there is a great deal of overlap between the borderline diagnosis and several of the other personality disorders, including paranoid, antisocial, narcissistic, histrionic, and schizotypal personality disorders (Nurnberg et al., 1991). Indeed, the majority of persons diagnosed with borderline personality disorder will also meet the diagnostic criteria for at least one other personality disorder.

People with borderline personality disorder also tend to receive diagnoses of one of the acute disorders, including substance abuse, depression, and generalized anxiety disorder; simple phobias; agoraphobia; posttraumatic stress disorder; panic disorder; or somatization disorder (Fabrega et al., 1991; Weissman, 1993b). About 6 percent of people with this disorder die by suicide (see Perry, 1993). The greatest risk of suicide appears to be in the first year or two after people are diagnosed with borderline personality disorder. This may be because people are often not diagnosed with this disorder until a crisis brings them to the attention of the mental-health system.

Epidemiological studies suggest that between 1 and 2 percent of the population develops borderline personality disorder in their lives (Weissman, 1993b). In clinical settings, borderline personality disorder is much more often diagnosed in women than in men and somewhat more commonly diagnosed in people of color than in Whites and in people in lower socioeconomic classes than in other classes (Fabrega et al., 1991; Swartz et al., 1990). People with this disorder are high users of outpatient mental-health services; one community study found that 50 percent had used some form of mental-health service in the past 6 months (Swartz et al., 1990). Follow-up studies of people treated as inpatients for borderline personality disorder suggest that about 50 percent continue meet the diagnostic criteria for the disorder 7 years later (Links, Heslegrave, & van Reekum, 1998). The more severe people's symptoms of the disorder at the time of treatment, the more likely the disorder is to be chronic.

Theories of Borderline Personality Disorder

Several family history studies of borderline personality disorder have been conducted, and the evidence that this specific disorder is transmitted genetically is mixed (Dahl, 1993; Nigg & Goldsmith, 1994). There are

Suicide attempts and self-mutilation are common among people with borderline personality disorder.

high rates of mood disorders in the families of persons diagnosed with borderline personality disorder, however (Kendler et al., 1993). People with borderline personality disorder also show some of the same sleep abnormalities as do people with mood disorders (see Weston & Siever, 1993). Most researchers do not suggest that borderline personality disorder is simply a type of affective disorder, but there clearly are links between the two disorders.

Impulsive behaviors in people with borderline personality disorder are correlated with low levels of serotonin (see Weston & Siever, 1993). Recall that impulsive behaviors in people with antisocial personality disorder have also been linked to low serotonin levels. This suggests that low serotonin is not associated with one diagnostic category but with the category of impulsive behaviors.

Psychoanalytic theorists, particularly those in the objects relations school (see Chapter 2), have been extremely interested in borderline personality disorder (see Kernberg, 1979; Klein, 1952). They suggest that persons with this disorder have very poorly developed views of the self and others, stemming from poor early relationships with caregivers. The early caregivers of people with borderline personality disorder may have encouraged the children's dependence on them early in life. They may have punished the children's attempts at individuation and separation, so the children never learned to fully differentiate their views of themselves and their views of others. This makes them extremely reactive to others' opinions of them and to the possibility of being abandoned by others. When they perceive others as rejecting them, they reject themselves and may engage in self-punishment or self-mutilation. They also have never been able to integrate the positive and negative qualities of either their self-concept or their concept of others, because their early caregivers were comforting and rewarding when they remained dependent and compliant toward them but hostile and rejecting when they tried to individuate from them. They tend to see themselves and other people as either "all good" or "all bad" and vacillate between these two views. This process is referred to as **splitting**. The instability in borderline persons' emotions and interpersonal relationships is due to splitting—their emotions and their perspectives on their interpersonal relationships reflect their vacillation between the "all good" and the "all bad" self and the "all good" and "all bad" other.

Another influential theorist, Marcia Linehan (1987), focuses on deficit in the ability to regulate their emotions seen in borderline personality disorder, which is probably physiologically based. Their extreme emotional reactions to situations lead to their impulsive actions. In addition, borderline persons have histories of significant others discounting and criticizing their emotional experiences, which make it even harder for them to learn appropriate emotion-regulation skills and to understand and accept their emotional reactions to events. Borderline persons come to rely on others to help them cope with difficult situations but do not have enough self-confidence to ask for help from others in mature ways. Thus, they become manipulative and indirect in trying to gain support from others.

Finally, research suggests that many, but not all, persons with borderline personality disorder have histories of physical and sexual abuse during childhood (Zanarini, 1997). Patty, whom we met earlier, is one of these people, as she describes here.

Voices

My father liked to joke that he should write a book on discipline because he knew how to raise disciplined kids. He never did write that book, though, because if anyone had known what methods he used to discipline me and my siblings, he would have been arrested. His favorite method of discipline was simply whipping us. Not the kind of hand-spanking on the bottom that other kids sometimes got from their parents. Father had a special belt he kept especially for discipline. It was wide and leather, with a pointy metal piece on the end. When we would do something really bad, like not get all A's on our report card, he would pull out the belt. He would make us strip naked and go down into the basement. While he told us how stupid we were and how we were never going to amount to anything, he whipped us with that belt. If you tried to protect yourself or move away, he'd grab you by the arm and hold you with one hand while he whipped you with the other. Or sometimes he'd punch you

down onto the floor and hold you down with his foot. He made all the kids watch while one kid was being beaten, so we'd all "learn a lesson."

Father also liked to teach us lessons by locking us away in a particular closet. Once he kept me locked in the closet for three days when I had worn a dress to school that he thought was indecent. He told me I needed the time to think about how I had disgraced him by looking like a slut. When you were in the closet, you weren't allowed to have any food or to come out to go to the bathroom. When he let you out of the closet, he'd get down on his hands and knees and sniff around for urine smells, to see if you'd gone pee in the closet. If he thought he smelled urine, you'd get a beating when you got out.

He beat my mother, too, but somehow I never felt sorry for her. I only felt a combination of rage and contempt. The rage was because she didn't protect us kids from my father. Sure, she'd bandage our wounds after a beating, and warn us when Father was in a particularly angry mood. But once Father started beating us, she disappeared. I also felt contempt for my mother because of her weakness, which kept her from leaving my father, or killing him in his sleep, which is what I would have preferred.

Abuse like this could lead to the problems in self-concept that most theorists suggest is at the core of this disorder.

Treatment for Borderline Personality Disorder

Therapists from all different theoretical perspectives acknowledge the importance of remaining aware of the borderline client's tendency either to idealize a therapist or to completely reject a therapist and of maintaining some emotional distance from the client's effusive praise or damning criticisms. The borderline client finds it very difficult to trust anyone, including a therapist, and is hypersensitive to signs of rejection. It is very important for the therapist to be honest, straightforward, and clear in communicating with the borderline client and to avoid or quickly clarify any misunderstandings that arise in the therapeutic relationship. The therapist must also set limits on the client's behaviors, particularly aggressive behaviors during therapy sessions or frequent requests for special treatment. Change can be slow with borderline clients, and the drop-out rate of borderline clients from therapy is on the order of 60 percent (Shea, 1993).

Drug treatments for persons with borderline personality disorder have focused on reducing their symptoms of anxiety and depression through antianxiety

PUSHING THE BOUNDARIES

Innovative Therapy for Borderline Personality Disorder

One of the most challenging aspects of conducting therapy with people with borderline personality disorder is their tendency to engage in splitting—idealizing the therapist at one moment and deriding the therapist in the next moment. Two therapists in Washington, D.C., decided that, rather than fighting the tendency of their borderline patients to split, they would use that tendency as part of the therapy. Here is their description of their technique (reprinted from the APA Monitor Web site, http://www.apa.org).

For years, Jean Carter, PhD, had been struggling to surmount the recurring conflicts with her patient Marcy (a pseudonym). But like many clients with borderline personality disorder (BPD), Marcy remained mired in profound splitting in the therapy, at times idealizing Carter, but—at the slightest provocation—abruptly and angrily deprecating her.

"I began to think that maybe she was right, that I didn't understand her, that I was a failure as a therapist," Carter says about one of Marcy's many complaints. "And I'd done a lot of effective work with borderlines, so this was a real blow to me."

So the Washington, D.C., psychologist teamed

up with colleague Bruce Wine, PhD, to try a fresh approach in Marcy's treatment. Wine had been helping Carter conduct adjunct couples therapy with Marcy and her husband. Since Marcy seemed to take a strong liking to Wine in those sessions, the two therapists each began conducting separate individual sessions with Marcy: Wine saw her once a week and Carter met with her twice weekly. Wine became an empathic-yet-objective listener for Marcy's complaints about Carter. And he gradually helped Marcy integrate her anger and affection toward Carter, rather than alternate between the extremes of those emotions.

Wine says. "With me, she could look at how her struggles with Jean paralleled other parts of her life—like her relationship with her husband and kids. We were actually engaging the split, rather than enabling it."

Thus, Carter and Wine developed what they believe is a potent treatment model for patients prone to the extreme and destructive splitting between negative and positive emotions toward others.

Carter and Wine are not the first psychologists to use a team approach to treating BPD. In fact,

drugs and antidepressants and on controlling their impulsive behaviors with serotonin reuptake inhibitors. Some studies of antidepressants find that people with borderline personality disorder do not improve and some actually become worse on tricyclic antidepressants (Links et al., 1990; Soloff et al., 1989). The serotonin reuptake inhibitor fluoxetine (Prozac) appears to be effective in treating depressed mood and reducing impulsive behaviors in borderline personality disorder (Coccaro & Siever, 1995).

Antipsychotic drugs are sometimes used with people with severe borderline personality disorder, particularly when they exhibit signs of psychosis. The neurological side effects of the phenothiazines (see Chapter 10) lead many people to discontinue taking

these drugs (Soloff et al., 1993). Studies of the atypical antipsychotic, clozapine, have suggested that this drug may relieve psychotic-like symptoms and other symptoms of borderline personality disorder in many people with the diagnosis (Benedetti et al., 1998).

Psychodynamic treatment for people with borderline personality disorder involves helping clients clarify feelings, confronting them with their tendency to split images of the self and other, and interpreting clients' transference relationships with therapists (Kernberg, 1989). Many people with borderline personality disorder will at times become extremely angry toward their therapists, as they move from idealizing to devaluing them. Therapists can use such times to help clients understand their splitting defenses and to set clear limits

Continued

dialectical behavioral therapy (DBT), the only psychosocial intervention for BPD to be demonstrated in controlled trials, involves multiple therapists working with the patient.

Each therapist helps the patient get along with the other therapists, explains Marsha Linehan, PhD, a University of Washington psychologist who developed DBT and has extensively tested it.

But the parallel treatment model is distinctive in the way it replicates the family structure for the patient.

"The formulation we're offering is a much more realistic setting—like a two-parent family," Wine says. "Think about a 3-year-old saying 'I hate Mommy,' to Daddy. And Daddy says, 'It sounds like you're pretty mad. Tell me what happened.' "

Carter and Wine admit that their approach is a sharp contrast from the conventional clinical approach to splitting.

"There's a lot of caution from other therapists when we talk about this," Carter says. "It runs so counter to the traditional approach that says you shouldn't allow splitting—that it's pathological and will destroy the therapy."

Instead, the clinicians view the drastic black-and-white thinking as a coping mechanism that the patient won't easily extinguish. A client is likely to become even more rageful or withdrawn when the therapist tries to challenge, rather than validate, that coping strategy, they posit.

"What we've done is shift the whole paradigm, saying that splitting is a natural, developmental process rather than a defense to be ignored or gotten rid of," Carter says. "And we have to respect that this is the best the patient can do at the time."

The model may appear to be costlier than conventional therapy, because two therapists are being paid to treat a single patient. But the approach actually shortens the duration of therapy, Carter says, in part because it deters the "therapist-hopping" characteristic of many patients prone to dramatic splitting behavior, Carter says. Such clients are more apt to stick with their therapy, rather than leave when a conflict arises, if they know another party will validate and help them understand their negative feelings toward their therapist, she explains.

"Otherwise, they either drop you or you end up referring them to someone else," she says. "And that just allows them to enact the same sort of splitting all over again. They're back to square one."

Although she ended therapy three years ago, Marcy still keeps in touch with Carter. And she reports that she's now able to replicate with her husband and children what she learned with Carter and Wine: She's learned that love and anger don't have to be mutually exclusive.

---

on the clients' behaviors. *Pushing the Boundaries:* Innovative Therapy for Borderline Personality Disorder describes two therapists attempt to use co-therapy to deal with splitting in a borderline client. Clients may also be taught more adaptive means of solving everyday problems so that the world does not appear so overwhelming. Self-destructive tendencies are addressed, with therapists helping clients identify the feelings leading to these acts and develop healthy ways of coping with these feelings.

Cognitive behavior therapies, such as Linehan's dialectical behavior therapy (see Chapter 9), focus on helping clients gain a more realistic and positive sense of self, learn adaptive skills for solving problems and regulating emotions, and correct dichotomous thinking (Beck & Freeman, 1990; Linehan, 1987; Millon et al., 2000). Therapists will teach clients to monitor self-disparaging thoughts and black-or-white evaluations of people and situations and to challenge these thoughts and evaluations. Therapists will also help clients learn appropriate assertiveness skills for close relationships so that they can express their needs and feelings in a mature manner. Clients may learn how to control impulsive behavior by monitoring the situations most likely to lead to such behaviors and learning alternative ways to handle such situations. Studies have found that dialectical behavioral therapy significantly reduces suicidal behaviors and the need for hospitalization in people with borderline personality disorder (Linehan et al., 1991).

Flamboyance is one symptom of histrionic personality disorder.

Histrionic Personality Disorder

Histrionic personality disorder shares features with borderline personality disorder, including rapidly shifting emotions and intense and unstable relationships. However, whereas people with borderline personality disorder are often self-effacing in an attempt to win favor from others, people with histrionic personality disorder always want to be the center of attention. The borderline person may desperately cling to others in self-doubt and need, but the histrionic person simply wants the attention of others. They pursue others' attention by being highly dramatic, being overtly seductive, and emphasizing the positive qualities of their physical appearance. They tend to speak in global terms. Others see them as self-centered and shallow, unable to delay gratification, demanding and overly dependent. Debbie is a person diagnosed with histrionic personality disorder (Beck & Freeman, 1990, pp. 211–212).

CASE STUDY

Debbie was a 26-year-old woman who worked as a sales-clerk in a trendy clothing store and who sought therapy for panic disorder with agoraphobia. She dressed flamboyantly, with an elaborate and dramatic hairdo. Her appearance was especially striking, since she was quite short (under 5 feet tall) and at least 75 pounds overweight. She wore sunglasses indoors throughout the evaluation and constantly fiddled with them, taking them on and off nervously and waving them to emphasize a point. She cried loudly and dramatically at various points in the interview, going through large numbers of tissue. She continually asked for reassurance. ("Will I be OK?" "Can I get over this?") She talked nonstop throughout the evaluation. When gently interrupted by the evaluator, she was very apologetic, laughing and saying, "I know I talk too much"; yet she continued to do so throughout the session.

Between 1.3 and 2.1 percent of the population will develop this disorder at sometime in their lives, and the vast majority of persons diagnosed with this disorder are women (Weissman, 1993b). Persons with this disorder are more likely to be separated or divorced than married. They tend to make more medical visits than the average person, and there is an increased rate of suicide gestures and threats in this group (Nestadt et al., 1990). Persons with this disorder most often seek treatment for depression or anxiety (Fabrega et al., 1991).

Theories of Histrionic Personality Disorder

Family history studies indicate that histrionic personality disorder clusters in families along with borderline personality disorder, antisocial personality disorder, and somatization disorder (Dahl, 1993). It is unclear whether these disorders are genetically related or the results of processes within the family or environment.

Psychodynamic theorists see this disorder as the result of deep dependency needs and repression of emotions, stemming from poor resolution of either the oral stage or the Oedipal stage (Fenichel, 1945; Kernberg, 1975; Millon et al., 2000). Attention-seeking results from the need for approval from others. The shallowness of thought and emotional involvement with others reflects the histrionic person's repression of her own feelings and needs.

Cognitive theories suggest that the underlying assumption driving the histrionic person's behavior is, "I am inadequate and unable to handle life on my own" (Beck & Freeman, 1990). Although this assumption is shared by persons with other disorders, particularly depression, the histrionic person responds to this assumption differently from persons with other disorders. Specifically, he or she works to get other people to care for her by seeking their attention and approval.

Theodore Millon and colleagues (2000) argue that histrionic adults may have been born with a high level of energy and need for stimulation. If they were exposed to a series of brief, highly charged, and irregular sources of stimulation, such as a succession of different caretakers in infancy, they may have developed an expectation or need for short, concentrated periods of stimulus from a variety of people. In other words, they may have developed a pattern of intense stimulation-seeking, reliance on others for stimulation, and intolerance for boredom. Their dramatic behaviors and emotional shallowness may have evolved from this pattern. In addition, histrionic people may have learned that parental approval was contingent on some sort of performance, such as "looking pretty" or performing well in some artistic endeavor. They seldom received negative reinforcement from their parents but had to "do something" to get their parents' attention and receive praise.

Treatment for Histrionic Personality Disorder

Psychodynamic treatments focus on uncovering histrionic persons' repressed emotions and needs and helping them express these emotions and needs in more socially appropriate ways. Cognitive therapy focuses on identifying histrionic people's assumptions that they cannot function on their own and helping them formulate goals and plans for their lives that do not rely on the approval of others (Beck & Freeman, 1990). Therapists attempt to help clients tone down their dramatic evaluations of situations by challenging these evaluations and suggesting more reasonable evaluations.

Narcissistic Personality Disorder

The characteristics of **narcissistic personality disorder** appear similar to the characteristics of histrionic personality disorder. In both disorders, individuals act in a dramatic and grandiose manner, seek admiration from others, and are shallow in their emotional expressions and relationships with others. However, whereas people with histrionic personality disorder look to others for approval, persons with narcissistic personality disorder rely on their own self-evaluations and see dependency on others as weak and dangerous. They are preoccupied with thoughts of their own self-importance and with fantasies of power and success and view themselves as above most others. In interpersonal relationships, they make unreasonable demands for others to follow their wishes, ignore the needs and wants of others, exploit others to gain power, and are arrogant and demeaning.

CASE STUDY

David was an attorney in his early 40s when he sought treatment for depressed mood. He cited business and marital problems as the source of his distress and wondered if he was having a midlife crisis.

David had grown up in a comfortable suburb of a large city, the oldest of three children and the only son of a successful businessman and a former secretary. Always known to have a bit of a temper, David usually provoked his parents and his sisters into giving in to his wishes. Even if they didn't give in to his demands, he reported that he usually went ahead and did what he wanted anyway. David spoke of being an "ace" student and a "super" athlete but could not provide any details that would validate a superior performance in these areas. He also recollected that he had his pick of girlfriends, as most women were "thrilled" to have a date with him.

David went to college, fantasizing about being famous in a high-profile career. He majored in communications, planning to go on to law school and eventually into politics. He met his first wife during college, the year she was the university homecoming queen. They married shortly after their joint graduation. He then went on to law school, and she went to work to support the couple.

During law school, David became a workaholic, fueled by fantasies of brilliant work and international recognition. He spent minimal time with his wife and, after their son was born, even less time with either of them. At the same time, he continued a string of extramarital affairs, mostly brief sexual encounters. He spoke of his wife in an annoyed, devaluing way, complaining about how she just did not live up to his expectations. He waited until he felt reasonably secure in his first job so that he could let go of her financial support and then he sought a divorce. He continued to see his son occasionally, but he rarely paid his stipulated child support.

After his divorce, David decided that he was totally free to just please himself. He loved spending all his money on himself, and he lavishly decorated his condominium and bought an attention-getting wardrobe. He constantly sought the companionship of attractive women. He was very successful at making initial contacts and getting dates, but he rarely found anyone good enough to date more than once or twice. Sometimes he played sexual games to amuse himself, such as seeing how fast he could make sexual contact or how many women would agree to have sex with him. He eventually married Susan, the daughter of a well-known politician, and was presently unhappy with her and what she expected of him. He thought that she was lucky to have him and therefore did not really have the right to make demands. He knew that there would be plenty of other, prettier women who would be glad to cater to his needs.

At work, David believed that because he was "different" from other people, they had no right to criticize him. But he had every right to criticize others. He also believed that other people were weak and needed contact with someone like him in order to bring direction or pleasure into their lives. He saw no problem in taking advantage of other people if they were "stupid" enough to allow him to do so.

David felt better when someone flattered him; when he was in a group social situation where he could easily grab the center of attention; and when he could fantasize about obtaining a high-level position, being honored for his great talent, or just being fabulously weathy. (Adapted from Beck & Freeman, 1990, pp. 245–247)

Narcissists can be extremely successful in societies that reward self-confidence and assertiveness, such as the United States (Millon et al., 2000). When narcissists grossly overestimate their abilities, however, they can make poor choices in their careers and may experience many failures. In addition, narcissists annoy other people and can alienate the important people in their lives. Narcissists seek treatment most often for depression and for trouble adjusting to life stressors (Fabrega et al., 1991).

Epidemiological studies suggest that narcissistic personality disorder is rare, with a lifetime prevalence of less than 1 percent (Gunderson, Ronningstam, & Smith, 1995; Weissman, 1993b). It is more frequently diagnosed in men.

Theories of Narcissistic Personality Disorder

Sigmund Freud (1914) viewed narcissism as a phase that all children pass through before transferring their love for themselves to significant others. Children could become fixated in this narcissistic phase, however, if they experienced caregivers as untrustworthy and decided that they could only rely on themselves or if they had parents who indulged them and instilled in them a grandiose sense of their abilities and worth (see also Horney, 1939). Later psychodynamic writers (Kernberg, 1998; Kohut, 1971) argued that the narcissist actually suffers from low self-esteem and feelings of emptiness and pain as a result of rejection from parents and that narcissistic behaviors are reaction formations against these problems with self-worth.

From the vantage point of social learning theory, Millon (1969) traced the origin of the narcissistic style to unrealistic overvaluation of a child's worth by parents. The child is unable to live up to his parents' evaluations of himself, but he continues to act as if he is superior to others and to demand that others see him as superior. Similarly, Beck and Freeman (1990) argued that some narcissists develop assumptions about their self-worth that are unrealistically positive as the result of indulgence and overvaluation by significant others during childhood. Other narcissists develop the belief that they are unique or exceptional in reaction to being singled out as "different" from others due to ethnic, racial, or economic status or as a defense against rejection by important people in their lives.

Treatment for Narcissistic Personality Disorder

People with narcissistic personality disorder do not tend to seek treatment, except when they develop depression or are confronted with severe interpersonal problems (Beck & Freeman, 1990). They generally see any problems they encounter as due to the weaknesses of others, rather than their own weaknesses. Cognitive techniques can help these clients develop more sensitivity to the needs of others and more realistic expectations of their own abilities by learning to challenge their initially self-aggrandizing ways of interpreting situations (Millon et al., 2000). Such self-challenging doesn't come easily for these people, however, and narcissistic clients often do not remain in therapy once

People with narcissistic personality disorder take great pride in their appearance, possessions, and status.

their acute symptoms or interpersonal problems decrease, however.

Summing Up

- People with the dramatic-emotional personality disorders—antisocial, borderline, histrionic, and narcissistic personality disorders—have histories of unstable relationships and emotional experiences and of behaving in dramatic and erratic ways.
- People with antisocial personality disorder regularly violate the basic rights of others and often engage in criminal acts.
- Antisocial personality disorder may have strong biological roots but is also associated with harsh and nonsupportive parenting.
- People with borderline personality disorder vacillate between "all good" and "all bad" evaluations of themselves and others.
- People with histrionic and narcissistic personality disorders act in flamboyant manners. People with histrionic personality disorder are overly dependent and solicitious of others, whereas people with narcissistic personality disorder are dismissive of others.
- None of these personality disorders responds consistently well to current treatments.

⟳ THE ANXIOUS-FEARFUL PERSONALITY DISORDERS

The **anxious-fearful personality disorders**—avoidant personality disorder, dependent personality disorder, and obsessive-compulsive personality disorder—are all characterized by a chronic sense of anxiety or fear-fulness and behaviors intended to ward off feared situations (see *Concept Review:* The Anxious-Fearful Personality Disorders). What is feared is different in each of the three disorders but people with any one of these three disorders are nervous and not terribly happy.

Avoidant Personality Disorder

Avoidant personality disorder has been studied more than the other two anxious-fearful personality disorders. People with avoidant personality disorder are extremely anxious about being criticized by others and so they avoid interactions with others in which there is any possibility of being criticized. They might choose occupations that are socially isolated, such as being park rangers in the wilderness. When they must interact with others, people with avoidant personality disorder are restrained and nervous and hypersensitive to signs of being evaluated or criticized. They are terrified of saying something silly or doing something that might embarrass themselves. They tend to be depressed and lonely. But though they may crave relationships with others, they feel unworthy of these relationships and so isolate themselves.

CASE STUDY

A 27-year-old, single, male bookkeeper was referred to a consulting psychologist because of a recent upsurge in anxiety that seemed to begin when a group of new employees was assigned to his office section. He feared that he was going to be fired, though his work was always highly commended. A clique had recently formed in the office, and, though very much wanting to be accepted into this "in group," the patient hesitated to join the clique unless explicitly asked to do so. Moreover, he "knew he had nothing to offer them" and thought that he would ultimately be rejected anyway.

The patient spoke of himself as having always been a shy, fearful, quiet boy. Although he had two "good friends" whom he continued to see occasionally, he was characterized by fellow workers as a loner, a nice young man who usually did his work efficiently but on his own. They noted that he always ate by himself in the company cafeteria and never joined in the "horsing around." (Spitzer et al., 1981, p. 59)

About 1 percent of people will eventually be diagnosed with avoidant personality disorder, with no strong gender differences in the prevalence of the disorder (Fabrega et al., 1991; Weissman, 1993b). People with this disorder are prone to chronic dysthymia and to bouts of major depression and severe anxiety (Fabrega et al., 1991). There is obvious overlap between the characteristics for avoidant personality disorder and for social phobia (see Chapter 6), but there is also a clear distinction. People with avoidant personality disorder have a general sense of inadequacy and a pervasive and general fear of being criticized that leads them to avoid most types of social interactions. People with social phobia tend to fear specific social situations in which they will be expected to perform (e.g., giving a talk in class) and do not tend to have a general sense of inadequacy. People with schizoid personality disorder

CONCEPT REVIEW

The Anxious-Fearful Personality Disorders

People with the anxious-fearful personality disorders are chronically anxious.

Label	Key Features	Similar Disorders on Axis I
Avoidant personality disorder	Pervasive anxiety, sense of inadequacy, fear of being criticized, which leads to avoidance of social interactions and nervousness	Social phobia
Dependent personality disorder	Pervasive selflessness, need to be cared for, fear of rejection, leading to total dependence on and submission to others	Separation anxiety disorder Dysthymic disorder
Obsessive-compulsive personality disorder	Pervasive rigidity in one's activities and interpersonal relationships, including emotional constriction, extreme perfectionism, and anxiety about even minor disruptions in one's routine	Obsessive-compulsive disorder

Source: DSM-IV, APA, 2000.

People with avoidant personality disorder may choose professions that allow them to avoid other people.

also withdraw from social situations, but unlike persons with avoidant personality disorder, they do not view themselves as inadequate and incompetent.

Theories of Avoidant Personality Disorder

Family history studies show that avoidant personality disorder is more common in the first-degree relatives of people with the disorder than in the relatives of normal control groups (Dahl, 1993). Studies have not been done to determine whether this is due to a genetic transmission of the disorder or to certain family environments. However, studies of temperamental differences between very young children suggest that some children may be born with a shy, fearful temperament that causes them to avoid most other people (Pilkonis, 1995).

People with avoidant personality disorder may have habitually high levels of physical arousal that make them hypersensitive to their environment and particularly to possible threats (Millon et al., 2000). As infants, these hypersensitive persons may have been experienced by their parents as troublesome, whining, and difficult to manage. If their parents reacted to the infants with frequent frustration, anger, and criticism, the infants may have begun to develop low self-regard and a sensitivity to criticism. The avoidant personality pattern may be more likely to develop if parental rejection takes the form of belittlement, depreciation, and humiliation of the child and if the child is biologically prone to being apprehensive (Millon et al., 2000).

Similarly, cognitive theorists suggest that people with avoidant personality disorder developed dysfunctional beliefs about being worthless as a result of rejection by important others early in life (Beck & Freeman, 1990). They contend that the children whose parents reject them conclude, "I must be a bad person

for my mother to treat me so badly," "I must be different or defective," and, "If my parents don't like me, how could anyone?" (p. 261). They assume that they will be rejected by others as they were rejected by their parents and thus avoid interactions with others. Their thoughts are of this sort: "Once people get to know me, they see I'm really inferior." When they must interact with others, they are unassertive and nervous because they think, "I must please this person in every way or she will criticize me." They also tend to discount any positive feedback they receive from others, believing that others are just being nice or do not see how incompetent they really are.

Treatment for Avoidant Personality Disorder

Cognitive and behavioral therapies have proven helpful for people with avoidant personality disorder (Shea, 1993). These therapies have included graduated exposure to social settings, social skills training, and challenging of negative automatic thoughts about social situations. Persons receiving these therapies show increases in the frequency and range of social contacts, decreases in avoidance behaviors, and increases in comfort and satisfaction in social activities (Alden, 1989; Cappe & Alden, 1986; Stravynski, Marks, & Yule, 1982).

Dependent Personality Disorder

People with **dependent personality disorder** are also anxious about interpersonal interactions, but their anxiety stems from a deep need to be cared for by others rather than a concern that they will be criticized. Their desire to be loved and taken care of by others leads persons with dependent personality disorder to deny any of their own thoughts and feelings that might displease others, to submit to even the most unreasonable demands, and to frantically cling to others. People with this personality disorder cannot make decisions for themselves and do not initiate new activities except in an effort to please others. In contrast to avoidant personalities, who avoid relationships, dependent personalities can only function within a relationship. They deeply fear rejection and abandonment and may allow themselves to be exploited and abused rather than lose relationships.

Some children may be born with a shy temperament.

CASE STUDY

Francesca was in a panic because her husband seemed to be getting increasingly annoyed with her. Last night he became very angry when Francesca asked him to cancel an upcoming business trip because she was terrified of being left at home alone. In a rage, her husband shouted, "You can't ever be alone! You can't do anything by yourself! You can't even decide what to have for dinner by yourself! I'm sick of it. Grow up and act like an adult!"

It was true that Francesca had a very difficult time making decisions for herself. While she was in high school, she couldn't decide which courses to take and would talk with her parents and friends for hours about what she should do, finally doing whatever her best friend or her mother told her to do. When she graduated from high school, she didn't feel smart enough to go to college, even though she had good grades in high school. She drifted into a job because her best friend had a job with the same company, and she wanted to remain close to that friend. The friend eventually dumped Francesca, however, because she was tired of Francesca's incessant demands for reassurance. Francesca would frequently buy gifts for the friend and offer to do the friend's laundry or cooking, in obvious attempts to win the friend's favor. But Francesca would also keep the friend for hours in the evening, asking her whether she thought Francesca had made the right decision about some trivial issue, such as what to buy her mother for Christmas, and how she thought Francesca was performing on the job.

Soon after her friend dumped her, Francesca met her husband, and when he showed some interest in her, she quickly tried to form a close relationship with him. She liked the fact that he seemed strong and confident, and when he asked her to marry him, Francesca thought that perhaps finally she would feel safe and secure. But especially since he has begun to get angry with her frequently, Francesca has been worrying constantly that he is going to leave her.

Between 1.6 percent and 6.7 percent of people will develop dependent personality disorder at sometime in their lives (Weissman, 1993b). Higher rates of the disorder are found when self-report methods are used than when structured clinical interviews are used, suggesting that many people feel they have this disorder, when clinicians would not diagnose the

disorder in them. More women than men are diagnosed with this disorder in clinical settings (Fabrega et al., 1991). Periods of major depression and chronic anxiety are common in people with the disorder (Fabrega et al., 1991; Millon et al., 2000).

Dependent personality disorder runs in families, but again it is unclear whether this is due to genetics or to family environments (Dahl, 1993). Children with histories of anxiety about separation from their parents or of chronic physical illness appear more prone to develop dependent personality disorder (APA, 2000).

Theories of Dependent Personality Disorder

Psychoanalytic theorists see dependent personality disorder as the outcome of fixation at the oral stage of psychosexual development (see Chapter 2). The caregivers of people who develop this disorder either withheld the nurturance these people needed during this stage, or required dependent behavior from them in exchange for nurturance. As a result, they did not develop a healthy sense of self separate from the nurturance they receive from others.

Millon et al., (2000) suggest that, as children, persons with dependent personality disorder were gentle but fearful and had warm but overprotective parents. They did not learn to overcome their fearfulness and to be assertive but instead became more and more dependent on others. If such children also have aggressive or abusive siblings or experiences with peers that make them feel unattractive or inadequate, feelings of self-doubt will increase and dependent behaviors may be reinforced by overprotective parents.

Treatment for Dependent Personality Disorder

Unlike people with many of the other personality disorders, persons with dependent personality disorder frequently seek treatment (Millon et al., 2000). Psychodynamic treatment focuses, of course, on helping clients gain insight into the early experiences with caregivers that led to their dependent behaviors through the use of free association, dream interpretation, and interpretation of the transference process. Nondirective and humanistic therapies may be helpful in fostering autonomy and self-confidence in persons with dependent personality disorder (Millon et al., 2000).

Cognitive-behavioral therapy for dependent personality disorder includes behavioral techniques designed to increase assertive behaviors and decrease anxiety and cognitive techniques designed to challenge assumptions about the need to rely on others (Beck & Freeman, 1990). Clients might be given graded exposure to anxiety-provoking situations, such as requesting help from a salesperson. Clients may also be taught relaxation skills so they can overcome anxiety enough to engage in homework assignments. They and their therapists might develop a hierarchy of increasingly difficult independent actions that the clients gradually attempt on their own, beginning with deciding what to have for lunch and ending with deciding what job to take. After making each decision, clients are encouraged to recognize their competence and challenge the negative thoughts they had about making the decision.

Regardless of what type of psychotherapy is used with clients with dependent personality disorder, therapists must be careful not to reinforce clients' tendency to see therapists as all-powerful people who will provide them with everything they need and to remain passive and submissive in therapy (Beck & Freeman, 1990; Millon et al., 2000). Clients must be gently encouraged to assume responsibility for their own recovery and to practice assertiveness skills within the context of the therapist-client relationship. Group therapy can be a useful means by which to teach dependent clients skills of assertiveness and decision making and to enhance their confidence in social situations (Millon et al., 2000).

Obsessive-Compulsive Personality Disorder

The characteristics of self-control, attention to detail, perseverance, and reliability are highly valued in many societies, including U.S. society. Some people, however, carry these traits to an extreme and become rigid, perfectionist, dogmatic, ruminative, and emotionally blocked. These people are said to have **obsessive-compulsive personality disorder.** The

"Ronald is extremely *compulsive."*
© Sidney Harris

obsessive-compulsive personality disorder shares features with obsessive-compulsive disorder (see Chapter 7), but obsessive-compulsive personality disorder represents a more generalized way of interacting with the world than does obsessive-compulsive disorder, which often involves only specific and constrained obsessional thoughts and compulsive behaviors.

People with obsessive-compulsive personality disorder often seem grim and austere, tensely in control of their emotions, and lacking spontaneity (Millon et al., 2000). They are workaholics and see little need for leisure activities or friendships. Other people experience them as stubborn, stingy, possessive, moralistic, and officious. They tend to relate to others in terms of rank or status and will be ingratiating and deferential to "superiors" but dismissive, demeaning, or authoritarian toward "inferiors." Although they are extremely concerned with efficiency, their perfectionism and obsessions about following rules often interfere with their completion of tasks.

CASE STUDY

Ronald Lewis is a 32-year-old accountant who is "having trouble holding on to a woman." He does not understand why, but the reasons become very clear as he tells his story. Mr. Lewis is a remarkably neat and well-organized man who tends to regard others as an interference to the otherwise mechanically perfect progression of his life. For many years he has maintained an almost inviolate schedule. On weekdays he arises at 6:47, has two eggs soft-boiled for 2 minutes, 45 seconds, and is at his desk at 8:15. Lunch is at 12:00, dinner at 6:00, bedtime at 11:00. He has separate Saturday and Sunday schedules, the latter characterized by a methodical and thorough trip through *The New York Times*. Any change in schedule causes him to feel varying degrees of anxiety, annoyance, and a sense that he is doing something wrong and wasting time.

Orderliness pervades Mr. Lewis's life. His apartment is immaculately clean and meticulously arranged. His extensive collections of books, records, and stamps are all carefully catalogued, and each item is reassuringly always in the right and familiar place. Mr. Lewis is highly valued at his work because his attention to detail has, at times, saved the company considerable embarrassment. . . . His perfectionism also presents something of a problem, however. He is the slowest worker in the office and probably the least productive. He gets the details right but may fail to put them in perspective. His relationships to coworkers are cordial but formal. He is on a "Mr. and Ms." basis with people he has known for years in an office that generally favors first names.

Mr. Lewis's major problems are with women and follow the same repetitive pattern. At first, things go well. . . . Soon, however, he begins to resent the intrusion upon his schedule a woman inevitably causes. This is most strongly illustrated in the bedtime arrangements. Mr. Lewis is a light and nervous sleeper with a rather elaborate routine preceding his going to bed. He must spray his sinuses, take two aspirin, straighten up the apartment, do 35 sit-ups and read two pages of the dictionary. The sheets must be of just the right crispness and temperature and the room must be noiseless. Obviously, a woman sleeping over interferes with his inner sanctum and, after sex, Mr. Lewis tries either to have the woman go home or sleep in the living room. No woman has put up with this for very long. (Spitzer et al., 1983, pp. 63–64)

Between 1.7 and 6.4 percent of the population eventually develops obsessive-compulsive personality disorder, and it is more common in men than women (Fabrega et al., 1991; Weissman, 1993b).

Theories of Obsessive-Compulsive Personality Disorder

There are no family history, twin, or adoption studies specifically focusing on obsessive-compulsive personality disorder. Perhaps surprisingly, family history and twin studies of obsessive-compulsive disorder do not tend to find a link between this disorder and obsessive-compulsive personality disorder (Insel, Hoover, & Murphy, 1983; Torgersen, 1980).

Early psychodynamic theorists attributed this personality disorder to fixation at the anal stage of development because the patient's parents were overly strict and punitive during toilet training (Freud, 1908/1963). Harry Stack Sullivan (1953) argued that

obsessive-compulsive personalities arise when children grow up in homes where there is much anger and hate that is hidden behind superficial love and niceness. The children do not develop interpersonal skills and instead avoid intimacy and follow rigid rules to gain a sense of self-esteem and self-control.

Millon and colleagues (2000) argue that people with this personality disorder had parents who were overcontrolling and punitive when they made mistakes but did not praise or reward them when they did well. Strict limits were set on their behaviors, and as they entered the stage of life when they attempted to assert their desires and resist their parents, the parents responded with firm and harsh discipline. They subsequently retreated and submerged their desire for independence and autonomy, strictly following their parents' rules in order to avoid punishment. They may begin to doubt their own abilities because they have not had the opportunity to test them. Instead, they search for a set of rules and regulations established by others to guide their behaviors.

Treatment for Obsessive-Compulsive Personality Disorder

Supportive therapies may assist people with this disorder in overcoming the crises that bring them in for treatment, and behavioral therapies can be used to decrease compulsive behaviors in persons with this disorder (Beck & Freeman, 1990; Millon et al., 2000). For example, a client may be given the assignment to alter his usual rigid schedule for the day, first by simply getting up 15 minutes later than he usually does and then gradually changing additional elements of his schedule. The client may be taught to use relaxation techniques to overcome anxiety created by alterations in the schedule. He might also write down the automatic negative thoughts he has about changes in the schedule ("Getting up 15 minutes later is going to put my entire day off"), and in the next therapy session, he and the therapist might discuss the evidence for and against these automatic thoughts.

Summing Up

- People with the anxious-fearful personality disorders—avoidant, dependent, and obsessive-compulsive personality disorders—are chronically fearful or concerned.

- People with avoidant personality disorder worry about being criticized.

- People with dependent personality disorder worry about being abandoned.

- People with obsessive-compulsive personality disorder are locked into rigid routines of behavior and become anxious when their routines are violated.

- Some children may be born with temperamental predispositions toward shy and avoidant behaviors, or childhood anxiety may contribute to dependent personalities.

- These disorders may also arise from lack of nurturing parenting and basic fears about one's ability to function competently.

⟲ ALTERNATIVE CONCEPTUALIZATIONS OF PERSONALITY DISORDERS

The DSM-IV scheme for conceptualizing and categorizing personality disorders was intentionally atheoretical. That is, the authors of DSM-IV sought to describe the personality disorders that had been observed in clinical practice and research, independent of any theoretical conceptualization of personality that suggests what personality disorders should exist in humans. Many theorists have criticized this lack of theory in the DSM-IV, however, saying that it impedes the progress of research on personality disorders because a good theory of personality disorders suggests what specific hypotheses about these disorders researchers should be testing. Several theoretical schemes for the personality disorders have been suggested (e.g., Becker, 1998; Cloninger, 1987; Millon et al., 2000; Strack & Lorr, 1994). We discuss two of these that have been the focus of considerable research in recent years.

Five-Factor Model

One of the leading theories of "normal" personality is the **five-factor model,** which posits that any individual's personality is organized along five broad dimensions or factors of personality, often referred to as the Big 5: neuroticism, extraversion, openness to experience, agreeableness, and conscientiousness (see *Concept Review:* Big 5 Personality Factors; Costa & McCrae, 1992). Considerable research does suggest that these five dimensions capture a great deal of the variation in people's personality, and that the personality traits these dimensions describe are strongly influenced by genetics (Costa & Widiger, 1994; Jang et al., 1998). In turn, the DSM-IV personality disorders can be conceptualized along these five dimensions (Widiger et al., 1994). For example, people with antisocial personality disorder can be characterized as high on antagonism

---

CONCEPT REVIEW

The Big 5 Personality Factors

The Big 5 Factor of personality posits that all personality can be characterized by combinations of the five personality factors described in this table.

Factor	Key Characteristics
Neuroticism	Individuals high on neuroticism are chronically anxious, hostile, depressed, self-conscious, impulsive, and have poor coping skills; people low on neuroticism lack these problems.
Extraversion	Individuals high on extraversion are sociable, active, talkative, interpersonally oriented, optimistic, fun-loving and affectionate; people low on extraversion (referred to as introverts) are reserved, sober, aloof, independent, and quiet.
Openness to experience	Individuals high on this factor actively seek and appreciate experiences for their own sake, are curious, imaginative, and willing to entertain new and unconventional ideas; people low on this factor are conventional in their beliefs and attitudes, conservative in tastes, dogmatic, rigid in their beliefs, set in their ways, and emotionally unresponsive.
Agreeableness	Individuals high on this factor are softhearted, good-natured, trusting, helpful, forgiving, and altruistic; people low on this factor are cynical, rude, suspicious, uncooperative, irritable, and can be manipulative, vengeful, and ruthless.
Conscientiousness	Individuals high on this factor are organized, reliable, hard-working, self-directed, punctual, scrupulous, ambitious, and persevering; people low on this factor are aimless, unreliable, lazy, careless, lax, negligent, and hedonistic.

Source: Costa & McCrae, 1992.

and low on conscientiousness. People with dependent personality disorder can be characterized as high on agreeableness and high on neuroticism.

One advantage of translating the DSM-IV personality disorders into the Big 5 personality traits is that research on gender differences in the Big 5 can be used to make hypotheses about what kind of gender differences are likely to occur in the personality disorders (Corbitt & Widiger, 1995). For example, women tend to score higher on both neuroticism and agreeableness than men, and if dependent personality disorder is an extreme version of this personality constellation, then we would expect women to be diagnosed with this personality disorder more than men, as they are (Widiger et al., 1994). On the other hand, the five-factor model would suggest that there should be a personality disorder characterized by antagonistic close-mindedness, and because men tend to score higher on both antagonism and close-mindedness, this personality disorder should be more frequently diagnosed in men than in women (Widiger, 1998).

There is no personality disorder in the DSM-IV for antagonistic close-mindedness, however. Thus, the five-factor model suggests a new personality disorder that could be the focus of new research, and also suggests some hypotheses about the distribution of this disorder in males versus females. It is this guiding of research that is provided by a theory such as the five-factor model that leads many researchers to argue that DSM-IV should not be so atheoretical.

Interpersonal Circumplex Model

Another dimensional approach to personality is the **interpersonal circumplex model** (Leary, 1957; Kiesler, 1986; Wiggins, 1982). The interpersonal circumplex model derives from interpersonal theories of normal and abnormal behavior, such as the theory of Henry Stack Sullivan (see Chapter 2; Pincus, 1994). According to this model, personality can be captured by two primary dimensions: dominance versus submission, and nurturance versus cold-heartedness. Figure 12.1 illustrates how crossing these two dimensions creates eight octants in a circumplex that represent blends of these two dimensions. Thus, a person who is high on dominance and high on nurturance is gregarious and extraverted, whereas a person who is high on dominance and high on cold-heartedness is arrogant and calculating. At least 6 of the 11 personality disorders listed in the DSM-IV can be easily reconceptualized via the interpersonal circumplex (see Figure 12.2; Gurtman, 1994; Wiggins & Pincus, 1994). For example, people with avoidant personality disorder score near the extreme of the submissiveness dimension, whereas people with schizoid personality disorder score in between submis-

siveness and cold-heartedness, and people with antisocial personality disorder score at the extreme of the cold-heartedness dimension.

Both the five-factor model and the interpersonal circumplex model are dimensional models of personality and personality disorders—they characterize personality along a discrete number of dimensions and view personality disorders as extremes of these dimensions. In contrast, the DSM-IV and some other models of personality disorders are categorical—they view personality disorders qualitatively, not just quantitatively, different from normal personality (see Davis &

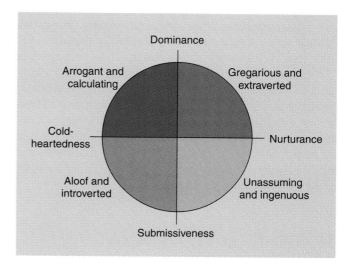

FIGURE 12.1 The Interpersonal Circumplex Model of Personality. The interpersonal circumplex model of personality holds that most personality characteristics represent a cross of the dimensions of nurturance and dominance.

Source: Wiggins & Pincus, 1994.

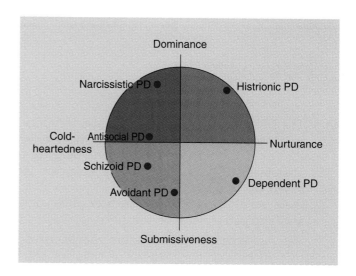

FIGURE 12.2 Personality Disorders on the Interpersonal Circumplex. At least six of the DSM-IV personality disorders can be characterized along the dimensions in the interpersonal circumplex (PD = personality disorder).

Source: Gurtman, 1994.

Millon, 1998). Critics of dimensional models note that redefining personality disorders in light of theories of normal personality does not avoid the difficult questions of where we should draw cut-offs between what is normal and what is pathological. In addition, just because dimensional models like the five-factor model and the circumplex model describe normal personality well, this does not mean that they describe personality disorders well (Davis & Millon, 1998). Dimensional models are usually based on extensive empirical research on people in the general population and they may be unlikely to capture the personality characteristics of that small portion of the population that has extreme personality disturbances.

These debates about the appropriate conceptualization and categorization of personality disorders are likely to continue for many years. These debates are difficult to resolve in part because it is inherently difficult to "carve nature at the joints" and derive accurate ways of describing personality and its variants. These debates are also difficult to resolve because the personality disorders do not represent discrete and acute sets of symptoms, as do many of the Axis I disorders, but appear to be chronic, pervasive, and amorphous by their very nature.

☉ BIO-PSYCHO-SOCIAL INTEGRATION

Although empirical research on the personality disorders is too lacking to allow for a clear integration of biological, psychological, and social factors impinging on these disorders, some theoretical models have attempted this integration and are serving as the basis for current research (Millon et al., 2000; Siever & Davis, 1991). At the root of many of the personality disorders may be a biological predisposition to a certain kind of temperament: an anxious and fearful temperament in the case of avoidant and schizotypal personality disorders, an impulsive and aggressive temperament in the case of borderline and antisocial personality disorders, and a labile, overly emotional temperament in the case of borderline and histrionic personality disorders. Children born with any of these temperaments are difficult to parent effectively, but if parents can be supportive of them and still set appropriate limits on their behavior, the children may never develop severe enough behavioral or emotional problems to be diagnosed with a personality disorder. If parents are unable to counteract children's temperamental vulnerabilities or if they exacerbate these vulnerabilities by engaging in harsh, critical, and unsupportive parenting or overprotective and indulgent parenting, then the children's temperamental vulnerabilities may grow into severe behavioral and emotional problems. These problems will influence how others—teachers, peers, and eventually employers and mates—interact with individuals, perhaps in ways that further exacerbate their temperamental vulnerabilities. Thus, out of the interaction between a child's biologically based temperament and the reactions of others to that temperament may emerge a lifelong pattern of dysfunction that we call a personality disorder.

Chapter Summary

- The DSM-IV divides the personality disorders into three clusters: the odd-eccentric disorders, the dramatic-emotional disorders, and the anxious-fearful disorders. This organization is based on symptom clusters. It assumes that there is a dividing line between normal personality and pathological personality.

- The odd-eccentric disorders are characterized by odd or eccentric patterns of behavior and thought, including paranoia, extreme social withdrawal or inappropriate social interactions, and magical or illusory thinking. This group of disorders, particularly schizotypal personality disorder, may be linked to schizophrenia genetically and may represent mild variations of schizophrenia. Studies of persons seeking therapy show that these disorders are more common in men than in women, although it is not clear why this is true. People with these disorders tend to have poor social relationships and are at increased risk for some acute psychiatric disorders, especially depression and schizophrenia.

- Psychoanalytic theorists view paranoid personality disorder as the result of the use of projection as a defense and schizoid personality disorder as the result of extremely dysfunctional parent-child relationships in which the child did not learn to give or receive love. Cognitive theorists view each of the odd-eccentric personality disorders as the result of particular cognitive distortions.

- Psychoanalytic and cognitive therapies have been devised for these disorders, but they have not been empirically tested for their efficacy. Neuroleptic drugs appear to reduce the odd thinking of people with schizotypal personality disorder.

- The dramatic-emotional personality disorders include four disorders characterized by dramatic, erratic, and emotional behavior and interpersonal relationships: antisocial personality disorder, histrionic personality disorder, borderline personality disorder, and narcissistic personality disorder. Persons with these disorders tend to be manipulative, volatile, and uncaring in social relationships and prone to impulsive behaviors.

- Antisocial personality disorder is one of the most common personality disorders and is more common in men than in women. There is substantial support for a genetic influence on antisocial behaviors, and some studies suggest that people with this personality disorder may suffer from low levels of serotonin, low levels of arousability, an attention deficit disorder, and extreme problems in inhibiting impulsive behaviors. These people tend to have had harsh and inconsistent parenting and to develop a set of assumptions about the world that promotes aggressive responding. Psychotherapy is not considered extremely effective for people with antisocial personality disorder. Lithium and the serotonin reuptake inhibitors may help to control their impulsive behaviors.

- People with borderline personality disorder show lability in their moods, self-concept, and interpersonal relationships. This disorder is more common in women than in men. People with the disorder may suffer from low levels of serotonin, which lead to impulsive behaviors. There is little evidence that borderline personality disorder is transmitted genetically, but the family members of people with this disorder show high rates of mood disorders.

- Psychoanalytic theorists argue that this disorder is the result of poorly developed and integrated views of the self, which result from poor early relationships with caregivers. Cognitive theorists see this disorder as stemming from deficits in self-concept. Many people with

this disorder were the victims of physical and sexual abuse in childhood. Drug treatments have not proven very effective for this disorder. Psychoanalytic and cognitive therapies focus on establishing a stronger self-identity in people with this disorder.

- Histrionic and narcissistic personality disorders are both characterized by dramatic self-presentations and unstable personal relationships. The person with histrionic personality disorder looks to others for approval, whereas the person with narcissistic personality disorder relies on his or her own self-evaluations.

- Psychoanalytic theorists see histrionic personality disorder, which is more common in women, as the result of deep dependency needs and repression of emotion, and they see narcissistic personality disorder, which is more common in men, as the result of either fixation at a self-centered stage of self-concept or as a reaction formation against feelings of low self-worth. Cognitive theorists see these disorders as the result of assumptions about one's worth relative to other people.

- The anxious-fearful personality disorders include three disorders characterized by anxious and fearful emotions and chronic self-doubt, leading to maladaptive behaviors: dependent personality disorder, avoidant personality disorder, and obsessive-compulsive personality disorder.

- Dependent personality disorder is more common in women, obsessive-compulsive personality disorder is more common in men, and avoidant personality disorder is equally common in men and women. Dependent and avoidant personality disorders tend to run in families, but it is not clear whether this is due to genetics or to family environments.

- Psychoanalysts view dependent personality disorder as the result of fixation at the oral stage of development and obsessive-compulsive personality disorder as the result of fixation at the anal stage of development. Cognitive theorists suggest that avoidant personality disorder results from beliefs about being worthless as the result of rejection by others in early life, that dependent personality disorder results from feelings of inadequacy plus parental overprotection, and that obsessive-compulsive disorder results from harsh discipline and parental criticism and beliefs that one must be perfect to be loved.

- Several alternative models of the personality disorders have been developed. Two prominent models are based on normal theories of personality. The five-factor model of personality suggests that there are five basic traits that describe most of personality: neuroticism, extraversion, openness to experience, agreeableness, and conscientiousness. Personality disorders may be extreme variants of these traits. The interpersonal circumplex theory suggests that personality can be conceptualized as a cross between two dimensions: dominance versus submission, and nurturance versus cold-heartedness. Again, personality disorders may be extreme variants of the traits resulting from the intersection of these two dimensions.

Key Terms

personality 404

personality trait 404

personality disorder 404

odd-eccentric personality disorders 409

paranoid personality disorder 409

schizoid personality disorder 411

schizotypal personality disorder 412

dramatic-emotional personality disorders 415

antisocial personality disorder 415

serotonin 418

executive functions 419

borderline personality disorder 421

splitting 423

histrionic personality disorder 426

narcissistic personality disorder 427

anxious-fearful personality disorders 428

avoidant personality disorder 429

dependent personality disorder 430

obsessive-compulsive personality disorder 432

five-factor model 434

interpersonal circumplex model 435

Critical Thinking Questions

1. Can you think of any occupations in which people with paranoid personality disorder might do well? Or do you think their paranoia would be dysfunctional in any occupation? Explain.

2. If schizoid people generally are not distressed by their own behavior and can function reasonably well in society, what criteria are used to label schizoid personality a disorder?

3. Some people argue that criminals who have been in jail for a very long time and are now elderly should be released, even if they have not finished serving their sentences, because the statistics suggest they will have "outgrown" their antisocial tendencies. How do you feel about this argument?

4. If a criminal could prove he has antisocial personality disorder, do you think this should absolve him or her in any way from responsibility for criminal acts?

5. Given the family dynamics that may contribute to the development of borderline personality disorder, do you think family therapy would be helpful in treating people with this disorder? Or might they do better in a therapy that did not include other family members?

Daniel Nevins
In the Fields

Youth, even in its sorrows, always has a brilliancy of its own.

—*Victor Hugo, "Saint Denis,"* Les Miserables
(1962; translated by Charles E. Wilbour)

CHAPTER
13

Childhood Disorders

CHAPTER OVERVIEW
Behavior Disorders

The behavior disorders include attention-deficit/hyperactivity disorder, conduct disorder, and oppositional defiant disorder. Children with attention-deficit/hyperactivity disorder have trouble maintaining attention and controlling impulsive behavior and are hyperactive. Children with conduct or oppositional defiant disorder engage in frequent antisocial or defiant behavior.

Viewpoints:
Is ADHD a Fad Diagnosis?

Separation Anxiety Disorder

One of the most common emotional disorders of childhood is separation anxiety disorder, in which children are extremely anxious about any separation from their primary caregivers. Behavioral and cognitive therapies are often used to treat this disorder.

Pushing the Boundaries:
Massage Therapy

Elimination Disorders

The two elimination disorders are enuresis—uncontrolled wetting—and encopresis—uncontrolled bowel movements. The most effective treatment is a behavioral technique that teaches children to awaken at night when they need to go to the bathroom.

Disorders of Cognitive, Motor, and Communication Skills

Disorders of cognitive, motor, and communication skills involve deficits and delays in the development of fundamental skills. These include learning disorders, motor skills disorder, and the communication disorders.

Mental Retardation

Children with mental retardation have deficits in cognitive skills that can range from mild to severe. A number of genetic factors and biological traumas in the early years of life can contribute to mental retardation. Sociocultural factors, such as poverty or lack of good education, can also contribute to mental retardation.

Autism

Autism is characterized by a wide array of deficits in communication and social interactions. Autism has biological roots but often responds well to behavioral interventions. Autism is one of a group of disorders called the pervasive developmental disorders, which involve severe and lasting impairment in several areas of development, including social interactions, communication with others, everyday behaviors, interests, and activities.

Extraordinary People:
Thinking in Pictures

Bio-Psycho-Social Integration
Chapter Summary
Key Terms
Critical Thinking Questions

We like to think of childhood as a time relatively free from stress, when boys and girls can enjoy the simple pleasures of everyday life and are immune from major psychological problems. Yet nearly 20 percent of children and almost 40 percent of adolescents suffer from significant emotional or behavioral disorders (Kessler et al., 1994; Newman et al., 1996; Roberts, Attkisson, & Rosenblatt, 1998). Thus, a substantial minority of children and adolescents are not living carefree existences; instead, they are experiencing distressing symptoms severe enough to warrant attention from mental-health professionals.

For some children, psychological symptoms and disorders are linked to major stressors in their environment. A large and growing number of children in the United States and in other countries are faced with severe circumstances that could overwhelm the coping capacities of adults. In the United States, about one in four children is the victim of severe physical abuse each year, and about one in five children lives below the poverty line (Flisher et al., 1997; Wolfner & Gelles, 1993). Children living in the inner city, particularly in the projects where poor families often are housed, are often exposed to violence. For example, in one study of fifth-grade children in a poor area of New Orleans, Louisiana, 91 percent reported witnessing some sort of violence in the last year; 26 percent of the children had witnessed a shooting, 40 percent had seen dead bodies in their neighborhoods, and 49 percent had seen someone wounded. Over half of the children had been the

Children, particularly those in urban areas, may be exposed to tremendous violence even at a young age.

victims of violence (Osofsky et al., 1993). Another study of drive-by shootings in Los Angeles found that in one year, 677 adolescents had been shot at, 429 had suffered gunshot wounds, and 36 had died from their injuries (Hutson, Anglin, & Pratts, 1994).

Children facing any one of these major stressors or risks are more likely than other children to have significant psychological problems (Compas, 1987; Flisher et al., 1997). A young girl named Melanie who lives in a violence-torn inner-city neighborhood described a recurrent dream (Plantenga, 1991, p. 27):

Voices

I am coming out of a supermarket and a man
is carrying a gun and tells me to give
him all my money. I give him my purse
and my jewelry, but he still shoots me.
And then I find myself in a funeral home. I
see my mom, my dad and my brother
crying and the rest of my family. I go up to
the coffin and see a person who reminds
me of me. I see myself. I start to cry and I
wake up.

Sadly, most children who face one such stressor are beset by multiple stressors. For example, children in poverty are more likely than other children to witness or be the victims of violence, to use illicit drugs, to engage in unprotected sexual intercourse, and to face racial and ethnic discrimination and harassment. These stressors appear to have a cumulative effect on children's risk for psychological problems: The more stressors a child encounters, the more likely he or she is to experience severe psychological symptoms (Osofsky et al., 1993).

What is remarkable is that many, perhaps most, children who face major stressors do *not* develop severe psychological symptoms or disorders. These children have been referred to as *resilient* or *invulnerable* children (Garmezy, 1991; Masten et al., 1993). We do not know exactly what makes these children so resilient in the face of stress, but having at least one healthy and competent adult that a child can rely on in his or her daily life seems to help. For example, studies of homeless children suggest that those who have high-quality interactions with a parent are no more likely to develop psychological problems than are children who are not homeless (Masten et al., 1993). Conversely, many children who develop psychological disorders do not have any major stressors in their lives to which the development of the disorders can be linked. These children may come from privileged backgrounds in which they have not been exposed to any traumas or chronic problems.

Children who have supportive adults in their lives appear more resilient to stress.

It seems that among children, as among adults, most psychological disorders are the result of multiple factors, such as biological predispositions plus environmental stressors. One biological factor that has been implicated in the development of many psychological disorders in children is temperament. *Temperament* refers to a child's arousability and general mood. Children with "difficult" temperaments are highly sensitive to stimulation, become upset easily, and have trouble calming themselves when upset. They also tend to have generally negative moods and trouble adapting to new situations, particularly social situations (Thomas & Chess, 1984). Children with difficult temperaments are more likely than other children to have both minor and major psychological problems during childhood and later in life (Rutter, 1987).

Temperament probably has strong biological roots, including genetic roots (Campos et al., 1989). The link between temperament and the development of psychological problems is not exclusively biological, however. Children with difficult temperaments elicit more negative interactions from others, including their parents. Adults act less affectionately toward children with difficult temperaments, and other children are more likely to be hostile toward these children. It may be the negative environments children with difficult temperaments create for themselves that contribute to psychological problems rather than the temperaments per se. Conversely, children with difficult temperaments who receive high-quality parenting are not at high risk for psychological problems, whereas children with difficult temperaments who are part of dysfunctional families are at high risk (Rutter, 1987).

In this chapter, we review the roles that biology and psychosocial factors play in the development of specific psychological disorders in children. There are a large number of disorders that can be diagnosed in children. The *Concept Review:* Disorders of Childhood (p. 444) lists several disorders that are usually first diagnosed in childhood or infancy. In addition to these disorders, several disorders we have already discussed, especially depression (see Chapter 8) and the anxiety disorders (see Chapters 6 and 7), can also occur for the first time during childhood or adolescence.

We focus on some of the most common and severe of the disorders that usually begin in infancy or childhood. First, we discuss the behavioral disorders, specifically attention-deficit/hyperactivity disorder, conduct disorder, and oppositional defiant disorder. Children with these disorders have trouble paying attention and controlling socially inappropriate behaviors. Then we turn to an anxiety disorder that is prevalent in children, separation anxiety disorder.

The third group of disorders we discuss is the elimination disorders, enuresis and encopresis. Children with these disorders have trouble controlling bladder and bowel movements far beyond the age at which most children learn to control them. The fourth is disorders of cognitive, motor and social skills, and the fifth is mental retardation. Finally, the sixth group is pervasive developmental disorders. Within this sixth group, we focus on autism.

The study of childhood disorders has expanded greatly in the last two decades and has grown into a new field known as *developmental psychopathology.* Developmental psychopathologists try to understand when children's behaviors cross the line from the normal perturbations of childhood into unusual or abnormal problems that merit concern. Most children have transient emotional or behavioral problems sometime during childhood. That is, most children will go through periods in which they are unusually fearful or easily distressed or engage in behaviors such as lying or stealing, but these periods pass relatively quickly and are often specific to certain situations. Differentiating these normal periods of distress from signs of a developing psychological disorder is not easy. Developmental psychopathologists also try to understand the impact of normal development on the shape and form that abnormal behaviors will take. That is, children's levels of cognitive, social, and emotional development can affect the types of symptoms they will show. These developmental considerations make the assessment, diagnosis, and treatment of childhood disorders quite challenging, but helping disturbed children overcome their problems and get back on the path to healthy development can be highly rewarding.

☺ BEHAVIOR DISORDERS

The *behavior disorders* have been the focus of a great deal of the research on children's disorders, probably because children with these disorders are quite difficult to

CONCEPT REVIEW

Disorders of Childhood

These disorders have their first onset in childhood.

Category	Specific Disorders
Behavior disorders	Attention-deficit/hyperactivity disorder Conduct disorder Oppositional defiant disorder
Elimination disorders	Eneuresis Encopresis

Disorders in cognitive, motor, and social skills	Learning disorders
	    Reading disorder
	    Mathematics disorder
	    Disorder of written expression
	Motor skills disorder
	    Developmental coordination disorder
	Communication disorders
	    Expressive language disorder
	    Phonological disorder
	    Stuttering

Mental retardation	Mild, moderate, severe, and profound mental retardation
Pervasive developmental disorders	Autism Rett's disorder Childhood disintegrative disorder Asperger's disorder
Tic disorders	Tourette's disorder Chronic motor or focal tic disorder Transient tic disorder
Feeding and eating disorders	Pica Rumination disorder Feeding disorder of infancy or early childhood
Other disorders	Separation anxiety Selective mutism Reactive attachment disorder Stereotypic movement disorder

deal with, and these children's behaviors can exact a heavy toll on society. The three behavior disorders we discuss are attention-deficit/hyperactivity disorder, conduct disorder, and oppositional defiant disorder. These are distinct disorders, but they often co-occur in the same child (see *Concept Review:* Behavior Disorders).

Attention-Deficit/Hyperactivity Disorder

"Pay attention! Slow down! You're so hyper today!" These are phrases that most children hear their parents saying to them at least occasionally. A major focus of socialization is helping children learn to pay attention, control their impulses, and organize their behaviors so that they can accomplish long-term goals. Some children have tremendous trouble learning these skills, however, and may be diagnosed with **attention-deficit/hyperactivity disorder,** or **ADHD** (see Table 13.1, p. 446). Eddie is a young boy with ADHD (adapted from Spitzer et al., 1994, pp. 351–352):

CASE STUDY

Eddie, age 9, was referred to a child psychiatrist at the request of his school because of the difficulties he creates in class. His teacher complains that he is so restless that his

CONCEPT REVIEW

Behavior Disorders

The behavioral disorders involve extreme inattention, hyperactivity, and socially inappropriate behavior.

Disorder	Symptoms	Proposed Etiologies	Treatments
Attention-deficit/hyperactivity disorder (ADHD)	Inattention, hyperactivity, impulsivity	1. Immaturity of brain, particularly frontal lobes, caudate nucleus, and corpus callosum 2. Genetic predisposition 3. Prenatal and birth complications 4. Disrupted families	1. Stimulant drugs (e.g., Ritalin) 2. Behavior therapy focused on reinforcing attentive, goal-directed behaviors and extinguishing impulsive and hyperactive behaviors
Conduct disorder	Behaviors that violate the basic rights of others and the norms for social behavior	1. Genetic predisposition 2. Deficits in brain regions involved in planning and controlling behavior 3. Difficult temperament 4. Lower physiological arousal to punishment 5. Serotonin imbalances 6. Higher testosterone 7. Poor parental supervision, parental uninvolvement, parental violence 8. Delinquent peer groups. 9. Cognitions that promote aggression	1. Antidepressants, neuroleptics, stimulants, and lithium 2. Cognitive-behavior therapy focused on changing hostile cognitions, teaching children to take others' perspectives, and teaching problem-solving skills
Oppositional defiant disorder	Argumentativeness, negativity, irritability, defiance; but behaviors not as severe as in conduct disorder	Same as conduct disorder, see Figure 13.1 for developmental progression	Same as conduct disorder

classmates are unable to concentrate. He is hardly ever in his seat and mostly roams around the class, talking to other children while they are working. When the teacher is able to get him to stay in his seat, he fidgets with his hands and feet and drops things on the floor. He never seems to know what he is going to do next and may suddenly do something quite outrageous. His most recent suspension from school was for swinging from the fluorescent light fixture over the blackboard. Because he was unable to climb down again, the class was in an uproar.

His mother says that Eddie's behavior has been difficult since he was a toddler and that, as a 3-year-old, he was unbearably restless and demanding. He has always required little sleep and been awake before anyone else. When he was small, "he got into everything," particularly in the early morning, when he would awaken at 4:30 A.M. or 5:00 A.M. and go downstairs by himself. His parents would awaken to find the living room or kitchen "demolished." When he was 4 years old, he managed to unlock the door of the apartment and wander off into a busy main street but, fortunately, was rescued from oncoming traffic by a passerby.

Eddie has no interest in TV and dislikes games or toys that require any concentration or patience. He is not popular with other children and at home prefers to be outdoors, playing with his dog or riding his bike. If he does play with toys, his games are messy and destructive, and his mother cannot get him to keep his things in any order.

Eddie's difficulties in paying attention and his impulsivity go far beyond what is normal for a child his age. Most elementary school–aged children can sit still for some period of time, like to engage in at least some games that require patience and concentration, and can inhibit their impulses to jump up in class and

TABLE 13.1
DSM-IV
Symptoms of Attention-Deficit/Hyperactivity Disorder (ADHD)

The symptoms of attention-deficit/hyperactivity disorder fall into three clusters: inattention, hyperactivity, and impulsivity.

Inattention

Does not pay attention to details and makes careless mistakes

Has difficulty sustaining attention

Does not seem to be listening when others are talking

Does not follow through on instructions or finish tasks

Has difficulty organizing behaviors

Avoids activities that require sustained effort and attention

Loses things frequently

Is easily distracted

Is forgetful

Hyperactivity

Fidgets with hands or feet and squirms in seat

Is restless, leaving his or her seat or running around when it is inappropriate

Has difficulty engaging in quiet activities

Impulsivity

Blurts out responses while others are talking

Has difficulty waiting his or her turn

Reprinted with permission from the *Diagnostic and Statistical Manual of Mental Disorders*, Fourth Edition. Copyright 2000 American Psychiatric Association.

Children usually have a great deal of energy and enthusiasm for life, which can make it difficult to define hyperactivity in children.

are rejected outright by other children (Hinshaw & Melnick, 1995). When interacting with their peers, children with ADHD are disorganized and never finish anything. They are intrusive, irritable, and demanding. They want to play by their own rules and have explosive tempers so when things do not go their way, they may become physically violent (Whalen & Henker, 1998). Here is how the classmates of hyperactive boys describe them (Henker & Whalen, 1989, p. 216):

> They can't sit still; they don't pay attention to the teacher; they mess around and get into trouble; they try to get others into trouble; they are rude; they get mad when they don't get their way; and they say they can beat everybody up.

The behavioral problems of some children with ADHD are so severe that the children may also be diagnosed with a **conduct disorder.** As we discuss shortly, children with conduct disorders grossly violate the norms for appropriate behavior toward others by acting in uncaring and even violent ways. Between 45 and 60 percent of children with ADHD develop conduct disorders, abuse drugs, or become juvenile delinquents (Barkley et al., 1990; Gittelman et al., 1985).

ADHD has become a popular diagnosis to give to children who are disruptive in school or at home, and the media attention on ADHD over the last few years has made it seem that there is an epidemic of this disorder. We discuss the controversy over the "fad" of ADHD in *Viewpoints:* Is ADHD a Fad Diagnosis? However, various epidemiological studies indicate that only 1 to 7 percent of children develop ADHD (Hinshaw,

talk to other children or to walk out into busy traffic. Eddie cannot do any of these things. His behavior has a character of being driven and disorganized, following one whim and then the next.

Children like Eddie often do poorly in school. Because they cannot pay attention or quell their hyperactivity, they do not learn the material they are being taught and thus perform below their intellectual capabilities (Whalen & Henker, 1998). In addition, 20 to 25 percent of children with ADHD may have serious learning disabilities that make it doubly hard for them to concentrate in school and to learn (Barkley, 1990).

Children with ADHD also have extremely poor relationships with other children and, like Eddie, often

VIEWPOINTS

Is ADHD a Fad Diagnosis?

Attention-deficit/hyperactivity disorder is now the most widely diagnosed mental disorder of childhood. The number of children diagnosed with ADHD skyrocketed in the early 1900s, more than doubling between 1990 and 1995 (Zito et al., 1998), and has continued to increase since then. In turn, the number of children taking Ritalin increased by 250 percent in the 1990s. Some studies suggest that as many as 12 percent of boys are on Ritalin currently, and the number of girls taking the drug is continuing to increase.

It is ADHD the fad diagnosis of the last decade? Those who would answer "yes" to this question argue that schools and teachers are too motivated to label children, especially energetic boys, as having ADHD and to get them on Ritalin so that they can control these children better. These children are taken to pediatricians, who are not trained adequately in diagnosing ADHD, and who largely take the teachers' and parents' word that the child is hyperactive and has attention problems, and the pediatrician prescribes Ritalin.

It is difficult to gather evidence for these views, but the large discrepancies across cities and geographic regions in the number of children diagnosed with ADHD and prescribed Ritalin certainly seem suspicious. In 1995, the number of people taking Ritalin in Virginia was 2.4 times higher than in neighboring West Virginia, and nearly 4 times higher than in California. Even within states, there are discrepancies across counties in Ritalin consumption. For example, in 1991, 4.1 percent of 6- to 12-year-old boys in New York were taking Ritalin, but consumption rates across counties varied by a factor of 10 in some cases (Carlson, 2000).

Many adults are now diagnosing themselves as having ADHD (Kelly & Ramundo, 1995; Hallowell &

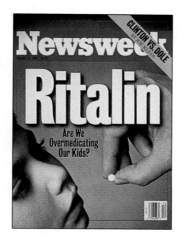

Some people think that attention deficit/hyperactivity disorder is being over diagnosed, and too many children are being prescribed Ritalin and other stimulant drugs.

Ratey, 1994). However, some studies have suggested that the full syndrome of ADHD in adulthood is quite rare, and ADHD is probably being overdiagnosed currently in adults (Feehan, McGee, & Williams, 1993; Mannuzza et al., 1998). Critics of the "adult ADHD movement" argue that these adults, many of whom have had long histories of underachievement and poor relationships, are using the diagnosis of ADHD to relieve their guilt and responsibility for their problems.

On the other side of the debate are those who argue that the increase in diagnoses of ADHD and the use of Ritalin reflects an increased public awareness of this disorder and realization that effective treatments are available. In 1991, the U.S. government designated ADHD as a handicapping condition, and directed educational institutions to establish screening and diagnostic procedures for ADHD. Thus, for the first time, children who were previously just considered "problems" were recognized as having a treatable mental disorder, and given special education and services. Similarly, the increase in diagnoses of ADHD in adults reflects the fact that childhood disorders, including ADHD, tended to be underdiagnosed in previous decades, so many adults who had ADHD as children were not diagnosed.

Clearly, it is important for parents, educators, and mental-health specialists to continue to engage in this debate and search for the truth. Stimulant drugs do have side effects, and thus should only be prescribed to children who have a valid diagnosis of ADHD. On the other hand, children with ADHD should not be deprived of treatments that could improve their school performance, social relationships, and self-esteem.

1994; McGee et al., 1990). Boys are about three times more likely than girls to develop ADHD in childhood and early adolescence (Cohen, Cohen, Kasen, Velez, Hartmark, Johnson et al., 1993). ADHD is found across most cultures and ethnic groups.

The long-term outcomes for children with ADHD vary considerably. The symptoms of ADHD persist from childhood into adolescence for about two-thirds of these children (Hinshaw, 1994; Mannuzza et al., 1998). As adults, children were diagnosed with ADHD are at increased risk for antisocial personality disorder, substance abuse, marital problems, traffic accidents, legal infractions, and frequent job changes (Mannuzza et al., 1998). Those children who develop serious conduct problems in addition to ADHD fare worse and tend to have criminal behavior, drug abuse, and emotional problems as adults (Moffitt, 1990). However, many children "grow out" of ADHD. By early adulthood, their symptoms of ADHD have passed and they go on to lead normal and healthy lives (Mannuzza et al, 1998).

Biological Contributors to ADHD

ADHD was formerly referred to as *minimal brain damage*, under the assumption that these children's attentional deficits and hyperactivity were due to some sort of mild brain damage. Most children who develop ADHD, however, have no histories of brain injury, and most children with some brain injury do not develop ADHD.

Modern studies have shown, however, that ADHD children differ from children with no psychological disorders on a variety of measures of neurological functioning and cerebral blood flow (Barkley, 1996). The areas of the brain most likely involved in ADHD include the frontal lobes, the caudate nucleus within the basal ganglia, the corpus callosum which connects the two lobes of the brain, and the pathways between these structures (Whalen & Henker, 1998). Each of these brain areas and pathways plays an important role in the deployment of attention, the regulation of impulses and the planning of complex behavior. One hypothesis is that children with ADHD are neurologically immature—their brains are slower in developing than are other children's—and this is why they are unable to maintain attention and control their behavior at a level that is appropriate for their age. This immaturity hypothesis helps to explain why the symptoms of ADHD decline with age in many children.

ADHD runs in families. Between 10 and 35 percent of the immediate family members of children with ADHD are also likely to have the disorder (Barkley, 1996; Biederman et al., 1986, 1990). Several other disorders also tend to run in the families of children with

ADHD, including antisocial personality disorder, alcoholism, and depression (Barkley, 1991; Faraone et al., 1991). Twin studies and adoption studies also suggest that genetic factors play a role in vulnerability to ADHD (Eaves et al., 1997; Gilger et al, 1992; Nadder et al., 1998; Rhee et al., 1999), although it is not clear exactly what aspects of the ADHD syndrome are inherited, whether they be problems with attention, hyperactivity, impulsivity, or aggressivity.

Children with ADHD often have histories of prenatal and birth complications, including maternal ingestion of large amounts of nicotine or barbiturates during pregnancy, low birth weight, premature delivery, and difficult delivery leading to oxygen deprivation (Anastopoulos & Barkley, 1988; Sprich-Buckminster et al., 1993). Some investigators suspect that moderate-to-severe drinking by mothers during pregnancy can lead to the kinds of problems in inhibiting behaviors seen in children with ADHD. As preschoolers, some of these children were exposed to high concentrations of lead, when they ingested lead-based paint (Fergusson, Horwood, & Lynskey, 1993). The popular notion that hyperactivity in children is caused by dietary factors, such as the consumption of large amounts of sugar, has not been supported in controlled studies (Whalen & Henker, 1998).

Psychological and Sociocultural Contributors to ADHD

Children with ADHD are more likely than children without psychological disturbances to belong to families in which there are frequent disruptions, such as changes in residence or parental divorce (Barkley et al., 1990). Their fathers are more prone to antisocial and criminal behavior, and their interactions with their mothers are often marked with hostility and conflict (Barkley et al., 1990). Some investigators argue that there is a nongenetic form of ADHD that is caused by environmental adversity (Bauermeister et al., 1992). Others argue, however, that both ADHD and difficult family environments are the result of genetic predispositions to "externalizing behaviors" (see Barkley, 1996).

Treatments for ADHD

The most common treatment for ADHD in children is stimulant drugs, such as methylphenidate (trade name Ritalin) and dextroamphetamine (trade name Dexedrine). It may seem odd to give a stimulant drug to a hyperactive child, but between 70 and 85 percent of ADHD children respond to these drugs with *decreases* in demanding, disruptive, and noncompliant behavior (Gadow, 1992). They also show increases in positive mood, in the ability to be goal-directed, and in the quality of their interactions with others (Berman, Douglas, & Barr, 1999).

The effects of stimulant drugs on the behavior of ADHD children are not as paradoxical as it might seem on the surface. Several neurological studies of children with ADHD show that they suffer from underarousal rather than overarousal of areas of the brain involved in attention (Barkley, 1996). This underarousal may make it impossible for children to maintain attention, which then may lead to their hyperactive behavior as a by-product, just as some people become hyperactive when they are sleepy and desperately trying to stay awake. Stimulant drugs may bring these children's levels of arousal in these key areas up to normal levels. In addition, children without ADHD who are given stimulant drugs also show increases in attention and decreases in disruptive behavior (Rapport et al., 1987).

Unfortunately, the gains made by ADHD children when treated with stimulants alone are short term (Whalen & Henker, 1998). Longer-term gains can be had by combining stimulant therapy with behavioral therapy that focuses on reinforcing attentive, goal-directed, and prosocial behaviors and extinguishing impulsive and hyperactive behaviors (DuPaul & Barkley, 1993). Parents may be taught behavioral methods for promoting positive behaviors and extinguishing maladaptive behaviors in their children. In addition, parents' own psychological problems and the impairments in parenting skills that these problems create may be the focus of psychosocial interventions for children with ADHD.

An ADHD child and his parents might design a contract that says that every time the child complies with a request from his parents to wash his hands, to set the dinner table, and to put away his toys, he earns a chip. At the end of each week, he can exchange his chips for toys or fun activities. Each time the child refuses to comply, however, he loses a chip. If the child throws a tantrum or becomes aggressive, he must go to his room for a time out. Such techniques can help parents break the cycle of arguments with their children that lead to escalations in the children's behaviors that, in turn, lead to more arguments and perhaps physical violence. These techniques also help children learn to anticipate the consequences of their behaviors and make less impulsive choices about their behaviors.

Several studies suggest that the combination of stimulant therapy and psychosocial therapy is more likely to lead to both short-term and long-term improvements than either type of therapy alone (DuPaul & Hoff, 1998). Interventions that focus on promoting parental competence and on treating aggression and defiance in ADHD children very early in childhood appear to lead to the most positive long-term outcomes (Fischer et al., 1993).

Conduct Disorder and Oppositional Defiant Disorder

Have you ever lied? Have you ever stolen something? Have you ever hit someone? Most of us would have to answer "yes" to some and probably all of these questions. Many fewer of us would answer "yes" to the following questions:

- Have you ever pulled a knife or a gun on another person?

- Have you ever forced someone into sexual activity?

- Have you ever deliberately set fire with the hope of doing serious damage to someone else's property?

- Have you ever broken into someone else's car or house with the intention of stealing?

Children who have **conduct disorder** often answer "yes" to these questions and engage in other serious trangressions of societal norms for behavior (see Table 13.2, p. 450). These children have chronic patterns of unconcern for the basic rights of others. Consider the following case of a boy named Phillip (from Jenkins, 1973, pp. 60–64):

CASE STUDY

Phillip, age 12, was suspended from a small-town Iowa school and referred for psychiatric treatment by his principal, who sent along the following note with Phillip:

This child has been a continual problem since coming to our school. He does not get along on the playground because he is mean to other children. He disobeys school rules, teases the patrol children, steals from the other children, and defies all authority. Phillip keeps getting into fights with other children on the bus.

He has been suspended from cafeteria privileges several times for fighting, pushing, and shoving. After he misbehaved one day at the cafeteria, the teacher told him to come up to my office to see me. He flatly refused, lay on the floor, and threw a temper tantrum, kicking and screaming.

The truth is not in Phillip. When caught in actual misdeeds, he denies everything and takes upon himself an air of injured innocence. He believes we are picking on him. His attitude is sullen when he is refused anything. He pouts, and when asked why he does these things, he points to his head and says, "Because I'm not right up here."

This boy needs help badly. He does not seem to have any friends. His aggressive behavior prevents the children from liking him. Our school psychologist tested Phillip, and the results indicated average intelligence, but his school achievement is only at the third- and low fourth-grade level.

TABLE 13.2

DSM-IV
Symptoms of Conduct Disorder

The symptoms of conduct disorder include behaviors that violate the basic rights of others and the norms for appropriate social behavior.

Bullies, threatens, or intimidates others

Initiates physical fights

Uses weapons in fights

Engages in theft and burglary

Is physically abusive to people and animals

Forces others into sexual activity

Lies and breaks promises often

Violates parents' rules about staying out at night

Runs away from home

Sets fires deliberately

Vandalizes and destroys others' property deliberately

Often skips school

Reprinted with permission from the *Diagnostic and Statistical Manual of Mental Disorders*, Fourth Edition. Copyright 2000 American Psychiatric Association.

Children with conduct problems are prone to interpreting the incorrect actions of others as intentional acts of aggression.

We all have known bullies and children who often get into trouble. Only 3 to 7 percent of children exhibit behaviors serious enough to qualify for a diagnosis of conduct disorder, however (Offord, 1997; Robins, 1991). Still, the behaviors of children with conduct disorder exact a high cost to society. For example, the cost of vandalism to schools by juveniles in the United States is estimated to be over $600 million per year. Juveniles account for almost 20 percent of all violent-crime arrests (*Newsweek*, August 2, 1993). About half of all adolescent boys and 25 percent of adolescent girls report being attacked by someone else at school (Offord, 1997).

Unfortunately, many children with conduct disorder continue to have serious difficulty conforming to societal norms in adolescence and adulthood (Offord et al., 1992). As adolescents, about half of them engage in criminal behavior and drug abuse. As adults, about 75 to 85 percent of them are chronically unemployed, have histories of unstable personal relationships, frequently engage in impulsive physical aggression, or are spouse abusers (Lahey & Loeber, 1997). Between 35 and 40 percent of them will be diagnosed with antisocial personality disorder as adults.

The DSM-IV recognizes a less severe pattern of chronic misbehavior than is seen in conduct disorder. This less severe pattern is known as **oppositional**

defiant disorder. Children with oppositional defiant disorder may be argumentative, negative, irritable, and defiant, but they do not engage in acts as serious as those of children with conduct disorder (see Table 13.3), as can be seen in the case of 9-year-old Jeremy (adapted from Spitzer et al., 1994, p. 343):

CASE STUDY

Jeremy has been difficult to manage since nursery school. The problems have slowly escalated. Whenever he is without close supervision, he gets into trouble. At school, he teases and kicks other children, trips them, and calls them names. He is described as bad-tempered and irritable, even though at times he seems to enjoy school. Often he appears to be deliberately trying to annoy other children, though he always claims that others have started the arguments. He does not become involved in serious fights but does occasionally exchange a few blows with another child.

Jeremy sometimes refuses to do what his two teachers tell him to do, and this year has been particularly difficult with one who takes him in the afternoon for arithmetic, art, and science lessons. He gives many reasons why he should not have to do his work and argues when told to do it. At home, Jeremy's behavior is quite variable. On some days he is defiant and rude to his mother, needing to be told to do everything several times before he will do it, though eventually he usually complies. On other days he is charming and volunteers to help, but his unhelpful days predominate. His mother says, "The least little thing upsets him, and then he shouts and screams." Jeremy is described as spiteful and mean with his younger brother, Rickie. His mother also comments that he tells many minor lies though, when pressed, is truthful about important things.

TABLE 13.3
DSM-IV
Symptoms of Oppositional Defiant Disorder

The symptoms of oppositional defiant disorder are not as severe as the symptoms of conduct disorder but have their onset at an earlier age, and oppositional defiant disorder often develops into conduct disorder.

Often loses temper

Often argues with adults

Often refuses to comply with requests or rules

Deliberately tries to annoy others

Blames others for his or her mistakes or misbehaviors

Is touchy or easily annoyed

Is angry and resentful

Is spiteful or vindictive

Reprinted with permission from the *Diagnostic and Statistical Manual of Mental Disorders*, Fourth Edition. Copyright 1994 American Psychiatric Association.

As was the case with Jeremy, the onset of symptoms of oppositional defiant disorder often occurs very early in life, during toddler and preschool years. Many children with oppositional defiant disorder seem to outgrow their behaviors by late childhood or early adolescence. A subset of children with oppositional defiant disorder, particularly those who tend to be aggressive, go on to develop conduct disorder in childhood and adolescence. Indeed, it seems that almost all children who develop conduct disorder during elementary school have had symptoms of oppositional defiant disorder in the earlier years of their lives (Loeber et al., 1995).

Boys are about three times more likely than girls to be diagnosed with conduct disorder or oppositional defiant disorder (Cohen et al., 1993). This may be because the causes of these disorders are more frequently present in boys than in girls. It may also be because aggressive and antisocial behaviors are tolerated more in boys than in girls, so boys may more frequently than girls develop extremes of these behaviors.

Some researchers have suggested that antisocial aggressive behavior is not more rare in girls than in boys—it just looks different (Crick & Grotpeter, 1995; Zoccolillo, 1993). Girls' aggression is more likely to be indirect and verbal rather than physical and to involve alienation, ostracism, and character defamation of others. Girls exclude their peers, gossip about them, and collude with others to damage the social status of their targets.

It is clear, however, that girls with conduct and oppositional defiant disorders, like boys with these disorders, are at risk for severe problems throughout their lives. Long-term studies of girls diagnosed with conduct disorders find that, as adolescents and adults, they show high rates of depression and anxiety disorders, severe marital problems, criminal activity, and early unplanned pregnancies (Kovacs, Krol, & Voti, 1994; Loeber & Keenan, 1994). Girls with conduct disorders are more likely than boys with these disorders to marry partners who themselves engage in antisocial behaviors (Robins, 1991).

Biological Contributors to Conduct and Oppositional Defiant Disorder

Antisocial behavior clearly runs in families. Children with conduct disorder are much more likely than children without this disorder to have parents with antisocial personalities (Edelbrock et al., 1995; Lahey et al., 1988). Their fathers are also highly likely to have histories of criminal arrest and alcohol abuse, and their mothers tend to have histories of depression (Lahey et al., 1988; Robins, 1991).

Twin studies indicate that both conduct disorder and oppositional defiant disorder are heritable (Eaves et al., 1997). Conduct disorder that persists into adulthood and involves violent criminal behavior seems to have especially strong genetic roots (Frick, 1998; Rutter et al., 1990). Adoption studies have focused primarily on criminal behavior rather than on conduct disorders, and find that the criminal records of adopted sons are more similar to the records of their biological fathers than to their adoptive fathers (Mednick, Moffitt, & Stack, 1987).

Some researchers have suggested that children with conduct disorders have fundamental neurological deficits in the brain systems involved in planning and controlling behavior (Seguin et al., 1995). One piece of evidence that neurological deficits play a role in the development of conduct disorder is the fact that many children with conduct disorder also have attention-deficit/hyperactivity disorder (Moffitt & Silva, 1988). Recall that children with ADHD have trouble maintaining attention and tend to be irritable and impulsive in their actions. These problems can lead to the development of conduct disorder when they bring about failure in school and therefore to rejection of school and to poor peer relationships and rejection by peers. One source of the neurological deficits these children suffer may be exposure to neurotoxins and drugs while in the womb or during preschool years (Loeber, 1990). These neurological deficits then lead to oppositional behavior in early childhood, followed by increasingly more aggressive and severe antisocial behavior as the child ages.

Another clue that biological factors are involved in conduct disorder is that there are often signs of trouble in diagnosed children even in infancy. Children who develop conduct disorders tend to have been difficult babies and toddlers, at least by their parents' reports (Henry et al., 1996; Shaw, Keenan, & Vondra, 1994; Shaw & Winslow, 1997). They were irritable and demanding and did not comply with their parents' requests. They were impulsive, seemed to have little control over their behaviors, and responded to frustration with aggression. This correlation suggests that diagnosed children are born with a particular kind of difficult temperament that portends the antisocial behaviors they will engage in as older children (Seguin et al., 1995).

One way that children learn to control their behavior is by associating punishment with misbehavior and rewards with good behavior. Children with conduct disorders may have more difficulty learning from punishments and rewards because they tend to become less physiologically aroused than other children by reinforcements and punishments they receive for their behaviors (Quay, 1993; Raine, Venables, & Williams, 1996). Dan Olweus (1986) found that boys who were prone to unprovoked aggression, impulsivity, and acting-out behaviors had lower levels of adrenaline in their blood than did boys who were not prone to these behaviors. Olweus suggested that boys with low levels of adrenaline become easily bored and experience a craving for stimulation, for thrills and sensations. Strong stimuli are not experienced as aversive or disturbing by these boys, making them more likely to take risks. When they engage in aggressive behavior, they may feel pleasant arousal and excitement and thus may seek out situations that foster aggressive behaviors.

The role of serotonin in violent behavior has been the focus of many recent studies (Berman, Kavoussi, & Coccaro, 1997). One study of a large community-based sample found that young men whose blood serotonin levels were high relative to other men their age were much more likely to have committed a violent crime (Moffitt et al., 1998). Serotonin levels were not correlated with propensity to violence in women, however.

Finally, a popular theory of aggressive behavior is that it is linked to the hormone testosterone. Although it is clear that high levels of testosterone are associated with aggressivity in animals, few studies of this association have been done in humans. In one study of 58 boys 15 to 17 years of age, Olweus (1986) found that boys who were more prone to verbal and physical aggression in response to provocation and who were more impatient and irritable had higher blood levels of testosterone. A link between testosterone and aggression in humans has not been consistently found, however (Brain & Susman, 1997).

Although children who develop conduct disorders may have some biological predisposition to these disorders, they are unlikely to develop them unless they are also exposed to environments that promote antisocial behavior (Cadoret & Cain, 1980; Cloninger & Gottesman, 1987). The characteristics of such environments are described in the next section.

Sociocultural Contributors to Conduct and Oppositional Defiant Disorder

Conduct disorders and oppositional defiant disorders are found more frequently in children in lower socioeconomic classes and in urban areas than in children in higher socioeconomic classes and rural areas (Loeber, 1990; Offord, Alder, & Racine, 1986). This may be because a tendency toward antisocial behavior runs in families, families with members who engage in antisocial behavior may experience "downward social drift": The adults in these families cannot maintain good jobs, and thus the families tend to decline in socioeconomic status. Alternately, this tendency may be due to differences between socioeconomic groups in some of the environmental causes of antisocial behavior, such as poverty and poor parenting.

The quality of parenting children receive, particularly children with vulnerability to hyperactivity and conduct disturbances, is strongly related to whether they develop the full syndrome of conduct disorder (Loeber, 1990; Shaw & Winslow, 1997). One of the best predictors of children's conduct disturbances is parental supervision: Children who frequently are unsupervised or poorly supervised for long periods of time (e.g., left home alone for several hours or even days at a time) are much more likely to develop patterns of delinquent behaviors than are children who are seldom unsupervised. A related variable is parental uninvolvement: Children whose parents are not involved in their everyday lives—for example, children whose parents do not know who their friends are or what they are doing in school—are more likely to develop conduct disturbances. When parents of children with conduct disturbances do interact with their children, these interactions often are characterized by hostility, physical violence, and ridicule (Dishion & Patterson, 1997). The picture one gets of these families is one in which parents frequently ignore the children or are absent from home, but then when children transgress in some way, the parents lash out at the children violently (Lochman, White, & Wayland, 1991). These parents are more likely to give severe physical punishments to boys than to girls, which may partially account for the higher rate of conduct disturbances in boys (Lytton & Romney, 1991).

Children living in such families may turn to their peers for validation and to escape their parents. Unfortunately, these peer groups may be comprised of other children with conduct disturbances. Deviant peer

Children whose parents use aggression to punish them may learn to be aggressive themselves.

groups tend to encourage delinquent acts, even providing opportunities for such acts (Dishion & Patterson, 1997). For example, the members of a peer group of adolescents may dare a new member to commit a robbery to "show he is a man" and provide him with a weapon and a getaway car to commit the robbery. Children who become part of deviant peer groups are especially likely to begin abusing alcohol and illicit drugs which, in turn, leads to increases in deviant acts (McBride, Joe, & Simpson, 1991). Conversely, adolescents and young adults with conduct disturbances who form close relationships with others who do not have such problems are much more likely to "grow out" of their conduct disturbances. For example, young delinquent men who marry young women with no history of conduct problems tend to cease their delinquent acts and never engage in such acts again (Sampson & Laub, 1992).

The biological factors and family factors that contribute to conduct disorders may often coincide, sending a child on a trajectory toward antisocial behaviors that is difficult to stop (see Figure 13.1, p. 454; Loeber, 1990; Reid & Eddy, 1997). As noted earlier, the neuropsychological problems associated with antisocial behaviors are linked to maternal drug use, poor prenatal nutrition, pre- and postnatal exposure to toxic agents, child abuse, birth complications, and low birth weight (Moffitt, 1993). Infants and toddlers with these neuropsychological problems are more irritable, impulsive, awkward, overreactive, and inattentive than their peers and slower learners. This makes them difficult for parents to care for, and they are thus at increased risk for maltreatment and neglect. Added to this, the parents of these children are likely to be teenagers and to have psychological problems of their own that contribute to ineffective, harsh, or inconsistent parenting. Thus, children may carry a biological predisposition to disruptive, antisocial behaviors and may experience parenting that contributes to these behaviors. In a study of 536 boys, Terri Moffitt (1990) found that those who had both neuropsychological deficits and adverse home environments scored higher on an aggression scale than did those boys with only neuropsychological deficits or adverse home environments.

Cognitive Contributors to Conduct Disorder

Children with conduct disorder tend to process information about social interactions in ways that promote aggressive reactions to these interactions (Crick & Dodge, 1994). They enter social interactions with assumptions that other children will be aggressive toward them, and they use these assumptions rather than cues from the specific situations to interpret the actions of their peers (Dodge & Schwartz, 1997). For example, when another child accidentally bumps into him, a child with a conduct disorder will assume that the bumping was intentional and meant to provoke a fight. In addition, conduct-disordered children tend to believe that any negative actions peers might take against them, such as taking their favorite pencils, are intentional rather than accidental. When deciding upon what action to take in response to a perceived provocation by a peer, children with conduct disturbances tend to think of a narrow range of responses, usually including aggression (Pettit, Dodge, & Brown, 1988; Rubin, Daniels-Bierness, & Hayvren, 1982; Spivack & Shure, 1974). When pressed to consider responses other than aggression, these children generate ineffective or vague responses and often consider responses other than aggression to be useless or unattractive (e.g., Crick & Ladd, 1990).

Children who think about their social interactions in these ways are likely to engage in aggressive behaviors toward others. They then may be retaliated against: Other children will hit them, parents and teachers will punish them, and others will perceive them negatively. In turn, these actions by others may feed the children's assumptions that the world is against them, causing them to misinterpret future actions by others. A cycle of interactions can be built that maintains and encourages aggressive, antisocial behaviors in such children (see Figure 13.2, p. 455). Again, the best evidence that thinking patterns are causes of antisocial behavior in children rather than just correlates comes from studies showing that changing aggressive children's thinking patterns can change their tendencies to act aggressively. Let us turn to these interventions and other interventions for children with conduct disorder.

Drug Therapies for Conduct Disorder

Children with severely aggressive behavior have been prescribed a variety of drugs, although the efficacy of most drugs has not been tested adequately in

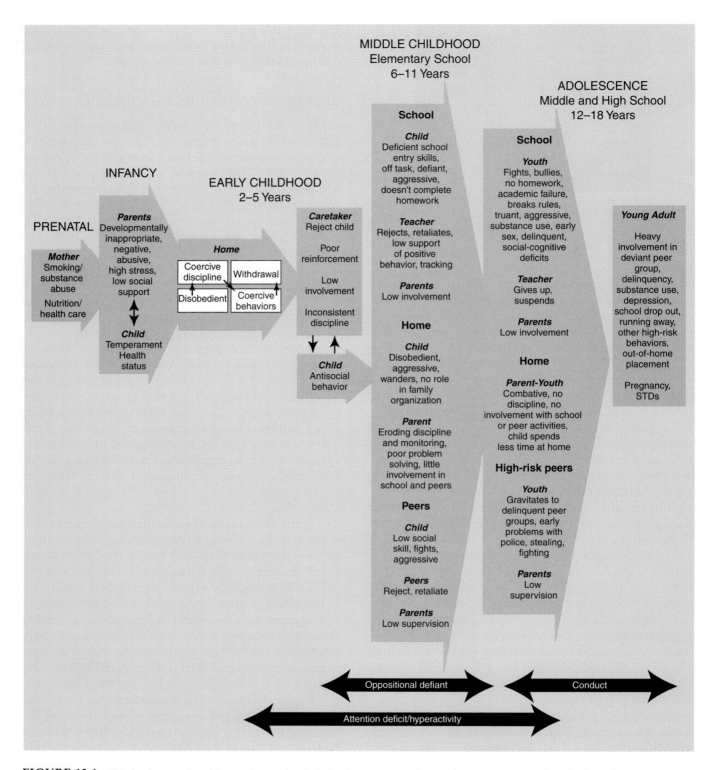

FIGURE 13.1   This developmental model suggests several biological and environmental factors come together to create behavioral disorders.

From J.B. Reid and J.M. Eddy, "The Prevention of Antisocial Behavior: Some Considerations in the Search for Effective Interventions" in D.M. Stoff, et al., (Eds.), *Handbook of Antisocial Personality Disorder.* Copyright © 1997 John Wiley & Sons, Inc.

controlled studies (Karper & Krystal, 1997). Antidepressant drugs, particularly the serotonin reuptake inhibitors, may help to reduce irritable and agitated behavior in children (Zubieta & Alessi, 1992). Children with conduct disorder are sometimes prescribed neuroleptic drugs, and controlled studies suggest that these drugs suppress aggressive behavior in these children (Gadow, 1992). It is unclear whether the drugs have any effect on the other symptoms of conduct disorder, such as lying and stealing. Children with both conduct disorder and attention-deficit/hyperactivity disorder are frequently prescribed stimulant drugs, and these drugs also suppress aggressive behaviors (Karper & Krystal, 1997). Finally, controlled studies suggest that lithium may be an effective treatment for children with aggressive conduct disorder (Campbell et al., 1995).

Psychological and Sociocultural Therapies for Conduct Disorder

Most therapies for conduct disorder are derived from social learning theory (see Chapter 2) and focus on changing the children's ways of interpreting interpersonal interactions, teaching them to take the perspectives of others and care about those perspectives, teaching them to use "self-talk" as a way of controlling impulsive behaviors, and teaching them more adaptive ways of solving conflicts than aggression (Lochman, White, & Wayland, 1991; Reid & Eddy, 1997; Southam-Gerow & Kendall, 1997).

Cognitive-Behavioral Therapy: Teaching Problem-Solving Skills

The first step in this therapy is to teach children to recognize situations that trigger anger or aggressive behaviors or in which they tend to be impulsive. This is done through observing children in their natural settings and then pointing out to them situations in which they misbehaved or seemed angry, discussing hypothetical situations and how the children would react to them, and having children keep diaries of their feelings and behaviors. The children also are taught to analyze their thoughts in these situations and to consider alternative ways of interpreting situations. Their assumptions that other children or adults act meanly toward them intentionally are challenged, and they are helped to take other people's perspectives on situations. Next, the children may be taught to use "self-talk" to help them avoid negative reactions to situations: They learn to talk to themselves in difficult situations, repeating phrases that help them calm themselves, and consider adaptive ways of coping with situations. For example,

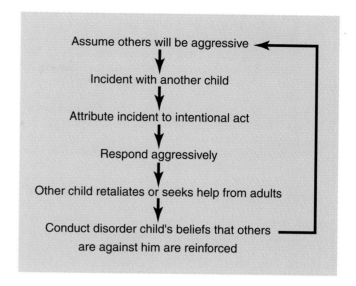

FIGURE 13.2   Feedback between Cognitions, Behaviors, and Others' Responses in Conduct Disorder. This feedback loop between a child's cognitions, behaviors, and the responses of others can develop into conduct disorder.

a child who tends to respond to provocation by others by immediately beginning to hit and kick might learn to say to himself,

> Slow down, slow down, slow down. Breathe deeply. Count to five. Slow down, slow down, slow down— Think about what to do. Don't want to get mad. Slow down, slow down.

Adaptive problem-solving skills are taught by discussing real and hypothetical problem situations with children and helping the children generate a variety of positive solutions to the problems. These solutions might be modeled by therapists and then practiced by the children in role plays. For example, if a therapist and child are discussing how to respond to another child who has cut in line in the lunchroom at school, the therapist might initially model an assertive (rather than aggressive) response, such as saying, "I would like you to move to the back of the line," to the cutting child. Then, the child in therapy might practice the assertive response and perhaps also pretend to be the child cutting in line in order to gain some perspective on why the child might do this.

Cognitive-Behavioral Therapy in a Group Setting

Cognitive-behavioral therapies for children with conduct disturbances often are applied in group settings. Lochman and colleagues (1991, pp. 50-51) provided the following example of how group therapy can be especially effective:

In a recent group session, Bob began talking about an incident that had led to a 5-day suspension from school the prior week. Rather than continue with the scheduled group activity, the bulk of the session was spent in group problem solving about this situation. Bob described how the incident began when he and another boy disagreed over who could sit on a cushion in the library. After a brief exchange of insults took place, the two boys were quiet for the remainder of the library period. However, as the class left the library, Bob got up in the other boy's face and reinitiated the verbal assaults in a more provocative way. When the boy responded with verbal insults, Bob knocked him down and kept hitting him until he was pulled away by the assistant principal. The group discussion included a focus on perspective taking with regard to the other boy's intentions, which did not initially appear to be as purposefully malevolent as Bob had perceived, and with regard to the assistant principal's intentions. In a spirited discussion, the group noted the assistant principal may have been either mean or trying to protect the combatants when he grabbed Bob and swung him around (most group members eventually decided he was trying to be protective). After several other ways of handling the initial "cushion" problem were suggested to Bob, Bob asked each of the group members how he or she would have handled it. When the group member with the most streetwise demeanor suggested a nonconfrontational solution, Bob tentatively decided to try that strategy in the next conflict. Notable aspects of this discussion included how assaultive incidents often escalate from trivial initial problems, how Bob had great difficulty letting his anger dissipate after the initial provocation, how Bob's anger disrupted his ordinarily adequate social cognitions through preemptive processing, and how the group members were instrumental in providing training in social perspective taking and social problem solving.

Bob was probably more willing to consider a nonconfrontational solution to his problem because it came from one of his peers, an especially "cool" peer, rather than from an adult. All the group members had the opportunity to learn to generate alternative interpretations and solutions to this problem in the nonthreatening context of helping Bob.

Some psychosocial therapies for children with conduct disorder also include parents, particularly if the family dynamics are supporting the children's conduct disorder (Reid & Eddy, 1997). Parents are taught to reinforce positive behaviors in their children and discourage aggressive or antisocial behaviors. Parents are also taught strategies similar to the ones already described for controlling their own angry outbursts and discipline techniques that are not violent. Unfortunately, it can be difficult to get the parents who need the most improvement in parenting skills to participate in therapy (Chamberlain & Rosicky, 1995).

Studies of the therapies based on social learning theory suggest that they can be very effective in reducing aggressive and impulsive behavior in children, particularly interventions made in the home, in the classroom, and in peer groups (see Borduin et al., 1995; Lochman, White, & Wayland, 1991; Reid & Eddy, 1997). Unfortunately, many children relapse into conduct disturbances after a while, particularly if their parents have poor parenting skills, alcoholism or drug abuse, or other psychopathology. Interventions are most likely to have long-term positive effects if they are begun early in a disturbed child's life (Estrada & Pinsof, 1995). Booster sessions of additional therapy sometime after a course of initial therapy has been completed also help a child avoid relapsing into conduct disturbance (Lochman, White, & Wayland, 1991).

Ethnic/Racial Differences in Interventions for Antisocial Behavior

It appears that the criminal justice system deals differently with ethnic minority adolescents who commit antisocial behaviors than with White adolescents who behave in antisocial ways (Tolan & Gorman-Smith, 1997). Researchers examined the case records of all adolescents who were sent to correctional schools or to state psychiatric hospitals in one area of Connecticut over a year (Lewis, Balla, & Shanok, 1979). The adolescents sent to psychiatric hospitals and those sent to jail were just as likely to have histories of violence and had equal levels of emotional problems. However, the adolescents sent to jail were much more likely to be African American than White, whereas those sent to psychiatric hospitals were much more likely to be White than African American. It appears that disturbed African American adolescents are incarcerated whereas disturbed Whites are hospitalized.

Summing Up

- The behavior disorders include attention-deficit/hyperactivity disorder, conduct disorder, and oppositional defiant disorder.
- Children with attention-deficit/hyperactivity disorder are inattentive, impulsive, and overactive. They often do not do well in school, and their relationships with their peers are extremely impaired.
- Many children with attention-deficit/hyperactivity disorder grow out of this disorder, but some continue to show the symptoms into adulthood, and they are at high risk for conduct problems and emotional problems throughout their lives.
- The two therapies that are effective in treating ADHD are stimulant drugs and behavioral

therapies that teach children how to control their behaviors.

- Children with conduct disorder engage in behaviors that severely violate societal norms, including chronic lying, stealing, and violence toward others.

- Children with oppositional defiant disorder engage in less severe antisocial behaviors that indicate a negativistic, irritable approach to others.

- Some children outgrow oppositional defiant disorder, but a subset develop full conduct disorder.

- Children who develop conduct disorder often continue to engage in antisocial behaviors into adulthood and have high rates of criminal activity and drug abuse.

- Neurological deficits may be involved in conduct disorder. These deficits may make it more difficult for children with this disorder to learn from reinforcements and punishments and to control their behaviors.

- Children with conduct disorder also tend to have parents that are neglectful much of the time and violent when annoyed with them.

- Children with conduct disorder tend to think about interactions with others in ways that contribute to their aggressive reactions.

⊙ SEPARATION ANXIETY DISORDER

Children can suffer from depression, panic attacks, obsessive-compulsive disorder, generalized anxiety disorder, posttraumatic stress disorder, and phobias. The childhood versions of most of these disorders have been described in the chapters on the individual disorders. One emotional disorder that is specific to childhood is **separation anxiety disorder** (see Table 13. 4).

Many infants, if separated from their primary caregivers, become anxious and upset. They cry loudly and cannot be consoled by anyone but their primary caregivers. This is a normal consequence of an infant's development of the understanding that objects (including mother and father) continue to exist even when they are not in direct sight and the infant's attachment to the caregivers. With development, however, most infants come to understand that their caregivers will return and find ways to comfort themselves while their caregivers are away so that they are not excessively anxious.

Some children continue to be extremely anxious when separated from their caregivers, even into childhood and adolescence. They may refuse to go to school because they fear the separation from their caregivers.

TABLE 13.4
DSM-IV Symptoms of Separation Anxiety Disorder

Children who show much more than the usual anxiety when separated from caregivers may be diagnosed with separation anxiety disorder.

Excessive distress when separated from home or caregivers, or is anticipating separation

Persistent and excessive worry about losing, or harm coming to, caregivers

Persistent reluctance or refusal to go to school or elsewhere because of fear of separation

Excessively fearful about being alone

Reluctance to go to sleep without caregivers nearby

Repeated nightmares involving themes of separation

Repeated complaints of physical symptoms when separation from caregivers occurs or is anticipated

Reprinted with permission from the *Diagnostic and Statistical Manual of Mental Disorders*, Fourth Edition. Copyright © 2000 American Psychiatric Association.

They cannot sleep at night unless they are with their caregivers. They have nightmares with themes of separation. They may follow their caregivers around the house to be with them. If they are separated from their caregivers, they worry tremendously that something bad will happen to the caregivers. They have exaggerated fears of natural disasters (e.g., tornadoes, earthquakes) and of robbers, kidnappers, and accidents. They may have stomachaches and headaches and become nauseous and vomit if forced to separate from their caregivers. Younger children may cry unconsolably. Older children may avoid activities, such as being on a baseball team, that might take them away from their caregivers, preferring to spend all the time possible with their caregivers.

Many children go through short episodes of a few days of these symptoms after traumatic events, such as getting lost in a shopping mall or the hospitalization of parents for sudden illness. Separation anxiety disorder is not diagnosed unless a child shows symptoms for at least 4 weeks and the symptoms significantly impair the child's ability to function in everyday life. Children with this disorder may be very shy, sensitive, and demanding of adults.

About 2 to 4 percent of preadolescents experience separation anxiety disorder (Anderson et al., 1987; Bowen, Offord, & Boyle, 1990). It is much more common in girls than in boys. Left untreated, this disorder can recur frequently throughout childhood and adolescence, significantly interfering with the child's academic

Some separation anxiety is normal in young children, but other children are excessively anxious about leaving their caregivers.

progress and peer relationships. One study examined the adult outcomes of children with separation anxiety who had refused to go to school because of their anxiety and compared them to people with no psychiatric disorders as children. The investigators found that those who had had separation anxiety disorder had more psychiatric problems as adults than the comparison group, were more likely to continue to live with their parents even though they were adults, and were less likely to have married and had children (Flakierska-Praquin, Lindstrom, & Gillberg, 1997).

Biological Contributors to Separation Anxiety

Biological factors may be involved in the development of separation anxiety disorder (see *Concept Review:* Proposed Etiologies and Treatments for Separation Anxiety Disorder). Children with this disorder tend to have family histories of anxiety disorders (Silverman & Ginsberg, 1998). There may be a particularly strong link between separation anxiety and panic attacks. The symptoms that children with separation anxiety disorder experience when separated from their parents resemble those of a panic attack. Children with separation anxiety disorder appear at increased risk for developing panic disorder as adults. The children of parents with panic disorder are three times more likely to develop separation anxiety disorder than are the children of parents without panic disorder (Weissman et al., 1984). Twin studies suggest that separation anxiety disorder is heritable, but possibly only in girls, not boys (Eaves et al., 1997).

Earlier we discussed the role of difficult temperament in the development of conduct disorder. A different kind of temperament is implicated in the development of anxiety disorders in children. Kagan and colleagues (1987) suggest that some children are born high in behavioral inhibition—they are shy, fearful, and irritable as toddlers, and cautious, quiet, and introverted as school-age children. These children tend to avoid or withdraw from novel situations, are clingy with parents, and become excessively aroused when exposed to unfamiliar situations. Some studies suggest that children high on behavioral inhibition as infants are at increased risk to develop anxiety disorders in childhood (Biederman et al., 1990, 1993b). These children's parents also are prone to anxiety disorders, particularly panic disorder, and often have a history of anxiety disorders that dates back to their own childhood. Thus, behavioral inhibition may be an early marker of a risk for anxiety disorders in children that they inherited from their parents.

Psychological and Sociocultural Contributors to Separation Anxiety

Children may learn to be anxious from their parents or as an understandable response to their environments, as well. In some cases, separation anxiety disorder develops following traumatic events, such as the following:

CASE STUDY
In the early morning hours, 7-year-old Maria was abruptly awakened by a loud rumbling and violent shaking. She sat upright in bed and called out to her 10-year-old sister, Rosemary, who was leaping out of her own bed 3 feet away. The two girls ran for their mother's bedroom as their toys and books plummeted from shelves and dresser tops. The china hutch in the hallway teetered in front of them and then fell forward with a crash, blocking their path to their mother's room. Mrs. Marshall called out to them to go back and stay in their doorway. They knew the doorway was a place you were supposed to go during an earthquake, so they huddled there together until the shaking finally stopped. Mrs. Marshall climbed over the hutch and broken china to her daughters. Although they were all very shaken and scared, they were unhurt.

Two weeks later, back at school, Maria began to complain every morning of stomachaches, headaches, and dizziness, asking to stay home with her mother. After 4 days, when a medical examination revealed no physical problems, Maria was told she must return to school. She protested tearfully, but her mother insisted, and Rosemary promised to hold her hand all the way to school. In the classroom, Maria could not concentrate on her schoolwork and was often out of her seat looking out the window in the direction of home. She told her teacher she needed to go home to see if her mother was okay. When

CONCEPT REVIEW

Proposed Etiologies and Treatments for Separation Anxiety Disorder

Biological and environmental factors may contribute to separation anxiety disorder, which is often treated with cognitive-behavior therapy.

Proposed Etiologies	Description
Biological predisposition	May be genetic predisposition to anxiety disorders, including separation anxiety and panic attacks.
Behavioral inhibition	Children are born with an inhibited, fearful temperament.
Traumatic and uncontrollable events	Some children develop separation anxiety after a traumatic event; studies of nonhuman primates show that chronic uncontrollability can contribute to anxiety.
Parenting experiences	Parents may encourage fearful behavior and not encourage appropriate independence.

Treatment	Description
Cognitive-behavioral therapy	Children are taught self-talk to challenge negative thoughts and relaxation to quell anxiety; periods of separation from parents are increased gradually; parents are taught to model and reinforce nonanxious behavior.

she was told she couldn't go home, she began to cry and shake so violently the school nurse called Mrs. Marshall, who came and picked Maria up and took her home. The next morning, Maria's protests grew stronger and she refused to go to school until her mother promised to go with her and sit in her classroom for the first hour. When Mrs. Marshall began to leave, Maria clung to her, crying, pleading for her not to leave, and following her into the hallway. The next day, Maria refused to leave the house for her Brownie meeting and her dancing lessons or even to play in the front yard. She followed her mother around the house and insisted on sleeping with her at night. "I need to be with you, Mommy, in case something happens," she declared.

Parents may contribute to the development of a separation anxiety disorder in their children by being overprotective and modeling anxious reactions to separations from their children (Kendall, 1992). The families of children with separation anxiety tend to be especially close-knit, not encouraging developmentally appropriate levels of independence in the children.

Some of the best evidence that environmental and parenting factors can influence the development of anxiety disorders in youngsters comes from studies of nonhuman primates (Mineka, Gunnar, & Champoux, 1986; Suomi, 1999). Mineka and colleagues found that rhesus monkeys who were given adequate

food and water from ages 2 to 6 months, but could not control their access to food and water, developed a fearfulness and became generally inhibited in their behavior. Other monkeys given the same amount of food and water, but under conditions that they could exert some control over, did not become fearful. This suggests that some human children who are raised in conditions over which they have little control may develop anxiety symptoms.

Moreover, Suomi (1999) found that, although some rhesus monkeys seem to be born behaviorally inhibited, the extent to which they develop serious signs of fearfulness and anxiety later in life depends on the parenting they receive. Those who are raised by anxious mothers, who also are inhibited and inappropriately responsive to the infants, are prone to develop monkey-versions of anxiety disorders. Those who are raised by calm, responsive mothers who model appropriate reactions to stressful situations, typically are not any more likely to develop anxiety problems as adolescents or adults than those who are not born behaviorally inhibited.

Treatments for Separation Anxiety

Cognitive and behavioral therapies are most often used to treat separation anxiety disorder (Silverman & Ginsburg, 1998). Children might be taught relaxation exercises to practice during periods of separation from their parents. Their fears about separation are challenged, and they are taught to use "self-talk" to calm themselves when they become anxious. As therapy progresses, periods of separation from their parents are increased in number and duration. Parents must be willing to participate in the therapy and to cope with their children's (and their own) reactions to attempts to increase periods of separation. Parents may need to be taught to model nonanxious reactions to separations from their children and to reinforce nonanxious behavior in their children. Controlled clinical trials of this type of therapy show that it can be effective in the short term, and maintain its effects in the long term (Kendall & Southam-Gerow, 1996). For example, Mark Dadds and colleagues (1999) provided a 10-week school-based intervention for anxiety-ridden children and their parents, and found that these children were much less likely than a control group who received no intervention to be diagnosed with separation anxiety or another anxiety disorder over the 2 years following the intervention (see Figure 13.3).

Here is how Maria was treated for her separation anxiety:

Studies of monkeys confirm that both biological and parenting factors contribute to problems with anxiety.

CASE STUDY

Mrs. Marshall was instructed to take Maria to school and leave four times during the period she was there. Initially, Mrs. Marshall left for 30 seconds each time. Over time, she gradually increased the amount of time and distance she was away while Maria remained in the classroom. Maria was given a sticker at the end of the school day for each time she remained in her seat while her mother was out of the room. In addition, she was praised by her teacher and her mother, and positive self-statements (e.g., "My mommy will be okay; I'm a big girl and I can stay at school") were encouraged. No response was made when Maria failed to stay in her chair. Maria could exchange her stickers for prizes at the end of each week.

At home, Mrs. Marshall was instructed to give minimal attention to Maria's inquiries about her well-being and to ignore excessive, inappropriate crying. Eventually, Maria was given a sticker and praise each morning for sleeping in her own bed.

The first few times Mrs. Marshall left the classroom, Maria followed her out. Soon she stayed in her chair and received stickers. At home, she remained in her own bed the first night, even though she was told she only had to stay 2 hours to earn her sticker. At her own request, she returned to Brownie meetings and attended summer camp.

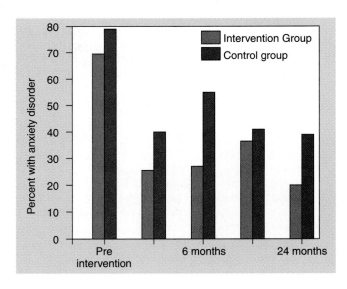

FIGURE 13.3 Effects of Cognitive-Behavioral Therapy for Separation Anxiety Disorder. Schoolchildren with separation anxiety and other anxiety disorders and their parents were given a 10-week cognitive-behavioral intervention. These children were less likely than a control group of children over the next 2 years to be diagnosed with an anxiety disorder.

Source: Dadds et al., 1999.

Many different kinds of drugs are used in the treatment of childhood anxiety disorders, including antidepressants, antianxiety drugs such as the benzodiazepines, stimulants, and antihistamines. Research on the efficacy of drug therapies for separation anxiety disorder is very limited (Silverman & Ginsburg, 1998).

A fascinating new therapy for children with anxiety symptoms, and a wide range of other symptoms, is massage therapy. As we discuss in *Pushing the Boundaries:* Massage Therapy, it has been shown to be effective in a number of controlled studies.

PUSHING THE BOUNDARIES

Massage Therapy

Massage therapy is one of the oldest forms of medical treatment. It was first described in China during the second century B.C. and became popular around the same time in India and Egypt (Field, 1998). In modern times, techniques like massage therapy have been replaced with pharmaceuticals. Still, among proponents of "alternative medicine," massage is still commonly used to treat a variety of ailments, including anxiety.

Is massage therapy useful? Dr. Tiffany Field and her colleagues at the Touch Research Institute at the University of Miami School of Medicine have embarked on a program of research to scientifically test the efficacy of massage in the treatment of certain disorders. They define massage as the manipulation of deep tissue with the presumed stimulation of pressure receptors. They have focused on disorders or conditions that they theorized could be positively affected by such techniques, by facilitating physical growth, reducing pain, increasing alertness, diminishing stress, anxiety, and depression, and enhancing immune function (Field, 1998).

One application of massage therapy is in the treatment of autistic children. As noted in this chapter, autistic children often do not like to be touched. But as Temple Grandin explains (see *Extraordinary People:* Thinking in Pictures), many autistic children respond well to predictable, high-pressure stimulation. It seems to reduce anxiety and help to calm them. In one study, autistic children were either given regular massages or were simply held by their teacher for the same period of time. The children given massages showed a decrease in their off-task behavior in the classroom, fewer autistic behaviors (such as stereotyped behaviors), and greater relatedness to their teachers than the children who were only held (Field, Lasko, Mundy, Henteleff, Talpins, & Dowling, 1997).

What is the mechanism for the effects of massage therapy, particularly across such a wide variety of conditions? The answer is not known yet, but it seems likely that reductions in stress-related hormones and in subjective states of anxiety and depression play an important role. The old notion that massage increases blood flow has not been consistently supported in recent studies (Field, 1998). It is likely that some of the positive effects of

massage for children actually come from improvements in the relationship between the children and their parents, who are delivering the massage. Parents who provide massages to their children in these studies report their own anxiety and depression levels decrease, and they feel they are having a more positive role in their child's illness than before (Field, Hernandez-Reif, Shaw, LaGreca, Schanberg, & Kuhn, 1997). This may lead to a general improvement in the home environment and family life that has widespread effects on children's well-being.

Many studies of massage therapy have focused on children who have failed to grow normally because of prematurity, exposure to cocaine or HIV, or other conditions. In these studies, children are randomly assigned to receive regular massages from their parents or to be in a control group that receives attention but no massage. In one study of preterm infants in a neonatal intensive care unit, infants given 15-minute massages three times a day for 10 days gained 47% more weight than control infants. The infants receiving massage were also hospitalized for six days less at a hospital cost savings of $10,000 per infant (Field et al., 1986; Scafidi et al., 1990). Measures of norepinephrine and epinephrine revealed more normal developmental increases over the period of the study in the massaged infants than the control infants, and the massaged infants had better scores on measure of neonatal behavior. At age 1 year, the massaged infants still weighed more than the control infants and performed better on measures of mental, motor, and behavioral development. Similar results have been obtained for infants exposed to cocaine or HIV in the womb (Scafidi & Field, 1996, Wheeden et al., 1993).

Full-term infants also seem to benefit from massage. In one study of full-term 1- to 3-month-old infants born to adolescent mothers, infants were given either 15 minutes a day of massage or rocking for a total of 12 days over a 6-week period. During the massage sessions, the massaged infants spent more time in active alert states, cried less, and had lower salivary cortisol levels suggesting lower stress levels. At the end of the 6-week treatment, the massaged infants gained more weight, improved on emotionality, sociability and soothability, showed better

Continued

face-to-face interactions, had decreased urinary stress hormones, and had increased serotonin levels, compared to the control infants (Field, et al., 1996).

Children with juvenile rheumatoid arthritis often suffer chronic pain. Antiinflamatory agents can relieve the pain but only so much, and some drugs are addictive. One study had parents provide their arthritic children with daily massages and found that these children experienced less anxiety, showed lower stress hormones, and reported less pain over a one-month period compared to children who received only training in muscle relaxation (Field, Hernandez-Reif, Seligman et al., 1997). Positive results of massage therapy have also been found with children with asthma, in reducing stress hormones and subjective states of anxiety that can trigger asthma attacks (Field et al., 1998).

Whatever the mechanisms, if massage therapy continues to be shown to reliably improve children's functioning across certain conditions, it represents an inexpensive and safe form of intervention.

Summing Up

- Children can suffer from all the emotional disorders, including depression and all the anxiety disorders. Separation anxiety disorder is one disorder specific to children.

- Children with separation anxiety disorder are excessively fearful about separation from primary caregivers. They may become extremely agitated or ill when they anticipate separation, and curtail usual activities to avoid separation.

- Separation anxiety disorder may be inherited as part of a larger predisposition to anxiety disorders, particularly panic attacks.

- Children who are behaviorally inhibited as infants appear at risk for separation anxiety disorder as adults.

- Parents may enhance a vulnerability to separation anxiety disorder by their reactions to children's distress.

- Cognitive-behavioral therapies can help children with separation anxiety disorder quiet their anxieties and resume everyday activities.

⊙ ELIMINATION DISORDERS

CASE STUDY
On the morning of her third birthday, Gretchen walked into the kitchen and announced to her mother, "I'm a big girl now, and I'm going to wear big girl underpants. No more diapers." She indeed did wear "big girl underpants" that day, and although she had a couple of accidents during the day, at bedtime Gretchen was extremely proud of herself for being such a big girl. Within a few weeks, she was able to wear big girl underpants all day without any accidents.

Most children gain sufficient control over their bladder and bowel movements by about age 4 that they no longer need to wear diapers during the day or night. Like Gretchen, many children view the ability to control their bladder and bowel movements as a marker of their passage into being "big boys or girls." It is understandable, then, that children who lose this control, particularly when they are far past the preschool years and into middle childhood, can experience shame and distress. These children might be diagnosed with one of the two **elimination disorders,** enuresis or encopresis (see *Concept Review:* Elimination Disorders).

Enuresis

Occasional wetting of the bed at night is common among elementary school children, particularly during times of stress. Children over age 5 are diagnosed with **enuresis** when they have wet the bed or their clothes at least twice a week for three months (APA, 2000). Most children with enuresis wet only at night. A subset wet during the daytime only, most often at school. These children may be socially anxious about using the public toilets at school or prone to becoming

Children are very proud of themselves when they learn to control their bowel and bladder movements, thus loss of control can be very distressing.

relatives who had the disorder. Some of these children may have inherited a biological vulnerability to the disorder in the form of unusually small bladders or lower bladder threshold for involuntary voiding. A variety of other biological mechanisms for enuresis have been suggested, but none have received consistent empirical support (Ondersma & Walker, 1998).

Psychodynamic and family systems theorists suggest that enuresis is due to conflicts and anxiety due to disruptions or dysfunction in the family (Olmos de Paz, 1990). For example, some children develop enuresis when new babies are born in their families, perhaps because they feel threatened by the attention their parents are giving to the new babies and resentful toward the new babies but cannot express feelings freely. Finally, behaviorists suggest that enuresis may be due to lax or inappropriate toilet training, that enuretic children never learned appropriate bladder control and thus have recurrent problems during childhood (Erickson, 1992).

Children with enuresis are usually taken to their pediatrician rather than a mental-health specialist, and physicians overwhelmingly prescribe antidepressants to treat enuresis (Ondersma & Walker, 1998). Tricyclic antidepressants, particularly imipramine, are commonly used. It is not clear how these drugs affect wetting, but it may be that increases in norepinephrine help in control of the bladder. About half of children treated with imipramine show reductions in wetting, but up to 95 percent relapse once the medication is discontinued (Ondersma & Walker, 1998). In addition, the tricyclic antidepressants have dangerous side effects in children, including sleep disturbances, tiredness,

preoccupied with other things they are doing. Thus, they do not use the toilet as they need to and tend to have wetting accidents. Enuresis is relatively common, as disorders go, among young children, but the prevalence decreases with age. About 15 to 20 percent of 5-year-olds are enuretic at least once per month, but by adolescence, the prevalence of enuresis decreases to about 1 percent (Ondersma & Walker, 1998).

Enuresis runs in families, and approximately 75 percent of children with enuresis have biological

CONCEPT REVIEW

Elimination Disorders

The elimination disorders involve uncontrolled wetting and defecation far beyond the age at which children usually gain control over these functions.

Disorder	Symptoms	Proposed Etiologies	Treatments
Enuresis	Unintended urination at least 2 times per week for 3 months; child over 5 years of age	1. Genetic vulnerability 2. Conflicts or anxiety 3. Lax or inappropriate toilet training	1. Antidepressant drugs, synthetic antidiuretic hormone 2. Bell and pad behavioral method
Encopresis	Unintended defecation at least 1 time per month for 3 months; child over 4 years of age	Usually begins after episodes of severe constipation; changes in colon reduce ability to know when to use toilet, leading to accidents	1. Medication to clear out colon, laxatives or mineral oil to soften stools, increase in dietary fiber 2. Behavioral contracting to increase appropriate toilet use and diet change, and teaching children relaxation methods

gastrointestinal distress, and cardiac irregularities. Overdoses of the tricyclics can be fatal.

Synthetic antidiuretic hormone (ADH) has emerged as the drug of choice for nighttime enuresis (Ondersma & Walker, 1998). This drug concentrates urine, thereby reducing urine output from the kidney to the bladder. It reliably reduces nighttime wetting, but again children typically relapse back into wetting once the medication is discontinued.

A behavioral method referred to as the **bell and pad method** is a reliable and long-term solution to enuresis. A pad is placed under the child while she sleeps. This pad has a sensory device to detect even small amounts of urine. If the child wets during her sleep, then a bell connected to the pad rings and awakens the child. Through classical conditioning, the child learns to wake up when she has a full bladder and needs to urinate. The bell and pad method is highly effective (Friman & Warzak, 1990; Whelan & Houts, 1990).

Encopresis

Encopresis is a more rare disorder than enuresis, involving repeated defecation into clothing or onto the floor. To be diagnosed with encopresis, children must have at least one such event a month for at least three months and must be at least 4 years of age. Only about 2 to 3 percent of 7-year-olds has encopresis, and it is more common in boys than in girls (Ondersma & Walker, 1998).

Encopresis usually begins after one or more episodes of severe constipation. Constipation may result from environmental factors, such as withholding bowel movements during toilet training or refusing to use the toilet during school, a genetic predisposition toward decreased bowl motility, food intolerance, or certain medications (Stark et al., 1997). Constipation can cause distention of the colon, decreasing the child's ability to detect the urge to have a bowel movement, fecal hardening and buildup in the colon, and subsequent leakage of fecal material. The child may then increase the problem by avoiding using the toilet because of large or painful bowel movements, which in turn makes him or her more insensitive to fecal matter in the colon and thus more unable to know when it is time to use the toilet.

Encopresis is typically treated by a combination of medications to clear out the colon, laxatives or mineral oil to soften stools, recommendations to increase dietary fiber, and encouragement to the child to sit on the toilet a certain amount of time each day (Levine, 1982). This medical management strategy works for 60 to 80 percent of children with encopresis. Stark and colleagues (1997) used a behavioral treatment program for a group of encopretic children who did not respond to medical management. This behavioral program included contracting around toileting behaviors and diet, the use of rewards for appropriate toilet usage, and teaching the children relaxation techniques. In addition, all the children went through the standard medical procedures described above once again. Eighty-six percent of the children stopped soiling by the end of the treatment and did not require further treatment.

Summing Up

- Enuresis is persistent uncontrolled wetting by children who have previously attained bladder control.
- Enuresis runs in families and has been attributed to a variety of biological mechanisms. Psychodynamic theories attribute it to emotional distress. Behavioral theories attribute it to poor toilet training.
- Antidepressants help to reduce enuresis in the short term, but not in the long term, and carry significant side effects.
- Behavioral methods that help the child learn to awaken and go to the bathroom can help to reduce nighttime enuresis.
- Encopresis is persistent uncontrolled soiling by children who have previously attained control of defecation.
- Encopresis typically begins after one or more episodes of constipation, which create distention in the colon and decrease a child's ability to detect needed bowel movements.
- Medical management and behavioral techniques can help reduce encopresis.

◑ DISORDERS OF COGNITIVE, MOTOR, AND COMMUNICATION SKILLS

Beginning from the first day home from the hospital, parents eagerly track their children's development, watching for the emergence of cognitive skills, motor skills, and social skills. The first responsive smile from a child, the first tentative steps, and the first babbling words are occasions for major celebrations. Although most parents become anxious at one time or another when it seems their children are not developing some skill "on time" (or perhaps even ahead of other children), their fears usually are allayed as their children's skills eventually emerge.

CONCEPT REVIEW	
Disorders of Cognitive, Motor, and Communication Skills	
These disorders involve deficits in specific skills.	
Disorder	**Description**
Learning Disorders:	
Reading disorder (dyslexia)	Deficits in ability to read
Mathematics disorder	Deficits in mathematics skills
Disorder of written expression	Deficits in the ability to write
Motor Skills Disorder:	
Developmental coordination disorder	Deficits in ability to walk, run, hold on to objects
Communication Disorders:	
Expressive language disorder	Deficits in the ability to express oneself through language
Mixed receptive-expressive language disorder	Deficits both in the ability to express oneself through language and to understand the language of others
Phonological disorder	Use of speech sounds inappropriate for age or dialect
Stuttering	Severe problems in word fluency

Sometimes, though, important skills do not emerge or develop fully in a child. A child might not learn to crawl or walk until many months after most children do. Another child might have severe trouble with reading or arithmetic, despite having good teachers. Approximately 20 percent of children have significant impairment in important learning, motor, or communication skills (APA, 2000). These problems are more common in boys than in girls. They can greatly affect a child's achievement in school and can lower self-esteem and well-being. When deficits in fundamental skills are severe enough to interfere with a child's progress, the child may be diagnosed with a learning disorder, motor skills disorder, or communication disorder (see *Concept Review:* Disorders of Cognitive, Motor, and Communication Skills).

Learning Disorders

Three specific **learning disorders** are described in the DSM-IV. These disorders are only diagnosed when a child's performance on standardized tests of these skills is significantly below that expected for his or her age, schooling, and overall level of intelligence. **Reading disorder,** also known as dyslexia, involves deficits in the ability to read. This disorder is usually apparent by the fourth grade. About 4 percent of children in the United States have reading disorder. **Mathematics disorder** involves deficits in the ability to learn math. This

may include problems in understanding mathematical terms, in recognizing numerical symbols, in clustering objects into groups, in counting, and in following mathematical principles. Although many of us feel that we are not great at math, deficits in math skills severe enough to warrant this diagnosis occur in only about 1 percent of children. The disorder is usually apparent at about second or third grade. **Disorder of written expression** involves deficits in the ability to write. Children with this disorder have severe trouble spelling, constructing a sentence or paragraph, or writing legibly. This disorder is rare.

Children with learning disorders can become demoralized and disruptive in class. If their learning disorder is never treated, they are at high risk for school drop-out, with as many as 40 percent never finishing high school (APA, 2000). As adults, they may have problems getting and keeping good jobs. The emotional side-effects of learning disorders may also affect their social relationships. On the other hand, many children overcome learning disorders. Nelson Rockefeller, former governor of New York and former vice president of the United States, suffered from reading disorder.

Motor Skills Disorder

The one **motor skills disorder,** called **developmental coordination disorder,** involves deficits in fundamental motor skills, such as walking or running or holding on to objects. This disorder is not diagnosed if a child's motor skills deficits are due to a medical condition such as cerebral palsy or muscular dystrophy, or to some more serious mental disorder, such as autism. A young child with developmental coordination disorder may be clumsy, and very slow in achieving major milestones such as walking, crawling, sitting, tying shoelaces, or zipping pants. Older children may be unable to assemble puzzles, build models, play ball, or write their names. This is a relatively common disorder, with as many as 6 percent of children between 5 and 11 years of age suffering from it (APA, 2000).

Communication Disorders

The **communication disorders** involve deficits in the ability to communicate verbally, because of a severely limited vocabulary, severe stuttering, or the inability to articulate words correctly. Children with **expressive language disorder** may have a limited vocabulary, difficulty in learning new words, difficulty in retrieving words or the right word, and poor grammar. They may use a limited variety of sentence types (only questions or declarations), omit critical parts of sentences, or use words in unusual orders. Some children with this disorder show signs of it from a very early age, while others develop language normally for a while but then begin to show signs of the disorder. Between 3 to 7 percent of children may be affected by this disorder (APA, 2000). Some children also have problems in understanding language produced by others, as well as in expressing their own thoughts. These children are said to have a **mixed receptive-expressive language disorder.**

Children with **phonological disorder** do not use speech sounds that are appropriate for their age or dialect. They may substitute one sound for another (e.g., use a *t* for *k* sound) or omit certain sounds (such as final consonants on words). Their words come out sounding like baby talk. They may say *wabbit* for *rabbit*, or *bu* for *blue*. Approximately 2 to 3 percent of 6- to 7-year-olds have moderate-to-severe phonological disorder. The prevalence falls to 0.5 percent by age 17 (APA, 2000). Finally, children who suffer from **stuttering** have significant problems in speech fluency often including frequent repetitions of sounds or syllables (such as, "I-I-I-I see him."). The severity of their speech problems can vary from situation to situation, but is usually worse when they are under pressure to speak well, as when giving a verbal report. The onset of stuttering is often gradual, and almost always occurs before the age of 10 (APA, 2000). As many as 80 percent of children who stutter recover on their own by age 16. Others, however, go on to stutter as adults. Stuttering can reduce a child's self-esteem and cause him or her

Learning disorders can lead to frustration and low self-esteem.

to limit goals and activities. The more aware the child is of stuttering, the more nervous he or she may become, which then just increases the stuttering.

The causes of these disorders of cognitive, motor, and communication skills are not well understood. Genetic factors are implicated in several of the disorders, especially stuttering and reading disorder. These disorders may also be linked to lead poisoning, birth defects, sensory dysfunction, or impoverished environments.

Treatment of these disorders usually involves therapies designed to build and correct missing skills, such as speech therapy for the communication disorders, reading therapy for dyslexia, and physical therapy for motor skills disorder. Recently, the use of computerized exercises has proven useful in helping children with communication and learning disorders learn to read and communicate normally (Merzenich et al., 1996).

Summing Up

- Disorders of cognitive, motor, and communication skills include the learning disorders, motor skills disorder, and communication disorders.

- Learning disorders include reading disorder (inability to read, also known as dyslexia), mathematics disorder (inability to learn math), and disorder of written expression (inability to write).

- The motor skills disorder is developmental coordination disorder, which involves deficits in fundamental motor skills.

- Communication disorders include expressive language disorder (inability to express oneself through language), mixed receptive-expressive language disorder (inability to express oneself through language or to understand the language of others), phonological disorder (use of speech sounds inappropriate for the age and dialect), and stuttering (deficits in word fluency).

- Some of these disorders, particularly reading disorder and stuttering, may have genetic roots. Many other factors have been implicated in these disorders, but they are not well understood.

- Treatment usually focuses on building skills in problem areas through specialized training, and now the use of computerized exercises.

MENTAL RETARDATION

Mental retardation involves deficits in a wide range of skills. It is defined as significantly subaverage intellectual functioning. A child's level of intellectual functioning may be assessed by standardized tests, usually referred to as *IQ tests* (see Chapter 4 for a discussion of these tests). Low scores on an IQ test do not, by themselves, warrant a diagnosis of mental retardation. This diagnosis requires that a child also show significant problems in performing the tasks of daily life. Specifically, in order to be diagnosed as mentally retarded, a child must show deficits, relative to other children that age, in at least two of the following skill areas (see Table 13.5): communication, self-care, home living, social and interpersonal interactions, use of community resources (e.g., riding a bus), self-direction, functional academic, work, or leisure activities, or protection of one's own health and safety.

The severity of mental retardation varies greatly. Children with *mild mental retardation* can feed and dress themselves with minimal help, may have average motor skills, and can learn to talk and write in simple terms. They can get around their own neighborhoods well, although they may not be able to venture beyond their neighborhoods without help. If they are put in special education classes that address their specific deficits, they can achieve a high school education and become self-sufficient. As adults, they can shop for specific items and cook simple meals for themselves. They may be employed in unskilled or semiskilled jobs. Their scores on IQ tests tend to be between about 50 and 70.

TABLE 13.5

DSM IV
Criteria for Diagnosing Mental Retardation

The diagnosis of mental retardation requires that a child show both poor intellectual functioning and significant defects in everyday skills.

A. Significantly subaverage intellectual functioning, indicated by an IQ of approximately 70 or below

B. Significant deficits in at least two of the following areas:
   1. communication
   2. self-care
   3. home living
   4. social or interpersonal skills
   5. use of community resources
   6. self-direction
   7. academic skills
   8. work
   9. leisure
   10. health
   11. personal safety

C. Onset before age 18

Reprinted with permission from the *Diagnostic and Statistical Manual of Mental Disorders*, Fourth Eidition. Copyright © 2000 American Psychiatric Association.

Children with *moderate mental retardation* typically have significant delays in language development, such as using only 4 to 10 words by the age of 3. They may be physically clumsy and thus have some trouble dressing and feeding themselves. They typically do not achieve beyond the second-grade level in academic skills but, with special education, can acquire simple vocational skills. As adults, they may not be able to travel alone or shop or cook for themselves. Their scores on IQ tests tend to be between about 35 and 50.

Children with *severe mental retardation* have very limited vocabularies and speak in two- to three-word sentences. They may have significant deficits in motor development and may play with toys inappropriately (e.g., banging two dolls together rather than having them interact symbolically). As adults, they can feed themselves with spoons and dress themselves if the clothing is not complicated with many buttons or zippers. They cannot travel alone for any distance and cannot shop or cook for themselves. They may be able to learn some unskilled manual labor, but many do not. Their IQ scores tend to run between 20 and 35.

Children and adults with *profound mental retardation* are severely impaired and require full-time custodial care. They cannot dress themselves completely. They may be able to use spoons, but not knives or forks.

They tend not to interact with others socially, although they may respond to simple commands. They may achieve vocabularies of 300 to 400 words as adults. Persons with profound mental retardation often suffer from frequent illnesses and their life expectancy is shorter than normal. Their IQ scores tend to be under 20.

Experts on mental retardation divide this disorder into two types: *organic retardation* and *cultural-familial retardation* (Hodapp, Burack, & Zigler, 1998). In cases of organic retardation, there is clear evidence of a biological cause for the disorder, and the level of retardation tends to be more severe. In cases of cultural-familial retardation, there is less evidence for the role of biology and more evidence for the role of environment in the development of the disorder. The severity of the retardation tends to be less severe, and there is a good chance that, with the right intervention, the child will eventually develop normal abilities (see Table 13.6).

Biological Causes of Mental Retardation

There are a large number of biological factors that can cause mental retardation, including chromosomal and gestational disorders, exposure to toxins prenatally and in early childhood, infections, physical trauma, metabolism and nutrition problems, and gross brain disease (see *Concept Review:* Factors Associated with Mental Retardation). We examine these factors first and then turn to the sociocultural factors implicated in mental retardation.

Genetic Contributors to Mental Retardation

Intellectual skills are at least partially inherited. The IQs of adopted children correlate much more strongly with those of their biological parents than with those of their adoptive parents. Similarly, the IQs of monozygotic twins are much more strongly correlated than are the IQs of dizygotic twins, even when the twins are reared apart (Scarr, Weinberg, & Waldman, 1993; Simonoff, Bolton, & Rutter, 1998). Families of children who are mentally retarded tend to have high incidences of a variety of intellectual problems, including the different levels of mental retardation and autism (Camp et al., 1998).

Two metabolic disorders that are genetically transmitted and that cause mental retardation are **phenylketonuria (PKU)** and **Tay-Sachs disease.** PKU is carried by a recessive gene and occurs in about 1 in 20,000 births. Children with PKU are unable to metabolize phenylalanine, an amino acid. As a result, phenylalanine and its derivative, phenyl pyruvic acid, build up in the body and cause permanent brain damage.

Children who do not have access to good nutrition, good schools, and a learning environment in the home, can develop cultural-familial forms of mental retardation.

Fortunately, an effective treatment is available, and children who receive this treatment from an early age can develop an average level of intelligence. If untreated, children with PKU typically have IQs below 50.

Tay-Sachs disease also is carried by a recessive gene and occurs primarily in Jewish populations. It usually does not appear until a child is between 3 and 6 months. At this point, a progressive degeneration of the nervous system begins, leading to mental and physical deterioration. These children usually die before the age of 6 years, and there is no effective treatment for this disease.

Several types of chromosomal disorders can lead to mental retardation. Recall from Chapter 2 that children are born with 23 pairs of chromosomes. Twenty-two of these pairs are known as *autosomes*, and the 23rd pair is the sex chromosomes. One of the best-known causes of mental retardation is **Down syndrome,** which is caused when chromosome 21 is present in triplicate rather than in duplicate (for this reason, Down syndrome is also referred to as *Trisomy 21*). Down syndrome occurs in about 1 in every 800 children born in the United States. From childhood, almost all people with Down syndrome are mentally retarded, although the level of their retardation can vary from mild to profound. Children with Down syndrome have round, flat faces and almond-shaped eyes, small noses, slightly protruding lips and tongues, and short square hands. They tend to be short in stature and

TABLE 13.6

Comparisons of Children with Organic and Cultural-Familial Mental Retardation

Children with organic mental retardation often have an earlier onset of problems, clear histories of biological abnormalities, more severe impairments, and worse prognosis than do children with cultural-familial mental retardation.

Organic Mental Retardation	Cultural-Familial Retardation
It is typically diagnosed in infancy.	It is typically diagnosed at school age.
There is a clear history or indicators of a biological abnormality.	There may be no history or indicators of biological abnormality.
The severity of retardation is profound, severe, or moderate.	The severity of retardation is often mild.
Impairments are generalized across situations.	Impairments are specific to certain situations.
Parents and siblings are likely to have intellectual functioning similar to that of the general population.	Parents and siblings are more likely to have mild retardation.
Socioeconomic status is representative of that of the general population.	Occurs often in lower socioeconomic groups.
Physical health is poorer than in the general population.	Physical health is about the same as that in the general population.
Treatments can improve functioning but not cure the condition.	Treatments may cure the condition entirely.

Source: MacMillan, Gresham, and Siperstein, 1993.

CONCEPT REVIEW

Factors Associated with Mental Retardation

A large number of factors my contribute to mental retardation.

Predisposing Factor	Examples of Specific Disorders or Conditions	Approximate % of this Population with Mental Retardation
Hereditary disorders	Down syndrome, Tay-Sachs disease, fragile X syndrome, phenylketonuria	5%
Early alterations of embryonic development	Down syndrome related to trisomy 21, prenatal exposure to toxins (e.g., maternal alcohol consumption or substance abuse)	30%
Later pregnancy and perinatal problems	Fetal malnutrition, placental insufficiency, prematurity, hypoxia, low birth weight, intracranial hemorrhage	10%
Acquired childhood diseases/accidents	Infections (e.g., meningitis, encephalitis), malnutrition, head trauma (e.g., car or household accidents, child abuse), poisoning (e.g., lead, mercury), environmental deprivation (psychosocial disadvantage, neglect)	5%
Environmental influences and other mental disorders	Deprivation, child abuse, severe mental disorders	15–20%
Unknown		30–40%

somewhat obese. Many of these children have congenital heart defects and gastrointestinal difficulties. As adults, they seem to age more rapidly than normal, and their life expectancy is shorter than average. People with Down syndrome have plaques and tangles on the neurons in their brains that resemble those found in Alzheimer's disease. About 25 to 40 percent of them lose their memories and the ability to care for themselves in adulthood.

Fragile X syndrome, which is the second most common cause of mental retardation in males after Down syndrome, is caused when a tip of the X chromosome breaks off. This syndrome is characterized by severe to profound mental retardation, speech defects, and severe deficits in interpersonal interactions. Males with Fragile X syndrome have large ears, long faces, and enlarged testes. Two other chromosomal abnormalities that cause mental retardation are **Trisomy 13** (chromosome 13 is present in triplicate) and **Trisomy 18** (chromosome 18 is present in triplicate). Both of these disorders lead to severe retardation and shortened life expectancy. The risk of having a child with Down syndrome or any other chromosomal abnormalities increases the older a woman is when she becomes pregnant. This may be because the older a mother is, the more likely her chromosomes are to have degenerated or been damaged by toxins.

The Prenatal Environment: Drugs and Alcohol

The intellectual development of a fetus can be profoundly affected by the quality of its prenatal environment. When a pregnant woman contracts the rubella virus (German measles), the herpes virus, or syphilis, there is a risk of physical damage to the fetus that can cause mental retardation. Chronic maternal disorders such as high blood pressure and diabetes can interfere with fetal nutrition and brain development and therefore affect the intellectual capacities of the fetus, although if these disorders are effectively treated throughout the pregnancy, the risk of damage to the fetus is low.

Most drugs that a pregnant woman takes can pass through the placenta to the fetus. It is estimated that 325,000 babies born in the United States each year were exposed to illicit drugs prenatally (Gonzalez & Campbell, 1994). Much media attention has been focused on "crack babies," infants born to women who smoked crack while pregnant. Any form of cocaine constricts the mother's blood vessels, leading to reduced oxygen and blood flow to the fetus, possibly resulting in brain damage and retardation. Crack babies tend to be less alert than other babies, and not as responsive, either emotionally or cognitively. They are more excitable and less able to regulate their sleep-wake patterns. They tend to be irritable and distractible (Napiorkowski et al., 1996; Tronick et al., 1996). Studies suggest that mothers who take cocaine during pregnancy differ in many ways from mothers who do not: They are older, more socially disadvantaged, and more likely to use tobacco, alcohol, marijuana, and other illicit drugs (Tronick et al., 1996). These other risk factors, in addition to exposure to cocaine, may severely impair intellectual growth in the children of these mothers.

Fetuses whose mothers abuse alcohol during pregnancy are at increased risk for mental retardation and a collection of physical defects known as **fetal alcohol syndrome** (Fried & Watkinson, 1990). Children with fetal alcohol syndrome have an average IQ of only 68, along with poor judgment, distractibility, difficulty in perceiving social cues, and the inability to learn from experience. As adolescents, their academic functioning is only at the second- to fourth-grade level, and they have great trouble following directions. It is estimated that about 1 in 700 children in the United States is born with fetal alcohol syndrome (Streissguth, Randels, & Smith, 1991). Abel Dorris was one such child:

> ## CASE STUDY
> Abel Dorris was adopted when he was 3 years old by Michael Dorris. Abel's mother had been a heavy drinker throughout the pregnancy and after Abel was born and later died at age 35 of alcohol poisoning. Abel had been born almost seven weeks premature, with low birthweight. He had been abused and malnourished before being removed to a foster home. At age 3, Abel was small for his age, not yet toilet-trained, and could only speak about 20 words. He had been diagnosed as mildly retarded. His adoptive father hoped that, in a positive environment, Abel could catch up.
>
> Yet, at age 4, Abel was still in diapers and weighed only 27 pounds. He had trouble remembering the names of other children and his activity level was unusually high. When alone, he would rock back and forth rhythmically. At age 4, he suffered the first of several severe seizures, which caused him to lose consciousness for days. No drug treatments seemed to help.
>
> When he entered school, Abel had trouble learning to count, to identify colors, and to tie his shoes. He had a short attention span and difficulty following simple instructions. Despite devoted teachers, when he finished elementary school, Abel still could not add, subtract, or identify his place of residence. His IQ was measured in the mid-60s.
>
> Eventually, at age 20, Abel entered a vocational training program and moved into a supervised home. His main preoccupations were his collections of stuffed animals, paper dolls, newspaper cartoons, family photographs, and old birthday cards. At age 23, he was hit by a car and killed. (Adapted from Dorris, 1989; Lyman, 1997).

Children born to mothers who drank only moderately during pregnancy may have intellectual deficits that are subtler than those found in fetal alcohol syndrome. One study of 44 babies born to White, middle-class mothers, found that those whose mothers drank even moderately while pregnant were more irritable at 1 year of age and had lower scores on tests of cognitive development than those whose mothers did not drink during pregnancy (O'Connor, Sigman, & Kasari, 1993). Presently, it is not known whether there is a safe amount of alcohol that a woman can ingest during pregnancy.

The First Years of Life: Shaken Baby Syndrome

Severe head traumas that damage children's brains can lead to mental retardation. **Shaken baby syndrome** is caused when a baby is shaken violently, leading to

intracranial injury and retinal hemorrhages (Caffey, 1972). Babies' heads are relatively large and heavy compared to the rest of their bodies, and their neck muscles are too weak to control their heads when they are shaken back and forth in whiplash fashion. The rapid movement of their heads when shaken can lead to their brains being bruised from being banged against the skull wall. Bleeding can also occur in and around the brain and behind the eyes. This can lead to seizures, partial or total blindness, paralysis, mental retardation, or death. Although violent shaking of a baby sometimes is part of a pattern of physical abuse by a parent, it often happens innocently when a frustrated parent does not know that shaking a baby can lead to permanent brain damage, as in the following case of a father of a young infant:

> ### CASE STUDY
> Jill's mother was very ill, so she left me with the baby for the day while she went to her mother's house to help her. About 2 o'clock, the baby started crying for some reason. I changed him, I fed him, I rocked him, I sang to him. Nothing would quiet him down. He kept crying and crying, for hours. Finally, around 6 P.M., I got so overwhelmed with his crying that I just shook him, hard, but only for a few seconds. He immediately quieted down, so I thought I had done the right thing. I put him to bed and he seemed to sleep peacefully. But then we had trouble waking him for his feeding. The next day he was listless, just like a rag doll. Jill rushed him to the doctor. They did a series of tests and said that he might have brain damage! That was 4 years ago. Since then, he has been delayed in many areas of his development. The doctors say he will never be normal. I just wish I had known that you aren't supposed to shake a baby.

Young children face a number of other hazards in addition to shaken baby syndrome. Exposure to toxic substances, such as lead, arsenic, and mercury, during early childhood can lead to mental retardation by damaging specific areas of the brain. The importance of protecting children from accidental ingestion of these substances cannot be understated. Children can also incur brain damage, leading to mental retardation, through accidents, including traffic accidents in cars in which they are not properly buckled.

Sociocultural Contributors to Mental Retardation

Children who have either organic or cultural-familial mental retardation are more likely to come from low socioeconomic groups (Camp et al., 1998; Brooks-Gunn, Klebanov, & Duncan, 1996). This may be because their

"Please don't shake them — you might break them."

[Pat Kratus- U. of M. Football Defensive Tackle]

Hey man, you don't know your own strength!
When I'm on the playing field, brute force is key, but I know that when it comes to babies and children, easy does it. Shaking a baby even for a few seconds can kill or seriously hurt her or him. If a crying baby gets you down, hand him off to someone you trust and take a time out. Taking care of a child is one play you don't want to fumble.

Washtenaw Area Council for Children and Children's Trust Fund—
working together to prevent child abuse and neglect, and to strengthen families.
(734) 761-7071. Ad funded by the Kiwanis Club of Ann Arbor.

Children's Trust Fund

Football player Pat Kratus participated in an ad campaign to make people aware of the dangers of shaking babies and young children.

parents are also mentally retarded and thus have not been able to acquire well-paying jobs. The social disadvantages of being poor may also contribute to lower than average intellectual development. Poor mothers are less likely to receive good prenatal care, increasing the risk of their children being born prematurely. Children living in lower socioeconomic areas are at increased risk for exposure to lead, because old, run-down buildings often have lead paint, which chips off and is ingested by the children. Poor children are concentrated in the inner city, in poorly funded schools, and this is especially true for poor minority children. Poor children who have lower IQs receive less favorable attention from teachers and fewer learning opportunities, especially if they are also minorities (Alexander, Entwisle, & Thompson, 1987). Poor children are less likely to have parents who read to them, who encourage academic success, and who are involved in their schooling. These factors may directly affect a child's intellectual development, and may exacerbate biological conditions that interfere with a child's cognitive development (Camp et al., 1998).

Treatments for Mental Retardation

Interventions for mentally retarded children must be comprehensive, intensive, and probably long term to show benefits (Singh, Oswald, & Ellis, 1998). The *Concept Review:* Treatments for Mental Retardation summarizes these treatments.

Behavioral Strategies

Typically, a child's parents or caregivers are enlisted in treatment, and taught new skills for enhancing the child's positive behaviors and reducing negative behaviors. Behavioral strategies are often used to help mentally retarded children and adults learn new skills, from identifying colors correctly to dressing themselves to a vocational skill. The desired behavior may be modeled in incremental steps and rewards are given to the child or adult as he or she comes closer and closer to mastering the skill. Behavioral strategies can also help to reduce self-injurious behaviors and other maladaptive behaviors. Behavioral methods do not simply focus on isolated skills, but are typically integrated in a comprehensive program designed to maximize a retarded individual's ability to integrate into the community.

Drug Therapy

Medications are used to reduce seizures, which are common among people with mental retardation, to help control aggressive or self-injurious behavior, and

---

CONCEPT REVIEW

Treatments for Mental Retardation

Comprehensive treatment programs for mental retardation involve biological, behavioral, and sociocultural interventions.

Behavioral Strategies:

Caregivers taught skills for enhancing the child's positive behaviors and reducing negative behaviors

Desired behaviors modeled in incremental steps; rewards given to the child as he or she masters the skill

Self-injurious behavior extinguished

Drug Therapies:

Neuroleptic medications to reduce aggressive and antisocial behavior

Atypical antipsychotics to reduce aggression and self-injury

Antidepressant medications to reduce depression, improve sleep, reduce self-injury

Sociocultural Programs:

Early intervention programs including comprehensive services addressing physical, developmental, and educational needs, and training parents

Mainstreaming children into regular classrooms

Group homes that provide comprehensive services to adults

Institutionalization of children or adults with severe physical handicaps or behavioral problems

---

to help improve their mood (Singh, Oswald, & Ellis, 1998). Neuroleptic medications (see Chapter 10) can reduce aggressive, destructive, and antisocial behavior. The potential for neurological side effects has made these medications controversial. The newer atypical antipsychotics, such as risperidone, have been shown to reduce aggression and self-injurious behavior in adults with mental retardation without inducing serious neurological side effects (Cohen et al., 1998). Antidepressant medications can reduce depressive symptoms, improve sleep patterns, and possibly help in controlling self-injurious behavior in mentally retarded individuals (Singh, Oswald, & Ellis, 1998).

Sociocultural Programs

Sociocultural programs have focused on intervening early in a child's life, integrating the child into the mainstream of other children where possible, group homes that provide comprehensive care, and institutionalization when necessary.

Early intervention programs Many experts recommend beginning comprehensive interventions with children at risk for mental retardation from the first days of life. These interventions include intensive one-on-one interventions with children to enhance their development of basic skills, measures to reduce social conditions that might interfere with the children's development, such as child abuse, malnutrition, or exposure to toxins, and providing children with adequate medical care.

One such program is the Infant Health and Development Program (Gross, Brooks-Gunn, & Spiker, 1992). The focus of this program was children born with a birth weight of 2,500 grams or less and a gestational age of 37 completed weeks or less. A total of 985 infants, across eight sites in the United States, were enrolled in the program. Two-thirds of these infants were randomly assigned to receive high-quality pediatric care for high-risk infants, the other third received same pediatric care plus an early education intervention program. The intervention involved three components. First, specially trained counselors conducted visits to the child's home during the first three years of the child's life, providing support to the mothers, and fostering parent-child activities that would enhance children's development. Mothers were given training in good parenting practices and in ways of facilitating their children's cognitive development. For example, mothers were taught ways of calming their babies (who tended to be irritable), ways to provide appropriate levels of stimulation and opportunities for self-motivated actions and explorations, and ways of reducing stress in their environments and in their babies' environments. Second, the children in the intervention condition went daily to a child development center with specially trained teachers who worked to overcome the children's intellectual and physical deficits. Third, parent support groups were started to help parents cope with the stresses of parenting.

At 36 months of age, the children in the intervention group were significantly less likely to have IQ scores in the retarded range than were those in the control group who received only medical care (The Infant Health and Development Program, 1990). Among infants with birth weights between 2,001 and 2,500 grams, the effects of the program were especially strong: At age 36 months, they had IQ scores an average of 13 points higher than infants in the control group with similar birth weights. Infants with birth weights under 2,000 grams also benefited from the program, but to a lesser degree: their 36-month IQ scores were an average of 6.6 points higher than control group infants with similar birth weights. Both the "heavier" and "lighter" birth weight groups in the intervention condition also showed fewer behavioral and emotional problems at 36 months than the children in the control groups.

The "heavier" birth weight children continued to show benefits in cognitive development from the intervention at 60 months and 96 months of age, compared to the control groups (Brooks-Gunn, Klebanov, & Liaw, 1995). Differences between the intervention groups and the control groups in behavioral and emotional problems had disappeared by this age, however. Thus, as has been the case with many early intervention programs, benefits are seen in the short term, but without continuation of the intervention, these benefits often diminish with time.

What accounted for the positive effects of the intervention? The home environments of the children in the intervention improved significantly (Berlin et al., 1998; McCormick et al., 1998). There were more learning materials available and their mothers more actively stimulated the children's learning. The mothers of the children in the intervention program were better at assisting their children in problem-solving, remaining more responsive and persistent with their children. In turn, these children showed more enthusiasm and involvement in learning tasks. In addition, the mothers in the intervention program reported better mental health than the mothers in the control group. The mothers in the intervention group were also less likely to use harsh disciplinary strategies with their children than the mothers in the control group. All of these factors were associated with the better outcomes of the children in the intervention groups.

Mainstreaming Controversy exists over whether mentally retarded children should be placed in special education classes or *mainstreamed*—that is, put into regular classrooms. Special education classes can concentrate

Many people with Down syndrome are being mainstreamed into jobs in the community.

on retarded children's needs, providing them with extra training in skills they lack. Some critics of these classes, however, argue that they stigmatize children and provide them with an education that asks less of them than what they are able to achieve. Critics also have charged that minority children often are placed inappropriately in special education classes because they score lower on culturally biased achievement tests or IQ tests. However, placing retarded children in a classroom with children of average intelligence can put the retarded children at certain disadvantages. One study found that retarded children were viewed by the other children in their classrooms negatively. Zigler and Hodapp (1991) argue that retarded children who are mainstreamed may often not receive the special training they need. However, studies of the academic progress of retarded children in special education programs and in regular classrooms tend to find little difference in the performance of these two groups.

Group homes Many retarded adults live in group homes where they are given assistance in the tasks of daily living (e.g., cooking, cleaning) and training in vocational and social skills. They may work in sheltered workshops during the day, doing unskilled or semi-skilled labor. Increasingly, they are being mainstreamed into the general workforce, often in service-related jobs (e.g., in fast-food restaurants, or as baggers in grocery stores). Community-based programs for retarded adults have shown to be effective in enhancing their social and vocational skills in some studies of specific programs.

Institutionalization In the past, most retarded children were institutionalized for life. Institutionalization is less common these days, but retarded children with severe physical handicaps or with significant behavior problems, such as problems controlling aggression, may still be institutionalized (Blacher, Hanneman, & Rousey, 1992). African American and Latino families are less likely to institutionalize their retarded children than are White families (Blacher, Hanneman, & Rousey, 1992). This may be because African American and Latino families are less likely than White families to have the financial resources to place their children in high-quality institutions. It may also be because there is a stronger emphasis placed on caring for ill or disabled family members within the family in African American and Latino cultures than in White culture.

Summing Up

- Mental retardation is defined as subaverage intellectual functioning, indexed by an IQ score of under 70 and deficits in adaptive behavioral functioning.

- There are four levels of mental retardation, ranging from mild to profound.

- A number of biological factors are implicated in mental retardation, including metabolic disorders (PKU, Tay-Sachs disease); chromosomal disorders (Down syndrome, Fragile X, Trisomy 13 and Trisomy 18); prenatal exposure to rubella, herpes, syphilis, or illicit drugs (especially alcohol); premature delivery; and head traumas (such as those arising from being violently shaken).

- There is some evidence that intensive and comprehensive educational interventions, administered very early in an affected child's life, can help to decrease the level of mental retardation.

- Controversy exists over whether mentally retarded children should be put in special education classes with other mentally retarded children or mainstreamed into normal classrooms.

◑ AUTISM

The **pervasive developmental disorders** are characterized by severe and lasting impairment in several areas of development, including social interactions, communication with others, everyday behaviors, interests, and activities. The pervasive developmental disorder that is probably most familiar to you is **autism**—a disorder in which children show deficits in social interaction, communication, and their activities and interests. Many autistic children also show at least mild levels of mental retardation.

Other disorders in this category include **Asperger's disorder,** which is characterized by deficits in social skills and activities similar to those in autism, but which does not involve deficits in language or basic cognitive skills (see *Concept Review:* Pervasive Developmental Disorders). **Rett's disorder** and **childhood disintegrative disorder** are two pervasive developmental disorders in which children appear to develop normally for a while and then show apparently permanent loss of basic skills in social interactions, language, and/or movement. By far, autism has been studied more than the other pervasive developmental disorders, and we focus on autism for the remainder of this chapter.

Autism affects many aspects of a child's development: communication skills, social interactions, cognitive skills, and motor development (see Table 13.7). The most salient features of autism, however, are the impairments in social interaction (Kanner, 1943). Some autistic children seem to live in worlds of their own, uninterested in other children or in their own caregivers. Richard is a child with autism (adapted from Spitzer et al., 1994, pp. 336–337):

CONCEPT REVIEW

Pervasive Developmental Disorders

The pervasive developmental disorders are characterized by severe and lasting deficits in several areas of development.

Disorder	Description
Autism	Deficits in social interactions, in communication, including significant language deficits, and in activities and interests
Asperger's disorder	Deficits in social interactions and in activities and interests, but not in language and or basic cognitive skills
Rett's disorder	Apparently normal development through first 5 months of life and normal head circumference at birth, but then deceleration of head growth between 5 and 48 months, loss of motor and social skills already learned, and poor development of motor skills and language
Childhood disintegrative disorder	Apparently normal development for first 2 years, followed by significant loss of previously acquired skills between age 2 and 10, and abnormalities of functioning in social interactions, communication, and activities

TABLE 13.7
DSM-IV
Symptoms of Autism

The symptoms of autism include a range of deficits in social interactions, communication, and activities. To be diagnosed with autism, children must show these deficits before the age of 3.

Deficits in Social Interactions

Little use of nonverbal behaviors that indicate a social "connection," such as eye-to-eye gazes, facial reactions to others (smiling or frowning at others' remarks as appropriate), body postures that indicate interest in others (leaning toward a person who is speaking), or gestures (waving goodbye to a parent)

Failure to develop peer relationships as other children do

Little expression of pleasure when others are happy

Little reciprocity in social interactions

Deficits in Communication

Delay in, or total absence of, spoken language

In children who do speak, significant trouble in initiating and maintaining conversations

Unusual language, including repetition of certain phrases and pronoun reversal

Lack of make-believe play or imitation of others at a level appropriate for the child's age

Deficits in Activities and Interests

Preoccupation with certain activities or toys and compulsive adherence to routines and rituals

Stereotyped and repetitive movements, such as hand flapping and head banging

Preoccupation with parts of objects (such as the arm of a doll instead of the whole doll) and unusual uses of objects (lining up toys in rows instead of playing "pretend" with them)

CASE STUDY

Richard, age 3 1/2, appeared to be self-sufficient and aloof from others. He did not greet his mother in the mornings or his father when he returned from work, though, if left with a baby-sitter, he tended to scream much of the time. He had no interest in other children and ignored his younger brother. His babbling had no conversational intonation. At age 3 he could understand simple practical instructions. His speech consisted of echoing some words and phrases he had heard in the past, with the original speaker's accent and intonation; he could use one or two such phrases to indicate his simple needs. For example, if he said, "Do you want a drink?" he meant he was thirsty. He did not communicate by facial expression or use gesture or mime, except for pulling someone along with him and placing his or her hand on an object he wanted.

He was fascinated by bright lights and spinning objects and would stare at them while laughing, flapping his hands, and dancing on tiptoe. He also displayed the same movements while listening to music, which he liked from infancy. He was intensely attached to a miniature car, which he held in his hand, day and night, but he never played imaginatively with this or any other toy. He could assemble jigsaw puzzles rapidly (with one hand because of the car held in the other), whether the picture side was exposed or hidden. From age 2 he had collected kitchen utensils and arranged them in repetitive patterns all over the floors of the house. These pursuits, together with occasional periods of aimless running around, constituted his whole repertoire of spontaneous activities.

The major management problem was Richard's intense resistance to any attempt to change or extend his interests. Removing his toy car, disturbing his puzzles or patterns, even retrieving, for example, an egg whisk or a spoon for its legitimate use in cooking, or trying to make him look at a picture book precipitated temper tantrums that could last an hour or more, with screaming, kicking, and the biting of himself or others. These tantrums could be cut short by restoring the status quo. Otherwise, playing his favorite music or going for a long car ride were sometimes effective.

His parents had wondered if Richard might be deaf, but his love of music, his accurate echoing, and his sensitivity to some very soft sounds, such as those made by unwrapping chocolate in the next room, convinced them that this was not the cause of his abnormal behavior. Psychological testing gave Richard a mental age of 3 years in non–language-dependent skills (such as assembling objects) but only 18 months in language comprehension.

Deficits

Autistic children's deficits can be grouped into three categories. The first is deficits in *social interactions*, such as Richard's lack of interaction with his family members. Even as infants, children with autism seem not to connect with other people, including their parents. They may not smile and coo in response to their caregivers or initiate play with their caregivers, as most young infants do. They may not want to cuddle with their parents, even when they are frightened. While most infants love to gaze upon their caregivers as the caregivers gaze adoringly at them, autistic infants may hardly ever make eye-to-eye contact. When they are a bit older, autistic children may not be interested in playing with other children, preferring to remain in solitary play, as Richard did. Autistic children also do not seem to react to other people's emotions. It was formerly thought that autistic children were preoccupied with internal thoughts and fantasies, much as people with schizophrenia might be preoccupied with hallucinations and delusions. Indeed, autism in children formerly was considered a precursor to adult schizophrenia. Studies over the last few decades have shown, however, that autistic children do not develop the classic symptoms of schizophrenia as adults (e.g., they show no evidence of hallucinations and delusions) and that adults with schizophrenia do not have histories of full autistic disorder as young children. In addition, autism and schizophrenia do not co-occur in families at a high rate, suggesting that they have different genetic causes.

The second group of deficits in autism has to do with *communication*. Approximately 50 percent of autistic children do not develop useful speech (Gillberg, 1991). Those who do develop language may not use it as other children do. Richard showed several of the communication problems of autistic children. Rather than generating his own words, he simply echoed or repeated what he had just heard, in a phenomenon called **echolalia.** He reversed pronouns, using *you* when he meant *I.* When he did try to generate his own words or sentences, he did not modulate his voice for expressiveness, sounding almost like a voice-generating machine.

The third group of deficits concerns the type of *activities and interests* of autistic children. Rather than engaging in symbolic play with toys, they are preoccupied with one part of a toy or object, as Richard was preoccupied with his miniature car. They may engage in bizarre, repetitive behaviors with toys. For example, rather than using two dolls to play "dollies have tea," an autistic child might take the arm off one doll and simply pass it back and forth between her two hands. Routines and rituals are often extremely important to autistic children: When any aspect of the daily routine is changed—for example, if a child's mother stops at the bank on the way to school—they may fly into a rage. Some autistic children perform stereotyped and repetitive behaviors using some parts of their own bodies, such as incessantly flapping their hands or banging their heads against walls. These behaviors are sometimes referred to as *self-stimulatory behaviors*, under the assumption that autistic children engage in these behaviors for self-stimulation. It is not clear, however, that this is the true purpose behind these behaviors.

Some autistic children will hurt themselves by banging their heads against a wall, and thus must wear helmets to be protected against brain damage.

Autistic children often do poorly on measures of intellectual ability, such as IQ tests, with 66 percent scoring below 70 (Ritvo et al., 1989). The deficits of some autistic children, however, are confined to skills that require language and perspective-taking skills, and like Richard, they may score in the average range on subtests that do not require language skills. Much has been made in the popular press about the special talents that some otherwise retarded autistic children have, such as the ability to play music without having been taught or to draw extremely well or exceptional memory and mathematical calculation abilities as was depicted in the movie *Rain Man*. These persons are sometimes referred to as *idiot savants*. These cases are quite rare, however (Gillberg, 1991).

By definition, the symptoms of autism have their onset before the age of 3. However, children with autism are not simply delayed in their development of important skills. When they do develop language or social interaction patterns, there is a deviancy in the nature of these that is striking. It is important to note, though, that there is a wide variation in the severity and outcome of this disorder (Gillberg, 1991). Somewhere between 10 and 20 percent of autistic children "grow out" of autism and eventually are able to function well as adults, hold jobs, and sometimes have families (Gillberg, 1991; Gillbert & Steffenburg, 1987; Szatmari et al., 1989). A substantial portion of these people still have some problems with social interactions, however, remaining aloof and having trouble in normal conversation. One person who has autism as a child but who has thrived in spite of, or perhaps because of, it, is Temple Grandin, a professor of animal sciences at Colorado State University. Her experiences are described in *Extraordinary People:* Thinking in Pictures (p. 478).

About two-thirds of autistic people are severely handicapped throughout adult life and must remain completely dependent on families or institutions for daily care (Nordin & Gillberg, 1998). The remainder of autistic people function somewhere in between, perhaps living in residential facilities with other autistic individuals and a caretaking staff and working in simple jobs. By far, the best predictor of the outcome of autism is a child's IQ and amount of language development before the age of 6 (Nordin & Gillberg, 1998; Ritvo et al., 1989). Children who have IQs above 50 and communicative speech before age 6 have a much better prognosis than do those with IQs below 50 and no communicative speech before age 6.

The prevalence of autism is about 5 cases in 10,000 (Nordin & Gillberg, 1996). Boys outnumber girls about three to one. The prevalence of autism does not appear to vary by national origin, race/ethnicity, socioeconomic status, or parental education.

Contributors to Autism

Over the years, there has been a wide variety of theories of autism (see *Concept Review:* Contributors to Autism, p. 480). The psychiatrist who first described autism, Leo Kanner (1943), thought that autism was caused partly by biological factors and partly by poor parenting. He and later psychoanalytic theorists (Bettelheim, 1967) described the parents of autistic children as cold, distant, and uncaring (hence the description, "refrigerator mothers"). The autistic child's symptoms were seen as a retreat inward to a secret world of fantasies in response to unavailable parents. Research over the decades has clearly shown, though, that parenting practices play little or no role in the development of autism. If parents of autistic children differ psychologically at all from parents of nonautistic children, it is because of the stress that having an autistic child places on a parent.

Deficits in Theory of Mind

One of the leading theories of autism these days is that autistic children have deficits in theory of mind—the ability to understand that you and others have mental states and to use this understanding to interact and communicate with others (Baron-Cohen & Swettenham, 1997). Having a theory of mind is essential to comprehending, explaining, predicting, and manipulating the behavior of others. Most young children show signs of the development of a theory of mind by 18 months, by engaging in symbolic play, using objects to represent something other than what they really are (Lillard, 1993, 1996). By about age 3, children are able to understand the difference between their own mental states and those of others, they seem to understand

EXTRAORDINARY PEOPLE

Thinking in Pictures

D r. Temple Grandin, a professor of animal sciences at Colorado State University, has designed one-third of all livestock-handling facilities in the United States. She has published dozens of scientific papers and gives lectures throughout the world. Sometimes those lectures describe the new equipment and procedures she has designed for safer and more humane handling of animals. Sometimes, however, those lectures describe her life with autism.

As a young child, Grandin had all the classic symptoms of autism. When she was a baby, she had no desire to be held by her mother and struggled to get away, but was calm if left alone in a baby carriage. She seldom made eye contact with others, seemed to have no interest in people, and was constantly staring off into space. She frequently threw wild tantrums and smeared her feces around. If left alone she would rock back and forth or spin around indefinitely. She could sit for hours on the beach watching sand dribbling through her fingers, in a trance-like state. She still had not begun talking at age 2½. She was labeled as "brain damaged" because doctors 40 years ago did not know about autism.

Fortunately, Grandin's mother was dogged about finding good teachers, learning ways to calm her daughter, and encouraging her daughter to speak and engage in the social world. Grandin did learn to speak by the time she entered elementary school, although most of her deficits in social interactions remained. By the time she was 12 years old, Grandin scored 137 on an IQ test, but still was thrown out of a regular school because she didn't fit in. She persisted, however, and eventually went to college, earning a degree in psychology, and then to graduate school, where she earned a Ph.D. in animal sciences.

Grandin's book *Thinking in Pictures* (1995) provides remarkable insights into the motivations and experiences behind some of the strange symptoms of autism. She describes how she, like many people with autism, think visually instead of verbally:

Temple Grandin has written about her life with autism.

Today, everyone is excited about the new virtual reality computer systems in which the user wears special goggles and is fully immersed in video game action. To me, these systems are like crude cartoons. My imagination works like the computer graphics programs that created the lifelike dinosaurs in Jurassic Park. When I do an equipment simulation in my imagination or work on an engineering problem, it is like seeing it on a videotape in my mind. I can view it from any angle, placing myself above or below the equipment and rotating it at the same time. I don't need any fancy graphics program that can produce three-dimensional design simulations. I can do it better and faster in my head. (p. 21)

This ability to visualize has been of tremendous value in Grandin's career as a facilities designer. She can literally take a "cow's-eye view" of holding facilities and equipment, seeing what a cow sees as it is shuttled down a shoot, even before the equipment is built. This has led her to develop revolutionary new designs for this equipment that prevent animals from panicking and thus either hurting themselves, possibly fatally, or being exposed to cruel tactics such as electric cattle prods.

Thinking in pictures instead of words is part of what made it difficult to learn language, however. She was able to learn nouns relatively easily because she could visualize the objects to which these words referred. Other components of language were more difficult until she developed means of visualizing them, too:

I also visualize verbs. The word "jumping" triggers a memory of jumping hurdles at the mock Olympics held at my elementary school. Adverbs often trigger inappropriate images—"quickly" reminds me of Nestle's Quick—unless they are paired with a verb, which modifies my visual image. For example, "he ran quickly" triggers an animated image of Dick from the first grade reading book

Continued

running fast, and "he walked slowly" slows the image down. As a child, I left out words such as "is," "the," and "it," because they had no meaning by themselves. Similarly, words like "of" and "an" made no sense. Eventually, I learned how to use them properly, because my parents always spoke correct English and I mimicked their speech patterns. To this day certain verb conjugations, such as "to be," are absolutely meaningless to me. (pp. 30–31).

Grandin explains her desire not to be held as a child, her temper tantrums, and her retreat into rocking and staring, as due to massive sensory overload. She argues that many people with autism are hypersensitive to sensory input, and everyday sounds like a hairdryer or a balloon popping can be as painful and overwhelming as a jet engine roaring a few feet away. She was also hypersensitive to touch:

From as far back as I can remember, I always hated to be hugged. I wanted to experience the good feeling of being hugged, but it was just too overwhelming. It was like a great, all-engulfing tidal wave of stimulation, and I reacted like a wild animal. . . .

Many autistic children crave pressure stimulation even though they cannot tolerate being touched . . . I was one of these pressure seekers. When I was six, I would wrap myself up in blankets and get under sofa cushions, because the pressure was relaxing. I used to daydream for hours in elementary school about constructing a device that would apply pressure to my body. I visualized a box with an inflatable liner that I could lie in. It would be like being totally encased in inflatable splints. (pp. 62–63)

Later Grandin actually built such a "squeeze machine." Her teachers and counselors thought this was weird, but she continued to use the machine and over the years developed more and more sophisticated machines that she could control with hydraulics. She credits her squeeze machine not only with calming her persistent anxiety and panic attacks, but also with teaching her something about human relationships:

To have feelings of gentleness, one must experience gentle bodily comfort. As my nervous system learned to tolerate the soothing pressure from my squeeze machine, I discovered that the comforting feeling made me a kinder and gentler person. It was difficult for me to understand the idea of kindness until I had soothed myself. . . .

From the time I started using my squeeze machine, I understood that the feeling it gave me was one that I needed to cultivate toward other people. It was clear that the pleasurable feelings were those associated with love for other people. I built a machine that would apply the soothing, comforting contact that I craved as well as the physical affection I couldn't tolerate when I was young. I would have been as hard and unfeeling as a rock if I had not built my squeeze machine and followed through with its use. The relaxing feeling of being held washes negative thoughts away. I believe that the brain needs to receive comforting sensory input. Gentle touching teaches kindness. (pp. 82–83)

Understanding emotions and social relationships is still very difficult for Grandin, however. She explains,

I get great satisfaction out of doing clever things with my mind, but I don't know what it is like to feel rapturous joy. I know I am missing something when other people swoon over a beautiful sunset. Intellectually I know it is beautiful, but I don't feel it. The closest thing I have to joy is the excited pleasure I feel when I have solved a design problem. When I get this feeling, I just want to kick up my heels. I'm like a calf gamboling about on a spring day.

My emotions are simpler than those of most people. I don't know what complex emotion in a human relationship is. I only understand simple emotions, such as fear, anger, happiness, and sadness. I cry during sad movies, and sometimes I cry when I see something that really moves me. But complex emotional relationships are beyond my comprehension. (p. 89)

This often makes it difficult for Grandin to operate in the social world. She does not "read" other people well, and often finds herself offending people or being stared at for her social awkwardness.

Social interactions that come naturally to most people can be daunting for people with autism. As a child, I was like an animal that had no instincts to guide me; I just had to learn by trial and error. I was always observing, trying to work out the best way

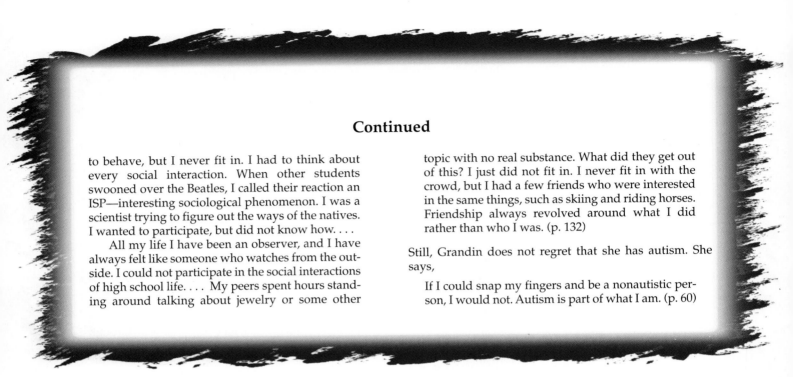

Continued

to behave, but I never fit in. I had to think about every social interaction. When other students swooned over the Beatles, I called their reaction an ISP—interesting sociological phenomenon. I was a scientist trying to figure out the ways of the natives. I wanted to participate, but did not know how. . . .

All my life I have been an observer, and I have always felt like someone who watches from the outside. I could not participate in the social interactions of high school life. . . . My peers spent hours standing around talking about jewelry or some other topic with no real substance. What did they get out of this? I just did not fit in. I never fit in with the crowd, but I had a few friends who were interested in the same things, such as skiing and riding horses. Friendship always revolved around what I did rather than who I was. (p. 132)

Still, Grandin does not regret that she has autism. She says,

If I could snap my fingers and be a nonautistic person, I would not. Autism is part of what I am. (p. 60)

CONCEPT REVIEW
Contributors to Autism

All of the modern theories of autism view it as the result of biological factors.

Contributor	Description
Deficits in theory of mind	Deficits in the ability to understand that you and others have mental states and to use this understanding to interact and communicate with others
Genetic predisposition	Predisposition to broad range of cognitive impairments
Chromosomal abnormalities	Possible aberrations on the long arm of chromosome 15, or in the number and structure of the sex hormones
Neurological deficits	Broad array of neurological problems seen, including seizure disorders
Prenatal and birth complications	Neurological deficits that could be caused by a number of complications
Neurotransmitter imbalances	Possible imbalances in serotonin and neorepinephrine

what others can perceive, and they know that people may differ in what they see, know, expect, like, and want (Yirmiya et al., 1998). By age 4 to 5, children understand false beliefs (e.g., that Mommy thinks they are hiding in the closet when they are really hiding in the bedroom), realize the distinction between appearance and reality, understand the concepts of desire and intention, and understand that people's actions are guided by their thoughts, beliefs, and desires (Flavell, 1992; Wellman, 1993).

Children with autism often fail tasks assessing theory of mind, even when they perform appropriately on other cognitive tasks for their age group (Yirmiya et al., 1998). The absence of a theory of mind may make it impossible for autistic children to understand and operate in the social world and communicate appropriately with others. Autistic children's strange play behavior—specifically the absence of symbolic play—may also represent an inability to understand anything but the concrete realities before them.

Biological Factors

Several biological factors have been implicated in the development of autism. Family and twin studies strongly suggest that genetics plays a role in the development of the disorder. Siblings of autistic children are 50 times more likely to also be autistic than are siblings of nonautistic children (Rutter et al., 1990; Szatmari et al., 1998). Twin studies show concordance rates for autism to be about 60 to 80 percent for monozygotic twins compared to 0 to 10 percent for dizygotic twins (Bailey et al., 1995). In addition, about 90 percent of the MZ twins of autistic children have some sort of significant cognitive impairment, compared to 10 percent of DZ twins. Finally, autistic children have a higher than average rate of other genetic disorders associated with cognitive impairment, including Fragile X syndrome and PKU (Szatmari et al., 1998). These data suggest that a general vulnerability to several types of cognitive impairment, only one of which is manifested as autism, runs in families.

Aberrations in almost all of the chromosomes have been found in studies comparing autistic and nonautistic individuals (Gillberg, 1998). The most frequently and consistently reported chromosomal abnormalities found in autism are aberrations on the long arm of chromosome 15, and abnormalities in the number and structure of the sex hormones.

It seems likely that neurological factors are involved in autism. The broad array of deficits seen in autism suggest disruption in the normal development and organization of the brain (Minshew, Sweeney, & Bauman, 1997). In addition, approximately 30 percent of autistic children develop seizure disorders by adolescence, suggesting a severe neurological dysfunction. Although neuroimaging research on autism is relatively new, studies have suggested that autistic people have increases in the volumes of the parietal, temporal, and occipital lobes of the cerebral cortex compared to nonautistic people (Minshew et al., 1997). These areas of the brain are involved in the deployment of attention and so-called "executive functions"—high-order cognitive planning and control of behavior—and thus dysfunction in these areas could reasonably be argued to lead to autistic symptoms. The direct connections between neurological dysfunction and autistic symptoms have not been made empirically yet, however.

Neuorological dysfunctions could be the result of genetic factors. Alternately, there is a higher than average rate of prenatal and birth complications among autistic children, complications that might have created neurological damage (Dykens & Volkmar, 1997). Finally, studies have found differences between autistic and nonautistic children in levels of the neurotransmitters serotonin and dopamine, although the meaning of these differences is not entirely clear (Anderson & Hoshino, 1997).

The variety of biological factors implicated in autism may indicate that there are several subtypes of autism, each of which has its own biological cause. With a disorder as rare as autism, it is difficult to study enough autistic children to discover subtypes. Ideally, recent advances in the technology of biomedical research, such as the use of magnetic resonance imagery and genetic mapping, will provide more detailed data on the biology of autism.

Treatments for Autism

A number of drugs have been shown to improve some symptoms autistic children have, such as overactivity, stereotyped behaviors, sleep disturbances, and tension (Gadow, 1992; McDougle, 1997). The serotonin reuptake inhibitors appear to reduce repetitive behavior and aggression, and improve social interactions in some people with autism (McDougle et al., 1998). The antipsychotic medications are used to reduce obsessive and repetitive behavior, and improve self-control in autistic individuals. Naltrexone, an opiate receptor antagonist, has been shown useful in reducing hyperactivity in some children with autism (McDougle, 1997). Finally, stimulants are used to improve attention. These drugs do not alter the basic autistic disorder, but they may make it easier for autistic persons to participate in school and in other interventions.

Psychosocial therapies for autism combine behavioral techniques and structured educational services. Modeling and reinforcement are used to teach autistic children to speak, to engage in social exchanges with others, and to reduce inappropriate behaviors (such as hand flapping). These techniques are often implemented in highly structured schools designed especially for autistic children. The specific deficits a child has in cognitive, motor, or social skills are targeted, and special materials that reduce possible distractions for autistic children (e.g., reading books that do not have words printed in bright colors) are used. The parents of autistic children may be taught to implement the techniques continually when the children are at home. One pioneering study showed that 47 percent of autistic children given this intensive behavioral treatment for at least 40 hours per week for at least 2 years achieved normal intellectual and educational functioning by age 7 compared to only 2 percent of autistic children who received only institutional care (Lovaas, 1987). Several other studies have shown remarkable improvements in cognitive skills and behavioral control in autistic children when they are treated with a comprehensive behavioral therapy administered both by their parents and in their school setting (Bregman & Gerdtz, 1997; Ozonoff & Cathcart, 1998; Schreibman & Charlop-Christy, 1998).

Summing Up

- The pervasive developmental disorders are characterized by severe and lasting impairment in several areas of development, including social interactions, communication with others, everyday behaviors, interests, and activities. They include Asperger's disorder, Rett's disorder, childhood disintegrative disorder, and autism.

- Autism is characterized by significant interpersonal, communication, and behavioral deficits.

- Two-thirds of autistic children score in the mentally retarded range on IQ tests.

- There is wide variation in the outcome of autism, although the majority of autistic children must have continual care as adults. The best predictors of a good outcome in autism are an IQ above 50 and language development before the age of 6.

- Biological causes of autism may include a genetic predisposition to cognitive impairment, central nervous system damage, prenatal complications, and neurotransmitter imbalances.

- Drugs reduce some behaviors in autism but do not eliminate the core of the disorder.

- Behavioral therapy is used to reduce inappropriate and self-injurious behaviors and to encourage prosocial behaviors in autistic children.

☉ BIO-PSYCHO-SOCIAL INTEGRATION

As noted earlier, the study of psychological disorders in children is often referred to as *developmental psychopathology*. This label explicitly recognizes that, in order to understand psychopathology in children, researchers must understand normal biological, psychological, and social development. Moreover, developmental psychopathologists are concerned with the interdependence of biological, psychological, and social development in children, recognizing that disruptions in any one of these three systems send perturbations through the other systems. The interdependence of these systems is probably even more true in children than in adults, because children are not mature enough to compartmentalize their troubles and are highly dependent on their caregivers and environment even for their most basic needs.

A nice example of the interplay between biology, psychology, and the social environment comes from a study of adopted children (Ge et al., 1996). Some of the adopted children in this study had biological parents who had antisocial personalities or histories of substance abuse; the other adopted children had biological parents with no histories of psychological problems. The children whose biological parents had histories of psychopathology were more likely than the other children to be hostile and antisocial themselves. Most researchers who do not adopt a bio-psycho-social approach to childhood disorders would stop with these results and declare the results clear evidence for the genetic inheritance of antisocial and hostile tendencies. The researchers in this study, however, went further and looked at the parenting behaviors of the children's adoptive parents. They found that the adoptive parents of the antisocial/hostile children were more harsh and critical in their parenting than were the adoptive parents of the children who were not antisocial and hostile. It appeared that the antisocial/hostile children drew out harsh and critical behaviors from their adoptive parents. The harsh and critical parenting these children received only exacerbated the children's antisocial behaviors. Thus, the children with biological parents who were antisocial or substance abusers appeared to have a genetic predisposition to being antisocial and hostile. Their genes also created an environment of parenting practices by their adoptive parents that contributed to more antisocial behavior on the part of the children. These children were on a developmental trajectory in which their biology and social environment were acting in synergy to lead them toward serious conduct disturbances. This kind of synergy between biology, psychology, and the social environment is the rule rather than the exception in the development of psychopathology, particularly in children.

Chapter Summary

- Nearly 20 percent of children and almost 40 percent of adolescents appear to suffer from serious psychological problems. For these children, some problems are linked to stressful events and others occur in the absence of stressful events, while other children exposed to stressful events appear to be resistant to the development of psychopathology.

- The behavioral disorders include attention-deficit/hyperactivity disorder (ADHD), conduct disorder, and oppositional defiant disorder. ADHD is characterized by inattentiveness, impulsivity, and hyperactivity. Children with ADHD do poorly in school and in peer relationships and are at increased risk for developing conduct disorder. ADHD is more common in boys than in girls. Biological factors that have been implicated in the development of ADHD include genetics, exposure to toxins prenatally and early in childhood, and abnormalities in neurological functioning. In addition, children with ADHD often come from families in which there are many disruptions, although it is not clear if this is a cause or just a correlate of ADHD. Treatment for ADHD usually involves stimulant drugs and behavior therapy designed to decrease children's impulsivity and hyperactivity and help them control aggression.

- Conduct disorder is characterized by extreme antisocial behavior and the violation of other people's rights and of social norms. Conduct disorder is more common in boys than in girls and is highly stable across childhood and adolescence. As adults, people who had conduct disorder are at increased risk for criminal behavior and a host of problems in fitting into society. The milder form of conduct disorder is oppositional defiant disorder. Genetics and neurological problems leading to attention deficits are implicated in the development of conduct disorder. In addition, children with conduct disorder tend to have parents who are harsh and inconsistent in their discipline practices and who model aggressive, antisocial behavior. Psychologically, children with conduct disorder tend to process information in ways that are likely to lead to aggressive reactions to others' behaviors. The treatment for conduct disorder is most often cognitive-behavioral, focusing on changing children's ways of interpreting interpersonal situations and helping them control their angry impulses. Neuroleptic drugs and stimulant drugs are also sometimes used to treat conduct disorder.

- Children can develop all the major emotional disorders (mood disorders, anxiety disorders), but separation anxiety is one disorder relatively unique in childhood. The symptoms of separation anxiety include chronic worry about separation from one's parents or about parents'

well-being, dreams and fantasies about separation from parents, refusal to go to school, and somatic complaints. This disorder is more common in girls. The disorder runs in families, which may suggest either that genetics plays a role in its development or that parents model anxious behavior for their children. Separation anxiety often arises following major traumas, particularly if parents are anxious and overprotective of their children. The therapy for separation anxiety follows behaviorist principles and involves relaxation training and increasing periods of separation from parents.

- The elimination disorders are enuresis, the repeated wetting of clothes or bed linens in children over the age of 5, and encopresis, repeated defecation in the clothes or on the floor in children over the age of 4. Enuresis is more common and has been studied more extensively than encopresis and has been linked to psychological stress, inappropriate or lax toilet training, and genetics. Enuresis is often treated with the bell and pad method, which helps children learn to awaken when their bladders are full so they can go to the bathroom. Antidepressants are also used to treat enuresis, but their effects disappear when the children stop taking them. Encopresis most often begins after episodes of constipation. It is treated by medical management and encouraging regular toilet-sitting.

- Disorders of cognitive, motor, and communication skills involve deficits and delays in the development of fundamental skills. Learning disorders include reading disorder (inability to read, also known as dyslexia), mathematics disorder (inability to learn math), and disorder of written expression (inability to write). The motor skills disorder is developmental coordination disorder, which involves deficits in fundamental motor skills. Communication disorders include expressive language disorder (inability to express oneself through language), mixed receptive-expressive language disorder (inability to express oneself through language or to understand the language of others), phonological disorder (use of speech sounds inappropriate for the age and dialect), and stuttering (deficits in word fluency). Some of these disorders, particularly reading disorder and stuttering, may have genetic roots. Many other factors have been implicated in these disorders, but they are not well understood. Treatment usually focuses on building skills in problem areas through specialized training, and now the use of computerized exercises.

- Mental retardation is defined as subaverage intellectual functioning, indexed by an IQ score below 70 and deficits in adaptive behavioral functioning. There are four levels of mental retardation, ranging from mild to profound. A number of biological factors are implicated in mental retardation, including metabolic disorders (PKU, Tay-Sachs disease); chromosomal disorders (Down syndrome, Fragile X, Trisomy 13 and Trisomy 18); prenatal exposure to rubella, herpes, syphilis, or illicit drugs (especially alcohol), premature delivery; and head traumas (such as those arising from being violently shaken as an infant). There is some evidence that intensive and comprehensive educational interventions, administered very early in an affected child's life, can help to decrease the level of mental retardation. Controversy exists over whether mentally retarded children should be put in special education classes with other mentally retarded children or mainstreamed into normal classrooms.
- The pervasive developmental disorders are characterized by severe and lasting impairment in several areas of development, including social interactions, communication with others, everyday behaviors, interests, and activities. They include Asperger's disorder, Rett's disorder, childhood disintegrative disorder, and autism. Autism is characterized by significant interpersonal, communication, and behavioral deficits. Two-thirds of autistic children score in the mentally retarded range on IQ tests. There is wide variation in the outcome of autism, although the majority of people with autism must have continual care even as adults. The best predictors of a good outcome in autism are an IQ above 50 and language development before the age of 6. Biological causes of autism may include a genetic predisposition to cognitive impairment, central nervous system damage, prenatal complications, and neurotransmitter imbalances. Drugs reduce some behaviors in autism but do not eliminate the core of the disorder. Behavioral therapy is used to reduce inappropriate and self-injurious behaviors and to encourage prosocial behaviors.

Key Terms

Critical Thinking Questions

1. Children are even more likely than adults to be diagnosed with multiple psychological disorders if they are diagnosed with any disorders at all. What are some possible explanations for this greater likelihood?

2. In what kind of environments might children with ADHD pay better attention and better control their behaviors? What kind of environments might exacerbate attentional and behavioral problems in these children?

3. Do you think society should insist that troubled children get treatment even if their parents object to it?

4. Some political leaders have advocated treating juveniles who commit crimes more like adults, in terms of the types of correctional facilities they are sent to and the lengths of their sentences. Given what you have learned about conduct disorder and juvenile delinquency, what do you think about this argument?

5. Should mental retardation be considered a psychiatric diagnosis, given its strong biological roots? Why or why not?

6. Which childhood behavior problems do you think would pose the greatest difficulty in establishing when the problem crosses the line from a "normal" problem of children to a psychological disorder?

John S. Bunker
Wednesday's Child

We love good looks rather than what is practical,
Though good looks may prove destructive.

—La Fontaine, "The Stag and His Reflection," Fables

(1668–1694; translated by Marianne Moore)

CHAPTER 14

Eating Disorders

CHAPTER OVERVIEW

Taking Psychology Personally:
Is There Such a Thing as a Healthy Diet?

Anorexia Nervosa

Anorexia nervosa is a disorder in which people refuse to a maintain body weight that is healthy and normal for their age and height. They have distorted body images and intense fears of becoming fat, and women with anorexia lose their menstrual periods. People with the restricting type of anorexia nervosa refuse to eat in order to prevent weight gain. People with the binge/purge type periodically engage in bingeing and then purge to prevent weight gain.

Bulimia Nervosa

Bulimia nervosa is characterized by uncontrolled binge eating, followed by behaviors designed to prevent weight gain, such as purging, fasting, and excessive exercising. People with the purging type of bulimia nervosa use self-induced vomiting, diuretics, or laxatives to prevent weight gain. People with the nonpurging type use fasting and exercise to prevent weight gain. Binge-eating disorder is a provisional category in the DSM-IV. People with this disorder regularly binge eat but do not engage in behaviors to compensate for the binges.

Understanding Eating Disorders

Societal pressures to be thin may play a role in the development of the eating disorders. Eating disorders may sometimes develop as a way of coping with negative emotions, or as the result of rigid, dichotomous thinking. Adolescent females who develop eating disorders often appear to come from families that are overcontrolling, require "perfection," and do not allow the expression of negative feelings. Although some women who develop eating disorders have histories of sexual abuse, sexual abuse seems to be a general risk factor for psychological problems rather than a specific risk factor for eating disorders. Eating disorders may be, in part, heritable. The families of people with eating disorders also tend to have high rates of depression. People with eating disorders may have disruptions in the hypothalamus, a part of the brain involved in the regulation of eating and emotions.

Extraordinary People:
Diana, Princess of Wales

Treatments for Eating Disorders

People with anorexia nervosa must often be hospitalized and forced to gain weight. Then behavior therapy and family therapy are used to try to help them overcome their disordered eating behaviors and attitudes. Cognitive-behavioral therapy, interpersonal therapy, and supportive-expressive therapy have proven useful in the treatment of bulimia nervosa. Antidepressants are helpful in reducing bingeing and purging and in enhancing a sense of control in people with bulimia nervosa. Antidepressants may also prove useful in treating anorexia nervosa, although there are few studies of their effectiveness to date. Prevention programs for eating disorders are popular, but their effects are unclear.

Bio-Psycho-Social Integration
Chapter Summary
Key Terms
Critical Thinking Questions

Voices

Dear Diary: This morning I had a half of a grapefruit for breakfast, and some coffee—no sugar or cream. For lunch, I had an apple and a diet soda. For dinner, I had some plain white rice and a salad with just some lemon squeezed over it. So I was feeling really good about myself, really virtuous. That is, until Jackie came over, and completely messed up my day. She brought over a movie to watch, which was fine. But then she insisted on ordering a pizza. I told her I didn't want any, that I wasn't hungry (which was a lie, because I was starving). But she ordered it anyway. The pizza arrived, and I thought I could be good and not have any. But it was just sitting there on the table, and I couldn't think of anything except having some. I couldn't concentrate on the movie. I kept smelling the pizza and feeling the emptiness in my stomach. Like a weakling, I reached out and got one piece, a small piece. It was ice cold by then, and kind of greasy, but I didn't care. I ate that piece in about 5 seconds flat. Then I had another piece. And another. I stopped after four pieces. But I still couldn't pay attention to the movie. All I could think about was what a pig I was for eating that pizza, and how I'll never lose the 10 pounds I need to lose to fit into a size smaller dress. Jackie's gone now, and I still keep thinking about how ugly and fat I am, and how I have no willpower. I didn't deserve to have that pizza tonight, because I haven't lost enough weight this month. I'm going to have to skip breakfast and lunch tomorrow, and exercise for a couple of hours, to make up for being a complete pig tonight.

This passage from a young woman's diary probably sounds familiar to many students. Surveys in the United States, Europe, Australia, New Zealand, and Israel have found that the majority of young women and about one-third of young men feel they are overweight and wish they could lose at least a few pounds (see Figure 14.1; Garner & Wooley, 1991; Horm & Anderson, 1993; Sasson, Lewin & Roth, 1995).

At any given time, about 45 percent of women and 25 percent of men in the United States are on diets to control their weight (Williamson et al., 1992). Thirty-one percent of American women between the ages of 19 and 39 diet at least once per month, and 16 percent are perpetual dieters. People are starting to diet at younger ages: Over 70 percent of American girls have dieted by the age of 10 (Hawkins, Turell, & Jackson, 1983). Dieting is hard, however, and almost everyone who loses weight through dieting gains it all back

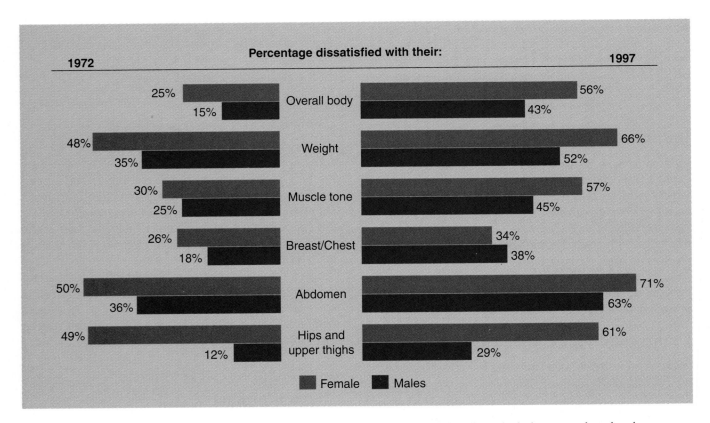

FIGURE 14.1   Our Growing Dissatisfaction with Our Bodies. Surveys over the last few decades have shown that both women and men have become more dissatisfied with their bodies.

Adapted from Garner, Cooke, & Marano, 1997, p. 42; Rodin, 1992, p. 57.

and often more. Many people spend their lives losing and gaining back tens of pounds in a cycle of "yo-yo" dieting. One famous example is the television star Oprah Winfrey, who lost 67 pounds in a heavily publicized liquid fast diet. On her television show, she wheeled 67 pounds of beef fat around the stage in a little red wagon to illustrate what she had left behind. Within a year, however, Winfrey had gained 90 pounds. In *Taking Psychology Personally:* Is There Such a Thing as a Healthy Diet? we discuss attempts to define a healthy diet.

Some people turn to more unconventional means of controlling their weight. Each year, over 100,000 people in the United States have their jaws wired to prevent them from eating or have liposuction performed to surgically remove fat (LaRosa, 1991). In all, Americans spend over $30 billion per year on weight-loss products, including $8 billion per year on spas and exercise clubs, $382 million on diet books, $10 billion on diet soft drinks, and billions of dollars on low-calorie foods and artificial sweeteners. To put this into perspective, consider that the federal govern-

TAKING PSYCHOLOGY PERSONALLY

Is There Such a Thing as a Healthy Diet?

The prevalence of obesity in developed countries has risen since the early 1900s, largely as a result of decreased physical activity and increases in the fat content of our diets (Brownell & Wadden, 1992). Recent estimates by the Centers for Disease Control show that one in five Americans is overweight (defined as being at least 20 percent above a healthy weight for one's height and frame), and 3 percent are at least 100 pounds overweight.

People who are obese have an increased risk of hypertension, diabetes, and cardiovascular disease (Bray, 1986; Pi-Sunyer, 1991). For example, one study followed over 100,000 American women, 30 to 55 years of age, for 8 years and found that those who were 30 percent or more overweight were 300 percent more likely to develop heart disease (Manson et al., 1990). On the other hand, studies of obese people indicate that losing as little as 10 percent of body weight can reduce high blood pressure, reduce cardiovascular disease, and improve diabetes (Blackburn & Kanders, 1987; Wing et al., 1987).

Unfortunately, the diets we use to lose weight can sometimes be as unhealthy as carrying the extra weight. For example, although the high-protein, low-carbohydrate diets that have been popular in recent years can help people lose weight, they can increase risk of cardiovascular disease. In addition, there is some evidence that "yo-yo" dieting (losing and then gaining back large amounts of weight) leads to substantial health problems (Garner & Wooley, 1991). In a long-term study of about 5,000

residents of Boston, researchers found that people whose weight fluctuated frequently or by many pounds had a 50 percent higher risk of heart disease than did those whose weight remained stable. Dieting tends to lower a person's metabolic rate. As a result, once the person begins gaining weight again, it is more likely that this weight will be stored as fat. In turn, the higher a person's percentage of body fat for his or her weight, the more at risk he or she is for heart disease. Some researchers have argued that the health risks that are typically associated with obesity may actually be due to yo-yo dieting by obese people (Garner & Wooley, 1991), but other researchers disagree (Stunkard & Smoller, 1996).

The other big problem with diets is that many people who develop eating disorders begin their dysfunctional patterns simply by going on diets (Abbott et al., 1998; Fairburn et al., 1997). Their diets may be innocuous at first, the type of diets most people think are safe and healthy, such as diets that are low in fats and high in fruits and vegetables. The diets may then become more and more extreme, perhaps because the simple and healthy diets do not achieve the desired weight loss.

Even moderate dieting can create a set of psychological and physiological conditions that make it difficult for an individual to maintain healthy eating patterns. Dieting creates chronic frustration, irritability, and emotional reactivity, which can make people more impulsive in their eating patterns (Federoff, Polivy, & Herman, 1997; Herman & Polivy, 1975). Dieting also changes people's

Continued

ability to read their bodies' cues about hunger and satiety and people's attitudes toward food. In a classic study, researchers compared the eating patterns of chronic dieters and of people not dieting. These people were brought into a laboratory and first asked to drink either two milkshakes, one milkshake, or no milkshake. Then they were asked to try three flavors of ice cream and rate the ice cream. People who were not dieting decreased the amount of ice cream they ate as a function of how many milkshakes they had consumed before the rating task: The more milkshakes they had consumed during the "preload," the less ice cream they ate during the rating task. Chronic dieters, however, ate more ice cream during the rating task if they had consumed milkshakes during the preload; those who had consumed two milkshakes during the preload ate even more ice cream during the rating task than did those who had consumed only one milkshake (Herman & Mack, 1975). Dieters develop beliefs that if they violate their diets in any way, they might as well violate them totally and binge. In addition, dieting may enhance the physiological appeal of "forbidden" foods, making it difficult to resist them especially after a taste or smell of them. People actually prefer sweet-tasting foods more when they are on diets than when they are not (Rodin, Slowchower, & Fleming, 1977).

Another physiological explanation is that each person has a "natural" weight that her body will fight to maintain, even if she attempts to lose weight (Keesey, 1986). This natural weight is often referred to as a **set point.** The set point is determined in part by a person's metabolic rate, which is known to be heavily influenced by genetics (Bouchard et al., 1989). When a person diets, her metabolic rate actually slows down, reducing her body's need for food. Unfortunately, the slowing of the metabolic rate also means that the body is not using up the food she consumes as quickly, making it more likely that this food will turn to fat even though she may be eating much less food than usual. The implication of this *set point theory* is that permanently changing weight may require some people to be on highly restrictive diets permanently.

People rarely stay on restrictive diets or keep their weight off after diets, however. In 1992, *Consumer Reports* did a survey of 95,000 of its readers who had tried to lose weight in the previous three years (*Consumer Reports*, June 1993). One in five of these readers had joined commercial weight-loss programs, such as Weight Watchers. Interestingly, 25 percent of these people who had joined

commercial weight loss programs were not even moderately overweight at the start. On average, the people who joined commercial weight-loss programs lost 10 to 20 percent of their starting weight, but they gained back half that weight in six months and two-thirds of the weight in two years. Only 25 percent of them kept the weight off for more than two years.

What's an overweight person to do then? Exercise is one thing. Exercise may be the one way people can overcome the effects of dieting on metabolic rates and keep their weight off (Jeffery et al., 1998). People who exercise regularly increase their basal metabolic rate, so the body burns more calories even when at rest. Thus, people who exercise may be able to maintain lower weights even without continuing to restrict the amount of food they eat. In addition, several studies now show that moderate exercise (i.e., the equivalent of 30 to 60 minutes per day of brisk walking, either in small spurts or all at once) is associated with substantial decreases in health risks and mortality, even among people with genetic predispositions to major diseases, people who smoke, and people who are overweight (Blair, Lewis & Booth, 1989; Paffenberger et al., 1986). So even if people do not lose weight through exercise, they may be improving their health and increasing their longevity.

Obesity experts also agree that decreasing the intake of fats and salt and increasing the intake of complex carbohydrates have positive health effects, even if they do not lead to weight loss. Most of us can reduce fats in our diet by switching from whole milk to skim and from high-fat meats to lower-fat meats and fish and by using low-fat dressings and spreads. We can increase carbohydrates by snacking on fruits, vegetables, and whole grains rather than on fatty foods such as potato chips and cookies.

Overweight people who want to lose weight might consider trying to achieve "reasonable" weight loss rather than "ideal" weights (Brownell & Wadden, 1992). The effects of biological factors such as genetics on weight may be strong enough that overweight people can never achieve the "ideal" weights they wish to achieve, at least not without chronic self-starvation. Many overweight people find themselves bingeing out of hunger or frustration or yo-yo dieting, both of which harm their self-esteem and possibly their health. If overweight people can adopt healthier diets, exercise regularly, and stabilize at weights that are reasonable given their family backgrounds and their histories of weight loss and gain, both their physical and psychological health may improve.

Talk-show host Oprah Winfrey has gained attention for her repeated efforts to lose weight and keep it off.

ment spends about $30 billion per year on all - education, training, employment, and social services programs.

Why do people care so much about their weight? There are health concerns that drive the attempt to lose weight. Being overweight can contribute to serious diseases like high blood pressure, heart disease, and diabetes and overweight people have shorter life spans than do people who are not overweight. However, the driving force behind most people's attempts to eat less and lose weight is the desire to be more attractive and increase self-esteem. Food has become more than something we eat to maintain healthy bodies or because it tastes good and exercise is not just something we do to improve our health. What we eat and how much we exercise have become linked to feelings of worth, merit, guilt, sin, rebelliousness, and defiance. Weight and how attractive we feel become an integral part of our self-esteem.

For some people, concerns about eating and weight become so overwhelming and behaviors oriented toward eating or avoiding eating get so out of control that they are said to have eating disorders. There are three specific types of eating disorders: anorexia nervosa, bulimia nervosa, and binge-eating disorder. *Anorexia nervosa* is characterized by a pursuit for thinness that leads people to starve themselves. *Bulimia nervosa* is characterized by a cycle of bingeing followed by extreme behaviors to prevent weight gain, such as self-induced vomiting. People with *binge-eating disorder* regularly binge but do not engage in behaviors to purge what they eat. The eating disorders are the focus of this chapter.

Traditionally, women have felt more pressure than men to be very thin (see Figure 14.2, p. 492), and we will see that the eating disorders are much more

common among women than men. In recent years, however, there has been increasing emphasis on men attaining a super-fit look, having lean lower bodies and strong, toned upper bodies. The number of articles in men's magazines on achieving such a look has risen dramatically and male television stars reach stardom in part because they have this look (Nemeroff et al., 1994). Obviously, this look is more difficult to attain for some men than for others.

Some men do develop eating disorders. Men who develop eating disorders generally display the same symptoms as do women who develop the disorders, including body dissatisfaction and the use of purging and excessive exercise to control their weight. Also, both men and women with eating disorders have high rates of comorbid depression and substance abuse (Olivardia et al., 1995; Striegel-Moore et al., 1998).

There are some differences between men and women with eating disorders. Men are more likely than women to have histories of being overweight and of bingeing before their anorexia or bulimia nervosa developed (Andersen, 1990). There is some evidence that homosexual men are more likely than heterosexual men to have eating disorders but there are no differences between lesbians and heterosexual women in the prevalence of eating disorders (Andersen, 1990; Schneider, O'Leary, & Jenkins, 1995). It may be that the gay male culture encourages concern with weight

There is increasing pressure in pop culture for men to be lean and super-fit.

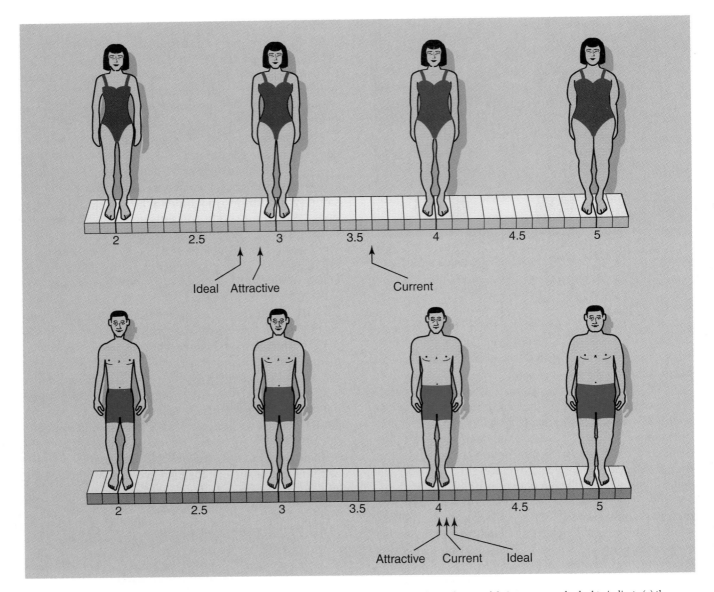

FIGURE 14.2 Women's and Men's Body Images. Female and male undergraduates were shown figures of their own sex and asked to indicate (a) the figure that looked most like their current shape, (b) their ideal figure, and (c) the figure they felt would be most attractive to the opposite sex. Men selected very similar figures for all three choices, but women selected very different figures for their current figure and either their ideal figure or the figure they thought would be most attractive.

control as much as do the cultures of both lesbians and heterosexual women.

In this chapter, we first explore the diagnosis and epidemiology of the eating disorders. Next, we review what we know about the causes of eating disorders. Societal pressures to be thin may create maladaptive attitudes toward weight and body shape in many people, but clearly most people do not develop full eating disorders. We discuss the psychological and biological factors that may lead some people to develop eating disorders. Then we discuss the most effective treatments for the eating disorders. Some progress has been made in developing effective treatments, especially for bulimia nervosa.

☉ ANOREXIA NERVOSA

Starving yourself, perhaps even to death, while remaining convinced that you are fat, is so self-destructive and incomprehensible that some theorists have argued it is a form of psychosis. People with **anorexia nervosa** starve themselves, subsisting on little or no food for very long periods of time, yet remain sure that they still need to lose more weight.

Diagnosis, Prevalence, and Prognosis

The diagnosis of anorexia nervosa requires that a person refuse to maintain a body weight that is healthy and normal for his or her age and height (see Table 14.1). The DSM-IV criteria for anorexia nervosa require that a person's weight be at least 15 percent below the minimum healthy weight for his or her age and height (APA, 2000). Often an anorexic's weight is much below this. For example, a 5 foot 6 inch young woman with anorexia may weigh 95 pounds, when the healthy weight for a woman this height is between 120 and 159 pounds. In girls and women who have begun menstruating, the weight loss causes them to stop having menstrual periods, a condition known as **amenorrhea.** Despite being emaciated, people with anorexia nervosa have intense fears of becoming fat. They have very distorted images of their bodies, often believing they are fat and need to lose more weight. The self-evaluations of anorexics hinge entirely on their weight and their control over their eating. They believe they are only good and worthwhile when they have complete control over their eating and when they are losing weight. The weight loss causes people with anorexia to be chronically fatigued, yet they will drive

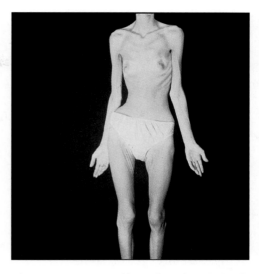

People with anorexia are emaciated but still see themselves as fat.

themselves to exercise excessively and to keep up a grueling schedule at work or school.

People with anorexia often develop elaborate rituals around food, as writer Marya Hornbacher describes in her autobiography, *Wasted* (1998, p. 254–255):

Voices

I would spread my paper out in front of me, set the yogurt aside, check my watch. I'd read the same sentence over and over, to prove that I could sit in front of food without snarfing it up, to prove it was no big deal. When five minutes had passed, I would start to skim my yogurt . . . You take the edge of your spoon and run it over the top of the yogurt, being careful to get only the melted part. Then let the yogurt drip off until there's only a sheen of it on the spoon. Lick it—wait, be careful, you have to only lick a teeny bit at a time, the sheen should last at least four or five licks, and you have to lick the back of the spoon first, then turn the spoon over and lick the front, with the tip of your tongue. Then set the yogurt aside again. Read a full page, but don't look at the yogurt to check the melt progression. Repeat. Repeat. Do not take a mouthful, do not eat any of the yogurt unless it's melted. Do not fantasize about toppings, crumbled Oreos, or chocolate sauce. Do not fantasize about a sandwich. A sandwich would be so *complicated.*

Types of Anorexia

Hornbacher describes one of the two types of anorexia, the restricting type (see *Concept Review:* Comparisons of Eating Disorders, p. 494). People with the **restricting type of anorexia nervosa** simply refuse to eat as a way of preventing weight gain. Some anorexics who are restrictors attempt to go for days without eating anything. Most will eat very small amounts of food each

TABLE 14.1
DSM IV
Diagnostic Criteria for Anorexia Nervosa

The DSM-IV specifies that both intentional extreme weight loss and distorted thoughts about one's body are key features of anorexia nervosa.

A. Refusal to maintain body weight at or above a minimally normal weight for age and height (e.g., weight loss leading to a weight at least 15% below minimum healthy body weight, or failure to make expected weight gain during a period of growth, resulting in a weight at least 15% below minimum healthy body weight)

B. Intense fear of gaining weight or becoming fat, despite being underweight

C. Distortions in the perception of one's body weight or shape, undue influence of body weight or shape on self-evaluation, or denial of the seriousness of the current low body weight

D. In females who have reached menarche, amenorrhea (absence of at least three consecutive menstrual cycles)

Reprinted with permission from the *Diagnostic and Statistical Manual of Mental Disorders*, Fourth Edition. Copyright © 2000 American Psychiatric Association.

CONCEPT REVIEW

Comparisons of Eating Disorders

The different eating disorders vary on these characteristics.

Symptom	AN*— Restricting Type	AN— Binge/Purge Type	BN*— Purging Type	BN— Nonpurging Type	Binge-Eating Disorder
Body weight	Must be < 15% underweight	Must be < 15% underweight	Often normal or somewhat overweight	Often normal or somewhat overweight	Often significantly overweight
Body image	Severely disturbed	Severely disturbed	Overconcern with weight	Overconcern with weight	Often disgusted with overweight
Binges	No	Yes	Yes	Yes	Yes
Purges or other compensatory behaviors	No	Yes	Yes	No	No
Sense of lack of control over eating	No	During binges	Yes	Yes	Yes
Amenorrhea in females	Yes	Yes	Not usually	Not usually	No

*AN refers to anorexia nervosa and BN to bulimia nervosa.

day, in part simply to stay alive and in part because of pressures from others to eat. Hornbacher survived for months on one cup of yogurt and one fat-free muffin per day. Daphne, in the case study below, also has the restricting type of anorexia nervosa.

CASE STUDY

Daphne is 5 foot 11 inches tall and weighs 102 pounds. She has felt "large" since her height soared above her schoolmates in the fifth grade. She has been on some type of diet ever since. During her junior year in high school, Daphne decided that she had to take drastic measures to lose more weight. She began by cutting her calorie intake to about 1,000 calories per day. She lost several pounds but not fast enough for her liking. So she cut her intake to 500 calories per day. She also began a vigorous exercise program of cross-country running. Each day, Daphne would not let herself eat until she had run at least 10 miles. Then she would have just a few vegetables and a handful of Cheerios. Later in the day, she might have some more vegetables and some fruit, but she would wait until she was so hungry that she was faint. Daphne dropped to 110 pounds and she stopped menstruating. Her mother expressed some concern about how little Daphne was eating, but since her mother tended to be overweight, she did not discourage Daphne from dieting. When it came time to go to college, Daphne was excited but also frightened, because she had always been a star student in high school and wasn't sure she could maintain her straight A's in college. In the first examination period

in college, Daphne got mostly A's but one B. She felt very vulnerable, like a failure, and like she was losing control. She also was unhappy with her social life which, by the middle of the first semester, was going nowhere. Daphne decided that things might be better if she lost more weight. So she cut her food intake to two apples and a handful of Cheerios each day. She also ran at least 15 miles each day. By the end of fall semester, she was down to 102 pounds. She was also chronically tired, had trouble concentrating, and occasionally fainted. Still, when Daphne looked in the mirror, she saw a fat, homely young woman who needed to lose more weight.

The other type of anorexia nervosa is the **binge/purge type,** in which people periodically engage in bingeing or purging behaviors (e.g., self-induced vomiting or the misuse of laxatives or diuretics). This disorder is different from bulimia nervosa, which we discuss shortly, in at least two ways (see *Concept Review:* Comparisons of Eating Disorders). First, people with the binge/purge type of anorexia will continue to be at least 15% below a healthy body weight, whereas people with bulimia nervosa are typically normal weight or somewhat overweight. Second, women with binge/purge anorexia will often develop amenorrhea, whereas women with bulimia nervosa usually do not. Often a person with the binge/purge type of anorexia nervosa will not engage in real binges in which she

TABLE 14.2

Common Medical Complications of Anorexia Nervosa

Anorexia is a dangerous disorder.

Cardiovascular Complications	**Dental Problems**
Slowness of heart rate Irregular heart beat Fluid in the sac enclosing the heart Heart failure	Decalcification Tooth decay
	Endocrine Complications
Metabolic Complications	Amenorrhea Lack of sexual interest Impotence
Yellowing of the skin Impaired taste Hypoglycemia	
	Gastrointestinal Complications
Fluid and Electrolyte Complications	Salivary gland swelling Acute expansion of the stomach Constipation
Dehydration Weakness Tetanus	
	General Complications
Hematological Complications	Weakness Hypothermia
Susceptibility to bleeding Anemia	

Source: Brownell & Foryet, 1986.

eats large amounts of food, but if she eats even a small amount of food, she feels like she has binged and will purge this food.

People with the restricting type of anorexia are more likely than those with the binge/purge type to have deep feelings of mistrust of others and a tendency to deny they have a problem. Binge/purge anorexics are more likely to have problems with unstable moods and controlling their impulses, with alcohol and drug abuse, and with self-mutilation (Garner, Garfinkel, & O'Shaughnessy, 1985). They also tend to have more chronic courses of their disorder.

About 1 percent of people will develop anorexia nervosa at some time in their lives, and between 90 and 95 percent of people diagnosed with anorexia nervosa are female (Fairburn, Welch, & Hay, 1993; Strober, 1986). Anorexia nervosa usually begins in adolescence, between the ages of 15 and 19 (Striegel-Moore, 1995). The course of the disorder varies greatly from person to person. Long-term studies suggest that as many as half of the women who develop anorexia nervosa recover within four years, but perhaps 30 percent still are severely underweight four years after the onset of the disorder. The remaining women achieve only intermediate levels of recovery over the four years (Hsu, Crisp, &

Harding, 1979; Morgan, Purgold, & Wellbourne, 1983; Morgan & Russell, 1975; Szmukler & Russell, 1986).

Anorexia nervosa is a very dangerous disorder physiologically. The death rate among anorexics is 15 percent. Table 14.2 lists just some of the possible physical complications caused by prolonged starvation. Some of the most serious consequences of anorexia are the cardiovascular complications, including bradycardia (extreme slowing of heart rate), arrhythmia (irregular heart beat), and heart failure. Another potentially serious complication of anorexia is acute expansion of the stomach, to the point of rupturing. Kidney damage has been seen in some anorexic patients, and impaired immune system functioning may make anorexics more vulnerable to severe illnesses.

Cultural Differences

There may be some cultural differences in the symptoms of eating disorders. Whereas fear of becoming fat is one of the defining features of eating disorders among White Europeans and Americans, studies of eating disorder patients in China, Hong Kong, and India find no preoccupation with becoming fat (Khandelwal & Saxena, 1990; Lee, 1995). Anorexic patients in these countries also do not have the distorted body images that are characteristic of anorexia in the United States and Europe and will readily admit that they are very thin. Nonetheless, they stubbornly refuse to eat, as is illustrated by the case of this Chinese woman (adapted from Sing, 1995, pp. 27–29):

CASE STUDY

Miss Y, aged 31, was 5 foot 3 inches. She had formerly weighed 110 pounds but now weighed 48 pounds. Her anorexia began four years previously, when she was suddenly deserted by her boyfriend, who came from a neighboring village. Greatly saddened by his departure for England, Miss Y started to complain of abdominal discomfort and reduced her food intake. She became socially withdrawn and unemployed.

At her psychiatric examination, she wore long hair and was shockingly emaciated—virtually a skeleton. She had sunken eyes, hollow cheeks, and pale, cold skin. She recognized her striking wasting readily but claimed a complete lack of hunger and blamed the weight loss on an unidentifiable abdominal problem. Her concern over the seriousness of her physical condition was perfunctory. When asked whether she consciously tried to restrict the amount she ate, she said, "No." When questioned why she had gone for periods of eight or more waking hours without eating anything, she said it was because she had no hunger and felt distended, pointing to the lower left side of her abdomen. All physical examinations revealed no biological source for her feelings of distension, however.

Miss Y was often in a low mood and became transiently tearful when her grief over the broken relationship was acknowledged. However, she resisted all attempts to discuss this loss in detail and all other psychological and medical treatments. Miss Y later died of cardiac arrest. Postmortem examination revealed no specific pathology other than multiple organ atrophy due to starvation.

If Asians who develop anorexia do not tend to be pursuing thinness and recognize they are too thin, this suggests that the triggers for anorexia nervosa in Asia may be different from those in Europe and the United States. Just what those triggers are for Asian anorexics is not clear, however.

Historical Perspectives on Anorexia Nervosa

There are accounts of self-induced starvation dating from as early as the Middle Ages (Strober, 1986). For example, a nun in Leichester, England, circa 1225, apparently ingested nothing but the wine and wafers of the Eucharist for 7 years. The earliest comprehensive description of a syndrome that sounds much like anorexia is credited to Richard Morton in 1694. He described women patients who had decreased appetite, amenorrhea, and aversions to food and were emaciated and hyperactive. Morton was intrigued by the apparent indifference these patients showed to their malnourishment and poor health:

CASE STUDY

Mr. Duke's Daughter in St. Mary Axe, in the Year 1684 and the eighteenth Year of her Age, in the month of July fell into a total suppression of her Monthly Courses from a multitude of Cares and Passions of her Mind, but without any Symptom of the Green-Sickness following upon it. From which time her Appetite began to abate, and her Digestion to be bad; her flesh also began to be flaccid and loose, and her looks pale . . . the Winter following, this consumption did seem to be not a little improved; for that she was wont both Day and Night to the injuries of the Air, which was at that time extreamly cold . . . So from that time loathing all sorts of Medicaments, she wholly neglected the care for her self for two full Years, till at last being brought to the last degree of a Marasmus, or Consumption, and thereupon subjects to Frequent Fainting Fits, she apply'd herself to me for advice.

I do not remember that I did ever in all my Practice see one, that was conversant with the Living so much wasted with the greatest degree of Consumption (like a Skeleton only clad with skin) yet there was no Fever, but on the contrary a coldness of the whole Body . . . (Quoted in Bliss & Branch, 1960, pp. 10–11)

In the latter part of the nineteenth century, Sir William Gull and Charles Lasegue published accounts of anorexic patients, bringing the condition to the widespread attention of the European medical establishment. In 1874, Gull coined the term *anorexia nervosa* for this condition. Gull noted that the onset of the disorder was usually in adolescence and that the disorder was much more likely seen in females than in males. In his 1873 report on "anorexia hysterique," Lasegue noted that girls with this disorder often express morbid beliefs about food being dangerous, that they are characterized by self-doubt and the need for approval from others, and that they seem driven to activity despite being terribly malnourished. Lasegue also described the interactions that arise between an anorexic girl and her family:

> The family has but two methods at its service which it always exhausts—entreaties and menaces, and which both serve as a touchstone. The delicacies of the table are multiplied in the hope of stimulating the appetite; but the more the solicitude increases, the more the appetite diminishes . . . (pp. 265–266)

The psychoanalyst Hilde Bruch was most influential in the modern conceptualization of anorexia. In 30 years of clinical practice with anorexic patients, Bruch (1970) came to see this disorder as caused by feelings of passivity, ineffectiveness, and lack of control, brought about by maladaptive family dynamics. The anorexic's "relentless pursuit of thinness" helped her gain a sense of efficacy and control over herself and over her relationship with her family. This theory of anorexia nervosa is discussed more later.

Summing Up

- Anorexia nervosa is characterized by self-starvation, a distorted body image, intense fears of becoming fat, and in women, amenorrhea.

- People with the restricting type refuse to eat in order to prevent weight gain.

- People with the binge/purge type periodically engage in bingeing and then purge to prevent weight gain.

- The lifetime prevalence of anorexia is about 1 percent, with 90 to 95 percent of cases being female.

- Anorexia usually begins in adolescence, and the course is variable from one person to another.

- It is a very dangerous disorder, and the death rate among anorexics is 15 percent.

- There may be cultural differences in the manifestation of anorexia nervosa.

☺ BULIMIA NERVOSA

The core characteristics of **bulimia nervosa** are uncontrolled eating or **bingeing**, followed by behaviors designed to prevent weight gain from the binges (see Table 14.3). The behaviors people with bulimia use to control their weight include self-induced vomiting; the abuse of laxatives, diuretics, or other purging medications; fasting; and excessive exercise. As with anorexics, the self-evaluations of people with bulimia nervosa are heavily influenced by their body shapes and weights. When they are thin, they feel like a "good person." Bulimics do not tend to show gross distortions in their body images as anorexics do, however. Whereas an anorexic woman who is absolutely emaciated will look in the mirror and see herself as obese, bulimics have more realistic perceptions of their actual body shapes. Still, bulimics are constantly dissatisfied with their shapes and weights and concerned about losing weight.

People with bulimia nervosa are distinguished from people with the binge/purge type of anorexia nervosa primarily by their body weight: The criteria for binge/purge anorexia require that a person be at least 15 percent below normal body weight, whereas there are no weight criteria for bulimia nervosa. People with the restricting type of anorexia nervosa also differ from people with bulimia nervosa in that they do not engage in binges—restrictors severely limit their food

---

TABLE 14.3
DSM IV
Diagnostic Criteria for Bulimia Nervosa

People with bulimia nervosa regularly binge-eat and then attempt to prevent gaining weight from their binge.

A. Recurrent episodes of binge eating, characterized by both of the following:
1. eating, in a discrete period of time (such as within a 2-hour period) an amount of food that is definitely larger than most people would eat during a similar period of time and under similar circumstances
2. a sense of lack of control over eating during the episode

B. Recurrent inappropriate behaviors to prevent weight gain, such as self-induced vomiting; misuse of laxatives, diuretics, enemas, or other medications; fasting; or excessive exercise.

C. The binge eating and inappropriate purging behaviors both occur, on average, at least twice a week for 3 months.

D. Self-evaluation is unduly influenced by body shape and weight.

Reprinted with permission from the *Diagnostic and Statistical Manual of Mental Disorders,* Fourth Edition. Copyright © 2000 American Psychiatric Association.

---

intake all of the time (see *Concept Review:* Comparisons of Eating Disorders, p. 494).

Self-induced vomiting is the behavior people associate most often with bulimia. Many bulimics are discovered by family members, roommates, and friends when they are caught vomiting or when they leave messes after they vomit. In one sorority, the frequent purging behavior of the members was discovered in a particularly odd way:

CASE STUDY
At first it seemed like a minor, if mystifying, problem: In the spring of 1996, plastic sandwich bags began disappearing by the hundreds from the kitchen of a sorority house at a large northeastern university. When the sorority's president investigated, she found a disturbing explanation: The bags, filled with vomit, were hidden in a basement bathroom. "I was shocked," says the president (who later learned that the building's pipes, eroded by gallons of stomach acid, would have to be replaced). "Yet in a way it made sense." Most of her 45 housemates, she recalls, worried about weight. "It was like a competition to see who could eat the least. At dinner they would say, 'All I had today was an apple,' or 'I haven't had anything.' It was surreal." (Hubbard et al., *People Magazine,* April 12, 1999, p. 52).

Some social settings may increase risk for eating disorders.

Dentists also discover bulimics because frequent vomiting can rot teeth from exposure to stomach acid. People who use self-induced vomiting or purging medications are said to have a **purging type of bulimia nervosa.** The cycle of bingeing and then purging or other compensatory behaviors to control weight becomes a way of life, as in the case of Alice:

CASE STUDY

Alice is a single 17-year-old who lives with her parents, who insisted that she be seen because of binge eating and vomiting. She achieved her greatest weight of 180 pounds at 16 years of age. Her lowest weight since she reached her present height of 5'9" has been 150 pounds, and her present weight is about 160 pounds. Alice states she has been dieting since age ten and says she has always been . . . slightly chubby. At age 12 she started binge eating and vomiting. She was a serious competitive swimmer at that time, and it was necessary for her to keep her weight down. She would deprive herself of all food for a few days and then get an urge to eat. She could not control this urge, and would raid the refrigerator and cupboards for ice cream, pastries, and other desserts. She would often do this at night, when nobody was looking, and would eat, for example, a quart of ice cream, an entire pie, and any other desserts she could find. She would eat until she felt physical discomfort and then she would become depressed and fearful of gaining weight, following which she would self-induce vomiting. When she was 15 she was having eating binges and vomiting four days a week. Since age 13 she has gone through only one period of six weeks without gaining weight or eating binges and vomiting . . . (Spitzer et al., 1981, p. 146)

People who use excessive exercise or fasting to control their weight but do not engage in purging are said to have a **nonpurging type of bulimia nervosa.** Bulimics who use excessive exercise to control their weight can easily hide their bulimia if they are part of a group that values exercise, like students on a college campus. The following passage was written by a male psychologist who developed the nonpurging type of bulimia nervosa over a period of years (Wilps, 1990, pp. 19–21). This man grew up viewing food as a source of comfort and bingeing as a way of escaping from overbearing and disapproving parents. He would fast for a day or more after a binge to control his weight. As the pressures of his job and a failed marriage increased, his bulimic pattern of bingeing and then fasting grew more serious:

Voices

I would sigh with relief when Sunday evening came, since I had no work responsibilities until the next morning, and I would have just returned my son to his mother's custody. I would then carefully shop at convenience stores for "just right" combinations of cheese, lunch meats, snack chips, and sweets such as chocolate bars. I would also make a stop at a neighborhood newsstand to buy escapist paperback novels (an essential part of the binge) and then settle down for a three-hour session of reading and slow eating until I could barely keep my eyes open. My binges took the place of Sunday dinner, averaging approximately 6,000 kilocalories in size. Following the binge, my stomach aching with distension, I would carefully clean my teeth, wash all the dishes, and fall into a drugged slumber.

I would typically schedule the following day as a heavy working day with evening meetings in order to distract myself from increasing hunger as I fasted. I began running . . . I would typically run for one hour, four to five days per week, and walked to work as a further weight control measure. . . .

As time went on, I increased the frequency of these binges, probably because of the decreasing structured demands for my time. They went from weekly to twice per week, then I was either bingeing or fasting with no normal days in my week at all. My sleep patterns were either near-comatose or restless, with either sweating after a binge or shivering after a fast. I became increasingly irritable and withdrawn . . . prompting increased guilt on my part that I resented the intrusion of my friends, my patients, and even my son into my cycle. . . .

The nadir of my life as a bulimic occurred when I found myself calling patients whom I had scheduled for evening appointments, explaining to them that I was ill, then using the freed evening for bingeing . . . I was physically exhausted most of the time, and my hands, feet, and abdomen were frequently puffy and edematous, which I, of course, interpreted as gain in body fat and which contributed to my obsession with weight and food. I weighed myself several times per day in various locations, attending to half pound variations as though my life depended on them.

Binge-Eating

The concept of a binge is central to several of the eating disorders. The definition of a binge has actually been a matter of controversy among clinicians, however (Fairburn & Wilson, 1993). In addition, it is clear that some people binge eat and do not purge or engage in other behaviors to compensate for the binge.

Defining the Binge

The DSM-IV defines a binge as occurring in a discrete period of time, such as an hour or two, and involving eating an amount of food that is definitely larger than most people would eat during a similar period of time and in similar circumstances. There are tremendous variations among people with eating disorders in the sizes of their binges, however. The average binge is about 1,500 calories. Less than a third of binge episodes contain more than 2,000 calories; one-third of the binge episodes contain only 600 calories, and many people will say that they consider eating just one piece of cake a binge. What makes that a binge for a person with an eating disorder is the sense that they have no control over their eating, that they feel compelled to eat even though they are not hungry. The DSM-IV recognizes this aspect of binges, and the criteria for a binge include a sense of lack of control over eating.

Binge-Eating Disorder

The DSM-IV mentions one further eating disorder, called **binge-eating disorder.** This disorder resembles bulimia nervosa in many ways, except that the person with binge-eating disorder does not regularly engage in purging, fasting, or excessive exercise to compensate for his or her binges. Binge-eating disorder is not one of the officially recognized forms of eating disorders in the DSM-IV, largely because the authors of the DSM-IV felt there has been too little research on this disorder to sanction the diagnosis. Rather, the diagnostic criteria for binge-eating disorder were placed in the appendix of the DSM-IV for further study. People with binge-eating disorder may eat continuously throughout the day with no planned mealtimes. Others engage in discrete binges on large amounts of food, often in response to stress and feelings of anxiety or depression. They may eat very rapidly and be almost in a daze as they eat, as this man describes:

Voices

"The day after New Year's Day I got my check cashed. I usually eat to celebrate the occasion, so I knew it might happen. On the way to the bank I steeled myself against it. I kept reminding myself of the treatment and about my New Year's resolution about dieting. . . .

"Then I got the check cashed. And I kept out a hundred. And everything just seemed to go blank. I don't know what it was. All of my good intentions just seemed to fade away. They just didn't seem to mean anything anymore. I just said, 'What the hell,' and started eating, and what I did then was an absolute sin."

He described starting in a grocery store where he bought a cake, several pieces of pie, and boxes of cookies. Then he drove through heavy midtown traffic with one hand, pulling food out of the bag with the other hand and eating as fast as he could.

After consuming all of his groceries, he set out on a furtive round of restaurants, staying only a short time in each and eating only small amounts. Although in constant dread of discovery, he had no idea what "sin" he felt he was committing. He knew only that it was not pleasurable. "I didn't enjoy it at all. It just happened. It's like a part of me just blacked out. And when that happened there was nothing there except the food and me, all alone."

Finally he went into a delicatessen, bought another $20 worth of food and drove home, eating all the way, "until my gut ached."

(Stunkard, 1993, pp. 20–21)

People with this binge-eating disorder are often significantly overweight and say they are disgusted with their bodies and ashamed of their bingeing. They typically have histories of frequent dieting, joining weight-control programs, and family obesity (Fairburn et al., 1997). As many as 30 percent of people currently in weight-loss programs may have binge-eating disorder. In contrast, only about 2 percent of the general population has the disorder (Spitzer et al., 1992).

As with anorexia and bulimia nervosa, binge-eating disorder is more common in women than in men, in both the general community and among people in weight-loss programs. People with binge-eating disorder have high rates of depression and anxiety and possibly more alcohol abuse and personality disorders (Castonguay, Eldredge, & Agras, 1995; Telch & Stice, 1998).

Prevalence and Prognosis of Bulimia Nervosa

In the 1970s, the popular media in the United States and Europe became intrigued by the binge/purge cycle of bulimia and gave it much attention. Questionnaires like the one in Figure 14.3 were developed to assess eating-disordered behaviors and attitudes. It was said that there was an epidemic of bulimia on college campuses, with as many as 25 percent of college

Eating Disorder Inventory						
	Always	Usually	Often	Sometimes	Rarely	Never
I think my stomach is too big.						
I eat when I am upset.						
I stuff myself with food.						
I think about dieting.						
I think that my thighs are too large.						
I feel ineffective as a person.						
I feel extremely guilty after overeating.						
I am terrified of gaining weight.						
I get confused as to whether or not I am hungry.						
If I gain a pound, I worry that I will keep gaining.						
I have the thought of trying to vomit in order to lose weight.						
I eat or drink in secrecy.						

FIGURE 14.3 Checking Your Own Attitudes Toward Eating. Psychologist David Garner and colleagues (1984) developed the Eating Disorder Inventory to assess people's attitudes and behaviors toward eating and their bodies. People who score higher on this questionnaire are more prone to eating disorders. As you read through these items, think about whether you would say each one is true of you always, usually, often, sometimes, rarely, or never. If you find you have answered "usually" or "always" to many of these items, you might want to reconsider your attitudes toward food and your body, and perhaps talk to someone you trust about them.

women using self-induced vomiting to control their weight. Researchers at the University of Pennsylvania investigated this claim in a study of 942 male and 994 female students. They asked the students how frequently they engaged in the behaviors and thoughts required for the diagnosis of bulimia. Many more students engaged in periodic binges than in self-induced vomiting. Among the women, 32 percent engaged in binges at least twice per month, but only 3 percent reported feeling out of control over their eating during those binges. Only 3 percent of the women reported engaging in vomiting after a binge at least once a month; only 1 percent engaged in bingeing and then vomiting twice per week, as required for a diagnosis of bulimia. Among the men, 29 percent engaged in binges at least twice per month, but only about 1 percent reported feeling out of control over their eating. Only 0.3 percent met the criteria for bulimia (Schotte & Stunkard, 1987). Similarly, in a nationwide sample of 1,007 college students, only 1.0 percent of the women and 0.2 percent of the men met the diagnostic criteria for bulimia (Drewnowski, Hopkins, & Kessler, 1988). Thus, although unnecessary concerns about weight control may be common among college students,

particularly women students, the full syndrome of bulimia, as defined by clinicians, is relatively uncommon (Schotte & Stunkard, 1987).

The onset of bulimia nervosa most often occurs between the ages of 15 and 29 (Striegel-Moore, 1995). The long-term course of bulimia nervosa, left untreated, is unclear. A year-long study of bulimia nervosa on a college campus found that 44 percent of women diagnosed as bulimic in the fall of the academic year were still classified as bulimic in the spring of that year (Drenowski, Yee, & Krahn, 1988). The majority of the remaining women who had been diagnosed as bulimic in the fall still showed some symptoms of bulimia nervosa in the spring, although they did not meet the full diagnostic criteria.

Many people with bulimia nervosa are of normal weight or slightly overweight. You might conclude, then, that bulimia is not a physically dangerous disorder as is anorexia. Although the death rate among bulimic patients is not as high as among anorexic patients, bulimia also has serious medical complications (see Table 14.4). One of the most serious complications is the imbalance in the body's electrolytes that results from fluid loss following excessive and chronic

TABLE 14.4

Medical Complications of Bulimia Nervosa

Although bulimia nervosa is not as likely to be lethal as anorexia nervosa, it still creates a number of medical complications.

Renal Complications	Laxative Abuse Complications
Dehydration Kidney disease	Reduction of blood calcium Tetanus Softening of the bones Skin pigmentation Reduction in magnesium levels Fluid retention Malabsorption syndromes Colon abnormalities
Gastrointestinal Complications	
Gastric dilation Inflammation of the salivary gland Elevations of the enzyme amylase Pancreatic disease	**Other Abnormalities**
Electrolyte Abnormalities	Susceptibility to bleeding Electroencephalogram abnormalities Abnormal thyroid hormone and growth hormone responses
Excess uric acid in the blood Lowered potassium levels Alkalosis Acidosis	
Dental Problems	
Tooth decay Enamel erosion	

Source: Brownell & Foreyt, 1986.

vomiting, laxative abuse, and diuretic abuse. Electrolytes are biochemicals that help to regulate the heart, and imbalances in electrolytes can lead to heart failure.

Summing Up

- Bulimia nervosa is characterized by uncontrolled bingeing followed by behaviors designed to prevent weight gain from the binges.

- People with the purging type use self-induced vomiting, diuretics, or laxatives to prevent weight gain.

- People with the nonpurging type use fasting and exercise to prevent weight gain.

- The definition of a binge has been controversial, but the DSM-IV specifies that it must involve the consumption of an unusually large amount of food in a short time, and a sense of lack of control.

- Binge-eating disorder is a provisional category in the DSM-IV. People with this disorder regularly binge eat but do not engage in behaviors to compensate for the binges.

- Although overconcern with weight and occasional bingeing is common among college students, the prevalence of the full syndrome of bulimia nervosa is only about 1.0 percent in women and 0.2 percent in men.

- The onset of bulimia nervosa is most often in adolescence, and its course, if left untreated, is unclear.

- Although people with bulimia nervosa do not tend to be severely underweight, there are a variety of possible medical complications of the disorder.

☉ UNDERSTANDING EATING DISORDERS

A number of sociocultural, psychological, and biological factors have been implicated in the development of the eating disorders (see *Concept Review:* Contributors to the Eating Disorders). It is likely that it takes an accumulation of several of these factors for any individual to develop an eating disorder, as we discuss in the Bio-Psycho-Social Integration at the end of this chapter. In this section, however, we consider each of these factors, and the evidence regarding each factor, separately.

CONCEPT REVIEW
Contributors to the Eating Disorders

A number of sociocultural, psychological, and biological factors have been said to contribute to the eating disorders.

Sociocultural and Psychological Factors:

Pressures to be thin

Cultural norms of attractiveness

Use food as a way of coping with negative emotions

Overconcern with others' opinions

Rigid, dichotomous thinking style

Family dynamics characterized by overcontrolling parents who do not allow expression of emotion

History of sexual abuse

Biological Factors:

Genetic predisposition to eating disorders

Predisposition to depression

Dysregulation of hypothalamus

Serotonin deficiency

Sociocultural and Psychological Factors

Societal pressures to be thin and attractive probably play a role in the eating disorders. Many people who are exposed to these pressures do not develop eating disorders, however. Certain psychological factors may also need to come into play for an eating disorder to develop.

Social Pressures and Cultural Norms

The prevalence of eating disorders, particularly binge-eating disorder and bulimia nervosa, appears to have increased in the United States and Europe over the last few decades (Striegel-Moore, 1995; Stunkard, 1997). In contrast, eating disorders are uncommon in many less developed countries (Davis & Yager, 1992; McCarthy, 1989; Pate et al., 1992; Sobal & Stunkard, 1989). Psychologists have linked the historical and cross-cultural differences in the prevalence of eating disorders to differences in the standards of beauty for women held at different historical times and in different cultures (Garner & Garfinkel, 1980; McCarthy, 1990; Sobal & Stunkard, 1989). When the most wealthy and influential members of a society value thinness, eating disorders tend to be more prevalent. When a heavier weight is seen as more beautiful, eating disorders are uncommon, but obesity is common. People in less developed countries may view heaviness as beautiful because only wealthy people have the means to obtain food and become obese.

Standards of beauty The ideal shape for women in the United States and Europe has become thinner and thinner over the last few decades. Models in fashion magazines, winners of the Miss America and Miss Universe pageants, and Barbie dolls—all icons of beauty for women—have been getting thinner (see Figure 14.4; Agras & Kirkley, 1986; Garner & Garfinkel, 1980; Wiseman et al., 1992). Indeed, the average model in a fashion magazine these days is pencil thin, with a figure that is physically unattainable by the majority of adult women.

Pressures to be thin do not come just from the media and marketers of Barbie dolls. Studies of adults' perceptions of each other show that women who are thin are rated as more feminine and attractive than are women who are heavier (e.g., Guy, Rankin, & Norvell, 1980). Similarly, women who dare to eat as much food as they wish in public settings (such as a dormitory cafeteria) are rated as less attractive than are women who eat less (Rolls, Fedoroff, & Guthrie, 1991). Women pick up on these cues and change their behavior in many ways to conform to societal expectations. For example, women eat less in situations in which they wish to appear desirable and feminine or in situations in which they want to show superiority over other women or compete with other women (Mori, Chaiken, & Pliner, 1987; Pliner & Chaiken, 1990). Many students can attest to the competitions that arise between friends sitting around a dinner table watching what each other eats, comparing calorie counts, and berating the "weaklings" or "traitors" who have dessert.

As we have noted, both anorexia nervosa and bulimia nervosa are much more common in females than in males. This gender difference has largely been attributed to the fact that thinness is more valued and encouraged in females than in males. For example, studies of popular women's and men's magazines find 10 times more diet articles in women's magazines than in men's magazines (Andersen & DiDomenico, 1992;

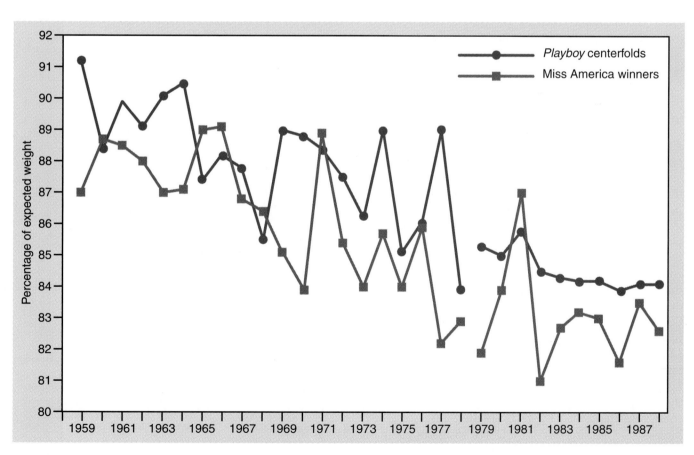

FIGURE 14.4 Our Changing Beauty Standards. In the period from 1959 to 1978, the average weight of women who were *Playboy* centerfolds or won the Miss America contest became lower and lower, relative to what would be expected for a woman of their height.

From C.V. Wiseman, et al., "Cultural Expectations of Thinness in Women: an Update" in *International Journal of Eating Disorders*, 11. Copyright © 1992 John Wiley & Sons, Inc.

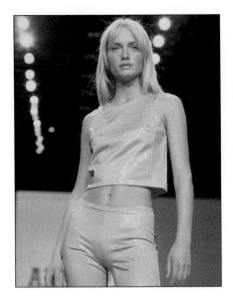

Fashion models have figures that are physically unattainable by the average woman, yet they set the standards for beauty.

Nemeroff et al., 1994). Half of all women report frequent dissatisfaction with their appearance, whereas fewer than one-third of men report the same (*Time Magazine*, June 3, 1996). In recent years, women's magazines have moved somewhat away from articles on dieting only toward articles on fitness and exercise (Nemeroff et al., 1994). Unfortunately, however, women's motivations for exercise are still more likely to be for weight control than are men's motivations, and exercising for weight control is more likely to contribute to eating-disordered behavior than is exercising for health (McDonald & Thompson, 1992).

Athletes and eating disorders One group that appears to be at increased risk for unhealthy eating habits and full-blown eating disorders is athletes, especially those in sports in which weight is considered an important factor in competitiveness, such as gymnastics, ice skating, dancing, horse racing, wrestling, and bodybuilding. Researchers in Norway assessed all 522 elite female athletes between the ages of 12 and 35 in that country for the presence of eating disorders and found that those in sports classified as "aesthetic" or "weight dependent," including diving, figure skating, gymnastics, dance, judo, karate, and wrestling, were most likely to have anorexia or bulimia nervosa (see Table 14.5; Sundgot-Borgen, 1994). When those women athletes with eating disorders were asked about the triggers for their eating disorders, many said that they felt that the physical changes of puberty came too early for them and decreased their competitive edge, so they had started dieting severely to try to maintain their prepubescent figures (see Table 14.6 for other triggers). The case of Heidi, described here by her therapist, illustrates several of these triggers (adapted from Pipher, 1994, pp. 165–168):

CASE STUDY

Heidi arrived in my office after gymnastics practice. Blond and pretty, she was dressed in a shiny red-and-white warm-up suit. We talked about gymnastics, which Heidi had been involved in since she was six. At that time, she was selected to train with the university coaches. Now she trained four hours a day, six days a week. She didn't expect to make an Olympic team, but she anticipated a scholarship to a Big-8 school.

Heidi glowed when she talked about gymnastics, but I noticed her eyes were red and she had a small scar on the index finger of her right hand. (When a hand is repeatedly stuck down the throat, it can be scarred by the acids in the mouth.) I wasn't surprised when she said she was coming in for help with bulimia.

Heidi said, "I've had this problem for two years, but lately it's affecting my gymnastics. I am too weak, particularly on the vault, which requires strength. It's hard to concentrate.

"I blame my training for my eating disorder," Heidi continued. "Our coach has weekly weigh-ins where we count each others' ribs. If they are hard to count we're in trouble."

Heidi explained that since puberty she had had trouble keeping her weight down. After meals, she was nervous that she'd eaten too much. She counted calories; she was hungry but afraid to eat. In class she pinched the fat on her side and freaked out.

I asked when it started.

"After my thirteenth birthday things got tough. I graduated from my neighborhood school and moved into a consolidated school. I made friends there, but I felt under more pressure. School was harder; gymnastics was harder. I gained weight when I started my periods. Coach put me on a diet."

Bodybuilding is an increasingly popular sport, but bodybuilders routinely have substantial weight

TABLE 14.5
Rates of Eating Disorders in Elite Women Athletes

Sports that emphasize weight are especially likely to encourage eating disorders.

Sport	Percent with an Eating Disorder
Aesthetic sports (e.g., figure skating, gymnastics)	35
Weight-dependent sports (e.g., judo, wrestling)	29
Endurance sports (e.g., cycling, running, swimming)	20
Technical sports (e.g., golf, high jumping)	14
Ball game sports (e.g., volleyball, soccer)	12

Source: Data from Sundgot-Borgen, 1994.

TABLE 14.6
Triggers Mentioned by Athletes with Eating Disorders for the Development of Their Eating Disorders

Athletes have many pressures that might contribute to eating disorders.

Trigger	Percent Mentioning
Prolonged periods of dieting/weight fluctuation	37
New coach	30
Injury/illness	23
Casual comments by others about weight	19
Leaving home/failure at school or work	10
Problem in relationship	10
Family problems	7
Illness/injury to family members	7
Death of significant other	4
Sexual abuse	4

Source: Data from Sundgot-Borgen, 1994.

fluctuations as they try to shape their bodies for competition and then binge in the off-seasons. For example, one study of male bodybuilders found that 46 percent reported bingeing after most competitions, and 85 percent reported gaining significant weight (an average of 15 pounds) in the off-season. Then they dieted to prepare for competition, losing an average of 14 pounds. A parallel study of female bodybuilders and weight lifters found that 42 percent reported having been anorexic at some time in their lives, 67 percent were terrified of being fat, and 58 percent were obsessed with food (Anderson et al., 1995).

Amateur athletes are also at increased risk for disordered eating behaviors. A survey of 4,551 readers of *Runner's World* magazine found that most of the women and many of the men reported dissatisfaction with their bodies, uncontrolled eating, and a preoccupation with food and eating (see Table 14.7; Brownell, Rodin, & Wilmore, 1992). Thus, although participation in athletics is good for the body and soul of many people, it is associated with disordered eating behaviors and attitudes for some people.

Socioeconomics and ethnicity Within the United States and Europe, there may be differences among socioeconomic and ethnic groups in the prevalence of eating disorders. Some studies find that eating disorders are more common among the upper and middle classes than among lower socioeconomic classes. This association between socioeconomic status and eating disorders is found among Caucasians and among African Americans and Hispanics. Perhaps because African Americans and Hispanics are more likely than Caucasians to be in lower socioeconomic groups, the overall rates of eating disorders are lower in African Americans and Hispanics than in Caucasians (Gray, Ford, & Kelly, 1987; Gross & Rosen, 1988; Pate et al., 1992). Other researchers have argued that the rate of eating disorders is lower in African Americans and Hispanics because they do not accept the thin ideal that is promoted in White culture (Osvold & Sodowsky, 1993). Finally, some researchers have suggested that African American adolescent girls are more focused than White adolescent girls on work and adult responsibilities, so they are less likely to become preoccupied with physical appearance and dieting than are White girls. The rates of eating disorders in ethnic minority groups in the United States have been rising in recent years, however, and some studies show equal rates across all socioeconomic and ethnic groups in the United States (Davis & Yager, 1992; Pate et al., 1992; Wilfley et al., 1996).

Emotions and Cognitions

Some theorists have examined the maladaptive cognitions about food that characterize people with eating

Sports that require certain body shapes or weights, such as gymnastics or body building, seem to breed eating disorders.

TABLE 14.7

Body Weight and Dieting Concerns in 4,551 Respondents to Survey in *Runner's World* Magazine

Question	Percent Giving this Response	
	Females (N = 1,911)	Males (N = 2,640)
Do you consciously watch your weight? ("often" or "always")	73	64
How satisfied are you with your current body size and shape? ("moderately satisfied" or worse)	57	37
How easy or difficult is it for you to maintain optimal weight? ("somewhat" or "very difficult")	52	39
Do you ever feel out of control while you are eating or have the feeling that you won't be able to stop eating? ("sometimes," "often," or "always")		
While in training	43	33
While not training	59	46
In the days before a race	30	20
After a race	38	44
Have you ever eaten a large amount of food rapidly and felt that this incident was excessive and out of control (aside from holiday feasts)	64	45
Questions From Easting Attitudes Test		
("often," "usually," or "always")		
I am terrified about being overweight	48	22
I find myself preoccupied with food	36	16
I feel extremely guilty after eating	20	7
I am preoccupied with a desire to be thinner	48	24
I give too much time and thought to be food	35	13

From K.D. Brownell, et al., *Eating, Body Weight, and Performance in Athletes: Disorders of Modern Society,* 1992. Copyright © 1992 Lea & Febiger. Reprinted by permission of Lippincott Williams & Wilkins.

Teenagers often feel great pressure to look like the models in magazines or fitness experts in work-out videos.

disorders. The use of food to cope with painful emotions has also been the subject of recent research.

The following passage written by a young woman with bulimia nervosa describes some of the possible emotional underpinnings of eating disorders:

Voices

I remember deciding not too long ago that if I could just stop bingeing and start eating right, my life would be "perfect." If I could just get control over food, I told myself, bulimia would disappear from my mind and from my life. How very wrong I was.

At that point, I was dealing with my bulimia in the same way as a doctor who would treat a sick person's sneezes rather than her cold. I was trying to treat the symptom of bulimia (overeating) rather than the disease itself.

Bulimia does not deal with food or overeating or bingeing. Food is not the problem. I believe, however, that bulimia does deal with hunger. Each binge is a signal that the bulimic is starving to death and is desperately seeking nourishment. This hunger, however, is one that does not come from physical emptiness but rather arises from an emptiness deep within a person, an emptiness of self. Food is not the problem behind the hunger, and food is not the answer.

I do not deny that I am hungry when my binge voice starts screaming in my ear. I immediately admit that I am terribly hungry. But I then ask myself, "What am I hungry for?" Rarely am I hungry for food. Food is instead a way of feeding emotional hungers that I otherwise do not know how to feed.

Sometimes I realize I am hungry for the approval of others. Sometimes my hunger is for the company of another person when I am lonely. Sometimes my hunger comes from the deprived little girl that still lives within me. Physical hunger is rarely a part of my binge voice. Food is not my problem. Control over food is not my problem. My emotional hungers and my inability to feed those hungers in the right way is my problem.

Never will I be able to eat enough food to fill hungers that are not really crying out for food. I will never get enough of what I do not really want or need. It is only by feeding my true hungers and shedding my food security blanket that I can feel nourished and satisfied. Only when I stop starving myself to death by gorging myself with food will I fully live.

The emotional hungers this young bulimic woman describes are common to people with eating disorders. The need for approval from others, low self-esteem, and frequent feelings of depression and anxiety characterize people with bulimia nervosa, anorexia nervosa, and binge-eating disorder (Fairburn et al., 1997; Herman & Polivy, 1988). Bingeing may develop as a way of coping with negative emotions (Bulik et al., 1997; Heatherton & Baumeister, 1991; Polivy & Herman, 1993). People who binge tend to be more prone to anxiety, emotionally unstable, and impulsive than are people with restricting anorexia nervosa or no eating disorders. They are easily upset by stressful situations and tend to engage impulsively in bingeing in response to emotional distress (Hsu, 1990). One of the most famous bulimics in recent history, the late Princess of Wales, Diana, said that she used food to cope with the painful emotions she had as a result of her failed marriage. Her struggle with bulimia is discussed in the *Extraordinary People:* Diana, Princess of Wales (p. 508).

EXTRAORDINARY PEOPLE

Diana, Princess of Wales

Perhaps the most famous person to suffer from bulimia nervosa, Diana, Princess of Wales, shocked the world when she made her suffering public. Never before had a member of the British royal family been so open, particularly about symptoms that could be diagnosed as a psychological disorder. After the birth of her first son, William, Diana suffered a postpartum depression (see Chapter 8). She attributed this depression to an accumulation of great changes in her life—her marriage at 19 to the Prince of Wales, her difficult pregnancy, which came early in that marriage, the tremendous media attention given her, the early signs that her marriage was falling apart. Diana felt she had little support from her husband or family, however, in fighting this depression and thus began to cope with her pain in maladaptive ways. Here is her story of how her bulimia developed, as told to a BBC interviewer in November 1995 (British Broadcasting Corporation).

Princess Diana was a public figure who openly discussed her eating disorders.

- **Diana:** When no one listens to you, or you feel no one's listening to you, all sort of things start to happen. For instance, you have so much pain inside yourself that you try and hurt yourself on the outside because you want help, but it's the wrong help you're asking for. People see it as crying wolf or attention-seeking, and they think because you're in the media all the time you've got enough attention. But I was actually crying out because I wanted to get better in order to go forward and continue my duty and my role as wife, mother, Princess of Wales. So yes, I did inflict upon myself. I didn't like myself,

I was ashamed because I couldn't cope with the pressures.

- **Question:** What did you actually do?

- **Diana:** Well, I just hurt my arms and my legs; and I work in environments now where I see women doing similar things and I'm able to understand completely where they're coming from.

- **Question:** What was your husband's reaction to this, when you began to injure yourself in this way?

- **Diana:** Well, I didn't actually always do it in front of him. But obviously anyone who loves someone would be very concerned about it.

- **Question:** Did he understand what was behind the physical act of hurting yourself, do you think?

- **Diana:** No but then not many people would have taken the time to see that.

- **Question:** Were you able to admit that you were in fact unwell, or did you feel compelled simply to carry on performing as the Princess of Wales?

- **Diana:** I felt compelled to perform. Well, when I say perform, I was compelled to go out and do my engagements and not let people down and support them and love them. And in a way by being out in public they supported me, although they weren't aware just how much healing they were giving me, and it carried me through.

- **Question:** But did you feel that you had to maintain the public image of a successful Princess of Wales?

- **Diana:** Yes I did, yes I did.

Continued

- **Question:** The depression was resolved, as you say, but it was subsequently reported that you suffered bulimia. Is that true?
- **Diana:** Yes, I did. I had bulimia for a number of years. And that's like a secret disease. You inflict it upon yourself because your self-esteem is at a low ebb, and you don't think you're worthy or valuable. You fill your stomach up four or five times a day—some do it more—and it gives you a feeling of comfort. It's like having a pair of arms around you, but it's temporarily, temporary. Then you're disgusted at the bloatedness of your stomach, and then you bring it all up again. And it's a repetitive pattern which is very destructive to yourself.
- **Question:** How often would you do that on a daily basis?
- **Diana:** Depends on the pressures going on. If I'd been on what I call an awayday, or I'd been up part of the country all day, I'd come home feeling pretty empty, because my engagements at that time would be to do with people dying, people very sick, people's marriage problems, and I'd come home and it would be very difficult to know how to comfort myself having been comforting lots of other people, so it would be a regular pattern to jump into the fridge. It was a symptom of what was going on in my marriage. I was crying out for help, but giving the wrong signals, and people were using my bulimia as a coat on a hanger: they decided that was the problem—Diana was unstable.
- **Question:** Instead of looking behind the symptom at the cause.
- **Diana:** Uh, uh.
- **Question:** What was the cause?
- **Diana:** The cause was the situation where my husband and I had to keep everything together because we didn't want to disappoint the public, and yet obviously there was a lot of anxiety going on within our four walls.

- **Question:** Do you mean between the two of you?
- **Diana:** Uh, uh.
- **Question:** And so you subjected yourself to this phase of bingeing and vomiting?
- **Diana:** You could say the word subjected, but it was my escape mechanism, and it worked, for me, at that time.
- **Question:** Did you seek help from any other members of the Royal Family?
- **Diana:** No. You, you have to know that when you have bulimia you're very ashamed of yourself and you hate yourself, so—and people think you're wasting food—so you don't discuss it with people. And the thing about bulimia is your weight always stays the same, whereas with anorexia you visibly shrink. So you can pretend the whole way through. There's no proof. . . .
- **Question:** How long did this bulimia go on for?
- **Diana:** A long time, a long time. But I'm free of it now.
- **Question:** Two years, three years?
- **Diana:** Mmm. A little bit more than that.

Although Diana's life was extraordinary by any standards, the development of her bulimia contains themes that are terribly common. She suffered symptoms of depression but she felt she had to be "perfect" at all times and show no weakness, even to her immediate family. The bulimia became a "release valve" for her negative emotions, but further damaged her self-esteem and sense of control. Diana perceived her family as unsupportive and overcontrolling, and felt unable to reach out to them directly, so used the bulimic behaviors as "cries for help."

As most of the world knows, Diana and her husband Charles divorced in 1996. She continued to live a glamorous life with the elite of Europe, and to be a devoted mother to her sons, William and Harry, until her death in a car crash in 1997.

Other research confirms that people with eating disorders are more concerned with the opinions of others, are more conforming to others' wishes, and are more rigid in their evaluations of themselves and others than are other people (Striegel-Moore, Silberstein, & Rodin, 1993; Strober, 1981; Vitousek & Manke, 1994). Studies of the cognitions of people with eating disorders show that they have a dichotomous thinking style, in which everything is either all good or all bad. For example, if they eat one cookie, they may think that they have blown their diets and might as well eat the whole box of cookies. They will say they cannot break their rigid eating routines or they will completely lose control over their eating. They obsess over their eating routines and plan their days down to the smallest detail around these routines.

Family Dynamics

A pioneer in the study of eating disorders is Hilde Bruch (1973, 1982). Her theory is most concerned with girls who develop anorexia nervosa, although it has also been used to understand the development of bulimia nervosa and binge-eating disorder. Bruch noted that anorexia nervosa often occurs in girls who have been unusually "good girls," high achievers, dutiful and compliant daughters who are always trying to please their parents and others by being "perfect." These girls tend to have parents who are overinvested in their daughters' compliance and achievements, who are overcontrolling, and who will not allow the expression of feelings, especially negative feelings. This certainly would seem to describe Diana's life as the Princess of Wales. Another pioneer in theorizing about anorexia, Salvador Minuchin, describes the families of anorexics as **enmeshed families** (Minuchin, Rosman, & Baker, 1978). There is extreme interdependence and intensity in the family interactions, so that the boundaries between the identities of individual family members are weak and easily crossed.

Throughout their daughters' lives, these parents are ineffective and inappropriate in their parenting, responding primarily to the parents' own schedules and needs rather than to their daughters' needs for food or comfort (Bruch, 1973). As a result, the daughters do not learn to identify and accept their own feelings and desires. Instead, they learn to monitor closely the needs and desires of others and to comply with others' demands, as we can see in the case of Rachel and her family.

CASE STUDY

Rachel is a 16-year-old with anorexia nervosa. Her parents are highly educated and very successful, having spent most of their careers in the diplomatic corps. Rachel, her two brothers, and her parents are "very close, as are many families in the diplomatic corps, because we move so much," although the daily care of the children has always been left to nannies. The children had to follow strict rules for appropriate conduct both in the home and outside. These rules were partly driven by the requirements of families of diplomats to "be on the best behavior" in their host country and partly driven by Rachel's parents' very conservative religious beliefs. Rachel, as the only daughter in the family, had always to behave like "a proper lady" to counteract the stereotype of American girls as brash and sexually promiscuous. All the children were required to act mature beyond their years, controlling any emotional outbursts, taking defeats and disappointments without complaint, and happily picking up and moving every couple of years when their parents were reassigned to another country.

Rachel's anorexic behaviors began when her parents announced they were leaving the diplomatic corps to return to the United States. Rachel had grown very fond of their last post in Europe, because she had finally found a group of friends that she liked *and* her parents approved of, and she liked her school. She had always done well in school but often had hated the harshly strict schoolteachers. In her present school, she felt accepted by her teachers as well as challenged by the work. When Rachel told her parents she would like to finish her last year of high school in this school rather than go to the United States with them, they flatly refused to even consider it. Rachel tried to talk with her parents, suggesting she stay with the family of one of her friends, who was willing to have her, but her parents cut her off and told her they would not discuss the idea further. Rachel became sullen and withdrawn and stopped eating shortly after the family arrived in the United States.

As a result of such family dynamics, anorexic girls have fundamental deficits in their senses of self and identities. They experience themselves as always acting in response to others rather than in response to their own wishes and needs. They do not accurately identify their own feelings or desires and thus do not cope appropriately with distress. They do not even accurately identify bodily sensations such as hunger, and this may contribute greatly to their ability to starve themselves for long periods of time.

Why do eating disorders often develop in adolescence? One of the important tasks of adolescence is separation and individuation from one's family. Girls from these families deeply fear separation because they have not developed the ability to act and think independently of their families. They also fear involvement with peers, especially sexual involvement, because they do not understand their feelings or trust their judgment. Yet they recognize at some level their need to separate from their families and take their place among their peers. They harbor rage against their parents for their overcontrol. They become angry, negativistic, defiant, and distrustful. They also discover that controlling their food intake both gives them some sense of control over their lives and elicits concern from their parents. The rigid control of their bodies provides a sense of power over the self and the family that the girls have never had before. It also provides a way of avoiding peer relationships—the girl dons the persona of an anorexic, sickly, distant, untouchable, and superior in her self-control. Other psychoanalytic theorists have taken this argument further to suggest that the anorexic girl is primarily avoiding sexual maturity and relationships by stopping pubertal maturation by self-starvation (Lerner, 1986).

Why would girls but not boys in such families develop eating disorders? It may be because, in general, parents tend to appreciate the need for boys to separate from the family in adolescence and give them the freedom to separate. Especially in these enmeshed families, parents are terrified of their girls' independence; the mothers of these girls may need their daughters to remain dependent because their own identities are tied too closely to their daughters (Bruch, 1973; Palazzoli, 1974). Thus, there are tremendous pressures on girls to remain enmeshed with their families, but boys have more opportunity to break free and build their own identities.

Research has confirmed that the families of girls with eating disorders have high levels of conflict, that expression of negative emotions is discouraged in the families, and that control and perfectionism are key themes in the families (Attie & Brooks-Gunn, 1989; Pike & Rodin, 1991; Strauss & Ryan, 1987). These negative characteristics are not specific to the families of girls with eating disorders, however. They are also prevalent in the families of children with depression, anxiety disorders, and several other forms of psychopathology. What may be crucial in the development of anorexia nervosa is the girls' lack of awareness of their own bodily sensations, which allows them to ignore even the most severe hunger pangs (Leon et al., 1995). Girls who come from these troubled families but are not able to completely ignore their hunger may fall into a binge/purge form of anorexia nervosa, or into bulimia nervosa.

Unfortunately, the majority of studies of the families and personality characteristics of anorexics and bulimics have compared people who already have eating disorders with those who do not (Vitousek & Manke, 1994). As a result, we do not know to what extent these family and personality characteristics are causes of anorexia or bulimia. The controlling nature of parents' behaviors toward their children may be a consequence as well as a cause of the disorder—parents are exerting control to try to save their children's lives. Similarly, many of the personality characteristics of people with eating disorders may be consequences as well as causes of the disorder. Studies of normal people who engage in self-starvation as part of an experiment show that depression, anxiety, rigidity, obsessiveness, irritability, concrete thinking, and social withdrawal appear after a few weeks of self-starvation (Keys, Brozek, Henschel, Mickelson, & Taylor, 1950). The success of psychological therapies for eating disorders, which we discuss later, provides more evidence that psychological factors are implicated in the development or at least the maintenance of these disorders.

Is sexual abuse a factor? A controversial theory that has gained much attention is that the eating disorders often result from experiences of sexual abuse (see Pope & Hudson, 1992). This theory has been controversial because it stemmed from clinical reports of high rates of sexual abuse among persons seeking therapy for eating disorders rather than from controlled studies and because it has led some therapists to urge their clients with eating disorders to search through their pasts for memories of childhood sexual abuse and then take action against their abusers as part of their therapy. Proponents of this theory argue that survivors of sexual abuse develop eating disorders as a symbol of self-loathing and a way of making themselves unattractive in an attempt to prevent further sexual abuse.

In recent years, several careful studies have been done to examine the rates of sexual abuse among women and men with eating disorders and to compare these rates to those of people with other psychological disorders and people with no disorders (Bulik et al., 1997; Kinzl et al., 1994; Pope & Hudson, 1992; Rorty, Yager, & Rossotto, 1994; Welch & Fairburn, 1994). These studies have found that although people with eating disorders tend to have higher rates of sexual abuse than people with no psychological disorders, they do not tend to have higher rates of sexual abuse than do people with other psychological disorders, such as depression or anxiety. Thus, sexual abuse seems to be a general risk factor for psychological problems, including eating disorders, depression, and anxiety, rather than a specific risk factor for eating disorders.

Twin studies suggest that eating behaviors and weight are partially controlled by genetics

Biological Theories of the Eating Disorders

As is the case with most psychological disorders, anorexia and bulimia nervosa tend to run in families (Kassett et al., 1988; Strober, 1991). One twin study of bulimia nervosa showed a concordance rate among female monozygotic twins of 23 percent, compared to a concordance rate of 9 percent in female dizygotic twins (Kendler et al., 1991). A more recent study of bingeing and vomiting behaviors estimated that 46 percent of the variation in bingeing behaviors and 72 percent of the variation in vomiting behaviors were due to genetics (Sullivan, Bulik, & Kendler, 1998). A twin study of anorexia nervosa showed a concordance rate among female MZ twins of 56 percent, compared to a concordance rate of 5 percent in female DZ twins (Holland et al., 1984). These data suggest that the eating disorders may be, at least in part, heritable.

The families of people with anorexia and bulimia also have higher than normal rates of depression (Kassett et al., 1988; Kendler et al., 1991). This has led some theorists to argue that the eating disorders are variants of mood disorders. That is, people with eating disorders may have underlying mood disorders that they manifest through bulimia nervosa or anorexia nervosa. Indeed, as many as 75 percent of people with eating disorders can also be diagnosed with mood disorders (APA, 2000). Fueling this perspective is the fact that some of the biological therapies for mood disorders also help to relieve eating disorders in some patients, as we discuss in a later section.

It may not be useful to consider the eating disorders only as manifestations of some other underlying disorders, however, because the eating disorders have

unique characteristics that must be addressed in therapy even if a patient has a mood disorder as well as an eating disorder (Wilson, 1993). In addition, even if some people with mood disorders develop eating disorders, we would need to understand why these people developed eating disorders while most people with mood disorders do not.

Much of the current research on biological causes of bulimia and anorexia is focusing on the systems in the body that regulate appetite, hunger, satiety, initiation of eating, and cessation of eating. The **hypothalamus** plays a central role in regulating eating (Blundell & Hill, 1993). It receives messages about the body's recent food consumption and nutrient level and sends messages to cease eating when the body's nutritional needs are met. These messages are carried by a variety of neurotransmitters, including norepinephrine, serotonin, and dopamine, and a number of hormones such as cortisol and insulin. Disordered eating behavior might be caused by imbalances or dysregulation in any of the neurochemicals involved in this system or by structural or functional problems in the hypothalamus. For example, if this system were disrupted, it could cause the individual to have trouble detecting hunger accurately or to stop eating when full, which are both characteristics of people with eating disorders.

There are pieces of evidence that people with eating disorders do have disruptions in the hypothalamus (Study Group on Anorexia Nervosa, 1995). Anorexic persons show lowered functioning of the hypothalamus and abnormalities in the levels or regulation of several different hormones important to the functioning of the hypothalamus (Fava et al., 1989; Mitchell, 1986). It is unclear whether these are causes or consequences of the self-starvation of anorexia. Some studies find that anorexics continue to show abnormalities in hypothalamic and hormonal functioning and in neurotransmitter levels after they gain some weight, whereas others studies show these abnormalities disappear with weight gain.

Many bulimic persons show abnormally low levels of the neurotransmitter **serotonin** (Mitchell & deZwaan, 1993). Wurtman and others (Wurtman, 1987; Wurtman & Wurtman, 1984) have suggested that this deficiency in serotonin causes the body to crave carbohydrates. Indeed, bulimics often binge on high-carbohydrate foods. Bulimic persons may then take up self-induced vomiting or other types of purges in order to avoid gaining weight from eating carbohydrates. Some studies also find that bulimics have lower than normal levels of **norepinephrine** (Fava et al., 1989). Again, however, it is not clear whether low levels of these neurotransmitters are causes of the bingeing of bulimia or the consequences of the disordered eating patterns of bulimics.

Thus, a number of biological abnormalities are associated with anorexia nervosa and bulimia nervosa. These abnormalities could contribute to disordered eating behavior by causing the body to crave certain foods or by making it difficult for a person to read the body's signals of hunger and fullness. Just why people with eating disorders also develop distorted body images and the other cognitive and emotional problems seen in the eating disorders is not clear, however. In addition, many of the biological abnormalities seen in the eating disorders could be the consequences rather than the causes of the disorders.

Summing Up

- Cultural and societal norms regarding beauty may play a role in the eating disorders. Eating disorders are more common in groups that consider extreme thinness attractive than in groups that consider a heavier weight attractive.

- Eating disorders develop as means of gaining some control or coping with negative emotions. In addition, people with eating disorders tend to show rigid, dichotomous thinking.

- People who develop eating disorders come from families that are overcontrolling and perfectionistic but discourage the expression of negative emotions.

- People who are so unaware of their own bodily sensations that they can starve themselves may develop anorexia nervosa. People who remain aware of their bodily sensations and cannot starve themselves but who are prone to anxiety and impulsivity may develop binge-eating disorder or bulimia nervosa.

- Girls may be more likely than boys to develop eating disorders in adolescence because girls are not given as much freedom as boys to develop independence and their own identities.

- People with eating disorders are more likely than people without eating disorders to have a history of sexual abuse, but a history of sexual abuse is also common among people with several other disorders.

- There is evidence that both anorexia nervosa and bulimia nervosa are heritable.

- Depression also runs in the families of people with eating disorders. Many theorists believe that the eating disorders should not be considered just a variant of depression, however.

- Eating disorders may be tied to dysfunction in the hypothalamus, a part of the brain that helps to regulate eating behavior.

- Some studies show abnormalities in levels of the neurotransmitters serotonin and norepinephrine in people with eating disorders.

☉ TREATMENTS FOR EATING DISORDERS

Fortunately, significant progress has been made in recent years in the treatment of the eating disorders. Below we discuss several psychotherapies and biological treatments that have proven successful either in the treatment of anorexia or bulimia, or both (see *Concept Review:* Treatments for Eating Disorders, p. 514). Then we discuss new research on the effectiveness of prevention programs for the eating disorders.

Psychotherapy for Anorexia Nervosa

It can be very difficult to engage a person with anorexia nervosa in psychotherapy. Because the anorexic client often feels that others try to control her and that she must maintain absolute control over her own behaviors, she can be extremely resistant to attempts by a therapist to change her behaviors or attitudes. Thus, regardless of what type of psychotherapy a therapist uses with an anorexic client, much work must be done to win the client's trust and participation in the therapy and to maintain this trust and participation as the client begins to gain that dreaded weight.

Winning the anorexic's trust can be especially difficult if the therapist is forced to hospitalize her because she has lost so much weight that her life is in danger. Yet hospitalization and forced refeeding are

CONCEPT REVIEW

Treatments for Eating Disorders

A number of treatments for the eating disorders have been developed in recent years.

Treatment	Description
In Treating Anorexia Nervosa:	
1. Hospitalization and refeeding	1. Patient is hospitalized and forced to ingest food to prevent death from starvation.
2. Behavior therapy	2. Rewards are made contingent upon eating. Relaxation techniques are taught.
3. Help the patient accept and value their emotions	3. Cognitive or supportive-expressive techniques are used to help the patient explore emotions and issues underlying behavior.
	4. Raise the family's concern about anorexic behavior. Confront family's tendency to be overcontrolling and have excessive expectations.
In Treating Bulimia Nervosa:	
1. Cognitive-behavioral therapy	1. Teach the client to recognize cognitions around eating and confront maladaptive cognitions. Introduce "forbidden foods" and regular diet, and help the client confront irrational cognitions about these.
2. Interpersonal therapy	2. Help the client identify interpersonal problems associated with bulimic behaviors, such as problems in a marriage, and deal with these problems more effectively.
3. Supportive-expressive therapy	3. Provide support and encouragement for the client's expression of feelings about problems associated with bulimia in a nondirective manner.
4. Tricyclic antidepressants and serotonin reuptake inhibitors.	4. These drugs may help to reduce impulsive eating and negative emotions that drive bulimic behaviors.

often necessary to save an anorexic's life. Because people with anorexia nervosa typically do not seek treatment themselves, they often do not come to the attention of therapists until they are so emaciated and malnourished that they have a medical crisis (such as cardiac problems) or their families fear for their lives. The first job of the therapist is obviously to help save the anorexic's life. Because the anorexic will not eat voluntarily, this may mean hospitalizing her and feeding her intravenously. During the hospitalization, the therapist will begin the work of engaging the anorexic in facing and solving the psychological issues causing her to starve herself.

Individual Therapy

Individual therapy with anorexic persons often focuses on their inability to recognize and trust their own feelings, with the goal of building their self-awareness and independence from others (Bruch, 1973). This can be very difficult, because many anorexic clients are resistant to therapy and suspicious of therapists, whom they think are just other people trying to control their lives. Other anorexic clients may be engaged in therapy but look to therapists to define their feelings for them, just as their parents have done for years. Therapists must convey to clients that their feelings are their own, valuable and legitimate, and the proper focus of attention in therapy. Only when clients can learn to read their feelings accurately will they also read their sensations of hunger and fullness accurately and be able to respond to them.

Behavior therapy is often used in the treatment of anorexia. Rewards are made contingent upon the anorexic gaining weight. If the client is hospitalized, certain privileges in the hospital are used as rewards, such as watching television, going outside the hospital, or receiving visitors. The client may also be taught relaxation techniques that she can use as she becomes extremely anxious about ingesting food. Studies suggest that the majority of anorexic patients benefit from behavior therapies, gaining weight to within 15 percent of normal body weight (Agras, 1987). The relapse rate with behavior therapies alone is very high, however, and most anorexic patients return to their anorexic eating patterns soon after therapy ends or they are released from the hospital, unless they are engaged in other therapies that confront some of the emotional issues accompanying their anorexia.

Family Therapy

In **family therapy**, the anorexic and her family are treated as a unit (Minuchin, Rosman & Baker, 1978). With some families, therapists must first raise the parents' level of anxiety about their daughters' eating disorders because the parents have been implicitly or explicitly supporting the daughters' avoidance of food. Therapists will identify patterns in the families' interactions that are contributing to the anorexics' sense of being controlled, such as being overprotective while not allowing their daughters the right to express their own needs and feelings. Parents' unreasonable expectations for their daughters are confronted, and families are helped to develop healthy ways of expressing and resolving conflict between the members.

One study of 50 anorexic girls and their families found that family therapy was successful with 86 percent of the cases (Minuchin, Rosman & Baker, 1978). These successful girls had normal eating patterns and good relations at home and at school even 2 1/2 years after treatment. This study focused on young girls (of an average age of 14 years) who had only shown anorexic symptoms for a short time. Other studies suggest that anorexics who have shown symptoms for much longer and who are older when they enter treatment are not as likely to benefit from family therapy (Dare et al., 1990).

Psychotherapy can help many anorexic people, but it typically is a long process, often taking years for the anorexic to fully recover. Along the way, many anorexics who have an initial period of recovery, with restoration of their weights to normal levels and their eating to healthy patterns, relapse into bulimic or anorexic behaviors. They often continue to have self-esteem deficits, family problems, and periods of depression and anxiety (Eckert et al., 1995). Most therapists combine techniques from different modes of therapy to meet the individual needs of anorexic people. Even multi-method inpatient treatment programs do not consistently overcome anorexia, and graduates of these programs often continue to show severely restrained eating, perfectionism, and low body weight (Sullivan et al., 1998). The difficulty in helping anorexic people to fully recover may indicate the depth of the psychological issues driving self-starvation.

Psychotherapy for Bulimia Nervosa

Treatment for bulimia nervosa is different from treatment for anorexia nervosa in many ways. First, by the time a person with anorexia nervosa obtains treatment, she may be near death, so extreme measures may need to be taken to save her life, such as hospitalization and forced refeeding. This is less likely to be the case for a person with bulimia nervosa. Second, the psychological issues of anorexia and bulimia can be different. For people with anorexia, these issues often have to do with family dynamics, concerns about losing control, and a greatly distorted body image. For people with bulimia, psychological issues may involve learning to cope more effectively with emotions, learning to control binge and purge behaviors, and learning more adaptive ways to think about food and one's body.

Parents can have a positive impact on children's eating behaviors, particularly when the children are young.

Cognitive-behavioral, interpersonal, and short-term psychodynamic therapies have all proven effective in the treatment of bulimia nervosa (Agras, 1993; Fairburn & Hay, 1992; Garner & Garfinkel, 1997). Most controlled studies of psychotherapy for eating disorders have focused on **cognitive-behavioral therapy** for bulimia (Agras, 1993; Fairburn & Hay, 1992; Wilson & Fairburn, 1998). This therapy is based on the view that the bulimic's extreme concerns about shape and weight are the central features of the disorder. The therapist teaches the client to monitor the cognitions that accompany her eating, particularly her binge episodes and her purging episodes (Wilson, Fairburn, & Agras, 1997). Then the therapist helps the client confront these cognitions and develop more adaptive attitudes toward her weight and body shape. An interchange between a therapist and client might go like this:

Voices

Therapist: What were you thinking just before you began to binge?

Client: I was thinking that I felt really upset and sad about having no social life. I wanted to eat just to feel better.

Therapist: And as you were eating, what were you thinking?

Client: I was thinking that the ice cream tasted really good, that it was making me feel good. But I was also thinking that I shouldn't be eating this, that I'm bingeing again. But then I thought that my life is such a wreck that I deserve to eat what I want to make me feel better.

Therapist: And what were you thinking after you finished the binge?

Client: That I was a failure, a blimp, that I have no control, that this therapy isn't working.

Therapist: Okay, let's go back to the beginning. You said you wanted to eat because you thought it would make you feel better. Did it?

Client: Well, like I said, the ice cream tasted good and it felt good to indulge myself.

Therapist: But in the long run did bingeing make you feel better?

Client: Of course not. I felt terrible afterward.

Therapist: Can you think of anything you might say to yourself the next time you get into such a state, where you want to eat in order to make yourself feel better?

Client: I could remind myself that I'll only feel better for a little while, but then I'll feel terrible.

Therapist: How likely do you think it is that you'll remember to say this to yourself?

Client: Not very likely.

Therapist: Is there any way to increase the likelihood?

Client: Well, I guess I could write it on a card or something and put the card near my refrigerator.

Therapist: That's a pretty good idea. What else could you do to prevent yourself from eating when you feel upset? What other things could you do to relieve your upset, other than eat?

Client: I could call my friend Keisha and talk about how I feel. Or I could go for a walk—someplace away from food—like up in the hills where it's so pretty. Walking up there always makes me feel better.

Therapist: Those are really good ideas. It's important to have a variety of things you can do, other than eat, to relieve bad moods.

The behavioral components of this therapy involve introducing "forbidden foods" (such as bread) back into the client's diet and helping her to confront her irrational thoughts about these foods, such as "if I have just one doughnut, I'm inevitably going to binge." Similarly, the client is taught to eat three healthy meals a day and to challenge the thoughts she has about these meals and the possibility of gaining weight. Cognitive-behavioral therapy for bulimia usually lasts about 3 to 6 months and involves 10 to 20 sessions.

Controlled studies of the efficacy of cognitive-behavioral therapy for bulimia find that about one-half of clients completely stop the binge/purge cycle (Wilson et al., 1997). Clients undergoing this therapy also show a decrease in depression and anxiety, an increase in social functioning, and a lessening of concern about dieting and weight. Comparisons to drug therapies show that cognitive-behavioral therapy is at least as effective as drug therapies in the short term and more likely to prevent relapse in the long term than are the drug therapies (Fairburn & Hay, 1992).

Other studies of the treatment of bulimia have compared cognitive-behavioral therapy to **interpersonal therapy,** to **supportive-expressive psychodynamic therapy,** and to behavior therapy without a focus on cognitions (Fairburn et al., 1991; Fairburn et al., 1995; Garner et al., 1993; Wilson et al., 1999). In the interpersonal therapy, client and therapist discuss interpersonal problems that are related to the client's eating disorder, and the therapist works actively with the client to develop strategies to solve these interpersonal problems. In supportive-expressive therapy, the therapist encourages the client to talk about problems related to the eating disorder, especially interpersonal problems, but in a highly nondirective manner. In behavior therapy, the client is taught how to monitor her food intake, is reinforced for introducing avoided foods into her diet, and is taught coping techniques for avoiding bingeing. In the studies, all the therapies resulted in significant improvement in the clients' eating behaviors and emotional well-being, with the cognitive-behavioral and interpersonal therapy clients showing the greatest and most enduring improvements. Cognitive-behavioral therapy was better than the other therapies in eliminating disturbed attitudes toward shape and weight and extreme attempts to diet. Clients receiving interpersonal therapy showed the greatest improvements in their relationships. Thus, it appears that cognitive-behavioral therapy and interpersonal therapy may be effective therapies for bulimia. Recent studies have also suggested that cognitive-behavioral therapy is effective in the treatment of binge-eating disorder (Carter & Fairburn, 1998).

Biological Therapies

Recall that many people with eating disorders are also depressed or have histories of depression in their families. This connection to depression has led many psychiatrists to use antidepressant drugs to treat the eating disorders, particularly bulimia nervosa (Fairburn & Hay, 1992; Mitchell & Zwaan, 1993). **Tricyclic antidepressants** are superior to placebos in reducing bingeing and vomiting and in enhancing a sense of control in bulimics (e.g., McCann & Agras, 1990). Bulimic patients often continue to engage in severe dieting, however, and relapse into the binge/purge cycle shortly after stopping the drugs (Mitchell & deZwaan, 1993). The monoamine oxidase (MAO) inhibitors also have proven more effective than placebos in the treatment of bulimia but are not typically prescribed because they require severe dietary restrictions to prevent side effects. The selective **serotonin reuptake inhibitors,** such as fluoxetine (trade name Prozac), have been the focus of much research on biological treatments for the eating disorders. In a large multicenter study of 387 persons with bulimia, the median reduction in the bingeing frequency of persons taking fluoxetine was 67 percent, compared to only 33 percent in the group receiving placebos (Fluoxetine Bulimia Nervosa Collaborative [FBNC] Study Group, 1992). Another large multicenter study of people with binge-eating disorder found that the serotonin reuptake inhibitor fluvoxamine (Luvox) was much better than placebo in reducing binge-eating (Hudson et al., 1998).

Tricyclic antidepressants and MAO inhibitors have not proven effective in the treatment of anorexia in controlled clinical trials (Advokat & Kutlesic, 1995; Gadow, 1992). Small-scale studies of fluoxetine, a serotonin reuptake inhibitor, suggest that it may be helpful in treating anorexia (Gwirtsman et al., 1990; Kaye et al., 1991). The one available placebo-controlled study of fluoxetine showed that it was not helpful in the treatment of anorexia (Attia et al., 1998).

Prevention Programs for Eating Disorders

Many colleges and universities have implemented programs to try to counteract the obsession with food and thinness among their students, and to try to get students with eating disorders into therapy. A poll of America's 490 largest colleges and universities found that 69 percent have professionals on their staffs who specialize in diagnosing and treating eating disorders (Hubbard et al., 1999). One of the most popular programs for eating disorders is the student-led outreach program. Typically two or three students who have had an eating disorder make presentations to other students, in dormitories, sororities or fraternities, or as part of classes. These students define and describe eating disorders, and talk about their own experiences with the disorders and with treatment. Their hope is that they can bring a discussion of eating disorders and maladaptive eating behaviors and attitudes out in the open so that students can be more comfortable resisting social pressures around food and seeking help for food-related problems.

But do these programs work? A group of researchers at Stanford University attempted to find out (Mann et al., 1997). They surveyed most of the women in one first-year class about their food-related attitudes and behaviors, shortly after the women began school. The student group that led dormitory programs on food issues, called Body Image, Food and Self-Esteem, agreed to conduct its programs in a randomly selected half of the dormitories with first-year students during the first few months of the school year. Thus, about half of the first-year women were exposed to their program and about half of them were not. Then, about halfway into the school year, the researchers surveyed all the first-year women in the study again to determine any changes in their food-related attitudes and behaviors.

There were changes in the women's attitudes and behaviors, but these changes were quite surprising. The women who had seen the Body Image, Food and Self-Esteem program actually showed greater *increases* in symptoms of eating disorders, and *decreases* in body dissatisfaction than the women who had not seen the program. Basically, it seemed that the student-led program backfired, increasing the very problems it was trying to prevent.

The researchers suggested that one of the problems with programs such as this is that they have multiple goals that are not compatible with each other. One goal is to inform students who know nothing about eating disorders, and are not engaging in eating disordered behaviors, about these disorders in hopes that this prevents them from falling into eating-disordered behaviors. This is known as primary prevention—preventing a disorder before it happens. The second goal has to do with secondary prevention—getting people who are already engaging in eating-disordered behavior into treatment. Program leaders attempt to destigmatize eating-disordered behavior so that women who are engaging in such behaviors feel less ashamed and more comfortable in seeking help. They often do this by discussing how common eating-disordered behaviors are, and how they overcame their eating disorders. Unfortunately, the secondary prevention efforts may be undermining the primary prevention efforts. That is, when students who are not yet engaging in eating-disordered behavior hear how common this behavior is, and see the program leaders talk about how they have overcome their eating disorders, they may see eating disordered behavior as more acceptable.

The researchers concluded that student-led programs on eating disorders can make an important contribution to mental-health efforts on college campuses. The messages these programs deliver must be carefully thought through, however, and it may be necessary to have two kinds of programs—primary prevention programs aimed at students who have not fallen into eating disordered behavior yet, and secondary programs for students who are already having food-related problems.

Summing Up

- People with anorexia nervosa often must be hospitalized because they are so emaciated and malnourished that they are in a medical crisis.

- Behavior therapy for anorexia nervosa involves making rewards contingent upon the client eating. Clients may be taught relaxation techniques to handle their anxiety about eating.

- Family therapy focuses on understanding the role of anorexic behaviors in the family unit. Therapists challenge parents' attitudes toward their anorexic children's behaviors and try to help the family find more adaptive ways of interacting with each other.

- Individual therapy for anorexia may focus on helping clients identify and accept their feelings and to confront their distorted cognitions about their bodies.

- Psychotherapy can be helpful for anorexia but is usually a long process and the risk for relapse is high.

- Several studies show that cognitive-behavioral therapy, which focuses on the bulimics distorted cognitions about eating, is effective in the treatment of bulimia.

- Interpersonal therapy, which focuses on the quality of a client's relationships, and supportive expressive psychodynamic therapy, can be effective in the treatment of bulimia.

- Tricyclic antidepressants and serotonin reuptake inhibitors have been shown to be helpful in the treatment of bulimia. The MAO inhibitors can also be helpful, but are not usually prescribed because they require dietary restrictions to avoid side effects.

- Antidepressants have not proven as useful in the treatment of anorexia nervosa, but some small studies suggest the serotonin reuptake inhibitors may be helpful.

- Prevention programs can help to make students more aware of eating disorders and available treatments, but may backfire if the prevention message is not carefully tailored for audiences with different needs.

⟲ BIO-PSYCHO-SOCIAL INTEGRATION

Several experts have suggested that a group of biological, psychological, and social factors interact to create the eating disorders (Agras & Kirkley, 1986; Garner & Garfinkel, 1985; Polivy & Herman, 1993; Striegel-Moore, 1993). Any one of these factors alone may not be enough to push a woman or a man to develop anorexia or bulimia nervosa, but when combined they may.

First, societal pressures for thinness clearly provide a potent impetus for the development of unhealthy attitudes toward eating, especially for women. If these pressures were simply toward achieving a healthy weight and maintaining fitness, they would not be so dangerous. However, as we discussed earlier, the ideal weight for women promoted by beauty symbols in developed countries is much lower than that considered healthy and normal for the average woman. While the ideal weight promoted in these symbols has been getting thinner over the last few decades, the average person in the developed countries has been getting heavier, in part because of the increase in fat in the diet of young people, who eat a great deal of take-out and highly processed foods. Thus, many people find themselves constantly fighting to avoid gaining weight and never quite achieving the slim figures that they wish they had.

Second, biological factors may interact with these societal pressures to make some people more likely than others to develop eating disorders. People who develop eating disorders may have biological predispositions to being overweight or to having poorly regulated eating patterns. They find it extremely difficult to keep weight off without chronically being on severe diets. The societal message that "thin is good" is especially cruel for these people. They want to believe that they can look like the models in fashion magazines if they just try hard enough, when it may be biologically impossible for them to achieve this look and remain physically or psychologically healthy.

Another biological factor that may predispose some people to acquiesce to the pressures to diet and be thin is a tendency toward anxiety or mild depression. As noted earlier, many people with eating disorders, especially bulimics, are easily distressed and emotionally labile and tend to eat impulsively in response to their moods. Although problems in mood in people with eating disorders may be the results of environmental circumstances or of the stresses of having eating disorders, they may also be biologically caused in at least some people who develop eating disorders.

Personality factors may also interact with societal pressures to be thin and/or with the biological predispositions described to lead some people to develop eating disorders. Perfectionism, all-or-nothing thinking, and low self-esteem may make people more likely to engage in extreme measures to control their weight in response to unwelcome weight gains or in an attempt to achieve some ideal of attractiveness and therefore increase their self-esteem. These personality characteristics will be more likely to develop in children whose parents are lacking in affection and nurturance and, at the same time, controlling and demanding of perfection.

Thus, it may take some mixture of these factors rather than any single one to lead someone to develop a full eating disorder.

Chapter Summary

- The eating disorders include anorexia nervosa, bulimia nervosa, and binge-eating disorder.

- Anorexia nervosa is characterized by self-starvation, a distorted body image, intense fears of becoming fat, and amenorrhea. People with the restricting type of anorexia nervosa refuse to eat in order to prevent weight gain. People with the binge/purge type periodically engage in bingeing and then purge to prevent weight gain. The lifetime prevalence of anorexia is about 1 percent, with 90 to 95 percent of cases being female. Anorexia nervosa usually begins in adolescence, and the course is variable from one person to another. It is a very dangerous disorder, and the death rate among anorexics is 15 percent.

- Bulimia nervosa is characterized by uncontrolled bingeing, followed by behaviors designed to prevent weight gain from the binges. People with the purging type use self-induced vomiting, diuretics, or laxatives to prevent weight gain. People with the nonpurging type use fasting and exercise to prevent weight gain. Although overconcern with weight and occasional bingeing is common among college students, the prevalence of the full syndrome of bulimia nervosa is only about 1.0 percent in women and 0.2 percent in men. The onset of bulimia nervosa is most often in adolescence. Although bulimics do not tend to be underweight, there are several dangerous medical complications in bulimia nervosa.

- People with binge-eating disorder engage in bingeing but not in purging or behaviors designed to compensate for the binges. It is more common in women than in men, and people with the disorder tend to be significantly overweight. Binge-eating disorder is not officially recognized by the DSM-IV, but the diagnostic criteria were placed in an appendix for further study.

- Sociocultural theorists have noted that eating disorders may be more common among cultures in which thinness is considered attractive. This helps to account for historical, gender, and cross-cultural trends in the rates of eating disorders.

- Difficulties in coping with negative emotions and a rigid, dichotomous thinking style may contribute to the development of the eating disorders.

- The families of girls with eating disorders may be overcontrolling, overprotective, and hostile and do not allow the expression of feelings. In adolescence, these girls may develop eating disorders as a way of exerting control.

- Sexual abuse is a risk factor for eating disorders as well as for several other psychological problems.

- The biological factors implicated in the development of the eating disorders include genetics, dysregulation of hormonal and neurotransmitter systems, and generally lower functioning in the hypothalamus.

- Behavior therapy and family therapy do seem to be effective treatments for anorexia. Cognitive-behavioral therapy has proven as effective as drug therapy in reducing the symptoms of bulimia and more effective in preventing relapse. Interpersonal therapy, supportive expressive therapy, and behavior therapy also appear to be effective for bulimia nervosa. Antidepressants are effective in treating bulimia, but the relapse rate is high. Drug therapies have not proven effective for anorexia.

Key Terms

set point 490

anorexia nervosa 492

amenorrhea 493

restricting type of anorexia nervosa 493

binge/purge type of anorexia nervosa 494

bulimia nervosa 497

bingeing 497

purging type of bulimia nervosa 498

nonpurging type of bulimia nervosa 498

binge-eating disorder 499

enmeshed families 510

hypothalamus 512

serotonin 513

norepinephrine 513

behavior therapy 514

family therapy 515

cognitive-behavioral therapy 516

interpersonal therapy 516

supportive-expressive psychodynamic therapy 516

tricyclic antidepressants 517

selective serotonin reuptake inhibitors 517

Critical Thinking Questions

1. Do you think the diagnostic criteria for anorexia nervosa and bulimia nervosa should be narrow so that only the most severe behaviors are given a diagnosis or broad so that more moderate types of disordered eating meet the criteria for a diagnosis?

2. Are there any acceptable ways that society might reduce the emphasis in the media on attractiveness? Do you think these ways would help to reduce disordered eating behaviors?

3. How do you feel about forced hospitalization and refeeding of people with anorexia nervosa? Would you feel differently if the anorexic person was you, a close friend, or your daughter?

4. There is a high relapse rate in eating disorders, even among people who have been treated for these disorders. Why might relapse rates be particularly high for the eating disorders?

Diana Ong
Shadow of Her Former Self

I don't know whether it's normal or not, but sex has always been something that I take seriously. I would put it higher than tennis on my list of constructive things to do.

—*Art Buchwald,* Leaving Home: A Memoir *(1993)*

CHAPTER
15

Sexual Disorders and Gender Identity Disorder

CHAPTER OVERVIEW

Sexual Dysfunctions

The most common sexual disorder is a sexual dysfunction. The sexual dysfunctions include disorders of sexual desire, sexual arousal, orgasm, and sexual pain. Occasional problems in all of these areas are very common. These problems are given a diagnosis when they are persistent, they cause individuals significant distress, and they interfere with people's intimate relationships. The sexual dysfunctions can have a host of biological causes, including undiagnosed diabetes, drug use, and hormonal and vascular abnormalities. Possible psychological causes include relationship concerns, traumatic experiences, maladaptive attitudes and cognitions, and an upbringing or cultural milieu that devalues or degrades sex. When a sexual dysfunction has a biological cause, treating the biological cause may reduce the sexual dysfunction. A number of drugs are now available that treat some of the sexual dysfunctions. Psychological treatments for sexual dysfunctions focus on the personal concerns of the individual with the dysfunction and on the conflicts between the individual and his or her partner. Sex therapy can decrease people's inhibitions about sex and teach them new techniques for optimal sexual enjoyment.

Taking Psychology Personally
Practicing Safe Sex

Pushing the Boundaries
New Theories of Sexual Orientation

Paraphilias

People with paraphilias prefer sexual activities that involve nonhuman objects, nonconsenting adults, the suffering or humiliation of oneself or one's partner, or children. The paraphilias include fetishism, transvestism, sexual sadism and masochism, voyeurism, exhibitionism, frotteurism, and pedophilia. Most paraphilics do not seek treatment for their behavior. Aversion therapy and desensitization therapy may be useful for some paraphilics.

Gender Identity Disorder

Gender identity is one's perception of oneself as male or female. A person with gender identity disorder believes he or she was born with the wrong sex's genitals and is fundamentally a person of the opposite sex. Gender identity disorder in adulthood is also referred to as *transsexualism*. Some transsexuals undergo sex change operations and hormonal treatments.

Extraordinary People
Jayne Thomas, Ph.D.

Bio-Psycho-Social Integration
Chapter Summary
Key Terms
Critical Thinking Questions

CASE STUDY

Mallory is distraught. She is very attracted to a man she recently met, named Tom, and he is also attracted to her. They have been on a few dates, and last night they returned to Mallory's apartment and began to make love. Although Mallory was extremely excited about having intercourse with Tom and Tom was a good lover, Mallory did not have an orgasm during intercourse. This was not the first time Mallory did not have an orgasm during a sexual encounter with a man she found attractive, and she is beginning to think there is something wrong with her.

CASE STUDY

Philip likes shoes—women's black patent leather shoes, to be exact. He has hundreds of pairs, which he keeps in a special room in his house. Many nights he will go to that room, undress partially or totally, and lie amid the shoes as he masturbates. He reaches orgasm quickly and experiences a deep sense of sexual pleasure.

CASE STUDY

David is a pedophile—he prefers to have sex with young children. He was recently arrested when a young boy that David was supposed to be tutoring in mathematics told his parents that David had tried to touch his penis. Under interrogation, David broke down and admitted that he had fondled or exposed himself to a dozen young children and had attempted intercourse with one young girl.

CASE STUDY

Joanne was born with the genitals of a male, but for as long as she can remember, she has considered herself female. She dresses in women's clothes, she wears women's makeup, her voice sounds like a woman's, and thanks to several surgeries and hormonal treatments, she now has a vagina and breasts instead of a penis.

Although the behaviors and concerns of these four people vary greatly, all of them are suffering from some kind of *sexual disorder*. The one underlying commonality to all the sexual disorders is that they involve sexual behaviors or beliefs that are a source of distress to the individual suffering the disorder or to people around him or her. Sexual disorders fall into three distinct categories. First, sexual dysfunctions involve problems in experiencing sexual arousal or carrying through with a sexual act to the point of sexual satisfaction. Mallory is suffering from a common sexual dysfunction known as *inhibited orgasm*. Second, paraphilias involve sexual activities that are focused on nonhuman objects, children or nonconsenting adults,

or on suffering or humiliation. There are several types of paraphilias, and they vary in the severity of their impact on other people. Fetishes like Philip's shoe fetish are relatively benign in that they usually do not affect anyone except the person with the fetish. However, paraphilias that involve nonconsenting adults or children, like David's pedophilia, clearly are not benign. Third, gender identity disorder, also known as *transsexualism*, involves the belief that one has been born with the body of the wrong gender. People with this disorder, like Joanne, feel trapped in the wrong body, wish to be rid of their genitals, and want to live as a member of the other gender.

In this chapter, we discuss specific sexual disorders within each of these three categories. We begin with some of the most common disorders that both men and women suffer: sexual dysfunctions. Then we move to the paraphilias, which are less common and primarily experienced by men. Finally, we discuss the most uncommon sexual disorder, gender identity disorder.

⑤ SEXUAL DYSFUNCTIONS

The **sexual dysfunctions** are a set of disorders in which people have trouble engaging in and enjoying sexual relationships with other people. In order to understand the sexual dysfunctions, it is important first to understand something about the human sexual response—what happens in our bodies when we feel sexually aroused, when we engage in sexual intercourse or other forms of sexual stimulation, and when we reach orgasm.

The Sexual Response Cycle

Before the work of William Masters and Virginia Johnson in the 1950s and 1960s, we knew little about what happened in the human body during sexual arousal and activity. Masters and Johnson (1970) observed people engaging in a variety of sexual practices in a laboratory setting and recorded the physiological changes that occurred during sexual activity.

Thanks to the work of Masters and Johnson and later researchers, we now know that the sexual response cycle can be divided into five phases: desire, excitement or arousal, plateau, orgasm, and resolution. **Sexual desire** is the urge to engage in any type of sexual activity. The **arousal phase** or *excitement phase* consists of a psychological experience of arousal and pleasure and the physiological changes known as *vasocongestion* and *myotonia*. **Vasocongestion** is the filling of blood vessels and tissues with blood, also known as *engorgement*. In males, erection of the penis is caused

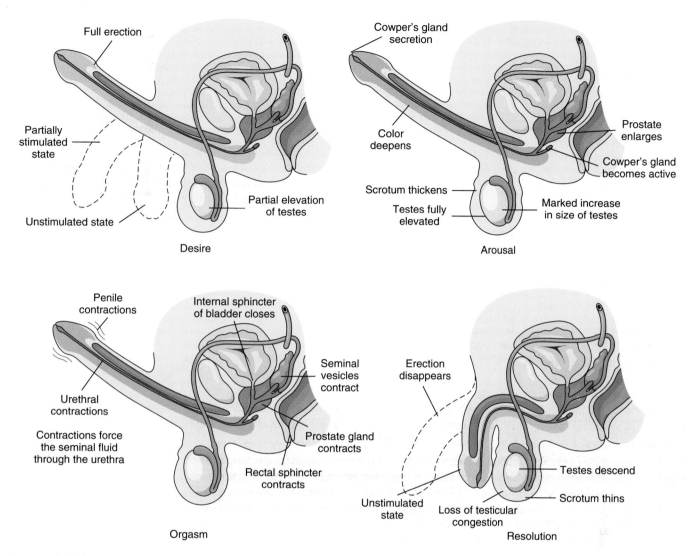

FIGURE 15.1   The Male Sexual Response Cycle. Males experience characteristic changes in physiology during each phase of their sexual response cycle.
Source: Adapted from Hyde, 1990, p. 199.

by increases in the flow of blood into the arteries of the penis, accompanied by decreases in the outflow of blood from the penis through the veins. In females, vasocongestion causes the clitoris to enlarge, the labia to swell, and the vagina to moisten. **Myotonia** is muscular tension. During the excitement phase, many muscles in the body may become more tense, culminating in the muscular contractions known as *orgasm*.

Following the excitement phase is the **plateau phase.** During this period, excitement remains at a high but stable level. This period is pleasurable in itself and some people try to extend this period as long as possible before reaching orgasm. During both the excitement and plateau phases, the person may feel tense all over, the skin is flushed, salivation increases, the nostrils flare, the heart pounds, breathing is heavy, and the person may be oblivious to external stimuli or events.

The excitement and plateau phases are followed by **orgasm.** Physiologically, orgasm is the discharge of the neuromuscular tension built up during the excitement and plateau phases. Both males and females experience a sense of the inevitability of orgasm just before it happens.

In males, orgasm involves rhythmic contractions of the prostate, seminal vesicles, vas deferens, and the entire length of the penis and the urethra, accompanied by the ejaculation of semen (see Figure 15.1). In males, a *refractory period* follows ejaculation. During this period, the male cannot achieve full erection and another orgasm regardless of the type or intensity of sexual stimulation. The refractory period may last anywhere from a few minutes to several hours.

In females, orgasm generally involves rhythmic contractions of the orgasmic platform (see Figure 15.2, p. 526) and more irregular contractions of the uterus,

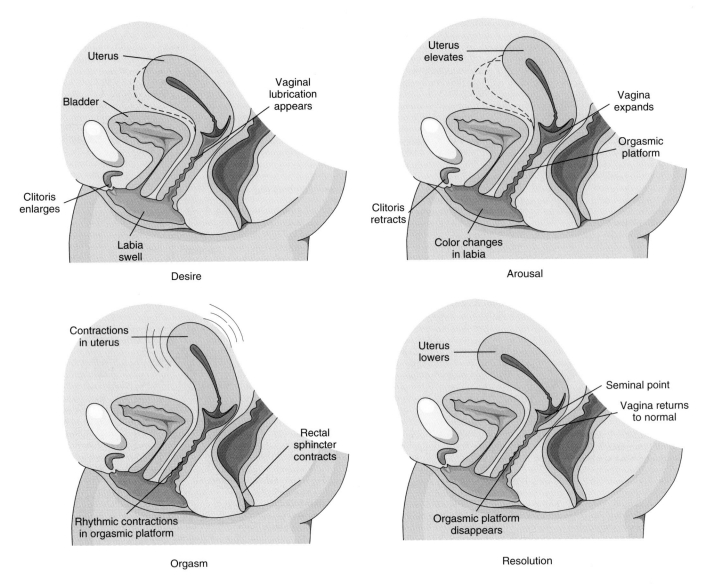

FIGURE 15.2   The Female Sexual Response Cycle. At each phase of the sexual response cycle in females, there are characteristic changes in physiology.
Source: Adapted from Hyde, 1990, p. 200.

which are not always felt. Because females do not have a refractory period, they are capable of experiencing additional orgasms immediately following a previous one. However, not all women want to have multiple orgasms or find it easy to be aroused to multiple orgasms.

Following orgasm, the entire musculature of the body relaxes and men and women tend to experience a state of deep relaxation, the stage known as **resolution.** A man loses his erection, and a woman's orgasmic platform subsides.

Both males and females experience these same five phases, regardless of whether orgasm is brought on by masturbation, coitus (insertion of the male penis into the female vagina), or some other activity. There are some differences between the male and female sexual responses, however (Masters, Johnson, & Kolodny, 1993). First, there is greater variability in the female

response pattern than in the male response pattern. Sometimes the excitement and plateau phases will be short for a female and she will reach a discernible orgasm quickly. At other times, the excitement and plateau phases are longer, and she may or may not experience a full orgasm. Second, as noted, there typically is a refractory period following orgasm for males but not for females. This refractory period in males becomes longer with age and after successive orgasms during a sexual experience.

If you are sexually active, you may or may not have recognized all these phases in your own sexual response cycle. People vary greatly in the length and distinctiveness of each phase. For example, some people do not notice a distinct plateau phase and feel they go straight from excitement to orgasm. Being aware of how your body reacts to sexual stimulation can help you

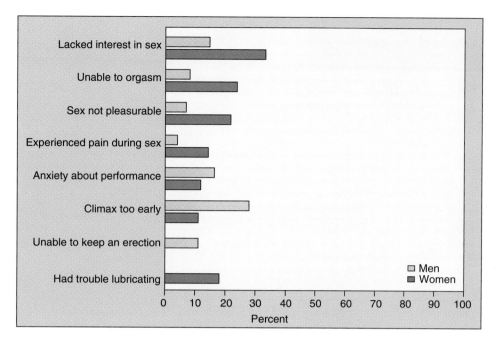

FIGURE 15.3   Percent of People Who Have Had a Sexual Difficulty in the Last Year. A national survey found that many people report having had one or more sexual difficulties in the last year.

Source: Michael et al., 1994, p. 126.

TABLE 15.1		
Responses to the Question, "How Often Do You Think About Sex?"		
A national survey found large variation in how often people think about sex and great differences between men and women.		
	"Every day" or "several times a day"	**"A few times a month" or "a few times a week"**	**"Less than once a month" or "never"**
Men	54%	43%	4%
Women	19	67	14

From *Sex in America* by Michael et al. Copyright © 1994 by CSG Enterprises, Inc., Edward O. Laumann, Robert T. Michael, and Gina Kolata. By permission of Little, Brown and Company.

recognize what helps you get the most pleasure from sexual activity and what interferes with that pleasure.

Occasional, transient problems in sexual functioning are extremely common (see Figure 15.3). To qualify for a diagnosis of a sexual dysfunction, a person must be experiencing a problem that causes significant distress or interpersonal difficulty. The DSM-IV divides sexual dysfunctions into four categories: sexual desire disorders, sexual arousal disorders, orgasmic disorders, and sexual pain disorders (see *Concept Review:* Sexual Dysfunction Disorders, p. 528). In reality, these dysfunctions overlap greatly, and many people who seek treatment for a sexual problem have more than one of these dysfunctions (Segraves & Segraves, 1991).

Sexual Desire Disorders

An individual's level of sexual desire is basically how much he or she wants to have sex. Sexual desire can be manifested in one's sexual thoughts and fantasies, one's interest in initiating or participating in sexual activities, and one's awareness of sexual cues from others (Schiavi & Segraves, 1995). People vary tremendously in their levels of sexual desire, and an individual's level of sexual desire can vary greatly across time (see Tables 15.1 and 15.2).

Lack of sexual desire is the most common complaint of people seeking sex therapy (Segraves & Segraves, 1991). Problems of sexual desire were not

CONCEPT REVIEW

Sexual Dysfunction Disorders

The DSM-IV defines a number of sexual dysfunction disorders.

Sexual Desire Disorders:	**Description:**
Hypoactive sexual desire disorder	Persistent lack of sexual fantasies and desire for sexual activity
Sexual aversion disorder	Persistent and extreme aversion to genital sexual contact with a sexual partner

Sexual Arousal Disorders:	
Female sexual arousal disorder	In women, recurrent inability to attain or maintain the swelling-lubrication response of sexual excitement
Male erectile disorder	In men, recurrent inability to attain or maintain an erection until the completion of sexual activity

Orgasmic Disorders:	
Female orgasmic disorder	In women, recurrent delay in or absence of orgasm following sexual excitement
Premature ejaculation	In men, inability to delay ejaculation as desired
Male orgasmic disorder	In men, recurrent delay in or absence of orgasm following sexual excitement

Sexual Pain Disorders:	
Dyspareunia	Genital pain associated with intercourse
Vaginismus	In women, involuntary contractions of the muscles surrounding the vagina that interferes with sexual functioning

Sexual Dysfunction Due to a Medical Condition:
One of the above sexual dysfunctions, due to a verified medical condition

Substance-Induced Sexual Dysfunction:
Sexual dysfunction as the result of substance use

Source: DSM-IV, APA, 2000.

recognized as common, nor as separate disorders, by sex therapists in the first several decades of modern research on sexual disorders, however (Kaplan, 1995). Masters and Johnson, the pioneers of research on sexuality, did not include sexual desire disorders in their initial studies of sexual problems. They saw lack of sexual desire as a consequence of other problems in sexual functioning. The expectation was that treating these sexual dysfunctions would bring back sexual desire.

Another pioneer in sex research, Helen Singer Kaplan was one of the first to recognize sexual desire disorders as a separate problem. She writes:

I first became aware of the existence of disorders of sexual desire in the early seventies as a consequence of analyzing our treatment failures. As I reviewed the charts, it became clear that we had

TABLE 15.2

How Often Do People Have Sex?

A national survey of adults in the United States found a great deal of variation in how frequently people had sex.

	Percentage Reporting	
	Men	**Women**
Two to three times per week	30	26
A few times per month	36	37
A few times per year or not at all	27	30

From E. O. Laumann et al., *The Social Organization of Sexuality: Sexual Practices in the United States.* Copyright © 1994 University of Chicago Press, Chicago, IL.

failed to recognize a considerable subgroup of patients who had little or no desire for sex or for sex with their partners. These patients had developed impotence or orgasmic disorders mainly because they had tried to make love without feeling lust or desire, and we had been trying to treat these secondary genital dysfunctions without being aware of the underlying desire disorders. This meant that some of our so-called "resistant" patients were not resistant to sex therapy at all. We had simply been treating them for the wrong thing! (Kaplan, 1995, p. 2)

Kaplan and other influential theorists (Kaplan, 1977; Masters, Johnson & Kolodny, 1979) published their research on problems of sexual desire in the late 1970s, and by the publication of the third edition of the DSM in 1980, these disorders had their own diagnostic category in the official nomenclature.

The percentage of people seeking therapy who report problems of sexual desire has increased sharply in the last 20 to 30 years (Kaplan, 1995; Leiblum & Rosen, 1988). Although the reasons for this increase are not clear, there are a number of possibilities. First, media attention to sexual desire disorders leads people to recognize that they have a problem that therapists can treat, and thus to seek treatment. Second, as the population ages, the likelihood of sexual desire problems due to hormonal changes of age increases. Third, anxieties over AIDS and other sexually transmitted diseases may be lowering some people's sexual desire (Kaplan, 1995). In *Taking Psychology Personally:* Practicing Safe Sex, we discuss how to protect oneself from sexually transmitted diseases, thereby improving sexual satisfaction. Fourth, adults, particularly women, may be carrying more roles and may be more burdened by these roles than in years past, leading to fatigue and burn-out that saps sexual desire (Michael

TAKING PSYCHOLOGY PERSONALLY

Practicing Safe Sex

One of the most common causes of low sexual desire or problems in sexual functioning is fear—fear of being hurt, getting pregnant or causing someone else to become pregnant, or of getting a sexually transmitted disease (STD). Here, we discuss how to practice safe sex. Practicing safe sex cannot protect you against violence by a partner, or from developing a sexual dysfunction. It can decrease your risk of pregnancy and sexually transmitted diseases, however, which can improve your sexual satisfaction and protect your health.

Sexually transmitted diseases such as AIDS (acquired immune deficiency syndrome), chlamydia, herpes, genital warts, gonorrhea, and syphilis often have no obvious signs or symptoms, so you cannot know if a potential sexual partner has one by just looking at him or her. Thus, it is essential to practice safe sex if you are going to be sexually active.

What does practicing safe sex mean? Here are some general tips*:

1. Have monogamous sexual relationships: Have sex with only one person who, in turn, is having sex only with you. If you or your partner change sexual partners frequently, your risk of contracting a sexually transmitted disease is increased.

2. Know your partner's sexual history before you engage in sexual activity. It can be very difficult to talk about your partner's history or your own. Volunteer information about your own history and then ask your partner about his or hers. Persist if your partner tries to brush your concerns aside and be prepared to postpone or refuse sexual contact if your partner will not answer your questions.

3. Avoid sexual activity if you or your partner might have been exposed to any sexually transmitted disease. Most of the sexually transmitted diseases can be treated medically, and sex can be resumed when the disease is cured or under control.

Continued

4. Wash your genitals after sexual contact; it helps to reduce risk but does not eliminate it.

5. Urinate immediately after intercourse to help flush out some germs.

6. Do not have sex under the influence of alcohol or other drugs. Drugs can lead you to practice unsafe sex, can lead to misunderstandings between partners about what sexual activities are acceptable, and can impair your ability to resist unwanted sexual activities.

7. Use condoms for vaginal and anal intercourse:

   • Use a condom EVERY time you have sex.

   • Put condoms on during foreplay, before there is any preejaculatory fluid.

   • After ejaculation and before the penis relaxes, remove the condom by holding it around the base and withdrawing it from the penis.

   • Use another condom if sex is repeated.

   • Store condoms in a cool, dry place (not a wallet or the glove compartment of a car).

   • Never test condoms by inflating them or stretching them.

   • Never use oil-based lubricants like petroleum jelly (Vaseline) on condoms.

   • Never reuse condoms.

8. Oral sex can also spread STDs. Males should wear condoms during oral sex. Partners performing oral sex on women should use dental dams or other latex barriers to protect their mouths from direct exposure to vaginal fluids.

Many people do not practice safe sex because they feel it will reduce spontaneity and excitement in sexual encounters. However, condom use can be eroticized so that it becomes a part of foreplay. Also, knowing that you are practicing safe sex can reduce fear and therefore increase your ability to enjoy sexual encounters. Most importantly, protecting yourself from sexually transmitted diseases, particularly AIDS, should always be a higher priority than having a little more spontaneity in any given sexual encounter.

*Adapted from "Breaking the STD Chain," distributed by Cowell Student Health Center and the Office of Residential Education, Stanford University.

---

et al., 1994). People who lack sexual desire can be diagnosed with one of two *sexual desire disorders*: hypoactive sexual desire disorder and sexual aversion disorder.

Hypoactive Sexual Desire Disorder

People with **hypoactive sexual desire disorder** have little desire for sex—they do not fantasize about sex or initiate sexual activity—and this lack of sexual desire is causing them marked distress or interpersonal difficulty. In some rare cases, people report never having had much interest in sex, either with other people or privately, as in viewing erotic films, masturbation, or fantasy. In most cases of hypoactive sexual desire, the individual used to enjoy sex but has lost interest in it, despite the presence of a willing and desirable partner. A diagnosis of hypoactive sexual desire is not given if the individual's lack of desire is the result of transient circumstances in his or her life, such as being too busy or fatigued from overwork to care about sex. Also, a diagnosis of sexual desire disorder is not given if lack of desire is actually caused by one of the other problems in sexual functioning, such as the inability to achieve orgasm or pain during intercourse. In such cases, the diagnosis a person receives focuses on the primary dysfunction rather than on the lack of desire that is the result of the primary dysfunction.

Inhibited desire can be either generalized to all partners or situations or specific to certain partners or

People can differ in their desire for sexual interactions with one another.

types of stimulation. A person who has had little desire for sexual activity most of his or her life would have a *generalized sexual desire disorder.* A person who lacks desire to have sex with his or her partner, but has sexual fantasies about other people, may be diagnosed with a *situational sexual desire disorder.* Obviously, the judgment about when a person's sexual desire has been too low for too long is a subjective one. Often, people seek treatment for lack of sexual desire primarily because their partner's sexual desire appears to be considerably greater than their own and the difference is causing conflict in the relationship (Masters, Johnson & Kolodny, 1993).

Women and men differ somewhat in their experience of hypoactive sexual desire (Kelly, 1998). Men with this disorder tend to be older (average age 50) than women with the disorder (average age 33). Women with hypoactive sexual desire are more likely than men to report anxiety, depression, and life stress. Finally, hypoactive sexual desire is more often connected to problems in relationships for women than for men.

Sexual Aversion Disorder

The other type of sexual desire disorder is **sexual aversion disorder.** People with this disorder do not simply have a passive lack of interest in sex; they actively avoid sexual activities. When they do engage in sex, they may feel sickened by it or experience acute anxiety. Some people experience a generalized aversion to all sexual activities, including kissing and touching. Women may be more prone to this disorder than men (Kaplan, 1995).

Sexual aversion disorder in women is frequently tied to sexual assault experiences, as in the case of Norma (adapted from Spitzer et al., 1994, p. 213):

Sexual Arousal Disorders

People with **sexual arousal disorders** do not experience the physiological changes that make up the excitement or arousal phase of the sexual response cycle. **Female sexual arousal disorder** involves a recurrent inability to attain or maintain the swelling-lubrication response of sexual excitement. **Male erectile disorder** involves the recurrent inability to attain or maintain an erection until the completion of sexual activity.

Much less is known about female sexual arousal disorder than about male erectile disorder (which is commonly referred to as *impotence*). In general, women's sexual problems have been researched less than men's (Andersen & Cyranowski, 1995). Female sexual arousal disorder is probably common, however. A national survey found that 19 percent of women reported lubrication difficulties during sexual activity (Michael et al., 1994).

Men with the *primary* or *lifelong* form of male erectile disorder have never been able to sustain erections for a desired period of time. Men with the *secondary* or *acquired* form of the disorder were able to sustain erections in the past but no longer can. Occasional problems in gaining or sustaining erections are very common, with as many as 30 million men in the United States having erectile problems at some time in their lives. Such problems do not constitute a disorder until they become persistent and significantly interfere with a man's interpersonal relationships or cause him distress. Only 4 to 9 percent of men will have problems sufficient to warrant a diagnosis of male erectile disorder (Spector & Carey, 1990). Paul Petersen is one of these men (adapted from Spitzer et al., 1994, pp. 198–199):

CASE STUDY

Paul and Petula Petersen have been living together for the last 6 months and are contemplating marriage. Petula describes the problem that has brought them to the sex therapy clinic.

"For the last 2 months he hasn't been able to keep his erection after he enters me."

The psychiatrist learns that Paul, age 26, is a recently graduated lawyer, and that Petula, age 24, is a successful buyer for a large department store. They both grew up in educated, middle class, suburban families. They met through mutual friends and started to have sexual intercourse a few months after they met and had no problems at that time.

Two months later, Paul moved from his family home into Petula's apartment. This was her idea, and Paul was unsure that he was ready for such an important step. Within a few weeks, Paul noticed that although he continued to be sexually aroused and wanted intercourse, as soon as he entered his partner, he began to lose his erection and could not stay inside. They would try again, but by then his desire had waned and he was unable to achieve another erection. Petula would become extremely angry with Paul, but he would just walk away from her.

The psychiatrist learned that sex was not the only area of contention in the relationship. Petula complained that Paul did not spend enough time with her and preferred to go to baseball games with his male friends. Even when he was home, he would watch all the sports events that were available on TV and was not interested in going to foreign movies, museums, or the theater with her. Despite these differences, Petula was eager to marry Paul and was pressuring him to set a date.

Orgasmic Disorders

Women with **female orgasmic disorder,** or *anorgasmia*, experience a recurrent delay in or complete absence of orgasm after having reached the excitement phase of the sexual response cycle. The DSM-IV specifies that this diagnosis should be made only when a woman is unable to achieve orgasm despite receiving adequate stimulation. In truth, many women treated for this disorder (and many women who do not experience orgasms but do not seek treatment) are able to achieve orgasm with certain types of stimulation, particularly clitoral stimulation, but simply cannot achieve orgasm with the type of stimulation they receive from their partners. Studies estimate that 10 percent of women in the United States have never had orgasms during sexual intercourse. About 15 percent of premenopausal

and 37 percent of postmenopausal women report usually having some problems reaching orgasm during sexual stimulation (Rosen & Leiblum, 1995; Spector & Carey, 1990). In contrast, about 75 percent of men always have orgasms during sexual stimulation.

The most common form of orgasmic disorder in males is **premature ejaculation.** Men who have this disorder persistently ejaculate with minimal sexual stimulation before they wish to ejaculate. Between 30 and 40 percent of men have significant trouble delaying ejaculation at will (Spector & Carey, 1990). Again, it is obviously a judgment call about when premature ejaculation becomes a sexual dysfunction. Premature ejaculation must cause significant distress or interpersonal problems before it is considered a disorder. Some men seeking treatment for this problem simply cannot prevent ejaculation before their partner reaches orgasm. Others do after very little stimulation, long before their partners are fully aroused. Men with significant problems in premature ejaculation seem not to experience the plateau phase of the sexual response cycle.

Men with premature ejaculation resort to applying desensitizing creams to their penises before sex, wearing multiple condoms, distracting themselves by doing complex mathematical problems while making love, not allowing their partners to touch them, and masturbating multiple times shortly before having sex in an attempt to delay their ejaculations (Althof, 1995). These tactics are generally unsuccessful and can make their partners feel shut out of the sexual encounter, as in the following account (McCarthy, 1989, pp. 151–152):

CASE STUDY

Bill and Margaret were a couple in their late 20s who had been married for 2 years. Margaret was 27 and the owner of a hair-styling studio. Bill was 29 and a legislative lobbyist for a financial institution. This was a first marriage for both. They had had a rather tumultuous dating relationship before marriage. Margaret had been in individual and group therapy for 1½ years at a university counseling center before dropping out of school to enroll in a hair-styling program. During their dating period, Margaret reentered individual therapy, and Bill, who had never participated in therapy, attended five conjoint sessions. That therapist helped Bill and Margaret deal with issues in their relationship and increased their commitment to marrying. However, the therapist made an incorrect assumption in stating that with increased intimacy and the commitment of marriage, the ejaculatory control problem would disappear. . . .

Margaret saw the early ejaculation as a symbol of lack of love and caring on Bill's part. As the problem continued over the next 2 years, Margaret became increasingly frustrated and withdrawn. She demonstrated her displeasure by resisting his sexual advances, and their intercourse frequency decreased from three or four times

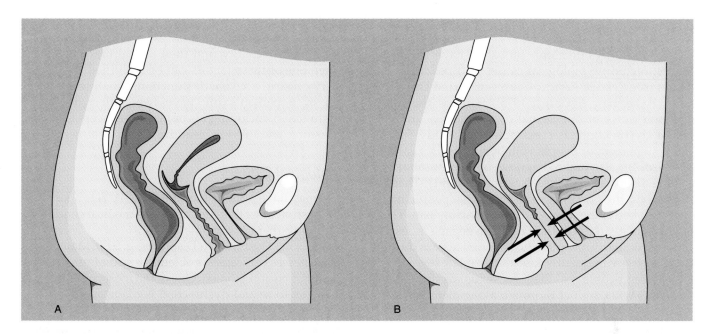

FIGURE 15.4   Vaginismus. Vaginismus is an involuntary constriction of the outer vaginal muscles, prohibiting intercourse. The drawing on the left (**A**) illustrates the relaxed vagina, while the drawing on the right (**B**) illustrates vaginismus.

per week to once every 10 days. A sexual and marital crisis was precipitated by Margaret's belief that Bill was acting more isolated and distant when they did have intercourse. When they talked about their sexual relationship, it was usually in bed after intercourse, and the communication quickly broke down into tears, anger, and accusations. Bill was on the defensive and handled the sexual issue by avoiding talking to Margaret, which frustrated her even more.

Unbeknownst to Margaret, Bill had attempted a do-it-yourself technique to gain better control. He had bought a desensitizing cream he'd read about in a men's magazine and applied it to the glans of his penis 20 minutes before initiating sex. He also masturbated the day before couple sex. During intercourse he tried to keep his leg muscles tense and think about sports as a way of keeping his arousal in check. Bill was unaware that Margaret felt emotionally shut out during sex. Bill was becoming more sensitized to his arousal cycle and was worrying about erection. He was not achieving better ejaculatory control, and he was enjoying sex less. The sexual relationship was heading downhill, and miscommunication and frustration were growing.

Men with **male orgasmic disorder** experience a recurrent delay in or absence of orgasm following the excitement phase of the sexual response cycle. In most cases of this disorder, a man cannot ejaculate during intercourse but can ejaculate with manual or oral stimulation. About 4 to 10 percent of men report persistent problems in reaching orgasm (Spector & Carey, 1990).

Sexual Pain Disorders

The final two sexual dysfunctions are **dyspareunia** and **vaginismus.** Dyspareunia is genital pain associated with intercourse. It is rare in men, but in community surveys 10 to 15 percent of women report frequent pain during intercourse (Laumann et al., 1994). In women, the pain may be superficial during intromission or deep during penile thrusting. Dyspareunia in women can be the result of dryness of the vagina caused by antihistamines or other drugs, infection of the clitoris or vulval area, injury or irritation to the vagina, and tumors of the internal reproductive organs. In men, dyspareunia may involve painful erections or pain during thrusting.

Vaginismus only occurs in women and involves the involuntary contraction of the muscles surrounding the outer third of the vagina when vaginal penetration with a penis, finger, tampon, or speculum is attempted (see Figure 15.4). Women with vaginismus may experience sexual arousal and have orgasms when their clitoris is stimulated. But when a penis or other object is inserted into the vagina, the muscles surrounding its opening contract involuntarily. In other women with this disorder, even the anticipation of vaginal insertion may result in this muscle spasm. It is estimated that 2 to 3 percent of women experience vaginismus (Kolodny, Masters & Johnson, 1979). Vaginismus is the major cause of unconsummated marriages, and is one of the sexual dysfunctions for which heterosexual couples are more likely to seek treatment.

Causes of Sexual Dysfunctions

Most sexual dysfunctions probably have multiple causes, including biological causes and psychosocial causes (see *Concept Review:* Causes of Sexual Dysfunctions; Ackerman & Carey, 1995). Perhaps the most common cause of one sexual dysfunction is another sexual dysfunction. For example, one study found about 40 percent of people with hypoactive sexual desire disorder also had a diagnosis of an arousal or orgasmic disorder (Segraves & Segraves, 1991). That is, even when they do engage in sex, these people have difficulty becoming aroused or reaching orgasm. This, in turn, greatly reduces their desire to engage in sexual activity. Similarly, people who experience pain during sexual activity frequently lose all desire for sex.

When people seek help for sexual dysfunctions, clinicians will conduct thorough assessments of their medical conditions, the drugs they are taking, the characteristics of their relationships, their attitudes toward their sexuality, and their sexual practices. Even when one of these factors can be identified as the primary cause of a sexual dysfunction, usually several areas of a person's life have been affected by the dysfunction, including his or her self-concept and relationships, and need to be addressed in treatment.

Biological Causes

You may have noticed that the DSM-IV sets apart sexual dysfunctions that are caused by medical conditions by giving them a separate diagnosis (see *Concept Review:* Sexual Dysfunction Disorders, p. 527). Many medical illnesses can cause problems in sexual functioning in both men and women. One of the most common contributors to sexual dysfunction is diabetes, which can

---

CONCEPT REVIEW

Causes of Sexual Dysfunctions

A host of biological, psychological, and sociocultural factors can contribute to sexual dysfunctions.

Biological Causes	Psychological Causes	Sociocultural Causes
Medical conditions:	Psychological disorders	Relationship problems
Diabetes	Depression	Lack of communication
Cardiovascular disease	Anxiety disorders	Differences in sexual expectations
Multiple sclerosis	Schizophrenia	Conflicts unrelated to sex
Renal failure	Attitudes and cognitions	Trauma
Vascular disease	Beliefs that sex is "dirty" or	Cultural taboos against sex
Spinal cord injury	"disgusting"	
Autonomic nervous system injury	Performance anxiety	
Prescription drugs		
Antihypertensive medications		
Antipsychotic medications		
Antidepressant medications		
Lithium		
Tranquilizers		
Recreational drugs		
Marijuana		
Cocaine		
Amphetamines		
Nicotine		
Alcohol		
In men:		
Low levels of androgen hormones or high levels of estrogen and prolactin		
Genital or urinary tract infections		
Peyronie's disease		
In women:		
Low levels of estrogen		
Vaginal dryness or irritation		
Injuries during childbirth		

lower sexual drive, arousal, enjoyment, and satisfaction, especially in men (Schiavi et al., 1995). Diabetes often goes undiagnosed, so people may believe that psychological factors are causing their sexual dysfunctions, when the cause is really undiagnosed diabetes.

Other diseases that are common causes of sexual dysfunction, particularly in men, are cardiovascular disease, multiple sclerosis, renal failure, vascular disease, spinal cord injury, and injury of the autonomic nervous system by surgery or radiation (APA, 2000; Kelly, 1998). As many as 40 percent of cases of male erectile disorder are caused by one of these medical conditions. In men with cardiovascular disease, sexual dysfunction can be caused directly by the disease, which can, for example, reduce the functioning of the vascular system. Sexual dysfunction may be a psychological response to the presence of the disease; for example, a man who recently had a heart attack may fear he will have another if he has sex, and thus he loses his desire for sex.

In men, abnormally low levels of the androgen hormones, especially testosterone, or high levels of the hormones estrogen and prolactin can cause sexual dysfunction. In women, hormones do not seem to have a consistent, direct effect on sexual desire. For example, levels of most reproductive hormones change in women over the menstrual cycle, but there is no consistent effect of these hormones on sexual desire—simply, there is variance among women in what parts of their menstrual cycles they feel the most sexual desire (Beck, 1995; Schiavi & Segraves, 1995). Hormones may have an indirect effect on sexual desire by affecting sexual arousal, however. Low levels of estrogen can cause decreases in vasocongestion and vaginal lubrication, leading to diminished sexual arousal, pain during sexual activity, and, therefore, lowered sexual desire (Sherwin, 1991). Levels of estrogen drop greatly at menopause, and thus postmenopausal women often complain of lowered sexual desire and arousal. Similarly, women who have had radical hysterectomies, which remove the main source of estrogen, the ovaries, can experience reductions in both sexual desire and arousal.

Vaginal dryness or irritation, which causes pain during sex and therefore lowers sexual desire and arousal, can be caused by radiation therapy, endometriosis, antihistamines, douches, tampons, vaginal contraceptives, and infections such as vaginitis or pelvic inflammatory disease. Injuries during childbirth that have healed poorly, such as a poorly repaired episiotomy, can cause coital pain in women (Masters, Johnson & Kolodny, 1993). Biological causes of dyspareunia in men include genital or urinary tract infections, especially prostatitis, and a rare condition called *Peyronie's disease*, which causes deposits of fibrous tissue in the penis.

Sexual desire, arousal, and activity tend to decrease in men with age, although many men remain sexually active well into their eighties (Schiavi, 1990). It becomes more difficult, however, for many men to maintain erections as they grow old, and thus the incidence of erectile dysfunctions increases with age in men (Rosen, 1996). In many of these cases, the cause of the erectile dysfunction was probably not age per se but one of the medical conditions already listed, which are more common in older men than in younger men. It may also be that normal declines with age in the functioning of the testes, in the production of testosterone, and in the functioning of the vascular system contribute to erectile problems in older men (Schiavi, 1990).

Several prescription drugs can diminish sexual drive and arousal and interfere with orgasm. These include antihypertensive drugs taken by people with high blood pressure, antipsychotic drugs, antidepressants, lithium, and tranquilizers. Indeed, one of the most common side effects of the widely used antidepressants known as serotonin reuptake inhibitors is sexual dysfunction (Schiavi & Segraves, 1995).

Many recreational drugs, including marijuana, cocaine, amphetamines, and nicotine, can impair sexual functioning (Schiavi & Segraves, 1995). Even though people often drink alcohol to make them feel more sexy and uninhibited, even small amounts of alcohol can significantly impair sexual functioning, and chronic alcoholics often have diagnosable sexual dysfunctions (Schiavi, 1990). When a sexual dysfunction is caused by substance use, it is given the diagnosis of

Although many people drink alcohol to decrease their sexual inhibitions, alcohol can also decrease sexual performance.

substance-induced sexual dysfunction (see *Concept Review:* Sexual Dysfunction Disorders, p. 527).

How can you know if a sexual dysfunction is caused by biological factors or has psychological causes? Certainly, the presence of one of the known biological causes of sexual dysfunctions is a clue that the cause of the dysfunction may be biological; similarly, if dysfunction immediately follows a psychological trauma, there is an increased likelihood that it is psychologically caused. There are some differences among the patterns of symptoms and the courses of biological and psychological sexual dysfunctions as well (Ackerman & Carey, 1995). Biologically caused dysfunctions tend to be global and consistent, whereas psychological disorders are more likely to be situational and inconsistent, occurring, for example, only with certain partners or specific types of sexual activity. Psychological dysfunctions tend to begin suddenly whereas biologically caused disorders tend to begin more gradually (unless they directly follow accidents or surgery).

For a man with erectile dysfunction, one of the best ways to know if the dysfunction has biological causes is to determine whether he has erections during sleep, as healthy men do. If he is having nocturnal erections, then chances are that his erectile problems have psychological origins, at least in part. If he is not having nocturnal erections, then chances are the erectile problems have biological causes (Ackerman & Carey, 1995). One sign that a man is having nocturnal erections is that he consistently awakens in the morning with an erection. A more thorough assessment of nocturnal erections can be done with devices that directly measure men's erections (Tiefer & Melman, 1989). These devices, which can be used at home, have Velcro straps that are wrapped around the man's penis before he goes to sleep. The straps have three connectors that snap with defined penile pressure. A more accurate way of determining if a man is having nocturnal erections is with the help of a sleep laboratory, where strain gauges are attached to the base of the penis to record the magnitude, duration, and pattern of erections, while electroencephalographs record his pattern of sleep.

Women also experience cyclic episodes of vasocongestion during sleep, which can be monitored to determine if a woman experiencing arousal problems has a biological disorder. Vasocongestion in women can be measured with a vaginal photoplethysmograph, a tampon-shaped device inserted into a woman's vagina that records the changes that accompany vasocongestion.

In sum, a number of medical conditions, drugs, and the physiological changes of normal aging can affect sexual desire, arousal, and orgasm. It is critical at the outset of any treatment program to determine if any of these factors are contributing to a sexual dysfunction.

Psychological Causes

Our emotional well-being and our beliefs and attitudes about sex greatly influence our sexuality.

Psychological disorders A number of other psychological disorders can cause sexual dysfunction. Loss of sexual functioning is a common symptom in depression. The depressed person may have no desire for sex, or may experience any of the problems in sexual arousal and functioning we have discussed. Unfortunately, as we have noted, the medications used to treat depression often induce problems in sexual functioning. Similarly, people with an anxiety disorder, such as generalized anxiety disorder, panic disorder, or obsessive-compulsive disorder may find their sexual desire and functioning waning. Loss of sexual desire and functioning are very common among people with schizophrenia.

Attitudes and cognitions People who have been taught that sex is dirty, disgusting, sinful, or a "necessary evil" may understandably lack desire to have sex. They may also know so little about their own bodies and sexual responses that they do not know how to make sex pleasurable. Such is the case with Mrs. Booth (adapted from Spitzer et al., 1994, pp. 251–252).

CASE STUDY

Mr. and Mrs. Booth have been married for 14 years and have three children, ages 8 through 12. They are both bright and well-educated. Both are from Scotland, from which they moved 10 years ago because of Mr. Booth's work as an industrial consultant. They present with the complaint that Mrs. Booth has been able to participate passively in sex "as a duty" but has never enjoyed it since they have been married.

Before their marriage, although they had had intercourse only twice, Mrs. Booth had been highly aroused by kissing and petting and felt she used her attractiveness to "seduce" her husband into marriage. She did, however, feel intense guilt about their two episodes of premarital intercourse; during their honeymoon, she began to think of sex as a chore that could not be pleasing. Although she periodically passively complied with intercourse, she had almost no spontaneous desire for sex. She never masturbated, had never reached orgasm, thought of all variations such as oral sex as completely repulsive, and was preoccupied with a fantasy of how disapproving her family would be if she ever engaged in any of these activities.

Mrs. Booth is almost totally certain that no woman she respects in any older generation has enjoyed sex and that despite the "new vogue" of sexuality, only sleazy, crude women let themselves act like "animals." These beliefs have led to a pattern of regular but infrequent sex that at best is accommodating and gives little or no pleasure to her or her husband. Whenever Mrs. Booth comes close to having a feeling of sexual arousal, numerous negative thoughts come into her mind such as, "What am I, a tramp?"; "If I like this, he'll just want it more often"; and "How could I look at myself in the mirror after something like this?" These thoughts almost inevitably are accompanied by a cold feeling and an insensitivity to sensual pleasure. As a result, sex is invariably an unhappy experience. Almost any excuse, such as fatigue or being busy, is sufficient for her to rationalize avoiding intercourse.

Women with severely negative attitudes toward sex like Mrs. Booth's also tend to experience dyspareunia and vaginismus because they have been taught that sex is painful and frightening (Rosen & Leiblum, 1995). Although attitudes toward sex such as Mrs. Booth's may be declining in modern countries among younger people, many younger and older women still report a fear of "letting go" that interferes with orgasm (Heiman & Grafton-Becker, 1989; Tugrul & Kabakci, 1997). They say they fear losing control or acting in some way that will embarrass them. This fear of loss of control may result from distrust of one's partner, a sense of shame about sex, a poor body image, and a host of other factors.

Another set of attitudes that interferes with sexual functioning appears to be rampant among middle-aged and younger adults. These attitudes are often referred to as *performance concerns* or **performance anxiety** (LoPiccolo, 1992; Masters & Johnson, 1970). People worry so much about whether they are going to be aroused and have orgasms that this worry interferes with sexual functioning: "What if I can't get an erection? I'll die of embarrassment!" "I've got to have an orgasm, or he'll think I'm frigid!" "Oh my god, I just can't get aroused tonight!" These worried thoughts are so distracting that people cannot focus on the pleasure that sexual stimulation is giving them and thus do not become as aroused as they want to or need to in order to reach orgasm (see Figure 15.5, p 538; Barlow, Sakheim, & Beck, 1983; Cranston-Cuebas & Barlow, 1990). In addition, many people engage in *spectatoring*: They anxiously attend to reactions and performance during sex as if they were spectators (Masters & Johnson, 1970). Spectatoring distracts from sexual pleasure and interferes with sexual functioning. Unfortunately, people who have had some problems in sexual functioning only develop more performance concerns, which then further interfere with their functioning. By the time they seek treatment for sexual dysfunction, they may be so anxious about "performing" sexually that they avoid all sexual activity.

Performance anxiety may also make some men reach orgasm *too* fast. Men with premature ejaculation problems may be so anxious about performing well that they do not pay attention to their level of sexual arousal and do not modulate their levels of self-stimulation

or stimulation from their partners enough to control when ejaculation occurs (Grenier & Byers, 1995; Kaplan, 1974; McCarthy, 1989.) Transient problems with premature ejaculation can be caused by anxiety-provoking stressors men encounter on the job or in other areas of their lives, anxiety about being with new sexual partners, or anxiety caused by problems maintaining erections or preventing ejaculation in recent sexual encounters.

More chronic problems can develop from the way young men learn about their own sexual responses during adolescence. Most males, perhaps 90 percent, have their first orgasmic experience during masturbation as adolescents (McCarthy, 1989). Masturbation is usually practiced in an intense, rapid manner, where the only focus is on ejaculation. Many young men do not view masturbation as a positive, healthy exercise in which they are learning about their bodies. Rather, they feel guilty or embarrassed and anxious about being caught masturbating, so they hurry through it, not paying attention to their bodies' levels of arousal and not learning anything about ejaculatory control. In partner sex, they can become aroused without much stimulation from their partners and may fear ejaculating before their partners becomes aroused. Thus, they avoid allowing partners to stimulate them and focus instead on stimulating their partners as quickly as possible so that they can have intercourse. As a result, they come to associate high levels of arousal with anxiety over premature ejaculation, and this anxiety only increases the chance of premature ejaculation.

With experience and maturity, most males gain ejaculatory control through a number of processes, as described by Barry McCarthy (1989, p. 146): "(1) a regular rhythm of being sexual; (2) increased comfort with practice; (3) a more give-and-take 'pleasuring process' rather than goal-oriented foreplay; (4) allowance of more time for the variety of sensations in the sexual experience; (5) greater intimacy and security resulting in increased sexual comfort; (6) partner encouragement for a slower, more tender, rhythmic sexual interchange; and (7) shift of intercourse positions and/or thrusting movements." Men who do not go through the process of gaining ejaculatory control may develop premature ejaculation disorder.

Sociocultural Factors

Although our internal psychological states and beliefs play important roles in our sexuality, sex is largely an interpersonal activity, and one that societies attempt to control. Thus, sociocultural factors also play important roles in people's sexual interests and activities.

Relationship problems Problems in intimate relationships are extremely common among people with

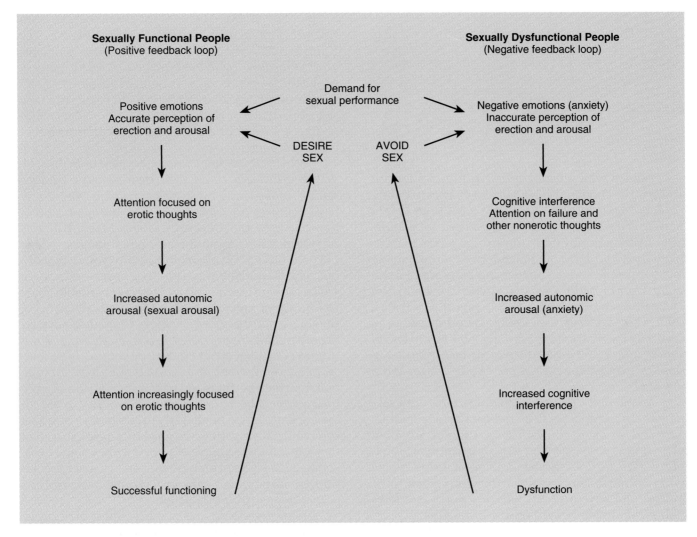

Sexually Functional People
(Positive feedback loop)

Sexually Dysfunctional People
(Negative feedback loop)

Demand for
sexual performance

Positive emotions
Accurate perception of
erection and arousal

DESIRE
SEX

AVOID
SEX

Negative emotions (anxiety)
Inaccurate perception of
erection and arousal

Attention focused on
erotic thoughts

Cognitive interference
Attention on failure and
other nonerotic thoughts

Increased autonomic
arousal (sexual arousal)

Increased autonomic
arousal (anxiety)

Attention increasingly focused
on erotic thoughts

Increased cognitive
interference

Successful functioning

Dysfunction

FIGURE 15.5   This model shows how anxiety and cognitive interference can produce erectile dysfunction and other sexual disorders.
Source: Barlow, 1986.

sexual dysfunctions. Sometimes these problems are the consequences of sexual dysfunctions, as when a couple cannot communicate about the sexual dysfunction of one of the partners and grow distant from each other. Relationship problems can be direct causes of sexual dysfunctions as well (Beck, 1995).

Conflicts between partners may be about their sexual activities. One partner may want to engage in a type of sexual activity that the other partner is not comfortable with, or one partner may want to engage in sexual activity much more often than the other partner. People with inhibited desire, arousal, or orgasm often have sexual partners who do not know how to arouse them or are not concerned with their arousal and focus on only themselves. Partners often do not communicate with each other about what is arousing, so even if both partners intend to please the other, they do not know what their partner wants them to do (Ackerman & Carey, 1995; Speckens et al., 1995).

Anorgasmia in women is especially likely to be tied to lack of communication between a woman and a male partner about what the woman needs to reach orgasm (Hurlbert, 1991). In sexual encounters between men and women, men still tend to decide when to initiate sex, how long to engage in foreplay, when to penetrate, and what position to use during intercourse. A man's pattern of arousal is often not the same as a woman's pattern of arousal, and he may be making these decisions on the basis of his level of arousal and needs for stimulation rather than hers. Most women have difficulty reaching orgasm by coitus alone and need oral or manual stimulation of the clitoris to become aroused enough to reach orgasm (Hite, 1976; Kaplan, 1974). Many men and women do not know this, however, or believe that men should be able to bring women to orgasm by penile insertion and thrusting alone. Many women thus never receive the stimulation they need to be sufficiently aroused to orgasm. They may feel inhibited from telling their partners that they would like them to stimulate their clitoris more, because they are afraid of hurting their partners' feelings or angering them, or because they believe they do not have the right to ask for the kind of stimulation they want. Some women may fake orgasms to protect their partners' egos. Often their partners know that they are not fully satisfied, however. Communication between partners may break down further, and sex may become a forum for hostility rather than pleasure.

Conflicts between partners that are not directly about their sexual activity can affect their sexual relationship as well, as we saw in the case of Paul and Petula Peterson earlier in this chapter (Beck, 1995; Rosen & Leiblum, 1995). Anger, distrust, and lack of respect for one's partner can greatly interfere with sexual desire and functioning. When one partner suspects that the other partner has been unfaithful or is losing interest in the relationship, all sexual interest may disappear. Often there is an imbalance of power in relationships, and people feel exploited, subjugated, and underappreciated by their partners, leading to problems in their sexual relationships (Rosen & Leiblum, 1995).

One study of men and women seeking treatment for hypoactive sexual desire disorder found that the women are more likely than men to report problems in their marital relationships, other stressful events in their lives, and higher levels of psychological distress (Donahey & Carroll, 1993). Men seeking treatment are more likely than women to be experiencing other types of sexual dysfunction in addition to low sexual desire, such as erectile dysfunction. Thus, for men, it appeared that issues of sexual functioning precipitate their entry into treatment, whereas for women, lack of sexual desire is linked to a broader array of psychosocial problems.

Trauma Reductions in sexual desire and functioning often follow personal traumas, such as the loss of a loved one, the loss of a job, or the diagnosis of severe illness in one's child. Unemployment in men is often tied to declines in sexual desire and functioning (Morokoff & Gilliland, 1993). Traumas such as unemployment can challenge a person's self-esteem and self-concept interfering with his or her sexual self-concept. Traumas can also cause a person to experience a depression that includes a loss of interest in most pleasurable activities, including sex. In such cases, clinicians will typically focus on treatment of the depression, with the expectation that sexual desire will resume once the depression has lifted.

As noted earlier, one type of personal trauma that is often associated with sexual desire disorders in women is sexual assault (Becker, 1989). A woman who has been raped may lose all interest in sex and be disgusted or extremely anxious when anyone, particularly a man, touches her. Her sexual aversion may be tied to a sense of vulnerability and loss of control or to a conditioned aversion to all forms of sexual contact (Leiblum & Rosen, 1989). In addition, male partners of women who have been raped sometimes cannot cope with the rapes and withdraw from sexual encounters with them. This may be more common among men who accept rape myths such as "Women who get raped were asking for it," and "Women enjoy being raped." Women rape survivors may thus feel victimized yet again, and their interest in sex may decline even further.

Cross-cultural differences Other cultures recognize types of sexual dysfunction not recognized in the DSM-IV. For example, both the traditional Chinese medical system and the Ayurvedic medical system, which is native to India, teach that loss of semen is detrimental to a man's health (Dewaraja & Sasaki, 1991). Masturbation is strongly discouraged, because it results in semen loss without the possibility of conception. A depersonalization syndrome known as *Koro*, thought to result from semen loss, has been reported among Malaysians, Southeast Asians, and southern Chinese. This syndrome involves an acute anxiety state, with a feeling of panic and impending death, and a delusion that the penis is shrinking into the body and disappearing. The patient or his relatives may grab and hold the penis until the attack of Koro is ended to stop the penis from disappearing into the body.

In Polynesian culture, there is no word for erection problems in men (Mannino, 1999). If a man does not have an erection, it is assumed that he does not want sex. In some African cultures, the preference is for women's vaginas to be dry and tight for sexual intercourse (Brown, Ayowa, & Brown, 1993). Several herbal treatments are used to achieve this dryness.

In surveys in the United States, less well-educated and poorer men and women tend to experience more sexual dysfunctions, including pain during sex, not finding sex pleasurable, inability to reach orgasm, lacking interest in sex, and climaxing too early and, for men, trouble in maintaining erections (Laumann et al., 1994). People in lower educational and income groups may have more sexual dysfunctions because they are under more psychological stress, their physical health is worse, or they have not had the benefit of educational programs that teach people about their bodies and healthy social relationships.

Treatment of Sexual Dysfunctions

The proper treatment for a sexual dysfunction obviously is one that is directed at the primary cause of the dysfunction. Because most dysfunctions have multiple

TABLE 15.3

Medical and Surgical Treatments for Male Erectile Disorder

A number of interventions can overcome male erectile disorder.

Treatments	How They Work	Effectiveness
Medications		
Oral medications		
Viagra, Vasomax	Relax muscles that surround small blood vessels in the penis, allowing dilation so blood can flow more freely	Effective
Yohimbine	Possible involvement of neurotransmitters	Modest improvement in some men
Injections	Injections of smooth muscle relaxants into penis	Moderately effective in most cases but high attrition rate
Topical creams	Topical cream or ointment with vasoactive properties	Uncertain efficacy
Surgery		
Vascular surgery	Unblocks blood vessels that supply the penis	May have limited short-term benefit
Semirigid surgical prosthesis	Surgical implantation of silicone rods into the penis	Moderately effective Low partner satisfaction ratings
Inflatable prosthesis	Surgical implantation of an inflatable device	Highly effective High patient and partner satisfaction ratings
Other		
Vacuum pump	Vacuum constriction device creates vacuum when held over the penis	Effective

Source: Kelly, 1998, Table 15.3, p. 470; Rosen, 1996, Table 1, p. 502.

causes, however, most treatments must involve a combination of approaches, often including biological interventions, direct sex therapy focusing on the sexual practices of a client and his or her partner, and psychosocial therapy focusing on problems in a relationship or the concerns of an individual client.

Biological Therapies

If a sexual dysfunction is the direct result of another medical condition, such as diabetes, treating the medical condition will often reduce the sexual dysfunction. Similarly, adjusting the dosage of medications that are contributing to a sexual dysfunction or getting a person to stop using recreational drugs that are causing a sexual dysfunction can often cure the dysfunction (Rosen & Ashton, 1993).

There are a number of biological treatments available for men with male erectile disorder (see Table 15.3).

A number of drugs have proven useful for the treatment of this disorder (Segraves & Segraves, 1998). The one that has received the most media attention in recent years is Viagra (generic name, sildenafil). Viagra is a selective inhibitor of cyclic guanosine monophosphate-specific phosphodiesterase type 5, which plays a critical role in erections. Both in men whose erectile dysfunction has no known organic causes, and in men whose erectile dysfunction is caused by medical conditions such as spinal cord injury, Viagra restores erectile functioning and improves sexual desire and satisfaction in the majority (Derry et al., 1998).

Two other drugs, yohimbine and apomorphine, can also help men with erectile dysfunction increase their ability to have erections (Rosen & Ashton, 1993; Segraves & Segraves, 1998). Interestingly, yohimbine comes from the bark of the yohimbe tree, which Africans have chewed for centuries to increase their sexual desire and functioning.

As we noted, some antidepressants, particularly the popular serotonin reuptake inhibitors, can cause sexual dysfunctions. Other drugs can be used, in conjunction with these antidepressants, to reduce the sexual side effects of the antidepressants. One drug that has proven helpful in this regard is bupropion, which goes by the trade names of Wellbutrin or Zyban (Ashton & Rosen, 1998). Viagra may also help men whose erectile dysfunction is caused by taking antidepressants, thereby allowing them to continue taking the antidepressants without losing sexual functioning (Balon, 1998). Some antidepressants can help to treat certain types of sexual dysfunction: The antidepressant drugs clomipramine (trade name Anafranil) and sertraline (trade name Zoloft) can be useful in reducing premature ejaculation in men (Althof, 1995).

When drugs do not cure erectile disorders, other biological or technical interventions are possible (Segraves & Segraves, 1998). Several drugs can cause penile rigidity when injected into the penis. There are mechanical devices that can cause blood to rush into the penis, causing an erection (von Buhler, 1998). The penis is placed in a tube in which a vacuum is created by the device, blood rushes into the penis, and a constricting band at the base of the penis prevents blood from rushing out. Other prosthetic devices can be surgically implanted into the penis to make it erect. One prosthetic is a pair of rods inserted into the penis. The rods create a permanent erection that can be bent up or down against the body. Another type is a hydraulic inflatable device, which allows a man to create an erection by pumping saline into rods inserted in the penis and then to relieve the erection by pumping out the saline.

Women with vaginal dryness may find that using vaginal lubricants significantly increases their ability to become sexually aroused. Hormone replacement therapy can be very effective for men whose low levels of sexual desire or arousal are linked to low levels of testosterone or for women whose low sexual desire or arousal, or dyspareunia, are linked to low levels of estrogen (Schiavi & Segraves, 1995; Schiavi et al., 1997).

Sex Therapy

When a sexual dysfunction seems to be due, at least in part, to inadequate sexual practices of the client and his or her partner, then sex therapy focusing on these practices can be useful. Some people have never learned what practices give them or their partners pleasure or have fallen out of the habit of engaging in these practices. Sex therapy teaches these practices and helps partners develop a regular pattern of satisfying sexual encounters (see *Concept Review:* Sex Therapy).

CONCEPT REVIEW

Sex Therapy

Sex therapy is designed to help individuals learn what their bodies need for sexual satisfaction.

Sensate Focus Therapy:

Phase One: Gentle nongenital touching, focusing on pleasurable sensations and communication.

Phase Two: Stimulation of partner's breasts and genitals without intercourse.

Phase Three: Intercourse with focus on enhancing and sustaining pleasure, not orgasm and performance.

Stop-Start Technique (for premature ejaculation):

Phase One: Stimulation of the man's penis stops just before he ejaculates; he relaxes and concentrates on bodily sensations until arousal passes.

Phase Two (if female partner involved): The woman inserts the man's penis into her vagina but remains quiet.

Phase Three: The female partner creates some thrusting motion with slow, long strokes.

Squeeze Technique (for premature ejaculation):

The man's partner stimulates him to erection, but then applies a firm squeeze to his penis to reduce erection. Exercise continues until the man learns to control ejaculation.

Relaxation Technique (for vaginismus):

The woman is taught to relax the muscles at the opening of her vagina; gradually she inserts larger dilators while practicing relaxation exercises and becoming accustomed to the feel of the object in her vagina.

Sex therapy often includes teaching or encouraging clients to masturbate (Morokoff & LoPiccolo, 1986). The goals of masturbation are for the people to explore their own bodies to discover what is arousing, and to become less inhibited about their own sexuality. Then individuals are taught to communicate what they have learned they need to partners. This technique can be especially helpful for anorgasmic women who often have never masturbated and have little knowledge of what they need to become aroused.

Sensate focus therapy One of the mainstays of sex therapy is **sensate focus therapy** (Masters & Johnson, 1970). In this therapy, one partner is active, carrying out a set of exercises to stimulate the other partner, while the other partner is the passive recipient, focusing on the pleasure that the exercises bring. Then the partners switch roles, so that each spends time being both the giver and recipient of the stimulation. The exercises should be carried out at quiet, unhurried times that are planned for by the partners. In the early phases of this therapy, partners are instructed *not* to be concerned about or even attempt intercourse. Rather, they are told to focus intently on the pleasure created by the exercises. These instructions are meant to reduce performance anxiety and concern about achieving orgasm.

In the first phase of sensate focus therapy, partners spend time gently touching each other but not around the genitals. They are instructed to focus on the sensations and to communicate with each other about what does and does not feel good. The goal is to have the partners spend intimate time together communicating, without pressure for intercourse. This first phase may continue for several weeks, until partners feel comfortable with the exercise and have learned what gives each of them pleasure.

In the second phase of sensate focus therapy, partners spend time directly stimulating each others' breasts and genitals but still without attempting to have intercourse. If the problem is a female arousal disorder, a woman will guide her partner to stimulate her in arousing ways. It is acceptable for a woman to be aroused to orgasm during these exercises, but the partners are instructed not to attempt intercourse until she regularly becomes fully aroused by her partner during sensate focus exercises. If the problem is a male erectile disorder, a man will guide his partner in touching him in ways that feel arousing. If he has an erection, he is to let it come and go naturally; intercourse is forbidden until he is able to have erections easily and frequently during the sensate focus exercises. Throughout these exercises, the partner with the problem is instructed to be selfish and to focus only on the arousing sensations and on communicating with his or her partner about what feels good. The touching should proceed in a relaxed and nondemanding atmosphere. Once the

In sensate focus therapy, people are encouraged to spend time exploring what sexually arouses each other without feeling pressured to reach orgasm.

partner with the problem regularly experiences arousal with genital stimulation, the partners may begin having intercourse, but the focus remains on enhancing and sustaining pleasure, rather than on orgasm or performance.

Techniques for treating premature ejaculation Two techniques are useful in helping a man with premature ejaculation to gain control over his ejaculations: the stop-start technique (Semans, 1956) and the squeeze technique (Masters & Johnson, 1970). The **stop-start technique** can be carried out either through masturbation or with a partner. In the first phase, the man is told to stop stimulating himself or to tell his partner to stop stimulation just before ejaculatory inevitability. He then relaxes and concentrates on the sensations in his body until his level of arousal declines. At that point he or his partner can resume stimulation, again stopping before the point of ejaculatory inevitability. If stimulation stops too late and the man ejaculates, he is encouraged not to feel angry or disappointed but to enjoy the ejaculation and reflect on what he learned about his body and then resume the exercise. If a man is engaging in this exercise with a female partner, they are instructed not to engage in intercourse until he has sufficient control over his ejaculations during her manual stimulation of him.

In the second phase of this process, when a female partner is involved, the man lies on his back with his female partner on top of him, and she inserts his penis into her vagina but then remains quiet. Most men with premature ejaculation have intercourse only in the man-on-top position, with quick and short thrusting during intercourse that makes it very difficult for them to exert control over their ejaculations. The goal is for the man to enjoy the sensation of being in the woman's vagina without ejaculating. During the exercise, he is encouraged to touch or massage his partner and to communicate with her about what each is experiencing. If he feels he is reaching ejaculatory inevitability, he can request that she dismount and lie next to him until his arousal subsides. The partners are encouraged to engage in this exercise for at least 10 to 15 minutes, even if they must interrupt it several times to prevent him from ejaculating.

In the third phase of the stop-start technique, she creates some thrusting motion while still on top of him but using slow, long strokes. The partners typically reach orgasm and experience the entire encounter as highly intimate and pleasurable. Female partners of men with premature ejaculation often have trouble reaching orgasm themselves because the men lose their erections after ejaculating long before the women are highly aroused, and tension is high between the partners during sex. The stop-start technique can create encounters in which female partners receive the stimulation they need to reach orgasm as well.

The **squeeze technique** is used somewhat less often because it is harder to teach to partners (McCarthy, 1989). The man's partner stimulates him to an erection, and then when he signals that ejaculation is imminent, the partner applies a firm but gentle squeeze to his penis, either at the glans or at the base, for 3 to 4 seconds. This results in a partial loss of erection. The partner can then stimulate him again to the point of ejaculation and use the squeeze technique to stop the ejaculation. The goal of this technique, as with the stop-start technique, is for the man with a premature ejaculation disorder to learn to identify the point of ejaculatory inevitability and to control his arousal level at that point.

Techniques for treating vaginismus Vaginismus is often treated by deconditioning the woman's automatic tightening of the muscles of her vagina (Leiblum, Pervin, & Campbell, 1989). She is taught about the muscular tension at the opening of her vagina and the need to learn to relax those muscles. In a safe setting, she is instructed to insert her own fingers into her vagina. She examines her vagina in a mirror and practices relaxation exercises. She may also use silicon or metal vaginal dilators made for this exercise. Gradually, she inserts larger and larger dilators, as she practices relaxation exercises and becomes accustomed to the feel of the dilator in her vagina. If she has a partner, his or her fingers may be used instead of the dilator. If the woman has a male partner, eventually she guides his penis into her vagina, while remaining in control.

Couples Therapy

Many couples who know how to have pleasurable sex with each other never get around to it or stop giving their sexual relationship the attention it needs, leading to declines in sexual desire.

> ### CASE STUDY
> Felicia, a middle-aged, upper-middle-class woman, lives with her husband and young son in a luxurious apartment on the Upper East Side of Manhattan. She seems to have it all—a lucrative job, a loving husband, an affluent lifestyle. However, she confessed, she does not have a very active sex life. "My husband and I are very easy with each other," she said. "But the truth is, I seldom feel like doing it. I'm exhausted all the time. So I've got two vibrators. Frankly, I can't remember when the last time I used them was. We make love now, maybe twice a month, if we're lucky. When I fall in bed, I crave sleep, not sex." (Michael et al., 1994, p. 2)

Some couples in long-standing relationships have abandoned the *seduction rituals*—those activities that arouse sexual interest in both partners—they followed when they were first together (McCarthy, 1997; Verhulst & Heiman, 1988). Couples in which both partners work may be particularly prone to try to squeeze in sexual encounters late at night when both partners are very tired and not very interested in sex. These encounters may be rushed or not fully satisfying and lead to a gradual decline in interest for any sexual intimacy. A therapist may encourage a couple to set aside enough time so that they can engage in seduction rituals and satisfying sexual encounters (McCarthy, 1997). For example, partners may decide to hire a babysitter for their children, have a romantic dinner out, and then go to a hotel where they can have sex without rushing or being interrupted by their children.

Partners often differ in their *scripts* for sexual encounters—their expectations about what will take place during a sexual encounter and about what each partner's responsibilities are. Resolving these differences in scripts may be a useful goal in therapy. For example, if a woman lacks desire for sex because she feels her partner is too rough during sex, a therapist may encourage the partner to slow down and show the woman the kind of gentle intimacy she needs to enjoy sex. In general, therapists will help partners understand what each other wants and needs from sexual interactions and negotiate mutually acceptable and satisfying repertoires of sexual exchange.

When the conflicts between partners involve matters other than their sexual practices, such as an imbalance of power, distrust or hostility, or disagreements over important values or decisions, the therapist will focus on these conflicts primarily and the sexual dysfunction only secondarily. Some therapists use cognitive-behavioral interventions, some use psychodynamic interventions, and some use interventions

Busy people often find little time or energy to engage in seduction rituals with their partners.

based on family systems therapy. All of these interventions may have some benefit, although little research has been done to evaluate their effectiveness (Rosen & Leiblum, 1995).

Individual Psychotherapy

Although many therapists prefer to treat people with sexual dysfunctions as members of relationships, this is not always possible. The partner of a person with a dysfunction may refuse to participate in treatment or a person with a dysfunction may not have a partner.

Cognitive-behavioral interventions are being used increasingly to address attitudes and scripts that interfere with sexual functioning (LoPiccolo & Stock, 1986; McCarthy, 1997; Rosen & Leiblum, 1995). For example, a man who fears that he will embarrass himself by not sustaining an erection in a sexual encounter may be challenged to examine the evidence for this having happened to him in the past. If this were a common occurrence for this man, his therapist would explore the cognitions surrounding the experience and help the man challenge these cognitions and practice more positive cognitions.

Psychodynamic therapies are used to explore the childhood experiences that contributed to people's negative attitudes toward sex (Kaplan, 1974). For example, some psychodynamic theorists believe that women with vaginismus and dyspareunia are overidentifed with their mothers and have not yet reached the level of personal autonomy they should have reached during adolescence (Hiller, 1996). These women reject involvement in sexual relationships by literally closing their vaginas or experiencing pain during intercourse because they unconsciously equate engaging in intercourse as a rejection of their mothers.

Psychotherapy with these women focuses on making the link between their vaginismus and their relationships with their mothers, as in the following case (adapted from Hiller, 1996, pp. 69–70).

CASE STUDY

Sally and Ivan, both in their mid-20s, had been married for a year when their physician referred Sally for painful intercourse, which had led to the marriage barely being consummated. Although they had known each other for 4 years, penetration was not attempted until after the wedding. On the few occasions when they tried, the internal pain was too severe for it to be continued.

Both Sally and Ivan were only children of unstable marriages, although neither set of parents had divorced. Sally felt very close to her mother, who confided in her, especially about the fights and marital disharmonies that were regular features of family life. She was acutely aware of wanting to be available when her mother was upset and never wanting to hurt her by letting her know there were differences between them. At the same time, Sally sensed that this prevented her growing, developing, and expressing her own emotions.

Sally believed that her parents' sexual contact had stopped around the time she started school. She was brought up very strictly with the message that boys were only after one thing and that sex before marriage was wrong; otherwise, sexual topics were completely avoided.

Exploring the intense emotional bond with her mother in individual sessions, Sally realized that she had always wanted her mother to feel they were part of one another. This strong mother-daughter tie not only conflicted with her developmental needs but also restricted Sally's involvement with her father—a liked and respected figure—for fear of letting her mother down. I suggested that the anxiety about opening things up with her mother had manifested itself in her ability to open herself up—to expand her own inner space—to allow sexual intercourse to be part of her life when it was no longer part of her mother's life. It seemed as if Sally's lack of full genital arousal maintained the exclusive link of female dependency, thereby preventing the creating of a new (sexual) link with her partner that would represent abandonment of her mother and repeat her earlier loss of significant female relationships. When Sally eventually told her mother about the sexual difficulty and her own therapy, it emerged that her mother had been sexually abused in her teens; she realized she needed help but so far lacked the confidence to embark on therapy for her own marital and sexual problems. Discussing their separate needs for professional help lifted the burden of responsibility from Sally, communication between them became more open.

The focus of couple work with Sally and Ivan was on enabling them to take in a different psychological perspective on their penetration difficulties, in order to counteract their sense of failure and helplessness. Directive intervention, initially involving sensual and sexual pleasuring, facilitated a pattern of foreplay that heightened awareness of their own arousal and the other's needs in the present. During this process, Sally's increased arousal and awareness of emotional change evoked anxiety about being different from her mother and therefore being unloved. Ivan appreciated that Sally needed to address these issues as therapy progressed. Later he became anxious himself, when sexual intimacy moved on to genital stimulation, about failing Sally again by not being able to penetrate. The emerging anxieties were addressed in joint therapy in combination with a behaviorally oriented approach to increasing sexual intimacy. Eventually, comfortable and pleasurable intercourse took place.

Whether a therapist uses a cognitive-behavioral, a psychodynamic, or some other therapeutic approach to addressing the psychological issues involved in a sexual dysfunction, direct sex therapy using the behavioral techniques described earlier often is also a part of therapy. In cognitive-behavioral therapy, the client's cognitions while engaging in new sexual exercises can be evaluated and used as a focus of therapy sessions (McCarthy, 1997). For example, a woman who is learning how to masturbate for the first time may realize that she has thoughts such as "I'm going to get caught and I'll be so embarrassed"; "I shouldn't be doing this, this is sinful"; and "Only pathetic people do this," while masturbating. A therapist can then help the woman address the accuracy of these thoughts and decide whether she wants to maintain this attitude toward masturbation. If the woman is in psychodynamic therapy, the therapist might explore the origins of the woman's attitudes about masturbation in her early relationships. Thus, the behavioral techniques of sex therapy not only directly teach the client new sexual skills but also provide material for discussion in therapy sessions.

Sociocultural Issues

Most of the treatments described assume that the client is in a heterosexual relationship, but sexual dysfunctions can arise in the context of homosexual relationships as well. The sexual issues gay, lesbian, and bisexual people face can be different from those faced by heterosexuals. Lesbians tend not to complain of dyspareunia or vaginismus as often as do heterosexual women but may be more likely to have aversions to oral sex (Nichols, 1989). Gay men in sex therapy often report an aversion toward anal eroticism.

Many of the problems in sexual functioning experienced by gay, lesbian, and bisexual people, however, may have to do with society's attitudes toward them, and the particular stressors they face. Many gay men have lost partners and friends to AIDS, and grief and depression can impair sexual functioning. The fear of contracting the human immunodeficiency virus (HIV) can also heighten sexual anxiety and dampen sexual desire. Gay, lesbian, and bisexual people must constantly deal with homophobia. Society's negative attitudes toward them, and the fear of violence due to homophobia, can also affect sexual well-being.

Some of the sexual therapy treatments described can readily be adapted for gay, lesbian, and bisexual couples and the types of sex that they practice. Therapists must also be sensitive to the psychological conflicts and stresses these clients face as a result of society's rejection of their lifestyle (Nichols, 1989). Therapists must also be aware of their own biases against homosexuality and their wrong assumptions. In *Pushing the Boundaries:* New Theories of Sexual Orientation (p. 546), we describe how psychologists' understanding of homosexuality has evolved over the last few decades.

The treatments for the sexual dysfunctions must also take into account the religious, moral, and cultural values that clients have concerning sex. The treatments

Sexual dysfunctions can also arise in the context of gay, lesbian, and bisexual relationships.

PUSHING THE BOUNDARIES

New Theories of Sexual Orientation

Not that long ago, homosexuality was considered a psychological disorder. With the publication of the third edition of the DSM in 1980, an official shift occurred in psychologists' and psychiatrists' views on homosexuality. The DSM-III specified that homosexuality was not to be considered a disorder unless an individual felt uncomfortable about his or her sexual orientation and wished to change it (so-called ego-dystonic homosexuality). Later revisions of the DSM dropped all references to any form of homosexuality as a disorder.

Still, many people—professionals and laypeople alike—wonder about the "causes" of homosexuality. In fact, the common question "What causes homosexuality?" is scientifically misconceived because it implicitly assumes that heterosexuality needs no explanation or that its causes are self-evident. Freud himself did not agree: "[heterosexuality] is also a problem that needs elucidation and is not a self-evident fact based upon an attraction that is ultimately of a chemical nature" (1905/1962, pp. 11–12).

The determinants of sexual orientation—specifically homosexuality—are currently the subject of debate in both the behavioral sciences and the public arena. At issue, once again, is the nature-nurture question: Is an adult's sexual orientation primarily determined by innate biological influences such as genes or by earlier life experiences? Evidence for a genetic link comes from studies of identical and fraternal twins. In a study of gay men who had twin brothers, it was found that 52 percent of their identical twin brothers were also gay compared with only 22 percent of their fraternal twin brothers (Bailey & Pillard, 1991). In a comparable study of lesbians, 48 percent of their identical twin sisters were also lesbian, compared with only 16 percent of fraternal twin sisters (Bailey et al.,

1993). These patterns show that there is a correlation between genetic factors and sexual orientation.

But we need to observe two cautions. First, a correlation does not necessarily imply that there is a direct cause-and-effect relationship. As we shall see below, the genes could be influencing some intermediate personality variable that is more directly the precursor of sexual orientation. Second, the percentages themselves reveal that genes cannot be the entire story. If you knew that a man was gay or that a woman was lesbian and you guessed that a genetic clone of this individual—his or her identical twin—would also be gay or lesbian, you would only be right about half the time (i.e., 52 percent of the time for the gay man and 48 percent for the lesbian woman). This is no better than a coin flip.

The most extensive study of sexual orientation and childhood experiences is an intensive, large-scale interview study of approximately 1,000 homosexual and 500 heterosexual men and women living in the San Francisco Bay area (Bell, Weinberg, & Hammersmith, 1981). The study uncovered one—and only one—major factor that predicted a homosexual orientation in adulthood for both men and women: childhood gender nonconformity, the degree to which a child has sex-atypical activity and playmate preferences. For example, 63 percent of both gay men and lesbians said that they had not enjoyed play activities typical of their sex during childhood, compared with only 10 to 15% of heterosexual men and women. Gay men and lesbians were also more likely to report that more than half of their childhood friends had been of the opposite sex.

The results of this study also disconfirmed several common theories about the childhood antecedents of a homosexual orientation. For example, contrary to Freud's

described tend to be based on the assumption that men and women should have sex when they wish and enjoy it each time they have it. This assumption is not shared by persons of all backgrounds. Inhibitions about sex based on religious or cultural teachings are

often seen as the causes of sexual dysfunctions by sex therapists. At the very least, cultural inhibitions against talking about sex can get in the way of therapy. The experienced therapist works within the values framework of the sexual partners, first finding out

Continued

psychoanalytic theory, an individual's identification with the opposite-sex parent while growing up appears to have no significant effect on whether he or she turns out to be homosexual or heterosexual. In fact, no family-related factors were strongly related to sexual orientation for either men or women.

The study also disconfirmed theories based on processes of learning or conditioning, (including the common notion that an individual can become gay by being seduced by a person of the same sex or by having an admired teacher, parent, clergyperson, or TV character who is openly gay). For example, gay men and lesbians were no more likely than their heterosexual counterparts to report having their first sexual encounter with a person of the same sex. Moreover, they neither lacked heterosexual experiences during their childhood and adolescent years nor found such experiences unpleasant. In fact—contrary to learning or conditioning theories—sexual feelings tended to precede rather than follow sexual experiences. Gay men and lesbians typically experienced same-sex attractions about 3 years before they had engaged in same-sex sexual activity.

Finally, it is clear from all the studies that one's sexual orientation is not simply a matter of choice. Gay men and lesbians do not choose to have erotic feelings toward persons of the same sex any more than heterosexual persons choose to have erotic feelings toward persons of the opposite sex. Behavioral scientists do disagree over the nature-nurture question—whether the major determinants of sexual orientation are rooted in biology or experience—but the public often misconstrues the question to be whether sexual orientation is determined by variables beyond the individual's control or is freely chosen. That is not the same question.

A recent theory attempts to integrate all the findings we have reviewed here. It is called the Exotic-Becomes-Erotic (EBE) theory of sexual orientation (Bem, 1996). The central proposition of the theory is that individuals can become erotically attracted to a class of individuals from whom they felt different during childhood.

The theory proposes, first, that biological factors such as genes or prenatal hormones do not influence adult sexual orientation directly but, rather, influence a child's temperaments and personality traits. As we have noted throughout this book, there is good evidence that most personality traits have a genetic component, including such childhood temperaments as aggression and activity level.

A child's temperament predisposes him or her to enjoy some activities more than others. One child will enjoy rough-and-tumble play and competitive team sports (male-typical activities); another will prefer to socialize quietly or play jacks or hopscotch (female-typical activities). Thus, depending on the sex of the child, he or she will be genetically predisposed to be gender conforming or gender nonconforming. Children will also prefer to play with peers who share their activity preferences; for example, the child who enjoys baseball or football will selectively seek out boys as playmates. Gender-conforming children will feel different from opposite-sex peers, and gender-nonconforming children will feel different from same-sex peers. In the San Francisco study, 70 to 71 percent of the gay men and lesbians reported that they had felt different from their same-sex peers during childhood for gender-related reasons, compared with fewer than 8 percent of heterosexual men and women who did so.

These feelings of being different produce heightened physiological arousal in the presence of peers from whom he or she feels different. This arousal is transformed in later years into erotic arousal or attraction. For people who develop a homosexual orientation, this arousal occurs in the presence of members of their own sex. For people who develop a heterosexual orientation, this arousal occurs in the presence of members of the opposite sex.

EBE theory is new and has not been extensively tested; it may well be wrong. But it provides an excellent illustration of how biological and environmental variables might interact to produce a complex human motivation like sexual orientation.

what is in their current repertoire of sexual activity and then building on that according to their comfort.

Finally, many cultures have their own folk remedies for sexual dysfunctions (Kelly, 1998; Mannino, 1999). In Africa, impotent men drink potions and engage in ritual ceremonies to overcome their dysfunction. Hashish is the cure for sexual dysfunction in males in Morocco, whereas women who are anorgasmic are encouraged to take a younger lover or have a lesbian relationship. In Thailand, men drink a tonic made of the bile of a cobra, the blood of a monkey, and local liquor. In India, they apply an herb to the penis that is a potent irritant. In other parts of the world, the testes and penises of seals or tigers are consumed to overcome erectile problems in men. Traditional Chinese healers use a number of herbal preparations, and acupuncture to treat sexual dysfunctions.

Summing Up

- The sexual response cycle includes five phases: desire, excitement or arousal, plateau, orgasm, and resolution.
- People with disorders of sexual desire have little or no desire to engage in sex. These disorders include hypoactive sexual desire disorder and sexual aversion disorder.
- People with sexual arousal disorders do not experience the physiological changes that make up the excitement or arousal phase of the sexual response cycle. These disorders include female sexual arousal disorder and male erectile disorder.
- Women with female orgasmic disorder do not experience orgasm or have greatly delayed orgasm after reaching the excitement phase. Men with premature ejaculation reach ejaculation before they wish. Men with male orgasmic disorder have a recurrent delay in or absence of orgasm following sexual excitement.
- The two sexual pain disorders are dyspareunia, genital pain associated with intercourse, and vaginismus, involuntary contraction of the vaginal muscles in women.
- Biological causes of sexual dysfunctions include undiagnosed diabetes or other medical conditions, prescription or recreational drug use, and hormonal or vascular abnormalities.
- Psychological causes include other psychological disorders and maladaptive attitudes and cognitions (especially performance concerns).
- Sociocultural causes include problems in intimate relationships, traumatic experiences, and an upbringing or cultural milieu that devalues or degrades sex.
- When the cause of a sexual dysfunction is biological, treatments that eradicate the cause can cure the sexual dysfunction. Alternately, drug therapies or prostheses can be used.
- Sex therapy corrects the inadequate sexual practices of a client and his or her partner. The techniques of sex therapy include sensate focus therapy, teaching masturbation, the stop-start and squeeze techniques, and deconditioning of vaginal contractions.
- Couples therapy focuses on decreasing conflicts between couples over their sexual practices or over other areas of their relationship.
- Individual psychotherapy helps people recognize conflicts or negative attitudes behind their sexual dysfunctions and resolve these.

PARAPHILIAS

People find all sorts of creative ways to fulfill their sexual needs and desires while remaining within the limits set on sexual behavior by their society. Some examples in Western culture might include the use of erotic fantasies, pictures or stories, or sex toys to enhance arousal while engaging in masturbation or sexual encounters with others. People vary greatly in what they do and do not find arousing (see Table 15.4). One person may find oral sex the most stimulating form of activity while another person may be repulsed by oral sex. One man may become extremely aroused

---

TABLE 15.4
What Kinds of Sexual Practices Do People Find Appealing?

A national survey of 18- to 44-year-olds found that many different sexual practices appeal to people, with men finding more activities appealing than women do.

	Percent saying "very appealing"	
	Men	**Women**
Vaginal intercourse	83	78
Watching partner undress	50	30
Receiving oral sex	50	33
Giving oral sex	37	19
Group sex	14	1
Anus stimulated by partner's fingers	6	4
Using dildos/vibrators	5	3
Watching others do sexual things	6	2
Having a same-gender sex partner	4	3
Having sex with a stranger	5	1

Source: Michael et al., 1994.

CONCEPT REVIEW

The Paraphilias

The paraphilias are sexual activities that involve nonhuman objects, nonconsenting adults, suffering or humiliation of one's partner, or children.

Diagnosis	Description
Fetishism	Person uses inanimate objects as the preferred or exclusive source of sexual arousal
Transvestitism	Fetish in which a heterosexual man dresses in women's clothing as his primary means of becoming sexually aroused
Sexual sadism	Sexual gratification obtained through inflicting pain and humiliation on one's partner
Sexual masochism	Sexual gratification obtained through experiencing pain and humiliation at the hands of one's partner
Voyeurism	Obtainment of sexual arousal by compulsively and secretly watching another person undressing, bathing, engaging in sex, or being naked
Exhibitionism	Obtainment of sexual gratification by exposing one's genitals to involuntary observers
Frotteurism	Obtainment of sexual gratification by rubbing one's genitals against or fondling the body parts of a nonconsenting person
Pedophilia	Adult obtainment of sexual gratification by engaging in sexual activities with young children

Source: DSM-IV, APA, 2000.

while watching a wet T-shirt contest, and another man may experience such a contest as silly. One woman may find men with beards extremely sexy, while another woman may dislike facial hair on men.

Most of the time, these variations in preferences about sexually arousing stimuli simply provide spice to life. Societies have always drawn lines, however, between what types of sexual activities they will allow and what types they will not allow. Judgments about what are acceptable sexual activities vary by culture and across historical periods. In Western cultures prior to this century and in some Islamic nations today, men are prohibited from seeing most of women's bodies except their faces and hands, for fear that viewing women's legs and perhaps even their arms or their hair could sexually arouse men.

Although we may like to think that in modern Western culture, we only disallow those sexual behaviors that are truly "sick," our judgments about what are normal and abnormal sexual behaviors are still subjective and culturally specific. Consider the following series of behaviors exhibited by three men. The first man goes to a public beach to watch women in skimpy bikinis. The second man pays to see a female topless dancer in a nightclub. The third man stands outside a woman's bedroom window at night secretly watching her undress. The behavior of the first man is not only allowed, but it is promoted in many movies, television shows, and commercials. The behavior of the second man is a form of allowed sexual commerce.

Only the behavior of the third man is prohibited both by modern cultural norms and by laws. Yet all three men had the intention of viewing women's partially or fully nude bodies because they found such activity sexually arousing.

Atypical sexual behaviors that are considered disorders by the DSM-IV are called **paraphilias** (Greek for *besides* and *love*). These behaviors have also been referred to as *perversions*, *deviations*, and *variations* by some. When people with paraphilias violate laws, they are referred to as *sex offenders*. The paraphilias are sexual activities that involve (1) nonhuman objects, (2) nonconsenting adults, (3) suffering or humiliation of oneself or one's partner, or (4) children (see *Concept Review: The Paraphilias*).

Many people have occasional paraphilic fantasies. For example, one study of men's sexual fantasies found that 62 percent fanaticized having sex with a young girl, 33 percent fantasized raping a woman, 12 percent fantasized being humiliated during sex, 5 percent fantasized having sexual activity with an animal, and 3 percent fantasized having sexual activity with a young boy (Crepault & Couture, 1980). In a study of male college undergraduates, 21 percent reported being sexually attracted to children, 9 percent fantasized having sex with children, 5 percent masturbated to fantasies of having sex with children, and 7 percent indicated they would become sexually involved with children if they could be assured they would never be discovered (Briere & Runtz, 1989).

Most of these men would not be diagnosed with paraphilias because their fantasies were not the primary focus of their sexual arousal and they reported making no attempts to act out these fantasies.

For persons diagnosed with paraphilias, atypical sexual acts are their primary forms of sexual arousal. They often feel compelled to engage in their paraphilias, even though they know they could be punished by law. Their partners in sexual acts are merely vehicles to act out their paraphilic fantasies, not individuals with personalities, needs, or rights. Some paraphilics will pay prostitutes to help them act out their fantasies, because it is difficult to find willing partners. Other paraphilics will force their fantasies on unwilling victims.

As noted at the beginning of this chapter, the paraphilias differ greatly in how severely they affect people other than the paraphilics. We begin our discussion of the paraphilias with the one that is most benign: fetishism. People with *fetishes* do not typically impose their atypical sexual practices on other people; indeed, the focus of their sexual activities are nonhuman objects. The second set of paraphilias we discuss, *sadism* and *masochism*, are less benign because they hold the potential for physical harm, even if both partners are engaging in the sexual activity willingly. The third set of paraphilias—*voyeurism, exhibitionism,* and *frotteurism*—are not benign because, by definition, they require victims. Finally, the most severe paraphilia is *pedophilia,* because the victims of pedophiles are the most powerless victims: children.

Fetishism

Fetishism involves the use of inanimate objects as the preferred or exclusive source of sexual arousal or gratification. Soft fetishes are objects that are soft, furry, or lacy, such as frilly women's panties, stockings, or garters. Hard fetishes are objects that are smooth, harsh, or black, such as spike-heeled shoes, black gloves, and garments made of leather or rubber. These soft and hard objects are somewhat arousing to many people and, indeed, are promoted as arousing by their manufacturers. For most people, however, the objects simply add to the sexiness of the people wearing them, and their desire is for sex with those people. For the person with a fetish, the desire is for the object itself.

CASE STUDY
A 32-year-old, single, male, freelance photographer presented with the chief complaint of "abnormal sex drive." The patient related that although he was somewhat sexually attracted by women, he was far more attracted by "their panties."

To the best of the patient's memory, sexual excitement began at about age 7, when he came upon a pornographic magazine and felt stimulated by pictures of partially nude women wearing panties. His first ejaculation occurred at 13 via masturbation to fantasies of women wearing panties. He masturbated into his older sister's panties, which he had stolen without her knowledge. Subsequently, he stole panties from her friends and from other women he met socially. He found pretexts to "wander" into the bedrooms of women during social occasions and would quickly rummage through their possessions until he found a pair of panties to his satisfaction. He later used these to masturbate into and then "saved them" in a "private cache." The pattern of masturbating into women's underwear had been his preferred method of achieving sexual excitement and orgasm from adolescence until the present consultation.

The patient first had sexual intercourse at 18. Since then he had had intercourse on many occasions, and his preferred partner was a prostitute paid to wear panties, with the crotch area cut away, during the act. On less common occasions when sexual activity was attempted with a partner who did not wear panties, his sexual excitement was sometimes weak.

The patient felt uncomfortable dating "nice women" as he felt that friendliness might lead to sexual intimacy and that they would not understand his sexual needs. He avoided socializing with friends who might introduce him to such women. He recognized that his appearance, social style, and profession all resulted in his being perceived as a highly desirable bachelor. He felt anxious and depressed because his social life was limited by his sexual preference. (Adapted from Spitzer et al., 1994, p. 247)

Transvestic Fetishism

One elaborate form of fetishism is **transvestism,** also referred to as *cross-dressing*, in which heterosexual men dress in women's clothing as their primary means of becoming sexually aroused. They may surreptitiously wear only one women's garment, such as a pair of women's panties, under their business suits. The complete cross-dresser fully clothes himself in women's garments and applies makeup and a wig. Some men engage in cross-dressing alone, and others participate in transvestite subcultures, in which groups of men gather for drinks, meals, and dancing, while elaborately dressed as women.

CASE STUDY
Mr. A., a 65-year-old security guard, is distressed about his wife's objections to his wearing a nightgown at home in the evening, now that his youngest child has left home. His appearance and demeanor, except when he is dressing in women's clothes, are always masculine, and he is

Transvestites gain sexual pleasure by dressing in the clothes of the opposite sex.

exclusively heterosexual. Occasionally, over the past 5 years, he has worn an inconspicuous item of female clothing even when dressed as a man, sometimes a pair of panties, sometimes an ambiguous pinkie ring. He always carries a photograph of himself dressed as a woman.

His first recollection of an interest in female clothing was putting on his sister's bloomers at age 12, an act accompanied by sexual excitement. He continued periodically to put on women's underpants—an activity that invariably resulted in an erection, sometimes a spontaneous emission, and sometimes masturbation but never accompanied by fantasy. Although he occasionally wished to be a girl, he never fantasized himself as one. During his single years he was always attracted to women but was shy about sex. Following his marriage at age 22, he had his first heterosexual intercourse.

His involvement with female clothes was of the same intensity even after his marriage. Beginning at age 45, after a chance exposure to a magazine called *Transvestia*, he began to increase his cross-dressing activity. He learned there were other men like himself, and he became more and more preoccupied with female clothing in fantasy and progressed to periodically dressing completely as a woman. More recently he has become involved in a transvestite network, writing to other transvestites contacted through the magazine and occasionally attending transvestite parties. These parties have been the only times that he has cross-dressed outside his home.

Although still committed to his marriage, sex with his wife has dwindled over the past 20 years as his waking thoughts and activities have become increasingly centered on cross-dressing. Over time this activity has become less eroticized and more an end in itself, but it still is a source of some sexual excitement. He always has an increased urge to dress as a woman when under stress; it has a tranquilizing effect. If particular circumstances prevent him from cross-dressing, he feels extremely frustrated. (Adapted from Spitzer et al., 1994, pp. 257–258)

Some clinicians question whether fetishism should qualify as a psychiatric diagnosis or should simply be considered a variation in human sexual activity. Many, perhaps most, fetishists do not seek therapy or feel particularly disturbed about their behavior, and in most cases, the behavior is socially harmless because it is done in private and does not involve the infliction of harm on others. Fetishism is one of the most common secondary diagnoses of persons with other types of paraphilias, however (Abel & Osborn, 1992). That is, many people who have fetishes also engage in other atypical sexual practices, including pedophilia, exhibitionism, and voyeurism. Thus, for some people, fetishes are part of a larger pattern of atypical sexual behaviors including behaviors that have victims.

Sexual Sadism and Sexual Masochism

Sexual sadism and **sexual masochism** are two separate diagnoses, although sadistic and masochistic sexual practices often are considered together as a pattern referred to as **sadomasochism.** The sexual sadist gains sexual gratification by inflicting pain and humiliation on his or her sex partner. The sexual masochist gains sexual gratification by suffering pain or humiliation during sex. Some people occasionally engage in moderately sadistic or masochistic behaviors during sex or simulate such behaviors without actually carrying through with the infliction of pain or suffering. Persons who are diagnosed as sexual sadists or masochists engage in these behaviors as their preferred or exclusive form of sexual gratification.

Sadomasochistic practices may be considered just another form of sexual practice by some people, but they can be dangerous.

The sexual rituals of sadists and masochists typically involve practices of bondage and domination. One partner is bound, gagged, and immobilized and then is subjected by the other partner to sexual acts, beatings, whippings, electrical shock, burning, cutting, stabbing, strangulation, torture, mutilation, and even death. The partner who is the victim in such encounters may be a masochist and a willing victim or may be a nonconsenting victim on whom the sadist carries out his or her wishes. A variety of props may be used in such encounters, including black leather garments, chains, shackles, whips, harnesses, and ropes. Men are much more likely than women to enjoy sadomasochistic sex, both in the roles of sadist and of masochist (Breslow, Evans, & Langlers, 1985). Some women find such activities exciting, but many consent to them only to please their partners or because they are paid to do so, and some are unconsenting victims of sadistic men.

Although sadomasochistic sex between consenting adults typically does not result in physical injury, the activities can get out of control or go too far. Particularly dangerous activities are those known as *auto-erotic asphyxiation*, which involve sexual arousal by oxygen deprivation, obtained by hanging, by putting plastic bags or masks over the head, or by severe chest compression (Uva, 1995). Accidents and equipment failure can result in permanent injury or death.

Voyeurism, Exhibitionism, and Frotteurism

Voyeurism involves secretly watching another person undressing, bathing, doing things in the nude, or engaged in sex as a preferred or exclusive form of sexual arousal. For a diagnosis to be made, the voyeuristic behavior must be repetitive over 6 months and compulsive. The person being observed must be unaware of it

and would be upset if he or she knew about it. Almost all voyeurs are men who watch women. They typically masturbate while watching or shortly after watching women. Part of what makes the behavior exciting is the danger of being caught and the knowledge that the women would be frightened or angry if they knew they were being watched.

> ## CASE STUDY
>
> Benjamin is a peeper. At night he takes out his high-powered binoculars and goes to the roof of his apartment building. From there, he can see into the windows of several other apartments in neighboring buildings. Most nights, he observes at least one event that causes him to be extremely sexually aroused. It might be a woman undressing or taking a bath, a couple engaged in foreplay or intercourse, or an individual masturbating alone. Benjamin will usually masturbate with one hand as he watches through the binoculars with the other hand, until he ejaculates.

Exhibitionism is in some ways the mirror image of voyeurism. The exhibitionist obtains sexual gratification by exposing his or her genitals to involuntary observers who are usually complete strangers. In the vast majority of cases, the exhibitionist is a man who bares all to surprised women. He typically confronts women in a public place, such as a park, a bus, or a subway, either with his genitals already exposed or by flashing open his coat to expose his bare genitals. He then may begin to openly masturbate. His arousal comes from observing the victim's surprise, fear, or disgust or from a fantasy that his victim is becoming sexually aroused. His behavior is often compulsive and impulsive: He feels a sense of excitement, fear, restlessness, and sexual arousal and then feels compelled to find relief by exhibiting himself.

Voyeurs gain sexual pleasure by watching an unknowing victim undress, bathe, or engage in sex.

> ## CASE STUDY
>
> A 27-year-old engineer requested consultation at a psychiatric clinic because of irresistible urges to exhibit his penis to female strangers. At age 18, for reasons unknown to himself, he first experienced an overwhelming desire to engage in exhibitionism. He sought situations in which he was alone with a woman he did not know. As he approached her, he would become sexually excited. He would then walk up to her and display his erect penis. He found that her shock and fear further stimulated him, and usually he would then ejaculate. He also fantasized past encounters while masturbating.
>
> He feels guilty and ashamed after exhibiting himself and vows never to repeat it. Nevertheless, the desire often overwhelms him, and the behavior recurs frequently, usually at periods of tension. (Adapted from Spitzer et al., 1994, pp. 117–118)

Exhibitionists are more likely than most sex offenders to get caught, in part because of the public nature of their behavior but also because some of them seem to invite arrest by doing things like repeatedly returning to places where they have already exhibited themselves. It may be that the danger of being caught heightens their arousal. Exhibitionists are also likely to continue their behavior after having been caught.

Frotteurism is another paraphilia that often co-occurs with voyeurism and exhibitionism. The frotteurist gains sexual gratification by rubbing against and fondling parts of the body of a nonconsenting person. Often, the frotteurist engages in this behavior in public places, such as on a bus or subway. Most frotteurists are young men between 15 and 25 years of age, but little else is known about this disorder.

Pedophilia

The most troubling and most common paraphilia is **pedophilia.** Pedophiles are sexually attracted to children and prefer to engage in sex with children rather than with other adults. The diagnosis of pedophilia generally requires that the sexual encounters be with children under the age of 13 and initiated by persons 16 years old or older and at least 5 years older than the children. Laws in most of the United States, however, define child molesting or statutory rape to include adults having sex with persons under the age of 18 (Green, 1993).

Sexual encounters between pedophiles and their child victims are often brief, although they may recur frequently. The contact most often consists of the pedophile exposing and touching the child's genitals (Abel & Osborn, 1992). Other pedophiles perform fellatio (orally stimulating the penis) or cunnilingus (orally stimulating the female genitals) on children or penetrate children's vaginas, mouths, or anuses with their fingers, foreign objects, or penises. Pedophiles often threaten children with harm, physically restrain them, or tell them that they will punish them or loved ones of the children if the children do not comply with the pedophiles' wishes. Pedophiles may try to convince children that they are only showing love to the children through their actions (McConaghy, 1998).

Most pedophiles are heterosexual men abusing young girls (Cole, 1992; Finkelhor, 1984). Homosexual men who are pedophiles typically abuse young boys. Women can be pedophiles, but this is much more rare. Sexual abuse of children is not a rare occurrence. The number of children abused in the United States is estimated to be over 400,000 per year (Finkelhor & Dzuiba-Leatherman, 1994). About 60 percent of these children are under 12 years of age. Only about 1 in 10 of these cases is reported to the authorities (Maletzky, 1998).

Most abusers are family members or acquaintances of the children. Some predatory pedophiles develop elaborate plans for gaining access to the children, such as winning the trust of their mothers or marrying their mothers, trading children with other pedophiles, or in rare cases, abducting children or adopting children from foreign countries (McConaghy, 1998).

CASE STUDY

Dr. Crone, a 35-year-old, single, child psychiatrist, has been arrested and convicted of fondling several neighborhood girls, ages 6 to 12. Friends and colleagues were shocked and dismayed, as he had been considered by all to be particularly caring and supportive of children.

Dr. Crone's first sexual experience was at age 6, when a 15-year-old female camp counselor performed fellatio on him several times over the course of the summer—an experience that he had always kept to himself. As he grew older, he was surprised to notice that the age range of girls who attracted him sexually did not change, and he continued to have recurrent erotic urges and fantasies about girls between the ages of 6 and 12. Whenever he masturbated, he would fantasize about a girl in that age range, and on a couple of occasions over the years, he had felt himself to be in love with such a youngster.

Intellectually, Dr. Crone knew that others would disapprove of his many sexual involvements with young girls. He never believed, however, that he had caused any of these youngsters harm, feeling instead that they were simply sharing pleasurable feelings together. He frequently prayed for help and that his actions would go undetected. He kept promising himself that he would stop, but the temptations were such that he could not. (Adapted from Spitzer et al., 1994, pp. 187–188)

Mental-health experts are divided over whether pedophiles should be viewed primarily as persons with a psychiatric disorder that needs treating or as criminals who should be incarcerated (McConaghy, 1998). Even those who view pedophilia primarily as a disorder to be treated tend to agree that pedophiles should be prevented from their behaviors, often through incarceration. Some clinicians, however, feel unable to empathize with pedophiles to the point of being able to treat them and believe that the resources of the mental-health system should be directed toward the victims of the pedophiles rather than the pedophiles themselves.

The impact on the child victim of the pedophile can be great. The most frequent symptoms shown by sexually abused children are fearfulness, posttraumatic stress disorder, conduct disorder and hyperactivity, sexualized behaviors (promiscuity and sexual behavior inappropriate for their ages), and poor self-esteem (Kendall-Tackett, Williams, & Finkelhor, 1993; McConaghy, 1998). More severe symptoms are experienced by children who endure frequent abuse over a

---

CONCEPT REVIEW

Causes of Paraphilias

Each of the major psychological approaches to abnormality has something to say about paraphilias.

Theory	Description	Paraphilia Best Explained
Psychodynamic theory	Fixation at early psychosexual stage or regression to that stage	All paraphilias
Behavioral theory	Arousal is classically conditioned to a previously neutral stimulus	All paraphilias
Social learning theory	Children whose parents engaged in aggressive, sexual behaviors with them learned to engage in impulsive, aggressive, sexualize acts toward others	All but fetishes
Cognitive theory	Distorted cognitions and assumptions about sexuality lead to deviant sexual behavior	All but fetishes

---

long period, who are penetrated by perpetrators, who are abused by family members (typically fathers or stepfathers), and whose mothers do not provide them with support upon learning of the abuse. About two-thirds of victimized children show significant recovery from their symptoms within 12 to 18 months following cessation of the abuse, but significant numbers of abused children continue to experience psychological problems even into adulthood (Burnam et al., 1988; Kendall-Tackett, Williams & Finkelhor, 1993).

Causes of Paraphilias

Many of the paraphilias may have similar causes, which may account for the fact that many paraphilics engage in a number of different paraphilic behaviors (see *Concept Review*: Causes of Paraphilias). Over 90 percent of paraphilics are men (McConaghy, 1998). This may be because paraphilic behavior often involves the acting out of hostile or aggressive impulses, which may be more common in men than in women and certainly are more socially sanctioned for men than for women. Attempts to link paraphilic behavior, particularly sexually aggressive paraphilias, to testosterone abnormalities have met with limited success (Langevin, 1992). Similarly, although some studies have found links between other hormones or endocrine abnormalities and paraphilias, no consistent biological cause of the paraphilias has been found (Maletzky, 1998). Alcohol and drug abuse are common among paraphilics (Langevin, 1992). These substances may disinhibit the paraphilic so that he acts out his fantasy. The abuse may also be the consequence of knowing one has unacceptable sexual desires and activities or part of a deeper psychological disturbance that also leads to the paraphilia.

Freud viewed paraphilias as the result of arrested psychological development or regression to childhood forms of sexual arousal (Freud, 1905). He argued that children could be sexually aroused by a myriad of people and objects but that, through proper socialization, they learn to repress their sexual desires for anything except other people. Persons with paraphilias either had been fixated at an early stage of sexual development or regressed back to an earlier stage. Psychoanalyst Robert Stoller (1975) argued that the paraphilias are symbolic reenactments of childhood traumas in which the paraphilic is unconsciously taking revenge on adults who inflicted harm on him as a child.

Behavioral theories of the paraphilias view them as the results of chance classical conditioning (McGuire, Carlisle, & Young, 1965). An adolescent male might be masturbating and notice a picture of a horse on the wall in the room. He fleetingly considers what it might be like to have sex with a horse and becomes more aroused at this thought. The next time he masturbates, he might be more drawn to the picture of the horse because it was arousing the last time and begin to incorporate fantasies about horses into his masturbatory fantasies. If this fantasy becomes so strongly associated with sexual arousal for him, he may find ways to act out the fantasy and thus have a fetish. Because men masturbate more than do women, men would be more likely to develop unusual associations with masturbation and thus to develop paraphilias.

These classic behavioral theories have been supplemented with principles of social learning theory (see Chapter 2), which suggest that the larger environment of a child's home and culture influence his or her tendency to develop deviant sexual behavior. Children whose parents frequently use physical punishment on them and who engage in aggressive, often sexual, contact with each other are more likely to engage in impulsive, aggressive, perhaps sexualized acts toward others as they grow older. Many pedophiles have poor interpersonal skills, and feel intimidated when interacting sexually with adults. Others harbor strong hostility toward women and carry out this hostility in antisocial acts toward children (Langevin, 1992). One study found that four of five pedophiles were sexually abused as children (Groth, 1979). They may have learned that it was acceptable for adults to sexually abuse children or may be acting out their childhood traumas in an attempt to gain mastery over those traumas or inflict harm on others the way they were harmed.

Cognitive theorists have also identified a number of distortions and assumptions that paraphilics have about their behaviors and the behaviors of their victims (see Table 15.5; Maletzky, 1998). These distortions may have been learned from parents' deviant messages about sexual behavior. They serve to justify the paraphilics victimization of others.

Treatments for the Paraphilias

Most paraphilics do not seek treatment for their behaviors. Treatment is often forced upon those who engage in illegal acts (voyeurism, exhibitionism, frotteurism, pedophilia) after they are arrested for breaking the law by engaging in their behaviors. Simple incarceration does little to change these behaviors, and the recidivism rate among convicted sex offenders is very high.

Drastic biological interventions have been tried, primarily with pedophiles and men who commit rape. These formerly included surgery on the centers of the brain thought to control sexual behavior and surgical castration of the testes. Castration certainly lowers recidivism rates among paraphilics who have committed sexual crimes (Bradford, 1995a). It is a drastic approach to treatment, however. These days, sex offenders might be offered antiandrogen drugs that suppress the functioning of the testes, thereby reducing the production

TABLE 15.5

Distortions, Assumptions, and Justifications in Sexual Paraphilias

Paraphilics may engage in cognitions that provide a rationale for their behaviors.

Category	Pedophilia	Exhibitionism	Rape
Misattributing blame	"She started it by being too cuddly." "She would always run around half dressed."	"She kept looking at me like she was expecting it." "The way she was dressed, she was asking for it."	"She was saying 'no' but her body said 'yes.'"
Minimizing or denying sexual intent	"I was teaching her about sex . . . better from her father than someone else."	"I was just looking for a place to pee." "My pants just slipped down."	"I was just trying to teach her a lesson . . . she deserved it."
Debasing the victim	"She'd had sex before with her boyfriend." "She always lies."	"She was just a slut anyway."	"The way she came on to me at the party, she deserved it." "She never fought back . . . she must have liked it."
Minimizing consequences	"She's always been real friendly to me, even afterward." "She was messed up even before it happened."	"I never touched her so I couldn't have hurt her." "She smiled so she must have liked it."	"She'd had sex with hundreds of guys before. It was no big deal."
Deflecting censure	"This happened years ago . . . why can't everyone forget about it?"	"It's not like I raped anyone."	"I only did it once."
Justifying the cause	"If I wasn't molested as a kid, I'd never have done this."	"If I knew how to get dates, I wouldn't have to expose."	"If my girlfriend gave me what I want, I wouldn't be forced to rape."

of testosterone and possibly reducing the sex drive. These drugs are typically used in conjunction with psychotherapy and can be useful for hypersexual men who are motivated to change their behavior (Cole, 1992). Follow-up studies have shown that paraphilics treated with antiandrogen drugs do show great reductions in their paraphilic behavior (Bradford, 1995a). These drugs can have significant side effects, however, and reduce overall sexual drive for the individual. Difficult ethical questions arise when the use of these drugs is part of a deal struck with a sex offender for a lighter sentence or parole.

Insight-oriented therapies alone have not proven extremely successful in changing paraphilics' behavior. Behavior modification therapies are commonly used to treat paraphilics and can be successful if paraphilics are willing to change their behavior. **Aversion therapy** is used to extinguish paraphilics' sexual responses to objects or situations they find arousing. During such therapy, paraphilics might receive painful but harmless electric shocks while viewing photographs of what arouse them (such as children) or while actually touching objects that arouse them (such as women's panties). **Desensitization** procedures may be used to reduce paraphilics' anxiety about engaging in normal sexual encounters with other adults. For example, paraphilics might be taught relaxation exercises, which they then use to control their anxiety as they gradually build up fantasies of interacting sexually with other adults in ways that are fulfilling to them and their partners (Maletzky, 1998).

Cognitive therapy is sometimes used to help predatory paraphilics (i.e., pedophiles, exhibitionists, voyeurs) identify and challenge thoughts and situations that trigger their behaviors and serve as justifications of their behaviors, such as those seen in Table 15.5 (p. 555) (Maletzky, 1998; McConaghy, 1998). Part of the work with predatory paraphilics involves empathy training—getting the paraphilic to understand the impact of his behavior on his victims and care about it. Five components of empathy training include (a) encouraging identification with the victim, (b) getting the client to take responsibility for his acts, (c) encouraging acceptance of the harm created by the acts, (d) encouraging the client to reverse roles with the victim, and (e) encouragement of empathy with the victim (Maletzky, 1998).

With nonpredatory paraphilics (e.g., people with fetishes), cognitive interventions may be combined with behavioral interventions designed to help them learn more appropriate ways of approaching and interacting with people they find attractive, in socially acceptable ways (Cole, 1992). Role-plays might be used to allow the paraphilic practice in initiating contact and eventually negotiating a positive sexual encounter with another person. Finally, group therapy in which paraphilics come together to support each other through changes in their behavior can be helpful.

Outcome studies comparing these treatments with control groups that receive no treatment have not been done for most types of therapy because of ethical concerns. There are several studies, however, that have followed paraphilics after receiving treatment, usually consisting of a comprehensive program of various psychosocial interventions, that suggest these treatments are useful (Maletzky, 1998). Table 15.6 summarizes the outcomes of over 7,000 people with paraphilia treated in a clinic that emphasized cognitive and behavioral interventions. Successful treatment was defined as completing all treatment sessions, reporting no deviant sexual behavior upon follow-up sessions up to 5 years after treatment, and no legal charges for sexual offenses during the follow-up period.

Summing Up

- The paraphilias are a group of disorders in which people's sexual activity is focused on (1) nonhuman objects, (2) nonconsenting adults, (3) suffering or humiliation of oneself or one's partner, or (4) children.

- Fetishism involves the use of inanimate objects (such as panties or shoes) as the preferred or exclusive source of sexual arousal or gratification. One elaborate fetish is transvestism, in which a man dresses in the clothes of a woman to sexually arouse himself.

- Voyeurism involves observing another person nude or engaging in sexual acts, without that person's knowledge or consent, in order to become sexually aroused.

- Exhibitionism involves exposing oneself to another without his or her consent, in order to become sexually aroused.

- Frotteurism involves rubbing up against another without his or her consent, in order to become sexually aroused.

- Sadism and masochism involve physically harming another or allowing oneself to be harmed for sexual arousal.

- Pedophilia involves engaging in sexual acts with a child.

- Most paraphilics are men. Their behavior may represent the acting out of hostile or aggressive impulses.

- Behavioral theories suggest that paraphilics' sexual preferences are the results of chance classical conditioning.

TABLE 15.6

Treatment Outcomes for Paraphilias (n = 7,156)

The data below suggest that cognitive behavioral treatment may help to reduce paraphilic behavior.

Category	N	Percentage meeting criteria for success*
Situational pedophilia, heterosexual	3,012	96.6
Predatory pedophilia, heterosexual	864	88.3
Situational pedophilia, homosexual	717	91.8
Predatory pedophilia, homosexual	596	80.1
Exhibitionism	1,130	95.4
Voyeurism	83	93.9
Public masturbation	77	94.8
Frotteurism	65	89.3
Fetishism	33	94.0
Transvestic fetishism	14	78.6

From "The Paraphilias: Research and Treatment" by Barry M. Maletzky, from *A Guide to Treatments That Work*, edited by Peter Nathan and Jack Gorman, copyright © 1998 by Peter E. Nathan and Jack M. Gorman. Used by permission of Oxford University Press, Inc.

*Treatment success was defined as (1) completing all treatment sessions, (2) reporting no deviant sexual behavior at any follow-up sessions, (3) demonstrating no deviant sexual arousal at any follow-up session, (4) no repeat legal charges for a sexual crime at any follow-up session. Follow-up sessions occurred at 6, 12, 24, 36, 48, and 60 months after the end of active treatment.

- Treatment of the paraphilias can include biological interventions to reduce sexual drive, behavioral interventions to decondition arousal to paraphillic objects, and training in interpersonal and social skills.

☺ GENDER IDENTITY DISORDER

For most people, their perception of themselves as male or female, referred to as **gender identity,** is a fundamental component of their self-concept. Gender identity differs from **gender role,** which is a person's belief about how he or she should behave as a male or female in society. Many females choose to engage in behaviors considered part of the masculine gender role, such as playing aggressive sports or pursuing competitive careers, but still have a fundamental sense of themselves as female. Similarly, many males choose to engage in behaviors considered part of the feminine gender role, such as caring for children or cooking and sewing, but still have a fundamental sense of themselves as male.

Gender identity and gender roles differ from **sexual orientation,** which is one's preference for sexual partners of the opposite sex or of the same sex. Most gay men have a fundamental sense of themselves as male and therefore male gender identities; most lesbians have a fundamental sense of themselves as female and therefore female gender identities. Although gay men and lesbians are often portrayed as violating stereotypic gender roles, many adhere to traditional roles for their genders, except in their choices of sexual partners.

Gender identity disorder is diagnosed when individuals believe that they were born with the wrong sex's genitals and are fundamentally persons of the opposite sex (see Table 15.7, p. 559). In *Extraordinary People:* Jayne Thomas, Ph.D., page 558, we meet a successful psychologist who had gender identity disorder and dealt with it by changing her sex.

Gender identity disorder of childhood is a rare condition in which a child persistently rejects his or her anatomic sex and desires to be or insists he or she is a member of the opposite sex. Girls with this disorder seek masculine-type activities and male peer groups to a degree far beyond that of a "tomboy." Sometimes these girls will express the belief that they will eventually grow penises. Boys with the disorder seek feminine-type activities and female peer groups and tend to begin cross-dressing in girls' clothes at a very early age (Bradley, 1995). They express disgust with their penises and wish they would disappear (Green, 1986). Boys with gender identity disturbances are more likely to be brought by their parents for counseling than are girls with the disturbance, probably because parents are more concerned about violations of gender roles in boys than in girls.

EXTRAORDINARY PEOPLE

Jayne Thomas, Ph.D.

Professor Jayne Thomas teaches courses on human sexuality in southern California. This psychologist brings a unique perspective to her research and teaching because she has lived both as a man and a woman. Here she describes her experience with gender identity disorder in her own words:

The "Glass Ceiling," male bashing, domestic violence, nagging, PMS, and Viagra are among the important issues addressed in the Human Sexuality classes I instruct. As both a researcher and participant in my area of specialization, I see many of these topics aligning themselves along gender lines. Ironically, I am able to both see and not see the distinctions. Certainly women have bumped up against the "glass ceiling" (some have only smudged this barrier while others have effectively broken through this metaphorical limitation to women's success in the workplace). And most assuredly men have often found themselves "bashed" by frustrated and angry women intent upon extracting a pound of flesh for centuries of felt persecution and unjust treatment. I must add that, having lived my life in both the gender roles of man and woman, I offer a rather unique perspective of masculinity and femininity.

Gender Identity Disorder

Gender Identity Disorder (GID) is defined by the American Psychiatric Association (1994) as a "strong and persistent cross-gender identification [accompanied by] a persistent discomfort with his or her sex or sense of appropriateness in the gender role of that sex" (page 537). All of my life I harbored the strongest conviction that I was inappropriately assigned to the wrong gender—that of a man—when inside I knew myself to be a woman.

Psychologist Jayne Thomas instructs courses in psychology in Southern California at Los Angeles Mission College offering her unique perspective on masculinity and femininity—as she has lived both as a man and a woman.

Even so (and like so many other GID's) I continued a lifelong struggle with this deeply felt mistake. I was successful in school, became a national swimming champion, received my college degrees, married twice (fathering children in both marriages), and was respected as a competent and good man in the workplace. However, in my heart the persistent unrelenting wrongfulness of my life continued to be felt. Not until my fourth decade was I able to confront my gender issue.

Jay Thomas, Ph.D., underwent gender reassignment and officially became Jayne Thomas, Ph.D., in November of 1985— what transpired in the ensuing years for Jayne has afforded her the most enlightening of glimpses into the plight of humankind. As teachers, we are constantly being taught by those we purport to instruct. My students, knowing my background (I share who I am when it is appropriate to do so), find me accessible in ways that many professors are not.

Granted, I am continually asked those titillating questions that one watching *Geraldo* might ask, and we do have fun with those answers (several years ago I even appeared on a few of the Geraldo Rivera shows). My students, however, are able to take our discussions beyond the sensational and often superficial into a more meaningful dialogue regarding gender differences in society and the workplace, sexual harassment, power and control issues in relationships, and what it means to be a man or woman in today's world.

Challenging Both the Masculine and Feminine

Iconoclastically, I try to challenge both the masculine and feminine. "I know something that none of you women know or will ever know in your lifetime." I am able to provocatively address the females in my audiences as

Continued

Jayne. "I once lived as a man and have been treated by society as an equal. You never have nor will you ever experience such equality." Or, when a male student once came to my assistance in a classroom, fixing an errant video playback machine and then strutting peacock-like back to his seat as only a satisfied male can, I teasingly commented to a nearby female student, "I used to be able to do that."

Having once lived as a man and now as a woman, I can honestly state that I see profound differences in our social/psychological/biological beingness as man and woman. I have now experienced many of the ways in which women are treated as less than men. Jay worked as a consultant to a large financial firm in Los Angeles and continued in that capacity following her gender shift. Not surprisingly the world presented itself in a different perspective. As Jay, technical presentations to management had generally been received in a positive manner, and credit for my work was fully acknowledged. Jayne now found management less accessible, credit for her efforts less forthcoming, and, in general, found herself expending a greater effort to be well prepared for each meeting than she ever had when male. As a man, her forceful and impassioned presentations were an asset; as a woman they definitely seemed a liability. On one occasion, as Jayne, when I passionately asserted my position regarding what I felt to be an important issue, my emotion and disappointment in not getting my point across (my voice must have shown my frustration) was met with a nearby colleague (a man) reaching to touch my arm with words of reassurance, "There, there, relax and take it easy, it will be alright." Believe me; that never would have happened in that way to Jay. There was also an occasion when I had worked most diligently on a briefing to management only to find the company vice president more interested in the fragrance of my cologne than my technical agenda.

Certainly there are significant differences in the treatment of men and women, and yet I continue to be impressed with how similar the two genders are. Although I have made this seemingly enormous change in lifestyle (and it is immense in so many ways), I continue as the same human being, perceiving the same world through these same sensory neurons. The difference—I now find myself a more comfortable and serene being, than the paradoxical woman in a man's body, now that my anatomy and gender have attained congruence.

Adjusting the Shifting Gender Roles

Does the shifting of gender role create difficulties in the GID's life? Most assuredly it does. Family and intimate relationships rank highest among those issues most problematic for the transitioning individual to resolve. When one shifts gender role, the effects of such a change are global; as ripples in a pond, the transformation radiates outward impacting all that have touched the GID's life. My parents had never realized that their eldest son was dealing with such a lifelong problem. Have they accepted or do they fully understand the magnitude of my issue? I fear not. After almost fifteen years of having lived as a female, my father continues to call me by my male name. I do not doubt my parents' or children's love for me, but so uninformed are we as a society of the true significance of gender identity that a clear understanding seems light years away. Often I see my clients losing jobs, closeness with family members, visitation rights with their children, and generally becoming relegated to the role of societal outcast. Someone once stated that "Everyone is born unique, but most of us die copies"—a great price my clients often pay for personal honesty and not living their lives a version of how society deems they should.

Having lived as man and woman in the same lifetime one personal truth seems clear. Rather than each gender attempting to change and convert the other to their own side, as I often see couples undertaking to accomplish (women need to become more logical and men should learn to better share their emotions), we might more productively come together in our relationships, building upon our gender uniqueness and strengths. Men and women have different perspectives, which can each be used to successfully address life's issues.

TABLE 15.7
DSM-IV
Criteria for Diagnosis of Gender Identity Disorder

People with gender identity disorder believe they were born with the wrong sex's body and are truly members of the other sex.

A. Strong and persistent identification with the other sex. In children, this is manifested by four or more of the following:

1. repeatedly stated desire to be, or insistence that he or she is, the other sex.

2. in boys, preference for cross-dressing or simulating female attire; in girls, insistence on wearing only stereotypical masculine clothing.

3. strong and persistent preferences for cross-sex roles in play and in fantasies.

4. intense desire to participate in the stereotypical games and pastimes of the other sex.

5. strong preference for playmates of the other sex.

In adolescents or adults, identification with the other sex may be manifested with symptoms such as the stated desire to be the other sex, frequently passing as the other sex, desire to live or be treated as the other sex, or the conviction that he or she has the typical feelings or reactions of the other sex.

B. Persistent discomfort with his or her sex and sense of inappropriateness in the gender role of that sex.

C. Disturbance is not concurrent with a physical intersex condition, and causes significant distress or problems in functioning.

Reprinted with permission from the *Diagnostic and Statistical Manual of Mental Disorders*, Fourth Edition. Copyright © 2000 American Psychiatric Association.

Gender identity disorder in adulthood is often referred to as **transsexualism.** Transsexuals experience a chronic discomfort and sense of inappropriateness with their gender and genitals, wish to be rid of them, and want to live as members of the opposite sex. Transsexuals will often dress in the clothes of the opposite sex, but unlike the transvestite, they do not do this to gain sexual arousal. They simply believe they are putting on the clothes of the gender they really belong to. Transsexuals who can afford it may seek sex-change operations. The sexual preferences of transsexuals vary. Some are asexual, having little interest in either sex, some are heterosexual, and some are homosexual. Transsexualism is rare, with an estimated prevalence of 1 per 30,000 males and 1 per 100,000 females (Bradley & Zucker, 1997; Katchadourian, 1989). Many transsexuals are so disturbed by their misassignment of gender that they develop alcohol and drug-abuse problems and other psychological disorders, but these seem to be consequences rather than causes of their transsexualism (Roback & Lothstein, 1986).

CASE STUDY

Stephanie was 30 when she first attended our clinic. She gave a history of conviction that she was, in fact, male and wished to rid herself of identifiably female attributes and acquire male traits and features. She said she had been cross-living and employed as a male for about 1 year, following the breakdown of a 10-year marriage. She was taking testosterone prescribed by her family physician. She presented at our clinic with a request for removal of her uterus and ovaries.

She did not give a childhood history of tomboy attitudes, thoughts, or behavior. She said social interaction with other children, boys or girls, was minimal. Desperate for a friend, she fantasized "an articulate and strong" boy, exactly her own age, named Ronan. They were always together and they talked over everything: thoughts and feelings and the events of her life. Cross-dressing in her father's clothing also began during childhood. There was no history of sexual arousal associated with or erotic fantasy involving cross-dressing.

Puberty at age 12 and the accompanying bodily changes apparently did not overly distress Stephanie. Sexual and romantic feelings focused on "slender, feminine-appearing men." At 16, Stephanie met such a man and they were together for 2 years. Her next romantic involvement was with a "male bisexual transvestite." Sexual interaction according to Stephanie, included experimentation with drugs and "role reversals." She and her partner cross-dressed, and Stephanie took the dominant and active role. During vaginal sex, she imagined herself as a male with another male.

At 19, she met a slender, good-looking man. They were compatible and married soon after. The marriage was a success. Stephanie's preferred position for intercourse was with both kneeling, she behind her husband, rubbing her pubic area against him while masturbating him. She would imagine she had a penis and was penetrating him.

Stephanie's marriage broke down after the couple's business failed. She decided to live full-time in the male role as Jacob. While on the West Coast, she started treatment with male hormones. She moved back east and presented at our clinic for assessment. She saw herself as a male, primarily attracted to gay or gay-appearing males. She was uninterested in relationships with women, except perhaps as purely sexual encounters of short duration. (Adapted from Dickey & Stephens, 1995, pp. 442–443)

Causes of Gender Identity Disorder

The genetic sex of an individual is determined at conception by the chromosomes received from the mother and father, but sexual development from that point on is influenced by many factors (Becker & Kavoussi, 1996). For the first few weeks of gestation, the gonads and internal and external genital structures are neither male nor female. If the Y chromosome is present, the gonads of the embryo will differentiate into testes. Then they will secrete testosterone, and male genitalia will develop in the fetus. If the Y chromosome is not present, the gonads will develop into ovaries, which will not secrete androgen, and female genitalia will develop.

Biological theories of gender identity disorder have focused on the effects of prenatal hormones on brain development (Bradley, 1995b; Bradley & Zucker, 1997). Although several different specific mechanisms have been implicated, in general these theories suggest that people who develop gender identity disorder were exposed to unusual levels of hormones that influence later gender identity and sexual orientation by influencing the development of the hypothalamus and other brain structures involved in sexuality. These brain/hormone theories were bolstered when reports were published in the early 1990s of differences between homosexual and heterosexual men in the anterior hypothalamus (LeVay, 1993). To date, these reports have not been well replicated by other investigators, however. The relevance of studies of biological factors in homosexuality to gender identity disorder is not always clear, as well.

One of the few studies directly focusing on transsexuals found significant differences between male transsexuals and a group of normal men in a cluster of cells in the hypothalamus called the bed nucleus of stria terminalis (Zhou et al., 1995). This cluster of cells was half as large in the transsexuals as in the normal men. Typically, this cluster of cells is smaller in women's brains than in men's, and the male transsexuals' cluster of cells was close to the size usually found in women's brains. This cluster of cells is known to play a role in sexual behavior, at least in male rats. Thus, it may be that the size of this cell cluster in the hypothalamus plays a role in gender identity disorder, at least in men.

Another group of studies that suggested that prenatal hormones play a role in gender identity disorder focused on girls who were exposed to elevated levels of testosterone in utero. Most of these girls are born with some degree of masculinazation of their genitalia, which is treated early in infancy through surgical correction and hormone replacement, then they are raised as girls. Studies have suggested that these girls tend to have more "tomboyish" or masculine behavior than other girls (Berenbaum & Hines, 1992; Slijper et al., 1998). In addition, more of these girls have a homosexual or bisexual sexual orientation than girls not exposed to testosterone in utero (Dittman et al., 1992; Money & Schwartz, 1977). Most of these girls do identify themselves as female, but they are at increased risk for gender identity disorder (Slijper et al., 1998). This lends some support to a prenatal hormone theory of gender identity disorder, although in general, the evidence has been somewhat weak (Bradley & Zucker, 1997).

Most of the psychosocial theories of gender identity disorder focus on the role parents play in shaping their children's gender identity. Parents encourage children to identify with one sex or the other, by reinforcing "gender-appropriate" behavior and punishing "gender-inappropriate" behavior. From early infancy, they buy male or female clothes for their children and sex-stereotyped toys (dolls or trucks). They will encourage or discourage rough-and-tumble play or playing with dolls. In a long-term study of a large sample of boys with gender identity disorder, Green (1986) found that their parents were less likely than the parents of normal boys to discourage cross-gender behaviors. That is, these boys were not punished, subtly or overtly, for engaging in feminine behavior such as playing with dolls or wearing dresses as much as boys who did not have gender identity disorder. Further, boys who were highly feminine (although did not necessarily have gender identity disorder) tended to have mothers who had wanted a girl rather than a boy, saw their baby sons as girls, and dressed their baby sons as girls. When the boys were older, their mothers tended to prohibit rough-and-tumble play, and the boys had few opportunities to have male playmates. About one-third of these boys had no father in the home, and those who did have fathers in the home tended to be very close to their mothers.

Other studies suggest that another factor in gender identity disorder, in addition to the reinforcements parents give for gender identification in their children, is parental psychopathology (Bradley, 1995b; Marantz & Coates, 1991). Significant percentages of the parents of children with gender identity disorder suffer from depression, severe anxiety, or personality disorders. It may be that these parents create a difficult emotional atmosphere in the home which makes the child anxious and unsure of himself. Then, if the parent reinforces the child for cross-gendered behavior, the child may be especially likely to adopt a cross-gendered identity as a way of pleasing parents and reducing his own anxiety.

In general, however, the evidence for various theories of gender identity disorder has been weak. Most theorists believe that gender identity is the result of a number of biological and social factors, including chromosomes, hormones, and socialization. Gender identity disorder could result from variations in development of any of these factors.

Treatments for Gender Identity Disorder

Therapists who work with people with gender identity disorder tend not to try to "cure" them by convincing them to accept the body with which they were born and the gender associated with that body (Bradley, 1995b). This tactic simply does not work with most people with gender identity disorder. The therapist will help these individuals clarify their gender identity and sexual orientation. Some people with gender identity disorder choose to undergo gender reassignment treatment, which provides them with the genitalia and secondary sex characteristics (e.g., breasts) of the gender with which they identify. Gender reassignment cannot change their chromosomes, however, nor can it allow people born male to have children eventually or people born female to impregnate a woman.

Gender reassignment requires a series of surgeries and hormone treatments, often taking 2 or more years. Before undertaking any of these medical procedures, patients are usually asked to dress and live in their new gender for a year or two, to ensure that they are confident about their decisions before proceeding. Then a lifetime of hormone treatments is begun. Male-to-female transsexuals take estrogen, which fosters the development of female secondary sex characteristics. This drug causes fatty deposits to develop in the breasts and hips, softens the skin, and inhibits growth of a beard. Female-to-male transsexuals take androgens, which promote male secondary sex characteristics. This drug causes the voice to deepen, hair to become distributed in a male pattern, fatty tissue in the breast to recede, and muscles to enlarge. The clitoris may grow larger.

Gender reassignment surgery is primarily cosmetic. In male-to-female surgery, the penis and testicles are removed, and tissue from the penis is used to create an artificial vagina. The construction of male genitals for a female-to-male reassignment is technically more difficult. First, the internal sex organs (ovaries, fallopian tubes, uterus) and any fatty tissue remaining in the breasts are removed. The urethra is rerouted through the enlarged clitoris, or an artificial penis and scrotum are constructed from tissue taken from other parts of the body. This penis allows for urination while standing, but cannot achieve a natural erection. Other procedures, such as artificial implants, may be used to create an erection.

Gender reassignment surgery has always been controversial. Some follow-up studies suggest that when patients are carefully selected for such sex reassignment procedures based on their motivation for change and their overall psychological health and given psychological counseling to assist them through the change, the outcome tends to be positive (Bradley & Zucker, 1997; Lindemalm, Korlin, & Uddenberg, 1986). Although many of these patients are unable to experience orgasm during sex, most are satisfied with their sex lives and are psychologically well adjusted to their new genders. Other studies suggest, however, that outcomes of this procedure are often not positive (Meyer & Reter, 1979).

Summing Up

- Gender identity disorder is diagnosed when individuals believe they were born with the wrong sex's genitals and are fundamentally persons of the opposite sex. This disorder in adults is also called transsexualism.
- Biological theories suggest that unusual exposure to prenatal hormones affects the development of the hypothalamus and other brain structures involved in sexuality, leading to gender identity disorder.
- Socialization theories suggest that parents of children (primarily boys) with gender identity disorder did not socialize "gender-appropriate" behaviors. Other theories suggest that parents of children who develop this disorder have high rates of psychopathology.
- Some people with this disorder undergo gender reassignment treatment to change their genitalia, and live as a member of the sex they believe they are.

☉ BIO-PSYCHO-SOCIAL INTEGRATION

Nowhere is the interplay of biological, psychological, and social forces more apparent than in matters of sexuality. Biological factors influence gender identity, sexual orientation, and sexual functioning. These factors can be greatly moderated by psychological and social factors, however. The meaning to people of a sexual dysfunction, an unusual sexual practice, or an atypical gender identity is heavily influenced by their attitudes toward their sexuality and by the reactions they get from people around them. In addition, as we saw with sexual dysfunctions, purely psychological and social conditions can cause a person's body to stop functioning as it normally would.

Chapter Summary

- The sexual response cycle can be divided into the desire, excitement, plateau, orgasm, and resolution phases. Sexual desire is manifested in sexual thoughts and fantasies, initiation of or participation in sexual activities, and awareness of sexual cues from others. The excitement phase consists of a psychological experience of arousal and pleasure and the physiological changes known as *vasocongestion* (filling of blood vessels and tissues with blood) and *myotonia* (muscle tension). During the plateau phase, excitement remains at a high but stable level. The excitement and plateau phases are followed by orgasm, which involves the discharge of the built-up neuromuscular tension. In males, orgasm involves rhythmic contractions of the prostate, seminal vesicles, vas deferens, and the entire length of the penis and urethra, accompanied by the ejaculation of semen. Males experience a refractory period following orgasm during which they cannot be aroused to another orgasm. In females, orgasm involves rhythmic contractions of the orgasmic platform and more irregular contractions of the uterus. Females do not have a refractory period. Following orgasm, the entire musculature of the body relaxes, and men and women tend to experience a state of deep relaxation, the stage known as *resolution*.

- Occasional problems with sexual functioning are extremely common. To qualify for a diagnosis of a sexual dysfunction, a person must be experiencing a problem that causes significant distress or interpersonal difficulty, that is not the result of another Axis I disorder, and that is not due exclusively to the direct effects of substance use or medical illness. The psychological factors leading to sexual dysfunction most commonly involve negative attitudes toward sex, traumatic or stressful experiences, or conflicts with sexual partners. A variety of biological factors, including medical illnesses, side effects of drugs, nervous system injury, and hormonal deficiencies, can cause sexual dysfunctions.

- Sexual desire disorders (hypoactive sexual desire disorder and sexual aversion disorder) are among the most common sexual dysfunctions. Persons with these disorders experience chronically lowered or absent desire for sex. The sexual arousal disorders include female sexual arousal disorder and male erectile disorder (formerly called *impotence*). Women with female orgasmic disorder experience a persistent or recurrent delay in or complete absence of orgasm, after having reached the excitement phase of the sexual response cycle. Men with premature ejaculation persistently experience ejaculation (after minimal sexual stimulation) before, on, or shortly after penetration and before they wish it. Men with male orgasmic disorder experience a persistent or recurrent delay in or absence of orgasm following the excitement phase of the sexual response cycle. The sexual pain disorders include dyspareunia, which is genital pain associated with intercourse, and vaginismus, in which a woman experiences involuntary contraction of the muscles surrounding the outer third of the vaginal when the vagina is penetrated.

- Fortunately, most of the sexual dysfunctions can be treated successfully. The psychological treatments combine psychotherapy focused on the personal concerns of the individual with the dysfunction and on the conflicts between the individual and his or her partner and sex therapy designed to decrease inhibitions about sex and to teach new techniques for optimal sexual enjoyment. One important set of techniques is sensate focus exercises. First, partners spend time gently touching each other, focusing on the sensations and communicating what feels good, without touching the genitals. Second, partners spend time in direct genital stimulation but without attempting to have intercourse. Third, partners begin having intercourse but remaining focused on enhancing and sustaining pleasure rather than on orgasm and performance.

- Men with premature ejaculation can be helped with the stop-start technique or the squeeze technique. In the stop-start technique, a man repeatedly halts stimulation of his penis just before ejaculation until he can control his level of arousal and the timing of ejaculation. In the squeeze technique, a man's partner squeezes the base or top section of his penis just before ejaculation, again until the man learns to control his level of arousal and timing of ejaculation.

- The paraphilias are a group of disorders in which the focus of the individual's sexual urges and activities are (1) nonhuman objects, (2) nonconsenting adults, (3) suffering or humiliation of oneself or one's partner, or (4) children. Pedophiles seek sexual gratification with young children. Most pedophiles are heterosexual men seeking sex with young girls. Many pedophiles have poor interpersonal skills, feel intimidated when interacting sexually with adults, and are victims of childhood sexual abuse. Others harbor strong hostility toward women and carry out this hostility in antisocial acts toward children. The impact of sexual abuse by a pedophile on a child is great, sometimes extending throughout the child's life.

- Voyeurism involves secretly watching another person undressing, bathing, doing things in the nude, or engaged in sex as a preferred or exclusive form of sexual arousal. To qualify for a diagnosis, the voyeuristic behavior must be repetitive and compulsive. The person being observed must be unaware of it and would be upset if he or she knew about it. Almost all voyeurs are men who watch women. Voyeurs typically masturbate during or shortly after watching women.

- Exhibitionism is in some ways the mirror image of voyeurism. The exhibitionist obtains sexual gratification by exposing his or her genitals to involuntary observers who are usually complete strangers. In the vast majority of cases, the exhibitionist is a man who bares all to surprised women. He typically confronts women in public places, such as a park, a bus, or a subway, either with his genitals already exposed or by flashing open his coat to expose his bare genitals. He then may begin to openly masturbate. His arousal comes from observing the victim's surprise, fear, or disgust. His behavior is often compulsive and impulsive: He feels a sense of excitement, fear, restlessness, and sexual arousal and then feels compelled to find relief by exhibiting himself.

- Frotteurism is another paraphilia that often co-occurs with voyeurism and exhibitionism. The frotteurist gains sexual gratification by rubbing against and fondling parts of the body of a nonconsenting person. In order to qualify for a diagnosis, this behavior has to be repetitive and compulsive and represent a preferred way of gaining sexual gratification.

- The sexual sadist gains sexual gratification by inflicting pain and humiliation on his or her sex partner. The sexual masochist gains sexual gratification by suffering pain or humiliation during sex. Some people occasionally engage in moderately sadistic or masochistic behaviors during sex or simulate such behaviors without actually carrying through with the infliction of pain or suffering. Persons who are diagnosed as sexual sadists or masochists engage in these behaviors as their preferred or exclusive forms of sexual gratification. The sexual rituals of sadists and masochists typically involve practices of bondage and domination.

- The final type of paraphilia is fetishism, which involves the use of isolated body parts or inanimate objects as the preferred or exclusive sources of sexual arousal or gratification. A particular form of fetish is transvestism, in which an individual dresses in clothes of the opposite sex (usually involving a man dressing in women's clothes) in order to become sexually aroused.

- Gender identity disorder is diagnosed when an individual believes that he or she was born with the wrong sex's genitals and is fundamentally a person of the opposite sex. Gender identity disorder of childhood is a rare condition in which a child persistently rejects his or her anatomic sex and desires to be or insists he or she is a member of the opposite sex. Gender identity disorder in adulthood is referred to as *transsexualism*. Transsexuals experience a chronic discomfort and sense of inappropriateness with their gender and genitals, wish to be rid of them, and want to live as members of the opposite sex. Transsexuals will often dress in the clothes of the opposite sex, but unlike transvestites, they do not do this to gain sexual arousal.

Key Terms

sexual dysfunction 524

sexual desire 524

arousal phase 524

vasocongestion 524

myotonia 525

plateau phase 525

orgasm 525

resolution 526

hypoactive sexual desire disorder 530

sexual aversion disorder 531

sexual arousal disorders 531

female sexual arousal disorder 531

male erectile disorder 531

female orgasmic disorder 532

premature ejaculation 532

male orgasmic disorder 533

dyspareunia 533

vaginismus 533

substance-induced sexual dysfunction 536

performance anxiety 537

sensate focus therapy 542

stop-start technique 542

squeeze technique 543

paraphilias 549

fetishism 550

transvestism 550

sexual sadism 551

sexual masochism 551

sadomasochism 551

voyeurism 552

exhibitionism 552

frotteurism 553

pedophilia 553

aversion therapy 556

desensitization 556

gender identity 557

gender role 557

sexual orientation 557

gender identity disorder 557

transsexualism 560

Critical Thinking Questions

1. If you were the parent of a teenager, how would you talk with your teenager about sex to help him or her develop a healthy perspective on sex?

2. If a person with a fetish such as a shoe fetish never harms anyone else and is not distressed about his or her behavior, should he or she be diagnosed with a psychological disorder?

3. What kinds of personality characteristics might differentiate people who find sadomasochistic practices sexually arousing from people who do not?

4. If pedophiles do have a psychological disorder, should they be held criminally responsible for their behaviors? How should they be dealt with if caught?

George E. Dunne
The Ferryman's

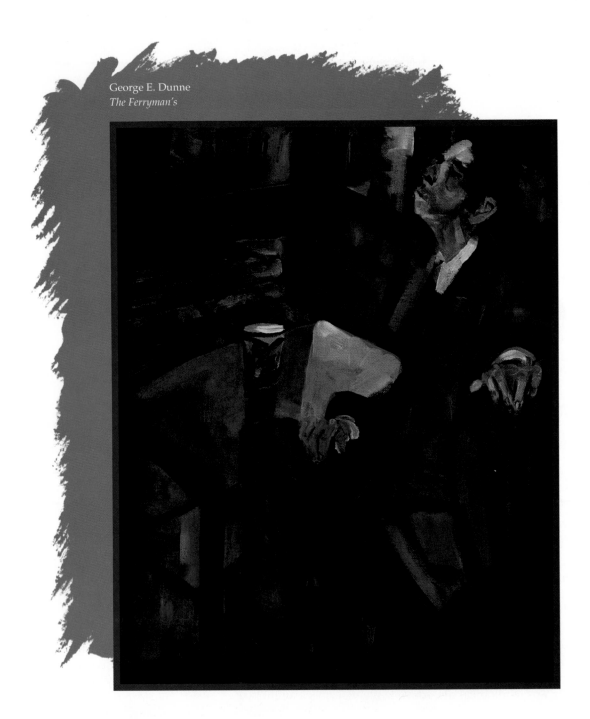

Refrain to-night,
And that shall lend a kind of easiness
To the next abstinence; the next more easy;
For use almost can change the stamp of nature.

—William Shakespeare, Hamlet *(3:4:165; 1600)*

CHAPTER 16

Substance-Related Disorders

CHAPTER OVERVIEW

Defining Substance-Related Disorders

Substance intoxication and withdrawal are characteristic behavioral and physical symptoms resulting from substance use. Substance abuse and dependence are diagnosed when substance use significantly interfers with an individual's functioning. Dependence also may involve the development of tolerance to substances.

Depressants

The depressants include alcohol, benzodiazepines, barbiturates, and inhalants. They produce the symptoms of depression and cognitive impairment.

Taking Psychology Personally:
Tips for Responsible Drinking

Stimulants

The stimulants—cocaine, amphetamines, nicotine, and caffeine—activate the central nervous system and parts of the brain that register pleasure.

Opioids

The opioids—morphine and heroin—cause euphoria, lethargy, unconsciousness, and seizures, and can be highly addictive.

Extraordinary People:
Celebrity Drug Abusers

Hallucinogens and PCP

The hallucinogens and PCP produce perceptual illusions and distortions and symptoms ranging from a sense of peace and tranquillity to feelings of unreality and violence.

Cannabis

Cannabis creates a high feeling, cognitive and motor impairments, and in some people hallucinogenic effects.

Theories of Substance Use, Abuse, and Dependence

Biological theories attribute vulnerability to substance disorders largely to genetic predispositions. Psychosocial theories focus on environmental reinforcements and beliefs that support substance use.

Pushing the Boundaries:
Finding the Gene for Smoking

Treatment for Substance-Related Disorders

Detoxification is the first step in treatment. Drugs may aid in withdrawal and abstinence. Alcoholics Anonymous is a widely used treatment. Behavioral and cognitive treatments extinguish substance use behaviors and change thoughts that motivate substance use.

Bio-Psycho-Social Integration
Chapter Summary
Key Terms
Critical Thinking Questions

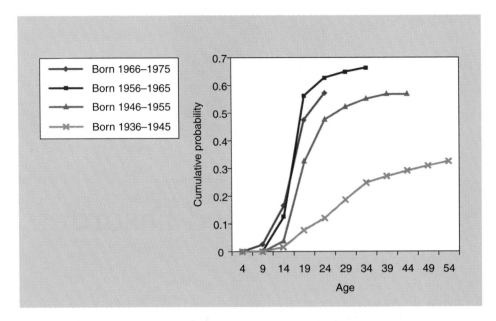

FIGURE 16.1   Cumulative Probability of Using Illegal Drugs in Four Generations. People born in more recent generations are much more likely to have used an illegal drug at some time in their lives than people born in earlier generations.

Source: Warner et al., 1995, Figure 1, p. 223.

A **substance** is any natural or synthesized product that has psychoactive effects—it changes perceptions, thoughts, emotions, and behaviors. Some of the substances we discuss in this chapter are cocaine, heroin, and amphetamines. These are popularly referred to as *drugs*, and people who have problems as a result of taking these drugs are often referred to as **drug addicts.** We use the more neutral term *substance*, however, because some of the disorders we discuss in this chapter involve substances that you might not normally think of as drugs, such as nicotine and alcohol. Also, as we see, a person need not be physically dependent on a substance, as is implied by the term *addict*, in order to have problems resulting from taking the substance.

The prevalence of illegal substance use and abuse increased substantially in the last four decades. People who were teenagers in the 1960s and more recent generations are much more likely to have tried illegal substances such as marijuana, cocaine, or heroin at some time in their lives than their parents or grandparents (see Figure 16.1). In the mid-1990s, fully one-half of the U.S. population admitted to having tried an illegal substance at some time in their lives, and an average of 15 percent had used one in the past year (see Figure 16.2; Warner et al., 1995). Most people who ever use an illegal substance do so before the age of 20. Surveys find that about 20 percent of adolescents have tried an illegal substance by age 17, and 46 percent of young adults have tried an illegal substance by the age of 25 (NIDA, 1995; Warner et al., 1995).

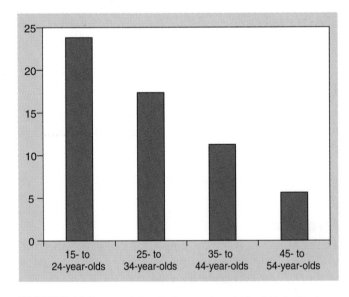

FIGURE 16.2   Use of Illegal Substances in a 12-Month Period in the United States. This figure shows the percentage of the U.S. population that used an illegal substance or used a prescription medication against a physician's instructions in the previous 12 months.

Source: Warner et al., 1995, Table 2, p. 222.

Much substance use by adolescents and young adults is experimental—typically, young people try alcohol or marijuana and maybe even heroin or cocaine a few times but do not use them chronically or continue to use them as they grow older. Some substances, however, have such powerful reinforcing effects on the brain that many people who try these substances, even experimentally, find themselves craving more of the substances and have a difficult time resisting taking the substances. In addition, some people have a greater vulnerability to becoming "hooked" psychologically or physically on substances, so even a little experimentation may be very dangerous for them.

☉ SOCIETY AND SUBSTANCE USE

Societies differ in their attitudes about substances with psychoactive effects, some seeing use as a matter of individual choice and others seeing it as a grave public health and security concern. These attitudes are reflected in different laws and approaches to treatment (Goldstein, 1994; MacCoun, 1998). Many Muslim countries following Islamic law strictly prohibit alcohol and enforce penalties against people caught using this or any other substance. When the Communists took over China in the late 1940s, they made it a major goal to eradicate the widespread use of opium. Traffickers were executed, and users were sent to the countryside for rehabilitation and reeducation. Today, antidrug laws are still strictly enforced, and punishments for the use or sale of illicit substances remain severe.

In Great Britain, substance addiction is considered a medical disease, and abusers and dependents are treated by physicians. Although traffickers in illegal substances are aggressively prosecuted by the British government, users of illegal substances are more often referred for treatment than arrested for possession of substances. Heroin use is as prevalent as it is in the United States, but physicians in Great Britain are more comfortable with long-term methadone maintenance than are physicians in the United States.

The Dutch make a distinction in their law enforcement between "soft" drugs (such as cannabis) and "hard" drugs (such as cocaine and heroin). Although both types of substances are illegal, possession, use, and sale of cannabis is rarely prosecuted, whereas the importing, manufacture, and sale of the hard substances are subject to heavy penalties that are enforced. The Dutch system is based on the belief that enforcing a strict prohibition of softer drugs would drive users underground, where they would come into contact with persons trafficking in harder drugs and be more likely to begin using these drugs.

Zurich, Switzerland, became famous for its "needle park," where the sale and use of substances including heroin and cocaine were carried out in the open and allowed by authorities, while a doctor employed by the government stood by in a small kiosk to handle any emergencies and to distribute clean needles for injection of substances. Opponents of the park argued that it made it extremely easy for troubled young people to become part of the drug scene and generally legitimized illicit drug use. In 1992, the park was closed because of evidence that addicts from around Europe had poured into the city and crime had soared.

Within the United States, attitudes toward substance use have varied greatly over time and across different subgroups. The American ambivalence toward alcohol use is nicely illustrated in a letter written by former Congressman Billy Mathews in response to a question from one of his constituents: "Dear Congressman, how do you stand on whiskey?" Because the congressman did not know how the constituent stood on alcohol, he fashioned the following safe response (quoted in Marlatt et al., 1993, p. 462):

> My dear friend, I had not intended to discuss this controversial subject at this particular time. However, I want you to know that I do not shun a controversy. On the contrary, I will take a stand on any issue at any time, regardless of how fraught with controversy it may be. You have asked me how I feel about whiskey. Here is how I stand on the issue.
>
> If when you say whiskey, you mean the Devil's brew; the poison scourge; the bloody monster that defiles innocence, dethrones reason, destroys the home, creates misery, poverty, fear; literally takes the bread from the mouths of little children; if you mean the evil drink that topples the Christian man and woman from the pinnacles of righteous, gracious living into the bottomless pit of degradation and despair, shame and helplessness and hopelessness; then certainly, I am against it with all of my power.
>
> But, if when you say whiskey, you mean the oil of conversation, the philosophic wine, the ale that is assumed when great fellows get together, that puts a song in their hearts and laughter on their lips, and the warm glow of contentment in their eyes; if you mean Christmas cheer; if you mean that stimulating drink that puts the spring in the old gentlemen's step on a frosty morning; if you mean the drink that enables the man to magnify his joy and his happiness and to forget, if only for a little while, life's great tragedies and heartbreaks and sorrows; if you mean that drink, the sale of which pours into our Treasury untold millions of dollars which are used to provide tender care for little crippled children, our blind, our deaf, our pitiful aged and infirm; to build highways, hospitals, and schools; then certainly, I am in favor of it. This is my stand, and I will not compromise. Your congressman.

Many substances come from plants and have been used for medicinal purposes for centuries. As long ago as 1500 B.C., natives in the Andes highlands chewed coca leaves to increase their endurance (Co-cores, Pottash, & Gold, 1991). Coca leaves can be manufactured into cocaine. Cocaine was used legally throughout Europe and then America into the twentieth century to relieve fatigue and was an ingredient in the original Coca-Cola drink and over 50 other widely available drinks and elixirs.

Opium, a milky juice produced from the poppy plant, has been used for hundreds of years to relieve pain, particularly in Asian and European countries. The leaves of a plant called *khat* have been chewed in parts of eastern Africa, the Middle East, and South America for hundreds of years to produce a sense of well-being and relief from fatigue. Today, modern derivatives of khat are used to make amphetamines, a class of drugs used to treat attention-deficit/hyperactivity disorder, narcolepsy, and obesity and included in over-the-counter cold remedies and appetite suppressants for weight control.

Substances have also been used for religious ceremonies to produce psychological changes important for the ceremonies. For example, the peyote cactus contains a substance that, when chewed, causes people to experience visual hallucinations, in the form of brightly colored lights, or vivid kaleidoscopic visions of geometric forms or of animals and people. The Aztecs and other native groups in Mexico and the Kiowa, Comanche, and other native groups in the United States and Canada have used peyote as part of religious rituals for hundreds of years.

When substances are used not as part of medical treatments or religious or ceremonial rituals but by individuals to change their moods, thoughts, and perceptions, other members of society begin to get nervous. This is because some individuals have great difficulty in using substances in moderation and begin to build their lives around using the substances. Their use of substances may lead to significant problems in their abilities to function in their daily lives—they may shirk their job and family responsibilities, they may act impulsively or bizarrely, and they may endanger their own lives and the lives of others. Such a person is said to have a **substance-related disorder.**

Societies have strong motivations for regulating the use of psychoactive substances. In the United States alone, the use of psychoactive substances for nonmedicinal and nonreligious purposes costs society over $200 billion a year in accidents, crime, health care costs, and lost productivity (Goldstein, 1994). Illnesses and accidents associated with alcohol alone result in about $6 billion in inpatient hospital costs and nearly $2 billion in outpatient medical costs. Alcohol is associated with over half of the deaths due to traffic accidents and homicides, and 30 percent of all suicides (Hunt, 1998).

DEFINING SUBSTANCE-RELATED DISORDERS

There are four substance-related conditions recognized by the DSM-IV: *substance intoxication, substance withdrawal, substance abuse,* and *substance dependence* (see *Concept Review:* Definitions of Substance Intoxication, Withdrawal, Abuse, and Dependence). In the first part of this chapter, we discuss the criteria for each of these conditions. In the remainder of this chapter, we discuss how these conditions are manifested in the context of the substances most commonly linked to them. These substances can be grouped into the following categories: (1) central nervous system depressants, including alcohol, barbiturates, benzodiazepines, and inhalants; (2) opioids, including heroin and morphine; (3) central nervous system stimulants, including cocaine, amphetamines, nicotine, and caffeine; (4) hallucinogens, phencyclidine (PCP); and (5) cannabis. Intoxication, withdrawal, abuse, and dependence can occur with most although not all of these substances (see Table 16.1).

There are many other substances used for intoxicating effects that more rarely lead to substance-related disorders (see Table 16.2). Although most people exposed to the substances listed in Table 16.2 either experience no psychoactive effects or only mild and transient effects, some people experience significant problems in cognition and mood, anxiety, hallucinations, delusions, and seizures when exposed. These people may be given the diagnosis of *other substance-related disorder.*

After we discuss specific substances and the disorders associated with them, we discuss theories of why some people are more prone than others to develop substance-related disorders, examining gender and cultural differences. Then we discuss what treatments are available for people with substance-related disorders. Most of these theories and treatments focus on people with alcohol-related disorders but have been adapted for people with other disorders.

Intoxication

Substance intoxication is a set of behavioral and psychological changes that occur as a direct result of the physiological effects of a substance on the central nervous system. When people are intoxicated, their perceptions change and they may see or hear strange things. Their attention is often diminished or they are easily distracted. Their good judgment is gone and they may be unable to "think straight." They cannot control their bodies as well as they normally can, and they may stumble or be too slow or awkward in their

CONCEPT REVIEW

Definitions of Substance Intoxication, Withdrawal, Abuse, and Dependence

These definitions of substance intoxication, withdrawal, abuse, and dependence apply across a variety of substances, but the specific symptoms will depend on the substance used.

Substance intoxication	Experience of significant maladaptive behavioral and psychological symptoms due to the effect of a substance on the central nervous system
Substance withdrawal	Experience of clinically significant distress in social, occupational, or other areas of functioning due to the cessation or reduction of substance use
Substance abuse	Diagnosis given when recurrent substance use leads to significant harmful consequences (see Table 16.3)
Substance dependence	Diagnosis given when substance use leads to physiological dependence or significant impairment or distress (see Table 16.4)

Source: DSM-IV, APA, 2000.

TABLE 16.1

DSM-IV Diagnosis for Each Class of Substances

	Intoxication	Withdrawal	Abuse	Dependence
Alcohol	X	X	X	X
Barbiturates	X	X	X	X
Benzodiazepines	X	X	X	X
Inhalants	X		X	X
Cocaine	X	X	X	X
Amphetamines	X	X	X	X
Caffeine	X			
Opioids	X	X	X	X
Hallucinogens	X		X	X
Phencyclidine	X		X	X
Cannabis	X		X	X
Nicotine		X		X

TABLE 16.2

DSM-IV
Other Substances That Can Lead to Substance Use Disorders

Anesthetics or analgesics	Muscle relaxants
Anticholinergic agents	Nonsteroidal anti-inflammatory medications
Anticonvulsants	Antidepressant medications
Antihistamines	Lead
Blood pressure medications	Rat poisons with strychnine
Antimicrobial medications	Pesticides
Anti-Parkinsonian medications	Nerve gas
Corticosteroids	Antifreeze
Gastrointestinal medications	Carbon monoxide or dioxide

reactions. They often either want to sleep a lot or not at all. Their interpersonal interactions change—they may become more gregarious than usual, more withdrawn, or more aggressive and impulsive. People begin to be intoxicated soon after they begin ingesting a substance, and the more they ingest, the more intoxicated they become. Intoxication begins to decline as the amount of substance in people's blood or tissue declines, but symptoms of intoxication may last for hours or days after the substance is no longer detectable in the body.

The specific symptoms of intoxication depend on what substance is taken, how much is taken, how long the substance has been ingested, and the user's tolerance for the substance. Short-term or acute intoxication can produce different symptoms from chronic intoxication. For example, the first time people take a moderate dose of cocaine, they may be outgoing, friendly, and very upbeat. With chronic use over days or weeks, they may begin to withdraw socially and become less gregarious. People's expectations about a substance's effects can also influence the types of symptoms shown. People who expect marijuana to make them relaxed may experience relaxation, whereas people who are frightened of the disinhibition that marijuana creates may experience anxiety, as happened with the woman in the following case study (adapted from Spitzer et al., 1994, pp. 204–205):

Each substance causes characteristic symptoms of intoxication and most cause symptoms of withdrawal.

CASE STUDY

In the middle of a rainy October night, a family doctor in a Chicago suburb was awakened by an old friend who begged him to get out of bed and come quickly to a neighbor's house, where he and his wife had been visiting. The caller, Lou Wolff, was very upset because his wife, Sybil, had smoked some marijuana and was "freaking out."

The doctor arrived at the neighbor's house to find Sybil lying on the couch looking quite frantic, unable to get up. She said she was too weak to stand, that she was dizzy, was having palpitations, and could feel her blood "rushing through [her] veins." She kept asking for water because her mouth was so dry she could not swallow. She was sure there was some poison in the marijuana.

Sybil, age 42, was the mother of three teenage boys. She worked as a librarian at a university. She was a very controlled, well-organized woman who prided herself on her rationality. It was she who had asked the neighbors to share some of their high-quality homegrown marijuana with her, because marijuana was a big thing with the students and she "wanted to see what all the fuss was about."

Her husband said that she took four or five puffs on a joint and then wailed, "There's something wrong with me. I can't stand up." Lou and the neighbors tried to calm her, telling her she should just lie down and she would soon feel better; but the more they reassured her, the more convinced she became that something was really wrong with her.

The doctor examined her. The only positive findings were that her heart rate was increased and her pupils dilated. He said to her, "For heaven's sake, Sybil, you're just a little stoned. Go home to bed."

Sybil did go home to bed, where she stayed for 2 days, feeling "spacey" and weak but no longer terribly anxious. She recovered completely and vowed never to smoke marijuana again.

The environment or setting in which the substance is taken can influence the types of symptoms people develop. For example, when people consume a few alcoholic drinks at a party, they may become uninhibited and loud, but when they consume the same amount at home alone, they may become simply tired and depressed. The environment in which people become intoxicated can also influence how maladaptive the intoxication is: People who only drink alcohol at home may be at less risk for causing harm to themselves or others than are people who typically drink at bars and drive home under the influence of alcohol.

Most people have been intoxicated, usually with alcohol, at some time in their lives. The diagnosis of substance intoxication is only given when the behavioral and psychological changes the person experiences are significantly maladaptive in that they cause substantial disruption in the person's social and family relationships, cause occupational or financial problems, or place the individual at significant risk for adverse effects, such as traffic accidents, severe medical complications, or legal problems.

Withdrawal

Substance withdrawal involves a set of physiological and behavioral symptoms that result when people who have been using substances heavily for prolonged periods of time stop using the substances or greatly reduce their use. The symptoms of withdrawal from a given substance are typically the opposite of the symptoms of intoxication with the same substance. The diagnosis of substance withdrawal is not made unless the withdrawal symptoms cause significant distress or impairment in a person's everyday functioning. For example, although the symptoms of caffeine withdrawal (nervousness, headaches) are annoying to many people, they do not typically cause significant impairment in people's functioning or great distress, and thus caffeine withdrawal is not included as a diagnostic category in the DSM-IV.

The symptoms of withdrawal can begin a few hours after a person stops ingesting a substance or substances that break down quickly in the body, such as alcohol and heroin. The more intense symptoms of withdrawal usually end within a few days to a few weeks. However, withdrawal symptoms, including seizures, may develop several weeks after a person stops taking high doses of substances that take a long time to completely eliminate from the body, such as some antianxiety substances. In addition, subtle physiological signs of withdrawal, such as problems in attention, perception, or motor skills, may be present for many weeks or months after a person stops using a substance.

Abuse

The diagnosis of **substance abuse** is given when a person's recurrent use of a substance results in significant harmful consequences. There are four categories of

People dependent on a substance may do anything—including engage in prostitution—to get money to buy their substance.

TABLE 16.3
DSM-IV
Criteria for Diagnosing Substance Abuse

The criteria for substance abuse require repeated problems as a result of the use of a substance.

One or more of the following occurs during a 12-month period, leading to significant impairment or distress:

1. failure to fulfill important obligations at work, home, or school as a result of substance use

2. repeated use of the substance in situations in which it is physically hazardous to do so

3. repeated legal problems as a result of substance use

4. continued use of the substance despite repeated social or legal problems as a result of use

Reprinted with permission from the *Diagnostic and Statistical Manual of Mental Disorders*, Fourth Edition. Copyright © 1994 American Psychiatric Association.

harmful consequences that suggest substance abuse (see Table 16.3; APA, 2000). First, the individual *fails to fulfill important obligations* at work, school, or home. He or she may fail to show up at work or for classes, be unable to concentrate and therefore perform poorly, and perhaps even take the substance at work or at school. Second, the individual *repeatedly uses the substance in situations in which it is physically hazardous to do so*, such as while driving a car or a boat. Third, the individual *repeatedly has legal problems as a result of substance use*, such as arrests for possession of illegal substances or for drunk driving. Fourth, the individual *continues to use the substance even though he or she has repeatedly had social or legal problems as a result of the use*. A person has to show repeated problems in at least one of these categories within a 12-month period to qualify for a diagnosis of substance abuse. For some people, abuse of a particular group of substances evolves into dependence on those substances. In such cases, the diagnosis of substance dependence preempts the diagnosis of substance abuse, since dependence is considered a more advanced condition than abuse. Some individuals abuse substances for years without ever becoming dependent on them, however.

Dependence

The diagnosis of **substance dependence** is closest to what people often refer to as *drug addiction* (see Table 16.4, p. 574). A person is *physiologically dependent* on a substance when he or she shows either tolerance or withdrawal from the substance. **Tolerance** is present when a person experiences less and less effect from the same dose of a substance and needs greater and

TABLE 16.4
DSM-IV
Criteria for Diagnosing Substance Dependence

Substance dependence often involves evidence of physiological dependence plus repeated problems due to use of the substance.

Maladaptive pattern of substance use, leading to three or more of the following:

1. tolerance, as defined by either

    a. the need for markedly increased amounts of the substance to achieve intoxication or desired effect

    b. markedly diminished effect with continued use of the same amount of the substance

2. withdrawal, as manifested by either

    a. the characteristic withdrawal syndrome for the substance

    b. the same or a closely related substance is taken to relieve or avoid withdrawal symptoms

3. the substance is often taken in larger amounts or over a longer period than was intended

4. there is a persistent desire or unsuccessful efforts to cut down or control substance use

5. a great deal of time is spent in activities necessary to obtain the substance, use the substance, or recover from its effects

6. important social, occupational, or recreational activities are given up or reduced because of substance use

7. the substance use is continued despite knowledge of having a persistent or recurrent physical or psychological problem caused by or exacerbated by the substance

Reprinted with permission from the *Diagnostic and Statistical Manual of Mental Disorders*, Fourth Edition. Copyright © 2000 American Psychiatric Association.

greater doses of a substance in order to achieve intoxication. People who have smoked cigarettes for years often smoke more than 20 cigarettes a day, when that same amount would have made them violently ill when they first began smoking. A person who is highly tolerant to a substance may have a very high blood level of the substance without being aware of any effects of the substance. For example, people who are highly tolerant to alcohol may have blood alcohol levels far above those used in the legal definition of intoxication but show few signs of alcohol intoxication. The risk of tolerance varies greatly from one substance to the next. Alcohol, opioids, stimulants, and nicotine have high risks of tolerance, whereas cannabis and PCP appear to have lower risks of tolerance.

People who are physiologically dependent on substances will often show severe withdrawal symptoms when they stop using the substances. The symptoms may be so severe that the substances must be withdrawn gradually in order to prevent the symptoms from becoming overwhelming or dangerous. These people may take the substances to relieve or avoid withdrawal symptoms. For example, a person dependent on alcohol may have a drink first thing in the morning to relieve a hangover.

Physiological dependence (i.e., evidence of tolerance or withdrawal) is not required for a diagnosis of substance dependence, however. The diagnosis can be given when a person compulsively uses a substance, despite experiencing significant social, occupational, psychological, or medical problems as a result of that use.

Most people who are dependent on a substance crave the substance and will often do almost anything to get the substance (steal, lie, prostitute themselves) when the craving is strong. Their entire lives may revolve around obtaining and ingesting the substance. They may have attempted repeatedly to cut back on or quit using the substance, only to find themselves compulsively taking the substance again. Lucy is physically and psychologically dependent on both heroin and crack cocaine (adapted from Inciardi, Lockwood, & Pottieger, 1993, pp. 160–161).

CASE STUDY
By the time Lucy was 18, she was heavily addicted to heroin. Her mother took her to a detoxification program. After the 21-day regimen, Lucy was released but immediately relapsed to heroin use. By age 24, Lucy was mainlining heroin and turning tricks regularly to support both her and a boyfriend's drug habits. Lucy's boyfriend admitted himself to a drug rehabilitation program. When he completed his treatment stay, they both stopped their heroin use. However, they began snorting cocaine. Lucy

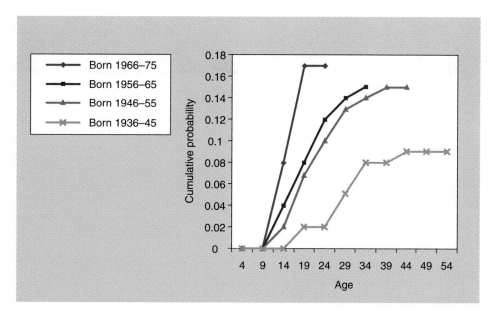

FIGURE 16.3 Cumulative Probability of Substance Dependence Among People Who Have Used Substances in Four Generations. People born in more recent generations are much more likely to be dependent on a substance if they have used substances at all than people born in earlier generations.
Source: Warner et al., 1995, Figure 2, p. 224.

left this boyfriend not too long afterwards. She went to work in a massage parlor, and the other women there introduced her to crack. This was 1984 and Lucy was 30 years old, a veteran drug addict and prostitute.

Lucy left the massage parlor and began working on the streets. Her crack use increased continually until 1986, when she tried to stop. In her opinion, crack was worse than heroin, so she started injecting narcotics again. But she never stopped using crack.

Because of her crack use, Lucy began doing things she had never even contemplated before, even while on heroin. For instance, she had anal sex and she sold herself for less money than ever before. She even began trading sex for drugs rather than money. Lucy also regularly worked in crack houses. She described them as "disgusting" and crowded. People would smoke and have sex in the same room in front of other people. Lucy insisted that her crack-house tricks rent rooms for sex, refusing to have sex in front of others. After having sex, Lucy would return to the stroll. Lucy would have five to seven customers a night, and most of the sex was oral. During this time, Lucy either stayed with her sister or slept in cars.

The way a substance is administered can be an important factor in determining how rapidly a person will become intoxicated and the likelihood that it will produce withdrawal symptoms or lead to abuse or dependence. Routes of administration that produce rapid and efficient absorption of the substance into the bloodstream lead to more intense intoxication and a greater likelihood of dependence. These include intravenous injection of the substance, smoking the

substance, or snorting the substance. These routes of administration are also more likely to lead to overdose. Some substances act more rapidly on the central nervous system and thus lead to faster intoxication and thus are more likely to lead to dependence or abuse. Finally, substances whose effects wear off quickly are more likely to lead to dependence or abuse than are substances whose effects are longer lasting.

Just as the rate of illegal substance use has increased in recent decades, the rate of substance dependence has as well (Warner et al., 1995). Figure 16.3 shows the cumulative probability of dependence on an illegal substance for four generations. Clearly, more recent generations are not only using more drugs, they are more likely to become dependent on drugs.

Let us turn now to discussing what intoxication, withdrawal, abuse, and dependence look like for the substances associated with substance disorders in the DSM-IV, beginning with the depressants, which include alcohol, benzodiazepines, barbiturates, and the inhalants.

☾ DEPRESSANTS

The depressants slow the activity of the central nervous system. In moderate doses, they make people relaxed and somewhat sleepy, reduce concentration, and impair thinking and motor skills. In heavy doses, they can induce stupor (see *Concept Review:* Intoxication with and Withdrawal from Depressants, p. 576).

CONCEPT REVIEW

Intoxication with and Withdrawal from Depressants

The depressants are among the most widely used substances.

Drug	Intoxication Symptoms	Withdrawal Symptoms
Alcohol, benzodiazepines, and barbiturates	Behavioral changes (e.g., inappropriate sexual or aggressive behavior, mood lability, impaired judgment) Slurred speech Incoordination Unsteady gait Nystagmus Attention and memory problems Stupor or coma	Autonomic hyperactivity (e.g., sweating or pulse rate greater than 100) Hand tremor Insomnia Nausea or vomiting Transient hallucinations or illusions Psychomotor agitation Anxiety Grand mal seizures
Inhalants	Behavioral changes (e.g., belligerence, assaultiveness, apathy, impaired judgment) Dizziness Involuntary rapid eyeball movements Incoordination Slurred speech Unsteady gait Lethargy Depressed reflexes Psychomotor retardation Tremor Muscle weakness Blurred vision Stupor or coma Euphoria	Not a diagnosis in DSM-IV

Source: DSM-IV, APA, 2000.

Alcohol

Alcohol is a classic central nervous system depressant, but its effects on the brain come in two distinct phases. In low doses, alcohol causes many people to feel more self-confident, more relaxed, and perhaps slightly euphoric. They may be less inhibited, and it may be this disinhibitory effect that many people find attractive. Indeed, people who do not experience the disinhibitory effects of alcohol tend not to drink at all (De-Wit, Pierri, & Johanson, 1989). At increasing doses, however, alcohol induces many of the symptoms of depression, including fatigue and lethargy, decreased motivation, sleep disturbances, depressed mood, and confusion. Also, although many people take alcohol to feel more sexy (mainly by reducing their sexual inhibitions), even low doses of alcohol can severely impair sexual functioning.

People who are intoxicated with alcohol slur their words, walk with unsteady gaits, have trouble paying attention or remembering things, and are slow and awkward in their physical reactions. They may act inappropriately, becoming aggressive, saying rude things, or taking off their clothes in public. Their moods may swing from exuberance to despair. With extreme intoxication, they may fall into stupors or comas. They will often not recognize they are intoxicated or may flatly deny it even though it is obvious. Once sober, they may have amnesia, known as a **blackout,** for the events that occurred while they were intoxicated.

One critical determinant of how quickly people become intoxicated with alcohol is whether their stomachs are full or empty. When the stomach is empty, alcohol is more quickly delivered from the stomach to the small intestine, where it is rapidly absorbed into the body. The person with a full stomach may drink significantly more drinks before reaching a dangerous blood-alcohol level or showing clear signs of intoxication. People in countries, such as France, where alcohol is almost always consumed with meals show lower rates of alcohol-related substance disorders than do people in countries such as the United States, where alcohol is often consumed on empty stomachs.

The legal definition of alcohol intoxication is much more narrow than the criteria for a diagnosis of alcohol intoxication. Most states in the United States consider a person to be under the influence of alcohol if his or her blood-alcohol level is above 0.05 or 0.10. As Table 16.5 (p. 578) indicates, it does not take very many drinks for most people to reach this blood-alcohol level. Deficits in attention, reaction time, and coordination arise even with the first drink and can interfere with the ability to operate a car or machinery safely and other tasks requiring a steady hand, coordination, clear thinking, and clear vision. These deficits are not always readily observable, even to trained observers (Winger, Hofman, & Woods, 1992). People often leave parties or bars with blood-alcohol levels well above the legal limit and dangerous deficits in their ability to drive, without appearing drunk.

Drinking large quantities of alcohol can result in death, even in people who are not chronic abusers of alcohol. About one-third of these deaths occur as a result of respiratory paralysis, usually as a result of a final large dose of alcohol in people who are already intoxicated. Alcohol can also interact fatally with a number of substances (Winger, Hofman, & Woods, 1992).

Most deaths due to alcohol, however, come from automobile accidents, private plane and boat accidents, and drownings. Nearly half of all fatal automobile accidents and deaths due to falls or fires and over a third of all drownings are alcohol related (Hunt,

1998). More than half of all murderers and their victims are believed to be intoxicated with alcohol at the time of the murders, and people who commit suicide often do so under the influence of alcohol.

In *Taking Psychology Personally:* Tips for Responsible Drinking (p. 579), we draw upon successful college-based programs to discuss the responsible use of alcohol.

Many people who have "a few too many" one night experience the next day what is commonly referred to as a *hangover*, including nausea, vomiting, headaches, and feelings of fatigue and dysphoria. These are symptoms of withdrawal from alcohol. Other symptoms are sweating and a fast pulse, hand tremors, insomnia, transient hallucinations or illusions, agitation, anxiety, and seizures. As we discuss shortly, people who are dependent on alcohol can experience life-threatening withdrawal symptoms.

Alcohol Abuse and Dependence

People given the diagnosis of **alcohol abuse** use alcohol in dangerous situations (such as when driving), fail to meet important obligations at work or at home as a result of their alcohol use, and have recurrent legal or social problems as a result of their alcohol use. People given the diagnosis of **alcohol dependence** typically have all the problems of an alcohol abuser, plus they may show physiological tolerance to alcohol; they spend a great deal of time intoxicated or withdrawing from alcohol, they often organize their lives around drinking, and they continue to drink despite having significant social, occupational, medical, or legal problems that result from drinking. The characteristics of alcohol

Drinking alcohol with food leads to slower absorption of the alcohol.

TABLE 16.5

Relationships Between Sex; Weight, Oral Alcohol Consumption, and Blood-Alcohol Level

It doesn't take very many drinks for most people to reach the blood-alcohol level of 0.05 or 0.10, which are the legal definitions of intoxication in most states.

Absolute Alcohol (ounces)	Beverage Intake*	Blood-Alcohol Level (percent)					
		Female (100 lb.)	Male (100 lb.)	Female (150 lb.)	Male (150 lb.)	Female (200 lb.)	Male (200 lb.)
1/2	1 oz spirits† 1 glass wine 1 can beer	0.045	0.037	0.03	0.025	0.022	0.019
1	2 oz. spirits 2 glasses wine 2 cans beer	0.090	0.075	0.06	0.050	0.045	0.037
2	4 oz. spirits 4 glasses wine 4 cans beer	0.180	0.150	0.12	0.100	0.090	0.070
3	6 oz. spirits 6 glasses wine 6 cans beer	0.270	0.220	0.18	0.150	0.130	0.110
4	8 oz. spirits 8 glasses wine 8 cans beer	0.360	0.300	0.24	0.200	0.180	0.150
5	10 oz. spirits 10 glasses wine 10 cans beer	0.450	0.370	0.30	0.250	0.220	0.180

Source: Data from Ray & Ksir, 1993, p. 194.
*In 1 hour.
†100-proof spirits

dependence match what most people associate with the label *alcoholism*. Table 16.6 (p. 580) lists a variety of problems experienced by people who abuse or are dependent on alcohol.

There are at least three distinct patterns of alcohol use by alcohol abusers and dependents. Some people drink large amounts of alcohol every day and plan their days around their drinking. Others abstain from drinking for long periods of time and then go on binges that may last days or weeks. They may stop drinking when faced with crises they must deal with, such as illnesses of their children, or with threats of sanctions for drinking, such as threats of being fired. When they begin drinking again, they may be able to control their drinking for a while, but it may soon escalate until severe problems develop. Still others are sober during the weekdays but drink heavily during the evenings or perhaps only on weekends. Nick and his buddies fit into this third group:

CASE STUDY

Nick began drinking in high school, but his drinking escalated when he moved away from his parents' home to go to college. After just a couple of weeks at college, Nick became friends with a group of guys who liked to party really hard on the weekends. On Thursday nights they would begin to drink beer, often getting quite drunk. They would get a little loud and obnoxious, and sometimes their neighbors in the dormitory would complain to the resident assistant of the dorm about them. They would typically sleep off their hangovers on Friday, missing classes, and then begin drinking again Friday afternoon. They would continue to drink through Saturday, stopping finally on Sunday to sleep and recover.

Nick was able to keep a decent grade average through his first year in college, despite missing many classes. In his sophomore year, however, the classes in his major were getting harder. Nick's drinking was also getting more out of hand. He still would abstain from drinking from about Sunday afternoon until noon on Thursday. But when he would go get the keg of beer for his group of

TAKING PSYCHOLOGY PERSONALLY

Tips for Responsible Drinking

Here are some tips for reducing your own drinking and for preventing problems due to drinking at social events, from the work of Alan Marlatt and colleagues (1998).

1. Set a limit on how much you will drink before you go to a party or other social function. You might want to use Table 16.5 to set your drink limit so that you do not exceed a low-to-moderate blood-alcohol limit. Tell a friend what your limit is and get a commitment from that friend that he or she will help you stick to that limit.

2. Alternate between alcohol and nonalcoholic beverages at the party.

3. Eat foods high in protein and carbohydrates before the party and at the party.

4. Designate someone in your group to drive; that person should drink *no* alcoholic beverages at the party.

5. If you are throwing the party, have plenty of non-alcoholic beverages and attractive food and try to focus the party on music or something other than alcohol consumption.

6. If someone at the party appears to be very intoxicated, encourage him or her to stop drinking. Try not to let him or her drive away from the party; call a taxi or have someone who has not been drinking drive him or her home.

7. If a person passes out after drinking heavily, lay the person on his or her side rather than on his or her back, in case of vomiting. Call medical personnel.

8. If you get drunk at a party, after you have recovered, review the reasons for your overdrinking. Were you trying to get rid of a bad mood? Were you nervous and trying to relax? Did certain people push you to drink? Did you tell yourself that you were not drinking that much? Try to develop concrete, realistic plans for avoiding in future situations the reasons you overdrank.

buddies on Thursday afternoon, he'd also pick up a few fifths of vodka or whatever hard liquor was the cheapest. His buddies would stick to the beer, but Nick would mix the beer with shots of hard liquor and was usually extremely drunk by dinner on Thursday. He started getting really mean and stupid when he was drunk. He punched a hole in the wall of his dorm room one night, and when the resident assistant came up to investigate what was going on, he threatened her, saying he would "smack her across the room" if she didn't shut up and leave. That got him kicked out of his dormitory and off campus. Nick didn't mind being away from the "geeks" who studied all the time and liked having his own apartment where his buddies could come to drink. Nick remained intoxicated from Thursday afternoon until Sunday morning, drinking all day and evening, except when he was passed out. He

usually slept through most of his classes on Monday, and even when he did go, he was so hungover that he couldn't pay attention. His grades were falling, and even his drinking buddies were getting disgusted with Nick's behavior.

Binge drinking on college campuses is common. One study of students at a large public university in the midwest found that 45 percent said they engage in binge drinking, defined as five or more drinks in one setting for males and four or more for females, at least occasionally (Wahlberg, 1999). Binge drinking is especially common among members of fraternities and sororities, with 76 percent of students saying they

TABLE 16.6

Problems Indicated by People Who Are Diagnosed with Alcohol Abuse or Dependence

People with alcohol abuse or dependence typically have many problems due to their alcohol use.

Symptom	Percent Saying Yes
Family objected to respondent's drinking	62
Thought himself or herself an excessive drinker	59
Consumed a fifth of liquor in one day	70
Engaged in daily or weekly heavy drinking	80
Told physician about drinking	22
Friends or professionals said drinking too much	39
Wanted to stop drinking but couldn't	21
Made efforts to control drinking	19
Engaged in morning drinking	21
Had job troubles due to drinking	15
Lost job	7
Had trouble driving	35
Was arrested while drinking	31
Had physical fights while drinking	50
Had two or more binges	29
Had blackouts while drinking	57
Had any withdrawal symptom	28
Had any medical complication	22
Continued to drink with serious illness	14
Couldn't do ordinary work without drinking	12

Source: Data from J. E. Helzer, Bucholz, & Robins, 1992.

Heavy drinking can be part of the culture of a peer group, but can still lead to alcohol abuse and dependence in some members.

subtypes of alcohol dependence have different causes and prognoses. One reliable distinction is between alcoholics who also have antisocial personalities, and alcoholics who do not have antisocial personalities (Babor & Dolinsky, 1988; Zucker et al., 1996). Antisocial alcoholics have more severe symptoms of alcoholism, tend to remain alcoholic for longer, have poorer social functioning, more marital failures, and heavier drug involvement compared to non-antisocial alcoholics (Zucker et al., 1996). Antisocial alcoholics are more likely to come from families with alcoholism and begin drinking earlier than non-antisocial alcoholics. In turn, the children of antisocial alcoholics are more likely to have behavioral problems than the children of non-antisocial alcoholics (Puttler et al., 1998).

Another distinction that has been made is between negative affect alcoholism and other alcoholisms (Colder & Chassin, 1993; Turnbull & Gomberg, 1990). People with negative affect alcoholism tend to have had depressive and anxiety symptoms in childhood and adolescence, and to have only begun severe alcohol use and abuse in adulthood. This pattern appears to be more common in women than in men.

Alcohol withdrawal People who are dependent on alcohol can experience severe alcohol withdrawal symptoms, which can be divided into three stages (Winger et al., 1992). The first stage, which usually begins within a few hours after drinking has been stopped or sharply curtailed, includes tremulousness (the "shakes"), weakness, and profuse perspiration. A person may complain of anxiety (the "jitters"), headache, nausea, and abdominal cramps. He or she may begin to retch and vomit. The person's face is flushed, and he or she is restless and easily startled but alert. The person's EEG pattern may be mildly abnormal. He or she may begin to "see" or "hear" things, at first only with

binge drink, and 15 percent having engaged in binge drinking at least six times in the previous two weeks.

Family members, friends, and business associates often recognize when an individual is abusing or dependent on alcohol, and they confront the individual. Sometimes this leads the individual to seek help, but denial is strong among alcoholics, and one confrontation or even a series of confrontations often does not motivate an alcohol abuser to change his or her behavior or seek help.

There is increasing evidence that alcohol dependence is a heterogeneous disorder, and that different eyes shut but with time also with eyes open. People whose dependence on alcohol is relatively moderate may only experience this first stage of withdrawal, and the symptoms may disappear within a few days.

The second stage of withdrawal involves convulsive seizures, which may begin as early as 12 hours after stopping drinking but more often appear during the second or third day. The third phase is characterized by **delirium tremens,** or **DTs.** Auditory, visual, and tactile hallucinations occur. The person may also develop bizarre delusions that are terrifying, such as the belief that monsters are attacking. He or she may sleep little and become severely agitated, continuously active, and completely disoriented. Fever, profuse perspiration, and an irregular heartbeat may develop. Delirium tremens is a fatal condition in approximately 10 percent of cases; death may occur from hyperthermia (greatly increased body temperature) or collapse of the peripheral vascular system. Fortunately, only about 11 percent of individuals with alcohol dependence ever experience seizures or DTs (Schuckit et al., 1995). Seizures and DTs are more common among people who drink large amounts in single sittings and who have additional medical illnesses.

People who make it through the entire withdrawal syndrome can show complete recovery from the withdrawal symptoms. The following is a case study of a man going through delirium tremens after prolonged alcohol dependence, presented by the groundbreaking psychiatrist Emil Kraepelin to medical students in the nineteenth century (Spitzer et al., 1981, pp. 304–305):

CASE STUDY

The innkeeper, aged thirty-four, whom I am bringing before you to-day was admitted to the hospital only an hour ago. He understands the questions put to him, but cannot quite hear some of them, and gives a rather absentminded impression. He states his name and age correctly. . . . Yet he does not know the doctors, calls them by the names of his acquaintances, and thinks he has been here for two or three days. It must be the Crown Hotel, or, rather, the "mad hospital." He does not know the date exactly.

. . . He moves about in his chair, looks round him a great deal, starts slightly several times, and keeps on playing with his hands. Suddenly he gets up, and begs to be allowed to play on the piano for a little at once. He sits down again immediately, on persuasion, but then wants to go away "to tell them something else that he has forgotten." He gradually gets more and more excited, saying that his fate is sealed; he must leave the world now; they might telegraph to his wife that her husband is lying at the point of death. We learn, by questioning him, that he is going to be executed by electricity, and also that he will be shot. "The picture is not clearly painted," he says; "every moment someone stands now here, now there, waiting for me with a revolver. When I open my eyes,

they vanish." He says that a stinking fluid has been injected into his head and both his toes, which causes the pictures one takes for reality; that is the work of an international society, which makes away with those "who fell into misfortune innocently through false steps." With this he looks eagerly at the window, where he sees houses and trees vanishing and reappearing. With slight pressure on his eyes, he sees first sparks, then a hare, a picture, a head, a washstand-set, a half-moon, and a human head, first dully and then in colours. If you show him a speck on the floor, he tries to pick it up, saying that it is a piece of money. If you shut his hand and ask him what you have given him, he keeps his fingers carefully closed, and guesses that it is a lead-pencil or a piece of indiarubber. The patient's mood is half apprehensive and half amused. His head is much flushed, and his pulse is small, weak, and rather hurried. His face is bloated and his eyes are watery. His breath smells strongly of alcohol and acetone. His tongue is thickly furred, and trembles when he puts it out, and his outspread fingers show strong, jerky tremors. The knee-reflexes are somewhat exaggerated.

Long-term effects of alcohol abuse Heavy and prolonged use of alcohol can have toxic effects on several systems of the body, including the stomach, esophagus, pancreas, and liver (Winger, Hofman, & Woods, 1992). One of the most common medical conditions associated with alcohol abuse and dependence is low-grade hypertension. This factor, combined with increases in triglycerides and low-density lipoprotein (or "bad") cholesterol, puts alcohol abusers at increased risk for heart disease.

Alcohol abusers and dependents are often malnourished, in part because chronic alcohol ingestion decreases the absorption of critical nutrients from the gastrointestinal system and in part because they tend to "drink their meals." Some alcohol abusers show chronic thiamine deficiencies, which can lead to several disorders of the central nervous system, including numbness and pain in the extremities, deterioration in muscles, and loss of visual acuity for both near and far objects (Martin & Bates, 1998)

Alcohol-induced persisting amnesic disorder, a permanent cognitive disorder caused by damage to the central nervous system, consists of two syndromes. **Wernicke's encephalopathy** involves mental confusion and disorientation and, in severe states, coma. **Korsakoff's psychosis** involves a loss of memory for recent events and problems in recalling distant events. The person may confabulate, telling implausible stories in an attempt to hide his or her ability to remember. **Alcohol-induced dementia** is the loss of intellectual abilities, including memory, abstract thinking, judgment, or problem solving, often accompanied by personality changes, such as increases in paranoia. This syndrome is found in approximately 9 percent of chronic alcohol abusers or dependents and is the second most common cause of adult dementia (Winger, Hofman & Woods, 1992). More subtle deficits due to central nervous system damage are observed in many chronic alcohol abusers, even after they have stopped using alcohol (Martin & Bates, 1998).

Children of mothers who chronically ingest large amounts of alcohol while pregnant may be born with **fetal alcohol syndrome** (Streissguth et al., 1999). This syndrome is characterized by retarded growth, facial abnormalities, central nervous system damage, mental retardation, motor abnormalities, tremors, hyperactivity, heart defects, and skeletal anomalies (see also Chapter 13). Although the risk of fetal alcohol syndrome is highest among women who are chronic, heavy alcohol users while pregnant, particularly those who abuse alcohol during their first trimester, even moderate intake of alcohol may affect the fetus during any point of pregnancy.

Cultural Differences in Alcohol Disorders

There are marked differences across cultures in the use of alcohol and in rates of alcohol-related problems (see Table 16.7). Low rates of alcohol-related problems in China and Taiwan may be due in part to the absence, in 50 percent of people of Asian descent, of an enzyme that eliminates the first breakdown product of alcohol, acetaldehyde. When these individuals consume alcohol, they experience a flushed face and heart palpitations, and the discomfort of this effect often leads them to avoid alcohol altogether. The low rates of alcohol-related disorders in Asia have also been attributed to

the Confucian moral ethic, which discourages drunken behavior, and to the fact that alcohol is seen as appropriate for meals and ceremonial occasions but not for personal indulgence (Helzer & Canino, 1992).

In recent years, however, there have been substantial increases in alcohol use and related problems among businessmen in Asia. This may explain, in part, the high rates of alcohol-related problems in South Korea (see Table 16.7), where drinking among business associates after work is common. These nightly parties often involve drinking contests lasting until some of the contestants have to be carried home.

Although the United States may not have the highest rates of alcohol dependence in the world, alcohol dependence and abuse are the most common disorders in the United States, with about 24 percent of the population reporting symptoms that qualify them for a diagnosis of dependence or abuse at some time in their lives (Kessler et al., 1994; note that Table 16.7 lists lifetime prevalences for alcohol dependence only). There are substantial differences among ethnic groups within the United States in alcohol use and abuse. Notice in Table 16.8 the much higher rate of alcohol abuse and dependence in Mexican Americans born in the United States than in those who immigrated to the United States. Some theorists have argued that the more an immigrant group becomes assimilated to dominant U.S. culture, the more at risk they are for mental-health problems in general and particularly for the common mental-health problems of this culture (see Gaw, 1993). This is because assimilation robs immigrants of their ties to their heritage and extended social networks and leads immigrants to identify with a culture that will never accept them fully. Mexican Americans born in the United States tend to be more assimilated than are more recent immigrants to the United States, and this may help to explain why they show greater rates of alcohol-related problems.

Differences between White and African American rates of alcohol problems in the United States vary by age and gender (Zucker, 1998). As can be seen in Figure 16.4, there are much higher rates of alcohol problems in young White males than in African American males but higher rates among older African American men than older White men. The rates among African American and White women are similar at all ages.

One group in the United States that appears at high risk for alcohol abuse and dependence are Native Americans (Manson et al., 1992). For example, a study of adult members of a Pacific Northwest reservation community found that 27 percent qualified for a diagnosis of alcohol dependence. Deaths related to alcohol are as much as five times more common among Native Americans than in the general U.S. population (Manson et al., 1992). Hospital records indicate that alcohol-related illnesses are three times higher among Native

TABLE 16.7

Lifetime Prevalence of Alcohol Dependence in Various Cultures

The rates of alcohol dependence vary greatly across cultures.

Culture	Percentage
South Korea	22.00
New Zealand	19.00
Canada	18.00
Germany	13.00
Puerto Rico	13.00
Mainland United States	8.00
Taiwan	6.00
China	0.45

Source: Data from J. E. Helzer, Bucholz, & Robins, 1992.

TABLE 16.8

Drinking Patterns of Some Groups in the United States (Percentages of People)

Heavy drinkers are those who regularly consumed seven or more drinks at least one evening a week for a period of several months but who never had any social, legal, or medical problems related to alcohol or any withdrawal symptoms. Problem drinkers are those who have had at least one alcohol-related problem in their lives but who have not had enough to qualify for a diagnosis of alcohol abuse or dependency.

	Total Abstention	Social Drinkers	Heavy Drinkers	Problem Drinkers	Abuse/ Dependency
Mexican Americans born in the United States	7	52	3	14	23
Immigrant Mexican Americans	23	44	1	19	13
Puerto Ricans	20	69	7	10	13

Source: Data from G. J. Canino, Burnam, & Chetano, 1992.

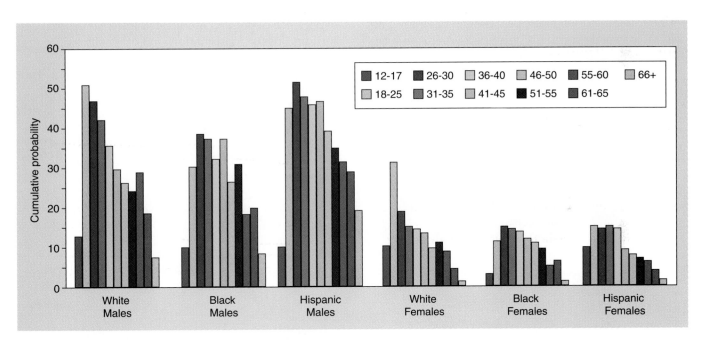

FIGURE 16.4 Percentage of the U.S. Population Reporting Four or More Drinks on a Single Day in Past 30 Days.
Source: Zucker, 1998.

Americans than among all people in the United States and twice the rates for other ethnic minority groups in the United States. The higher rates of alcohol-related problems among Native Americans have been tied to their excessive rates of poverty and unemployment, lower education, and greater sense of helplessness and hopelessness.

Gender and Age Differences in Alcohol Disorders

In a community survey done in the United States, 72 percent of adult men said they had consumed at least one alcoholic beverage in the last year, compared to 62 percent of adult women (NIDA, 1995). About 11 percent of American men and 4 percent of American women meet the criteria for alcohol dependence in any given year (Kessler et al., 1994). Males are more likely than females to drink in all cultures, but the size of the gender difference differs by culture (see Figure 16.5, p. 584; Helzer & Canino, 1992). The gender gap in alcohol use is much greater among men and women who subscribe to traditional gender roles, which condone drinking for men but not for women (Huselid & Cooper, 1992). Similarly, in ethnic minority groups of the United States in which traditional gender roles are more widely accepted, such as Hispanics and recent Asian immigrants, the gender gap in drinking is greater than it is among Whites, due largely to high percentages of women in the minority groups completely abstaining from alcohol.

Elderly people are less likely than others to abuse or be dependent on alcohol, probably for several reasons. First, with age, the liver metabolizes alcohol at a slower rate, and the lower percentage of body water increases the absorption of alcohol. As a result, older people can become intoxicated faster and experience the negative effects of alcohol more severely and quickly. Second, as people grow older, they may become more mature in their choices, including the choice about drinking alcohol to excess. Third, older people have grown up under stronger prohibitions against alcohol use and abuse and in a society in which there was more stigma associated with alcoholism, leading them to curtail their use of alcohol more than younger people do. Finally, people who have used alcohol excessively for many years may die from alcohol-related diseases before they reach old age.

Recent studies of adolescents and young adults find widespread abuse of alcohol (Lewinsohn, Rohde, & Seeley, 1996; Nelson & Wittchen, 1998), particularly among males. For example, one study of over 3,000 14- to 24-year-olds found that 15 percent of the males and about 5 percent of the females could be diagnosed with alcohol abuse according to the DSM-IV (Nelson & Wittchen, 1998). Alcohol dependence was lower, with about 10 percent of the males and 3 percent of the females qualifying for the diagnosis. Over time, about half of the adolescents and young adults who abused alcohol stopped abusing alcohol, but abusers of alcohol were much more likely than nonabusers to become dependent on alcohol eventually.

Benzodiazepines, Barbiturates, and Inhalants

Three other groups of substances that, like alcohol, depress the central nervous system are benzodiazepines, barbiturates, and inhalants. Intoxication with and withdrawal from these substances are quite similar to alcohol intoxication and withdrawal. Users initially may feel euphoric and become disinhibited but then experience depressed moods, lethargy, perceptual distortions, loss of coordination, and other signs of central nervous system depression.

Benzodiazepines (such as Xanax, Valium, Halcion, and Librium) and **barbiturates** (such as Quaalude) are legally manufactured and sold by prescription, usually for the treatment of anxiety and insomnia. In the United States, approximately 90 percent of people hospitalized for medical care or surgery are prescribed

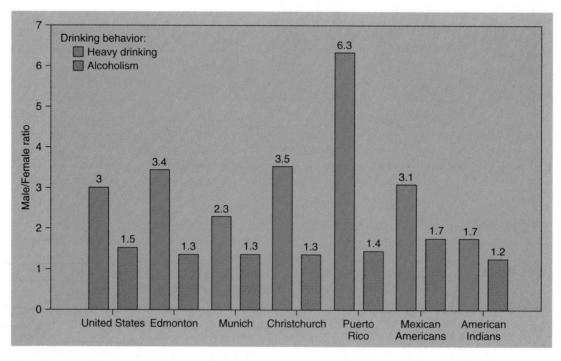

FIGURE 16.5 Male-to-Female Ratios for People Who Drink Heavily or Are Alcoholics, Across Cultures. Males are more likely than females to be heavy drinkers or alcoholics in most cultures, but the male-to-female ratio varies by culture.

Source: Helzer & Canino, 1992.

Some women begin taking sedatives by prescription but increase their use dramatically and become physically dependent on these drugs.

sedatives. Large quantities of these substances end up on the illegal black market, however. These substances are especially likely to be taken in combination with other psychoactive substances to produce greater highs or feelings of euphoria or to relieve the agitation created by other substances (Schuckit, 1995).

There are two common patterns in the development of benzodiazapine or barbiturate abuse and dependence (Schuckit, 1995; Sowers, 1998). The most common pattern is followed by the teenager or young adult who begins using these substances "recreationally," often at "bring your own drug" parties, to produce a sense of well-being or euphoria but then escalates to chronic use and physiological dependence. This pattern is especially likely among persons who already have other substance-abuse problems with alcohol, opioids, cocaine, amphetamines, or other substances.

A second pattern is seen in people, particularly women, who initially use sedatives under physicians' care for anxiety or insomnia but then gradually increase their use as tolerance develops, without the knowledge of their physicians. They may obtain prescriptions from several different physicians or even photocopy their prescriptions. When confronted about their sedative use and dependency, they may deny that they use the drugs to produce euphoria or that they are dependent on the sedatives.

Barbiturates and benzodiazepines cause decreases in blood pressure, respiratory rate, and heart rate. In overdose, they can be extremely dangerous and even fatal. Death can occur from respiratory arrest or cardiovascular collapse. Overdose is especially likely to occur when these substances (particularly the benzodiazepines) are taken in combination with alcohol.

Inhalants are solvents such as gasoline, glue, paint thinners, and spray paints. Users may inhale vapors directly from the cans or bottles containing the substances, soak rags with the substances and then

hold the rag to their mouths and noses, or place the substances in paper or plastic bags and then inhale the gases from the bags. The chemicals reach the lungs, bloodstream, and brain very rapidly (Hartman, 1998).

The greatest users of inhalants are young boys between 10 and 15 years of age (Schuckit, 1995). Twenty percent of American high school students have reported experimenting with inhalants at least once during high school. One group that appears especially prone to using inhalants is Native American teenagers. Some studies have found that nearly all children on some Native American reservations have experimented with gasoline inhaling. Hispanic American teenagers also appear to have higher rates of inhalant use than other groups of teenagers in the United States, and it is estimated that 500,000 children in Mexico City are addicted to inhalants (Hartman, 1998). Males are more likely than females to use inhalants.

Chronic users of inhalants may have a variety of respiratory irritations and rashes due to the inhalants. Inhalants can cause permanent damage to the central nervous system, including degeneration and lesions of the brain (Hartman, 1998). Recurrent use can also cause hepatitis and liver and kidney disease. Death can occur from depression of the respiratory or cardiovascular systems; *sudden sniffing death* is due to acute irregularities in the heartbeat or loss of oxygen (Dinwiddie, 1998). Sometimes users suffocate themselves when they go unconscious with plastic bags filled with inhalants firmly placed over their noses and mouths. Users can also die or become seriously injured when the inhalants cause them to have delusions that they can do fantastic things like fly, and they jump off cliffs or tall buildings to try it.

Sniffing inhalants like paint thinner is highly dangerous, but unfortunately it is quite common among young people.

Summing Up

- At low doses, alcohol produces relaxation and a mild euphoria. At higher doses, it produces the classic signs of depression and cognitive and motor impairment.

- A large proportion of deaths due to accidents, murders, and suicides are alcohol-related.

- Alcohol withdrawal symptoms can be mild or so severe as to be life threatening.

- Alcohol abusers and dependents experience a wide range of social and interpersonal problems and are at risk for many serious health problems.

- Persons of Asian descent typically are less prone to alcohol-related problems, although exceptions to this include Native Americans and Koreans. Women drink less alcohol than do men in most cultures and are less likely to have alcohol-related disorders than are men.

- Benzodiazepines and barbiturates are sold legally by prescription for the treatment of anxiety and insomnia. Inhalants are solvents such as gasoline or paint thinner.

- These substances can cause an initial rush plus a loss of inhibitions. These pleasurable sensations are then followed by depressed mood, lethargy, and physical signs of central nervous system depression. Benzodiazepines and barbiturates are dangerous in overdose and when mixed with other substances.

- Inhalants can cause permanent organ and brain damage and accidental deaths due to suffocation or dangerous delusional behavior.

◑ STIMULANTS

The stimulants are drugs that activate the central nervous system, causing feelings of energy, happiness, power, a decreased desire for sleep, and a diminished appetite (see *Concept Review: Intoxication with and Withdrawal from Stimulants*). Cocaine and the amphetamines are the two types of stimulants associated with severe substance-related disorders. Both substances are used by people to get a psychological lift or rush. Both substances cause dangerous increases in blood pressure and heart rate, changes in the rhythm and electrical activity of the heart, and constriction of the blood vessels, which can lead to heart attacks, respiratory arrest, and seizures. In the United States, toxic reactions to cocaine and amphetamines account for 40 percent of all substance-related cases seen in hospital emergency rooms and for 50 percent of sudden deaths in which substances were involved (Goldstein, 1994). These substances are costly, both to users and to society.

Caffeine and nicotine are also stimulants, and can result in diagnosable substance-related disorders. Although the psychological effects of caffeine and nicotine are not as severe as those of cocaine and the amphetamines, these drugs, particularly nicotine, can have long-term negative effects, so we discuss them as well.

Cocaine

Cocaine is a white powder extracted from the coca plant and one of the most highly addictive substances known. People can snort the powder, which causes its effects on the brain to be quickly felt. In the 1970s, freebase cocaine appeared when users developed a method for separating the most potent chemicals in cocaine by heating it with ether. This produced a cocaine base, or freebase, that is even more powerful. It is usually smoked in a water pipe, or mixed in a tobacco or marijuana cigarette. Crack is a form of freebase cocaine that is boiled down into tiny chunks or rocks, which are usually smoked.

Cocaine activates those parts of the brain that register reward or pleasure (Gatley et al., 1998). It produces a sudden rush of intense euphoria, followed by great self-esteem, alertness, energy, and a general feeling of competence, creativity, and social acceptability. Users often do not feel drugged. Instead, they feel they have become the people they always wanted to be (Winger, Hofman & Woods, 1992). When taken at high doses or chronically, however, cocaine leads to grandiosity, impulsiveness, hypersexuality, compulsive behavior, agitation, and anxiety, reaching the point of panic and paranoia. After stopping use of the substance, users may feel exhausted and depressed and sleep a great deal. Users also feel an intense craving for more of the substance, both for its physiological and psychological effects.

Many cocaine abusers and dependents started with heavy alcohol or marijuana use and then graduated to "harder" substances, including cocaine (Denison et al., 1998; Miller, 1991). The extraordinarily rapid and strong effects of cocaine on the brain's reward centers, however, seem to make this substance more likely than most illicit substances to result in patterns of abuse and dependence even among people who have never been heavy users of any other substances (Winger, Hofman & Woods, 1992).

CASE STUDY
Dr. Arnie Rosenthal is a 31-year-old white male dentist, married for 10 years with two children. His wife insisted

CONCEPT REVIEW

Intoxication with and Withdrawal from Stimulants

The stimulants activate the central nervous system.

Drug	Intoxication Symptoms	Withdrawal Symptoms
Cocaine and amphetamines	Behavioral changes (e.g., euphoria or affective blunting; changes in sociability; hypervigilance; interpersonal sensitivity; anxiety, tension, or anger; impaired judgment) Rapid heartbeat Dilation of pupils Elevated or lowered blood pressure Perspiration or chills Nausea or vomiting Weight loss Psychomotor agitation or retardation Muscular weakness Slowed breathing Chest pain Confusion, seizures, coma	Dysphoric mood Fatigue Vivid, unpleasant dreams Insomnia or hypersomnia Increased appetite Psychomotor retardation or agitation
Nicotine	Not a diagnosis in DSM-IV	Dysphoria or depressed mood Insomnia Irritability, frustration or anger Anxiety Difficulty concentrating Restlessness Decreased heart rate Increased appetite or weight gain
Caffeine	Restlessness Nervousness Excitement Insomnia Flushed face Frequent urination Stomach upset Muscle twitching Rambling flow of thought or speech Rapid heartbeat Periods of inexhaustibility Psychomotor agitation	(Provisional diagnosis in DSM-IV) Marked fatigue or drowsiness Marked anxiety or depression Nausea or vomiting

Source: DSM-IV, APA, 2000.

he see a psychiatrist because of uncontrolled use of cocaine, which over the past year had made it increasingly difficult for him to function as a dentist. During the previous 5 years he used cocaine virtually every day, with only occasional periods of abstinence of 1 or 2 weeks. For the past 4 years he wanted to stop cocaine use, but his desire was overridden by a "compulsion" to take the drug. He estimates having spent $12,000 to $15,000 on cocaine during the past year.

The patient's wife, who accompanied him to the interview, complained primarily about her husband's lack of energy and motivation, which started with his drug use 5 years ago. She complained that "he isn't working; he has no interests outside of me and the kids—not even his music—and he spends all of his time alone watching TV." She is also bothered by his occasional temper outbursts, but that is less troubling to her. . . .

During his second year in dental school he got married, while being supported comfortably by his in-laws. After having been married 1 year he began using marijuana, smoking a joint each day upon coming home from school, and spent the evenings "staring" at TV. When he graduated from dental school his wife was pregnant, and he was "scared to death" at the prospect of being a father. His deepening depression was characterized by social isolation, increased loss of interests, and frequent temper outbursts. He needed to be intoxicated with marijuana, or occasionally sedatives, for sex, relaxation, and socialization. Following the birth of the child he "never felt so crazy," and his marijuana and sedative use escalated. Two years later, a second child was born. Dr. Rosenthal was financially successful, had moved to an expensive suburban home with a swimming pool, and had two cars and "everything my parents wanted for me." He was 27 years old, felt he had nothing to look forward to, felt painfully isolated, and the drugs were no longer providing relief.

He tried cocaine for the first time and immediately felt good. "I was no longer depressed. I used cocaine as often as possible because all my problems seemed to vanish, but I had to keep doing it. The effects were brief and it was very expensive, but I didn't care. When the immediate effects wore off, I'd feel even more miserable and depressed so that I did as much cocaine as I was able to obtain." He is now continuously nervous and irritable. Practicing dentistry has become increasingly difficult. (Adapted from Spitzer et al., 1983, pp. 81–83)

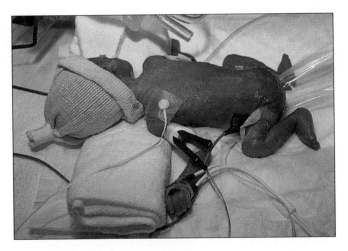

The babies of mothers who take high levels of crack during pregnancy are at increased risk for being born prematurely and having major birth defects.

Because cocaine has a short half-life, its effects wear off quickly. This means the person dependent on cocaine must take frequent doses of the substance to maintain a high. In addition, tolerance to cocaine can develop, so that the individual must obtain larger and larger amounts of cocaine to experience any high. Cocaine dependents will spend huge amounts of money on the substance and may become involved in theft, prostitution, or drug dealing to obtain enough money to purchase cocaine. The desperation to obtain cocaine seen in many frequent users also can lead them to engage in extremely dangerous behaviors. Many cocaine users contract HIV, the virus that causes AIDS, by sharing needles with infected users or by having unprotected sex in exchange for money or more cocaine. Said one woman crack user (Inciardi, Lockwood, & Pottieger, 1993, p. 139),

Voices

If I pulled out a condom in a crack house, I'd be laughed at. If I started to take it out of the wrapper, it would be slapped out of my hand. If I tried to put it on a man's [penis], I'd be slapped across the face, or worse. If I get AIDS, who cares anyway, really?

Another tragic consequence of cocaine use is its effects on fetuses. Cocaine easily crosses the placenta so that even pregnant women who only occasionally use cocaine put their fetuses at risk. It causes irregularities

in placental blood flow, spontaneous abortions, and premature labor and delivery. In addition, pregnant women who are chronic cocaine abusers often are malnourished and abusing other substances, further putting their fetuses at risk. Babies whose mothers have used cocaine tend to be hyperirritable; have small head circumferences; weigh less than normal; and have higher rates of physical malformations, learning disabilities, neurological impairments, and sudden infant death (Napiorkowski et al., 1996; Tronick et al., 1996).

Although cocaine began as a wealthy person's substance because of its high cost, a sharp reduction in the cost of cocaine in the 1970s led to its widespread use at all socioeconomic levels. Almost 25 percent of people under the age of 35 have tried cocaine at least once in their lives (NIDA, 1995). Although the monetary cost of cocaine has decreased in recent decades, the human cost of cocaine has risen dramatically. Between 1976 and 1986, cocaine-related emergency room visits, deaths, and admissions to cocaine treatment programs multiplied by 15 (Cocores, Pottash, & Gold, 1991).

Fortunately, the use of cocaine has fallen since the mid-1980s. Whereas in 1979, 9 percent of young people said they were using cocaine at least once a month, by the mid-1990s, this number had dropped to less than 2 percent (Goldstein, 1994; Kendler & Prescott, 1998b; NIDA, 1995). This decline may have to do, in part, with antidrug campaigns in schools and in the media and with highly publicized deaths of rock stars and athletes due to cocaine overdose. Decline has occurred primarily among casual users of cocaine; chronic abusers and dependents have continued to use cocaine. There is also some evidence that the use of crack has not fallen off in recent years.

Amphetamines

The U.S. pharmaceutical industry manufactures 8 to 10 billion doses of amphetamines annually, under names such as Dexedrine and Benzedrine (Miller, 1991). The drugs are most often swallowed as pills, but can be injected intraveneously, and methamphetamine can be snorted or smoked. These drugs were initially introduced as antihistamines, but people soon recognized their stimulant effects. These days, many people use them to combat depression or chronic fatigue from overwork or simply to boost their self-confidence and energy (Miller, 1991). They are also a component of diet drugs. Finally, stimulants such as Ritalin are used to treat attention-deficit/hyperactivity disorder in children, as we discussed in Chapter 13. Many of these drugs are used appropriately under the supervision of physicians, but a great many doses are diverted from prescription use to illegal use and abuse.

The amphetamines have their effects by causing the release of the neurotransmitters dopamine and norepinephrine and blocking reuptake of these neurotransmitters. The symptoms of intoxication with **amphetamines** are similar to the symptoms of cocaine intoxication: euphoria, self-confidence, alertness, agitation, paranoia (Wyatt & Ziedonis, 1998). Like cocaine, amphetamines can produce perceptual illusions that are frightening. The movement of other people and objects may seem distorted or exaggerated. Users may hear frightening voices making derogatory statements about them, see sores all over their bodies, or feel snakes crawling on their arms. They may have delusions that they are being stalked. They may act out violently against others as a result of their paranoid delusions. Some amphetamine users are aware that these experiences are not real, but some lose their reality-testing and develop *amphetamine-induced psychotic disorders.*

CASE STUDY

An agitated 42-year-old businessman was admitted to the psychiatric service after a period of 2½ months in which he found himself becoming increasingly distrustful of others and suspicious of his business associates. He was taking their statements out of context, "twisting" their words, and making inappropriately hostile and accusatory comments; he had, in fact, lost several business deals that had been "virtually sealed." Finally, he fired a shotgun into the backyard late one night when he heard noises that convinced him that intruders were about to break into his house and kill him.

One and one-half years previously, he had been diagnosed as having narcolepsy because of daily irresistible sleep attacks and episodes of sudden loss of muscle tone, and he had been placed on an amphetaminelike stimulant, methylphenidate. His narcolepsy declined and he was able to work quite effectively as the sales manager of a small office-machine company and to participate in an active social life with his family and a small circle of friends.

In the 4 months before this admission, he had been using increasingly large doses of methylphenidate to maintain alertness late at night because of an increasing amount of work that could not be handled during the day. He reported that during this time he could often feel his heart race and he had trouble sitting still. (Adapted from Spitzer et al., 1994, pp. 139–140)

Legal problems for amphetamine abusers typically arise because of aggressive or inappropriate behavior while intoxicated or as a result of buying the drug illegally. Tolerance to amphetamines develops quickly, so frequent users can become physically dependent on the drug in a short period. They may switch from swallowing pills to injecting amphetamines intravenously. Some go on a speed run, in which they inject amphetamines frequently over several days, without eating or sleeping. When a speed run ends, they crash into a physical and emotional depression that can be so severe that they may become suicidal. Acute withdrawal symptoms typically subside within a few days, but the chronic user may experience mood instability, memory loss, confusion, paranoid thinking, and perceptual abnormalities for weeks, months, and perhaps even years. Most often they battle the withdrawal symptoms with another speed run.

Amphetamines are increasingly used in the workplace by people trying to keep up with the rapid pace of today's work world. Employers may even provide the amphetamines to employees to keep them working and increase their productivity. When the employees finally go home, they may use depressants such as alcohol to come down off the speed. Although the amphetamines may have the desired effects on employee morale and productivity in the short run, over time people become irritable and hostile, and need more and more of the amphetamines to avoid withdrawal effects. Their health will decline, as well as their personal relationships. In California, emergency room admissions for amphetamine abuse have skyrocketed in recent years.

Nicotine

All of the substances we have discussed thus far, except alcohol and the inhalants, are illegal for nonprescription use, and there are many laws regulating the use of alcohol. One of the most addictive substances

Our fast-paced technological world has created a high-stress environment for many workers.

we know, however, is fully legal for use by adults and readily available for use by adolescents.

Nicotine is an alkaloid found in tobacco. Cigarettes are the most popular "nicotine delivery device." Cigarettes deliver nicotine to the brain within a few seconds after a person begins smoking (Goldstein, 1998). In the United States, 72 percent of adults have smoked cigarettes at some time in their lives, and 32 percent currently smoke. Smoking usually begins in the early teens. Among people who continue to smoke through age 20, 95 percent become regular, daily smokers. In general, the use of tobacco has declined in the United States and other industrialized countries over the last few decades. In contrast, its use is increasing in developing countries (Giovini et al., 1994).

Nicotine operates on both the central and peripheral nervous systems. It results in the release of several biochemicals that may have direct reinforcing effects on the brain, including dopamine, norepinephrine, serotonin, and the endogenous opioids. Although people often say they smoke to reduce stress, the physiological effects of nicotine actually resemble the fight-or-flight syndrome—several systems in the body are aroused in preparation to fight or flee a stressor, including the cardiovascular and respiratory systems. The subjective sense that smoking may reduce stress may actually reflect the reversal of tension and irritability that builds in smokers between cigarettes because they are addicted to the nicotine (Parrott, 1998). In other words, nicotine addicts need nicotine to remain feeling normal because of the effects of nicotine on the body and brain.

In 1964, on the basis of a review of 6,000 empirical studies, the Surgeon General of the United States concluded that smoking, particularly cigarette smoking, caused lung cancer, bronchitis, and probably coronary heart disease. Mortality rates for smokers are 70 percent greater than for nonsmokers. This means that a person between 30 and 35 years of age who smokes two packs of cigarettes a day will die 8 to 9 years earlier than will a nonsmoker. The chief causes of increased mortality rates among smokers are coronary heart disease, lung cancer, emphysema, and chronic

Smoking usually begins in the teen years, and 95 percent of people who continue to smoke through age 20 become regular daily users.

bronchitis. Tobacco use accounts for 19 percent of all deaths in the United States (Goldstein, 1998). The babies of women who smoke while pregnant are smaller at birth. The longer a person smokes and the more he or she smokes per day, the greater the health risks.

Increasing attention is being paid to the effects of passive smoking—unintentionally inhaling the smoke from nearby smokers' cigarettes. This smoke contains more toxins than does the smoke that the smoker actively inhales, although the passive smoker does not inhale the smoke in concentrations as high as the smoker does. Children of parents who smoke have 30 to 80 percent more chronic respiratory problems than do nonsmokers and nearly 30 percent more hospitalizations for bronchitis and pneumonia (Winger, Hofman & Woods, 1992).

Tobacco manufacturers have tried to claim that nicotine is "not an addictive drug," but it causes most of the core symptoms of physiological and psychological dependence. The best evidence of nicotine dependence is the presence of tolerance to the substance and withdrawal symptoms after quitting. Chronic heavy smokers become so tolerant to nicotine that they show no adverse physiological reactions to a dosage of nicotine that would have made them violently nauseous when they first began smoking. When they try to stop smoking or are prohibited from smoking for an extended period (such as at work or on an airplane), they show severe withdrawal symptoms: They are depressed, irritable, angry, anxious, frustrated, restless, and hungry; they have trouble concentrating; and they desperately crave another cigarette. These symptoms are immediately relieved by smoking another cigarette, another sign of physiological dependence.

Because nicotine is relatively cheap and available, people who are nicotine dependent do not tend to spend large amounts of time trying to obtain nicotine. They may, however, become panicked if they run out of cigarettes and replacements are not available. They may also spend large amounts of their day engaged in smoking or chewing tobacco and continue to use nicotine even though it is damaging their health (such as after they have been diagnosed with emphysema). They may skip social or recreational activities as a result of their habit. For example, people may turn down dinner invitations at the homes of friends who do not allow smoking. Or they may stop playing tennis because they have trouble breathing. With the increasing restrictions on smoking in the workplace, nicotine dependents may even begin to turn down or switch jobs to avoid these restrictions.

Over 70 percent of people who smoke say they wish they could quit (Goldstein, 1998). Quitting is difficult, however, in part because the withdrawal syndrome is so difficult to withstand. Only about 3 to 5 percent of smokers who attempt to quit smoking are still abstinent after one year (Lichtentstein & Glasgow, 1992). The craving for cigarettes can remain long after smokers have stopped smoking: 50 percent of people who quit smoking report they have desired cigarettes in the last 24 hours (Goldstein, 1994). Fortunately, one of the new heterocyclic antidepressants, bupropion (trade names Wellbutrin and Zyban) can significant reduce craving for nicotine and help smokers stop smoking permanently (Goldstein, 1998).

There are increasing calls for the U.S. government to declare nicotine a drug much like marijuana and other substances that produce psychological changes and physiological dependence and are detrimental to health. Such a declaration would then lead to strict governmental regulation of the sale and use of tobacco. Antismoking advocates argue that nicotine dependence is a negative psychological and physiological condition just as bad as other substance dependencies. Moreover, between the effects of secondary smoke and the health care dollars spent treating diseases due to smoking, nicotine dependence exacts a much bigger toll on people who are not nicotine dependent than do most other substance dependencies. Opponents of the antismoking movement argue that nicotine is not truly

Programs to prevent and reduce smoking have become quite creative in recent years.

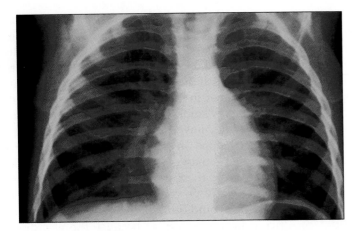
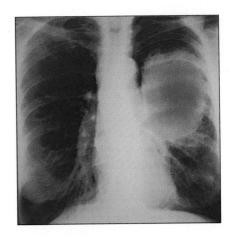

Smoking is the leading cause of cancer. The lungs on the left are healthy. The lungs on the right are from a smoker and show cancer.

a psychoactive substance—nicotine does not cause great changes in mood, thought, or perceptions as does cannabis, cocaine, heroin, or for that matter, alcohol. The negative health effects of smoking are the smoker's business only. People do many things that are not good for their health—they eat high-cholesterol foods, they sit in the sun without sunscreen—but these activities are not regulated by the government. This debate is likely to rage for some time to come, particularly given the issues of personal freedom and the massive amounts of money involved.

Caffeine

Caffeine is by far the most heavily used stimulant drug. Seventy-five percent of caffeine is ingested through coffee (Chou, 1992). The average American drinks about two cups of coffee per day, and a cup of brewed coffee has about 100 milligrams of caffeine. Other sources of caffeine include tea (about 40 milligrams of caffeine per 6 ounces), caffeinated soda (45 milligrams per 12 ounces), over-the-counter analgesics and cold remedies (25 to 50 milligrams per tablet), weight-loss drugs (75 to 200 milligrams per tablet), and chocolate or cocoa (5 milligrams per chocolate bar).

Caffeine stimulates the central nervous system, increasing levels of dopamine, norepinephrine, and serotonin. It causes metabolism, body temperature, and blood pressure to increase. Our appetite wanes and we feel more alert. But in doses equivalent to just two to three cups of coffee, caffeine can cause a number of unpleasant symptoms, including restlessness, nervousness, and hand tremors. We may experience an upset stomach and feel our heart beating rapidly or irregularly. We may have trouble going to sleep later on, and need to urinate frequently. These are symptoms of *caffeine intoxication*. Extremely large doses of caffeine

can cause extreme agitation, seizures, respiratory failure, and cardiac problems. The DSM-IV specifies that a diagnosis of caffeine intoxication should only be given if an individual experiences significant distress or impairment in functioning as a result of the symptoms. For example, someone drinking too much coffee for several days in a row during exam week might be so agitated he cannot sit through exams and so shaky he cannot drive a car.

Some heavy coffee drinkers joke that they are "caffeine addicts." Actually, they cannot be diagnosed with caffeine dependence disorder according to the DSM-IV, because to date there is little evidence that dependence on the drug causes significant social and occupational problems. Still, caffeine users can develop tolerance to caffeine and undergo withdrawal symptoms if they stop ingesting caffeine. They may find that they have to have several cups of coffee in the morning to feel "normal" and if they do not get their coffee, will experience significant headaches, fatigue, and anxiety.

Having friends who will engage in activities that do not involve alcohol can help an alcoholic avoid temptations to drink.

Summing Up

- Cocaine and amphetamines produce a rush of euphoria, followed by increases in self-esteem, alertness, and energy. With chronic use, however, they can lead to grandiosity, impulsiveness, hypersexuality, agitation, and paranoia.

- Withdrawal from cocaine and amphetamines causes symptoms of depression, exhaustion, and an intense craving for more of the substances.

- Cocaine seems particularly prone to lead to dependence, because it has extraordinarily rapid and strong effects on the brain and its effects wear off quickly.

- The intense activation of the central nervous system caused by cocaine and amphetamines can lead to a number of cardiac, respiratory, and neurological problems, and these substances are responsible for a large percentage of substance-related medical emergencies and deaths.

- Nicotine is an alkaloid found in tobacco, and affects the release of several neurochemicals in the body. Nicotine subjectively reduces stress but causes physiological arousal similar to that seen in the fight-or-flight response.

- Smoking is associated with higher rate of heart disease, lung cancer, emphysema, and chronic bronchitis, and substantially increases mortality rates.

- The majority of people who smoke wish they could quit, but have trouble doing so, in part because tolerance develops to nicotine and withdrawal symptoms are difficult to tolerate.

- Caffeine is the most commonly used stimulant drug. Caffeine intoxication can cause agitation, tremors, heart irregularities, and insomnia. People can develop tolerance and withdrawal from caffeine.

☺ OPIOIDS

Morphine, heroin, codeine, and methadone are all known as **opioids.** They derive from the sap of the opium poppy, which has been used for thousands of years to relieve pain. Our bodies actually produce natural opioids, some of which are called *endorphins* and *enkaphalins,* to cope with pain. For example, a sports injury induces the body to produce endorphins to reduce the pain of the injury to avoid shock. Doctors may also prescribe synthetic opioids, such as Percodan, Demerol, or Darvon, to help with pain.

Morphine was widely used as a pain-reliever in the nineteenth century, until it was discovered that it was highly addictive. Heroin was developed from morphine in the late nineteenth century, and used for a time for medicinal purposes. By 1917, however, it was clear that heroin and all opioids had dangerous addictive properties and the U.S. Congress passed a law to make heroin illegal and to ban the other opioids except for specific medical needs. Heroin remained widely available on the street, however. There was an explosion of heroin use during the Vietnam War, when young soldiers facing horrific circumstances found heroin cheap and easy to obtain in Vietnam. Fortunately, most of these soldiers stopped using heroin once they returned to the United States. But those who had experience with IV drugs or opioids before going to Vietnam tended to come back physically dependent on the drugs, which they continued to use when they returned to the United States. Current use of heroin expands and contracts with the price and availability of the drug on the street (Schuckit, 1995). When the drug is cheap and highly available, "epidemics" of use occur.

When used illegally, opioids are often injected directly into veins (*mainlining*), snorted, or smoked. The initial symptom of opioid intoxication is often euphoria (see *Concept Review:* Intoxication with and Withdrawal from Opioids, p. 594). People describe a sensation in the abdomen like a sexual orgasm, referring to it as a *thrill, kick,* or *flash* (Winger, Hofman, & Woods, 1992). They may have a tingling sensation and a pervasive sense of warmth. Their pupils dilate, and they pass into a state of drowsiness during which time they are lethargic, their speech is slurred, and their mind may be clouded. They may experience periods of light sleep, with vivid dreams. Pain is reduced. A person in this state is referred to as being *on the nod.*

Severe intoxication with opioids can lead to unconsciousness, coma, and seizures. These substances

Heroin is often injected directly into the veins.

CONCEPT REVIEW

Intoxication with and Withdrawal from Opioids

The opioids include morphine and heroin.

Drug	Intoxication Symptoms	Withdrawal Symptoms
Opioids	Behavioral changes (e.g., initial euphoria followed by apathy, dysphoria, psychomotor agitation or retardation, impaired judgment) Constriction of pupils Drowsiness or coma Slurred speech Attention and memory problems Hallucinations or illusions	Dysphoric mood Nausea or vomiting Muscle aches Tearing or nasal mucus discharge Dilation of pupils Goose bumps Sweating Diarrhea Yawning Fever Insomnia

can suppress the part of the brain stem controlling the respiratory and cardiovascular systems to the point of death. Basically, people stop breathing and their heart stops pumping. The drugs are especially dangerous when used in combination with depressants such as alcohol and sedatives. Comedian Chris Farley is just one of the celebrities who died of an overdose of opioids, mixed with cocaine and other drugs, as we discuss in *Extraordinary People:* Celebrity Drug Abusers.

Withdrawal symptoms can include dysphoria, anxiety, and agitation; an achy feeling in the back and legs; increased sensitivity to pain; and craving for more opioids. The person may be nauseous and vomit and have profuse sweating and goose bumps, diarrhea, and fever. These symptoms usually come on within 8 to 16 hours of the last use of morphine or heroin and peak within 36 to 72 hours. In chronic or heavy users, the symptoms may continue strongly for 5 to 8 days and in a milder form for weeks to months.

There are at least two pathways to opioid abuse and dependence (Schuckit, 1995). The first is a medical pathway. People may be prescribed opioids to treat chronic pain disorders, but become physically dependent on the drugs. Another type of medical pathway is the illegal use of these drugs by physicians and nurses, who obtain them on the job and use them to cope with the stress of their job.

The majority of people who develop opioid abuse or dependence begin using these drugs after having used alcohol, marijuana, and related drugs, and perhaps some of the depressants and stimulants. The first use of heroin is typically in the late teen years, after people have experimented with several of these other drugs (Schuckit, 1995). They may become psychologically dependent on the effects of the drugs first,

and then later become physiologically dependent. Once they are physiologically dependent, IV heroin users need to "shoot up" every four to six hours to avoid physical withdrawal. This is enormously expensive, but makes it almost impossible to hold a regular job. As a result, many people dependent on opioids turn to stealing, prostitution, and other crimes to get money for the drug. Heavy users often have a police record by their early twenties.

One of the greatest risks to opioid abusers and dependents is the risk of contracting HIV through contaminated needles or unprotected sex, which many opioid abusers engage in exchange for more substance. In some areas of the United States, up to 60 percent of chronic heroin users have HIV. Intravenous users also can contract hepatitis, tuberculosis, serious skin abscesses, and deep infections.

Summing Up

- The opioids include heroin, morphine, codeine, and methadone.
- They cause an initial rush or euphoria followed by a drowsy, dream-like state. Severe intoxication can cause respiratory and cardiovascular failure.
- Withdrawal symptoms can include dysphoria, anxiety, and agitation; an achy feeling in the back and legs; increased sensitivity to pain; and craving for more opioids.
- Opioid users who inject drugs can contract HIV and a number of other disorders by sharing needles.

EXTRAORDINARY PEOPLE

Celebrity Drug Abusers

Comedian Chris Farley was at the height of his career. This veteran of Chicago's famed Second City was catapulted to stardom when he landed a slot on *Saturday Night Live*. There his slapstick and baudy routines made him an instant favorite, and drew comparisons to one of his heroes, John Belushi. Like Belushi, Farley was overweight (weighing nearly 300 pounds) and had an "in your face" style of comedy. Also like Belushi, Farley lived hard and fast, abusing alcohol, cocaine, heroin, and other drugs. After *Saturday Night Live*, Farley moved on to star in movies such as *Tommy Boy* and *Black Sheep* and *Beverly Hills Ninja*.

On December 18, 1997, Chris Farley was found dead at the age of 33 in his condominium on the sixtieth floor of the John Hancock Building in Chicago. He had spent the night drinking, drugging, and debauching with friends, reportedly hiring "party girls" to do lap dances and strip for him. An autopsy later showed that he had overdosed on morphine and cocaine. There were also traces of marijuana in his urine. The coroner noted that heart disease, possibly due to Farley's excessive weight, also contributed to his death, and that his liver showed clear evidence of damage from chronic heavy alcohol use.

Without much trouble, many of us could name a number of other celebrities who abuse illicit drugs, or have died from drug overdoses: Marilyn Monroe, Elvis Presley, John Belushi, River Phoenix, Dana Plato. Comedian Richard Prior was permanently disfigured in an explosion while he was freebasing cocaine. You'd think that these high-profile celebrity deaths and debacles would discourage drug use by fans. As guitarist Keith Richards of the Rolling Stones said, "I used to know a few guys that did drugs all the time, but they're not alive anymore. . . . And you get the message after you've been to a few funerals."

But what message do fans, especially young fans, get from celebrities who use, and die from, drugs? It's easy to dismiss the celebrity drug deaths as the result of out-of-control excess by spoiled rich people who can't manage their drug use. The drug-related antics of people like Chris Farley seem so outrageous that we can easily believe we'd never fall into such behavior.

Yet, celebrity drug users—the ones who are alive—also can serve as models for cool and hip behavior. Many openly admit their drug use on talk shows and say little about the harm drugs are doing to their minds, bodies, and careers. They make snide jokes about their attempts to "get on the wagon." Alcohol and even illicit drug use is a staple of popular movies, where the star characters use these substances to cope with stress, to increase their sex appeal, and as part of everyday life. Certainly there are celebrities who have quit using drugs and who use their fame to campaign against drug use, especially by youth. But the overwhelming message that comes down in popular media is one that promotes alcohol and drug use. What is extraordinary about celebrity drug users is their power to shape popular opinion about drug use and abuse.

Chris Farley, John Belushi, and River Phoenix abused cocaine and other substances and died of overdoses.

☾ HALLUCINOGENS AND PCP

Most of the substances we have discussed so far can produce perceptual illusions and distortions when taken in large doses. The hallucinogens and PCP produce perceptual changes even in small doses (see *Concept Review:* Intoxication with Hallucinogens and PCP). A clear withdrawal syndrome from the hallucinogens and PCP has not been documented, so the DSM-IV does not currently recognize withdrawal from these drugs as a diagnosis.

The **hallucinogens** are a mixed group of substances including LSD (lysergic acid diethylamide),

CONCEPT REVIEW

Intoxication with Hallucinogens and PCP

The hallucinogens and PCP cause a variety of perceptual and behavioral changes.

Drug	Intoxication Symptoms
Hallucinogens	Behavioral changes (e.g., marked anxiety or depression, feeling that others are talking about you, fear of losing your mind, paranoia, impaired judgment) Perceptual changes while awake (e.g., intensification of senses, depersonalization, illusions, hallucinations) Dilation of pupils Rapid heartbeat Sweating Palpitations Blurring of vision Tremors Incoordination
PCP	Behavioral changes (e.g., belligerence, assaultiveness, impulsiveness, unpredictability, psychomotor agitation, impaired judgment) Involuntary rapid eyeball movement Hypertension Numbness Loss of muscle coordination Problems speaking due to poor muscle control Muscle rigidity Seizures or coma Exceptionally acute hearing Perceptual disturbances

Source: DSM-IV, APA, 2000.

MDMA (also called *ecstasy*), and peyote. Perhaps the best-known hallucinogen is LSD, which was first synthesized in 1938 by Swiss chemists. It was not until 1943 that the substance's psychoactive effects were discovered, when Dr. Albert Hoffman accidentally swallowed a minute amount of LSD and experienced visual hallucinations similar to those in schizophrenia. He later purposefully swallowed a small amount of LSD and reported the effects (Hoffman, 1968, pp. 185–186):

Voices

As far as I remember, the following were the most outstanding symptoms: vertigo, visual disturbances; the faces of those around me appeared as grotesque, colored masks; marked motor unrest, alternating with paresis; an intermittent heavy feeling in the head, limbs, and the entire body, as if they were filled with metal; cramps in the legs, coldness, and loss of feeling in the hands; a metallic taste on the tongue; dry constricted sensation in the throat; feeling of choking; confusion alternating between clear recognition of my condition, in which state I sometimes observed, in the manner of an independent, neutral observer, that I shouted half insanely or babbled incoherent words. Occasionally, I felt as if I were out of my body.

The doctor found a rather weak pulse but an otherwise normal circulation.

Six hours after ingestion of the LSD my condition had already improved considerably. Only the visual disturbances were still pronounced. Everything seemed to sway and the proportions were distorted like the reflections in the surface of moving water. Moreover, all objects appeared in unpleasant, constantly changing colors, the predominant shades being sickly green and blue. When I closed my eyes, an unending series of colorful, very realistic and fantastic images surged in upon me. A remarkable feature was the manner in which all acoustic perceptions (e.g., the noise of a passing car) were transformed into optical effects, every sound causing a corresponding colored hallucination constantly changing in shape and color like pictures in a kaleidoscope.

As Hoffman describes, one of the symptoms of intoxication from LSD and other hallucinogens is synethesia, the overflow from one sensory modality to another. People say they hear colors and see sounds. Time seems to pass very slowly. The boundaries between oneself and the environment seem gone. Moods may shift from depression to elation to fear. Some people become anxious, even panicked. Others feel a sense of detachment, and a great sensitivity for art, music, and feelings. These experiences led to these drugs being labeled psychedelic, from the Greek words for "soul" and "to make manifest." LSD was used in the 1960s as part of the consciousness-expanding movement. More recently, the hallucinogen known as ecstasy is used by people who believe it enhances insight, improves relationships, and enhances mood.

The hallucinogens are dangerous drugs, however. Although LSD was legal for use in the early 1960s, by 1967, reports of "bad acid trips," or "bummers," became common, particularly in the Haight-Ashbury district of San Francisco, where many LSD enthusiasts from around the United States congregated (Smith & Seymour, 1994). The symptoms included severe anxiety, paranoia, and loss of control. Some people on bad trips would walk off roofs or jump out windows, believing they could fly, or walk into the sea, believing they were "one with the universe." For some people, the anxiety and hallucinations caused by hallucinogens are so severe that they become psychotic and require hospitalization and long-term treatment. Some people experience flashbacks to their psychedelic experiences long after the drug has worn off. These flashbacks can be extremely distressing.

The most recent pattern of use for hallucinogens in the last few years has been as part of "raves" (Morrison, 1998). Raves began in Europe in the 1980s. These events, which are often sponsored by club owners or businesspeople, are held in warehouses, basements, tenements, and other large spaces. Participants ingest hallucinogens and then spend the night listening and dancing to "techno music." After the drug effects disappear, people are usually exhausted and may spend several hours sleeping. One of the greatest health concerns during raves is dehydration, so some rave organizers encourage participants to drink fluids and take breaks from the dancing. Agitation and paranoia can set into the crowd, creating the possibility of a chaotic scene that can result in injury.

Phenylcyclidine (PCP), also known as *angel dust*, *PeaCePill*, *Hog*, and *Tranq*, is manufactured as a powder to be snorted or smoked. Although PCP is not classified as a hallucinogen, it has many of the same effects. At lower doses, it produces a sense of intoxication, euphoria or affective dulling, talkativeness, lack of concern, slowed reaction time, vertigo, eye twitching, mild hypertension, abnormal involuntary movements, and weakness. At intermediate doses, it leads to disorganized thinking, distortions of body image (such as feeling one's arms do not belong to the rest of one's body), depersonalization, and feelings of unreality. A user may become hostile, belligerent, and even violent (Morrison, 1998). At higher doses, it produces amnesia and coma; analgesia sufficient to allow surgery; seizures; severe respiratory problems; hypothermia; and hyperthermia. The effects of phenylcyclidine begin immediately after injection, snorting, or smoking, reaching a peak within minutes. The symptoms of

severe intoxication can persist for several days. As a result, people with PCP intoxication are often misdiagnosed as having psychotic disorders not related to substance use.

As with the substances we have discussed so far, hallucinogen or PCP abuse is diagnosed when individuals repeatedly fail to fulfill major role obligations at school, work, or home due to intoxication with these drugs. They may use the drugs in dangerous situations (such as while driving a car), and may have legal troubles due to possession of the drugs. Particularly because these drugs can cause paranoia or aggressive behavior, people who use them frequently may find their work and social relationships being affected.

Summing Up

- The hallucinogens create perceptual illusions and distortions, sometimes fantastic, sometimes frightening. Some people feel more sensitive to art, music, and others. They also create mood swings and paranoia. Some people experience frightening flashbacks to experiences under the hallucinogens.

- PCP causes euphoria or affective dulling, abnormal involuntary movements, and weakness at low doses. At intermediate doses, it leads to disorganized thinking, depersonalization, feelings of unreality, and aggression. At higher doses, it produces amnesia and coma; analgesia sufficient to allow surgery; seizures; severe respiratory problems; hypothermia; and hyperthermia.

☉ CANNABIS

The leaves of the **cannabis** (or hemp) plant can be cut, dried, and rolled into cigarettes or inserted into food and beverages. It is the most widely used illicit substance in the world. In North America, the result is known as *marijuana*, *pot*, *grass*, *reefer*, and *Mary Jane*. It is called *ganja* in Jamaica, *kif* in North Africa, *dagga* in South Africa, *bhang* in India and the Middle East, and *macohna* in South America (Winger, Hofman & Woods, 1992). Hashish is a dried resin extract from the cannabis plant sold in cubes in America.

Cannabis is the most commonly used illegal drug in the United States, with nearly half the population reporting they have used this drug at some time in their lives, and 7 percent use it monthly (Anthony, Warner, & Kessler, 1994; NIDA, 1995). Teenagers are especially heavy users of marijuana, with about 20 percent saying they have used it in the last month. The use of cannabis has increased in recent years, and the potency of

Cannabis is the most commonly used illegal drug in the United States.

Drug	Intoxication Symptoms
Cannabis	Behavioral changes (e.g., impaired motor coordination, euphoria, anxiety, sensation of slowed time, impaired judgment) Red eyes Increased appetite Dry mouth Rapid heartbeat

Source: DSM-IV, APA, 2000.

cannabis has become greater as well. About 7 percent of the population would qualify for a diagnosis of cannabis abuse, and 2 to 3 percent of the population would qualify for a diagnosis of cannabis dependence (Kendler & Prescott, 1998a).

The symptoms of cannabis intoxication may develop within minutes if the cannabis is smoked, but may take a few hours to develop if taken orally (see *Concept Review:* Intoxication with Cannabis). The acute symptoms will last 3 to 4 hours, but some symptoms may linger or recur for 12 to 24 hours. Intoxication with cannabis usually begins with a "high" feeling of well-being, relaxation, and tranquillity. Users may feel dizzy, sleepy, or "dreamy." They may become more aware of their environments, and everything may seem funny. They may become grandiose or lethargic. People who are very anxious, depressed, or angry may become more so under the influence of cannabis.

The cognitive symptoms of cannabis intoxication are negative. People may believe they are thinking profound thoughts, but their short-term memories will be impaired to the point that they cannot remember thoughts long enough to express them in sentences (de Wit, Kirk, & Justice, 1998). Thus, they will perform poorly on a wide range of tests, and may not be able to hold a conversation. Motor performance is also impaired. People's reaction times are slower, their concentration and judgment are deficient, and as a result, they are at risk for accidents.

Cannabis has hallucinogenic effects at moderate to large doses. Users experience perceptual distortions, feelings of depersonalization, and paranoid thinking. Some people experience frank hallucinations and delusions. The changes in perceptions may be experienced as pleasant by some but as very frightening by others. Some users may have severe anxiety episodes resembling panic attacks (Phariss, Millman, & Beeder, 1998).

Physiological symptoms of cannabis intoxication include increases in heart rate, an irregular heartbeat, increases in appetite, and dry mouth. Cannabis smoke is irritating and thus increases the risk of chronic cough, sinusitis, bronchitis, and emphysema. It contains even larger amounts of known carcinogens than does tobacco, so it creates a high risk for cancer. Chronic use of cannabis lowers sperm count in men and may cause irregular ovulation in women.

In part because of the increased potency of cannabis, many people who formerly might have been casual users of cannabis, including high school students, have developed problems with abuse and dependence. They may smoke marijuana often enough that their school performance suffers, their lives revolve around smoking, and they have frequent accidents as the result of intoxication. Physical tolerance to cannabis can develop, so users need greater amounts to avoid withdrawal symptoms. The symptoms of withdrawal can include loss of appetite, hot flashes, a runny nose, sweating, diarrhea, and hiccups.

In recent years, several groups have advocated the legalization of marijuana cigarettes for medical uses (Grinspoon & Bakalar, 1995). THC, the active compound in cannabis, can help relieve nausea in cancer patients undergoing chemotherapy and increase appetite in AIDS patients. It also helps in the treatment of asthma and glaucoma. THC can be given in pill form, but some people argue that the level of THC that enters the body is more controllable when it is taken in a marijuana cigarette. People who ingest THC in pill form do not risk the respiratory damage due to the smoke from marijuana cigarettes, however.

Summing Up

- Cannabis creates a high feeling, cognitive and motor impairments, and in some people hallucinogenic effects.

- Cannabis use is high and significant numbers of people, especially teenagers, have impaired performance at school or on the job, and in relationships as a result of chronic use. Marijuana use can also lead to a number of physical problems, especially respiratory problems.

⊙ THEORIES OF SUBSTANCE USE, ABUSE, AND DEPENDENCE

All the substances we have discussed in this chapter affect several biochemicals in the brain, and these chemicals can have direct reinforcing effects on the brain. One area of the brain that may be intimately involved in the effects of psychoactive substances is the **mesolimbic dopamine system** (see Figure 16.6). This system is activated by natural rewards of many kinds, such as the taste of good food and the physical pleasure accompanying sexual stimulation. The same system is activated much more intensely by the psychoactive substances that people abuse or become dependent upon, such as cocaine, amphetamines, and heroin. The activation of this system actually disposes people to want to repeat the events that caused its activation. This occurs when a small bite of tasty food whets one's appetite. It also occurs when one hit of crack causes a user to want another hit (Berridge & Valenstein, 1991).

When the mesolimbic dopamine system is activated by a psychoactive substance, the brain may try to balance this state of activation with processes that have effects that are the opposite of those of the psychoactive substance. These processes are often referred to as *opponent processes* (Solomon, 1980). These opponent processes may remain active even after a person stops taking a psychoactive substance and may cause many of the symptoms of withdrawal.

Chronic use of psychoactive substances may produce permanent changes in the mesolimbic dopamine system, causing craving for these substances even after withdrawal symptoms pass. The repeated use of substances like cocaine, heroin, and amphetamines causes the neurons in the mesolimbic dopamine system to become hyperactive or sensitized. This sensitization can be permanent, so that these neurons will be activated more highly by subsequent exposure to the psychoactive substance or by stimuli that are associated with the substance (such as the pipe that a cocaine user formerly used to smoke crack). Subjectively, this creates a chronic and strong craving for the substance, which is made worse every time a former user comes into contact with stimuli that remind him or her of the substance. This can create a powerful physiological motivation for relapsing back into substance abuse and dependence (Robinson & Berridge, 1993). Susan, who was dependent on cocaine and alcohol but has been abstinent for 3 months, describes this phenomenon:

Voices

Right now, I mean, I wanna go out and—I mean I want a line so bad, you know, I can taste it. Right now. I know I'm not supposed to. I just want it, though. Coke.

(Engel, 1989, p. 40)

Thus, the substances we have discussed in this chapter have powerful effects on the brain, in both the short term and the long term, that can make these substances hard for people to resist once they have used them. Substances like cocaine that have especially

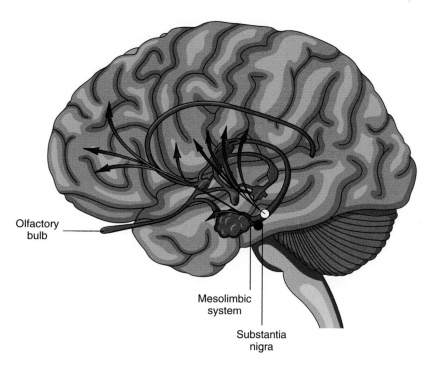

FIGURE 16.6 The Mesolimbic Dopamine System. The mesolimbic dopamine system may be the "reward center" of the brain where pleasure and displeasure arising from many sources (including psychoactive drugs) is registered.

rapid and powerful effects on the brain but that also wear off very quickly create great risk for dependency. Even people trying a substance casually can find the rapid, intense, but short-lived high so compelling that they crave more and soon increase their use.

Clearly, however, most people never even try most of the substances discussed in this chapter, and of those who do try them, most do not abuse them or become dependent on them. We turn now to other theories of substance abuse and dependence that have tried to explain differences between people in vulnerability to substance-related disorders. Most theories of substance-related disorders have focused on alcohol abuse and dependence, probably because alcohol-related disorders are more widespread than the other disorders. Thus, much of our discussion of theories will be concerned with the development of alcohol abuse and dependence. Several of these theories have been applied to explain the development of abuse and dependence on disorders other than alcohol, however, and we note these as we go along.

For years, alcoholism and other drug addictions were considered the result of a moral deficiency. Alcoholics and drug addicts were simply weak, bad people who would not exert control over their impulses. Since the 1960s, that view has largely been replaced by the **disease model** of alcoholism and drug addiction, which views these disorders as incurable physical diseases, like epilepsy or diabetes (Jellinek, 1960). This model has been supported somewhat by research on the genetics and biology of alcoholism and drug addiction, but there clearly are social and psychological forces that make some people more prone to these disorders than are others. In this section, we discuss the biological, social, and psychological factors that increase people's vulnerability to substance abuse and dependence.

Biological Theories

Three types of biological theories have been prominent in the literature on substance-related disorders. First, many theorists attribute vulnerability to these disorders to genetics. Second, people who become substance dependent or abusive may react differently physiologically to substances from those who do not. Third, some theorists have argued that alcoholism, and perhaps other forms of substance dependence, really represent an underlying biological depression.

Genetic Factors

Family history, adoption, and twin studies all suggest that genetics may play a substantial role in at least some forms of alcohol dependency and drug addiction

(Bierut et al., 1998; Kendler, Davis, & Kessler, 1997; McGue, 1999; Merikangas, Dierker, & Szatmari, 1998). For example, the relatives of people with substance-related disorders are eight times more likely to also have a substance disorder than the relatives of people with no substance-related disorder (Merikangas et al., 1998). The particular substance being used tends to run in families, be it alcohol, cocaine, cannabis, or opioids, and so on. Families that use one substance, however, are more likely to use multiple substances.

Twin studies have clearly shown that a substantial portion of the family transmission of substance abuse and dependence is due to genetics (Kendler & Prescott, 1998b; Lerman et al., 1999; Pomerleau & Kardia, 1999; Prescott & Kendler, 1999). For example, in a study of over 3,000 male twins, Prescott and Kendler (1999) found concordance rates for alcohol dependence among monozygotic twins of .48, compared to .32 among dizygotic twins. Evidence of heritability was strong only for early-onset alcoholism (with onset of first symptoms before age 20) but not for late-onset alcoholism.

The evidence for a genetic transmission of alcoholism and drug addiction has been much more consistent for males than for females (Bierut et al., 1998; Jang, Livesley, & Vernan, 1997). Several studies of female twins have found no evidence for a genetic contribution to female alcoholism (McGue, 1999; McGue, Pickens, & Svikis, 1992). Some recent studies have suggested that genetics are involved in female alcoholism. Certain environmental circumstances, such as sexual abuse, are stronger predictors of alcoholism in women than in men, however (McGue, 1999). Researchers are currently debating whether the contributors to alcoholism and other drug dependencies are different, at least in magnitude, for women and men.

Biological theorists interested in nicotine addiction have recently made advances in identifying genetic factors that may influence an individual's vulnerability. This research is highlighted in *Pushing the Boundaries: Finding the Gene for Smoking*.

Alcohol Reactivity

When given moderate doses of alcohol, the sons of alcoholics, who are presumably at increased risk for alcoholism, experience less intoxication, subjectively, in their cognitive and motor performance and on some physiological indicators than do the sons of nonalcoholics (Schuckit & Smith, 1996, 1997). At high doses of alcohol, however, the sons of alcoholics are just as intoxicated, by both subjective and objective measures, as are the sons of nonalcoholics. This lower reactivity to moderate doses of alcohol among sons of alcoholics may lead them to drink substantially more before they

PUSHING THE BOUNDARIES

Finding the Gene for Smoking

People start smoking cigarettes because they succumb to peer pressure and media images that say smoking is cool; then they continue smoking because they become physically addicted to the nicotine. Right? Although societal messages and the addictive properties of nicotine no doubt play roles in people's smoking behavior, there are clearly many more factors involved. Recent research on smoking has focused on genetic contributors to smoking behavior and the risk of nicotine addiction (Pomerleau & Kardia, 1999).

The first reports suggesting that genes play a role in smoking actually were published over 40 years ago by Fisher (1958), who found that the concordance rate for smoking behavior was significantly higher in monozygotic twins than in dizygotic twins. Several subsequent publications confirmed this finding (Carmelli et al., 1992; Eaves & Eysenck, 1980; Hannah, Hopper, & Mathews, 1984; Health & Martihn, 1993; Hughes, 1986). Hughes (1986) summarized the data from 18 twin studies of smoking and concluded that 53 percent of the variation in smoking behavior was attributable to genetic causes.

Just how genes might affect smoking behavior was not known, however, until advanced technologies for genetic research began to be applied in studies of smoking. This new research is focusing on the neurotransmitter dopamine because the reinforcing properties of nicotine are probably due, in part, to the fact that nicotine stimulates dopamine release and inhibits the reuptake of dopamine, thereby increasing levels of dopamine at the synapse (Perkins & Stitzer, 1998). Genetic variation in the dopamine receptor gene (labeled DRD2) and the

dopamine transporter gene (labeled SLC6A3) may influence concentrations of dopamine at the synapse and responses to dopamine, thereby influencing how reinforcing nicotine is (Pomerleau & Kardia, 1999). People with certain polymorphisms in the DRD2 or SLC6A3 genes that result in more dopamine at the synapse appear less likely to become smokers than people without these polymorphisms (Lerman et al., 1999). In addition, smokers with the SLC6A3 polymorphism are more likely to quit smoking than those without it (Sabol et al., 1999).

This is likely to be only one of many pathways by which genes influence smoking (Pomerleau & Kardia, 1999). For example, there are nicotinic acetylcholine receptors that are the point of entry for nicotine into the central nervous system and moderate the reinforcing effects of nicotine (Picciotto et al., 1998). Presently, there are no genetic probes available to study polymorphisms in these nicotine receptors in humans, but this seems a good target for future research. In addition, it is clear that cigarette smoking and nicotine dependence are much more common among people with serious psychiatric disorders, such as schizophrenia and depression, than among people without psychiatric disorders (Pomerleau, 1997). Whether this is due to genetic factors common both to smoking behavior and psychiatric disorder, or other causes is currently unclear.

The hope of investigators in this area is that greater understanding of the genetics of smoking behavior will lead to better identification of people at risk and the development of better treatments, including new drugs, to help people stop smoking.

begin to feel drunk; as a result, they may not learn to recognize subtle, early signs of intoxication and may not learn to quit drinking before they become highly intoxicated. They may also develop high physiological tolerance for alcohol, which leads them to ingest more and more alcohol to achieve any level of subjective intoxication. Long-term studies of men with low reactivity to

moderate doses of alcohol show that they are significantly more likely to become alcoholics over time than are men with greater reactivity to moderate doses of alcohol (Schuckit, 1998; Schuckit & Smith, 1997). The low-reactivity men are especially likely to develop alcohol problems if they encounter significant stress, or have a tendency toward poor behavioral control.

Women may be less prone than men to alcoholism because they are much *more* sensitive than men to the intoxicating effects of alcohol (Lex, 1995). At a given dose of alcohol, about 30 percent more of the alcohol will enter a woman's bloodstream than a man's, because women have less of an enzyme that neutralizes and breaks down alcohol. Thus, a woman will experience the subjective and overt symptoms of alcohol intoxication at lower doses than a man will and may experience more severe withdrawal symptoms (i.e., hangovers) if she drinks too much. These factors may lead many women to drink less than men do. Women who do abuse alcohol, however, may be at more risk for negative health effects of alcohol than are men, because their blood concentrations of alcohol are higher than those of men who abuse.

Alcoholism as a Form of Depression

As many as 70 percent of people with alcohol dependency have depressive symptoms severe enough to interfere with daily living (Schuckit, 1991). In addition, early family history studies suggested that alcohol-related disorders and unipolar depression run together in families, with alcoholism more prevalent in male relatives and unipolar depression more prevalent in female relatives (Winokur & Clayton, 1967). These trends led some researchers to argue that alcoholism and depression are genetically related or perhaps one disorder and that many male alcoholics are actually depressed and denying their depression or "self-medicating" with alcohol (see Williams & Spitzer, 1983).

Although many people with alcohol-related problems appear to use alcohol to cope with daily stresses and emotional distress, it is probably not wise to consider alcoholism simply another form of depression for several reasons. First, although the children of alcoholics do have higher rates of depression than do the children of nonalcoholics, these depressions might result more from the stresses of having alcoholic parents than from genetics (Schuckit, 1995). Second, several family history studies have failed to find higher rates of alcoholism among the offspring of depressed people than among the offspring of nondepressed people, as one would suspect if depression and alcoholism were genetically related (Merikangas, Weissman, & Pauls, 1985). Third, because alcohol is a central nervous system depressant, it can cause the classic symptoms of depression. In addition, the social consequences of alcohol abuse and dependency (loss of relationships, loss of job) can cause depressions. Thus, when depression and alcohol dependency co-occur in individuals, the depression is just as likely to be a consequence as a cause of the alcohol dependency. Indeed, large epidemiological studies find that the odds of depression preceding alcoholism are equal to the odds that alcoholism will precede depression (Swendsen et al., 1998). Fourth, studies show that adolescents who are depressed are not more likely to become alcoholics than are adolescents who are not depressed, as we might expect if alcoholism is often a response to depression (Schuckit, 1995). Fifth, simply prescribing antidepressant medications to a person with alcohol abuse or dependency is not enough to help him or her overcome the alcohol-related problems in the long run (Schuckit, 1995). The risk of relapse is high unless he or she also undergoes treatment directly targeted at the drinking. Sixth, depression among alcoholics usually disappears once they become abstinent, even without any antidepressant treatment, again suggesting that the depression is secondary to the alcoholism, rather than its cause (Brown et al., 1995). Seventh, alcoholism and other drug addictions co-occur with a wide range of other psychological disorders in addition to depression, including bipolar disorder, the personality disorders, anxiety disorders, schizophrenia, and in people who have been physically or sexually abused (Schuckit et al., 1998).

Behavioral and Cognitive Theories

Children and adolescents learn alcohol-related behaviors from the modeling of their parents and important others in their culture. Studies of children of alcoholics find that even as preschoolers, they are more likely than other children to be able to identify alcoholic drinks and were more likely to view alcohol use as a normal part of daily life (Zucker et al., 1995). Children of parents who abuse alcohol by frequently getting drunk or driving while intoxicated learn that these are acceptable behaviors and are thus more likely to engage in them as well (Chassin et al., 1999). Because alcohol-related problems are more common among males than females, most of the adults modeling the inappropriate use of alcohol will be male. In turn, because children are more likely to learn from adults who are similar to themselves, male children and male adolescents may be more likely to learn these behaviors from the adults in their world than are female children and female adolescents. Thus, maladaptive patterns of alcohol use may be passed down through the males in a family through modeling.

The cognitive theories of alcohol abuse have focused on people's expectations for the effects of alcohol and their beliefs about the appropriateness of using alcohol to cope with stress (Marlatt et al., 1988). People who expect alcohol to reduce their distress, and who do not have other, more adaptive means of coping available to them (such as problem solving or turning to others for support) are more likely than others to drink alcohol when they are upset and more likely to have social problems related to drinking. For example, one study found that both men and women who believed that alcohol helped them relax and handle stress better and who tended to cope with stressful situations with avoidance rather than problem solving drank more often and had more drinking-related problems (Cooper et al., 1992). In long-term studies of sons of alcoholics mentioned above, those men who used alcohol to cope and who expected alcohol to relax them, were more likely to develop alcohol abuse or dependence, whether or not they had low reactivity to low doses of alcohol (Schuckit, 1998). When we explore treatment, we review therapies that try to change people's beliefs about alcohol as a coping tool and to give people more appropriate strategies for coping with their problems.

Sociocultural Approaches

Voices

It was great being stoned. It was, you know, it was great. I just could evade all the bull—and just be stoned, do anything stoned. I just wanted to block everything out, is basically what it was.

(Engel, 1989, p. 27)

The reinforcing effects of substances—the highs that stimulants produce, the calming and "zoning out" effects of the depressants and opioids—all may be more attractive to people under great psychological stress, particularly those under chronic stress. Thus, we see higher rates of substance abuse and dependence among people facing severe chronic stress—people living in poverty and with few hopes, women in abusive relationships, adolescents whose parents fight frequently and violently (Stewart, 1996; Zucker, Chermack, & Curran, 1999). For these people, the effects of substances may be especially reinforcing. Plus, they may see few costs to becoming dependent on substances because they feel they have little to lose.

Chronic stress combined with an environment that supports and even promotes the use of substances as an escape is a recipe for widespread substance abuse and dependence. Such was the situation for soldiers fighting in the Vietnam War. The conditions under which they fought and lived created chronic stress. Illegal drugs, especially heroin and marijuana, were readily available, and the culture of the 1960s supported drug experimentation. Only 1 percent of soldiers who

Children may learn health-related behaviors from their parents.

served in Vietnam had been dependent on heroin or other hard substances before the war. During the war, half the soldiers used these substances at least occasionally, and 20 percent were dependent on them. Fortunately, once these soldiers left that environment and returned home, their substance use dropped to the same level it was before they went to Vietnam (Robins, Helzer, & Davis, 1975).

Some people cannot leave their stress behind because the stress is present where they live. Indeed, many people dependent on substances were introduced to these substances by their family members and grew up in horrible conditions from which everyone around them was using substances to escape (Zucker, Fitzgerald, & Moses, 1995).

CASE STUDY

LaTisha, 35 years old when interviewed, was born and raised in Miami. Her mother was a barmaid and she never knew her father. She grew up with two brothers and four sisters, all of whom have different fathers. Her mother used pills during LaTisha's childhood, particularly Valium.

LaTisha took her first alcoholic drink when she was 12, introduced to her by her mother. However, she didn't drink regularly until she was 17, although she started sniffing glue at age 13. LaTisha's mother often brought men home from the bar to have sex with them for money.

At 14, LaTisha's mother "turned her out" (introduced her to prostitution) by setting her up with "dates" from the bar. LaTisha was not aware until years later that the men had been paying her mother. LaTisha also recalls having been sexually abused by one of her mother's male friends when she was about 8.

When LaTisha was 16, her older brother returned home from the army. He and his friends would smoke marijuana. In an attempt to "be with the crowd," LaTisha also began smoking marijuana. At a party, her brother introduced her to "downers"—prescription sedatives and tranquilizers. LaTisha began taking pills regularly, eventually taking as many as 15 a day for about a year and a half. She was most often using both Valium and Quaalude.

By 17, LaTisha's brother had introduced her to heroin. Almost immediately, she began speedballing—injecting as well as snorting heroin, cocaine, and various amphetamines. During all the phases of LaTisha's injection-substance use, sharing needles was common. By age 24, LaTisha was mainlining heroin and turning tricks every day. (Adapted from Inciardi, Lockwood, & Pottieger, 1993, pp. 160–161).

It does not take conditions as extreme as LaTisha's to create an atmosphere that promotes substance use and abuse. More subtle environmental reinforcements and punishments for substance use and abuse clearly influence people's substance use habits. Some societies discourage any use of alcohol, often as part of religious beliefs, and alcohol abuse and dependence in these societies are rare. Other societies, including many European cultures, allow drinking of alcohol but strongly discourage excessive drinking or irresponsible behavior while intoxicated. Alcohol-related disorders are less common in these societies than in those with few restrictions, either legal or cultural, on alcohol use (Winger, Hofman & Woods, 1992).

Gender Differences

Most of the theories about the gender differences in substance use disorders have focused on differences in the reinforcements and punishments for substance use between men and women and their resulting attitudes toward their own use (see Gomberg, 1994; Lex, 1995). Substance use, particularly alcohol use, is much more acceptable for men than for women in many societies. Heavy drinking is part of what "masculine" men do and it is modeled by heroes and cultural icons. However, until quite recently, heavy drinking was a sign that a woman was "not a lady." Societal acceptance of heavy drinking by women has increased in recent generations and so has the rate of alcohol use in young women.

Men and women have also tended to have different expectations about the effects of alcohol and perhaps other substances that influence their use. Men are more likely than women to have positive expectations about alcohol helping them cope and to use alcohol to cope. Indeed, some laboratory studies find that women often expect alcohol to interfere with their ability to cope with difficult situations and avoid alcohol when they must deal with stressful situations. Thus, differences between men and women both in expectations about alcohol and the use of alcohol to cope may contribute to the gender differences in alcohol-related problems (Cooper et al., 1992).

When women do become substance abusers, their patterns of use and reasons for use tend to differ from men's. Whereas men tend to begin using substances in the context of socializing with male friends, women are most often initiated into substance use by family members, partners, or lovers (Boyd & Guthrie, 1996; Gomberg, 1994; Inciardi, Lockwood, & Pottieger, 1993). One study found that 70 percent of female crack users were living with men who were also substance users, and many were living with multiple abusers (Inciardi, Lockwood, & Pottieger, 1993).

Summing Up

- Psychoactive substances have powerful effects on the parts of the brain that register reward and pleasure, including the mesolimbic dopamine system. Repeated use of a substance may sensitize this system, causing craving for more of the substance.

- Some types of alcoholism, particularly among males, may be genetically transmitted. Men genetically predisposed to alcoholism are less sensitive to the effects of low doses of alcohol. One reason women may be less prone to alcoholism is that their bodies are more reactive to low doses of alcohol.

- Some theorists view alcoholism as a form of depression, although the prevailing evidence suggests that alcoholism and depression are distinct disorders.

- Behavioral theories of alcoholism note that people are reinforced or punished by other people for their alcohol-related behaviors.

- Cognitive theories argue that people who develop alcohol-related problems have strong expectations that alcohol will help them feel better and cope better when they face stressful times.

- Sociocultural theorists note that alcohol and drug use increases among people under severe stress.

In addition, the gender differences in substance-related disorders may be tied to different reinforcements and punishments for men and women for using substances.

☉ TREATMENT FOR SUBSTANCE-RELATED DISORDERS

Historically, treatments for substance-related disorders have been based on the disease model, which states that these disorders are medical diseases (MacCoun, 1998). The disease model suggests that biological treatments are most appropriate. It also suggests that people with these disorders have no control over their use of substances because of their disease, and thus must avoid all use of the substances. Thus, Alcoholics Anonymous, which focuses on helping alcoholics accept that they have a disease and completely abstain from drinking, is based on a disease model, and is the most widely prescribed intervention for proponents of biological perspectives on alcoholism.

More recently, psychological interventions have been based on a harm-reduction approach to treatment (Marlatt, 1998). Proponents of this approach focus on the psychological and sociocultural factors that lead people to use substances inappropriately, and on helping people gain control over their use of substances through behavioral and cognitive interventions. The harm-reduction model does not presume that people must avoid all use of substances—for example, that alcoholics must never take another drink. As a result, it has been severely criticized by strong proponents of the disease model.

Whether an individual clinician follows the disease model or the harm-reduction model of intervention, he or she will most often recommend **detoxification** as the first step to any treatment program. Detoxification is especially important when the substance being used can cause permanent organ or brain damage or is frequently lethal, such as cocaine, amphetamines, and inhalants. Basically, individuals are assisted to stop using the substance, then the substance is allowed to eliminate from the body. Many detoxification programs are in hospitals and clinics, so that physicians can monitor individuals through withdrawal from the drug, making them more comfortable, and intervening if their life is in danger.

Once people stop using the substance and are through the withdrawal process, a variety of biological and psychosocial therapies are used to help them prevent relapse. These therapies are often combined in comprehensive substance treatment programs. People check themselves into these programs where they remain for a few weeks or months until they feel they have gained control over their substance use and dependence.

Biological Treatments

Medications can be used to help wean individuals off a substance, to reduce their desire for a substance, and to maintain their use of substances at a controlled level.

Antianxiety Drugs, Antidepressants, and Antagonists

Although many substance-dependent people can withstand withdrawal symptoms with emotional support, for other people the symptoms are so severe that medications may be prescribed to reduce these symptoms (O'Brien & McKay, 1998; Schuckit, 1996). For people who are alcohol dependent, a benzodiazepine, which has depressant effects similar to those of alcohol, can be prescribed to reduce symptoms of tremor and anxiety, decrease pulse and respiration rates, and stabilize blood pressure. The dosage of the drug is decreased each day so that a patient withdraws from the alcohol slowly but does not become dependent on the benzodiazepine.

Antidepressants are also used to help people weather the withdrawal syndrome so as to continue abstaining from substance use (O'Brien & McKay, 1998; Schuckit, 1996). The serotonin reuptake inhibitors can help to reduce impulsive consumption of alcohol and craving for alcohol. Antidepressant drugs are sometimes used to treat alcoholics or drug addicts who are depressed, but the efficacy of these drugs in treating either the alcohol or drug problems or the depression in the absence of psychotherapy has not been consistently supported (Schuckit, 1996).

Antagonist drugs block or change the effects of the addictive drug, reducing the desire of the addict for the drug. **Naltrexone** and **naloxone** are opioid antagonists—they block the effects of opioids like heroin. Heroin dependents are also given other drugs that reduce the reinforcing effects of heroin and thus reduce their desire for the heroin. If a person takes heroin while on naltrexone or naloxone, he or she will not experience the positive effects of the heroin. This, theoretically, can reduce desire for the drug and therefore use of the drug. The opioid antagonists must be administered very carefully, however, because they can cause severe withdrawal reactions in people addicted to opioids.

Naltrexone has also proven useful in blocking the high that can be caused by alcohol. Alcoholics on naltrexone report that their craving for alcohol is diminished and they drink less (Croop, Faulkner, & Labriola,

1997). Naltrexone may block the effects of alcohol as well as opioids because it affects the mesolimbic area of the brain, which is involved in the psychoactive effects of most drugs.

One drug that can make alcohol actually punishing is **disulfiram,** commonly referred to as *Antabuse* (Schuckit, 1996). Just having one drink can make a person taking disulfiram feel sick and dizzy, and make him vomit, blush, and even faint. People must be very motivated to agree to remain on disulfiram, and it only works to reduce alcohol consumption as long as they take it.

Methadone Maintenance Programs

Gradual withdrawal from heroin can be achieved with the help of a synthetic drug known as **methadone.** This is an opioid itself, but it has less potent and longer-lasting effects than heroin when taken orally. The heroin dependent will take methadone while discontinuing use of heroin. The methadone will help reduce the extreme negative withdrawal symptoms from heroin. Individuals who take heroin while on methadone do not experience the intense psychological effects of heroin because methadone blocks receptors for heroin. While the goal of treatment is eventually to withdraw individuals from methadone, some patients continue to use methadone for years, under physicians' care, rather than taper off their use. These **methadone maintenance programs** are controversial. Some people believe that they allow the heroin dependent simply to transfer dependency to another substance that is legal and provided by a physician. Other people believe that methadone maintenance is the only way to keep some heroin dependents from going back on the street and becoming readdicted. Studies following patients in methadone maintenance programs do find they are much more likely than patients who try to withdraw from heroin without methadone to remain in psychological treatment and they are less likely to relapse into heroin use or to become reinvolved in criminal activity (O'Brien & McKay, 1998).

Behavioral and Cognitive Treatments

Behavioral Treatments

Behavioral treatments based on **aversive classical conditioning** are sometimes used to treat alcohol dependency and abuse, either alone or in combination with biological or other psychosocial therapies (Finney & Moos, 1998; Schuckit, 1995). Drugs like disulfiram (Antabuse) that make the ingestion of alcoholic unpleasant or toxic are given to alcoholics. If they take

Behavioral interventions help alcoholics learn to inhibit their impulses to drink.

drinks of alcohol, the drug interacts with the alcohol to cause nausea and vomiting. Eventually, through classical conditioning, alcoholics develop conditioned responses to the alcohol, namely nausea and vomiting. They then learn to avoid the alcohol, through operant conditioning, in order to avoid the aversive response to the alcohol. Studies have shown such aversive conditioning to be effective in reducing alcohol consumption, at least in the short term (Schuckit, 1995). "Booster" sessions are often needed to reinforce the aversive conditioning, however, because it tends to weaken with time.

An alternative is **covert sensitization therapy** in which alcoholics use imagery to create associations between thoughts of alcohol use and thoughts of highly unpleasant consequences of alcohol use. An example of a sensitization scene that a therapist might take a client through begins as follows (Rimmele, Miller, & Dougher, 1989, p. 135):

Voices

You finish the first sip of beer, and you . . . notice a funny feeling in your stomach. . . . Maybe another drink will help. . . . As you tip back . . . that funny feeling in your stomach is stronger, and you feel like you have to burp. . . . You swallow again, trying to force it down, but it doesn't work. You can feel the gas coming up. . . . You swallow more, but suddenly your mouth is filled with a sour liquid that burns the back of your throat and goes up your nose. . . . [You] spew the liquid all over the counter and sink. . . .

The imagery gets even more graphic from there. Covert sensitization techniques seem effective in creating conditioned aversive responses to the sight and smell of alcohol and in reducing alcohol consumption.

Finally, as noted earlier, some alcoholics develop classically conditioned responses to the environmental cues often present when they drink. For example, when they see or smell their favorite alcoholic beverages, they begin to salivate and report cravings to drink. These conditioned responses increase the risk of relapse among alcoholics who are abstinent or trying to quit drinking. A behavioral therapy known as **cue exposure and response prevention** is used to extinguish this conditioned response to cues associated with alcohol intake (Rankin, Hodgson, & Stockwell, 1983). Alcoholics are exposed to their favorite types of alcohol, encouraged to hold glasses to their lips, and smell the alcohol but are prohibited or strongly encouraged not to drink any of the alcohol. Eventually, this procedure has been shown to reduce the desire to drink and increase the ability to avoid drinking when the opportunity arises (Rankin, Hodgson & Stockwell, 1983). The procedure probably should be coupled with instructions on strategies for coping with and removing oneself from tempting situations as we discuss next.

Cognitive Treatments

Interventions based on the cognitive models of alcohol abuse and dependency help clients identify those situations in which they are most likely to drink and lose control over their drinking and their expectations that alcohol will help them cope better with those situations (Marlatt & Gordon, 1985). Therapists then work with clients to challenge these expectations by reviewing the negative effects of alcohol on their behavior. For example, a therapist may focus on a recent party at which a client was feeling anxious and thus began to drink heavily. The therapist might have the client recount the embarrassing and socially inappropriate behaviors he engaged in while intoxicated, to challenge the notion that the alcohol helped him cope effectively with his party anxiety. Therapists also help clients learn to anticipate and reduce stress in their lives and to develop more adaptive ways of coping with stressful situations, such as seeking the help of others or active problem solving. Finally, therapists help clients learn to say, "No thanks," when offered drinks and to deal effectively with social pressure to drink by using assertiveness skills.

The following is an excerpt from a discussion between a therapist and a client with alcohol-related problems in which the therapist is helping the client generate strategies for coping with the stress of a possible job promotion (adapted from Sobell & Sobell, 1978, pp. 97–98). The therapist encourages the client to brainstorm coping strategies, without evaluating them for the moment, so that the client feels free to generate as many possible strategies as he can.

Voices

Client: I really want this job, and it'll mean a lot more money for me, not only now but also at retirement. Besides, if I refused the promotion, what would I tell my wife or my boss?

Therapist: Rather than worrying about that for the moment, why don't we explore what kinds of possible behavioral options you have regarding this job promotion. Remember, don't evaluate the options now. Alternatives, at this point, can include anything even remotely possible; what we want you to do is come up with a range of possible alternatives. You don't have to carry out an alternative just because you consider it.

Client: You know, I could do what I usually do in these kinds of situations. In fact, being as nervous as I've been these past couple of months, I've done that quite often.

Therapist: You mean drinking?

Client: Yeah, I've been drinking quite heavily some nights when I get home, and my wife is really complaining.

Therapist: Well, OK, drinking is one option. What other ways could you deal with this problem?

Client: Well, I could take the job, and on the side I could take some night courses in business at a local college. That way I could learn how to be a supervisor. But, gee, that would be a lot of work. I don't even know if I have the time. Besides, I don't know if they offer the kind of training I need.

Therapist: At this point, it's really not necessary to worry about how to carry out the options but simply to identify them. You're doing fine. What are some other ways you might handle the situation?

Client: Well, another thing I could do is to simply tell the boss that I'm not sure I'm qualified and either tell him that I don't want the job or ask him if he could give me some time to learn my new role.

Therapist: OK. Go on, you're doing fine.

Client: But what if the boss tells me that I have to take the job, I don't have any choice?

Therapist: Well, what general kinds of things might happen in that case?

Client: Oh, I could take the job and fail. That's one option. I could take the job and learn how to be a supervisor. I could refuse the job, risk being fired, and maybe end up having to look for another job. You know, I could just go and talk to my supervisor right now and explain the problem to him and see what comes of that.

Therapist: Well, you've delineated a lot of options. Let's take some time to evaluate them before you reach any decision.

The therapist then helps the client evaluate the potential effectiveness of each option and anticipate any potential negative consequences of each action. The client decides to accept the promotion but take some courses at the local college to increase his business background. The therapist discusses with the client the stresses of managing a new job and classes, and they generate ways the client can manage these stresses other than by drinking.

In most cases, therapists using these cognitive-behavioral approaches encourage clients to abstain from alcohol, especially when clients have histories of frequent relapses into alcohol abuse. When clients' goals are to learn to drink socially and therapists believe clients have the capability to achieve these goals, then therapists may focus on teaching clients to engage in social, or controlled, drinking.

The Controlled Drinking Controversy

The notion that some alcoholics can learn to engage in controlled, social drinking directly clashes with the idea that alcoholism is a biological disease and that if an alcoholic takes even one sip of alcohol he or she will lose all control and plunge back into full alcoholism. In 1973, researchers Mark and Linda Sobell published one of the first studies showing that a cognitive-behaviorally oriented controlled drinking program could work for alcoholics, perhaps even better than a traditional abstinence program. They found that the alcoholics who had had their controlled drinking intervention were significantly less likely than alcoholics in the abstinence program to relapse into severe drinking, and were significantly more likely to be functioning well over the 2 years following treatment.

These findings were assailed by proponents of the alcohol-as-a-disease model. For example, Pendery, Maltzman, and West (1982) published a 10-year follow-up of the alcoholics in the Sobells' controlled drinking group in the journal *Science*, based on interviews with these alcoholics and family members, and investigations of public records. Pendery and colleagues report that 40 percent of the men in the Sobells' controlled drinking treatment group were drinking excessively, 20 percent were dead from alcohol-related causes, 30 percent had given up attempts at controlled drinking in favor of becoming abstinent, and only 5 percent were engaging in controlled drinking. Subsequently, the TV program *60 Minutes* did a segment on the evils of controlled drinking treatments, which was introduced with Harry Reasoner standing at the graveside of one of the people from the Sobells' study who had died. The Sobells were publicly charged with fraud. Multiple investigations of the Sobells' work followed, including one by the U.S. Congress, interrupting their research for years. They were eventually cleared of any wrongdoing.

In a response to the Pendery and colleagues' article titled "Aftermath of a Heresy," Mark and Linda So-

bell (1984) detail the many flaws in the Pendery article, the greatest of which was the lack of any information on the outcomes of the alcoholics who had been in the abstinence program in the Sobells' original study. They noted that claims that 30 percent of the men in their controlled drinking group were abstinent and 5 percent were engaging in controlled drinking suggest a much better long-term outcome for these men than other studies have suggested is true of alcoholics who are treated by abstinence programs. The Sobells were able to track down the mortality rates of the men in the abstinence treatment group in their study. Whereas Pendery and colleagues had reported that 20 percent of the men in the controlled drinking treatment group had died over the 10 years after the study, the Sobells found that 30 percent of the men in the abstinence treatment groups had died in the same 10 years, with all but one of these deaths directly attributable to alcohol.

Subsequent research by the Sobells and many others has shown that controlled drinking programs can work, at least for people with mild to moderate alcohol problems or dependence (see Marlatt, 1998; and Sobell & Sobell, 1995 for reviews). People who have had many alcohol-related problems generally have trouble with controlled social drinking and must remain abstinent in order to avoid relapse into alcohol dependency.

Relapse Prevention

Unfortunately, the relapse rate for people undergoing any kind of treatment for alcohol abuse and dependency is high. The **abstinence violation effect** is a powerful contributor to relapse. There are two components to the abstinence violation effect. The first is a sense of conflict and guilt when an alcoholic who has been abstinent violates the abstinence and has a drink. He or she may then continue to drink to try to suppress the conflict and guilt. The second is a tendency to attribute the violation of abstinence to a lack of willpower and self-control rather than to situational factors. Thus, the person may think, "I'm an alcoholic and there's no way I can control my drinking. The fact I had a drink proves this." This type of thinking may pave the way to continued, uncontrolled drinking.

Relapse prevention programs teach alcoholics to view slips as temporary and situationally caused. Therapists work with clients to identify high-risk situations for relapse and to avoid those situations or exercise effective coping strategies for the situations. For example, a client may identify parties as high-risk situations for relapse. If she decides to go to a party, she may first practice with her therapist assertiveness skills for resisting pressure from friends to drink and write down other coping strategies she can use if she feels tempted to drink, such as starting a conversation with a supportive friend or practicing deep breathing exercises. She may also decide that if the temptation to drink becomes too great, she will ask a supportive friend to leave the party with her and go somewhere for coffee, until the temptation to drink passes.

Only about 10 percent of people who are alcohol dependents or abusers ever seek treatment. Another 40 percent may recover on their own, often as the result of maturation or positive changes in their environment (such as getting a good job or getting married to a supportive person) that help them and motivate them to get control of their drinking (Sobell & Sobell, 1995). The remainder of people with significant alcohol problems continue to have these problems throughout their lives. Some of these people become physically ill or completely unable to hold jobs or maintain their relationships. Others are able to hide or control their alcohol abuse and dependency enough to keep their jobs and may be in relationships with people who facilitate their alcohol dependency. Often they will have periods, sometimes long periods, of abstinence, but then, perhaps when facing stressful events, they will begin drinking again. This is why preventing the development of alcohol abuse and dependency and other substance-related problems is so important.

Sociocultural Approaches

Many sociocultural approaches involve self-help groups in which members who share a substance-related disorder help each other to overcome the disorder. The most famous of these groups is Alcoholics Anonymous. In addition, researchers are attempting to design preventative interventions to reduce the impact of alcohol and other substances on people's lives, and prevent the development of serious substance-related problems. Finally, clinicians are becoming increasingly sensitive to gender and cultural differences in the appropriate treatments for substance-related disorders.

Alcoholics Anonymous

Alcoholics Anonymous (AA) is an organization created by and for people with alcohol-related problems. Its philosophy is based on the disease model of alcoholism, which views alcoholism as a disease that causes alcoholics to lose all control over their drinking once they have the first drink. The implication of this model is that the only way to control alcoholism is to completely abstain from any alcohol. AA prescribes 12 steps that alcoholics must take toward recovery. The first step is for alcoholics to admit they are alcoholics and powerless to control the effects of alcohol. AA encourages members to seek help from a higher power and to admit to their weaknesses and ask for forgiveness. The goal for all members is complete abstinence.

Group members provide moral and social support for each other and make themselves available to each other in times of crisis. Once they are able, group members are expected to devote themselves to helping other alcoholics. AA believes that people are never completely cured of alcoholism—they are always "recovering alcoholics" with the potential of falling back into alcohol dependency with one drink. AA meetings include testimonials from recovering alcoholics about their paths into alcoholism, such as the one below, which are meant to motivate others to abstain from alcohol (Spitzer et al., 1983, pp. 87–89):

Voices

"I am Duncan. I am an alcoholic. . . . I know that I will always be an alcoholic, that I can never again touch alcohol in any form. It'll kill me if I don't keep away from it. In fact, it almost did. . . . I must have been just past my 15th birthday when I had that first drink that everybody talks about. And like so many of them—and you—it was like a miracle. With a little beer in my gut, the world was transformed. I wasn't a weakling anymore, I could lick almost anybody on the block. And girls? Well, you can imagine how a couple of beers made me feel, like I could have any girl I wanted. So, like so many of you, my friends in the Fellowship, alcohol became the royal road to love, respect, and self-esteem. If I couldn't feel good about myself when I wasn't drinking, if I felt stupid or lazy or ugly or misunderstood, all I had to do was belt down a few and everything got better. Of course, I was fooling myself, wasn't I, because I was as ugly and dumb and lazy when I was drunk as when I was sober. But I didn't know it."

Duncan paused, wiped his brow, then started in again. "Though it's obvious to me now that my drinking even then, in high school, and after I got to college, was a problem, I didn't think so at the time. After all, everybody was drinking and getting drunk and acting stupid, and I didn't really think I was different. A couple of minor auto accidents, one conviction for drunken driving, a few fights—nothing out of the ordinary, it seemed to me at the time. True, I was drinking quite a lot, even then, but my friends seemed to be able to down as much beer as I did. I guess the fact that I hadn't really had any blackouts and that I could go for days without having to drink reassured me that things hadn't gotten out of control. And that's the way it went, until I found myself drinking even more—and more often—and suffering more from my drinking, along about my third year of college. . . . [Eventually] I did cut down on my drinking by half or more. I only drank on weekends—and then only at night. And I set more-or-less arbitrary limits on how much I would drink, as well as where and when I would drink. And that got me through the rest of college and, actually, through law school as well. I'd drink enough to get very drunk once or twice a week, but only on weekends, and then I'd tough it out through the rest of the week.

"[Later] on, the drinking began to affect both my marriage and my career. With enough booze in me and under the pressures of guilt over my failure to carry out my responsibilities to my wife and children, I sometimes got kind of rough physically with them. I would break furniture, throw things around, then rush out and drive off in the car. I had a couple of wrecks, lost my license for two years because of one of them. Worst of all was when I tried to stop. By then I was totally hooked, so every time I tried to stop drinking, I'd experience withdrawal in all its horrors. I never had DTs, but I came awfully close many times, with the vomiting and the 'shakes' and being unable to sit still or to lie down. And that would go on for days at a time. . . .

"Then, about four years ago, with my life in ruins, my wife given up on me and the kids with her, out of a job, and way down on my luck, the Fellowship and I found each other. Jim, over there, bless his heart, decided to sponsor me—we'd been friends for a long time, and I knew he'd found sobriety through this group. I've been dry now for a little over two years, and with luck and support, I may stay sober. I've begun to make amends for my transgressions, I've faced my faults squarely again instead of hiding them with booze, and I think I may make it."

The practices and philosophies of AA do not appeal to everyone. The emphases on one's powerlessness, need for a higher power, and complete abstinence turn many people away. In addition, many people who subscribe to AA's philosophy still find it difficult to maintain complete abstinence and "fall off the wagon" at various times throughout their lives. However, many people have found AA very helpful in their recovery from alcohol abuse and dependency, and AA remains the most common source of treatment for people with alcohol-related problems. There are about 23,000 chapters of AA across 90 countries, and it is estimated that 800,000 people currently attend meetings of AA (Goodwin, 1988). Recent evaluations of 12-Step programs like AA have found that they are as effective as the behavioral and cognitive programs we describe below in the treatment of alcoholism (Finney & Moos, 1998). Narcotics Anonymous is an organization similar in structure and purpose to AA that focuses on people

who abuse substances other than (or in addition to) alcohol.

Prevention Programs for College Students

In the United States, young adults between 18 and 24 years of age have the highest rates of alcohol consumption and make up the largest proportion of problem drinkers of any age group. College students are even more likely than their peers who are not in college to drink. Among college students, 73 to 98 percent drink alcohol, in response to easy access to alcohol, social activities that focus on drinking, and peer pressure to drink. One survey of 17,000 college students found that 50 percent of the men and 39 percent of the women reported binge drinking at least once in the previous 2 weeks (Wechsler et al., 1994). As many as 20 to 25 percent of college students report having experienced alcohol-related problems, such as the inability to complete schoolwork or an alcohol-related accident, and alcohol-related accidents are the leading causes of death in college students (Marlatt et al., 1993). Heavy drinking is also associated with acute alcohol toxicity (which can be lethal), date rape, unsafe sexual activity, vandalism, and impaired academic performance. The pattern of drinking among college students has shifted so that a greater percentage of students abstain completely from alcohol, but those who do drink are more likely to be heavy drinkers (Marlatt et al., 1993). These heavy drinkers are most likely to be binge drinkers, who drink large quantities of alcohol on weekends, typically at social events, often with the intention of getting drunk.

Many colleges are developing programs to reduce drinking and drinking-related problems among students. These programs often emphasize the health-related consequences of drinking, but such long-term concerns do not tend to impress young people who are more likely to be focused on the short-term gains of alcohol use. Simply providing information about the dangers of alcohol abuse and trying to invoke fear of these dangers have little effect. Some college counselors refer students with drinking problems to abstinence programs, such as Alcoholics Anonymous, but college students often find the focus on admitting one's powerlessness and the principle of lifelong abstinence so unattractive that they will not attend these programs. Finally, many colleges try to provide alternative recreational activities that do not focus on alcohol. In general, however, such prevention programs designed to stop drinking altogether have had limited success (Moskowitz, 1989).

Psychologist Alan Marlatt and colleagues at the University of Washington (Marlatt, 1998; Marlatt et al., 1998) have argued that a more credible approach to college drinking is to recognize alcohol use as normative behavior among young adults and to focus education on the immediate risks of excessive use of alcohol (such as alcohol-related accidents) and on the payoffs of moderation (such as avoidance of hangovers). They view young drinkers as relatively inexperienced in regulating their use of alcohol and as in need of skills training to prevent abuse of alcohol. Learning to drink safely is compared to learning to drive safely; one must learn to anticipate hazards and avoid "unnecessary accidents."

Based on this harm reduction model, they designed the Alcohol Skills Training Program (ASTP), and targeted heavy-drinking college students for intervention. In eight weekly sessions of 90 minutes, participants are first taught to be aware of their drinking habits, including when, where, and with whom they are most likely to overdrink, by keeping daily records of their alcohol consumption and the situations in which they drink. They are also taught to calculate their own blood-alcohol levels; it often comes as a surprise to people how few drinks it takes to be legally intoxicated. Next, participants' beliefs about the "magical" effects of drinking on social skills and sexual prowess are challenged. They discuss the negative effects of alcohol on social behaviors, on the ability to drive, and on weight gain, and they discuss hangovers. Participants are encouraged to set personal goals for limiting alcohol consumption, based on their maximum blood-alcohol levels and their desires to avoid the negative effects of alcohol. They learn skills for limiting consumption, such as alternating alcoholic and nonalcoholic beverages and selecting drinks based on quality rather than quantity (e.g., buying two good beers rather than a six-pack of generic beer). In later sessions, members are taught to consider alternatives to drinking alcohol to reduce negative emotional states, such as using relaxation exercises or meditation or reducing sources of stress in their lives. Finally, in role-plays, participants are taught skills for avoiding "high-risk situations" in which they are likely to overdrink and for resisting peer pressure to drink.

Evaluations of ASTP have shown that participants do decrease alcohol consumption and problems and increase their social skills in resisting alcohol abuse (Fromme et al., 1994; Marlatt, Baer, & Larimer, 1995). ASTP was designed for a group format, and the use of group pressure to encourage change in individuals and as a forum for role-playing has many advantages. One study suggested that ASTP could be delivered in a written form as a self-help manual with positive effects equal to those of the group administration (Baer et al., 1992).

In a recent study, Marlatt and colleagues (1998) attempted to intervene with high-risk drinkers when they might be most open to intervention, in their first year of college. They identified a group of high school students who were about to matriculate into the University of Washington, and who were already drinking at least monthly and consuming at least five to six drinks in one sitting, or who reported frequent alcohol-related problems. These high-risk students were then randomly assigned to receive either a one-session intervention based on the Alcohol Skills Training Program, or no intervention, some time in January through March of their first year of college. Both groups of students were followed for the next two years. Over that two years, the intervention group showed less drinking overall and fewer harmful consequences of drinking (e.g., getting into alcohol-related accidents) over the subsequent two years than did the comparison group. In addition, approximately 90 percent of those receiving the intervention said it was helpful and that they would recommend it to friends. The work of Marlatt and colleagues suggests that problem drinkers of college age can learn to reduce their intake of alcohol and the harmful consequences of alcohol consumption if they receive nonconfrontational training on the skills necessary for harm reduction.

Gender-Sensitive Treatment Programs

The differences in the contexts for men's and women's substance abuse suggest the need for different approaches to treating men and women (Beckman, 1994). For men, treatment may need to focus on challenging the societal supports for their substance use and their view that substance use is an appropriate way to cope. It may also need to focus on men's tendency to act in aggressive and impulsive ways, particularly when intoxicated. For women, treatment may need to focus more on issues of self-esteem and powerlessness and on helping them remove themselves from abusive environments.

Some therapists feel it is harder to treat women substance users than men substance users (see Beckman, 1994). Women who violate social norms so greatly as to become substance abusers may have more severe underlying emotional problems than do men who become substance abusers. In addition, because women substance abusers typically are living with partners and other family members who are also substance abusers, they may not have the necessary support from their environments to stop their substance use. Rarely do husbands or boyfriends participate in the treatment of woman substance users. In contrast, women partners often participate in male substance abusers' treatment (Higgins et al., 1994). Women substance abusers also tend to cut themselves off from women friends, hiding their substance use and feeling they are not like other women (Henderson & Boyd, 1996).

As substance use among women increases, however, treatment programs will have to become more sensitive to the differences in patterns and motives of substance use in women and men and design their programs to meet the need of both genders.

Summing Up

- Detoxification is the first step in treating substance-related disorders.

- Antianxiety and antidepressant drugs can help ease the withdrawal symptoms from other substances. Antagonist drugs can block the effects of substances, reducing desire for the drug, or making the ingestion of the drug aversive.

- Methadone maintenance programs substitute methadone for heroin in the treatment of heroin addicts. These programs are controversial, but may be the only way some heroin addicts will get off the streets.

- Behavioral therapies based on aversive classical conditioning are sometimes used to treat alcoholism.

- Treatments based on social learning and cognitive theories focus on training the alcoholic in more adaptive coping skills and challenging his or her positive expectations about the effects of alcohol.

- The most common treatment for alcoholism is Alcoholics Anonymous, a self-help group that encourages alcoholics to admit their weaknesses and call on a higher power and other group members to help them remain completely abstinent from alcohol. A related group called *Narcotics Anonymous* is available for people dependent on other substances.

- Prevention programs for college students aim to teach them responsible use of alcohol.

- Different treatments may be needed for men and women that take into account the different contexts for their substance use.

☉ BIO-PSYCHO-SOCIAL INTEGRATION

The substances we have discussed in this chapter are powerful biological agents. They affect the brain directly, producing changes in mood, thoughts, and perceptions. Some people may find these changes more positive or rewarding than other people do because they are genetically or biochemically predisposed to do so. The rewards and punishments in the environment can clearly affect an individual's choice to pursue the effects of substances, however. Even many long-term chronic substance abusers can abstain from using if they can decide to abstain and receive the strong environmental support for abstention.

The biological and psychosocial pressures that lead some people to develop substance use disorders often co-occur. For example, people who grow up with alcoholic parents may have biological vulnerabilities to alcoholism, but they also may think that drinking is an appropriate way to cope with distress, and tend have chaotic childhoods. They are more likely to have grown up in poverty and in neighborhoods that socialize drinking (Zucker, Chermack & Curran, 1999). In turn, heavy drinkers are more likely to marry other heavy drinkers. They may support each other in drinking, and create a biological and psychosocial environment for their children that promotes alcohol abuse and dependence. Thus, the cycle of familial transmission of alcohol abuse and dependence has intersecting biological and psychosocial components.

Chapter Summary

- A substance is any natural or synthesized product that has psychoactive effects. The five groups of substances most often leading to substance disorders are (1) central nervous system depressants, including alcohol, barbiturates and benzodiazepines, and inhalants; (2) central nervous system stimulants, including cocaine, amphetamines, nicotine, and caffeine; (3) opioids; (4) hallucinogens, phencyclidine; and (5) cannabis.

- Substance intoxication is indicated by a set of behavioral and psychological changes that occur as a direct result of the physiological effects of a substance on the central nervous system. Substance withdrawal involves a set of physiological and behavioral symptoms that result from the cessation of or reduction in heavy and prolonged use of a substance. The specific symptoms of intoxication and withdrawal depend on the substance being used, the amount of the substance ingested, and the method of ingestion. Substance abuse is indicated when an individual shows persistent problems in one of four categories: (1) failure to fulfill major role obligations at work, school, or home; (2) substance use in situations in which such use is physically hazardous; (3) substance-related legal problems; and (4) continued substance use despite social or interpersonal problems. Substance dependence is characterized by a maladaptive pattern of substance use leading to significant problems in a person's life and usually leading to tolerance to the substance, withdrawal symptoms if the substance is discontinued, and compulsive substance-taking behavior.

- Routes of administration that produce rapid and efficient absorption of a substance into the bloodstream (i.e., intravenous injection, smoking, snorting) lead to a more intense intoxication, a greater likelihood of dependence, and a greater risk of overdose. Substances that act more rapidly on the central nervous system and whose effects wear off more quickly (e.g., cocaine) and that lead to faster intoxication are more likely to lead to dependence or abuse.

- At low doses, alcohol produces relaxation and a mild euphoria. At higher doses, it produces the classic signs of depression and cognitive and motor impairment. A large proportion of deaths due to accidents, murders, and suicides are alcohol related. Alcohol withdrawal symptoms can be mild or so severe as to be life threatening. Alcohol abusers and dependents experience a wide range of social and interpersonal problems and are at risk for many serious health problems. Women drink less alcohol than men do in most cultures and are less likely to have alcohol-related problems than are men. Persons of Asian descent typically are less prone to alcohol-related problems.

- Benzodiazepines and barbiturates are sold by prescription for the treatment of anxiety and insomnia. One pattern of the development of abuse of or dependence on these substances is reflected by the teenager or young adult who begins using the substances recreationally to produce a sense of well-being or euphoria but then escalates to chronic use and physiological dependence. A second pattern is shown by individuals who begin to use substances under physicians' care for insomnia or anxiety but then escalate their usage without the knowledge of their physicians.

- The inhalants are volatile agents that people sniff to produce a sense of euphoria, disinhibition,

and increased aggressiveness or sexual performance. The greatest users and abusers of inhalants are young boys, particularly Native American teenagers and Hispanic teenagers. Inhalants are extremely dangerous because they can cause permanent brain damage even with casual use, several major diseases, and suffocation when the user goes unconscious with the plastic bag used for inhaling still over his or her head.

- Cocaine activates those parts of the brain that register reward or pleasure and produces a sudden rush of euphoria, followed by increased self-esteem, alertness, and energy and a greater sense of competence, creativity, and social acceptability. The user may also experience frightening perceptual changes. The withdrawal symptoms from cocaine include exhaustion, need for sleep, and depression. The extraordinarily rapid and strong effects of cocaine on the brain's reward centers seem to make this substance more likely than most illicit substances to result in patterns of abuse and dependence.

- The amphetamines are readily available by prescription for the treatment of certain disorders but often end up in the black market and used by people to help them keep going through the day or to counteract the effects of depressants or heroin. They can make people feel euphoric, invigorated, self-confident, and gregarious, but they also can make people restless, hypervigilant, anxious, and aggressive and can result in several dangerous physiological symptoms and changes.

- The opioids are a group of substances developed from the juice of the poppy plant. The most commonly used illegal opioid is heroin. The initial symptom of opioid intoxication is euphoria; it is followed by a sense of drowsiness, lethargy, and periods of light sleep. Severe intoxication can lead to respiratory difficulties, unconsciousness, coma, and seizures. Withdrawal symptoms include dysphoria, anxiety, agitation, sensitivity to pain, and craving for more substance.

- The hallucinogens, phenylcyclidine, and cannabis all produce perceptual changes that can include sensory distortions and hallucinations. For some people, these are pleasant experiences, but for others, they can be extremely frightening. Similarly, some people experience a sense of euphoria or relaxation while on these substances, and others become anxious and agitated.

- Nicotine is another widely available substance. While legal, it causes cancer, bronchitis, and coronary heart disease in users and a range of birth defects in the children of women who smoke when pregnant. People can become physiologically dependent on nicotine and undergo difficult withdrawal symptoms when they stop smoking.

- The disease model of alcoholism views alcoholism as a biological disorder in which the individual has no control over his or her drinking and therefore must remain abstinent. Other theorists see alcoholism along a continuum of drinking habits, as modifiable through therapy. There is evidence that some types of alcoholism among males may be genetically transmitted and that men genetically predisposed to alcoholism are less sensitive to the effects of low doses of alcohol. Some theorists view alcoholism as a form of depression, although the prevailing evidence suggests that alcoholism and depression are distinct disorders.

- Behavioral theories of alcoholism note that people are also reinforced or punished by other people for their alcohol-related behaviors. Cognitive theories argue that people who develop alcohol-related problems have strong expectations that alcohol will help them feel better and cope better when they face stressful times.

- Medications can be used to ease the symptoms of withdrawal from many substances and to reduce craving for substances. The symptoms of withdrawal from opioids can be so severe that dependents are given a drug called *methadone* to curtail the symptoms as they try to discontinue use of heroin. Methadone also blocks the effects of subsequent doses of heroin, reducing people's desire to obtain heroin. Methadone maintenance programs, which continue to administer methadone to former heroin dependents, are controversial.

- The most common treatment for alcoholism is Alcoholics Anonymous, a self-help group that encourages alcoholics to admit their weaknesses and call on a higher power and other group members to help them remain completely abstinent from alcohol. Behavioral therapies based on aversive classical conditioning are sometimes used to treat alcoholism. Alcoholics in these therapies use a drug that makes them ill if they ingest alcohol or use imagery to develop a conditioned aversive response to the sight and smell of alcohol. Treatments based on social learning and cognitive theories focus on training alcoholics in more adaptive coping skills and challenging their positive expectations about the effects of alcohol. Many therapists in the behavioral and cognitive tradition reject the disease model of alcoholism and suggest that some alcoholics may learn to engage in controlled social drinking.

Key Terms

substance 568

drug addicts 568

substance-related disorder 570

substance intoxication 570

substance withdrawal 573

substance abuse 573

substance dependence 573

tolerance 573

blackout 576

alcohol abuse 577

alcohol dependence 577

delirium tremens (DTs) 581

alcohol-induced persisting amnesic disorder 581

Wernicke's encephalopathy 581

Korsakoff's psychosis 581

alcohol-induced dementia 581

fetal alcohol syndrome 582

benzodiazepines 584

barbiturates 584

inhalants 585

cocaine 586

amphetamines 589

nicotine 590

caffeine 592

opioids 593

hallucinogens 596

phenylcyclidine (PCP) 597

cannabis 597

mesolimbic dopamine system 599

disease model 600

detoxification 605

antagonist drugs 605

Critical Thinking Questions

1. All of the psychosocial interventions for substance abuse put the major responsibility for stopping substance use on the individual. What are the pros and cons of this?

2. Given what you know about other substances and the disorders related to them, do you think nicotine is like these other substances and should be regulated by the government? Why or why not?

3. What theories of or perspectives on substance abuse and dependence are reflected in the current drug policies of this country?

Daniel Nevins
The Dream Tree

If the mind, which rules the body, ever forgets itself so far as to trample upon its slave, the slave is never generous enough to forgive the injury; but will rise and smite its oppressor.

—*Longfellow,* Hyperion *(1839)*

CHAPTER 17

Psychology and Physical Health

CHAPTER OVERVIEW
Stress and Health

Our bodies have a natural physiological response to stress, known as the fight-or-flight response. In the short term, this physiological response is adaptive because it helps the body fight or flee from a threat. When this physiological response is prolonged, however, it causes wear and tear on the body, potentially contributing to ulcers, asthma, headaches, coronary heart disease, high blood pressure, and impairment of the immune system. Events that are perceived as stressful by people are often uncontrollable, are unpredictable, or challenge the limits of our abilities and threaten our self-concepts.

Sleep and Health

Stress can also affect health indirectly by leading people to engage in less healthy behaviors, such as not sleeping enough. Some people develop sleep disorders, which the DSM-IV divides into four categories: sleep disorders due to another mental disorder, sleep disorders due to a general medical condition, substance-induced sleep disorders, and primary sleep disorders. The most well-known primary sleep disorder is insomnia.

Personality and Health

Some personality styles that have been linked to poor physical health include dispositional pessimism, the Type A behavior pattern, the repressive coping style,

and John Henryism. Each of these may contribute to poor health by causing a chronic hyperarousal of the fight-or-flight response or by causing people to engage in unhealthy behaviors.

Extraordinary People:
Norman Cousins, Healing Through Laughter

Interventions to Improve Health

Health psychologists have designed a variety of cognitive and behavioral interventions to improve people's physical health, including guided mastery techniques that help people learn healthy behaviors, techniques to reduce catastrophizing cognitions, biofeedback, and time-management techniques. Sociocultural interventions for health focus on helping people use or change their social environment to improve their health.

Taking Psychology Personally:
How Can You Reduce Your Stress Level?

Viewpoints:
Is Religion Good for Your Health?

Bio-Psycho-Social Integration

Chapter Summary
Key Terms
Critical Thinking Questions

"You're making yourself sick with worry." "If he doesn't slow down, he's going to have a heart attack." "She's so stressed out that she's going to have a stroke."

How many times have we heard or said similar things? Is it true that psychological factors, such as worry or stress, can affect physical health? An entire new field of psychology, known as **health psychology,** has developed over the last 20 or so years to investigate the effects of psychological factors on physical illness. Health psychologists are concerned with the roles of personality factors, coping styles, stressful events, and health-related behaviors (such as maintaining a good diet) in the development and progress of physical disease. They also study whether changing a person's psychology—for example, by teaching stress-reduction techniques—can influence the course of a physical disease and whether diseases can be prevented by helping people adopt healthy lifestyles and attitudes about the world.

The field of health psychology is new, but the questions of whether and how the mind can affect the body and the body affect the mind have been debated for centuries. Such questions are often referred to as the **mind-body question**. Biological theories of mental illness, ranging from the ancient theories through the modern theories of the effects of neurotransmitters and genetics, all suggest that the body has a direct effect on the workings of the mind. There are also ancient theories suggesting that the mind has a direct effect on the workings of the body, such as theories that physical illnesses are the result of sin or possession by spirits. In Eastern medicine to this day, there continues to be an emphasis on the importance of a positive mental state and psychological balance on physical health. In Western medicine, however, the technological advances in identification and treatment of the physical causes of disease have led to a dominance of biological models of disease.

In recent decades, interest in the impact of psychological factors has begun to reemerge. There are three models for how psychological factors affect physical disease that drive most of the work in health psychology (see Figure 17.1).

The *direct effects model* suggests that psychological factors, such as stressful experiences or certain personality characteristics, directly cause changes in the physiology of the body that in turn cause or exacerbate disease. As we discuss in detail shortly, our bodies have a characteristic physiological response to certain types of stresses or challenges. In the short run, this physiological response is adaptive, but if it is greatly prolonged, it can cause damage to several systems of the body that may then cause or exacerbate disease.

The *interactive model* suggests that psychological factors must interact with a preexisting biological vulnerability to a disease in order for an individual to develop the disease. According to this model, prolonged stress or a maladaptive personality style will contribute to disease only in people who already have biological vulnerability to the disease or perhaps have already developed mild forms of the disease.

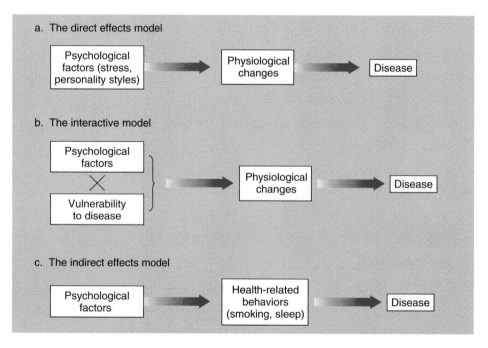

FIGURE 17.1   Three Models for the Effects of Psychological Factors on Disease. These three models posit quite different pathways by which psychological factors such as stress or personality style might affect physical disease.

The *indirect effects model* suggests that psychological factors affect disease largely by influencing whether people engage in health-promoting behaviors. For example, our diets, the amount of exercise we get, and whether we smoke, can all influence our vulnerability to certain diseases like heart disease or lung cancer and can influence the progression of many diseases once we have developed them. People under stress or with certain personality characteristics may be less prone to engage in healthy behaviors and more prone to engage in unhealthy behaviors. Thus, according to this model, psychological factors do not directly affect health but affect health indirectly by influencing health-related behaviors.

As already suggested, the two types of psychological factors focused on in many health psychology models are *stress* and *personality styles*. We begin this chapter by discussing the body's natural physiological reactions to stress and how these reactions can go awry and contribute to the development of disease or hasten the progression of disease. We also discuss one of the main casualties of stress: sleep. Then we discuss personality characteristics that may affect health either directly or indirectly. Finally, we discuss interventions to help people change their attitudes and behaviors in ways that may help them prevent disease or slow existing disease.

The same physiological systems are aroused whether we voluntarily expose ourselves to danger or are exposed involuntarily.

⟲ STRESS AND HEALTH

When the body faces any type of stressor—a saber-toothed tiger, a burglar with a gun, a first bungee jump—it mobilizes to handle the stressor. The liver releases extra sugar (glucose) to fuel muscles, and hormones are released to stimulate the conversion of fats and proteins to sugar. The body's metabolism increases in preparation for expending energy on physical action. Heart rate, blood pressure, and breathing rate increase, and the muscles tense. At the same time, certain unessential activities, such as digestion, are curtailed. Saliva and mucus dry up, thereby increasing the size of air passages to the lungs. The body's natural painkillers, endorphins, are secreted, and the surface blood vessels constrict to reduce bleeding in case of injury. The spleen releases more red blood cells to help carry oxygen.

Most of these physiological changes result from activation of two systems controlled by the hypothalamus, the autonomic nervous system (in particular the sympathetic division of this system) and the adrenal-cortical system (a hormone-releasing system). These physiological responses have developed through evolution to prepare the body to flee a threat or to fight it (e.g., to run away from the saber-toothed tiger or to

attack it) and thus have been labeled the **fight-or-flight response.** They are very adaptive when the stressor or threat is immediate and fight or flight is possible and useful. When a stressor is chronic and a person or animal cannot fight it or flee from it, then the chronic arousal of these physiological responses can be severely damaging to the body (see Sapolsky, 1992).

In groundbreaking work that continues to be influential today, researcher Hans Selye (1979) described the physiological changes we just discussed as part of a **general adaptation syndrome** that all organisms show in response to stress. The general adaptation syndrome consists of three phases (Figure 17.2, p. 620). In the first phase, known as alarm, the body mobilizes to confront a threat, by triggering sympathetic nervous system activity. In the second phase, known as resistance, the organism makes efforts to cope with the threat, by fleeing it or fighting it. The third phase, exhaustion, occurs if the organism is unable to flee from or fight the threat and depletes physiological resources while trying to do so.

Selye argued that a wide variety of physical and psychological stressors triggers this response pattern.

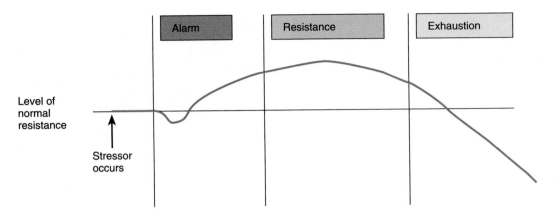

FIGURE 17.2   The General Adaptation Syndrome. According to Hans Selye, the body reacts in three phases to a stressor. In the first phase, alarm, the body mobilizes to confront the threat, which temporarily expends resources and lowers resistance. In the resistance phase, the body is actively confronting the threat and resistance is high. If the threat continues, the body moves into exhaustion.

He also argued that repeated or prolonged exhaustion of physiological resources, due to exposure to prolonged stressors that one cannot flee from or fight, is responsible for a wide array of physiological diseases. He conducted laboratory studies in which he exposed animals to several types of prolonged stressors—such as extreme cold and fatigue—and found that, regardless of the stress, certain bodily changes inevitably occurred: enlarged adrenal glands, shrunken lymph nodes, and stomach ulcers (Selye, 1979).

Selye's work inspired the development of the field of health psychology. Although some of Selye's specific hypotheses have not been supported in subsequent work, his general assertion that stress is an important determinant of the degree of physiological damage in several diseases has been supported (Overmier & Murison, 1998). Before we consider the impact of stress on specific diseases, however, we must define stress.

CONCEPT REVIEW

Characteristics of Stressful Events

These three factors influence whether an event is perceived as stressful.

Characteristic	Examples
Uncontrollable	Natural disasters, bereavement, many personal illnesses
Unpredictable	Earthquakes, some job layoffs, many accidents
Challenge capabilities or self-concepts	Exams, new relationships, a tough new job

Characteristics of Stressful Events

Stress is a term that is used loosely in both the popular media and in professional circles. Psychologists have identified three characteristics of events that contribute to their being perceived as stressful: their *controllability*, their *predictability*, and their *level of challenge or threat* to one's capabilities or self-concept (see *Concept Review: Characteristics of Stressful Events*).

Controllability

CASE STUDY

Tyron was busily doing his job welding small parts onto the frame of a car in the factory where he worked. His foreman told him that the boss wanted to see him. When he entered the boss's office, Tyron knew the news wasn't good. "Tyron," the boss said, "I'm afraid that the plant is undergoing some downsizing. Your job has been eliminated. You've been a good worker, but the new owners of the company want to automatize production in the plant as much as possible and yours is one of the jobs that a computer can do faster and cheaper than a person. I'm sorry to have to give you this news. You can finish out the month here and then you'll get a month's severance pay."

Tyron was stunned. He couldn't talk, he couldn't move. There had never been any indication that the new owners were thinking of firing people. When he was able to think again after several moments, Tyron felt angry, helpless, like the whole world had fallen in on him.

Uncontrollable negative events, such as the loss of a job, sudden death of a loved one, or loss of one's home to a natural disaster, are perceived by most people as stressful. Indeed, any negative event is perceived as more stressful if it is uncontrollable. For example, in one experimental study participants were

Uncontrollable events, such as being laid off a job, are perceived as stressful by many people.

shown vivid photographs of victims of violent deaths. One group of participants, the experimental group, could terminate their viewing by pressing a button. The other group, the control group, could not terminate their viewing by pressing a button. Both groups of participants saw the same photographs for the same duration of time. The level of anxiety in both groups was measured by their galvanic skin response (GSR), a drop in the electrical resistance of the skin that is an index of physiological arousal. The experimental group showed much less anxiety while viewing the photographs than did the control group, even though the only difference between the groups was their control over their viewing (Geer & Maisel, 1972).

Similarly, a person who has a traffic accident because he or she was not wearing glasses while driving may experience the accident as less stressful than if he or she had not perceived a reason for the accident. An accident that happens because a person forgot to wear glasses can presumably be prevented from happening again by the person wearing glasses. An accident that appears to have no explanation cannot be prevented from happening again in the future.

Unpredictability

Another factor that makes some events especially stressful is unpredictability. Tyron was stunned by his layoff in part because he did not see it coming. Again, experimental studies have confirmed that unpredictable events are more stressful than predictable events. These studies show that both rats and human subjects prefer mild but painful electric shocks or loud bursts of noise that are preceded by a warning tone (and therefore predictable) to electric shocks or noise

that are preceded by no warning tone (Abbott, Schoen, & Badia, 1984; Glass & Singer, 1972; Katz & Wykes, 1985). Having sufficient warning of upcoming aversive events may allow people to prepare themselves in ways that reduce the impact of events. For example, knowing that he is about to receive a shot allows a patient to begin distracting himself or practicing breathing exercises to reduce the pain of the shot.

Another reason predictable aversive events may be less stressful is that with predictable events, people know they can relax until they get the warning that the events are about to occur. With unpredictable events, people feel they can never relax because the events may occur at any time; thus, they remain anxious all the time. This explanation has been called the **safety signal hypothesis** (Seligman & Binik, 1977). For example, perhaps a woman's boss occasionally flies into a rage, criticizing her in front of others. If these outbursts are completely unpredictable, then the employee is always on guard and may chronically feel stressed. If, however, she knows these outbursts only happen around the end of each fiscal quarter when her boss is upset because he has to prepare a fiscal account for the firm, then she can relax to some extent during the remainder of the fiscal year. We discussed safety signals previously in Chapter 6, when we noted that people with panic disorder often have certain situations—such as being in their home or being with a trusted friend—in which they feel safe from a panic attack. Being in situations that provide safety signals helps them actually avoid panic attacks.

One group of people who often feel they are facing events that are both uncontrollable and unpredictable are patients awaiting surgical procedures. They may be terrified that something will go wrong during surgery or that they will be in severe pain or disabled following surgery. Their fears about surgical procedures and about their prognoses are often overblown, based on imagined worst-case scenarios or horror stories that other people have told them or that they have heard on the news. Dozens of studies, sparked by seminal work by psychologist Irving Janis (1958), have now shown that giving surgical patients information about what will happen during surgical procedures, the pain or disability they can expect after procedures, and ways to reduce pain or overcome disability greatly improves their adjustment to surgery (see Taylor, 1999). Patients given such information experience less distress before and after surgery, are able to leave the hospital sooner, require less medication, and may experience less pain than patients not given the information. Preoperative information appears to give patients a sense that they can control certain aspects of their experience—for example, by engaging in breathing exercises to reduce their pain—and anticipate what will happen. Similar interventions have

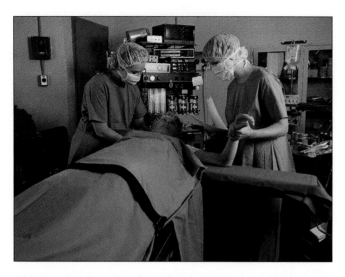

Giving people information about what they can expect and how they can cope following surgery can quicken their recovery.

been used with success with women in childbirth and persons undergoing invasive medical procedures, such as chemotherapy or cardiac catheterization (Ludwick-Rosenthal & Neufeld, 1988).

Challenge or Threat to Capabilities and Self-Concept

Even events that are controllable and predictable may be perceived as stressful if they challenge the limits of one's capabilities and threaten one's self-concept. One example is final exam week in college. Even students who know they can do well on their exams and have a good idea of what they must study for exams tend to experience final exams as stressful. They may have to work much harder and for longer hours during exams than at other times of the year and must perform at the peak of their intellectual capabilities even though they may be very weary. Although they are capable of doing well on the exams, their concept of themselves as competent may be threatened by the possibility of doing poorly on the exams.

Any change in life that requires numerous readjustments—even positive changes—can challenge the limits of our capabilities or challenge our self-concepts and thus can be perceived as stressful (Holmes & Rahe, 1967). For example, most people think of marriage as a positive event, but it requires many readjustments in daily life and a change in people's concepts of themselves as they change from single individuals to lifetime partners of other people. However, negative events are more likely than positive events to be perceived as stressful and to have impacts on physical and psychological health (e.g., Sarason, Johnson, & Siegel, 1978). This may be because, although some positive events require people to make adjustments and to

change their self-concepts, these changes tend to be for the better: Those affected are gaining something from the events and from the new roles they are taking. In contrast, negative events often involve loss and can threaten self-esteem or sense of mastery of the world (Thoits, 1986).

Stress and Ulcers, Asthma and Headaches

Ulcers, asthma, and chronic headaches are some of the diseases that health psychologists focused on in the early years of this field. **Ulcers** are holes, or lesions, in the wall of the stomach (gastric ulcers) or of the duodenum (peptic ulcers). These holes cause burning sensations and pain in the stomach, vomiting, and stomach bleeding. Ulcers are relatively common, with 5 to 10 percent of Americans experiencing them. They can be fatal, and more than 6,000 people die from ulcers each year. The physiological contributors to ulcers include bacterial infections, excessive secretions of gastric juices, and a weak lining of the stomach or duodenum. Early in the history of health psychology, researchers suggested that there also was a ulcer-prone personality—that specific personality characteristics caused ulcers. People with an ulcer-prone personality had intense feelings of anger or anxiety that they could not express, and a dependent personality (Tennant, 1988; Weiner et al., 1957; Wolff & Wolff, 1947). Subsequent research has not consistently supported the notion that these personality characteristics are important predictors of ulcers (for reviews, see Overmier & Murison, 1998; Taylor, 1999). Research has suggested, however, that chronically high levels of stress, particularly uncontrollable or unpredictable stress, can worsen an ulcer (Overmier & Murison, 1998).

Asthma is an extremely common disease, with approximately 15 million people in the United States suffering asthma (Weiss, 1997). One-third of asthma sufferers are children, and about two-thirds of these are boys. By adolescence, however, girls are more prone to asthma than boys (Sweeting, 1995). Asthma causes the airways (the trachea and bronchi) to constrict, making it hard to breathe. Most asthma attacks begin suddenly. The individual has a sense of tightness in the chest, wheezes, coughs, and expectorates sputum. Asthma attacks can be very frightening, because the sufferer feels he or she is suffocating, and may panic. An attack may last an hour or continue for several hours. The physiological causes of asthma include allergies, a slow-acting sympathetic nervous system, respiratory infections that weaken the lungs, and a genetic predisposition to a slow-responding sympathetic nervous system. Again, health psychologists formerly thought that specific personality characteristics, such as dependency and chronic anxiety, caused asthma. And again, the research testing these theories has been inconsistent (Overmier & Murison, 1998). Negative emotion, often due to stressful circumstances, can precipitate asthma attacks, however (Hyland, 1990).

Finally, *chronic headaches,* including **migraines,** have long been a focus of health psychology. **Muscle contraction headaches,** also called *tension headaches,* are one form of chronic headache caused when the muscles surrounding the skull contract, constricting the blood vessels. This results in pain at the back or front of the head or at the back of the neck. Migraine headaches often begin with the experience of an aura, or warning sensation that the headache is coming, along with dizziness, nausea, and "seeing" bright lights. They progress to an intense ache in the head, often on one side. Migraines occur when the blood vessels in the brain first constrict, reducing the flow of blood to parts of the brain, and then dilate, so that blood flows rapidly, stimulating neuron endings and causing pain. Approximately 12 million people in America experience migraines. Serotonin deficiencies have been implicated in headaches, and serotonin reuptake inhibitors are sometimes prescribed to headache sufferers. Personality factors that have been shown to predict the experience of headaches include a passive personality, and chronic feelings of helplessness, hostility, and distress (Marazziti et al., 1995; Merikangas, Stevens, & Angst, 1993). Stressful experiences also contribute to headaches (Overmier & Murison, 1998).

Stress and Coronary Heart Disease

CASE STUDY

Orrin was so mad he could scream. He had been told at 3:00 that afternoon to prepare a report on the financial status of his division of the company in time for a 9:00 A.M. meeting of the board of directors the next morning. On the way home from work, some idiot rear-ended him at a stop light and caused several hundred dollars in damages to his new car. When he got home from work, there was a message from his wife saying she had been delayed at work and would not be home in time to cook dinner for the children, so Orrin would have to do it. Then at dinner, Orrin's 12-year-old son revealed that he had flunked his math exam that afternoon.

After finishing the dishes, Orrin went to his study to work on the report. The kids had the TV on so loud he couldn't concentrate. Orrin yelled to the kids to turn off the TV but they couldn't hear him. Furious, he stalked into the family room and began yelling at the children about the television and anything else that came to his mind.

Then, suddenly, Orrin began to feel a tremendous pressure on his chest, as if a truck were driving across it.

Coronary heart disease occurs when blood vessels supplying the heart are blocked by plaque; complete blockage causes a myocardial infarction—a heart attack.

Pain shot through his chest and down his left arm. Orrin felt dizzy and terrified. He collapsed onto the floor. His 7-year-old began screaming. Luckily, his 12-year-old called 911 for an ambulance.

Orrin was having a *myocardial infarction*—a heart attack. A myocardial infarction is one endpoint of **coronary heart disease,** or **CHD.** CHD occurs when the blood vessels that supply the heart muscles are narrowed or closed by the gradual buildup of a hard, fatty substance called *plaque,* blocking the flow of oxygen and nutrients to the heart. This can lead to pain, called *angina pectoris,* that radiates across the chest and arm. When the oxygen to the heart is completely blocked, it can cause a myocardial infarction.

Coronary heart disease is the leading cause of death and chronic illness in the United States today, accounting for 40 percent of all deaths, most before the age of 75 (American Heart Association, 1993). CHD is also a chronic disease, and millions of people live daily with its symptoms. Men are more prone to CHD than are women, but CHD is still the leading cause of death of women. People with family histories of CHD are more susceptible to CHD. CHD has been linked to high blood pressure, high serum cholesterol, diabetes, smoking, and obesity.

People who live in chronically stressful environments over which they have little control appear to be at increased risk for CHD. For example, one study followed about 900 middle-aged men and women for over 10 years, tracking the emergence of coronary heart disease (Karasek, Russell, & Theorell, 1982). These people worked in a variety of jobs, and the researchers categorized these jobs in terms of how demanding they were and how much control they allowed a worker. Over the 10 years of this study, workers in jobs that were highly demanding but low in control had a risk of coronary heart disease that was 1½ times greater than that of those in other occupations.

The stress of being an immigrant to a new country, particularly a poor immigrant, may contribute to CHD and other illness, as we see in this case study (Mathews, 1996):

> ## CASE STUDY
> Heliodoro Bravo worked so hard for so long that, when he dropped dead 2 weeks ago at age 39, what his wife did made sense to their friends: She kept the family restaurant open and kept working.
>
> No time off for a funeral. Only a few scattered hours to mourn. She says she could not even spare the days or money to accompany his body to Mexico, where her husband's parents had a service and burial. "We have always had to go forward, to support the family," says Filomena Bravo, 41. "We always work and work, because we have to pay the bills. We never rest."
>
> "At first, I was astonished to see the Bravos' restaurant open the day he died," said Manuel Alban, publisher of the Spanish-language weekly *El Heraldo*. "But in our community, it was not really a surprise, because if you don't sell, you don't eat."

The impact on physical health of being an immigrant varies greatly depending on the type of setting a person moves to, however. Some immigrants are able to move with family members into ethnic communities within their new country that provide them with some continuity of culture and help them to adapt. These persons are not at higher risk for CHD or other illness, whereas immigrants who do not have social support systems in their new country may be at increased risk (Kuo & Tsai, 1986).

Stress and Hypertension

Hypertension, or high blood pressure, is a condition in which the supply of blood through the vessels is excessive, putting pressure on the vessel walls. Chronic high blood pressure can cause hardening of the arterial walls and deterioration of the cell tissue, leading eventually to coronary artery disease, kidney failure, and stroke. Approximately 60 million people in the United States have hypertension, and about 16,000 die each year due to hypertensive heart disease. Genetics appear to play a role in the predisposition to hypertension (Smith et al., 1987), but only about 10 percent of cases of hypertension can be traced to genetics or to specific organic causes, such as kidney dysfunction. The other 90 percent of cases are known as essential hypertension, meaning the causes are unknown.

Because part of the body's response to stress—the fight-or-flight response—is to increase blood pressure, it is not surprising that people who live in chronically stressful circumstances are more likely to develop hypertension (James, Hartnett, & Kalsbeek, 1983). As an example, persons who move from quiet rural settings to crowded and noisy urban settings show increases in rates of hypertension.

One group that lives in chronically stressful settings and has particularly high rates of hypertension is low-income African Americans. They often do not have adequate financial resources for daily living, are poorly educated and have trouble finding good employment, live in neighborhoods racked with violence, and are frequently exposed to racism. All these conditions have been linked to higher blood pressure. In addition, African Americans may be genetically prone to a particular pattern of cardiovascular response to stress that contributes to the development of hypertension (Anderson et al., 1989; Light & Sherwood, 1989).

Persons with hypertension and the children of parents with hypertension tend to show a stronger blood pressure response to a wide variety of stressors. In experimental situations, solving arithmetic problems and immersing their hands in ice water, people with no personal or family histories of hypertension show much less response than those with a history of hypertension (Harrell, 1980). In addition, it takes longer for the blood pressure of persons with hypertension to return to normal following stressors than it does the blood pressure of those without hypertension. This suggests that hypertensives and persons with family/genetic histories of hypertension may have heightened physiological reactivity to stress. If these persons are exposed to chronic stress, then their chronically elevated blood pressure can lead to hardening and narrowing of the arteries, which creates a physiologically based hypertension (Harrell, 1980). Low-income African Americans may have both this physiological predisposition to heightened reactivity to stress *and* chronic exposure to stressful environments, making them doubly vulnerable to hypertension.

Stress and the Immune System

The **immune system** protects the body from disease-causing microorganisms. This system affects our susceptibility to infections, diseases, allergies, cancer, and autoimmune disorders, such as AIDS, in which the immune cells attack normal tissues of the body. There are many components of the immune system and its response to foreign invaders to the body that cause disease. One of the fastest-growing areas of health psychology is *psychoneuroimmunology,* the study of the effects of psychological factors on **immunocompetence,** the functioning of the immune system (see Maier, Watkins, & Fleshner, 1994). Stress may affect the immune system through several mechanisms. In particular, some of the biochemicals released as part of the fight-or-flight response, such as the corticosteroids, may suppress the immune system.

The most controlled research linking stress and immune system functioning has been conducted with animals. They are experimentally exposed to stressors and then the functioning of their immune system is measured directly. Studies have shown that **lymphocytes,** cells of the immune system that attack viruses, are suppressed in animals that have been exposed to loud noise, electric shock, separation from their mothers as infants, separation from peers, and a variety of other stressors (Maier, Watkins & Fleshner, 1994).

Animals are most likely to show impairment of their immune system if exposed to stressors that are uncontrollable. In one experiment, one group of rats were subjected to electric shock that they could turn off by pressing a lever (Laudenslager et al., 1983). Another group received an identical sequence of shocks but could not control the shocks by pressing the lever. A third group received no shock. The investigators examined how well the rats' T-cells multiplied when challenged by invaders. *T-cells* are lymphocytes that secrete chemicals that kill harmful cells, such as cancer cells. They found that the T-cells in the rats who could control the shock multiplied as well as did those in rats who were not shocked at all (see Figure 17.3). T-cells in rats exposed to uncontrollable shock multiplied only weakly, however. In another study following the same experimental design, investigators implanted tumor cells into rats, gave them controllable or uncontrollable shocks, and examined whether the rats' natural defenses rejected the tumors. Only 27 percent of the rats given uncontrollable shock rejected the tumors, whereas 63 percent of the rats given controllable shock rejected the tumors (Visintainer, Volpicelli, & Seligman, 1982).

Uncontrollable stress also is related to impaired immune system functioning in humans (Benschop et al., 1998). In a particularly elegant study, investigators exposed about 400 healthy volunteers to a nasal wash containing one of five cold viruses or an innocuous salt solution (Cohen, Tyrrel, & Smith, 1991). Each participant was assigned a stress score ranging from 3 (lowest stress) to 12 (highest stress), based on the number of stressful events they had experienced in the past year, the degree to which they felt able to cope with daily demands, and their frequency of negative emotions such as anger and depression. The participants were examined daily for cold symptoms and for the presence of cold viruses or virus-specific antibodies in their

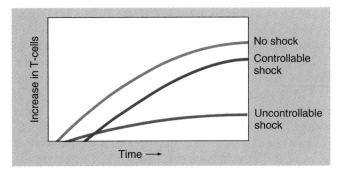

FIGURE 17.3 The Effects of Controllable and Uncontrollable Shock on Rats' Immune Systems. Rats given uncontrollable shock showed less increase in T-cells, which kill harmful cells, than did rats given controllable shock or no shock.

Source: Laudenslager et al., 1983.

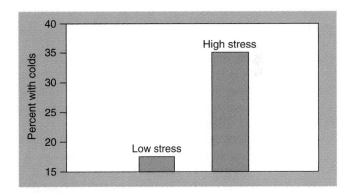

FIGURE 17.4 The Development of Colds in People with High Stress and Low Stress in Their Lives. People who were leading highly stressful lives were much more likely to develop colds than were people leading low-stress lives when exposed to a cold virus.

Source: Cohen, Tyrrel & Smith, 1991.

upper respiratory secretions. The majority of the volunteers exposed to the virus showed some signs of infection, but only about one-third developed colds. Volunteers who reported the highest stress in their lives were more likely to develop infections and much more likely to develop actual colds than those with the lowest stress scores (see Figure 17.4).

Most other studies of humans simply have compared the immunocompetence of persons undergoing particular stressors with that of persons not undergoing these stressors (see Cohen, 1996). For example, a study of people who survived Hurricane Andrew in 1992 found that those who experienced more damage to their home or whose lives were more threatened by the storm showed poorer immune system functioning than people whose homes and lives had been safer (Ironson et al., 1997). Similarly, following the 1994 Northridge earthquake in the Los Angeles area, people whose lives had been more severely disrupted showed more decline in immune system functioning than those who had not experienced as much stress as a result of the earthquake (Solomon et al., 1997). People who worried more about the impact of the earthquake on their lives were especially likely to show detriments in *natural killer cells,* a type of T-cell that seeks out and destroys cells that have been infected with a virus (Segerstrom et al., 1998).

More common events have also been linked to deficits in immune system functioning. Students often complain that they become ill during exam times, and studies have verified the idea that college students and medical students are more prone to infectious illness during exam periods than at other times of the academic year (Glaser et al., 1986). Negative interpersonal events seem particularly prone to affect immune system functioning. Married couples who have more conflictual interactions with each other show poorer immunological functioning than married couples with fewer conflictual interactions (Kiecolt-Glaser et al., 1997). Studies of men whose wives have died from breast cancer show that their immune system functioning declines in the month following their wives' deaths and in some cases remains low for a year thereafter (Schleifer et al., 1979).

Men and women who have recently been separated or divorced show poorer immune functioning than matched control subjects who are still married (Kiecolt-Glaser et al., 1987, 1988). However, the partner who has more control over the divorce or separation—that is, the partner who initiated the divorce or separation—shows better immune system functioning and better health than does the partner who has less control over the divorce or separation. This is one example of how perceptions of the controllability of a stressor can influence the impact of that stressor on health (see also Brosschot et al., 1998).

Several studies have examined whether stress can contribute to the development or progression of cancer in humans (see O'Leary, 1990, and Taylor, 1999, for reviews). The results of these studies have been mixed, some showing that people who are more stressed are more vulnerable to develop cancer or have faster progressions of their cancer than people who are less stressed. Again, it may be that people's perceptions or appraisals of stressors and not the presence of stressors alone determine the impact of the stressors on immune system functioning. For example, one study of women with breast cancer found that those who felt they had little control over their cancer and over other aspects of their lives were more likely to develop new tumors over a five-year period than women who felt more in control, even though the two groups of women did not differ in the type or initial seriousness of their cancers (Levy & Heiden, 1991). Similarly, although studies have not shown conclusively that stress

contributes to the progression of acquired immune deficiency syndrome (AIDS), perceptions of control may be related to the progression of this disease (O'Leary, 1990). We explore these studies in more detail later in this chapter when we discuss the role of personality factors in health.

Summing Up

- Three characteristics of stressful events are that they are uncontrollable, unpredictable, and they challenge our capabilities and self-concept.
- Health psychologists formerly thought that ulcers, asthma, and chronic headaches were due to specific personality characteristics. Research support for these views have been inconsistent, but stress and distress can worsen these diseases in people who already have them.
- There is substantial evidence that stress, particularly uncontrollable stress, increases risks for coronary heart disease and hypertension, probably through chronic hyperarousal of the body's fight-or-flight response.
- There is mounting evidence from animal and human studies that stress may also impair the functioning of the immune system, possibly leading to higher rates of infectious diseases.

SLEEP AND HEALTH

In 1993, the National Commission on Sleep Disorders Research estimated that at least one-third of U.S. adults suffer from chronic sleep disturbances, especially chronic sleep deprivation due to busy schedules. Over the past century, the average night's sleep time has declined by more than 20 percent as people try to fit more and more into the 24-hour day. The costs of sleep disorders and sleepiness to society include lost lives, lost income, disabilities, accidents, and family dysfunction. For example, each year in the United States, there are 200,000 sleep-related automobile accidents, and 5,000 of these accidents are fatal. Twenty percent of automobile drivers admit to having fallen asleep at the wheel at least once. Some of the most serious disasters in modern history have been caused by mistakes made by sleepy people (Mitler & Miller, 1995). In 1979, the worst nuclear plant accident in the United States resulted from fatigued workers at Three Mile Island failing to respond to a mechanical problem at the plant. In 1986, the world's worst nuclear disaster happened in Chernobyl in the former Soviet Union while a test was being conducted by an exhausted team of engineers.

Teenagers and young adults often do not get as much sleep as they need, because their social lives keep them up late at night.

Young adults will sleep on average 8.6 hours per day when they have no environmental influences to interfere with sleep patterns. Yet most young adults sleep 7.5 or fewer hours per day. Similarly, most middle-aged adults seem to need at least 7 or 8 hours of sleep per day, but on average get less than 7 hours per day. People who work rotating shifts or in jobs demanding long periods of activity, including nurses, doctors, firefighters, police, and rescue personnel, are often chronically sleep deprived. Even when they have time to sleep, they have trouble doing so, because their bodies' natural rhythms that promote sleep are disrupted by their irregular schedules. The effects of sleep deprivation are cumulative: One builds up an increasing "sleep debt" for every 24-hour period in which one does not get adequate sleep.

Sleep Deprivation

Lack of sleep can impair health. In addition to the increased risk of accidents due to sleepiness, lack of sleep also appears to impair the immune system (Hall et al., 1998). People who sleep fewer than 6 hours per night have a 70 percent higher mortality rate than do those sleeping at least 7 or 8 hours per night (Kryger, Roth, & Dement, 1994). This is true both for men and for women, for people of many ethnicities, and for people with many different health backgrounds. People who work rotating shifts have higher rates of illness, including cardiovascular and gastrointestinal disease, than do people who do not work shifts.

Sleep deprivation also has a number of psychological effects. Cognitive impairments caused by sleep deprivation include impairments in memory, learning, logical reasoning, arithmetic skills, complex verbal processing, and decision making. For example, reducing your amount of sleep to 5 hours per night for just two nights significantly reduces performance on math problems and creative thinking tasks. Thus, staying up to study for exams for just a couple of nights can significantly impair your ability to do as well as possible on those exams. Sleep deprivation also causes irritability, emotional ups and downs, and perceptual distortions such as mild hallucinations (Dinges & Broughton, 1989).

How can people reduce sleepiness and the effects of sleep deprivation? First of all, by getting enough sleep. Although the social lives of college students often begin at 10 P.M. or later, it is important to keep in mind that the sleep lost on the weekend can affect performance and health for the rest of the week. Students who have families and/or jobs are especially prone to skipping sleep in order to get everything done. Good time-management skills can help people find more time in their days to accomplish all their tasks without having to give up much sleep (tips on time management are given near the end of this chapter). Avoiding alcohol and caffeine in the evening can also help people fall asleep and sleep well when they do go to bed.

Sleep experts emphasize the value of naps during the day, particularly for people who have trouble getting as much sleep as they need during the night. Many people naturally need a short nap in the middle of the day (typically about 8 hours after they have awakened from the night's sleep) to restore them to optimal functioning. The best length for a nap varies from person to person but usually is between 15 and 30 minutes. The important thing is to sleep long enough to restore your energy and attention but not long enough to make you groggy for the rest of the day.

In addition to its direct positive effects on health, getting adequate sleep helps people feel more in control of the stressful events that befall them during the day. When we are alert and rested, challenging events may not seem so overwhelming because we can marshal our best coping responses. Indeed, when we are rested, we may be better able to prevent stressful events from ever happening because we are alert enough to anticipate them and to take action before they occur. Thus, sleep has both direct effects on our health and indirect effects by enhancing our ability to prevent or cope with stressful events.

Sleep Disorders

Some people experience so much difficulty in sleeping that they may be diagnosed with a sleep disorder. The DSM-IV recognizes four general types of sleep disorders (see *Concept Review:* Four Groups of Sleep Disorders). **Sleep disorders related to another mental disorder** involve sleep disturbances that are directly attributable to psychological disorders such as depression or anxiety. **Sleep disorders due to a general medical condition** involve sleep disturbances that result from the physiological effects of a medical condition. Many medical conditions can disturb sleep, including degenerative neurological illnesses (such as Parkinson's disease), cerebrovascular disease (such as vascular lesions to the upper brain stem), endocrine conditions (such as hypo- or hyperthyroidism), viral and bacterial infections (such as viral encephalitis), pulmonary diseases (such as chronic bronchitis), and pain from musculoskeletal diseases (such as rheumatoid arthritis or fibromyalgia). **Substance-induced sleep disorders** involve sleep disturbances due to use of substances, including prescription medications (such as medications that control hypertension or cardiac arrhythmias) and nonprescription substances (such as alcohol and caffeine). The fourth category of sleep disorders is **primary sleep disorders.** These are further subdivided into **dyssomnias** (see *Concept Review:* Dyssomnias), which involve abnormalities in the amount, quality, or timing of sleep, and **parasomnias** (see *Concept Review:* Parasomnias), which involve abnormal behavioral and physiological events occurring during sleep.

Insomnia

Probably the most familiar dyssomnia is **insomnia,** difficulty in initiating or maintaining sleep, or sleep that chronically does not restore your energy and alertness. People with insomnia usually report a combination of difficulty falling asleep and intermittent wakefulness during the night. A vicious cycle often develops in people with insomnia. The longer they lie in bed, unable to go to sleep, the more distressed and aroused they become. This arousal makes it even more difficult for

Insomnia is one of the most common sleep disorders.

CONCEPT REVIEW

Four Groups of Sleep Disorders

The DSM-IV divides the sleep disorders into these four categories.

Diagnostic Group	Definition
Sleep disorder due to another mental disorder	Sleep disturbance resulting from a diagnosable mental disorder, such as depression or anxiety
Sleep disorder due to a general medical condition	Sleep disturbance resulting from the direct physiological effects of a medical condition, such as arthritis or chronic bronchitis
Substance-induced sleep disorder	Sleep disturbance due to concurrent use, or recent discontinuation of use, of a prescription or nonprescription medication
Primary sleep disorder	Sleep disturbance *not* due to a diagnosable mental disorder, medical condition, or substance

Source: DSM-IV, APA, 2000.

them to fall asleep. Their arousal then becomes conditioned to their environment—to their bed and bedroom, so that their arousal levels go up when they try to go to bed the next night. In addition, they may consciously worry about having trouble falling asleep, which adds more to their arousal level. Often, people with insomnia will report that they sleep better when they are in unfamiliar settings, such as hotel rooms. In contrast, people without insomnia report they sleep worse in unfamiliar settings (Hauri & Fisher, 1986).

Occasional problems with insomnia are extremely common, with as many as 50 percent of adults reporting they have had insomnia sometime in their lives, and one in three adults complaining they have had insomnia in the last year (Nowell et al., 1998). Complaints of insomnia increase with age, but decrease with

CONCEPT REVIEW

Dyssomnias

These are the primary sleep disorders known as dyssomnias. Each condition must not be due to a general medical condition or substance use, and must cause significant impairment in functioning, to be diagnosed.

Type	Definition
Primary insomnia	Difficulty initiating or maintaining sleep, or nonrestorative sleep, for at least 1month
Primary hypersomnia	Excessive sleepiness for at least 1 month as evidenced by either prolonged sleep episodes or daytime sleep episodes that occur almost daily
Narcolepsy	Irresistible attacks of refreshing sleep that occur daily over at least 3 months, plus either cataplexy or recurrent intrusions of elements of rapid eye movement (REM) sleep
Breathing-related sleep disorder	Sleep disruption, leading to excessive sleepiness or insomnia, that is due to a sleep-related breathing condition such as apnea
Circadian rhythm sleep disorder	Sleep disruption leading to excessive sleepiness or insomnia that is due to a mismatch between the sleep-wake schedule required by a person's environment and his or her circadian sleep-wake pattern

Source: DSM-IV, APA, 2000.

CONCEPT REVIEW

Parasomnias

These are the primary sleep disorders known as parasomnias. Each condition must not be due to a general medical condition or substance use, and must cause significant impairment in functioning, to be diagnosed.

Type	Definition
Nightmare disorder	Repeated awakenings with detailed recall of extended and extremely frightening dreams, usually involving threats to survival, security, or self-esteem. On awakening, the person is alert and oriented.
Sleep terror disorder	Repeated abrupt awakenings beginning with a panicky scream; intense fear and signs of autonomic arousal; relative unresponsiveness to efforts of others to comfort the person; no detailed dream is recalled and there is amnesia for the episode.
Sleepwalking disorder	Repeated episodes of rising from the bed during sleep and walking about; while sleepwalking, the person has a blank, staring face, is relatively unresponsive to others, and can be awakened only with great difficulty; on awakening, the person has amnesia for the episode; within several minutes after awakening, there is no impairment of mental activity or behavior, although there may initially be a short period of confusion and disorientation.

Source: DSM-IV, APA, 2000.

socioeconomic status. To be diagnosed with primary insomnia, people must have symptoms of insomnia for at least one month, and the sleep disturbance must cause significant distress or impairment in their functioning. In addition, the insomnia must not be due to another mental disorder, to a medical condition, or to substance use. It is unclear how prevalent diagnosable insomnia is in the general population, but one long-term study of young adults found that 9 percent reported chronic insomnia (Angst et al., 1989).

Several different medications are used in the treatment of insomnia, including antidepressants, antihistamines, tryptophan, delta-sleep-inducing peptide (DSIP), melatonin, and benzodiazepines. All of these have proven effective in at least some studies, although the number of studies done on most of these agents is small. The agents that have proven most reliably effective are the benzodizepines and zolpidem (trade name Ambien), while those that have the least clear benefit include the antihistamines and tryptophan (Nowell et al., 1998).

Many studies have focused on behavioral interventions for insomnia. **Stimulus-control therapy** involves a set of instructions designed to curtail behaviors that might interfere with sleep and to regulate sleep-wake schedules (Bootzin & Perlis, 1992). These include:

1. Go to bed only when sleepy.
2. Use the bed and bedroom only for sleep and sex, not for reading, television watching, eating, or working.
3. Get out of bed and go to another room if you are unable to sleep for 15 to 20 minutes, and do not return to bed until you are sleepy.
4. Get out of bed at the same time each morning.
5. Don't nap during the day.

Sleep restriction therapy involves initially restricting the amount of time insomniacs can try to sleep in the night (Spielman, Saskin, & Thorpy, 1987). Once their sleep becomes more efficient, then the amount of time they are allowed to spend in bed is gradually increased, until they reach the greatest total amount of sleep possible while maintaining efficient sleep. In addition, people are often taught relaxation exercises (see Chapter 6) and are given education about the role of diet, exercise, and substance use on sleep. Cognitive-behavioral interventions may be used to help counteract people's maladaptive cognitions about sleep, such as "There's no way I can go to sleep quickly." Although these behavioral and cognitive interventions typically take longer to begin working with insomniacs than the drug therapies, they tend to have more long-lasting effects (Nowell et al., 1998).

Other Sleep Disorders

Primary **hypersomnia** is just the opposite of insomnia. People with hypersomnia are chronically sleepy and sleep for long periods at a time. They may sleep 12 hours at a stretch and still wake up sleepy. A nap during the day may last for an hour or more, and the individual may wake up unrefreshed. If their environment is not stimulating (e.g., they are sitting in a boring lecture), they are sure to fall asleep. They may even fall asleep at the wheel while driving. To qualify for a diagnosis, the hypersomnia must be present for at least a month and must cause significant distress or impairment in functioning. Again, the prevalence of hypersomnia in the general population is not known, but about 5 to 16 percent of people who go to sleep disorders clinic are diagnosed with primary hypersomnia (APA, 2000).

Narcolepsy involves irresistible attacks of sleep, lasting at least three months. These sleep attacks are most likely to come during low-stimulation, low-activity situations, but may also come while the person is carrying on a conversation or driving a car. Sleep episodes general last 10 to 20 minutes, but can last up to an hour, and people may dream during the episodes. People will wake up from these sleep attacks refreshed, but then will become sleepy again after several hours, and may report chronic sleepiness. If untreated, people with narcolepsy typically have two to six episodes of sleep per day.

In addition to sleepiness, people diagnosed with narcolepsy must experience (1) cataplexy, or (2) recurrent intrusions of elements of rapid eye movement (REM) sleep into the transition between sleep and wakefulness. **Cataplexy** is episodes of sudden loss of muscle tone lasting from a few seconds to minutes, and occurs in about 70 percent of people with narcolepsy (APA, 2000). They may suddenly drop objects, buckle at the knees, or even fall to the ground. Cataplexy is usually triggered by a strong emotion, such as anger or surprise. The intrusions of REM sleep often involve the experience of intense dreamlike imagery just before falling asleep or just after awakening. Sometimes these hallucinations are accompanied by a sense of paralysis, so people report seeing or hearing unusual things but being unable to move. Narcolepsy most often starts in adolescence, and is quite rare, affecting less than one-half of one percent of the general population (APA, 2000).

The most common **breathing-related sleep disorder** is obstructive *sleep apnea*, which involves repeated episodes of upper-airway obstruction during sleep. People with sleep apnea typically snore loudly, go silent and do not breathe for several seconds at a time, then gasp for air. Apnea occurs in up to 10 percent of the population, and can begin throughout the life span. It is most common, however, in overweight, middle-aged men, and prepubertal children with enlarged tonsils.

There are several other primary sleep disorders (described in *Concept Review:* Parasomnias and *Concept Review:* Dyssomnias). Occasional problems with the symptoms of these disorders are very common. For example, most children have occasional nightmares, but the prevalence of diagnosable levels of these disorders in the population is quite low.

Summing Up

- The sleep disorders are divided into sleep disorders due to other mental disorders, medical conditions, or substances, and primary sleep disorders.

- The primary sleep disorders are further divided into dyssomnias and parasomnias.

- The most common dyssomnia is insomnia. Hypersomnia, narcolepsy, and breathing-related sleep disorder are also dyssomnias.

- The parasomnias include nightmare disorder, sleep terror disorder, and sleepwalking disorder. Many people experience symptoms of these disorders occasionally, but only a small percentage of the population ever develops one of these sleep disorders.

- Sleep disorders, particularly insomnia, can be treated with a variety of drugs, or through behavioral and cognitive-behavioral therapies that change sleep-related behavior and thinking patterns.

⊙ PERSONALITY AND HEALTH

In recent years, psychologists have explored certain personality characteristics and coping strategies that seem to be associated with an increased risk for a variety of diseases. Individuals with these characteristics or strategies appraise a wider range of events as stressful or do not readily engage in behaviors that reduce the stressfulness of events. Thus, these people are more chronically stressed, and their bodies are more chronically in the fight-or-flight response described earlier in this chapter.

Pessimism and Health

In Chapter 8, we explored the relationship between pessimism and vulnerability to depression. Other research has linked pessimism to poor physical health as well (for reviews, see Taylor, 1999; Taylor et al., in press). One study found that students who were more pessimistic reported more illness and made more visits to the student health center than did students who were more optimistic (Peterson, 1988). Pessimists' vulnerability to illness does not end with college, however. In a long-term study of men in the Harvard classes of 1939 to 1940, men who were pessimistic when they were in college were more likely to develop physical illness over the subsequent 35 years than were men who were more optimistic (Peterson, Seligman, & Vaillant, 1988; see also Peterson et al., 1988; see also Peterson et al., 1998). Other studies have found that pessimists recover more slowly from coronary bypass surgery and have more severe anginal pain than optimists (Fitzgerald et al., 1993; Scheier, et al., 1989). Pessimistic cancer patients are more likely to die during the first few years after their diagnosis than optimists (Schulz et al., 1996).

How does pessimism affect health? People who are pessimistic tend to feel they have less control over their lives than people who are more optimistic and therefore may appraise more events as stressful. Thus, pessimism may contribute to poor health by causing chronic arousal of the body's fight-or-flight response, resulting in the type of physiological damage discussed earlier (see Figure 17.5). Several studies have found evidence for this. In one, the blood pressure of pessimists and optimists was monitored daily for three days. The pessimists had chronically higher blood pressure levels than the optimists across the three days (Raikkonen et al., 1999). Another study found that

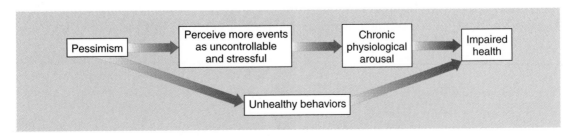

FIGURE 17.5 Pathways by Which Pessimism Might Impair Health. People who are pessimistic may appraise more events as uncontrollable and stressful, which then leads to chronic arousal of the fight-or-flight syndrome, which impairs health. They may also engage in more unhealthy behaviors that impair health.

EXTRAORDINARY PEOPLE

Norman Cousins, Healing Through Laughter

In 1964, Norman Cousins, a successful writer at the *Saturday Review*, was diagnosed with ankylosing spondylitis, a collagen disease that is painful and usually lethal. He traced the origins of his disease to a recent trip to Moscow, where he had been exposed to fumes from diesel trucks and jet engines repeatedly over several weeks. He believed he had been in a state of adrenal exhaustion at the time, lowering his resistance and making it possible for the deadly disease he now had to set in. After many medical tests and days in the hospital, doctors gave him a 1 in 500 chance of living.

Cousins refused to believe that he would succumb to the disease and set out to find a course of action that might reverse the progression of his disease. His 1979 book *Anatomy of an Illness* describes his use of comedy and movies to raise his levels of positive emotions and thereby affect the functioning of his adrenal and endocrine systems. Cousins eventually recovered from his illness, and became known for his views that laughter cured his fatal disease.

Although many scientists criticized Cousins' conclusions about the role of laughter in his recovery, Cousins objected that these criticisms tended to oversimplify his theorizing about the role of positive emotions in recovery,

and the scientific evidence that positive emotions have healing powers. After returning to his career as a writer for several years, Cousins spent the last 12 years of his life at the UCLA Medical School working with researchers to find scientific proof for his beliefs. It is clear that Cousins played a pivotal role in the movements toward more holistic approaches to patient care by physicians and hospitals.

Here is an excerpt of an essay Cousins wrote, based on his experience (Cousins, 1985):

A good place to begin, I thought, was with amusing movies. Allen Funt, producer of the spoofing television program "Candid Camera," sent films of some of his "CC" classics, along with a motion-picture projector. The nurse was instructed in its use.

It worked. I made the joyous discovery that ten minutes of genuine belly laughter had an anesthetic effect and would give me at least two hours of pain-free sleep. When the painkilling effect of the laughter wore off, we would switch on the motion-picture projector again, and not infrequently, it would lead to another pain-free sleep interval. Sometimes the nurse read to me out of a trove of humor books. Especially useful were E. G. and

older adults who were pessimistic showed poorer immune system functioning on two biological indices than those were optimistic, even after the researchers statistically controlled for differences between pessimists and optimists on current health, depression, medication, sleep, and alcohol use (Kamen-Siegel et al., 1991). Similarly, a study of gay men who were HIV-positive found that those who blamed themselves for negative events showed more decline in immune functioning over 18 months than those who engaged in less self-blaming attributions (Segerstrom et al., 1996).

A pessimistic outlook may also impair health by leading people to engage in unhealthy behaviors. In the work with gay men just mentioned, researchers found that, among both the HIV-positive and HIV-negative

men, those who were more pessimistic in their outlooks were less likely to be engaging in healthy behaviors, such as maintaining proper diets, getting enough sleep, and exercising (Taylor et al., 1992). These behaviors were particularly important for the HIV-positive men, because engaging in these healthy behaviors can reduce the risk of developing AIDS. Thus, a pessimistic outlook may affect health directly by causing hyperarousal of the body's physiological response to stress or indirectly by reducing positive coping strategies and, more specifically, reducing healthy behaviors.

In *Extraordinary People:* Norman Cousins, Healing Through Laughter, we highlight a renowned writer who was stricken with a lethal disease, and who decided to use comedy to make himself more optimistic

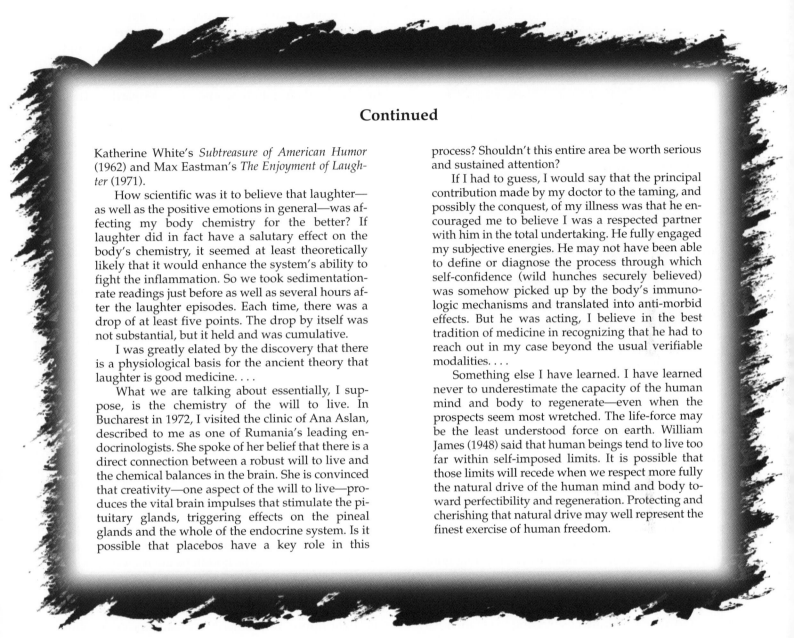

Continued

Katherine White's *Subtreasure of American Humor* (1962) and Max Eastman's *The Enjoyment of Laughter* (1971).

How scientific was it to believe that laughter—as well as the positive emotions in general—was affecting my body chemistry for the better? If laughter did in fact have a salutary effect on the body's chemistry, it seemed at least theoretically likely that it would enhance the system's ability to fight the inflammation. So we took sedimentation-rate readings just before as well as several hours after the laughter episodes. Each time, there was a drop of at least five points. The drop by itself was not substantial, but it held and was cumulative.

I was greatly elated by the discovery that there is a physiological basis for the ancient theory that laughter is good medicine. . . .

What we are talking about essentially, I suppose, is the chemistry of the will to live. In Bucharest in 1972, I visited the clinic of Ana Aslan, described to me as one of Rumania's leading endocrinologists. She spoke of her belief that there is a direct connection between a robust will to live and the chemical balances in the brain. She is convinced that creativity—one aspect of the will to live—produces the vital brain impulses that stimulate the pituitary glands, triggering effects on the pineal glands and the whole of the endocrine system. Is it possible that placebos have a key role in this process? Shouldn't this entire area be worth serious and sustained attention?

If I had to guess, I would say that the principal contribution made by my doctor to the taming, and possibly the conquest, of my illness was that he encouraged me to believe I was a respected partner with him in the total undertaking. He fully engaged my subjective energies. He may not have been able to define or diagnose the process through which self-confidence (wild hunches securely believed) was somehow picked up by the body's immunologic mechanisms and translated into anti-morbid effects. But he was acting, I believe in the best tradition of medicine in recognizing that he had to reach out in my case beyond the usual verifiable modalities. . . .

Something else I have learned. I have learned never to underestimate the capacity of the human mind and body to regenerate—even when the prospects seem most wretched. The life-force may be the least understood force on earth. William James (1948) said that human beings tend to live too far within self-imposed limits. It is possible that those limits will recede when we respect more fully the natural drive of the human mind and body toward perfectibility and regeneration. Protecting and cherishing that natural drive may well represent the finest exercise of human freedom.

and upbeat so that his body could fight his disease better. Although researchers disagree on whether laughter truly cured Cousins, his account of his attempt to overcome disease through laughter has inspired many other disease sufferers and researchers.

Type A Pattern and Health

Like the word *stress*, the term **Type A behavior pattern** is used more or less loosely to describe friends, colleagues, and family members. Let us try to pin down the definition of this important personality style.

The Type A pattern was initially identified by two physicians, Meyer Friedman and Ray Rosenman, who noticed that the chairs in the waiting room of their offices seemed to wear out terribly quickly (Friedman & Rosenman, 1974). Specifically, the edges of the seats would become threadbare, as if their patients were sitting on the edges, anxiously waiting to spring up. These patients were most frequently cardiology patients who had histories of coronary artery disease. Friedman and Rosenman eventually described a personality pattern seen in many of their cardiology patients, which was given the label Type A behavior pattern.

The three components of the Type A pattern, according to these physicians, are a sense of time urgency, easily aroused hostility, and competitive achievement strivings (see *Concept Review:* Type A and Type B Pat-

People with the Type A behavior pattern are always doing several things at once, trying to cram more and more activity into each day.

terns). People who are Type A are always in a hurry, setting unnecessary deadlines for themselves, and trying to do multiple things at once. They are competitive, even in situations in which it is ridiculous to be competitive. For example, they will rush to be the first in line at a restaurant or at the movies, even when the wait would be only two or three minutes if they were last in line. They are also chronically hostile and will fly into a rage with little provocation. Persons who are not Type A are referred to as *Type B*. They are able to relax without feeling guilty, are able to work without feeling pressured or becoming impatient, and are not easily aroused to hostility.

Although we tend to think of Type A people as angry and aggressive, always fighting to get their way and to accomplish a great deal, there is evidence that

they are often anxious and depressed and that these negative emotions may contribute to their risk of disease (Booth-Kewley & Friedman, 1987). Type As may be anxious and depressed because they tend to be dissatisfied with their careers, they tend to spend little time with their families, and thus jeopardize their home lives, and their social lives in general are not as satisfying as they might be. Regardless of the source of their negative emotions, it appears that these emotions are risk factors for both coronary heart disease and death as the result of a variety of other diseases.

Type A Personality and Coronary Heart Disease

One of the most compelling studies to demonstrate the relationship between Type A behavior and coronary heart disease followed more than 3,000 healthy, middle-aged men for 8½ years (Rosenman et al., 1976). At the beginning of the study, the men were evaluated for the Type A pattern by means of a cleverly structured interview. The interview was designed to be irritating. The interviewer kept the participant waiting without explanation and then asked a series of questions about being competitive, hostile, and pressed for time: Do you ever feel rushed or under pressure? Do you eat quickly? Would you describe yourself as ambitious and hard driving or relaxed and easygoing? Do you resent it if someone is late? The interviewer interrupted subjects, asked questions in a challenging manner, and threw in non sequiturs. A participant's level of Type A behavior was determined more on the way he behaved in answering the questions and responding to the interviewer's rudeness than on his answers to the questions themselves. For example, a man was labeled as extremely Type A if he spoke loudly in an explosive manner, talked over the interviewer so as not to be interrupted, appeared tense and tight-lipped, and described hostile incidents with great emotional intensity. The Type B men tended to sit

CONCEPT REVIEW

Type A and Type B Patterns

The Type A behavior pattern is characterized by time urgency, hostility, and competitiveness, whereas the Type B behavior pattern is characterized by a relaxed, non-hostile approach to life.

	Type A	Type B
Personality Characteristics	Time urgency Easily aroused hostility Competitive	Not constantly in a hurry Can relax without feeling guilty Not easily hostile Not overly competitive
Heart Attack Rate	Twice that of Type B	Half that of Type A

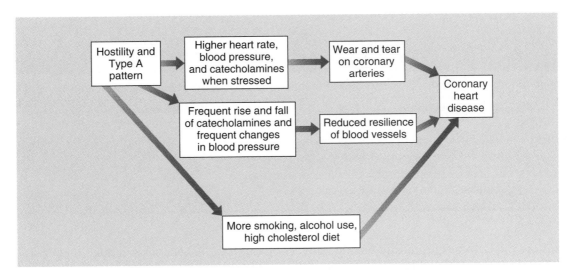

FIGURE 17.6 Pathways by Which Hostility and the Type A Behavior Pattern May Contribute to Coronary Heart Disease. People who are chronically hostile or have the Type A behavior pattern may have chronic or intermittent hyperarousal, which negatively affects the heart, and engage in several behaviors known to increase risk of coronary heart disease.

in a relaxed manner, spoke slowly and softly, were easily interrupted, and smiled often.

Over the 8½ years of the study, Type A men had twice as many heart attacks or other forms of coronary heart disease than did Type B men. These results held up even after diet, age, smoking, and other variables associated with coronary heart disease were taken into account. Other studies have confirmed this twofold risk and linked Type A behavior to heart disease in both men and women (Haynes, Feinleib, & Kannel, 1980). In addition, Type A behavior correlates with severity of coronary artery blockage as determined at autopsy or in X-ray studies of the inside of coronary blood vessels (Friedman et al., 1968; Williams et al., 1988). Based on such evidence, the American Heart Association classified Type A behavior as a risk factor for coronary heart disease in 1981.

More recent research suggests that the definition of Type A behavior, as originally formulated, is too diffuse. Time urgency and competitiveness do not appear to be the variables that best predict coronary heart disease. Instead, the crucial variable may be hostility, particularly a cynical form of hostility characterized by suspiciousness, resentment, frequent anger, antagonism, and distrust of others (Barefoot et al., 1989; Miller et al., 1996). Indeed, a person's chronic level of hostility seems to be a better predictor of heart disease than does his or her classification as Type A or Type B (Booth-Kewley & Friedman, 1987; Dembroski et al., 1985; Thoresen, Telch, & Eagleston, 1981). For example, a 25-year study of 118 male lawyers found that those who scored high on hostility traits on a personality inventory taken in law school were five times more likely to die before the age of 50 than were classmates who were not hostile (Barefoot et al., 1989). Similarly, in a study of physicians, hostility scores obtained in medical school predicted the incidence of coronary heart disease as well as mortality from all causes (Barefoot, Dahlstrom, & Williams, 1983). In both studies, the relationship between hostility and illness was independent of the effects of smoking, age, and high blood pressure.

How does Type A behavior, or more specifically hostility and related negative emotions, lead to coronary heart disease? Again, one mechanism may have to do with overarousal of the sympathetic nervous system (see Figure 17.6). Hostile people show greater physiological arousal in the anticipation of stressors and in the early stages of dealing with stressors (Benotsch, Christensen, & McKelvey, 1997; Lepore, 1995): Their heart rates and blood pressures are higher and they have greater secretion of the stress-related biochemicals known as *catecholamines*. They also show slower returns to baseline levels of sympathetic nervous system activity following stressors than do non-hostile people. This hyperreactivity may cause wear and tear on the coronary arteries, leading to coronary heart disease. Alternately, the excessive secretion of catecholamines in response to stress seen in hostile people may exert a direct chemical effect on blood vessels. The frequent rise and fall of levels of catecholamines may cause frequent changes in blood pressure that reduce the resilience of the blood vessels (Wright, 1984). Hostile people may also engage in behaviors that increase their propensity to heart disease, including smoking, heavy drinking, and maintaining high-cholesterol diets (Folsom et al., 1985).

Gender Differences

Although hostility and the Type A behavior pattern has been linked to coronary heart disease in both men and women, men are more likely to be classified as

CONCEPT REVIEW

Ineffective Coping Strategies

Two ineffective coping strategies that have been linked to illness are a repressive coping style and John Henryism.

	Repressive Coping	John Henryism
Characteristics	Inability to admit to negative emotions; lack of awareness of one's negative emotions	Constantly battling against obstacles that may be insurmountable
Link to illness	Higher levels of cortisol, autonomic arousal; may damage immune and cardiovascular systems	Correlated with hypertension

Type A and more likely to be chronically hostile than are women (Barefoot et al., 1987; Haynes, Feinleib, & Kannel, 1980). Men also are more likely than women to carry three other risk factors for CHD: smoking, hypertension, and elevated cholesterol. In turn, men have a much greater rate of CHD than do women: Heart attacks account for 41 percent of the difference between men and women in mortality in early and middle adulthood (Lerner & Kannel, 1986). Men's greater tendency to be Type A and hostile may be the result of biological predisposition to physiological reactivity: In several studies, men, particularly Type A men, have been shown to be more physiologically reactive to stressors than have women (see Weidner & Collins, 1993). Most of these studies have used male-stereotyped tasks to induce stress in subjects, however. When more female-stereotyped tasks are used to induce stress (such as taking one's child to the pediatrician), gender differences in physiological reactivity are not found (Weidner & Collins, 1993).

Alternately, because many of the components of the Type A pattern, such as competitiveness and aggressiveness, are behaviors that are valued in males, some men may be reinforced for these behaviors and thus adopt them. Weidner and colleagues (1988) found that sons of Type A fathers were more likely to develop the Type A pattern themselves, perhaps by modeling their fathers' behaviors and by being reinforced for imitating their fathers. Studies of the interactions between Type A children and their parents suggest that Type A children are repeatedly urged by their parents to try harder and to do better but are not given praise when they do well, are often harshly criticized for not performing better than others, and are not given concrete criteria to determine when they have been successful. Thus, they may not learn personal standards to evaluate their own achievements and thus always push harder to do more and do better.

Fortunately, as we discuss later in this chapter, Type A behavior appears to be changeable through cognitive and behavioral therapies. People who reduce their Type A behaviors reduce their risk of coronary heart disease considerably.

Ineffective Coping Strategies

A great deal of the research on personality and health has focused on the role of specific coping strategies in maintaining physiological arousal, and thus damaging health (see *Concept Review:* Ineffective Coping Strategies).

Repressive Coping

Type A people are constantly showing their hostile feelings, much to others' dismay. Some people have the opposite tendency—to bottle up and repress all negative emotions. A person with a **repressive coping style** does not admit when he or she is upset and may not even be aware of his or her own negative emotions.

Some studies suggest that repressive coping is detrimental to physical health. Laboratory studies find that repressors have higher base levels of cortisol, a hormone that is secreted in response to stress (Brown et al., 1996). Repressors also evidence greater autonomic arousal (heart rate, galvanic skin response) while completing sentences with sexual or aggressive content than do people with nonrepressive coping styles (Weinberger, Schwartz, & Davidson, 1979). Repressors are not aware that they are physiologically aroused chronically or in response to challenging tasks, however.

As noted repeatedly in this chapter, chronic physiological arousal or reactivity to situations can cause damage to both the immune and cardiovascular systems. Some naturalistic studies have found links between repressive coping and diseases of the immune or cardiovascular system. For example, studies of students and of elderly adults have found that repressive coping is associated with poorer immune system functioning (Jamner, Schwartz, & Leigh, 1988).

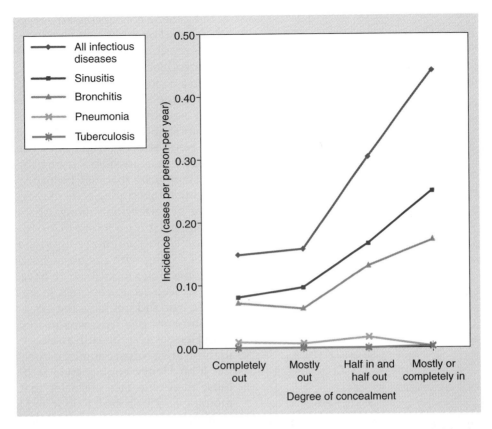

FIGURE 17.7   Infectious Diseases as a Function of Concealing One's Sexual Orientation. Homosexual men who concealed their homosexuality from others were more prone to several infectious diseases.

Source: Cole et al., 1996.

Repressing important aspects of your identity may also be bad for your health. One intriguing study showed that gay men who conceal their homosexual identity from others may suffer health consequences (Cole, Kemeny, Taylor, & Visscher, 1996). Those men who concealed their homosexuality were about three times more likely to develop cancer and several infectious diseases (pneumonia, bronchitis, sinusitis, and tuberculosis) over a five-year period than men who were open about their homosexuality (see Figure 17.7). All of these men were HIV-negative. But another study by this same research group focused on HIV-positive gay men and found that those who concealed their homosexuality showed faster progression of the HIV infection than those who did not conceal their identity (Cole et al., 1995). The differences in health between the men who were "out" and those who were "closeted" did not reflect differences in health care behaviors (smoking or exercise). It may be that chronic inhibition of one's identity, like chronic inhibition of emotions, can lead directly to health changes.

In contrast, talking about important issues in one's life and about negative emotions appears to have positive health benefits. In a large series of studies,

Pennebaker (1990) has found that having people reveal personal traumas in diaries or essays improves people's health. For example, in one study, 50 healthy undergraduates were randomly assigned to write either about the most traumatic and upsetting events in their lives or about trivial topics for 20 minutes on each of four consecutive days. Blood samples were taken from the students the day before they began writing and the last day of writing, and six weeks after writing, and tested for several markers of immune system functioning. The number of times the students visited the college health center over the six weeks after the writing task were also recorded and compared to the number health center visits the students had made before the study. As Figures 17.8, page 638, shows, students who revealed their personal traumas in essays had a more positive immune system functioning and a greater decline in health center visits than the control group who wrote about trivial events (Pennebaker, Kiecolt-Glaser & Glaser, 1988).

Repressive coping styles may be detrimental to health because repressors have no outlets for their negative emotions—they do not recognize them or will not admit to them, so they cannot let go of them. In turn,

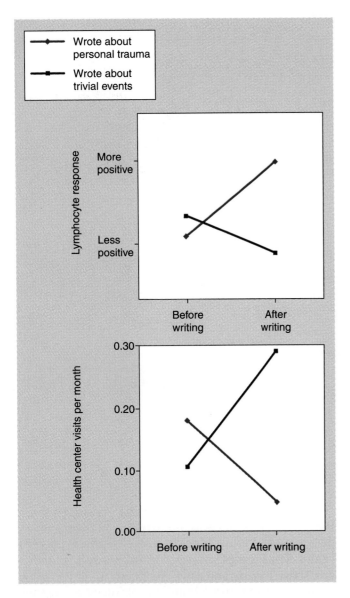

FIGURE 17.8 Students' Health After Writing About Traumas or Trivialities. Students who revealed personal traumas in a series of essays had stronger immune system functioning and fewer health care visits than students who only wrote about trivial events in their essays.

Adapted from Pennebaker, Kiecolt-Glaser, & Glaser, 1988.

this may cause the chronic physiological arousal that impairs health. In addition, it may take a great deal of unconscious psychological and physiological work to constantly repress one's emotions, which may take its toll on health.

John Henryism

In general, research has shown that engaging in active strategies to solve one's problems and overcome obstacles is associated with more positive mental and physical health (Billings & Moos, 1981). There is an exception

to this general conclusion, however. A group of studies has focused on a phenomenon known as **John Henryism.** According to the story, John Henry was an uneducated black laborer who beat a mechanical steam drill in a contest to see which could complete the most work in the shortest period of time. Although John Henry won the battle, he dropped dead after the contest. James and colleagues (1983, 1984) coined the term John Henryism for a pattern of active coping with stressors that involves trying harder and harder against obstacles that may be insurmountable and suggested that this coping style may be linked to the high rate of hypertension among African American men. Subsequent studies found that African American men in lower socioeconomic groups who had a John Henry way of coping with the obstacles they faced were almost three times more likely to have hypertension than were African American men in lower socioeconomic classes who did not have the same active coping pattern. In contrast, there was no relationship between John Henryism and health among White men of either high or low socioeconomic status. This suggests that the John Henry coping style is dangerous only for those men who face obstacles that are nearly insurmountable. This research on John Henryism raises the troubling possibility that men who are trying to overcome with hard work and persistence the oppression and hardship they were born into may be putting their health at risk.

Summing Up

- People who are chronically pessimistic may show poorer physical health because they appraise more events as uncontrollable or because they engage in poorer health-related behaviors.

- People with the Type A behavior pattern are highly competitive, time urgent, and hostile. The Type A behavior pattern significantly increases risk for coronary heart disease. The most potent component of this pattern is hostility, which alone significantly predicts heart disease.

- People with repressive coping styles deny their negative emotions and may be at increased risk for poor health.

- John Henryism is a coping style in which people work diligently against tremendous obstacles but apparently put their physical health at risk in doing so.

⊙ INTERVENTIONS TO IMPROVE HEALTH

Most of the interventions designed to improve health have (1) provided people with new health-related skills and opportunity to practice these skills or (2) attempted to challenge and change negative, self-defeating cognitions that contribute to the development of illness or interfere with recovery or adaptation to illness. We discuss four types of interventions that have proven useful in improving people's health.

Behavioral and Cognitive Interventions

Many of the behavioral and cognitive techniques we have described as useful in the treatment of psychological disorders can help people learn new skills and attitudes that also improve their physical health (see *Concept Review:* Behavioral and Cognitive Interventions, p. 640).

Guided Mastery Techniques

When told what they have to do to protect or improve their health, people often feel unable or unwilling to engage in these behaviors. **Guided mastery techniques** provide people with explicit information about how to engage in positive health-related behaviors and with opportunities to engage in these behaviors in increasingly challenging situations (Taylor, 1999). The goals are to increase people's skills at engaging in the behaviors and their beliefs that they can engage in the behaviors. For example, a guided mastery program for teaching women how to negotiate safe sexual practices in sexual encounters with men might begin with information on condom use. A counselor might then model how a woman can tell a man that she wants him to use a condom when they have sex. The women would watch the counselor and then practice insisting on condom use in role-plays with the counselor or other group participants. In these role-plays, the women would be presented with increasingly difficult challenges to their insistence on condom use, feedback on effective means for meeting these challenges, and practice in meeting these challenges. The women might also be taught techniques for determining when it was useless to argue with their partners any longer about condom use and skills for withdrawing from sexual encounters in which their partners wanted to practice unsafe sex.

African American men who find themselves chronically fighting nearly insurmountable obstacles to their achievement may be at increased risk for hypertension.

Guided mastery techniques have been successfully used in AIDS prevention programs with African American female and male adolescents (Jemmott & Jemmott, 1992). In the programs with the young women, researchers gave participants information about the cause, transmission, and prevention of AIDS. The young women then participated in guided mastery exercises to increase their skills and self-confidence for negotiating condom use by their male partners. The young women were also given instruction on how to eroticize condom use—how to incorporate putting on condoms in foreplay and intercourse in ways that increase positive attitudes toward condoms. Compared to young women who received only information and not guided mastery exercises, these young women showed a greater sense of efficacy in negotiating condom use, more positive expectations for sexual enjoyment with condoms, and stronger intentions to use condoms. These effects were found in a similar program with sexually active African American female adolescents drawn from the inner city (Jemmott & Jemmott, 1992). In a program with African American male adolescents, young men also were first given information about the cause, transmission, and prevention of AIDS. Then they participated in guided mastery exercises that taught them how to negotiate condom use with their partners and to eroticize condom use. Follow-up assessments showed that, compared to those in a control group, the adolescents who participated in the program were more knowledgeable about risks for AIDS, less accepting of risky practices, and engaged in lower-risk sexual behavior with fewer sexual partners (Jemmott et al., 1992). Thus, enhancing

CONCEPT REVIEW

Behavioral and Cognitive Interventions

Behavioral and cognitive techniques designed to treat psychological disorders have also proven effective in helping people change maladaptive health-related behaviors.

Intervention	Description	Example
Guided mastery techniques	Provide explicit information on how to engage in positive behaviors and opportunities to practice these behaviors in challenging situations	Teach a woman the importance of condom use to safe sex and how to persuade male partner to use condoms; use role-plays to allow the woman to practice persuasion techniques.
Reducing catastrophizing cognitions	Provide basic education about illness to reduce concern; identify irrational thoughts about illness and teach the person to challenge them and be more realistic; help the person engage in positive coping	Reduce a surgical patient's concern by providing information on success of surgery; identify irrational concerns about postoperative disability and challenge with realistic information; help the patient identify resources for coping, such as aides.
Biofeedback	Helps the person identify signs that bodily processes are going awry, and ways of controlling them, often through relaxation	A hypertension patient is hooked up to machine that emits a tone whenever blood pressure is above a certain level; the patient learns to relax to reduce blood pressure when a tone sounds.
Time management	Teach the person to reduce obligations, prioritize and schedule important activities, break tasks into easier chunks, and reward self for accomplishments	A working mother with migraines reduces unnecessary obligations (e.g., always being the mother to drive on field trips), prioritizes activities with her child and at work, and rewards herself with an evening out with friends.

people's skills to engage in healthy behaviors seems to increase their self-efficacy for engaging in these behaviors and, in turn, increases their intentions to engage in these behaviors and their actual enacting of the behaviors.

Reducing Catastrophizing Cognitions

Many people believe the worst when they are told that they have a serious illness, regardless of what they are told by their physicians about their prognoses. These catastrophizing cognitions cause great distress and can lead people to be fatalistic and to not comply with treatments or engage in behaviors that could prevent future illnesses. Consider, for example, a man who is expected to recover fully from a minor heart attack. Despite assurances, the man believes that his physician is trying to shield him from the truth and that he is doomed to die of another heart attack at any minute. This fatalistic attitude leads the man to ignore his physician's advice to quit smoking, reduce the fat in his diet, and begin to exercise regularly. He decides that all of these changes in his behaviors will do no good, so he will just do what he wants until the inevitable next heart attack kills him. Another man is

told he has prostate cancer but that surgeons should be able to remove all the cancer in a routine surgery. Still, upon hearing the word *cancer*, he imagines certain death. He becomes so anxious that his blood pressure rises and he begins having panic attacks. These panic attacks interfere with his preparation for surgery and recovery after the surgery.

Psychologists working with patients who are catastrophizing their illnesses often begin with basic education about their illnesses—the prevalence of the illnesses, the standard procedures for treating the illnesses, the average prognosis for the illnesses, and differences between patients in prognoses. This education is tailored to the individual patient, in an attempt to make sure that the patient understands all the physician has told him or her about the illness and prognosis. This can be very helpful, because physicians are not always good at speaking to patients about their illnesses in simple, straightforward, understandable language. Much of the catastrophic thinking is often a result of misunderstanding what they have been told by their physicians.

Psychologists also use standard cognitive therapy techniques to challenge these thoughts (see Chapter 5). For example, a patient who has breast cancer believes that the lumpectomy will disfigure her to such a degree that her husband will no longer love her and will leave her. Her psychologist helps her assess the evidence for this belief, by convincing her to talk directly with her husband about her fears. The husband says that he is completely supportive of his wife, that he will love her no matter what surgery she has, and that her fears of his leaving are completely unfounded. Of course, there is always the chance that a patient's fears are realistic—that the husband really is having doubts about his ability to support his wife through her surgery—or that a patient does have an illness that is likely to take her life. In such cases, psychologists help patients accept and cope with this reality, find support in friends and other family members, and get their affairs in order should death come quickly.

A study demonstrated the efficacy of challenging patients' catastrophizing cognitions about their illnesses (Greene & Blanchard, 1994). The patients in this study had irritable bowel syndrome (IBS), a widespread, chronic illness of the lower gastrointestinal (GI) tract, characterized by abdominal pain or extreme abdominal tenderness and diarrhea or constipation. No drug treatments have proven effective for this condition. In this study, patients with IBS were randomly assigned either to intensive, individualized cognitive therapy (10 sessions over eight weeks) or to eight weeks of daily GI symptom reporting. In the cognitive therapy, therapists challenged the patients' negative and irrational cognitions about their condition. Many of these cognitions involved hypervigilance to symptoms and catastrophizing about those symptoms. For example, a patient constantly presses against her abdomen. Finding certain areas of tenderness, she panics, believing she is beginning to have another episode. The therapist helps this patient identify her beliefs and fears about her illness and the ways these fears can exacerbate the illness. The patient is also taught to "decenter" by labeling her negative self-statements and thereby gaining distance from these thoughts. Finally, the therapist encourages her to challenge negative beliefs by engaging in behaviors that disconfirmed their beliefs (e.g., going out in the evening even though she believes that it may trigger a new episode). After treatment, 80 percent of the patients receiving cognitive therapy showed significant improvement in their symptoms of IBS compared to only 10 percent of the patients who simply monitored their symptoms. In the cognitive therapy group, reduction in IBS symptoms was related to reductions in negative, catastrophizing thoughts and to reduction in depression and anxiety. The effects of the cognitive therapy remained strong three months following the treatment. Thus, this study demonstrated that cognitive therapy aimed at catastrophizing cognitions not only produced reductions in psychological distress over the illness but also reductions in the actual symptoms of this chronic illness.

Biofeedback

Biofeedback has been used to treat a wide variety of health problems—most frequently migraine headaches, chronic pain, and hypertension (Taylor, 1999). Biofeedback actually involves several techniques designed to help people change bodily processes by learning to identify signs that the processes are going awry and then learning ways of controlling the processes. For example, a person with hypertension might be hooked up to a machine that converts his heartbeats to tones. He sits quietly listening to his heart rate and trying various means to change his heart rate, such as breathing slowly or concentrating on a pleasant image. The goal in biofeedback is for people to detect early signs of dysfunction in their bodies, such as signs that their blood pressure is rising, and to use techniques they learned while hooked up to machines to control their bodies even when they are independent of the machines. Several controlled studies have found that biofeedback training can significantly reduce blood pressure among people with hypertension (Glasgow, Gaader, & Engel, 1982; Glasgow, Engle & D'Lugoff, 1989; Nakao et al., 1997)

Biofeedback also seems to be successful in reducing tension-related headaches (Gannon et al., 1987). Headache sufferers learn to detect when they are tensing the muscles in their heads. They then use techniques for reducing this tension, thus relieving their headaches. Biofeedback is used for migraine sufferers to increase the blood flow to the body's periphery, thereby decreasing the blood flow to the head and reducing pressure on the arteries. Migraine patients are hooked up to machines that give them temperature readings to their heads and to their fingers. They are taught to relax fully and to notice the effects that relaxation has on their temperatures. Then they may be encouraged to increase the temperatures of their fingers, using the feedback of the machines as an aid. It is not clear just how patients do this—it is a matter of using trial and error to find some way of changing their temperatures. Eventually, patients attempt to use these techniques to control headaches at home. When they feel headaches coming on, they then concentrate warming up their fingers to divert blood flow from the arteries in their heads to the periphery (see Turk, Meichenbaum, & Berman, 1979).

Although biofeedback can be successful in treating hypertension and pain conditions such as headaches, it is not clear that it works the way its proponents believe it works (Turk, Meichenbaum, & Berman, 1979). For example, although biofeedback can reduce migraine headaches, the evidence that it does

Biofeedback helps people learn to detect when bodily processes are going awry and to counteract these processes.

so by temperature control is mixed. In addition, biofeedback appears to be no more successful than simple relaxation techniques in reducing headaches, pain, and hypertension (see Chapter 6 for a detailed description of relaxation techniques.) Indeed, biofeedback may work largely because individuals often learn relaxation techniques as a part of biofeedback training. Relaxation techniques have the advantage over biofeedback of being much less expensive and time-consuming to learn.

Time Management

There are hundreds of books on time management, most of which have been published in the last 25 years. As the pace of life in the industrialized world has quickened, the number of activities people try to jam into each day has expanded greatly. The recommendations of time-management experts generally fall into four categories: prioritizing, breaking tasks into small chunks, scheduling, and rewarding oneself.

The first step of time management is determining what activities are worth one's time and what activities are not. Time-management experts often distinguish between *important* activities and *urgent* activities. Important activities are activities that have to do with one's central values or goals in life. For example, if one of a person's central goals in life is to become an expert car mechanic and eventually own her own car repair shop, then important activities for her might be taking a course on car repair at the community college, ap-

prenticing at a local car repair shop, or investigating how to buy into a car repair franchise.

Urgent activities are those that beg to be done *now*. Sometimes these activities are also important activities. For example, if a person's central goal is to become a car mechanic and the deadline for signing up for the course on car repair at the community college is today, then going to the college and signing up today is both an important and an urgent activity. Often, however, urgent activities are not important activities. For example, talking on the phone to a salesperson trying to sell life insurance is an urgent activity (at least the salesperson tries to stress that it is), but it is not an important activity for a person who already has life insurance and whose 2-year-old child is about to pull over the bookshelf. Many of the activities that get labeled urgent involve responding to other people who want one's time or attention *now* but could just as easily be dealt with later. We often make activities into urgent activities when we are trying to avoid important activities that we do not want to do. Cleaning your dormitory room suddenly becomes an urgent activity during exam week. Answering letters ignored for months suddenly becomes an urgent activity when you must decide what courses to take next year. Calling your "best friend" for the first time in a year suddenly becomes an urgent activity when a paper is due the next morning at 9 A.M.

It is crucial to decide what activities are important. Determining important activities requires a clear set of goals and values. What would we like to

It may be tempting to clean a messy room rather than tackling more important activities.

accomplish in the next month, in the next six months, in the next year, in the next five years? The answers to these questions indicate what our primary goals are, and the activities that help us accomplish these goals are important activities. Which people in our lives do we care about most? Which organizations (e.g., church) or activities (e.g., horseback riding) are most central to our lives? The answers to these questions can help us recognize some of our core values, and the activities that further these values are important activities.

The second step in time management is to break large activities or tasks into smaller ones. It is important to have both distal goals (long-term goals) and proximal goals (short-term goals that move one closer to long-term goals). Any large goal or activity, such as becoming an expert car mechanic, can be broken into a series of smaller activities. These smaller activities are steps that must be taken to accomplish long-term goals. Long-term goals can be overwhelming and demoralizing, but breaking these goals into smaller activities can make the tasks seem more manageable. One time management book recommends breaking tasks into five-minute chunks, if possible (Lakein, 1973). Once that is done, a person can coax himself into getting engaged in the activity by saying to himself, "I'll only work on this for five minutes—I can stand that." Once he has accomplished one five-minute task, however, he may find himself so engaged in the activity that he moves on to the next five-minute task and then the next, and soon he has spent an hour on his important activity.

The third step in time management is scheduling important activities. Most of us have to-do lists, and some of us live by them. The to-do lists are often filled with urgent but unimportant activities (*pick up laundry, return five phone calls to unfamiliar people, wash the car*). If important activities do show up on the list, they are often in the form of monolithic tasks, such as *write term paper, look for a new job,* or *save money.* The activities that should be on the to-do list are the important activities broken down into their small components, which was done in step two. So rather than listing *write term paper* on the list, one should write, *discuss ideas for term paper with professor, look in library listings for pertinent materials,* and *begin outline.* It helps to schedule specific times to do these important small activities. So one might write, *after class on Thursday, talk with professor about ideas for term paper,* or *look in library listings on Saturday afternoon for pertinent materials.* When scheduling an important activity for a specific time, it is important to be ruthless about protecting that time from other urgent but unimportant activities, such as chatty phone calls from friends one sees every day. This is not to say that people should schedule every minute of their days. However, scheduling important activities increases the likelihood that they will be accomplished. This also reduces the stress of worrying about whether these tasks can be completed.

A fourth and final step in time management is establishing rewards for accomplishing short-term and long-term goals. Few of us can keep up a grueling pace of working on our important activities without taking

TAKING PSYCHOLOGY PERSONALLY

How Can You Reduce Your Stress Level?

If you are a college student, how can you use the stress-management techniques to reduce the stress in your life and possibly improve your health and well-being? The first step involves self-monitoring—monitoring your reactions to events over the course of your day to determine which ones you experience as stressful. You may think that you do not need to do this—that it is obvious what is stressful in your life, such as exams or having too much work to do. However, it is important to do a more fine-grained analysis of exactly what aspects of events make you feel most stressed and/or the cognitions you are having about those events that are increasing your stress level. Keeping a diary or daily log of your emotions and the situations and thoughts connected to those emotions can help. You might discover that it is not exams in general that you are experiencing as stressful but an upcoming math exam in particular. You might further discover that certain cognitions such as "My parents will kill me if I don't do well in math," or "I'm an older student so I can't learn this new math like the younger students," are elevating your stress about the exam.

If you identify any cognitions that are contributing to your stress, then use cognitive therapy techniques to challenge these cognitions and determine if they are realistic and the only ways to view your situation. Remember that the four main questions that cognitive therapists ask are (1) what is the evidence for your viewpoint, (2) are there other ways of viewing the situation, (3) what's the worst that could happen in this situation, and (4) how could I cope if the worst-case scenario came true? For example, let us say that you are an older person returning to college after a long absence, and you believe that you are incapable of learning math in the way it is taught these days. First, ask yourself what is the evidence for your viewpoint. Have you been completely unable to comprehend anything the professor has taught in this math class? Do your problems have anything to do with your age or are some of the young people in this class also having trouble? Ideally, you will discover evidence against your assumption that you are completely incapable of learning math, which then will lead you to the next question: What is an alternative way of viewing this situation? Is it possible that there are specific skills that you are lacking rather than competence in math? Is it possible that the professor is not very good at teaching math and that the problem lies with her rather than with your capabilities? Although you cannot learn specific new skills or improve your

occasional breaks and patting ourselves on the back for our accomplishments. These pats on the back may involve doing something social with a close friend, indulging in a favorite meal or dessert, or going for a walk in a beautiful place. The key is that we recognize in some way that accomplishing even small activities related to our most important goals is laudable and that we give ourselves praise for this.

Some of us need to reduce the number of activities we try to accomplish in our lives, even if all these activities are important ones. We may be able to reduce the number of important activities we jam into our lives by asking for help from others or by hiring help if we can afford it. For example, a single mother who works full-time might hire someone to clean her house if she can afford it, so that she can spend more of her time away from work with her children. However, we must give up certain goals and activities, in recognition that only a limited number of things can get done well. In *Taking Psychology Personally:* How Can You Reduce Your Stress Level?, we discuss additional ways that college students can reduce stress in their lives.

Interventions for the Type A Behavior Pattern

Many of the interventions we have discussed in this chapter, including biofeedback, cognitive therapy, and

Continued

professor's teaching overnight, discovering that the problem is not your general incompetence but something more amenable to change can reduce your sense of stress.

The third question to ask yourself is, What is the worst thing that could happen? The answer in this case is probably that you could flunk the course. What is the consequence of flunking the course? If it is not a required course, then probably the worst thing that could happen would be that you would not know math as well as you might. If it is a required course, then it is time to move to the fourth and final question: How do you cope with the worst-case scenario? Perhaps you could find an alternative course that is not as difficult but would still meet the requirement or get some tutoring over the summer and retake the course next fall. If these are not possible coping strategies, then you may need to think of strategies to cope with the reality of your flunking the course, such as changing your major. It can be quite helpful to go through these questions with a trusted friend who can help you generate challenges to your negative cognitions and coping strategies for dealing with the situations that might arise should the worst-case scenario come true.

Time management is an especially important component of stress reduction for college students. Students who are living away from home for the first time may not have the structure and discipline imposed on their lives that their parents provided when they were living at home. At the same time, they may be facing much larger workloads and more difficult course material than they ever dreamed of in high school. The time-management

strategies discussed earlier in this chapter can go a long way toward structuring their lives around the important activities of doing well in school as well as enjoying a social life. Scheduling of important activities is particularly important for college students who are prone to procrastination. In a college atmosphere, there are endless distractions that can make it easy to put off doing homework assignments or preparing for examinations. Only by scheduling specific times for doing schoolwork and refusing to succumb to these distractions during those times can some college students keep up with their work. Procrastinator college students are very prone to developing the belief that they do their best work when under the pressure of a deadline. This belief is almost always a fantasy that simply justifies procrastination. It is very seldom the case that good papers are written or exams are properly studied for under the influence of sleep deprivation and panic.

Time management is also especially important for students who must work while going to school. Interestingly, these students sometimes are natural time managers and find it easy to impose discipline and schedules on themselves, in part because they have been forced to learn these skills to survive. One type of activity these students sometimes find hardest to work into their schedules are leisure activities that are relaxing and can serve to reward them for all their hard work. These activities are just as important as activities related to school or work, because they can help students keep their stress down and can help them keep a healthy perspective on school and work.

time-management training, have been used to help people with the Type A behavior pattern change their behaviors and their attitudes toward themselves and the world and thereby reduce their risk of coronary heart disease. In one study, 1,000 men who had suffered heart attacks were assigned to a cognitive-behavioral treatment to reduce Type A behavior, or to a control group that received no treatment (Friedman et al., 1986). The men in the treatment group were helped to reduce their sense of time urgency by practicing standing in line (a situation Type A individuals find extremely irritating). While standing, they were encouraged to use the opportunity to reflect on things they did not normally have time to think about, to watch

people, or to strike up conversations with strangers. Treatment also included learning to express themselves without exploding in anger and to alter certain specific behaviors (such as interrupting the speech of others or talking or eating hurriedly). Therapists helped the subjects reevaluate basic beliefs, such as the notion that success depends on the quality of work produced, that might drive much of a Type A person's urgent and hostile behavior. Finally, subjects found ways to make home and work environments less stressful, such as by reducing the number of unnecessary social engagements. When researchers followed up on the treatment and control subjects 4½ years later, they found that the treatment subjects were only about half as likely to have experienced second heart attacks as were the control subjects.

Sociocultural Interventions

Other interventions to improve health focus on helping people use and change their social environment.

Seeking Social Support

One strategy for coping with negative emotions that appears to help people adjust both emotionally and physically to stressors is seeking emotional support from others. A wide variety of studies have found that people who seek and receive positive emotional support from others show more positive health outcomes, both on microlevel measures such as natural killer cell activity, and on macrolevel outcomes, such as the progression of major diseases (Uchino, Cacioppo, & Kiecolt-Glaser, 1996). For example, a study of women who had just received surgery for breast cancer found that those who actively sought social support from others had higher natural killer cell activity (Levy et al., 1990). In a large series of studies, James Pennebaker (1990) found that people who simply reveal personal traumas, such as being raped or losing a spouse to suicide, to supportive others tend to show more positive physical health both shortly after traumas and in the long run.

Some studies suggest that support groups can improve the physical health, as well as the well-being of cancer patients.

Unfortunately, not all interactions with people are supportive ones. Some friends or relatives can be burdens instead of blessings in times of stress. The quality of the social support a person receives from others following a stressor is more important than the quantity of support received (Rook, 1984). Persons who have a high degree of conflict in their social networks tend to show poorer physical and emotional health following major stressors, such as bereavement (Windholz, Marmar, & Horowitz, 1985). Conflictual social relationships may affect physical health through the immune system. A study of newlywed couples found that those who became hostile and negative toward each other while discussing marital problems showed more decrements in four indicators of immune system functioning than did couples who remained calm and nonhostile in discussing marital problems. Couples who became hostile during these discussions also showed elevated blood pressure for longer periods of time than did those who did not become hostile (Kiecolt-Glaser et al., 1993). Thus, the old prescription of talking through troubles with others may only be good if those others can be emotionally supportive when needed.

Psychologists can work with people facing stress and illness to help them identify their sources of positive social support and use these resources better. This might involve helping people organize their time so they have opportunities for quiet walks or evenings with a friend. Or a psychologist might help an individual whose relationships with important others are conflictual to deal more effectively with those relationships, so they are a source of strength, rather than a burden.

Some people use religious groups as a source of social support. As we discuss in *Viewpoints: Is Religion Good for Your Health?*, new research on the links between religion and health is causing psychologists to rethink their previously negative attitudes toward religion. Another source of social support can be support groups of people who face similar stressors.

Support Groups

Many people facing stressors, including physical illness, seek support from support groups. A provocative study of breast cancer patients found evidence that support groups may not only help women cope emotionally with their cancer but may also prolong the lives of these women (Spiegel et al., 1989). Several years ago, researchers began a study in which they randomly assigned women with advanced breast cancer either to a series of weekly support groups or to no support groups. All the women received standard medical care for their cancer. The focus in the groups was on facing death and learning to live one's remaining days to the

VIEWPOINTS

Is Religion Good for Your Health?

P sychologists have had an ambivalent relationship with religion. William James, a founder of modern psychology, noted that religion can be sick or healthy, debilitating or vitalizing. Certainly, religious doctrines and beliefs have been the justification for many horrible deeds across history and in our recent times. Recently, however, psychologists have been forced to reevaluate their opinions about the effects of religion because of a number of studies showing that religion benefits both physical and mental health.

Actively religious people show lower mortality rates from a variety of diseases than nonreligious people (Oman & Reed, 1998; Strawbridge et al., 1997). They are generally in better physical health when they are alive (Grosse-Holforth et al., 1996; Koenig et al., 1997). People who are religious also tend to score better than nonreligious people on measures of mental health (for reviews, see Ellison & Levin, 1998; Koenig, 1998; Myers, 1992). Religious beliefs may impact health because they influence health behaviors (Gorsuch, 1995). Many religions have prohibitions against unhealthy behaviors, such as excessive drinking and drug-taking and smoking, and religious people do smoke and drink less than nonreligious people (e.g., Koenig, George, Cohen, Hays, Larson, & Blazer, 1998). In addition, positive social support is linked to better health, and religious groups offer social support to their members.

Other psychologists, however, argue that religious beliefs do not help people cope with adversity—they lead people to accept adversity as "God's will" rather than doing what they can to overcome that adversity (Ellis, 1995). And, they say, if religious people look healthier in some studies, it is only because they are more prone to deny their psychological problems, or because these studies were biased in favor of finding a positive relationship between religion and health. It is true that many of the studies on religion and health done over the years were conducted by people who had a stake in the outcome of the study—religious people who wanted to find a positive relationship, or nonreligious people who wanted to find a negative relationship.

Increasingly, however, good research is being done by researchers who are not invested in finding either that religion is good or bad for people's health. As that research accumulates, we may begin to understand how religion affects people's health. Is it the social support that religious communities provide? Do religious doctrines simply prescribe healthier behaviors? Is there something truly health-promoting in believing in a higher power?

fullest. The researchers did not expect they could alter the course of the cancer; they only wanted to improve the quality of life for women with advanced cancer. They were quite surprised when, 48 months after the study began, all of the women who had not been in the support groups were dead from their cancer and a third of the women in the support groups were still alive. The average survival from the time the study began for the women in the support groups was about 40 months, compared to about 19 months for the women who were not in the support groups. There were no differences between the groups other than their participation in the weekly support meetings that could explain the differences in the average survival times. It appears that the support groups actually increased the number of months that the women in the support group lived (for similar results, see Fawzy et al., 1990; Richardson et al., 1990).

What can account for this? The women in the support groups had lower levels of emotional distress and they learned how to control their physical pain better than the women who did not participate in the support groups. This lowering of distress may have improved the functioning of their immune systems. The mechanisms by which lowering of distress can affect immune functioning are not yet known, but one possibility is that reducing distress reduces levels of stress-related hormones, including the corticosteroids. In turn, excessive levels of corticosteroids promote the growth of some cancers (Spiegel, 1996).

Summing Up

- Guided mastery techniques help people learn positive health-related behaviors, by teaching them the most effective ways of engaging in these behaviors and giving them opportunity to practice the behaviors in increasingly challenging situations.

- Cognitive-behavioral techniques can be used to challenge catastrophizing cognitions people may have about illnesses that maintain high states of physiological arousal.

- Biofeedback is used to help people learn to control their own negative physiological responses.

- Time-management techniques can help people reduce the overall levels of stress in their lives, thereby improving their health.

- A variety of cognitive-behavioral techniques have been combined into an effective treatment package to reduce the Type A behavior pattern and the risk of further coronary disease in men.

- Seeking social support is one coping strategy associated with better health, as long as others provide positive social support rather than social conflict.

- Support groups are one source of social support for some people. Some research suggests that they can improve both psychological and physical well-being.

◑ BIO-PSYCHO-SOCIAL INTEGRATION

The field of health psychology is based on the notion that the body, the mind, and the environment are intimately connected. Psychological and social factors can have direct effects on the physiology of the body and indirect effects on health by leading people to engage in either health-promoting or health-impairing behaviors. It is clear that our physical health affects our emotional health and self-concept. People with life-threatening or debilitating physical illnesses are at much increased risk for depression and other emotional problems. At a more subtle level, physiology may influence many characteristics we think of as personality, such as how quick we are to react with anger when someone confronts us or how adaptable we are to new situations. Thus, health psychologists begin with the assumption that biology, psychology, and social environment have reciprocal influences on each other. Then they attempt to characterize these influences and determine their importance.

Chapter Summary

- Health psychologists are concerned with the roles of personality factors, coping styles, stressful events, and health-related behaviors on the development of physical disease and on the progress of disease once it begins. There are three models for explaining how psychological factors affect health. The direct effects model suggests that psychological factors, such as stressful experiences or certain personality characteristics, directly cause changes in the physiology of the body that, in turn, cause or exacerbate disease. The interactive model suggests that psychological factors must interact with preexisting biological vulnerability to disease in order for a disease to develop. The indirect effects model suggests that psychological factors affect disease largely by influencing whether people engage in health-promoting behaviors.

- The three characteristics of events that contribute to their being perceived as stressful are their controllability, their predictability, and their level of challenge or threat to the limits of one's capabilities. Stress can have a direct effect on health by causing chronic arousal of the physiological responses that make up the fight-or-flight response. These physiological responses result from the activation of the sympathetic nervous system and the adrenal-cortical system. Although these physiological changes are useful in helping the body fight or flee from a threat, they can cause damage to the body if they are chronically aroused due to stress. Diseases that can result from such chronic arousal include coronary heart disease, hypertension, and possibly impairment of the immune system.

- One activity that many of us give up when we are under stress is sleep. There is increasing evidence, however, that the amount and quality of sleep we get on a daily basis have a significant impact on our physical health and our psychological functioning. Some people develop sleep disorders. Dyssomnias, such as insomnia, involve abnormalities in the amount, quality, or timing of sleep. Parasomnias, such as sleep walking disorder, involve abnormal behavioral and psychological events occurring during sleep.

- Pessimism is a personality characteristic that has been linked to poor health. The Type A behavior pattern is strongly related to high risk for coronary heart disease and possibly also to other diseases. People who have the Type A pattern have a sense of time urgency, are easily made hostile, and are competitive in many situations. The component of this pattern that has been most consistently linked to coronary heart disease is a cynical form of hostility. Another important aspect of personality is the way individuals cope with difficult situations. Two coping strategies that are linked to poor health are repressive coping and John Henryism.

- Guided mastery techniques have been effective in increasing self-efficacy for engaging in healthy behaviors and in increasing the actual conduct of healthy behaviors. These techniques include the use of modeling and role-playing to provide people with new skills and opportunities to practice those skills in increasingly challenging circumstances. Cognitive techniques are used to help patients reduce catastrophizing cognitions about their illnesses and stress-inducing self-expectations. Biofeedback is sometimes used to help people gain control over bodily processes that contribute to disease. It is unclear how biofeedback works, but it has been shown to be useful in reducing hypertension and headaches. Finally, time-management techniques can help people reduce stress in their lives by identifying important activities, breaking these activities into smaller chunks, scheduling the activities, and rewarding themselves for accomplishing the activities.

- These cognitive and behavioral techniques have been combined to reduce the health-damaging behaviors and cognitions of people with the Type A behavior pattern. One study showed that Type A men who underwent cognitive therapy were significantly less likely to have future myocardial infarctions than were Type A men who did not undergo cognitive therapy.

- Sociocultural interventions focus on changing and using people's social networks to improve their health. Seeking social support is a positive coping strategy for health. Some research suggests support groups may improve physical well-being. Religious people are more healthy than nonreligious people, possibly because they have better social support.

Key Terms

health psychology 618

mind-body question 618

fight-or-flight response 619

general adaptation syndrome 619

stress 620

safety signal hypothesis 621

ulcers 622

asthma 622

migraines 623

muscle contraction headaches 623

coronary heart disease (CHD) 623

hypertension 624

immune system 624

immunocompetence 625

lymphocytes 625

sleep disorders related to another mental disorder 628

sleep disorders due to a general medical condition 628

substance-induced sleep disorders 628

primary sleep disorders 628

dyssomnias 628

parasomnias 628

insomnia 628

stimulus-control therapy 630

Critical Thinking Questions

1. Is having complete control over everything in your life necessarily nonstressful? Why or why not?

2. What might be the benefits of the Type A behavior pattern for people with this pattern?

3. How would you differentiate between repressors who deny they experience distress and people who really do not experience much distress?

4. What do you think might be the most difficult aspects of Type A behavior for a therapist to change?

Deborah Schneider
Untitled #4

Men are not prisoners of fate, but only prisoners of their own minds.

—*Franklin D. Roosevelt, Pan American Day Address (1939)*

CHAPTER 18

The Cognitive Disorders: Dementia, Delirium, and Amnesia

CHAPTER OVERVIEW

Dementia

Dementia is characterized by memory loss, deterioration in language and the ability to engage in voluntary behaviors, and failure to recognize objects or people. The most common cause of dementia is Alzheimer's disease, but it can also be caused by several other medical conditions and is an effect of chronic intoxication with alcohol and other toxic substances. There is no effective treatment for dementia, but memory aids and drugs to increase cognitive functioning and reduce distress can help.

Extraordinary People:
Elegy for Iris

Pushing the Boundaries:
The Implications of Genetic Testing for Alzheimer's Disease

Taking Psychology Personally:
Tips for the Caregivers of Dementia Patients

Delirium

The symptoms of delirium involve disorientation, recent memory loss, and clouding of consciousness. Medical conditions, surgery, many different drugs, high fever, and infections are just some of the causes of delirium. Delirium must be treated quickly to prevent brain damage.

Amnesia

The amnesic disorders can involve retrograde amnesia, which is a loss of memory for past events, and anterograde amnesia, which is the inability to learn new information. Amnesia can result from some medical illnesses, brain damage due to injury, and long-term substance abuse.

Bio-Psycho-Social Integration
Chapter Summary
Key Terms
Critical Thinking Questions

CASE STUDY

Mariel is a 29-year-old, single, Puerto Rican woman. She has no children and lives with her mother and aunt in the Bronx. Since June 1993, she has been unemployed and supported by her family. Mariel was found to be HIV-positive 8 years ago when she was donating blood. She contracted the virus when raped at age 17 by a family friend. The offender later died of AIDS. For the last 2 years, Mariel was living and working as a store clerk in Puerto Rico. When she developed *Pneumocystis carinii* pneumonia, her mother insisted that she come back to New York City to obtain better medical care.

In the hospital, Mariel was referred for a psychiatric consultation because she was found wandering in a corridor distant from her room. When the psychiatrist arrived in her room, he found her lying on her bed with half her body outside the covers, rocking back and forth while clutching a pink teddy bear, appearing to stare at the television expressionlessly. When asked a series of questions about where she was, what day it was, and so on, she answered correctly, indicating she was oriented to the time and place. But her responses were greatly delayed, and it was almost impossible to engage her in conversation. She said she wanted to leave the hospital to find a place to think. Her mother reported that Mariel had told her she wanted to die.

Over the next few days in the hospital, Mariel became increasingly withdrawn. She would sit motionless for hours, not eating voluntarily, and did not recognize her mother when she came to visit. At times, Mariel would become agitated and appear to be responding to visual hallucinations. When asked to state where she was and her own birthdate, Mariel did not answer and either turned away or became angry and agitated.

As the pneumonia subsided, these acute psychological symptoms dissipated. But Mariel continued to be inattentive, apathetic, and withdrawn and to take a long time to answer simple questions. Suspecting depression, the psychiatrists prescribed an antidepressant medication, but it had little effect on Mariel's symptoms. After being discharged from the hospital, Mariel showed increasing trouble in expressing herself to her mother and in remembering things her mother had told her. She would spend all day in her room, staring out the window, with little interest in the activities her mother would suggest to her.

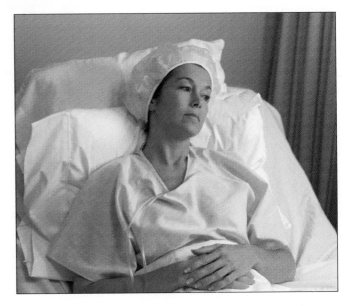

A variety of medical conditions can create cognitive impairment in young or old people.

The impairments that Mariel is experiencing are common in the advanced stages of HIV disease. As we discuss in this chapter, HIV disease is just one of several progressive diseases that inflict damage on the brain, causing a variety of cognitive and emotional deficits. Mariel shows symptoms of two types of disorders, dementia and delirium. *Dementia* is characterized by the gradual and usually permanent decline of intellectual functioning. In contrast, *delirium* involves a more acute and usually transient disorientation and memory loss.

Dementia and delirium are two of the three disorders often referred to as the **cognitive disorders.** The third cognitive disorder is *amnesia*. These disorders are characterized by impairments in cognition caused by a medical condition (such as HIV) or by substance intoxication or withdrawal. The impairments in cognition include memory deficits, language disturbance, perceptual disturbance, impairment in the capacity to plan and organize, and failure to recognize or identify objects. These disorders were formerly called *organic brain disorders*. This label was discontinued in the DSM-IV, however, because it implies that other disorders are *not* caused by biological factors, when it is clear that many disorders recognized by the DSM-IV have biological causes.

The cognitive impairments seen in dementia, delirium, and amnesia can also occur in other psychological disorders. For example, people with schizophrenia have language impairments and perceptual disturbances. People with depression may have problems with concentration and memory. Dementia, delirium, and amnesia are diagnosed when cognitive impairments appear to be the results of nonpsychiatric medical diseases or substance intoxication or withdrawal but not when the cognitive impairments appear only to be symptoms of other psychiatric disorders, such as schizophrenia or depression.

We tend to think of dementia, and to some extent delirium, as disorders of the elderly. Indeed, we will see that the elderly are much more likely to show these disorders than younger people. But as Mariel's story illustrates, these disorders can occur in people of all ages. Similarly, the other psychological disorders we have discussed in this book, including the mood disorders, anxiety disorders, schizophrenia, and so on, can occur in the elderly, just as they can occur in younger people.

We have discussed elderly people's experience of these disorders in earlier chapters on these disorders.

In this chapter, we review the symptoms and causes of, and treatments for dementia, delirium, and amnesia. We begin with dementia, a disorder that typically involves irreversible loss of intellectual functioning and can devastate the lives of the people suffering from it and their families.

☉ DEMENTIA

CASE STUDY

Aside from sustaining a head injury of uncertain significance while a young man in the service, Mr. Abbot B. Carrington had no medical or psychiatric problems until the age of 56. At that time, employed as an officer of a bank, he began to be forgetful. For example, he would forget to bring his briefcase to work or he would misplace his eyeglasses. His efficiency at work declined. He failed to follow through with assignments. Reports that he prepared were incomplete.

Although still friendly and sociable, Mr. Carrington began to lose interest in many of his usual activities. He ignored his coin collection. He no longer thoroughly perused *The Wall Street Journal* each day. When he discussed economics, it was without his previous grasp of the subject. After about a year of these difficulties, he was gradually eased out of his responsible position at the bank and eventually retired permanently.

At home, he tended to withdraw into himself. He would arise early each morning and go for a long walk, occasionally losing his way if he reached an unfamiliar neighborhood. He needed to be reminded constantly of the time of day, of upcoming events, and of his son's progress in college. He tried to use electric appliances without first plugging them into the socket. He shaved with the wrong side of the razor. Mostly, he remained a quiet, pleasant, and tractable person, but sometimes, particularly at night, he became exceptionally confused, and at these times he might be somewhat irritable, loud, and difficult to control.

Approximately 2 years following the onset of these symptoms, he was seen by a neurologist, who conducted a detailed examination of his mental status. The examiner noted that Mr. Carrington was neatly dressed, polite, and cooperative. He sat passively in the office as his wife described his problems to the doctor. He himself offered very little information. In fact, at one point, apparently bored by the proceedings, he unceremoniously got up from his chair and left the room to wander in the corridor. He did not know the correct date or the name and location of the hospital in which he was being examined. Mr. Carrington was then told the date and place, but 10 minutes later he had forgotten this information. Although a presidential election campaign was then in progress, he did not know the names of the candidates. Despite his background in banking and economics, he could not give any relevant information concerning inflation, unemployment, or the prime

lending rate. When questioned about the events of his own life, Mr. Carrington was also frequently in error. He confused recent and remote events. For example, he thought his father had recently died, but in fact this had occurred many years earlier. He could not provide a good description of his occupation.

The patient's speech was fluent and well articulated, but vague and imprecise. He used long, roundabout, cliché-filled phrases to express rather simple ideas. Sometimes he would use the wrong word, as when he substituted *prescribe* for *subscribe*. Despite his past facility with figures, he was unable to do simple calculations. With a pencil and paper, he could not copy two-dimensional figures or a cube. When instructed to draw a house, he drew a succession of attached squares. Asked to give a single word that would define the similarity between an apple and an orange, he replied, "round." He interpreted the proverb, "People who live in glass houses shouldn't throw stones" to mean that "People don't want their windows broken." He seemed to have little insight into his problem. He appeared apathetic rather than anxious or depressed. (Adapted from Spitzer et al., 1981, pp. 243–244)

Mr. Carrington was slowly losing his ability to remember the most fundamental facts of his life, to express himself through language, and to carry out basic activities of everyday life. This is the picture of **dementia,** the most common cognitive disorder.

Dementia most commonly occurs in late life. The estimated prevalence of the most common type of dementia—that due to Alzheimer's disease—is 2 to 5 percent in people over 65 years of age (Aguero-Torres, Fratiglioni, & Winblad, 1998; APA, 2000). The prevalence of most types of dementia increases with age, with an estimated prevalence of 20 percent in people over 85 years of age. Notice, however, that the vast majority of older people do not suffer from dementia. Severe cognitive decline is not an inevitable part of old age.

The amount of news coverage on dementia has increased substantially in recent years, and at times it seems that there is an epidemic of this disorder. Three factors have probably contributed to the increased public attention to dementia. First, there have been substantial advances in our understanding of some types of dementia in the last decade, which have made the news, and which we review shortly. Second, in previous generations, people died of heart disease, cancer, and infectious diseases at younger ages and, therefore, did not reach the age at which dementia often has its onset. These days, however, people are living long enough for dementia to develop and affect their functioning. Third, as the baby-boomer generation ages, the number of people who reach the age at which dementia typically emerges is increasing. Indeed, the number of people with dementia is expected to double in the next 50 years due to the aging of the general population (Max, 1993). The cost to society in health care and to individuals in time spent caring for demented family members is likely to be staggering.

Symptoms of Dementia

There are five types of cognitive deficits in dementia (see Table 18.1). The most prominent is a *memory deficit*, which is required for the diagnosis of dementia. In the early stages of dementia, the memory lapses may be similar to those that we all experience from time to time—forgetting the name of someone we know casually, our own phone number, or what we went into the next room to get. Most of us eventually remember what we temporarily forgot, either spontaneously or by tricks that jog our memories. The difference with dementia is that memory does not return spontaneously and may not respond to reminders or other memory cues.

People in the early stages of dementia may repeat questions because they do not remember asking them moments ago or they do not remember getting answers. They will misplace items, such as keys or wallets, frequently. They may try to compensate for the memory loss. For example, they may carefully write down their appointments or things they need to do. Eventually, however, they forget to look at their calendars or lists. As the memory problems become more apparent, they may become angry when asked questions or make up answers in an attempt to hide memory loss. Later, as dementia progresses, they may become lost in familiar surroundings and be unable to find their way unaccompanied.

Losses in executive functioning can make it difficult for a person to accomplish tasks that require much planning and coordination, like preparing an elaborate family dinner.

Eventually, long-term memory also becomes impaired. People with dementia will forget the order of major events in their lives, such as graduation from college, marriage, and the birth of their children. After a time, they will be unable to recall the events at all and may not even know their own names.

The second type of cognitive impairment is a *deterioration of language*, known as **aphasia.** People with dementia will have tremendous difficulty producing the names of objects or people and may often use terms like *thing* or vague references to *them* to hide their inability to produce names. If asked to identify a cup, for example, they may say that it is a *thing for drinking*, but be unable to name it as a cup. They may be unable to understand what another person is saying, and to follow simple requests such as "Turn on the lights and shut the door." In advanced stages of dementia, people may exhibit **echolalia**—simply repeating back what they hear—or **palialia**—simply repeating sounds or words over and over.

The third cognitive deficit is **apraxia,** an impaired ability to execute common actions, such as waving good-bye or putting on a shirt. This deficit is not caused by problems in motor functioning (i.e., moving the arm), in sensory functioning, or in comprehending what action is required. People with dementia simply are unable to carry out actions that are requested of them or that they wish to carry out.

The fourth cognitive deficit is **agnosia,** the failure to recognize objects or people. People with dementia may not be able to identify common objects such as chairs or tables. At first, they will fail to recognize casual friends or distant family members. With time,

---

TABLE 18.1
DSM-IV
Major Symptoms of Dementia

Dementia is characterized by permanent loss of basic cognitive functions.

Memory impairment, including impaired ability to learn new information or to recall previously learned information

Aphasia (language disturbance)

Apraxia (inability to carry out motor activities despite intact motor function)

Agnosia (failure to recognize or identify objects despite intact sensory functioning)

Disturbance in executive functioning (such as planning, organizing, sequencing, and abstracting information)

Reprinted with permission from the *Diagnostic and Statistical Manual of Mental Disorders*, Fourth Edition. Copyright © 2000 American Psychiatric Association.

they may not recognize their spouses or children or even their own reflections in a mirror.

The fifth cognitive deficit is a *loss of executive functioning*. Executive functioning is the ability to plan, initiate, monitor, and stop complex behaviors. Cooking Thanksgiving dinner requires executive functioning. Each menu item (i.e., the turkey, the stuffing, the pumpkin pie) requires different ingredients and preparation. The cooking of different menu items must be coordinated so that all the items are ready at the same time. People in the early stages of dementia may attempt to cook Thanksgiving dinner but forget important components (like the turkey) or fail to coordinate the dinner, burning certain items while other items remain uncooked. People in later stages of dementia will be unable even to plan or initiate a complex task such as this.

Deficits in executive functioning also involve problems in the kind of abstract thinking required to evaluate new situations and respond appropriately to these situations. For example, when Mr. Carrington was presented with the proverb, "People who live in glass houses shouldn't throw stones," he was unable to interpret the abstract meaning of the proverb and instead interpreted it concretely to mean, "People don't want their windows broken."

In addition to having these cognitive deficits, people with dementia often show changes in emotional and personality functioning. Shoplifting, exhibitionism, and wandering into traffic are common occurrences caused by declines in judgment and the ability to control impulses. People with dementia may become depressed when they recognize their cognitive deterioration. Often, however, they do not recognize or admit to their cognitive deficits. This can lead them to take unrealistic or dangerous actions, such as driving a car when they are too impaired to do so safely. People with dementia may become paranoid and angry with family members and friends, whom they see as thwarting their desires and freedoms. They may accuse others of stealing the belongings they have misplaced. They may believe that others are conspiring against them—the only conclusion left for them when they simply do not remember conversations in which they agreed to some action (such as starting a new medication or moving into a treatment facility for people with dementia). Violent outbursts are not unusual.

Types of Dementia

Dementia has several causes (see Figure 18.1). The most common cause is Alzheimer's disease. Great strides are being made in our understanding of Alzheimer's dementia, and we discuss this disorder in detail next. Dementia can also be caused by cerebrovascular disease (blockage of blood to the brain), by head injury, by several progressive diseases like Parkinson's disease and HIV disease, and by chronic drug abuse. We discuss each of these as well (see *Concept Review: Types of Dementia*, p. 658).

Dementia of the Alzheimer's Type

In 1995, the family of former President Ronald Reagan announced that he had been diagnosed with Alzheimer's disease. Although the family decided to maintain their privacy concerning the specific manifestations of the disease, their announcement of Reagan's diagnosis helped to bring attention to this disease, which affects nearly 4 million Americans (Max, 1993). More recently, famed writer Iris Murdoch suffered

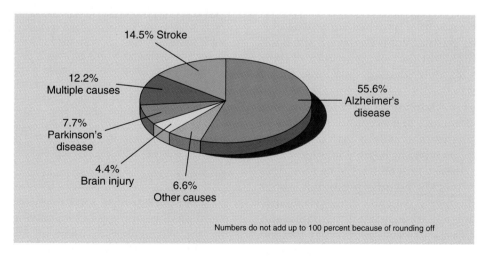

FIGURE 18.1   The Leading Causes of Dementia. Alzheimer's disease causes over half of all cases of dementia. Other causes of dementia are chronic alcoholism, nutritional deficiencies, and metabolic imbalances.

Source: Max, 1993.

Former President Ronald Reagan has been diagnosed with Alzheimer's disease.

CONCEPT REVIEW
Types of Dementia

Dementia can be caused by a number of progressive diseases, as well as by repeated head injury.

Alzheimer's type

Vascular dementia

Dementia due to head injury

Dementia associated with other medical conditions
  Parkinson's disease
  HIV disease
  Huntington's disease
  Pick's disease
  Creutzfeldt-Jakob disease
  Other medical conditions
  Chronic heavy use of alcohol, inhalants, and
  sedative drugs

from Alzheimer's dementia, and her story was eloquently told by her partner, John Bayley, in the book *Elegy for Iris.* We highlight the poignant story of their love, and Murdoch's deterioration, in *Extraordinary People:* Elegy for Iris.

Dementia due to **Alzheimer's disease** is the most common type of dementia and accounts for 55 to 80 percent of all dementias (Chun et al., 1998). Alzheimer's dementias typically begin with mild memory loss, but as the disease progresses, the memory loss and disorientation quickly become profound. About two-thirds of Alzheimer's patients show psychiatric symptoms, including agitation, irritability, apathy, and dysphoria. As the disease worsens, people may become violent, and experience hallucinations and delusions. The disease usually begins after the age of 65, but there is an early-onset type of Alzheimer's disease that tends to progress more quickly than the late-onset type that

develops after age 65. On average, people with this disease die within 8 to 10 years of its diagnosis, usually as the result of physical decline or independent diseases common in old age, such as heart disease.

Alzheimer's disease exacts a heavy toll on the family members of patients as well as on the patients (Dunkin & Anderson-Hanley, 1998). Medical and custodial care for an Alzheimer's patient averages about $47,000 per year (in 1990 dollars), with family members shouldering the majority of this financial burden (Max, 1993). The primary caregiver to an Alzheimer's patient is most often a woman—the daughter, daughter-in-law, or wife of the patient (Dunkin & Anderson-Hanley, 1998). Often this primary caregiver will also be raising her own children and trying to hold down a job. This is the *sandwich generation* of women, caught in the middle of caring for young children and for elderly parents or parents-in-law. These primary caregivers show higher rates of depression, anxiety, and physical illness than do controls (Dunkin & Anderson-Hanley, 1998; Gallagher-Thompson, Lovett, & Rose, 1991). Some caregivers become so frustrated with their demented family members that they resort to violence and abuse of the family members. Here is an example:

CASE STUDY
Mr. E was a 60-year-old caregiver of a rather frail younger brother (Robert) who had been diagnosed with dementia. Robert had been an alcoholic earlier in life and was the type of person who settled disagreements with verbal and/or physical abuse. Mr. E and his brother had begun sharing a household following the deaths of both their wives about 5 years before. Shortly thereafter, Robert was diagnosed with Alzheimer's disease and eventually developed substantial cognitive and physical deficits. Mr. E felt guilty about doing anything other than keeping his brother in the home with him, although Robert's disabilities were very distressing to him and Robert's increasing hostility and angry verbal outbursts were hard to handle. At the same time, Mr. E was developing a romantic interest and resented not being able to follow through with that as he pleased; instead he felt quite inhibited by his brother's presence in his home. The situation gradually worsened to the point where the two brothers were given to frequent angry outbursts leading, at times, to Mr. E hitting Robert. Afterwards he would feel extremely guilty about this and concerned that he might lose control during one of these episodes and actually hurt his brother. (Adapted from Gallagher-Thompson, Lovett, & Rose, 1991, pp. 68–69)

Support groups for caregivers and therapy focused on developing problem-solving skills for managing the Alzheimer's patient at home have proven effective in reducing caregivers' emotional problems and feelings of burden. For example, Mr. E joined an anger management class and learned new ways of interpreting and reacting to his brother's behaviors. He

EXTRAORDINARY PEOPLE

Elegy for Iris

When she was a young woman, teaching philosophy at Oxford, Iris Murdoch met John Bayley, a recent graduate in English. They fell in love, married two years later, and settled in Oxford, where John eventually taught and became an eminent literary critic. Iris went on to write a total of 26 novels and several textbooks on philosophy and to be considered one of the greatest writers of the twentieth century. She received honorary doctorates from many major universities and was named a Dame of the British Empire. These two intellectual giants shared a life and love that was extraordinary for its passion, its intimacy and its fun.

John Bayley writes:

The more I got to know Iris during the early days of our relationship, the less I understood her. Indeed, I soon began not to want to understand her. I was far too preoccupied at the time to think of such parallels, but it was like living in a fairy story—the kind with sinister overtones and not always a happy ending—in which a young man loves a beautiful maiden who returns his love but is always disappearing into some unknown and mysterious world, about which she will reveal nothing. (Bayley, 1999, p. 45–46)

The tragedy that John Bayley expected to happen eventually did, although not until he and Iris Murdoch had been married nearly 40 years. In 1994, Murdoch developed Alzheimer's disease. This brilliant novelist and philospher was reduced to grunts, squeaks, and murmers, asking the same questions over and over, and not being able to care for her own basic needs.

Bayley's account of his life with Murdoch after she developed Alzheimer's disease, published in *Elegy for Iris* (1999), describes not only his suffering as he lost this brilliant woman and partner to the disease. It also is full of his continuing love for her and fascination with her. Below are several passages from this wonderful love story:

Alzheimer's is, in fact, like an insidious fog, barely noticeable until everything around has disap-

peared. After that, it is no longer possible to believe that a world outside the fog exists. (p. 281)

The sense of someone's mind. Only now an awareness of it; other minds are usually taken for granted. I wonder sometimes if Iris is secretly thinking: How can I escape? What am I to do? Has nothing replaced the play of her mind when she was writing, cogitating, living in her mind? I find myself devoutly hoping not. (p. 228)

Our mode of communication seems like underwater sonar, each bouncing pulsations off the other, then listening for an echo. The baffling moments at which I cannot understand what Iris is saying, or about whom or what—moments which can produce tears and anxieties, though never, thank goodness, the raging frustration typical of many Alzheimer's sufferers—can sometimes be dispelled by embarking on a jokey parody of helplessness, and trying to make it mutual, both of us at a loss of words. (pp. 51–52)

The face of an Alzheimer's patient has been clinically described as the "lion face." An apparently odd comparison, but in fact a very apt one. The features settle into a leonine impassivity which does remind one of the king of beasts, and the way his broad expressionless mask is represented in painting and sculpture. . . . The face of the Alzheimer's sufferer indicates only an absence: It is a mask in the most literal sense.

That is why the sudden appearance of a smile is so extraordinary. The lion face becomes the face of the Virgin Mary, tranquil in sculpture and painting, with a gravity that gives such a smile its deepest meaning. (pp. 53–54)

This terror of being alone, of being cut off for even a few seconds from the familiar object, is a feature of Alzheimer's. If Iris could climb inside my skin now, or enter me as if I had a pouch like a kangaroo, she

Continued

would do so. She has no awareness of what I am doing, only an awareness of what I am. The worlds and gestures of love still come naturally, but they cannot be accompanied by that wordless communication which depends on the ability to use words. (p. 127)

The horrid wish, almost a compulsion at some moments, to show the other how bad things are. Force her to share the knowledge, relieve what seems my isolation.

I make a savage comment today about the grimness of our outlook. Iris looks relieved and intelligent. She says, "But I love you." (p. 233)

"When are we going?"
"I'll tell you when we go."
Iris always responds to a jokey tone. But it is sometimes hard to maintain. Violent irritation possesses me and I shout out before I can stop myself, "Don't keep asking me when we are going!" . . .

Her face just crumples into tears. I hasten to comfort her, and she always responds to comfort. We kiss and embrace now much more than we used to. (p. 235)

[A lady] told me in her own deliberately jolly way that living with an Alzheimer's victim was like being chained to a corpse [and] went on to an even greater access of desperate facetiousness, saying, "And, as you and I know, it's a corpse that complains all the time."

I don't know it. In spite of her anxious and perpetual queries, Iris seems not to know how to complain. She never has. Alzheimer's, which can accentuate personality traits to the point of demonic parody, has only been able to exaggerate a natural goodness in her.

On a good day, her need for a loving presence, mutual pattings and murmurs, has something angelic about it; she seems herself in the presence found in an ikon. It is more important for her still on days of silent tears, a grief seemingly unaware of that mysterious world of creation she has lost, and yet aware that something is missing. (pp. 76–77)

There are so many doubts and illusions and concealments in any close relationship. Even in our present situation, they can come as an unexpected shock. Iris's tears sometimes seem to signify a whole inner world which she is determined to keep from me and shield me from. There is something ghastly in the feeling of relief that this can't be so; and yet the illusion of such an inner world still there—if it is an illusion—can't help haunting me from time to time. There are moments when I almost welcome it. Iris has always had—must have had—so vast and rich and complex an inner world, which it used to give me immense pleasure not to know anything about. Like looking at a map of South Africa as a child and wondering about the sources of the Amazon, and what unknown cities might be hidden there in the jungle. Have any of those hidden places survived in her? (pp. 258–259)

Life is no longer bringing the pair of us "closer and closer apart," in the poet's tenderly ambiguous words. Every day we move closer and closer together. We could not do otherwise. There is a certain comic irony—happily, not darkly comic—that after more than forty years of taking marriage for granted, marriage has decided it is tired of this, and is taking a hand in the game. Purposefully, persistently, involuntarily, our marriage is now getting somewhere. It is giving us no choice—and I am glad of that.

Every day, we are physically closer; and Iris's little "mouse cry," as I think of it, signifying loneliness in the next room, the wish to be back beside me, seems less and less forlorn, more simple, more natural. She is not sailing into the dark: The voyage is over, and under the dark escort of Alzheimer's she has arrived somewhere. So have I. (pp. 265–266)

Iris Murdoch died in February 1999, just a few months after *Elegy for Iris* was published.

read about Alzheimer's disease and learned to challenge his beliefs that his brother was intentionally acting in ways to annoy him. He learned to walk away from his brother's angry outbursts. He found other resources in the community to help him care for his brother so that he could pursue his own interests more fully.

Brain abnormalities in Alzheimer's This type of dementia was first described in 1906 by Alois Alzheimer.

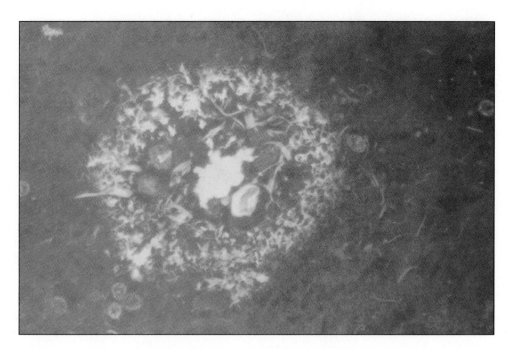

FIGURE 18.2   Plaques in the Brains of Alzheimers' Patients. The brains of Alzheimers' patients show plaques surrounded by abnormal axons and dendrites and degenerating neural cell bodies.

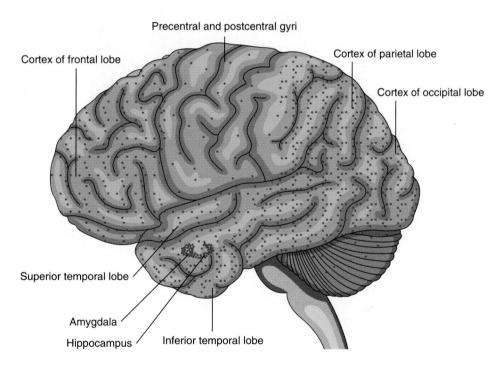

FIGURE 18.3   Brain Regions Most Affected in Dementia. The brains of people with Alzheimer's disease have plaques of amyloid beta-protein, indicated here by dots, in specific brain areas.

Source: Selkoe, 1992.

He observed severe memory loss and disorientation in a 51-year-old female patient. Following her death at age 55, an autopsy revealed that filaments within nerve cells in her brain were twisted and tangled (see Figure 18.2). These **neurofibrillary tangles** are common in the brains of Alzheimer's patients but rare in people without cognitive disorders (Beatty, 1995).

Another brain abnormality seen in Alzheimer's disease is **plaques.** These are deposits of a class of protein called **amyloid** that accumulate in the spaces between cells of the cerebral cortex, hippocampus, and other areas of the brain structures critical to memory and cognitive functioning (see Figure 18.3; Selkoe, 1992).

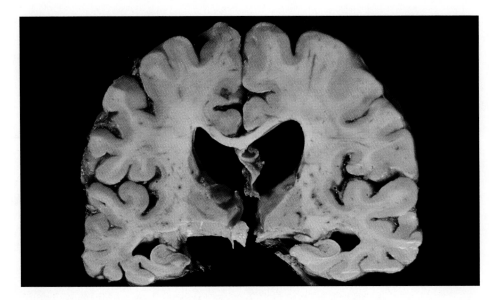

FIGURE 18.4   Cortical Atrophy in Alzheimer's Disease. Alzheimer's patients show widespread atrophy or shrinkage in the cortex and enlargement in the ventricular areas of the brain.

Source: Beatty, 1995.

There is extensive cell death in the cortex of Alzheimer's patients, resulting in shrinking of the cortex and enlargement of the ventricles of the brain (see Figure 18.4). The remaining cells lose much of their dendrites—the branches of cells that link one cell to other cells (see Figure 18.5). The end result of all these brain abnormalities is profound memory loss and inability to coordinate one's activities.

Typically, Alzheimer's disease cannot be definitively diagnosed until the patient has died and a brain autopsy is performed. The tangles and plaques can only be detected through a microscope. Advances in neuroimaging techniques (PET, MRI, and CT scans) promise the potential of diagnosing Alzheimer's disease in live patients, however (Zakzanis, 1998). For example, one study used MRI and single-photon emission computed tomography (SPECT) to examine structural deterioration and diminished blood flow in the brains of people suspected to have Alzheimer's disease and healthy people the same age and gender. These two neuroimaging procedures correctly identified all of the patients later confirmed to have had Alzheimer's (Pearlson et al., 1992).

Causes of Alzheimer's   What causes the brain deterioration of Alzheimer's disease? This is an area of tremendous research activity, and new answers to this question emerge each day. Alzheimer's disease has been attributed to viral infections, immune system dysfunction, exposure to toxic levels of aluminum, deficiencies of the vitamin folate, and head traumas (Small, 1998).

Much of the current research, however, has focused on genes that might transmit a vulnerability to this disorder and on the amyloid proteins that form the

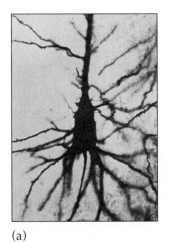   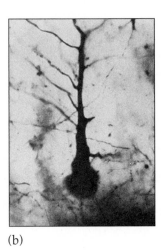

(a)   (b)

FIGURE 18.5   Loss of Neuronal Dendrites in Alzheimer's Disease. In panel (a) are dendrites in the brain of a healthy person. In panel (b) are shrunken and deteriorated dendrites in the brain of an Alzheimer's patient.

Source: Beatty, 1995.

plaques found in the brains of almost all Alzheimer's patients. Family history studies suggest that 25 to 50 percent of relatives of patients with Alzheimer's disease eventually develop the disease, compared to only about 10 percent of family members of elderly people without Alzheimer's disease (Plassman & Breitner, 1996). Several different genes have been linked to Alzheimer's disease (Small, 1998). A defective gene on chromosome 19 is associated with an increased risk for the late-onset form of Alzheimer's disease, which is the most common form. This gene appears to be responsible for a rare protein known as ApoE4. ApoE4 is one of a group of proteins that transport cholesterol through the blood. ApoE4 binds to the amyloid protein and may play a role in the regulation of amyloid protein (see Small, 1998). One study found that 64 percent of people with late onset Alzheimer's disease had the ApoE4 gene compared to only 31 percent of people without Alzheimer's disease (Schmechal, Saunders, & Strittmatter, 1993). Another study found that people with two copies of the ApoE4 gene (one on both of their chromosome 19s) were eight times more likely to have Alzheimer's disease than were people with no copies of the ApoE4 gene on either of their chromosome 19s (Corder, Saunders, & Strittmatter, 1993).

Other genes are implicated in the development of less common forms of Alzheimer's disease, which begin in middle age and are more strongly familial. The first of these genes is on chromosome 21 (Bird et al., 1998). The first clue that a defective gene on chromosome 21 may be linked with Alzheimer's disease came from the fact that people with Down syndrome are more likely than people in the general population to develop Alzheimer's disease in late life. Down syndrome is caused by an extra chromosome 21. Researchers hypothesized that the gene responsible for some forms of Alzheimer's disease may be on chromosome 21 and that people with Down syndrome are more prone to Alzheimer's disease because they have an extra chromosome 21 (Mayeux, 1996). This hypothesis has been supported by linkage studies of families with high rates of Alzheimer's disease. These studies have found links between the presence of the disease and the presence of an abnormal gene on chromosome 21 (see Goate et al., 1991; St. George-Hyslop et al., 1987, 1990). In turn, this abnormal gene on chromosome 21 is near the gene responsible for producing a precursor of the amyloid protein, known as the amyloid precursor protein gene or APP gene. It may be that defects along this section of chromosome 21 cause an abnormal production and buildup of amyloid proteins in the brain, resulting in Alzheimer's disease.

A defective gene on chromosome 14 has been linked to early-onset Alzheimer's disease (Sherrington, Rogaev, & Liang, 1995). This discovery is especially exciting because this defective chromosome 14 gene may be implicated in almost 80 percent of early onset Alzheimer's disease. This gene appears to be responsible for a protein on the membranes of cells, known as S182. The link between S182 and the amyloid protein or other processes responsible for Alzheimer's disease is not yet known. Finally, another gene, E5-1, on chromosome 1, was recently linked to Alzheimer's disease (Lendon, Ashall, & Goate, 1997).

People with Alzheimer's disease also show deficits in a number of neurotransmitters, including acetylcholine, norepinephrine, serotonin, and somatostatin (a corticotropin-releasing factor), and peptide Y (Small, 1998). The deficits in acetylcholine are particularly noteworthy because this neurotransmitter is thought to be critical in memory function. The degree of cognitive decline seen in patients with Alzheimer's is significantly correlated with the degree of deficits in acetylcholine (Perry et al., 1978). In turn, drugs that enhance levels of acetylcholine can slow the rate of cognitive decline in some Alzheimer's sufferers.

We will likely know much more about the causes of Alzheimer's disease in the next few years, because the technologies to study the genetic and neurological processes of the disease are advancing rapidly and because many researchers are pursuing investigation of this disorder. As many as 9 million people in the United States alone may suffer from Alzheimer's disease by the year 2040 (Max, 1993). We can hope that, by then, we will understand the disorder well enough to treat it effectively. In *Pushing the Boundaries:* The Implications of Genetic Testing for Alzheimer's Disease (p. 664), we describe new tests that indicate whether an individual carries a genetic predisposition and explore the implications of these tests, given that there currently is no effective treatment for Alzheimer's.

Vascular Dementia

The second most common type of dementia, after Alzheimer's dementia, is **vascular dementia** (formerly called *multi-infarct dementia*). To be diagnosed with vascular dementia, a person must have symptoms or laboratory evidence of **cerebrovascular disease.** Cerebrovascular disease occurs when the blood supply to areas of the brain is blocked, causing tissue damage in the brain. Neuroimaging techniques such as PET and MRI can detect areas of tissue damage and reduced blood flow in the brain, confirming cerebrovascular disease (see Figure 18.6, p. 664).

Sudden damage to an area of the brain due to blockage of blood flow or hemorrhaging is called a **stroke.** Vascular dementia can occur after one large stroke or an accumulation of small strokes. Cerebrovascular disease can also be caused by high blood pressure and the accumulation of fatty deposits in the arteries, which block blood flow to the brain. It can also be a complication of diseases that inflame the brain and head injuries. The specific cognitive deficits and emotional changes a person experiences will depend on the extent and location of tissue damage to the brain (Desmond & Tatemichi, 1998).

Although cognitive impairment is common following a stroke, one large study found that only 26 percent of stroke patients developed cognitive deficits severe enough to qualify for a diagnosis of dementia (Desmond & Tatemichi, 1998). A greater risk of developing dementia was seen in stroke patients who were older (over 80 years of age versus under 80 years of age), who had less education, who had a previous history of strokes, and who had diabetes. The finding

PUSHING THE BOUNDARIES

The Implications of Genetic Testing for Alzheimer's Disease

P redictive testing for certain early-onset forms of Alzheimer's disease already exists, allowing people to know if they have the genetic markers that indicate a high risk for this disorder. These forms of Alzheimer's disease are rare, however, making these tests useful to a small minority of people (Lannfelt et al., 1995). Still, the race is on among researchers and biotechnology companies to develop genetic tests for other, more common forms of Alzheimer's disease. Many people, especially relatives of people with Alzheimer's disease, want genetic tests that can indicate their risk for the disease. For example, one survey of the New York City Alzheimer's Association chapter found that about 64 percent of respondents were interested in predictive testing for Alzheimer's (Friend, 1996). What are the implications of genetic testing for Alzheimer's disease?

If reliable and valid tests for common forms of Alzheimer's disease can be found, these tests may further research on the factors that cause the disease. For example, research could focus on the characteristics that distinguish people with the "Alzheimer's gene" who eventually go on to develop the disorder and those who have the gene but do not go on to develop the disorder, to better understand protective factors against development of the disorder in high-risk people. On a personal level, people who know from genetic testing that they are at increased risk for Alzheimer's disease can be more proactive in ensuring that they have the resources to be cared for well if they do develop the disease.

There are many possible pitfalls to genetic testing, however. First and foremost, there are no cures for Alzheimer's disease presently. Some people may become despondent upon finding they test positive for the target gene, even when told that this gene only increases their risk of Alzheimer's disease, and does not determine that they will develop the disease (Lannfelt et al., 1995). Second, there is the potential for abuse of information about people's genetic status by employers, insurance companies, and others (Lerman et al., 1996). As Nelkin (1992, p. 183) stated, "In the context of growing economic competition,

that greater education protected against the development of dementia corresponds with findings in studies of Alzheimer's disease.

Even stroke patients who do not immediately develop dementia are at increased risk for developing dementia compared to people the same age who do not suffer a stroke. Follow-ups of stroke victims who remained free of dementia in the 3 months after their stroke found that about one-third of them developed dementia within the next 52 months, compared to 10 percent of a control group (Desmond & Tatemichi, 1998). Those patients most likely to develop dementia eventually tended to have additional strokes over this time, some of which were obvious and some of which were "silent" and only detected later. In addition, patients who had medical events or conditions that caused widespread oxygen or blood deficiency, such as seizures, cardiac arrhythmias, congestive heart failure, and pneumonia, were more likely to develop dementia.

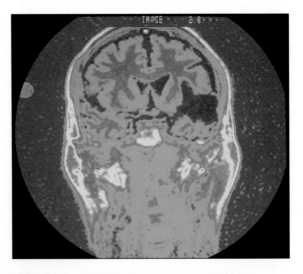

FIGURE 18.6 Tissue Damage Following a Stroke. This magnetic resonance image shows the tissue damage following a stroke (dark blue areas).
Source: Beatty, 1995.

Continued

screening techniques that identify those predisposed to genetic disease can become a cost-effective way to control absenteeism, reduce compensation claims, and avoid future medical costs for workers and their families."

Lessons can be learned from studies of the impact of genetic testing on people at risk for Huntington's disease (HD). This disease is a simple genetic disorder, and children of HD patients have at least a 50 percent risk of developing the disorder. Highly accurate predictive genetic testing is available for the disorder. Testing positive for the genetic mutation that causes HD means that an individual is 99 percent likely to develop the disorder (Benjamin et al., 1994). Studies of people with a family history of HD find that, although most say they are interested in having the test, only about 10 percent go through with testing (Quaid & Morris, 1993). People who chose not to take the test often said they feared the psychological burden of a positive test result. They were also concerned that their insurance company might discover that they tested positive and cancel their insurance. A. Wexler (1995, p. 235), in a memoir of the family most responsible for the discovery of the HD gene, noted:

> The media, and sometimes the doctors and counselors who administered the test, engaged in subtle psychological pressure, portraying those who took

the test as somehow stronger, braver, and more optimistic than those of us who chose not to know. But isn't it also possible that those of us who opt not to know are more able to live with uncertainty and ambiguity? As (my sister) Nancy says, the test does not really resolve the uncertainty, because you still don't know when the symptoms appear, only that they will come at some time in the future. But it could be years, decades away, and by then you will have lost all that time.

Some people want to know, however, and follow-ups of people who chose to take the HD gene test find that, regardless of the test outcome, many become less distressed when they finally know their genetic status (Brandt & Codori, 1995; Wiggins et al., 1992).

Thus, it is clear that different people react differently to genetic testing. To date, there is little knowledge of why some people desire genetic testing and some do not, and why some people are devastated by the results of genetic testing and others are relieved (Roberts, 1999). Understanding the different psychological reactions to genetic testing is clearly an important focus for future research, however, because tests for many genetically transmitted medical and psychiatric disorders are currently under development.

Dementia Due to Head Injury

CASE STUDY

A 41-year-old factory worker named Leland was returning home along a rural road one night after work. A drunk driver ran a stop sign and collided at a high rate of speed with the driver's side of Leland's car. Leland was not wearing a seat belt. The collision sent Leland hurling through the windshield and onto the pavement. He lived but sustained substantial injuries to the frontal lobe of his brain as well as many broken bones and cuts. Leland was unconscious for over 2 weeks and then spent another 2 months in the hospital recovering from his injuries.

When he returned home to his family, Leland was not himself. Before the accident he was a quiet man who doted on his family and frequently displayed a wry sense of humor. After the accident, Leland was sullen and chronically irritable. He would scream at his wife or children for the slightest annoyance. He even slapped his

wife once when she confronted him about his verbal abuse of the children.

Leland did not fare much better at work. He found he now had great trouble concentrating on his job, and he could not follow his boss's instructions. When his boss approached Leland about his inability to perform his job, Leland could not express much about the trouble he was having. He became angry at his boss and accused him of wanting to fire him. Leland had always been much liked by his coworkers, and they welcomed him back after the accident with sincere joy. But soon he began to lash out at them as he was at his wife and children. He accused a close friend of stealing from him.

These symptoms continued acutely for about 3 months. Gradually they declined. Finally, about 18 months after the accident, Leland's emotional and personality functioning appear to be "back to normal." His cognitive functioning also improved greatly, but he still found it more difficult to pay attention and to complete tasks than he did before the accident.

TABLE 18.2
Symptoms of Frontal Lobe Injuries

Social and Behavioral Changes

Disorderliness, suspiciousness, argumentativeness, disruptiveness, and anxiousness

Apathy, lack of concern for others

Uncharacteristic lewdness, inattention to personal appearance or hygiene

Intrusiveness, boisterousness, pervasive profanity, talking loudly

Risk taking, poor impulse control, increase alcohol use

Affective Changes

Apathy, indifference, shallowness

Lability of affect, irritability, mania

Inability to control rage and violent behavior

Intellectual Changes

Reduced capacity to use language, symbols, and logic

Reduced ability to use mathematics, to calculate, to process abstract information, and to reason

Diminished ability to focus, to concentrate, or to be oriented in time and place

Source: Beatty, 1995.

Leland's symptoms are characteristic of people with traumatic brain injury (see Table 18.2). He showed changes both in his cognitive abilities and in his usual emotional and personality functioning Fortunately, Leland's symptoms subsided after several months. Many victims of brain injury never fully recover (Beatty, 1995).

Brain damage can be caused by penetrating injuries, such as those caused by gunshots, or closed head injuries, typically caused by blows to the head. The most common causes of closed head injuries are motor vehicle accidents, followed by falls, blows to the head during violent assault, and sports injuries. Dementias that follow single closed head injuries, such as Leland's, are more likely to dissipate with time than are dementias that follow repeated closed head injuries, such as those experienced by boxers. Young men are most likely to suffer dementia due to head injury because they take more risks associated with head injuries than do other groups.

Dementia pugilistica is a type of dementia due to repetitive head injuries (Jordan, 1998). It was first described in boxers, but has been seen frequently in professional football, soccer, and ice hockey players. Dementia pugilistica is characterized by the cognitive symptoms of dementia we have described thus far, various personality changes such as excessive jealousy and rage, plus extrapyradimal symptoms, such as

those in Parkinson's disease (see below). In one study of ex-professional boxers, 17 percent had clinical evidence of central nervous system damage attributable to boxing (Roberts, 1969). About half of these men showed some signs of impairment in intellectual functioning, and about 30 percent showed severe cognitive impairment.

Dementia Associated with Other Medical Conditions

A variety of other serious medical conditions can produce dementia. We discuss the most common ones here, including Parkinson's disease, HIV disease, and Huntington's disease. Dementia can also be caused by two rare diseases, Pick's disease, and Creutzfeldt-Jakob disease, brain tumors, endocrine conditions (such as hypothyroidism), nutritional conditions (deficiencies of thiamine, niacin, and vitamin B12), infectious conditions (syphilis), and other neurological diseases (such as multiple sclerosis). In addition, chronic heavy use of alcohol, inhalants, and the sedative drugs, especially in combination with nutritional deficiencies, can cause brain damage and dementia. As many as 10 percent of chronic alcohol abusers may develop dementia (Winger, Hofman, & Woods, 1992). Alcohol-related dementia usually has a slow, insidious

People engaged in sports like boxing or who do not wear helmets while riding bicycles are at risk for brain injuries that can lead to severe cognitive deficits.

onset. It may be slowed with nutritional supplements but is often irreversible.

Parkinson's disease *Parkinson's disease* is a degenerative brain disorder that affects about 1 of every 100,000 people (Mayeux et al., 1992). The primary symptoms of Parkinson's disease are tremors, muscle rigidity, and the inability to initiate movement. About 40 percent of Parkinson's disease patients also develop dementia in the advanced stages of the disorder (Mayeux et al., 1992). Parkinson's disorder results from the death of cells in the brain that produce the neurotransmitter dopamine. The death of these cells can be caused by certain drugs or by inflammation of the brain, but the cause of Parkinson's disease is often unclear.

HIV disease The *human immunodeficiency virus (HIV)*, the virus that causes AIDS, can cause dementia. HIV probably enters the brain in the early stages of the infection (Price, 1998). People's memory and concentration become impaired. Their mental processes slow—they may have difficulty following conversations or plots in movies or may take much longer to organize their thoughts and complete simple, familiar tasks. Their behaviors may change—they may withdraw socially, become indifferent to familiar people and responsibilities, and lose their spontaneity. They may complain of fatigue, depression, irritability, agitation, emotional instability, and reduced sex drive. Sometimes, although rarely, they may experience hallucinations or delusions. Weakness in the legs or hands, clumsiness, loss of balance, and lack of coordination are common complaints. People may trip more frequently, drop things, or have difficulty writing or eating. If the dementia progresses, the deficits become more global and more severe. Speech becomes increasingly impaired, as does the understanding of language. The ability to walk is lost, and people are confined to bed, often with indifference to their surroundings and their illness.

The course of HIV dementia varies from person to person, as does the speed with which it progresses.

The San Diego HIV Neurobehavioral Research Center (HNRC) Group has termed the earlier, less severe symptoms of HIV-associated dementia *mild neurocognitive disorder (MND)*. In order to receive a diagnosis of MND, an HIV-infected person must exhibit defects in two or more cognitive areas with mild interference in social/occupational functioning. It is estimated that approximately 50 percent of persons with AIDS will meet the criteria for MND (Heaton et al., 1996).

HIV-associated dementia is diagnosed when the deficits and symptoms become more severe and global, with significant disruption of daily activities and functioning. Epidemiological studies estimate that anywhere from 7 to 66 percent of HIV-infected persons will become demented (Day et al., 1992; McArthur et al., 1993). It is possible that the development of treatments, such as the antiviral agent azidovudine (AZT), may have the effect of decreasing the rates of dementia among HIV-infected persons by slowing the progression of the disease.

Huntington's disease *Huntington's disease* is a rare genetic disorder that afflicts people early in life, usually between the ages of 25 and 55. People with this disorder develop severe dementia and chorea—irregular jerks, grimaces, and twitches. Huntington's disease is transmitted by a single dominant gene on chromosome 4 (Gusella et al., 1993). If one parent has the gene, his or her children have a 50 percent chance of developing the disorder. There are many neurotransmitter changes in the brains of people with Huntington's disease. It is not yet clear which of these changes is responsible for the chorea and the dementia seen in the disorder.

Treatment for Dementia

To date, there are few widely successful treatments for dementia. People with Alzheimer's disease have reduced levels of the neurotransmitter acetylcholine in their brains, which may contribute to their cognitive impairments. Some Alzheimer's patients show improvement in cognitive functioning when given drugs that increase levels of acetylcholine, such as tacrine and donepezil (Gottlieb & Kumar, 1993; Rabins, 1998). These drugs can induce nausea and gastrointestinal distress, however. Because Parkinson's disease is associated with too little dopamine in the brain, some Parkinson's patients are given drugs that increase levels of dopamine and thus experience some relief from their symptoms. For both these diseases, however, the drugs do not work for all patients and have only temporary effects.

A great deal of media attention has been given lately to the role of antioxidants in slowing cognitive decline in Alzheimer's disease. Antioxidants include natural products such as vitamin E and manufactured products such as a selective monoamine oxidase-B inhibitor known as selegiline. A few controlled trials have shown that Alzheimer's patients given antioxidants showed slower rates of decline than those given placebo treatment, although they did not show improvement in cognitive functioning (Sano et al., 1997). Ginkgo biloba, a plant extract sold without prescription, has been shown to stabilize and improve cognitive functioning in some Alzheimer's patients (see Le Bars et al., 1997). Antioxidants may work by reducing levels of monamine oxidase-B in the brain, which normally increase with aging, but increase at excessive rates among people with Alzheimer's disease, particularly in the hippocampus, causing cell damage (Thal, 1998).

Many of the other drugs used to treat people with dementia are meant to treat secondary symptoms of the disorder, rather than the primary cognitive symptoms. Antidepressant and antianxiety drugs may be used to help control the emotional symptoms of people with dementia. Antipsychotic drugs may help to control hallucinations and delusions and agitation (Rabins, 1998). Finally, some studies suggest that two types of drugs can help to protect against the development of Alzheimer's disease—nonsteroidal anti-inflammatory

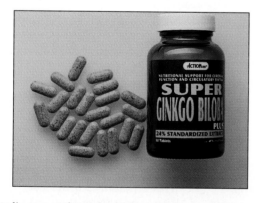

Some studies suggest that ginkgo biloba can improve cognitive functioning in Alzheimers' patients.

drugs such as aspirin, and estrogen replacement therapies for women (Thal, 1998).

Behavioral therapies can be helpful in controlling patients' angry outbursts and emotional instability (Rovner et al., 1996). Often, family members are given training in behavioral techniques to help them manage patients at home. These techniques not only reduce stress and emotional distress among caregiving family members, but may also result in lower behavioral problems in the demented family members (Dunkin & Anderson-Hanley, 1998). In *Taking Psychology Personally:* Tips for the Caregivers of Dementia Patients, we describe a variety of strategies families of people with dementia can reduce stress for themselves and their demented family member.

The Impact of Gender and Culture on Dementia

There are more elderly women than men with dementia, particularly Alzheimer's dementia (Gao et al., 1998). This simply may be because women tend to live longer than men and thus live long enough to develop age-related dementias. Among people with dementia, women tend to show greater decline in language skills than do men, even though among people without dementia, women tend to score better on tests of language skills than do men (Buckwalter et al., 1993). The reason for the greater impact of dementia on language in women compared to men is unknown. Some researchers have speculated that language skills are distributed across both sides of the brain in women but more localized in the left side of the brain for men, and this somehow makes women's language skills more vulnerable to the effects of dementia.

In general, African Americans are more frequently diagnosed with dementia than are Whites. The types of dementias that African Americans and Whites develop differ, however (Chun et al., 1998). African Americans are more likely than Whites to be diagnosed with vascular dementia. This may be because African Americans have higher rates of hypertension and cardiovascular disease, which contribute to vascular dementia. In contrast, Whites may be more likely than African Americans to have dementias due to Alzheimer's disease and Parkinson's disease. The genetic factors leading to these diseases may be more prevalent in Whites than in African Americans.

Perhaps the greatest cross-cultural issue in dementia is the impact of culture and education on the validity of instruments used to assess cognitive impairment. One of the most common paper-and-pencil assessment tools is the Mini-Mental State Examination (Folstein, Folstein, & McHugh, 1975). Some items from

TAKING PSYCHOLOGY PERSONALLY

Tips for the Caregivers of Dementia Patients

There is a good chance that at some time in your life you will be a caregiver to a family member with dementia or some other disease that reduces intellectual and physical functioning. This may be your parent, a loved one who sustains a head injury or has AIDS, or when you are older, your spouse or partner. The Alzheimer's Association has published many practical tips on managing life with a loved one with Alzheimer's disease. These tips are useful for caregivers of anyone who is debilitated by cognitive and emotional deficits. Some of these tips follow. For further information, contact the Alzheimer's Association at 70 E. Lake Street, Chicago, IL 60601-5997 or phone (800) 621-0379.

Activities

People with dementia can have trouble concentrating, following instructions, and initiating or following through with plans. This can lead them to become completely inactive and isolated. Here are some tips for helping your loved one remain as active and involved with others as possible.

Build in structure. Do not be afraid to give activities structure and routine. It is fine for the person to do the same thing at the same time every day. If he has a sense of routine, there is a greater chance that he will look forward to an activity with a positive attitude.

Be flexible. Adjust to the person's level of ability and look for hidden messages. When the person insists that she does not want to do something, it might be her way of telling you that she cannot do it or fears doing it. If an individual patient has problems with one part of a task such as separating dishes and putting them into a cabinet, you might want to take over part of the task and ask the person to hand you dishes one by one.

Stress involvement. Emphasize activities that help the individual feel like a valued part of the household and experience a feeling of success and accomplishment. Working along with you on such tasks as setting the table, wiping counter-

tops, folding napkins, or emptying wastebaskets will help the person feel useful and sociable.

Do not forget the family. Plan for social activities such as family picnics or birthday parties, but make special allowances for the person with the disease. Allow for frequent rest periods and try to prevent family members from overwhelming the individual.

Focus on enjoyment, not achievement. Help the individual find activities that build on remaining skills and talents. A person who was once a professional artist might become frustrated over the declining quality of her work when engaged in an art activity, but someone who never pursued art as a career might enjoy a new opportunity for self-expression.

Understand combativeness. When a person with dementia becomes combative, angry, or agitated, it may be because of frustration. The individual may feel that he is being pushed to do something that simply cannot be done.

Be on the lookout for frustration. Look for early signs of frustration in such activities as bathing, dressing, or eating and respond in a calm and reassuring tone.

Do not take aggression and combativeness personally. Keep in mind that the person is not necessarily angry at you. Instead, she may misunderstand the situation or be frustrated with her own disabilities.

Avoid teaching. Offer encouragement, but keep in mind the person's capabilities and do not expect more than he can do. Avoid elaborate explanations or arguments.

Learn from previous experiences. Try to avoid situations or experiences that make the person combative. For example, if the individual tires easily when she visits with family members, you might want to limit the length of these visits. Try

Continued

to identify early signs of agitation. For example, outbursts are sometimes preceded by restlessness, frustration, fidgeting, or blushing.

Restructure tasks and the person's environment. Simplify tasks or plan more difficult tasks for the time of day when the person is at his best. Allow the person to make some choices but limit the total number of choices. Having too many decisions to make about what to eat or wear might be confusing or overwhelming. Break down each task into small steps and allow the person to complete one step at a time. Keep the environment calm, quiet, and clutter free.

Feelings

The person with dementia is often on an emotional roller coaster as she attempts to understand and cope with the effects of the disease. Family members can help her express her emotions and cope with them in constructive ways. They can also avoid interactions that induce anger, shame, or sadness in the person with dementia.

Treat the patient as a person. Through words and touch, try to do everything you can to relate to this individual as a valued human being with emotional and spiritual needs. People with dementia are often hurt when caregivers talk about them as if they are not present. Avoid talking about the person in his presence; assume that he understands everything you are saying.

Communicate slowly and calmly. Speak in simple sentences. Slow down your rate of speech and lower the pitch of your voice. Give the person with dementia time to hear your words and prepare a response. Keep in mind that it can take up to a minute for the person with this disease to respond. Keep communication on an adult-to-adult level. Avoid baby talk or demeaning expressions.

Be positive, optimistic, and reassuring to the person. Use comforting and noncontrolling statements. Try to identify feelings rather than argue about facts. For example, instead of arguing with the person about going outside, you can agree by saying, "Yes, it would be fun to go outside." Or put limits on the request by saying, "I want to go outside, too. Let's do it after we eat. I'm hungry!" Give praise for the simplest achievements and successes.

Tell the person what to expect. Prepare the person for what is about to happen. Instead of pulling the patient out of the chair or pushing the patient across the room, say, "We need to get up now." Then gently assist the person out of the chair or across the room.

Help the person remain independent. Avoid taking responsibilities away from the person. Do not assume that the person cannot perform certain tasks; put the emphasis on what the person can do.

---

this questionnaire are presented in Figure 18.7. People with low levels of education tend to perform more poorly on this questionnaire than do people with more education, whether or not they have dementia (Murden et al., 1991). This may lead to some elderly people with poor education being misdiagnosed as having dementia.

Indeed, studies in the United States, Europe, Israel, and China show that people with low levels of education are more likely to be diagnosed with dementia than are people with more education (Katzman, 1993; Stern et al., 1994). The relationship between lower education and dementia is not just a factor of the

measures used to assess dementia, however. Neuroimaging studies of people with dementia find that those with less education show more of the brain deterioration associated with dementia than do those with more education. It may be that people with more education have a higher socioeconomic status, which in turn provides them with better nutrition and health care that protect them against the conditions contributing to Alzheimer's disease. A fascinating long-term study of nuns, however, suggested that it is something about the cognitive skills that are enhanced by education that helps to protect against Alzheimer's disease (Snowdon et al., 1996). This study found that nuns

Mini-Mental State Examination
(Add points for each correct response.)

Orientation

			Score	Points
1. What is the		Year?	——	1
		Season?	——	1
		Date?	——	1
		Day?	——	1
		Month?	——	1
2. Where are we?		State?	——	1
		County?	——	1
		Town or city?	——	1
		Hospital?	——	1
		Floor?	——	1

Registration

3. Name three objects, taking one second to say each. Then ask the patient all three after you have said them. Give one point for each correct anwer. Repeat the answers until patient learns all three.   ——   3

Attention and calculation

4. Serial sevens. Give one point for each correct answer. Stop after five answers.
   Alternate: Spell WORLD backwards.   ——   5

Recall

5. Ask for names of three objects learned in Q.3. Give one point for each correct answer.   ——   3

Language

6. Point to a pencil and a watch. Have the patient name them as you point.   ——   2
7. Have the patient repeat 'No ifs, ands or buts.'   ——   1
8. Have the patient follow a three-stage command: 'Take a paper in your right hand. Fold the paper in half. Put the paper on the floor.'   ——   3
9. Have the patient read and obey the following: 'CLOSE YOUR EYES.' (Write it in large letters.)   ——   1
10. Have the patient write a sentence of his or her choice. (The sentence should contain a subject and an object, and should make sense. Ignore spelling errors when scoring.)   ——   1
11. Enlarge the design printed below to 1.5 cm per side, and have the patient copy it. (Give one point if all sides and angles are preserved and if the intersecting sides form a quadrangle.)   ——   1

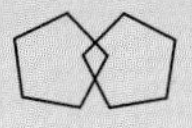

—————— = Total 30

FIGURE 18.7   The Mini-Mental State Examination. The Mini-Mental State Examination is one of the most commonly used tests to assess patients' cognitive functioning and orientation.

Source: Folstein, Folstein, & McHugh, 1975.

who had greater linguistic skills early in life were less likely to develop Alzheimer's disease in late life. Education and more generally cognitive activity throughout one's life may actually increase brain resources in ways that forestall the development of dementia in people prone to the disorder.

Summing Up

- Dementia is typically a permanent deterioration in cognitive functioning, often accompanied by emotional changes.

- The five types of cognitive impairments in dementia are memory impairment, aphasia, apraxia, agnosia, and loss of executive functioning.

- The most common type of dementia is due to Alzheimer's disease.

- The brains of Alzheimer's patients show neurofibrillary tangles, plaques made up of amyloid protein, and cortical atrophy.

- Recent theories of Alzheimer's disease focus on three different genes that might contribute to the buildup of amyloid in the brains of Alzheimer's disease patients.

TABLE 18.3
DSM-IV
Diagnostic Criteria for Delirium

Delirium is characterized by disorientation, recent memory loss, and clouding of consciousness.

Disturbance of consciousness, such as reduced clarity of awareness of the environment, with reduced ability to focus, sustain, or shift attention

Change in cognition (such as memory deficit, disorientation, language disturbance) or development of a perceptual disturbance that is not accounted for by a dementia

Disturbance develops over a short period of time, usually hours to days, and tends to fluctuate during the course of the day

Evidence that the disturbance is caused by the direct physiological consequences of a medical condition

Reprinted with permission from the *Diagnostic and Statistical Manual of Mental Disorders*, Fourth Edition. Copyright © 1994 American Psychiatric Association.

- Dementia can also be caused by cerebrovascular disorder, head injury, and progressive disorders such as Parkinson's disease, HIV disease, Huntington's disease, Pick's disease, Creutzfeldt-Jakob disease, and a number of other medical conditions. Finally, chronic drug abuse and the nutritional deficiencies that often accompany it can lead to dementia.

- There is no effective treatment for dementia, although drugs help to reduce the cognitive symptoms and accompanying depression, anxiety, and psychotic symptoms, in some patients.

- Gender, culture, and education all play roles in vulnerability to dementia.

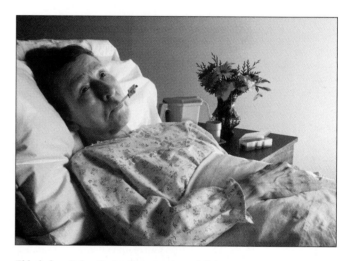

Elderly hospital patients often experience delirium.

⊙ DELIRIUM

Delirium is characterized by disorientation, recent memory loss, and a clouding of consciousness (see Table 18.3). A delirious person will have difficulty focusing, sustaining, or shifting attention. These signs arise suddenly, within several hours or days. They fluctuate over the course of a day and often become worse at night, a condition known as *sundowning*. The duration of these signs is short—rarely more than a month. Delirious patients are often agitated or frightened. They may also experience disrupted sleep-wake cycles, incoherent speech, illusions, and hallucinations.

The signs of delirium usually follow a common progression. Disorientation about time is typically the first sign to appear: If asked, the patient does not know the time of day or the current year or will say it is 6:00 A.M. when it is 6:00 P.M. As the delirium worsens, the person's orientation to place becomes disrupted; for

example, the patient may think she is in her childhood home when she is actually in the hospital. If undetected, the delirium progresses, and the person's orientation to familiar people becomes distorted. For example, a delirious patient will misidentify his wife or fail to recognize his child. Immediate memory is the first to be affected, followed by intermediate memory (memories of events occurring in the last 10 minutes), and finally remote or distant memory. When intervals of these symptoms alternate with intervals of lucid functioning and the symptoms become worse at night, a diagnosis of delirium is likely. If the person is not disoriented (to time, place, or person) or recent memory loss is absent, then a diagnosis of delirium is unlikely.

The onset of delirium may be very dramatic, as when a normally quiet person becomes suddenly loud, verbally abusive, and combative or when a compliant hospital patient tries to pull out his IVs and will not be

TABLE 18.4

Substances That Can Induce Delirium

A wide range of substances can cause delirium.

Alcohol	Antimicrobials	Inhalants
Amphetamines	Antiparkinsonian drugs	Muscle relaxants
Anesthetics	Cannabis	Opioids
Analgesics	Carbon dioxide	Organophosphate insecticides
Antiasthmatic agents	Carbon monoxide	Phencyclidine
Anticholinesterase	Cocaine	Psychotropic medications with anticholinergic side effects
Anticonvulsants	Corticosteroids	
Antihistamines	Gastrointestinal medications	Sedatives, hypnotics, and anxiolytics
Antihypertensive and cardiovascular medications	Hallucinogens	Volatile substances such as fuel or paint

Source: Data from DSM-IV, APA, 2000.

calmed by family or medical staff. Sometimes, though, the onset of delirium is subtle and manifests as an exaggerated form of an individual's normal personality traits. For example, a perfectionist nurse recovering from surgery may complain loudly and harshly about the "inadequate" care she is receiving from the attending nurses. It would be easy for attending staff to regard her irritability as consistent with her personality style and her recovery: "She must be feeling better, she's beginning to complain." In this type of case, the delirium may go unrecognized until severe symptoms of delirium emerge.

Sometimes delirious patients just appear confused. People who know them well say, "He just doesn't seem like himself." These delirious patients may call acquaintances by the wrong names, or forget how to get to familiar locations; for example, they may not remember where their rooms are. In cases like these, often the first indication of delirium comes from the observations of family or medical staff. They will notice that the person seems calm during the day but agitated at night. It is important to monitor such a patient around the clock. Detecting delirium may require frequent testing of the person's orientation. Close monitoring is also important because, with delirium, accidents such as falling out of bed or stepping into traffic are common.

Delirium typically is a signal of some serious medical condition. When it is detected and the underlying medical condition treated, delirium is temporary and reversible. The longer delirium continues, however, the more likely the person will suffer permanent brain damage, because the causes of delirium, if left untreated, can induce permanent changes in the functioning of the brain.

Causes of Delirium

There are many causes of delirium. For most patients, an underlying medical, surgical, chemical, or neurological problem causes the delirium. Delirium can be caused by a stroke, congestive heart failure, an infectious disease, a high fever, and HIV infection. Drug intoxication or withdrawal can lead to delirium. Other possible causes include fluid and electrolyte imbalances, illicit drugs, medications, and toxic substances (see Table 18.4).

Delirium is probably the most common psychiatric syndrome found in a general hospital, particularly in older people. About 10 percent of older people are delirious upon admission to the hospital for a serious illness, and another 10 to 15 percent develop delirium while in the hospital. Older people often experience delirium following surgery (Fisher & Flowerdew, 1995). The delirium may be the result of the medical disorder of the patient or the effects of medications. It may also result from sensory isolation. There is a syndrome known as *ICU/CCU psychosis* that occurs in intensive care and cardiac care units (Maxmen & Ward, 1995). When patients are kept in unfamiliar surroundings that are strange and monotonous, they may hear noises from machines as human voices, see the walls quiver, or hallucinate that someone is tapping them on the shoulder.

Among the elderly, a high mortality rate is associated with delirium (Byrne, 1994). Typically, this is because the underlying condition or cause of the delirium is very serious. Between 15 and 40 percent of delirious hospital patients die within 1 month as compared to half that rate in nondelirious patients.

Some people are at increased risk for delirium. Risk factors include age (the older the person, the higher the risk), gender (males are more at risk than females), preexisting brain damage or dementia (Gustafson et al., 1991; Lipowski, 1990; Schor, Levkoff, & Lipsitz, 1992; Williams-Russo et al., 1992). African Americans have higher rates of delirium than Whites. This may be because African Americans are less likely to have health insurance, so they do not receive early medical care for serious illnesses. As a result, their illnesses may be more likely to become severe enough to cause delirium.

There are very few data on the prevalence of delirium in the United States (Byrne, 1994). One large epidemiological study of mental disorders in Boston found six cases of delirium in the total sample of 829 adults (Folstein et al., 1991). Most of these people were over the age of 55. Delirium in these six cases was related to multiple medications, visual impairment, diabetes, brain disease, incontinence, and diuretic use or a combination of these causes. Among nursing home residents, approximately 6 percent have been reported to be delirious (Beinenfeld and Wheeler, 1989).

Treatment of Delirium

It is extremely important that delirium be recognized and treated quickly. If a delirious person is not already hospitalized, an immediate referral to a physician should be made. The first priority is to keep patients alive and to prevent brain damage by removing or alleviating the causes of the delirium. It may also be necessary to prevent people from harming themselves (Maxmen & Ward, 1995). Often, nursing care is required to monitor people's states and to prevent them from wandering off, tripping, or ripping out intravenous tubes and to manage their behavior if they should become noncompliant or violent. In some instances, restraints are necessary.

Psychotropic medications (usually antipsychotics) in small doses initially can help to relieve the patient of psychotic symptoms until the cause of the delirium can be identified and treated (Cole et al., 1998; Sipahimalinai & Masand, 1998). In addition, delirious patients should be oriented frequently—they can be helped by numerous brief contacts with family and staff, reassuring them that they are safe, by having them repeat the date and time, by informing them where they are and who the people around him are,

and by giving them detailed descriptions of whatever procedures may be taking place. It may be helpful to place clocks, calendars, and photographs of family members in patients' rooms.

Summing Up

- Delirium is characterized by disorientation, recent memory loss, and clouding of consciousness.
- The onset of delirium can be either sudden or slow.
- The many causes of delirium include medical diseases, the trauma of surgery, illicit drugs, medications, high fever, and infections.
- Delirium must be treated immediately by treating its underlying causes, to prevent brain damage and to prevent people from hurting themselves.

☉ AMNESIA

CASE STUDY

A 46-year-old divorced housepainter is admitted to the hospital with a history of 30 years of heavy drinking. He has had two previous admissions for detoxification, but his family states that he has not had a drink in several weeks, and he shows no signs of alcohol withdrawal. He looks malnourished, however, and appears confused and mistakes one of his physicians for a dead uncle.

Within a week, the patient seems less confused and can find his way to the bathroom without direction. He remembers the names and birthdays of his siblings but has difficulty naming the past five presidents. More strikingly, he has great difficulty in retaining information for longer than a few minutes. He can repeat a list of numbers immediately after he has heard them, but a few minutes later does not recall being asked to perform the task. Shown three objects (keys, comb, ring), he cannot recall them 3 minutes later. He does not seem worried about this. Asked if he can recall the name of his doctor, he replies, "Certainly," and proceeds to call the doctor "Dr. Masters" (not his name), and he claims to have met him in the Korean War. He tells a long untrue story about how he and Dr. Masters served as fellow soldiers. (Adapted from Spitzer et al., 1981, pp. 41–42)

In dementia and delirium, people show multiple cognitive deficits, including memory deficits, language deficits, disorientation, inability to recognize objects or people, and inability to think abstractly or plan and carry through with an activity. In **amnesic disorders,** only memory is affected. A person with **amnesia** will be impaired in the ability to learn new information (**anterograde amnesia**) or to recall previously learned

People with amnesia can have trouble learning new information or remembering old information.

information or past events (**retrograde amnesia**). Amnesic disorders often follow periods of confusion and disorientation and delirium.

The patterns of amnesia represented in television shows and soap operas—with people suddenly losing their memories for everything they previously knew—are unrealistic. Commonly, people with amnesia can remember events from the distant past but not from the recent past. For example, a 60-year-old patient may be able to tell where he went to high school and college but be unable to remember that he was admitted to the hospital yesterday. He will also forget meeting his doctor from one day to the next. In profound amnesia, a person may be completely disoriented about place or time, but rarely does an amnesic person forget his or her own identity.

Often, people with amnesia do not realize they have profound memory deficits and will deny evidence of these deficits. They may seem unconcerned with obvious lapses in memory or may make up stories to cover their lapses in memory, as did the housepainter. They may become agitated with others who point out their memory lapses. They may even accuse others of conspiring against them.

Amnesia can be caused by brain damage due to strokes, head injuries, chronic nutritional deficiencies, exposure to toxins (such as through carbon monoxide poisoning), and chronic substance abuse. *Korsakoff's syndrome* is an amnesic disorder caused by damage to the thalamus, a part of the brain that acts as a relay station to other parts of the brain. Chronic and heavy alcohol use is associated with Korsakoff's syndrome, probably because the alcoholic neglects nutrition and thus develops thiamin deficiencies (see Chapter 16).

The course of amnesic disorders depends on the cause. If, for example, a stroke occurs in the hippocampus, the memory loss that results will include events after the date of the stroke. Memories prior to the stroke will remain intact. If the memory loss is caused by alcohol or other toxins, it is often more broad and the onset can be insidious. For some people, remote memory may also become impaired.

The first step in the treatment of amnesic disorders is to remove, if possible, any conditions contributing to the amnesia, such as alcohol use or exposure to toxins. In addition, attention to nutrition and treatment of any accompanying health condition (e.g., hypertension) can help to prevent further deterioration. Lastly, because new surroundings and routines may prove too difficult or impossible for the amnesic person to learn, the environment should be kept as familiar as possible. Often, as with dementia, it can be helpful to have clocks, calendars, photographs, labels, and other kinds of reminders prominent.

Summing Up

- The amnesic disorders are characterized only by memory loss.

- Retrograde amnesia is loss of memory for past events, and anterograde amnesia is the inability to remember new information.

- Amnesia can be caused by brain damage due to strokes, head injuries, chronic nutritional deficiencies, exposure to toxins (such as through carbon monoxide poisoning), and chronic substance abuse.

- Treatment of amnesia can involve removal of the agents contributing to the amnesia and helping the person develop memory aids.

☉ BIO-PSYCHO-SOCIAL INTEGRATION

The fact that deterioration or damage to the brain can cause not only cognitive deficits but also personality changes is strong evidence that biological factors have significant impact on psychological characteristics. Do psychological or social factors also have an impact on the cognitive disorders, which by definition, are biologically caused? The answer seems to be "yes." For example, many people in the early stages of dementia become paranoid, irritable, and impulsive. These symptoms may be especially pronounced in people who, even before they developed dementia, were somewhat paranoid, irritable, or impulsive. Social environment can greatly affect the severity of cognitive deficits. If a person who is easily confused or forgetful is further stressed by family members who frequently become annoyed with him or her or expect too much of him or her, then the cognitive deficits can become even more severe. Thus, even though the cognitive disorders are rooted in medical disease or chronic intoxi- cation with substances like alcohol, there are several ways in which psychosocial factors can influence the severity and manifestation of these disorders.

Chapter Summary

- Dementia is typically a permanent deterioration in cognitive functioning, often accompanied by emotional changes. The five types of cognitive impairments in dementia are memory impairment, aphasia, apraxia, agnosia, and loss of executive functioning. The most common type of dementia is due to Alzheimer's disease. The brains of Alzheimer's patients show neurofibrillary tangles, plaques made up of amyloid protein, and cortical atrophy. Recent theories of Alzheimer's disease focus on three different genes that might contribute to the buildup of amyloid protein in the brains of Alzheimer's patients.

- Dementia can also be caused by cerebrovascular disorder, head injury, and progressive disorders such as Parkinson's disease, HIV disease, Huntington's disease, Pick's disease, and Creutzfeldt-Jakob disease. Finally, chronic drug abuse and the nutritional deficiencies that often accompany it can lead to dementia. There is no effective treatment for dementia, although drugs help to reduce the cognitive symptoms and accompanying depression, anxiety, and psychotic symptoms in some patients.

- Delirium is characterized by disorientation, recent memory loss, and clouding of consciousness. Delirium typically is a signal of a serious medical condition, such as a stroke, congestive heart failure, infectious disease, or high fever, or of drug intoxication or withdrawal. It is a common syndrome in hospitals, particularly among elderly surgery patients. Treating delirium involves treating the underlying condition leading to the delirium and keeping the patient safe until the symptoms subside.

- In amnesic disorders, only patients' memories are affected. Anterograde amnesia is the most common form of amnesia and is characterized by the inability to learn or retain new information. Retrograde amnesia is the inability to recall previously learned information or past events. Amnesic disorders can be caused by strokes, head injuries, chronic nutritional deficiencies, exposure to toxins, and chronic substance abuse. The course and treatment of amnesic disorders depend on the cause.

Key Terms

cognitive disorders 654

dementia 655

aphasia 656

echolalia 656

palialia 656

apraxia 656

agnosia 656

Alzheimer's disease 658

neurofibrillary tangles 661

plaques 661

amyloid 661

vascular dementia 663

cerebrovascular disease 663

stroke 663

delirium 672

amnesic disorders 674

amnesia 674

anterograde amnesia 674

retrograde amnesia 675

Critical Thinking Questions

1. If the cognitive disorders, by definition, are caused by medical conditions or substance intoxication but not by emotional distress or other psychological problems, should they be considered psychological disorders? Why or why not?

2. What are some of the potential benefits of developing neuroimaging techniques to diagnose Alzheimer's disease if there currently are no effective treatments for the disorder?

3. Why might men be more prone to delirium than women?

4. Most people have complete amnesia for events that happened before they were about 3 years of age. Why might this be true?

Paul Klee
Sun and Moon (Subtitled Starker Traum)

All, too, will bear in mind this sacred principle, that though the will of the majority is in all cases to prevail, that will to be rightful must be reasonable; that the minority possess their equal rights, which equal law must protect, and to violate would be oppression.

—Thomas Jefferson, First Inaugural Address (1801)

CHAPTER
19

Mental Health, Social Policy, and the Law

CHAPTER OVERVIEW
Judgments About People Accused of Crimes

Mental-health professionals are called upon to help determine if accused people are competent to stand trial and if accused people were "sane" at the time crimes were committed. The insanity defense has undergone many changes in recent history, often in response to its use in high-profile crimes. It is based on the notion that a person who was mentally incapacitated at the time of a crime should not be held responsible for the crime.

Involuntary Commitment and Civil Rights

People can be committed involuntarily to psychiatric facilities if they are gravely disabled by psychological disorders or are imminent dangers to themselves or others. These criteria are difficult to apply accurately and consistently. The deinstitutionalization movement led to many long-term psychiatric patients being released, but unfortunately, community-based facilities for helping these people are often inadequate.

Pushing the Boundaries:
Mental-Health Care for Pregnant Prison Inmates

Clinicians' Duties to Clients and Society

Some specific duties clinicians have are the duties to provide competent and appropriate treatment; to avoid multiple relationships, especially sexual relationships, with clients; and to protect clients' confidentiality. Client confidentiality can be broken, however, when clients are threatening others or abusing children or elderly people.

Taking Psychology Personally:
Guidelines for Ethical Service to Culturally Diverse Populations

Family Law and Mental-Health Professionals

Three areas of family law in which mental-health professionals are increasingly involved are child custody disputes between divorcing parents, child maltreatment cases, and adult accusations about their molestation during childhood.

Viewpoints:
The Repressed Memory Debate

Bio-Psycho-Social Integration
Chapter Summary
Key Terms
Critical Thinking Questions

CASE STUDY

A 60-year-old man wanders the streets as the temperature plummets below freezing, talking to imaginary creatures and stripping off his warm clothes. When asked if he wants shelter or food, he curses and turns away. The police apprehend the man and bring him to court. A psychologist is asked to determine whether the man is such a danger to himself that he should be held against his will.

CASE STUDY

The parents of two young children are going through a bitter divorce, each claiming that he or she should have custody of the children because the other is an incompetent and abusive parent. The court asks a social worker to assist in determining the best custody arrangement for the children.

CASE STUDY

A middle-aged man kills three people in a shooting rampage. When arrested, he says that he was obeying voices telling him to shoot "sinners." A psychiatrist is asked to evaluate whether this man is telling the truth.

CASE STUDY

A college student who has been depressed for some time begins to remember events from her childhood that suggest she may have been sexually abused by her father. She seeks out a therapist to determine if these memories are real.

Situations such as these raise fundamental questions about society's values: Do people have the right to conduct their lives as they wish, even if their behaviors pose a risk to their own health and well-being? Under what conditions should people be absolved of responsibility for behaviors that harm others? Does society have a right or an obligation to intervene in troubled families? Should the diagnosis of a psychological disorder entitle a person to special services and protection against discrimination? Questions such as these are concerned with the values of personal freedom, the obligation of society to protect its vulnerable members, the right of society to protect itself against the actions of individuals, and the sanctity of the family.

Mental-health professionals are increasingly being brought into such situations to help individuals and society make judgments about the appropriate actions to take. It would be nice if mental-health professionals could simply turn to the research literature for "objective" information that indicates which judgment is best in each situation. Frequently, however, there is no re-

search literature relevant to a situation or the research holds conflicting messages. Moreover, at its best, research can only tell us what is *likely* to be right or true in a given situation but not what is *definitely* right or true. That is, the predictions we can make from the research literature are probabilistic—they tell us how likely people are to do something but not that they definitely will do something. Also, we are limited in our ability to generalize from the research literature to individual cases. Finally, because most of such judgments involve conflicts between different values, ethical principles, or moral principles, research and clinical judgment can only tell us so much about the right resolution.

This chapter is about the interface between psychology and the law. Because the law has tended to regard at least some psychological disorders as medical illnesses or diseases, we use the phrase **mentally ill** throughout this chapter. We have refrained from using this phrase in most previous chapters because it connotes a medical view of psychological problems, which is only one of several ways to view psychological problems. We shall see, however, that the law is inconsistent in its view of psychological disorders, and this view has changed quite frequently.

We first examine how the law regards people charged with crimes who might have psychological disorders. Mental-health professionals help legal authorities decide when people's psychological disorders make them incompetent to stand trial and when they should be considered not guilty by reason of insanity. Then we discuss when a person can be held in a mental-health facility against his or her will—a procedure known as *civil commitment*. Over the last 50 years, the criteria for commitment and the rights of committed patients have changed greatly. Next, we discuss certain duties that courts and professional organizations have argued clinicians have toward clients and society: the duty to provide competent treatment, the duty to avoid multiple relationships with clients, the duty to maintain clients' confidentiality, the duty to protect persons their clients are threatening to harm, and the duty to report suspected child or elder abuse. Finally, we end with a discussion of three areas in which mental-health professionals are increasingly becoming involved: child custody disputes in divorce proceedings, child maltreatment cases, and claims by adults that they have recovered repressed memories of childhood sexual abuse.

○ JUDGMENTS ABOUT PEOPLE ACCUSED OF CRIMES

Two critical judgments that mental-health professionals are asked to make about people accused of

Judgments of competency to stand trial are some of the most common judgments made in courts, and psychologists often play a role in these judgments.

crimes are whether they are competent to stand trial and whether they were sane at the time the crimes were committed. Mental-health professionals actually do not make the final judgments about the dispensation of people accused of crimes; they only make recommendations to the court. Their recommendations can be influential in judges' or juries' decisions, however.

Competency to Stand Trial

One of the fundamental principles of law is that, in order to stand trial, accused individuals must have a rational understanding of the charges against them and the proceedings of the trial and must be able to participate in their defense. People who do not have an understanding of what is happening to them in a courtroom and who cannot participate in their own defense are said to be **incompetent to stand trial.** Incompetence may involve impairment in several capacities, including the capacity to understand information, to think rationally about alternative courses of action, to make good choices, and to appreciate one's situation as a criminal defendant (Hoge, Bonnie, Poythress, Monahan, Eisenberg, & Feucht-Havia, 1997).

Impaired competence may be a common problem: Defense attorneys suspect impaired competence in their clients in up to 10 percent of cases. Although only a handful of these clients are referred for formal evaluation, still between 24,000 and 60,000 evaluations of criminal defendants for "competence to stand trial" are performed every year in the United States (MacArthur Research Network on Mental Health and

the Law, 1998). Competency judgments are thus some of the most frequent types of judgments that mental-health professionals are asked to make for courts. Judges appear to value the testimony of mental-health experts concerning defendants' competency and rarely rule against the experts' recommendations. As a result, the consequences of competency judgments for defendants are great. If they are judged incompetent, trials are postponed as long as there is some reason to believe that they will become competent in the foreseeable future, and defendants may be forced to receive treatment. Incompetent defendants who are wrongly judged competent may not contribute adequately to their defense and may be wrongly convicted and incarcerated. Defendants who are suspected to be incompetent are described by their attorneys as much less helpful in establishing the facts of their case and much less actively involved in making decisions about their defense (MacArthur Research Network on Mental Health and the Law, 1998).

Not surprisingly, defendants with long histories of psychiatric problems, particularly schizophrenia or psychotic symptoms, are more likely to be referred for competency evaluations (Nicholson & Kugler, 1991). Defendants referred for competency evaluations also tend to have lower levels of education and to be poor, unemployed, and unmarried. Over half have been accused of violent offenses. Women and members of ethnic minority groups are more likely to be judged incompetent than are men or Whites (Nicholson & Kugler, 1991). Women and ethnic minority persons who commit crimes may be more likely to have severe psychological problems that make them incompetent to stand trial than do men or Whites who commit crimes. On the other hand, evaluators may have lower thresholds for judging women and ethnic minorities incompetent. In addition, when evaluators do not speak the same languages as ethnic minority defendants, the defendants may not understand the evaluators' questions, evaluators may not understand the defendants' answers to questions, and evaluators may tend to interpret this lack of communication as an indication of defendants' incompetence to stand trial.

Psychologists have developed tests of cognitive abilities important to following legal proceedings, and people who perform poorly on these tests are more likely to be judged incompetent to stand trial. These tests have not been widely used, however. Instead, judgments of incompetence are usually given to people who have existing diagnoses of psychotic disorders or who have symptoms indicating severe psychopathology, such as gross disorientation, delusions, hallucinations, and thought disorder (Nicholson & Kugler, 1991).

TABLE 19.1

Comparison of Public Perceptions of the Insanity Defense with Actual Use and Results

The public perceives that many more accused persons use the insanity defense successfully than is actually the case.

	Public Perception	Reality
Percentage of felony indictments for which an insanity plea is made	37%	1%
Percentage of insanity pleas resulting in "not guilty by reason of insanity"	44%	26%
Percentage of persons "not guilty by reason of insanity" sent to mental hospitals	51%	85%
Percentage of persons "not guilty by reason of insanity" set free	26%	15%
Conditional release		12%
Outpatient treatment		3%
Unconditional release		1%
Length of confinement of persons "not guilty by reason of insanity" (in months)		
All crimes	21.8	32.5
Murder		76.4

Source: Data from Silver, Cirincione, & Steadman, 1994.

Insanity Defense

Insanity is actually a legal term rather than a psychological or medical term, and it has been defined in various ways, as we explore shortly. All of these definitions reflect the fundamental doctrine that people cannot be held fully responsible for their acts if they were so mentally incapacitated at the time of the acts that they could not conform to the rules of society. Note that people do not have to be chronically insane for the insanity defense to apply. They only have to be judged to have been insane at the time they committed the acts. Obviously, this can be a difficult judgment to make.

The **insanity defense** has been one of the most controversial applications of psychology to the law. The lay public often thinks of the insanity defense as a means by which guilty people "get off." When the insanity defense has been used successfully in celebrated cases, as when John Hinckley successfully used this defense after shooting former President Ronald Reagan and the president's press secretary Jim Brady, there have been calls to eliminate the insanity defense altogether (Steadman et al., 1993). Indeed, these celebrated cases have often led to reappraisals of the insanity defense and redefinitions of the legal meaning of insanity, as we consider next.

The insanity defense is used much less often than the public tends to think. As is shown in Table 19.1, fewer than 1 in 100 defendants in felony cases file insanity pleas, and of these only 26 percent result in acquittal (Silver, Cirincione, & Steadman, 1994). Thus, only about 1 in 400 people charged with a felony is judged not guilty by reason of insanity. About two-thirds of these people have diagnoses of schizophrenia, and most have histories of psychiatric hospitalizations and previous crimes (McGreevy, Steadman, & Callahan, 1991).

Almost 90 percent of the people who are acquitted after pleading the insanity defense are male, and two-thirds of them are White (McGreevy, Steadman, & Callahan, 1991). The reasons men and Whites are more likely to successfully plead the insanity defense are unclear but may have to do with their greater access to competent attorneys who can effectively argue the insanity defense. In the last decade or two, as society has become more aware of the plight of abused and battered women, increasing numbers of women are pleading the insanity defense after injuring or killing partners who had been abusing them for years. One case is that of Lorena and John Bobbitt. According to Lorena Bobbitt, her husband John Bobbitt had sexually and emotionally abused her for years. One night in 1994, John Bobbitt came home drunk and raped Lorena Bobbitt. In what her attorneys described as a brief psychotic episode, Lorena Bobbitt cut off her husband's penis and threw it away. Lorena Bobbitt was acquitted of charges of malicious injury by reason of temporary insanity. She was referred to a mental institution for further evaluation and released a few months later.

Another controversial application of the insanity defense by women has been its use by women who have committed infanticide, supposedly as the result of psychotic postpartum depression (Williamson, 1993). Severe postpartum depression with psychotic symptoms is very rare and violence by these women against their newborns is even more rare (Nolen-Hoeksema, 1990). When such violence does occur, some courts have accepted that the mothers' behaviors are the result of the postpartum psychosis and have judged these women not guilty by reason of insanity.

Even when a defendant is judged not guilty by reason of insanity, it usually is not the case that he or she "gets off." Of those people acquitted because of insanity, about 85 percent are still sent to mental hospitals, and all but 1 percent are put under some type of supervision and care. Of those who are sent to mental hospitals, the average length of stay (or incarceration) in the hospital is almost three years when all types of crimes are considered, and over six years for those who had been accused (and acquitted by reason of insanity) of murder. John Hinckley, who shot former President Reagan in 1981, has been incarcerated in St. Elizabeth's Hospital since he was found not guilty by reason of insanity. Some states require that people judged not guilty by reason of insanity cannot be incarcerated in mental institutions for longer than they would have served prison sentences if they had been judged guilty of their crimes, but not all states have this rule. Thus, there is little evidence that the insanity defense is widely used to help people avoid incarceration for their crimes.

Insanity Defense Rules

There are five rules that have been used in modern history to evaluate defendants' pleas that they should be judged not guilty by reason of insanity (see *Concept Review: Insanity Defense Criteria*).

M'Naghten Rule The first is the **M'Naghten Rule.** Daniel M'Naghten lived in England in the mid-1800s and had the delusion that the English Tory party was persecuting him. He set out to kill the Tory prime minister but mistakenly shot the prime minister's secretary. At his trial, the jury judged M'Naghten not guilty by reason of insanity. There was a public outcry at this verdict, leading the House of Lords to formalize a rule for when a person could be absolved from responsibility for his or her acts because of a mental disorder. This rule became known as the M'Naghten Rule, and it still is used in many jurisdictions today:

> To establish a defense on the ground of insanity, it must be clearly proved that at the time of committing the act, the party accused was labouring under such a defect of reason, from disease of the mind, as not to know the nature and quality of the act he was doing, or if he did know it, that he did not know he was doing what was wrong.

The M'Naghten rule reflects the doctrine that a person must have a "guilty mind"—in Latin, *mens rea*—or the intention to commit the illegal act in order to be held responsible for the act.

It might seem that applying the M'Naghten Rule is a straightforward matter—one simply determines whether a person suffers from a disease of the mind and whether during the crime he or she understood that his or her actions were wrong. Unfortunately, it is not that simple. A major problem in applying the M'Naghten Rule emerges in determining what is

CONCEPT REVIEW

Insanity Defense Criteria

Five different criteria have been used for determining whether an individual was insane at the time he or she committed and therefore whether he or she should not be held responsible for the crime.

Rule	The individual is not held responsible for a crime if
M'Naghten Rule	At the time of the crime, the individual was so affected by a disease of the mind that he or she did not know the nature of the act he or she was committing or did not know it was wrong.
Irresistible Impulse Rule	At the time of the crime, the individual was driven by an irresistible impulse to perform the act or had a diminished capacity to resist performing the act.
Durham Rule	The crime was a product of a mental disease or defect.
ALI Rule	At the time of the crime, as a result of mental disease or defect, the person lacked substantial capacity either to appreciate the criminality (wrongfulness) of the act or to conform his or her conduct to the law.
American Psychiatric Association Definition	At the time of the crime, as a result of mental disease or mental retardation, the person was unable to appreciate the wrongfulness of his or her conduct.

meant by a "disease of the mind." The law has been unclear and inconsistent in what disorders it recognizes as diseases of the mind. The most consistently recognized diseases are psychoses. It has been relatively easy for the courts and the public to accept that someone experiencing severe delusions and hallucinations is suffering from a disease and, at times, may not know right from wrong. However, defendants have argued that several other disorders, such as alcoholism, severe depression, and posttraumatic stress disorder, are diseases of the mind that impair judgments of right and wrong. It is much more difficult for courts, the lay public, and mental-health professionals to agree on these claims.

A second major problem is that the M'Naghten Rule requires that a person did not know right from wrong at the time of the crime in order to be judged not guilty by reason of insanity. This is a difficult judgment to make because it is a retrospective judgment. Even when everyone agrees that a defendant suffers from a severe psychological disorder, this does not necessarily mean that, at the time of the crime, he or she was incapable of knowing "right from wrong" as the M'Naghten Rule requires. For example, the serial killer Jeffrey Dahmer, who tortured, killed, dismembered, and ate his victims, clearly seemed to have a psychological disorder. Nevertheless, the jury denied his insanity defense in part because he took great care to hide his crimes from the local police, suggesting that he knew what he was doing was "wrong" or against the law.

Irresistible impulse rule The second rule used to judge the acceptability of the insanity defense is the **irresistible impulse rule.** First applied in Ohio in 1934, the irresistible impulse rule broadened the conditions

Serial killer Jeffrey Dahmer clearly had psychological problems, but his insanity defense was not accepted because he took care to hide his crimes from the police, suggesting he knew what he was doing was wrong.

under which a criminal act could be considered the product of insanity to include "acts of passion." Even if a person knew the act he was committing was wrong, if he was driven by an irresistible impulse to perform the act or had a diminished capacity to resist performing the act, then he could be absolved of responsibility for performing the act. One of the most celebrated applications of the notion of diminished capacity was the "Twinkie Defense" of Dan White. In 1979, Dan White assassinated San Francisco mayor George Moscone and a city council member named Harvey Milk. White argued that he had had diminished capacity to resist the impulse to shoot Moscone and Milk due to the psychological effects of extreme stress and the consumption of large amounts of junk food. Using a particularly broad definition of diminished capacity in force in California law at the time, the jury convicted White of manslaughter instead of first-degree murder. Variations of the "Twinkie Defense" have rarely been attempted since White's trial.

The Durham Rule In 1954, Judge David Bazelon further broadened the criteria for the legal definition of insanity in his ruling on the case *Durham v. United States*, which produced the third rule for defining insanity, the **Durham Rule.** According to the Durham Rule, the insanity defense could be accepted for any crimes that were the "product of mental disease or mental defect." This allowed defendants to claim that the presence of any disorder recognized by mental-health professionals could be the "cause" of their crimes. The Durham Rule did not require that defendants show they were incapacitated by their disorders or that they did not understand that their acts were illegal. The Durham Rule was eventually dropped by almost all jurisdictions by the early 1970s.

The ALI Rule The fourth rule for deciding the acceptability of the insanity defense comes from the American Law Institute's Model Penal Code. Motivated by dissatisfaction with the existing legal definitions of insanity, a group of lawyers, judges, and scholars associated with the American Law Institute worked to formulate a better definition, which eventually resulted in what is known as the **ALI Rule:**

> A person is not responsible for criminal conduct if at the time of such conduct as the result of mental disease or defect he lacks substantial capacity either to appreciate the criminality (wrongfulness) of his conduct or to conform his conduct to the requirements of the law.

This rule is broader than the M'Naghten Rule because it requires only that the defendant have a lack of appreciation of the criminality of his or her act, not an absence of understanding of the criminality of the act. The defendant's inability to conform his or her conduct to the requirements of the law could come from the emotional symptoms of a psychological disorder as well as from the cognitive deficits caused by the disorder. This expanded understanding incorporates some of the crimes recognized by the irresistible impulse doctrine. The ALI Rule is clearly more restrictive than the Durham Rule, however, because it requires some lack of appreciation of the criminality of one's act rather than merely the presence of a mental disorder. The ALI Rule further restricted the types of mental disorders that could contribute to a successful insanity defense:

> As used in this Article, the term "mental disease or defect" does not include an abnormality manifested only by repeated criminal or otherwise antisocial conduct.

This further restriction prohibited defense attorneys from arguing that a defendant's long history of antisocial acts was itself evidence of the presence of a mental disease or defect. Further, in 1977, in the case *Barrett v. United States*, it was ruled that "temporary insanity created by voluntary use of alcohol or drugs" also did not qualify a defendant for acquittal by reason of insanity.

The ALI Rule was widely adopted in the United States, including in the jurisdiction in which John Hinckley was tried for shooting Ronald Reagan. Hinckley had a long-standing diagnosis of schizophrenia, and an obsession with the actress Jodi Foster. Letters he wrote to Foster before shooting Reagan indicated that he committed the act under the delusion that this would impress Foster and cause her to return his love. Hinckley's defense attorneys successfully argued that he had a diminished capacity to understand the wrongfulness of shooting Reagan or to conform his behaviors to the requirements of the law. The public outcry over the judgment that Hinckley was "not guilty by reason of insanity" initiated another reappraisal of the legal definition of insanity and the use of the insanity defense (Steadman et al., 1993).

American Psychiatric Association definition This reappraisal led to the fifth legal redefinition of insanity, the **Insanity Defense Reform Act,** put into law by Congress in 1984. The Insanity Defense Reform Act adopted a legal definition of insanity proposed by the **American Psychiatric Association definition of insanity** in 1983. This definition dropped the provision in the ALI Rule that absolved people of responsibility for criminal acts if they were unable to conform their behavior to the law and retained the wrongfulness criterion initially proposed in the M'Naghten Rule. This definition reads as follows:

> A person charged with a criminal offense should be found not guilty by reason of insanity if it is shown that, as a result of mental disease or mental retardation, he was unable to appreciate the

John Hinckley was judged not guilty by reason of insanity for shooting President Ronald Reagan. This judgment inspired a reappraisal of the insanity defense.

wrongfulness of his conduct at the time of his offense.

This definition now applies in all cases tried in federal courts and in about half the states. Also following the Hinckley verdict, most states now require that a defendant pleading not guilty by reason of insanity prove he or she was insane at the time of the crime. Previously, the burden of proof had been on the prosecution to prove that the defendant was sane at the time the crime was committed (Steadman et al., 1993).

Problems with the Insanity Defense

Mental-health professionals tend to be strong proponents of the notion that psychological disorders can impair people's ability to follow the law. They believe that this should be taken into consideration when judging an individual's responsibility for his or her actions. Cases that are built on the insanity defense often use mental-health professionals to provide expert opinions in such cases. Despite their expertise, mental-health professionals often disagree about the nature and causes of psychological disorders, the presence or absence of psychological disorders, and the evaluation of defendants' states of mind at the time crimes were committed. Usually lawyers on both sides of the case will find mental-health professionals who support their point of view, and the two professionals are inevitably in disagreement with each other. This disagreement leads to confusion in judges, juries, and the public.

Mental-health professionals have also raised concerns about the rules used to determine the acceptability

Susan Smith drowned her two young sons in 1994. Although she had a troubled history, the public was not prepared to excuse her act because of her history.

of the insanity defense. Behind these rules is the assumption that most people, including most people with psychological disorders, have free will and can usually choose how they will act in any given situation. Many current models of both normal and abnormal behavior suggest that people are not that much in control of their behaviors. Because of biological predispositions, early life experiences, or disordered patterns of thinking, people often act in irrational and perhaps uncontrolled ways. This view makes it more difficult to say when a person should or should not be held responsible for his or her behaviors.

Guilty but Mentally Ill

In a sixth and most recent reform of the insanity defense, some states have adopted as an alternative to the verdict "not guilty by reason of insanity" the verdict **guilty but mentally ill (GBMI).** Defendants convicted as guilty but mentally ill are incarcerated for the normal terms designated for their crimes, with the expectation that they will also receive treatment for their mental illness. Proponents of the GBMI argue that it recognizes the mental illness of defendants while still holding them responsible for their actions. Critics argue that the GBMI verdict is essentially a guilty verdict and a means of eliminating the insanity defense (Tanay, 1992). In addition, juries may believe they are ensuring that a person gets treatment by judging him or her guilty but mentally ill, but there are no guarantees that a person convicted under GBMI will receive treatment. In most states, it is left up to legal authorities to decide whether to incarcerate these people in mental institutions or prisons and, if they are sent to prisons, whether to provide them with treatment for their mental illness.

Summing Up

- One judgment mental-health professionals are asked to make is about an accused person's competency to stand trial.

- Another judgment is whether the accused person was "sane" at the time he or she committed a crime.

- The insanity defense has undergone many changes over recent history, often in response to its use in high-profile crimes.

- Five different rules have been used to evaluate the acceptability of a plea of not guilty by reason of insanity: the M'Naghten Rule, the irresistible impulse rule, the Durham Rule, the ALI Rule, and the American Psychiatric Association definition.

- All of these rules require that the defendant be diagnosed with a "mental disease" but do not clearly define *mental disease*.

- Most of these rules also require that the defendant has been unable to understand the criminality of his or her actions or conform his or her actions to the law in order to be judged not guilty by reason of insanity.

- Many states have introduced the alternative verdict of "guilty but mentally ill."

⊙ INVOLUNTARY COMMITMENT AND CIVIL RIGHTS

In the best circumstances, people who need treatment for psychological disorders will seek it themselves.

They will work with mental-health professionals to find the medication or psychotherapy that helps to reduce their symptoms and keeps their disorder under control. Many people who have serious psychological problems do not recognize their need for treatment, however, or may refuse treatment for a variety of reasons. For example, a woman with persecutory delusions and hallucinations may fear treatment, believing that doctors are part of the conspiracy against her. A man in a manic episode may like many of the symptoms he is experiencing—the high energy, inflated self-esteem, and grandiose thoughts—and not want to take medication that will reduce these symptoms. The teenager who is abusing illegal drugs may believe that it is his right to do so and that there is nothing wrong with him. Can these people be forced into mental institutions and to undergo treatment against their will? These are the questions we address in this section.

Civil Commitment

Prior to 1969, in the United States the **need for treatment** was sufficient cause to hospitalize people against their will and force them to undergo treatment. Such involuntary hospitalization is called **civil commitment.** All that was needed for civil commitment was a certificate signed by two physicians stating that a person needed treatment and was not agreeing to it voluntarily. The person could then be confined, often indefinitely, without advice of an attorney, a hearing, or any appeal. In Great Britain and several other countries around the world, need for treatment still is one criterion for civil commitment.

Since 1969, however, the need for treatment alone is no longer sufficient legal cause for civil commitment in most states in the United States. This change came about as part of the patients' rights movement of the 1960s, in which concerns were raised about the personal freedom and civil liberties of mental patients (Holstein, 1993; Mulvey, Geller, & Roth, 1987). Opponents of the civil commitment process argued that it allowed people to be incarcerated simply for having "alternative lifestyles" or different political or moral values (Szasz, 1963, 1977). Certainly there were many cases in the former Soviet Union and other countries of political dissidents being labeled mentally ill and in need of treatment and then being incarcerated in prisons for years. In the United States, there also were disturbing cases of the misuse of civil commitment proceedings. For example, Mrs. E. P. W. Packard was one of several women involuntarily hospitalized by their husbands for holding "unacceptable" and "sick" political or moral views (Weiner & Wettstein, 1993). Mrs. Packard remained hospitalized for three years until she won her release and then began crusading against civil commitment.

Criteria for Involuntary Commitment

The three criteria currently used in the United States and in many other countries to commit someone to a psychiatric facility against his or her will are (1) grave disability, (2) dangerousness to self, and (3) dangerousness to others. In addition, most states require that the danger people pose to themselves or to others be *imminent*—if they are not immediately incarcerated, they or someone else will likely be harmed in the very near future. Finally, all persons committed to psychiatric facilities must be diagnosed with mental disorders.

Grave disability The **grave disability** criterion requires that people be so incapacitated by mental disorders that they cannot care for their basic needs of food, clothing, and shelter. This criterion is, in theory, much more severe than the need for treatment criterion, because it requires that the person's survival be in immediate danger because of illness. At least 30 states in the United States use the grave disability criterion in civil commitment hearings, and in those states, about 80 percent of persons involuntarily committed are committed on the basis of grave disability (Turkheimer & Parry, 1992).

One might think that the grave disability criterion could be used to hospitalize homeless people on the streets who appear to be psychotic and do not seem able to take care of their basic needs. This is what former New York Mayor Ed Koch thought in the bitter winter of 1988, when he invoked the legal principle of *parens patriae* (sovereign as parent) to have mentally ill homeless people picked up from the streets of New York and taken to mental-health facilities. Mayor Koch argued that it was the city's duty to protect these mentally ill homeless people from the ravages of the winter

One ethical question facing society is whether we have an obligation to provide mental health services to people who cannot take care of themselves.

weather because they were unable to do it for themselves. One of the homeless people who was involuntarily taken to a psychiatric facility was 40-year-old Joyce Brown, who was subsequently given a diagnosis of paranoid schizophrenia. Brown had been living on the streets on and off for years, despite efforts by her family to get her into psychiatric treatment. She refused treatment of any kind. When Brown was involuntarily hospitalized in the winter of 1988 as part of Koch's campaign, she and the American Civil Liberties Union contested her commitment and won her release on the grounds that the city had no right to incarcerate Brown if she had no intention of being treated.

One of the legal precedents of Joyce Brown's release is *Donaldson v. O'Connor* (1975). Kenneth Donaldson had been committed to a Florida state hospital for 14 years. It was Donaldson's father who originally had him committed, believing that Donaldson was delusional and therefore a danger to himself. At the time, Florida law allowed people to be committed if their mental disorders might impair their ability to manage their finances or protect themselves against being cheated by others. Throughout his hospitalization, Donaldson refused medication because it violated his Christian Science beliefs. The superintendent, O'Connor, considered this refusal to be a symptom of Donaldson's mental disorder. Even though Donaldson had been caring for himself adequately before his hospitalization and had friends who offered to help care for him if he was released from the hospital, O'Connor and the hospital continually refused Donaldson's requests for release. Donaldson sued, on the grounds that he had received only custodial care during his hospitalization and that he was not a danger to himself. He requested to be released to the care of his friends and family. The Supreme Court agreed and ruled that "a State cannot constitutionally confine . . . a nondangerous individual, who is capable of surviving safely in freedom by himself or with the help of willing and responsible family and friends."

In practice, however, most persons involuntarily committed because of grave disability do not have the American Civil Liberties Union championing their rights or the personal wherewithal to file suit. Often, these are people with few financial resources, friends, or families, who have long histories of serious mental illness. The elderly mentally ill are especially likely to be committed because of grave disability (Turkheimer & Parry, 1992). Often, these people are committed to psychiatric facilities because there are not enough less restrictive treatment facilities available in their communities, and their families do not have the ability to care for them.

Dangerousness to self The criterion of **dangerousness to self** is most often invoked when it is believed that a person is imminently suicidal. In such cases, the person is often held in an inpatient psychiatric facility for a few days while undergoing further evaluation and possibly treatment. Most states allow short-term commitments without a court hearing in emergency situations such as this. All that is needed is a certification by the attending mental-health professionals that the individual is in imminent danger to him- or herself. If the mental-health professionals judge that the person needs further treatment but the person does not voluntarily agree to treatment, they can go to court to ask that the person be committed for a longer period of time.

Dangerousness to others **Dangerousness to others** is the third criterion under which people can be committed involuntarily. If a mentally ill person is going to hurt another if set free, then society has claimed the right to protect itself against this person by holding her against her will. This may seem completely justified. Yet the appropriateness of this criterion rests on our being able to predict who will be dangerous and who will not. Some research has suggested that predictions of dangerousness tend to be wrong more often than they are correct (McNiel & Binder, 1991; Monahan & Walker, 1990). As a tragic example, the serial killer Jeffrey Dahmer was arrested and jailed in 1988 for sexually molesting a 13-year-old boy. He was released in 1990 with only a limited follow-up by mental-health professionals, despite concerns raised by his family about his mental health. Dahmer proceeded to drug, molest, kill, and dismember at least 17 additional victims over the next few years before being apprehended.

Some studies suggest that, given enough information, mental-health professionals can make short-term predictions about which individuals are most likely to be violent that are better than chance (Gardner et al., 1996; Lidz, Mulvey, & Gardner, 1993). Three of the best predictors of violence over the short term are a past history of violence, antisocial personality disorder, and substance abuse (Bonta, Law, & Hanson, 1998; Monahan, 1997; Mulvey, 1994).

Violence Among People with Mental Disorders

Are people with psychological disorders more likely to be violent than people without disorders? Until recently, sufficient research had not been done to answer this question. But as part of the Research Network on Mental Health and the Law funded by the John D. and Catherine T. MacArthur Foundation, some answers are emerging (Steadman et al., 1998; for other important research in this area, see Hodgins, 1992; Link, Andrews, & Cullen, 1992; Swanson et al., 1990; Swanson et al., 1996; Teplin, Abram, & McClelland, 1994).

These researchers followed 1,136 men and women with mental disorders for one year after being

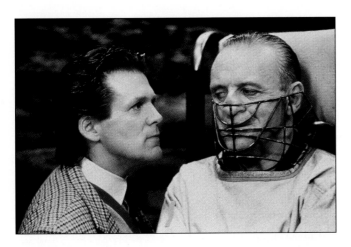

Movies and television give a distorted picture of violence among people with psychological disorders.

discharged from a psychiatric hospital, monitoring their own self-reports of violent behaviors, reports in police and hospital records, and reports by other informants, such as family members. Their records of violent activity were compared to those of 519 people living in the same neighborhoods in which the former patients resided after their hospital discharge. The community group was interviewed only once, at the end of the year-long study, and asked about violent behavior in the past 10 weeks. Serious violent acts were defined as battery that resulted in physical injury, sexual assaults, assaultive acts that involved the use of a weapon, or threats made with a weapon in hand.

The likelihood that the former patients would commit a violent act was strongly related to their diagnosis and whether they had a substance abuse problem. About 18 percent of the former patients who had diagnoses of a major mental disorder (e.g., schizophre-

nia, major depression, other psychotic disorder) *without* a history of substance abuse committed a serious violent act in the year following discharge, compared to 31 percent of those with a major mental disorder *and* a history of substance abuse, and 43 percent of those with a diagnosis of an "other" mental disorder (i.e., a personality or adjustment disorder) *and* a co-occurring substance abuse problem. The researchers were somewhat surprised to find that the former patients were most likely to commit a violent act in the first couple of months following their discharge, and less likely as the year wore on (see Figure 19.1). They suggested that patients may still be in crisis shortly after their hospitalization, and it takes some months for social support systems and treatment to begin to affect their behavior.

The rate of violence in the community sample was also strongly related to whether individuals had a history of substance abuse: 11 percent of those with a substance abuse problem committed a violent act during the year of the study, compared to 3 percent of those with no substance abuse problem. Although the overall rate of violence in the community sample was lower than in the patient sample, this difference was statistically significant only when the researchers considered violence by the former patients shortly after their discharge. By the end of that year, the former patients were no more likely to commit a violent act than the community comparison group (see Figure 19.1).

The targets of violence by both the former patients and the community comparisons were most often family members, followed by friends and acquaintances. The former patients were actually somewhat less likely than the comparison group to commit a violent act against a stranger (13.8 percent of the acts committed by former patients versus 22.2 percent of acts committed by the comparison group).

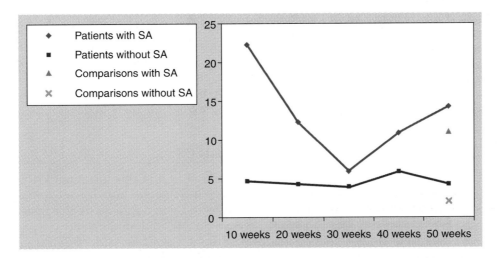

FIGURE 19.1   Likelihood of Violence. Note: SA refers to substance abuse. This figure presents the percent of patients with or without a substance abuse problem, and community comparisons with or without a substance abuse problem, who committed a violent act in the previous 10 weeks.

Source: Steadman et al., 1998.

The rates of violence committed in this study may seem high, for both the patient group and the comparison group. The patient group probably represents people with more serious psychological disorders, who are facing acute crises in their lives. The comparison group was largely from low socioeconomic backgrounds and in impoverished neighborhoods. These contextual factors may account for the relatively high rate of violence.

The researchers who conducted this study emphasized that their data show how inappropriate it is to consider "former mental patients" a homogeneous group of people who are all prone to violence. The presence of substance abuse problems was a strong predictor of violent behavior both in this group and in a group of people who had not been mental patients. Moreover, the majority of people with serious mental disorders did not commit any violent acts in the year after their discharge, particularly against random strangers, as media depictions of "former mental patients" often suggest.

Other research has suggested that violence by mentally ill women tends to be *underestimated* by clinicians (Coontz, Lidz, & Mulvey, 1994). Clinicians do not expect mentally ill women to be violent to the same degree that they expect mentally ill men to be violent. As a result, they do not probe mentally ill women for evidence regarding violence as much as they probe mentally ill men. In reality, however, mentally ill women are as likely to commit violent acts toward others as are mentally ill men. The victims of mentally ill women's violent acts are most likely to be family members; mentally ill men also are most often violent toward family members, but they commit violent acts against strangers more often than do mentally ill women (Newhill, Mulvey, & Lidz, 1995).

Racial stereotypes lead people to expect that mentally ill persons from ethnic minority groups are more likely to commit acts of violence than are White mentally ill people. There are, however, no differences among the ethnic groups in rates of violence among mentally ill people (Mulvey, 1995). Thus, new research is clarifying the true rates of violence among the mentally ill, and some predictors of violence in this group. Judgments about the dangerousness of any individual person with a mental disorder, however, remain highly subjective.

Prevalence of Involuntary Commitment

How often are people involuntarily committed to a psychiatric facility? There are sparse data to answer this question, but the available studies suggest that about one in four admissions to inpatient psychiatric facilities in the United States are involuntary, and about 15 to 20 percent of inpatient admissions in Euro-

---

TABLE 19.2
Frequency of Involuntary Admissions to Psychiatric Facilities

These data reveal the percentage of all admissions to various types of psychiatric facilities that involve involuntary commitments. Data are from the United States in 1986.

Type of Facility	Percent of All Admissions That Are Involuntary
State and county hospitals	61.6%
Multiservice mental-health organizations (e.g., community mental health centers)	46.1%
Private psychiatric hospitals	15.6%
Non-federal general hospitals	14.8%
Veterans Administration hospitals	5.6%

Source: Monahan et al., in press.

---

pean countries are involuntary (Monahan et al., in press). Admissions to state and county mental hospitals are much more likely to be involuntary than admissions to other types of hospitals (see Table 19.2).

These numbers probably underestimate the number of people coerced into mental-health care, because parents or legal guardians often "volunteer" a protesting child or incompetent adult for admission (Monahan et al., in press). One study found that nearly half of adults admitted to inpatient psychiatric facilities voluntarily said that someone other than they had initiated coming to the hospital; 14 percent of the patients were under the custody of someone else at the time they were admitted (Hoge et al., 1997). Nearly 40 percent of the legally voluntary patients believed they would have been involuntarily committed if they had not "volunteered" to be hospitalized. Some of the patients felt they had been coerced by their own therapists, who did not include them in the admission process:

Voices

I talked to him this morning. I said, "You . . . didn't even listen to me. You . . . call yourself a counselor. . . . Why did you decide to do this instead of . . . try to listen to me and understand . . . what I was going through." And he said, "Well, it doesn't matter, you know, you're going anyway." . . . He didn't listen to what I had to say. . . . He didn't listen to the situation. . . . He had decided before he ever got to the house . . .

that I was coming up here. Either I come freely or the officers would have to subdue me and bring me in.

(Monahan et al., in press)

Patients involuntarily committed often may need treatment that they cannot acknowledge they need. About half of patients who feel coerced into treatment eventually acknowledge that they needed treatment, but about half continue to believe they did not need treatment (MacArthur Research Network on Mental Health and the Law, 1998).

Procedurally, most states now mandate that persons being considered for involuntary commitment have the right to a public hearing, the right to counsel, the right to call and confront witnesses, the right to appeal decisions, and the right to be placed in the least restrictive treatment setting. In practice, however, attorneys and judges typically defer to the judgment of mental-health professionals about a person's mental illness and meeting of the criteria for commitment (Turkheimer & Parry, 1992). Thus, even the attorneys who are supposed to be upholding an individual's rights tend to acquiesce to the judgment of mental-health professionals, particularly if the attorney is court appointed, as is often the case. Again, it appears that many attorneys who are going along with the commitment of their clients are doing so because they believe the clients need treatment and that there are not enough facilities in the community to provide this treatment (Turkheimer & Parry, 1992).

Civil Rights

People who have been committed to a mental institution often feel that they have given up all their civil rights. But numerous court cases over the years have established that these people retain most of their civil rights, and have certain additional rights due to their committed status.

Right to Treatment

One fundamental right of people who have been committed is the **right to treatment.** In the past, mental patients, including those involuntarily committed and those who sought treatment voluntarily, were often warehoused. The conditions in which they lived were appalling, with little stimulation or pleasantries, let alone treatment for their disorders. In *Wyatt v. Stickney* (1972), patient Ricky Wyatt and others filed a class action suit against a custodial facility in Alabama, charging that they received no useful treatment and lived in minimally acceptable living conditions. They won

their case. A federal court ruled that the state could not simply shelter patients who had been civilly committed but had to provide them with active treatment.

The right to treatment for prison inmates Many prison inmates have severe mental disorders. For example, one study of all women felons ($n = 805$) entering prison in North Carolina in 1991 and 1992 found that 64 percent had a lifetime history of a major psychiatric disorder, including major depression, an anxiety disorder, a substance use disorder, or a personality disorder, and 46 percent had suffered such a disorder in the previous six months (Jordan et al., 1996). In addition, nearly 80 percent of these women had been exposed to an extreme trauma, such as sexual abuse, at some time in their lives. Another study of 1,272 women jail detainees awaiting trial in Chicago found that over 80 percent had a lifetime history of some psychiatric disorder, and 70 percent were symptomatic within the previous six months (Teplin, Abram, & McClelland, 1996). In both studies, the most common diagnosis the women received was a substance abuse or dependence diagnosis, but substantial percentages of the women also had major depression and/or a borderline or antisocial personality disorder. Studies of male prison inmates also find that over 50 percent can be diagnosed with a mental disorder, most often a substance use disorder or antisocial personality disorder (Collins & Schlenger, 1983; Hodgins & Cote, 1990; Neighbors et al., 1987).

Numerous court decisions have mandated that prison inmates receive necessary mental-health services just as they should receive necessary medical services. Most inmates with mental disorders do not receive services, however. A study of male inmates found that only 37 percent of those with schizophrenia or a major mood disorder received services while in jail

Many prison inmates suffer from psychological disorders, but few receive adequate treatment.

(Teplin, 1990), and a study of female inmates found that only 23.5 percent suffering schizophrenia or a major mood disorder received services in jail (Teplin, Abram, & McClelland, 1997). Depression in inmates is particularly likely to go unnoticed and untreated. Yet, suicide is the second most frequent cause of death among jail detainees, accounting for 39 percent of all inmate deaths (Patterson, 1994).

The services inmates do receive are often minimal. Drug treatments may involve only the provision of information about drugs and perhaps allowing Alcoholics Anonymous or Narcotics Anonymous to hold meetings in the prison. Treatment for schizophrenia or depression may involve only occasional visits with a prison physician who prescribes a standard drug treatment but does not have the time or expertise to follow individuals closely.

Comprehensive treatment programs focusing on the special needs of prison inmates with mental disorders have been proven successful at reducing symptoms of mental disorder, substance abuse, and recidivism. Many of these treatment programs are focused on male inmates, because they outnumber female inmates greatly. The female inmate population has grown more rapidly than the male inmate population in the last decade, however, more than tripling in that time frame (Teplin, Abram & McClelland, 1997). Female inmates may have different needs for services compared to male inmates, for several reasons. Female inmates may be more likely than male inmates to have a history of sexual and physical abuse that needs to be addressed in treatment. Female inmates are more likely than male inmates to be suffering from depression or anxiety. And female inmates are more likely than male inmates to have children for whom they will become caregivers once they are released from prison. In *Pushing the Boundaries:* Mental-Health Care for Pregnant Prison Inmates, we highlight one new program designed to meet the special needs of women inmates with children.

Right to Refuse Treatment

Another basic right is the **right to refuse treatment.** One of the greatest fears of people committed against their will is that they will be given drugs or other treatments that rob them of their consciousness, their personality, and their free will. Many states now do not allow mental institutions or prisons to administer treatments without the informed consent of patients. **Informed consent** means that a patient accepts treatment after receiving a full and understandable explanation of the treatment being offered and making a decision based on his or her own judgment of the risks and benefits of the treatment. The right to refuse treatment is not recognized in some states, however, and in

most states, this right can be overruled in many circumstances. Particularly if a patient is psychotic or manic, it may be judged that he or she cannot make a reasonable decision about treatment, and thus the decision must be made by others. The simple fact that patients have a psychiatric diagnosis, particularly if it is a diagnosis of schizophrenia, is enough to declare them incompetent to make decisions about their treatment in some jurisdictions (Grisso & Appelbaum, 1998). Yet, studies using reliable measures of patients' abilities to make rational decisions suggest that as many as 75 percent of those with schizophrenia and 90 percent of those with depression have adequate decision-making capacity (Grisso & Appelbaum, 1995).

Patients' psychiatrists and perhaps families may seek court rulings allowing them to administer treatment even if patients refuse treatment. Judges most often agree with the psychiatrists' or families' requests to force treatment on patients (Hargreaves et al., 1987). Most cases in which patients refuse treatment never get to court, however. Clinicians and family members pressure and persuade patients to accept treatment, and eventually, most patients agree to treatment after initially refusing it (Cleveland et al., 1989; MacArthur Research Network on Mental Health and the Law, 1998).

Deinstitutionalization

The patients' rights movement was aimed at stopping the warehousing and dehumanizing of mental patients and reestablishing their personal freedoms and basic legal rights. Patients' rights advocates argued that these patients could recover more fully or live more satisfying lives if they were integrated into the community, with the support of community-based treatment facilities. Many of these patients would continue to need around-the-clock care, but it could be given in halfway houses and group homes based in neighborhoods, rather than in large, impersonal institutions. Thousands of mental patients were released from mental institutions. The number of patients in large state psychiatric hospitals decreased by 75 percent over the period of this movement (Kiesler & Sibulkin, 1987). Many former mental patients who had lived for years in cold, sterile facilities, receiving little useful care, experienced dramatic increases in the quality of life upon their release.

Unfortunately, the resources to care for all the mental patients released from institutions were never adequate. There were not enough halfway houses built or community mental-health centers funded to serve the thousands of men and women who were formerly institutionalized or who would have been if the movement had not happened. Instead, these men and women

PUSHING THE BOUNDARIES

Mental-Health Care for Pregnant Prison Inmates

An innovative program in Michigan called Women and Infants at Risk (WIAR) is seeking to meet the special needs of one group of female inmates—women with substance use disorders who are pregnant while in prison. Very often these women deliver their babies in prison and then the babies are taken away to foster homes within days of their birth. This program removes these women from the general prison population and places them in a more homelike setting where they live together during the last trimester of the pregnancy and at least four months after they deliver their baby. The women are given prenatal and postnatal medical care. They attend parenting classes and are helped to form a positive bond and habits with their babies. They are helped to achieve their high school diploma if they do not already have it and receive help in increasing their employability once they are released. They are given intensive psychotherapy for substance abuse and other mental-health problems (a great many of the women have been sexually abused and suffer stress disorders). And they are linked with community services before and after they are discharged to help them live healthy, drug-free lives with their children.

Evaluations of this program are currently under way. It has already seen many individual successes, as well as failures. For many of these women who are at very high risk for drug use, success needs to be measured differently from the "happily ever after" scenario we might hope is possible. One example is Mary (Pimlott, personal communication, April 1999). At 38 years old, after several years of drug use and prostitution, she entered the WIAR program. Mary gave birth to a healthy son, obtained her GED, obtained employment, and completed the program. For two and a half years she maintained her own apartment, a job, and motherhood. A year ago, on her birthday, a party turned into a week-long binge. The baby-sitter caring for her son turned him into protective services and he was held in a residential facility. Mary returned to the streets and was arrested, and her son was put in a foster home. With remarkable courage, Mary got herself into one treatment center, then another. She contacted the foster agency and began weekly visitation with her son. She was able to support the foster mother's efforts and taught her son to call her "Mama Ginger." Since she wasn't yet allowed solitary visits with her son, she bought tickets to the circus for him and his foster family so he wouldn't miss it. Today, Mary has been drug free for six months, has regained weekend visits with her son, is working full time, and has just purchased an automobile. She attends weekly counseling sessions and support groups, beginning to look at the sexual abuse and incest issues that have been very difficult for her, and is waiting for a hearing that will determine if she has earned the right to be a full-time mother again. Mary is a success because she has the will to succeed and the courage to keep trying even after she fails. Mary remains in contact with the Women and Infants at Risk program, knowing if she needs help, they will be there.

began living in nursing homes or other types of group homes, where they received little mental-health treatment, or with their families, who were often ill-equipped to handle serious mental illness (Bachrach, 1987). Some of these people began living on the streets. This situation continues today.

Certainly not all homeless people are mentally ill, but estimates of the rates of serious mental illness among the homeless are typically around 20 to 30 percent (Koegel, Burnam, & Farr, 1988). In emergencies, these people end up in general or private hospitals that are often not equipped to treat them appropriately (Kiesler & Sibulkin, 1983).

Thus, **deinstitutionalization** began with laudatory goals, but many of these goals were never fully reached, leaving many people who would formerly have been institutionalized in mental hospitals no better off. In recent years, the financial strains on local, state, and federal governments have led to the closing of many more community mental-health centers.

One fundamental right of people committed to a mental-health facility is the right to be treated rather than just warehoused.

National Alliance for the Mentally Ill

One of the strongest advocacy groups for people with mental disorders is the National Alliance for the Mentally Ill, known as NAMI. NAMI began in 1979 when 254 people met in Madison, Wisconsin, to talk about how to help themselves and their relatives with mental disorders. The parents of people with mental disorders had suffered blame by the psychiatric community and ostracization by other family members and their communities. The sufferers of mental disorders (whom NAMI calls consumers) endured constant discrimination and lack of effective treatment. The early founders of NAMI wanted to band together to educate the public, fight discrimination, and advocate for more effective research and treatment on mental disorders. In that weekend, a grass roots family movement was born. By 1980, NAMI was incorporated and had begun making connections with other family support groups across the nation.

Today, NAMI has over 1,200 state and local affiliates and over 203,000 members across the United States, Canada, Puerto Rico, and American Samoa. It has become the nation's leading grass roots, self-help, and family advocacy organization dedicated to improving the lives of people with severe mental disorders. It remains an organization run by and for "consumers." Only people with mental disorders and their family members are elected to the NAMI Board of Directors, although mental-health professionals can become associates of NAMI.

NAMI's current Campaign to End Discrimination is a five-year effort to educate the public, challenge negative stereotypes, confront discrimination, and demand fair social policies for people with mental disorders. For example, NAMI works with the producers and directors of movies and television to overcome sensational depictions of people with mental disorders as wild and dangerous. It lobbies legislators to see that a fair share of public dollars go to research on the causes and treatments for mental disorders. It also uses public education campaigns to help people recognize how common mental disorders are, and to learn about the available treatments for mental disorders. NAMI takes a biological perspective on serious mental disorders such as schizophrenia and mood disorders, viewing them as "no-fault brain diseases."

Local chapters of NAMI also continue to provide front-line support services for consumers and their family members. Support groups are provided so families can talk about the effects of mental disorders on individuals and the families with people who understand. Referrals to mental-health specialists can be obtained for people who are just beginning to seek treatment or need a different kind of treatment. Some local chapters provide speakers who will talk with community groups or classes about mental disorders. For more information about NAMI, visit their Web site at www.NAMI.org, call 1-800-950-NAMI, or call your local chapter of NAMI listed in the phone book.

Summing Up

- People can be held in mental-health facilities involuntarily if they are judged to have grave disabilities that make it difficult for them to meet their own basic needs or that pose imminent danger to themselves or to others. Each of the criteria used to make such judgments has its flaws, however, creating concerns about the appropriateness of civil commitment.

- Short-term commitments can occur without court hearings on the certification of mental-health professionals that individuals are in emergency situations. Such commitments are most likely to happen for individuals who are actively suicidal.

- Longer-term commitments require court hearings. Patients have the rights to have attorneys and to appeal rulings.

- Other basic rights of patients are the right to be treated while being hospitalized and the right to refuse treatment (at least in some states).

- The deinstitutionalization movement was intended to stop the warehousing of mental patients and to reintegrate them into society through community-based mental-health centers. Thousands of patients were subsequently released from long-term mental institutions, but unfortunately, not enough community mental-health centers were built and funded to serve all these people's needs.

- The National Alliance for the Mentally Ill is a patients' advocacy group that works to educate the public on mental disorders and increase resources for patients and their families.

☺ CLINICIANS' DUTIES TO CLIENTS AND SOCIETY

The clinician's primary responsibility to the client is a *duty to provide competent and appropriate treatment* for the client's problems. There are a number of other duties of clinicians that deserve special mention (see *Concept Review: Clinicians' Duties*).

First, according to the ethical guidelines that clinicians are expected to follow, there is a *duty not to become involved in multiple relationships* with clients. Thus, therapists should avoid becoming involved in business or social relationships with clients, and therapists should not treat members of their own families. Such multiple relationships can cloud therapists' judgments about the best treatment for their clients. Of great concern is potential sexual involvement of therapists with clients. No matter how egalitarian a therapist is, the relationship between a therapist and client is always a relationship of power. The client comes to the therapist, vulnerable and seeking answers. The therapist is in a position to exploit the client's vulnerability. Current professional guidelines for psychologists and psychiatrists assert that it is almost never acceptable for a

---

CONCEPT REVIEW
Clinicians' Duties

Clinicians have a number of duties to the clients they serve.

To provide competent and appropriate treatment for client's problems

Not to become involved in multiple relationships with clients

To protect client confidentiality

To protect persons who might be in danger because of their clients

To report suspected child abuse

To report suspected abuse of elderly persons

To provide ethical service to culturally diverse populations

---

therapist to become sexually involved with a client, even if the client seems to be consenting to such a liaison voluntarily. Further, a therapist must not become intimately involved with a client for at least two years after the therapeutic relationship has ended. Sexual contact between a therapist and client is not just unethical—it is a felony in some states.

The vast majority of cases of sexual liaisons between therapists and clients involve male therapists and female clients. Older studies asking therapists (anonymously) if they had ever had sexual contact with their clients suggested that as many as 12 percent of male therapists and three percent of female therapists had, at some time in their careers, had such relationships with clients (Holroyd & Brodsky, 1977). Fortunately, the rates of such abuse have decreased dramatically in more recent surveys, which suggest that about 1 to 4 percent of male therapists and less than 1 percent of female therapists have had sexual liaisons with clients (Borys & Pope, 1989; Pope, Tabachnick, & Keith-Spiegel, 1987). The decrease in rates of such liaisons is probably due to a number of factors, including the criminalization of the act, malpractice suits brought against therapists who have become sexually involved with clients, and increased sensitivity to the wrongness of such relationships among professionals and the organizations that govern them. On the other hand, therapists may be simply less willing to admit to having sexual relationships with their clients now than they were in previous years due to the increased sanctions against such relationships.

Second, therapists have a *duty to protect client confidentiality*. Therapists must not reveal information

TAKING PSYCHOLOGY PERSONALLY

Guidelines for Ethical Service to Culturally Diverse Populations

I n this chapter, we have discussed several sets of guidelines that professional organizations such as the American Psychological Association and the American Psychiatric Association have put forward to guide the conduct of members of their profession. We quote here some guidelines from the American Psychological Association for ethical conduct by psychologists treating culturally diverse populations (Office of Ethnic Minority Affairs, 1993). These guidelines are meant to inspire psychologists to provide the best possible service and treatment to people who are of ethnicities or cultures different from those of the psychologists. For those of you hoping to become psychologists, these guidelines provide a sense of the competencies you will be expected to gain in your training. For those of you being treated by psychologists, the guidelines provide some expectations you may have of your psychologists, particularly if they are from different ethnicities or cultures.

1. Psychologists educate their clients to the processes of psychological intervention, such as goals and expectations; the scope and, where appropriate, legal limits of confidentiality; and the psychologists' orientations.

2. Psychologists are cognizant of relevant research and practice issues as related to the population being served.

a. Psychologists acknowledge that ethnicity and culture impact on behavior and take those factors into account when working with various ethnic/racial groups.

b. Psychologists seek out educational and training experiences to enhance their understanding and thereby address the needs of these populations more appropriately and effectively. These experiences include cultural, social, psychological, political, economic, and historical material specific to the particular ethnic group being served.

c. Psychologists recognize the limits of their competencies and expertise. Psychologists who do not possess knowledge and training about an ethnic group seek consultation with, and/or make referrals to, appropriate experts as necessary.

d. Psychologists consider the validity of a given instrument or procedure and interpret resulting data, keeping in mind the cultural and linguistic characteristics of the person being assessed. . . .

3. Psychologists recognize ethnicity and culture as significant parameters in understanding psychological processes.

---

about their clients, including clients' identities, to anyone except with the clients' permission or under special circumstances. One of those special circumstances occurs when the therapist believes the client needs to be committed involuntarily and must convince a court of this.

Another condition under which therapists can violate their clients' confidentiality happens when they believe clients may harm other people. Based on the decision in *Tarasoff v. Regents of the University of California* (1974), in many jurisdictions clinicians now have a *duty*

to protect persons who might be in danger because of their clients. Tatiana Tarasoff was a student at the University of California at Berkeley in the late 1960s. A graduate student named Prosenjit Poddar was infatuated with Tarasoff, who had rejected him. Poddar told his therapist in the student counseling service that he planned to kill Tarasoff when she returned from vacation. The therapist informed the campus police, who picked Poddar up for questioning. Poddar agreed to leave Tarasoff alone, and the campus police released him. Two months later, Poddar killed Tarasoff. Tarasoff's parents

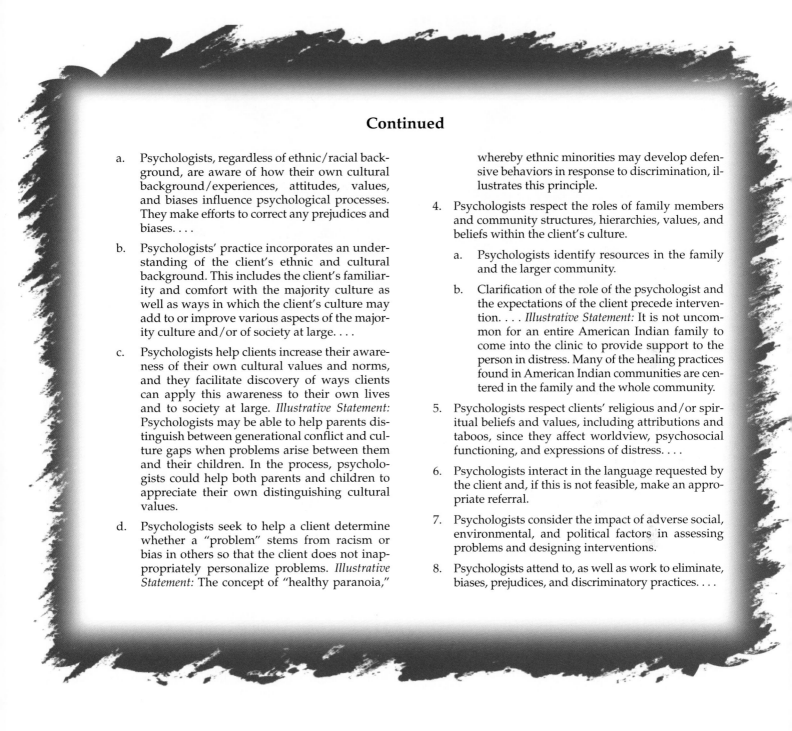

Continued

a.   Psychologists, regardless of ethnic/racial background, are aware of how their own cultural background/experiences, attitudes, values, and biases influence psychological processes. They make efforts to correct any prejudices and biases. . . .

b.   Psychologists' practice incorporates an understanding of the client's ethnic and cultural background. This includes the client's familiarity and comfort with the majority culture as well as ways in which the client's culture may add to or improve various aspects of the majority culture and/or of society at large. . . .

c.   Psychologists help clients increase their awareness of their own cultural values and norms, and they facilitate discovery of ways clients can apply this awareness to their own lives and to society at large. *Illustrative Statement:* Psychologists may be able to help parents distinguish between generational conflict and culture gaps when problems arise between them and their children. In the process, psychologists could help both parents and children to appreciate their own distinguishing cultural values.

d.   Psychologists seek to help a client determine whether a "problem" stems from racism or bias in others so that the client does not inappropriately personalize problems. *Illustrative Statement:* The concept of "healthy paranoia,"

whereby ethnic minorities may develop defensive behaviors in response to discrimination, illustrates this principle.

4.   Psychologists respect the roles of family members and community structures, hierarchies, values, and beliefs within the client's culture.

a.   Psychologists identify resources in the family and the larger community.

b.   Clarification of the role of the psychologist and the expectations of the client precede intervention. . . . *Illustrative Statement:* It is not uncommon for an entire American Indian family to come into the clinic to provide support to the person in distress. Many of the healing practices found in American Indian communities are centered in the family and the whole community.

5.   Psychologists respect clients' religious and/or spiritual beliefs and values, including attributions and taboos, since they affect worldview, psychosocial functioning, and expressions of distress. . . .

6.   Psychologists interact in the language requested by the client and, if this is not feasible, make an appropriate referral.

7.   Psychologists consider the impact of adverse social, environmental, and political factors in assessing problems and designing interventions.

8.   Psychologists attend to, as well as work to eliminate, biases, prejudices, and discriminatory practices. . . .

sued the university, arguing that the therapist should have protected Tarasoff from Poddar. The California courts agreed and established that therapists have a duty to warn persons who are threatened by their clients during therapy sessions and to take actions to protect these persons.

In addition, in most states, therapists have a *duty to report suspected child abuse* to the proper authorities even when such reports violate their clients' confidentiality. These authorities then are required to investigate these reports and determine whether to file

charges and to remove children from potentially abusive situations. In some states, therapists also have a *duty to report suspected abuse of elderly persons.* Confidentiality is considered by therapists one of the most fundamental rights of clients, but in these cases, the courts have ruled that confidentiality must be broken to protect innocent people that clients might harm or are harming.

Finally, in recent years, a new duty has been added to the clinicians' obligations: *to provide ethical service to culturally diverse populations.* We highlight this duty in

Therapists have duties to provide appropriate treatment for their clients, to avoid multiple relationships with clients, and to protect clients' confidentiality.

the *Taking Psychology Personally:* Guidelines for Ethical Service to Culturally Diverse Populations (p. 696).

Summing Up

- First and foremost, clinicians have a duty to provide competent care to their clients.
- Clinicians must also avoid multiple relationships with their clients, particularly sexual relationships.
- They must protect their clients' confidentiality, except under special circumstances. One of these occurs when therapists believe clients need to be committed involuntarily.
- Two other duties therapists have to society require them to break clients' confidentiality: the duty to protect people clients are threatening to harm and the duty to report suspected child or elder abuse.
- Recently, clinicians have been charged to provide ethical service to diverse populations.

☉ FAMILY LAW AND MENTAL-HEALTH PROFESSIONALS

In years past, the law had little to say about what could and could not happen within a family. Husbands could beat their wives, parents could beat their children, and the courts tended to turn away from intervening in the "sanctity of the family." Wife battering and child abuse certainly still go on without sufficient intervention by law authorities, but there have been remarkable increases in the rights of individual family members to be protected against the abuses of other family members. Thus, for example, rape within a marriage is now illegal in most jurisdictions, and the law puts limits on the ways that parents can punish or discipline their children. Amidst this revolution in the rights of individual family members has been tremendous change in the structure of families and in what units are recognized as families. The high divorce rate now means that a large percentage of children will live much of their childhood in single-parent homes with parents who have remarried or with their divorced biological parents in complicated joint custody arrangements. In addition, many types of nontraditional families are gaining legal recognition, including gay and lesbian couples and cohabiting (but not married) heterosexual couples and their children.

These many changes in family life and in laws regarding families have led to increases in the number and complexity of court cases requiring decisions that can greatly affect the individual families involved and set precedents that will affect families. Increasingly, the courts have turned to mental-health professionals for assistance in formulating and carrying out laws regarding families and children. Here we consider three areas where mental-health professionals have become heavily involved: child custody disputes between divorcing parents, child maltreatment cases, and charges by adults of sexual abuse during their childhood.

Child Custody Disputes

Ninety percent of the time, parents who are divorcing can agree on the custody arrangements for their children without taking disputes to court (Melton & Wilcox, 1989). If parents cannot agree, however, the court must help determine how much authority each parent will have in decisions for the children and how much contact each parent will have with the children. These decisions obviously can have tremendous impact on a child's daily life. They can determine where a child lives, the financial resources available to the child, the religion the child is raised in, the type of school the child attends, and of course, how much the child sees each parent. The decisions can also have great impact on the lives of the parents. In addition to determining how much contact parents will have with their children, courts can put restraints on parents' freedom to make certain decisions for their children, such as parents' ability to practice Christian Science (which discourages medical intervention for many illnesses) or to move a child to another state where a noncustodial parent will not be able to see the child.

The law requires that custody decisions be made "in the best interest of the child." Determining what custody arrangements are in the best interest of the child can be very difficult. Each parent will often try to convince a judge that he or she is the better parent and that the child would prefer to be with him or her. Each parent can bring family members, friends, and hired mental-health professionals to court to try to convince a judge to rule in his or her favor. In the midst of all this highly charged, conflicting information, judges often rely on their own intuitions or theories about what is best for children (Thompson, Tinsley, Scalora, & Parke, 1989).

Alternately, many states have designated preferred types of custody arrangements in the belief that children usually respond best to a particular type of custody. For example, the presumption in the law used to be that mothers were the best caregivers for their children. In custody disputes mothers almost always received custody of their children. The prevailing view today is that access to both parents is best for most children, so many states are mandating joint custody of children. Another recent trend is to award grandparents visitation rights to children, even when opposed by children's parents. Once again, this is based on a belief that children usually benefit from exposure to their grandparents (Thompson, Tinsley, Scalora, & Parke, 1989). Although it would be nice if such mandates were based on solid psychological research, most of the time they are the results of waves of enthusiasm for what "everybody knows" will benefit children and families (Melton & Wilcox, 1989). Moreover, these mandates do not reflect the complexity and idiosyncrasies of individual cases. Studies of the wholesale application of the joint custody mandate in California found that, although many children benefit from exposure to both parents, many children suffer as a result of joint custody (Maccoby & Mnookin, 1992). In particular, children whose parents fought constantly while they were married often continue in such joint custody arrangements to be caught in their parents' conflicts, as their parents are forced to deal with each other to comply

Therapists are often involved in child custody disputes, interviewing parents and children to obtain information that can be used to settle the dispute.

with the arrangements. These children might have been better served by single-parent custody arrangements.

Mental-health professionals are increasingly being asked to assist courts in making custody decisions. As noted, sometimes mental-health professionals are hired by the parents in dispute, but sometimes mental-health professionals are brought in by the courts to make independent assessments of what would be "in the best interest of the child." Table 19.3 lists some of the guidelines that the American Psychological Association (1994)

TABLE 19.3
Guidelines for Expert Evaluators in Child Custody Proceedings

These guidelines are meant to help mental-health professionals in their evaluations of child custody cases.

1. The child's interests and well-being are paramount. Parents competing for custody, as well as others, may have legitimate concerns, but the child's best interests must prevail.

2. The focus of the evaluation is on parenting capacity of the parents, the psychological and developmental needs of the child, and the resulting fit.

3. The role of the psychologist is as a professional expert. The psychologist does not act as a judge, who makes the ultimate decision applying the law to all relevant evidence. Neither does the psychologist act as an advocating attorney, who strives to present his or her client's best possible case. The psychologist, in a balanced, impartial manner, informs and advises the court and the prospective custodians of the child of the relevant psychological factors pertaining to the custody issue.

4. Psychologists generally avoid conducting child custody evaluations in a case in which they served in therapeutic roles for the children or their immediate families or in which they had other involvements that could compromise their own objectivity.

5. The psychologist refrains from drawing conclusions not adequately supported by the data. The psychologist strives to acknowledge to the court any limitations in the methods or data used.

6. The psychologist engaging in child custody evaluations is aware of how biases regarding age, gender, race, ethnicity, national origin, religion, sexual orientation, disability, language, culture, and socioeconomic status may interfere with an objective evaluation and recommendations. The psychologist recognizes and strives to overcome any such biases or withdraws from the evaluation.

From American Psychological Association, 1994, Guidelines for Expert Evaluations in Child Custody Proceedings.

---

recommends that psychologists follow when acting as expert evaluators in child custody proceedings.

This last guideline listed in Table 19.3 recognizes that all of us, including mental-health professionals, have implicit assumptions about what constitutes good parenting, and these assumptions are influenced by the culture in which we are raised. Thus, a person raised in a somewhat stoic, emotionally unexpressive household or culture may be uncomfortable with parents who are highly expressive toward their children, including openly expressing both praise and criticism. If this expressiveness is characteristic of the culture from which the parents and children come, it may be inappropriate for the mental-health professional to judge this as "bad parenting." In addition, expectations for how a parent should act toward a child are heavily influenced by the parent's gender. A mother who works 60 to 80 hours per week in a high-pressure job may be judged more harshly as neglecting her children than a father who works 60 to 80 hours in a similar job. Mental-health professionals must be vigilant that such assumptions or biases do not contaminate their evaluations of parents in custody disputes.

As we shall see, these issues and ethical guidelines also pertain to a mental-health professional's role in evaluating children and adults involved in child maltreatment cases.

Child Maltreatment Cases

Psychologists and other mental-health professionals are now involved in every phase of child maltreatment cases. The most recent and controversial change in mental-health professionals' roles in child maltreatment cases is the use of mental-health professionals to investigate the claims of maltreatment or to determine if maltreatment is likely to happen in the future. A psychologist may interview all the parties involved in a case. The psychologist may administer psychological tests to the parents and children. Then the psychologist may act as an expert witness in court, testifying on what is known about such cases from the research literature.

Although mental-health professionals are accustomed to interviewing children and parents in these highly sensitive cases because they have experience working with troubled children and families, there have been several cases in which mental-health professionals appear to have asked leading questions in their interviews, particularly of children, which then have contaminated the evidence for a trial. For example, charges were brought against teachers at the McMartin Preschool in California for sexually molesting children in their care. The charges began with one child reporting strange activities at the preschool. Then the other children were interviewed by members of the local police force, members of the prosecutor's office, and mental-health professionals. Videotapes of these interviews suggest that some of the children were pressured into "reporting" sexual activities at the preschool. They were told that other children had already admitted that these activities had happened and that these were the "good children." The interviewers made it clear that as soon as a child said what the interviewers were looking for, the interview would be over. At times, words were put directly into the children's mouths. All of this was done by adults who truly believed that abuse had happened and wanted to apprehend and punish the people who had perpetrated the abuse. Eventually, many of the children reported extraordinary and bizarre sexual encounters with their preschool teachers. In the end, however, most of the charges had to be dropped against the adults because the evidence was so contaminated by the interview techniques used in the early investigation that it could not be believed.

Other concerns have been raised about mental-health professionals providing expert testimony in child maltreatment trials and other types of trials (Melton & Limber, 1989). The least controversial role mental-health professionals can play as expert witnesses is to explain behaviors of children or adults that might seem confusing or conflicting with their claims. For example, in child maltreatment cases, children often will not report their abuse to adults until long after the abuse has occurred or has begun, they are often vague or give conflicting information in their reports, and they often retract their accusations when they see the consequences of these accusations. These behaviors might suggest that such children are lying about the accusations. A psychologist can point out (usually for the prosecution) that children who have been abused often exhibit these kinds of behaviors, so they do not necessarily indicate that children are lying.

More concerns have been raised about mental-health professionals giving expert opinions about whether the accused fits the profile of the "typical" abuser or the child fits the profile of a "typical" abused child (Melton & Limber, 1989). First, the presence of a similarity between an individual adult or child and some profile does not necessarily mean that an individual is an abuser or is abused. Conversely, if an adult or a child does not fit the abuser or abused profile, it does not necessarily mean that no abuse took place. Second, the profiles described in such testimony are often based on clinical experience rather than on firm research. The statement by an expert witness that someone fits the profile of an abuser or the abused can be taken more seriously than it should by juries and judges who do not understand the probabilistic nature of the kinds of predictions mental-health professionals can make. A example of controversy over a psychologist providing expert testimony came in the trial of

O. J. Simpson for the murders of Nicole Brown Simpson and Ronald Goldman. After interviewing Simpson for 80 hours, a psychologist was willing to testify for the defense that Simpson did not fit the profile of a battering husband with the potential to kill his wife. This psychologist was heavily criticized, in part because her willingness to testify about whether Simpson met the profile of a violent, battering man raised all the concerns mentioned here.

In recent years, there has been a great deal of discussion and research on proper techniques for interviewing children involved in court cases and on the ethical obligations of mental-health professionals serving as expert witnesses. Although some tragic mistakes have been made and there is still much to be learned, mental-health professionals do play important and worthwhile roles in legal proceedings, especially those involving families. Mental-health professionals have experience in talking with distressed children and adults about sensitive topics. They may be able to gather more information more objectively because of this expertise, without further traumatizing the children and adults being interviewed.

The Repressed/Recovered/False Memory Debate

There has been a profound increase in the last 20 years in public and professional awareness of the sexual and physical abuse of women and children. As a society, we are admitting it happens too frequently, and we are beginning to do something about it. Currently, one of the greatest controversies in clinical psychology is centered on claims by adults that they were abused as children but repressed the memories of the abuse for years, only to recover these memories as adults. This phenomenon is variously referred to as the **repressed memory debate**, the *recovered memory debate*, and the *false memory debate*. An example of a claim of a repressed memory follows (Harvey & Herman, 1994, pp. 300–301; this is a compilation of several different cases):

CASE STUDY

Emily B. is a 45-year-old married woman. She and her husband recently relocated to the Boston area where she'd grown up. Emily has two siblings and an aging paternal aunt in this area. She was referred to psychotherapy by a local psychiatric emergency service, where she appeared in a state of confusion and despair following a reunion with her sister, whom she had not seen for many years. . . .

Emily is the youngest of three children raised by their father and two paternal aunts following their mother's untimely death when Emily was 4 years old. The aunts were extraordinarily severe in their approach to punishment and discipline. Emily recalls that she and her siblings were frequently beaten with belts and "other objects," locked in closets, blindfolded for long periods of time, deprived of food, and subjected to verbal assaults and humiliation. Their father did not engage in this abuse, but he also did not protect them. At some point in her childhood—"maybe I was 10 or 11, but maybe I was younger than that"—Emily's father began molesting her. Once the abuse began, it escalated to include oral, anal, and vaginal penetration, and by the time she was 13, it assumed violent and sadistic proportions. As far as Emily knows now, the abuse continued until she ran away at age "15 or 16."

When Emily left home, she cut off all contact with her family. By the time she met and married her husband, she had "completely forgotten" the sexual abuse. "I never forgot the beatings, though." Among the major precipitants to Emily's remembrance of the sexual abuse are her return to the geographic area in which she was raised and her renewed contact with an older sister. It was while visiting this sister and hearing "one family horror story after another" that Emily began feeling extremely agitated and fearful. One night, she was awakened with terrifying dreams and for several days afterward was flooded with memories of her father's abuse. Since then, Emily has spent a great deal of time with her sister and has confirmed many of her new memories. She has learned that her sister and brother were also sexually abused by their father.

In thousands of such cases in the United States, Canada, and Europe, the adults who have remembered such experiences have filed suit against the people they believe abused then. Often, such suits are encouraged by therapists who view this as part of the therapy of empowerment (Bass & Davis, 1988). Many courts will waive the statute of limitations to allow the accused to be tried for such crimes, even though they may have occurred decades ago.

On one side of the controversy over these claims are mental-health professionals who believe it is their role to promote the welfare of the women who have been abused by helping them recover their memories of abuse and resolve their feelings about these memories any way possible. On the other side of the controversy are mental-health professionals who argue there is little or no scientific evidence that repression exists and that many claims of the recovery of repressed memories are due to clients succumbing to suggestions by their therapists (Loftus & Ketcham, 1994). That is, at a time when clients are vulnerable and seeking answers for their current psychological distress, their therapists pressure them directly or indirectly to "recall" memories of the abuse. The clients confabulate— they fill in and create memories of abuse when, in reality, they were never abused. In *Viewpoints: The*

Repressed Memory Debate, we describe the evidence for and against both sides of this debate.

It is important to remember that in the midst of this controversy are women in pain over what they believe happened to them long ago and families that have been torn apart by allegations of sexual abuse. This is an area where fundamental issues in the science and practice of psychology collide with fundamental issues in the law about how to weigh conflicting and indefinite evidence.

Summing Up

- Psychologists and other mental-health professionals can provide a number of services in family law courts hearing cases of custody disputes, charges of child maltreatment, or charges by adults that they were sexually abused as children.

- Mental-health professionals can help to investigate cases, employing proper interviewing techniques with great caution to obtain information that is as objective as possible without further traumatizing the parties involved.

- They can act as expert witnesses, providing the court with information about research relevant to a case.

- They can assist in getting family members into appropriate treatment if necessary after a case is decided.

- In each of these areas of involvement, however, there are pitfalls to avoid. In interviewing people for a case, the mental-health professional must be careful not to be overly suggestive, leading a person to fabricate a story that is not true or to misremember events.

- In giving expert testimony, the mental-health professional must not overstate the research evidence pertinent to a case or make inappropriate generalizations from the research to a specific case being tried.

- In assisting parties in getting treatment, the mental-health professional must follow all the ethical guidelines of clinicians, including that of not being involved in multiple relationships with the parties.

- Child custody, child maltreatment, and repressed memory cases create highly charged atmospheres with great potential for further harm of the children and adults involved. Mental-health professionals must act with the greatest objectivity and skill to help reduce this harm rather than add to it.

VIEWPOINTS

The Repressed Memory Debate

Do some child abuse victims repress memories of their abuse, only to recover these memories in adulthood? Or are their recovered memories actually false memories, created by the suggestions of a zealous therapist and the needs of a vulnerable client? These questions have been referred to as the repressed memory debate.

Both sides in this debate can marshal evidence in support of their views. Most of the evidence for the phenomenon of repressed memories comes from studies of people who are known to have been abused or who self-report abuse. Researchers then typically look for evidence that these people have forgotten or repressed their abuse at some time in the past. For example, Williams (1995) surveyed 129 women who had documented histories of having been sexually abused sometime between 1973 and 1975. These women, who were between 10 months and 12 years old at the time of their abuse, were interviewed about 17 years after their abuse. Williams found that 49 of these 129 women had no memory of or had forgotten about the abuse events that were documented. Briere and Conte (1993) located 450 therapy patients who identified themselves as abuse victims. Briere and Conte asked these people if there had ever been a time before their eighteenth birthdays when they "could not remember" their abuse. Fifty-nine percent answered "yes" to this question. As a final example, Herman and Harvey (1997) examined interviews of 77 women who had reported memories of childhood trauma and found that 17 percent spontaneously reported they had had some delayed recall of the trauma and 16 percent said there had been a period of complete amnesia following the trauma.

Nonbelievers in repressed memories have raised questions about the methods and conclusions of these studies (Loftus, Garry, & Feldman, 1994; Pope et al., 1998). For example, regarding the Williams (1995) study, it turns out that 33 of the 49 women who said they could not remember the specific abuse incidents they were asked about could remember other abuse incidents during their childhoods. Thus, they had not completely forgotten or repressed all memories of abuse; they simply could not remember the specific incident about which they were being asked. Williams did not give any additional information about

the 16 women who could remember no incidents of molestation in their childhoods. They may have been too young to remember these incidents—memory for anything that happens before the age of about 3 tends to be very bad.

Regarding the Briere and Conte study, concerns have been raised about the question they asked their subjects, which required them to report if there ever was a time before they were 18 years old when they could not remember the abuse that occurred. Answering this question requires some fancy retrospection: People were asked not only to remember times when they did not remember events but also to determine whether during those times, they might have been unable to remember events if they had tried. It is not clear that the subjects of this study understood all these nuances in the question they were being asked. A greater problem with this study is that all of the subjects identified themselves, before the study began, as having recovered repressed memories of sexual abuse.

Nonbelievers in repressed memories also cite numerous studies from the literature on eyewitness identification and testimony indicating that people can be made to believe that events occurred when, in fact, they never did (Ceci & Bruck, 1995; Loftus, 1993; Read & Lindsay, 1997). For example, Elizabeth Loftus and her colleagues developed a method for instilling a specific childhood memory of being lost on a specific occasion at the age of 5 (Loftus & Pickrell, 1995). This method involved a trusted family member engaging the subject in a conversation about the time he or she was lost (Loftus, 1993, p. 532):

Chris (14 years old) was convinced by his older brother Jim that he had been lost in a shopping mall when he was 5 years old. Jim told Chris this story as if it were the truth: "It was 1981 or 1982. I remember that Chris was 5. We had gone shopping in the University City shopping mall in Spokane. After some panic, we found Chris being led down the mall by a tall, oldish man (I think he was wearing a flannel shirt). Chris was crying and holding the man's hand. The man explained that he had found Chris walking around crying his eyes out just a few moments before and was trying to help him find his parents."

Continued

Just two days later, Chris recalled his feelings about being lost: "That day I was so scared that I would never see my family again. I knew that I was in trouble." On the third day, he recalled a conversation with his mother: "I remember Mom telling me never to do that again." On the fourth day: "I also remember that old man's flannel shirt." On the fifth day, he started remembering the mall itself: "I sort of remember the stores." In his last recollection, he could even remember a conversation with the man who found him: "I remember the man asking me if I was lost." . . .

A couple of weeks later, Chris described his false memory and he greatly expanded on it. "I was with you guys for a second and I think I went over to look at the toy store, the Kay-bee Toy and uh, we got lost and I was looking around and I thought, 'Uh-oh, I'm in trouble now.' You know. And then I . . . I thought I was never going to see my family again. I was really scared you know. And then this old man, I think he was wearing a blue flannel, came up to me. . . . He was kind of old. He was kind of bald on top. . . . He had like a ring of gray hair . . . and he had glasses."

Other studies have found that repeatedly asking adults about childhood events that never actually happened leads a substantial percentage (perhaps 20 to 40 percent) eventually to "remember" these events and even explain them in detail (Hyman & Billings, 1998; Schachter, 1999). In addition, Mazzoni and Loftus (1998) found that if a psychologist suggests that an individual's dreams reflect repressed memories of childhood events, a majority of subjects subsequently report that the events depicted in their dreams actually happened.

Critics of this line of work question the application of these studies to claims of repressed memories of sexual abuse (Gleaves & Freyd, 1997). They argue that people might be willing to go along with experimenters or therapists who try to convince them that they were lost in a shopping mall as a child, but it is unlikely that people would be willing to go along with therapists or experimenters trying to convince them they were sexually abused if this abuse did not happen. Abuse is such a terrible thing to remember, and the social consequences of admitting the abuse and confronting the abuser are so negative that people simply would not claim it were true if it were not true.

Freyd (1996) further argues that childhood abuse and incest are exactly the kinds of events that might be blocked, repressed, or forgotten for some period of time because they so greatly violate a child's expectations that caregiving adults can be trusted and the child's desperate need to trust adults. To survive, the child may dissociate from the ongoing experience of abuse and thus form no explicit memory of the abuse, although an implicit memory lays blocked from consciousness. Freyd links this betrayal trauma theory to basic research in cognitive and perceptual psychology on the formation and retrieval of memories.

The repressed memory debate will not go away or be resolved soon. It is one of the most contentious issues currently in clinical and research psychology.

⊙ BIO-PSYCHO-SOCIAL INTEGRATION

There has been perhaps less integration of biological, social, and psychological viewpoints in the law's approach to issues of mental health than in the mental-health field itself. The rules governing the insanity defense suggest that the law takes a biological perspective on psychological disorders, conforming to the belief that a mental disease is like a medical disease. Similarly, civil commitment rules require certification that a person has a mental disorder or disease before he or she can be committed, further legitimizing psychiatric diagnostic systems that are based on medical models.

The patients' rights movement was led, in part, by people who believed that there was no such thing as a mental disorder and that people said to have such disorders were the victims of their culture's intolerance of anyone different. These critics focused on the social forces driving people's lawful and unlawful behaviors and called upon society to change its behavior and stop treating mental patients as diseased children in need of care by the state.

In each of the areas discussed in this chapter, however, there are mental-health professionals advocating a more integrated and complex view of mental disorders than that traditionally held by the law. These professionals are trying to educate judges, juries, and laypeople that some people have biological, psychological, or social predispositions to disorders and that other biological, psychological, or social factors can interact with predispositions to trigger the onset of disorders or trigger certain manifestations of disorders. What is most difficult to explain is the probabilistic nature of the predictions we can make about mental disorders and the behavior of people with these disorders. That is, a predisposition or certain recent life experiences may make it more likely that a person will develop a disorder or engage in a specific behavior (such as a violent behavior), but they do not determine the disorder or the specific behavior. We all prefer to have predictions about the future that are definite, especially when we are making decisions that will determine a person's freedom or confinement. That kind of definitiveness is not possible, however, given our present knowledge of the ways biological, psychological, and social forces interact to influence people's behavior.

Chapter Summary

- One of the fundamental principles of law is that, in order to stand trial, an accused individual must have a reasonable degree of rational understanding of the charges against her and the proceedings of the trial and must be able to participate in her defense. People who do not have an understanding of what is happening to them in a courtroom and who cannot participate in their own defense are said to be incompetent to stand trial. Defendants who have histories of psychotic disorders, who have current symptoms of psychosis, or who perform poorly on tests of important cognitive skills may be judged incompetent to stand trial.

- Five different rules for judging the acceptability of the insanity defense have been used in recent history: the M'Naghten Rule, the irresistible impulse rule, the Durham Rule, the ALI Rule, and the American Psychiatric Association definition. Each of these rules requires that the defendant be diagnosed with a mental disorder, and most of the rules require it be shown that the defendant did not appreciate the criminality of his or her act or could not control his or her behaviors at the time of the crime. A new verdict, guilty but mentally ill, has been introduced following public uproar over recent uses of the insanity defense in high-profile cases. Persons judged guilty but mentally ill are confined for the duration of a regular prison term but with the presumption that they will be given psychiatric treatment. Mental-health professionals have raised a number of concerns about the insanity defense. It requires post hoc judgments of a defendant's state of mind at the time of the crime. In addition, the rules governing the insanity defense presume that people have free will and usually can control their actions. These presumptions contradict some models of normal and abnormal behavior that suggest that behavior is strongly influenced by biological, psychological, and social forces.

- Civil commitment is the procedure through which a person may be committed for treatment in a mental institution against his or her will. In most jurisdictions, three criteria are used to determine whether individuals may be committed: if they suffer from grave disability that impairs their ability to care for their own basic needs, if they are imminent dangers to themselves, or if they are imminent dangers to others. Each of these criteria requires a subjective judgment on the part of clinicians and often predictions about the future that clinicians may not be that good at making. In particular, the prediction of who will pose a danger to others in the future is a difficult one to make, and it is often made incorrectly.

- When being considered for commitment, patients have the right to an attorney, to a public hearing, to call and confront witnesses, to appeal decisions, and to be placed in the least restrictive treatment setting. (The right to a hearing is often waived for short-term commitments in emergency settings.) Once committed, patients have the right to be treated and the right to refuse treatment.

- The goal of the deinstitutionalization movement was to move mental patients from custodial mental-health facilities, where they were isolated and received little treatment, to community-based mental-health centers. Thousands of patients were released from mental institutions. Unfortunately, community-based mental-health centers have never been fully funded or supported, leaving many former mental patients with few resources in the community.

- Mental-health professionals have a number of duties to their clients and to society. They have a duty to provide competent care, to avoid multiple relationships with clients, and to uphold clients' confidentiality, except in unusual circumstances. They have a duty to warn people whom their client is threatening and to report suspected child or elder abuse.

- Mental-health professionals are becoming increasingly active in family law cases, including child custody disputes, cases of child maltreatment, and charges by adults that they were sexually molested as children. In child custody disputes, the law and professional guidelines require that decisions be made in the best interest of the child. Mental-health professionals are often asked by courts to make objective evaluations of the parenting capabilities of both parents and about what would be the best "fit" between parent and child. In child maltreatment cases, mental-health professionals must take care not to contaminate the testimony of witnesses, especially children, by being overly suggestive or pressuring witnesses to provide certain types of evidence. Concerns have been raised about mental-health professionals acting as expert witnesses in such cases, particularly when they provide opinions about whether the accused or the victims fit "typical" profiles of accused people or victims. Finally, there is a recent wave of charges being brought by adults against people they believe sexually abused them in childhood. Their memories of this abuse were repressed most of their lives. These memories are variously known as *repressed memories, recovered memories,* or *false memories.* Believers in repressed memories argue that the experience of child abuse is so terrible that the mind protects itself by repressing memories of the abuse. People who recover memories of abuse as adults must be helped to work through these memories and often to confront their abusers. Nonbelievers in repressed memories argue that there is little scientific evidence for the phenomenon of repression and that false memories of abuse are being created in vulnerable clients by their therapists. Mental-health professionals can be found on both sides of this debate.

Key Terms

Critical Thinking Questions

1. What should happen to someone who continues to be incompetent to stand trial for months or even years after a crime was committed?

2. What accounts for the widespread belief in the lay public that many criminals plead the insanity defense successfully and "get off"?

3. Should all committed patients be allowed to refuse all kinds of treatment?

4. Why might it be that women and minorities who are judged incompetent to stand trial are more seriously disturbed than are White males who are judged incompetent to stand trial?

5. Should research findings have a strong effect on legal rulings or is each case so individual and idiosyncratic that we cannot apply general research findings to these individual cases? Why?

6. Given that it is often difficult to objectively determine the truth of accusations of abuse, should we be inclined to believe the accuser or the accused who says she or he did not commit the abuse?

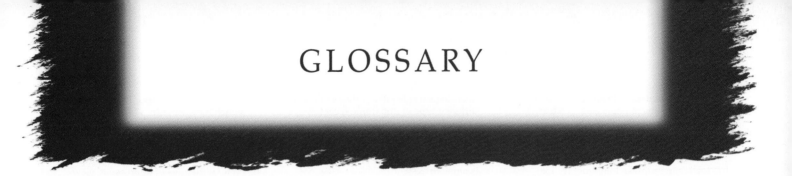

GLOSSARY

A

abstinence violation effect what happens when a person attempting to abstain from alcohol use ingests alcohol and then endures conflict and guilt by making an internal attribution to explain why he or she drank, thereby making him or her more likely to continue drinking in order to cope with the self-blame and guilt (p. 608)

acculturation extent to which a person identifies with his or her group of origin and its culture or with the mainstream dominant culture (p. 100)

acute stress disorder disorder similar to posttraumatic stress disorder but occurs within one month of exposure to the stressor and does not last more than four weeks; often involves dissociative symptoms (p. 218)

adoption study study of the heritability of a disorder by finding adopted people with a disorder and then determining the prevalence of the disorder among their biological and adoptive relatives, in order to separate out contributing genetic and environmental factors (p. 41)

adrenal-cortical system neuroendocrine system controlling the hypothalamus, important in the body's adjustment to emergency situations (p. 178)

affective flattening negative symptom of schizophrenia that consists of a severe reduction or complete absence of affective responses to the environment (p. 337)

agnosia impaired ability to recognize objects or people (p. 656)

agoraphobia anxiety disorder characterized by fear of places and situations in which it would be difficult to escape such as enclosed places, wide open spaces, and crowds (p. 192)

agranulocytosis condition characterized by a deficiency of granulocytes, which are substances produced by the bone marrow and fight infection; 1–2% of people who take clozapine develop this condition (p. 361)

akathesis agitation caused by neuroleptic drugs (p. 360)

akinesia condition marked by slowed motor activity, a monotonous voice, and an expressionless face, resulting from taking neuroleptic drugs (p. 360)

alcohol abuse diagnosis given to someone who uses alcohol in dangerous situations, fails to meet obligations at work or at home due to alcohol use, and has recurrent legal or social problems as a result of alcohol use (p. 577)

alcohol dependence diagnosis given to someone who has a physiological tolerance to alcohol, spends a lot of time intoxicated or in withdrawal, or continues to drink despite significant legal, social, medical, or occupational problems that result from alcohol (often referred to as alcoholism) (p. 577)

alcohol-induced dementia loss of intellectual abilities, including memory, abstract thinking, judgment, and problem solving, often accompanied by changes in personality, such as increases in paranoia (p. 581)

alcohol-induced persisting amnesic disorder permanent cognitive disorder caused by damage to the central nervous system, consisting of Wernicke's encephalopathy and Korsakoff's psychosis (p. 581)

ALI Rule legal principle stating that a person is not responsible for criminal conduct if he or she lacks the capacity to appreciate the criminality (wrongfulness) of the act or to conform his or her conduct to the requirements of the law as a result of mental disease (p. 684)

alogia deficit in both the quantity of speech and the quality of its expression (p. 338)

alternate form reliability extent to which a measure yields consistent results when presented in different forms (p. 104)

altruistic suicide suicide committed by people who believe that taking their own lives will benefit society (p. 309)

Alzheimer's disease progressive neurological disease that is the most common cause of dementia (p. 658)

amenorrhea cessation of the menses (p. 493)

American Psychiatric Association definition of insanity definition of insanity stating that people cannot be held responsible for their conduct if, at the time they commit crimes, as the result of mental disease or mental retardation they are unable to appreciate the wrongfulness of their conduct (p. 685)

amnesia impairment in the ability to learn new information or to recall previously learned information or past events (p. 674)

amnesic disorders cognitive disorders involving deficits in the ability to learn new information and recall previously learned information (p. 674)

amphetamines stimulant drugs that can produce symptoms of euphoria, self-confidence, alertness, agitation, paranoia, perceptual illusions, and depression (p. 589)

amyloid class of proteins that can accumulate between cells in areas of the brain critical to memory and cognitive functioning (p. 661)

anal stage psychosexual stage that occurs between the ages of 18 months to 3 years; focus of gratification is the anus, and children are interested in toilet activities; parents can cause children to be fixated in this stage by being too harsh and critical during toilet training (p. 48)

analogue study study that creates conditions in the laboratory meant to represent conditions in the real world (p. 80)

animal studies studies that attempt to test theories of psychopathology using animals (p. 84).

animal type phobias extreme fear of specific animals that may induce immediate and intense panic attacks and cause the individual to go to great lengths to avoid the animals (p. 194)

anomic suicide suicide committed by people who experience a severe disorientation and role confusion because of a large change in their relationship to society (p. 309)

anorexia nervosa eating disorder in which people fail to maintain body weights that are normal for their ages and heights and suffer from fears of becoming fat, distorted body images, and amenorrhea (p. 492)

antagonist drugs drugs that block or change the effects of an addictive drug, reducing desire for the drug (p. 605)

anterograde amnesia deficit in the ability to learn new information (pp. 384, 674)

antianxiety drugs drugs used to treat anxiety, insomnia, and other psychological symptoms (p. 140)

anticonvulsant drugs class of drugs used to treat mania and depression (pp. 140, 284)

antidepressant drugs drugs used to treat the symptoms of depression, such as sad mood, negative thinking, and disturbances of sleep and appetite; three common types are monoamine oxidase inhibitors, tricyclics, and serotonin reuptake inhibitors (p. 138)

antipsychotic drugs drugs used to treat psychotic symptoms such as delusions, hallucinations, and disorganized thinking (pp. 138, 284)

antisocial personality disorder pervasive pattern of criminal, impulsive, callous, and/or ruthless behavior, predicated upon disregard for the rights of others and an absence of respect for social norms (p. 415)

anxiety syndrome encompassing a range of symptoms including somatic, emotional, cognitive, and behavioral symptoms (p. 178)

anxiety sensitivity belief that bodily symptoms have harmful consequences (p. 185)

anxious-fearful personality disorders category including avoidant, dependent, and obsessive-compulsive personality disorders that is characterized by a chronic sense of anxiety or fearfulness and behaviors intended to ward off feared situations (p. 428)

aphasia impaired ability to produce and comprehend language (p. 656)

applied tension technique technique used to treat blood-injection-injury phobias in which the therapist teaches the client to increase his or her blood pressure and heart rate, thus preventing the client from fainting (p. 202)

apraxia impaired ability to initiate common voluntary behaviors (p. 656)

arousal phase in the sexual response cycle, psychological experience of arousal and pleasure as well as physiological changes, such as the tensing of muscles and enlargement of blood vessels and tissues (also called the excitement phase) (p. 524)

Asperger's disorder pervasive developmental disorder characterized by deficits in social skills and activities; similar to autism, but does not include deficits in language or cognitive skills (p. 474)

assessment process of gathering information about a person's symptoms and their possible causes (p. 96)

asthma condition in which the airways (the trachea and bronchi) constrict, making it hard to breathe (p. 622)

ataque de nervios attack of the nerves, syndrome in Hispanic cultures that closely resembles anxiety and depressive disorders (p. 210)

attention-deficit/hyperactivity disorder (ADHD) syndrome marked by deficits in controlling attention, inhibiting impulses, and organizing behavior to accomplish long-term goals (p. 444)

atypical antipsychotics new drugs that seem to be even more effective in treating schizophrenia than phenothiazines without the same

neurological side effects; they bind to a different type of dopamine receptor than other neuroleptic drugs (p. 360)

auditory hallucination auditory perception of phenomena that is not real, such as hearing a voice when one is alone (p. 334)

autism childhood disorder marked by deficits in social interaction (such as a lack of interest in one's family or other children), communication (such as failing to modulate one's voice to signify emotional expression), and activities and interests (such as engaging in bizarre, repetitive behaviors) (p. 474)

automatic thoughts thoughts that come to mind quickly and without intention, causing emotions such as fear or sadness (p. 207)

aversion therapy treatment that involves the pairing of unpleasant stimuli with deviant or maladaptive sources of pleasure in order to induce an aversive reaction to the formerly pleasurable stimulus (p. 556)

aversive classical conditioning pairing of alcohol with a substance that will interact with it to cause nausea or vomiting (such as disulfiram) in order to make alcohol itself a conditioned stimulus to be avoided (p. 606)

avoidant personality disorder pervasive anxiety, sense of inadequacy, and fear of being criticized that leads to the avoidance of most social interactions with others and to restraint and nervousness in social interactions (p. 429)

avolition inability to persist at common goal-directed activities (p. 338)

B

barbiturates drugs used to treat anxiety and insomnia that work by suppressing the central nervous system and decreasing the activity level of certain neurons (pp. 140, 584)

behavior genetics study of the processes by which genes affect behavior and the extent to which personality and abnormality are genetically inherited (p. 38)

behavioral therapy type of psychotherapy that involves the use of reinforcement and punishment to overcome a patient's undesirable behaviors (p. 285)

behavior therapy type of therapy that focuses on changing a person's specific behaviors by replacing unwanted behaviors with desired behaviors (pp. 148, 514)

behavioral assessment in behavior therapy, the therapist's assessment of the clients' adaptive and maladaptive behaviors and the triggers for these behaviors (p. 148)

behavioral assignments giving a client "homework" to practice new behaviors or gather new information between therapy sessions (p. 153)

behavioral observation method for assessing the frequency of a client's

behaviors and the specific situations in which they occur (p. 114)

behavioral theories theories that focus on an individual's history of reinforcements and punishments as causes for abnormal behavior (p. 51)

behavioral theories of depression view that depression results from negative life events that represent a reduction in positive reinforcement; sympathetic responses to depressive behavior then serve as positive reinforcement for the depression itself (p. 268)

behaviorism study of the impact of reinforcements and punishments on behavior (p. 23)

bell and pad method treatment for enuresis in which a pad placed under a sleeping child to detect traces of urine sets off a bell when urine is detected, awakening the child to condition him or her to wake up and use the bathroom before urinating (p. 464)

benzodiazepines drugs that reduce anxiety and insomnia (pp. 140, 187, 584)

bingeing eating a large amount of food in one sitting (p. 497)

binge-eating disorder eating disorder in which people compulsively overeat either continuously or on discrete binges but do not behave in ways to compensate for the overeating (p. 499)

binge/purge type of anorexia nervosa type of anorexia nervosa in which periodic bingeing or purging behaviors occur along with behaviors that meet criteria for anorexia nervosa (p. 494)

biological approach view that biological factors cause and should be used to treat abnormality (p. 30)

bipolar disorder disorder marked by cycles between manic episodes and depressive episodes; also called manic-depression (p. 248)

bipolar I disorder form of bipolar disorder in which the full symptoms of mania are experienced while depressive aspects may be more infrequent or mild (p. 256)

bipolar II disorder form of bipolar disorder in which only hypomanic episodes are experienced, and the depressive component is more pronounced (p. 256)

blackout amnesia for events that occurred during one's intoxication (p. 576)

blood-injection-injury type phobias extreme fear of seeing blood or an injury or receiving an injection or other invasive medical procedures, which causes a drop in heart rate and blood pressure and fainting (p. 195)

body dysmorphic disorder syndrome involving obsessive concern over some part of the body the individual believes is defective (p. 397)

borderline personality disorder syndrome characterized by rapidly shifting and unstable mood, self-concept, and interpersonal relationships as well as impulsive behavior and transient dissociative states (p. 421)

breathing-related sleep disorders type of dyssomnia that involves repeated episodes of upper-airway obstruction during sleep; obstructive sleep apnea (p. 630)

bulimia nervosa eating disorder in which people engage in bingeing (episodes involving a loss of control over eating and consumption of an abnormally large amount of food) as well as behave in ways to prevent weight gain from the binges, such as self-induced vomiting, excessive exercise, or abuse of purging drugs (such as laxatives) (p. 497)

buspirone new drug that appears to alleviate symptoms of general anxiety for some, but has very few side effects and is unlikely to lead to physical dependence (p. 208)

butyrophenone class of drug that can reduce psychotic symptoms; includes the drug haloperidol (Haldol) (p. 138)

C

caffeine a chemical compound with stimulant effects (p. 592)

calcium channel blockers class of drugs used to treat mania and depression (pp. 140, 284)

cannabis substance that causes feelings of well-being, perceptual distortions, and paranoid thinking (p. 597)

case study in-depth analysis of an individual (p. 72)

castration anxiety boys' fear that their fathers will retaliate against them by castrating them; this fear serves as motivation for them putting aside their desires for their mothers and aspiring to become like their fathers (p. 48)

catalepsy condition characterized by trancelike states and a waxy rigidity of the muscles (p. 249)

cataplexy episodes of sudden loss of muscle tone lasting from a few seconds to minutes (p. 630)

catatonia disorder of movement involving immobility or excited agitation, often accompanied by speech disturbances (pp. 249, 335)

catatonic excitement state of constant agitation and excitability (p. 335)

catharsis expression of emotions connected to memories and conflicts which leads to the release of energy used to keep these memories in the unconscious (pp. 22, 44, 146)

caudate nucleus part of the basal ganglia which is involved in carrying the impulses to the thalamus that direct primitive patterns of primitive behavior, such as aggression, sexuality, and bodily excretion (p. 239)

causal attribution explanation for why an event occurred (pp. 53, 270)

central core part of brain that includes brain stem and regulates basic life processes (p. 35)

cerebrovascular disease a disease that occurs when the blood supply to the brain is blocked, causing tissue damage to the brain (p. 663)

cerebrum part of the brain that regulates complex activities such as speech and analytical thinking (p. 35)

childhood disintegrative disorder pervasive developmental disorder in which children develop normally at first and later show permanent loss of basic skills in social interactions, language, and/or movement (p. 474)

chlorpromazine an antipsychotic drug (pp. 137, 359)

civil commitment forcing a person into a mental health facility against his or her will (p. 687)

classical conditioning form of learning in which a neutral stimulus becomes associated with a stimulus that naturally elicits a response, thereby making the neutral stimulus itself sufficient to elicit the same response (p. 51)

client-centered therapy (CCT) Carl Rogers's form of psychotherapy that consists of an equal relationship between therapist and client as the client searches for his or her inner self, receiving unconditional positive regard and an empathic understanding from the therapist (pp. 56, 148)

clozapine one of the newest, most effective drugs for schizophrenia. It does not block neuroreceptors like neuroleptics, but instead appears to bind to a newly discovered type of dopamine receptor, labeled D4 (p. 352)

cocaine central nervous system stimulant that causes a rush of positive feelings initially but that can lead to impulsiveness, agitation, and anxiety and that can cause withdrawal symptoms of exhaustion and depression (p. 586)

cognitions thoughts or beliefs (pp. 24, 53)

cognitive-behavioral therapy treatment that works by changing negative patterns of thinking and by solving concrete problems through brief sessions in which a therapist helps a client challenge negative thoughts, consider alternative perspectives, and take effective actions (pp. 286, 516)

cognitive disorders dementia, delirium, or amnesia characterized by impairments in cognition (such as deficits in memory, language, or planning) and caused by a medical condition or by substance intoxication or withdrawal (p. 654)

cognitive theories theories that focus on belief systems and ways of thinking as causes for abnormal behavior (p. 53)

cognitive therapy therapeutic approach that focuses on changing people's maladaptive thought patterns (p. 151)

communication deviance vague and indefinite communications including misperceptions and misinterpretations, odd or inappropriate word usage, and fragmented and disruptive interactions (p. 355)

communication disorder developmental disorder involving deficits in communication abilities, such as

stuttering or poor articulation (p. 466)

community mental-health centers clinic that provides mental-health care based in the community through teams of social workers, therapists, and physicians who coordinate care (p. 158)

community mental-health movement movement that attempted to provide coordinated mental-health services to people in community-based centers; initiated in 1963 by President John Kennedy (p. 158)

compulsions repetitive behaviors or mental acts that the individual feels he or she must perform (p. 234)

computerized tomography (CT) method of analyzing brain structure by passing narrow X-ray beams through a person's head from several angles to produce measurements from which a computer can construct an image of the brain (p. 105)

concordance rate probability that both twins will develop a disorder if one twin has the disorder (p. 41)

concurrent validity extent to which a test yields the same results as other measures of the same phenomenon (p. 103)

conditioned response (CR) in classical conditioning, response that first followed a natural stimulus but that now follows a conditioned stimulus (p. 51)

conditioned stimulus (CS) in classical conditioning, previously neutral stimulus that when paired with a natural stimulus becomes itself sufficient to elicit a response (p. 51)

conditions of worth set of external standards some people feel they must meet in order to be acceptable (p. 205)

conduct disorder syndrome marked by chronic disregard for the rights of others, including specific behaviors such as stealing, lying, and engaging in acts of violence (p. 446)

conscious mental contents and processes of which we are actively aware (p. 46)

construct validity extent to which a test measures only what it is intended to measure (p. 103)

content validity extent to which a measure assesses all the important aspects of a phenomenon that it purports to measure (p. 103)

context environment and circumstances in which a behavior occurs (p. 5)

contingencies of self worth "if-then" rules concerning self-worth, such as "I'm nothing if a person I care about doesn't love me" (p. 275)

continuous reinforcement schedule system of behavior modification in which certain behaviors are always rewarded or punished, leading to rapid learning of desired responses (p. 52)

continuous variable factor that is measured along a continuum (such as 0–100) rather than falling into a discrete category (such as "diagnosed with depression") (p. 74)

control group in an experimental study, group of subjects whose experience resembles that of the experimental group in all ways, except that they do not receive the key manipulation (p. 80)

control theory cognitive theory that explains people's variance in behavior in certain domains in terms of their beliefs that they can or cannot effectively control situations in that domain (p. 54)

conversion disorder syndrome marked by a sudden loss of functioning in some part of the body, usually following an extreme psychological stressor (p. 388)

coronary heart disease (CHD) chronic illness that is the leading cause of death in the United States, occurring when the blood vessels that supply the heart with oxygen and nutrients are narrowed or closed by plaque, resulting in a myocardial infarction (heart attack) when closed completely (p. 623)

correlation coefficient statistic used to indicate the degree of relationship between two variables (p. 75)

correlational study method in which researchers assess only the relationship between two variables and do not manipulate one variable to determine its effects on another variable (p. 74)

cortisol hormone that helps the body respond to stressors, inducing the "fight or flight" response (pp. 179, 266)

course length of time that a disorder typically lasts and the likelihood that the client will relapse following the current episode of the disorder (p. 120)

covert sensitization therapy pairing of mental images of alcohol with other images of highly unpleasant consequences resulting from its use in order to create an aversive reaction to the sight and smell of alcohol and reduce drinking (p. 606)

crisis intervention programs that help people who are highly suicidal and refer them to mental-health professionals (p. 316)

cross-sectional study study that examines people at one point in time, but does not follow them over time (p. 75)

cue exposure and response prevention therapy to reduce relapse among alcoholics by tempting them with stimuli that induce cravings to drink while preventing them from actually drinking, allowing them to habituate to the cravings and reduce temptation (p. 607)

cultural relativism view that norms among different cultures set the standard for what counts as normal behavior, which implies that abnormal behavior can only be defined relative to these norms; no universal definition of abnormality is therefore possible; only definitions of abnormality relative to a specific culture are possible (p. 5)

cyclothymic disorder milder but more chronic form of bipolar disorder that consists of alternation between

hypomanic episodes and mild depressive episodes over a period of at least two years (p. 256)

D

dangerousness to others legal criterion for involuntary commitment that is met when a person would pose a threat or danger to other people if not incarcerated (p. 685)

dangerousness to self legal criterion for involuntary commitment that is met when a person is imminently suicidal or a danger to him- or herself as judged by a mental health professional (p. 688)

day treatment centers centers where people with mental-health problems can obtain treatment all day, including occupational and rehabilitative therapies, but live at home at night (p. 158)

death darers individuals who are ambivalent about dying and take actions that increase their chances of death, but do not guarantee they will die (p. 301)

death ignorers individuals that intend to end their lives but do not believe this means the end of their existence (p. 301)

death initiators individuals that intend to die, but believe that they are simply speeding up an inevitable death (p. 301)

death seekers individuals that clearly and explicitly seek to end their lives (p. 300)

defense mechanisms strategies the ego uses to disguise or transform unconscious wishes (p. 46)

degradation process in which the receiving neuron releases an enzyme into the synapse, breaking down neurotransmitters into other biochemicals (p. 36)

deinstitutionalization movement in which thousands of mental patients were released from mental institutions; a result of the patients' rights movement that was aimed at stopping the dehumanizing of mental patients and restoring their basic legal rights (p. 693)

delirium cognitive disorder that is acute and usually transient, including disorientation and memory loss (p. 672)

delirium tremens (DTs) symptoms that result during severe alcohol withdrawal, including hallucinations, delusions, agitation, and disorientation (p. 581)

delusion of reference false belief that external events, such as people's actions or natural disasters, relate somehow to one's self (p. 331)

delusions fixed beliefs with no basis in reality (pp. 250, 330)

delusions of thought control idea that someone else has the power to determine what one feels by means of facial expression, gesture or posturing (p. 332)

demand characteristics factors in an experiment that suggest to participants how the experimenter would like them to behave (p. 80)

dementia cognitive disorder in which a gradual and usually permanent decline of intellectual functioning occurs; can be caused by medical condition, substance intoxication, or withdrawal (p. 655)

dependent personality disorder pervasive selflessness, need to be cared for, and fear of rejection that lead to total dependence on and submission to others (p. 430)

dependent variable factor that one seeks to predict (p. 69)

depersonalization disorder syndrome marked by frequent episodes of feeling detached from one's own body and mental processes, as if one were an outside observer of oneself; symptoms must cause significant distress or interference with one's ability to function. (p. 386)

depression state marked by either a sad mood or a loss of interest in one's usual activities, as well as feelings of hopelessness, suicidal ideation, psychomotor agitation or retardation, and trouble concentrating (p. 248)

depressive realism phenomenon whereby depressed people make more realistic judgments as to whether they can control actually uncontrollable events than do nondepressed people, who exhibit an illusion of control over the same events (p. 271)

desensitization treatment used to reduce anxiety by rendering a previously threatening stimulus innocuous by repeated and guided exposure to the stimulus under nonthreatening circumstances (p. 556)

detoxification first step in treatment for substance-related disorders in which a person stops using the substance and allows it to fully exit the body (p. 605)

developmental coordination disorder disorder involving deficits in the ability to walk, run, or hold on to objects (p. 465)

diagnosis label affixed to a set of symptoms that tend to occur together (p. 96)

Diagnostic and Statistical Manual of Mental Disorders (DSM) official manual for diagnosing mental disorders in the United States, containing a list of specific criteria for each disorder, how long a person's symptoms must be present to qualify for a diagnosis, and requirements that the symptoms interfere with daily functioning in order to be called disorders (p. 118)

dialectical behavior therapy cognitive-behavioral intervention aimed at problem-solving skills, interpersonal skills, and managing negative emotions (p. 318)

dichotomous thinking inflexible way of thinking in which everything is viewed in either/or terms (p. 314)

differential diagnosis determination of which of two or more possible diagnoses is most appropriate for a client (p. 98)

discomfort criterion for abnormality that suggests that only behaviors that cause a person great distress should be labeled as abnormal (p. 8)

disease model view that alcoholism (or drug addiction) is an incurable physical disease, like epilepsy or diabetes, and that only total abstinence can control it (p. 600)

disorder of written expression developmental disorder involving deficits in the ability to write (p. 465)

disorganized schizophrenia syndrome marked by incoherence in cognition, speech, and behavior as well as flat or inappropriate affect (also called hebephrenic schizophrenia) (p. 341)

dissociation process whereby different facets of an individual's sense of self, memories, or consciousness become split off from one another (p. 372)

dissociative amnesia loss of memory for important facts about a person's own life and personal identity, usually including the awareness of this memory loss (p. 384)

dissociative fugue disorder in which a person moves away and assumes a new identity, with amnesia for the previous identity (p. 382)

dissociative identity disorder (DID) syndrome in which a person develops more than one distinct identity or personality, each of which can have distinct facial and verbal expressions, gestures, interpersonal styles, attitudes, and even physiological responses (p. 376)

dissociative symptoms symptoms involved in acute stress disorder that indicate a detachment from the trauma and from ongoing events (p. 218)

disulfiram drug that produces an aversive physical reaction to alcohol and is used to encourage abstinence; commonly referred to as Antabuse (p. 606)

dizygotic (DZ) twins twins who average only 50 percent of their genes in common because they developed from two separate fertilized eggs (p. 41)

Dodo bird verdict conclusion that psychotherapy is not better than other types of therapies; all types of therapies are seen as equally effective (p. 163)

dopamine neurotransmitter in the brain, excess amounts of which have been thought to cause schizophrenia (pp. 262, 351)

double bind position parents (especially mothers) who later become schizophrenic place children in by communicating conflicting messages (e.g., being verbally abusive to the child while also being physically comforting); children learn not to trust their own feelings and develop distorted views of themselves in these situations (p. 355)

double depression disorder involving a cycle between major depression and dysthymic disorder (p. 251)

double-blind experiment study in which both the researchers and the participants are unaware of which experimental condition the participants are in, in order to prevent demand effects (p. 82)

Down syndrome chromosomal disorder in which chromosome 21 is present in triplicate and causes mental retardation; often characterized by flat-round faces, almond-shaped eyes, short statures, rapid aging, and memory loss (p. 468)

dramatic-emotional personality disorders category including antisocial, borderline, narcissistic, and histrionic personality disorders that is characterized by dramatic and impulsive behaviors that are maladaptive and dangerous (p. 415)

drug addicts people who are physically dependent on substances and who suffer from withdrawal when not taking the substances (p. 568)

Durham Rule legal principle stating that the presence of mental disorder is sufficient to absolve a criminal of responsibility for a crime (p. 684)

dyspareunia genital pain associated with sexual intercourse (p. 533)

dyssomnia primary sleep disorder that involves abnormalities in the amount, quality, or timing of sleep (p. 625)

dysthymic disorder type of depression that is less severe than major depression but more chronic; diagnosis requires the presence of a sad mood or anhedonia, plus two other symptoms of depression, for at least two years during which symptoms do not remit for two months or longer (p. 250)

E

echolalia occurrence in which a person repeats what he or she just heard instead of generating his or her own words; a communication deficit associated with autism (pp. 342, 476, 656,)

echopraxia repetitive imitation of another person's movements (p. 342)

ego part of the psyche that channels libido into activities in accordance superego and within the constraints of reality (p. 44)

egoistic suicide suicide committed by people who feel alienated from others and lack social support (p. 309)

Electra complex girls' realization during the phallic stage that they don't have a penis, and their horror at the discovery; they realize that their mothers also don't have penises, and disdain females for this deficit; an attraction for the father ensues, following the belief that he can provide a penis (p. 48)

electroconvulsive therapy (ECT) treatment for depression that involves the induction of a brain seizure by passing electrical current through the patient's brain while he or she is anesthetized (pp. 141, 281)

electroencephalogram (EEG) graph of the electrical activity in the brain, recorded from electrodes placed on the surface of the scalp (p. 106)

elimination disorders disorders in which a child shows frequent uncontrolled urination or defecation far beyond the age at which children usually develop control over these functions (p. 462)

emergency reaction bodily response enabling humans to fight off or flee from threats to their safety; quick energy is needed and supplied with the release of glucose and hormones (p. 178)

encopresis diagnosis given to children who are at least 4 years old and who defecate inappropriately at least once a month for 3 months (p. 464)

endocrine system system of glands that produces many different hormones (pp. 35, 37)

enlarged ventricles fluid-filled spaces in the brain that are larger than normal and suggest atrophy or deterioration in other brain tissue (p. 349)

enmeshed families family in which there is extreme interdependence in family interactions, so that the boundaries between the identities of individual members are weak and easily crossed (p. 510)

enuresis diagnosis given to children over 5 years of age who wet the bed or their clothes at least twice a week for 3 months (p. 462)

event-related potential (ERP) EEG measure of the brain's electrical activity (potentials) as it corresponds to stimuli (events) in the environment (p. 106)

executive functions functions of the brain that involve the ability to sustain concentration, use abstract reasoning and concept formation, anticipate, plan, program and initiate purposeful behavior, self-monitor, and shift from maladaptive patterns of behavior to more adaptive ones (p. 419)

exhibitionism obtainment of sexual gratification by exposing one's genitals to involuntary observers (p. 552)

existential anxiety universal human fear of limits and the responsibilities of one's existence (p. 205)

existential theory view that upholds personal responsibility for discovering one's personal values and meanings in life and then living in accordance with them; people face existential anxiety due to awareness of their life's finitude, and must overcome both this anxiety and obstacles to a life governed by the meanings they give to it, in order to achieve mental health and avoid maladaptive behavior (p. 55)

experimental group in an experimental study, group of participants that receives the key manipulation (p. 80)

experimental study study in which the independent variables are directly manipulated and the effects on the dependent variable are examined (p. 79)

expressed emotion family interaction style in which families are overinvolved with each other, overprotective of the disturbed family member, voice self-sacrificing attitudes to the disturbed family member, while simultaneously being critical, hostile, and resentful of this member (p. 355)

expressive language disorder disorder involving deficits in the ability to express oneself through language (p. 466)

external validity extent to which a study's results can be generalized to phenomena in real life (p. 77)

extinction abolition of a learned behavior (p. 52)

F

face validity extent to which a measure seems to measure a phenomenon on face value, or intuition (p. 103)

factitious disorder by proxy disorder in which the individual creates an illness in another individual in order to gain attention (p. 387)

factitious disorders disorders marked by deliberately faking physical or mental illness to gain medical attention (p. 386)

family history study study of the heritability of a disorder involving identifying people with the disorder and people without the disorder and then determining the disorder's frequency within each person's family (p. 40)

family systems theories theories that see the family as a complex system that works to maintain the status quo (p. 61)

family systems therapy psychotherapy that focuses on the family, rather than a single individual, as the source of problems; family therapists challenge communication styles, disrupt pathological family dynamics, and challenge defensive conceptions in order to harmonize relationships among all members and within each member (pp. 61, 156)

family therapy type of psychotherapy in which the patient and his or her family are treated as a unit (p. 515)

feedback loops system in which changes in one element result in changes in a second element, then the changes in the second element feedback to change the first element again (p. 31)

female orgasmic disorder in women, recurrent delay in or absence of orgasm after having reached the excitement phase of the sexual response cycle (also called anorgasmia) (p. 532)

female sexual arousal disorder in women, recurrent inability to attain or maintain the swelling-lubrication response of sexual excitement (p. 531)

fetal alcohol syndrome occurs when a mother abuses alcohol during pregnancy; causes lowered IQ, increased risk for mental retardation, distractibility, and difficulties with learning from experience (pp. 470, 582)

fetishism paraphilia in which a person uses inanimate objects as the preferred or exclusive source of sexual arousal (p. 550)

fight-or-flight response physiological changes in the human body that occur in response to a perceived threat, including secretion of glucose, endorphins, and hormones as well as elevation of heart rate, metabolism, blood pressure, breathing, and muscle tension (pp. 178, 619)

five-factor model personality theory that posits that any individual's personality is organized along five broad dimensions of personality: neuroticism, extraversion, openness to experience, agreeableness, and conscientiousness (p. 434)

flooding behavioral technique in which a client is intensively exposed to the feared object until the anxiety diminishes (pp. 150, 202)

formal thought disorder state of highly disorganized thinking (also known as loosening of associations) (p. 355)

Fragile X syndrome chromosomal disorder in which the tip of the X chromosome breaks off, causing severe to profound mental retardation, speech defects, and severe deficits in interpersonal interactions (p. 470)

free association method of uncovering unconscious conflicts in which the client is taught to talk about whatever comes to mind, without censoring any thoughts (p. 145)

frontal cortex largest brain region in humans; it facilitates the planning and production of thoughts, language, emotional expression, and action (p. 350)

frotteurism obtainment of sexual gratification by rubbing one's genitals against or fondling the body parts of a nonconsenting person (p. 553)

G

gamma-aminobutyric acid (GABA) neurotransmitter that carries inhibiting messages from one neuron to another (p. 208)

gender identity disorder condition in which a person believes that he or she was born with the wrong sex's genitals and is fundamentally a person of the opposite sex (p. 557)

gender identity one's perception of oneself as male or female (p. 557)

gender role what society considers to be the appropriate set of behaviors for males or females (p. 557)

gender role expectations expectations for an individual's behavior based on societal norms for that individual's gender (p. 6)

general adaptation syndrome physiological changes that occur when an organism reacts to stress; includes the stages of alarm, resistance, and exhaustion (p. 619)

general paresis disease that leads to paralysis, insanity, and eventually death; discovery of this disease helped to establish a connection between biological diseases and mental disorders (p. 21)

generalizability extent to which the results of a study generalize to, or inform us about, people other than those who were studied (p. 73)

generalized anxiety disorder (GAD) anxiety disorder characterized by chronic anxiety in daily life (p. 204)

genital stage psychosexual stage that occurs around the age of 12, when children's sex drives reemerge; if a child has successfully resolved the phallic stage, interest in sex turns toward heterosexual relationships (p. 48)

global assumptions fundamental beliefs that encompass all types of situations (p. 54)

glove anesthesia state in which people lose all feeling in one hand as if they were wearing a glove that wiped out all physical symptoms (p. 389)

glutamate neurotransmitter involved in bipolar disorder (p. 263)

grandiose delusions elevated thinking about the self, ideas of omnipotence and the taking of credit for occurrences not personally facilitated (p. 331)

grave disability legal criterion for involuntary commitment that is met when a person is so incapacitated by a mental disorder that he or she cannot care for his or her own basic needs such as food, clothing, or shelter and his or her survival is threatened as a result (p. 687)

group comparison study study that compares two or more distinct groups on some variable of interest (p. 74)

group therapy therapy conducted with groups of people rather than one-on-one between a therapist and client (p. 157)

guided mastery techniques interventions designed to increase health-promoting behaviors by providing explicit information about how to engage in these behaviors as well as opportunities to engage in these behaviors in increasingly challenging situations (p. 639)

guilty but mentally ill (GBMI) verdict that requires a convicted criminal to serve the full sentence designated for his or her crime, with the expectation that he or she will also receive treatment for mental illness (p. 686)

H

halfway houses organizations that offer people with long-term mental-health problems a structured, supportive environment to live in while they reestablish a job and ties to their friends and family (p. 158)

hallucinations perceptual experiences that are not real (pp. 250, 334)

hallucinogens substances, including LSD and MDMA, that produce perceptual illusions and distortions even in small doses (p. 596)

health psychology study of the effects of psychological factors on health (p. 618)

histrionic personality disorder syndrome marked by rapidly shifting moods, unstable relationships, and an intense need for attention and approval, which is sought by means of overly dramatic behavior, seductiveness, and dependence (p. 426)

homeostasis status quo, or a point of equilibrium (p. 61)

hopelessness sense that the future is bleak and there is no way of making it more positive (p. 313)

human laboratory study experimental study involving human participants; see also experimental study (p. 80)

humanistic theory view that people strive to develop their innate potential for goodness and self-actualization; abnormality arises as a result of societal pressures to conform to unchosen dictates that clash with a person's self-actualization needs and from an inability to satisfy more basic needs, such as hunger (p. 55)

humanistic therapy type of therapy in which the goal is to help the client discover his or her place in the world and to accomplish self-actualization through self-exploration; is based on the assumption that the natural tendency for humans is toward growth (p. 147)

hypersomnia type of dyssomnia that involves being chronically sleepy and sleeping for long periods at a time (p. 630)

hypertension condition in which the blood supply through the blood vessels is excessive and can lead to deterioration of the cell tissue and hardening of the arterial walls but cannot be traced to genetics or a specific organic cause (p. 624)

hypoactive sexual desire disorder condition in which a person's desire for sex is diminished to the point where it causes him or her significant distress or interpersonal difficulties and is not due to transient life circumstances or other sexual dysfunction (p. 530)

hypochondriasis syndrome marked by chronic worry that one has a physical symptom or disease that one clearly does not have (p. 396)

hypothalamic-pituitary-adrenal axis (HPA axis) three key components of the neuroendocrine system which work together in a feedback system interconnected with the limbic system and the cerebral cortex (p. 266)

hypothalamus component of the central core that regulates eating, drinking, sex, and basic emotions; abnormal behaviors involving any of these activities may be the result of dysfunction in the hypothalamus (pp. 35, 178, 512)

hypothesis testable statement about two or more variables and the relationship between them (p. 69)

hysterical disorders syndrome in which people lose functioning or feeling in some part of the body due to psychological, rather than biological, causes (p. 22)

I

id most primitive part of the unconscious that consists of drives and impulses seeking immediate gratification (p. 44)

immune system system that protects the body from disease-causing microorganisms and affects our susceptibility to diseases (p. 624)

immunocompetence estimation of the robustness or vulnerability of the immune system (p. 625)

implosive therapy see flooding (p. 150)

in vivo exposure technique of behavioral therapy in which clients are encouraged to experience the stimuli that they fear directly (p. 150)

incidence number of new cases of a disorder that develop during a specified period of time (p. 121)

incompetent to stand trial legal status of an individual who lacks a rational understanding of the charges against him or her, an understanding of the proceedings of his or her trial, or the ability to participate in his or her own defense (p. 681)

independent variable factor that is manipulated by the experimenter or used to predict the dependent variable (p. 70)

informed consent procedure (often legally required prior to treatment administration) in which a patient receives a full and understandable explanation of the treatment being offered and makes a decision about whether to accept or refuse the treatment (p. 692)

inhalants solvents such as gasoline, glue, or paint thinner that one inhales to produce a high and that can cause permanent central nervous system damage as well as hepatitis and liver and kidney disease (p. 585)

insanity legal term denoting a state of mental incapacitation during the time a crime was committed (p. 681)

insanity defense occurrence in which people accused of a crime state that they cannot be held responsible for their illegal acts because they were mentally incapacitated at the time of the act (p. 682)

Insanity Defense Reform Act 1984 law that affects all federal courts and about half of the state courts that finds a person not guilty by reason of insanity if it is shown that, as a result of mental disease or mental retardation, the accused was unable to appreciate the wrongfulness of his or her conduct at the time of the offense (p. 685)

insomnia type of dyssomnia that involves difficulty in initiating or maintaining sleep; chronically nonrestorative sleep (p. 628)

intelligence test test to assess a person's intellectual strengths and weaknesses (p. 105)

internal reliability extent to which a measure yields similar results among its different parts as it measures a single phenomenon (p. 104)

internal validity extent to which all factors that could extraneously affect a study's results are controlled within a laboratory study (p. 80)

interpersonal circumplex model personality theory that is based on the idea that personality is made up of two primary dimensions: dominance vs. submission and nurturance vs. cold-heartedness; these dimensions cross to create eight octants in a circumplex that represent how the two dimensions blend together to form an individual's personality (p. 435)

interpersonal theories of depression theories that view the causes of depression as rooted in interpersonal relationships (p. 275)

interpersonal therapy (IPT) more structured and short-term version of psychodynamic therapy (pp. 57, 154, 289, 516)

interrater reliability extent to which an observational measure yields similar results across different judges (also called interjudge reliability) (p. 104)

interview method for gathering information from a client and/or his or her family in which a therapist asks questions and examines the content of answers as well as nonverbal behaviors (p. 101)

introject to internalize moral standards because following them makes us feel good and reduces anxiety (p. 45)

introjected hostility Freud's theory explaining how depressive people, being too frightened to express their rage for their rejection outwardly, turn their anger inward on parts of their own egos; their self-blame and punishment is actually blame and punishment intended for others who have abandoned them (p. 272)

irresistible impulse rule legal principle stating that even a person who knowingly performs a wrongful act can be absolved of responsibility if he or she is driven by an irresistible impulse to perform the act or had a diminished capacity to resist performing the act (p. 684)

J

John Henryism pattern of active coping with stressors by trying harder and harder against obstacles that may be insurmountable (p. 638)

K

Korsakoff's psychosis alcohol-induced permanent cognitive disorder involving deficiencies in one's ability to recall both recent and distant events (p. 581)

L

la belle indifference feature of conversion disorders involving an odd lack of concern about one's loss of functioning in some area of one's body (p. 388)

latency stage period of psychosexual development following the phallic stage in which libidinal drives are quelled and children's energy turns

skills such as walking or holding onto objects (p. 465)

muscle contraction headaches one form of chronic headache caused when the muscles surrounding the skull contract, constricting the blood vessels, resulting in pain at the back or front of the head or at the back of the neck (p. 623)

myotonia in the sexual response cycle, muscular tension in the body that culminates in contractions during orgasm (p. 525)

N

naloxone drug that blocks the positive effects of heroin and can lead to a decreased desire to use it (p. 605)

naltrexone drug that blocks the positive effects of alcohol and heroin and can lead to a decreased desire to drink or use substances (p. 605)

narcissistic personality disorder syndrome marked by grandiose thoughts and feelings of one's own worth as well as an obliviousness to others' needs and an exploitive, arrogant demeanor (p. 427)

narcolepsy type of dyssomnia that involves irresistible attacks of sleep (p. 630)

natural environmental type phobia extreme fear of events or situations in the natural environment that causes impairment in one's ability to function normally (p. 195)

natural theories group of theories based on the belief that mental disorders are caused by the breakdown of systems of the body and can be cured through restoring the body to good health (p. 10)

nature-nurture question debate over the causes of psychological disorders (are disorders caused by something in the biology of the person or in the history of events to which the person was exposed?); debate implies that the cause of disorder has to be either biological or psychological and that it cannot be both (p. 30)

need for treatment legal criterion operationalized as a signed certificate by two physicians stating that a person requires treatment but will not agree to it voluntarily; formerly a sufficient cause to hospitalize the person involuntarily and force him or her to undergo treatment (p. 687)

negative symptoms in schizophrenia, deficits in functioning that indicate the absence of a capacity present in normal people, such as affective flattening (also called Type II symptoms) (p. 330)

neurofibrillary tangles twists or tangles of filaments within nerve cells, especially prominent in the cerebral cortex and hippocampus, common in the brains of Alzheimer's disease patients (p. 661)

neuroleptics drugs used to treat psychotic symptoms (pp. 137, 351)

neuropsychological test test of cognitive, sensory, and/or motor skills that attempts to differentiate people with deficits in these areas from normal subjects (p. 104)

neurosis set of maladaptive symptoms caused by unconscious anxiety (p. 180)

neurotic anxiety anxiety that occurs when we are repeatedly prevented from expressing our id impulses (p. 205)

neurotic paradox a psychoanalytic term for a condition in which an individual's way of coping with unconscious concerns creates even more problems in that individual's life (p. 6)

neurotransmitters biochemicals released from a sending neuron that transmit messages to a receiving neuron in the brain and nervous system (p. 35)

nicotine alkaloid found in tobacco; operates on both the central and peripheral nervous systems resulting in the release of several biochemicals including dopamine, norepinephrine, serotonin, and the endogenous opioids (p. 590)

nonpurging type of bulimia nervosa type of bulimia nervosa in which bingeing is followed by excessive exercise or fasting to control weight gain (p. 498)

norepinephrine neurotransmitter that is involved in the regulation of mood (pp. 182, 262, 513)

null hypothesis alternative to the primary hypothesis, stating that there is no relationship between the independent variable and the dependent variable (p. 69)

O

object relations school group of modern psychodynamic theorists who believe that one develops a self-concept and appraisals of others in a four-stage process during childhood and retains them throughout adulthood; psychopathology consists of an incomplete progression through these stages or an acquisition of poor self-and-other concepts (p. 49)

observational learning learning that occurs when a person observes the rewards and punishments of another's behavior and then behaves in accordance with the same rewards and punishments (p. 53)

obsessions uncontrollable, persistent thoughts, images, ideas, or impulses that an individual feels intrude upon his or her consciousness and that cause significant anxiety or distress (p. 234)

obsessive-compulsive disorder (OCD) anxiety disorder characterized by obsessions (persistent thoughts) and compulsions (rituals) (p. 234)

obsessive-compulsive personality disorder pervasive rigidity in one's activities and interpersonal relationships that includes qualities such as emotional constriction, extreme perfectionism, and anxiety resulting from even slight disruptions in one's routine ways (p. 432)

odd-eccentric personality disorders category including paranoid, schizotypal, and schizoid personality disorders that is marked by chronic odd and/or inappropriate behavior with mild features of psychosis and/or paranoia (p. 409)

Oedipus complex major conflict of male sexual development during which boys are sexually attracted to their mothers and hate their fathers as rivals (p. 48)

operant conditioning form of learning in which behaviors lead to consequences that either reinforce or punish the organism, leading to an increased or decreased probability of a future response (p. 51)

operationalization specific manner in which one measures or manipulates variables in a study (p. 70)

opioids substances, including morphine and heroin, that produce euphoria followed by a tranquil state; that in severe intoxication can lead to unconsciousness, coma, and seizures; and that can cause withdrawal symptoms of emotional distress and severe nausea, sweating, diarrhea, and fever (p. 593)

oppositional defiant disorder syndrome of chronic misbehavior in childhood marked by belligerence, irritability, and defiance, though not to the extent found in a diagnosis of conduct disorder (p. 450)

oral stage earliest psychosexual stage lasting for the first 18 months of life; libidinal impulses are best satisfied through the stimulation of the mouth area, including actions such as feeding or sucking; major issues of concern are dependence and the reliability of others (p. 46)

organic amnesias caused by brain injury resulting from disease, drugs, accidents (blows to head), or surgery (p. 384)

orgasm the discharge of neuromuscular tension built up during sexual activity; in men, entails rhythmic contractions of the prostate, seminal vesicles, vas deferens, and penis and seminal discharge; in women, entails contractions of the orgasmic platform and uterus (p. 525)

P

pain disorder syndrome marked by the chronic experience of acute pain that appears to have no physical cause (pp. 181, 393)

palialia repetition of sounds and words over and over (p. 656)

panic attacks short, intense periods during which an individual experiences physiological and cognitive symptoms of anxiety, characterized by intense fear or discomfort (p. 181)

panic disorder disorder characterized by recurrent, unexpected panic attacks (p. 181)

paranoid personality disorder chronic and pervasive mistrust and suspicion of other people that are unwarranted and maladaptive (p. 409)

paranoid schizophrenia syndrome marked by delusions and hallucinations that involve themes of persecution and grandiosity (p. 341)

paraphilias atypical sexual activities that involve one of the following: (1) nonhuman objects, (2) nonconsenting adults, (3) suffering or humiliation of oneself or one's partner, or (4) children (p. 549)

parasomnia primary sleep disorder that involves abnormal behavioral and physiological events occurring during sleep (p. 628)

partial reinforcement schedule form of behavior modification in which a behavior is rewarded or punished only some of the time (p. 52)

pedophilia adult obtainment of sexual gratification by engaging in sexual activities with young children (p. 553)

penis envy wish to have the male sex organ (p. 48)

performance anxiety anxiety over sexual performance that interferes with sexual functioning (p. 537)

perinatal hypoxia oxygen deprivation during labor and delivery; an obstetrical complication that may be especially important in neurological development (p. 351)

persecutory delusion false, persistent belief that one is being pursued by other people (p. 331)

personality habitual and enduring ways of thinking, feeling, and acting that make each of us unique and different from every other person (p. 404)

personality disorder chronic pattern of maladaptive cognition, emotion, and behavior that begins in adolescence or early adulthood and continues into later adulthood (p. 404)

personality inventories questionnaires that assess people's typical ways of thinking, feeling, and behaving; used to obtain information about people's well-being, self-concept, attitudes, and beliefs (p. 109)

personality trait complex pattern of thought, emotion, and behavior that is stable across time and many situations (p. 404)

person-centered therapy see humanistic therapy (p. 147)

pervasive developmental disorders disorders that are characterized by severe and persisting impairment in several areas of development (p. 474)

phallic stage psychosexual stage that occurs between the ages of 3 to 6; focus of pleasure is the genitals; important conflicts of sexual development emerge this time, differing for boys and girls (p. 48)

phenothiazines drugs that reduce the functional level of dopamine in the brain, and also tend to reduce symptoms of schizophrenia (pp. 137, 351)

phenylcyclidine (PCP) substance that produces euphoria, slowed reaction times, and involuntary movements at low doses; disorganized thinking, feelings of unreality, and hostility at intermediate doses; and

amnesia, analgesia, respiratory problems, and changes in body temperature at high doses (p. 597)

phenylketonuria (PKU) genetically transmitted metabolic disorder that causes mental retardation; involves the inability to metabolize phenylalanine, the buildup of phenyl pyruvic acid in the body, and permanent brain damage (p. 468)

phonological disorder disorder involving use of speech sounds inappropriate for age or dialect (p. 466)

pituitary major endocrine gland which lies partly on the outgrowth of the brain and just below the hypothalamus; produces the largest number of different hormones and controls the secretion of other endocrine glands (p. 37)

placebo control group in a therapy outcome study, group of people whose treatment is an inactive substance (to compare with the effects of a drug) or a non-theory-based therapy providing social support (to compare with the effects of psychotherapy) (p. 82)

plaques deposits of amyloid protein that accumulate in the extracellular spaces of the cerebral cortex, hippocampus, and other forebrain structures in people with Alzheimer's disease (p. 661)

plateau phase in the sexual response cycle, period between arousal and orgasm during which excitement remains high but stable (p. 525)

pleasure principle drive to maximize pleasure and minimize pain as quickly as possible (p. 44)

point prevalence number of people who have a disorder at one given point in time (p. 120)

polygenic combination of many genes, each of which makes a small contribution to an inherited trait (p. 40)

positive symptoms in schizophrenia, hallucinations, delusions, and disorganization in thought and behavior (also called Type I symptoms) (p. 330)

positron emission tomography (PET) method of localizing and measuring brain activity by detecting photons that result from the metabolization of an injected isotope (p. 105)

posttraumatic stress disorder (PTSD) anxiety disorder characterized by (a) repeated mental images of experiencing a traumatic event, (b) emotional numbing and detachment, and (c) hypervigilance and chronic arousal (p. 216)

preconscious area of the psyche that contains material from the unconscious before it reaches the conscious mind (p. 45)

predictive validity extent to which a measure accurately forecasts how a person will think, act, and feel in the future (p. 103)

predisposition tendency to develop a disorder which must interact with other biological, psychological, or environmental factors for the disorder to develop (p. 40)

prefrontal lobotomy type of psychosurgery in which the frontal lobes of the brain are severed from the lower centers of the brain in people suffering from psychosis (p. 141)

premature ejaculation inability to delay ejaculation after minimal sexual stimulation or until one wishes to ejaculate, causing significant distress or interpersonal problems (p. 532)

premenstrual dysphoric disorder syndrome in which a woman experiences an increase in depressive symptoms during the premenstrual period and relief from these symptoms with the onset of menstruation (p. 267)

prepared classical conditioning theory that evolution has prepared us to be easily conditioned to fear objects or situations that were dangerous in ancient times (p. 200)

prevalence number of people who have a disorder during a specified period of time (p. 120)

primary prevention stopping the development of psychological disorders before they start (p. 159)

primary process thinking wish fulfillment, or fantasies, humans use to conjure up desired objects or actions; an example is a hungry infant imagining its mother's breast when she is not present (p. 44)

primary sleep disorders sleep disorders that include dyssomnias and parasomnias (p. 628)

probands people who have the disorder under investigation in a family history study (p. 40)

prodromal symptoms in schizophrenia, experience of milder symptoms prior to an acute phase of the disorder, during which behaviors are unusual and peculiar but not yet psychotic or completely disorganized (p. 340)

projective test presentation of an ambiguous stimulus, such as an inkblot, to a client, who then projects unconscious motives and issues onto the stimulus in his or her interpretation of its content (p. 112)

prototypes images of the self and others in relation to the self formed from experiences with family during childhood (p. 58)

psychic epidemic phenomenon in which large numbers of people begin to engage in unusual behaviors that appear to have a psychological origin (p. 15)

psychoanalysis form of treatment for psychopathology involving alleviating unconscious conflicts driving psychological symptoms by helping people gain insight into their conflicts and finding ways of resolving these conflicts (pp. 22, 44, 147)

psychodynamic theories label for group of theories developed by Freud's followers, but usually differing somewhat from Freud's original theories (pp. 43, 49)

psychodynamic therapy therapy focused on uncovering and resolving unconscious conflicts that drive psychological symptoms (pp. 145, 289)

psychogenic amnesias loss of memory in the absence of any brain injury or disease, and thought to have psychological causes (p. 384)

psychological approach or theories approach to abnormality that focuses on personality, behavior, and ways of thinking as possible causes of abnormality (p. 30)

psychological theories theories that view mental disorders as caused by psychological processes, such as beliefs, thinking styles, and coping styles (p. 10)

psychopathology symptoms that cause mental, emotional, and/or physical pain (p. 4)

psychosexual stages developmental process children pass through; in each stage sex drives are focused on the stimulation of certain areas of the body and particular psychological issues can arouse anxiety (p. 46)

psychosis experiences that involve a loss of contact with reality as well as an inability to differentiate between reality and one's subjective state (p. 326)

psychosomatic disorders syndromes marked by identifiable physical illness or defect caused at least partly by psychological factors (p. 386)

psychosurgery rare treatment for mental disorders in which a neurosurgeon attempts to destroy small areas of the brain thought to be involved in a patient's symptoms (p. 141)

psychotherapy treatment for abnormality that consists of a therapist and client discussing the client's symptoms and their causes; the therapist's theoretical orientation determines the foci of conversations with the client (p. 134)

purging type of bulimia nervosa type of bulimia nervosa in which bingeing is followed by the use of self-induced vomiting or purging medications to control weight gain (p. 498)

R

random assignment assignment of participants in an experiment to groups based on a random process (p. 80)

random sample sample for a study that is generated by methods that ensure it is a random selection of the population (p. 77)

rapid cycling bipolar disorder diagnosis given when a person has four or more cycles of mania and depression within a single year (p. 257)

reading disorder developmental disorder involving deficits in reading ability (p. 465)

realistic anxiety anxiety that occurs when we face a real danger or threat such as a tornado (p. 205)

reality principle idea that the ego seeks to satisfy our needs within the realities of society's rules, rather than following the abandon of the pleasure principle (p. 44)

reflection method of responding in which the therapist expresses his or her attempt to understand what the client is experiencing and trying to communicate (p. 148)

reformulated learned helplessness theory view that people who attribute negative events to internal, stable, and global causes are more likely than other people to experience learned helplessness deficits following such events and are thus predisposed to depression (p. 270)

relapse prevention programs treatments that seek to offset continued alcohol use by identifying high-risk situations for those attempting to stop or cut down on drinking and teaching them either to avoid those situations or to use assertiveness skills when in them, while viewing setbacks as temporary (p. 608)

reliability degree of consistency in a measurement—that is, the extent to which it yields accurate measurements of a phenomenon across several trials, different populations, and in different forms (p. 103)

replicate to repeat a study and obtain the same results (p. 73)

representative sample subgroup taken from a larger population of interest that is similar to the larger sample regarding the prevalence of factors that might affect the results of a study, such as gender, ethnicity, education level, and age (p. 77)

repressed memory debate controversy among psychologists over the existence or nonexistence of repression, the possibility of repressed memories and implanted memories, and the admissibility to legal cases of claims based on such theories (p. 701)

repression defense mechanism in which the ego pushes anxiety-provoking material back into the unconscious (p. 44)

repressive coping style tendency to expunge negative emotions from one's awareness, at times to a point at which one is unaware that one is experiencing them at all (p. 636)

residual schizophrenia diagnosis made when a person has already experienced a single acute phase of schizophrenia but currently has milder and less debilitating symptoms (p. 342)

residual symptoms in schizophrenia, experience of milder symptoms following an acute phase of the disorder, during which behaviors are unusual and peculiar but not psychotic or completely disorganized (p. 340)

resistance in psychodynamic therapy, material that a client finds difficult or impossible to address; client's resistance signals an unconscious conflict that the therapist then tries to interpret (pp. 101, 145)

resolution in the sexual response cycle, state of deep relaxation following orgasm in which a man loses his erection and a woman's orgasmic platform subsides (p. 526)

response shaping technique used in behavior therapy in which a person's behavior problems are changed to desirable behaviors through operant conditioning (p. 150)

restricting type of anorexia nervosa type of anorexia nervosa in which weight gain is prevented by refusing to eat (p. 493)

retrograde amnesia deficit in the ability to recall previously learned information or past events (pp. 384, 675)

Rett's disorder pervasive developmental disorder in which children develop normally at first and later show permanent loss of basic skills in social interactions, language, and/or movement (p. 474)

reuptake process in which the sending neuron reabsorbs some of the neurotransmitter in the synapse, decreasing the amount left in the synapse (p. 36)

right to refuse treatment right, not recognized by all states, of involuntarily committed people to refuse drugs or other treatment (p. 692)

right to treatment fundamental right of involuntarily committed people to active treatment for their disorders rather than shelter alone (p. 692)

risperidone atypical antipsychotic; is a serotonin receptor antagonist and a weak blocker of dopamine receptors; has a faster onset than clozapine and does not induce tardive dyskinesia; however, it can induce sedation, hypotension, weight gain, seizures, and concentration problems (p. 361)

role play technique used in behavioral therapy in which the client and the therapist take on the roles of people involved with the client's maladaptive behaviors; the therapist observes the client's behavior in the role play to assess what aspects of that behavior need to change (p. 148)

rumination the tendency to focus on one's personal concerns and feelings of distress repetitively and passively (p. 269)

S

sadomasochism pattern of sexual rituals between a sexually sadistic "giver" and a sexually masochistic "receiver" (p. 551)

safety signal hypothesis hypothesis that people associate certain signals with the absence of anxiety symptoms and can relax when those signals are present (pp. 199, 621)

sample group of people taken from a population of interest who participate in a study (p. 77)

schizoid personality disorder syndrome marked by chronic lack of interest in and avoidance of interpersonal relationships as well as emotional coldness in interactions with others (p. 411)

schizophrenia disorder consisting of unreal or disorganized thoughts and perceptions as well as verbal, cognitive, and behavioral deficits (p. 326)

schizophrenogenic mothers mothers exhibiting parenting styles that have been described to cause children to become schizophrenic; these mothers are described as dominant, cold, and rejecting of their children (p. 353)

schizotypal personality disorder chronic pattern of inhibited or inappropriate emotion and social behavior as well as aberrant cognitions and disorganized speech (p. 412)

scientific method method of obtaining and evaluating information relevant to a problem in a systematic way (p. 69)

seasonal affective disorder (SAD) disorder identified by a two-year period in which a person experiences major depression during winter months and then recovers fully during the summer; some people with this disorder also experience mild mania during summer months (p. 251)

secondary prevention detecting psychological disorders in their earliest stages and providing treatment designed to reduce their development (p. 159)

secondary process thinking rational deliberation, as opposed to the irrational thought of primary process thinking (p. 44)

selective serotonin reuptake inhibitors (SSRIs) class of antidepressant drugs (pp. 139, 186, 280, 317, 517)

self-actualization person's fulfillment of his or her potential for love, creativity, and meaning (p. 56)

self-efficacy beliefs beliefs that one can engage in the behaviors necessary to overcome a situation (p. 24)

self-help groups groups that form to help each other with a common problem (p. 157)

self-monitoring method of assessment in which a client records the number of times per day that he or she engages in a specific behavior and the conditions surrounding the behavior (p. 114)

sensate focus therapy treatment for sexual dysfunction in which partners alternate between giving and receiving stimulation in a relaxed, openly communicative atmosphere, in order to reduce performance anxiety and concern over achieving orgasm by learning each partner's sexual fulfillment needs (p. 542)

separation anxiety disorder syndrome of childhood and adolescence marked by the presence of abnormal fear or worry over becoming separated from one's caregiver(s) as well as clinging behaviors in the presence of the caregiver(s) (p. 457)

serotonin neurotransmitter that is involved in the regulation of mood and impulsive responses (pp. 262, 418, 513)

set point natural body weight determined by a person's metabolic rate, diet, and genetics (p. 490)

sexual arousal disorders conditions in which people do not experience the physiological changes that make up the excitement or arousal phase of the sexual response cycle (p. 531)

sexual aversion disorder condition in which a person actively avoids sexual activities and experiences sex as unpleasant or anxiety provoking (p. 531)

sexual desire in the sexual response cycle, urge or inclination to engage in sexual activity (p. 524)

sexual dysfunction problems in experiencing sexual arousal or carrying through with sexual acts to the point of sexual arousal (p. 524)

sexual masochism sexual gratification obtained through experiencing pain and humiliation at the hands of one's partner (p. 551)

sexual orientation one's preference for partners of the same or opposite sex with respect to attraction and sexual desire (p. 557)

sexual sadism sexual gratification obtained through inflicting pain and humiliation on one's partner (p. 551)

shaken baby syndrome caused when a baby is shaken; can lead to a bruised brain, bleeding around the brain and/or eyes, seizures, partial blindness, paralysis, mental retardation, or death (p. 471)

situational type phobias extreme fear of situations such as public transportation, tunnels, bridges, elevators, flying, driving, and enclosed spaces (p. 195)

sleep disorders due to general medical conditions sleep disturbances that are caused by the physiological effects of a medical condition (p. 628)

sleep disorders related to another mental disorder sleep disturbances that are caused by psychological disorders such as depression or anxiety (p. 628)

sleep restriction therapy treatment for insomnia that involves initially restricting the amount of time that insomniacs can try to sleep at night (p. 630)

social approach approach to abnormality that focuses on interpersonal relationships, culture, society, and the environment as possible causes of abnormality (p. 30)

social learning theory theory that people learn behaviors by imitating and observing others and learning about the rewards and punishments that follow behaviors (p. 52)

social phobia extreme fear of being judged or embarrassed in front of people that causes the individual to avoid social situations (p. 195)

social selection explanation of the effects symptoms of schizophrenia have on a person's life and the resulting tendency to drift downward in social class, as compared to family of origin (p. 356)

social skills training technique often used in behavior therapy to help people with problems in interacting and communicating with others (p. 150)

social structural theories theories that focus on environmental and societal demands as causes of abnormal behavior (p. 62)

somatization disorder syndrome marked by the chronic experience of unpleasant or painful physical symptoms for which no organic cause can be found (p. 392)

somatoform disorders disorders marked by unpleasant or painful physical symptoms that have no apparent organic cause and that are often not physiologically possible, suggesting that psychological factors are involved (p. 386)

specific phobia extreme fear of a specific object or situation that causes an individual to routinely avoid that object or situation (p. 194)

splitting in object relations theory, phenomenon wherein a person fails to resolve stages two or three of the self-concept acquisition process and splits conceptions of self and others into either all-good or all-bad categories, neglecting to recognize people's mixed qualities (pp. 49, 423)

squeeze technique sex therapy technique for premature ejaculation (p. 543)

statistical significance indication of how likely it is that a study's result occurred only by chance (p. 76)

stimulus-control therapy behavioral intervention for insomnia that involves a set of instructions designed to reduce behaviors that might interfere with sleep and to regulate sleep-wake schedules (p. 630)

stop-start technique sex therapy technique for premature ejaculation (p. 542)

stress reaction to events that are perceived as uncontrollable, unpredictable, challenging, and/or threatening (p. 620)

stress-management interventions strategy that teaches clients to overcome problems in their lives that are increasing their stress (p. 230)

stroke sudden damage to the brain due to blockage of blood flow or hemorrhaging (p. 663)

structured interview meeting between a clinician and a client or a client's associate(s) in which the clinician asks questions that are standardized, written in advance, and asked of every client (p. 101)

stuttering severe problems in word fluency (p. 466)

subintentional deaths acts in which individuals indirectly contribute to their own deaths (p. 301)

substance naturally occurring or synthetically produced product that alters perceptions, thoughts, emotions, and behaviors when ingested, smoked or injected (p. 568)

substance abuse diagnosis given when a person's recurrent substance use leads to significant harmful consequences, as manifested by a failure to fulfill obligations at work, school, or home, the use of substances in physically hazardous situations, legal problems, and continued use despite social and legal problems (p. 573)

substance dependence diagnosis given when a person's substance use leads to physiological dependence or significant impairment or distress, as manifested by an inability to use the substance in moderation; decline in social, occupational, or recreational activities; or spending large amounts of time obtaining substances or recovering from their effects (p. 573)

substance intoxication experience of significantly maladaptive behavioral and psychological symptoms due to the effect of a substance on the central nervous system that develops during or shortly after use of the substance (p. 570)

substance P amino acid neurotransmitter that is involved in emotion and pain (pp. 140, 263)

substance withdrawal experience of clinically significant distress in social, occupational, or other areas of functioning due to the cessation or reduction of substance use (p. 573)

substance-induced sexual dysfunction problems in sexual functioning that are caused by substance use (p. 536)

substance-induced sleep disorders sleep disturbances that are caused by the use of substances, including prescription medications (p. 628)

substance-related disorder inability to use a substance in moderation and/or the intentional use of a substance to change one's thoughts, feelings, and/or behaviors, leading to impairment in work, academic, personal, or social endeavors (p. 570)

suffocation false alarm theory theory that people with panic disorders have an oversensitivity to sensations of suffocation, making them vulnerable to panic attacks (p. 184)

suicide purposeful taking of one's own life (p. 300)

suicide clusters when two or more suicides or attempted suicides nonrandomly occur closely together in space or time (p. 310)

suicide contagion phenomenon in which the suicide of a well-known person is linked to the acceptance of suicide by people who closely identify with that individual (p. 310)

suicide hot lines form of crisis intervention that is done over the phone (p. 316)

superego part of the unconscious that consists of absolute moral standards internalized from one's parents during childhood and one's culture (p. 45)

supernatural theories set of theories that sees mental disorders as the result of supernatural forces, such as divine intervention, curses, demonic possession, and/or personal sins; mental disorders can be cured through religious rituals, exorcisms, confessions, and/or death (p. 10)

supportive-expressive psychodynamic therapy type of therapy in which the therapist is highly nondirective when he or she encourages the clients to talk about their problems (p. 516)

sympathetic division of the autonomic nervous system acts directly on smooth muscles and internal organs to produce body changes including increased heart rate, elevated blood pressure, and dilated pupils (p. 178)

symptom questionnaire questionnaire that assesses what symptoms a person is experiencing (p. 109)

synapse space between the sending neuron and the receiving neuron into which neurotransmitters are first released (also known as the synaptic gap) (p. 36)

syndrome set of symptoms that tend to occur together (p. 118)

systematic desensitization type of behavior therapy that attempts to reduce client anxiety through relaxation techniques and progressive exposure to feared stimuli (pp. 149, 191, 229)

T

tardive dyskinesia neurological disorder marked by involuntary movements of the tongue, face, mouth, or jaw, resulting from taking neuroleptic drugs (p. 360)

Tay-Sachs disease genetically transmitted disease that causes the degeneration of the nervous system and mental and physical deterioration (p. 468)

test-retest reliability index of how consistent the results of a test are over time (p. 103)

theoretical approach set of assumptions about the likely causes of abnormality and appropriate treatments (p. 30)

therapeutic alliance during therapy the therapist is empathetic and supportive of the client in order to create a relationship of trust with the client and encourage the exploration of difficult issues (p. 147)

therapy outcome study experimental study that assesses the effects of an intervention designed to reduce psychopathology in an experimental group, while performing no intervention or a different type of intervention on another group (p. 82)

third variable factor that affects levels of the dependent variable and confounds the results of a study if it is not appropriately controlled for or eliminated (p. 76)

thought-stopping strategy that involves finding ways to stop intrusive thoughts (p. 230)

token economy application of operant conditioning in which patients receive tokens for exhibiting desired behaviors that are exchangeable for privileges and rewards; these tokens are withheld when a patient exhibits unwanted behaviors (p. 150)

tolerance the condition of experiencing less and less effect from the same dose of a substance (p. 573)

transference in psychodynamic therapy, client's reaction to the therapist as if the therapist were an important person in his or her early development; the client's feelings and beliefs about this other person are transferred onto the therapist (p. 146)

transsexualism condition of chronic discomfort with one's gender and genitals as well as a desire to be rid of one's genitals and to live as a member of the opposite sex (p. 558)

transvestism fetish in which a heterosexual man dresses in women's clothing as his primary means of becoming sexually aroused (p. 550)

trephination procedure in which holes were drilled in the skulls of people displaying abnormal behavior to allow evil spirits to depart their bodies; performed in the Stone Age (p. 11)

tricyclic antidepressants class of antidepressant drugs (pp. 138, 186, 279, 517)

Trisomy 13 chromosomal abnormality in which chromosome 13 is present in triplicate; causes severe mental retardation and shortened life expectancy (p. 470)

Trisomy 18 chromosomal abnormality in which chromosome 18 is present in triplicate; causes severe mental retardation and shortened life expectancy (p. 470)

twin study study of the heritability of a disorder by comparing concordance rates between monozygotic and dizygotic twins (p. 41)

Type A behavior pattern personality pattern characterized by time urgency, hostility, and competitiveness (p. 633)

U

ulcers holes, or lesions, in the wall of the stomach (gastric ulcers) or of the duodenum (peptic ulcers) that cause burning sensations and pain in the stomach, vomiting, and stomach bleeding (p. 622)

unconditional positive regard essential part of humanistic therapy; the therapist expresses that he or she accepts the client no matter how unattractive, disturbed, or difficult the client is (p. 148)

unconditioned response (UR) in classical conditioning, response that naturally follows when a certain stimulus appears, as a dog salivating when it smells food (p. 51)

unconditioned stimulus (US) in classical conditioning, stimulus that naturally elicits a reaction, as food elicits salivation in dogs (p. 51)

unconscious area of the psyche where memories, wishes, and needs are stored and where conflicts among the id, ego, and superego are played out (p. 45)

undifferentiated schizophrenia diagnosis made when a person experiences schizophrenic symptoms, such as delusions and hallucinations, but does not meet criteria for paranoid, disorganized, or catatonic schizophrenia (p. 342)

unipolar depression type of depression consisting of depressive symptoms but without manic episodes (p. 248)

unstructured interview meeting between a clinician and a client or a client's associate(s) that consists of open-ended, general questions that are particular to each person interviewed (p. 101)

unusualness criterion for abnormality that suggests that abnormal behaviors are rare or unexpected (p. 7)

V

vaginismus in women, involuntary contractions of the muscles surrounding the outer third of the vagina that interfere with penetration and sexual functioning (p. 533)

validity degree of correspondence between a measurement and the phenomenon under study (p. 102)

variable measurable factor or characteristic that can vary within an individual, between individuals, or both (p. 69)

vascular dementia second most common type of dementia, associated with symptoms of cerebrovascular disease (tissue damage in the brain due to a blockage of blood flow) (p. 663)

vasocongestion in the sexual response cycle, filling of blood vessels and tissues with blood, leading to erection of the penis in males and enlargement of the clitoris, swelling of the labia, and vaginal moistening in women (also called engorgement) (p. 524)

visual hallucination visual perception of something that is not actually present (p. 334)

voyeurism obtainment of sexual arousal by compulsively and secretly watching another person undressing, bathing, engaging in sex, or being naked (p. 552)

vulnerability-stress model comprehensive model of the many factors that lead some people to develop a given mental disorder (p. 31)

W

wait list control group in a therapy outcome study, group of people that functions as a control group while an experimental group receives an intervention and then receives the intervention itself after a waiting period (p. 82)

Wernicke's encephalopathy alcohol-induced permanent cognitive disorder involving mental disorientation and confusion and, in severe states, coma (p. 581)

word salad speech that is so disorganized that a listener cannot comprehend it (p. 355)

working through method used in psychodynamic therapy in which the client repeatedly goes over and over painful memories and difficult issues as a way to understand and accept them (p. 146)

REFERENCES

A

Abbott, B. B., Schoen, L. S., & Badia, P. (1984). Predictable and unpredictable shock: Behavioral measures of aversion and physiological measures of stress. *Psychological Bulletin, 96,* 45–71.

Abbott, D. W., De Zwaan, M., Mussell, M. P., Raymond, N. C., Seim, H. C., Crow, S. J., Crosby, R. D., & Mitchell, J. E. (1998). Onset of binge eating and dieting in overweight women: Implications for etiology, associated features and treatment. *Journal of Psychosomatic Research, 44,* 367–374.

Abel, G. G., & Osborn, C. (1992). The paraphilias: The extent and nature of sexually deviant and criminal behavior. *Psychiatric Clinics of North America, 15,* 675–687.

Abplanalp, J. M., Haskett, R. F., & Rose, R. M. (1979). Psychoendocrinology of the menstrual cycle: I. Enjoyment of daily activities and moods. *Psychosomatic Medicine, 41,* 587–604.

Abramowitz, J. S. (1997). Effectiveness of psychological and pharmacological treatments for obsessive-compulsive disorder: A quantitative review. *Journal of Consulting & Clinical Psychology, 65,* 44–52.

Abramson, L. Y., Metalsky, G. I., & Alloy, L. B. (1989). Hopelessness depression: A theory-based subtype of depression. *Psychological Review, 96,* 358–372.

Abramson, L. Y., Seligman, M. E. P., & Teasdale, J. (1978). Learned helplessness in humans: Critique and reformulation. *Journal of Abnormal Psychology, 87,* 49–74.

Achenbach, T. M., & Edelbrock, C. (1983). *Manual for the child behavior checklist and revised child behavior profile.* Burlington, VT: Queen City Printers.

Achenbach, T. M., McConaughy, S. H., & Howell, C. T. (1987). Child/adolescent behavioral and emotional problems: Implications of cross-informant correlations for situational specificity. *Psychological Bulletin, 101,* 213–232.

Ackerman, M. D., & Carey, M. P. (1995). Psychology's role in the assessment of erectile dysfunction: Historical perspectives, current knowledge, and methods. *Journal of Consulting & Clinical Psychology, 63,* 862–876.

Advokat, C., & Kutlesic, V. (1995). Pharmacotherapy of the eating disorders: A commentary. *Neuroscience & Biobehavioral Reviews, 19,* 59–66.

Agras, S., Sylvester, D., & Oliveau, D. (1969). The epidemiology of common fears and phobia. *Comprehensive Psychiatry, 10,* 151–156.

Agras, W. S. (1987). *Eating disorders: Management of obesity, bulimia, and anorexia nervosa.* New York: Pergamon Press.

Agras, W. S. (1993). Short term psychological treatments for binge eating. In C. G. Fairburn & G. T. Wilson (Eds.), *Binge eating: Nature, assessment & treatment* (pp. 270–286). New York: Guilford.

Agras, W. S., & Kirkley, B. G. (1986). Bulimia: Theories of etiology. In K. D. Brownell & J. P. Foreyt (Eds.), *Handbook of eating disorders: Physiology, psychology, and treatment of obesity, anorexia, and bulimia* (pp. 367–378). New York: Basic Books.

Aguero-Torres, H., Fratiglioni, L., & Winblad, B. (1998). Natural history of Alzheimer's disease and other dementias: Review of the literature in the light of the findings from the Kungholmen Project. *International Journal of Geriatric, 13,* 755–766.

Akhtar, S., Wig, N. N., Varma, V. K., Pershad, D., & Verma, S. K. (1975). A phenomenological analysis of symptoms in obsessive-compulsive neurosis. *British Journal of Psychiatry, 127,* 342–348.

Alden, L. (1989). Short-term structured treatment for avoidant personality disorder. *Journal of Consulting & Clinical Psychology, 57,* 756–764.

Alexander, K. L., Entwisle, D. R., & Thompson, M. S. (1987). School performance, status relations, and the structure of sentiment: Bringing the teacher back in. *American Sociological Review, 52,* 665–682.

Allderidge, P. (1979). Hospitals, madhouses and asylums: Cycles in the care of the insane. *British Journal of Psychiatry, 134,* 321–334.

Allgood-Merten, B., Lewinsohn, P. M., & Hops, H. (1990). Sex differences and adolescent depression. *Journal of Abnormal Psychology, 99,* 55–63.

Allison, J., Blatt, S. J., & Zimet, C. N. (1968). *The interpretation of psychological tests.* New York: Harper & Row.

Alloy, L. B., & Abramson, L. Y. (1979). Judgment of contingency in depressed and nondepressed students: Sadder but wiser? *Journal of Experimental Psychology: General, 108,* 441–485.

Alloy, L. B., Abramson, L. Y., & Francis, E. L. (1999). Do negative cognitive styles confer vulnerability to depression? *Current Directions in Psychological Science, 8,* 128–132.

Althof, S. E. (1995). Pharmacologic treatment of rapid ejaculation. *Psychiatric Clinics of North America, 18,* 85–94.

American Heart Association. (1997). *Heart and stroke facts.* Dallas: Author.

American Psychiatric Association. (1983). *Diagnostic and statistical manual of mental disorders* (3rd ed.). Washington, DC: Author.

American Psychiatric Association. (1994). *Diagnostic and statistical manual of mental disorders* (4th ed.). Washington, DC: American Psychiatric Press.

American Psychiatric Association. (2000). *Diagnostic and statistical manual of mental disorders* (4th ed.—Revised text). Washington, DC: American Psychiatric Press.

American Psychiatric Association. (1998). Practice guidelines for the treatment of patients with panic disorder. (Vol. 155 suppl.). Washington, DC: American Psychiatric Press.

American Psychological Association. (1994). Guidelines for child custody evaluations in divorce proceedings. *American Psychologist, 49,* 677–680.

American Psychological Association. (1994). *Publication manual* (4th ed.). Washington, DC: American Psychological Association.

Anastopoulos, A. D., & Barkley, R. A. (1988). Biological factors in attention deficit-hyperactivity disorder. *Behavior Therapist, 11,* 47–53.

Andersen, A. E. (Ed.). (1990). *Males with eating disorders.* New York: Brunner/Mazel.

Andersen, A. E., & DiDomenico, L. (1992). Diet vs. shape content of popular male and female magazines: A dose-response relationship to the incidence of eating disorders? *International Journal of Eating Disorders, 11,* 283–287.

Andersen, B. L., & Cyranowski, J. M. (1995). Women's sexuality: Behaviors, responses, and individual difference. *Journal of Consulting & Clinical Psychology, 63,* 891–906.

Anderson, E. M., & Lambert, M. J. (1995). Short-term dynamically oriented psychotherapy: A review and meta-analysis. *Clinical Psychology Review, 15,* 503–514.

Anderson, G. M., & Hoshino, Y. (1997). Neurochemical studies of autism. In D. J. Cohen & F. R. Volkmar (Eds.), *Handbook of autism and pervasive developmental disorders* (pp. 325–343). Toronto: Wiley.

Anderson, G., Yasenik, L., & Ross, C. A. (1993). Dissociative experiences and disorders among women who identify themselves as sexual abuse survivors. *Child Abuse & Neglect, 17,* 677–686.

Anderson, J. C., Williams, S. M., McGee, R., & Silva, P. A. (1987). DSM-III disorders in preadolescent children: Prevalence in a large sample from the general population. *Archives of General Psychiatry, 44,* 69–76.

Anderson, N. B., Lane, J. D., Taguchi, F., & Williams, R. B. (1989). Patterns of cardiovascular responses to stress as a function of race and parental hypertension in men. *Health Psychology, 8,* 525–540.

Anderson, R. E., Bartlett, S. J., Morgan, G. D., & Brownell, K. D. (1995). Weight loss, psychological, and nutritional patterns in competitive male body builders. *International Journal of Eating Disorders, 18,* 49–57.

Andreasen, N. C. (1997). Linking mind and brain in the study of mental illnesses: A project for a scientific psychopathology. *Science, 275,* 1586–1593.

Andreasen, N. C., Flaum, M., Schultz, S., & Duzyurek, S. (1997). Diagnosis, methodology, and subtypes of schizophrenia. *Neuropsychobiology, 35,* 61–63.

Andreasen, N. C., Flaum, M., Swayze, V. W., Tyrrell, G., & Arndt, S. (1990). Positive and negative symptoms in schizophrenia: A critical reappraisal. *Archives of General Psychiatry, 47,* 615–621.

Andreasen, N. C., Rezai, K., Alliger, R., & Swayze, V. W. (1992). Hypofrontality in neuroleptic-naive patients and in patients with chronic schizophrenia: Assessment with xenon 133 single-photon emission computed tomography and the Tower of London. *Archives of General Psychiatry, 49*, 943–958.

Andreasen, N. C., Swayze, V. W., Flaum, M., & Alliger, R. (1990). Ventricular abnormalities in affective disorder; Clinical and demographic correlates. *American Journal of Psychiatry, 147*, 893–900.

Andrews, J. A., & Lewinsohn, P. M. (1992). Suicidal attempts among older adolescents: Prevalence and co-occurrence with psychiatric disorders. *Journal of the American Academy of Child & Adolescent Psychiatry, 32*, 655–662.

Angold, A., & Worthman, C. W. (1993). Puberty onset of gender differences in rates of depression: A developmental, epidemiological and neuroendocrine perspective. *Journal of Affective Disorders, 29*, 145–158.

Angold, A., Costello, E. J., & Worthman, C. M. (1998). Puberty and depression: The roles of age, pubertal status, and pubertal timing. *Psychological Medicine, 28*, 51–61.

Angst, J. (1998). Treated versus untreated major depressive episodes. *Psychopathology, 31*, 37–44.

Angst, J., Vollrath, M., Koch, R., & Dobler-Mikola, A. (1989). The Zurich Study: VII. Insomnia: Symptoms, classification and prevalence. *European Archives of Psychiatry & Clinical Neuroscience, 238*, 285–293.

Anonymous. (1983). First-person account. *Schizophrenia Bulletin, 9*, 152–155.

Anonymous. (1992). First-person account: Portrait of a schizophrenic. *Schizophrenia Bulletin, 18*, 333–334.

Anthony, J. C., Warner, L. A., & Kessler, R. C. (1994). Comparative epidemiology of dependence on tobacco, alcohol, controlled substances, and inhalants: Basic findings from the National Comorbidity Survey. *Experimental Clinical Psychopharmacology, 2*, 244–268.

Aponte, J. F., Rivers, R. Y., & Wohl, J. (Eds.) (1995). *Psychological interventions and cultural diversity.* Boston: Allyn & Bacon.

Arieti, S. (1955). *Interpretation of schizophrenia.* New York: R. Brunner.

Arieti, S., & Bemporad, J. R. (1980). The psychological organization of depression. *American Journal of Psychiatry, 137*, 1360–1365.

Armsden, G. C., McCauley, E., Greenberg, M. T., Burke, P. M., & Mitchell, J. R. (1990). Parent and peer attachment in early adolescent depression. *Journal of Abnormal Child Psychology, 18*, 683–697.

Ashton, A. K., & Rosen, R. (1998). Bupropion as an antidote for serotonin reuptake inhibitor–induced sexual dysfunction. *Journal of Clinical Psychiatry, 59*, 112–115.

Astin, John A. (1998). Why patients use alternative medicine: Results of a national study. *Journal of the American Medical Association, 279*, 1548–1553.

Atkinson, D. R., & Hackett, G. (1998). *Counseling diverse populations* (2nd ed.). Boston: McGraw-Hill.

Atkinson, R. L., Atkinson, R. C., Smith, E. E., Bem, D. J., & Nolen-Hoeksema, S. (2000). *Hilgard's introduction to psychology* (13th ed.). Fort Worth: Harcourt.

Attia, E., Haiman, C., Walsh, T., & Flater, S. R. (1998). Does fluoxetine augment the inpatient treatment of anorexia nervosa? *American Journal of Psychiatry, 155*, 548–551.

Attie, I., & Brooks-Gunn, J. (1989). Development of eating problems in adolescent girls: A longitudinal study. *Development Psychology, 25*, 70–79.

B

Babor, T. F., & Dolinsky, Z. S. (1988). Alcoholic typologies: Historical evolution and empirical evaluation of some common classification schemes. In R. M. Rose & J. Barrett (Eds.), *Alcoholism: Origins and outcome* (pp. 245–266). New York: Raven Press.

Bachrach, H. M., Galatzer-Levy, R., Skolnikoff, A., & Waldron, S. (1991). On the efficacy of psychoanalysis. *Journal of the American Psychoanalytic Association, 39*, 871–916.

Bachrach, L. L. (1987). Asylum for chronic mental patients. *New Directions for Mental Health Service, 35*, 5–12.

Baer, J. S., Marlatt, G. A., Kivlahan, D. R., & Fromme, K. (1992). An experimental test of three methods of alcohol risk reduction with young adults. *Journal of Consulting & Clinical Psychology, 60*, 974–979.

Bailey, A., Le Couteur, A., Gottesman, I., Bolton, P., Simonoff, E., Yuzda, E., & Rutter, M. (1995). Autism as a strongly genetic disorder: Evidence from a British twin study. *Psychological Medicine, 25*, 63–77.

Bailey, J. M., & Pillard, R. C. (1991). A genetic study of male sexual orientation. *Archives of General Psychiatry, 48*, 1089–1096.

Bailey, J. M., Pillard, R. C., Neale, M. C., & Agyei, Y. (1993). Heritable factors influence sexual orientation in women. *Archives of General Psychiatry, 50*, 217–223.

Balderer, G., & Borbely, A. A. (1985). Effect of valerian on human sleep. *Psychopharmacology, 87*, 406–409.

Baldessarini, R. J., & Tondo, L. (1999). Antisuicidal effect of lithium treatment in major mood disorders. In D. G. Jacobs (Ed.), *The Harvard Medical School guide to suicide assessment and intervention* (pp. 355–371). San Francisco: Jossey-Bass.

Ballenger, J. C. (1995). Benzodiazepines. In A. F. Schatzberg & C. B. Nemeroff (Eds.), *The American Psychiatric Press textbook of psychopharmacology.* Washington, DC: American Psychiatric Press.

Ballenger, J. C., Burrows, G. D., Dupont, R. L., & Lesser, I. M. (1988). Alprazolam in panic disorder and agoraphobia: Results from a multicenter trial. *Archives of General Psychiatry, 45*, 413–422.

Balon, R. (1998). Fluoxamine-induced erectile dysfunction responding to sildenafil. *Journal of Sex and Marital Therapy, 24*, 313–317.

Bandura, A. (1969). *Principles of behavior modification.* New York: Holt, Rinehart & Winston.

Bandura, A. (1977). Self-efficacy: Toward a unifying theory of behavioral change. *Psychological Review, 84*, 191–215.

Bandura, A. (1986). *Social foundations of thought and action.* Englewood Cliffs, NJ: Prentice Hall.

Bandura, A. (1995). *Self-efficacy in changing societies.* New York: Cambridge University Press.

Banich, M. T., Stolar, N., Heller, W., & Goldman, R. B. (1992). A deficit in right-hemisphere performance after induction of a depressed mood. *Neuropsychiatry, Neuropsychology, & Behavioral Neurology, 5*, 20–27.

Barber, J. P., & DeRubeis, R. J. (1989). On second thought: Where the action is in cognitive therapy for depression. *Cognitive Therapy & Research, 13*, 441–457.

Barefoot, J. C., Dahlstrom, W. G., & Williams, R. B. (1983). Hostility, CHD incidence, and total mortality: A 25-yr follow-up study of 255 physicians. *Psychosomatic Medicine, 45*, 59–63.

Barefoot, J. C., Dodge, K. A., Peterson, B. L., Dahlstrom, W. G., & Williams, R. B., Jr. (1989). The Cook-Medley Hostility scale: Item content and ability to predict survival. *Psychosomatic Medicine, 51*, 46–57.

Barefoot, J. C., Siegler, I. C., Nowlin, J. B., & Peterson, B. L. (1987). Suspiciousness, health, and mortality: A follow-up study of 500 older adults. *Psychosomatic Medicine, 49*, 450–457.

Barkley, R. A. (1990). *Attention-deficit hyperactivity disorder: A handbook for diagnosis and treatment.* New York: Guilford Press.

Barkley, R. A. (1991). Attention deficit hyperactivity disorder. *Psychiatric Annals, 21*, 725–733.

Barkley, R. A. (1996). Attention deficit/hyperactivity disorder. In E. J. Mash & R. A. Barkley (Eds.), *Child psychopathology* (pp. 63–112). New York: Guilford Press.

Barkley, R. A., Fischer, M., Edelbrock, C. S., & Smallish, L. (1990). The adolescent outcome of hyperactive children diagnosed by research criteria: I. An 8-year prospective follow-up study. *Journal of the American Academy of Child & Adolescent Psychiatry, 29*, 546–557.

Barlow, D. H. (1986). Causes of sexual dysfunction: The role of anxiety and cognitive interference. *Journal of Consulting & Clinical Psychology, 54*, 140–148.

Barlow, D. H. (1988). *Anxiety and its disorders: The nature and treatment of anxiety and panic.* New York: Guilford Press.

Barlow, D. H., Brown, T. A., & Craske, M. G. (1994). Definitions of panic attacks and panic disorder in the DSM-IV: Implications for research. *Journal of Abnormal Psychology, 103*, 553–564.

Barlow, D. H., & Craske, M. G. (1994). *Mastery of your anxiety and panic (MAP II).* Albany, NY: Graywind Publications.

Barlow, D. H., Craske, M. G., Cerny, J. A., & Klosko, J. S. (1989). Behavioral treatment of panic disorder. *Behavior Therapy, 20*, 261–282.

Barlow, D. H., Sakheim, D. K., & Beck, J. G. (1983). Anxiety increases sexual arousal. *Journal of Abnormal Psychology, 92*, 49–54.

Baron, M., Gruen, R., Asnis, L., & Lord, S. (1985). Familial transmission of schizotypal and borderline personality disorders. *American Journal of Psychiatry, 142*, 927–934.

Baron, M., Perlman, R., & Levitt, M. (1980). Paranoid schizophrenia and platelet MAO activity. *American Journal of Psychiatry, 137*, 1465–1466.

Baron, P., & Peixoto, N. (1991). Depressive symptoms in adolescents as a function of personality factors. *Journal of Youth and Adolescence, 20*, 493–500.

Baron-Cohen, S., & Swettenham, J. (1997). Theory of mind in autism: Its relationship to executive function and central coherence. In D. J. Cohen & F. R. Volkmar (Eds.), *Handbook of autism and pervasive developmental disorders* (pp. 880–893). Toronto: Wiley.

Barondes, S. H. (1993). *Molecules and mental illness.* New York: Scientific American Library.

Barsky, A. J. (1992). Amplification, somatization, and the somatoform disorders. *Psychosomatics, 33*, 28–34.

Barsky, A. J., Wyshak, G., & Klerman, G. L. (1992). Psychiatric comorbidity in DSM-III-R hypochondriasis. *Archives of General Psychiatry, 49*, 101–108.

Basoglu, M., & Mineka, S. (1992). The role of uncontrollable and unpredictable stress in post-traumatic stress responses in torture survivors. In M. Basoglu (Ed.), *Torture and its consequences: Current treatment approaches* (182–225). Cambridge, England: Cambridge University Press.

Basoglu, M., Mineka, S., Paker, M., Aker, T., Livanou, M., & Goek, S. (1997). Psychological preparedness for trauma as a protective factor in survivors of torture. *Psychological Medicine, 27*, 1421–1433.

Bass, E., & Davis, L. (1988). *The courage to heal: A guide for women survivors of child sexual abuse.* New York: Harper & Row.

Bateson, G., Jackson, D. D., Haley, J., & Weakland, J. (1956). Toward a theory of schizophrenia. *Behavioral Science, 1*, 251–264.

Bauermeister, J. J., Alegria, M., Bird, H. R., Rubio-Stipec, M. et al. (1992). Are attentional-hyperactivity deficits unidimensional or multidimensional syndromes? Empirical findings from a community survey. *Journal of the American Academy of Child & Adolescent Psychiatry, 31,* 423–431.

Baxter, L., Schwartz, J., Bergman, K., & Szuba, M. (1992). Caudate glucose metabolic rate changes with both drug and behavior therapy for obsessive-compulsive disorder. *Archives of General Psychiatry, 49,* 681–689.

Baxter, L. R., Jr., Phelps, M. E., Mazziotta, J. C., Schwartz, J. M., Gerner, R. H., Selin, C. E., & Sumida, R. M. (1985). Cerebral metabolic rates for glucose in mood disorders: Studies with positron emission tomography and fluorodeoxyglucose F 18. *Archives of General Psychiatry, 42,* 441–447.

Baxter, L. R., Schwartz, J. M., Guze, B. H., & Bergman, K. (1990). PET imaging in obsessive compulsive disorder with and without depression. *Journal of Clinical Psychiatry, 51,* 61–69.

Bayley, J. (1999). *Elegy for Iris.* New York: St. Martin's Press.

Beatty, J. (1995). *Principles of behavioral neuroscience.* Dubuque, IA: Wm. C. Brown.

Bebbington, P. E. (1998). Sex and depression. *Psychological Depression, 28,* 1–8.

Beck, A. T. (1967). *Depression: Clinical, experimental, and theoretical aspects.* New York: Harper & Row.

Beck, A. T. (1976). *Cognitive therapy and the emotional disorders.* New York: International Universities Press.

Beck, A. T. (1997). Cognitive therapy: Reflections. In J. K. Zeig (Ed.), *The evolution of psychotherapy: The third conference.* New York: Brunner/Mazel.

Beck, A. T., & Beck, R. W. (1972). Screening depressed patients in family practice: A rapid technique. *Postgraduate Medicine, 52,* 81–85.

Beck, A. T., & Emery, G. (1985). *Anxiety disorders and phobias: A cognitive perspective.* New York: Basic Books.

Beck, A. T., & Freeman, A. M. (1990). *Cognitive therapy of personality disorders.* New York: Guilford Press.

Beck, A. T., Rush, A. J., Shaw, B. F., & Emery, G. (1979). *Cognitive therapy of depression.* New York: Guilford Press.

Beck, A. T., Steer, R. A., Kovacs, M., & Garrison, B. (1985). Hopelessness and eventual suicide: A 10-year prospective study of patients hospitalized with suicidal ideation. *American Journal of Psychiatry, 142,* 559–563.

Beck, A. T., Ward, C. H., Mendelson, M., Moch, J. E., & Erbaugh, J. (1962). Reliability of psychiatric diagnosis: II. A study of consistency of clinical judgments and ratings. *American Journal of Psychiatry, 119,* 351–357.

Beck, A. T., Weissman, A., Lester, D., & Trexler, L. (1974). The measurement of pessimism: The Hopelessness Scale. *Journal of Consulting & Clinical Psychology, 42,* 861–865.

Beck, J. G. (1995). Hypoactive sexual desire: An overview. *Journal of Consulting & Clinical Psychology, 63,* 919–927.

Becker, J. V. (1989). Impact of sexual abuse on sexual functioning. In S. R. Leiblum & R. C. Rosen (Eds.), *Principles and practice of sex therapy: Update for the 1990s* (pp. 298–318). New York: Guilford Press.

Becker, J. V., & Kavoussi, R. J. (1996). Sexual and gender identity disorders. In R. E. Hales & S. C. Yudofsky (Eds.), *The American Psychiatric Press synopsis of psychiatry.* Washington, DC: American Psychiatric Press.

Becker, P. (1998). Special feature: A multifacet circumplex model of personality as a basis for the description and therapy of personality disorders. *Journal of Personality Disorders, 12,* 213–225.

Beckman, L. J. (1994). Treatment needs of women with alcohol problems. *Alcohol Health & Research World, 18,* 206–211.

Beels, C. C., & McFarlane, W. R. (1982). Family treatments of schizophrenia: Background and state of the art. *Hospital & Community Psychiatry, 33,* 541–550.

Beinenfeld, D., & Wheeler, B. G. (1989). Psychiatric services to nursing homes: A liaison model. *Hospital & Community Psychiatry, 40,* 793–794.

Beiser, M. (1988). Influences of time, ethnicity, and attachment on depression in Southeast Asian refugees. *American Journal of Psychiatry, 145,* 46–51.

Beitman, B. D. (1992). Integration through fundamental similarities and useful differences among the schools. In J. C. Norcross (Ed.), *Handbook of psychotherapy integration* (pp. 202–230). New York: Basic Books.

Belcher, J. R. (1988). The future role of state hospitals. *Psychiatric Hospitals, 19,* 79–83.

Bell, A. P., Weinberg, M. S., & Hammersmith, S. K. (1981). *Sexual preference: Its development in men and women.* Bloomington: Indiana University Press.

Bell, C. J., & Nutt, D. J. (1998). Serotonin and panic. *British Journal of Psychiatry, 172,* 465–471.

Bellack, A. S., Morrison, R. L., & Mueser, K. T. (1992). Behavioral interventions in schizophrenia. In S. M. Turner, K. S. Calhoun, & H. E. Adams (Eds.), *Handbook of clinical behavior therapy* (pp. 135–154). New York: Wiley.

Bem, D. J. (1996). Exotic becomes erotic: A developmental theory of sexual orientation. *Psychological Review, 103,* 320–335.

Bemporad, J. (1995). Long-term analytic treatment of depression. In E. E. Beckham & W. R. Leber (Eds.), *Handbook of depression,* (2nd ed., pp. 391–403). New York: Guilford Press.

Bender, L. (1938). *A visual motor gestalt test and its clinical use.* New York: The American Orthopsychiatric Association.

Benedetti, F., Sforzini, L., Colombo, C., Maffei, C., & Smeraldi, E. (1998). Low-dose clozapine in acute and continuation treatment of severe borderline personality disorder. *Journal of Clinical Psychology, 59,* 103–107.

Benjamin, C. M., Adam, S., Wiggins, S., Theilman, J. L., Copley, T. T., Bloch, M., Squitieri, F., McKellin, W., Cox, S., Brown, S. A., Kremer, H. P. H., Burgess, M., Meschino, W., Summers, A., Macgregor, D., Buchanan, J., Greenberg, C., Carson, N., Ives, E., Frecker, M., Welch, J. P., Fuller, A., Rosenblatt, D., Miller, S., Dufrasne, S., Roy, M., Andermann, E., Prevost, C., Khalifa, M., Girard, K., Taylor, S., Hunter, A., Goldsmith, C. Whelan, D., Eisenberg, D., Soltan, H., Kane, J., Shokeir, M. H. K., Gibson, A., Cardwell, S., Bamforth, S., Grover, S., Suchowersky, O., Klimek, M., Garber, T., Gardner, H. A., MacLeod, P., & Hayden, M. R. (1994). Proceed with care: Direct predictive testing for Huntington's disease. *American Journal of Human Genetics, 55,* 606–617.

Bennett, A. E. (1947). Mad doctors. *Journal of Nervous & Mental Disorders, 29,* 11–18.

Benotsch, E. G., Christensen, A. J., & McKelvey, L. (1997). Hostility, social support, and ambulatory cardiovascular activity. *Journal of Behavioral Medicine, 20,* 163–176.

Benschop, R. J., Habaaij, L., Oostveen, F. G., Vingerhoets, A. J. J. M., & Ballieux, R. E. (1998). The influence of psychological stress on immunoregulation of latent Epstein-Barr virus. *Stress Medicine, 14,* 21–29.

Benton, M. K., & Schroeder, H. E. (1990). Social skills training with schizophrenics: A meta-analytic evaluation. *Journal of Consulting & Clinical Psychology, 58,* 741–747.

Berenbaum, S. A., & Hines, M. (1992). Early androgens are related to childhood sex-typed toy preferences. *Psychological Science, 3,* 203–206.

Bergman, A. J., Harvey, P. D., Roitman, S. L., Mohs, R. C., Marder, D., Silverman, J. M., & Siever, L. J. (1998). Verbal learning and memory in schizotypal disorder. *Schizophrenia Bulletin, 24,* 635–641.

Berlin, L. J., Brooks-Gunn, J., McCartoon, C., & McCormick, M. C. (1998). The effectiveness of early intervention: Examining risk factors and pathways to enhanced development. *Preventive Medicine, 27,* 238–245.

Berman, A. L., & Jobes, D. A. (1995). Suicide prevention in adolescents (age 12–18). *Suicide & Life-Threatening Behavior, 25,* 143–154.

Berman, K. F., Torrey, E. F., Daniel, D. G., & Weinberger, D. R. (1992). Regional cerebral blood flow in monozygotic twins discordant and concordant for schizophrenia. *Archives of General Psychiatry, 49,* 927–934.

Berman, M. E., Kavoussi, R. J., & Coccaro, E. F. (1997). Neurotransmitter correlates of human aggression. In D. M. Stoff, J. Breiling, & J. D. Maser (Eds.), *Handbook of antisocial personality disorder* (pp. 305–314). New York: Wiley.

Berman, T., Douglas, V. I., & Barr, R. G. (1999). Effects of methylphenidate on complex cognitive processing in attention-deficit/hyperactivity disorder. *Journal of Abnormal Psychology, 108,* 90–105.

Bernheim, K. F. (1997). *The Lanahan cases and readings in abnormal behavior.* Baltimore, MD: Lanahan.

Bernstein, D. P., Useda, D., & Siever, L. J. (1995). Paranoid personality disorder. In W. J. Livesley (Ed.), *The DSM-IV personality disorders* (pp. 45–57). New York: Guilford Press.

Berridge, K. C., & Valenstein, E. S. (1991). What psychological process mediates feeding evoked by electrical stimulation of the lateral hypothalamus? *Behavioral Neuroscience, 105,* 3–14.

Bettelheim, B. (1967). *The empty fortress: Infantile autism and the birth of the self.* New York: Free Press.

Beutler, L. E., Crago, M., & Arizmendi, T. G. (1986). Therapist variables in psychotherapy process and outcome. In S. L. Garfield & A. E. Bergen (Eds.), *Handbook of psychotherapy and behavior change* (Vol. 3, pp. 257–310). New York: Wiley.

Beutler, L. E., Daldrup, R., Engle, D., & Guest, P. D. (1988). Family dynamics and emotional expression among patients with chronic pain and depression. *Pain, 32,* 65–72.

Beyond Prozac. (1994, February 7). *Newsweek,* p. 123.

Bibring, E. (1953). The mechanism of depression. In P. Greenacre (Ed.), *Affective disorders* (pp. 13–48). New York: International Universities Press.

Biederman, J., Rosenbaum, J. F., Bolduc-Murphy, E. A., Faraone, S. V., Chaloff, J., Hirshfeld, D. R., & Kagan, J. (1993a). A three year follow-up of children with and without behavioral inhibition. *Journal of the American Academy of Child & Adolescent Psychiatry, 32,* 814–821.

Biederman, J., Rosenbaum, J. F., Bolduc-Murphy, E. A., Faraone, S. V., Chaloff, J., Hirshfeld, D. R., & Kagan, J. (1993b). Behavioral inhibition as a temperamental risk factor for anxiety disorders. *Child & Adolescent Psychiatric Clinics of North America, 2,* 667–684.

Biederman, J., Rosenbaum, J. F., Hirshfeld, D. R., Faraone, V., Bolduc, E., Gersten, M., Meminger, S., & Reznick, S. (1990). Psychiatric correlates of behavioral inhibition in young children of parents with and without psychiatric disorders. *Archives of General Psychiatry, 47,* 21–26.

Bierut, L. J., Dinwiddie, S. H., Begleiter, H., Crowe, R. R., Hesselbrock, V., Nurnberger, J. I., Porjesz, B., Schuckit, M. A., & Reich, T. (1998). Familial transmission of substance dependence: Alcohol, marijuana, cocaine, and habitual smoking. *Archives of General Psychiatry, 55,* 982–988.

Billett, R. A., Richter, M. A., & Kennedy, J. L. (1998). Genetics of obsessive-compulsive disorder. In R. P. Swinson (Ed.), *Obsessive-compulsive disorder: Theory, research, and treatment* (pp. 181–206). New York: Guilford Press.

Billings, A., & Moos, R. H. (1981). The role of coping responses and social resources in attenuating the stress of life events. *Journal of Behavioral Medicine, 4,* 157–189.

Bird, T. D., Lampe, T. H., Wijsman, E. M., & Schellenberg, G. D. (1998). Familial Alzheimer's: Genetic studies. In M. F. Folstein (Ed.), *Neurobiology of primary dementia* (pp. 27–42). Washington, DC: American Psychiatric Press.

Birmaher, B., Ryan, N. D., Williamson, D. E., & Brent, D. A. (1996). Childhood and adolescent depression: A review of the past 10 years: Part I. *Journal of the American Academy of Child & Adolescent Psychiatry, 35,* 1427–1439.

Blacher, J. B., Hanneman, R. A., & Rousey, A. B. (1992). Out-of-home placement of children with severe handicaps: A comparison of approaches. *American Journal on Mental Retardation, 96,* 607–616.

Blackburn, G. L., & Kanders, B. S. (1987). Medical evaluation and treatment of the obese patient with cardiovascular disease. *American Journal of Cardiology, 60,* 55G–58G.

Blair, A. J., Lewis, J., & Booth, D. A. (1989). Behavior therapy for obesity: The role of clinicians in the reduction of overweight. *Counseling Psychology Quarterly, 2,* 289–301.

Blake, P., Pincus, J., & Buckner, C. (1995). Neurologic abnormalities in murderers. *Neurology, 45,* 1641–1647.

Blanchard, E. B., Hickling, E. J., Taylor, A. E., & Loos, W. R. et al. (1996). Who develops PTSD from motor vehicle accidents. *Behavior Research & Therapy, 34,* 1–10.

Blanchard, J. J., & Neale, J. M. (1992). Medication effects: Conceptual and methodological issues in schizophrenia research. *Clinical Psychology Review, 12,* 345–361.

Blatt, S. J., & Zuroff, D. C. (1992). Interpersonal relatedness and self-definition: Two prototypes for depression. *Clinical Psychology Review, 12,* 527–562.

Blazer, D. G., George, L., & Hughes, D. (1991). The epidemiology of anxiety disorders. In C. Salzman & B. Liebowitz (Eds.), *Anxiety disorders in the elderly* (pp. 17–30). New York: Springer-Verlag.

Blazer, D. G., Kessler, R. C., & Swartz, M. (1998). Epidemiology of recurrent major and minor depression with a seasonal pattern: The National Comorbidity Study. *British Journal of Psychiatry, 172,* 164–167.

Blazer, D. G., Kessler, R. C., McGonagle, K. A., & Swartz, M. S. (1994). The prevalence and distribution of major depression in a national community sample: The National Comorbidity Study. *American Journal of Psychiatry, 151,* 979–986.

Bleuler, E. (1924). *Textbook of psychiatry.* New York: Macmillan.

Bliss, E. L. (1980). Multiple personalities: A report of 14 cases with implications for schizophrenia and hysteria. *Archives of General Psychiatry, 37,* 1388–1397.

Bliss, E. L. (1986). *Multiple personality, allied disorders, and hypnosis.* New York: Oxford University Press.

Bliss, E. L., & Branch, C. H. H. (1960). *Anorexia nervosa; its history, psychology, and biology.* New York: Hoeber.

Blundell, J. E., & Hill, A. (1993). Binge eating: Psychobiological mechanisms. In C. G. Fairburn & G. T. Wilson (Eds.), *Binge eating:*

Nature, assessment, and treatment (pp. 206–226). New York: Guilford Press.

Boffeli, T. J., & Guze, S. B. (1992). The simulation of neurologic disease. *Psychiatric Clinics of North America, 15,* 301–310.

Bograd, M. (1988). Feminist perspectives on wife abuse: An introduction. In K. Yllo & M. Bograd (Eds.), *Feminist perspectives on wife abuse* (pp. 11–27). Newbury Park, CA: Sage.

Bohart, A. C. (1995). The person-centered psychotherapies. In A. S. Gurman (Ed.), *Essential psychotherapies: Theory and practice* (pp. 55–84). New York: Guilford Press.

Bohart, A. C. (1990). Psychotherapy integration from a client-centered perspective. In G. Lietaer (Ed.), *Client-centered and experiential psychotherapy in the nineties* (pp. 481–500). Leuven, Belgium: Leuven University Press.

Bondolfi, G., Dufour, H., Patris, M., May, J. P., Billeter, U., Eap, C. B., & Bauman, P. (1998). Risperidone versus clozapine in treatment-resistant chronic schizophrenia: A randomized double-blind study. *American Journal of Psychiatry, 155,* 449–504.

Bonta, J., Law, M., & Hanson, K. (1998). The prediction of criminal and violent recidivism among mentally disordered offenders: A meta-analysis. *Psychological Bulletin, 123,* 123–142.

Booth-Kewley, S., & Friedman, H. S. (1987). Psychological predictors of heart disease: A quantitative review. *Psychological Bulletin, 101,* 343–362.

Bootzin, R. R., & Perlis, M. L. (1992). Nonpharmacologic treatments of insomnia. *Journal of Clinical Psychiatry, 53,* 37–41.

Borduin, C. M., Mann, B. J., Cone, L. T., Henggeler, S. W., Fucci, B. R., Blaske, D. M., & Williams, R. A. (1995). Multisystemic treatment of serious juvenile offenders: Long-term prevention of criminality and violence. *Journal of Consulting & Clinical Psychology, 63,* 569–578.

Borkovec, T. D. (1994). The nature, functions, and origins of worry. In G. C. L. Davey & F. Tallis (Eds.), *Worrying: Perspectives on theory, assessment, and treatment* (pp. 5–34). Sussex, England: Wiley.

Borkovec, T. D., & Costello, E. (1993). Efficacy of applied relaxation and cognitive-behavioral therapy in the treatment of generalized anxiety disorder. *Journal of Consulting & Clinical Psychology, 61,* 611–619.

Borkovec, T. D., & Hu, S. (1990). The effect of worry on cardiovascular response to phobic imagery. *Behaviour Research & Therapy, 28,* 69–73.

Borkovec, T. D., & Mathews, A. M. (1988). Treatment of nonphobic anxiety disorders: A comparison of nondirective, cognitive, and coping desensitization therapy. *Journal of Consulting & Clinical Psychology, 56,* 877–884.

Borkovec, T. D., & Roemer, L. (1994). Generalized anxiety disorder. In M. Hersen (Ed.), *Handbook of prescriptive treatments for adults* (pp. 261–281). New York: Plenum.

Borkovec, T. D., & Whisman, M. A. (1996). Psychosocial treatment for generalized anxiety disorder. In M. R. Mavissakalian (Ed.), *Long-term treatments of anxiety disorders* (pp. 171–199). Washington, DC: American Psychiatric Press.

Bornstein, P. E., Clayton, P. J., Halikas, J. A., Maurice, W. L., & Robins, E. (1973). The depression of widowhood after thirteen months. *British Journal of Psychiatry, 122,* 561–566.

Borys, D. S., & Pope, K. S. (1989). Dual relationships between therapist and client: A national study of psychologists, psychiatrists, and social workers. *Professional Psychology: Research & Practice, 20,* 283–293.

Bouchard, T. J. (1994). Genes, environment, and personality. *Science, 264,* 1700–1701.

Bouchard, T. J., Lykken, D. T., McGue, M., & Segal, N. L. (1990). Sources of human psychological differences: The Minnesota study of twins reared apart. *Science, 250,* 223–228.

Bourden, K., Boyd, J., Rae, D., & Burns, B. (1988). Gender differences in phobias: Results of the EAC community survey. *Journal of Anxiety Disorders, 2,* 227–241.

Bourin, M., Baker, G. B., & Bradwejn, J. (1998). Neurobiology of panic disorder. *Journal of Psychosomatic Research, 44,* 163–180.

Bouwer, C., & Stein, D. J. (1998). Use of selective serotonin reuptake inhibitor citalopram in the treatment of generalized social phobia. *Journal of Affective Disorders, 49,* 79–82.

Bowen, R. C., Offord, D. R., & Boyle, M. H. (1990). The prevalence of overanxious disorder and separation anxiety disorder: Results from the Ontario Child Health Study. *Journal of the American Academy of Child & Adolescent Psychiatry, 29,* 753–758.

Bower, G. H. (1981). Mood and memory. *American Psychologist, 36,* 129–148.

Bowlby, J. (1969). *Attachment and loss.* London: Hogarth Press.

Bowlby, J. (1982). *Attachment and loss* (2nd ed.). New York: Basic Books.

Boyd, C. J., & Guthrie, B. (1996). Women, their significant others, and crack cocaine. *The American Journal on Addictions, 5,* 156–166.

Bradford, J. M. (1995a). Pharmacological treatment of paraphilias. In J. M. Oldham & M. B. Riba (Eds.), *Review of psychiatry* (Vol. 14, pp. 755–778). Washington, DC: American Psychiatric Press.

Bradley, S. J. (1995a). Psychosexual disorders in adolescence. In J. M. Oldham & M. B. Riba (Eds.), *Review of psychiatry* (Vol. 14, pp. 735–754). Washington, DC: American Psychiatric Press.

Bradley, S. J. (1995b). Psychosexual disorders in adolescence. In J. M. Oldham & M. B. Riba (Eds.), *Review of psychiatry* (Vol. 14, pp. 735–754). Washington, DC: American Psychiatric Press.

Bradley, S. J. & Zucker, K. J. (1997). Gender identity disorder: A review of the past 10 years. *Journal of the American Academy of Child & Adolescent Psychiatry, 36,* 872–880.

Braginsky, B. M., Braginsky, D. D., & Ring, K. (1969). *Methods of madness: The mental hospital as last resort.* New York: Holt.

Brain, P. F., & Susman, E. J. (1997). Hormonal aspects of aggression and violence. In D. M. Stoff, J. Breiling, & J. D. Maser (Eds.), *Handbook of antisocial personality disorder* (pp. 314–323). New York: Wiley.

Brandt, J., & Codori, A. M. (1995). Three year longitudinal follow-up after predictive testing for Huntington's disease (poster abstract). *American Journal of Human Genetics, 57,* A291.

Braun, B. G. (Ed.). (1986). *Treatment of multiple personality disorder.* Washington, DC: American Psychiatric Press.

Bray, G. A. (1986). Effects of obesity on health and happiness. In K. D. Brownell & J. P. Foreyt (Eds.), *Handbook of eating disorders: Physiology, psychology, and treatment of obesity, anorexia, and bulimia* (pp. 3–44). New York: Basic Books.

Brazier, M. (1960). *The electrical activity of the nervous system: A textbook for students.* London: Pitman Medical Publishing.

Breggin, P. R. (1991). *Toxic psychiatry: Why therapy, empathy, and love must replace the drugs, electroshock, and biochemical theories of the "new psychiatry."* New York: St. Martin's Press.

Breggin, P. R. (1997). *Brain-disabling treatments in psychiatry: Drugs, electroshock, and the role of the FDA.* New York: Springer.

Bregman, J. D., & Gerdtz, J. (1997). Behavioral interventions. In D. J. Cohen & F. R. Volkmar (Eds.), *Handbook of autism and pervasive developmental disorders* (pp. 606–630). Toronto: Wiley.

Breier, A. (1995). Serotonin, schizophrenia and antipsychotic drug action. *Schizophrenia Research, 14*, 187–202.

Breier, A., Schreiber, J. L., Dyer, J., & Pickar, D. (1991). National Institutes of Mental Health longitudinal study of chronic schizophrenia: Prognosis and predictors of outcome. *Archives of General Psychiatry, 48*, 239–246.

Breier, A., Schreiber, J. L., Dyer, J., & Pickar, D. (1992). Course of illness and predictors of outcome in chronic schizophrenia: Implications for pathophysiology. *British Journal of Psychiatry, 161*, 38–43.

Bremner, J. D. (1998). Neuroimaging of posttraumatic stress disorder. *Psychiatric Annals, 28*, 445–450.

Bremner, J. D., Southwick, S. M., & Charney, D. S. (1999). The neurobiology of posttraumatic stress disorder: An integration of animal and human research. In P. A. Saigh (Ed.), *Posttraumatic stress disorder: A comprehensive text.* (pp. 103–143). Boston: Allyn & Bacon.

Brems, C., & Schlottmann, R. S. (1988). Gender-bound definitions of mental health. *The Journal of Psychology, 122*, 5–14.

Brent, D. A., Kerr, M. M., Goldstein, C., Bozigar, J., Wartella, M., & Allan, M. J. (1989). An outbreak of suicide and suicidal behavior in a high school. *Journal of the American Academy of Child & Adolescent Psychiatry, 28*, 918–924.

Brent, D. A., Kupfer, D. J., Bromet, E. J., & Dew, M. A. (1988). The assessment and treatment of patients at risk for suicide. In A. J. Frances & R. E. Hales (Eds.), *American Psychiatric Press review of psychiatry,* (Vol. 7,). Washington, DC: American Psychiatric Press.

Brent, D. A., Moritz, G., Bridge, J., Perper, J., et al. (1996). Long-term impact of exposure to suicide: A three-year controlled follow-up. *Journal of the American Academy of Child & Adolescent Psychiatry, 35*, 646–653.

Brent, D. A., Perper, J. A., Allman, C. J., Moritz, G. M., Wartella, M. E., & Zelenak, J. P. (1991). The presence and accessibility of firearms in the homes of adolescent suicide: A case-control study. *Journal of the American Medical Association, 266*, 2989–2995.

Breslow, N., Evans, L., & Langley, J. (1985). On the prevalence and roles of females in the sadomasochistic subculture: Report of an empirical study. *Archives of Sexual Behavior, 14*, 303–317.

Brewin, C. R., MacCarthy, B., Duda, K., & Vaughn, C. E. (1991). Attribution and expressed emotion in the relatives of patients with schizophrenia. *Journal of Abnormal Psychology, 100*, 546–554.

Briere, J., & Conte, J. R. (1993). Self-reported amnesia for abuse in adults molested as children. *Journal of Traumatic Stress, 6*, 21–31.

Briere, J., & Runtz, M. (1989). University males' sexual interest in children: Predicting potential indices of "pedophilia" in a nonforensic sample. *Child Abuse & Neglect, 13*, 65–75.

British Broadcasting Corporation (1995). *The Panorama Interview with the Princess of Wales.* London, England.

Bromberger, J. T., & Matthews, K. A. (1996). A longitudinal study of the effects of pessimism, trait anxiety, and life stress on depressive symptoms in middle-aged women. *Psychology & Aging, 11*, 207–213.

Brooks-Gunn, J., Klebanov, P. K., & Duncan, G. J. (1996). Ethnic differences in children's intelligence test scores: Role of economic deprivation, home environment, and maternal characteristics. *Child Development, 67*, 396–408.

Brooks-Gunn, J., Klebanov, P. K., & Liaw, F. (1995). The learning, physical, and emotional environment of the home in the context of

poverty: The Infant Health and Development Program. *Children & Youth Services Review, 17*, 251–276.

Brosschot, J. F., Godaert, G. L. R., Benschop, R. J., Olff, M., Ballieux, R. E., & Heijnen, C. J. (1998). Experimental stress and immunological reactivity: A closer look at perceived uncontrollability. *Psychosomatic Medicine, 60*, 359–361.

Broverman, I. K., Vogel, S. R., Clarkson, F. E., & Rosenkrantz, P. S. (1970). Sex-role stereotypes and clinical judgment on mental health. *Journal of Consulting & Clinical Psychology, 34*, 1–7.

Brown, G. W., Birley, J. L., & Wing, J. K. (1972). Influence of family life on the course of schizophrenic disorders: A replication. *British Journal of Psychiatry, 121*, 241–258.

Brown, J. E., Ayowa, O. B., & Brown, R. C. (1993). Dry and tight: Sexual practices and potential risks in Zaire. *Social Science & Medicine, 37*, 989–994.

Brown, L. L., Tomarken, A. J., Orth, D. N., & Loosen, P. T. (1996). Individual differences in repressive-defensiveness precit basal salivary cortisol levels. *Journal of Personality & Social Psychology, 70*, 362–371.

Brown, S. A., Inaba, R. K., Gillin, J. C., & Schuckit, M. A. (1995). Alcoholism and affective disorder: Clinical course of depressive symptoms. *American Journal of Psychiatry, 152*, 45–52.

Browne, A. (1993). Violence against women by male partners: Prevalence, outcomes, and policy implications. *American Psychologist, 48*, 1077–1087.

Browne, A., & Williams, K. R. (1993). Gender, intimacy, and lethal violence: Trends from 1976–1987. *Gender & Society, 7*, 78–98.

Brownell, K. D., & Foreyt, J. P. (Eds.). (1986). *Handbook of eating disorders.* New York: Basic Books.

Brownell, K. D., & Rodin, J. (1994). The dieting maelstrom: Is it possible and advisable to lose weight? *American Psychologist, 49*, 781–791.

Brownell, K. D., Rodin, J., & Wilmore, J. H. (1992). *Eating, body weight, and performance in athletes: Disorders of modern society.* Philadelphia: Lea & Febiger.

Brownell, K. D., & Wadden, T. A. (1992). Etiology and treatment of obesity: Understanding a serious, prevalent, and refractory disorder. *Journal of Consulting & Clinical Psychology, 60*, 505–517.

Bruce, T. J., Spiegel, D. A., & Hegel, M. T. (1999). Cognitive-behavioral therapy helps prevent relapse and recurrence of panic disorder following alprazolam discontinuation: A long-term follow-up of the Peoria and Dartmouth studies. *Journal of Consulting & Clinical Psychology, 67*, 151–156.

Bruch, H. (1970). Instinct and interpersonal experience. *Comprehensive Psychiatry, 11*, 495–506.

Bruch, H. (1973). *Eating disorders: Obesity, anorexia nervosa, and the person within.* New York: Basic Books.

Bruch, H. (1982). Anorexia nervosa: Therapy and theory. *American Journal of Psychiatry, 139*, 1531–1538.

Bruch, M. A., & Cheek, J. M. (1995). Developmental factors in childhood and adolescent shyness. In R. G. Heimberg, M. R. Liebowitz, D. A. Hope, & F. R. Schneier (Eds.), *Social phobia: Diagnosis, assessment, and treatment.* New York: Guilford Press.

Brugha, T. S., Sharp, H. M., Cooper, S. A., Weisender, C., Britto, D., Shrikwin, R., Sherrif, T., & Kirwan, P. H. (1998). The Leicester 500 Project. Social support and the development of postnatal depressive symptoms, a prospective cohort survey. *Psychological Medicine, 28*, 63–79.

Buchanan, R. W., Breier, A., Kirkpatrick, B., Ball, P., & Carpenter, W. T. (1998). Positive and negative symptom response to clozapine in schizophrenic patients with and without the deficit syndrome. *American Journal of Psychiatry, 155*, 751–760.

Buchsbaum, M. S. (1984). The Genain quadruplets: Electrophysiological, positron emission, and X-ray tomographic studies. *Psychiatry Research, 13*, 95–108.

Buchsbaum, M. S., Haier, R. J., Potkin, S. G., & Nuechterlein, K. (1992). Fronostriatal disorder of cerebral metabolism in never-medicated schizophrenics. *Archives of General Psychiatry, 49*, 935–942.

Buchsbaum, M. S., Someya, T., Wu, J. C., Tang, C. Y., & Bunney, W. E. (1997). Neuroimaging bipolar illness with positron emission tomography and magnetic resonance imaging. *Psychiatric Annals, 27*, 489–495.

Buckley, P. F. (1998). Structural brain imaging in schizophrenia. *Psychiatric Clinics of North America, 21*, 77–92.

Buckley, P. F., & Meltzer, H. Y. (1995). Treatment of schizophrenia. In A. F. Schatzberg & C. B. Nemeroff (Eds.), *The American Psychiatric Press textbook of psychopharmacology* (pp. 615–640). Washington, DC: American Psychiatric Press.

Buckwalter, J., Sobel, E., Dunn, M. E., & Diz, M. M. (1993). Gender differences on a brief measure of cognitive functioning in Alzheimer's disease. *Archives of Neurology, 50*, 757–760.

Bugental, J. F. T. (1997). There is a fundamental division in how psychotherapy is conceived. In J. K. Zeig (Ed.), *The evolution of psychotherapy: The third conference.* New York: Brunner/Mazel.

Bulik, C. M., Sullivan, P. F., Fear, J., & Pickering, A. (1997). Predictors of the development of bulimia nervosa in women with anorexia nervosa. *Journal of Nervous & Mental Disease, 185*, 704–707.

Bulman, R. J., & Wortman, C. G. (1977). Attributions of blame and coping in the "real world": Severe accident victims react to their lot. *Journal of Personality & Social Psychology, 35*, 351–363.

Bunney, W. E., & Davis, J. M. (1965). Norepinephrine in depressive reactions: A review. *Archives of General Psychiatry, 13*, 483–493.

Burke, K. C., Burke, J. D., Regier, D. A., & Rae, D. S. (1990). Age at onset of selected mental disorders in five community populations. *Archives of General Psychiatry, 47*, 511–518.

Burnam, M. A., Stein, J. A., Golding, J. M., & Siegel, J. M. (1988). Sexual assault and mental disorders in a community population. *Journal of Consulting & Clinical Psychology, 56*, 843–850.

Burnette, E. (1997). Community psychologists help South Africans mend. *APA Monitor, 28*. On the web at: www.apa.org/monitor/sep97/safrica.html

Burns, D. (1980). *Feeling good: The new mood therapy.* New York: Morrow.

Burns, D., & Nolen-Hoeksema, S. (1991). Coping styles, homework assignments and the effectiveness of cognitive-behavioral therapy. *Journal of Consulting & Clinical Psychology, 59*, 305–311.

Burns, D. D., & Nolen-Hoeksema, S. (1992). Therapeutic empathy and recovery from depression in cognitive-behavioral therapy: A structural equation model. *Journal of Consulting & Clinical Psychology, 60*, 441–449.

Burr, J. A., Hartman, J. T., & Matteson, D. W. (1999). Black suicide in U.S. metropolitan areas: An examination of the racial inequality and social integration-regulation hypotheses. *Social Forces, 77*, 1049–1081.

Bursik, R. J. J., & Grasmick, H. G. (1993). *Neighborhoods and crime: The dimensions of effective community control.* New York: Lexington Books.

Busfield, J. (1986). *Managing madness: Changing ideas and practice.* London: Hutchinson.

Butcher, J. N. (1990). *The MMPI-2 in psychological treatment.* New York: Oxford University Press.

Butler, G., Fennell, M., Robson, P., & Gelder, M. (1991). Comparison of behavior therapy and cognitive behavior therapy in the treatment of generalized anxiety disorder. *Journal of Consulting & Clinical Psychology, 59,* 167–175.

Butzlaff, R. L., & Hooley, J. M. (1998). Expressed emotion and psychiatric relapse. *Archives of General Psychiatry, 55,* 547–552.

Byrne, E. J. (1994). *Confusional states in older people.* Boston: E. Arnold.

C

Cade, J. (1949). Lithium salts in the treatment of psychotic excitement. *Medical Journal of Australia, 36,* 349–352.

Cade, J. (1979). *Mending the mind: A short history of twentieth century psychiatry.* Melbourne: Sun Books.

Cadoret, R. J., & Cain, C. A. (1980). Sex differences in predictors of antisocial behavior in adoptees. *Archives of General Psychiatry, 37,* 1171–1175.

Cadoret, R. J., & Stewart, M. A. (1991). An adoption study of attention deficit/hyperactivity/aggression and their relationship to adult antisocial personality. *Comprehensive Psychiatry, 32,* 73–82.

Caffey, J. (1972). On the theory and practice of shaking infants. *American Journal of Diseases of Children, 124,* 161–172.

Cameron, N., & Rychlak, J. F. (1985). *Personality development and psychopathology: A dynamic approach.* Boston: Houghton Mifflin.

Camp, B. W., Broman, S. H., Nichols, P. L., & Leff, M. (1998). Maternal and neonatal risk factors for mental retardation: Defining the "at-risk" child. *Early Human Development, 50,* 159–173.

Campbell, M., Adams, P. B., Small, A. M., Kafantaris, V., Silva, R. R., Shell, J., Perry, R., & Overall, J. E. (1995). Lithium in hospitalized aggressive children with conduct disorder: A double-blind and placebo-controlled study. *Journal of the American Academy of Child & Adolescent Psychiatry, 34,* 445–453.

Campbell, M., Perry, R., & Green, W. H. (1984). Use of lithium in children and adolescents. *Psychosomatics, 25,* 95–106.

Campos, J. J., Campos, R. G., & Barrett, K. C. (1989). Emergent themes in the study of emotional development and emotion regulation. *Developmental Psychology, 25,* 394–402.

Canetto, S. S., & Lester, D. (1995). Gender and the primary prevention of suicide mortality. *Suicide & Life Threatening Behavior, 25,* 58–69.

Canino, G. J., Burnam, A., & Caetano, R. (1992). The prevalence of alcohol abuse and/or dependence in two Hispanic communities. In J. E. Helzer & G. J. Canino, (Eds.), *Alcoholism in North America, Europe, and Asia* (pp. 131–155). New York: Oxford University Press.

Canino, G. J., Rubio-Stipec, M., & Bravo, M. (1988). Psychiatric diagnostic nosology in transcultural epidemiology research. *Acta Psiquiatrica Psicologica de America Latina, 34,* 251–259.

Cannon, T. D. (1996). Abnormalities of brain structure and function in schizophrenia: Implications for etiology and pathophysiology. *Annals of Medicine, 28,* 533–539.

Cannon, T. D. (1998). Genetic and perinatal influences in the etiology of schizophrenia: A neurodevelopmental model. In M. F. Lenzenweger (Ed.), *Origins and development of schizophrenia: Advances in experimental psychopathology,* (pp. 67–92). Washington, DC: American Psychological Association.

Cannon, T. D., Kapiro, J., Lonnqvist, J., Huttunen, M., & Koskenvuo, M. (1998). The genetic epidemiology of schizophrenia in a Finnish twin cohort. *Archives of General Psychiatry, 55,* 67–74.

Cannon, T. D., Mednick, S. A., Parnas, J., Schulsinger, F., Praestholm, J., & Vestergaard, A. (1993). Developmental brain abnormalities in the offspring of schizophrenic mothers: I. Contributions of genetic and perinatal factors. *Archives of General Psychiatry, 50,* 551–564.

Cannon, T. D., Rosso, I. M., Bearden, C. E., Sanchez, L. E., & Hadley, T. (1999). A prospective cohort study of neurodevelopmental processes in the genesis and epigenesis of schizophrenia. *Development & Psychopathology, 11,* 467–485.

Caplan, P. J., & Gans, M. (1991). Is there empirical justification for the category of "self-defeating personality disorder"? *Feminism & Psychology, 1,* 263–278.

Cappe, R. F., & Alden, L. E. (1986). A comparison of treatment strategies for clients functionally impaired by extreme shyness and social avoidance. *Journal of Consulting & Clinical Psychology, 54,* 796–801.

Carey, G., & Goldman, D. (1997). The genetics of antisocial behavior. In D. M. Stoff, J. Breiling, & J. D. Maser (Eds.), *Handbook of antisocial personality disorder* (pp. 243–254). New York: Wiley.

Carlson, C. (2000). ADHD is overdiagnosed. In R. L. Atkinson, R. C. Atkinson, E. E. Smith, D. J. Bem, & Nolen-Hoeksema, S. *Hilgard's introduction to psychology,* (13th ed., p. 562). Ft. Worth: Harcourt.

Carmelli, D. S., Swan, G. E., Robinette, D., & Fabsitz, R. (1992). Genetic influence on smoking: A study of male twins. *New England Journal of Medicine, 327,* 829–833.

Carnelley, K. B., Pietromonaco, P. R., & Jaffe, K. (1994). Depression, working models of others, and relationship functioning. *Journal of Personality & Social Psychology, 66,* 127–140.

Carson, N. D., & Johnson, R. E. (1985). Suicidal thoughts and problem-solving preparation among college students. *Journal of College Student Personnel, 26,* 484–487.

Carter, J. C., & Fairburn, C. G. (1998). Cognitive-behavioral self-help for binge eating disorder: A controlled effectiveness study. *Journal of Consulting & Clinical Psychology, 66,* 616–623.

Carter, M. M., Hollon, S. D., Carson, R. S., & Shelton, R. C. (1995). Effects of a safe person on induced distress following a biological challenge in panic disorder with agoraphobia. *Journal of Abnormal Psychology, 104,* 156–163.

Caspi, A. (1993). Why maladaptive behaviors persist: Sources of continuity and change across the life course. In D. C. Funder (Ed.), *Studying lives through time: Personality and development* (pp. 343–376). Washington, DC: American Psychological Association.

Caspi, A. (in press). Personality development across the life course. In N. Eisenberg (Ed.), *Handbook of child psychology: Vol. 3. Social, emotional, and personality development.* New York: Wiley.

Caspi, A., & Moffitt, T. E. (1991). Individual differences are accentuated during periods of social change: The sample case of girls at puberty. *Journal of Personality & Social Psychology, 61,* 157–168.

Castiglioni, A. (1946). *Adventures of the mind.* (1st American ed.). New York: Alfred A. Knopf.

Castonguay, L. G., Eldredge, K. L., & Agras, W. S. (1995). Binge eating disorder: Current state and future directions. *Clinical Psychology Review, 15,* 865–890.

Ceci, S. J., & Bruck, M. (1995). *Jeopardy in the courtroom.* Washington, DC: American Psychological Association.

Cervantes, R. C., Salgado de Snyder, V. N., & Padilla, A. M. (1989). Posttraumatic stress in immigrants from Central America and Mexico. *Hospital & Community Psychiatry, 40,* 615–619.

Chamberlain, P., & Rosicky, J. G. (1995). The effectiveness of family therapy in the treatment of adolescents with conduct disorders and delinquency. *Journal of Marital & Family Therapy, 21,* 441–459.

Chambless, D. C., Cherney, J., Caputo, G. C., & Rheinstein, B. J. (1987). Anxiety disorders and alcoholism: A study with inpatient alcoholics. *Journal of Anxiety Disorders, 1,* 29–40.

Chambless, D. L., & Hollon, S. D. (1998). Defining empirically supported therapies. *Journal of Consulting & Clinical Psychology, 66,* 7–18.

Champion, L. A., Goodall, G., & Rutter, M. (1995). Behavior problems in childhood and stressors in early adult life: I. A 20-year follow-up of London school children. *Psychological Medicine, 25,* 231–246.

Chapman, L. J., Edell, W. S., & Chapman, J. P. (1980). Physical anhedonia, perceptual aberration, and psychosis proneness. *Schizophrenia Bulletin, 6,* 639–653.

Chapman, T. F., Manuzza, S., & Fyer, A. J. (1995). Epidemiology and family studies of social phobia. In R. G. Heimberg, M. R. Liebowitz, D. A. Hope, & F. R. Schneier (Eds.), *Social phobia: Diagnosis, assessment, and treatment* (pp. 21–40). New York: Guilford Press.

Charney, D. S., Southwick, S. M., Krystal, J. H., Deutch, A. Y., Murburg, M. M., & Davis, M. (1994). Neurobiological mechanisms of PTSD. In M. M. Murburg (Ed.), *Catecholamine function in posttraumatic stress disorder: Emerging concepts* (pp. 131–158). Washington, DC: American Psychiatric Press.

Charney, D. S., Woods, S. W., Krystal, J. H., Nagy, L. M., & Heninger, G. R. (1992). Noradrenergic neuronal dysregulation in panic disorder: The effects of intravenous yohimbine and clonidine in panic disorder patients. *Acta Psychiatrica Scandinavica, 86,* 273–282.

Chassin, L., Pitts, S. C., DeLucia, C., & Todd, M. (1999). A longitudinal study of children of alcoholics: Predicting young adult substance use disorders anxiety, and depression. *Journal of Abnormal Psychology, 108,* 106–119.

Chaturvedi, S. K. (1987). Family morbidity in chronic pain patients. *Pain, 30,* 159–168.

Chemtob, C. M., Bauer, G. B., Neller, G., Hamada, R., Glisson, C., & Stevens, V. (1990). Posttraumatic stress disorder among Special Forces Vietnam veterans. *Military Medicine, 155,* 16–20.

Chodorow, N. (1978). *The reproduction of mothering.* Berkeley: University of California Press.

Chou, T. (1992). Wake up and smell the coffee: Caffeine, coffee, and the medical consequences. *Western Journal of Medicine, 157,* 544–553.

Chun, M. R., Schofield, P., Stern, Y., Tatemichi, T. K., & Mayeux, R. (1998). The epidemiology of dementia among the elderly: Experience in a community-based registry. In M. F. Folstein (Ed.), *Neurobiology of primary dementia* (pp. 1–26). Washington, DC: American Psychiatric Press.

Cicchetti, D., & Rogosch, F. A. (1996). Equifinality and multifinality in developmental psychopathology. *Development & Psychopathology, 8,* 597–600.

Cicchetti, D., & Toth, S. L. (1998). The development of depression in children and adolescents. *American Psychologists, 53,* 221–241.

Clark, D. A., & DeSilva, P. (1985). The nature of depressive and anxious, intrusive thoughts:

Distinct or uniform phenomena? *Behaviour Research & Therapy, 23,* 383–393.

Clark, D. A., & Purdon, C. (1993). New perspectives for a cognitive theory of obsessions. *Australian Psychologist, 28,* 161–167.

Clark, D. M. (1988). A cognitive model of panic attacks. In S. Rachman & J. D. Maser (Eds.), *Panic: Psychological perspectives* (pp. 71–89). Hillsdale, NJ: Erlbaum.

Clark, D. M., Salkovskis, P. M., Hackmann, A., Middleton, H., Anastasiades, P., & Gelder, M. (1994). A comparison of cognitive therapy, applied relaxation, and imipramine in the treatment of panic disorder. *British Journal of Psychiatry, 164,* 759–769.

Clark, D. M., Salkovskis, P. M., Hackmann, A., Wells, A., Ludgate, J., & Gelder, M. (1999). Brief cognitive therapy for panic disorder: A randomized controlled trial. *Journal of Consulting & Clinical Psychology, 67,* 583–589.

Clark, L. A., Watson, D., & Mineka, S. (1994). Temperament, personality, and the mood and anxiety disorders. *Journal of Abnormal Psychology, 103,* 103–116.

Cleckley, H. M. (1941). *The mask of sanity: An attempt to reinterpret the so-called psychopathic personality.* St. Louis: C. V. Mosby.

Cleveland, S., Mulvey, E. P., Appelbaum, P. S., & Lidz, C. W. (1989). Do dangerousness-oriented commitment laws restrict hospitalization of patients who need treatment? A test. *Hospital & Community Psychiatry, 40,* 266–271.

Cloninger, C. R. (1987). A systematic method for clinical description and classification of personality variants: A proposal. *Archives of General Psychiatry, 44,* 573–588.

Cloninger, C. R., & Gottesman, I. I. (1987). Genetic and environmental factors in antisocial behavior disorders. In S. A Mednick, T. E. Moffitt, & S. A. Stack (Eds.), *The causes of crime: New biological approaches* (pp. 92–109). New York: Cambridge University Press.

Cloninger, R., Bayon, C., & Przybeck, T. (1997). Epidemiology and axis I comorbidity of antisocial personality. In D. M. Stoff, J. Breiling, & J. D. Maser (Eds.), *Handbook of antisocial personality disorder* (pp. 12–21). New York: Wiley.

Coccaro, E. F., & Kavoussi, R. J. (1997). Fluoxetine and impulsive aggressive behavior in personality-disordered subjects. *Archives of General Psychiatry, 54,* 1081–1088.

Coccaro, E. F., & Siever, L. J. (1995). The psychopharmacology of personality disorders. In F. E. Bloom & D. J. Kupfer (Eds.), *Psychopharmacology: The fourth generation of progress* (pp. 1567–1578). New York: Raven Press.

Cocores, J., Pottash, A. C., & Gold, M. S. (1991). Cocaine. In N. S. Miller (Ed.), *Comprehensive handbook of drug and alcohol addiction* (pp. 341–352). New York: Marcel Dekker.

Coffey, C. E. (1987). Cerebral laterality and emotion: The neurology of depression. *Comprehensive Psychiatry, 28,* 197–219.

Coffey, L. E., Wilkinson, W. E., Weiner, R. D., & Ritchie, J. C. (1993). The dexamethasone suppression test and quantitative cerebral anatomy in depression. *Biological Psychiatry, 33,* 442–449.

Cohen, P., Cohen, J., Kasen, S., Velez, C. N., Hartmark, C., Johnson, J., Rojas, M., Brook, J., & Streuning, E. L. (1993). An epidemiological study of disorders in late adolescence: I. Age- and gender-specific prevalence. *Journal of Child Psychology & Psychiatry, 6,* 851–867.

Cohen, S. (1996). Psychological stress, immunity, and upper respiratory infections. *Current Directions in Psychological Science, 5,* 86–90.

Cohen, S., Tyrrell, D. A., & Smith, A. P. (1991). Psychological stress and susceptibility to the common cold. *The New England Journal of Medicine, 325,* 606–612.

Cohen, S. A., Ohrig, K., Lott, R. S., & Kerrick, J. M. (1998). Risperidone for aggression and self-injurious behavior in adults with mental retardation. *Journal of Autism & Developmental Disorders, 28,* 229–233.

Cohen-Cole, S. A., & Stoudemire, A. (1987). Major depression and physical illness. *Psychiatric Clinics of North America, 10,* 1–17.

Cohen-Sandler, R., Berman, A. L., & King, R. A. (1982). Life stress and symptomatology: Determinants of suicidal behavior in children. *Journal of American Academy of Child Psychiatry, 21,* 178–186.

Colas, E. (1998). *Just checking: Scenes from the life of an obsessive-compulsive.* New York: Pocket Books.

Colby, D. M. (1981). Modeling a paranoid mind. *Behavioral & Brain Sciences, 4,* 515–560.

Colder, C. R., & Chassin, L. (1993). The stress and negative affect model of adolescent alcohol use and the moderating effects of behavioral undercontrol. *Journal of Studies on Alcohol, 54,* 326–333.

Cole, D. A., Martin, J. M., Peeke, L. G., Seroczynski, A. D., & Hoffman, K. (1998). Are cognitive errors of underestimation predictive or reflective of depressive symptoms in children: A longitudinal study. *Journal of Abnormal Psychology, 107,* 481–496.

Cole, M. G., & Bellavance, F. (1997). The prognosis of depression in old age. *American Journal of Geriatric Psychiatry, 5,* 4–14.

Cole, S. W., Kemeny, M. E., Taylor, S. E., & Visscher, B. R. (1996). Elevated physical health risk among gay men who conceal their homosexual identity. *Health Psychology, 15,* 243–251.

Cole, S. W., Kemeny, M. E., Taylor, S. E., Visscher, B. R., & Fahey, J. L. (1995). Psychological inhibition and the accelerated course of HIV infection in gay men who conceal their homosexual identity. *Psychosomatic Medicine, 57,* 68.

Cole, W. (1992). Incest perpetrators: Their assessment and treatment. *Psychiatric Clinics of North America, 15,* 689–701.

Collins, J. J., & Schlenger, W. E. (Nov. 9–13, 1983). The prevalence of psychiatric disorder among admissions to prison (Ed.). Paper presented at the American Society of Criminology 35th Annual Meeting, Denver, CO.

Compas, B. E. (1987). Stress and life events during childhood and adolescence. *Clinical Psychology Review, 7,* 275–302.

Compton, W. M., Helzer, J. E., Hwu, H., Yeh, E., McEvoy, L., Tipp, J. E., & Spitznagel, E. L. (1991). New methods in cross-cultural psychiatry: Psychiatric illness in Taiwan and the United States. *American Journal of Psychiatry, 148,* 1697–1704.

Consumer Reports. (1993, June). Diets: What works—what doesn't. *Consumer Reports,* 347–357.

Consumer Reports. (1995, November). Mental health: Does therapy help? *Consumer Reports,* 734–739.

Coons, P. M. (1980). Multiple personality: Diagnostic considerations. *Journal of Clinical Psychiatry, 41,* 330–336.

Coons, P. M. (1984). *Childhood antecedents of multiple personality.* Paper presented at the Meeting of the American Psychiatric Association, Los Angeles, CA.

Coons, P. M. (1986). Treatment progress in 20 patients with multiple personality disorder. *The Journal of Nervous & Mental Disease, 174,* 715–721.

Coons, P. M. (1994). Confirmation of childhood abuse in child and adolescent cases of multiple personality disorder and dissociative disorder not otherwise specified. *Journal of Nervous & Mental Disease, 182,* 461–464.

Coons, P. M., Cole, C., Pellow, T. A., & Milstein, V. (1990). Symptoms of posttraumatic stress disorder and dissociation in women victims of abuse. In R. P. Kluft (Ed.), *Incest-related syndromes of adult psychopathology* (pp. 205–226). Washington, DC: American Psychiatric Press.

Coons, P. M., & Milstein, V. (1986). Psychosexual disturbances in multiple personality: Characteristics, etiology, and treatment. *Journal of Clinical Psychiatry, 47,* 106–110.

Coons, P. M., & Milstein, V. (1990). Self-mutilation associated with dissociative disorders. *Dissociation: Progress in the Dissociative Disorders, 3,* 81–87.

Coontz, P. D., Lidz, C. W., & Mulvey, E. P. (1994). Gender and the assessment of dangerousness in the psychiatric emergency room. *International Journal of Law & Psychiatry, 17,* 369–376.

Cooper, M. L., Russell, M., Skinner, J. B., Frone, M. R., & Mudar, P. (1992). Stress and alcohol use: Moderating effects of gender, coping, and alcohol expectancies. *Journal of Abnormal Psychology, 101,* 139–152.

Corbitt, E. M., & Widiger, T. A. (1995). Sex differences among the personality disorders: An exploration of the data. *Clinical Psychology: Science & Practice, 2,* 225–238.

Corder, E. H., Saunders, A. M., & Strittmatter, W. J. (1993). Gene dose of apolipoprotein E type 4 allele and the risk of Alzheimer's disease in late onset families. *Science, 261,* 921–923.

Cornblatt, B., Obuchowski, M., Andreasen, A., & Smith, C. (1998). High-risk research in schizophrenia: New strategies, new designs. In M. F. Lenzenweger & R. H. Dworkin (Eds.), *Origins of the development of schizophrenia* (pp. 349–383). Washington, DC: American Psychological Association.

Coryell, W. (1998). The treatment of psychotic depression. *Journal of Clinical Psychiatry, 59* (Suppl. 1), 22–27.

Coryell, W., Scheftner, W., Keller, M., & Endicott, J. (1993). The enduring psychosocial consequences of mania and depression. *American Journal of Psychiatry, 150,* 720–727.

Costa, E. (1985). Benzodiazepine-GABA interactions: A model to investigate the neurobiology of anxiety. In A. H. Tuma & J. Maser (Eds.), *Anxiety and the anxiety disorders.* Hillsdale, NJ: Erlbaum.

Costa, P. T., & McCrae, R. R. (1992). The five-factor model of personality and its relevance to personality disorders. *Journal of Personality Disorders, 6,* 343–359.

Costa, P. T., & Widiger, T. A. (Eds.). (1994). *Personality disorders and the five-factor model of personality.* Washington, DC: American Psychological Association.

Cott, J. (1995a). Medicinal plants and dietary supplements: Sources for innovative treatments or adjuncts? *Psychopharmacology, 31,* 131–137.

Cott, J. (1995b). Natural product formulations available in Europe for psychotropic indications. *Psychopharmacology, 31,* 745–751.

Cott, J. M., & Fugh-Berman, A. (1998). Is St. John's Wort (*hypericum perforatum*) an effective antidepressant? *Journal of Nervous & Mental Disease, 186,* 500–501.

Coulton, C. J., Korbin, J. E., Su, M., & Chow, J. (1995). Community level factors and child maltreatment rates. *Child Development, 66,* 1262–1276.

Cousins, N. (1985). Anatomy of an illness (as perceived by the patient). In A. Monat & R. S. Lazarus (Eds.), *Stress and coping: An anthology* (pp. 55–66). New York: Columbia University Press.

Coyne, J. C., & Gotlib, I. H. (1983). The role of cognition in depression: A critical appraisal. *Psychological Bulletin, 94*, 472–505.

Craig, T. K., Boardman, A. P., Mills, K., & Daly-Jones, O. (1993). The South London Somatisation Study: I. Longitudinal course and the influence of early life experiences. *British Journal of Psychiatry, 163*, 579–588.

Craighead, W. E., Craighead, L. W., & Ilardi, S. S. (1998). Psychosocial treatments for major depressive disorder. In P. E. Nathan (Ed.), *A guide to treatments that work* (pp. 226–239). New York: Oxford University Press.

Craighead, W. E., Meyers, A. W., & Craighead, L. W. (1985). A conceptual model for cognitive-behavior therapy with children. *Journal of Abnormal Child Psychiatry, 13*, 331–342.

Cranston-Cuebas, M. A., & Barlow, D. H. (1990). Cognitive and affective contributions to sexual functioning. *Annual Review of Sex Research, 1*, 119–161.

Craske, M. G., & Barlow, D. H. (1993). Panic disorder and agoraphobia. In D. H. Barlow (Ed.), *Clinical handbook of psychological disorders: A step-by-step treatment manual* (2nd ed., pp. 1–47). New York: Guilford Press.

Craske, M. G., Brown, T. A., & Barlow, D. H. (1991). Behavioral treatment of panic disorder: A two-year follow-up. *Behavior Therapy, 22*, 289–304.

Creer, C., & Wing, J. K. (1974). *Several relatives mentioned*. London: Institute of Psychiatry.

Crepault, C., & Couture, M. (1980). Men's erotic fantasies. *Archives of Sexual Behavior, 9*, 565–581.

Crick, N. R., & Dodge, K. A. (1994). A review and reformulation of social information-processing mechanisms in children's social adjustment. *Psychological Bulletin, 115*, 74–101.

Crick, N. R., & Grotpeter, J. K. (1995). Relational aggression, gender, and social-psychological adjustment. *Child Development, 66*, 710–722.

Crick, N. R., & Ladd, G. W. (1990). Children's perceptions of the outcomes of social strategies: Do the ends justify being mean? *Developmental Psychology, 26*, 612–620.

Crits-Christoph, P. (1992). The efficacy of brief dynamic psychotherapy: A meta-analysis. *American Journal of Psychiatry, 149*, 151–158.

Crits-Christoph, P. (1997). Limitations of the dodo bird verdict and the role of clinical trials in psychotherapy research: Comment on Wamplod et al. (1997). *Psychological Bulletin, 122*, 216–220.

Crits-Christoph, P., & Barber, J. P. (Eds.). (1991). *Handbook of short-term dynamic psychotherapy*. New York: Basic Books.

Crits-Christoph, P., Baranackie, K., Kurcias, J. S., & Beck, A. T. (1991). Meta-analysis of therapist effects in psychotherapy outcome. *Psychotherapy Research, 1*, 81–91.

Crits-Christoph, P., Luborsky, L., & Barber, J. (1990). Overview of psychodynamic treatment. In M. E. Thase (Ed.), *Handbook of outpatient treatment of adults: Nonpsychotic mental disorders* (pp. 51–70). New York: Plenum.

Cromwell, R. L., & Snyder, C. R. (Eds.). (1993). *Schizophrenia: Origins, processes, treatment, and outcome*. New York: Oxford University Press.

Cronbach, L. J., & Meehl, P. E. (1955). Construct validity in psychological tests. *Psychological Bulletin, 52*, 281–302.

Croop, R. S., Faulkner, E. B., & Labriola, D. F. (1997). The safety profile of naltrexone in the treatment of alcoholism. *Archives of General Psychiatry, 54*, 1130–1135.

Crosby, A. E., Cheltenham, M. P., & Sacks, J. J. (1999). Incidence of suicidal ideation and behavior in the United States, 1994. *Suicide and Life-Threatening Behavior, 29*, 131–140.

Cross-National Collaborative Group (1992). The changing rate of major depression. *Journal of the American Medical Association, 268*, 3098–3105.

Crowe, R. R. (1990). Panic disorder: Genetic considerations. *Journal of Psychiatric Research, 24*, (Suppl. 2), 129–134.

Curtis, J. (1998). *"Do not grieve for me," James Whale: A new world of gods and monsters* (pp. 384–385). Boston: Faber & Faber.

Cutler, S. E., & Nolen-Hoeksema, S. (1991). Accounting for sex differences in depression through female victimization: Childhood sexual abuse. *Sex Roles, 24*, 425–438.

D

D'Andrea, M., & Daniels, J. (1995). Helping students learn to get along: Assessing the effectiveness of a multicultural developmental guidance project. *Elementary School Guidance & Counseling, 30*, 143–154.

Dadds, M. R., Holland, D. E., Barrett, P. M., & Spence, S. H. (1999). Early intervention and prevention of anxiety disorders in children: Results at 2-year follow-up. *Journal of Consulting & Clinical Psychology, 67*, 145–150.

Dahl, A. A. (1993). The personality disorders: A critical review of family, twin, and adoption studies. *Journal of Personality Disorders* (Spr. Suppl. 1), 86–99.

Dain, N. (1980). *Clifford W. Beers, advocate for the insane*. Pittsburgh: University of Pittsburgh Press.

Damasio, H., Grabowski, T., Frank, R., Galaburda, A. M., & Damasio, A. R. (1994). The return of Phineas Gage: Clues about the brain from the skull of a famous patient. *Science, 264*, 1102–1105.

Dana, R. H. (1995). *Multicultural assessment perspectives for professional psychology*. Boston: Allyn & Bacon.

Dana, R. H. (1998). *Understanding cultural identity in intervention and assessment*. Thousand Oaks, CA: Sage.

Dare, C., Eisler, I., Russell, G. F., & Szmukler, G. I. (1990). The clinical and theoretical impact of a controlled trial of family therapy in anorexia nervosa. *Journal of Marital & Familial Therapy, 16*, 39–57.

Davis, C., & Yager, J. (1992). Transcultural aspects of eating disorders: A critical literature review. *Culture, Medicine & Psychiatry, 16*, 377–394.

Davis, K. L., Kahn, R. S., Ko, G., & Davidson, M. (1991). Dopamine in schizophrenia: A review and conceptualization. *American Journal of Psychiatry, 148*, 1474–1486.

Davis, R. D., & Millon, T. (1993). The five-factor model for personality disorders: Apt or misguided? *Psychological Inquiry, 4*, 104–109.

Day, J. J., Grant, I., Atkinson, J. H., & Brysk, L. T. (1992). Incidence of AIDS dementia in a two-year follow-up of AIDS and ARC patients on an initial Phase II AZT placebo-controlled study: San Diego cohort. *Journal of Neuropsychiatry & Clinical Neurosciences, 4*, 15–20.

de Wit, H., Kirk, J. M., & Justice, A. (1998). Behavioral pharmacology of cannabinoids. In R. E. Tarter (Ed.), *Handbook of substance abuse: Neurobehavioral pharmacology* (pp. 131–146). New York: Plenum.

Deakin, J. W., & Graeff, F. G. (1991). 5-HT and mechanisms of defense. *Journal of Psychopharmacology, 5*, 305–315.

DeHeer, N. D., Wampold, B. E., & Freund, R. D. (1992). Do sex-typed and androgynous subjects prefer counselors on the basis of gender or effectiveness? They prefer the best. *Journal of Counseling Psychology, 39*, 175–184.

Delay, J., Deniker, P., & Harl, J. M. (1952). Traitement des etats d'excitation et d'agitation par une methode medicamenteuse derivee de l'hibernotherapie. *Annuls Medicine Psychologie, 110*, 262–267.

DeLeon, P. H., & Wiggins, J. G., Jr. (1996). Prescription privileges for psychologists. *American Psychologist, 51*, 225–229.

Dell, P. F. (1998). Axis II pathology in outpatients with dissociative identity disorder. *Journal of Nervous & Mental Disease, 186*, 352–356.

Dell, P. F., & Eisenhower, J. W. (1990). Adolescent multiple personality disorder: A preliminary study of eleven cases. *Journal of the American Academy of Child & Adolescent Psychiatry, 29*, 359–366.

Dembroski, T. M., MacDougall, J. M., Williams, J. M., & Haney, T. L. (1985). Components of Type A hostility and anger: Relationship to angiographic findings. *Psychosomatic Medicine, 47*, 219–233.

Denison, M. E., Paredes, A., Bacal, S., & Gawin, F. H. (1998). Psychological and psychiatric consequences of cocaine. In R. E. Tarter (Ed.), *Handbook of substance abuse: Neurobehavioral pharmacology* (pp. 201–213). New York: Plenum.

Derry, F. A., Dinsmore, W. W., Fraser, M., Gardner, B. P., Glass, C. A., Maytom, M. C., & Smith, M. D. (1998). Efficacy and safety of oral sildenafil (Viagara) in men with erectile dysfunction caused by spinal cord injury. *Neurology, 51*, 1629–1633.

DeRubeis, R. J., Gelfand, L. A., Tang, T. Z., & Simons, A. D. (1999). Medications versus cognitive behavior therapy for severely depressed outpatients: Mega-analysis of four randomized comparisons. *American Journal of Psychiatry, 156*, 1001–1013.

deSilva, P., Rachman, S., & Seligman, M. (1977). Prepared phobias and obsessions. *Behaviour Research & Therapy, 15*, 65–77.

Desmond, D. W., & Tatemichi, T. K. (1998). Vascular dementia. In M. F. Folstein (Ed.), *Neurobiology of primary dementia* (pp. 167–190). Washington, DC: American Psychiatric Press.

Deutsch, A. (1937). *The mentally ill in America: A history of their care and treatment from colonial times*. Garden City, NY: Doubleday, Doran & Company.

De-Veaugh-Geiss, J., Moroz, G., Biederman, J., & Cantwell, D. P. (1992). Clomipramine hydrochloride in childhood and adolescent obsessive compulsive disorder: A multicenter trial. *Journal of the American Academy of Child & Adolescent Psychiatry, 31*, 45–49.

Dewaraja, R., & Sasaki, Y. (1991). Semen-loss syndrome: A comparison between Sri Lanka and Japan. *American Journal of Psychotherapy, 45*, 14–20.

DeWit, H., Pierri, J., & Johanson, C. E. (1989). Assessing individual differences in ethanol preference using a cumulative dosing procedure. *Psychopharmacology, 98*, 113–119.

Dickey, R., & Stephens, J. (1995). Female-to-male transsexualism, heterosexual type: Two cases. *Archives of Sexual Behavior, 24*, 439–445.

Dickinson, E. (1955). *Poems: Including variant readings critically compared with all known manuscripts*. Cambridge, MA: Belknap Press.

Diekstra, R., & Garnefski, N. (1995). On the nature, magnitude, and causality of suicidal behavior: An international perspective. *Suicide & Life Threatening Behavior, 25*, 36–57.

Diekstra, R. F., Kienhorst, C. W. M., & de Wilde, E. J. (1995). Suicide and suicidal behaviour among adolescents. In M. Rutter & D. J. Smith (Eds.), *Psychological disorders in young people*. Chichester, England: Wiley.

Dinges, D. F., & Broughton, R. J. (Eds.). (1989). *Sleep and alertness: Chronobiological, behavioral, and medical aspects of napping*. New York: Raven Press.

Dinwiddie, S. H. (1998). Psychological and psychiatric consequences of inhalants. In R. E. Tarter (Ed.), *Handbook of substance abuse: Neurobehavioral pharmacology,* (pp. 269–279). New York, NY.

Dishion, T. J., & Patterson, G. R. (1997). The timing and severity of antisocial behavior: Three hypotheses within an ecological framework. In D. M. Stoff, J. Breiling, & J. D. Maser (Eds.), *Handbook of antisocial personality disorder* (pp. 205–217). New York: Wiley.

Dittman, R. W., Kappes, M. E., & Kappes, M. H. (1992). Sexual behavior in adolescent and adult females with congenital and adrenal hyperplasia. *Psychoneuroendocrinology, 17,* 153–170.

Dixon, J. F., & Hokin, L. E. (1998). Lithium acutely inhibits and chronically up-regulates and stabilizes glutamate uptake by presynaptic nerve endings in mouse cerebral cortex. *Neurobiology, 95,* 8363–8368.

Dobash, R. E., & Dobash, R. P. (1979). *Violence against wives: A case against patriarchy.* New York: Free Press.

Dobson, K. S. (1989). A meta-analysis of the efficacy of cognitive therapy for depression. *Journal of Consulting & Clinical Psychology, 57,* 414–419.

Dodge, K., & Schwartz, D. (1997). Social information processing mechanisms in aggressive behavior. In D. M. Stoff, J. Breiling, & J. D. Maser (Eds.), *Handbook of antisocial personality disorder* (pp. 171–180). New York: Wiley.

Doering, S., Muller, E., Kopcke, W., Pietcker, A., Gaebel, W., Linden, M., Muller, P., Muller-Spahn, F., Tegler, J., & Schussler, G. (1998). Predictors of relapse and rehospitalization in schizophrenia and schizoaffective disorder. *Schizophrenia Bulletin, 24,* 87–98.

Dohrenwend, B. P., Levav, I., Shrout, P. E., Link, B. G., Skodol, A. E., & Martin, J. L. (1987). Life stress and psychopathology: Progress on research begun with Barbara Snell Dohrenwend. *American Journal of Community Psychology, 15,* 677–715.

Dohrenwend, B. P., Levav, I., Shrout, P. E., Schwartz, S., Naveh, G., Link, B., Skodol, A., & Stueve, A. (1992). Socioeconomic status and psychiatric disorders: The causation-selection issue. *Science, 255,* 946–952.

Donahey, K. M., & Carroll, R. A. (1993). Gender differences in factors associated with hypoactive sexual desire. *Journal of Sex & Marital Therapy, 19,* 25–40.

Dornbusch, S. M., Carlsmith, J. M., Duncan, P. D., Gross, R. T., Martin, J. A., Ritter, P. L., & Siegel-Gorelick, B. (1984). Sexual maturation, social class, and the desire to be thin among adolescent females. *Developmental & Behavioral Pediatrics, 5,* 308–314.

Dorris, M. (1989). *The unbroken cord.* New York: Harper & Row.

Drewnowski, A., Hopkins, S. A., & Kessler, R. C. (1988). The prevalence of bulimia nervosa in the US college student population. *American Journal of Public Health, 78,* 1322–1325.

Drewnowski, A., Yee, D. K., & Krahn, D. D. (1988). Bulimia in college women: Incidence and recovery rates. 140th Annual Meeting of the American Psychiatric Association (1987, Chicago, Illinois). *American Journal of Psychiatry, 145,* 753–755.

Dubner, A. E., & Motta, R. W. (1999). Sexually and physically abused foster care children and posttraumatic stress disorder. *Journal of Consulting & Clinical Psychology, 67,* 367–373.

Duncan, R. D., Saunders, B. E., Kilpatrick, D. G., Hanson, R. F., & Resnick, H. S. (1996). Childhood physical assault as a risk factor for PTSD, depression, and substance abuse: Findings from a national survey. *American Journal of Orthopsychiatry, 66,* 437–448.

Dunkin, J. J., & Anderson-Hanley, C. (1998). Dementia caregiver burden: A review of the literature and guidelines for assessment and intervention. *Neurology, 51,* S53–S60.

DuPaul, G. J., & Barkley, R. A. (1993). Behavioral contributions to pharmacology: The utility of behavioral methodology in medication treatment of children with attention deficit hyperactivity disorder. *Behavior Therapy, 24,* 47–65.

DuPaul, G. J., & Hoff, K. E. (1998). Attention/concentration problems. In T. S. Watson & F. M. Gresham (Eds.), *Handbook of child behavior therapy* (pp. 99–126). New York: Plenum.

Durkheim, E. (1897). *Le suicide: Etude de sociologie.* Paris: F. Alcan.

Dutton, D. G. (1988). *The domestic assault of women: Psychological and criminal justice perspectives.* Boston: Allyn & Bacon.

Dykens, E. M., & Volkmar, F. R. (1997). Medical condition associated with autism. In D. J. Cohen & F. R. Volkmar (Eds.), *Handbook of autism and pervasive developmental disorders* (pp. 388–410). Toronto: Wiley.

E

Eaton, W. W., & Keyl, P. M. (1990). Risk factors for the onset of Diagnostic Schedule/DSM-III agoraphobia in a prospective, population-based study. *Archives of General Psychiatry, 47,* 819–824.

Eaton, W. W., Moortensenk, P. B., Herrman, H., & Freeman, H. (1992). Long-term course of hospitalization for schizophrenia: I. Risk for rehospitalization. *Schizophrenia Bulletin, 18,* 217–228.

Eaton, W. W., Thara, R., Federman, E., & Tien, A. (1998). Remission and relapse in schizophrenia: The Madras longitudinal study. *The Journal of Nervous & Mental Disease, 186,* 357–363.

Eaves, L. J., Silberg, J. L., Meyer, J. M., Maes, H. H., Simonoff, E., Pickles, A., Rutter, M., Neale, M. C., Reynolds, C. A., Erikson, M. T., Heath, A. C., Loeber, R., Truett, K. R., & Hewitt, J. K. (1997). Genetics and developmental psychopathology: 2. The main effects of genes and environment on behavior problems in the Virginia Twin Study of Adolescent Behavioral Development. *Journal of Child Psychology & Psychiatry, 38,* 965–980.

Eckert, E. D., Halmi, K. A., Marchi, P., & Grove, W. (1995). Ten-year follow-up of anorexia nervosa: Clinical course and outcome. *Psychological Medicine, 25,* 143–156.

Edelbrock, C., Rende, R., Plomin, R., & Thompson, L. A. (1995). A twin study of competence and problem behavior in childhood and adolescence. *Journal of Child Psychology & Psychiatry & Allied Disciplines, 36,* 775–785.

Edelmann, R. J. (1992). *Anxiety: Theory, research, and intervention in clinical and health psychology.* Chichester, NY: Wiley.

Edinger, D. (1963). *Bertha Pappenheim, Leben und Schriften.* Frankfurt: Ner-Tamid Verlag.

Egeland, J. A. (1986). Cultural factors and social stigma for manic-depression: The Amish Study. *The American Journal of Social Psychiatry, 6,* 279–286.

Egeland, J. A., Gerhard, D. S., Pauls, D. L., Sussex, J. N., Kidd, K. K., Allen, C. R., Hostetter, A. M., & Housman, D. E. (1987). Bipolar affective disorders linked to DNA markers on Chromosome 11. *Nature, 325,* 783–787.

Egeland, J. A., & Hostetter, A. M. (1983). Amish study: I. Affective disorders among the Amish, 1976–1980. *American Journal of Psychiatry, 140,* 56–61.

Egeland, J. A., Hostetter, A. M., & Eshleman, S. K. (1983). Amish study III: The impact of cultural factors on bipolar diagnosis. *American Journal of Psychiatry, 140,* 67–71.

Egeland, J. A., & Sussex, J. N. (1985). Suicide and family loading for affective disorders. *Journal of the American Medical Association, 254,* 915–918.

Ehlers, A. (1993). Interoception and panic disorder. *Advances in Behavior Research & Therapy, 15,* 3–21.

Ehlers, A. (1995). A 1-year prospective study of panic attacks: Clinical course and factors associated with maintenance. *Journal of Abnormal Psychology, 104,* 164–172.

Ehlers, A., & Breuer, P. (1992). Increased cardiac awareness in panic disorder. *Journal of Abnormal Psychology, 101,* 371–382.

Ehlers, A., Clark, D. M., Dunmore, E., Jaycox, L., Meadows, E., & Foa, E. (1998). Predicating response to exposure treatment in PTSD: The role of mental defeat and alienation. *Journal of Traumatic Stress, 11,* 457–471.

Ehlers, A., Mayou, R., & Bryant, B. (1998). Psychological predictors of chronic posttraumatic stress disorder after motor vehicle accidents. *Journal of Abnormal Psychology, 107,* 508–519.

Eisenberg, L. (1958). School phobia: A study in the communication of anxiety. *American Journal of Psychiatry, 114,* 712–718.

Elder, G. H., & Clipp, E. C. (1989). Combat experience and emotional health: Impairment and resilience in later life. *Journal of Personality, 57,* 311–341.

Elder, G. H., Liker, J. K., & Jaworski, B. J. (1984). Hardship in lives: Depression influences. In K. A. McCluskey & H. W. Reese (Eds.), *Life-span developmental psychology: Historical and generational effects.* Orlando, FL: Academic Press.

Elkin, I., Shea, T., Watkins, J. T., Imber, S. D., Sotsky, S. M., Collins, J. F., Glass, D. R., Pilkonis, P. A., Leber, W. R., Docherty, J. P., Fiester, S. J., & Parloff, M. B. (1989). National Institute of Mental Health treatment of depression collaborative research program: General effectiveness of treatments. *Archives of General Psychiatry, 46,* 971–982.

Ellason, J. W., & Ross, C. A. (1997). Two-year follow-up of inpatients with dissociative identity disorder. *American Journal of Psychiatry, 154,* 832–839.

Ellason, J. W., Ross, C. A., & Fuchs, D. L. (1995). Assessment of dissociative identity disorder with the Millon Clinical Multiaxial Inventory-II. *Psychological Reports, 76,* 895–905.

Ellason, J. W., Ross, C. A., & Fuchs, D. L. (1996). Lifetime axis I and II comorbidity and childhood trauma history in dissociative identity disorder. *Psychiatry, 59,* 255–266.

Ellis, A. (1995, March 6). Dogmatic devotion doesn't help, it hurts. *Insight.*

Ellis, A. (1997). The evolution of Albert Ellis and emotive behavior therapy. In J. K. Zeig (Ed.), *The rational evolution of psychotherapy: The third conference.* New York: Brunner/Mazel.

Ellis, A., & Harper, R. A. (1961). *A guide to rational living.* Englewood Cliffs, NJ: Prentice Hall.

Ellison, C. G., & Levin, J. S. (1998). The religion-health connection: Evidence, theory, and future directions. *Health Education & Behavior, 25,* 700–720.

Emmelkamp, P. M. (1982). *Phobic and obsessive-compulsive disorders.* New York: Plenum.

Emmelkamp, P. M. G. (1994). Behavior therapy with adults. In A. E. Bergin (Ed.), *Handbook of psychotherapy and behavior change* (4th ed., pp. 379–427). New York: Wiley.

Endicott, J. (1994). Differential diagnoses and comorbidity. In J. H. Gold & S. K. Severino (Eds.), *Premenstrual dysphorias* (pp. 3–17). Washington, DC: American Psychiatric Association Press.

Engel, J. (1989). *Addicted: Kids talking about drugs in their own words.* New York: T. Doherty.

Engels, G. I., Garnefski, N., & Diekstra, R. F. W. (1993). Efficacy of rational-emotive therapy: A quantitative analysis. *Journal of Consulting & Clinical Psychology, 61,* 1083–1090.

Ensminger, M. E. (1995). Welfare and psychological distress: A longitudinal study of African/American urban mothers. *Journal of Health & Social Behavior, 36,* 346–359.

Epstein, C. M., Figiel, G. S., McDonald, W. M., Amazon-Leece, J., & Figiel, L. (1998). Rapid rate transcranial magnetic stimulation in young and middle-aged refractory depressed patients. *Psychiatric Annals, 28,* 36–39.

Epstein, J., Saunders, B. E., & Kilpatrick, D. G. (1997). Predicting PTSD in women with a history of childhood rape. *Journal of Traumatic Stress, 10,* 573–588.

Erdelyi, M. H. (1992). Psychodynamics and the unconscious. *American Psychologist, 47,* 784–787.

Erickson, M. T. (1992). *Behavior disorders of children and adolescents.* Englewood Cliffs, NJ: Prentice Hall.

Erikson, K. T. (1976). *Everything in its path: Destruction of community in the Buffalo Creek flood.* New York: Simon & Schuster.

Erlenmeyer-Kimling, L., & Cornblatt, B. (1987). The New York High-Risk Project: A follow-up report. *Schizophrenia Bulletin, 13,* 451–461.

Erlenmeyer-Kimling, L., & Cornblatt, B. A. (1992). A summary of attentional findings in the New York High-Risk Project. *Journal of Psychiatry Research, 26,* 405–426.

Erlenmeyer-Kimling, L., Golden, R. R., & Cornblatt, B. A. (1989). A taxometric analysis of cognitive and neuromotor variables in children at risk for schizophrenia. *Journal of Abnormal Psychology, 98,* 203–208.

Erlenmeyer-Kimling, L., Roberts, S. A., Rock, D., Adamo, U. H., & Shapiro, M. B. (1998). Prediction from longitudinal assessments of high-risk children. In M. F. Lenzenweger & R. H. Dworkin (Eds.), *Origins of the development of schizophrenia* (pp. 427–445). Washington, DC: American Psychological Association.

Erlenmeyer-Kimling, L., Rock, D., Squires-Wheeler, E., & Roberts, S. (1991). Early life precursors of psychiatric outcomes in adulthood in subjects at risk for schizophrenia or affective disorders. *Psychiatry Research, 39,* 239–256.

Erlenmeyer-Kimling, L., Squires-Wheeler, E., Adamo, U. H., & Bassett, A. S. (1995). The New York High-Risk Project. *Archives of General Psychiatry, 52,* 857–865.

Escobar, J. I. (1993). Psychiatric epidemiology. In A. C. Gaw (Ed.), *Culture, ethnicity, and mental illness* (pp. 43–73). Washington, DC: American Psychiatric Press.

Escobar, J. I., Burnam, M. A., Karno, M., & Forsythe, A. (1987). Somatization in the community. *Archives of General Psychiatry, 44,* 713–718.

Escobar, J. I., Gara, M., Waitzkin, H., Cohen Silver, R., Holman, A., & Compton, W. (1998). DSM-IV hypochondriasis in primary care. *General Hospital Psychiatry, 20,* 155–159.

Estrada, A. U., & Pinsof, W. M. (1995). The effectiveness of family therapies for selected behavioral disorders of childhood. *Journal of Marital & Family Therapy, 21,* 403–440.

Evans, M. D., Hollon, S. D., DeRubeis, R. J., Piasecki, J. M., Grove, W. M., Garvey, M. J., & Tuason, V. B. (1992). Differential relapse following cognitive therapy and pharmacotherapy for depression. *Archives of General Psychiatry, 49,* 802–808.

Exner, J. E. (1993). *The Rorschach: A comprehensive system: Vol. 1. Basic foundations* (3rd ed.). New York: John Wiley & Sons.

Eysenck, H. J. (Ed.). (1967). *The biological basis of personality.* Springfield, IL: Charles C Thomas.

Eysenck, H. J. (1994). The biology of morality. In B. Puka (Ed.), *Defining perspectives in moral development.* New York: Garland.

F

Fabrega, H. (1993). Toward a social theory of psychiatric phenomena. *Behavioral Science, 38,* 75–100.

Fabrega, H. (1994). Personality disorders as medical entities: A cultural interpretation. *Journal of Personality Disorders, 8,* 149–167.

Fabrega, H., Ulrich, R., Pilkonis, P., & Mezzich, J. (1991). On the homogeneity of personality disorder clusters. *Comprehensive Psychiatry, 32,* 373–386.

Fagan, J. A., Stewart, D. K., & Hansen, K. V. (1983). Violent men or violent husbands? Background factors and situational correlates. In D. Finkelhor, R. J. Gelles, G. T. Hotaling, & M. A. Strauss (Eds.), *The dark side of families: Current family violence research.* Beverly Hills, CA: Sage.

Fahy, T. A. (1988). The diagnosis of multiple personality disorder: A critical review. *British Journal of Psychiatry, 153,* 597–606.

Fairbank, J. A., Hansen, D. J., & Fitterling, J. M. (1991). Patterns of appraisal and coping across different stressor conditions among former prisoners of war with and without posttraumatic stress disorder. *Journal of Consulting & Clinical Psychology, 59,* 274–281.

Fairburn, C., & Hay, P. J. (1992). Treatment of bulimia nervosa. *Annals of Medicine, 24,* 297–302.

Fairburn, C. G., Jones, R., Peveler, R. C., & Carr, S. J. (1991). Three psychological treatments for bulimia nervosa: A comparative trial. *Archives of General Psychiatry, 48,* 463–469.

Fairburn, C. G., Norman, P. A., Welch, S. L., O'Connor, M. E., Doll, H. A., & Peveler, R. C. (1995). A prospective study of outcome in bulimia nervosa and the long-term effects of three psychological treatments. *Archives of General Psychiatry, 52,* 304–312.

Fairburn, C. G., Welch, S. L., & Hay, P. J. (1993). The classification of recurrent overeating: The "binge eating disorder" proposal. Fifth International Conference on Eating Disorders (1992, New York). *International Journal of Eating Disorders, 13,* 155–159.

Fairburn, C. G., Welsh, S. L., Doll, H. A., Davies, B. A. & O'Connor, M. E. (1997). Risk factors for bulimia nervosa. *Archives of General Psychiatry, 54,* 509–517.

Fairburn, C. G. & Wilson, G. T. (1993). *Binge eating: Nature, assessment, and treatment.* New York: Guilford Press.

Fairweather, G. W., Sanders, D. H., Maynard, H., & Cressler, D. L. (1969). *Community life for the mentally ill: An alternative to institutional care.* Chicago: Aldine.

Faletti, M. V., Gibbs, J. M., Clark, C., Pruchno, R. A., & Berman, E. A. (1989). Longitudinal course of bereavement in older adults. In D. A. Lund (Ed.), *Older bereaved spouses: Research with practical applications* (pp. 37–51). New York: Taylor & Francis/Hemisphere.

Fallon, A. E., & Rozin, P. (1985). Sex differences in perceptions of desirable body shape. *Journal of Abnormal Psychology, 94,* 102–105.

Falloon, I. R., Brooker, C., & Graham-Hole, V. (1992). Psychosocial interventions for schizophrenia. *Behavior Change, 9,* 238–245.

Fals-Stewart, W., Marks, A. P., & Schafer, J. (1993). A comparison of behavioral group therapy and individual behavior therapy in treating obsessive-compulsive disorder. *Journal of Nervous & Mental Disease, 181,* 189–193.

Faraone, S. V., Biederman, J., Keenan, K., & Tsuang, M. T. (1991). A family-genetic study of girls with DSM-III attention deficit disorder. *American Journal of Psychiatry, 148,* 112–117.

Faraone, S. V., & Tsuang, M. T. (1990). Genetic transmission of major affective disorders: Quantitative models and linkage analyses. *Psychological Bulletin, 108,* 109–127.

Faustman, W. O., Bardgett, M., Faull, K. F., Pfefferbaum, A., & Csernansky, J. G. (1999). Cerebrospinal fluid glutamate inversely correlates with positive symptom severity in unmedicated male schizophrenic/ schizoaffective patients. *Biological Psychiatry, 45,* 68–75.

Fava, M., Copeland, P. M., Schweiger, U., & Herzog, D. B. (1989). Neurochemical abnormalities of anorexia nervosa and bulimia nervosa. *American Journal of Psychiatry, 146,* 963–971.

Fava, M., & Rosenbaum, J. F. (1995). Pharmacotherapy and somatic therapies. In E. E. Beckham & W. R. Leber (Eds.), *Handbook of depression* (2nd ed., pp. 280–301). New York: Guilford.

Fawcett, J., Busch, K. A., Jacobs, D., Kravitz, H. M., & Fogg, L. (1997). Suicide: A four-pathway clinical-biochemical model. *Annals of the New York Academy of Sciences, 836,* 288–301.

Fawzy, F. I., Fawzy, N. W., Hyun, C. S., Elashoff, R., Guthrie, D., Fahey, J. L., & Morton, D. L. (1993). Malignant melanoma: Effects of an early structured psychiatric intervention, coping, and affective state on recurrence and survival six years later. *Archives of General Psychology, 9,* 681–689.

Fedoroff, I. C., Polivy, J., & Herman, C. P. (1997). The effect of pre-exposure to food cues on the eating behavior of restrained and unrestrained eaters. *Appetite, 28,* 33–47.

Feehan, M., McGee, R., & Williams, S. (1993). Mental health disorders from age 15 to age 18 years. *Journal of the American Academy of Child & Adolescent Psychiatry, 32,* 1118–1126.

Fenichel, O. (1945). *The psychoanalytic theory of neurosis.* New York: W. W. Norton.

Fennell, M. J. V., & Teasdale, J. D. (1987). Cognitive therapy for depression: Individual differences and the process of change. *Cognitive Therapy & Research, 11,* 253–271.

Fenton, W. S., & McGlashan, T. H. (1994). Antecedents, symptom progression, and long-term outcome of the deficit syndrome in schizophrenia. *American Journal of Psychiatry, 151,* 351–356.

Fergusson, D. M., Horwood, J. L., & Lynskey, M. T. (1993). Early dentine lead levels and subsequent cognitive and behavioural development. *Journal of Child Psychology & Psychiatry & Allied Disciplines, 34,* 215–227.

Ferris, C. F., & de Vries, G. J. (1997). Ethological models for examining the neurobiology of aggressive and affiliative behaviors. In D. M. Stoff, J. Breiling, & J. D. Maser (Eds.), *Handbook of antisocial personality disorder* (pp. 255–268). New York: Wiley.

Field, T. (1998). Massage therapy effects. *American Psychologist, 53,* 1270–1281.

Field, T., Grizzle, N., Scafidi, F., Abrams, S., & Richardson, S. (1996). Massage therapy for infants of depressed mothers. *Infant Behavior & Development, 19,* 109–114.

Field, T., Henteleff, T., Hernandez-Reif, M., Martinez, E., Mavunda, K., Kuhn, C., & Schanberg, S. (1998). Children with asthma have improved pulmonary function after massage therapy. *Journal of Pediatrics, 132,* 854–858.

Field, T., Hernandez-Reif, M., Seligman, S., Krasnegor, J., Sunshine, W., Rivas-Chacon, R., Schanberg, S., & Kuhn, C. (1997). Juvenile rheumatoid arthritis: Benefits from massage therapy. *Journal of Pediatric Psychology, 22,* 607–617.

Field, T., Hernandez-Reif, M., Shaw, K. H., La Greca, A., Schanberg, S., & Kuhn, C. (1997). Glucose levels decreased after giving massage therapy to children with diabetes mellitus. *Diabetes Spectrum, 10,* 23–25.

Field, T., Lasko, D., Mundy, P., Henteleff, T., Talpins, S., & Dowling, M. (1997). Autistic children's attentiveness and responsivity improved after touch therapy. *Journal of Autism & Developmental Disorders, 27,* 329–334.

Field, T., Schanberg, S. M., Scafidi, F., Bauer, C. R., Vega-Lahr, N., Garcia, R., Nystrom, J., & Kuhn, C. M. (1986). Tactile/kinesthetic stimulation effects on preterm neonates. *Pediatrics, 77,* 654–658.

Figiel, G. S., Epstein, C. S., McDonald, W. M., Amazon-Leece, J., Figiel, L., Saldavia, A., & Glover, S. (1998). The use of rapid rate transcranial magnetic stimulation (rTMS) in refractory depressed patients. *The Journal of Neuropsychiatry & Clinical Neurosciences, 10,* 20–25.

Figley, C. R., & Leventman, S. (Eds.). (1980). *Strangers at home: Vietnam veterans since the war.* New York: Brunner/Mazel.

Figueira-McDonough, J. (1993). Residence, dropping out, and delinquency rates. *Deviant Behavior, 14,* 109–132.

Finkelhor, D. (1984). *Child sexual abuse: New theory and research.* New York: Free Press.

Finkelhor, D., & Dzuiba-Leatherman, J. (1994). Victimization of children. *American Psychologist, 49,* 173–183.

Finney, J. W., & Moos, R. H. (1998). Psychosocial treatments for alcohol use disorders. In P. E. Nathan (Ed.), *A guide to treatments that work* (pp. 156–166). New York: Oxford University Press.

Fischer, M., Barkley, R. A., Fletcher, K. E., & Smallish, L. (1993). The adolescent outcome of hyperactive children: Predictors of psychiatric, academic, social, and emotional adjustment. *Journal of the American Academy of Child & Adolescent Psychiatry, 32,* 324–332.

Fishbain, D. A., & Goldberg, M. (1991). The misdiagnosis of conversion disorder in a psychiatric emergency service. *General Hospital Psychiatry, 13,* 177–181.

Fisher, B. W., & Flowerdew, G. (1995). A simple model for predicting postoperative delirium in older patients undergoing elective orthopedic surgery. *Journal of the American Geriatrics Society, 43,* 175–178.

Fisher, R. A. (1958). *The cancer controversy.* London: Oliver & Boyd.

Fisher, S., Kent, T. A., & Bryant, S. G. (1995). Postmarketing surveillance by patient self-monitoring: Preliminary data for sertraline versus fluoxetine. *Journal of Clinical Psychiatry, 56,* 288–296.

Fitzgerald, L. F. (1993). Sexual harassment: Violence against women in the workplace. *American Psychologist, 48,* 1070–1076.

Fitzgerald, T. E., Tennen, H., Affleck, G., & Pransky, G. S. (1993). The relative importance of dispositional optimism and control appraisals in quality of life after coronary artery bypass surgery. *Journal of Behavioral Medicine, 16,* 25–43.

Flakierska-Praquin, N., Lindstrom, M., & Gilberg, C. (1997). School phobia with separation anxiety disorder: A comparative 20- to 29-year follow up study of 35 school refusers. *Comprehensive Psychology, 38,* 17–22.

Flisher, A. J., Kramer, R. A., Hoven, C. W., Greenwald, S., Alegria, M., Bird, H. R., Canino, G., Connell, R., & Moore, R. E. (1997). Psychosocial characteristics of physically abused children and adolescents. *Journal of the American Academy of Child & Adolescent Psychiatry, 36,* 123–131.

Fluoxetine Bulimia Nervosa Collaborative Study Group. (1992). Fluoxetine in the treatment of bulimia nervosa: A multicenter, placebo-controlled, double-blind trial. *Archives of General Psychiatry, 49,* 139–147.

Foa, E., & Kozak, M. (1993). Obsessive-compulsive disorder: Long-term outcome of psychological treatment. In M. Mavissakalian & R. Prien (Eds.), *Long-term treatment of anxiety disorders.* Washington, DC: American Psychiatric Press.

Foa, E. B., & Hearst-Ikeda, D. (1996). Emotional dissociation in response to trauma: An information-processing approach. In L. K. Michelson (Ed.), *Handbook of dissociation: Theoretical, empirical, and clinical perspectives* (pp. 207–224). New York: Plenum.

Foa, E. B., Dancu, C. V., Hembree, E., Jaycox, L. H., Anonymous, & Street, G. P. (1999). A comparison of exposure therapy, stress inoculation training, and their combination for reducing posttraumatic stress disorder in female assault victims. *Journal of Consulting & Clinical Psychology, 67,* 194–200.

Foa, E. B., Feske, U., Murdock, T. B., & Kozak, M. J. (1991). Processing threat-related information in rape victims. *Journal of Abnormal Psychology, 100,* 156–162.

Foa, E. B., Franklin, M. E., Perry, K. J., & Herbert, J. D. (1996). Cognitive biases in generalized social phobia. *Journal of Abnormal Psychology, 105,* 433–439.

Foa, E. B., & Jaycox, L. H. (1999). Cognitive-behavioral theory and treatment of posttraumatic stress disorder. In D. Spiegel (Ed.), *Efficacy and cost-effectiveness of psychotherapy* (pp. 23–61). Washington, DC: American Psychiatric Association.

Foa, E. D., & Riggs, D. S. (1995). Posttraumatic stress disorder following assault: Theoretical considerations and empirical findings. *Current Directions in Psychological Science, 4,* 61–65.

Folsom, A. R. (1985). Do Type A men drink more frequently than Type B men? Findings in the Multiple Risk Factor Intervention Trial (MRFIT). *Journal of Behavioral Medicine, 8,* 227–235.

Folstein, M. F., Bassett, S. S., Romanoski, A. J., & Nestadt, G. (1991). The epidemiology of delirium in the community: The Eastern Baltimore Mental Health Survey. *International Psychogeriatrics, 3,* 169–176.

Folstein, M. F., Folstein, S. E., & McHugh, P. R. (1975). Mini-mental state: A practical method for grading the cognitive state of patients for the clinician. *Journal of Psychiatric Research, 12,* 189–198.

Fonagy, P., Leigh, R., Steele, M., Steele, H., Kennedy, R., Mattoon, G., Target, M., & Gerber, A. (1996). The relation of attachment status, psychiatric classification and response to psychotherapy. *Journal of Consulting & Clinical Psychology, 64,* 22–31.

Forehand, R., Lautenschlager, G. J., Faust, J., & Graziano, W. G. (1986). Parent perceptions and parent-child interactions in clinic-referred children: A preliminary investigation of the effects of maternal depressive moods. *Behaviour Research & Therapy, 24,* 73–75.

Frances, A., Kahn, D., Carpenter, D., Docherty, J., & Donovan, S. (1998). The expert consensus guidelines for treating depression in bipolar disorder. *Journal of Clinical Psychiatry, 59* (Suppl. 4), 73–79.

Frances, A. J., First, M. B., & Pincus, H. A. (1995). *DSM-IV guidebook.* Washington, DC: American Psychiatric Press.

Frank, E. (1991). Interpersonal psychotherapy as a maintenance treatment for patients with recurrent depression. *Psychotherapy, 28,* 259–266.

Frank, E., Anderson, B., Reynolds, C. F., & Ritenour, A. (1994). Life events and the

research diagnostic criteria endogenous subtype: A confirmation of the distinction using the Bedford College methods. *Archives of General Psychiatry, 51,* 519–524.

Frank, E., Kupfer, D., Wagner, E., & McEachran, A. (1991). Efficacy of interpersonal psychotherapy as a maintenance treatment of recurrent depression: Contributing factors. *Archives of General Psychiatry, 48,* 1053–1059.

Frank, E., Kupfer, D. J., Perel, J. M., & Cornes, C. (1990). Three-year outcomes for maintenance therapies in recurrent depression. *Archives of General Psychiatry, 47,* 1093–1099.

Frank, J. (1973). *Persuasion and healing: A comparative study of psychotherapy.* Baltimore, MD: The Johns Hopkins University Press.

Frank, J. D. (1978). *Effective ingredients of successful psychotherapy.* New York: Brunner/Mazel.

Frankl, V. E. (1963). *Man's search for meaning: An introduction to logotherapy.* Boston: Beacon Press.

Fraser, M. W., Pecora, P. J., & Haapala, D. A. (Eds.). (1991). *Families in crisis: The impact of intensive family preservation services.* New York: A. de Gruyter.

Freeman, A., & Reinecke, M. A. (1995). Cognitive therapy. In A. S. Gurman (Ed.), *Essential psychotherapies: Theory and practice* (pp. 182–225). New York: Guilford Press.

Freeston, M. H., Ladouceur, R., Thibodeau, N., & Gagnon, F. (1992). Cognitive intrusions in a non-clinical population: II. Associations with depressive, anxious, and compulsive symptoms. *Behaviour Research & Therapy, 30,* 263–271.

Freud, S. (1905). *Collected works.* London: Hogarth Press.

Freud, S. (1909). *Analysis of a phobia of a five-year-old boy.* (Vol. III). New York: Basic Books.

Freud, S. (1914). *Psychopathology of everyday life.* (Authorized English ed.). New York: Macmillan.

Freud, S. (1917). Mourning and melancholia. *Collected works.* London: Hogarth Press.

Freud, S. (1920). *A general introduction to psychoanalysis.* New York: Boni & Liveright.

Freud, S. (1923). *The ego and id.* London: Hogarth Press.

Freud, S. (1924). The loss of reality in neurosis and psychosis. In *Sigmund Freud's collected papers* (Vol. 2, pp. 272–282). London: Hogarth Press.

Freud, S. (1958). The handling of dream-interpretation in psychoanalysis. In J. Strachey (Ed.), *The standard edition* (Vol. 12, pp. 89–96). London: Hogarth Press.

Freud, S. (1963). *Collected papers. With an introduction by the editor Philip Rieff.* New York: Collier Books.

Freyd, J. J. (1996). *Betrayal trauma: The logic of forgetting childhood abuse.* Cambridge, MA: Harvard University Press.

Frick, P. J. (1989). Conduct disorders. In T. H. Ollendick & M. Hersen (Eds.), *Handbook of child psychopathology* (pp. 213–239). New York: Plenum.

Frick, P. J. (1998). *Conduct disorders and severe antisocial behavior.* New York: Plenum.

Fried, P. A., & Watkinson, B. (1990). 36- and 48-month neurobehavioral follow-up of children prenatally exposed to marijuana, cigarettes, and alcohol. *Journal of Developmental & Behavioral Pediatrics, 11,* 49–58.

Friedman, M. (1998). Current and future drug treatment for posttraumatic stress disorder patients. *Psychiatric Annals, 28,* 461–468.

Friedman, M., & Rosenman, R. H. (1974). *Type A behavior and your heart.* New York: Knopf.

Friedman, M., Rosenman, R. H., Straus, R., Wurm, M., & Kositcheck, R. (1968). The relationship of behavior pattern A to the state of coronary vasculature. *American Journal of Medicine, 44*, 525–537.

Friedman, M., Thoresen, C. E., Gill, J. J., Ulmer, D., Powell, L. H., Price, V. A., Brown, B., Thompson, L., Rabin, D. D., Breall, W. S., Bourg, E., Levy, R., & Dixon, T. (1986). Alteration of Type A behavior and its effect on cardiac recurrences in post myocardial infarction patients: Summary results of the recurrent coronary prevention project. *American Heart Journal, 112*, 653–665.

Friend, T. (1996, May 13). Test identifies gene but can't predict disease. *USA Today*, A1–A2.

Friman, P. C., & Warzak, W. J. (1990). Nocturnal enuresis: A prevalent, persistent, yet curable parasomia. *Pediatrician, 17*, 38–45.

Fritz, G. K., Fritsch, S., & Hagino, O. (1997). Somatoform disorders in children and adolescents: A review of the past 10 years. *Journal of the American Academy of Child & Adolescent Psychiatry, 36*, 1329–1338.

Fromme, K., Marlatt, G. A., Baer, J. S., & Kivlahan, D. R. (1994). The Alcohol Skills Training Program: A group intervention for young adult drinkers. *Journal of Substance Abuse Treatment, 11*, 143–154.

Fromm-Reichmann, F. (1948). Notes on the development of treatments of schizophrenia by psychoanalytic psychotherapy. *Psychiatry, 2*, 263–273.

Fugh-Berman, A., & Cott, J. M. (1999). Dietary supplements and natural products as psychotherapeutic agents. *Psychosomatic Medicine, 61*, 712–728.

Futterman, A., Thompson, L., Gallagher-Thompson, D., & Ferris, R. (1995). Depression in late life: Epidemiology, assessment, etiology, and treatment. In E. E. Beckham & W. R. Leber (Eds.), *Handbook of depression* (2nd ed., pp. 494–525). New York: Guilford Press.

Fyer, A. J., Liebowitz, M. R., Gorman, J. M., & Campeas, R. (1987). Discontinuation of alprazolam treatment in panic patients. *American Journal of Psychiatry, 144*, 303–308.

Fyer, A. J., Mannuzza, S., Chapman, T. F., & Liebowitz, M. R. (1993). A direct interview family study of social phobia. *Archives of General Psychiatry, 50*, 286–293.

Fyer, A. J., Mannuzza, S., Gallops, M. S., & Martin, L. Y. (1990). Familial transmission of simple phobias and fears: A preliminary report. *Archives of General Psychiatry, 47*, 252–256.

G

Gadow, K. D. (1991). Clinical issues in child and adolescent psychopharmacology. *Journal of Consulting & Clinical Psychology, 59*, 842–852.

Gadow, K. D. (1992). Pediatric psychopharmacology: A review of recent research. *Journal of Child Psychology & Psychiatry & Allied Disciplines, 33*, 153–195.

Gallagher-Thompson, D., Lovett, S., & Rose, J. (1991). Psychotherapeutic interventions for stressed family caregivers. In W. A. Myers (Ed.), *New techniques in psychotherapy of older patients*. Washington, DC: American Psychiatric Press.

Ganley, A. L. (1989). Integrating feminist and social learning analyses of aggression: Creating multiple models for intervention with men who batter. In P. L. Caesar & K. L. Hamberger (Eds.), *Treating men who batter: Theory practice and programs* (pp. 196–235). New York: Springer.

Gannon, L. R., Haynes, S. N., Cuevas, J., & Chavez, R. (1987). Psychophysiological correlates of induced headaches. *Journal of Behavioral Medicine, 10*, 411–423.

Gao, S., Hendrie, H., Hall, K., & Hui, S. (1998). The relationship between age, sex, and the incidence of dementia and Alzheimer's disease: A meta-analysis. *Archives of General Psychiatry, 55*, 809–815.

Garb, H. N., Florio, C. M., & Grove, W. M. (1998). The validity of the Rorschach and the Minnesota Multiphasic Personality Inventory. *Psychological Science, 9*, 402–404.

Garbarino, J. (1995). *Raising children in a socially toxic environment*. San Francisco: Jossey-Bass.

Garbarino, J., & Sherman, D. (1980). High-risk neighborhoods and high-risk families: The human ecology of child maltreatment. *Child Development, 51*, 188–198.

Garber, J., Walker, L. S., & Zeman, J. (1991). Somatization symptoms in a community sample of children and adolescents: Further validation of the Children's Somatization Inventory. *Psychological Assessment, 3*, 588–595.

Gardner, W., Lidz, C. W., Mulvey, E. P., & Shaw, E. C. (1996). Clinical versus actuarial predictions of violence in patients with mental illnesses. *Journal of Consulting & Clinical Psychology, 64*, 602–609.

Garety, P. (1991). Reasoning and delusions. *British Journal of Psychiatry, 159*, 14–18.

Garfield, S. L. (1992). Eclectic psychotherapy: A common factors approach. In J. C. Norcross (Ed.), *Handbook of psychotherapy integration* (pp. 169–201). New York: Basic Books.

Garfield, S. L. (1994). Research on client variables in psychotherapy. In A. E. Bergin (Ed.), *Handbook of psychotherapy and behavior change* (4th ed., pp. 190–228). New York: Wiley.

Garland, A., Shaffer, D., & Whittle, B. (1989). A national survey of school-based, adolescent suicide prevention programs. *Journal of the American Academy of Child & Adolescent Psychiatry, 28*, 931–934.

Garland, A. F., & Zigler, R. (1993). Adolescent suicide prevention: Current research and social policy implications. *American Psychologist, 48*, 169–182.

Garmezy, N. (1991). Resilience and vulnerability to adverse developmental outcomes associated with poverty. *American Behavioral Scientist, 34*, 416–430.

Garner, D., Cooke, A. K., & Marano, H. E. (1997). The 1997 body image survey results. *Psychology Today*, 30–44.

Garner, D. M., & Garfinkel, P. E. (1980). Socio-cultural factors in the development of anorexia nervosa. *Psychological Medicine, 10*, 647–656.

Garner, D. M., & Garfinkel, P. E. (Eds.). (1985). *Handbook of psychotherapy for anorexia nervosa and bulimia*. New York: Guilford Press.

Garner, D. M., & Garfinkel, P. E. (Eds.). (1997). *Handbook for treatment for eating disorders* (2nd ed.). New York: Guilford Press.

Garner, D. M., Garfinkel, P. E., & O'Shaughnessy, M. (1985). The validity of the distinction between bulimia with and without anorexia nervosa. *American Journal of Psychiatry, 142*, 581–587.

Garner, D. M., Olmstead, M. P., & Polivy, J. (1984). *The EDI*. Odessa, FL: Psychological Assessment Resources.

Garner, D. M., Rockert, W., Davis, R., & Garner, M. V. (1993). Comparison of cognitive-behavioral and supportive-expressive therapy for bulimia nervosa. *American Journal of Psychiatry, 150*, 37–46.

Garner, D. M., & Wooley, S. C. (1991). Confronting the failure of behavioral and dietary treatments for obesity. *Clinical Psychology Review, 11*, 729–780.

Garrison, C. Z., Bryant, E. S., Addy, C. L., Spurrier, P. G., Freedy, J. R., & Kilpatrick, D. G. (1995). Posttraumatic stress disorder in adolescents after Hurricane Andrew. *Journal of the American Academy of Child & Adolescent Psychiatry, 34*, 1193–1201.

Gatley, S. J., Gifford, A. N., Volkow, N. D., & Fowler, J. S. (1998). Pharmacology of cocaine. In R. E. Tarter (Ed.), *Handbook of substance abuse: Neurobehavioral pharmacology* (pp. 161–185). New York: Plenum.

Gavin, A. (1985). Treatment outlines for the management of anxiety states: The Quality Assurance Project. *Australian & New Zealand Journal Psychiatry, 19*, 138–151.

Gaw, A. C. (Ed.). (1993). *Culture, ethnicity, and mental illness*. Washington, DC: American Psychiatric Press.

Ge, X., Conger, R. D., Cadoret, R. J., & Neiderhiser, J. M. (1996). The developmental interface between nature and nurture: A mutual influence model of child antisocial behavior and parent behaviors. *Developmental Psychology, 32*, 574–589.

Geer, J. H., & Maisel, E. (1972). Evaluating the effects of the prediction-control confound. *Journal of Personality & Social Psychology, 23*, 314–319.

Gelles, R. J., & Cornell, C. P. (1990). *Intimate violence in families* (2nd Edition). Newbury Park, CA: Sage.

George, M. S. (1998). Why would you ever want to? Toward understanding the antidepressant effect of prefrontal rTMS. *Human Psychopharmacology, 13*, 307–313.

George, M. S., Speer, A. M., Molloy, M., Nahas, Z., Teneback, C. C., Risch, S. C., Arana, G. W., Ballenger, J. C., & Post, R. M. (1998). Low frequency daily prefrontal rTMS improves mood in bipolar depression: A placebo-controlled case report. *Human Psychopharmacology, 13*, 271–275.

Gershon, E. S. (1990). Genetics. In F. K. Goodwin & K. R. Jamison (Eds.), *Manic-depressive illness* (pp. 373–401). New York: Oxford University Press.

Gershon, E. S., & Rieder, R. O. (1992). Major disorders of mind and brain. *Scientific American, 267*, 128.

Giles, J. (1994, April 18). The poet of alienation. *Newsweek, 123*, 46–47.

Gilger, J. W., Pennington, B. F., & DeFries, J. C. (1992). A twin study of the etiology of comorbidity: Attention-deficit hyperactivity disorder and dyslexia. *Journal of the American Academy of Child & Adolescent Psychiatry, 31*, 343–348.

Gillberg, C. (1991). Outcome in autism and autistic-like conditions. *Journal of the American Academy of Child & Adolescent Psychiatry, 30*, 375–382.

Gillberg, C. (1998). Chromosomal disorders in autism. *Journal of Autism & Developmental Disorders, 28*, 415–425.

Gillberg, C., & Steffenburg, S. (1987). Outcome and prognostic factors in infantile autism and similar conditions: A population-based study of 46 cases followed through puberty. *Journal of Autism & Developmental Disorders, 17*, 273–287.

Gillham, J. E., Reivich, K. J., Jaycox, L. H., & Seligman, M. E. P. (1995). Prevention of depressive symptoms in schoolchildren: Two-year follow-up. *Psychological Science, 6*, 343–351.

Gillis, L. S., Elk, R., Ben-Arie, O., & Teggin, A. (1982). The Present State Examination: Experiences with Xhosa-speaking psychiatric patients. *British Journal of Psychiatry, 141*, 143–147.

Ginns, E. I., Ott, J., Egeland, J. A., Allen, C. R., Fann, C. S. J., Pauls, D. L., Weissenbach, J., Carulli, J. P., Falls, K. M., Keith, T. P., & Paul S. (1996). A genome-wide search for chromosomal loci linked to bipolar affective disorder in the Old Order Amish. *Nature Genetics, 12*, 431–435.

Ginns, E. I., St. Jean, P., Philibert, R. A., Galdzicka, M., Damschroder-Williams, P., et al. (1998). A genome-wide search for chromosomal loci linked to mental health wellness in relatives at high risk for bipolar affective disorder among the Old Order Amish. *Proceedings of the National Academy of Sciences, USA, 95*, 15531–15536.

Giovini, G. A., Schooley, M. W., Zhu, B., Chrismon, J. H., Tomar, S. L., Peddicord, J. P., Merritt, R. K., Husten, C. G., & Eriksen, M. P. (1994). Surveillance for selected tobacco-use behaviors—United States, 1900–1994. *Morbidity & Mortality Weekly Report, 43*, 1–43.

Girelli, S. A., Resick, P. A., Marhoefer-Dvorak, S., & Hutter, C. K. (1986). Subjective distress and violence during rape: Their effects on long-term fear. *Violence & Victims, 1*, 35–46.

Girgus, J., & Nolen-Hoeksema, S. (in press). *Depression in childhood and adolescence*. New York: Oxford University Press.

Gittelman, R., Mannuzza, S., Shenker, R., & Bonagura, N. (1985). Hyperactive boys almost grown up: I. Psychiatric status. *Archives of General Psychiatry, 42*, 937–947.

Glaser, R., Rice, J., Speicher, C. E., Stout, J. C., & Kiecolt-Glaser, J. C. (1986). Stress depresses interferon production by leukocytes concomitant with a decrease in natural killer cell activity. *Behavioral Neuroscience, 100*, 675–678.

Glasgow, M. S., Engel, B. T., & D'Lugoff, B. C. (1989). A controlled study of a standardized behavioral stepped treatment for hypertension. *Psychosomatic Medicine, 51*, 10–26.

Glasgow, M. S., Gaader, K. R., & Engel, B. T. (1982). Behavioral treatment of high blood pressure: I. Acute and sustained effects of relaxation and systolic blood pressure biofeedback. *Psychosomatic Medicine, 44*, 155–170.

Glass, G. V., & Singer, J. E. (1972). *Urban stress: Experiments on noise and social stressors*. New York: Academic Press.

Glassman, A. (1969). Indoleamines and affective disorders. *Psychosomatic Medicine, 31*, 107–114.

Gleaves, D. H. (1996). The sociocognitive model of dissociative identity disorder: A reexamination of the evidence. *Psychological Bulletin, 120*, 42–59.

Gleaves, D. H., & Freyd, J. J. (1997, September). Questioning additional claims about the false memory syndrome epidemic. *American Psychologist*, 993–994.

Glick, I. D., Weiss, R. S., & Parkes, C. M. (1974). *The first year of bereavement*. New York: Wiley.

Goate, A., Chartier-Harlin, M.-C., Mullan, M., Brown, J., Crawford, F., Fidani, L., Giuffa, L., Haynes, A., Irving, N., James, L., et al. (1991). Segregation of a missense mutation in the amyloid precursor protein gene with familial Alzheimer's disease. *Nature, 349*, 704–706.

Goldberg, E. M., & Morrison, S. L. (1963). Schizophrenia and social class. *British Journal of Psychiatry, 109*, 785–802.

Goldman, S., & Beardslee, W. R. (1999). Suicide in children and adolescents. In D. G. Jacobs (Ed.), *The Harvard Medical School guide to suicide assessment and intervention*. (pp. 417–442). San Francisco: Jossey-Bass.

Goldstein, A. (1994). *Addiction: From biology to drug policy*. New York: W. H. Freeman.

Goldstein, G., & Hersen, M. (Eds.). (1990). *Handbook of psychological assessment*. Elmsford, NY: Pergamon Press.

Goldstein, J. M. (1995). The impact of gender on understanding the epidemiology of schizophrenia. In M. V. Seeman (Ed.), *Gender and psychopathology* (pp. 159–200). Washington, DC: American Psychiatric Press.

Goldstein, J. M. (1997). Sex differences in schizophrenia: Epidemiology, genetics, and the brain. *International Review of Psychiatry, 9*, 399–408.

Goldstein, J. M., Seidman, L. J., Goodman, J. M., Koren, D., Lee, H., Weintraub, S., & Tsuang, M. (1998). Are there sex differences in neuropsychological functions among patients with schizophrenia. *American Journal of Psychiatry, 155*, 1358–1364.

Goldstein, M. G. (1998). Bupropion sustained release and smoking cessation. *Journal of Clinical Psychology, 59* (Suppl. 4), 66–72.

Goldstein, M. J. (1987). The UCLA High-Risk Project. *Schizophrenia Bulletin, 13*, 505–514.

Goldstein, M. J., Talovic, S. A., Nuechterlein, K. H., & Fogelson, D. L. (1992). Family interaction versus individual psychopathology: Do they indicate the same processes in the families of schizophrenia? *British Journal of Psychiatry, 161*, 97–102.

Goleman, D. (1995). *Emotional intelligence*. New York: Bantam Books.

Goleman, G. (1993, December 3). Depression costs put at $43 billion. *New York Times*, A-10.

Gomberg, E. S. (1994). Risk factors for drinking over a woman's life span. *Alcohol Health & Research World, 18*, 220–227.

Gong-Guy, E. (1978). *The California Southeast Asian's mental health needs assessment* (California State Department Mental Health Contract #85-7628-2A-2, 1987): California State Department.

Gong-Guy, E. (1986). *Depression in students of Chinese and Japanese ancestry: An acculturation, vulnerability and stress model*. Unpublished dissertation, University of California, Los Angeles.

Gonzalez, N. M., & Campbell, M. (1994). Cocaine babies: Does prenatal exposure to cocaine affect development? *Journal of the American Academy of Child & Adolescent Psychiatry, 33*, 16–19.

Goodwin, D. W. (1988). *Alcohol and the writer*. Kansas City, MO: Andrews and McMeel.

Goodwin, F. K., & Jamison, K. R. (1990). *Manic-depressive illness*. New York: Oxford University Press.

Goodwin, F., & Ghaemi, S. (1998). Understanding manic-depressive illness. *Archives of General Psychiatry, 55*, 23–25.

Gorman, J. M., Liebowitz, M. R., Fyer, A. J., Fyer, M. R., & Klein, D. F. (1986). Possible respiratory abnormalities in panic disorder. *Psychopharmacological Bulletin, 221*, 797–801.

Gorman, J. M., Papp, L. A., & Coplan, J. D. (1995). Neuroanatomy and neurotransmitter function in panic disorder. In S. P. Roose & R. A. Glick (Eds.), *Anxiety as symptom and signal* (pp. 39–56). Hillsdale, NJ: Analytic Press.

Gorsuch, R. L. (1995). Religious aspects of substance abuse and recovery. *Journal of Social Issues, 51*, 65–83.

Gottesman, I., & Moldin, S. O. (1998). Genotypes, genes, genesis, and pathogenesis in schizophrenia. In M. F. Lenzenweger & R. H. Dworkin (Eds.), *Origins of the development of schizophrenia* (pp. 5–26). Washington, DC: American Psychological Association.

Gottesman, I. I. (1991). *Schizophrenia genesis: The origins of madness*. New York: W. H. Freeman.

Gottesman, I. I., & Shields, J. (1982). *Schizophrenia, the epigenetic puzzle*. New York: Cambridge University Press.

Gottlieb, G. L., & Kumar, A. (1993). Conventional pharmacologic treatment for patients with Alzheimer's disease. *Neurology, 43*, S56–S63.

Gottman, J. M., Jacobsen, N. S., Rushe, R. H., Shortt, J. W., Babcock, J., La Taillade, J. J., & Waltz, J. (1995). The relationship between heart rate reactivity, emotionally aggressive behavior and general violence in batterers. *Journal of Family Psychology, 9*, 227–248.

Graber, J. A., Brooks-Gunn, J., Paikoff, R. L., & Warren, M. P. (1994). Prediction of eating problems: An 8-year study of adolescent girls. *Developmental Psychology, 30*, 823–834.

Graber, J. A., Lewinsohn, P. M., Seeley, J. R., & Brooks-Gunn, J. (1997). Is psychopathology associated with the timing of pubertal development? *Journal of the American Academy of Child & Adolescent Psychiatry, 36*, 1768–1776.

Graeff, F. G., Guimaraes, F. S., Francisco, S., De Andrade, T. G. C. S., & Deakin, J. F. W. (1996). Role of 5-HT in stress, anxiety, and depression. *Pharmacology, Biochemistry, & Behavior, 54*, 129–141.

Grandin, T. (1995). *Thinking in pictures and my other reports from my life with autism*. New York: Vintage Books.

Grattan-Smith, P., Fairly, M., & Procopis, P. (1988). Clinical features of conversion disorder. *Archives of Disease in Childhood, 63*, 408–414.

Grau, L., & Padgett, D. (1988). Somatic depression among the elderly: A sociocultural perspective. *International Journal of Geriatric Psychiatry, 3*, 201–207.

Gray, E., & Cosgrove, J. (1985). Ethnocentric perception of childbearing practices in protective services. *Child Abuse and Neglect, 9*, 389–396.

Gray, J. A. (1987). *The psychology of fear and stress* (2nd ed.). Cambridge, England: Cambridge University Press.

Gray, J. J., Ford, K., & Kelly, L. M. (1987). The prevalence of bulimia in a black college population. *International Journal of Eating Disorders, 6*, 733–740.

Greaves, G. B. (1980). Multiple personality: 165 years after Mary Reynolds. *The Journal of Nervous & Mental Disease, 168*, 577–596.

Green, A. H. (1993). Child sexual abuse: Immediate and long-term effects and intervention. *Journal of the American Academy of Child & Adolescent Psychiatry, 32*, 890–902.

Green, B. L., Grace, M. C., Lindy, L. D., Titchener, J. L., & Lindy, J. G. (1983). Levels of functional impairment following a civilian disaster: The Beverly Hills Supper Club fire. *Journal of Consulting & Clinical Psychology, 51*, 573–580.

Green, B. L., Lindy, J. D., Grace, M. C. & Leonard, A. C. (1992). Chronic posttraumatic stress disorder and diagnostic comorbidity in a disaster sample. *Journal of Nervous & Mental Disease, 180*, 760–766.

Green, R. (1986). Gender identity in childhood and later sexual orientation: Follow-up of 78 males. *Annual Progress in Child Psychiatry & Child Development*, 214–220.

Greenberg, J., & Cheselka, O. (1995). Relational approaches to psychoanalytic psychotherapy. In A. S. Gurman (Ed.), *Essential psychotherapies: Theory and practice* (pp. 55–84). New York: Guilford Press.

Greenberg, L. S., Elliot, R., & Lietaer, G. (1994). Research on humanistic and experiential psychotherapies. In A. Bergin & S. Garfield (Eds.), *Handbook of psychotherapy and behavior change* (4th ed., pp. 509–542). New York: Wiley.

Greene, B., & Blanchard, E. B. (1994). Cognitive therapy for irritable bowel syndrome. *Journal of Consulting & Clinical Psychology, 62*, 576–582.

Gregory, R. J. (1999). *Foundations of intellectual assessment: The WAIS-III and other tests in clinical practice*. Boston: Allyn & Bacon.

Grenier, G., & Byers, E. S. (1995). Rapid ejaculation: A review of conceptual, etiological, and treatment issues. *Archives of Sexual Behavior, 24*, 447–472.

Griffith, E. E. H., & Baker, F. M. (1993). Psychiatric care of African Americans. In A. C. Gaw (Ed.), *Culture, ethnicity, and mental illness* (pp. 147–173). Washington, DC: American Psychiatric Press.

Grinspoon, L., & Bakalar, J. B. (1995). Marihuana as medicine: A plea for reconsideration. *Journal of the American Medical Association, 273*, 1875–1876.

Grisso, T., & Applebaum, P. S. (1995). The MacArthur Treatment Competence Study: III.

Abilities of patients to consent to psychiatric and medical treatments. *Law & Human Behavior, 19,* 149–174.

Grisso, T., & Applebaum, P. S. (1998). Assessing competence to consent to treatment: A guide for physicians and other health professionals. New York: Oxford University Press.

Grob, G. N. (1994). *The mad among us: A history of the care of America's mentally ill.* Cambridge, MA: Harvard University Press.

Gross, J., & Rosen, J. C. (1988). Bulimia in adolescents: Prevalence and psychosocial correlates. *International Journal of Eating Disorders, 7,* 51–61.

Gross, R. T., Brooks-Gunn, J., & Spiker, D. (1992). Efficacy of educational interventions for low birth weight infants: The Infant Health and Development Program. In S. L. Friedman & M. D. Sigman (Eds.), *The psychological development of low birth weight children: Advances in applied developmental psychology.* Norwood, NJ: Ablex.

Gross-Isseroff, R., Biegon, A., Voet, H., & Weizman, A. (1998). The suicide brain: A review of postmortem receptor/transporter binding studies. *Neuroscience & Biobehavioral Reviews, 22,* 653–661.

Grosse-Holforth, M., Pathak, A., Koenig, H. G., & Cohen, H. J. (1996). Medical illness, religion, health control, and depression of institutionalized medically ill veterans in long-term care. *International Journal of Geriatric Psychology, 11,* 613–620.

Groth, A. N. (1979). *Men who rape: The psychology of the offender.* New York: Plenum.

Grunwald, J. (1995). The European phytomedicines: Market figures, trends, analyses. *Herbalgram, 34,* 60–65.

Guarnaccia, P. J., Canino, G., Rubio-Stipec, M., & Bravo, M. (1993). The prevalence of *ataques de nervios* in the Puerto Rico Disaster Study: The role of culture in psychiatric epidemiology. *Journal of Nervous & Mental Disease, 181,* 157–165.

Guarnaccia, P. J., Guevara-Ramos, L. M., Gonzales, G., Canino, G. J., & Bird, H. (1992). Cross-cultural aspects of psychiatric symptoms in Puerto Rico. *Community & Mental Health, 7,* 99–110.

Guarnaccia, P. J., Rivera, M., Franco, F., Neighbors, C., & Allende-Ramos, C. (1996). The experiences of *ataques de nervios:* Toward an anthropology of emotions in Puerto Rico. *Culture, Medicine, & Psychiatry, 15,* 139–165.

Gunderson, J. G., Ronningstam, E., & Smith, L. E. (1995). Narcissistic personality disorder. In W. J. Livesley (Ed.), *The DSM-IV personality disorders* (pp. 201–212). New York: Guilford Press.

Gunderson, J. G., Zanarini, M. C., & Kisiel, C. L. (1995). Borderline personality disorder. In W. J. Livesley (Ed.), *The DSM-IV personality disorders* (pp. 141–157). New York: Guilford Press.

Gur, R. E., Cowell, P., Turetsky, B. I., Gallacher, F., Cannon, T., Bilker, W., & Gur, R. C. (1998). A follow-up magnetic resonance imaging study of schizophrenia. *Archives of General Psychiatry, 55,* 145–152.

Gurtman, M. B. (1994). The circumplex as a tool for studying normal and abnormal personality: A methodological primer. In S. Stack & M. Lorr (Eds.), *Differentiating normal and abnormal personality* (pp. 243–263). New York: Springer.

Gusella, J. F., MacDonald, M. E., Ambrose, C. M., & Duyao, M. P. (1993). Molecular genetics of Huntington's disease. *Archives of Neurology, 50,* 1157–1163.

Gustafson, Y., Brannstrom, B., Berggren, D., & Ragnarsson, J. I. (1991). A geriatric-anesthesiologic program to reduce acute confusional states in elderly patients treated for femoral neck fractures. *Journal of the American Geriatrics Society, 39,* 655–662.

Gutierrez, P. M., & Silk, K. R. (1998). Prescription privileges for psychologists: A review of the psychological literature. *Professional Psychology: Research & Practice, 29,* 213–222.

Guy, R. F., Rankin, B. A., & Norvell, M. J. (1980). The relation of sex role stereotyping to body image. *Journal of Psychology, 105,* 167–173.

Guze, B. H., & Gitlin, M. (1994). New antidepressants and the treatment of depression. *Journal of Family Practice, 38,* 49–57.

Guze, S. B. (1993). Genetics of Briquet's syndrome and somatization disorder: A review of family, adoption, and twin studies. Sanibel Island Symposium (1993, Ft. Myers, Florida). *Annals of Clinical Psychiatry, 5,* 225–230.

Gwirtsman, H. E., Guze, B. H., Yager, J., & Gainsley, B. (1990). Fluoxetine treatment of anorexia nervosa: An open clinical trial. *Journal of Clinical Psychiatry, 51,* 378–382.

H

Halford, W. K., & Hayes, R. (1991). Psychological rehabilitation of chronic schizophrenic patients: Recent findings on social skills training and family psychoeducation. *Clinical Psychology Review, 11,* 23–44.

Hall, M., Baum, A., Buysse, D. J., Prigerson, H. G., Kupfer, D. J., & Reynolds, C. F. I. (1998). Sleep as a mediator of the stress-immune relationship. *Psychosomatic Medicine, 60,* 48–51.

Hallowell, E. M., & Ratey, J. J. (1994). *Driven to distraction.* New York: Simon & Schuster.

Hambrecht, M., Maurer, K., Hafner, H., & Sartorius, N. (1992). Transnational stability of gender differences in schizophrenia: An analysis based on the WHO study on determinants of outcome of severe mental disorders. *European Archives of Psychiatry & Clinical Neuroscience, 242,* 6–12.

Hamilton, A. (1999, April 26). Virtually fearless. *Time, 153,* 110.

Hammen, C. (1991). Generation of stress in the course of unipolar depression. *Journal of Abnormal Psychology, 100,* 555–561.

Hammen, C. (1992). Cognitive, life stress, and interpersonal approaches to a developmental psychopathology model of depression. *Development & Psychopathology, 4,* 189–206.

Hammen, C. L., Burge, D., Daley, S. E., Davial, J., Paley, B., & Rudolph, K. D. (1995). Interpersonal attachment cognitions and prediction of symptomatic responses to interpersonal stress. *Journal of Abnormal Psychology, 104,* 436–443.

Hannah, M. C., Hopper, J. L., & Mathews, J. D. (1983). Twin concordance for a binary trait: I. Statistical models illustrated with data on drinking status. *Acta Geneticae Medicae et Gemellologiae: Twin Research, 32,* 127–137.

Hardie, E. A. (1997). Prevalence and predictors of cyclic and noncyclic affective change. *Psychology of Women Quarterly, 21,* 299–314.

Harding, C. M., Zubin, J., & Strauss, J. S. (1987). Chronicity in schizophrenia: Fact, partial fact, or artifact? *Hospital & Community Psychiatry, 38,* 477–486.

Hargreaves, W. A., Shumway, M., Knutsen, E. J., & Weinstein, A. (1987). Effects of the Jamison-Farabee consent decree: Due process protection for involuntary psychiatric patients treated with psychoactive medication. *American Journal of Psychiatry, 144,* 188–192.

Harrell, J. P. (1980). Psychological factors and hypertension: A status report. *Psychological Bulletin, 87,* 482–501.

Harrington, R., Rutter, M., & Fombonne, E. (1996). Developmental pathways in depression: Multiple meanings, antecedents, and endpoints. *Development & Psychopathology, 8,* 601–616.

Harris, M. J., Milich, R., Corbitt, E. M., & Hoover, D. W. (1992). Self-fulfilling effects of stigmatizing information on children's social interactions. *Journal of Personality & Social Psychology, 63,* 41–50.

Hart, S. D., & Hare, R. D. (1997). Psychopathy: Assessment and association with criminal conduct. In D. M. Stoff, J. Breiling, & J. D. Maser (Eds.), *Handbook of antisocial personality disorder* (pp. 22–35). New York: Wiley.

Harter, S. (1983). Developmental perspectives on the self-system. In P. H. Mussen (Ed.), *Handbook of child development* (pp. 275–385). New York: Wiley.

Hartman, D. E. (1998). Behavioral pharmacology of inhalants. In R. E. Tarter (Ed.), *Handbook of substance abuse: Neurobehavioral pharmacology.* (pp. 263–268). New York: Plenum.

Hartung, C. M., & Widiger, T. A. (1998). Gender differences in the diagnosis of mental disorders: Conclusions and controversies of the DSM-IV. *Psychological Bulletin, 123,* 260–278.

Harvey, A. G., & Rapee, R. M. (1995). Cognitive-behavior therapy for generalized anxiety disorder. *Psychiatric Clinics of North America, 4,* 859–870.

Harvey, M. R., & Herman, J. L. (1994). Amnesia, partial amnesia, and delayed recall among adult survivors of childhood trauma. *Consciousness & Cognition: An International Journal, 3,* 295–306.

Hauri, P., & Fisher, J. (1986). Persistent psychophysiologic (learned) insomnia. *Sleep, 9,* 38–53.

Hawkins, R. C., Turell, S., & Jackson, L. J. (1983). Desirable and undesirable masculine and feminine traits in relation to student's dieting tendencies and body image dissatisfaction. *Sex Roles, 9,* 705–718.

Haynes, S. G., Feinleib, M., & Kannel, W. B. (1980). The relationship of psychosocial factors to coronary heart disease in the Framingham study: III. Eight-year incidence of coronary heart disease. *American Journal of Epidemiology, 111,* 37–58.

Hayward, C., Killen, J. D., Wilson, D. M., & Hammer, L. D. (1997). Psychiatric risk associated with early puberty in adolescent girls. *Journal of the American Academy of Child & Adolescent Psychiatry, 36,* 255–262.

Hayward, C., Killen, J. D., Wilson, D. M., Hammer, L. D., Litt, I. F., Kraemer, H. C., Haydel, F., Varady, A., & Taylor, B. C. (1993, October). *Timing of puberty and onset of psychiatric symptoms.* Paper presented at the American Academy of Child and Adolescent Psychiatry, San Antonio, TX.

Heath, A. C. & Martin, N. G. (1993). Genetic models for the natural history of smoking: Evidence for a genetic influence on smoking. *Addictive Behaviors, 18,* 19–34.

Heatherton, T. F., & Baumeister, R. F. (1991). Binge-eating as escape from self-awareness. *Psychological Bulletin, 110,* 86–110.

Heaton, R. K., Marcotte, T. D., White, D. A., & Ross, D. (1996). Nature and vocational significance of neuropsychological impairment associated with HIV infection. *Clinical Neuropsychologist, 10,* 1–14.

Heide, F. J., & Borkovec, T. D. (1984). Relaxation-induced anxiety: Mechanisms & theoretical implications. *Behaviour Research & Therapy, 22,* 1–12.

Heikkinen, M., Aro, H., & Loennqvist, J. (1992). Recent life events and their role in suicide as seen by the spouses. *Acta Psychiatrica Scandinavica, 86,* 489–494.

Heiman, J. R., & Grafton-Becker, V. (1989). Orgasmic disorders in women. In S. R. Leiblum & R. C. Rosen (Eds.), *Principles and practice of sex therapy: Update for the 1990s* (pp. 51–88). New York: Guilford Press.

Heimberg, R. G., Juster, H. R., & Hope, D. A. (1995). Cognitive-behavioral group treatment: Description, case presentation, and empirical support. In M. B. Stein (Ed.), *Social phobia: Clinical and research perspectives* (pp. 293–321). Washington, DC: American Psychiatric Press.

Helgeson, V. S. (1994). Relation of agency and communion to well-being: Evidence and potential explanations. *Psychological Bulletin, 116,* 412–428.

Helms, J. E. (1992). Why is there no study of cultural equivalence in standardized cognitive ability testing? *American Psychologist, 47,* 1083–1101.

Helzer, J. E., & Canino, G. J. (1992). *Alcoholism in North America, Europe, and Asia.* New York: Oxford University Press.

Helzer, J. E., Bucholz, K., & Robins, L. N. (1992). Five communities in the United States: Results of the Epidemiologic Catchment Area Survey. In J. E. Helzer & G. J. Canino (Eds.), *Alcoholism in North America, Europe, and Asia.* New York: Oxford University Press.

Henderson, D., & Boyd, C. (1996). *All my buddies was male: Relationship issues of addicted women.* Unpublished manuscript.

Hendin, H. (1995). *Suicide in America.* New York: W. W. Norton.

Hendrick, V., Altshuler, L., & Suri, R. (1998). Hormonal changes in the postpartum and implications for postpartum depression. *Psychosomatics, 39,* 93–101.

Henker, B., & Whalen, C. K. (1989). Hyperactivity and attention deficits. *American Psychologist, 44,* 216–223.

Hennessy, K. D. (1997). Neglecting our common—and the public—interest. *American Psychologist, 52,* 272–273.

Henry, B., & Moffitt, T. E. (1997). Neuropsychological and neuroimaging studies of juvenile delinquency and adult criminal behavior. In D. M. Stoff, J. Breiling, & J. D. Maser (Eds.), *Handbook of antisocial personality disorder* (pp. 280–288). New York: Wiley.

Henry, B., Caspi, A., Moffitt, T. E., & Silva, P. A. (1996). Temperamental and familial predictors of violent and nonviolent criminal convictions: Age 3 to age 18. *Developmental Psychology, 32,* 614–623.

Herek, G. M. (1990). Gay people and government security clearances: A social science perspective. *American Psychologist, 45,* 1035–1042.

Herman, C. P., & Mack, D. (1975). Restrained and unrestrained eating. *Journal of Personality, 43,* 647–660.

Herman, C. P., & Polivy, J. (1975). Anxiety, restraint and eating disorder. *Journal of Abnormal Psychology, 84,* 666–672.

Herman, C. P., & Polivy, J. (1988). Psychological factors in the control of appetite. *Current Concepts in Nutrition, 16,* 41–51.

Herman, J. L., & Harvey, M. R. (1997). Adult memories of childhood trauma: A naturalistic clinical study. *Journal of Traumatic Stress, 10,* 557–571.

Heston, L. L. (1966). Psychiatric disorders in foster home reared children of schizophrenic mothers. *British Journal of Psychiatry, 112,* 819–825.

Higgins, S. T., Budney, A. J., Beckel, W. K., & Badger, G. J. (1994). Participation of significant others in outpatient behavioral treatment predicts greater cocaine abstinence. *American Journal of Drug & Alcohol Abuse, 20,* 47–56.

Hilgard, E. R. (1977/1986). *Divided consciousness: Multiple controls in human thought and action.* New York: Wiley.

Hilgard, E. R. (1992). Divided consciousness and dissociation. *Consciousness and Cognition: An International Journal, 1,* 16–31.

Hillbrand, M., Spitz, R. T., & VandenBos, G. R. (1997). Investigating the role of lipids in mood, aggression, and schizophrenia. *Psychiatric Services, 48,* 875–876.

Hiller, J. (1996). Female sexual arousal and its impairment: The psychodynamics of non-organic coital pain. *Sexual & Marital Therapy, 11,* 55–76.

Hinshaw, S. P. (1994). *Attention deficits and hyperactivity in children.* Thousand Oaks, CA: Sage.

Hinshaw, S. P., & Melnick, S. M. (1995). Peer relationships in boys with attention-deficit hyperactivity disorder with and without comorbid aggression. *Development & Psychopathology, 7,* 627–647.

Hirschfeld, R. (1994). Guidelines for the longterm treatment of depression. *Journal of Clinical Psychiatry, 55* (suppl. 12), 59–67.

Hirschfeld, R., Keller, M., Panico, S., Arons, B., Barlow, D., Davidoff, F., Endicott, J., Froom, J., Goldstein, M., Gorman, J., Guthrie, D., Marek, R., Maurer, T., Meyer, R., Phillips, K., Ross, J., Schwenk, T., Sharfstein, S., Thase, M., & Wyatt, R. (1997). The National Depressive and Manic-Depressive Association consensus statement on the undertreatment of depression. *Journal of the American Medical Association, 277,* 333–340.

Hirschfeld, R. M. A. (1996). Panic disorder: Diagnosis, epidemiology, and clinical course. *Journal of Clinical Psychology, 57* (Suppl. 10), 3–8.

Hite, S. (1976). *The Hite report: A nationwide study on female sexuality.* New York: Macmillan.

Hodapp, R. M., Burack, J. A., & Zigler, E. (1998). Developmental approaches to mental retardation: A short introduction. In J. A. Burack, R. M. Hodapp, & E. Zigler (Eds.), *Handbook of mental retardation and development* (pp. 3–19). New York: Cambridge University Press.

Hodgins, S. (1992). Mental disorder, intellectual deficiency, and crime: Evidence from a birth cohort. *Archives of General Psychiatry, 49,* 476–483.

Hodgins, S., & Cote, G. (1990). Prevalence of mental disorders among penitentiary inmates in Quebec. *Canadian Journal of Mental Health, 39,* 1–4.

Hoffman, A. (1968). Psychotomimetic agents. In A. Burger (Ed.), *Drugs affecting the central nervous system* (Vol. 2). New York: Marcel Dekker.

Hogarty, G. E., Anderson, C. M., Reiss, D. J., Kornblith, S. J., Greenwald, D. P., Jaund, C. D., & Madonia, M. J. (1986). Family psychoeducation, social skills training, and maintenance chemotherapy in the aftercare treatment of schizophrenia: I. One-year effects of a controlled study on relapse and expressed emotion. *Archives of General Psychiatry, 43,* 633–642.

Hogarty, G. E., Anderson, C. M., Reiss, D. J., Kornblith, S. J., Greenwald, D. P., Ulrich, R. F., & Carter, M. (1991). Family psychoeducation, social skills training, and maintenance chemotherapy in the aftercare treatment of schizophrenia: II. Two-year effects of a controlled study on relapse and adjustment. *Archives of General Psychiatry, 48,* 340–347.

Hogarty, G. E., Greenwald, D., Ulrich, R. F., Kornblith, S. J., DiBarry, A. L., Cooley, S., Carter, M., & Flesher, S. (1997a). Three-year trials of personal therapy among schizophrenic patients living with or independent of family: II. Effects of adjustment of patients. *American Journal of Psychiatry, 154,* 1514–1524.

Hogarty, G. E., Kornblith, S. J., Greenwald, D., DiBarry, A. L., Cooley, S., Ulrich, R. F., Carter, M., & Flesher, S. (1997b). Three-year trials of personal therapy among schizophrenic patients living with or independent of family: I. Description of study and effects on relapse rates. *American Journal of Psychiatry, 154,* 1504–1513.

Hoge, S. K., Bonnie, R. J., Poythress, N., Monahan, J., Eisenberg, M., & Feucht-Haviar, T. (1997). The MacArthur Adjudicative Competence Study: Development and validation of a research instrument. *Law and Human Behavior, 21,* 141–179.

Hoge, S. K., Poythress, N., Bonnie, R. J., Monahan, J., Eisenberg, M., & Feucht-Haviar, T. (1997). The MacArthur Adjudicative Competence Study: Diagnosis, psychopathology, and competence-related abilities. *Behavioral Sciences & the Law, 15,* 329–345.

Holden, C. (1980). Identical twins reared apart. *Science, 207,* 1323–1328.

Holland, A. J., Hall, A., Murray, R., Russell, G. F. M., & Crisp, A. H. (1984). Anorexia nervosa: A study of 34 twin pairs and one set of triplets. *British Journal of Psychiatry, 145,* 414–419.

Hollander, E., Neville, D., Frenkel, M., & Josephson, S. (1992). Body dysmorphic disorder: Diagnostic issues and related disorders. *Psychosomatics, 33,* 156–165.

Hollon, S. D. (1996). The efficacy and effectiveness of psychotherapy relative to medications. *American Psychologist, 51,* 1025–1030.

Hollon, S. D., DuRubeis, R. J., Evans, M. D., & Wiemer, M. J. (1992). Cognitive therapy and pharmacotherapy for depression: Singly and in combination. *Archives of General Psychiatry, 49,* 774–781.

Hollon, S. D., Shelton, R. C., & Loosen, P. T. (1991). Cognitive therapy and pharmacotherapy for depression. *Journal of Consulting & Clinical Psychology, 59,* 88–99.

Holmes, T. H., & Rahe, R. H. (1967). The social readjustment rating scale. *Journal of Psychosomatic Research, 11,* 213–218.

Holroyd, J. C., & Brodsky, A. M. (1977). Psychologists' attitudes and practices regarding erotic and nonerotic physical contact with patients. *American Psychologist, 32,* 843–849.

Holsboer, F. (1992). The hypothalamic-pituitary-adrenocortical system. In E. S. Paykel (Ed.), *Handbook of affective disorders* (pp. 267–287). New York: Guilford Press.

Holstein, J. A. (1993). *Court-ordered insanity: Interpretive practice and involuntary commitment.* New York: A. de Gruyter.

Hooley, J. M. (1998). Expressed emotion and psychiatric illness: From empirical data to clinical practice. *Behavior Therapy, 29,* 631–646.

Hooley, J. M., & Hiller, J. B. (1998). Expressed emotion and the pathogenesis of relapse in schizophrenia. In M. F. Lenzenweger & R. H. Dworkin (Eds.), *Origins of the development of schizophrenia* (pp. 447–468). Washington, DC: American Psychological Association.

Hooley, J. M., Richters, J. E., Weintraub, S., & Neale, J. M. (1987). Psychopathology and marital distress: The positive side of positive symptoms. *Journal of Abnormal Psychology, 96,* 27–33.

Hooper, J. (1999, February). A new germ theory. *The Atlantic Monthly,* 41–53.

Horm, J., & Anderson, K. (1993). Who in America is trying to lose weight? *Annals of Internal Medicine, 119,* 672–676.

Hornbacher, M. (1998). *Wasted.* New York: HarperPerennial.

Horney, K. (1934/1967). The overvaluation of love: A study of present-day feminine type. In H. Kelman (Ed.), *Feminine psychology* (pp. 182–213). New York: Norton.

Horney, K. (1939). *New ways in psychoanalysis.* New York: W. W. Norton.

Hornig, C. D., & McNally, R. J. (1995). Panic disorder and suicide attempt: A reanalysis of data from the Epidemiologic Catchment Area study. *British Journal of Psychiatry, 167,* 76–79.

Hornstein, N. L., & Putnam, F. W. (1992). Clinical phenomenology of child and adolescent dissociative disorders. *Journal of the American Academy of Child & Adolescent Psychiatry, 31,* 1077–1085.

Horowitz, M. J. (1976). *Stress response syndromes.* New York: Aronson.

Hsu, L. G. (1990). Experiential aspects of bulimia nervosa: Implications for cognitive behavioral therapy. *Behavior Modification, 14,* 50–65.

Hsu, L. K., Crisp, A. H., & Harding, B. (1979). Outcome of anorexia nervosa. *Lancet, 1,* 61–65.

Hubbard, K., O'Neill, A.-M., Cheakalos, C., Baker, K., Berenstein, L., Breu, G., Duffy, T., Fowler, J., Greissinger, L. K., Matsumoto, N., Smith, P., Weinstein, F., & York, M. (1999, April 12). Out of control. *People Magazine,* 52–69.

Hudson, J. I., McElroy, S. L., Raymond, N. C., Crow, S., Keck, P. E., Carter, W. P., Mitchell, J. E., Strakowski, S. M., Pope Jr., H. G., Coleman, B. S., & Jonas, J. M. (1998). Fluvoxamine in the treatment of binge-eating disorder: A multicenter placebo-controlled, double-blind trial. *American Journal of Psychiatry, 155,* 1756–1762.

Hugdahl, K., & Ohman, A. (1977). Effects of instruction on acquisition and extinction of electrodermal response to fear-relevant stimuli. *Journal of Experimental Psychiatry: Human Learning & Memory, 3,* 608–618.

Hughes, J. R. (1986). Genetics of smoking: A review. *Behavior Therapy, 17,* 335–345.

Humphreys, K. (1996). Clinical psychologists as therapists: History, future, and alternatives. *American Psychologist, 51,* 190–197.

Hunt, W. A. (1998). Pharmacology of alcohol. In R. E. Tarter, R. T. Ammerman, & P. J. Ott (Eds.), *Handbook of substance abuse: Neurobehavioral pharmacology* (pp. 7–21). New York: Plenum.

Hur, Y., Bouchard, T. J., Jr., & Eckert, E. (1998). Genetic and environmental influences on self-reported diet: A reared-apart twin study. *Physiology & Behavior, 64,* 629–636.

Hurlbert, D. F. (1991). The role of assertiveness in female sexuality: A comparative study between sexually assertive and sexually nonassertive women. *Journal of Sex & Marital Therapy, 17,* 183–190.

Huselid, R. F., & Cooper, M. L. (1992). Gender roles as mediators of sex differences in adolescent alcohol use and abuse. *Journal of Health & Social Behavior, 33,* 348–362.

Hutson, H. R., Anglin, D., & Pratts, M. J. (1994). Adolescents and children injured or killed in drive-by shootings in Los Angeles. *The New England Journal of Medicine, 330,* 324–327.

Hyde, J. S. (1990). *Understanding human sexuality.* New York: McGraw-Hill.

Hyland, M. E. (1990). The mood-peak flow relationship in adult asthmatics: A pilot study of individual differences and direction of causality. *British Journal of Medical Psychology, 63,* 379–384.

Hyman, I. E., & Billings, F. J. (1998). Individual differences and the creation of false childhood memories. *Memory, 6,* 1–20.

I

Inciardi, J. A., Lockwood, D., & Pottieger, A. E. (1993). *Women and crack cocaine.* New York: Macmillan.

The Infant Health and Development Program. (1990). Enhancing the outcome of low-birth-weight, premature infants: A multisite

randomized trial. *Journal of the American Medical Association, 263,* 3035–3042.

Insel, T. R. (Ed.). (1984). *New findings in obsessive-compulsive disorder.* Washington, DC: American Psychiatric Press.

Insel, T. R., Hoover, C., & Murphy, D. L. (1983). Parents of patients with obsessive-compulsive disorder. *Psychological Medicine, 13,* 807–811.

Ironside, R. N., & Batchelor, I. R. C. (1945). *Aviation neuro-psychiatry.* Baltimore: Williams & Wilkins.

Ironson, G., Wynings, C., Schneiderman, N., Baum, A., Rodriguez, M., Greenwood, D., Benight, C., Antoni, M., LaPerriere, A., Huang, H.-S., Klimas, N., & Fletcher, M. A. (1997). Posttraumatic stress symptoms, intrusive thoughts, loss and immune function after Hurricane Andrew. *Psychosomatic Medicine, 59,* 128–141.

Isometsa, E., Heikkinen, M., Henriksson, M., Aro, H., & Lonnqvist, J. (1995). Recent life events and completed suicide in bipolar affective disorder: A comparison with major depressive suicides. *Journal of Affective Disorders, 33,* 99–106.

J

Jablensky, A., (1989). Epidemiology and cross-cultural aspects of schizophrenia. *Psychiatric Annals, 19,* 516–524.

Jack, D. C. (1991). *Silencing the self: Women and depression.* New York: HarperPerennial.

Jack, R. (1992). *Women and attempted suicide.* Hillsdale, NJ: Erlbaum.

Jacobs, D., Blackburn, H., Higgins, M., Reed, D., Iso, H., McMillan, G., Neaton, J., Nelson, J., Potter, J., Rifkind, B., Rossouw, J., Shekelle, R., & Yusuf, S. (1992). Report of the conference on low blood cholesterol: Mortality associations. *Circulation, 86,* 1046–1060.

Jacobson, E. (1964). *The self and the object world.* New York: International Universities Press.

Jacobson, N. S. (1994). Rewards and dangers in researching domestic violence. *Family Process, 33,* 81–85.

Jacobson, N. S., Gottman, J. M., & Shortt, J. W. (1995). The distinction between type 1 an type 2 batterers—further consideration reply to Ornduff et al. (1995), Margolin et al. (1995), and Walker (1995). *Journal of Family Psychology, 9,* 272–279.

Jacobson, N. S., & Hollon, S. D. (1996). Cognitive-behavior therapy versus pharmacotherapy: Now that the jury's returned its verdict, it's time to present the rest of the evidence. *Journal of Consulting & Clinical Psychology, 64,* 74–80.

James, S. A., Hartnett, S. A., & Kalsbeek, W. D. (1983). John Henryism and blood pressure differences among black men. *Journal of Behavioral Medicine, 6,* 259–278.

James, S. A., LaCroix, A. Z., Kleinbaum, D. G., & Strogatz, D. S. (1984). John Henryism and blood pressure differences among black men: II. The role of occupational stressors. *Journal of Behavioral Medicine, 7,* 259–275.

James, W. (1890). *The principles of psychology.* New York: Henry Holt.

Jamison, K. R. (1993). *Touched with fire: Manic-depressive illness and the artistic temperament.* New York: Free Press.

Jamison, K. R. (1995a). Manic-depressive illness and creativity. *Scientific American, 272,* 62–67.

Jamison, K. R. (1995b). *An unquiet mind: A memoir of moods and madness.* New York: Alfred A. Knopf.

Jamison, K. R. (1999). *Night falls fast: Understanding suicide.* New York: Knopf.

Jamner, L. D., Schwartz, G. E., & Leigh, H. (1988). The relationship between repressive and defensive coping styles and monocyte, eosinophile, and serum glucose levels: Support for the opioid peptide hypothesis of repression. *Psychosomatic Medicine, 50,* 567–575.

Jang, K. L., McCrae, R. R., Angleitner, A., Riemann, R., & Livesley, W. J. (1998). Heritability of facet-level traits in a cross-cultural twin sample: Support for a hierarchical model of personality. *Journal of Personality & Social Psychology, 74,* 1556–1565.

Jang, K. L., Livesley, W. J., & Vernon, P. A. (1997). Gender-specific etiological differences in alcohol and drug problems: A behavioral genetic analysis. *Addiction, 92,* 1265–1276.

Jang, K. L., Paris, J., Zweig-Frank, H., & Livesley, W. J. (1998). Twin study of dissociative experience. *Journal of Nervous & Mental Disease, 186,* 345–351.

Janis, I. L. (1958). *Psychological stress: Psychoanalytic and behavioral studies of surgical patients.* New York: Wiley.

Janoff-Bulman, R. (1992). *Shattered assumptions: Toward a new psychology of trauma.* New York: Maxwell Macmillan International.

Janoff-Bulman, R., & Frieze, I. H. (1983). A theoretical perspective for understanding reactions to victimization. *Journal of Social Issues, 39,* 1–17.

Jarrett, R. B., Basco, M. R., Risser, R., Ramanan, J., Marwill, M., Kraft, D., & Rush, A. J. (1998). Is there a role for continuation phase cognitive therapy for depressed patients? *Journal of Consulting & Clinical Psychology, 66,* 1036–1040.

Jaycox, L. H., Reivich, K. J., Gillham, J., & Seligman, M. E. P. (1994). Preventing depressive symptoms in school children. *Behaviour Research & Therapy, 32,* 801–816.

Jeffery, R. W., Wing, R. R., Thorson, C., & Burton, L. R. (1998). Use of personal trainers and financial incentives to increase exercise in a behavioral weight-loss program. *Journal of Consulting & Clinical Psychology, 66,* 777–783.

Jellinek, E. (1960). *The disease concept of alcoholism.* Highland Park, NJ: Hillhouse.

Jemmott, J. B., Jemmott, L. S., Spears, H., & Hewitt, N. (1992). Self-efficacy, hedonistic expectancies, and condom-use intentions among inner-city black adolescent women: A social cognitive approach to AIDS risk behavior. *Journal of Adolescent Health, 13,* 512–519.

Jemmott, J. B., & Locke, S. E. (1984). Psychosocial factors, immunologic mediation, and human susceptibility to infectious diseases: How much do we really know? *Psychological Bulletin, 95,* 78–108.

Jemmott, L. S., & Jemmott, J. B. (1992). Increasing condom-use intentions among sexually active adolescent women. *Nursing Research, 41,* 273–279.

Jenike, M. A. (1992). Pharmacological treatment of obsessive compulsive disorders. *Psychiatric Clinics of North America, 15,* 895–919.

Jenkins, J. H., & Karno, M. (1992). The meaning of expressed emotion: Theoretical issues raised by cross-cultural research. *American Journal of Psychiatry, 149,* 9–21.

Jenkins, J. H., Kleinman, A., & Good, B. J. (1991). Cross-cultural studies of depression. In J. Becker (Ed.), *Psychosocial aspects of depression* (pp. 67–99). Hillsdale, NJ: Erlbaum.

Jenkins, R. L. (1968). The varieties of children's behavioral problems and family dynamics. *American Journal of Psychiatry, 124,* 1440–1445.

Jenkins, R. L. (1973). *Behavior disorders of childhood and adolescence.* Springfield, IL: Charles C Thomas.

Johannessen, D. J., Cowley, D. S., Walker, D. R., & Jensen, C. F. (1989). Prevalence, onset and clinical recognition of panic states in hospitalized male alcoholics. *American Journal of Psychiatry, 146,* 1201–1203.

Johnson, S. L., & Roberts, J. E. (1995). Life events and bipolar disorder: Implications from biological theories. *Psychological Bulletin, 117,* 434–449.

Joiner, T. E. (1999). The clustering and contagion of suicide. *Current Directions in Psychological Science, 8,* 89–92.

Jones, E. E., & Harris, V. A. (1967). The attribution of attitudes. *Journal of Experimental Social Psychology, 3,* 1–24.

Jones, P., & Cannon, M. (1998). The new epidemiology of schizophrenia. *Psychiatric Clinics of North America, 21,* 1–25.

Jordan, B. D. (1998). Dementia pugilistia. In M. F. Folstein (Ed.), *Neurobiology of primary dementia* (pp. 191–204). Washington, DC: American Psychiatric Press.

Jordan, B. K., Schlenger, W. E., Fairbank, J. A., & Caddell, J. M. (1996). Prevalence of psychiatric disorders among incarcerated women: II. Convicted felons entering prison. *Archives of General Psychiatry, 53,* 513–519.

Judd, L., Akiskal, H., Maser, J., Zeller, P. J., Endicott, J., Coryell, W., Paulus, M., Kunovac, J., Leon, A., Mueller, T., Rice, J., & Keller, M. (1998). A prospective 12-year study of subsyndromal and syndromal depressive symptoms in unipolar major depressive disorders. *Archives of General Psychiatry, 55,* 694–700.

Jun-mian, X. (1987). Some issues in the diagnosis of depression in China. *Canadian Journal of Psychiatry, 32,* 368–370.

K

Kagan, J., Reznick, J. S., & Snidman, N. (1987). The physiology and psychology of behavioral inhibition. *Child Development, 60,* 838–845.

Kamen-Siegel, L., Rodin, J., Seligman, M. E., & Dwyer, J. (1991). Explanatory style and cell-mediated immunity in elderly men and women. *Health Psychology, 10,* 229–235.

Kanner, L. (1943). Autistic disturbances of affective contact. *Nervous Child, 21,* 217–250.

Kanowski, S., Herrmann, W. M., Stephan, K., Wierich, W., & Hoerr, R. (1996). Proof of efficacy of the ginkgo biloba special extract EGb 761 in outpatients suffering from mild to moderate primary degenerative dementia of the Alzheimer type or multi-infarct dementia. *Pharmacopsychiatry, 29,* 47–56.

Kaplan, H. S. (1974). *The new sex therapy: Active treatment of sexual dysfunction.* New York: Brunner/Mazel.

Kaplan, H. S. (1977). Hypoactive sexual desire. *Journal of Sex & Marital Therapy, 3,* 3–9.

Kaplan, H. S. (1995). *The sexual desire disorders: Dysfunctional regulation of sexual motivation.* New York: Brunner/Mazel.

Kaplan, J. R., & Kaufmann, P. (1993). Low or lowered cholesterol and risk of death from suicide and trauma. *Metabolism, 42* (Suppl. 1), 45–56.

Kaplan, J. R., Muldoon, M. F., Manuck, S. B., & Mann, J. J. (1997). Assessing the observed relationship between low cholesterol and violence-related mortality: Implications for suicide risk. In Stoff, D. M. (Ed.), *The neurobiology of suicide: From the bench to the clinic* (pp. 57–80). New York: New York Academy of Sciences.

Kaplan, M. (1983). The issue of sex bias in DSM-III: Comments on the articles by Spitzer, Williams, and Kass. *American Psychologist, 38,* 802–803.

Karasek, R. A., Russell, R. S., & Theorell, T. (1982). Physiology of stress and regeneration in job related cardiovascular illness. *Journal of Human Stress, 8,* 29–42.

Karno, M., & Golding, J. M. (1991). Obsessive compulsive disorder. In L. R. Robins & D. A. Regier (Eds.), *Psychiatric disorders in America: The Epidemiologic Catchment Area Study.* New York: Maxwell Macmillan International.

Karno, M., Hough, R., Burnam, A., Escobar, J. I., Timbers, D. M., Santana, F., & Boyd, J. H. (1987). Lifetime prevalence of specific psychiatric disorders among Mexican Americans and non-Hispanic whites in Los Angeles. *Archives of General Psychiatry, 44,* 695–701.

Karno, M., & Jenkins, J. H. (1993). Cross-cultural issues in the course and treatment of schizophrenia. *Psychiatric Clinics of North America, 16,* 339–350.

Karper, L. P., & Krystal, J. H. (1997). Pharmacotherapy of violent behavior. In D. M. Stoff, J. Breiling, & J. D. Maser (Eds.), *Handbook of antisocial personality disorder* (pp. 436–444). New York: Wiley.

Kaslow, N. J., & Celano, M. P. (1995). The family therapies. In A. S. Gurman (Ed.), *Essential psychotherapies: Theory and practice* (pp. 343–403). New York: Guilford Press.

Kaslow, N. J., & Racusin, G. R. (1990). Family therapy or child therapy: An open or shut case. *Journal of Family Psychology, 3,* 273–289.

Kassett, J. A., Gwirtsman, H. E., Kaye, W. H., & Brandt, H. A. (1988). Pattern of onset of bulimic symptoms in anorexia nervosa. 140th Annual Meeting of the American Psychiatric Association (1987, Chicago, Illinois). *American Journal of Psychiatry, 145,* 1287–1288.

Katchadourian, H. A. (1989). *Fundamentals of human sexuality* (5th ed.). New York: Holt, Rinehart & Winston.

Katerndahl, D. A., & Realini, J. P. (1993). Lifetime prevalence of panic states. *American Journal of Psychiatry, 15,* 246–249.

Katz, R., & Wykes, T. (1985). The psychological difference between temporally predictable and unpredictable stressful events: Evidence for information control theories. *Journal of Personality & Social Psychology, 48,* 781–790.

Katzman, R. (1993). Education and the prevalence of dementia and Alzheimer's disease. *Neurology, 43,* 13–20.

Kavanagh, D. J. (1992). Recent developments in expressed emotion and schizophrenia. *British Journal of Psychiatry, 160,* 601–620.

Kaye, W. H., Weltzin, T. E., Hsu, H. G., & Bulik, C. M. (1991). An open trial of fluoxetine in patients with anorexia nervosa. *Journal of Clinical Psychiatry, 52,* 464–471.

Kazdin, A. E. (1986). Comparative outcome studies of psychotherapy: Methodological issues and strategies. *Journal of Consulting & Clinical Psychology, 54,* 95–105.

Kazdin, A. E. (1991). Effectiveness of psychotherapy with children and adolescents. *Journal of Consulting & Clinical Psychology, 59,* 785–798.

Kazdin, A. E., & Wilcoxon, L. A. (1976). Systematic desensitization and nonspecific treatment effects: A methodological evaluation. *Psychological Bulletin, 83,* 729–758.

Keane, T. M., Gerardi, R. J., Quinn, S. J., & Litz, B. T. (1992). Behavioral treatment of post-traumatic stress disorder. In S. M. Turner, K. S. Calhoun, & H. E. Adams (Eds.), *Handbook of clinical behavior therapy* (pp. 87–97). New York: Wiley.

Keane, T., Kolb, L. C., Kaloupek, D. G., Orr, S. P., Blanchard, E. B., Thomas, R. G., Hsieh, F. Y., & Lavori, P. W. (1998). Utility of measurement in the diagnosis of posttraumatic stress disorder: Results from a

Department of Veterans Affairs Cooperative Study. *Journal of Consulting & Clinical Psychology, 66,* 914–923.

Keck, P. E., McElroy, S. L., Strakowski, S., West, S., Sax, K., Hawkins, J., Bourne, M. L., & Haggard, P. (1998). 12-month outcome of patients with bipolar disorder following hospitalization or a manic or mixed episode. *American Journal of Psychiatry, 155,* 646–652.

Keesey, R. E. (1986). A set-point theory of obesity. In K. D. Brownell & J. P. Foreyt (Eds.), *Handbook of eating disorders* (pp. 45–62). New York: Basic Books.

Keller, M. B., & Baker, L. A. (1991). Bipolar disorder: Epidemiology, course, diagnosis, and treatment. *Bulletin of the Menninger Clinic, 55,* 172–181.

Keller, M. B., Kocsis, J. H., Thase, M. E., Gelenberg, A. J., Rush, A. J., Koran, L., Schatzberg, A., Russell, J., Hirschfeld, R., Klein, D., McCullough, J. P., Fawcett, J. A., Kornstein, S., LaVange, L., & Harrison, W. (1998). Maintenance phase drug efficacy of sertraline for chronic depression: A randomized controlled trial. *Journal of the American Medical Association, 280,* 1665–1672.

Kellermann, A. L., Rivara, F. P., Somes, G., & Reay, D. T. (1992). Suicide in the home in relation to gun ownership. *New England Journal of Medicine, 327,* 467–472.

Kelly, G. F. (1998). *Sexuality today: The human perspective.* New York: McGraw-Hill.

Kelly, K., & Ramundo, P. (1995). *You mean I'm not lazy, stupid, or crazy?!* New York: Charles Scribner's Sons.

Kendall, P. C. (1992). *Anxiety disorders in youth: Cognitive-behavioral interventions.* Boston: Allyn & Bacon.

Kendall, P. C., Hollon, S. D., Beck, A. T., Hammen, C. L., & Ingram, R. E. (1987). Issues and recommendations regarding use of the Beck Depression Inventory. *Cognitive Therapy & Research, 11,* 289–299.

Kendall, P. C., & Morris, R. J. (1991). Child therapy: Issues and recommendations. *Journal of Consulting & Clinical Psychology, 59,* 777–784.

Kendall, P. C., & Southam-Gerow, M. A. (1996). Long-term follow-up of a cognitive-behavioral therapy for anxiety disordered youths. *Journal of Consulting & Clinical Psychology, 64,* 724–730.

Kendall-Tackett, K. A., Williams, L. M., & Finkelhor, D. (1993). Impact of sexual abuse on children: A review and synthesis of recent empirical studies. *Psychological Bulletin, 113,* 164–180.

Kendler, K. (1998). Major depression and the environment: A psychiatric genetic perspective. *Pharmacopsychiatry, 31,* 5–9.

Kendler, K. & Karkowski-Shuman, L. (1997). Stressful life events and genetic liability to major depression: Genetic control of exposure to the environment? *Psychological Medicine, 27,* 539–547.

Kendler, K. S., Davis, C. G., & Kessler, R. C. (1997). The familial aggregation of common psychiatric and substance use disorders in the National Comorbidity Survey: A family history study. *British Journal of Psychiatry, 170,* 541–548.

Kendler, K. S., Gallagher, T. J., Abelson, J. M., & Kessler, R. C. (1996). Lifetime prevalence, demographic risk factors, and diagnostic validity of nonaffective psychosis as assessed in a U.S. community sample. *Archives of General Psychiatry, 53,* 1022–1031.

Kendler, K. S., MacLean, C., Neale, M., & Kessler, R. C. (1991). The genetic epidemiology of bulimia nervosa. *American Journal of Psychiatry, 148,* 1627–1637.

Kendler, K. S., McGuire, M., Gruenberg, A. M., & Walsh, D. (1994). Outcome and family study of the subtypes of schizophrenia in the west of Ireland. *American Journal of Psychiatry, 151,* 849–856.

Kendler, K. S., Neale, M. C., Kessler, R. C., & Heath, A. C. (1992). Major depression and generalized anxiety disorder: Same genes, (partly) different environments? *Archives of General Psychiatry, 49,* 716–722.

Kendler, K. S., Neale, M. C., Kessler, R. C., & Heath, A. C. (1993). Panic disorder in women: A population-based twin study. *Psychological Medicine, 23,* 397–406.

Kendler, K. S., Neale, M. C., Kessler, R. C., Heath, A. C., & Eaves, L. J. (1992). A population-based twin study of major depression in women. *Archives of General Psychiatry, 49,* 257–266.

Kendler, K. S., Neale, M. C., Kessler, R. C., Heath, A. C., & Eaves, L. J. (1993). A test of the equal-environment assumption in twin studies of psychiatric illness. *Behavior Genetics, 23,* 21–28.

Kendler, K. S., & Prescott, C. A. (1998a). Cannabis use, abuse, and dependence in a population-based sample of female twins. *American Journal of Psychiatry, 155,* 1016–1022.

Kendler, K. S., & Prescott, C. A. (1998b). Cocaine use, abuse, and dependence in a population-based sample of female twins. *British Journal of Psychiatry, 173,* 345–350.

Kendler, K. S., Walters, E. E., Neale, M. C., Kessler, R. C., Heath, A. C., & Eaves, L. J. (1995). The structure of the genetic and environmental risk factors for six major psychiatric disorders in women: Phobia, generalized anxiety disorder, panic disorder, bulimia, major depression, and alcoholism. *Archives of General Psychiatry, 52,* 374–383.

Kennedy, S., Javanmard, M., & Vaccarino, F. (1997). A review of functional neuroimaging in mood disorders: Positron emission tomography and depression. *Canadian Journal of Psychiatry, 42,* 467–475.

Kernberg, O. (1975). *Borderline conditions and pathological narcissism.* New York: Jason Aronson.

Kernberg, O. F. (1979). Psychoanalystic profile of the borderline adolescent. *Adolescent Psychiatry, 7,* 234–256.

Kernberg, O. F. (1989). *Psychodynamic psychotherapy of borderline patients.* New York: Basic Books.

Kernberg, O. F. (1998). Pathological narcissism and narcissistic personality disorder: Theoretical background and diagnostic classification. In E. F. Ronningstam (Ed.), *Disorders of narcissism* (pp. 29–58). Washington, DC: American Psychiatric Press.

Kessler, R. C., Davis, C. G., & Kendler, K. S. (1997). Childhood adversity and adult psychiatric disorder in the U.S. National Comorbidity Survey. *Psychological Medicine, 27,* 1101–1119.

Kessler, R. C., Downey, G., & Milavsky, J. R. (1988). Clustering of teenage suicides after television news stories about suicide. *American Journal of Psychiatry, 145,* 1379–1383.

Kessler, R. C., Frank, R. G., Edlund, M., Katz, S. J., Lin, E., & Leaf, P. (1997). Differences in the use of psychiatric outpatient services between the United States and Ontario. *The New England Journal of Medicine, 336,* 551–557.

Kessler, R. C., McGonagle, K. A., Zhao, S., Nelson, C. B, Hughes, M., Eshleman, S., Wittchen, H., & Kendler, K. S. (1994). Lifetime and 12-month prevalence of DSM-III-R psychiatric disorders in the United States: Results from the National Comorbidity Study. *Archives of General Psychiatry, 51,* 8–19.

Kessler, R. C., Olfson, M., & Berglund, P. A. (1998). Patterns and predictors of treatment contact after first onset of psychiatric disorders. *American Journal of Psychiatry, 155,* 62–69.

Kessler, R. C., Sonnega, A., Bromet, E., Hughes, M., & Nelson, C. B. (1995). Posttraumatic stress disorder in the National Comorbidity Survey. *Archives of General Psychiatry, 52,* 1048–1060.

Kessler, R. C., Stein, M. B., & Berglund, P. (1998). Social phobia subtypes in the National Comorbidity Survey. *American Journal of Psychiatry, 155,* 613–619.

Kety, S. S., Wender, P. H., Jacobsen, B., Ingraham, L. J., Jansson, L., Faber, B., & Kinney, D. K. (1994). Mental illness in the biological and adoptive relative of schizophrenic adoptees: Replication of the Copenhagen study in the rest of Denmark. *Archives of General Psychiatry, 51,* 442–455.

Keys, A., Brozek, J., Henschel, A., Mickelsen, O., & Taylor, H. L. (1950). *The biology of human starvation.* Minneapolis: Univ. of Minnesota Press, 1950.

Khandelwal, D. K., & Saxena, S. (1990). "Anorexia nervosa in adolescents of Asian extraction": Comment. *British Journal of Psychiatry, 157,* 784.

Kiecolt-Glaser, J. K., Fisher, L. D., Ogrocki, P., & Stout, J. C. (1987). Marital quality, marital disruption, and immune function. *Psychosomatic Medicine, 49,* 13–34.

Kiecolt-Glaser, J. K., Kennedy, S., Malkoff, S., & Fisher, L. (1988). Marital discord and immunity in males. *Psychosomatic Medicine, 50,* 213–229.

Kiecolt-Glaser, J. K., Malarkey, W. B., Chee, M., & Newton, T. (1993). Negative behavior during marital conflict is associated with immunological down-regulation. *Psychosomatic Medicine, 55,* 395–409.

Kiesler, C. A., & Sibulkin, A. E. (1983). Proportion of inpatient days for mental disorders: 1969–1978. *Hospital & Community Psychiatry, 34,* 606–611.

Kiesler, C. A., & Sibulkin, A. E. (1987). *Mental hospitalization: Myths and facts about a national crisis.* Beverly Hills, CA: Sage Publications.

Kiesler, D. J. (1986). The 1982 interpersonal circle: An analysis of DSM-III personality disorders. In T. Millon & G. L. Klerman (Eds.), *Contemporary directions in psychopathology.* New York: Guilford Press.

Kihlstrom, J. F. (1992). Dissociation and dissociations: A comment on consciousness and cognition. *Consciousness & Cognition: An International Journal, 1,* 47–53.

Kihlstrom, J. F., & Couture, L. J. (1992). Awareness and information processing in general anesthesia. *Journal of Psychopharmacology, 6,* 410–417.

Kihlstrom, J. F., Glisky, M. L., & Angiulo, M. J. (1994). Dissociative tendencies and dissociative disorders. *Journal of Abnormal Psychology, 103,* 117–124.

Kilpatrick, D. G., Veronen, L. J., & Resick, P. A. (1979). The aftermath of rape: Recent empirical findings. *American Journal of Orthopsychiatry, 49,* 658–669.

Kim, L. I. C. (1993). Psychiatric care of Korean Americans. In A. C. Gaw (Ed.), *Culture, ethnicity, and mental illness* (pp. 347–375). Washington, DC: American Psychiatric Press.

King, D. W., King, L. A., Foy, D. W., Keane, T. M., & Fairbank, F. A. (1999). Posttraumatic stress disorder in a national sample of female and male Vietnam veterans: Risk factors, war-zone stressors, and resilience-recovery variables. *Journal of Abnormal Psychology, 108,* 164–170.

King, N. H., Gullone, E., & Tonge, B. J. (1993). Self-reports of panic attacks and manifest anxiety in adolescents. *Behaviour Research and Therapy, 31,* 111–116.

Kinney, J., Haapala, D., & Booth, C. (1991). *Keeping families together: The homebuilders model.* New York: A. de Gruyter.

Kinzie, J. D., & Leung, P. K. (1993). Psychiatric care of Indochinese Americans. In A. C. Gaw (Ed.), *Culture, ethnicity, and mental illness* (pp. 281–304). Washington, DC: American Psychiatric Press.

Kinzl, J. F., Traweger, C., Guenther, V., & Biebl, W. (1994). Family background and sexual abuse associated with eating disorders. *American Journal of Psychiatry, 151,* 1127–1131.

Kirch, D. G. (1993). Infection and autoimmunity as etiologic factors in schizophrenia: A review and reappraisal. *Schizophrenia Bulletin, 19,* 355–370.

Kirk, S. A., & Kutchins, H. (1992). *The selling of DSM: The rhetoric of science in psychiatry.* New York: A. de Gruyter.

Kirkcaldie, M., Pridmore, S., & Reid, P. (1997). Bridging the skull: Electroconvulsive therapy (ECT) and repetitive transcranial magnetic stimulation (rTMS) in psychiatry. *Convulsive Therapy, 13,* 83–91.

Kirsch, I., & Lynn, S. J. (1998). Dissociation theories of hypnosis. *Psychological Bulletin, 123,* 100–115.

Klein, D. F. (1964). Delineation of two drug-responsive anxiety syndromes. *Psychopharmacologia, 5,* 397–408.

Klein, D. F. (1993). False suffocation alarms, spontaneous panics, and related conditions: An integrative hypothesis. *Archives of General Psychiatry, 50,* 306–317.

Klein, M. (1952). Notes on some schizoid mechanisms. In M. Klein, P. Heimann, S. Isaacs, & J. Riviere (Eds.), *Developments in psychoanalysis.* London: Hogarth Press.

Kleinman, A., & Good, B. (Eds.). (1985). *Culture and depression: Studies in the anthropology and cross-cultural psychiatry of affect and disorder.* Berkeley: University of California Press.

Kleinman, A., & Kleinman, J. (1985). Somatization: The interconnections in Chinese society among culture, depressive experiences, and meanings of pain. In A. Kleinman, & B. Good (Eds.), *Culture and depression* (pp. 429–490). Berkeley: University of California Press.

Klerman, G. L., & Weissman, M. M. (1989). Increasing rates of depression. *Journal of the American Medical Association, 261,* 2229–2235.

Klerman, G. L., Weissman, M. M., Rounsaville, B., & Chevron, E. (1984). *Interpersonal psychotherapy of depression.* New York: Basic Books.

Kline, P. (1993). *The handbook of psychological testing.* New York: Routledge.

Klosko, J. S., Barlow, D. H., Tassinari, R., & Cerny, J. A. (1990). A comparison of alprazolam and behavior therapy in treatment of panic disorder. *Journal of Consulting & Clinical Psychology, 58,* 77–84.

Kluft, R. P. (1985). The natural history of multiple personality disorder. In R. P. Kluft (Ed.), *Childhood antecedents of multiple personality* (pp. 197–238). Washington, DC: American Psychiatric Press.

Kluft, R. P. (1986). Preliminary observations on age regression in multiple personality disorder patients before and after integration. *American Journal of Clinical Hypnosis, 28,* 147–156.

Kluft, R. P. (1987). Unsuspected multiple personality disorder: An uncommon source of protracted resistance, interruption, and failure in psychoanalysis. *Hillside Journal of Clinical Psychiatry, 9,* 100–115.

Knutson, B., Wolkowitz, O. M., Cole, S. W., Chan, T., Moore, E. A., Johnson, R. C., Terpstra, J., Turner, R. A., & Reus, V. I. (1998). Selective alteration of personality and social behavior by serotonergic intervention. *American Journal of Psychiatry, 155,* 373–379.

Koegel, P., Burnam, M. A., & Farr, R. K. (1988). The prevalence of specific psychiatric disorders among homeless individuals in the inner city of Los Angeles. *Archives of General Psychiatry, 45,* 1085–1092.

Koenig, H. (Ed.). (1998). *Handbook of religion and mental health.* San Diego: Academic Press.

Koenig, H. G., George, L. K., Cohen, H. J., Hays, J. C., Larson, D. B., & Blazer, D. G. (1998). The relationship between religious activities and cigarette smoking in older adults. *Journals of Gerontology, Series A, Biological Sciences & Medical Sciences, 53A,* M426–M434.

Koenig, H. G., Hays, J. C., George, L. K., Blazer, D. G., Larson, D. B., & Landerman, L. R. (1997). Modeling the cross-sectional relationships between religion, physical health, social support, and depressive symptoms. *American Journal of Geriatric Psychology, 5,* 131–144.

Kohut, H. (1971). *The analysis of the self: A systematic approach to the treatment of narcissistic personality disorders.* New York: New York International Universities Press.

Kohut, H. (1984). *How does analysis cure?* Chicago: University of Chicago Press.

Kohut, H., & Wolf, E. S. (1978). The disorders of the self and their treatment: An outline. *International Journal of Psychoanalysis, 59,* 413–425.

Kolodny, R. C., Masters, W. H., & Johnson, V. E. (1979). *Textbook of sexual medicine.* Boston: Little, Brown.

Koopman, C., Classen, C., & Spiegel, D. A. (1994). Predictors of posttraumatic stress symptoms among survivors of the Oakland/Berkeley, California, firestorm. *American Journal of Psychiatry, 151,* 888–894.

Kopelman, M. D. (1987). Crime and amnesia: A review. *Behavioral Sciences & the Law, 5,* 323–342.

Koss, J. D. (1990). Somatization and somatic complaint syndromes among Hispanics: Overview and ethnopsychological perspectives. *Transcultural Psychiatric Research Review, 27,* 5–29.

Koss, M. P. (1993). Rape: Scope, impact, interventions, and public policy responses. *American Psychologist, 48,* 1062–1069.

Koss-Chioino, J. D. (1995). Traditional and folk approaches among ethnic minorities. In J. F. Aponte (Ed.), *Psychological interventions and cultural diversity* (pp. 145–163). Boston: Allyn & Bacon.

Kovacs, M., & Beck, A. T. (1977). An empirical approach toward definition of childhood depression. In J. G. Schulterbrandt (Ed.), *Depression in childhood: Diagnosis, treatment and conceptual models.* New York: Raven Press.

Kovacs, M., & Devlin, B. (1998). Internalizing disorders in childhood. *Journal of Child Psychology & Psychiatry & Applied Disciplines, 39,* 47–63.

Kovacs, M., Goldston, D., & Gatsonis, C. (1993). Suicidal behaviors and childhood-onset depressive disorders: A longitudinal investigation. *Journal of the American Academy of Child & Adolescent Psychiatry, 32,* 8–20.

Kovacs, M., Krol, R. S., & Voti, L. (1994). Early onset psychopathology and the risk for teenage pregnancy among clinically referred girls. *Journal of the American Academy of Child & Adolescent Psychiatry, 33,* 106–113.

Kraepelin, E. (1922). *Manic-depressive insanity and paranoia.* Edinburgh, Scotland: E. & S. Livingstone.

Kramer, M. S., Cutler, N., Feighner, J., Shrivastava, R., Carman, J., Sramek, J. J., Reines, S. A., Liu, G., Snavely, D., Wyatt-Knowles, E., Hale, J. J., Mills, S., MacCoss, M., Swain, C. J., Harrison, T., Hill, R. G.,

Hefti, G. C., Scolnick, E. M., Casieri, M. A., Chicchi, G. G., Sadowski, S., Williams, A. R., Hewson, L., Smith, D., Carlson, E. J., Hargreaves, R. J., & Rupniak, N. M. J. (1998). Distinct mechanism for antidepressant activity by blockade of central substance P receptors. *Science, 281,* 1640–1645.

Kramer, P. D. (1993). *Listening to Prozac.* New York: Viking.

Kring, A. M., & Neale, J. M. (1996). Do schizophrenic patients show a disjunctive relationship among expressive, experiential, and psychophysiological components of emotion? *Journal of Abnormal Psychology, 105,* 249–257.

Kroll, J. (1973). A reappraisal of psychiatry in the Middle Ages. *Archives of General Psychiatry, 29,* 276–283.

Krull, F., & Schifferdecker, M. (1990). Inpatient treatment of conversion disorder: A clinical investigation of outcome. 14th International Congress of Medical Psychotherapy: Training in medical psychotherapy: Cross-cultural diversity (1988, Lausanne, Switzerland). *Psychotherapy & Psychosomatics, 53,* 161–165.

Kryger, M. H., Roth, T., & Dement, W. C. (Eds.). (1994). *Principles and practice of sleep medicine.* Philadelphia: Saunders.

Krystal, H. (Ed.). (1968). *Massive psychic trauma.* New York: International Universities Press.

Kubler-Ross, E. (1969). *On death and dying.* New York: Macmillan.

Kuch, K., & Cox, B. J. (1992). Symptoms of PTSD in 124 survivors of the Holocaust. *American Journal of Psychiatry, 149,* 337–340.

Kuhn, R. (1958). The treatment of depressive states with G22355 (imipramine hydrochloride). *American Journal of Psychiatry, 115,* 459–464.

Kuiper, N. A., & Olinger, L. J. (1986). Dysfunctional attitudes and a self-worth contingency model of depression. *Advances in Cognitive-Behavioral Research & Theapy, 5,* 115–142.

Kuiper, N. A., Olinger, L., J., & MacDonald, M. R. (1988). Vulnerability and episodic cognitions in a self-worth contingency model of depression. In L. B. Alloy (Ed.), *Cognitive processes in depression* (pp. 289–309). New York: Guilford Press.

Kuo, W. H., & Tsai, Y. (1986). Social networking, hardiness and immigrant's mental health. *Journal of Health & Social Behavior, 27,* 133–149.

Kushner, H. I. (1995). Women and suicidal behavior: Epidemiology, gender and lethality in historical perspective. In S. S. Canetto & D. Lester (Eds.), *Women and suicidal behavior.* New York: Springer.

L

Laakmann, G., Schuele, C., Lorkowski, G., Baghai, R., Kuhn, K., & Ehrentraut, S. (1998). Buspirone and lorazepam in the treatment of generalized anxiety disorder in outpatients. *Psychopharmacology, 136,* 357–366.

LaFromboise, T. D., Trimble, J. E., & Mohatt, G. V. (1998). Counseling intervention and American Indian tradition: An integrative approach. In D. R. Atkinson (Ed.), *Counseling American minorities* (5th ed., pp. 159–182). Boston: McGraw-Hill.

LaGreca, A. M., Silverman, W. K., Vernberg, E. M., & Prinstein, M. J. (1996). Symptoms of posttraumatic stress in children after Hurricane Andrew: A prospective study. *Journal of Consulting & Clinical Psychology, 64,* 712–723.

LaGreca, A. M., Silverman, W. K., & Wasserstein, S. B. (1998). Children's predisaster functioning as a predictor of posttraumatic stress following Hurricane Andrew. *Journal of Consulting & Clinical Psychology, 66,* 883–892.

Lahey, B. B., & Loeber, R. (1997). Attention-deficit/hyperactivity disorder, oppositional defiant disorder, conduct disorder, and adult antisocial behavior: A life span perspective. In D. M. Stoff, J. Breiling, & J. D. Maser (Eds.), *Handbook of antisocial personality disorder* (pp. 51–59). New York: Wiley.

Lahey, B. B., Pelham, W. E., Schaughency, E. A., & Atkins, M. S. (1988). Dimensions and types of attention deficit disorder. *Journal of the American Academy of Child & Adolescent Psychiatry, 27,* 330–335.

Laing, R. D. (1971). *The divided self.* Harmondsworth: Penguin Books.

Lakein, A. (1973). *How to get control of your time and life.* New York: P. H. Wyden.

Lambert, M. C., Knight, F., Overly, K., Weisz, J. R., Desrosiers, M., & Thesiger, C. (1992). Jamaican and American adult perspectives on child psychopathology: Further exploration of the threshold model. *Journal of Consulting & Clinical Psychology, 60,* 146–149.

Lambert, M. J., & Bergen, A. E. (1994). The effectiveness of psychotherapy. In A. E. Bergen & S. L. Garfield (Eds.), *Handbook of psychotherapy and behavior change* (Vol. 4, pp. 143–189). New York: Wiley.

Lambert, M. T., & Silva, P. S. (1998). An update on the impact of gun control legislation on suicide. *Psychiatric Quarterly, 69,* 127–134.

Langevin, R. (1992). Biological factors contributing to paraphilic behavior. *Psychiatric Annals, 22,* 309–314.

Langevin, R., Wortman, G., Dickey, R., Wright, P., & Handy, L. (1988). Neuropsychological impairment in incest offenders. *Annals of Sex Research, 1,* 401–415.

Langone, J. (1985). The war that has no ending. *Discover, 6,* 44–54.

Lannfelt, L., Axelman, K., Lilius, L., & Basun, H. (1995). Genetic counseling in a Swedish Alzheimer family with amyloid precursor protein mutation. *American Journal of Human Genetics, 56,* 332–335.

LaRosa, J. (1991). *Dieter beware: The complete consumer guide to weight loss programs.* Valley Stream, NY: Marketdata Enterprises.

Lasegue, C. (1873). On hysterical anorexia. *Medical Times Gazette, 2,* 265–266.

Laudenslager, M. L., Ryan, S. M., Drugan, R. C., Hyson, R. L., & Maier, S. F. (1983). Coping and immunosuppression: Inescapable but not escapable shock suppresses lymphocyte proliferation. *Science, 221,* 569–570.

Laumann, E. O., Gagnon, J. H., Michael, R. T., & Michaels, S. (1994). *The social organization of sexuality: Sexual practices in the United States.* Chicago: University of Chicago Press.

Lawrie, S. M., & Abukmeil, S. S. (1998). Brain abnormality in schizophrenia: A systematic and quantitative review of volumetric magnetic resonance imaging studies. *British Journal of Psychiatry, 172,* 110–120.

Layton, M. (1995, May/June). Emerging from the shadows. *Networker,* 35–41.

Lazrove, S., Triffleman, E., Kite, L., McGlashan, T., & Rounsaville, B. (1998). An open trial of EMDR as treatment for chronic PTSD. *American Journal of Orthopsychiatry, 69,* 601–608.

Le Bars, P. L., Katz, M. M., Berman, N., Itil, T. M., Freedman, A. M., & Schatzberg, A. F. (1997). A placebo-controlled, double-blind, randomized trial of an extract of Ginkgo biloba for dementia. *Journal of the American Medical Association, 278,* 1327–1332.

Leary, T. (1957). *Interpersonal diagnosis of personality.* New York: Ronald.

Lee, S. (1995). Self-starvation in context: Towards a culturally sensitive understanding of anorexia nervosa. *Social Science & Medicine, 41,* 25–36.

Leenaars, A. A. (1988). *"I wish I could explain it," Suicide notes: Predictive clues and patterns* (pp. 247–248). New York: Human Sciences Press.

Leff, J., Sartorius, N., Jablensky, A., Korten, A., & Ernberg, G. (1992). The International Pilot Study of Schizophrenia: Five-year follow-up findings. *Psychological Medicine, 22,* 131–145.

Leff, J. P., & Vaughn, C. E. (1981). The role of maintenance therapy and relatives' expressed emotion in relapse of schizophrenia: A two-year follow-up. *British Journal of Psychiatry, 139,* 102–104.

Lehman, D. R., Wortman, C. B., & Williams, A. F. (1987). Long-term effects of losing a spouse or child in a motor vehicle crash. *Journal of Personality & Social Psychology, 52,* 218–231.

Leiblum, S. R., & Rosen, R. C. (1988). *Sexual desire disorders.* New York: Guilford Press.

Leiblum, S. R., Pervin, L. A., & Campbell, E. H. (1989). The treatment of vaginismus: Success and failure. In S. R. Leiblum & R. C. Rosen (Eds.), *Principles and practice of sex therapy: Update for the 1990s* (pp. 113–138). New York: Guilford Press.

Lemann, N. (1999, March 29). The IQ meritocracy. *Time, 153,* 115–116.

Lendon, C. L., Ashall, F., & Goate, A. M. (1997). Exploring the etiology of Alzheimer disease using molecular genetics. *Journal of the American Medical Association, 277,* 825–831.

Leon, A. C., Keller, M. B., Warshaw, M. S. S., Mueller, T. I., Solomon, D. A., Coryell, W., & Endicott, J. (1999). Prospective study of fluoxetine treatment and suicidal behavior in affectively ill subjects. *American Journal of Psychiatry, 156,* 195–201.

Leon, G. R., Fulkerson, J. A., Perry, C. L., & Early-Zald, M. B. (1995). Prospective analysis of personality and behavioral vulnerabilities and gender influences in the later development of disordered eating. *Journal of Abnormal Psychology, 104,* 140–149.

Lepore, S. J. (1995). Cynicism, social support and cardiovascular reactivity. *Health Psychology, 14,* 210–216.

Lerman, C., Caporaso, N. E., Audrain, J., Main, D., Bowman, E. D., Lockshin, B., Boyd, N. R., & Shields, P. G. (1999). Evidence suggesting the role of specific genetic factors in cigarette smoking. *Health Psychology, 18,* 14–20.

Lerman, C., Narod, S., Schulman, K., Hughes, C., Gomez-Caminero, A., Bonney, G., Gold, K., Trock, B., Main, D., Lynch, J., Fulmore, C., Snyder, C., Lemon, S. J., Conway, T., Tomin, P., Lenoir, G., & Lynch, H. (1996). BRCA1 testing in families with hereditary breast-ovarian cancer: A prospective study of patient decision making and outcomes. *Journal of the American Medical Association, 275,* 1885–1892.

Lerner, D. J., & Kannel, W. B. (1986). Patterns of coronary heart disease morbidity and mortality in the sexes: A 26-year follow-up of the Framington population. *American Heart Journal, 111,* 383–390.

Lerner, H. D. (1986). Current developments in the psychoanalytic psychotherapy of anorexia nervosa and bulimia nervosa. *Clinical Psychologist, 39,* 39–43.

Lerner, M. J. (1980). *The belief in a just world: A fundamental delusion.* New York: Plenum.

Lester, D. (1992). Suicide and disease. *Loss, Grief, & Care, 6,* 173–181.

LeVay, S. (1991). A difference in hypothalamic structure between heterosexual and homosexual men. *Science, 253,* 1034–1037.

LeVay, S. (1993). *The sexual brain.* Cambridge: MIT Press.

Levy, D., Kimhi, R., Barak, Y., Demmer, M., Harel, M., & Elizur, A. (1996). Brainstem auditory evoked potentials of panic disorder patients. *Neuropsychobiology, 33,* 164–167.

Levy, S. M., & Heiden, L. (1991). Depression, distress, and immunity: Risk factors for infectious disease. *Stress Medicine, 7,* 45–51.

Levy, S. M., Herberman, R. B., Whiteside, T., & Sanzo, K. (1990). Perceived social support

and tumor estrogen/ progesterone receptor status as predictors of natural killer cell activity in breast cancer patients. *Psychosomatic Medicine, 52,* 73–85.

Lewinsohn, P. M. (1974). A behavioral approach to depression. In R. J. Friedman & M. M. Katz (Eds.), *The psychology of depression: Contemporary theory and research.* Washington, DC: Winston-Wiley.

Lewinsohn, P. M., & Gotlib, I. H. (1995). Behavioral therapy and treatment of depression. In E. E. Beckham & W. R. Leber (Eds.), *Handbook of depression* (2nd ed., pp. 352–375). New York: Guilford.

Lewinsohn, P. M., Clark, G. N., Hops, H., & Andrews, J. (1990). Cognitive-behavioral treatment for depressed adolescents. *Behavior Therapy, 21,* 385–401.

Lewinsohn, P. M., Hops, H., Roberts, R. E., Seeley, J. R., & Andrews, J. (1993). Adolescent psychopathology: I. Prevalence and incidence of depression and other DSM-III—R disorders in high school students. *Journal of Abnormal Psychology, 102,* 133–144.

Lewinsohn, P. M., Muñoz, R. F., Youngren, M. A., & Zeiss, A. M. (1986). *Control your depression.* Englewood Cliffs, NJ: Prentice Hall.

Lewinsohn, P. M., Rohde, P., & Seeley, J. R. (1994). Psychosocial risk factors for future adolescent suicide attempts. *Journal of Consulting & Clinical Psychology, 62,* 297–305.

Lewinsohn, P. M., Rohde, P., Seeley, J. R. (1996). Alcohol consumption in high school adolescents: Frequency of use and dimensional structure of associated problems. *Addiction, 91,* 375–390.

Lewinsohn, P. M., Steinmetz, J. L., Larson, D. W., & Franklin, J. (1981). Depression-related cognitions: Antecedent or consequence? *Journal of Abnormal Psychology, 90,* 213–219.

Lewinsohn, P. M., Zinbarg, R., Seeley, J. R., Lewinsohn, M., & Sack, W. H. (1997). Lifetime comorbidity among anxiety disorders and between anxiety disorders and other mental disorders in adolescents. *Journal of Anxiety Disorders, 11,* 377–394.

Lewis, D. O., Balla, D. A., & Shanok, S. S. (1979). Some evidence of race bias in the diagnosis and treatment of the juvenile offender. *American Journal of Orthopsychiatry, 49,* 53–61.

Lewis, G., David, A., Andreasson, S., & Allebeck, P. (1992). Schizophrenia and city life. *Lancet, 340,* 137–140.

Lex, B. W. (1995). Alcohol and other psychoactive substance consumption in women and men. In M. V. Seeman (Ed.), *Gender and psychopathology* (pp. 311–358). Washington, DC: American Psychiatric Association Press.

Liberman, R. P. (1994). Psychosocial treatments for schizophrenia. *Psychiatry, 57,* 104–114.

Liberman, R. P., & Corrigan, P. W. (1993). Designing new psychosocial treatments for schizophrenia. *Psychiatry: Interpersonal & Biological Processes, 56,* 238–249.

Liberman, R. P., Putten, T. V., Marshall, B. D., Mintz, J., Bowen, L., Kuehnel, T. G., Aravagiri, A., & Marder, S. R. (1994). Optimal drug and behavior therapy for treatment-refractory schizophrenic patients. *American Journal of Psychiatry, 151,* 756–759.

Lichtenstein, E., & Glasgow, R. E. (1992). Smoking cessation: What have we learned over the past decade? *Journal of Consulting & Clinical Psychology: Special Issue: Behavioral medicine: An update for the 1990s, 60,* 518–527.

Lidz, C. W., Mulvey, E. P., & Gardner, W. (1993). The accuracy of predictions of violence to others. *Journal of the American Medical Association, 269,* 1007–1011.

Liebowitz, M. R., Schneier, F. R., Campeas, R., & Hollander, E. (1992). Phenelzine vs atenolol in social phobia: A placebo-controlled

comparison. *Archives of General Psychiatry, 49,* 290–300.

Light, K. C., & Sherwood, A. (1989). Race, borderline hypertension, and hemodynamic responses to behavioral stress before and after beta-adrenergic blockage. *Health Psychology, 8,* 577–595.

Lilienfeld, S. O., Lynn, S. J., Kirsch, I., Chaves, J. F., Sarvin, T. R., Ganaway, G. K., & Powell, R. A. (1999). Dissociative identity disorders and the sociocognitive model: Recalling the lessons of the past. *Psychological Bulletin, 125,* 507–523.

Lillard, A. S. (1993). Young children's conceptualization of pretend: Action or mental representational states? *Child Development, 64,* 372–386.

Lillard, A. S. (1996). Body or mind: Children's categorizing of pretense. *Child Development, 67,* 1717–1734.

Lin, K.-m., & Shen, W. W. (1991). Pharmacotherapy for Southeast Asian psychiatric patients. *Journal of Nervous & Mental Disease, 179,* 346–350.

Linde, K., Ramirez, G., Mulrow, C. D., Pauls, A., Weidenhammer, W., & Melchart, D. (1996). St. John's wort for depression: An overview and meta-analysis of randomized clinical trials. *British Medical Journal, 313,* 253–258.

Lindemalm, G., Korlin, D., & Uddenberg, N. (1986). Long-term follow-up of "sex change" in 13 male-to-female transsexuals. *Archives of Sexual Behavior, 15,* 187–210.

Linehan, M. M. (1973). Suicide and attempted suicide: Study of perceived sex differences. *Perceptual & Motor Skills, 37,* 31–34.

Linehan, M. M. (1987). Dialectical behavior therapy for borderline personality disorder: Theory and method. *Bulletin of the Menninger Clinic, 51,* 261–276.

Linehan, M. M. (1999). Standard protocol for assessing and treating suicidal behaviors for patients in treatment. In D. G. Jacobs (Ed.), *The Harvard Medical School guide to suicide assessment and intervention* (pp. 146–187). San Francisco: Jossey-Bass.

Linehan, M. M., Armstrong, H. E., Suarez, A., & Allmon, D. (1991). Cognitive-behavioral treatment of chronically parasuicidal borderline patients. *Archives of General Psychiatry, 48,* 1060–1064.

Linehan, M. M., Camper, P., Chiles, J. A., Strosahl, K., & Shearin, E. N. (1987). Interpersonal problem-solving and parasuicide. *Cognitive Therapy & Research, 11,* 1–12.

Link, B., Andrews, A., & Cullen, F. (1992). The violent and illegal behavior of mental patients reconsidered. *American Sociological Review, 57,* 275–292.

Links, P. S., Heslegrave, R., & van Reekum, R. (1998). Prospective follow-up study of borderline personality disorder: Prognosis, prediction of outcome, and axis II comorbidity. *Canadian Journal of Psychiatry, 43,* 265–270.

Links, P. S., Steiner, M., Boiago, I., & Irwin, D. (1990). Lithium therapy for borderline patients: Preliminary findings. *Journal of Personality Disorders, 4,* 173–181.

Linnoila, V. M., & Virkkunen, M. (1992). Aggression, suicidality, and serotonin. *Journal of Clinical Psychiatry, 53,* 46–51.

Lipowski, Z. J. (1990). *Delirium: Acute confusional states.* New York: Oxford University Press.

Lipschitz, D. S., Rasmusson, A. M., & Southwick, S. M. (1998). Childhood posttraumatic stress disorder: A review of neurobiologic sequelae. *Psychiatric Annals, 28,* 452–457.

Livesley, W. J., Schroeder, M. L., Jackson, D. N., & Jang, K. L. (1994). Categorical distinctions in the study of personality disorder: Implications for classification. *Journal of Abnormal Psychology, 103,* 6–17.

Livingston, R. (1993). Children of people with somatization disorder. *Journal of the American Academy of Child & Adolescent Psychiatry, 32,* 536–544.

Lochman, J. E., White, K. J., & Wayland, K. K. (1991). Cognitive-behavioral assessment and treatment with aggressive children. In P. Kendall (Ed.), *Therapy with children and adolescents: Cognitive behavioral procedures.* New York: Guilford Press.

Loebel, J. P., Loebel, J. S., Dager, S. R., Centerwall, B. S., & Reay, D. T. (1991). Anticipation of nursing home placement may be a precipitant of suicide among the elderly. *Journal of the American Geriatric Society, 39,* 407–408.

Loeber, R. (1990). Development and risk factors of juvenile antisocial behavior and delinquency. *Clinical Psychology Review, 10,* 1–41.

Loeber, R., & Farrington, D. P. (1997). Strategies and yields of longitudinal studies on antisocial behavior. In D. M. Stoff, J. Breiling, & J. D. Maser (Eds.), *Handbook of antisocial personality disorder* (pp. 125–139). New York: Wiley.

Loeber, R., & Keenan, K. (1994). Interaction between conduct disorder and its comorbid conditions. *Clinical Psychology Review, 14,* 497–523.

Loeber, R., Green, S. M., Keenan, K., & Lahey, B. B. (1995). Which boys will fare worse? Early predictors of the onset of conduct disorder in a six-year longitudinal study. *Journal of the American Academy of Child & Adolescent Psychiatry, 34,* 499–509.

Loftus, E. F. (1993). The reality of repressed memories. *American Psychologist, 48,* 518–537.

Loftus, E. F., & Ketchum, K. (1994). *The myth of repressed memory.* New York: St. Martin's Press.

Loftus, E. F., & Pickrell, J. E. (1995). The formation of fasle memories. *Psychiatric Annals, 25,* 720–725.

Loftus, E. F., Garry, M., & Feldman, J. (1994). Forgetting sexual trauma: What does it mean when 38% forget? *Journal of Consulting & Clinical Psychology, 62,* 1177–1181.

Long, P. W. (1996). Internet Mental Health. http://www.mentalhealth.com/.

Lopez, S. R., Nelson, K. A., Snyder, K. S., & Mintz, J. (1999). Attributions and affective reactions of family members and course of schizophrenia. *Journal of Abnormal Psychology, 108,* 307–314.

LoPiccolo, J. (1992). Paraphilias. *Nordisk Sexolgi, 10,* 1–14.

Lopiccolo, J., & Stock, W. E. (1986). Treatment of sexual dysfunction. *Journal of Consulting & Clinical Psychology, 54,* 158–167.

Lovaas, O. I. (1987). Behavioral treatment and normal educational and intellectual functioning in young autistic children. *Journal of Consulting & Clinical Psychology, 55,* 3–9.

Luborsky, L. (1973). Forgetting and remembering (momentary forgetting) during psychotherapy. In M. Mayman (Ed.), *Psychoanalytic research and psychological issues* (pp. 29–55). New York: International Universities Press.

Luborsky, L. (1984). *Principles of psychoanalytic psychotherapy: A manual for supportive-expressive treatment.* New York: Basic Books.

Luborsky, L., & Crits-Cristoph, P. (1990). *Understanding transference: The core conflictual relationship theme method.* New York: Basic Books.

Luborsky, L., Singer, B., & Luborsky, L. (1975). Comparative studies of psychotherapies: Is it true that "everyone has won and all must have prizes"? *Archives of General Psychiatry, 32,* 995–1008.

Ludwick-Rosenthal, R., & Neufeld, R. W. (1988). Stress management during noxious medical procedures: An evaluative review of outcome studies. *Psychological Bulletin, 104,* 326–342.

Ludwig, A. M. (1992). Creative achievement and psychopathology: Comparison among professions. *American Journal of Psychotherapy, 46,* 330–356.

Luria, A. R. (1973). *The working brain.* New York: Basic Books.

Luria, A. R. (1976). *Cognitive development: Its cultural and social foundations.* Cambridge, MA: Harvard University Press.

Luthar, S., & Blatt, S. J. (1995). Differential vulnerability of dependency and self-criticism among disadvantaged teenagers. *Journal of Research on Adolescence, 5,* 431–449.

Lydiard, R. B., Brawman-Mintzer, O., & Ballenger, J. C. (1996). Recent developments in the psychopharmacology of anxiety disorders. *Journal of Consulting & Clinical Psychology, 64,* 660–668.

Lykken, D. T., Bouchard, T. J., McGue, M., & Tellegen, A. (1993). Heritability of interests: A twin study. *Journal of Applied Psychology, 78,* 649–661.

Lyman, R. (1997, April 15). Michael Dorris dies at 52: Wrote of his son's suffering. *The New York Times,* 24.

M

MacArthur Research Network on Mental Health and the Law. (1998). Executive summary. Retrieved from http://ness.sys.Virginia.EDU/macarthur/violence.html

Maccoby, E. E., & Mnookin, R. H. (1992). *Dividing the child: Social and legal dilemmas of custody.* Cambridge, MA: Harvard University Press.

Maccoby, N., & Altman, D. G. (1988). Disease prevention in communities: The Stanford Heart Disease Prevention Program. In R. H. Price (Ed.), *Fourteen ounces of prevention: A casebook for practitioners* (pp. 165–174). Washington, DC: American Psychological Association.

MacCoun, R. J. (1998). Toward a psychology of harm reduction. *American Psychologist, 53,* 1199–1208.

Machover, K. A. (1949). *Personality projection in the drawing of the human figure: A method of personality investigation.* Springfield, IL: Charles C Thomas.

MacKinnon, D., Jamison, K. R., & DePaulo, J. R. (1997). Genetics of manic depressive illness. *Annual Review of Neuroscience, 20,* 355–373.

MacMillan, D. L., Gresham, F. M., & Siperstein, G. N. (1993). Conceptual and psychometric concerns about the 1992 AAMR definition of mental retardation. *American Journal on Mental Retardation, 98,* 325–335.

Madge, N., & Harvey, J. G. (1999). Suicide among the young—the size of the problem. *Journal of Adolescence, 22,* 145–155.

Magdol, L., Moffitt, T. E., Caspi, A., Newman, D. L., Fagan, J., & Silva, P. A. (1997). Gender differences in partner violence in a birth cohort of 21-year-olds: Bridging the gap between clinical and epidemiological approaches. *Journal of Consulting & Clinical Psychology, 65,* 68–78.

Maher, B. A. (1974). Delusional thinking and perceptual disorder. *Journal of Individual Psychology, 30,* 98–113.

Maher, W. B., & Maher, B. A. (1985). Psychopathology: I. From ancient times to eighteenth century. In G. A. Kimble & K. Schlesinger (Eds.), *Topics in the history of psychology* (Vol. 2,). Hillsdale, NJ: Erlbaum.

Mahler, M. (1968). On human symbiosis and the vicissitudes of individuation: Vol. I. Infantile psychosis. New York: International Universities Press.

Maier, S. F., Watkins, L. R., & Fleshner, M. (1994). Psychoneuroimmunology: The interface between behavior, brain, and immunity. *American Psychologist, 49,* 1004–1017.

Maj, M., Pirozzi, R., Magliano, L., & Bartoli, L. (1998). Long-term outcome of lithium prophylaxis in bipolar disorder: A 5-year prospective study of 402 patients at a lithium clinic. *American Journal of Psychiatry, 155,* 30–35.

Maletzky, B. (1998). The paraphilias: Research and treatment. In P. E. Nathan (Ed.), *A guide to treatments that work* (pp. 472–500). New York: Oxford University Press.

Maller, R. G., & Reiss, S. (1992). Anxiety sensitivity in 1984 and panic attacks in 1987. *Journal of Anxiety Disorders, 6,* 241–247.

Malone, K., & Mann, J. J. (1993). Serotonin and major depression. In J. J. Mann & D. J. Kupfer (Eds.), *Biology of depressive disorders: Part A. A systems perspective* (pp. 29–49). New York: Plenum.

Maltsberger, J. T. (1999). The psychodynamic understanding of suicide. In D. G. Jacobs (Ed.), *The Harvard Medical School guide to suicide assessment and intervention* (pp. 72–82). San Francisco: Jossey-Bass.

Mann, J. J., & Arango, V. (1999). The neurobiology of suicidal behavior. In D. G. Jacobs (Ed.), *The Harvard Medical School guide to suicide assessment and intervention* (pp. 98–114). San Francisco: Jossey-Bass.

Mann, T., Nolen-Hoeksema, S., Huang, K., Burgard, D., Wright, A., & Hanson, K. (1997). Are two interventions worse than none? Joint primary and secondary prevention of eating disorders in college females. *Health Psychology, 16,* 215–225.

Mannino, J. D. (1999). *Sexually speaking.* New York: McGraw-Hill.

Mannuza, S., Klein, R. G., Bessler, A., Malloy, P., & LaPadula, M. (1998). Adult psychiatric status of hyperactive boys grown up. *American Journal of Psychiatry, 155,* 493–498.

Manson, J. E., Colditz, G. A., Stampfer, M. J., Willett, W. C., Rosner, B., Monson, R. R., Speizer, F. E., & Hennekens, C. H. (1990). A prospective study of obesity and risk of coronary heart disease in women. *New England Journal of Medicine, 322,* 882–889.

Manson, S., Beals, J., O'Nell, T., Piasecki, J., Bechtold, D., Keane, E., & Jones, M. (1996). Wounded spirits, ailing hearts: PTSD and related disorders among American Indians. In A. J. Marsella, M. J. Friedman, E. T. Gerrity, & R. M. Scurfield (Eds.), *Ethnocultural aspects of posttraumatic stress disorder* (pp. 255–283). Washington, DC: American Psychiatric Press.

Manson, S. M. (1997). Cross-cultural and multiethnic assessment of trauma. In J. P. Wilson (Ed.), *Assessing psychological trauma and PTSD* (pp. 239–266). New York: Guilford Press.

Manson, S. M., Ackerson, L. M., Dick, R. W., & Baron, A. E. (1990). Depressive symptoms among American Indian adolescents: Psychometric characteristics of the Center for Epidemiologic Studies Depression Scale (CES-D). *Psychological Assessment, 2,* 231–237.

Manson, S. M., Shore, J. H., Baron, A. E., Ackerson, L., & Neligh, G. (1992). Alcohol abuse and dependence among American Indians. In J. E. Helzer & G. J. Canino (Eds.), *Alcoholism in North America, Europe, and Asia* (pp. 113–127). New York: Oxford University Press.

Manu, P., Lane, T. J., & Matthews, D. A. (1989). Somatization disorder in patients with chronic fatigue. *Psychosomatics, 30,* 388–395.

Manu, P., Lane, T. J., & Matthews, D. A. (1992). Chronic fatigue syndromes in clinical practice. *Psychotherapy & Psychosomatics, 58,* 60–68.

Marantz, S., & Coates, S. (1991). Mothers of boys with gender identity disorder: A comparison of matched controls. *Journal of the American Academy of Child & Adolescent Psychiatry, 30,* 310–315.

Marazziti, D., Toni, C. Bonuccelli, U., Pavese, N., Nuti, A., Muratorio, A., Cassano, G. B., & Akiskal, H. S. (1995). Headache, panic disorder and depression: Comorbidity or a spectrum? *Neuropsychobiology, 31,* 125–129.

March, J. S., Biederman, J., Wolkow, R., Safferman, A., Mardekian, J., Cook, E. H., Cutler, N. R., Dominguez, R., Ferguson, J., Muller, B., Riesenberg, R., Rosenthal, M., Sallee, F. E., & Wagner, K. D. (1998). Sertraline in children and adolescents with obsessive-compulsive disorder. *Journal of the American Medical Association, 280,* 1752–1756.

Marcos, L. R. (1979). Effects of interpreters on the evaluation of psychopathology in non-English-speaking patients. *American Journal of Psychiatry, 136,* 171–174.

Margraf, J. (1993). Hyperventilation and panic disorder: A psychophysiological connection. *Advances in Behaviour Research & Therapy, 15,* 49–74.

Margraf, J., Barlow, D. H., Clark, D. M., & Telch, M. J. (1993). Psychological treatment of panic: Work in progress on outcome, active ingredients, and follow-up. *Behaviour Research & Therapy, 31,* 1–8.

Markowitz, J. C., & Weissman, M. W. (1995). Interpersonal psychotherapy. In E. E. Beckham & W. R. Leber (Eds.), *Handbook of depression* (2nd ed., pp. 376–390). New York: Guilford.

Marks, I. M., & Swinson, R. (1992). Behavioral and/or drug therapy. In G. D. Burrows, S. M. Roth, & R. Noyes, Jr. (Eds.), *Handbook of Anxiety* (Vol. 5). Oxford: Elsevier.

Markus, H. R., & Kitayama, S. (1998). The cultural psychology of personality. *Journal of Cross-Cultural Psychology, 29,* 63–87.

Marlatt, G. A. (Ed.). (1998). *Harm reduction: Pragmatic strategies for managing high-risk behaviors.* New York: Guilford Press.

Marlatt, G. A., Baer, J. S., & Larimer, M. (1995). Preventing alcohol abuse in college students: A harm reduction approach. In G. M. Boyd, J. Howard, & R. A. Zucker (Eds.), *Alcohol problems among adolescents: Current directions in prevention research* (pp. 147–172). Hillsdale, NJ: Erlbaum.

Marlatt, G. A., & Gordon, J. R. (Eds.). (1985). *Relapse prevention: Maintenance strategies in the treatment of addictive behaviors.* New York: Guilford Press.

Marlatt, G. A., Abrams, D. B., & Lewis, D. C. (1998). *Harm reduction: Pragmatic strategies for managing high-risk behaviors.* New York: Guilford Press.

Marlatt, G. A., Baer, J. S., Donovan, D. M., & Kivlahan, D. R. (1988). Addictive behaviors: Etiology and treatment. *Annual Review of Psychology, 39,* 223–252.

Marlatt, G. A., Baer, J. S., Kivlahan, D. R., Dimeff, L. A., Larimer, M. E., Quigley, L. A., Somers, J. M., & Williams, E. (1998). Screening and brief intervention for high-risk college student drinkers: Results from a 2-year follow-up assessment. *Journal of Consulting & Clinical Psychology, 66,* 604–615.

Marlatt, G. A., Larimer, M. E., Baer, J. S., & Quigley, L. A. (1993). Harm reduction for alcohol problems: Moving beyond the controlled drinking economy. *Behavior Therapy, 24,* 461–503.

Martin, C. S., & Bates, M. E. (1998). Psychological and psychiatric consequences of alcohol. In R. E. Tarter, R. T. Ammerman, & P. J. Ott (Eds.), *Handbook of substance abuse: Neurobehavioral pharmacology* (pp. 33–50). New York: Plenum.

Martinez, C. (1993). Psychiatric care of Mexican Americans. In A. C. Gaw (Ed.), *Culture, ethnicity, and mental illness* (pp. 431–466). Washington, DC: American Psychiatric Association Press.

Martinez-Taboas, A. (1989). Preliminary observations on MPD in Puerto Rico. *Dissociation: Progress in the Dissociative Disorders, 2,* 128–131.

Maslow, A. H. (1954). *Motivation and personality.* New York: Harper & Row.

Masten, A. S., Miliotis, D., Graham-Bermann, S. A., & Ramirez, M. (1993). Children in homeless families: Risks to mental health and development. *Journal of Consulting & Clinical Psychology, 61,* 335–343.

Masters, K. (1996, July 15). It hurts so much. *Time,* 148.

Masters, W. H., & Johnson, V. E. (1970). *Human sexual inadequacy.* Boston: Little, Brown.

Masters, W. H., Johnson, V. E., & Kolodny, R. C. (1993). *Biological foundations of human sexuality.* New York: HarperCollins.

Masters, W. H., Johnson, V. E., & Kolodny, R. C. (Eds.). (1979). *Ethical issues in sex therapy & research.* Boston: Little, Brown.

Matarazzo, J. D. (1985). Psychotherapy. In G. A. Kimble & K. Schlesinger (Eds.), *Topics in the history of psychology.* Hillsdale, NJ: Erlbaum.

Mathews, A., & MacLeod, C. (1994). Cognitive approaches to emotion and emotional disorders. *Annual Review of Psychology, 45,* 25–50.

Mathews. (1996, July 30). *Baltimore Sun.*

Matthews, A., Mogg, K., Kentish, J., & Eysenck, M. (1995). Effect of psychological treatment on cognitive bias in generalized anxiety disorder. *Behavior Research & Therapy, 33,* 293–303.

Matthews, K. A., Wing, R. R., Kuller, L. H., & Meilhan, E. N. (1990). Influences of natural menopause on psychological characteristics and symptoms of middle-aged healthy women. *Journal of Consulting & Clinical Psychology, 58,* 345–351.

Max, W. (1993). The economic impact of Alzheimer's disease. *Neurology, 43,* S6–S10.

Maxmen, J. S., & Ward, N. G. (1995). *Essential psychopathology and its treatment.* New York: W. W. Norton.

May, R., & Yalom, I. (1995). Existential psychotherapy. In R. J. Corsini & D. Wedding (Eds.), *Current psychotherapies* (5th ed., pp. 363–402) . Itasca, IL: Peacock.

Mayeux, R. (1996). Understanding Alzheimer's disease: Expect more genes and other things. *Annals of Neurology, 39,* 689–690.

Mayeux, R., Denaro, J., Hemenegildo, N., & Marder, K. (1992). A population-based investigation of Parkinson's disease with and without dementia: Relationship to age and gender. *Archives of Neurology, 49,* 492–497.

Mazzoni, G., & Loftus, E. F. (1998). Dream interpretations can change beliefs about the past. *Psychotherapy, 35,* 177–187.

McArthur, J. C., Hoover, D. R., Bacellar, H., & Miller, E. N. (1993). Dementia in AIDS patients: Incidence and risk factors. *Neurology, 43,* 2245–2252.

McBride, A. A., Joe, G. W., & Simpson, D. D. (1991). Prediction of long-term alcohol use, drug use, and criminality among inhalant users. *Hispanic Journal of Behavioral Sciences, 13,* 315–323.

McBride, P., Brown, R. P., DeMeo, M., & Keilp, J. (1994). The relationship of platelet 5-HT-sub-2 receptor indices to major depressive disorder, personality traits, and suicidal behavior. *Biological Psychiatry, 35,* 295–308.

McCabe, S. B., & Gotlib, I. H. (1993). Interactions of couples with and without a depressed spouse: Self-report and observations of

problem-solving situations. *Journal of Social & Personal Relationship, 10,* 589–599.

McCarthy, B. W. (1989). Cognitive-behavioral strategies and techniques in the treatment of early ejaculation. In S. R. Leiblum & R. C. Rosen (Eds.), *Principles and practice of sex therapy: Update for the 1990s* (pp. 141–167). New York: Guilford Press.

McCarthy, B. W. (1997). Strategies and techniques for revitalizing a nonsexual marriage. *Journal of Sex & Marital Therapy, 23,* 231–240.

McCarthy, M. (1990). The thin ideal, depression and eating disorders in women. *Behaviour Research & Therapy, 28,* 205–215.

McClellan-Buchanan, G., & Seligman, M. E. P. (Eds.). (1995). *Explanatory style.* Hillsdale, NJ: Erlbaum.

McConaghy, N. (1998). Paedophila: A review of the evidence. *Australian & New Zealand Journal of Psychiatry, 32,* 252–265.

McCormick, M. C., McCarton, C., Brooks-Gunn, J., Belt, P., & Gross, R. T. (1998). The infant health development program: Interim summary. *Developmental & Behavioral Pediatrics, 19,* 359–370.

McDonald, K., & Thompson, J. K. (1992). Eating disturbance, body image dissatisfaction, and reasons for exercising: Gender differences and correlational findings. *International Journal of Eating Disorders, 11,* 289–292.

McDougle, C. J. (1997). Psychopharmacology. In D. J. Cohen & F. R. Volkmar (Eds.), *Handbook of autism and pervasive developmental disorders* (pp. 707–729). Toronto: Wiley.

McDougle, C. J., Brodkin, E. S., Naylor, S. T., Carlson, D. C., Cohen, D. J., & Price, L. H. (1998). Sertraline in adults with pervasive developmental disorders: A prospective open-label investigation. *Journal of Clinical Psychopharmacology, 18,* 62–66.

McElroy, S. L., Keck, P. E., Stanton, S. P., Tugrul, K. C., et al. (1996). A randomized comparison of divalproex oral loading versus haloperidol in the initial treatment of acute psychotic mania. *Journal of Clinical Psychiatry, 57,* 142–146.

McFarlane, W. R., Lukens, E., Link, B., & Dushay, R. (1995). Multiple-family groups and psychoeducation in the treatment of schizophrenia. *Archives of General Psychiatry, 52,* 679–687.

McGee, R., Feehan, M., Williams, S., & Partridge, F. (1990). DSM-III disorders in a large sample of adolescents. *Journal of the American Academy of Child & Adolescent Psychiatry, 29,* 611–619.

McGhie, A., & Chapman, J. (1961). Disorders in attention and perception in early schizophrenia. *Schizophrenia Bulletin, 34,* 103–116.

McGlashan, T. H. (1988). A selective review of recent North American long-term followup studies of schizophrenia. *Schizophrenia Bulletin, 14,* 515–542.

McGovern, C. M. (1985). *Masters of madness.* Hanover, NH: University Press of New England.

McGreevy, M. A., Steadman, H. J., & Callahan, L. A. (1991). The negligible effects of California's 1982 reform of the insanity defense test. *American Journal of Psychiatry, 148,* 744–750.

McGue, M. (1999). The behavioral genetics of alcoholism. *Current Directions in Psychological Science, 8,* 109–115.

McGue, M., & Bouchard, T. J. (1998). Genetic and environmental influences on human behavioral differences. *Annual Review of Neuroscience, 21,* 1–14.

McGue, M., Pickens, R. W., & Svikis, D. S. (1992). Sex and age effects on the inheritance of alcohol problems: A twin study. *Journal of Abnormal Psychology, 101,* 3–17.

McGuffin, P., & Katz, R. (1989). The genetics of depression and manic-depressive disorder. *British Journal of Psychiatry, 155,* 294–304.

McGuffin, P., Katz, R., & Rutherford, J. (1991). Nature, nurture and depression: A twin study. *Psychological Medicine, 21,* 329–335.

McGuire, R. J., Carlisle, J. M., & Young, B. G. (1965). Sexual deviation as conditioned behavior. *Behavior Research & Therapy, 2,* 185–190.

McIntosh, D. N., Silver, R. C., & Wortman, C. B. (1993). Religion's role in adjustment to a negative life event: Coping with the loss of a child. *Journal of Personality & Social Psychology, 65,* 812–821.

McIntosh, J. L. (1991). Epidemiology of suicide in the United States. In A. A. Leenaars (Ed.), *Life span perspectives of suicide: Time-lines in the suicide process.* New York: Plenum.

McIntosh, J. L. (1995). Suicide prevention in the elderly (age 65–99). *Suicide & Life-Threatening Behaviors, 25,* 180–192.

McMillan, T. M., & Rachman, S. J. (1987). Fearlessness and courage: A laboratory study of paratrooper veterans of the Falklands War. *British Journal of Psychology, 78,* 375–383.

McNally, R. J. (1994). *Panic disorder: A critical analysis.* New York: Guilford.

McNiel, D. E., & Binder, R. L. (1991). Clinical assessment of the risk of violence among psychiatric inpatients. *American Journal of Psychiatry, 148,* 1317–1321.

Mednick, B., Reznick, C., Hocevar, D., & Baker, R. (1987). Long-term effects of parental divorce on young adult male crime. *Journal of Youth & Adolescence, 16,* 31–45.

Mednick, S. A., Machon, R. A., Huttunen, M. O., & Bonett, D. (1988). Adult schizophrenia following prenatal exposure to an influenza epidemic. *Archives of General Psychiatry, 45,* 189–192.

Mednick, S. A., Moffitt, T. E., & Stack, S. A. (Eds.). (1987). *The causes of crime: New biological approaches.* New York: Cambridge University Press.

Mednick, S. A., Watson, J. B., Huttunen, M., Cannon, T. D., Katila, H., Machon, R., Mednick, B., Hollister, M., Parnas, J., Schulsinger, F., Sajaniemi, N., Voldsgaard, P., Pyhala, R., Gutkind, D., & Wang, X. (1998). A two-hit working model of the etiology of schizophrenia. In M. F. Lenzenweger & R. H. Dworkin (Eds.), *Origins of the development of schizophrenia* (pp. 27–66). Washington, DC: American Psychological Association.

Meichenbaum, D., & Jaremko, M. (Eds.). (1983). *Stress reduction and prevention.* New York: Plenum.

Mellor, J. E., Laugharne, J. D. E., & Peet, M. (1995). Schizophrenic symptoms and the dietary intake of n-3 fatty acids. *Schizophrenia Research, 18,* 85–86.

Melton, G. B., & Limber, S. (1989). Psychologists' involvement in cases of child maltreatment: Limits of role and expertise. *American Psychologist, 44,* 1225–1233.

Melton, G. B., & Wilcox, B. L. (1989). Changes in family law and family life: Challenges for psychology. *American Psychologist, 44,* 1213–1216.

Merikangas, K. R., Dierker, L. C., & Szatmari, P. (1998). Psychopathology among offspring of parents with substance abuse and/or anxiety disorders: A high-risk study. *Journal of Child Psychology & Psychiatry, 5,* 711–720.

Merikangas, K. R., Stevens, D. E., & Angst, J. (1993). Headache and personality: Results of a community sample of young adults. *Journal of Psychiatric Research, 27,* 187–196.

Merikangas, K. R., Stolar, M., Stevens, D. E., Goulet, J., Preisig, M. A., Fenton, B., Zhang, H., O'Malley, S. S., & Rounsaville, B. J. (1998). Familial transmission of substance use

disorders. *Archives of General Psychiatry, 55,* 973–979.

Merikangas, K. R., Weissman, M. M., & Pauls, D. L. (1985). Genetic factors in the sex ratio of major depression. *Psychological Medicine, 15,* 63–69.

Merzenich, M. M., Jenkins, W. M., Johnston, P., Schreiner, C., Miller, S. L., & Tallal, P. (1996). Temporal processing deficits of language-learning impaired children ameliorated by training. *Science, 271,* 77–81.

Meyer, J. K., & Reter, D. J. (1979). Sex reassignment: Follow-up. *Archives of General Psychiatry, 36,* 1010–1015.

Michael, R. T., Gagnon, J. H., Laumann, E., & Kolata, G. (1994). *Sex in America: A definitive survey.* Boston: Little, Brown.

Michelson, L. K., & Marchione, K. (1991). Behavioral, cognitive, and pharmacological treatments of panic disorder with agoraphobia: Critique and synthesis. *Journal of Consulting & Clinical Psychology, 59,* 100–114.

Milkowitz, D. J. (1996). Psychotherapy in combination with drug treatment for bipolar disorder. *Journal of Clinical Psychopharmacology, 16* (Suppl. 1), 56S–66S.

Miklowitz, D. J., Velligan, D. I., Goldstein, M. J., & Nuechterlein, K. H. (1991). Communication deviance in families of schizophrenic and manic patients. *Journal of Abnormal Psychology, 100,* 163–173.

Miller, I. W., Norman, W. H., & Keitner, G. I. (1989). Cognitive-behavioral treatment of depressed inpatients: Six- and twelve-month follow-up. *American Journal of Psychiatry, 146,* 1274–1279.

Miller, J. B. (1976). *Toward a new psychology of women.* Boston: Beacon Press.

Miller, N. S. (Ed.). (1991). *Comprehensive handbook of drug and alcohol addiction.* New York: Dekker.

Miller, S. D. (1989). Optical differences in cases of multiple personality disorder. *The Journal of Nervous & Mental Disease, 177,* 480–486.

Miller, T. Q., Smith, T. W., Turner, C. W., & Guijarro, M. L. (1996). Meta-analytic review of research on hostility and physical health. *Psychological Bulletin, 119,* 322–348.

Millon, T. (1969). *Modern psychopathology: A biosocial approach to maladaptive learning and functioning.* Philadelphia: W. B. Saunders.

Millon, T. (1981). *Disorders of personality: DSM-III.* New York: Wiley.

Millon, T., Davis, R., Millon, C., Escovar, L., & Meagher, S. (2000). *Personality disorders in modern life.* New York: Wiley.

Milne, A. A. (1961). *Winnie-the-Pooh.* New York: E. P. Dutton.

Mineka, S. (1985). Animal models of anxiety based disorders: Their usefulness and limitations. In A. H. Tuma & J. Maser (Eds.), *Anxiety and the anxiety disorders.* Hillsdale, NJ: Erlbaum.

Mineka, S., & Kelly, K. A. (1989). The relationship between anxiety, lack of control and loss of control. In A. Steptoe (Ed.), *Stress, personal control and health* (pp. 163–191). Chichester, England: Wiley.

Mineka, S., & Zinbarg, R. (1998). Experimental approaches to the anxiety and mood disorders. In J. G. Adair (Ed.), *Advances in psychological science: Vol. 1. Social, personal, and cultural aspects* (pp. 429–454). Hove, England: Psychology Press/Erlbaum Taylor & Francis.

Mineka, S., Davidson, M., Cook, M., & Keir, R. (1984). Observational conditioning of snake fear in rhesus monkeys. *Journal of Abnormal Psychology, 93,* 355–372.

Mineka, S., Gunnar, M., & Champoux, M. (1986). Control and early socioemotional development: Infant rhesus monkeys reared in controllable versus uncontrollable environments. *Child Development, 57,* 1241–1256.

Minshew, N. J., Sweeney, J. A., & Bauman, M. L. (1997). Neurological aspects of autism. In D. J. Cohen & F. R. Volkmar (Eds.), *Handbook of autism and pervasive developmental disorders* (pp. 344–369). Toronto: Wiley.

Mintz, L. I., Lieberman, R. P., Miklowitz, D. J., & Mintz, J. (1987). Expressed emotion: A call for partnership among relatives, patients, and professionals. *Schizophrenia Bulletin, 13,* 227–235.

Minuchin, S. (1981). *Family therapy techniques.* Cambridge, MA: Harvard University Press.

Minuchin, S., Rosman, B. L., & Baker, L. (1978). *Psychosomatic families: Anorexia nervosa in context.* Cambridge, MA: Harvard University Press.

Miranda, J., & Persons, J. B. (1988). Dysfunctional attitudes are mood-state dependent. *Journal of Abnormal Psychology, 97,* 76–79.

Mitchell, J. E. (1986). Anorexia nervosa: Medical and physiological aspects. In K. D. Brownell & J. P. Foreyt (Eds.), *Handbook of eating disorders* (pp. 247–265). New York: Basic Books.

Mitchell, J. E., & deZwaan, M. (1993). Pharmacological treatments of binge eating. In C. E. Fairburn & G. T. Wilson (Eds.), *Binge eating: Nature, assessment, & treatment* (pp. 250–269). New York: Guilford.

Mitler, M. M., & Miller, J. C. (1995). Some practical considerations and policy implications of studies and sleep patterns. *Behavioral Medicine, 21,* 184–185.

Modrow, J. (1995). *How to become a schizophrenic: The case against biological psychiatry* (2nd ed.). Everett, WA: Apollyon Press.

Moffitt, T. E. (1990). Juvenile delinquency and attention deficit disorder: Boys' developmental trajectories from age 3 to age 15. *Child Development, 61,* 893–910.

Moffitt, T. E. (1993). The neuropsychology of conduct disorder. *Development and Psychopathology, 5,* 135–151.

Moffitt, T. E., & Silva, P. A. (1988). Self-reported delinquency, neuropsychological deficit, and history of attention deficit disorder. *Journal of Abnormal Child Psychology, 16,* 553–569.

Moffitt, T. E., Brammer, G. L., Caspi, A., Fawcet, J. P., Raleigh, M., Yuwiler, A., & Silva, P. A. (1998). Whole blood serotonin relates to violence in an epidemiological study. *Biological Psychiatry, 43,* 446–457.

Mohler, H., Richards, J. G., & Wu, J. Y. (1981). Autoradiographic localization of benzodiazepine receptors in immunocytochemically identified Y-aminobutyric synapses. *Proceedings of the National Academy of Science USA, 78,* 1935–1938.

Monahan, J. (1997). Clinical and actuarial predictions of violence. In D. Faigman, D. Kaye, M. Saks, & J. Sanders (Eds.), *Modern scientific evidence: The law and science of expert testimony* (Vol. 1, pp. 300–318). St. Paul, MN: West.

Monahan, J., & Walker, L. (1990). *Social science in law: Cases and materials.* Westbury, NY: Foundation Press.

Monahan, J., Lidz, C. W., Hoge, S. K., Mulvey, E. P., Eisenberg, M. M., Roth, L. H., Gardner, W. P., & Bennett, N. (in press). Coercion in the provision of mental health services: The MacArthur studies. In J. Morrissey & J. Monahan (Eds.), *Research in community and mental health* (Vol. 10). Stamford, CT: JAI Press.

Money, J., & Schwartz, M. (1976). Fetal androgens in the early treated adrenogenital syndrome of 46 XX hermaphroditism: Influence on assertive and aggressive types of behavior. *Aggressive Behavior, 2,* 19–30.

Morey, L. C. (1988). A psychometric analysis of the DSM-III-R personality disorder criteria. *Journal of Personality Disorders, 2,* 109–124.

Morey, L. C. (1993). Psychological correlates of personality disorder. *Journal of Personality Disorders* (suppl.), 149–166.

Morgan, H. G., & Russell, G. F. M. (1975). Value of family background and clinical features as predictors of long-term outcome in anorexia nervosa: Four-year follow-up study of 41 patients. *Psychological Medicine, 5,* 355–371.

Morgan, H. G., Purgold, J., & Welbourne, J. (1983). Management and outcome in anorexia nervosa: A standardized prognostic study. *British Journal of Psychiatry, 143,* 282–287.

Morgenstern, H., & Glazer, W. M. (1993). Identifying risk factors for tardive dyskinesia among long-term outpatients maintained with neuroleptic medications: Results of the Yale Tardive Dyskinesia Study. *Archives of General Psychiatry, 50,* 723–733.

Mori, D., Chaiken, S., & Pliner, P. (1987). "Eating lightly" and the self-presentation of femininity. *Journal of Personality & Social Psychology, 53,* 693-702.

Morokoff, P. J., & Gillilland, R. (1993). Stress, sexual functioning, and marital satisfaction. *Journal of Sex Research, 30,* 43–53.

Morokoff, P. J., & LoPiccolo, J. (1986). A comparative evaluation of minimal therapist contact and 15-session treatment for female orgasmic dysfunction. *Journal of Consulting & Clinical Psychology, 54,* 294–300.

Morrison, N. K. (1998). Behavioral pharmacology of hallucinogens. In R. E. Tarter (Ed.), *Handbook of substance abuse: Neurobehavioral pharmacology* (pp. 229–240). New York: Plenum.

Moscicki, E. (1995). Epidemiology of suicidal behavior. *Suicide & Life-Threatening Behavior, 25,* 22–35.

Moskowitz, J. M. (1989). The primary prevention of alcohol problems: A critical review of the research literature. *Journal of Studies on Alcohol, 50,* 54–88.

Mueser, K. T., Bellack, A. S., Morrison, R. L., & Wade, J. H. (1990). Gender, social competence, and symptomatology in schizophrenia: A longitudinal analysis. *Journal of Abnormal Psychology, 99,* 138–147.

Mukherjee, S., Shukla, S., Woodle, J., Rosen, A. M., & Olarte, S. (1983). Misdiagnosis of schizophrenia in bipolar patients: A multiethnic comparison. *American Journal of Psychiatry, 140,* 1571–1574.

Mulvey, E. P. (1994). Assessing the evidence of a link between mental illness and violence. *Hospital & Community Psychiatry, 45,* 663–668.

Mulvey, E. P. (1995). Personal communication.

Mulvey, E. P., Geller, J. L., & Roth, L. H. (1987). The promise and peril of involuntary outpatient commitment. *American Psychologist, 42,* 571–584.

Munoz, R. F. (1997). The San Francisco Depression Prevention Research Project. In G. W. Albee (Ed.), *Primary prevention works* (pp. 380–400). Thousand Oaks, CA: Sage.

Munoz, R. F., Mrazek, P. J., & Haggerty, R. J. (1996). Institute of Medicine report on prevention of mental disorders: Summary and commentary. *American Psychologist, 51,* 1116–1122.

Murden, R. A., McRae, T. D., Kaner, S., & Bucknam, M. E. (1991). Mini-mental state exam scores vary with education in blacks and whites. *Journal of the American Geriatrics Society, 39,* 149–155.

Muris, P., Merckelbach, H., & Clavan, M. (1997). Abnormal and normal compulsions. *Behaviour Research & Therapy, 35,* 249–252.

Murphy, J. M. (1976). Psychiatric labeling in cross-cultural perspective. *Science, 191,* 1019–1028.

Murray, H. A. (1943). *Thematic apperception test manual.* Cambridge, MA: Harvard University Press.

Murrell, S. A., Himmelfarb, S., & Wright, K. (1983). Prevalence of depression and its correlates in older adults. *Journal of Epidemiology, 117,* 173–185.

Myers, D. G. (1992). The pursuit of happiness. New York: Morrow.

N

Nadder, T. S., Silberg, J. L., Eaves, L. J., Maes, H. H., & Meyer, J. M. (1998). Genetic effects on ADHD symptomatology in 7- to 13-year-old twins: Results from a telephone survey. *Behavior Genetics, 28,* 83–99.

Nakao, M., Nomura, S., Shimosawa, T., Yoshiuchi, K., Kumano, H., Kuboki, T., Suematsu, H., & Fujita, T. (1997). Clinical effects of blood pressure biofeedback treatment on hypertension by auto-shaping. *Psychosomatic Medicine, 59,* 331–338.

Napiorkowski, B., Lester, B. M., Freier, C., Brunner, S., Dietz, L., Nadra, A., & Oh, W. (1996). Effects of in utero substance exposure on infant neurobehavior. *Pediatrics, 98,* 71–75.

Narrow, W. E., Regier, D. A., Rae, D., Manderscheid, R. W., & Locke, B. Z. (1993). Use of services by persons with mental and addictive disorders. *Archives of General Psychiatry, 50,* 95–107.

Nasar, S. (1998). *A beautiful mind.* New York: Simon & Schuster.

National Depressive and Manic-Depressive Association. (1996). *Suicide and depressive illness.* Chicago: Author.

National Institute of Mental Health. (2000). *Suicide facts.* Washington, DC: Author. Retrieved January 26, 2000 from the World Wide Web: http://www.nimh.nih.gov/genpop/su_fact.htm

National Institute on Drug Abuse. (1995). *National household survey on drug abuse: Population estimates 1994* (SMA 95-3063). Research Triangle Park, NC: U.S. Department of Health and Human Services.

NCHS (1994). Advance report of final mortality statistics, 1992. (Monthly vital statistics report, 43). Hyattsville, MD: Public Health Service.

Neighbors, H. W. (1984). Professional help use among black Americans: Implications for unmet need. *American Journal of Community Psychology, 12,* 551–566.

Neighbors, H. W., Williams, D. H., Gunnings, T. S., Lipscomb, W. D., Broman, C., & Lepkowski, J. (1987). *The prevalence of mental disorder in Michigan prisons: Final report.* Ann Arbor, MI: Michigan Department of Corrections, University of Michigan, School of Public Health, Department of Community Health Programs, Community Mental Health Program.

Nelkin, D. (1992). The social power of genetic information. In D. J. Kevles & L. Hood (Eds.), *The code of codes: Scientific and social issues in the Human Genome Project* (pp. 177–190). Cambridge, MA: Harvard University Press.

Nelson, C. B., & Wittchen, H. (1998). DSM-IV alcohol disorders in a general population sample of adolescents and young adults. *Addiction, 93,* 1065–1077.

Nemeroff, C. B., & Schatzberg, A. F. (1998). Pharmacological treatment of unipolar depression. In P. E. Nathan (Ed.), *A guide to treatments that work* (pp. 212–225). New York: Oxford University Press.

Nemeroff, C. J., Stein, R. I., Diehl, N. S., & Smilack, K. M. (1994). From the Cleavers to the Clintons: Role choices and body orientation as reflected in magazine article content. *International Journal of Eating Disorders, 16,* 167–176.

Nestadt, G., Romanoski, A. J., Chahal, R., & Merchant, A. (1990). An epidemiological study of histrionic personality disorder. *Psychological Medicine, 20,* 413–422.

Neuchterlein, K. H., Dawson, M. E., Gitlin, M., Ventura, J., Goldstein, M. J., Snyder, K. S., Yee, C. M., & Mintz, J. (1992). Developmental processes in schizophrenic disorders: Longitudinal studies of vulnerability and stress. *Schizophrenia Bulletin, 18,* 387–420.

Neugebauer, R. (1979). Medieval and early modern theories of mental illness. *Archives of General Psychiatry, 36,* 477–483.

New York Times/CBS News Poll. (1999, October 20). Teen-ager's concerns. *New York Times,* A1.

Newhill, C. E., Mulvey, E. P., & Lidz, C. W. (1995). Characteristics of violence in the community by female patients seen in a psychiatric emergency service. *Psychiatric Services, 46,* 785–789.

Newman, D. L., Moffitt, T. E., Caspi, A., & Magdol, L. (1996). Psychiatric disorder in a birth cohort of young adults: Prevalence, comorbidity, clinical significance, and new case incidence from ages 11–21. *Journal of Consulting and Clinical Psychology, 64,* 552–562.

Newman, D. L., Tellegen, A., & Bouchard, T. J. (1998). Individual differences in adult ego development: Sources of influence in twins reared apart. *Journal of Personality & Social Psychology, 74,* 985–995.

Newman, J. P. (1989). Aging and depression. *Psychology & Aging, 4,* 150–165.

Newsweek. (1993, August 2).

Nichols, M. (1989). Sex therapy with lesbians, gay men, and bisexuals. In S. R. Leiblum & R. C. Rosen (Eds.), *Principles and practice of sex therapy: Update for the 1990s* (pp. 269–297). New York: Guilford Press.

Nicholson, R. A., & Kugler, K. E. (1991). Competent and incompetent criminal defendants: A quantitative review of comparative research. *Psychological Bulletin, 109,* 355–370.

Nicol-Smith, L. (1996). Causality, menopause, and depression: A critical review of the literature. *British Medical Journal, 313,* 1229–1232.

Nigg, J. T., & Goldsmith, H. H. (1994). Genetics of personality disorders: Perspectives from personality and psychopathology research. *Psychological Bulletin, 115,* 346–380.

Nilsson, A. (1999). Lithium therapy and suicide risk. *Journal of Clinical Psychiatry, 60* (Suppl. 2), 85–88.

Nolen-Hoeksema, S. (1990). *Sex differences in depression.* Stanford, CA: Stanford University Press.

Nolen-Hoeksema, S. (1995). Gender differences in coping with depression across the lifespan. *Depression, 3,* 81–90.

Nolen-Hoeksema, S., & Girgus, J. S. (1994). The emergence of gender differences in depression during adolescence. *Psychological Bulletin, 115,* 424–443.

Nolen-Hoeksema, S., & Larson, J. (1999). *Coping with loss.* Mahwah, NJ: Erlbaum.

Nolen-Hoeksema, S., & Morrow, J. (1991). A prospective study of depression and distress following a natural disaster: The 1989 Loma Prieta earthquake. *Journal of Personality & Social Psychology, 61,* 105–121.

Nolen-Hoeksema, S., Larson, J., & Grayson, C. (1999). Explaining the gender difference in depressive symptoms. *Journal of Personality & Social Psychology, 77,* 1061–1072.

Nolen-Hoeksema, S., Parker, L. E., & Larson, J. (1994). Ruminative coping with depressed mood following loss. *Journal of Personality & Social Psychology, 67,* 92–104.

Nopoulos, P., Flaum, M., & Andreasen, N. C. (1997). Sex differences in brain morphology in schizophrenia. *American Journal of Psychiatry, 154,* 1648–1654.

Norcross, J. C. (1997). Emerging breakthroughs in psychotherapy integration: Three predictions and one fantasy. *Psychotherapy, 34,* 86–90.

Norcross, J. C., & Goldfried, M. R. (Eds.) (1992). *Handbook of psychotherapy integration.* New York: Basic Books.

Nordin, V., & Gillberg, C. (1996). Autism spectrum disorders in children with physical or mental disability or both: 1. Clinical and epidemiological aspects. *Developmental Medicine & Child Neurology, 38,* 297–313.

Norman, R. M., & Malla, A. K. (1993). Stressful life events and schizophrenia: II. Conceptual and methodological issues. *British Journal of Psychiatry, 162,* 166–174.

Norris, F. H., & Uhl, G. A. (1993). Chronic stress as a mediator of acute stress: The case of Hurricane Hugo. *Journal of Applied Social Psychology, 23,* 1263–1284.

Nowell, P. D., Buysse, D. J., Morin, C. M., Reynolds III, C. F., & Kuper, D. J. (1998). Effective treatments for selected sleep disorders. In P. E. Nathan (Ed.), *A guide to treatments that work* (pp. 531–543). New York: Oxford University Press.

Nuechterlein, K. H., Asarnow, R. F., Subotnik, K. L., Fogelson, D. L., Ventura, J., Torquato, R. D., & Dawson, M. E. (1998). Neurocognitive vulnerability factors for schizophrenia: Convergence across genetic risk studies and longitudinal trait-state studies. In M. F. Lenzenweger & R. H. Dworkin (Eds.), *Origins of the development of schizophrenia* (pp. 299–327). Washington, DC: American Psychological Association.

Nuechterlein, K. H., Dawson, M. E., Gitlin, M., Ventura, J., Goldstein, M. J., Snyder, K. S., Yee, C. M., & Mintz, J. (1992). Developmental processes in schizophrenic disorders: Longitudinal studies of vulnerability and stress. *Schizophrenia Bulletin, 18,* 387–420.

Nurnberg, H. G., Raskin, M., Livine, P. E., & Pollack, S. (1991). The comorbidity of borderline personality disorder and other DSM-III-R Axis II personality disorders. *American Journal of Psychiatry, 148,* 1371–1377.

O

O'Brien, C. P., & McKay, J. R. (1998). Psycho-pharmacological treatments of substance use disorders. In P. E. Nathan (Ed.), *A guide to treatments that work* (pp. 127–155). New York: Oxford University Press.

O'Connor, K., Hallam, R., & Rachman, S. (1985). Fearlessness and courage: A replication experiment. *British Journal of Psychology, 76,* 187–197.

O'Connor, M. J., Sigman, M., & Kasari, C. (1993). Interactional model for the association among maternal alcohol use, mother-infant interaction, and infant cognitive development. *Infant Behavior & Development, 16,* 177–192.

Office of Ethnic Minority Affairs, American Psychological Association. (1993). Guidelines for providers of psychological services to ethnic, linguistic, and culturally diverse populations. *American Psychologist, 48,* 45–48.

Offord, D. R. (1997). Bridging development, prevention, and policy. In D. M. Stoff, J. Breiling, & J. D. Maser (Eds.), *Handbook of antisocial personality disorder* (pp. 357–364). New York: Wiley.

Offord, D. R., Alder, R. J., & Boyle, M. H. (1986). Prevalence and sociodemographic correlates of conduct disorder. *American Journal of Social Psychiatry, 4,* 272–278.

Offord, D. R., Boyle, M. H., Racine, Y. A., & Fleming, J. E. (1992). Outcome, prognosis, and risk in a longitudinal follow-up study. *Journal of the American Academy of Child & Adolescent Psychiatry, 31,* 916–923.

O'Hara, M. W., & Swain, A. M. (1996). Rates and risk of postpartum depression—a meta-analysis. *International Review of Psychiatry, 8,* 37–54.

O'Hara, M. W., Schlecte, J. A., Lewis, D. A., & Wright, E. (1991). Prospective study of post-partum blues: Biological and psychosocial factors. *Archives of General Psychiatry, 48,* 801–806.

Ohman, A., Fredrikson, M., Hugdahl, K., & Rimmo, P. (1976). The premise of equipotentiality in human classical conditioning: Conditioned electrodermal responses to potentially phobic stimuli. *Journal of Experimental Psychology: General, 105,* 313–337.

O'Leary, A. (1990). Stress, emotion, and human immune function. *Psychological Bulletin, 108,* 363–382.

Olfson, M., Marcus, S., Sackheim, H. A., Thompson, J., & Pincus, H. A. (1998). Use of ECT for the inpatient treatment of recurrent major depression. *American Journal of Psychiatry, 155,* 22–29.

Olin, S. S., Raine, A., Cannon, T. D., Parnas, J., Schulsinger, F., & Mednick, S. A. (1999). Childhood behavior precursors of schizotypal personality disorder. *Schizophrenia Bulletin, 23,* 93–103.

Olivardia, R., Pope, H. G., Mangweth, B., & Hudson, J. I. (1995). Eating disorders in college men. *American Journal of Psychiatry, 152,* 1279–1285.

Olmos de Paz, T. (1990). Working-through and insight in child psychoanalysis. *Melanie Klein & Object Relations, 8,* 99–112.

Olweus, D. (1986). Aggression and hormones: Behavioral relationship with testosterone and adrenaline. In D. Olweus, J. Block, & M. Radke-Yarrow (Eds.), *Development of antisocial and prosocial behavior: Research, theories, and issues.* Orlando, FL: Academic Press.

Oman, D., & Reed, D. (1998). Religion and mortality among the community dwelling elderly. *American Journal of Public Health, 88,* 1469–1475.

Ondersma, S. J., & Walker, C. E. (1998). Elimination disorders. In T. H. Ollendick & M. Hersen (Eds.), *Handbook of child psychopathology* (pp. 355–380). New York: Plenum.

Oquendo, M. A., Malone, K. M., Ellis, S. P., Harold, A. S., & Mann, J. J. (1999). Inadequacy of antidepressant treatment for patients with major depression who are at risk for suicidal behavior. *American Journal of Psychiatry, 156,* 190–194.

Oren, D. A., & Rosenthal, N. E. (1992). Seasonal affective disorders. In E. S. Paykel (Ed.), *Handbook of affective disorders* (pp. 551–567). New York: Guilford Press.

Orlinsky, D. E., & Howard, K. I. (1986). Process and outcome in psychotherapy. In S. L. Garfield & A. E. Bergin (Eds.), *Handbook of psychotherapy and behavior change* (3rd ed., pp. 344–347). New York: Wiley.

Orloff, L. M., Battle, M. A., Baer, L., & Ivanjack, L. (1994). Long-term follow-up of 85 patients with obsessive-compulsive disorder. *American Journal of Psychiatry, 151,* 441–442.

Orsillo, S. M., Weathers, F. W., Litz, B. T., Steinberg, H. R., Huska, J. A., & Keane, T. M. (1996). Current and lifetime psychiatric disorders among veterans with war zone–related posttraumatic stress disorder. *Journal of Nervous & Mental Disease, 184,* 307–313.

Osofsky, J. D., Wewers, S., Hann, D. M., & Fick, A. C. (1993). Chronic community violence: What is happening to our children? *Psychiatry: Interpersonal & Biological Processes, 56,* 36–45.

Ost, L. (1992). Blood and injection phobia: Background and cognitive, physiological, and behavioral variables. *Journal of Abnormal Psychology, 101,* 68–74.

Ost, L. (1996). Long-term effects of behavior therapy for specific phobia. In M. R. Mavissakalian & R. F. Prien (Eds.), *Long-term treatments of anxiety disorders* (pp. 121–170). Washington, DC: American Psychiatric Press.

Ost, L. S., & Sterner, U. (1987). Applied tension: A specific behavioral method for treatment of blood phobia. *Behaviour Research & Therapy, 25,* 25–29.

Osterweis, M., Soloman, F., & Green, M. (1984). *Bereavement: Reactions, consequences and care.* Washington, DC: National Academy Press.

Osvold, L. L., & Sodowsky, G. R. (1993). Eating disorders of white American, racial and ethnic minority American, and international women. Special issue: Multicultural health issues. *Journal of Multicultural Counseling & Development, 21,* 143–154.

Otto, M. W., Pollack, M. H., Meltzer-Brody, S., & Rosenbaum, J. F. (1992). Cognitive-behavioral therapy for benzodiazepine discontinuation in panic disorder patients. *Psychopharmacology Bulletin, 28,* 123–130.

Otto, M. W., Yeo, R. A., & Dougher, M. J. (1987). Right hemisphere involvement in depression: Toward a neuropsychological theory of negative affective experiences. *Biological Psychiatry, 22,* 1201–1215.

Overmier, J. B., & Murrison, R. (1998). Animal models reveal the "psych" in the psychosomatics of peptic ulcers. *Current Directions in Psychological Science, 6,* 180–184.

Overmier, J. B., & Seligman, M. E. (1967). Effects of inescapable shock upon subsequent escape and avoidance responding. *Journal of Comparative & Physiological Psychology, 63,* 28–33.

Ozonoff, S., & Cathcart, K. (1998). Effectiveness of a home program intervention for young children with autism. *Journal of Autism & Developmental Disorders, 28,* 25–32.

P

Paffenbarger, R. S., Hyde, R. T., Wing, A. L., & Hsieh, C. (1986). Physical activity, all-cause mortality, and longevity of college alumni. *New England Journal of Medicine, 314,* 605–613.

Palazzoli, M. S. (1974). *Self-starvation: From the intrapsychic to the transpersonal approach to anorexia nervosa* (A. Pomerans, Trans.). London: Chaucer.

Papp, L., Martinez, J. M., Klein, D. F., Coplan, J. D., Norman, R. G., Cole, R., de Jesus, M., Ross, D., Goetz, R., & Gorman, J. M. (1997). Respiratory psychophysiology of panic disorder: Three respiratory challenges in 98 subjects. *American Journal of Psychiatry, 154,* 1557–1565.

Pappenheim, B. (1936). Gebete. *Ausgewahlt und herausgegeben vom Judischen Frauenbund.* Berlin: Philo Verlag.

Parker, G., & Hadzi-Pavlovic, D. (1990). Expressed emotion as a predictor of schizophrenic relapse: An analysis of aggregated data. *Psychological Medicine, 20,* 961–965.

Parker, G., Johnston, P., & Hayward, L. (1988). Parental "expressed emotion" as a predictor of schizophrenic relapse. *Archives of General Psychiatry, 45,* 806–813.

Parker, K. C., Hanson, R., & Hunsley, J. (1988). MMPI, Rorschach, and WAIS: A meta-analytic comparison of reliability, stability, and validity. *Psychological Bulletin, 103,* 367–373.

Parkes, C. M. (1971). Psycho-social transitions: A field for study. *Social Science & Medicine, 5,* 101–115.

Parlee, M. B. (1994). Commentary on the literature review. In J. H. Gold & S. K. Severino (Eds.), *Premenstrual dysphorias* (pp. 149–167). Washington, DC: American Psychiatric Association Press.

Parrott, A. C. (1998). Nesbitt's Paradox resolved? Stress and arousal modulation during cigarette smoking. *Addiction, 93,* 27–39.

Parry, B. L. (1994). Biological correlates of premenstrual complaints. In J. H. Gold & S. K. Severino (Eds.), *Premenstrual dysphorias* (pp. 47–66). Washington, DC: American Psychiatric Association Press.

Pate, J. E., Pumariega, A. J., Hester, C., & Garner, D. M. (1992). Cross-cultural patterns in eating disorders: A review. *Journal of the American Academy of Child & Adolescent Psychiatry, 31,* 802–809.

Patterson, R. (1994). *Opening remarks.* Paper presented at the National Forum on Creating Jail Mental Health Services for Tomorrow's Health Care Systems, San Francisco.

Pauli, P., Dengler, W., Wiedemann, G., Montoya, P., Flor, H., Birbaumer, N., & Buchkremer, G. (1997). Behavioral and neurophysiological evidence for altered processing of anxiety-related words in panic disorder. *Journal of Abnormal Psychology, 106,* 213–220.

Pauls, D. A., Morton, L. A., & Egeland, J. A. (1992). Risks of affective illness among first-degree relatives of bipolar I old-order Amish probands. *Archives of General Psychiatry, 49,* 703–708.

Pavlov, I. P. (1927). *Conditioned reflexes: An investigation of the physiological activity of the cerebral cortex.* London: Oxford University Press.

Paykel, E. S. (1991). Stress and life events. In L. Davison & M. Linnoila (Eds.), *Risk factors for youth suicide.* New York: Hemisphere.

Peach, L., & Reddick, T. L. (1991). Counselors can make a difference in preventing adolescent suicide. *School Counselor, 39,* 107–110.

Pearce, J. (1978). The recognition of depressive disorder in children. *Journal of the Royal Society of Medicine, 71,* 494–500.

Pearlson, G. D., Harris, G. J., Powers, R. E., & Barta, P. E. (1992). Quantitative changes in mesial temporal volume, regional cerebral blood flow, and cognition in Alzheimer's disease. *Archives of General Psychiatry, 49,* 402–408.

Pearlstein, T., Stone, A., Lund, S., Scheft, H., Zlotnik, C., & Brown, W. (1997). Comparison of fluoxetine, bupropion, and placebo in the treatment of premenstrual dysphoric disorder. *Journal of Clinical Psychopharmacology, 17,* 261–266.

Pedersen, C. A., Stern, R. A., Pate, J., & Senger, M. A. (1993). Thyroid and adrenal measures during late pregnancy and the puerperium in women who have been major depressed or who become dysphoric postpartum. *Journal of Affective Disorders, 29,* 201–211.

Pendery, M. L., Maltzman, I. M., & West, L. J. (1982). Controlled drinking by alcoholics? New findings and a reevaluation of a major affirmative study. *Science, 217,* 169–175.

Pennebaker, J. W. (1990). *Opening up: The healing power of confiding in others.* New York: William Morrow.

Pennebaker, J. W., & O'Heeron, R. C. (1984). Confiding in others and illness rates among spouses of suicide and accidental-death victims. *Journal of Abnormal Psychology, 93,* 473–476.

Pennebaker, J. W., Kiecolt-Glaser, J. K., & Glaser, R. (1988). Disclosure of traumas and immune function: Health implications for psychotherapy. *Journal of Consulting & Clinical Psychology, 56,* 239–245.

Perkins, K. A., & Stitzer, M. (1998). Behavioral pharmacology of nicotine. In R. E. Tarter (Ed.), *Handbook of substance abuse: Neurobehavioral pharmacology* (pp. 299–317). New York: Plenum.

Perry, E. K., Tomlinson, B. E., Blessed, G., Bergmann, K., Gibson, P. H., & Perry, R. H. (1978). Correlation of cholinergic abnormalities with senile plaques and mental test scores in senile dementia. *British Medical Journal, 2,* 1457–1459.

Perry, J. C. (1993). Longitudinal studies of personality disorders. *Journal of Personality Disorders* (Suppl. 1), 63–85.

Perugi, G., Akiskal, H. S., Giannotti, D., Frare, F., Di Vaio, S., & Cassano, G. B. (1997). Gender-related differences in body dysmorphic disorder (dysmorphophobia). *Journal of Nervous & Mental Disease, 185,* 578–582.

Petersen, E. N. (1992). The pharmacology and toxicology of disulfiram and its metabolites. *Acta Psychiatrica Scandinavica, 86* (suppl. 369), 7–13.

Peterson, C. (1988). Explanatory style as a risk factor for illness. *Cognitive Therapy & Research, 12,* 119–132.

Peterson, C., & Seligman, M. E. (1984). Causal explanations as a risk factor for depression: Theory and evidence. *Psychological Review, 91,* 347–374.

Peterson, C., Seligman, M. E., & Vaillant, G. E. (1988). Pessimistic explanatory style is a risk factor for physical illness: A thirty-five-year longitudinal study. *Journal of Personality & Social Psychology, 55,* 23–27.

Peterson, C., Seligman, M. E. P., Yurko, K. H., Martin, L. R., & Friedman, H. S. (1998). Catastrophizing and untimely death. *Psychological Science, 9,* 127–130.

Peterson, G. (1991). Children coping with trauma: Diagnosis of "Dissociation Identity Disorder." *Dissociation: Progress in the Dissociation Disorders, 4,* 152–164.

Petronis, K. R., Samuels, J. F., Moscicki, E. K., & Anthony, J. C. (1990). An epidemiologic investigation of potential risk factors for suicide attempts. *Social Psychiatry & Psychiatric Epidemiology, 25,* 193–199.

Pettit, G. S., Dodge, K. A., & Brown, M. M. (1988). Early family experience, social problem solving patterns, and children's social competence. *Child Development, 59,* 107–120.

Pfeffer, C. R. (1985). Suicidal tendencies in normal children. *Journal of Nervous & Mental Disease, 173,* 78–84.

Phares, E. J. (1992). *Clinical psychology: Concepts, methods and profession.* Pacific Grove, CA: Brooks/Cole.

Phariss, B., Millman, R. B., & Beeder, A. B. (1998). Psychological and psychiatric consequences of cannabis. In R. E. Tarter (Ed.), *Handbook of substance abuse: Neurobehavioral pharmacology* (pp. 147–158). New York: Plenum.

Philibert, R. A., Egeland, J. A., Paul, S. M., & Ginns, E. I. (1997). The inheritance of bipolar affective disorder: Adundant genes coming together. *Journal of Affective Disorder, 43,* 1–3.

Phillips, D. P., & Carstensen, L. L. (1986). Clustering of teenage suicides after television news stories about suicide. *The New England Journal of Medicine, 315,* 685–689.

Phillips, D. P., & Carstensen, L. L. (1988). The effect of suicide stories on various demographic groups, 1968–1985. *Suicide & Life-Threatening Behavior, 18,* 100–114.

Phillips, D. P., Lesyna, K., & Paight, D. J. (1992). Suicide and the media. In R. W. Maris, A. L. Berman, J. T. Maltsberger, & R. I. Yufit (eds.), *Assessment and prediction of suicide* (pp. 499–519). New York: Guilford Press.

Phillips, K. A. (1991). Body dysmorphic disorder: The distress of imagined ugliness. *American Journal of Psychiatry, 148,* 1138–1149.

Phillips, K. A. (1992). "Body dysmorphic disorder: The distress of imagined ugliness": Reply. *American Journal of Psychiatry, 149,* 719.

Phillips, K. A., & Diaz, S. F. (1997). Gender differences in body dysmorphic disorder. *Journal of Nervous & Mental Disease, 185,* 570–577.

Phillips, K. A., Dwight, M. M., & McElroy, S. L. (1998). Efficacy and safety of fluvoxamine in body dysmorphic disorder. *Journal of Clinical Psychiatry, 59,* 165–171.

Picciotto, M. R., Zoli, M., Rimondi, R., Lena, C., Marubio, L. M., Pich, E. M., Fuxe, K., & Changeneux, J. P. (1998). Acetylcholine receptors containing the B2 subunit are involved in the reinforcing properties of nicotine. *Nature, 391,* 173–177.

Pike, K. M., & Rodin, J. (1991). Mothers, daughters, and disordered eating. *Journal of Abnormal Psychology, 100,* 198–204.

Pilkonis, P. A. (1995). Commentary on avoidant personality disorder: Temperament, shame, or both? In W. J. Livesley (Ed.), *The DSM-IV personality disorders* (pp. 234–238). New York: Guilford Press.

Pincus, A. L. (1994). The interpersonal circumplex and the interpersonal theory: Perspectives on personality and its pathology. In S. Stack & M. Lorr (Eds.), *Differentiating normal and abnormal personality* (pp. 114–136). New York: Springer.

Pipher, M. B. (1994). *Reviving Ophelia: Saving the selves of adolescent girls.* New York: Putnam.

Pi-Sunyer, F. X. (1991). Health implications of obesity. *The American Journal of Clinical Nutrition, 53,* 1595–1603.

Pitman, R. K. (1989). Posttraumatic stress disorder, hormones, and memory. *Biological Psychiatry, 26,* 221–223.

Plantenga, B. (1991). *Like open bright windows.* New York: Poets in Public Service.

Plassman, B. L., & Breitner, J. C. S. (1996). Recent advances in the genetics of Alzheimer's disease and vascular dementia with an emphasis on gene-environment interactions. *Journal of the American Geriatric Society, 44,* 1242–1250.

Plath, S. (1971). *The bell jar.* New York: Harper & Row.

Pliner, P., & Chaiken, S. (1990). Eating, social motives, and self-presentation in women and men. *Journal of Experimental Social Psychology, 26,* 240–254.

Polivy, J., & Herman, C. P. (1993). Etiology of binge eating: Psychological mechanisms. In C. G. Fairburn & G. T. Wilson (Eds.), *Binge eating: Nature, assessment, and treatment.* New York: Guilford Press.

Pomales, J., Claiborn, C. D., & LaFromboise, T. D. (1986). Effects of black students' racial identity on perceptions of white counselors varying in cultural sensitivity. *Journal of Counseling Psychology, 33,* 57–61.

Pomerleau, C. S. (1997). Co-factors for smoking and evolutionary psychobiology. *Addiction, 92,* 397–408.

Pomerleau, O., & Kardia, S. (1999). Introduction to the featured section: Research on smoking. *Health Psychology, 18,* 3–6.

Pope, H. G., & Hudson, J. I. (1992). Is childhood sexual abuse a risk factor for bulimia nervosa? *American Journal of Psychiatry, 149,* 455–463.

Pope, H. G., Hudson, J. I., Bodkin, J. A., & Oliva, P. (1998). Questionable validity of dissociative amnesia in trauma victims: Evidence from prospective studies. *British Journal of Psychiatry, 172,* 210–215.

Pope, K. S., Tabachnick, B. G., & Keith-Spiegel, P. (1987). Ethics of practice: The beliefs and behaviors of psychologists as therapists. *American Psychologist, 42*, 993–1006.

Post, R. M. (1992). Transduction of psychosocial stress into the neurobiology of recurrent affective disorder. *American Journal of Psychiatry, 149*, 999–1010.

Post, R. M., & Weiss, S. R. B. (1995). The neurobiology of treatment-resistant mood disorders. In F. E. Bloom & D. J. Kupfer (Eds.), *Psychopharmacology: The fourth generation of progress* (pp. 1155–1170). New York: Raven Press.

Post, R., Frye, M., Denicoff, K., Leverich, G., Kimbrell, T., & Dunn, R. (1998). Beyond lithium in the treatment of bipolar illness. *Neuropsychopharmacology, 19*, 206–219.

Power, K. G., Simpson, R. J., Swanson, V., & Wallace, L. A. (1990). A controlled comparison of cognitive-behavior therapy, diazepam, and placebo, alone and in combination, for the treatment of generalized anxiety disorder. *Journal of Anxiety Disorders, 4*, 267–292.

Prescott, C. A., & Kendler, K. S. (1999). Genetic and environmental contributions to alcohol abuse and dependence in a population-based sample of male twins. *American Journal of Psychiatry, 156*, 34–40.

Pribor, E. F., Yutzy, S. H., Dean, J. T, & Wetzel, R. D. (1993). Briquet's syndrome, dissociation, and abuse. *American Journal of Psychiatry, 150*, 1507–1511.

Price, R. W. (1998). Implications of the AIDS dementia complex viewed as an acquired genetic neurodegenerative disease. In M. F. Folstein (Ed.), *Neurobiology of primary dementia* (pp. 213–234). Washington, DC: American Psychiatric Press.

Pritchard, J. C. (1837). *A treatise on insanity and other diseases affecting the mind.* Philadelphia: Harwell, Barrington, and Harwell.

Prochaska, J. O. (1995). Common problems: Common solutions. *Clinical Psychology: Science & Practice, 2*, 101–105.

Putnam, F. W. (1991). Recent research on multiple personality disorder. *Psychiatric Clinics of North America, 14*, 489–502.

Putnam, F. W. (1996). Posttraumatic stress disorder in children and adolescents. In L. J. Dickstein, M. B. Riba, & J. M. Oldham (Eds.), *Review of psychiatry* (Vol. 15,). Washington, DC: American Psychiatric Press.

Putnam, F. W., & Lowenstein, R. J. (1993). Treatment of multiple personality disorder: A survey of current practices. *American Journal of Psychiatry, 150*, 1048–1052.

Putnam, F. W., Guroff, J. J., Silberman, E. K., & Barban, L. (1986). The clinical phenomenology of multiple personality disorder: Review of 100 recent cases. *Journal of Clinical Psychiatry, 47*, 285–293.

Puttler, L. I., Zucker, R. A., Fitzgerald, H. E., & Bingham, C. R. (1998). Behavioral outcomes among children of alcoholics during the early and middle childhood years: Familial subtype variations. *Alcoholism: Clinical & Experimental Research, 22*, 1962–1972.

Q

Quaid, K. A., & Morris, M. (1993). Reluctance to undergo predictive testing: The case of Huntington's disease. *American Journal of Medical Genetics, 45*, 41–45.

Quality Assurance Project (1990). Treatment outlines for paranoid, schizotypal, and schizoid personality disorders. *Australian & New Zealand Journal of Psychiatry, 24*, 339–350.

Quay, H. C. (1993). The psychobiology of undersocialized aggressive conduct disorder:

A theoretical perspective. *Development & Psychopathology, 5*, 165–180.

R

Rabins, P. V. (1998). Developing treatment guidelines for Alzheimer's disease and other dementias. *Journal of Clinical Psychiatry, 59* (Suppl. 11), 17–19.

Rachman, S. (1978). *Fear and courage.* San Francisco: W. H. Freeman.

Rachman, S. (1993). Obsessions, responsibility and guilt. *Behaviour Research & Therapy, 31*, 149–154.

Rachman, S., & DeSilva, P. (1978). Abnormal and normal obsessions. *Behaviour Research & Therapy, 16*, 233–248.

Rachman, S. J., & Hodgson, R. J. (1980). *Obsessions and compulsions.* Englewood Cliffs, NJ: Prentice-Hall.

Ragland, J. D., & Berman, A. L. (1990–1991). Farm crisis and suicide: Dying on the vine? *Omega Journal of Death & Dying, 22*, 173–185.

Raikkonen, K., Matthews, K. A., Flory, J. D., Owens, J. F., & Gump, B. B. (1999). Effects of optimism, pessimism, and trait anxiety on ambulatory blood pressure and mood during everyday life. *Journal of Personality & Social Psychology, 76*, 104–113.

Raine, A. (1997). Antisocial behavior and psychophysiology: A biological perspective. In D. M. Stoff, J. Breiling, & J. D. Maser (Eds.), *Handbook of antisocial personality disorder* (p. 289–304). New York: Wiley.

Raine, A., Venables, P. H., & Williams, M. (1996). Better autonomic conditioning and faster electrodermal half-recovery time at age 15 years as possible protective factors against crime at age 29 years. *Developmental Psychology, 32*, 624–630.

Rankin, H., Hodgson, R., & Stockwell, T. (1983). Cue exposure and response prevention with alcoholics: A controlled trial. *Behaviour Research & Therapy, 21*, 435–446.

Rapaport, J. L. (1989, March). The biology of obsessions and compulsions. *Scientific American*, 83–89.

Rapaport, J. L. (1990). *The boy who couldn't stop washing.* New York: Plume.

Rapaport, J. L. (1991). Recent advances in obsessive-compulsive disorder. *Neuropsychopharmacology, 5*, 1–10.

Rapee, R. M. (1994). Detection of somatic sensations in panic disorder. *Behaviour Research & Therapy, 32*, 825–831.

Rapee, R. M., & Barlow, D. H. (1993). Generalized anxiety disorder, panic disorder, and the phobias. In P. B. Sutker (Ed.), *Comprehensive handbook of psychopathology* (pp. 109–127). New York: Plenum.

Rapee, R. M., Brown, T. A., Antony, M. M., & Barlow, D. H. (1992). Response to hyperventilation and inhalation of 5.5% carbon dioxide-enriched air across the DSM-III-R anxiety disorders. *Journal of Abnormal Psychology, 101*, 538–552.

Rapoport, J. L. (1989). *The boy who couldn't stop washing.* Markham, Ontario: Penguin Books.

Rapport, M. D., Jones, J. T., DuPaul, G. J., Kelly, K. L., et al. (1987). Attention deficit disorder and methylphenidate: Group and single-subject analyses of dose effects on attention in clinic and classroom settings. *Journal of Clinical Child Psychology, 16*, 329–338.

Rasmussen, S. A., & Eisen, J. L. (1990). Epidemiology of obsessive compulsive disorder. *Journal of Clinical Psychiatry, 51* (Suppl. 2), 10–13.

Rasmussen, S. A., & Tsuang, M. T. (1984). The epidemiology of obsessive compulsive

disorder. *Journal of Clinical Psychiatry, 45*, 450–457.

Rasmussen, S. A., & Tsuang, M. T. (1986). Clinical characteristics and family history in DSM-III obsessive-compulsive disorder. *American Journal of Psychiatry, 143*, 317–322.

Rauch, S. L., Shin, L. M., & Pitman, R. K. (1998). Evaluating the effects of psychological trauma using neuroimaging techniques. In R. Yehuda (Ed.), *Psychological trauma* (pp. 67–96). Washington, DC: American Psychiatric Press.

Ray, O., & Ksir, C. (1993). *Drugs, society, and human behavior.* St. Louis: Mosby.

Read, J. D., & Lindsay, D. S. (Eds.). (1997). *Recollections of trauma: Scientific research and clinical practice.* New York: Plenum.

Redmond, D. E. (1985). Neurochemical basis for anxiety and anxiety disorders: Evidence from drugs which decrease human fear or anxiety. In A. H. Tuma & J. Maser (Eds.), *Anxiety and the anxiety disorders.* Hillsdale, NJ: Erlbaum.

Regier, D. A., Narrow, W. E., Rae, D. S., Manderscheid, R. W., Locke, B. Z., & Goodwin, F. K. (1993). The de facto U.S. mental and addictive disorders service system. *Archives of General Psychiatry, 50*, 85–94.

Rehm, L. P. (1977). A self-control model of depression. *Behavior Therapy, 8*, 787–804.

Reid, J. B., & Eddy, J. M. (1997). The prevention of antisocial behavior: Some considerations in the search for effective interventions. In D. M. Stoff, J. Breiling, & J. D. Maser (Eds.), *Handbook of antisocial personality disorder* (pp. 343–356). New York: Wiley.

Reid, R. L., & Yen, S. S. C. (1981). Premenstrual syndrome. *American Journal of Obstetrics & Gynecology, 1*, 85–104.

Reitan, R. M., & Davidson, L. A. (1974). *Clinical neuropsychology: Current status and applications.* Washington, DC: V. H. Winston & Sons.

Resick, P. A. (1993). The psychological impact of rape. *Journal of Interpersonal Violence, 8*, 223–255.

Resick, P. A., & Schnicke, M. K. (1992). Cognitive processing therapy for sexual assault victims. *Journal of Consulting & Clinical Psychology, 60*, 748–756.

Resnick, H. S., Kilpatrick, D. G., Dansky, B. S., & Saunders, B. E. (1993). Prevalence of civilian trauma and posttraumatic stress disorder in a representative national sample of women. *Journal of Consulting & Clinical Psychology, 61*, 984–991.

Rhee, S. H., Waldman, I. D., Hay, D. A., & Levy, F. (1999). Sex differences in genetic and environmental influences on DSM-III-R attention-deficit/hyperactivity disorder. *Journal of Abnormal Psychology, 108*, 24–41.

Richards, R., Kinney, D. K., Lunde, I., & Benet, M. (1988). Creativity in manic-depressives, cyclothymes, their normal relatives, and control subjects. *Journal of Abnormal Psychology, 97*, 281–288.

Richardson, J. L., Shelton, D. R., Krailo, M., & Levine, A. M. (1990). The effect of compliance with treatment in survival among patients with hematologic malignancies. *Journal of Clinical Oncology, 8*, 356.

Rief, W., Hiller, W., & Margraf, J. (1998). Cognitive aspects of hypochondriasis and the somatization syndrome. *Journal of Abnormal Psychology, 107*, 587–595.

Riley, W. T., Treiber, F. A., & Woods, M. G. (1989). Anger and hostility in depression. *Journal of Nervous & Mental Disease, 177*, 668–674.

Rimm, D. C., & Masters, J. C. (1979). *Behavior therapy: Techniques and empirical findings* (2nd ed.). New York: Academic Press.

Rimmele, C. T., Miller, W. R., & Dougher, M. J. (1989). Aversion therapies. In R. K. Hester & W. R. Miller (Eds.), *Handbook of alcoholism treatment approaches: Effective alternatives.* New York: Pergamon.

Ritvo, E. A., Jorde, L. B., Mason-Brothers, A., & Freeman, B. J. (1989). The UCLA-University of Utah epidemiologic survey of autism: Recurrence risk estimates and genetic counseling. *American Journal of Psychiatry, 146,* 1032–1036.

Rivera, G. (1988). Hispanic folk medicine utilization in urban Colorado. *Sociology & Social Research, 72,* 237–241.

Rivers, R. Y., & Morrow, C. A. (1995). Understanding and treating ethnic minority youth. In J. F. Aponte (Ed.), *Psychological interventions and cultural diversity* (pp. 164–180). Boston: Allyn & Bacon.

Roback, H. B., & Lothstein, L. M. (1986). The female mid-life sex change applicant: A comparison with younger female transsexuals and older male sex change applicants. *Archives of Sexual Behavior, 15,* 401–415.

Roberts, A. H. (1969). *Brain damage in boxers.* London: Pitman.

Roberts, J. E., Gotlib, I. H., & Kassel, J. D. (1996). Adult attachment security and symptoms of depression: The mediating roles of dysfunctional attitudes and low self-esteem. *Journal of Personality & Social Psychology, 60,* 310–320.

Roberts, J. S. (1999). *Medical decision-making in individuals at risk for Alzheimer's disease: The case of predictive testing.* Ann Arbor: University of Michigan.

Roberts, R. E., Attkisson, C. C., & Rosenblatt, A. (1998). Prevalence of psychopathology among children and adolescents. *American Journal of Psychiatry, 155,* 715–725.

Robins, L. N. (1991). Conduct disorder. *Journal of Child Psychology & Psychiatry & Allied Disciplines, 32,* 193–212.

Robins, L. N., & Regier, D. A. (Eds.). (1991). *Psychiatric disorders in America: The Epidemiologic Catchment Area Study.* New York: Free Press.

Robins, L. N., Helzer, J. E., Craghan, J., & Ratcliff, K. S. (1981). National Institute of Mental Health Diagnostic Interview Schedule: Its history, characteristics, and validity. *Archives of General Psychiatry, 38,* 381–389.

Robins, L. N., Helzer, J. E., & Davis, D. H. (1975). Narcotic use in Southeast Asia and afterward: An interview of 898 Vietnam returnees. *Archives of General Psychiatry, 32,* 955–961.

Robins, L. N., Helzer, J. E., Weissman, M. M., Orvaschel, H., Gruenberg, E., Burke, J. D., & Regier, D. A. (1984). Lifetime prevalence of specific psychiatric disorders in three sites. *Archives of General Psychiatry, 41,* 949–958.

Robinson, L. A., Berman, J. S., & Neimeyer, R. A. (1990). Psychotherapy for the treatment of depression: A comprehensive review of controlled outcome research. *Psychological Bulletin, 109,* 30–49.

Robinson, T. E., & Berridge, K. C. (1993). The neural basis of drug craving: An incentive-sensitization theory of addiction. *Brain Research Reviews, 18,* 247–291.

Rockney, R. M., & Lemke, T. (1992). Casualties from a junior-senior high school during the Persian Gulf War: Toxic poisoning or mass hysteria? *Journal of Developmental & Behavioral Pediatrics, 13,* 339–342.

Rodin, J. (1992). Sick of worrying about the way you look? Read this. *Psychology Today, 25,* 56–60.

Rodin, J., Slochower, J., & Fleming, B. (1977). Effects of degree of obesity, age of onset, and weight loss on responsiveness to sensory and external stimuli. *Journal of Comparative & Physiological Psychology, 91,* 586–597.

Roemer, L., Molina, S., & Borkovec, T. D. (1997). An investigation of worry content among generally anxious individuals. *The Journal of Nervous & Mental Disease, 185,* 314–319.

Rogers, C. R. (1951). *Client-centered therapy, its current practice, implications, and theory.* Boston: Houghton Mifflin.

Rogler, L. H. (1989). The meaning of culturally sensitive research in mental health. *American Journal of Psychiatry, 146,* 296–303.

Rogler, L. H. (1999). Methodological sources of cultural insensitivity in mental health research. *American Psychologist, 54,* 424–433.

Rollin, H. R. (1980). *Coping with schizophrenia.* London: Burnett Books.

Rolls, B. J., Fedoroff, I. C., & Guthrie, J. F. (1991). Gender differences in eating behavior and body weight regulation. Special Issue: Gender and health. *Health Psychology, 10,* 133–142.

Rook, K. (1984). The negative side of social interaction: Impact on psychological well-being. *Journal of Personality & Social Psychology, 46,* 1097–1108.

Rorty, M., Yager, J., & Rossotto, E. (1994). Childhood sexual, physical, and psychological abuse in bulimia nervosa. *American Journal of Psychiatry, 151,* 1122–1126.

Rosen, G. (1968). *Madness in society: Chapters in the historical sociology of mental illness.* Chicago: University of Chicago Press.

Rosen, J. C., & Ramirez, E. (1998). A comparison of eating disorders and body dysmorphic disorder on body image and psychological adjustment. *Journal of Psychosomatic Research: Special Issue: Current issues in eating disorder research, 44,* 441–449.

Rosen, L. N., Targum, S. D., Terman, M., Bryant, M. J., Hoffman, H., Kasper, S. F., Hamovit, J. R., Docherty, J. P., Welch, B., & Rosenthal, N. E. (1990). Prevalence of seasonal affective disorder at four latitudes. *Psychiatry Research, 31,* 131–144.

Rosen, R. C. (1996). Erectile dysfunction: The medicalization of male sexuality. *Clinical Psychology Review, 16,* 497–519.

Rosen, R. C., & Ashton, A. K. (1993). Prosexual drugs: Empirical status of the "new aphrodisiacs." *Archives of Sexual Behavior, 22,* 521–543.

Rosen, R. C., & Leiblum, S. R. (1995). Treatment of sexual disorders in the 1990s: An integrated approach. *Journal of Consulting & Clinical Psychology, 63,* 877–890.

Rosenbaum, M. (1980). The role of the term schizophrenia in the decline of the diagnoses of multiple personality. *Archives of General Psychiatry, 37,* 1383–1385.

Rosenblatt, P. (1983). *Bitter, bitter tears: Nineteenth century diarists and twentieth century grief theories.* Minneapolis: University of Minnesota Press.

Rosenhan, D. L. (1973). On being sane in insane places. *Science, 179,* 250–258.

Rosenman, R. H., Brand, R. J., Jenkins, C. D., Friedman, M., Straus, R., & Wrum, M. (1976). Coronary heart disease in the Western Collaborative Group Study: Final follow-up experience of 8 years. *Journal of the American Medical Association, 233,* 877–878.

Rosenstein, M. J., Milazzo-Sayre, L. J., & Manderscheid, R. W. (1989). Care of persons with schizophrenia: A statistical profile. *Schizophrenia Bulletin, 15,* 45–58.

Rosenthal, N. E. (1993). *Winter blues: Seasonal affective disorder: What it is and how to overcome it.* New York: Guilford Press.

Rosenthal, N. E. (1995, October 9–11). *The mechanism of action of light in the treatment of seasonal affective disorder.* Paper presented at the Biologic Effects of Light 1995, Atlanta.

Rosenzweig, S. (1936). Some implicit common factors in diverse methods in psychotherapy. *American Journal of Orthopsychiatry, 6,* 412–415.

Ross, C. A. (1989). *Multiple personality disorder: Diagnosis, clinical features, and treatment.* New York: Wiley.

Ross, C. A. (1991). Epidemiology of multiple personality disorder and dissociation. *Psychiatric Clinics of North America, 14,* 503–517.

Ross, C. A. (1997). *Dissociative identity disorder: Diagnosis, clinical features, and treatment of multiple personality.* Toronto: Wiley.

Ross, C. A., & Norton, G. R. (1989). Differences between men and women with multiple personality disorder. *Hospital & Community Psychiatry, 40,* 186–188.

Ross, C. A., Norton, G. R., & Fraser, G. A. (1989). Evidence against the iatrogenesis of multiple personality disorder. *Dissociation: Progress in the Dissociative Disorders, 2,* 61–65.

Ross, C. A., Norton, G. R., & Wozney, K. (1989). Multiple personality disorder: An analysis of 236 cases. *Canadian Journal of Psychiatry, 34,* 413–418.

Ross, C. E., & Mirowsky, J. (1984). Socially-desirable response and acquiescence in a cross-cultural survey of mental health. *Journal of Health & Social Behavior, 25,* 189–197.

Ross, L., & Nisbett, R. E. (1991). *The person and the situation: Perspectives of social psychology.* Philadelphia: Temple University Press.

Ross, L., Lepper, M. R., & Hubbard, M. (1975). Perseverance in self-perception and social preparation: Biased attributional processes in the debriefing paradigm. *Journal of Personality & Social Psychology, 32,* 880–892.

Rost, K., Zhang, M., Fortney, J., Smith, J., & Smith, R. (1998). Expenditures for the treatment of major depression. *American Journal of Psychiatry, 155,* 883–888.

Rothbaum, B. O. (1992). The behavioral treatment of trichotillomania. *Behavioural Psychotherapy, 20,* 85–90.

Rothbaum, B. O., & Foa, E. B. (1991). Exposure treatment of PTSD concomitant with conversion mutism: A case study. *Behavior Therapy, 22,* 449–456.

Rothbaum, B. O., Foa, E. D., Riggs, D. S., & Murdock, T. (1992). A prospective examination of post-traumatic stress disorder in rape victims. *Journal of Traumatic Stress, 5,* 455–475.

Rotter, J. B. (1954). *Social learning and clinical psychology.* Englewood Cliffs, NJ: Prentice Hall.

Rounsaville, B. J. (1978). Theories in marital violence: Evidence from a study of battered women. *Victimology, 3,* 11–31.

Rovner, B., Steele, C., Shmuely, Y., & Folstein, M. F. (1996). A randomized trial of dementia care in nursing homes. *Journal of the American Geriatric Society, 44,* 7–13.

Rowse, A. L. (1969). *The early Churchills.* Middlesex: Penguin Books.

Roy, A. (1983). Family history of suicide. *Archives of General Psychiatry, 40,* 971–974.

Roy, A. (1992). Genetics, biology, and suicide in the family. In R. W. Maris, A. L. Berman, J. T. Maltsberger, & R. I. Yufit (Eds.), *Assessment and prediction of suicide* (pp. 574–588). New York: Guilford Press.

Roy, A. (1995). Suicide. In H. I. Kaplan & B. J. Sadock (Eds.), *Comprehensive textbook of psychiatry* (6th ed., pp. 1739–1752). Baltimore: William & Wilkins.

Roy, A., Segal, N. L., & Sarchiapone, M. (1995). Attempted suicide among living co-twins of twin suicide. *American Journal of Psychiatry, 152,* 1075–1076.

Roy-Byrne, P. P., & Katon, W. (1997). Generalized anxiety disorder in primary care: The precursor/modifier pathway to increased health care utilization. *Journal of Clinical Psychiatry, 58* (Suppl. 3), 34–40.

Rubin, K. H., Daniels-Beirness, T., & Hayvren, M. (1982). Social and social-cognitive correlates of sociometric status in preschool and kindergarten children. *Canadian Journal of Behavioural Science, 14,* 338–349.

Rubinow, D. R., & Schmidt, P. J. (1989). Models for the development and expression of symptoms of premenstrual disorder. *Psychiatric Clinics of North America, 12,* 653–681.

Russell, D. E. H. (1982). *Rape in marriage.* New York: MacMillan.

Rutherford, M. J., Alterman, A. I., Cacciola, J. S., & Snider, E. C. (1995). Gender differences in diagnosing antisocial personality disorder in methadone patients. *American Journal of Psychiatry, 152,* 1309–1316.

Rutherford, M. J., Cacciola, J. S., Alterman, A. I., & McKay, J. R. (1996). Reliability and validity of the Revised Psychopathy Checklist in women methadone patients. *Assessment, 3,* 145–156.

Rutter, M. (1987). Temperament, personality and personality disorder. *British Journal of Psychiatry, 150,* 443–458.

Rutter, M. (1997). Antisocial behavior: Developmental psychopathology perspectives. In D. M. Stoff, J. Breiling, & J. D. Maser (Eds.), *Handbook of antisocial personality disorder* (pp. 115–124). New York: Wiley.

Rutter, M., Bolton, P., Harrington, R., & Couteur, A. I. (1990). Genetic factors in child psychiatric disorder: I. A review of research strategies. *Journal of Child Psychology & Psychiatry & Allied Disciplines, 31,* 3–37.

Rutter, M., MacDonald, H., Couteur, A. L., Harrington, R., Bolton, P., & Bailey, A. (1990). Genetic factors in child psychiatric disorders—II. Empirical findings. *Journal of Child Psychology & Psychiatry, 31,* 39–83.

Rutter, M., Tizard, J., & Whitmore, K. (Eds.). (1970). *Education, health, and behavior.* London: Longmans.

S

Sabol, S. Z., Nelson, M. L., Fisher, C., Gunzerath, L., Brody, C. L., Hu, S., Sirota, L. A., Marcus, S. E., Greenberg, B. D., Lucas, F. R., Benjamin, J., Murphy, D. L., & Hamer, D. H. (1999). A genetic association for cigarette smoking behavior. *Health Psychology, 18,* 7–13.

Sabri, O., Erkwoh, R., Schreckenberger, M., Owega, A., Sass, H., & Buell, U. (1997). Correlation of positive symptoms exclusively to hyperfusion or hypoperfusion of cerebral cortex in never-treated schizophrenics. *Lancet, 349,* 1735–1739.

Sacco, W. P., & Beck, A. T. (1995). Cognitive theory and therapy. In E. E. Beckham & W. R. Leber (Eds.), *Handbook of depression* (2nd ed., pp. 329–351). New York: Guilford.

Salkovskis, P. M. (1989). Cognitive-behavioral factors and the persistence of intrusive thoughts in obsessional problems. *Behaviour Research & Therapy, 27,* 677–682.

Salkovskis, P. M., Westbrook, D., Davis, J., Jeavons, A., & Gledhill, A. (1997). Effects of neutralizing on intrusive thoughts: An experiment investigating the etiology of obsessive-compulsive disorder. *Behaviour Research & Therapy, 35,* 211–219.

Salzman, C. (1999). Treatment of the suicidal patient with psychotropic drugs and ECT. In D. G. Jacobs (Ed.), *The Harvard Medical School guide to suicide assessment and intervention* (pp. 372–382). San Francisco: Jossey-Bass.

Salzman, C., Wolfson, A. N., Schatzberg, A., Looper, J., Henke, R., Albanese, M., Swartz, J., & Miyawaki, E. (1995). Effect of fluoxetine on anger in symptomatic volunteers with borderline personality disorder. *Journal of Clinical Psychopharmacology, 15,* 23–29.

Salzman, L. (1980). *Psychotherapy of the obsessive personality.* New York: Jason Aronson.

Sameroff, A. J., & Seifer, R. (1995). Accumulation of environmental risk and child mental health. In H. E. Fitzgerald (Ed.), *Children of poverty: Research, health, and policy issues* (pp. 233–258). New York: Garland.

Sampath, G., Shah, A., Krska, J., & Soni, S. D. (1992). Neuroleptic discontinuation in the very stable schizophrenic patient: Relapse rates and serum neuroleptic levels. *Human Psychopharmacology Clinical & Experimental, 7,* 255–264.

Sampson, R. J., & Laub, J. H. (1992). Crime and deviance in the life course. *Annual Review of Sociology, 18,* 63–84.

Samuels, J., & Nestadt, G. (1997). Epidemiology and genetics of obsessive-compulsive disorder. *International Review of Psychiatry, 9,* 61–72.

Sanders, S. K., & Shekhar, A. (1995). Regulation of anxiety by GABA-sub(A) receptors in the rat amygdala. *Pharmacology, Biochemistry & Behavior, 52,* 701–706.

Sanderson, W. C., Rapee, R. M., & Barlow, D. H. (1989). The influence of illusion of control on panic attacks induced via inhalation of 5.5% carbon dioxide-enriched air. *Archives of General Psychology, 46,* 157–162.

Sano, M., Ernesto, C., Thomas, R. G., & Klauber, M. R. (1997). A controlled trial of selegiline, alpha-tocopherol, or both as treatment for Alzheimer's disease. *The New England Journal of Medicine, 336,* 1216–1222.

Sarason, I. G., Johnson, J. H., & Siegel, J. M. (1978). Assessing the impact of life changes: Development of the Life Experiences Survey. *Journal of Consulting & Clinical Psychology, 46,* 932–946.

Sarbin, T. R. (1990). Toward the obsolescence of the schizophrenia hypothesis. *Journal of Mind & Behavior, 11,* 259–283.

Sarbin, T. R., & Juhasz, J. B. (1967). The historical background of the concept of hallucination. *Journal of the History of the Behavioral Sciences, 3,* 339–358.

Sasson, A., Lewin, C., & Roth, D. (1995). Dieting behavior and eating attitudes in Israeli children. *International Journal of Eating Disorders, 17,* 67–72.

Satir, V. (1967). Family systems and approaches to family therapy. *Journal of the Fort Logan Mental Health Center, 4,* 81–93.

Saunders, D. G. (1992). A typology of men who batter: Three types derived from cluster analysis. *American Journal of Orthopsychiatry, 62,* 264–275.

Saxena, S., & Prasad, K. V. (1989). DSM-III subclassification of dissociative disorders applied to psychiatric outpatients in India. *American Journal of Psychiatry, 146,* 261–262.

Saxena, S., Brody, A. L., Schwartz, J. M., & Baxter, L. R. (1998). Neuroimaging and frontal-subcortical circuitry in obsessive-compulsive disorder. *British Journal of Psychiatry, 173* (Suppl. 35), 26–37.

Scafidi, F., & Field, T. (1996). Massage therapy improves behavior in neonates born to HIV positive mothers. *Journal of Pediatric Psychology, 21,* 889–898.

Scafidi, F., Field, T., Schanberg, S., Bauer, C., Tucci, K., Roberts, J., Morrow, C., & Kuhn, C. M. (1990). Massage stimulates growth in preterm infants: A replication. *Infant Behavior & Development, 13,* 167–168.

Scarr, S., Weinberg, R. A., & Waldman, I. D. (1993). IQ correlations in transracial adoptive families. *Intelligence, 17,* 541–555.

Schacter, D. L. (1999). The seven sins of memory. *American Psychologist, 54,* 182–203.

Schafer, W. (1992). *Stress management for wellness.* Fort Worth: Holt, Rinehart & Winston.

Scheff, T. J. (1966). *Being mentally ill: Sociological theory.* Chicago: Aldine.

Scheier, M. F., Matthews, K. A., Owens, J. F., Magovern, G. J., Lefebvre, R. C., Abbott, R. A., & Carver, C. S. (1989). Dispositional optimism and recovery from coronary artery surgery: The beneficial effects on physical and psychological well-being. *Journal of Personality & Social Psychology, 57,* 1024–1040.

Schiavi, R. C. (1990). Sexuality and aging in men. *Annual Review of Sex Research, 1,* 227–249.

Schiavi, R. C., & Segraves, R. T. (1995). The biology of sexual dysfunction. *Psychiatric Clinics of North America, 18,* 7–23.

Schiavi, R. C., Stimmel, B. B., Mandeli, J., & Schreiner-Engel, P. (1995). Diabetes, psychological functioning, and male sexuality. *Journal of Psychosomatic Research, 39,* 305–314.

Schiavi, R. C., White, D., Mandeli, J., & Levine, A. (1997). Effect of testosterone administration on sexual behavior and mood in men with erectile dysfunction. *Archives of Sexual Behavior, 26,* 231–241.

Schildkraut, J. J. (1965). The catecholamine hypothesis of affective disorder: A review of supporting evidence. *American Journal of Psychiatry, 122,* 509–522.

Schleifer, S. J., Keller, S. E., McKegney, F. P., & Stein, M. (1979). *The influence of stress and other psychosocial factors on human immunity.* Paper presented at the 36th Annual Meeting of the Psychosomatic Society, Dallas, TX.

Schlenger, W. E., Kulka, R. A., Fairbank, J. A., & Hough, R. L. (1992). The prevalence of post-traumatic stress disorder in the Vietnam generation: A multimethod, multisource assessment of psychiatric disorder. *Journal of Traumatic Stress, 5,* 333–363.

Schmechel, D. E., Saunders, A. M., & Strittmatter, W. J. (1993). Increased amyloid b-peptide deposition in cerebral cortex as a consequence of apolipoprotein E genotype in late-onset Alzheimer disease. *Proceedings of the National Academy of Science of the United States of America, 90,* 9649–9653.

Schmidt, N. B., & Telch, M. J. (1997). Nonpsychiatric medical comorbidity, health perceptions, and treatment outcome in patients with panic disorder. *Health Psychology, 16,* 114–122.

Schneider, J. A., O'Leary, A., & Jenkins, S. R. (1995). Gender, sexual orientation, and disordered eating. *Psychology & Health, 10,* 113–128.

Schneier, F. R., Johnson, J., Hornig, C. D., & Liebowitz, M. R. (1992). Social phobia: Comorbidity and morbidity in an epidemiologic sample. *Archives of General Psychiatry, 49,* 282–288.

Schnurr, P. P., Hurt, S. W., & Stout, A. L. (1994). Consequences and methodological decisions in the diagnosis of late luteal phase dysphoric disorder. In J. H. Gold (Ed.), *Premenstrual dysphorias: Myths and realities* (pp. 19–46). Washington, DC: American Psychiatric Press.

Schor, J. D., Levkoff, S. E., & Lipsitz, L. A. (1992). Risk factors for delirium in hospitalized elderly. *Journal of the American Medical Association, 267,* 827–831.

Schotte, D. E., & Stunkard, A. J. (1987). Bulimia vs. bulimic behaviors on a college campus. *JAMA: Journal of the American Medical Association, 258,* 1213–1215.

Schreibman, L., & Charlop-Christy, M. H. (1998). Autistic disorder. In T. H. Ollendick & M. Hersen (Eds.), *Handbook of child psychopathology* (pp. 157–180). New York: Plenum.

Schuckit, M. A. (1991). A longitudinal study of children of alcoholics. In Galanter, M. (Ed.), *Recent developments in alcoholism, Vol. 9. Children of alcoholics* (pp. 5–19). New York: Plenum.

Schuckit, M. A. (1995). *Drug and alcohol abuse: A clinical guide to diagnosis and treatment*. New York: Plenum Medical Book Company.

Schuckit, M. A. (1996). Recent developments in the pharmacotherapy of alcohol dependence. *Journal of Consulting & Clinical Psychology, 64*, 669–676.

Schuckit, M. A. (1998). Biological, psychological, and environmental predictors of the alcoholism risk: A longitudinal study. *Journal of Studies on Alcohol, 59*, 485–494.

Schuckit, M. A., & Smith, T. L. (1996). An 8-year follow-up of 450 sons of alcoholic and control subjects. *Archives of General Psychiatry, 53*, 202–211.

Schuckit, M. A., & Smith, T. L. (1997). Assessing the risk for alcoholism among sons of alcoholics. *Journal of Studies on Alcohol, 58*, 141–145.

Schuckit, M. A., Daeppen, J. B., Tipp, J. E., Hesselbrock, M., & Bucholz, K. K. (1998). The clinical course of alcohol-related problems in alcohol dependent and nonalcohol dependent drinking men and women. *Journal of Studies in Alcohol, 59*, 581–590.

Schuckit, M. A., Tip, J. E., Reich, T., & Hesselbrock, V. M. (1995). The histories of withdrawal convulsions and delirium tremens in 1648 alcohol dependent subjects. *Addiction, 90*, 1335–1347.

Schulberg, H. C., Pilkonis, P. A., & Houck, P. (1998). The severity of major depression and choice of treatment in primary care practice. *Journal of Consulting & Clinical Psychology, 66*, 932–938.

Schulz, R., Bookwala, J., Knapp, J. E., Scheier, M., & Williamson, G. M. (1996). Pessimism, age, and cancer mortality. *Psychology & Aging, 11*, 304–309.

Schur, E. M. (1971). *Labeling deviant behavior: Its sociological implications*. New York: Harper & Row.

Schwartz, J., Stoessel, P. W., Baxter, L. R., Martin, K. M., & Phelps, M. C. (1996). Systemic changes in cerebral glucose metabolic rate after successful behavior modification treatment of obsessive-compulsive disorder. *Archives of General Psychiatry, 53*, 109–113.

Schweizer, E., & Rickels, K. (1997). Strategies for the treatment of generalized anxiety disorder in the primary care setting. *Journal of Clinical Psychiatry, 58*, 27–33.

Scull, A. (1993). *The most solitary of afflictions*. New Haven: Yale University Press.

Sechehaye, M. (1951). *Autobiography of a schizophrenic girl*. New York: Grune & Stratton.

Segerstrom, S. C., Solomon, G. F., Kemeny, M. E., & Fahey, J. L. (1998). Relationship of worry to immune sequelae of the Northridge earthquake. *Journal of Behavioral Medicine, 21*, 433–450.

Segerstrom, S. C., Taylor, S. E., Kemeny, M. E., Reed, G. M., & Visscher, B. R. (1996). Causal attributions predict rate of immune decline in HIV-seropositive gay men. *Health Psychology, 15*, 485–493.

Segraves, K. B., & Segraves, R. T. (1991). Multiple-phase sexual dysfunction. *Journal of Sex Education & Therapy, 17*, 153–156.

Segraves, R. T., & Segraves, K. B. (1998). Pharmacotherapy for sexual disorders: Advantages and pitfalls. *Sexual & Marital Therapy, 13*, 295–309.

Seguin, J. R., Pihl, R. O., Harden, P. W., & Tremblay, R. E. (1995). Cognitive and neuropsychological characteristics of physically aggressive boys. *Journal of Abnormal Psychology, 104*, 614–624.

Seiden, R. H. (1969, December). *Suicide among youth: A review of the literature, 1900–1967* (NIMH Bulletin of Suicidology, PHS publication number 1971). Washington, DC: National Institute of Mental Health.

Seligman, M. (1970). On the generality of the laws of learning. *Psychological Review, 77*, 406–418.

Seligman, M. E. (1993). *What you can change and what you can't: The complete guide to self-improvement*. New York: Alfred A. Knopf.

Seligman, M. E., & Maier, S. F. (1967). Failure to escape traumatic shock. *Journal of Experimental Psychology, 74*, 1–9.

Seligman, M. E. P. (1975). *Helplessness: On depression, development, and death*. San Francisco: Freeman, Cooper.

Seligman, M. E. P. (1995). The effectiveness of psychotherapy: The *Consumer Reports* study. *American Psychologist, 50*, 965–974.

Seligman, M. E. P. (1996). A creditable beginning. *American Psychologist, 51*, 1086–1088.

Seligman, M. E. P., & Binik, Y. M. (1977). The safety signal hypothesis. In H. Davis & H. Hurwitz (Eds.), *Pavlovian operant interactions*. Hillsdale, NJ: Erlbaum.

Selkoe, D. (1992). Aging brains, aging mind. *Scientific American, 267*, 134–142.

Selling, L. H. (1940). *Men against madness*. New York: Greenberg.

Selye, H. (1979). *The stress of life*. New York: McGraw-Hill.

Semans, J. (1956). Premature ejaculation. *Southern Medical Journal, 49*, 352–358.

Shadish, W. R., Montgomery, L. M., Wilson, P., Wilson, M. R., Bright, I., & Okwumabua, T. (1993). Effects of family and marital psychotherapies: A meta-analysis. *Journal of Consulting & Clinical Psychology, 61*, 992–1002.

Shaffer, D., Gould, M. S., Fisher, P., Moreau, D., Kleinman, M., & Flory, M. (1996). Psychiatric diagnosis in child and adolescent suicide. *Archives of General Psychiatry, 53*, 339–348.

Shalev, A. Y., Peri, T., Canetti, L., & Schreiber, S. (1996). Predictors of PTSD in injured trauma survivors: A prospective study. *American Journal of Psychiatry, 153*, 219–225.

Shapiro, D. (1965). *Neurotic styles*. New York: Basic Books.

Shapiro, F. (1995). *Eye movement desensitization and reprocessing: Basic principles, protocols, and procedures*. New York: Guilford Press.

Sharma, T., Lancaster, E., Lee, D., Lewis, S., Sigmundsson, T., Takei, N., Gurling, H., Barta, P., Pearlson, G., & Murray, R. (1998). Brain changes in schizophrenia: Volumetric MRI study of families multiply affected with schizophrenia—the Maudsley Family Study 5. *British Journal of Psychiatry, 173*, 132–138.

Shaw, D. S., & Winslow, E. B. (1997). Precursors and correlates of antisocial behavior from infancy to preschool. In D. M. Stoff, J. Breiling, & J. D. Maser (Eds.), *Handbook of antisocial personality disorder* (pp. 148–158). New York: Wiley.

Shaw, D. S., Keenan, K., & Vondra, J. I. (1994). Developmental precursors of externalizing behavior: Ages 1 to 3. *Developmental Psychology, 30*, 355–364.

Shea, M. T. (1993). Psychosocial treatment of personality disorders. *Journal of Personality Disorders* (Spr. Suppl.), 167–180.

Shea, M. T., Elkin, I., Imber, S. D., & Sotsky, S. M. (1992). Course of depressive symptoms over follow-up: Findings from the National Institute of Mental Health Treatment of Depression Collaborative Research Program. *Archives of General Psychiatry, 49*, 782–787.

Sheard, M. H., Marini, J. L., Bridges, C. I., & Wagner, E. (1976). The effect of lithium on impulsive aggressive behavior in man. *American Journal of Psychiatry, 133*, 1409–1413.

Shearin, E. N., & Linehan, M. M. (1989). Dialectics and behavior therapy: A metaparadoxical approach to the treatment of borderline personality disorder. In L. M. Ascher (Ed.), *Therapeutic paradox* (pp. 255–288). New York: Guilford Press.

Sheikh, J. I. (1992). Anxiety and its disorders in old age. In J. E. Birren, K. Sloan, & G. D. Cohen (Eds.), *Handbook of mental health and aging* (pp. 410–432). New York: Academic Press.

Sher, K. J., & Trull, T. J. (1994). Personality and disinhibitory psychopathology: Alcoholism and antisocial personality disorder. *Journal of Abnormal Psychology, 103*, 92–102.

Sherrington, R., Rogaev, E. I., & Liang, Y. (1995). Cloning of a gene bearing missense mutations in early-onset familial Alzheimer's disease. *Nature, 375*, 754–760.

Sherwin, B. B. (1991). The psychoendocrinology of aging and female sexuality. *Annual Review of Sex Research, 2*, 191–198.

Shin, L. M., Kosslyn, S. M., McNally, R. J., Alpert, N. M., Thompson, W. L., Rauch, S. L., Macklin, M. L., & Pitman, R. K. (1997). Visual imagery and perception in posttraumatic stress disorder: A positron emission tomographic investigation. *Archives of General Psychiatry, 54*, 233–241.

Shneidman, E. (1976). *Suicidology: Contemporary developments*. New York: Grune & Stratton.

Shneidman, E. S. (1963). Orientations toward death: Subintentioned death and indirect suicide. In R. W. White (Ed.), *The study of lives*. New York: Atherton.

Shneidman, E. S. (1979). A bibliography of suicide notes: 1856–1979. *Suicide & Life-Threatening Behavior, 9*, 57–59.

Shneidman, E. S. (1981). Suicide. *Suicide & Life-Threatening Behavior, 11*, 198–220.

Shneidman, E. S. (1993). *Suicide as psychache: A clinical approach to self-destructive behavior*. Northvale, NJ: Jason Aronson.

Shrestha, N. M., Sharma, B., Van Ommeren, M., Regmi, S., Makaju, R., Komproe, I., Shrestha, G. B., & de Jong, J. T. V. M. (1998). Impact of torture on refugees displaced within the developing world. *Journal of the American Medical Association, 280*, 443–448.

Shrout, P. E., Canino, G. J., Bird, H. R., & Rubio-Stipec, M. (1992). Mental health status among Puerto Ricans, Mexican Americans, and non-Hispanic whites. *American Journal of Community Psychology, 20*, 729–752.

Shuchter, S. R., & Zisook, S. (1993). The course of normal grief. In M. S. Stroebe (Ed.), *Handbook of bereavement: Theory, research, and intervention* (pp. 23–43). New York: Cambridge University Press.

Siever, L. J., & Davis, K. L. (1991). A psychobiological perspective on the personality disorders. *American Journal of Psychiatry, 148*, 1647–1658.

Siever, L. J., & Kendler, K. S. (1985). Paranoid personality disorder. In R. Michels, J. Cavenar, & H. Bradley (Eds.), *Psychiatry, Vol. 1. The personality disorders and neuroses* (pp. 1–11). New York: Basic Books.

Siever, L. J., Bernstein, D. P., & Silverman, J. M. (1995). Schizotypal personality disorder. In W. J. Livesley (Ed.), *The DSM-IV personality disorders* (pp. 71–90). New York: Guilford Press.

Siever, L. J., Keefe, R., Bernstein, D. P., & Coccaro, E. F. (1990). Eye tracking impairment in clinically identified patients with schizotypal personality disorder. *American Journal of Psychiatry, 147*, 740–745.

Siever, L. J., New, A. S., Kirrane, R., Novotny, S., Koenigsberg, H., & Grossman, R. (1998). New biological research strategies for personality disorders. In K. R. Silk (Ed.), *Biology of personality disorders* (pp. 27–61). Washington, DC: American Psychiatric Press.

Silver, E., Cirincione, C., & Steadman, H. J. (1994). Demythologizing inaccurate perceptions of the insanity defense. *Law & Human Behavior, 18*, 63–70.

Silver, R. L., & Wortman, C. B. (1980). Coping with undesirable life events. In J. Garber & M. E. P. Seligman (Eds.), *Human helplessness: Theory and applications* (pp. 279–375). New York: Academic Press.

Silver, R. L., Boon, C., & Stones, M. H. (1983). Searching for meaning in misfortune: Making sense of incest. *Journal of Social Issues, 39,* 81–101.

Silverman, W. K., & Ginsburg, G. S. (1995). Specific phobia and generalized anxiety disorder. In D. P. Cantwell (Ed.), *Anxiety disorders in children and adolescents* (pp. 151–180). New York: Guilford Press.

Silverman, W. K., & Ginsburg, G. S. (1998). Anxiety disorders. In T. H. Ollendick & M. Hersen (Eds.), *Handbook of child psychopathology* (pp. 239–268). New York: Plenum.

Simmons, R. G., & Blyth, D. A. (1987). *Moving into adolescence: The impact of pubertal change and school context.* Hawthorne, NY: Aldine De Gruyter.

Simonoff, E., Bolton, P., & Rutter, M. (1998). Genetic perspectives on mental retardation. In J. A. Burack, R. M. Hodapp, & E. Zigler (Eds.), *Handbook of mental retardation and development* (pp. 41–79). New York: Cambridge University Press.

Simons, J. A., & Helms, J. E. (1976). Influence of counselors' marital status, sex, and age on college and noncollege women's counselor preferences. *Journal of Counseling Psychology, 23,* 380–386.

Simopoulos, A. P. (1998). *The omega plan: The medically proven diet that restores your body's essential nutritional balance.* New York: Harper Collins.

Sing, L. (1995). Self-starvation in context: Towards a culturally sensitive understanding of anorexia nervosa. *Social Science & Medicine, 41,* 25–36.

Singer, M. T., & Wynne, L. C. (1965). Thought disorder and family relations of schizophrenics: IV. Results and implications. *Archives of General Psychiatry, 12,* 201–212.

Singh, N. N., Oswald, D. P., & Ellis, C. R. (1998). Mental retardation. In T. H. Ollendick & M. Hersen (Eds.), *Handbook of child psychopathology* (pp. 91–116). New York: Plenum.

Sipahimalani, A., & Masand, P. S. (1998). Olanzapine in the treatment of delirium. *Psychosomatics, 39,* 422–430.

Slater, L. (1998). *Prozac diary* (1st ed.). New York: Random House.

Slijper, F. M. E., Drop, S. L. S., Molenaar, J. C., & de Munick Keizer-Schrama, S. M. P. F. (1998). Long-term psychological evaluation of intersex children. *Archives of Sexual Behavior, 27,* 125–144.

Sloan, J. H., Rivara, F. P., Reay, D. T., Ferris, J. A., Path, M. R. C., & Kellerman, A. L. (1990). Firearm regulations and rates of suicide: A comparison of two metropolitan areas. *The New England Journal of Medicine, 322,* 369–373.

Small, G. W. (1998). The pathogenesis of Alzheimer's disease. *Journal of Clinical Psychiatry, 59,* 7–14.

Smith, D. E., & Seymour, R. B. (1994). LSD: History and toxicity. *Psychiatric Annals, 24,* 145–147.

Smith, H. (1995). *Unhappy children: Reasons and remedies.* London: Free Association Books.

Smith, M. L., Glass, G. V., & Miller, T. I. (1980). *The benefits of psychotherapy.* Baltimore: The Johns Hopkins University Press.

Smith, T. W., Turner, C. W., Ford, M. H., & Hunt, S. C. (1987). Blood pressure reactivity in adult male twins. *Health Psychology, 6,* 209–220.

Snowden, D. A., Kemper, S. J., Mortimer, J. A., Greiner, L. H., Wekstein, D. R., & Markesbery, W. R. (1996). Linguistic ability in early life and cognitive function and Alzheimer's disease in late life. *Journal of the American Medical Association, 275,* 528–532.

Snowden, L. R., & Cheung, F. K. (1990). Use of inpatient mental health services by members of ethnic minority groups. *American Psychologist, 45,* 347–355.

Sobal, J., & Stunkard, A. J. (1989). Socioeconomic status and obesity: A review of the literature. *Psychological Bulletin, 105,* 260–275.

Sobell, M. B., & Sobell, L. C. (1978). *Behavioral treatment of alcohol problems.* New York: Plenum.

Sobell, M. B., & Sobell, L. C. (1984). The aftermath of heresy: A response to Pendery et al.'s (1982) critique of "Individualized behavior therapy for alcoholics." *Behavior Research & Therapy, 22,* 413–440.

Sobell, M. B., & Sobell, L. C. (1995). Controlled drinking after 25 years: How important was the great debate? *Addiction, 90,* 1145–1153.

Soloff, P. H., Cornelius, J., George, A., Nathan, S., Perel, J. M., & Ulrich, R. F. (1993). Efficacy of phenelzine and haloperidol in borderline personality disorder. *Archives of General Psychiatry, 50,* 377–385.

Soloff, P. H., George, A., Nathan, R. S., & Schulz, P. M. (1989). Amitriptyline versus haloperidol in borderlines: Final outcomes and predictors of response. 140th Annual Meeting of the American Psychiatric Association (1987, Chicago). *Journal of Clinical Psychopharmacology, 9,* 238–246.

Solomon, G. F., Segerstrom, S. C., Grohr, P., Kemeny, M., & Fahey, J. (1997). Shaking up immunity: Psychological and immunologic changes following a natural disaster. *Psychosomatic Medicine, 59,* 114–127.

Solomon, K., & Hart, R. (1978). Pitfalls and prospects in clinical research on antianxiety drugs: Benzodiazepines and placebo: A research review. *Journal of Clinical Psychiatry, 39,* 823–831.

Solomon, R. L. (1980). The opponent-process theory of acquired motivation: The costs of pleasure and the benefits of pain. *American Psychologist, 35,* 691–712.

Southham-Gerow, M. A., & Kendall, P. C. (1997). Parent-focused and cognitive-behavioral treatments of antisocial youth. In D. M. Stoff, J. Breiling, & J. D. Maser (Eds.), *Handbook of antisocial personality disorder* (pp. 384–394). New York: Wiley.

Southwick, S. M., Bremner, D., Krystal, J. H., & Charney, D. S. (1994). Psychobiologic research in post-traumatic stress disorder. *Psychiatric Clinics of North America, 17,* 251–264.

Southwick, S. M., Yehuda, R., & Wang, S. (1998). Neuroendocrine alterations in posttraumatic stress disorder. *Psychiatric Annals, 28,* 436–442.

Sowers, W. (1998). Psychological and psychiatric consequences of sedatives, hypnotics, and anxiolytics. In R. E. Tarter (Ed.), *Handbook of substance abuse: Neurobehavioral pharmacology* (pp. 471–483). New York: Plenum.

Spanos, N. P. (1978). Witchcraft in histories of psychiatry: A critical analysis and an alternative conceptualization. *Psychological Bulletin, 85,* 417–439.

Spanos, N. P., Weekes, J. R., & Bertrand, L. D. (1985). Multiple personality: A social psychological perspective. *Journal of Abnormal Psychology, 94,* 362–376.

Speckens, A. E., Hengeveld, M. W., Nijeholt, G. L., & Van Hemert, A. M. (1995). Psychosexual functioning of partners of men with presumed non-organic erectile dysfunction: Causes or consequences of the disorder? *Archives of Sexual Behavior, 24,* 157–172.

Spector, I. P., & Carey, M. P. (1990). Incidence and prevalence of the sexual dysfunctions: A critical review of the empirical literature. *Archives of Sexual Behavior, 19,* 389–408.

Spiegel, D. (1991). Dissociation and trauma. In A. Tasman (Ed.), *American Psychiatric Press review of psychiatry* (Vol. 10, pp. 261–275). Washington, DC: American Psychiatric Press.

Spiegel, D. (1996). Cancer and depression. *British Journal of Psychiatry, 168,* 109–116.

Spiegel, D., Bollm, J. R., Kraemer, H. C., & Gottheil, E. (1989). Psychological support for cancer patients. *Lancet, II,* 1447.

Spiegel, D. A. (1998). Efficacy studies of alprazolam in panic disorder. *Psychopharmacology Bulletin, 43,* 191–195.

Spiegel, D. A., Bruce, T. J., Gregg, S. F. & Nuzzarello, A. (1994). Does cognitive behavior therapy assist slow-taper alprazolam discontinuation in panic disorder? *American Journal of Psychiatry, 151,* 876–881.

Spielman, A. J., Saskin, P., & Thorpy, M. J. (1987). Treatment of chronic insomnia by restriction of time in bed. *Sleep, 10,* 45–56.

Spierings, C., Poels, P. J., Sijben, N., Gabreels, F. J., & Renier, W. O. (1990). Conversion disorders in childhood: A retrospective follow-up study of 84 inpatients. *Developmental Medicine & Child Neurology, 32,* 865–871.

Spitzer, R. L. (1981). The diagnostic status of homosexuality in DSM-III: A reformulation of the issues. *American Journal of Psychiatry, 138,* 210–215.

Spitzer, R. L., & Williams, J. B. W., Gibbon, M., & First, M. (1992). The Structured Clinical Interview for DSM-III-R (SCID): I. History, rationale, and description. *Archives of General Psychiatry, 49,* 624–636.

Spitzer, R. L., Devlin, M., Walsh, B. T., Hasin, D., Wing, R., Marcus, M., Stunkard, A., Wadden, T., Yanovski, S., Agras, S., Mitchell, J., & Nonas, C. (1992). A multisite field trial of the diagnostic criteria. *International Journal of Eating Disorders, 11,* 191–203.

Spitzer, R. L., Gibbon, M., Skodol, A. E., Williams, J. B. W., & First, M. B. (Eds.). (1994). *DSM-IV case book: A learning companion to the Diagnostic and Statistical Manual of Mental Disorders, Fourth Edition.* Washington, DC: American Psychiatric Association Press.

Spitzer, R. L., Skodol, A. E., Gibbon, M., & Williams, J. B. W. (1981). *DSM-III case book: A learning companion to the Diagnostic and Statistical Manual of Mental Disorders* (3rd ed.). Washington, DC: American Psychiatric Association.

Spitzer, R. L., Skodol, A. E., Gibbon, M., & Williams, J. B. W. (1983). *Psychopathology, a case book.* New York: McGraw-Hill.

Spitzer, R. L., Williams, J. B. W., & Gibbon, M. (1987). *Structured clinical interview for DSM-III-R—Non-patient version (SCID-NP4/1/87).* New York: New York State Psychiatric Institute.

Spivack, G., & Shure, M. B. (1974). *Social adjustment of young children: A cognitive approach to solving real-life problems.* San Francisco, CA: Jossey-Bass.

Sprich-Buckminster, S., Biederman, J., Milberger, S., & Faraone, S. V. (1993). Are perinatal complications relevant to the manifestation of ADD? Issues of comorbidity and familiality. *Journal of the American Academy of Child & Adolescent Psychiatry, 32,* 1032–1037.

Sprock, J., Balshfield, R. K., & Smith, B. (1990). Gender weighting of DSM-III-R personality disorder criteria. *American Journal of Psychiatry, 147,* 586–590.

St. George-Hyslop, P. H., Tanzi, R. E., Polinsky, R. J., Haines, J. L., Nee, L., Watkins, P. C., & Meyers, R. H. (1987). The genetic defect causing familial Alzheimer's disease maps on chromosome 21. *Science, 235,* 885–890.

Stack, S. (1987). Celebrities and suicide: A taxonomy and analysis, 1948–1983. *American Sociological Review, 52*, 401–412.

Stack, S. (1991). Social correlates of suicide by age: Media impacts. In A. A. Leenaars (Ed.), *Life span perspectives of suicide* (pp. 187–213). New York: Plenum.

Stahl, S. M. (1998). Basic psychopharmacology of antidepressants: Part 1. Antidepressants have seven distinct mechanisms of action. *Journal of Clinical Psychiatry 59* (Suppl. 4), 5–14.

Stark, L. J., Opipari, L. C., Donaldson, D. L., Danovsky, M. B., Rasile, D. A., & DelSanto, A. F. (1997). Evaluation of a standard protocol for retentive encopresis: A replication. *Journal of Pediatric Psychology, 22*, 619–633.

Statham, D. J., Heath, A. C., Madden, P., Bucholz, K., Bierut, L., Dinwiddie, S. H., Slutske, W. S., Dunne, M. P., & Martin, N. G. (1998). Suicidal behavior: An epidemiological study. *Psychological Medicine, 28*, 839–855.

Stattin, H., & Magnusson, D. (1990). *Paths through life. Volume 2: Pubertal maturation in female development.* Hillsdale, NJ: Erlbaum.

Steadman, H. J., McGreevy, M. A., Morrissey, J. P., Callahan, L. A., Robbins, P. C., & Cirincione, C. (1993). *Before and after Hinckley: Evaluating insanity defense reform.* New York: Guilford Press.

Steadman, H. J., Mulvey, E. P., Monahan, J., Robbins, P. C., Applebaum, P. S., Grisso, T., Roth, L., & Silver, E. (1998). Violence by people discharged from acute psychiatric inpatient facilities and by others in the same neighborhoods. *Archives of General Psychiatry, 55*, 393–401.

Stein, M. D., O'Sullivan, P. S., Ellis, P., Perrin, H., et al. (1993). Utilization of medical services by drug abusers in detoxification. *Journal of Substance Abuse, 5*, 187–193.

Steinberg, M. (1990). Transcultural issues in psychiatry: The ataque and multiple personality disorder. *Dissociation: Progress in the Dissociative Disorders, 3*, 31–33.

Stengel, E. (1974). *Suicide and attempted suicide.* New York: Jason Aronson.

Stern, Y., Gurland, B., Tatemichi, T. K., & Tang, M. X. (1994). Influence of education and occupation on the incidence of Alzheimer's disease. *Journal of the American Medical Association, 271*, 1004–1010.

Sternberg, R. J. (1988). *The triarchic mind: A new theory of human intelligence.* New York: Viking Press.

Stevenson, H. W., Chen, C., & Lee, S. (1993). Motivation and achievement of gifted children in East Asia and the United States. *Journal for the Education of the Gifted, 16*, 223–250.

Stewart, S. H. (1996). Alcohol abuse in individuals exposed to trauma: A critical review. *Psychological Bulletin, 120*, 83–112.

Stoller, R. F. (1975). *Perversion: The erotic form of hatred.* New York: Pantheon Books.

Storr, A. (1988). *Churchill's black dog, Kafka's mice, and other phenomena of the human mind.* New York: Grove Press.

Strack, S., & Lorr, M. (Eds.). (1994). *Differentiating normal and abnormal personality.* New York: Springer.

Straus, M. A., & Gelles, R. J. (1990). *Physical violence in American families: Risk factors and adaptations to violence in 8,145 families.* New Brunswick, NJ: Transaction.

Strauss, J., & Ryan, R. M. (1987). Autonomy disturbances in subtypes of anorexia nervosa. *Journal of Abnormal Psychology, 96*, 254–258.

Strauss, J. S. (1969). Hallucinations and delusions as points on continua function: Rating scale evidence. *Archives of General Psychiatry, 21*, 581–586.

Stravynski, A., Marks, I., & Yule, W. (1982). Social skills problems in neurotic outpatients: Social skills training with and without cognitive modification. *Archives of General Psychiatry, 39*, 1378–1385.

Strawbridge, W. J., Cohen, R. D., Shema, S. J., & Kaplan, G. A. (1997). Frequent attendance at religious services and mortality over 28 years. *American Journal of Public Health, 87*, 957–961.

Streissguth, A. P., Barr, H. M., Bookstein, F. L., Sampson, P. D., & Olson, H. C. (1999). The long-term neurocognitive consequences of prenatal alcohol exposure: A 14-year study. *Psychological Science, 10*, 186–190.

Streissguth, A. P., Randels, S. P., & Smith, D. F. (1991). A test-retest study of intelligence in patients with fetal alcohol syndrome: Implications for care. *Journal of the American Academy of Child & Adolescent Psychiatry, 30*, 584–587.

Striegel-Moore, R. (1995). Psychological factors in the etiology of binge eating. *Addictive Behaviors, 20*, 713–723.

Striegel-Moore, R. H. (1993). Etiology of binge eating: A developmental perspective. In C. G. Fairburn & G. T. Wilson (Eds.), *Binge eating: Nature, assessment, and treatment* (pp. 144–172). New York: Guilford Press.

Striegel-Moore, R. H., Silberstein, L. R., & Rodin, J. (1993). The social self in bulimia nervosa: Public self-consciousness, social anxiety, and perceived fraudulence. *Journal of Abnormal Psychology, 102*, 297–303.

Striegel-Moore, R., Wilson, G. T., Wilfley, D. E., Elder, K. A., & Brownell, K. D. (1998). Binge eating in an obese community sample. *International Journal of Eating Disorders, 23*, 27–37.

Strober, M. (1981). The significance of bulimia in juvenile anorexia nervosa: An exploration of possible etiologic factors. *International Journal of Eating Disorders, 1*, 28–43.

Strober, M. (1986). Anorexia nervosa: History and psychological concepts. In K. D. Brownell & J. P. Foreyt (Eds.), *Handbook of eating disorders* (pp. 231–246). New York: Basic Books.

Strober, M. (1991). Family-genetic studies of eating disorders. Annual Meeting of the American Psychiatric Association Symposium: Recent advances in bulimia nervosa (1991, New Orleans, Louisiana). *Journal of Clinical Psychiatry, 52* (Suppl.), 9–12.

Stroebe, M., Gergen, M., Gergen, K., & Stroebe, W. (1992). Broken hearts or broken bonds: Love and death in historical perspective. *American Psychologist, 47*, 1205–1212.

Study Group on Anorexia Nervosa. (1995). Anorexia nervosa: Directions for future research. *International Journal of Eating Disorders, 17*, 235–241.

Stunkard, A. (1997). Eating disorders: The last 25 years. *Appetite, 29*, 181–190.

Stunkard, A. J. (1993). A history of binge eating. In C. G. Fairburn & G. T. Wilson (Eds.), *Binge eating: Nature, assessment, and treatment* (pp. 15–34). New York: Guilford Press.

Stunkard, A. J., & Smoller, J. W. (1996, January). Does dieting cause depression? *The Harvard Mental Health Letter, 8.*

Styron, W. (1990). *Darkness visible: A memoir of madness.* New York: Vintage Books.

Su, T., Schmidt, P., Danaceau, M., Tobin, M., Rosenstein, D. L., Murphy, D. L., & Rubinow, D. (1997). Fluoxetine in the treatment of premenstrual dysphoria. *Neuropsychopharmacology, 16*, 346–356.

Suddath, R. L., Christison, G. W., Torrey, E. F., & Casanova, M. F. (1990). Anatomical abnormalities in the brains of monozygotic twins discordant for schizophrenia. *New England Journal of Medicine, 322*, 789–794.

Sue, D. W., & Sue, D. (1990). *Counseling the culturally different: Theory and practice* (2nd ed.). New York: Wiley.

Sue, D. W., & Sue, D. (1999). *Counseling the culturally different: Theory and practice* (3rd ed.). New York: Wiley.

Sue, D. W., Carter, R. T., Casas, J. M., Fouad, N. A., Ivey, A. E., Jensen, M., LaFromboise, T., Manese, J. E., Ponterotto, J. G., & Vazquez-Nutall, E. (1998). *Multicultural counseling competencies: Individual and organizational development.* Thousand Oaks, CA: Sage.

Sue, S. (1998). In search of cultural competence in psychotherapy and counseling. *American Psychologist, 53*, 440–448.

Sue, S., & Zane, N. (1987). The role of culture and cultural techniques in psychotherapy: A critique and reformulation. *American Psychologist, 42*, 37–51.

Sugarman, D. B., & Hotaling, G. T. (1989). Dating violence: Prevalence, context, and risk markers. In M. A. Pirog-Good & J. E. Stets (Eds.), *Violence in dating relationships: Emerging social issues* (pp. 3–32). New York: Praeger.

Sullivan, H. S. (1953). *The interpersonal theory of psychiatry.* New York: Norton.

Sullivan, P. F., Bulik, C. M., & Kendler, K. S. (1998). Genetic epidemiology of bingeing and vomiting. *British Journal of Psychiatry, 173*, 75–79.

Sullivan, P. F., Bulik, C. M., Fear, J. L., & Pickering, A. (1998). Outcome of anorexia nervosa: A case-control study. *American Journal of Psychiatry, 155*, 939–946.

Sundgot-Borgen, J. (1994). Risk and trigger factors for the development of eating disorders in female elite athletes. *Medicine & Science in Sports & Exercise, 26*, 414–419.

Suomi, S. J. (1999). Developmental trajectories, early experiences, and community consequences: Lessons from studies with rhesus monkeys. In D. P. Keating (Ed.), *Developmental health and the wealth of nations: Social, biological, and educational dynamics* (pp. 185–200). New York: Guilford Press.

Sutker, P. B., Allain, A. N., & Winstead, D. K. (1993). Psychopathology and psychiatric diagnoses of World War II Pacific theater prisoners of war and combat veterans. *American Journal of Psychiatry, 150*, 240–245.

Sutker, P. B., Davis, J. M., Uddo, M., & Ditta, S. R. (1995). Assessment of psychological distress in Persian Gulf troops: Ethnicity and gender comparisons. *Journal of Personality Assessment, 64*, 415–427.

Sutker, P. B., Winstead, D. K., Galina, Z. H., & Allain, A. N. (1991). Cognitive deficits and psychopathology among former prisoners of war and combat veterans of the Korean conflict. *American Journal of Psychiatry, 148*, 67–72.

Swanson, J., Borum, R., Swartz, M., & Monahan, J. (1996). Psychotic symptoms and disorders and the risk of violent behavior in the community. *Criminal Behaviour & Mental Health, 6*, 309–329.

Swanson, J., Holzer, C., Ganju, V., & Jono, R. (1990). Violence and psychiatric disorder in the community: Evidence from the Epidemiologic Catchment Area Surveys. *Hospital and Community Psychiatry, 41*, 761–770.

Swartz, C. (1995). Setting the ECT stimulus. *Psychiatric Times, 12*(6). (Reprint addition)

Swartz, M., Blazer, D., George, L., & Winfield, I. (1990). Estimating the prevalence of borderline personality disorder in the community. *Journal of Personality Disorders, 4*, 257–272.

Swazey, J. P. (1974). *Chlorpromazine in psychiatry: A study of therapeutic innovation.* Cambridge, MA: MIT Press.

Swedo, S. E., Pietrini, P., Leonard, H. L., Schapiro, M. B., Rettew, D. C., Goldberger, E. L., Rapoport, S. I., Rapoport, J. L., & Grody, C. L. (1992). Cerebral glucose metabolism in childhood-onset obsessive-compulsive disorder: Revisualization during pharmacotherapy. *Archives of General Psychiatry, 49*, 690–694.

Sweeting, H. (1995). Reversals of fortune? Sex differences in health in childhood and adolescence. *Social Science & Medicine, 40*, 77–90.

Swendsen, J. D., Merikangas, K. R., Canino, G. J., Kessler, R. C., Rubio-Stipec, M., & Angst, J. (1998). The comorbidity of alcoholism with anxiety and depressive disorders in four geographic communities. *Comprehensive Psychiatry, 39*, 176–184.

Szasz, T. (1961). *The myth of mental illness.* New York: Hoeber-Harper.

Szasz, T. S. (1963). *Law, liberty, and psychiatry: An inquiry into the social uses of mental health practice.* New York: Collier Books.

Szasz, T. S. (1963). *The manufacture of madness.* New York: Harper & Row.

Szasz, T. S. (1971). The sane slave: An historical note on the use of medical diagnosis as justificatory rhetoric. *American Journal of Psychotherapy, 25*, 228–239.

Szasz, T. S. (1977). *Psychiatric slavery.* New York: Free Press.

Szatmari, P., Bartolucci, G., Bremner, R., & Bond, S. (1989). A follow-up study of high-functioning autistic children. *Journal of Autism & Developmental Disorders, 19*, 213–225.

Szatmari, P., Jones, M. B., Zwaigenbaum, L., & MacLean, J. E. (1998). Genetics of autism? Overview and new directions. *Journal of Autism & Developmental Disorders, 28*, 351–368.

Szmukler, G. I., & Russell, G. F. M. (1986). Bulimia: Medical and physiological aspects. In K. D. Brownell & J. P. Foreyt (Eds.), *Handbook of eating disorders* (pp. 283–300). New York: Basic Books.

T

Takahashi, Y. (1990). Is multiple personality disorder really rare in Japan? *Dissociation: Progress in the Dissociative Disorders, 3*, 57–59.

Takei, N., Kunugi, H., Nanko, S., Aoki, H., Iyo, R., & Kazamatsuri, H. (1994). Low serum cholesterol and suicide attempts. *British Journal of Psychiatry, 164*, 702–703.

Takei, N., Sham, P. C., O'Callaghan, E., & Murray, R. M. (1992). Cities, winter birth, and schizophrenia. *Lancet, 340*, 558–559.

Takei, N., Sham, P. C., O'Callaghan, R., Glover, G., et al. (1995). Early risk factors in schizophrenia: Place and season of birth. *European Psychiatry, 10*, 165–170.

Tanay, E. (1992). The verdict with two names. *Psychiatric Annals, 22*, 571–573.

Tanner, J. M. (1962). *Growth at adolescence: With a general consideration of the effects of heredity and environmental factors upon growth and maturation from birth to maturity.* Oxford: Blackwell Scientific Publications.

Tarrier, N., Pilgrim, H., Sommerfield, C., Faragher, B., Reynolds, M., Graham, E., & Barrowclough, C. (1999). A randomized trial of cognitive therapy and imaginal exposure in the treatment of chronic posttraumatic stress disorder. *Journal of Consulting & Clinical Psychology, 67*, 13–18.

Tateyama, M. Asai, M., Hashimoto, M., Bartels, M., & Kasper, S. (1998). Transcultural study of schizophrenic delusions: Tokyo versus Vienna versus Tuebingen (Germany).

Tateyama, M., Asai, M., Kamisada, M., Hashimoto, M., Bartels, M., & Heimann, H. (1993). Comparison of schizophrenia delusions between Japan and Germany. *Psychopathology, 26*, 151–158.

Taubes, G. (1994). Will new dopamine receptors offer a key to schizophrenia? *Science, 265*, 1034–1035.

Tavris, C. (1992). *The mismeasure of woman.* New York: Simon & Schuster.

Taylor, R. (1982). *Robert Schumann: His life and work.* London: Granada.

Taylor, S. E. (1991). *Health Psychology.* New York: McGraw-Hill.

Taylor, S. E., & Brown, J. D. (1988). Illusion and well-being: A social psychological perspective on mental health. *Psychological Bulletin, 103*, 193–210.

Taylor, S. E., Kemeny, M. E., Aspinwall, L. G., & Schneider, S. G. (1992). Optimism, coping, psychological distress, and high-risk sexual behavior among men at risk for acquired immunodeficiency syndrome (AIDS). *Journal of Personality & Social Psychology, 63*, 460–473.

Taylor, S. E. (1999). *Health Psychology.* San Francisco: McGraw-Hill.

Taylor, S., Kemeny, M. E., Reed, G. M., Bower, J., & Gruenewald, T. (in press). Psychological resources, positive illusions, and health. *American Psychologist.*

Telch, C. F., & Stice, E. (1998). Psychiatric comorbidity in women with binge eating disorder: Prevalence rates from a non-treatment-seeking sample. *Journal of Consulting & Clinical Psychology, 66*, 768–776.

Telch, M. J. (1988). Combined pharmacological and psychological treatment for panic sufferers. In S. Rachman & J. D. Maser (Eds.), *Panic: Psychological perspectives.* Hillsdale, NJ: Erlbaum.

Telch, M. J., Lucas, J. A., Schmidt, N. B., Hanna, H. H., LaNae, J. T., & Lucas, R. A. (1993). Group cognitive-behavioral treatment of panic disorder. *Behaviour Research & Therapy, 31*, 279–287.

Tellegen, A., Lykken, D. T., Bouchard, T. J., & Wilcox, K. J., Segal, N. L., & Rich, S. (1988). Personality similarity in twins reared apart and together. *Journal of Personality & Social Psychology, 54*, 1031–1039.

Telles, C. Karno, M., Mintz, J., Paz, G., Arias, M., Tucker, D., & Lopez, S. (1995). Immigrant families coping with schizophrenia. *British Journal of Psychiatry, 167*, 473–479.

Tennant, C. (1988). Psychosocial causes of duodenal ulcer. *Australian & New Zealand Journal of Psychiatry, 22*, 195–201.

Teplin, L. A. (1990). The prevalence of severe mental disorder among male urban jail detainers: Comparison with the Epidemiologic Catchment Area program. *American Journal of Public Health, 80*, 663–669.

Teplin, L. A., Abram, K. M., & McClelland, G. M. (1994). Does psychiatric disorder predict violent crime among released jail detainees? A six-year longitudinal study. *American Psychologist, 49*, 335–342.

Teplin, L. A., Abram, K. M., & McClelland, G. M. (1996). Prevalence of psychiatric disorders among incarcerated women. I. Pretrial jail detainees. *Archives of General Psychiatry, 53*, 505–512.

Teplin, L. A., Abram, K. M., & McClelland, G. M. (1997). Mentally disordered women in jail: Who receives services? *American Journal of Public Health, 87*, 604–609.

Teri, L., & Lewinsohn, P. M. (1986). Individual and group treatment of unipolar depression: Comparison of treatment outcome and identification of predictors of successful treatment outcome. *Behavior Therapy, 17*, 215–228.

Terr, L. C. (1981). Psychic trauma in children: Observations following the Chowchilla school-bus kidnapping. *American Journal of Psychiatry, 138*, 14–19.

Terr, L. C. (1983). Chowchilla revisited: The effects of psychic trauma four years after a school-bus kidnapping. *American Journal of Psychiatry, 140*, 1543–1550.

Test, M. A., & Stein, L. I. (1980). Alternative to mental hospital treatment: III. Social cost. *Archives of General Psychiatry, 37*, 409–412.

Thakker, J., & Ward, T. (1998). Culture and classification: The cross-cultural application of DSM-IV. *Clinical Psychology Review, 18*, 501–529.

Thal, L. J. (1998). Pharmacotherapy past and future. In M. F. Folstein (Ed.), *Neurobiology of primary dementia* (pp. 289–310). Washington, DC: American Psychiatric Press.

Tharp, R. G. (1991). Cultural diversity and treatment of children. *Journal of Consulting & Clinical Psychology, 59*, 799–812.

Thase, M. E., & Howland, R. H. (1995). Biological processes in depression: An updated review and integration. In E. E. Beckham & W. R. Leber (Eds.), *Handbook of depression* (2nd ed., pp. 213–279). New York: Guilford Press.

Thase, M. E., & Kupfer, D. J. (1996). Recent developments in the pharmacotherapy of mood disorders. *Journal of Consulting & Clinical Psychology, 64*, 646–659.

Thigpen, C. H., & Cleckley, H. M. (1957). *The three faces of Eve.* New York: McGraw-Hill.

Thoits, P. A. (1986). Multiple identities: Examining gender and marital status difference in distress. *American Sociological Review, 51*, 259–272.

Thom, M. (Ed.) (1987). *Letters to Ms.* New York: Henry Holt.

Thomas, A., & Chess, S. (1984). Genesis and evolution of behavioral disorders: From infancy to early adult life. *American Journal of Psychiatry, 141*, 1–9.

Thomas, E. L., & Robinson, H. A. (1982). *Improving reading in every class.* Boston: Allyn & Bacon.

Thompson, L. W., Gallagher, D., Cover, H., Gilewski, M., & Peterson, J. (1989). Effects of bereavement on symptoms of psychopathology in older men and women. In D. A. Lund (Ed.), *Older bereaved spouses: Research with practical applications* (pp. 17–24). New York: Taylor & Francis/Hemisphere.

Thompson, R. A., Tinsley, B. R., Scalora, M. J., & Parke, R. D. (1989). Grandparents' visitation rights: Legalizing the ties that bind. *American Psychologist, 44*, 1217–1222.

Thoresen, C. E., Telch, M. J., & Eagleston, J. R. (1981). Altering Type A behavior. *Psychosomatics, 8*, 472–482.

Thorpe, G. L., & Olson, S. L. (1997). *Behavior therapy: Concepts, procedures, and applications* (2nd ed.). Boston, MA: Allyn & Bacon.

Tiefer, L., & Melman, A. (1989). Comprehensive evaluation of erectile dysfunction and medical treatments. In S. R. Leiblum & R. C. Rosen (Eds.), *Principles and practice of sex therapy: Update for the 1990s* (pp. 207–236). New York: Guilford Press.

Tillich, P. (1952). Anxiety, religion, and medicine. *Pastoral Psychology, 3*, 11–17.

Tolan, P. H., & Gorman-Smith, D. (1997). Treatment of juvenile delinquency: Between punishment and therapy. In D. M. Stoff, J. Breiling, & J. D. Maser (Eds.), *Handbook of antisocial personality disorder* (pp. 405–415). New York: Wiley.

Tomasson, K., Kent, D., & Coryell, W. (1991). Somatization and conversion disorders: Comorbidity and demographics at presentation. *Acta Psychiatrica Scandinavica, 84*, 288–293.

Tondo, L., Baldessarini, R. J., Floris, G., & Rudas, N. (1997). Effectiveness of restarting lithium treatment after its discontinuation in bipolar I and bipolar II disorders. *American Journal of Psychiatry, 154*, 548–550.

Tondo, L., Jamison, K. R., & Baldessarini, R. J. (1997). Effect of lithium maintenance on suicidal behavior in major mood disorders. *Annals of the New York Academy of Sciences, 836,* 339–351.

Torgersen, S. (1980). The oral, obsessive, and hysterical personality syndromes: A study of hereditary and environmental factors by means of the twin method. *Archives of General Psychiatry, 37,* 1272–1277.

Torgersen, S. (1986). Genetic factors in moderately severe and mild affective disorders. *Archives of General Psychiatry, 43,* 222–226.

Torrey, E. F. (1995). *Surviving schizophrenia: A manual for families, consumers, and providers* (3rd ed.). New York: HarperPerennial.

Torrey, E. F. (1997). *Out of the shadows: Confronting America's mental illness crisis.* New York: Wiley.

Torrey, E. F., & Yolken, R. H. (1998). At issue: Is household crowding a risk factor for schizophrenia and bipolar disorder. *Schizophrenia Bulletin, 24,* 321–324.

Torrey, E. F., Bowler, A. E., & Clark, K. (1997). Urban birth and residence as risk factors for psychosis: An analysis of 1880 data. *Schizophrenia Research, 25,* 169–176.

Toth, S. L., & Cicchetti, D. (1996). Patterns of relatedness, depressive symptomatology, and perceived competence in maltreated children. *Journal of Consulting & Clinical Psychology, 64,* 32–41.

Toufexis, A. (1996, April 29). Why Jennifer Got Sick. *Time,* 70.

Toufexis, A. (1996, May 13). Diet pills are coming back. *Time, 147,* 78.

Trierweiler, S. J., & Stricker, G. (1998). *The scientific practice of professional psychology.* New York: Plenum.

Tronick, E. Z., Frank, D. A., Cabral, H., Mirochnick, M., & Zuckerman, B. (1996). Late dose-response effects of prenatal cocaine exposure on newborn neurobehavioral performance. *Pediatrics, 98,* 76–83.

True, W. R., Rice, J., Eisen, S. A., Heath, A. C., Goldberg, J., Lyons, M. J., & Nowak, J. (1993). A twin study of genetic and environmental contributions to liability for posttraumatic stress symptoms. *Archives of General Psychiatry, 50,* 257–264.

Tseng, W. (1973). The development of psychiatric concepts in traditional Chinese medicine. *Archives of General Psychiatry, 29,* 569–575.

Tsuang, M. T. (1983). Suicide in the relatives of schizophrenics, manics, depressives, and controls. *Journal of Clinical Psychiatry, 44,* 396–400.

Tsuang, M. T., Fleming, J. A., & Simpson, J. C. (1999). Suicide and schizophrenia. In D. G. Jacobs (Ed.), *The Harvard Medical School guide to suicide assessment and intervention* (pp. 287–299). San Francisco: Jossey-Bass.

Tugrul, C., & Kabakci, E. (1997). Vaginismus and its correlates. *Sexual & Marital Therapy, 12,* 23–34.

Tuma, J. M. (1989). Mental health services for children: The state of the art. *American Psychologist, 44,* 188–199.

Turk, D. C., & Ruby, T. E. (1992). Cognitive factors and persistent pain: A glimpse into Pandora's box. *Cognitive Therapy & Research, 16,* 99–122.

Turk, D. C., Meichenbaum, D. H., & Berman, W. H. (1979). Application of biofeedback for the regulation of pain: A critical review. *Psychological Bulletin, 86,* 1322–1338.

Turkat, I. D. (1985). *Behavioral case formulation.* New York: Plenum.

Turkheimer, E., & Parry, C. D. (1992). Why the gap? Practice and policy in civil commitment hearings. *American Psychologist, 47,* 646–655.

Turnbull, J. E., & Gomberg, E. S. (1990). The structure of depression in alcoholic women. *Journal of Studies on Alcohol, 51,* 148–155.

U

Uchino, B. N., Cacioppo, J. T., & Kiecolt-Glaser, J. K. (1996). The relationship between social support and physiological processes: A review with emphasis on underlying mechanisms and implications for health. *Psychological Bulletin, 119,* 488–531.

Uchino, B. N., Uno, D., & Holt-Lunstad, J. (1999). Social support, psychological processes, and health. *Current Directions in Psychological Science, 8,* 145–148.

Uva, J. L. (1995). Review: Autoerotic asphyxiation in the United States. *Journal of Forensic Sciences, 40,* 574–581.

V

Vaillant, G. E. (1985). An empirically derived hierarchy of adaptive mechanisms and its usefulness as a potential diagnostic axis. *Acta Psychiatrica Scandinavica, 71,* 171–180.

Valenstein, E. S. (1986). *Great and desperate cures: The rise and decline of psychosurgery and other radical treatments for mental illness.* New York: Basic Books.

Valenstein, R. S. (1998). *Blaming the brain: The truth about drugs and mental health.* New York: Free Press.

van Gorp, W. G., Altshuler, L., Theberge, D. C., Wilkins, J., & Dixon, W. (1998). Cognitive impairment in euthymic bipolar patients with and without prior alcohol dependence: A preliminary study. *Archives of General Psychiatry, 55,* 41–46.

Van Hemert, A. M., Hengeveld, M. W., Bolk, J. H., & Rooijmans, H. G. (1993). Psychiatric disorders in relation to medical illness among patients of a general medical outpatient clinic. *Psychological Medicine, 23,* 167–173.

van Ijzendoorn, M. H., & Bakermans-Kranenburg, M. J. (1996). Attachment representations in mothers, fathers, adolescents, and clinical groups: A meta-analytic search for normative data. *Journal of Consulting & Clinical Psychology, 64,* 8–21.

van Os, J., Wright, P., & Murray, R. M. (1997). Follow-up studies of schizophrenia: I. Natural history and non-psychopathological predictors of outcome. *European Psychiatry, 12* (Suppl. 5), 327–341.

Van Zandt, S., Mou, R., & Abbott, R. (1989). Mental and physical health of rural bereaved and nonbereaved elders: A longitudinal study. In D. A. Lund (Ed.), *Older bereaved spouses: Research with practical applications* (pp. 25–35). New York: Hemisphere.

Vaughn, C. E., & Leff, J. P. (1976). The influence of family and social factors on the course of psychiatric illness: A comparison of schizophrenic and depressed neurotic patients. *British Journal of Psychiatry, 129,* 125–137.

Vaszquez-Nuttall, E., Avila-Vivas, Z., & Morales-Barreto, G. (1984). Working with Latin American families. *Family Therapy Collections, 9,* 74–90.

Veith, I. (1965). *Hysteria: The history of a disease.* Chicago, IL: University of Chicago Press.

Ventura, J., Neuchterlein, K. H., Lukoff, D., & Hardesty, J. P. (1989). A prospective study of stressful life events and schizophrenic relapse. *Journal of Abnormal Psychology, 98,* 407–411.

Verhulst, J., & Heiman, J. (1988). A systems perspective on sexual desire. In S. R. Leiblum & R. C. Rosen (Eds.), *Sexual desire disorders* (pp. 243–270). New York: Guilford Press.

Veronen, L. J., & Kilpatrick, D. G. (1983). Stress management for rape victims. In D. Meichenbaum & M. E. Jaremko (Eds.), *Stress reduction and prevention.* New York: Plenum.

Viney, W., & Zorich, S. (1982). Contributions to the history of psychology: XXIX. Dorothea Dix and the history of psychology. *Psychological Reports, 50,* 211–218.

Visintainer, M. A., Volpicelli, J. R., & Seligman, M. E. (1982). Tumor rejection in rats after inescapable or escapable shock. *Science, 216,* 437–439.

Vitousek, K., & Manke, F. (1994). Personality variables and disorders in anorexia nervosa and bulimia nervosa. Special issue: Personality and psychopathology. *Journal of Abnormal Psychology, 103,* 137–147.

Volz, H.-P., & Kieser, M. (1997). Kava-kava extract WS 1490 versus placebo in anxiety disorders: A randomized placebo-controlled 25-week outpatient trial. *Pharmacopsychiatry, 30,* 1–5.

von Buhler, J. M. (1998). Vacuum and constriction devices for erectile disorder—an integrative view. *Sexual & Marital Therapy, 13,* 257–276.

Von Korff, M., Nestadt, G., Romanoski, A., Anthony, J., Eaton, W., Merchant, A., Chahal, R., Kramer, M., Folstein, M., & Gruenberg, E. (1985). Prevalence of treated and untreated DSM-III schizophrenia: Results of a two-stage community survey. *Journal of Nervous & Mental Disease, 173,* 577–581.

W

Wahlberg, D. (1999, October 21). Binge drinking remains problem. *Ann Arbor News,* A1.

Walker, L. E. A. (1994). Are personality disorders gender biased? In S. A. Kirk & S. D. Einbinder (Eds.), *Controversial issues in mental health* (pp. 22–29). New York: Allyn & Bacon.

Waller, S. J., Lyons, J. S., & Costantini-Ferrando, M. F. (1999). Impact of comorbid affective and alcohol use disorders on suicide ideation and attempts. *Journal of Clinical Psychology, 55,* 585–595.

Wampold, B. E., Mondin, G. W., Moody, M., Stich, F., Benson, K., & Ahn, H. (1997). A meta-analysis of outcome studies comparing bona fide psychotherapies: Empirically, "All must have prizes." *Psychological Bulletin, 122,* 203–215.

Wandersman, A., & Nation, M. (1998). Urban neighborhoods and mental health: Psychological contributions to understanding toxicity, resilience, and interventions. *American Psychologist, 53,* 647–656.

Wannan, G., & Fombonne, E. (1998). Gender differences in rates and correlates of suicidal behavior amongst child psychiatric outpatients. *Journal of Adolescence, 21,* 371–381.

Warga, C. (1988, September). You are what you think. *Psychology Today,* 54–58.

Warner, L. A., Kessler, R. C., Hughes, M., Anthony, J. C., & Nelson, C. B. (1995). Prevalence and correlates of drug use and dependence in the United States. *Archive of General Psychiatry, 52,* 219–229.

Watson, C. G. & Buranen, C. (1979). The frequencies of conversion reaction symptoms. *Journal of Abnormal Psychology, 88,* 209–211.

Watson, J. B. (1930). *Behaviorism.* Chicago: University of Chicago Press.

Watson, J. B., & Raynor, R. (1920). Conditioned emotional reactions. *Journal of Experimental Psychology, 3,* 1–14.

Wechsler, H., Davenport, A., Dowdall, G., Moeykens, B., & Castillo, S. (1994). Health and behavioral consequences of binge drinking in college: A national survey of students at 140 campuses. *Journal of the American Medical Association, 272,* 1672–1677.

Weeks, D., & James, J. (1995). *Eccentrics.* New York: Villard.

Wehr, T. A., & Rosenthal, N. E. (1989). Seasonality and affective illness. *American Journal of Psychiatry, 146,* 829–839.

Weidner, G., & Collins, R. L. (1993). Gender, coping, and health. In H. W. Krohne (Ed.), *Attention and avoidance* (pp. 241–265). Seattle: Hogrefe & Huber.

Weidner, G., Sexton, G., Matarazzo, J. D., & Pereira, C. (1988). Type A behavior in children, adolescents, and their parents. *Developmental Psychology, 24,* 118–121.

Weinberger, D. A., Schwartz, G. E., & Davidson, R. J. (1979). Low-anxious, high-anxious, and repressive coping styles: Psychometric patterns and behavioral and physiological responses to stress. *Journal of Abnormal Psychology, 88,* 369–380.

Weine, S. M., Becker, D. F., McGlashan, T. H., Laub, D., Lazrove, S., Vojvoda, D., & Hyman, L. (1995). Psychiatric consequences of "ethnic cleansing": Clinical assessments and trauma testimonies of newly resettled Bosnian refugees. *American Journal of Psychiatry, 152,* 536–542.

Weine, S. M., Vojvoda, D., Becker, D. F., McGlashan, T. H., Hodzic, E., Laub, D., Hyman, L., Sawyer, M., & Lazrove, S. (1998). PTSD symptoms in Bosnian refugees 1 year after resettlement in the United States. *American Journal of Psychiatry, 155,* 562–564.

Weiner, B. A., & Wettstein, R. M. (1993). *Legal issues in mental health care.* New York: Plenum.

Weiner, H., Thaler, M., Reiser, M. F., & Mirsky, I. A. (1957). Etiology of duodenal ulcer: I. Relation of specific psychological characteristics to rate of gastric secretion (serum pepsinogen). *Psychosomatic Medicine, 19,* 1–10.

Weisbrod, B. A., Test, M. A., & Stein, L. I. (1980). Alternative to mental hospital treatment: II. Economic benefit-cost analysis. *Archives of General Psychiatry, 37,* 400–405.

Weiss, B., & Weisz, J. R. (1995). Effectiveness of psychotherapy. *Journal of the American Academy of Child & Adolescent Psychiatry, 34,* 971–972.

Weiss, J. M. (1991). Stress-induced depression: Critical neurochemical and electrophysiological changes. In J. I. Madden (Ed.), *Neurobiology of learning, emotion, and affect* (pp. 123–154). New York: Raven Press.

Weiss, R. (1997, January 3). Study takes a new tack on asthma. *The Philadelphia Inquirer,* A1, A22.

Weissman, M., & Olfson, M. (1995). Depression in women: Implications for health care research. *Science, 269,* 799–801.

Weissman, M. M. (1993a). Family genetic studies of panic disorder. Conference on panic and anxiety: A decade of progress. *Journal of Psychiatric Research, 27* (suppl. 1), 69–78.

Weissman, M. M. (1993b). The epidemiology of personality disorders: A 1990 update. NIMH Conference: Personality disorders (1990, Williamsburg, Virginia). *Journal of Personality Disorders* (Spr. Suppl. 1), 44–62.

Weissman, M. M., Prusoff, B. A., Gammon, G. D., Merikangas, K. R., Leckman, J. F., & Kidd, K. K. (1984). Psychopathology in children (ages 6–18) of depressed and normal parents. *Journal of the American Academy of Child Psychiatry, 23,* 78–84.

Weissman, M. M., Wolk, S., Goldstein, R. B., Moreau, D., Adams, P., Greenwald, S., Klier, C. M., Ryan, N. D., Dahl, R. E., & Wickramaratne, P. (1999, May 12). Depressed adolescents grown up. *Journal of the American Medical Association, 281,* 1707–1713.

Weisz, J. R., Donenberg, G., Han, S., & Kauneckis, D. (1995). Child and adolescent psychotherapy outcomes in experiments versus clinics: Why the disparity? *Journal of Abnormal Child Psychology, 23,* 83–106.

Weisz, J. R., Weiss, B., Alicke, M. D., & Klotz, M. L. (1987). Effectiveness of psychotherapy with children and adolescents: A meta-analysis for clinicians. *Journal of Consulting & Clinical Psychology, 55,* 542–549.

Welch, S. L., & Fairburn, C. G. (1994). Sexual abuse and bulimia nervosa: Three integrated case control comparisons. 11th National Conference on Eating Disorders (1992, Columbus, Ohio). *American Journal of Psychiatry, 151,* 402–407.

Wender, P. H., Kety, S. S., Rosenthal, D., Schulsinger, F., Ortmann, J., & Lunde, I. (1986). Psychiatric disorders in the biological and adoptive families of adopted individuals with affective disorders. *Archives of General Psychiatry, 43,* 923–929.

Westen, D. (1998). The scientific legacy of Sigmund Freud: Toward a psychodynamically informed psychological science. *Psychological Bulletin, 124,* 333–371.

Westermeyer, J. (1993). Cross-cultural psychiatric assessment. In A. C. Gaw (Ed.), *Culture, ethnicity, and mental illness* (pp. 125–144). Washington, DC: American Psychiatric Press.

Westermeyer, J., Bouafuely, M., Neider, J., & Callies, A. (1989). Somatization among refugees: An epidemiologic study. *Psychosomatics, 30,* 34–43.

Weston, S. C., & Siever, L. J. (1993). Biologic correlates of personality disorders. NIMH Conference: Personality disorders (1990, Williamsburg, Virginia). *Journal of Personality Disorders* (Suppl. 1), 129–148.

Wexler, A. (1995). *Mapping fate: A memoir of family, risk, and genetic research.* New York: Times Books.

Whalen, C. K., & Henker, B. (1998). Attention-deficit/hyperactivity disorder. In T. H. Ollendick & M. Hersen (Eds.), *Handbook of child psychopathology* (pp. 181–212). New York: Plenum.

Wheeden, A., Scafidi, F. A., Field, T., Ironson, G., Bandstra, E., Schanberg, S., & Valdeon, C. (1993). Massage effects on cocaine-exposed preterm neonates. *Journal of Developmental & Behavioral Pediatrics, 14,* 318–322.

Whelan, J. P., & Houts, A. C. (1990). Effects of a waking schedule on primary enuretic children treated with full-spectrum home training. *Health Psychology, 90,* 164–176.

Widiger, T. A. (1998). Invited essay: Sex biases in the diagnosis of personality disorders. *Journal of Personality Disorders, 12,* 95–118.

Widiger, T. A., & Costa, P. T. (1994). Personality and personality disorders. Special Issue: Personality and psychopathology. *Journal of Abnormal Psychology, 103,* 78–91.

Widiger, T. A., & Spitzer, R. L. (1991). Sex biases in the diagnosis of personality disorder: Conceptual and methodological issues. *Clinical Psychological Review, 11,* 1–22.

Widiger, T. A., Mangine, S., Corbitt, E. M., Ellis, C. G., & Thomas, G. V. (1995). *Personality disorder interview-IV. A semistructured interview for the assessment of personality disorders.* Odessa, FL: Psychological Assessment Resources.

Widiger, T. A., Trull, T. J., Clarkin, J. F., Sanderson, C., & Costa, P. T. (1994). A description of the DSM-III-R and DSM-IV personality disorders with the five-factor model of personality. In P. T. Costa & T. A. Widiger (Eds.), *Personality disorders and the five-factor model of personality* (pp. 41–58). Washington, DC: American Psychological Association.

Wiggins, J. S. (1982). Circumplex models of interpersonal behavior in clinical psychology. In P. Kendall & J. Butcher (Eds.), *Handbook of research methods in clinical psychology.* New York: Wiley.

Wiggins, J. S., & Pincus, A. L. (1994). Personality structure and the structure of personality disorders. In P. T. Costa & T. A. Widiger (Eds.), *Personality disorders and the five-factor model of personality* (pp. 73–94). Washington, DC: American Psychological Association.

Wiggins, S., Whyte, P., Huggins, M., Adam, S., Theilman, J., Bloch, M., Sheps, S. B., Schechter, M. T., & Hayden, M. R. (1992). The psychological consequences of predictive testing for Huntington's disease. *The New England Journal of Medicine, 327,* 1401–1405.

Wikan, U. (1991). *Managing turbulent hearts.* Chicago: University of Chicago Press.

Wilfley, D. E., Schreiber, G. B., Pike, K. M., Striegel-Moore, R. H., Wright, D. J., & Rodin, J. (1996). Eating disturbance and body image: A comparison of a community sample of adult black and white women. *International Journal of Eating Disorders, 20,* 377–387.

Williams, J. B., & Spitzer, R. L. (1983). The issue of sex bias in DSM-III. *American Psychologist, 38,* 793–798.

Williams, L. M. (1995). Recovered memories of abuse in women with documented child sexual victimization histories. *Journal of Traumatic Stress, 8,* 649–673.

Williams, R. B., Barefoot, J. C., Haney, T. L., & Harrell, F. E. (1988). Type A behavior and angiographically documented coronary atherosclerosis in a sample of 2,289 patients. *Psychosomatic Medicine, 50,* 139–152.

Williamson, D. F., Serdula, M. K., Anda, R. F., & Levy, A. (1992). Weight loss attempts in adults: Goals, duration, and rate of weight loss. *American Journal of Public Health, 82,* 1251–1257.

Williamson, G. L. (1993). Postpartum depression syndrome as a defense to criminal behavior. *Journal of Family Violence, 8,* 151–165.

Williams-Russo, P., Urquhart, B. L., Sharrock, N. E., & Charlson, M. E. (1992). Post-operative delirium: Predictors and prognosis in elderly orthopedic patients. *Journal of the American Geriatrics Society, 40,* 759–767.

Wilps, R. F., Jr. (1990). Male bulimia nervosa: An autobiographical case study. In A. E. Andersen (Ed.), *Males with eating disorders* (pp. 9–29). New York: Brunner/Mazel.

Wilson, G. R., Loeb, K. L., Walsh, B. T., Labouvie, R., Petkova, E., Xinhua, L., & Waternaux, C. (1999). Psychological versus pharmacological treatments of bulimia nervosa: Predictors and processes of change. *Journal of Consulting & Clinical Psychology, 67,* 451–459.

Wilson, G. T. (1993). Psychological and pharmacological treatments of bulimia nervosa: A research update. *Applied & Preventive Psychology, 2,* 35–42.

Wilson, G. T., Fairburn, C. G. (1998). Cognitive treatments for eating disorders. *Journal of Consulting & Clinical Psychology, 61,* 261–269.

Wilson, G. T., & Fairburn, C. G., & Agras, W. S. (1997). Cognitive-behavioral treatment for anorexia nervosa. In D. M. Garner & P. E. Garfinkel (Eds.), *Handbook of treatment for eating disorders.* New York: Guilford Press.

Wilson, W. H., & Clausen, A. M. (1995). 18-month outcome of clozapine treatment for 100 patients in a state psychiatric hospital. *Psychiatric Services, 46,* 386–389.

Windholz, M. J., Marmar, C. R., & Horowitz, M. J. (1985). A review of the research on conjugal bereavement: Impact on health and efficacy of intervention. *Comprehensive Psychiatry, 26,* 433–447.

Wing, R. R., Epstein, L. H., Nowalk, M. P., & Scott, N. (1987). Family history of diabetes and its effect on treatment outcome in Type II diabetes. *Behavior Therapy, 18,* 283–289.

Winger, G., Hofmann, F. G., & Woods, J. H. (1992). *Handbook on drug and alcohol abuse.* New York: Oxford University Press.

Winokur, G., & Clayton, P. (1967). Family history studies: II. Sex differences and alcoholism in primary affective illness. *British Journal of Psychiatry, 113,* 973–979.

Wiseman, C. V., Gray, J. J., Mosimann, J. E., & Ahrens, A. H. (1992). Cultural expectations of thinness in women: An update. *International Journal of Eating Disorders, 11,* 85–89.

Wolfe, J., Erickson, D. J., Sharkansky, R. J., King, D. W., & King, L. A. (1999). Course and predictors of posttraumatic stress disorder among Gulf War veterans: A prospective analysis. *Journal of Consulting & Clinical Psychology, 67,* 520–528.

Wolff, S., & Wolff, H. G. (1947). An experimental study of changes in gastric function in response to varying life experiences. *Review of Gastroenterology, 14,* 419–426.

Wolfner, G. D., & Gelles, R. J. (1993). A profile of violence toward children: A national study. *Child Abuse & Neglect, 17,* 197–212.

Wolitzky, D. L. (1995). The theory and practice of traditional psychoanalytic psychotherapy. In A. S. Gurman (Ed.), *Essential psychotherapies: Theory and practice* (pp. 12–54). New York: Guilford Press.

Wollstonecraft, M. (1792). *A vindication of the rights of women.* London: J. Johnson.

Wolpe, J. (1969). *The practice of behavior therapy.* Elmsford, New York: Pergamon.

Wolpe, J. (1997). Thirty years of behavior therapy. *Behavior Therapy, 28,* 633–635.

Woolf, V. (1975–1980a). "I feel certain" Virginia Woolf, March 18, 1941. In N. Nicolson & J. Trautman (Eds.), *The letters* (Vol. 6, p. 481). London: Hogarth Press.

Woolf, V. (1975–1980b). "Dearest I want to tell you": Virginia Woolf, March 28, 1941. In N. Nicolson & J. Trautman (Eds.), *The letters* (Vol. 6, pp. 486–487). London: Hogarth Press.

Wortman, C., & Silver, R. (1987). Coping with irrevocable loss, in cataclysms, crises and catastrophes. In G. R. VandenBos & B. K. Bryant (Eds.), *Psychology in action* (pp. 189–235). Washington, DC: American Psychological Association.

Wright, R. A. (1984). Motivation, anxiety, and the difficulty of avoidant control. *Journal of Personality & Social Psychology, 46,* 1376–1388.

Wulsin, L. R., Vaillat, G. E., & Wells, V. E. (1999). A systematic review of the mortality of depression. *Psychosomatic Medicine, 61,* 6–17.

Wurtman, J. J. (1987). Disorders of food intake: Excessive carbohydrate snack intake among a class of obese people. *Annals of the New York Academy of Sciences, 499,* 197–202.

Wurtman, R. J., & Wurtman, J. J. (1984). Nutritional control of central neurotransmitters. In K. M. Pirke & D. Plogg (Eds.), *The psychobiology of anorexia nervosa.* Berlin: Springer-Verlag.

Wurtzel, E. (1995). *Prozac nation.* New York: Berkley.

Wyatt, S. A., & Ziedonis, D. (1998). Psychological and psychiatric consequences of amphetamines. In R. E. Tarter (Ed.), *Handbook of substance abuse: Neurobehavioral pharmacology* (pp. 529–544). New York: Plenum.

Y

Yalom, I. D. (1985). *The theory and practice of group psychotherapy* (3rd ed.). New York: Basic Books.

Yamamoto, J. (1970). Cultural factors in loneliness, death, and separation. *Medical Times, 98,* 177–183.

Yapko, M. D. (1997). *Breaking the patterns of depression.* New York: Golden Books.

Yehuda, R. (1998). Psychoneuroendocrinology of posttraumatic stress disorder. *Psychiatric Clinics of North America, 21,* 359–379.

Yirmiya, N., Erel, O., Shaked, M., & Solomonica-Levi, D. (1998). Meta-analysis comparing theory of mind abilities of individuals with autism, individuals with mental retardation, and normally developed individuals. *Psychological Bulletin, 124,* 283–307.

Yonkers, K. A. (1997). Anxiety symptoms and anxiety disorders: How are they related to premenstrual disorders. *Journal of Clinical Psychiatry, 58* (Suppl. 3), 62–67.

Yonkers, K. A., & Gurguis, G. (1995). Gender differences in the prevalence and expression of anxiety disorders. In M. V. Seeman (Ed.), *Gender and psychopathology* (pp. 113–130). Washington, DC: American Psychiatric Press.

Young, E., & Korzun, A. (1998). Psycho-neuroendocrinology of depression: Hypothalamic-pituitary-gonadal axis. *Psychiatric Clinics of North America, 21,* 309–323.

Z

Zakzanis, K. K. (1998). Quantitative evidence for neuroanatomic and neuropsychological markers in dementia of the Alzheimer's type. *Journal of Clinical & Experimental Neuropsychology, 20,* 259–269.

Zaleman, S. E. (1995). Neural basis of psychopathology. In S. H. Koslow, D. L. Meinecke, I. I. Lederhendler, H. Khachaturian, R. K. Nakamura, D. Karp, L. Vitkovic, D. L. Glanzman, & S. Zaleman (Eds.), *The neuroscience of mental health: II. A report on neuroscience research—status and potential for mental health and mental illness.* Rockville, MD: National Institute for Mental Health.

Zanarini, M. C. (Ed.). (1997). *Role of sexual abuse in the etiology of borderline personality disorder.* Washington, DC: American Psychiatric Press.

Zeitlin, H. (1986). *The natural history of psychiatric disorder in childhood.* New York: Oxford University Press.

Zelt, D. (1981). First person account: The Messiah quest. *Schizophrenia Bulletin, 7,* 527–531.

Zerbe, K. J. (1990). Through the storm: Psychoanalytic theory in the psychotherapy of anxiety disorders. *Bulletin of the Menninger Clinic, 54,* 171–183.

Zhou, J.-N., Hofman, M. A., & Swaab, D. F. (1995). No changes in the number of vasoactive intestinal polypeptide (VIP)-expressing neurons in the suprachiasmatic nucleus of homosexual men; comparison with vasopressin-expressing neurons. *Brain Research, 672,* 285–288.

Zigler, E., & Hodapp, R. M. (1991). Behavioral functioning in individuals with mental retardation. *Annual Review of Psychology, 42,* 29–50.

Zilboorg, G., & Henry, G. W. (1941). *A history of medical psychology.* New York: W. W. Norton.

Zimbardo, P. G., Andersen, S. M., & Kabat, L. G. (1981). Induced hearing deficit generates experimental paranoia. *Science, 212,* 1529–1531.

Zisook, S., & Downs, N. (1998). Diagnosis and treatment of depression in late life. *Journal of Clinical Psychiatry, 59* (Suppl. 4), 80–91.

Zisook, S., Shuchter, S. R., & Lyons, L. E. (1987). Predictors of psychological reactions during the early stages of widowhood. *Psychiatric Clinics of North America, 10,* 355–368.

Zito, J. M., Safer, D. J., Riddle, M. A., Johnson, R. E., Speedie, S. M., & Fox, M. (1998). Prevalence variations in psychotropic treatment of children. *Journal of Child & Adolescent Psychopharmacology, 8,* 99–105.

Zlotnik, C., Elkin, I., & Shea, M. T. (1998). Does the gender of a patient or the gender of a therapist affect the treatment of patients with major depression? *Journal of Consulting & Clinical Psychology, 66,* 655–659.

Zoccolillo, M. (1993). Gender and the development of conduct disorder. *Development & Psychopathology, 5,* 65–78.

Zoellner, L. A., Craske, M. G., & Rapee, R. M. (1996). Stability of catastrophic cognitions in panic disorder. *Behaviour Research & Therapy, 34,* 399–402.

Zorrilla, L. T., Cannon, T. D., Kronenberg, S., Mednick, S. A., Schulsinger, F., Parnas, J., Praestholm, J., & Vestergaard, A. (1997). Structural brain abnormalities in schizophrenia: A family study. *Biological Psychiatry, 42,* 1080–1086.

Zubieta, J. K., & Alessi, N. E. (1992). Acute and chronic administration of trazodone in the treatment of disruptive behavior disorders in children. *Journal of Clinical Psychopharmacology, 12,* 346–351.

Zucker, R. A. (1998). *Alcohol involvement over the life course* (Draft manuscript for Tenth Special Report to the U.S. Congress on Alcohol and Health 10). Ann Arbor: University of Michigan.

Zucker, R. A., Chermack, S. T., & Curran, G. M. (in press). Alcoholism: A lifespan perspective on etiology and course. In M. Lewis & A. J. Sameroff (Eds.), *Handbook of developmental psychopathology* (2nd ed.,). New York: Plenum.

Zucker, R. A., Ellis, D. A., Fitzgerald, H. E., Bingham, C. R., & Sanford, K. (1996). Other evidence for at least two alcoholisms: II. Life course variation in antisociality and heterogeneity of alcoholic outcome. *Development & Psychopathology, 8,* 831–848.

Zucker, R. A., Fitzgerald, H. E., & Moses, H. D. (1994). Emergence of alcohol problems and the several alcoholisms: A developmental perspective on etiologic theory and life course trajectory. In D. Cicchetti & D. J. Cohen (Eds.), *Developmental psychopathology* (Vol. 2, pp. 677–711). New York: Wiley.

Zucker, R. A., Kincaid, S. B., Fitzgerald, H. E., & Bingham, C. R. (1995). Alcohol schema acquisition in preschoolers: Differences between children of alcoholics and children of nonalcoholics. *Alcoholism: Clinical & Experimental Research, 19,* 1011–1017.

CREDITS

PHOTOGRAPHS

Chapter 1

Opener: *People Flying* by Peter Sickles. American/Superstock; **p. 5:** © VanBucher/Photo Researchers; **p. 6:** © Steve Lynch/Tony Stone Images; **p. 7:** Courtesy of Gary Holloway. Photo by Josef Astor; **p. 11 (top):** © Sandved B. Kjell/Visuals Unlimited; **p. 11 (bottom):** © The Granger Collection; **p. 13:** © Archivo Iconografico, S.A./CORBIS; **pp. 14–15:** © Corbis-Bettmann; **p. 16:** © US National Library of Medicine/Science Photo Library/Photo Researchers; **p. 17:** © National Library of Medicine/Photo Researchers; **Fig. 1.12:** © Belzeaux/Photo Researchers; **p. 20, p. 23 (left):** © The Granger Collection; **p. 23 (right):** © UPI/Corbis-Bettmann.

Chapter 2

Opener: *Heart of the Hunter* by Michelle Puleo, B. 1967, American, Private Collection/Superstock ; **Fig. 2.4:** From: Damasio H, Grabowski, T, Frank R, Galaburda A M, Damasio A R: The return of Phineas Gage: Clues about the brain from the skull of a famous patient. *Science*, 264:1102–1105, 1994. Department of Neurology and Image Analysis Facility, University of Iowa.; **Fig. 2.9:** © L. Willatt/East Anglian Regional Genetics Service/Science Photo Library/Photo Researchers; **p. 42:** © Enrico Ferorelli; **p. 44:** © Corbis/Bettmann; **p. 46:** © Barton Silverman/NYT Pictures; **p. 48:** © Dorothy Littell Greco/Image Works; **p. 49 (top):** © Wellcome Trust; **p. 49 (bottom):** © Otto Kernberg; **p. 50:** © Corbis-Bettmann; **p. 52:** © John Maier, Jr./Image Works; **p. 54:** © Christopher Bissell/Tony Stone Images; **p. 56:** National Library of Medicine; **p. 58:** © Sarah Putnam/The Picture Cube; **p. 59:** © Tamara Reynolds/Tony Stone Images; **p. 61:** © F. Pedrick/The Image Works; **p. 62:** © Joseph Nettis/Tony Stone Images.

Chapter 3

Opener: *Global Seat* by Christian Pierre. American. Private Collection/Superstock; **p. 68:** © 1999 TIME Inc. Reprinted by Permission.; **p. 73:** © Barry King/Gamma Liaison; **p. 76:** © Davis Barber/Photo Edit; **p. 80:** © Peter Cade/Tony Stone Images; **p. 82:** © Bill Aron/Photo Edit; **p. 83:** © Conor Caffrey/Science Photo Library/Photo Researchers; **p. 84:** © Robert Brenner/Photo Edit; **p. 88:** © Michael Newman/Photo Edit.

Chapter 4

Opener: *Essor* by Andre Rouillard, 1981/Superstock; **p. 99:** © Steven Peters/Tony Stone Images; **p. 100:** © Michael Newman/Photo Edit; **Fig. 4.3:** © Science Photo Library/Photo Researchers; **Fig. 4.4:** © Science Source/Photo Researchers; **Fig. 4.5:** © Science Photo Library/Photo Researchers; **Fig. 4.8:** © Will & Deni McIntyre/Photo Researchers; **p. 114:** © Jeff Greenberg/Photo Edit; **p. 115:** © Peter L. Chapman/Stock Boston; **p. 116:** © Lawrence Migdale/Stock Boston; **p. 117:** © Michael Newman/Photo Edit; **p. 128:** © Tim Davis/Photo Researchers.

Chapter 5

Opener: *Window of Opportunity* by Christian Pierre. American, Private Collection/Superstock; **p. 134:** © Jeff Isaac Greenberg/Photo Researchers; **Fig. 5.2:** © 1994 Newsweek, Inc. All rights reserved. Reprinted by permission.; **p. 141:** © Najlah Feanny/Stock Boston; **Fig. 5.3:** Courtesy of the Ad Council.; **p. 147:** © Bruce Ayres/Tony Stone Images; **p. 151:** © Stephen Agricola/Stock Boston; **p. 154:** © Bruce Ayres/Tony Stone Images; **p. 157:** © Bob Daemmrich/Stock Boston; **p. 161:** © Michael Grecco/Stock Boston; **p. 162:** © David R. Frazier/Photo Researchers; **p. 164:** © The Granger Collection.

Chapter 6

Opener: *Birddog* by Diana Ong, B. 1940, Private Collection/Superstock; **p. 178:** © Jack Spratt/The Image Works; **p. 182:** © David Young-Wolff/Photo Edit; **p. 191:** © Bill Bachmann/Photo Edit; **p. 194 (top left):** © Owen Franken/Stock Boston; **p. 194 (top right):** © John Elk III/Stock Boston; **p. 194 (bottom right):** © The Lippin Group/Shooting Star; **p. 195:** © John Cancalosi/Stock Boston; **p. 198:** © David Young-Wolff/Photo Edit; **p. 200:** © Corbis; **p. 206:** © Richard Hutchings/Photo Researchers; **p. 207:** © Zig Leszczynski/Animals Animals; **p. 210:** © Bob Daemmrich/Stock Boston.

Chapter 7

Opener: *Grey Clowns* by Diana Ong, B. 1940/Superstock; **p. 217:** © Catherine Ursillo/Photo Researchers; **p. 219 (top left):** © William Campbell/Peter Arnold; **p. 219 (top right):** © Peter Menzel/Stock Boston; **p. 219 (bottom right):** © Monika Anderson/Stock Boston; **p. 220:** © Hulton Getty/Liaison Agency; **p. 222:** © Express Newspapers/Archive Photos; **p. 223:** © Hodson/Spooner/Liaison Agency; **p. 225:** © Judith Calson/The Sacramento Bee/Sygma; **p. 226:** © Liaison Agency; **Fig. 7.3:** © Shin, L. M., Kosslyn, S. M., McNally, R. J., Alpert, N. M., Thompson, W. L., Rauch, S. L., Macklin, M. L., & Pitman, R. K. (1997). Visual imagery and perception in posttraumatic stress disorder: A positron emission tomographic investigation. *Archives of General Psychiatry*, 54, 233–241.; **p. 229:** © Rhoda Sidney/Stock Boston; **Fig. 7.4:** © Bremner, J. D. (1998). Neuroimaging of posttraumatic stress disorder. *Psychiatric Annuals*, 28, 445–450.; **p. 232:** © Dirck Halstead/Liaison Agency; **p. 235:** © Aaron Haupt/Stock Boston; **Fig. 7.7:** © Schwartz, J., Stoessel, P. W., Baxter, L. R., Martin, K. M., & Phelps, M. C. (1996) Systemic Changes in Cerebral Glucose Metabolic Rate After Successful Behavior Modification Treatment of Obsessive-Compulsive Disorder. *Archives of General Psychiatry*, 53, 109–113; **Fig. 7.6:** © Lewis Baxter/Peter Arnold.

Chapter 8

Opener: *Watching from the Steps* by Hyacinth Manning-Carner. *African American*, Private Collection/Superstock; **p. 249:** © Michelle Bridwell/Photo Edit; **p. 251:** © Frank Siteman/Stock Boston; **p. 257 (1–2):** © The Granger Collection; **p. 257 (3):** © Kobal Collection; **p. 257 (4):** © Darren McCollester/Liaison Agency; **Fig. 8.9:** © Monte S. Buchsbaum, M. D., M Sinai School of Medicine, New York, NY.;

Fig. 8.10: Courtesy, Dr. Lewis R. Baxter, Jr.; **p. 268:** © Jon Riley/Tony Stone Images; **p. 270:** © Toni Michaels; **p. 272:** © Stephen Agricola/Stock Boston; **p. 283:** © Will & Deni McIntyre/Photo Researchers; **p. 288:** © Bob Daemmrich/Stock Boston; **p. 291:** © David K. Crow/Photo Edit.

Chapter 9

Opener: *Florista* by Bernadita Zegers. Kactus Foto, Santiago, Chile/Superstock; **p. 301:** © AP/Wide World Photos; **p. 303:** © Natsuko Utsumi/Liaison Agency; **p. 309:** © Bob Daemmrich/Stock Boston; **p. 314:** © Barbara Stitzer/Photo Edit; **p. 315 (left):** © Corbis-Bettmann; **p. 315 (right):** © Alain Benainous/Liaison Agency; **p. 318:** © Michael Newman/Photo Edit; **p. 319:** © Richard Shock/Tony Stone Images.

Chapter 10

Opener: *My Dog and I Are One* by Patricia Schwimmer. Canadian/Superstock; **p. 331:** © Judy Allen-Newberry; **p. 334:** *The Green House* by Sandy Skoglund, 1990, American/Superstock; **p. 337:** © Grunnitu/Monkmeyer; **p. 338:** © Peter Southwick/Stock Boston; **p. 343:** © Reuters/Corbis-Bettmann; **p. 347:** Courtesy, The Genain Quadrulplets; **Fig. 10.5a–b, 10.6:** Courtesy, Dr. Nancy Andreasen; **Fig. 10.7:** © Dr. Dean Wong; **p. 354:** Courtesy, William Alanson White Institute of Psychiatry, *Psychoanalysis & Psychology*; **p. 359:** © Bob Daemmrich/Stock Boston; **p. 362:** © Peter Turnley/Corbis; **p. 363:** © Ed Lalio/Picture Cube.

Chapter 11

Opener: *Day Dream* by Daniel Nevins. American, Private Collection/Superstock; **p. 372:** © Phyllis Picardizd/Stock Boston; **p. 375:** © The Kobal Collection; **p. 377:** © Cindy Charles/Photo Edit; **p. 378:** © UPI/Corbis-Bettmann; **p. 381:** © Richard T. Nowitz/Photo Researchers; **p. 382:** © Corbis/Bettmann; **p. 385 (top):** © Bob Daemmrich/Stock Boston; **p. 385 (bottom):** © Jeffrey Markowitz/Sygma; **p. 387:** © AP Photo/Alan Diaz/Wide World Photos; **p. 390:** © The Granger Collection; **p. 392:** © Hank Morgan/Science Source/Photo Researchers; **p. 393:** © Charles Gupton/Stock Boston; **p. 395:** © Bob Daemmrich/Stock Boston; **p. 398:** © Phyllis Picardi/Stock Boston.

Chapter 12

Opener: *The Armour* by Gayle Ray. American/Superstock; **p. 408 (left):** © Tony Arruza/Tony Stone Images; **p. 408 (right):** © Kobal Collection; **p. 409:** © Bob Daemmrich/The Image Works; **p. 413:** © Stacy Pick/Stock Boston; **p. 416:** © UPI/Corbis-Bettmann; **p. 418:** © A. Ramey/Stock Boston; **p. 420:** © Labat/Jerrican/Photo Researchers; **p. 422:** © Fred R. Palmer/Stock Boston; **p. 426:** © Tordai/The Image Works; **p. 428:** © Dagmar Fabricius/Stock Boston; **p. 430:** © Walter Hodges/Tony Stone Images; **p. 431:** © Bob Daemmrich/The Image Works.

Chapter 13

Opener: *In The Fields* by Daniel Nevins. American, Private Collection/Superstock; **p. 442:** © AP

LINE ART & EXCERPTS

Chapter 1

p. 4: From Anonymous, (1992), First-person account: Portrait of a schizophrenic in *Schizophrenia Bulletin*, 18, 333–334. Reprinted by permission. **p. 4:** From *An Unquiet Mind* by Kay Redfield Jamison. Copyright © 1995 by Kay Redfield Jamison. Reprinted by permission of Alfred A. Knopf, a Division of Random House Inc.

Chapter 2

p. 30: From *The Lanahan Cases and Readings in Abnormal Behavior*, by Kayla F. Bernheim, pp. 34, 95–98, & 126–130. Copyright © 1997 by Lanahan Publishers, Inc., Baltimore, MD. Adapted and reprinted by permission of the Publisher. **p. 32:** From Damasio, H., Grabowski, T., Frank R., Galaburda, A. M., & Damasio, A. R., "The return of Phineas Cage: Clues about the brain from the skull of a famous patient, *Science*, 264, pp. 1102–1105, Copyright ©1994 American Association for the Advancement of Science. Reprinted with permission. p. 60: From *An Unquiet Mind* by Kay Redfield Jamison. Copyright ©1995 by Kay Redfield Jamison. Reprinted by permissions of Alfred A. Knopf, a Division of Random House Inc.

Chapter 3

p. 72: Case Study on Kurt Cobain; From Giles, J., "The Poet of Alienation" in *Newsweek*, Vol. 123, 4/18/94, pp. 46–47, © 1994 Newsweek, Inc. All rights reserved. Reprinted by permission. **p. 90:** From Andreasen, N. C., "Linking Mind and Brain in the Study of Mental Illnesses: A project for a scientific psychopathology" in *Science*, 275, pp. 1586–1593. Copyright © 1997 American Association for the Advancement of Science. Reprinted with permission.

Chapter 4

p. 96: From *An Unquiet Mind* by Kay Redfield Jamison. Copyright © 1995 by Kay Redfield Jamison. Reprinted by permissions of Alfred A. Knopf, a Division of Random House Inc. **Fig. 4.1:** From J. M. Sattler, *Assessment of Children*, 3rd edition. Copyright © J. M. Sattler. Reprinted by permission. **Fig. 4.2:** From Jackson Beatty, *Principles of Behavioral Neuroscience*. Copyright © 1995 McGraw-Hill Company. All Rights Reserved. Reprinted by permission. **Fig. 4.7:** Minnesota Multiphasic Personality Inventory (MMPI). Copyright © 1942, 1943, 1951, 1967 (renewed 1970), 1983. Reprinted by permission of the University of Minnesota. "MMPI" and "Minnesota Multiphasic Personality Inventory" are trademarks owned by the University of Minnesota. **pp. 120–121:** Based on John Bernedt in *The New Yorker Magazine*, January 19, 1995. Reprinted by permission of International Creative

Management. **p. 123:** From *The Lanahan Cases and Readings in Abnormal Behavior*, by Kayla F. Bernheim, pp. 34, 95–98, & 126–130. Copyright © 1997 by Lanahan Publishers, Inc., Baltimore, MD. Adapted and reprinted by permission of the Publisher.

Chapter 5

pp. 135–136: From *The Lanahan Cases and Readings in Abnormal Behavior*, by Kayla F. Bernheim, pp. 34, 95–98, & 126–130. Copyright © 1997 by Lanahan Publishers, Inc., Baltimore, MD. Adapted and reprinted by permission of the Publisher. **pp. 138–139:** From Kuhn, R. (1958) in *American Journal of Psychiatry*, 115, pp. 459–464. Copyright © 1958 the American Psychiatric Association. Reprinted with permission. **p. 148:** From Bohart, A. C. (1995) "The person-centered psychotherapies" in A. S. Gurman & B. M. Stanley (Eds.), Essential psychotherapies: Theory and practice (pp. 85–1270) **p. 153:** From Freeman, E., & Reinecke, M. A. (1995) "Cognitive therapy" in A. S. Gurman (Ed.), *Essential psychotherapies: Theory and practice* (pp. 203–204) **pp. 160–161:** From Sue, S. & Zane, N. in *American Psychologist*, 42, 37–51. Copyright © 1987 by the American Psychological Association. Reprinted by permission of American Psychological Association and Dr. Stanley Sue. **Fig. 5.4:** From M. E. P. Seligman, "The Effectiveness of Psychotherapy" in the Consumer Reports Study in *American Psychologist*, 50, 965–974. Copyright © 1995 by the American Psychological Association. Reprinted with permission. **pp. 167–169:** From Anonymous, (1992), First-person account: Portrait of a schizophrenic in *Schizophrenia Bulletin*, 18, 333–334. Reprinted with permission.

Chapter 6

Fig. 6.2: From C. J. Bell and D. J. Nutt, "Serotonin and Panic" in *British Journal of Psychiatry*, 172, 465–471. Copyright © 1998 Royal College of Psychiatrists, London. **p. 191:** From Hamilton, A. (April 26, 1999) "Virtually Fearless", *Time* 4/26/99, p. 110. © 1999 Time Inc. Reprinted by permission. **p. 196:** From Kinzie, J. D. & Leung, P .K., "Psychiatric care of Indochinese Americans" in A. C. Gaw (Eds.), *Culture, ethnicity, and mental illness*, pp. 281–304. Copyright © 1993 the American Psychiatric Association. Reprinted with permission. **p. 201:** From Silverman, W. K. & Ginsberg, G. S. (1995) "Specific phobia and generalized anxiety disorder" in D. P. Cantwell (Ed.) *Anxiety disorders in children and adolescents*, pp. 169–170. **p. 188:** Warga; From Warga, C. (1988) "You are what you think" in *Psychology Today*, p. 56. Reprinted with permission.

Chapter 7

p. 217: From *The Lanahan Cases and Readings in Abnormal Behavior*, by Kayla F. Bernheim, pp. 34, 95–98, & 126–130. Copyright © 1997 by Lanahan Publishers, Inc., Baltimore, MD. Adapted and reprinted by permission of the Publisher. **pp. 217–218:** From Berheim, 1997 (original source is Smith): From John Russell Smith, "Personal Responsibility and Traumatic Stress Reactions" in *Psychiatric Annals*, Vol. 12, no. 11, November 1982, pp. 1029–30. Reprinted by permission of Slack, Inc. **p. 222:** From Weine, S. M., Becker, D. F., McGlashan, T. H., Laub, D., Lazrove, S., Vojvoda, D., & Hyman, L. in *American Journal of Psychiatry*, 152, pp. 536–542. Copyright © 1995 the American Psychiatric Association. Reprinted by permission. **pp. 233–234:** From Burnette, E., "Community psychologists help South Africans mend", *APA Monitor*, September 1997 issue, p. 31. Copyright © 1997 by the American Psychological Association. Reprinted with permission. **pp. 230–231:** From Keane, T. M., Gerardi, R. J., Quinn, S. J., & Litz, B. T. "Behavioral treatment of post-traumatic stress disorder" in S. M. Turner, K. S. Calhoun, & H. E. Adams (Eds.), *Handbook of clinical behavior therapy*, pp. 87–97. Copyright © 1992 John Wiley & Sons, Inc. Reprinted by permission of John Wiley & Sons, Inc. **pp. 234–235, 237–238:** From *The Boy Who Couldn't Stop Washing* by Dr. Judith Rapoport, copyright © 1989 by Judith L. Rapoport, M.D. Used by permission of Dutton, a division of Penguin Putnam Inc. **pp. 236–237:** From *Just checking:*

Scenes from the life of an obsessive-compulsive by Emily Colas. Copyright © 1998 by Emily Colas. Reprinted with the permission of Pocket Books, a division of Simon & Schuster. **Fig. 7.5:** From J. L. Rapaport, "The Biology of Obsessions and Compulsions" in *Scientific American,* March 1989. Reprinted by permission of Neil O. Hardy, illustrator.

Chapter 8

p. 248: From *An Unquiet Mind* by Kay Redfield Jamison, pp. 35–38, 110. Copyright © 1995 by Kay Redfield Jamison. Reprinted by permission of Alfred A. Knopf, a Division of Random House Inc. and MacMillan UK. **p. 274:** From Bemporad, J. (1995), "Long-term analytic treatment of depression" in E. E. Beckham & W. R. Leber (Eds.) *Handbook of depression,* 2/e, pp. 391–403. **p. 278:** From Kleinman, A. & Kleinman, J. in A. Kleinman & B. Goods (Eds.) *Culture and depression,* pp. 454–455. Copyright © 1985 The Regents of the University of California. Reprinted with permission. **p. 288:** From Thorpe, G. & Olson, S. in *Behavior therapy: Concepts, procedures, and applications,* 2/e, pp. 217, 225–227. Copyright © 1997 by Allyn & Bacon. Reprinted by permission. **Fig. 8.6:** Adapted with permission of the Free Press, a division of Simon & Schuster, Inc., from *Touched With Fire: Manic-Depressive Illness and The Artistic Temperament* by Kay Redfield Jamison, PhD. Copyright © 1993 by Kay Redfield Jamison. **Fig. 8.8:** From E. E. Beckman and W. R. Leber, *Handbook of Depression.* Copyright © 1985 Guilford Publications. Reprinted by permission. **Fig. 8.13:** From Cross National Collaborative Group, "The Changing Rate of Major Depression" in *Journal of the American Medical Association* 168 (21): 3098–3105. Copyright © 1992, American Medical Association. **Fig. 8.16:** From J. E. Gillham, et al., "Prevention of Depressive Symptoms in School Children: Two-year Follow-up" in *Psychological Science,* 6, 343–351. Copyright © 1995 Blackwell Publishers, Malden, MA. Reprinted by permission.

Chapter 9

p. 298: From Parker, D. (1994) "Resume," copyright 1926, 1928, renewed 1954, © 1956 by Dorothy Oarker, from in *The Portable of Dorothy Parker* by Dorothy Parker. Used by permission of Viking Penguin, a division of Penguin Putnam Inc. **Fig. 9.1:** From The New York Times/CBS News poll, in the *New York Times,* October 20, 1991. Reprinted by permission of NYT Pictures. **Fig. 9.2:** From E. Moscicki, "Epidemiology of Suicidal Behavior" in *Suicide and Life-Threatening Behavior,* 25(1): 22–35. Copyright © 1995 Guilford Publications, Inc. Reprinted by permission. **Fig. 9.3:** From A. L. Berman and D. A. Jobes, *Adolescent Suicide: Assessment and Intervention.* Copyright © 1991 by the American Psychological Association. Reprinted with permission. **Fig. 9.4:** From R. Diekstra and N. Garnefski, "On the Nature, Magnitude, and Casualty of Suicidal Behavior" in *Suicide and Life-Threatening Behavior,* 25(1): 36–57. Copyright © 1995 Guilford Publications, Inc. Reprinted by permission. **p. 311:** From *An Unquiet Mind* by Kay Redfield Jamison. Copyright © 1995 by Kay Redfield Jamison. Reprinted by permissions of Alfred A. Knopf, a Division of Random House Inc.

Chapter 10

Fig. 10.2 and 10.4: From *Schizophrenia Genesis* by Gottesman. Copyright © 1991 by Iriving I. Gottesman. Used with permission by W. H. Freeman and Company. **Fig. 10.3:** From A. Jablensky, et al., "Epidemiology and Cross-Cultural Aspects of Schizophrenia" in *Psychiatric Annals,* 19(10): 521, October 1989. Reprinted by permission of SLACK Incorporated. **Fig. 10.10:** From G. E. Hogarty, et al., "Family Psychoeducation" in *Archives of General Psychiatry,* 43:633–642. Copyright © 1986 American Medical Association.

Chapter 11

p. 387: From Toufexis, A. (April 29, 1999) "Why Jennifer Got Sick", *Time* 4/29/99, p. 70. Copyright © 1999 Time Inc. Reprinted by permission.

Chapter 12

pp. 411, 426, 427: From Beck, A. T., & Freeman, A. M. (1990) Cognitive therapy of personality disorders, pp. 111–112, 211–212, 245–247. **pp. 411–12, 413, 429:** From Spitzer, R. L., Skodol, A. E., Gibbon, M., & Williams, J. B. W. in *DSM-III case book: A Learning Companion to the Diagnostic and Statistical Manual of Mental Disorders,* 3/e, pp. 95–96, 146, 243–244, 304–305. Copyright © 1981 the American Psychiatric Association. Reprinted by permission. **pp. 416–417, 432–433:** From Spitzer, R. L., Skodol, A. E., Gibbon, M., & Williams, J. B. W. in *Psychopathology, a Case Book,* 1983, pp. 63–68, 87–89. Reprinted by permission. **pp. 424–425:** From APA Monitor Web Site. Copyright © 1997 by the American Psychological Association. Reprinted with permission. **p. 434:** From Costa, P. T. & Widiger, T. A. (Eds.) "Personality disorders and the five-factor model of personality." Copyright © 1994 by the American Psychological Association. Reprinted with permission.

Chapter 13

pp. 444–445: From Spitzer, R. L., Skodol, A. E., Gibbon, M., & Williams, J. B. W. in *DSM-IV case book: A Learning Companion to the Diagnostic and Statistical Manual of Mental Disorders,* 4/e, pp. 351–352. Copyright © 1981 the American Psychiatric Association. Reprinted by permission. **p. 450:** From Spitzer, R. L., Skodol, A. E., Gibbon, M., & Williams, J. B. W. in *DSM-III case book: A Learning Companion to the Diagnostic and Statistical Manual of Mental Disorders,* 3/e, pp. 95–96. Copyright © 1981 the American Psychiatric Association. Reprinted by permission. **p. 456:** From Lochman, White & Wayland, "Cognitive-behavioral assessment and treatment with aggressive children" in Kendall (Ed.) *Child and adolescent therapy: Cognitive-behavioral procedures,* 1996 (xvii, 361), 50–51. **Fig. 13.3:** From Dadds, et al., "Early Intervention and Prevention of Anxiety Disorders in Children: Results at 2-Year Follow-Up" in *Journal of Consulting and Clinical Psychology.* Copyright © 1999 by the American Psychological Association. Reprinted by permission

Chapter 14

p. 493: From *Wasted: A memoir of anorexia and bulimia,* pp. 254–255 by Marya Hornbacher. Copyright © 1998 by Marya Hornbacher-Beard. Reprinted by permission of HarperCollins Publishers, Inc. **pp. 499–500:** From Stunkard, A. J. (1993) "A history of binge eating" in C. G. Fairburn & G. T. Wilson (Eds.), *Binge eating: Nature, assessment, and treatment,* pp. 20–21. **p. 498:** From Spitzer, R. L., Skodol, A. E., Gibbon, M., & Williams, J. B. W. in *DSM-III case book: A Learning Companion to the Diagnostic and Statistical Manual of Mental Disorders,* 3/e, p. 146. Copyright © 1981 the American Psychiatric Association. Reprinted by permission. **Fig. 14.2:** From "Use of the Danish Adoption Register for the Study of Obesity and Thinness" by A. Stunkard, T. Sorensen, and F. Schulsinger, in *The Genetics of Neurological and Psychiatric Disorders,* edited by S. Kety, ARNMD Series, Volume 60, 1980, p. 119. Copyright © 1983 by Raven Press. Reprinted by permission of Lippincott Williams & Wilkins. **pp. 508–509:** From BBC Panorama—An Interview with HRH the Princess of Wales, 20th November 1995. Reprinted with permission.

Chapter 15

pp. 531, 532, 536–537, 550–551, 552, 553: From Spitzer, R. L., Skodol, A. E., Gibbon, M., & Williams, J. B. W. in *DSM-IV case book: A Learning Companion to the Diagnostic and Statistical Manual of Mental Disorders,* 4/e, pp. 117–118, 187–188, 198–199, 213, 247, 251–252, 257–258. Copyright © 1981 the American Psychiatric Association. Reprinted with permission. **pp. 532–533:** From McCarthy, R. W. (1989) "Cognitive-behavioral strategies and techniques in the treatment of early ejaculation" in S. R. Leiblum, R. C. Rosen (Eds.), *Principles and practice of sex therapy: Update for the 1990's,* pp. 151–152. **pp. 544–545:** From Hiller, J. (1996) "Female sexual arousal and its impairment: The psychodynamics of non-organic coital pain" in *Sexual & Marital Therapy,* 11, 69–70. **pp. 560–561:** From Dickey, R., & Stephens, J. (1995) "Female-to-male transsexualism, heterosexual type: Two cases" in *Archives of Sexual behavior,* 24, 442–443 Kluwer Academic/Plenum Publishers. Reprinted by permission. **Fig. 15.1 and 15.2:** From J. S. Hyde, *Understanding Human Sexuality.* Copyright © 1990 McGraw-Hill Companies, Inc. All Rights Reserved. Reprinted with permission. **Fig. 15.4:** From G. F. Kelly, *Sexuality Today.* Copyright © 1998 McGraw-Hill Companies, Inc. All Rights Reserved. Reprinted with permission. **Fig. 15.5:** From J. S. Hyde and J. D. Delamater, *Understanding Human Sexuality,* 7th edition. Copyright © 2000 McGraw-Hill Companies, Inc. All Rights Reserved. Reprinted with permission.

Chapter 16

pp. 574–575, 603–604: From Inciardi, J. A., Lockwood, D., & Pottieger, A. E. in *Women and crack cocaine,* pp. 138–139, 160–163. Copyright © 1993 by Allyn & Bacon. Reprinted by permission. **pp. 572, 589:** From Spitzer, R. L., Skodol, A. E., Gibbon, M., & Williams, J. B. W. in *DSM-IV case book: A Learning Companion to the Diagnostic and Statistical Manual of Mental Disorders,* 4/e, pp. 139–140, 204–205. Copyright © 1981 the American Psychiatric Association. Reprinted by permission. **p. 581:** From Spitzer, R. L., Skodol, A. E., Gibbon, M., & Williams, J. B. W. in *DSM-III case book: A Learning Companion to the Diagnostic and Statistical Manual of Mental Disorders,* 3/e, pp. 304–305. Copyright © 1981 American Psychiatric Association. Reprinted by permission. **Fig. 16.1, 16.2, 16.3:** From L. A. Warner, et al., "Prevalence and Correlates of Drug Use and Dependence in the United States" in *Archives of General Psychiatry,* 52, 219–229. Copyright © 1995 American Medical Association. **pp. 609–610:** From Spitzer, R. L., Skodol, A. E., Gibbon, M., & Williams, J. B. W. in *Psychopathology, a Case Book,* 1983, pp. 87–89. Reprinted by permission.

Chapter 17

p. 624: From Joe Mathews in *The Baltimore Sun,* July 30, 1996. Reprinted with permission. **p. 632:** From *Stress and Coping: An Anthology.* eds. A. Monat and R. S. Lazarus, pp. 55–66. © 1985 Columbia University Press. Reprinted by permission of the publisher. **Fig. 17.7:** From S. W. Cole, et al., "Elevated Physical Health Risk Among Gay Men Who Conceal Their Homosexual Identity" in *Health Psychology,* 15, 243–251, 1996. Copyright © 1996 by the American Psychological Association. Reprinted by permission.

Chapter 18

p. 658: From Gallagher-Thompson, D., Lovett, S., & Rose, J., "Psychotherpaeutic interventions for stressed family caregivers" in W. A. Myers (Ed.), *New techniques in psychotherapy of older patients,* pp. 68–69. Copyright © 1991 the American Psychiatric Association. Reprinted by permission. **pp. 655, 674:** From Spitzer, R. L., Skodol, A. E., Gibbon, M., & Williams, J. B. W. in *DSM-III case book: A Learning Companion to the Diagnostic and Statistical Manual of Mental Disorders,* 3/e, pp. 41–42, 243–244. Copyright © 1981 the American Psychiatric Association. Reprinted by permission. **Fig. 18.7:** From M. F. Folstein, et al., "Mini-mental State: A Practical Method of Grading the Cognitive State of Patients for the Clinician" in *Journal of Psychiatric Research,* 12, 189–198. Copyright © 1975 Mini Mental LLC.

Chapter 19

pp. 696–697: From Guidelines for Ethical Service to Culturally Diverse Populations. Copyright © 1993 by the American Psychological Association. Reprinted with permission.

NAME INDEX

Note: Page numbers in *italics* indicate illustrations; page numbers followed by *t* indicate tables.

Note: Page numbers in *italics* indicate figures; page numbers followed by *t* indicate tables; page numbers followed by *n* indicate footnotes.

(Continued from inside front cover)

Anxiety Disorders

Panic Disorder without Agoraphobia
Panic Disorder with Agoraphobia
Agoraphobia without History of Panic
  Disorder
Specific Phobia
Social Phobia
Obsessive-Compulsive Disorder
Posttraumatic Stress Disorder
Acute Stress Disorder
Generalized Anxiety Disorder
Anxiety Disorders Due to a General Medical
  Condition
Substance-Induced Anxiety Disorder
Anxiety Disorder NOS

Somatoform Disorders

Somatization Disorder
Undifferentiated Somatoform
  Disorder
Conversion Disorder
Pain Disorder
Hypochondriasis
Body Dysmorphic Disorder
Somatoform Disorder NOS

Factitious Disorders

Factitious Disorder
Factitious Disorder NOS

Dissociative Disorders

Dissociative Amnesia
Dissociative Fugue
Dissociative Identity Disorder
Depersonalization Disorder
Dissociative Disorder NOS

Sexual and Gender Identity Disorders

Sexual Dysfunctions
  Sexual Desire Disorders
    Hypoactive Sexual Desire Disorder
    Sexual Aversion Disorder
  Sexual Arousal Disorders
    Female Sexual Arousal Disorder
    Male Erectile Disorder

Orgasmic Disorders
  Female Orgasmic Disorder
  Male Orgasmic Disorder
  Premature Ejaculation
Sexual Pain Disorders
  Dyspareunia
  Vaginismus
  Sexual Dysfunction Due to a General
    Medical Condition
  Substance-Induced Sexual Dysfunction
  Sexual Dysfunction NOS
Paraphilias
  Exhibitionism
  Fetishism
  Frotteurism
  Pedophilia
  Sexual Masochism
  Sexual Sadism
  Transvestic Fetishism
  Voyeurism
  Paraphilia NOS
Gender Identity Disorders
  Gender Identity Disorder in Children
  Gender Identity Disorder in Adolescents
    or Adults
  Gender Identity Disorder NOS
Other Sexual Disorder
  Sexual Disorder NOS

Eating Disorders

Anorexia Nervosa
Bulimia Nervosa
Eating Disorder NOS

Sleep Disorders

Primary Sleep Disorders
  Dyssomnias
    Primary Insomnia
    Primary Hypersomnia
    Narcolepsy
    Breathing-Related Sleep Disorder
    Circadian Rhythm Sleep Disorder
    Dyssomnia NOS
  Parasomnias
    Nightmare Disorder
    Sleep Terror Disorder
    Sleepwalking Disorder
    Parasomnia NOS

SEW EASY
EMBELLISHMENTS

Nancy Zieman

OXMOOR
HOUSE®

Sew Easy Embellishments

by Nancy Zieman
from the "Sewing with Nancy" series

Published by Oxmoor House, Inc., and Leisure Arts, Inc.

Library of Congress Catalog Number: 97-66727
Hardcover ISBN: 0-8487-1537-3
Softcover ISBN: 0-8487-1605-1
Manufactured in the United States of America
First Printing 1997

Editor-in-Chief: Nancy Fitzpatrick Wyatt
Senior Crafts Editor: Susan Ramey Cleveland
Senior Editor, Editorial Services: Olivia Kindig Wells
Art Director: James Boone

Sew Easy Embellishments

Editor: Lois Martin
Editorial Assistant: Cecile Y. Nierodzinski
Copy Editor: Anne S. Dickson
Designer: Emily Albright Parrish
Associate Art Director: Cindy Cooper
Production and Distribution Director: Phillip Lee
Associate Production Manager: Theresa L. Beste
Senior Photographer: John O'Hagan
Photo Stylists: Katie Stoddard, Linda Baltzell Wright
Illustrator: Rochelle Stibb
Editorial Assistance, Nancy's Notions: Betty Hanneman

We're Here for You!

We at Oxmoor House are dedicated to serving you with reliable information that expands your imagination and enriches your life. We welcome your comments and suggestions.
Please write us at:
Oxmoor House, Inc.
Editor, *Sew Easy Embellishments*
2100 Lakeshore Drive
Birmingham, AL 35209
To order additional publications, call 1-205-877-6560.

The editor thanks Allison D. Ingram for modeling the fashions in this book, Ann Marie Harvey for providing hands to photograph, and Mark McDowell of the Sewing Machine Mart in Homewood, Alabama, for lending the Pfaff sewing machines and sergers used in photography.

A Note from Nancy

Nancy Zieman, author, teacher, and business-woman, hosted her 15th season of "Sewing With Nancy" on the Public Broadcasting System in 1997.

If you're like me, one of the reasons you love sewing is that you can create one-of-a-kind garments and gifts. Discovering the right fabric to go with the perfect pattern is fun, but I find it even more satisfying to create a special embellishment that sets my project apart.

Sometimes, I need an embellishment I can stitch quickly and easily, adding it to a garment I've bought. When I have more time, I may create my own fabric or use my sewing machine to add silk-ribbon embroidery to a stitching project.

If you've never thought of yourself as a fashion designer, here's a chance to release your creativity! Just choose a technique from this book that looks like it would be fun for you, and gather your supplies and fabric. Take your time, and enjoy the sewing. You be the designer!

Contents

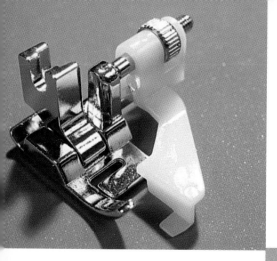

A built-in guide on the blindhem foot *(left and page 12)* keeps seam width even. Choosing the right thread *(right and page 14)* makes any project easier to stitch. ▶

Beginning with the right tools simplifies embellishing. From thread to presser feet to scissors, creative supplies enhance your sewing.

Creative Supplies

◀ A notch in the blade of buttonhole scissors *(left and page 9)* helps you cut precise openings. For a novel edge, try a pinking or a wave blade in your rotary cutter *(right and page 9)*. ▶

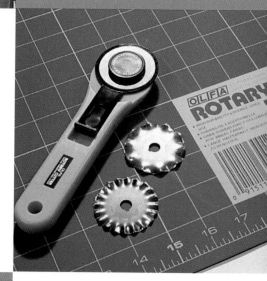

◀ Magnetic templates for a buttonhole foot *(left and page 12)* ensure that buttonholes are just the size needed.

Confetti Appliqué,
page 47

Specialized Notions

Choose from a wide assortment of tools and notions that make sewing easier.

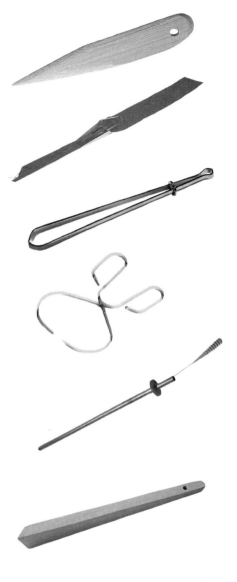

Bamboo Pointer & Creaser

Use the pointed end to turn collars, cuffs, lapels, or appliqués. Flip the tool over and use the curved, beveled end to temporarily press seams open.

Bias Tape Maker

Slip a bias strip into the wide end of this metal tool and pull the strip out as you press. You create single-fold bias tape with edges that are always uniform. Bias tape makers are available in a wide range of widths, from 6 mm to 50 mm.

Bodkin

This tweezerlike notion has special teeth that grasp your fabric or trim, making it easier for you to draw lace, ribbon, and elastic through a casing. Also handy for weaving.

Collar Point & Tube Turner

Turn lapel and collar points, pocket flaps, spaghetti straps, and belts using this scissorlike tool.

Fasturn®

Used for turning fabric tubes right side out, this specialty notion has two sections: a metal cylinder and a wire hook. Place a fabric tube over the cylinder, and use the hook to pull the fabric through the inside of the cylinder, turning the tube right side out. (See page 106 for diagrams of how to use this notion.) Also inserts cording.

Little Wooden Iron

A unique finger-pressing notion, this smoothly sanded hardwood tool is useful for opening seams and for pressing seams to the side when quilting. Choose a right- or left-handed iron, since the tool's pressing edge is made at an angle. The 5¼"-long (13 cm-long) Little Wooden Iron has a comfortable grasp.

Seam Sealant

Products like Fray Check™ and No-Fray reinforce and lock threads to prevent fraying of seams. Stabilize buttonholes with a drop of this clear-drying liquid.

Stiletto

Use this awl-like tool to ease fabric, lace, or ribbon under the presser foot as you sew or quilt. A stiletto also helps keep seam allowances in place as you stitch, straighten silk ribbon embroidery stitches, and turn appliqué points.

Cutting Tools

Choosing the right cutting tool gets your project off to a good start.

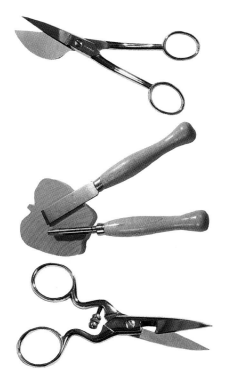

Appliqué Scissors

Use appliqué scissors for trimming close to edgestitching. The scissors' large bill lifts the fabric to be trimmed, and the curved handles ensure a comfortable hand position.

Buttonhole Cutter and Block

This tool helps you make neat, professional-looking buttonholes. The cutter has a hardwood handle with a hardened steel blade; the block comes in various shapes. Place the buttonhole over the block and cut with the cutter. If the buttonhole is smaller than the cutter, place half the buttonhole over the edge of the block, cut, and repeat for the second part.

Buttonhole Scissors

These handy scissors allow you to make precise buttonhole cuts. Adjust the screw at the handle of the scissors to hold them in a partially open position. This allows you to use part of the blade to make precise ½" to ¼" (1.3 cm to 3.8 cm) buttonhole cuts. Fabric in front of the buttonhole bunches safely in the reservoir at the base of the blade.

Dressmaker Shears

The term "shears" refers to blades of 8" or longer. Shears are available with or without bent handles. Use them for general sewing needs.

Pinking Shears

These shears with sawtooth edges cut decorative, ravel-resistant edges of seams and trim. When you cut curved seam allowances with pinking shears, you automatically reduce bulk in the finished seam.

Rotary Cutter

This special fabric cutting tool looks and works like a pizza cutter. Easy to grasp and comfortable to use, a rotary cutter has a round sharp blade attached to the end of a handle. The replaceable blades come with straight, wavy, or pinked edges. Rotary cutters were developed for quilting, since they can cut through several layers of fabric at once, but they're useful for other types of sewing as well.

Rotary Cutting Mat

Designed for use with rotary cutters, these mats protect your work surface and provide guides to make cutting straight edges and identical pieces fast and easy. The mat's cutting side is printed with hash marks every ¼", a 1" grid, and diagonal lines to help you cut triangles. The mats are sold in various sizes. Store mats flat to prevent warping.

Marking Tools

Top-quality sewing requires accuracy. The right marking tools will help you achieve it.

Chalk

This oil-free marking tool is available in several forms.

• A chalk wheel accurately transfers markings to fabric with a fine line of chalk. Fill the wheel with loose white chalk (for dark fabrics) or blue chalk (for light fabrics).

• Triangle Tailor's Chalk has a chalk base in a firm triangular form, and never leaves a stain. Use it to make crisp, accurate lines on all your sewing projects. Triangle Tailor's Chalk comes in red, yellow, white, and blue.

• A Soapstone Fabric Marker will not harm fabrics because it's made from natural soapstone. Soapstone marks are clearly visible, yet rub off easily when no longer needed. It does not show up on light-colored fabrics. This marker is adjustable and sharpens in a pencil sharpener.

Fabric Marking Pen

This pinpoint pen marks fine lines so you can trace small designs or mark complex patterns clearly. Fabric marking pens are available in air- and water-soluble form.

• The Wonder Marker's blue ink disappears with just a drop of water, making it a perfect marking tool to use on washable fabrics.

> ### Note from Nancy
> *Always test fabric markers on a scrap of the fabric you plan to use to be sure the marks come out. And remember that heat will set these marks. Remove the marks before pressing, and do not use hot water to remove water-soluble marks.*

Fabric Marking Pencil

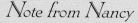

A super-thin lead pencil specifically designed for fabric, the fabric marking pencil is always sharp. Since it contains less graphite than a standard pencil, it resists smearing and washes out beautifully.

Gridded Paper

An iron-on paper with a ¼" grid, this paper bonds permanently to other paper and temporarily to fabric (without leaving a residue). Gridded paper is ideal for appliqué and stencilling.

Hot Tape™

No more pins or burned fingers as you position transfers, appliqué, and pleats! Hot Tape is an adhesive-backed, gridded tape that's heat resistant. Use it to create pleats or position appliqué. The tape peels off easily without any residue and may be reused. Note: Do not sew over tape because it gums up the needle.

Pattern Transfer Materials

Use a traditional sawtoothed tracing wheel and tracing/transfer paper to mark seam lines, trace quilting patterns, indicate appliqué positions, and more. The paper is reusable, wax-free, and carbonless, and marks from it erase, sponge off, or wash out. Tracing/transfer paper comes in a variety of colors.

- Pressure-fax® Transfer Pen & Paper is simple to use: just trace and rub. Use a transfer pen to trace your design onto the special paper. Then simply place the paper (image side down) over your fabric and rub with your fingernail, a spoon, or the Little Wooden Iron.
- The Fabric Pattern Transfer Kit™ includes everything you need to transfer silk-ribbon embroidery designs to fabric. Trace a design onto the transfer paper and place the traced design over fabric. Use the purple pen tip to retrace the design, which marks your fabric. The pen has a white tip to erase marks.

Pigma Permanent Marker

These pens work best on natural, untreated 100% cotton or cotton blends, where their marks dry quickly and will not fade, smear, or feather when dry. Pigma ink is waterproof. Use these pens to personalize heirloom treasures and draw details on projects.

Measuring Tools

For clothes to fit, quilts to go together without bunching, and home decorating projects to cover surfaces, you must measure carefully when you cut.

Quilting Rulers

These heavy-duty, clear acrylic rulers were developed for quilters to use with rotary cutters, but they're also useful in other sewing projects. Quilting rulers come in various sizes. The most popular ones are listed below.
- A 1" x 6" pocket-size ruler is convenient and versatile for quilting and sewing.
- Keep a 1" x 12½" ruler for quick measuring references.
- The larger 3" x 18" ruler is great for secondary cutting and for fine patchwork techniques. Use positions clearly marked on the ruler to cut accurate 30°, 45°, and 60° angles.

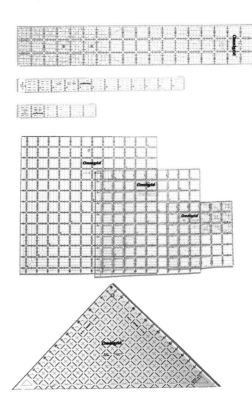

Quilting Squares

Quilting squares help you square-up quilt blocks. (See Crazy Patchwork with Decorative Stitching on page 68.) The squares come in 6", 9½", and 12½", and are marked with diagonal bias lines.

Half Squares

Use Half Squares to cut half-square triangles up to 8" in size.

Sewing Machine Feet

Matching the right presser foot to the job can save you hours of sewing time and simplify many stitching jobs.

Blindhem Foot

The blindhem foot is one of the most versatile presser feet in your accessory box. In addition to its traditional use for hemming woven and knit fabrics, this foot can help you apply patch pockets and appliqué, and makes straight edgestitching a breeze!

• You can move the adjustable guide closer to or farther from the left side of the foot to accommodate fabrics of various weights and textures.

• As stitches form, they pass over a metal pin (optional feature) at the center of the foot. This pin adds slack so that stitches are not too taut.

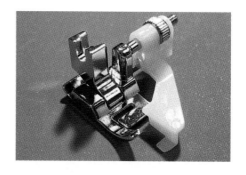

Buttonhole Foot

Whether your project calls for 2 or 12 buttonholes, it's easy to get identical buttonholes with smooth, uniform stitching every time you use a buttonhole foot.

• The top of this foot moves back and forth in a sliding tray attached to the bottom of the foot.

• Markings along one or both sides of the foot indicate buttonhole length.

• Toes at the front or back of foot accommodate cording for corded buttonholes.

• Buttonhole templates in ½", ⅝", ¾", ⅞", and 1" sizes fit into the back of this foot to determine quickly buttonhole length.

Conventional Foot

The conventional, or general purpose, presser foot is most commonly used for everyday sewing.

• The foot's wide opening is proportionate to the width of the machine's zigzag stitch. The width of the opening ranges from ⅛" to ¼" (4 mm to 9 mm), depending on the sewing machine.

• The throat plate used with the conventional foot has an opening of similar size so that the needle can easily enter the bobbin area to form a perfect stitch.

Note From Nancy
The presser feet pictured may not look exactly like the ones in your accessory box because each manufacturer has a different style. To identify your presser feet, check your sewing machine owner's manual, or compare the features listed in this section with your presser feet.

Cording Foot

The cording foot streamlines the process of making piping and couching multiple cords to fabric. It's usually available from your sewing machine dealer.

• The top of the cording foot looks much like the conventional foot with a wide opening for the zigzag stitch.

• The underside has a large, hollowed-out groove to accommodate cording, piping, or decorative trim, allowing the trim to lie flat and feed evenly under the foot.

Little Foot™

Accurate piecing is crucial for successful quiltmaking. The Little Foot makes it easy to get that accuracy.

• The right edge of the foot is precisely ¼" (6 mm) from the center needle position, providing an accurate mark for making a ¼" (6 mm) seam allowance.

• The left edge of the foot is precisely ⅛" (3 mm) from the center needle position, providing an accurate mark for making a ⅛" (3 mm) seam allowance.

• Red laser markings ¼" (6 mm) in front of and behind the needle serve as accurate reference points for starting, stopping, and pivoting.

Multicord Foot

If you've ever wrestled with an assortment of decorative threads, trying to keep them aligned as you couch them in place, this presser foot is for you. Use it to guide up to five decorative threads (some feet guide up to nine threads) through the slots and under the foot to create interesting embellishments.

• The multicord foot has five holes in front of the needle opening, three on the top row, and two on the bottom. Feet with nine holes have a third row with four openings.

• Holes accommodate cording or decorative thread.

• Optional: Use a Multiple Cording Guide to keep threads aligned as they feed through the machine. This guide keeps threads separated and controls the flow.

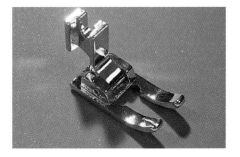

Open Toe or Embroidery Foot

This specialty presser foot lets you see more of the area around the needle when sewing decorative stitches or satin-stitching around appliqué.

• The toe area may be completely open or its center may be clear plastic. This makes it easy to see stitches as they form on fabric.

• The underside has a hollowed or grooved section that allows dense stitching to move smoothly under the foot without bunching under the needle.

Pintuck Foot

A must for creating pintucks, this presser foot has grooves that make it simple to guide and evenly space row after row of pintucks.

• The most distinctive feature of a pintuck foot is the series of grooves on the underside. Depending on the manufacturer, the foot may have five to nine grooves. These grooves provide channels or guides for previous rows of pintucking.

• By combining a pintuck foot with a double needle, you can quickly make straight, uniform pintucks.

• Optional: Insert a cording blade on the machine. This accessory, available for some machines, forces the fabric up into the pintuck foot, making the pintuck more pronounced.

Sequins 'N Ribbons™ Foot

Sew on sequins, ribbons, and even narrow elastic with this unique presser foot.

• An adjustable guide precisely positions the trim in front of the needle.

• Additional accessory guides are available for attaching ⅛" (3 mm) and ⅜" (1 cm) trims and elastics.

Thread

For successful sewing, there's more to choosing thread than just picking the right color.

Choose thread the same color or one shade darker than your fashion fabric. Thread appears lighter when sewn than it does on the spool. Match thread to the predominant or background color when working with prints, tweeds, or plaids.

If your stitches are not smooth and uniform, check the sewing machine needle for damage, size, and type. The needle should match the thread type, fabric, and sewing technique. The chart that follows includes descriptions of different thread types, their uses, fiber content, and size. Under the size column, the first number (Wt.) indicates the weight of the thread, and the second number (Ply) indicates the number of plies or strands used to make the thread. The larger the weight number, the finer the thread.

> ### Note From Nancy
> *Always use 3-ply thread for general-purpose sewing. Two-ply thread works well on sergers because serger seams have three or more threads each, which strengthens the seams. I do not recommend using serger thread on your sewing machine.*

Thread Type	Description	Uses	Fiber Content	Wt./Ply
All-purpose • Cotton-wrapped polyester core	Polyester core wrapped with fine cotton; less static than 100% polyester, easy to sew with, and withstands high temperatures; can rot or mildew; more durable than 100% cotton, with more stretch and strength	General sewing for most fabrics; avoid on leather, fur, suede, rainwear, and very lightweight fabrics	Cotton and polyester	50/3
• Long-staple polyester	High-quality polyester thread made with long fibers; stronger and more durable than cotton, and more resistant to abrasion and chemicals; may pucker seams and skip stitches in lightweight fabrics	General sewing for most fabrics, including leather, suede, and fur; avoid using on silk and lightweight fabrics	Polyester	50/3
Bobbinfil	Lightweight thread designed specifically for use in the bobbin	Machine embroidery, decorative stitching	100% polyester	70/none
Buttonhole Twist	Thick, heavy thread; sometimes called topstitching thread; less lustrous than silk	Embellishment, topstitching	Polyester or polyester core	40/3

Thread Type	Description	Uses	Fiber Content	Wt./Ply
Cotton	Lightweight thread, double mercerized for sheen and softness	Heirloom sewing, including smocking and embroidery	100% cotton	80/2
Decorative and embellishment threads and yarns	Variety of threads, usually made from cotton, wool, silk, linen, acrylic, or silk-and-wool blend; dry clean or prewash; some fibers may bleed	Surface embellishment, such as couching	Varies	Varies
Embroidery • Cotton	Soft matte finish for a natural appearance	Embroidery, lace-making, quilting	100% cotton	30/2
• Rayon	Brilliant, colorfast thread; available in solid and variegated colors	Decorative stitching, topstitching	100% viscose rayon	40/2, 30/2
Fusible	Adhesive coating on thread melts when pressed with warm iron	Basting; substitute for narrow strips of fusible web	Twisted polyester thread containing heat-activated fusible nylon filament	85/3
Jeans Stitch	Colorfast, durable thread	Topstitching, decorative stitching	Spun polyester	30/3
Lingerie/Bobbin	Extra-fine nylon thread with good stretch; black or white only	Bobbin thread for decorative stitching, machine embroidery, stretch seams	100% nylon with special twist that creates stretch as you sew	70 denier/2
Metallic	Shimmery foil-wrap bonded to thread core; available textured or smooth	Decorative stitching	Foil-wrapped core thread	40/2

Thread Type	Description	Uses	Fiber Content	Wt./Ply
Monofilament (Wonder Thread or Monofil)	Clear, lightweight, soft, single-strand nylon thread; appears invisible when used on the right side of fabric; available clear or smoke-colored	Appliqué, couching, attaching sequins, soft rolled hems, joining lace strips, soft seam finishes, setting pockets, serging	100% nylon filament	.004 size
Serger, All-purpose	Comparable to all-purpose sewing machine thread, except serger thread is 2-ply	Finishing edges, seaming fabrics	Polyester core wrapped with fine cotton or 100% polyester	40/2
Serger, Decorative • Decor 6	Satiny soft thread with extra thickness because plies have minimal twist	Decorative serging, surface embellishment	100% viscose rayon filament	4-ply
• Glamour	Brilliant, glittery durable thread	Decorative serging, surface embellishment	65% viscose rayon, 35% metallic polyester	8-ply
• Pearl Cotton	Very lustrous Egyptian cotton thread	Decorative serging and stitching (size 30/2 is too heavy for stitching on conventional machine)	100% Egyptian cotton, double mercerized for sheen	30/2, 60/2
• Pearl Rayon	Strong, brilliant, colorfast rayon thread; available in solid or variegated colors	Decorative serging, surface embellishment	100% viscose rayon filament	40/2
Silk	Very lustrous	Embellishment, topstitching	100% silk	Varies
Sliver	Thin, flat, ribbonlike polyester film; infused with metal to make it brilliantly reflective	Decorative sewing, serging	Polyester film metalized with aluminum	1/100" thick
Woolly Nylon	Super-stretchy thread used as an edge finish or in seams that require stretch	Serging swimwear, lingerie, baby clothes; especially effective for rolled edges	Texturized (unspun) 100% nylon	DNA

Needles

By choosing the correct needle type and size, you can avoid skipped stitches and fraying thread.

Hand-sewing Needles

• A **crewel needle** is sharp and of medium length, with an elongated eye. It's generally used for embroidery.

• A **double-eyed needle** has blunt tips with eyes on each end that make it useful for weaving threads or trim underneath stitches. Keep the ends of serged seams neat and secure by inserting the thread ends into either of the needle's eyes and threading the needle under the stitches of the seam. Pull the needle through, anchoring the thread ends so that they won't ravel.

Double-eyed needle

Use a double-eyed needle to thread ribbons under decorative serged stitches, to pinweave yarns and ribbons, and to place ribbons in heirloom sewing. Knitters and crocheters appreciate how easily the double-eyed needle secures yarn ends when they change colors or yarn skeins.

• **Sharps** are all-purpose, medium-length needles used for general sewing.

• A **tapestry needle** has a large oval eye and a rounded point. Use it for silk-ribbon embroidery and drawnwork.

• A **weaving needle's** flat shape and bent tip makes it easy to get under warp threads when weaving. This needle's large eye accommodates embellishment yarns, threads, and ribbons.

sharp

tapestry needle

weaving needle

• A **Trolley Needle™** Thread Controller is not actually a sewing needle, but a sewing guide. Slip a Trolley Needle onto your index finger like a thimble, and use it to ease seams and ruffles under the presser foot or hold ribbon flat while doing silk-ribbon embroidery by machine. You'll also find this a handy tool for positioning sequins and trims while you stitch.

Trolley Needle

Sewing Machine Needles

When choosing a sewing machine needle, you should consider the type and weight of fabric in your project, the type of thread you're using, and the kind of sewing you will be doing.

Some needles have special eyes to accommodate larger threads, others are sturdy enough to stitch heavy fabrics such as denim, and still others are best suited to delicate heirloom sewing on fine fabrics, such as batiste. The Guide to Sewing Machine Needles (on page 18) provides information on needle types, sizes, and appropriate uses.

A sewing machine needle has a shank, a shaft, an eye, and a point. The shank fits into your sewing machine's needle holder, and it has a rounded side and a flat side. The indentation behind the eye is called the scarf. The needle groove is on the same side of the needle as the rounded part of the shaft.

In sewing machine needles, higher numbers identify larger needles, so a size 110 denim needle is larger than a size 90 denim needle. Generally, the larger the needle, the heavier the fabric for which it's appropriate. Use smaller sizes with more delicate fabrics and larger sizes with heavier fabrics.

For double needles, the first size indicates the distance between the two needles, followed by the size of each needle. For example, a 2.0 mm/75 double needle has two size-75 needles that are 2.0 mm apart.

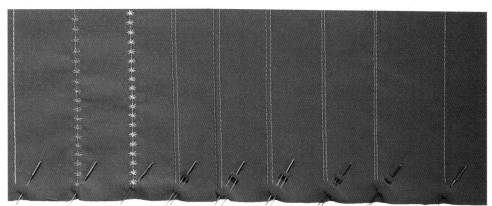
Machine needles and sample stitches shown left to right are: topstitching, metallic, embroidery, double stretch, double 4.0, double 3.0, double 2.0, double 1.6, and all-purpose.

Needle	Size	Description	Uses
Denim/Sharp	90, 100, 110	Very sharp point to ease penetration of dense fabrics	Denim, heavy corduroy, dense wool, canvas, heavy poplin or twill
Leather	80, 90	Wedge shape, knife-edge cutting point; not suited for synthetic suede or leather because slit made by needle eventually tears	Real leather or suede; not suitable for synthetic leather or suede
Machine Embroidery	75, 90	Slightly rounded point, long eye, and deep front groove; for use with decorative threads; protects delicate embroidery threads; avoids fraying and breaking	Knits and wovens
Metafil	80	Fine shaft, sharp point, and large, elongated eye; specialized scarf eliminates skipped stitches	Sewing with metallic and other decorative threads
Metallica	80	Large eye for easy threading and to accommodate heavier threads; large groove prevents shredding of threads	Sewing with metallic and other delicate threads
Microtex Sharps	60, 70, 80, 90	Slim, sharp point; very thin shaft for penetrating dense fabric surfaces	Microfiber fabrics such as Ultrasuede; heirloom sewing
Self-threading	90	Slit in side of eye for threading ease; weaker than conventional needles	Simplifies needle threading
Spring Denim/Sharp	100	Sharp point for penetrating dense fabrics; attached spring allows free-form sewing	Free-motion embroidery
Spring Machine Embroidery	75, 90	Same features as machine embroidery needle with an attached spring	Free-motion embroidery using decorative threads
Spring Machine Quilting	75, 90	Same features as machine quilting needle with an attached spring	Free-form quilting
Stretch	75, 90	Medium ballpoint; long, flat shank lets needle work close to bobbin; prevents skipped stitches	Size 75 for sewing lightweight knits, such as tricot, interlock, silk jersey, lycra, and Ultrasuede; size 90 for sewing lycra, Ultrasuede, and synthetic furs with knit backings
Topstitching	80, 90, 100	Extra-large eye; large groove accommodates topstitching thread	Sewing with heavier thread; embroidery with delicate and metallic threads
Universal	60, 70, 80, 90, 100, 110	Slightly rounded point, long needle scarf; all-purpose needle for sewing wovens, knits	Size 60 for silks; size 70 for lightweight fabrics; size 80 for medium-weight fabrics; size 90 for medium-weight to heavy fabrics; size 100 for heavy fabrics; size 110 for upholstery fabrics
Wing	100, 120	Wide, wing-shaped blades on each side create holes in fabric that look like entredeux trim	Hemstitch effect for heirloom sewing; best on natural fabrics, such as cotton, linen, silk, organdy
Double	1.6 mm/80 2.0 mm/80 3.0 mm/90 4.0 mm/90 6.0 mm/100 8.0 mm/100	Two universal needles on a crossbar; slightly rounded points	1.6 mm/80 and 2.0 mm/80 for pintucks, delicate heirloom sewing 3.0 mm/90 for hems, pintucks 4.0 mm/90 for decorative hems, surface embellishment 6.0 mm/100 for surface embellishment 8.0 mm/100 for adding texture to fabric
Double Machine Embroidery	2.0 mm/75 3.0 mm/75	Two machine embroidery needles on a crossbar; protects embroidery threads from fraying and breaking	Surface embellishment made with decorative threads
Double Metafil	3.0 mm/80	Two Metafil needles on a crossbar	Double stitching, embellishing with metallic threads
Double Wing	100	One wing needle and one universal needle on a crossbar	Special hemstitch effects and heirloom sewing on natural fabrics, such as cotton, linen, silk, organdy
Double Stretch	2.5 mm/75 4.0 mm/75	Two stretch needles on a crossbar; ballpoint prevents skipped stitches on knits	Pintucking, embroidery on knits, silk jersey, lycra, Ultrasuede
Triple	3.0 mm/80	Three universal needles on a single shaft	Decorative stitching

Interfacings

Interfacing should play a supporting role in almost every garment, adding stability and body.

Fusible Interfacings

The difference between fusible interfacing and fusible web is that fusible interfacing has adhesive on one side only, and fusible web has adhesive on both sides.

For sheer shaping of separates and dresses:
• Fabrics: sheer, lightweight; *batiste, chiffon, dimity, georgette, lawn, voile*
• Brands: Fusible Pellon® #906, Touch O'Gold™

For soft shaping of separates and dresses:
• Fabrics: drapable light- to medium-weight; *challis, jersey, single knits*
• Brands: Pellon® Easy Shaper #114ES, Fusible Pellon® #911FF, Soft 'N Silky™

For crisp shaping of separates and dresses:
• Fabrics: medium-weight; *broadcloth, chambray, cotton blends, gingham, lightweight denim, oxford cloth, poplin*
• Brands: Armo® ShirtShaper, Fusible Pellon® #931TD, Pellon® ShirTailor® #950F, Shape-up® Lightweight, Stacy® Shape

For allover shaping of coats, dresses, jackets, and suits:
• Fabrics: medium- to heavyweight; *corduroy, denim, flannel, linen, poplin, tweed, wool, wool blends*
• Brands: Armo® Fusi-Form™ Lightweights, SuitMaker™, Pellon® Sof-Shape® #880F, SofBrush™, SofTouch™

For crisp shaping of coats, dresses, jackets, and suits:
• Fabrics: medium- to heavyweight; *gabardine, mohair, synthetic leather, synthetic suede*
• Brands: Armo® Form-Flex™

Nonwoven, Armo® Fusi-Form™ Suitweight, Pellon® Pel-Aire® #881, Whisper Weft™

For knits only:
• Fabrics: *cotton/blended knits, double knits, jersey, lightweight velour, single knits, sweatshirt fleece, terry*
• Brands: Knit fuze®, Pellon® Stretch-Ease #921, Quick Knit™, SofKnit®, Stacy® Easy-Knit® #130EK

For crafts:
• Fabrics: all
• Brands: Pellon® Craft-Bond®

Fusible Webs

Woven or nonwoven fusible web has adhesive on both sides, and may have paper covering one side. You can also buy fusible thread and liquid fusible web, which acts like heat-activated fabric glue.

Paper-backed, no-sew fusible web
• Use for crafts, home-decorating projects; light- to medium-weight fabrics; dense web gums needle if stitched through
• Brands: HeatnBond® UltraHold, Pellon® Heavy Duty, Wonder-Under®

Paper-backed fusible web
• Use for appliqués, hems; light-, medium-, heavyweight fabrics; transfer designs onto paper backing, which acts as built-in pressing sheet; OK to sew through
• Brands: Aleene's Original Fusible Web™, Aleene's Ultra Hold Fusible Web™, HeatnBond® Lite, Pellon® Wonder-Under® Fusing Web, Stitch Witchery® Plus with Grid

Fusible web
• Use for appliqués, hems; light-, medium-, heavyweight fabrics
• Brands: Fine Fuse, Stitch Witchery®

Liquid fusible web
• Use for hems, appliqués, emblems, ribbons, other trims; reposition ribbons, appliqués before you heat-set liquid fusible; bottle's applicator tip makes it easy to control amount and placement
• Brands: Aleene's Liquid Fusible Web™, Liqui Fuse™ Liquid Fusible Web™

Fusible thread
• Use for basting zippers, hems; heat and steam from iron cause thread to fuse fabrics together
• Brands: Stitch 'n Fuse®, ThreadFuse™

Stabilizers

Stabilizers add body to fabric and prevent puckering, pulling, or tearing of stitches.

Iron-on stabilizer
• Use for appliqué, machine embroidery, especially on stretchy, delicate fabrics; iron on, then tear away
• Brands: Totally Stable

Liquid stabilizer
• Use for appliqué, machine embroidery; apply to fabric and let dry; wash away after stitching
• Brands: Perfect Sew

Tear-away stabilizer
• Use for appliqué, machine embroidery
• Brands: Pellon® Stitch-N-Tear®, Tear Easy Stabilizer®

Water-soluble stabilizer
• Use for machine embroidery on knit or woven fabrics; apply to right or wrong side of fabric; press away using a wet press cloth, or place project under water
• Brands: Avalon Soluble Stabilizer, Wash-Away Plastic Stabilizer

Stitch thread scraps and fabric bits into a Scribble Collage *(left and page 29)*. Zigzag over colorful thread in a simple design and you've added Basic Couching *(right and page 22)* to a vest. ▶

Using nothing more than a sewing machine or serger and thread, you can embroider, quilt, and even create custom fabric.

Versatile Threads

Easy hints, such as inserting decorative yarn through the top of an embroidery foot *(left and page 22)*, make these embellishments a snap. Fused braid and satin-stitched leaf ribs create this Pseudo Battenberg vest *(right and page 36)*. ▶

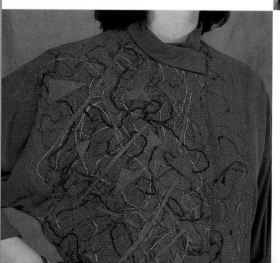

Place stabilizer on top of the area you plan to embellish and use metallic thread in a double needle to stitch the Windowpane Collage blouse *(left and page 27)*.

Top-Thread Sashiko Dress,
page 32

Couching

Zigzagging over thread, yarns, ribbon, decorative serger thread, or cording is a novel yet simple way to add highlights to fabric.

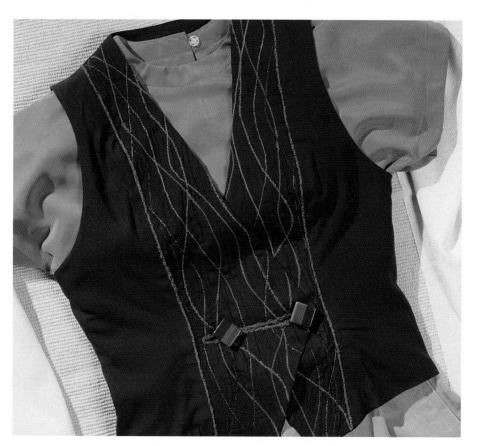

Couching techniques range from single-yarn to multiple-yarn or thread embellishments.

Gather Basic Supplies

Listed are general supplies for couching. Additional notions streamline specialized couching techniques; you'll find those listed with the specific technique.

❑ Monofilament thread
❑ Thread that matches fabric
❑ Decorative yarn
❑ Embroidery foot
❑ Metafil needle
❑ Iron-on stabilizer

Select Fabric

Choose a solid-colored fashion fabric to embellish that coordinates with the decorative yarns. See your pattern for fabric amount.

Get Ready

✔ Replace the conventional foot with an embroidery foot.
✔ Insert a metafil needle.
✔ Thread the top of the machine with monofilament thread.
✔ Use thread matched to the fabric in the bobbin.
✔ Set the machine for a medium-width and medium-length zigzag stitch.

Create Basic Couching

1. Use your pattern to cut out the fabric.
2. Back the fabric pieces with an iron-on stabilizer.
3. Insert decorative yarn through the top zigzag opening in the front of the embroidery foot.

Yarn placement in an embroidery foot

Note from Nancy

Inserting decorative yarn through the opening in the foot gives you greater control over the yarn when stitching a meandering pattern. To follow a specific design, simply place the yarn on the fabric and lower the presser foot over the yarn for easiest control.

4. Zigzag or couch over the decorative yarns, stitching in a meandering pattern. The zig should fall on one side of the yarn, and the zag on the other side.
5. Remove the stabilizer from the wrong side of the fabric.

Highlighted Couching

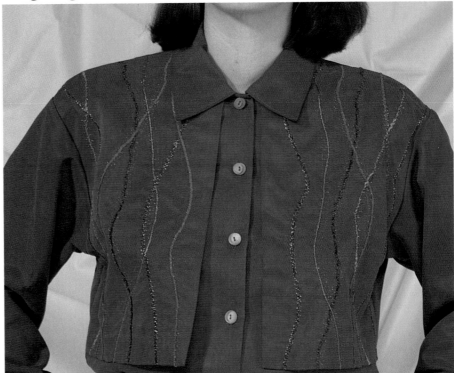

Gather Supplies

☐ Metallic or metallic ribbonlike thread

☐ Metallic needle

Get Ready

✔ Insert a metallic needle in your machine.

✔ Thread the top of your sewing machine with the metallic or metallic ribbonlike thread.

✔ Loosen the top tension by two notches or positions.

✔ Use thread matched to the fabric in the bobbin.

✔ Choose an airy, decorative stitch or a common utility stitch, such as blindhem, feather, or scribble stitch.

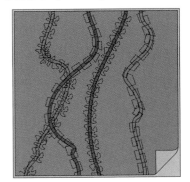

Decorative stitches used for couching

Create Highlighted Couching

Follow the instructions for Basic Couching. The elements of metallic threads and decorative stitches add interest to basic couching.

Quick-Twist Couching

Add variety and texture to fabric by couching over cording created by twisting together decorative threads.

Gather Supplies

❑ Cording foot
❑ Empty bobbin
❑ Decorative threads or yarns:
   Decorative serger thread
   Metallic threads
   Decorative yarns
❑ Monofilament or metallic thread for needle
❑ Thread for bobbin that matches the fabric

Get Ready

✔ Set up the sewing machine as detailed on page 22 in Get Ready for Basic Couching, except replace the embroidery foot with a cording foot.

Create Quick-Twist Couching

1. Quick-twist several strands of decorative thread to create cording.
• Cut several lengths of decorative thread or yarns at least four times the length needed for the finished cording.
• Insert a 3" to 4" (7.5 cm to 10 cm) piece of strong thread through the opening in a bobbin and tie the thread ends to form a lasso. Insert the decorative threads through the lasso; meet thread cut ends (*Photo A*). The doubled thread should be at least twice the length needed for the finished cording.
• Attach the bobbin to the sewing machine as if you were winding a bobbin. If necessary, disengage the fly wheel.
• Hold the cut ends of the threads vertically with one hand; lightly pinch the threads together at the bobbin (*Photo B*).

Quick-Twisting Cording

Photo A: Insert decorative threads through thread lasso on bobbin.

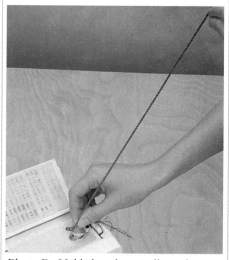

Photo B: Hold thread vertically and pinch together at bobbin.

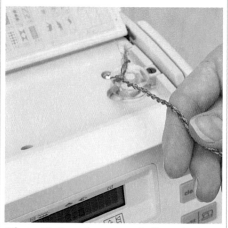

Photo C: Strands automatically twist into decorative cording.

Fringed Couching

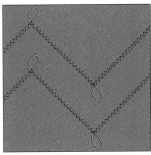

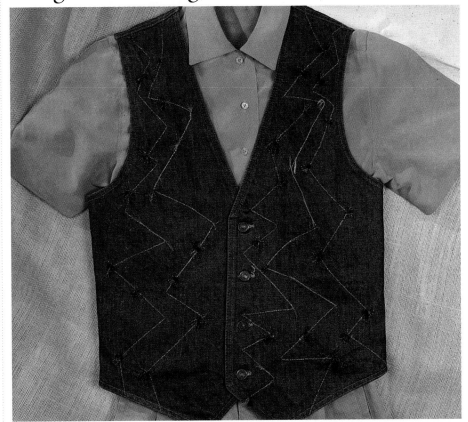

• Run the sewing machine as if winding the bobbin. The threads will twist together.

• When the threads are tightly twisted, meet the cut ends to the lasso and grasp the four strands together. Let go of the remaining thread end. The four strands will automatically twist together, creating thread that resembles heavy cording (*Photo C*).

• Clip the thread at the lasso. Remove the bobbin and reset the machine for stitching.

2. Couch over the quick-twist cording, using a zigzag stitch as described in Basic Couching.

1. Quick-twist two or more strands of thread together.

2. Couch over the threads as previously described.

3. Create fringed sections:

• Stop stitching with the needle down in the fabric (*Diagram A*).

• If your machine has a "needle up/down" feature, set the sewing machine so that the needle stops in the down position.

• Raise the presser foot. Wrap the quick-twist cording around the back of the needle, allowing a loop to form.

• Bring the quick twist to the front of the needle. Lower the presser foot and continue stitching, securing the loop to the fabric.

• Repeat, creating additional loops.

• After adding as many loops as desired, cut the loops, and the quick-twist cording will fringe (*Diagram B*).

Diagram A: Stop stitching with needle down.

Diagram B: Cut loops to create fringe.

Controlled Couching

Gather Supplies

❑ Water-soluble stabilizer
❑ Sequins 'N Ribbon™ Foot or cording foot
❑ Ribbon or sequins by the yard

Get Ready

✔ Replace the conventional foot with a ribbon or cording foot.
✔ Set up the sewing machine as for Basic Couching.
✔ Thread ribbon or sequins through the ribbon foot's accessory guide or under the opening of the cording foot.

Sequins 'N Ribbon foot

Note from Nancy
Before threading the sequins through the opening of the foot, brush the sequin strand with your finger to determine the smooth (napped) direction. Insert the strand in the guide so that you stitch in the direction of the nap.

Create Controlled Couching

1. Draw a design on a piece of water-soluble stabilizer.
2. Place the stabilizer over the right side of the fabric (*Diagram A*).

Carefully flip the fabric over to the wrong side. Press, using a steam iron, to fuse stabilizer to fabric. This fusing isn't permanent, but the stabilizer adheres long enough to prevent the fabric from shifting during stitching.
3. Couch over the ribbon or sequins. Zigzag, following the traced design on the stabilizer.
• If possible, adjust the machine so that the needle stops in the down position, making it easier to turn the fabric.
• Shorten the stitch length and stitch slower when couching in curved areas.
4. Carefully tear away large sections of the water-soluble stabilizer.
5. Remove the stabilizer from the interior of the design by spritzing with water. If the fabric or trim is not washable, press away the remaining stabilizer as follows.
• Cover design with a damp press cloth.
• Press, and the stabilizer will adhere to or be absorbed onto the press cloth (*Diagram B*).

• Repeat this process as necessary, rinsing out the press cloth between pressings.

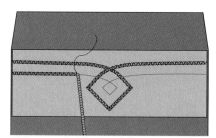

Diagram A: Place stabilizer over right side of fabric.

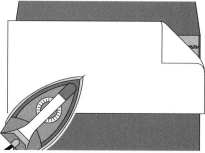

Diagram B: Remove stabilizer using a damp press cloth.

Thread Collages

Here is a thread lover's version of a collage!

Simply scatter a selection of threads and appliqué shapes on top of your fabric palette. Add stitching and you've made a one-of-a-kind embellishment.

Gather Supplies

❏ Threads for collage (choose your favorites):
   Ribbon Floss
   Embroidery threads
   Decorative serger threads
   Decorative yarns
❏ Metallic or machine embroidery thread for needle
❏ Thread that matches fabric for bobbin
❏ Paper-backed fusible web
❏ Water-soluble stabilizer
❏ 3.0 or 4.0 double needle
❏ Quilting bar

Select Fabric

Choose fashion fabric for the garment. See your pattern for amount.

Choose coordinating, tightly woven or nonraveling fabric scraps for appliqué. The garment shown features Ultrasuede appliqués.

Get Ready

✔ Insert the double needle in your machine.
✔ Thread two spools of metallic or machine embroidery thread on the top of the machine, threading them as one until they reach the needle. Then separate the threads and insert each through one needle.
✔ Use thread matched to the fashion fabric in the bobbin.
✔ Attach a quilting bar to the presser foot, setting the bar ¾" to 1" (2 cm to 2.5 cm) from the needle.

Note from Nancy

If you have only one spool of the color you're using, wind two bobbins. Use one as the bobbin thread as usual; use the other as the second thread spool on top of the machine.

Quilting bar attached to presser foot

Create a Windowpane Collage

1. Unwind the collage threads and place them on the fabric in a random arrangement, creating a pleasing abstract design *(Diagram A on page 28)*. Extend the threads to the seam lines of the garment section; you don't have to extend the threads into seam allowances.

Note from Nancy

Bobbins from previous projects are a great source of thread for these collages. When you unwind the tightly coiled thread, it has graceful curls and swirls.

2. Add geometric appliqués.

• Back coordinating fabric scraps with paper-backed fusible web.

• Cut the fabric into desired shapes.

• Place these appliqués within the thread arrangement.

• Press to fuse the appliqués in place *(Diagram B)*.

3. Place a layer of water-soluble stabilizer on top of the fabric. Pin securely in place *(Diagram C)*.

Note from Nancy

Stabilizers are traditionally placed under fabric for decorative stitching. However, by placing stabilizer on top of the collage, you hold the thread in position during stitching and also stabilize the area. The stabilizer also offers a convenient surface to mark the position for the first line of stitching.

4. Stitch a windowpane design over the positioned threads and fabrics.

• Mark one line on the water-soluble stabilizer. This line may be vertical, horizontal, or on the bias.

• Stitch along the marked line *(Diagram D)*.

• Align the edge of the quilting bar with the first row of stitching. Stitch additional rows parallel to the first row, spaced equally apart, guiding the quilting bar along the previously sewn row *(Diagram E)*.

• Repeat until you have stitched the entire piece.

• Mark one cross row at a 90° angle to the first rows and stitch along that row.

• Stitch additional cross rows until you have stitched the entire piece into a windowpane effect, again using the quilting bar as a guide *(Diagram F)*.

5. Remove the water-soluble stabilizer.

Stitching a Windowpane Collage

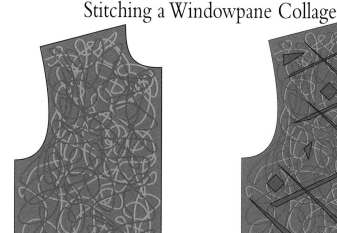

Diagram A: Place collage threads in a pleasing design.

Diagram B: Fuse geometric appliqués in place.

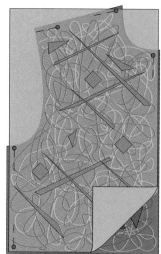

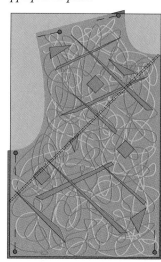

Diagram C: Pin stabilizer on top of collage.

Diagram D: Mark and stitch first line.

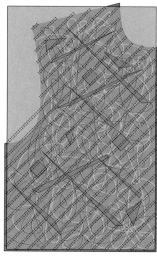

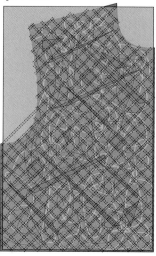

Diagram E: Stitch rows parallel to first stitching.

Diagram F: Complete windowpane grid of stitches.

Scribble Collage

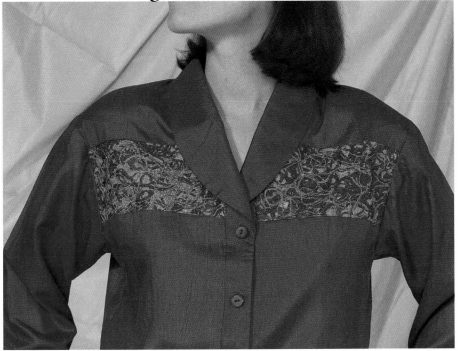
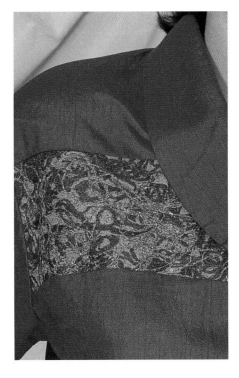

A thread collage takes on a different look when you substitute a sheer backing for the fashion fabric and replace the double-needle stitching with a scribble stitch. This collage application can give your project a dramatic look.

Gather Supplies

❑ Threads for collage (choose your favorites):
  Ribbon Floss
  Embroidery threads
  Decorative serger threads
  Decorative yarns
❑ Machine embroidery thread for needle
❑ Thread that matches fabric for bobbin
❑ Water-soluble stabilizer
❑ Machine embroidery needle and thread

Select Fabric

Select a lightweight fabric, such as organza or batiste, as the background fabric for the collage.

Get Ready

✔ Set the machine for a programmed scribble stitch (available on some sewing machines). A scribble stitch resembles a random stitch pattern. If your machine doesn't have this feature, select a wide zigzag or multiple-step zigzag stitch.
✔ Use the conventional presser foot.
✔ Insert a machine embroidery needle.
✔ Thread the machine with embroidery thread in the needle.
✔ Use thread matched to the fabric in the bobbin.

Create Scribble Collage

1. Create the collage over the lightweight fabric; cover it with water-soluble stabilizer.
2. Stitch over the thread collage with a scribble stitch or zigzag stitch (Diagram).
3. Remove the water-soluble stabilizer.

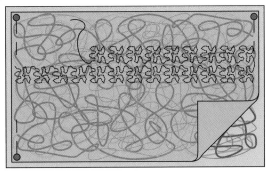

Diagram: Sew over thread collage using a scribble stitch or a random stitch pattern.

Create a Plaid

Stitching on the diagonal is a worry-free way to match plaids.
This creative embellishment takes time, but the results are well worth the effort!

Gather Supplies

- ❑ Iron-on stabilizer
- ❑ Quilting ruler
- ❑ Chalk
- ❑ Embroidery or metallic thread for needle
- ❑ Thread that matches fabric for bobbin
- ❑ Machine embroidery needle or metallic needle
- ❑ Embroidery or open toe foot

Select Fabric

Choose a solid-colored fabric. See your pattern for amount.

Get Ready

- ✔ Insert a machine embroidery needle or a metallic needle, depending upon which thread is used.
- ✔ Thread the top of the machine with decorative thread. Experiment with various threads.
- ✔ Use thread that matches the fabric in the bobbin.
- ✔ Loosen the top tension by two numbers or notches (for example, from 5 to 3).
- ✔ Replace the conventional presser foot with an embroidery or open toe foot.
- ✔ Set the machine for a decorative stitch.

Note from Nancy
Totally Stable is a paperlike stabilizer with a waxy coating on the wrong side. Ironing temporarily adheres the stabilizer to the fabric, yet Totally Stable tears away easily.

Create a Plaid

1. Press iron-on stabilizer to the wrong side of the fabric (*Diagram A*). Stabilizer prevents the fabric from shifting or moving during decorative stitching.

2. Grid the fabric.

- Press or use chalk to mark the lengthwise grain line on the right side of the fabric.

Note from Nancy
Use white chalk on dark fabric and blue or yellow chalk on light-colored fabric. Always test chalk marks on a scrap of fabric before marking your project to be sure they show up and that they will come out of the fabric when you finish stitching.

- Align the 45° angle on a quilting ruler with the lengthwise mark. Use chalk to mark the diagonal line (*Diagram B*). Retrace the line if needed to provide a heavy coating of chalk.
- Mark additional lines parallel to the first line, spaced 4½" (11.5 cm) apart, until you mark the entire fabric (*Diagram C*).
- Mark another set of lines at right angles to the first lines, again spaced 4½" (11.5 cm) apart. Be certain all lines have a heavy concentration of chalk.
- Stack the corresponding fabrics pieces, right sides together. Rub or hand-press the fabric until the chalk transfers to the second piece, creating a perfect mirror image (*Diagram D*).

Creating Plaid

Diagram A: Fuse stabilizer to wrong side of fabric.

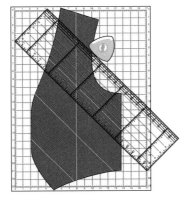

Diagram B: Use a quilting ruler and chalk to mark diagonal lines.

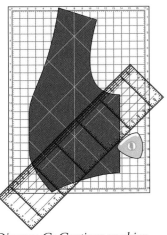

Diagram C: Continue marking until entire fabric is gridded.

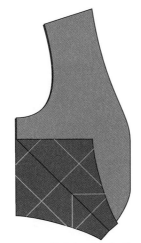

Diagram D: Transfer chalk pattern to unmarked garment piece.

Diagram E: Stitch design, using thread colors and stitches as determined from test strips.

Note from Nancy

If your decorative plaid design goes on only one piece of fabric, you don't need a heavy concentration of chalk to mark the decorative stitching lines.

• Rechalk lines on the fabric if necessary.

3. Plan the design by testing stitching strips.

• Cut 1" (2.5 cm) strips of the fashion fabric.

• Fuse stabilizer to the strips.

• Sew different decorative stitches on each strip. Stitches with geometric designs are especially suited for the plaid. Vary thread colors as you stitch the test strips.

• Arrange and rearrange the strips of the various colors and stitches until the design pleases you. Do this by placing the strips on the diagonal grid to determine the number and arrangement of stitches for the finished plaid. (It's like arranging puzzle pieces.)

4. Once you decide on the design, stitch the design on the fabric, using the threads and stitches from your puzzle arrangement *(Diagram E)*.

Note from Nancy

Don't be in a hurry to do this stitching. Creating the plaid is easy, but it is also time consuming. Take your time, and enjoy!

5. Remove the stabilizer when you have finished stitching.

6. Complete your garment or project following your pattern directions.

Sashiko

Create this Japanese hand embellishment entirely by machine.

When you machine-stitch Sashiko from the right side of fabric, the thread highlights are less pronounced than in traditional, hand-stitched Sashiko, because heavyweight thread cannot easily pass through a sewing machine needle. My variation lets you choose more dramatic threads, and it is the easiest way to machine-stitch Sashiko embellishments.

Gather Supplies

❑ Metallic or machine embroidery thread (two spools) for needle

❑ Thread that matches fabric for bobbin

❑ Water-soluble stabilizer

❑ Machine embroidery or metallic needle

Select Fabric

Choose a dark solid-colored fabric. (Denim is traditional.) Check your pattern for amount.

Get Ready

✔ Insert a metallic or machine embroidery needle that corresponds with the top thread.

✔ Use two strands of thread on top of the machine, threading them through the machine as if they were a single strand. I created the embellishment on the black evening dress using two spools of metallic thread.

✔ Use thread that matches the fabric in the bobbin.

✔ Loosen the top tension by one or two notches to keep the bobbin thread on the underside of the fabric. For example, adjust the tension from 5 to 3.

✔ Set the machine for a straightstitch.

Create Top-Thread Sashiko

1. Trace the design on a section of water-soluble stabilizer; pin or press the stabilizer to the right side of the fabric *(Diagram)*. The pattern I used appears on page 135.

2. Stitch the design.

• Practice stitching on a scrap to determine an appropriate stitch length.

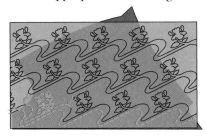

Diagram: Trace design on stabilizer and pin or press to right side of fabric.

Note from Nancy
Traditional Sashiko features a long running stitch. With the sewing machine, I use a medium-length stitch, because a longer stitch makes it more difficult to maneuver curves. As you stitch, sew at a slow, constant speed and turn the fabric with both hands, like turning a steering wheel. Practice on a scrap so that you get the feel of the stitching.

• Stitch continuously to complete the design. Adjust the machine to stop with the needle in the down position (if possible) to simplify the sewing process.

3. Remove the water-soluble stabilizer.

• Cut or tear away as much of the stabilizer as possible.

• To remove the remaining stabilizer and any residue from fabric that is washable, spritz the stabilizer with water.

• If the fabric isn't washable, place a very damp (almost wet) cloth over the stabilizer and press. The stabilizer adheres to and is absorbed into the press cloth. If necessary, rinse the press cloth and repeat until you remove all the stabilizer.

Bobbin-Work Sashiko

Gather Supplies

❑ All-purpose thread for the needle that matches the decorative bobbin thread

❑ Heavyweight thread, such as top-stitching thread, buttonhole twist, or jeans thread, for the bobbin

❑ Water-soluble stabilizer

❑ Topstitching needle, size 90 or 100

Select Fabric

Choose a dark solid-colored fabric. (Denim is traditional.) Check your pattern for amount.

Get Ready

✔ Insert the topstitching needle in your machine.

✔ Thread the top of the machine with all-purpose thread.

✔ Wind the bobbin with heavy-weight thread.

✔ Set machine for a straightstitch with a medium stitch length.

✔ Tighten the top tension by one or two notches so that the top thread stays on the surface of the fabric. For example, adjust the tension from 5 to 7.

Create Bobbin-Work Sashiko

1. Trace the Sashiko design onto a section of water-soluble stabilizer. Place the stabilizer on the wrong

side of the fabric; pin in place *(Diagram)*.

2. Stitch the Sashiko design from the wrong side.

• Practice stitching on a scrap to determine an appropriate stitch length.

• Stitch continuously to complete the design, sewing at a slow, constant speed to make maneuvering curves easier. Adjust the machine to stop with the needle in the down position (if possible) to simplify the sewing process.

3. Remove the stabilizer from the wrong side of the fabric after stitching is completed. Pull threads to the wrong side; tie and clip threads.

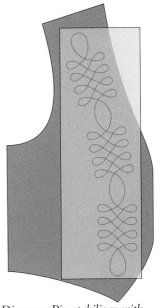

Diagram: Pin stabilizer with design to wrong side of fabric.

Rambling Pintucks with Trapunto

Create a dramatic effect by using pintucks to frame trapunto, a raised Italian quilting design.

Gather Supplies

- ❑ 3.0 and 4.0 double needles
- ❑ Pintuck foot
- ❑ Cording foot
- ❑ Batting or fiberfill
- ❑ Embroidery floss
- ❑ Serger looper threader
- ❑ Machine embroidery thread (two spools) for needle
- ❑ Thread that matches fabric for bobbin
- ❑ Thread to use as cording for pintucks such as pearl cotton or pearl rayon, serger thread, embroidery floss, or ⅛" (3 mm) cable cord

Select Fabrics

Choose a lightweight, drapable fabric. Check your pattern for amount.

Get Ready

- ✔ Insert the double needle in your machine.
- ✔ Thread two spools of machine embroidery thread on top of the machine, threading them as one until they reach the needle. Then separate the threads and insert each through its respective needle.
- ✔ Use thread matched to the fashion fabric in the bobbin.
- ✔ Replace the conventional foot with a pintuck foot.

Create Rambling Pintucks with Trapunto

1. Add the embellishment before cutting out the garment. Cut the fabric 3" to 4" (7.5 cm to 10 cm) wider than the pattern piece to allow for the width and length that the embellishment will take up.

2. Add dimension with trapunto.

• Determine approximately where you want to place the trapunto and mark with pins *(Diagram A)*.

• Cut a small section of quilt batting or fiberfill the size and shape of the trapunto design.

Note from Nancy
Try out various shapes before choosing a specific trapunto design. Small abstract or geometric shapes often are more attractive than large designs. In this instance, "less is best" is good advice.

• Place the batting on the wrong side of the fabric behind the pin-marked areas.

• Hand-baste around outer edges of the batting to create stitching guides *(Diagram B)*.

3. Use thread or cording to add dimension to the pintucks. Place lightweight cording, such as floss, serger thread, pearl cotton, or pearl rayon, in your lap. Insert the cording through the opening in the sewing machine throat plate, threading the cording from the underside and drawing the cord through to the back of the machine. As you stitch, the cording will automatically be included on the underside of the fabric, which will help raise the pintuck.

Note from Nancy
A serger looper threader makes this job easier. Insert the serger looper threader through the hole in the throat plate from the top, and pull the thread up from the bobbin area.

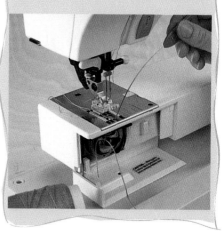

4. Begin stitching pintucks.

• Stitch the first row, gently turning the fabric to create a curved, rambling pattern. At the trapunto areas, sew next to the basting stitch to catch the edge of the batting and secure it in place *(Diagram C)*.

• Stitch another row, placing the first pintuck row in one of the pintuck foot's outer grooves.

• Stitch additional rows, generally sewing parallel to the first row. You can vary the distance between pintuck rows by placing previously stitched rows at different positions in the grooved foot.

5. Stitch the second side of the rambling pattern, making numerous rows of pintucks, following the same guidelines as for the first section *(Diagram D)*.

6. Add hand-stitched embellishments.
• Hand-stitch along the side of the pintucks, using heavier threads, such as silk floss or embroidery thread.
• Add French knots or other embroidery stitching as desired *(Diagram F)*.
7. Remove basting threads along the trapunto edges.
8. Back the fabric with a facing or lining.

Framing Trapunto with Pintucks

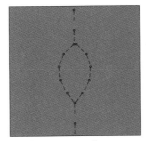

Diagram A: Mark trapunto design with pins.

Diagram B: Hand-baste to make stitching guides.

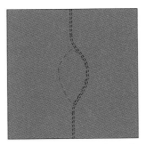

Diagram C: Sew through batting next to basting.

Diagram D: Add pintucks to opposite side of trapunto.

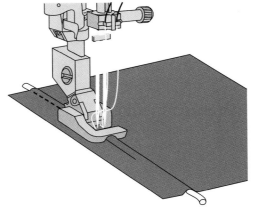

Diagram E: Exaggerate pintucks by stitching over cording.

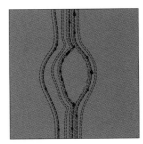

Diagram F: Add hand-embroidery stitches as desired.

Pseudo Battenberg

Duplicate any Battenberg design with thread, braid, and savvy zigzag stitching.

Gather Supplies

- ❑ Lightweight fusible interfacing
- ❑ Transfer pen and paper or dressmaker's tracing paper
- ❑ Embroidery needle or metallic needle
- ❑ Metallic or machine embroidery thread that matches or coordinates with braid for needle
- ❑ Lingerie/bobbin thread for bobbin
- ❑ Embroidery foot
- ❑ Liquid fusible web
- ❑ 4 mm–wide braid
- ❑ Press cloth

Select Fabrics

Choose a base color. Check your pattern for amount.

Get Ready

- ✔ Insert a needle that coordinates with the thread (metallic or machine embroidery).

- ✔ Thread the top of the machine with machine embroidery or metallic thread.
- ✔ Use a lightweight thread, such as lingerie/bobbin thread, in the bobbin.
- ✔ Replace the conventional presser foot with an embroidery foot. Loosen the top tension by two numbers or notches.
- ✔ Adjust the machine for a narrow zigzag. As a starting point, set the stitch width at 1 and the stitch length at .5. Test stitching on a scrap before stitching on the actual project.

Create Pseudo Battenberg

1. Fuse lightweight interfacing to the wrong side of the fabric for added support.

2. Transfer the design to the fabric in one of the following ways. The design I used appears on page 138.

- Trace the design on transfer paper using a transfer pen. Place the transfer paper face down on the fabric. Rub, pressing with your thumbnail or a tool like the Little Wooden Iron (*Diagram A*).

> *Note from Nancy*
> *I sometimes use the Fabric Pattern Transfer Kit to transfer designs to fabric. The kit includes two reusable Transfer Rice Paper sheets and a double-sided fabric transfer pen (the purple tip marks the fabric and the white tip erases the mark). Consider using this timesaving notion when transferring silk-ribbon embroidery patterns to fabric. Learn how to stitch silk-ribbon embroidery by machine in Chapter 6.*

- Trace the design onto tissue paper. Place dressmaker's tracing paper on top of the fabric, carbon side down, with the tissue tracing on top. Use a blunt pencil or fingernail to trace over the image (*Diagram B*).

> *Note from Nancy*
> *When you transfer the design, remember that you get the reverse, or mirror image, of the traced design. If you want the design to appear exactly like the original, flip the design so that you trace a mirror image. As always, test this or any transfer method on a fabric scrap before using it on the actual project.*

3. Satin-stitch the inside ribs or veins of the design.

• Stitch over one of the lines in the design. Raise the presser foot and advance the fabric to the next line without cutting the threads.

• After stitching all inside lines of one section, clip the top thread tails *(Diagram C)*.

4. Apply a fine line of liquid fusible web along the outer lines of the transferred design. Let dry *(Diagram D)*.

5. Place the braid over the liquid fusible web and cut the braid to size.

• Work on a padded pressing surface.

• Tuck the cut ends of the braid under a continuous strip of the braid.

• Shape the braid to conform to the design. *(Diagram E)*. If necessary, fold the braid back on itself to form tight angles or corners.

• Pin the braid to the fabric, using enough pins to hold the shape.

6. To position the braid temporarily, cover it with a press cloth and press 40 to 50 seconds, following manufacturers instructions. Remove pins.

7. Permanently stitch the braid to the fabric.

• Adjust machine for a zigzag slightly narrower than the braid.

• Zigzag down the center of the braid *(Diagram F)*.

Creating Pseudo Battenberg Designs

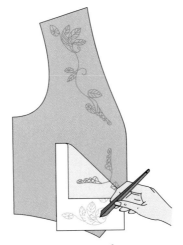

Diagram A: Use transfer paper to mark design.

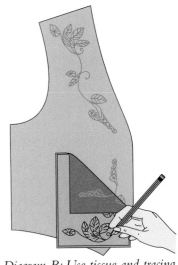

Diagram B: Use tissue and tracing paper to transfer design.

Diagram C: Satin-stitch inside details; clip thread tails.

Diagram D: Apply liquid fusible web to outer lines of design.

Diagram E: Place braid over fusible web, shaping to fit design.

Diagram F: Stitch down center of braid.

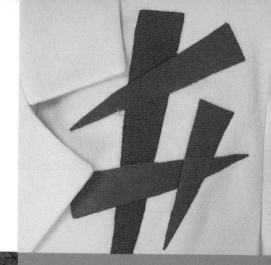

◀ Confetti appliqué *(left and page 47)* adds a casual look that's easy to make and fun to wear. Small shapes of Ultrasuede make a striking and easy accent for a jacket *(right and page 56).* ▶

Dress up even simple appliqués with metallic threads, or make the stitching almost invisible by using monofilament nylon thread.

Uncommon Appliqué

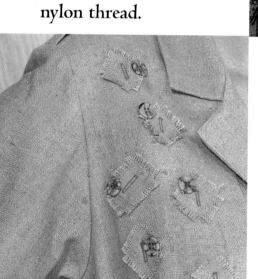

◀ Decorative buttons and buttonholes impart a folk-art look to fringed buttonhole appliqués *(left and page 52).* Ultrasuede on a pocket finishes off a simple outfit, such as this chambray shirt *(right and page 57).* ▶

◀ Liquid fabric solvent is the secret to quick and easy cutwork appliqué *(left and page 54).*

Framed-Stitch Appliqué,
page 58

Invisibly Stitched Appliqués

Create a machine-sewn embellishment that looks like you stitched it by hand.

This charming invisibly stitched option features the ever-popular Sunbonnet Sue design. Look for additional design choices in appliqué and quilting books.

Gather Supplies

- ❑ Conventional sewing machine foot
- ❑ Thread that matches the fabric for needle and bobbin
- ❑ Metafil needle
- ❑ Lightweight fusible interfacing
- ❑ Bamboo Pointer & Creaser
- ❑ Liquid fusible web
- ❑ Press cloth
- ❑ Embroidery or open toe foot
- ❑ Monofilament nylon thread

Select Fabrics

Choose fashion fabric. See your pattern for amount.

Choose cotton or cotton blend coordinating fabric scraps for appliqués.

Get Ready

- ✔ Attach the conventional foot (you will replace it with an embroidery or open toe foot later).
- ✔ Thread the needle and bobbin with all-purpose thread to match the fashion fabric.
- ✔ Insert a metafil needle.
- ✔ Set the machine for a straightstitch with a short length, approximately 15 stitches per inch.

Create Invisibly Stitched Appliqués

1. Trace the elements of the appliqué design to the nonfusible side of the interfacing, leaving ½" (1.3 cm) of

space between the designs. (See page 138 for our Sunbonnet Sue appliqué pattern.) Cut out pieces, allowing approximately ¼" (6 mm) seam allowances *(Diagram A)*.

2. Cut out the fabrics for the appliqués, approximately the same size as the interfacing pieces.

3. Meet the right side of the fabric to the nonfusible side of the interfacing. You may want to redraw the tracing on the fusible side of the interfacing. Stitch around the traced design with a short stitch length *(Diagram B)*.

See page 138 for our Sunbonnet Sue appliqué pattern.

Note from Nancy
A short stitch length makes it easier to stitch curves on small pieces. The shorter stitches reinforce the seam and give you greater accuracy when stitching a curve.

4. Trim the seam allowance to approximately ⅛" (3 mm).

5. Cut a slit in the center of the interfacing, taking care not to cut through the appliqué fabric *(Diagram C)*. Turn the appliqué right side out.

Invisibly Stitched Appliqué

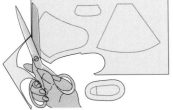

Diagram A: Cut out pattern, adding ¼" seam allowances.

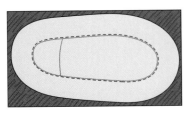

Diagram B: Stitch around traced design.

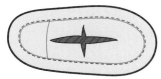

Diagram C: Slit interfacing; turn right side out.

Diagram D: Apply liquid fusible web to edges.

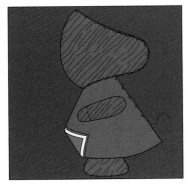

Diagram E: Stitch using monofilament thread.

6. Use a tool with a rounded point to obtain crisp edges on the appliqué. Roll the seam to the edge of the appliqué between your fingers, and press with the tip of the iron. The fusible interfacing adheres the two layers, giving sharp, crisp edges.

Note from Nancy
A Bamboo Pointer & Creaser is an ideal notion to use when turning appliqué pieces right side out. The rounded point easily brings the seam to the appliqué edge without making a hole in the appliqué.

7. Position the appliqué on the project.

No-sew Method Step 1: Apply a liquid fusible web around the edges of the appliqué *(Diagram D)*. Let dry. Speed the drying process with a hair dryer if desired.

Note from Nancy
Liqui Fuse Liquid Fusible Web is an ideal product to use to temporarily or even permanently attach appliqués. You can apply the gluelike liquid in a fine line, making it easier to create intricate designs.

No-sew Method Step 2: Place the appliqué on the project, positioning the background pieces on the design first and layering additional pieces to form the completed design. Cover with a press cloth; fuse the appliqué permanently in place. You don't need to do any stitching.

Stitching Method Step 1: Pin the appliqué to the base fabric, or use liquid fusible web to secure the appliqué.

Stitching Method Step 2: Position the background pieces first; then lay out the foreground pieces.

Stitching Method Step 3: Set the machine for a blindhem stitch with a length of 1.5 and a width of 2. Attach an embroidery or open toe foot. Insert a metafil needle and thread the needle with monofilament thread.

Note from Nancy
Always test machine settings on a fabric sample before stitching on a garment. You may need to adjust the stitch length, depending on how curved your appliqué edge is. The longer and straighter the edge, the longer the stitch length should be. You may also need to loosen the top tension so that the bobbin thread remains on the underside of the fabric.

Stitching Method Step 4: Stitch around the edges of the appliqué with the straight stitches falling on the base fabric at the edge of the appliqué and the zigzag stitches falling on the appliqué *(Diagram E)*. Because the thread is clear, the stitching is almost invisible.

Note from Nancy
An open toe foot has an extra-wide opening to make it easy to see the stitching area. This extra space is particularly helpful for blindhem stitching around an appliqué.

Invisibly Stitched Quilt Appliqués

This variation shows you how to stitch appliqués with points and corners. I chose a common quilt design, the six-pointed Morning Star, as the inspiration for this vest. I added the intertwining leaves using the same creative stitching technique.

Gather Supplies

Items listed on page 40, plus:
- ❑ Celtic Bias Bars
- ❑ Diamond-shaped template
- ❑ Quilting ruler
- ❑ Marking pencil
- ❑ Spray starch
- ❑ ¼"-wide (6 mm-wide) quilting foot (optional)

Select Fabrics

For the garment, choose fashion fabric. See your pattern for amount.

For star sections, choose an assortment of cotton or cotton blend scraps that coordinate with your fashion fabric.

For vines, choose an assortment of cotton or cotton blend scraps that contrast with your fashion fabric.

For lattice strips, choose black cotton or cotton blend scraps.

Get Ready

✔ Set up the sewing machine as detailed on page 40.

Create Vines and Lattice

1. Cut 1¼"-wide (3.2 cm-wide) black bias strips for the lattice.
2. Cut contrasting ¾"-wide (2 cm-wide) print bias strips for vines.
3. Fold strips wrong sides together, meeting lengthwise edges. Stitch narrow ⅛" (3 mm) seams *(Diagram A)*.
4. Press tubes using Celtic Bias Bars.

Note from Nancy
Usually we stitch seams with fabric right sides together. This time we stitch with wrong sides together, since you will not turn the strips. If you find it difficult to stitch ⅛" (3 mm) seams, cut the strips slightly wider and stitch ¼" (6 mm) seams first. Then trim seams to ⅛" (3 mm) using a rotary cutter or scissors.

Note from Nancy
Celtic Bias Bars are flexible aluminum bars that make it easy to press fabric tubes. Stitchers may use the bars, which are available in various widths, to create Celtic (bias-strip appliqué) designs and for stained-glass quilting. I find these bars helpful when creating bias strips, such as the ones in this embellishment.

- Insert a Celtic Bias Bar in the tube.
- Position the seam at the center of one side of the bar.
- Finger-press the seam to one side; steam-press. (Metal bars get hot when you press, so be careful!) The pressed seam will stay on the underside of the tube when the tube is stitched to the garment.

Create Six-pointed Star Sections

1. Cut 1¾" (4.5 cm) fabric strips.

2. Make a diamond template using the pattern on page 138, and cut six sections for the six-pointed star using the template *(Diagram B)*. Or cut diamonds using a quilting ruler specifically designed for creating a six-pointed star.

3. Prepare the fabric sections. Mark the starting and stopping points on the wrong side of each fabric section, ¼" (6 mm) from each corner. Be accurate, since these marks provide matching points when you join the sections. If you're using a template, poke a hole through the template at the seam intersection. Then use a marking pencil to transfer the position to the fabric *(Diagram C)*.

Spray-starch the fabric pieces to add body. This makes it easier to sew the sections together.

4. Join the fabric sections with ¼" (6 mm) seams, right sides together, beginning and ending at marks. Press the seam to one side *(Diagram D)*.

5. Finish the outer edges of the pieced sections.
- Cut a rectangle of fusible interfacing slightly larger than the pieced section.
- Pin the pieced section to the interfacing, right sides together. (Fusible side of interfacing faces out.) Stitch completely around the outer edges with a ¼" (6 mm) seam. Trim the seam allowance to approximately ⅛" (3 mm); angle-cut corners *(Diagram E)*.

6. Cut a slit in the center of the interfacing, taking care not to cut the appliqué fabric. Turn the appliqué right side out *(Diagram F)*.

7. Use a tool with a rounded point to help obtain crisp edges on the appliqué. Roll the seam to the edge of the appliqué between your fingers and then press with the tip of the iron. The fusible interfacing adheres the two layers, giving sharp, crisp edges.

8. Stitch design to the garment.
- Position background sections such as lattice and stems first.
- Stitch around both outer edges following the techniques for Invisibly Stitched Appliqués on page 41 *(Diagram G)*.
- Position foreground pieces (leaves and flowers) and stitch.

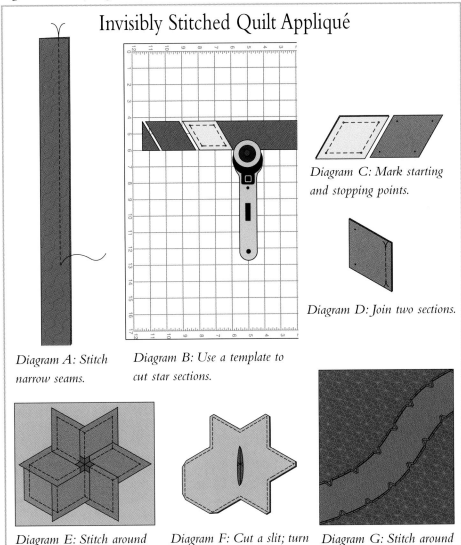

Invisibly Stitched Quilt Appliqué

Diagram A: Stitch narrow seams.

Diagram B: Use a template to cut star sections.

Diagram C: Mark starting and stopping points.

Diagram D: Join two sections.

Diagram E: Stitch around outer edge of star.

Diagram F: Cut a slit; turn star right side out.

Diagram G: Stitch around outer edges.

Monogram

What do the letters, or fonts, on your computer have in common with sewing?
A lot, when you use computer letters as stylized monograms to stitch on a project.

Gather Supplies

- ❏ Machine embroidery needle
- ❏ Machine embroidery thread
- ❏ Lingerie/bobbin thread
- ❏ Open toe or embroidery foot
- ❏ Gridded paper
- ❏ Tear-away or water-soluble stabilizer
- ❏ Ruler
- ❏ Appliqué scissors

Select Fabrics

Choose fashion fabric for your project. See your pattern for amount.

Choose contrasting or coordinating fabric for appliqué letters.

Get Ready

- ✔ Insert a machine embroidery needle in your machine.
- ✔ Thread the needle with machine embroidery thread and the bobbin with lingerie/bobbin thread.
- ✔ Replace the conventional foot with an open toe or embroidery foot.
- ✔ Loosen the upper tension by two positions or numbers (for example, from 5 to 3).
- ✔ Set the machine for a straightstitch with a short stitch length of 1.

Create Monogram Appliqués

1. Choose letters for the monogram using one of the following options:
- Use the alphabet on pages 140-141.
- Select letters from a printed alphabet, or print out letters using one of the fonts on a personal computer. Choose letters that are at least ¼" (6 mm) wide and styled without serifs (the

curved tails on some fonts). Serifs are difficult to appliqué.

2. Trace the letters on gridded paper, spacing the letters about ¼" (6 mm) apart *(Diagram A)*. If using letters from a personal computer, simply print out the name or monogram combination.

> ### Note from Nancy
> *I like to use a gridded craft and pattern paper such as Grid Works™ when tracing letters to paper. This paper has a waxy backing, so you can press it to a base fabric to prevent the paper from shifting while you stitch. Added stabilization is a bonus.*

3. Make a fabric sandwich.
- Place a layer of stabilizer on the underside of the fabric. Use either a tear-away stabilizer or a water-soluble stabilizer.

- For a centered monogram, fold the fashion fabric in half vertically; press to mark the center *(Diagram B)*. Position the fashion fabric over the stabilizer.
- Fold the fabric for the appliqué letters in half vertically; press to mark the center. If this fabric is lightweight, fuse a layer of lightweight fusible interfacing to the back of the fabric. Position this fabric over the fashion fabric, matching centers.
- Fold the paper with the traced or printed letters in half vertically to mark its center. Place the paper over the other layers, matching center marks *(Diagram C)*.
- Measure with a ruler to make certain the letters are aligned vertically and horizontally on the fashion fabric *(Diagram D)*. Once the letters are stitched, they're difficult to remove.

4. Straightstitch over each letter's traced outline through all four layers, using a short stitch length. Remove the paper after stitching around all letters *(Diagram E)*.

5. Trim the excess appliqué fabric, cutting very close to the stitching line, using one of the following techniques:
• Use conventional scissors. Bevel the blade by holding it flat against the fabric. Cut as close as possible to the stitching line, taking little snips as you trim around the curves *(Diagram F)*.
• Use appliqué scissors. The large bill lifts the fabric to be trimmed, and the curved handle ensures a comfortable hand position *(Diagram G)*.

6. Satin-stitch around the letters.
• Position the fabric so that the larger portion of the design is to the left of the machine.
• Adjust the machine for a narrow zigzag and a satin-stitch length of .5.
• Stitch so that one edge of the zigzag falls in the appliqué and the other edge falls just past the raw edge of it *(Diagram H)*.

Creating Monograms

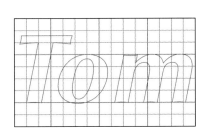

Diagram A: Trace letters on gridded paper.

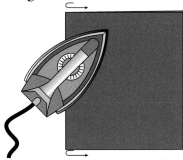

Diagram B: Fold and press fabric to mark center.

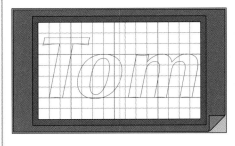

Diagram C: Match paper and fabric center marks.

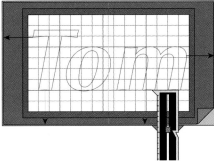

Diagram D: Use a ruler to check alignment of letters.

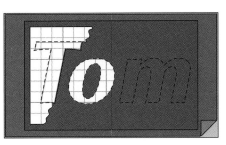

Diagram E: Straightstitch over each letter outline; remove paper.

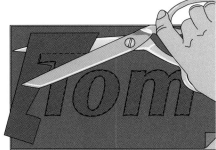

Diagram F: Trim excess appliqué fabric using conventional scissors.

Diagram G: Or use appliqué scissors to trim excess fabric.

Diagram H: Satin-stitch around edges of each letter.

• If possible, adjust the machine so that the needle stops in the down position for easy fabric turning.

• To stitch outside corners, zigzag to the corner, making sure the final stitch falls exactly at the corner *(Diagram I)*. Stop with the needle down in the out-side position. Raise the presser foot and pivot the fabric. Lower the presser foot and continue stitching *(Diagram J)*.

• To stitch inside corners, stitch to the corner and then sew several additional stitches, sewing beyond the corner the width of a zigzag stitch *(Diagram K)*. Stop with the needle down in the inside position. Raise the presser foot and pivot the fabric. Lower the foot and continue stitching *(Diagram L)*.

• Give the fabric a little nudge when beginning a line of stitching that crosses previous stitching. Stitches can bunch up at those points, so helping the fabric along produces a smoother completed stitching.

7. Remove the stabilizer after you finish all stitching.

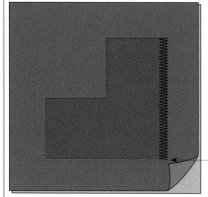

Diagram I: Make sure final stitch of an outside corner falls exactly at the corner.

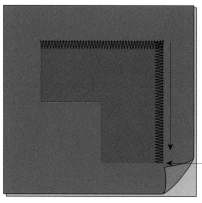

Diagram J: Pivot; stitch the next side.

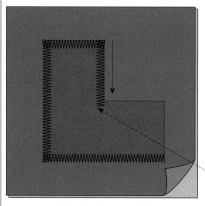

Diagram K: For inside corners, stitch beyond the corner the width of one zigzag stitch.

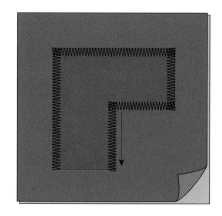

Diagram K: Pivot; stitch the next side.

Time-savers

🕐 If you use computer letters for your monograms, choose a sans serif (without serifs) typeface. Serifs are the short strokes on the ends of some styles of letters; these little strokes are difficult and timeconsuming to stitch around.

🕐 Choose a nonwoven or closely woven fabric for your monograms so that the fabric won't ravel. Ultrasuede and felt are good choices.

🕐 You can make felted wool from scraps or recycled clothing by washing the fabric in hot water and drying it on your dryer's hottest setting.

🕐 Be sure that the care instructions for monogram fabric you choose are compatible with the care instructions for your fashion fabric.

Confetti Appliqué

Cluster fabric scraps and add decorative stitching to create a unique look.

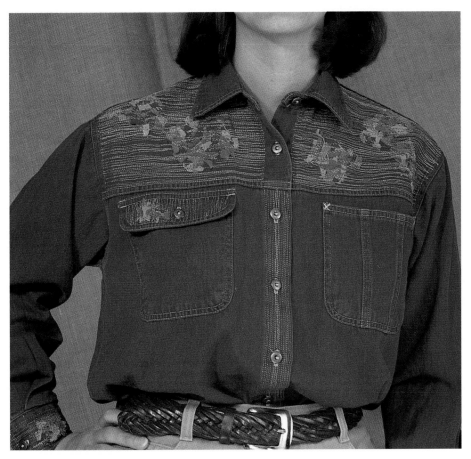

outline the area with a water-soluble marker to highlight the web, making it easier to see.

3. Using a rotary cutter and mat, cut fabric scraps into small pieces, varying the sizes and shapes.

4. Mound or cluster the confetti on the web. Add a few strands of embellishment thread if desired for interest. Cover with a press cloth and press *(Diagram A)*.

5. Dust off excess confetti (optional).

6. Zigzag randomly around the outer edges and over the entire piece to hold the tiny pieces in place *(Diagram B)*.

7. Change the machine stitch to a straightstitch and randomly stitch the area to add interest *(Diagram C)*.

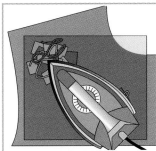

Diagram A: Arrange confetti on fusible web; press.

Diagram B: Zigzag randomly to hold tiny pieces in place.

Diagram C: Straightstitch over entire piece.

Gather Supplies

- ❏ Machine embroidery or metallic needle
- ❏ Machine embroidery thread or metallic thread for needle
- ❏ Thread that matches fashion fabric for bobbin
- ❏ Paper-backed fusible web
- ❏ Water-soluble fabric marker
- ❏ Rotary cutter and mat
- ❏ Press cloth

Select Fabrics

Choose a ready-made shirt or garment. Or choose a solid color fabric for your garment; see your pattern for amount.

   Gather scraps of fabric that contrast or coordinate with the garment fabric.

Get Ready

- ✔ Insert a metallic or machine embroidery needle.
- ✔ Thread the needle with two strands of embroidery or metallic thread, threading as one strand.
- ✔ Use thread matching the fashion fabric in the bobbin.
- ✔ Set the machine for a medium length and medium width zigzag stitch.

Create Confetti Appliqués

1. Cut paper-backed fusible web into geometric shapes and press to garment in desired areas.

2. Remove the paper backing and

Folk Art Appliqués

Add a touch of folk art to your next project by using plaid fabric for appliqués.

Gather Supplies

❑ Size 90 machine embroidery needle
❑ Machine embroidery thread (two spools) for needle
❑ Thread that matches the fashion fabric for the bobbin
❑ Lightweight paper-backed fusible web
❑ Wave or pinking shears or rotary cutter and mat (optional)
❑ Decorative yarns
❑ Large hand-sewing needles
❑ Permanent marking pen (optional)
❑ Heavyweight paper-backed fusible web
❑ Tear-away stabilizer

Select Fabrics

Choose a solid color for the base fabric. See your pattern for amount.

Choose a plaid fabric for appliqués.

Get Ready

✔ Insert the embroidery needle in your machine.

✔ Thread the top of the machine with two strands of machine embroidery thread, threading both strands as one. Thread the bobbin with thread to match the fabric.

✔ Adjust the sewing machine for a wide blanket stitch. Test stitching on a fabric scrap.

Note from Nancy
If your machine does not have a programmed blanket stitch, use the blindhem stitch. Adjust the width and length of the stitch until it resembles a traditional blanket stitch.

✔ Loosen the top tension by two numbers or notches (for example, from 5 to 3).

Create Plaid Appliqués

1. Trace the appliqué design onto the paper side of lightweight web.
2. Roughly cut out the design; fuse the web to the wrong side of the plaid fabric *(Diagram A)*.
3. Cut out the appliqué, following the traced design. For a folk art look, cut out the design using a wave or pinking blade *(Diagram B)*.
4. Peel off the paper backing and fuse the appliqué to the project.
5. Stitch around the appliqués using one or several of the following techniques.

Running Stitch
1. Thread decorative yarn through a large-eyed hand-sewing needle.
2. Sew a running stitch ¼" (6 mm) inside the raw edges.
3. Knot threads on either the right side or the wrong side of the fabric. Knots exposed on the right side are characteristic of folk art techniques and provide an additional embellishment *(Diagrams C and D)*.

Note from Nancy
Many decorative yarns are made of rayon. These yarns fray and are difficult to knot because the thread is slippery. Place a dab of a seam sealant, such as Fray Check, on the knot to prevent it from coming open (Diagram E). Dry the thread ends with the tip of the iron.

Pen Stitch

To "pen stitch," simply draw running stitches on fabric with a permanent fabric marking pen *(Diagram F)*. Since you don't secure pen-stitched appliqués with machine stitching, use a heavy-weight fusible web on your appliqués to provide a permanent no-sew bond.

Hand Blanket Stitch

1. Machine baste ¼" to ½" (6 mm to 1.3 cm) from edges of collars, pockets, and cuffs. This basting provides a stitching guide, which you will remove after you finish sewing.

2. Form a blanket stitch by anchoring the first stitch at the edge of the fabric.

3. Count over three or four basting stitches. For the next stitch and each succeeding one, insert the needle approximately ¼" (6 mm) from the fabric edge and ¼" (6 mm) from the preceding stitch, with the point of the needle toward you. Draw the point of the needle over the thread loop that forms *(Diagram G)*.

4. Repeat, always keeping the thread below the work and under the needle, forming a decorative thread along the project edge.

5. Remove the machine basting stitches when you finish the hand-stitching.

Machine Blanket Stitch

1. Back the fabric with a tear-away stabilizer.

2. Stitch with the straight stitches of the blanket stitch next to the outer edge of the appliqué and the zigzag stitches falling on the appliqué *(Diagram H)*.

Satin Stitch

1. Back the fabric with a stabilizer.

2. Set the machine for a satin stitch. Use only one thread in the top of the machine.

3. Stitch around the edges of the design *(Diagram I)*.

Creating Folk Art Appliqué

Diagram A: Fuse web to wrong side of fabric.

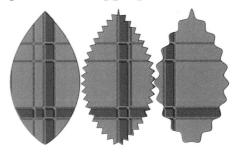

Diagram B: Cut appliqués as desired.

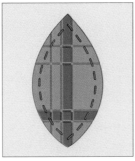

Diagram C: Sew a running stitch around raw edges.

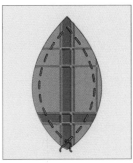

Diagram D: Leave knots on right side of fabric if desired.

Diagram E: Apply seam sealant to knots.

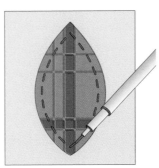

Diagram F: Draw running stitches using a fabric marker.

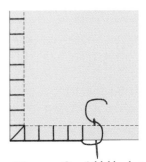

Diagram G: Add blanket stitches by hand.

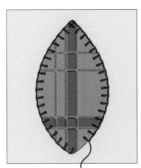

Diagram H: Sew blanket stitches by machine.

Diagram I: Satin-stitch appliqué edges.

Dimensional Appliqués

Instead of stitching one dimensional appliqués to your garment or project, make some of the appliqués look three-dimensional. It's a great folk art look.

Gather Supplies

❑ Paper-backed fusible web
❑ Buttons
❑ Embellishment yarns
❑ Large hand-sewing needles
❑ Machine embroidery thread for needle
❑ Thread that matches the fashion fabric for the bobbin

Create Dimensional Appliqués

1. Make square fringed flowers. Cut two 2" (5 cm) squares of plaid for each flower.

• Fringe the edges of the squares, and then place them on top of each other, offsetting the top square to create the look of flower petals *(Diagram A)*.

• Cut a 1½" (3.8 cm) plaid circle and fuse it to the top square *(Diagram B)*.

• Finish the edges of the circle using one of the techniques described on pages 48 and 49.

• Sew buttons to the center of the circle. Tie threads on the top of the button circle, leaving thread tails as accents *(Diagram C)*.

2. Make round flowers.

• Using fusible web, cut and fuse a 1½" (3.8 cm) fabric circle for the center of the flower and two petal shapes, each 1½" (3.8 cm) in length *(Diagram D)*.

• Finish the edges of the appliqués using one of the techniques described on pages 48 and 49.

• Sew buttons around the outer edge of the circle, fastening the threads on the wrong side of the fabric *(Diagram E)*.

• Secure knots with a seam sealant if desired.

Making Appliqué Dimensional

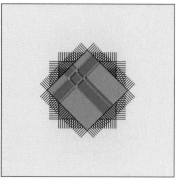

Diagram A: Place squares on top of each other, offsetting them.

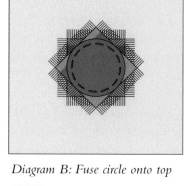

Diagram B: Fuse circle onto top square.

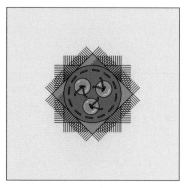

Diagram C: Sew buttons to "flower" center.

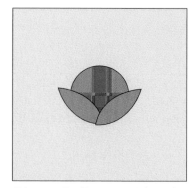

Diagram D: Fuse one circle and two leaves to make round flower.

Diagram E: Sew buttons around outer edge of flower.

Bias-Accent Appliqués

Combine bias strips with appliqués to simulate the look of stems and vines. What a simple yet interesting accent!

Gather Supplies

❑ Bias tape maker, ½" (1.3 cm) tape size
❑ Water-soluble basting tape

Create Bias-Accent Appliqués

1. Cut 1" (2.5 cm) bias strips of fabric.

2. Turn under the cut edges to form bias tape, using a bias tape maker. Insert the bias strip, wrong side up, through the wide end of the bias tape maker.

Using a safety pin or a straight pin, advance the fabric through the wide end of the tape maker. Fabric edges will fold to the middle as they come out the narrow end.

Press edges as they come from the tape maker.

> *Note from Nancy*
> To make bias tape without a bias tape maker, just press cut edges of a bias strip to the center (Diagram A).

3. Position the bias tape on the project using a water-soluble basting tape (Diagram B).

> *Note from Nancy*
> Wash-A-Way Basting Tape is ¼"-wide (6 mm-wide) water-soluble, double-sided tape. In difficult-to-pin areas, this product securely "bastes" fabric to fabric—an excellent notion to use when shaping the stems and vines of Folk Art Appliqués.

4. Stitch the bias to the project using one of the techniques described on pages 48 and 49.

Time-saver

🕐 For a true country look, eliminate the fusing from your appliqué. Without turning under raw edges, stitch the appliqués in place by hand or machine. The edges remain free.

Bias Appliqué

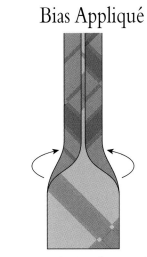

Diagram A: Press bias strip's cut edges to center.

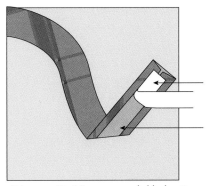

Diagram B: Use water-soluble basting tape to position bias tape.

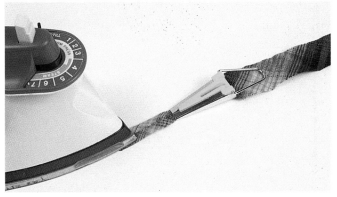

Bias Tape Maker

Fringed Buttonhole Appliqué

Add decorative buttonholes to fringed patches, and then highlight the patches with offset buttons. This makes an artistic combination of fabric, thread, and notions—something you can create, too!

Gather Supplies
- Lightweight fusible interfacing
- Rayon embroidery thread
- Machine embroidery needle
- Buttons

Select Fabrics

Choose fabric scraps to match your project, or use a coordinating or contrasting fabric for an accent.

Create Fringed Buttonhole Appliqués

1. Cut 1" to 1½" (2.5 cm to 3.8 cm) squares of woven fabric. Fringe the edges.

2. Stabilize the back of the buttonhole area with fusible interfacing.

3. Place the fringed rectangles on the project. You may want to pin them in place first until you're satisfied with the design.

4. Stitch buttonholes through all layers, using a machine embroidery needle and rayon embroidery thread. This lustrous thread adds another decorative element to the appliqué.

5. Add buttons, using the photo as a placement guide *(Diagram)*.

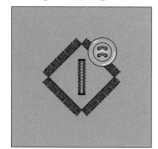

Add buttons to fringed appliqué.

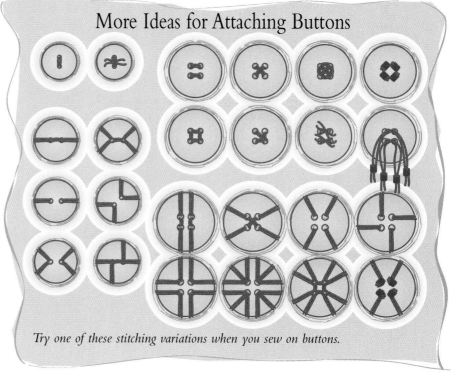

More Ideas for Attaching Buttons

Try one of these stitching variations when you sew on buttons.

Fringed Appliqués

Take advantage of a fabric's ability to ravel to add embellishments to projects.

Gather Supplies

Use the same supplies as for Fringed Buttonhole Appliqué on page 52.

Select Fabrics

Choose fabric scraps to match your project, or use a coordinating or contrasting fabric for an accent.

Create Fringed Appliqués

1. Cut fabric pieces for the appliqué, following the straight of grain. Geometric shapes, such as squares, rectangles, diamonds, and triangles, work best.

2. Fringe the outer edges of the shapes.

3. Add the fringed appliqués to the garment.

    Option 1: Insert the fringed shapes into seam lines.

    Option 2: Create a pseudo pin by combining a fringed section with several long threads. Fold fringed section or leave it flat as desired. Secure both to the garment with a button.

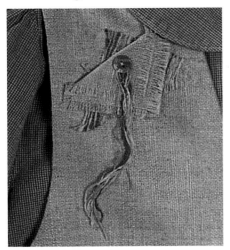

Time-savers

Take the time to plan your embellishment before you start sewing, and you'll save time in the long run. With fringed appliqué, for example, pin the appliqués into the seam line where you think you want them, and try on the garment section to see how they look. Then adjust the placement as needed. Stopping to try out the embellished garment takes less time than ripping out a seam and redoing it if you don't like the placement.

Some synthetic fabrics are not suitable for fringed appliqués because they ravel too much, and they wouldn't hold up in the laundry. If you're not sure how stable your fabric is, back the appliqué with fusible interfacing. Cut the interfacing the size and shape of your appliqué without the fringe.

Make a pseudo pin to embellish a purchased item. It's a quick way to personalize a denim jumper or a vest, using materials you already have in your sewing basket.

Cutwork Appliqué

You can create cutwork appliqué using a liquid fabric remover instead of cutting away the fabric.

Gather Supplies
- ❑ Size 90 (14) universal needle
- ❑ Open toe or embroidery foot
- ❑ 100% polyester or silk thread that matches or coordinates with the fashion fabric
- ❑ Tracing wheel and tracing paper
- ❑ Water-soluble stabilizer
- ❑ Liquid fabric remover

Select Fabrics
Choose a fabric with a plant origin (cotton, rayon, ramie, or linen). See your pattern for amount.

Note from Nancy
Common fabric removers, such as Fiber-Etch®, dissolve cotton, rayon, ramie, linen—all fibers of plant origin. To use this technique for cutwork, you must be sure that your fabric is plant-based and that your thread is not. It's critical to choose 100% polyester thread or silk thread in both the needle and bobbin when you use a liquid fabric remover. The non-plant-fiber thread acts as a barrier, keeping the liquid fabric remover from going beyond its intended boundaries.

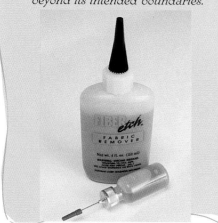

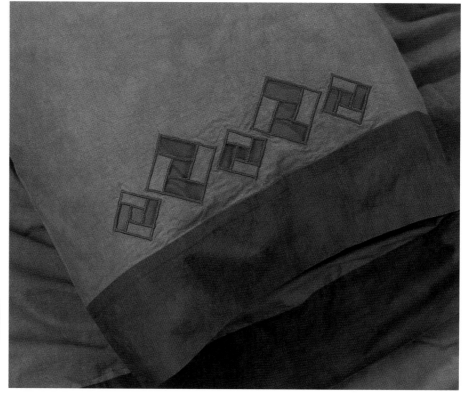

Get Ready
- ✔ Set the machine for a straightstitch.
- ✔ Insert a universal needle.
- ✔ Use a balanced thread tension.
- ✔ Replace the conventional presser foot with an open toe or embroidery foot.
- ✔ Use a 100% polyester or silk thread in both the bobbin and the needle of the machine.

Create Cutwork Appliqués
1. Choose an appliqué design that includes enclosed sections, or use the design on page 138.

2. Transfer the designs to the fabric using a tracing wheel and tracing paper.

3. Back the fabric with water-soluble stabilizer *(Diagram A)*.

4. Stitch around the traced designs with a straightstitch to ensure that the transfer markings do not rub off.

5. Set the machine for a satin stitch, using a stitch width of 3 and a stitch length of .5.

Note from Nancy
Make sure the stitches are not too narrow. This stitching establishes the boundaries of the design. If the stitches are too narrow, the liquid fabric remover may seep beyond them and dissolve fabric you need to keep.

6. Satin-stitch around the design, completely enclosing the area intended for the cutwork. Remove the stabilizer *(Diagram B)*.

7. Apply the liquid fabric remover within the enclosed areas next to the satin stitching that will feature the cutwork. Let dry *(Diagram C)*.

Note from Nancy
Try applying Fiber-Etch or another fabric remover with an applicator bottle that has a fine tip. I use the Great Little Liquid Bottle for the easiest application!

8. Cover with a press cloth and press until the cutwork areas change color.
9. Remove the marked sections. If the sections do not fall out of their own accord, rinse the design under running water. Cutwork areas will drop out of the fabric, leaving a clean edge *(Diagram D)*.

Note from Nancy
Try this creative option: Use liquid fabric remover to remove some portions of a fabric print, creating another cutwork lookalike. Satin-stitch around portions of the print, and then remove those areas using liquid fabric remover *(Diagram D)*.

Layered Cutwork

Gather Supplies
Use the same supplies listed for Cutwork Appliqué

Select Fabrics
Choose a fabric with a plant origin

Creating Cutwork Appliqué

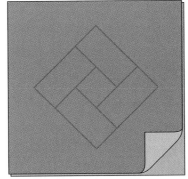

Diagram A: Trace designs onto fabric; back with water-soluble stabilizer.

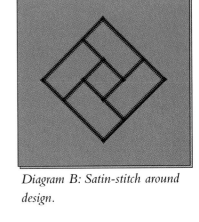

Diagram B: Satin-stitch around design.

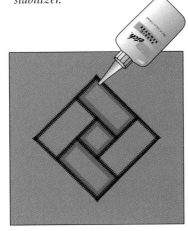

Diagram C: Apply liquid fabric remover.

Diagram D: Remove marked sections.

(cotton, rayon, ramie, or linen) as the fashion fabric. See your pattern for amount.

Choose synthetic fabric of contrasting or coordinating color. This fabric will appear through the openings in the cutwork appliqué after you move the fashion fabric.

Get Ready
✔ Use the same machine set-ups listed for Cutwork Appliqué.

Create Layered Cutwork
1. Transfer the design to the right side of the fashion fabric using a tracing wheel and tracing paper *(Diagram)*.

2. Behind the traced area, stack the fabrics in the following order: stabilizer on the bottom, synthetic fabric in the middle (right side up), and fashion fabric on top (right side up).
3. Follow steps 4 through 6 under Cutwork Appliqué. When you remove the fashion fabric portions, the synthetic fabric underneath appears.

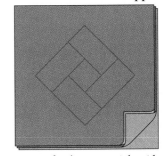

Diagram: Transfer design to right side of fabric.

Ultrasuede Appliqué

Nonravelling Ultrasuede is the perfect accent for appliqué projects.

Gather Supplies
- ❑ Metafil needle
- ❑ Monofilament nylon thread
- ❑ Lightweight paper-backed fusible web
- ❑ Press cloth
- ❑ Lightweight stabilizer

Select Fabrics

Choose a ready-made garment or fashion fabric. See your pattern for amount.

Use Ultrasuede fabric or scraps for appliqué shapes.

Get Ready
- ✔ Insert a Metafil needle in your machine.
- ✔ Thread the top of the machine with monofilament nylon thread.
- ✔ Adjust the machine for a blindhem stitch with a length of 1.5 and a width of 2.

Create Ultrasuede Appliqués

1. Position the appliqués.

> ### Note from Nancy
> Check the references on page 19 for fusible webs—they are not all alike! I recommend lightweight fusible web to combine with Ultrasuede. The heat and moisture of an iron have a hard time penetrating Ultrasuede. Lighter web melts more readily than traditional fusible web, making it a better match for Ultrasuede.

• Trace the appliqué design on the paper side of the fusible web.

• Press the fusible web to the Ultrasuede fabric and cut out the design.

• Position the design on the project. Cover with a press cloth and lightly fuse.

• Flip the project so that the right side faces the ironing board. Finish the fusing process.

> ### Note from Nancy
> Always do the final fusing from the wrong side when working with Ultrasuede. With the suede protected by the ironing board, you won't flatten the nap and create an iron imprint. Play it safe—press from the wrong side!

2. Back the fabric with a lightweight stabilizer.

3. Stitch the appliqué onto the garment, using the blindhem stitch; or simply edgestitch the design with a straightstitch.

> ### Note from Nancy
> If using the blindhem stitch, test stitch length and width on a sample, adjusting to accommodate the shape of the appliqués. Stitch so that the straightstitch runs along the edge of the appliqué and the zigzag of the blindhem stitch catches the appliqué.

Appliqué Collar Band

You can personalize or upgrade a plain purchased shirt by adding Ultrasuede. Stitch distinctive accents at the collar band, pocket and yoke.

Gather Supplies

In addition to the general supplies for Ultrasuede Appliqués, you need:
- ❑ Purchased shirt
- ❑ Tissue paper
- ❑ Tracing wheel (optional)
- ❑ Thread that matches the Ultrasuede and the shirt

Select Fabrics

Choose Ultrasuede for appliqués:
- 9" x 12" (23 cm x 30.5 cm) square for collar
- Scraps for designs

Create an Appliqué Collar Band

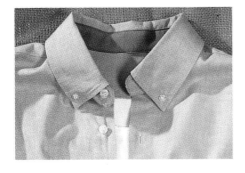

1. Create a pattern for the collar band, taking the pattern from the shirt itself.
- Place a layer of tissue paper, wider and longer than the collar band, on a padded surface.
- Position the shirt flat on top of the tissue paper, placing the center of the collar band at the center of the paper. Mold the fabric to meet the paper, making the collar as flat as possible.
- Transfer the collar band shape to the paper by poking a needle along the

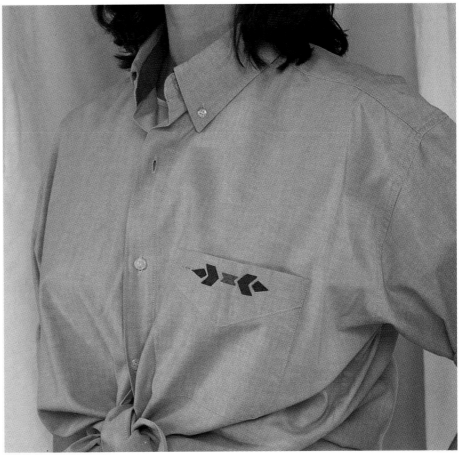

shirt seam line or tracing with a tracing wheel, piercing holes in the paper. You may have to do one section of the collar and then reposition the shirt to do another section.
- Connect the pierced dots with a pencil. If you prefer, you can make a pattern for half the collar, and then cut out the traced section on the fold to get a full pattern.

2. Cut out the collar band from Ultrasuede, using the newly created pattern.

> *Note from Nancy*
> Another fabric option is *Ultraleather*™. As the name implies, this fabric combines the feel and appearance of real leather with the easy-care qualities of a synthetic fabric.

3. Remove the button from the shirt collar band.

4. Pin the new collar band to the inside of the original collar band. Edgestitch in place using either monofilament nylon thread or thread that matches the collar band and shirt.

5. Attach the button to the collar band.

6. Prepare and apply appliqués from scraps, following instructions on page 56 (Diagram).

Diagram: Use Ultrasuede scraps for pocket appliqués.

Framed-Stitch Appliqué

Take an ordinary satin-stitched appliqué and make it dramatic by outlining the satin stitches with metallic thread.

Gather Supplies

❑ Machine embroidery needle
❑ Rayon machine embroidery thread to contrast with fashion fabric and appliqué
❑ Lingerie/bobbin thread or a thread to match the fabric
❑ Embroidery or open toe foot
❑ Lightweight stabilizer
❑ Metafil needle
❑ Metallic thread

Select Fabrics

For garment, choose a fashion fabric. Check your pattern for amount.

For appliqué, choose Ultrasuede fabric in a color that complements your fashion fabric.

Get Ready

✔ Insert machine embroidery needle. You'll replace it later with the Metafil needle.
✔ Thread the needle with machine embroidery thread.
✔ Use lingerie/bobbin thread or thread that matches the fabric in the bobbin.
✔ Set the machine for a satin stitch using a wide width. I used a stitch width of 4 and a stitch length of .5.
✔ Loosen the top tension by two numbers (for example, from 5 to 3).
✔ Replace the conventional foot with an embroidery or open toe foot.

Create Framed-Stitch Appliqué

1. Apply your Ultrasuede appliqué design to your garment, using the method described on page 56.
2. Back the appliqué area with a stabilizer. Satin-stitch around the outside edges of the appliqué (Diagram A).
3. Replace the embroidery needle with the Metafil needle. Thread the needle with metallic thread.
4. Set the machine for a triple stitch. Built into most sewing machines, this stitch takes two stitches forward and one stitch back. Select a regular stitch length.
5. Stitch around both edges of the satin stitching, forming a frame (Diagram B).

Framed-Stitch Appliqué

Diagram A: Satin-stitch around outside edges.

Diagram B: Straightstitch around both edges of satin stitching.

Ultrasuede Buttonhole Appliqué

Change an off-the-rack shirt into a one-of-a-kind creation by adding simple Ultrasuede appliqués over the buttonhole area.

Gather Supplies
❏ In addition to the general supplies listed under Ultrasuede Appliqué, you need paper.

Select Fabrics
Choose a ready-made garment, or buy fashion fabric and pattern. See your pattern for amount of fabric.

Choose Ultrasuede fabric for appliqués.

Get Ready
✔ Thread the needle with metallic or monofilament thread.
✔ Use thread to match the garment in the bobbin.
✔ Set the machine for a straightstitch.

Note from Nancy
Sometimes, the time-consuming part of the sewing process is deciding which design to use. Look through books for ideas, or create shapes of your own. Cut shapes from paper, and position them on the garment to see if you like the effect. I find geometric and abstract shapes very attractive for this creative embellishment.

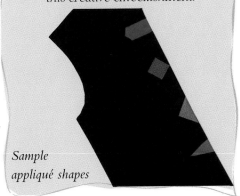

Sample appliqué shapes

Create Buttonhole Appliqué
1. Select an appliqué for the buttonhole area.
2. To position all elements correctly, make a test buttonhole using the appliqué and garment fabrics. If you can't use actual garment fabric, use a fabric of similar weight and color from your fabric stash.
3. Attach the appliqué using your favorite technique outlined earlier *(Diagrams A and B)*.

4. If you are stitching the appliqué to a ready-made garment, open the buttonhole after you finish the appliqué.
• Poke pins through the ends of the existing buttonholes to mark starting and stopping points *(Diagram C)*.
• Using a pair of small scissors, carefully open the buttonhole through the appliqué fabric, working from the right side of the fabric.
• Stitch around the buttonhole with a straightstitch or satin stitch.

Ultrasuede Buttonhole Appliqué

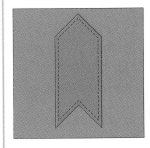

Diagram A: Straightstitch appliqué in place.

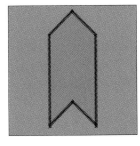

Diagram B: Or zizag or satinstitch appliqué in place.

Diagram C: Use pins to mark buttonhole placement.

Ultrasuede Toggles

Add an interesting design and create a closure in one simple yet creative step by making Ultrasuede toggles.

Gather Supplies
❑ Metafil needle
❑ Monofilament nylon thread
❑ Lightweight paper-backed fusible web
❑ Press cloth
❑ Lightweight stabilizer

Select Fabrics
Choose a ready-made garment or fashion fabric. See your pattern for amount.

Use Ultrasuede fabric or scraps for appliqué shapes.

Get Ready
✔ Insert a Metafil needle in your machine.
✔ Thread the top of the machine with monofilament nylon thread.

Create Toggles
1. Trace appliqué designs on the paper side of the fusible web. Abstract shapes or simple geometric shapes like the triangles pictured work well. Press fusible web to the Ultrasuede fabric and cut out the designs.
2. Pin the appliqué shapes on each side of the closure.
3. Cut narrow strips of suede 6" (15 cm) long.
4. Place the strips (one or more per side) under the center edge of the appliqués. Fuse the appliqués in place to serve as ties *(Diagram)*.
5. Stitch the appliqués in place using a straightstitch.
6. Tie knots or add beads to the ends of the suede ties.

Diagram: Fuse appliqués over tie strips.

Other ideas

Toggle Closure for a Handbag

Cutwork Applique Lapel

Confetti Applique on a Bodice

Ultrasuede Buttonhole Appliques

61

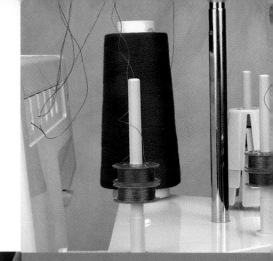

Put odd-sized fabric scraps to good use by crazy-quilting jacket lapels *(left and page 68)*. Wind bobbins and use these on a thread palette for small sections of serged patchwork *(page 67)*. ▶

When you sew patchwork, you actually create fabric. Embellish one area or stitch an entire garment using your new fabric.

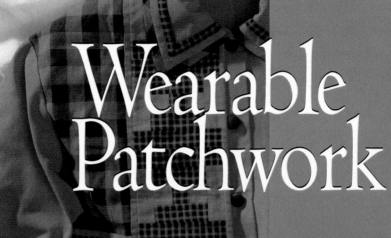

Wearable Patchwork

◀ Combine decorative stitching, pleats, and other techniques to make a delicate Heirloom Patchwork blouse *(left and page 80)*. Show off your serged seams by putting them on the outside of a Serged Patchwork vest *(right and page 66)*. ▶

◀ Add a Plaid Pinwheel block to the front of a jumper *(left and page 74)* or the back of a jacket, or make a slightly larger Plaid Pinwheel for a wall hanging *(page 76)*.

Fusible Patchwork
Vest, page 64

Fusible Patchwork

This embellishment is a great technique for beginners—you don't sew any seams!

Gather Supplies

❑ Fabric-marking pen
❑ Medium-weight fusible interfacing
❑ 4.0/90 double needle
❑ Thread
❑ Pinking shears or rotary cutter with a wave blade or a pinking blade and cutting mat
❑ Press cloth

Select Fabrics

For patchwork, use coordinating fabrics that are compatible in weight and care. Consider interlock knits, cottons, and synthetic suede, such as Ultrasuede and Ultrasuede Lite.

Buy narrow trim or create trim from a nonraveling fabric, such as interlock knit or synthetic suede.

Get Ready

✔ Set machine for a medium-width zigzag stitch.
✔ Use matching thread in needle and bobbin.

Create Fusible Patchwork

1. From fusible interfacing, cut the pattern pieces you plan to embellish, eliminating armhole, front, and lower-edge seam allowances *(Diagram A)*. Use light-colored interfacing with light-colored fabrics and dark interfacing with dark fabrics.

2. Use a fabric-marking pen to mark vertical and horizontal lines to serve as alignment points.

• Mark the center of the interfacing piece, following the lengthwise grain.

• Mark one horizontal line at right angles to the center line *(Diagram B)*.

• Place interfacing on ironing board, fusible side up.

3. Cut 3" (7.6 cm) squares of coordinating fabrics. I used 3" (7.5 cm) squares in the denim vest. Since the fabrics completely cover the interfacing foundation, you can use any size patchwork.

4. Arrange the squares on the interfacing, using marked lines as positioning guides. Place squares so their edges meet. Some of the squares will extend beyond the edge of the interfacing *(Diagram C)*.

5. Cover fabric squares with a press cloth. Following interfacing manufacturer's instructions, fuse with an iron, repositioning the iron until the entire piece is fused *(Diagram D)*.

> *Note from Nancy*
> *If your vest will have bias-bound edges like the denim one I made, trim the seam allowances from the outer edges of the front interfacing section and the back pattern piece. You only need the shoulder and side seams (Diagram A).*

> *Note from Nancy*
> *If you do not use a press cloth, any fusible interfacing not covered by fabric may end up on the bottom of your iron. If you use synthetic suede, test pressing on a sample to ensure that the heat of the iron does not flatten the nap.*

Making Fusible Patchwork

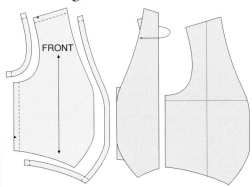

Diagram A: Eliminate pattern seam allowances.

Diagram B: Mark horizontal and vertical lines.

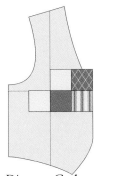

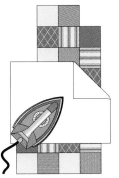

Diagram C: Arrange squares on interfacing.

Diagram D: Fuse entire piece.

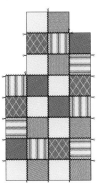

Diagram E: Zizag along all edges.

Diagram F: Place strips on vertical seams.

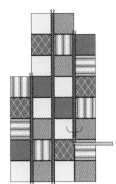

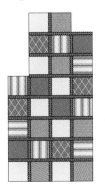

Diagram G: Stitch trim in place.

Diagram H: Place and stitch horizontal strips.

Stitching Options

Quick-Stitch Trim

6a. Zigzag along the lengthwise and crosswise edges of the squares with a long, wide stitch *(Diagram E)*. You won't see this stitching on the completed vest; it merely keeps the edges flat and makes it easier to apply the trim.

7a. Add trim to seams.

• Cut ½" (1.3 cm) strips of knit. You can cut the strip edges straight, wavy, or pinked, as you prefer. I cut the edges of the trim on the pictured vest using a rotary cutter with a pinking blade. I could have used pinking shears or a rotary cutter with a wave blade.

Rotary cutter with wave blade

• Position strips over lengthwise square intersections, covering the seams *(Diagram F)*.

• Insert the double needle. Thread both the needles and the bobbin with thread that matches the trim. Stitch the trim to the fusible patchwork *(Diagram G)*. As an option, straight-stitch along both edges of the strip using a single needle in your sewing machine.

• Repeat, positioning and stitching trim over crosswise square intersections *(Diagram H)*.

8a. Treat the newly created fusible patchwork as fabric. My denim vest is lined, and the edges are bound with bias strips of fabric.

Decorative Stitching

6b. Set up machine for decorative stitching.

• Insert a machine embroidery needle if you're using rayon thread; insert a metallic needle if using metallic thread.

• Thread the top of the machine with rayon or metallic thread; use all-purpose thread that matches the fabric in the bobbin.

• Adjust the machine for a decorative stitch and attach an embroidery foot.

• Loosen the top tension by two numbers or notches.

Note from Nancy
If you use synthetic suede for your patchwork, you can be especially creative in adding decorative stitching to the seamlines. With fabric that ravels, you'll need to use a dense decorative stitch, covering the seams completely. Since synthetic suede doesn't ravel, you can choose airy or dense decorative stitches. The choice is yours!

7b. Stitch over the butted edges of patchwork with a decorative stitch.
8b. Follow instructions in **8a**.

Time-savers

⏱ Use fused patchwork on one pattern piece only, such as one side of a vest, using a coordinating solid-color fabric for the other side and the back.

⏱ Cut larger fabric squares (but remember to keep your squares in proportion to your overall finished project).

⏱ Use the decorative stitching option for finishing. You save the time of cutting and applying the quick-stitch trim.

Serged Patchwork

Use your serger to create exciting patchwork.

Note from Nancy

Add interest to the stitching by blending several threads in each looper. To make this process easier, place a thread palette on a looper thread spindle, and feed two threads through each looper tension guide, treating them as a single thread. A thread palette is a plastic stand designed to fit over your serger spool holder. It feeds thread from up to five spools into the upper or lower loopers of your serger. You can also place the palette over a sewing machine cone thread stand to feed up to three types of thread into the upper part of your sewing machine.

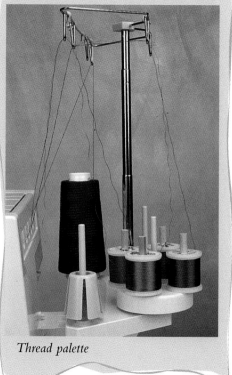

Thread palette

Gather Supplies

❑ For the upper and lower loopers, two spools each of rayon machine embroidery thread in two coordinating colors that highlight the fabrics

❑ For the needle, all-purpose serger thread that matches the fabric

❑ Thread palette

Select Fabrics

Choose two coordinating 100%-cotton, medium-weight fabrics with a small design.

Choose two 100%-cotton, medium-weight fabrics with a large design, in a color and style that are compatible with the first two.

Get Ready

✔ Adjust the serger for a balanced 3-thread overlock stitch, with normal stitch width and a short stitch length.

✔ Thread two coordinating rayon threads in both the upper and lower loopers; thread all-purpose serger thread in the needle.

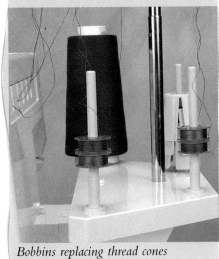

Bobbins replacing thread cones

Create Serged Patchwork

1. Cut 2½" to 3" (6.3 cm to 7.5 cm) crosswise strips of each large print and 1½" to 2" (3.8 cm to 5 cm) crosswise strips of each small print.

2. Serge the strips together.

• Match two strips of different widths, wrong sides together. Serge lengthwise edges *(Diagram A)*. The seam is exposed on the fabric's right side.

• Join additional strips in a random layout, alternating strip sizes and colors until the serged fabric is slightly longer than the pattern section.

• Press serged seams in one direction, pressing from the right side because seams are exposed.

3. Recut the newly formed serged strips (called "strata") crosswise into various sections ranging in width from 1" to 3" (2.5 cm to 7.5 cm). Vary widths to add interest *(Diagram B)*. Do not cut sections narrower than 1" (2.5 cm) or they will be too small after pieces are serged back together.

4. Serge the sections together.

• Invert one section; match it to a second section, wrong sides together. To accentuate a patchwork design, slightly offset the strips. Place the section with the seam allowances pressed upward on top *(Diagram C)*.

• Serge, using a small screwdriver, stiletto, or a Puts-it to keep the seams facing the correct direction.

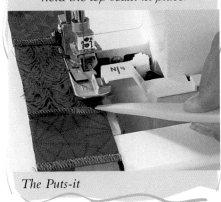

The Puts-it

• Add more sections, varying strip widths and inverting every other section, until you've created sufficient fabric to cut out pattern pieces *(Diagram D)*.

• Repeat for the other vest front. You don't have to create a mirror image of the design. The arrangement should be fun and free flowing.

5. Cut out the pattern pieces. Complete the project following your pattern instructions.

Creating Serged Patchwork

Diagram A: Serge 2 strips together.

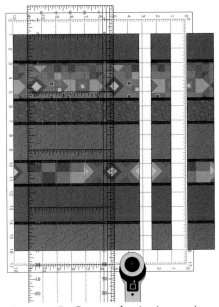

Diagram B: Cut serged strips into sections.

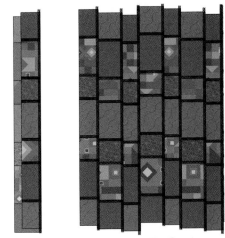

Diagram C: Serge 2 sections together.

Diagram D: Continue adding sections.

Crazy Patchwork with Decorative Stitching

*This jacket spotlights an attractive use of fabric scraps as well as
dramatic highlights of metallic threads.*

Gather Supplies

- ❏ All-purpose thread
- ❏ Metallic thread(s)
- ❏ Metallic needle, size 80 (12)
- ❏ Quilting ruler or 6" quilting square, or plastic template sheets
- ❏ Embroidery foot

Select Fabrics

Collect scraps of similar colors, or coordinate colored scraps of various cotton fabrics.

Buy 100%-cotton flannel or muslin to use as a stabilizer for the patchwork section.

Note from Nancy
Use flannel as a stabilizer to create interesting texture. After decoratively stitching the patchwork to flannel, wash the fabric. Flannel made from 100% cotton shrinks, adding dimension to patchwork.

Get Ready

- ✔ Set machine for a straightstitch.
- ✔ Use all-purpose thread in the needle and the bobbin that coordinates with the fabric scraps.

Create Crazy Patchwork

1. Cut fabric for crazy quilt blocks.
- For block centers, cut numerous polygon-shaped pieces with sides approximately 2" to 3" (5 cm to 7.5 cm). The number depends on the size of the finished project *(Diagram A)*. I cut 12 center sections for my jacket.
- Cut the remaining scraps into strips of various widths.
2. Stitch crazy quilt blocks using an adaptation of a Log Cabin technique.
- Place a center section on one of the fabric strips, right sides together, aligning one edge of the center section along the strip. Repeat, placing additional center sections along the strip. Allow space between center sections to provide room for cutting the strip into separate segments. *(Diagram B)*.
- Stitch the center sections to the strip with a narrow seam allowance.
- Open the fabric so that the right side faces up. Press or finger-press seam allowances in one direction.
- Cut the strips apart, extending and cutting along the line of the center section *(Diagram C)*.
- Place a second fabric strip on the bed of the sewing machine, right side up. Align the crazy pieces along one edge of that strip, right sides together, to determine spacing; again allow extra fabric between sections for angle

cuts. Stitch the strips together *(Diagram D)*. Open the fabrics so that right sides face up. Press seam allowances in one direction.

• Cut the sections following the angle of the crazy piece.

• Add subsequent strips so that the crazy piece forms a square shape. The shape will not be perfectly square, but you will trim it to the correct size and shape.

3. Cut a 6" (15 cm) template or use a 6"-square quilting ruler or a rotary-cutting ruler to trim crazy pieces to that size *(Diagram E)*.

Use your creativity in cutting these squares. Cant or tilt your template to cut some squares at an angle. Use larger squares (up to about 8" or 20.5 cm). Cut squares according to your personal preference.

4. Combine crazy quilt blocks to make fabric for your project.

• Seam the squares together to create a patchwork piece slightly larger than the pattern piece.

• Back the squares with a piece of 100%-cotton muslin or flannel (wrong sides facing) before you add decorative stitches, or use a stabilizer *(Diagram F)*.

5. Set up the machine for decorative stitching.

• Insert a metallic needle.

• Attach an embroidery foot.

• Use all-purpose thread to match your fabric in the bobbin and contrasting metallic thread in the needle to emphasize the stitches.

• Loosen the top tension by two numbers or notches.

6. Embellish the patchwork with decorative stitches.

• Select one or more decorative stitches. Stitch along seams of the crazy patchwork to embellish. This is an ideal project for a beginner. Just doodle at the machine, playing with the decorative stitches on the fabric like you might doodle with a pen on paper.

• Randomly stitch design(s) along the seams of the crazy piecing *(Diagram G)*.

• Change threads and stitch patterns as desired.

7. Wash the fabric. This causes the muslin or flannel layer to shrink and create attractive puckering.

8. Cut out the pattern shapes and construct the garment following your pattern instructions.

Stitching Crazy Patchwork

Diagram A: Cut pieces to make block centers.

Diagram B: Place blocks on strip.

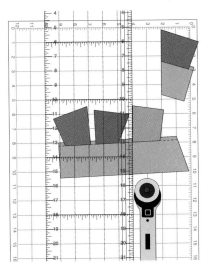

Diagram C: Cut strips apart.

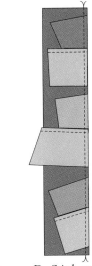

Diagram D: Stitch strips, open, and press.

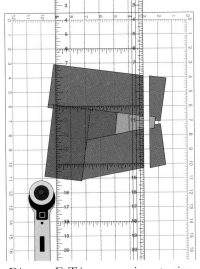

Diagram E: Trim crazy pieces to size.

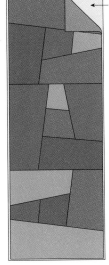

Diagram F: Back squares with stabilizer.

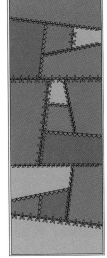

Diagram G: Use decorative stitches to sew.

Dimensional Patchwork

Use three different patchwork techniques to make this blouse, or try any one of them to make a pillow or a wall hanging.

Gather Supplies

❑ All-purpose thread
❑ Nylon thread
❑ Universal needle
❑ Metafil needle
❑ Rotary cutter, mat, and ruler

Select Fabric

Choose a base color; check your pattern for amount.

Buy ¼ yard (23 cm) each of two contrasting fabrics.

Get Ready

✔ Set up your sewing machine for a straightstitch and insert the universal needle.

✔ Use all-purpose thread in the needle and bobbin that coordinates with all fabrics.

Create Quarter-Circles

1. Cut circles and squares.

• Cut four 3" (7.5 cm) squares from the base fabric.
• Cut eight 3½" (9 cm) circles from contrasting fabric (two for each square).

Note from Nancy

Our instructions make 2½" (6.3 cm) finished squares. For other dimensions, be sure your circle diameter is ½" (1.3 cm) larger than your base square. For a 4" (10 cm) base square, cut 4½" (11.5 cm) circles.

2. Create quarter-circles.
• Join two circles, right sides together. Stitch around the outer edge with a ¼" (6 mm) seam.
• Nip the seam allowances (make ¼" or 6 mm clips) without cutting the stitching line. Or use pinking shears to grade and clip in one operation *(Diagram A)*.

• Fold the circle in half; press to mark. Fold in half again; press to mark the circle into quarters.
• Cut the circle into quarters along pressed lines. Turn each quarter right side out. Roll the edges with your fingers to get the seam exactly on the edge. Press *(Diagram B)*.

3. Position four quarter-circles on the right side of each base square, meeting the circle's cut edges to the square's corners. Machine-baste ⅛" (3 mm) from the edges *(Diagram C)*.

Creating Quarter-Circles

Diagram A: Nip seams or use pinking shears to grade seam.

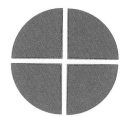

Diagram B: Cut circle into quarters and turn right side out.

Diagram C: Place quarter-circles on base square.

Create Quilting Strips

This quilting idea is a little more complex and requires more time than the previous technique, but the results are spectacular! Insert tucks of contrasting fabric between strips of the base fabric, then add directional stitching to produce this dramatic result.

1. Cut strips to make twists.
• Cut five 1¼" (3.2 cm) crosswise strips from base fabric.
• Cut four ¾" (2 cm) crosswise strips of each of *two* contrasting fabrics (eight strips total).

2. Stitch the twist strips.
• Meet ¾" (2 cm) strips of the contrasting fabrics, right sides together.
• Stitch one long edge with a ¼" (6 mm) seam; press *(Diagram D)*.
• Turn strip right side out, meeting cut edges.
• Repeat, stitching and pressing all four twist strips.

Note from Nancy
To get a sharp crease at the edge where the two fabrics are seamed, first press the seam flat and then press it open. This makes it much easier to position the stitching line precisely at the fold when you turn the strip right side out.

3. Join the twist and base strips.
• Place two base strips right sides together and sandwich a twist strip between them, meeting cut edges. Stitch a ¼" (6 mm) seam *(Diagram E)*.
• Repeat until all the twist strips and the base strips are stitched together *(Diagram F)*.
• Press all seams in one direction.

Note from Nancy
For the strips to twist, you must join each strip to a base strip with the same fabric facing up. Before you stitch, be sure that the same side of each twist faces the same direction.

4. Mark and stitch the twists.
• Square the end of the strip. Measure and mark a series of lines 1½" (3.8 cm) apart. Vary this measurement if you wish. For example, draw all lines only 1" (2.5 cm) apart to make twists more definite.
• Insert a Metafil needle and thread the needle with nylon thread. Match the bobbin thread to the fabric.
• Straightstitch the twists to the fabric, stitching from top to bottom on the first row and from bottom to top on the second row. Repeat, alternating stitching direction on each row *(Diagram G)*.

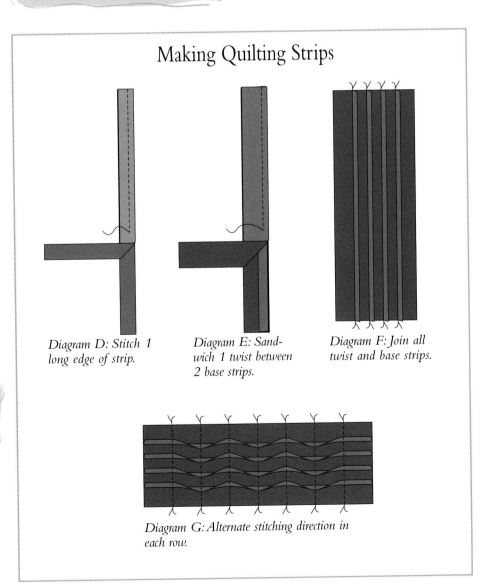

Making Quilting Strips

Diagram D: Stitch 1 long edge of strip.

Diagram E: Sandwich 1 twist between 2 base strips.

Diagram F: Join all twist and base strips.

Diagram G: Alternate stitching direction in each row.

Create Dimensional Right Triangles

1. Cut eight 3" (7.5 cm) squares from the base fabric.
2. Make right triangles from contrasting fabric.
• Cut eight 3" (7.5 cm) squares from the second contrasting fabric.
• Fold each contrasting square in half diagonally, wrong sides together, to create a right triangle *(Diagram H)*.
3. Place each right triangle on the right side of a base square, meeting cut edges. Machine-baste ⅛" (3 mm) from the edges *(Diagram I)*.

Making Dimensional Right Triangles

Diagram H: Fold square in half to form triangle.

Diagram I: Place triangle on base square and baste.

Put It All Together

The instructions tell you how I created the pieced fabric used for the purple-and-green blouse, but you can create other designs with the same pieces. Place the finished blocks on a flat surface and move them around until you're pleased with the look.

1. Arrange the quilt blocks.
• Meet four quarter-circles to create the center of the design.
• Place two dimensional triangles at each side, the top, and the bottom of the center square.
• Cut four 3" (7.5 cm) squares from the fabric you used to make the quarter-circles. Place these in the corners *(Diagram J)*.
• Cut the twist strip into blocks the length you want and arrange them along the quilt block sides. Mine are 10½" x 3½" (27 cm x 9 cm).
• Cut squares of contrasting fabric as needed to fill in the corners of your block. I used 3½" (9 cm) squares.
2. Assemble the block center (without the twist strips and outside corner blocks). *Use ¼" (6 mm) seam allowances throughout.*
• Join adjacent pairs of segments for the center portion, chain-piecing them together *(Diagram K)*.
• Join the paired segments to form vertical rows, chain-piecing them *(Diagram L)*.
• Press seams on adjacent blocks in opposite directions. This reduces bulk when seaming the horizontal rows.
• Join the horizontal seams, placing vertical rows with right sides together and matching seam intersections. Since the blocks are chain-pieced together like a honeycomb, matching is easy *(Diagram M)*.

Note from Nancy

Chain piecing, an assembly-line method of sewing, makes patchwork a lot faster. Stack blocks in pairs with right sides together. Join the two top blocks. Pick up the next pair, butt them to the first stitched blocks, and continue sewing. Repeat until you have butted and stitched together all blocks in a row.

4. Add the twist-strip border.
• Place a twist strip at each side of the block center, right sides together.
• Stitch a corner block to each end of the remaining two twist strips, right sides together.
• Place the remaining twist strips at the top and bottom of the block, matching seams, and stitch *(Diagram N)*.
6. Use the dimensional patchwork as part of your next sewing project.

Note from Nancy

For the purple-and-green blouse, I cut the block in half diagonally and featured one half on each side of the blouse front (Diagram O).

Joining Dimensional Patchwork Blocks

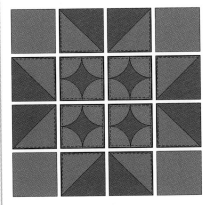

Diagram J: Arrange quilt blocks for center portion.

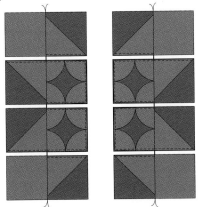

Diagram K: Join adjacent pairs of segments.

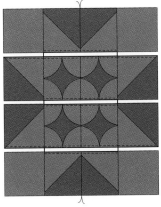

Diagram L: Join paired segments to form vertical rows.

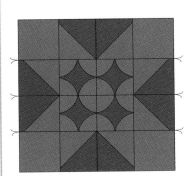

Diagram M: Join horizontal seams.

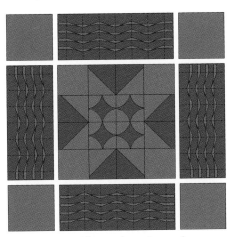

Diagram N: Place twist strips and corners around center block.

Diagram O: Cut the block diagonally to duplicate blouse on page 70.

More Ideas

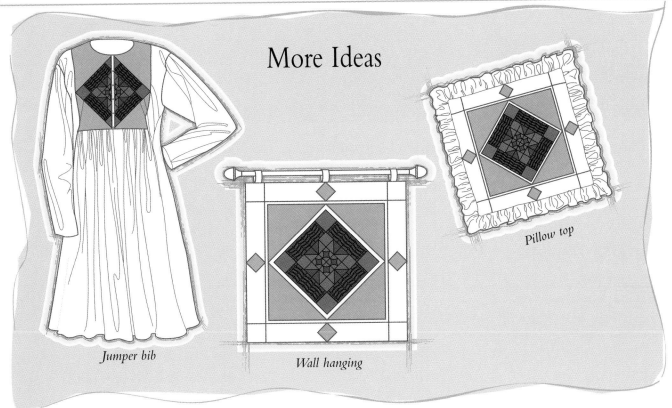

Jumper bib

Wall hanging

Pillow top

Plaidwork

Instead of using calicos and prints for patchwork, try plaids in traditional quilt patterns. I made Pinwheels, Seminole piecing, and Courthouse Steps.

Stitching traditional quilt patterns using plaid fabrics is a great way to experiment with the way colors, stripes, and designs work together. And best of all, there's no matching involved!

Plaid Pinwheel

Combine plaid fabric that has a dominant stripe with solid-colored fabric to create a design that seems to spin like a pinwheel!

Gather Supplies

- ❏ All-purpose thread
- ❏ Little Foot or other foot with ¼" (6 mm) marking
- ❏ Rotary cutter and mat
- ❏ Half-square ruler
- ❏ Quilting ruler
- ❏ Fusible interfacing

Select Fabrics

Choose equal yardage of two plaid fabrics and two coordinating solid-colored fabrics. For the pictured jumper, we used ⅛ yard (11.5 cm) of each fabric. Make sure one of your plaid fabrics has a dominant stripe.

Buy additional fabric for the back of the Pinwheel block and for completion of your project as your pattern requires.

Get Ready

- ✔ Set up your sewing machine for a straightstitch. Use thread in the needle and the bobbin that coordinates with all fabrics.
- ✔ Attach a foot that provides a guide for stitching a ¼" (6 mm) seam allowance.
- ✔ Or set up your serger for a 4-thread overlock stitch. Set seam width for ¼" (6 mm) and use all-purpose serger thread.

Note from Nancy

You need to maintain an accurate seam width. If your machine allows it, adjust your needle position so that it is precisely ¼" (6 mm) from the cut edges. Or use the Little Foot. This specialty presser foot has an accurate ¼" (6 mm) seam guide and is notched ¼" (6 mm) in front of and behind the center needle position. The notches provide an exact reference for starting, stopping, and pivoting.

Create Plaid Pinwheel

1. Cut and join fabric strips.

• Cut each fabric into 2" (5 cm) crosswise strips.

• Decide which plaid to match with each solid and use those pairings throughout.

• Match one plaid strip to one solid strip, right sides together. Stitch along *each* lengthwise edge with ¼" (6 mm) seam allowances *(Diagram A)*.

• Repeat, joining the remaining sets of fabrics.

2. Cut the joined strips into 16 right triangles, using a quilting ruler. For the jumper pinwheel design, I used 4 squares for the center blocks and 12 squares to surround the central blocks.

• Place the tip of the ruler at the top right end of the seamed strips. Align the 45°-angle marking on the ruler with one of the plaid lines, placing it parallel to the opposite lengthwise edge. Cut along the edge of the ruler *(Diagram B)*.

• Flip the ruler over, placing the outer edge of the ruler at the lower right edge of the strip and aligning the 45°-angle marking with a plaid line. Cut along the edge of the ruler. Repeat to cut 16 triangles *(Diagram C)*.

3. Open the right triangles.

• Remove the two or three stitches at the point of the triangle *(Diagram D)*.

• Press the seam toward the solid-colored fabric.

4. Arrange the quilt blocks into the Pinwheel pattern shown in *Diagram E;* stitch them together using the chain-stitching method detailed on page 76.

5. Back the block with fusible interfacing to cover the raw edges.

Making the Plaid Pinwheel

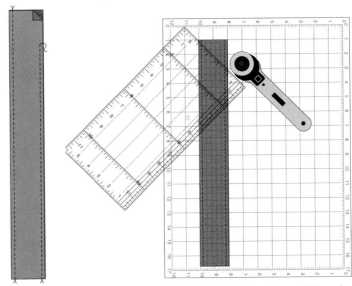

Diagram A: Stitch plaid strip to solid strip.

Diagram B: Cut strip at 45° angle.

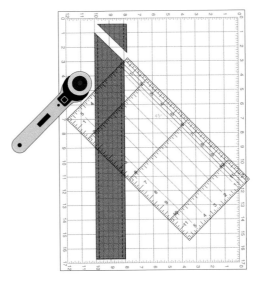

Diagram C: Flip ruler over to cut second 45° angle.

Diagram D: Remove stitches at triangle point.

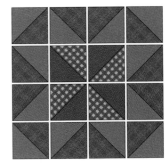

Diagram E: Assemble blocks into Pinwheel pattern.

Wall Hanging Option

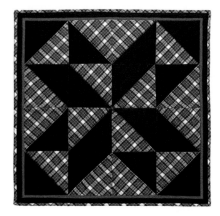

To sew a plaid Pinwheel wall hanging, use the instructions on pages 74 and 75, with the following variations.

• Buy 1 yard (.9 m) each of a plaid and a solid fabric. You'll need additional fabric for the backing, binding, and borders.

• Cut each fabric into four 6½" (16.5 cm) crosswise strips.

• Join one strip of each fabric, right sides together, stitching along both lengthwise edges with ¼" (6 mm) seam allowances.

• Cut strips using rotary cutting as detailed in Step 2 on page 75.

• Arrange blocks into a Pinwheel (photo and *Diagram E* on page 75).

• Add backing, batting, and borders. Quilt and bind as desired.

Note from Nancy
My staff quilted the layers using red thread and a zigzag stitch. These stitches add interest to the homespun look of the wall hanging.

Time-saver

Make more than one Pinwheel block at once. By cutting all the parts at the same time and chain-piecing them, you'll be through in less time than you would need to sew each project separately.

Seminole Plaidwork

Seminole patchwork requires piecing many small fabric scraps to make chevrons. By choosing plaid fabrics for Seminole piecing, you simplify the sewing. Because plaid combines colors and stripes, the chevron effect is built in, so you keep piecing to a minimum.

Select Fabrics

Choose three coordinating plaids: a small, a medium, and a large one.

Select a coordinating solid fabric.

Get Ready

Set up sewing machine or serger as detailed on page 74. See Get Ready for Plaid Pinwheel.

Create Seminole Plaidwork

1. Cut fabric strips. Adjust strip size if desired.

• Cut 3" (7.5 cm) crosswise strips of the three coordinating plaids.

• Cut 2" (5 cm) strips of the coordinating solid fabric *(Diagram A)*.

2. Join the fabric strips.

• Stitch strips together with ¼" (6 mm) seam allowances, alternating plaid and solid strips.

• Continue adding strips until the pieced section is approximately 4" (10 cm) longer than the pattern piece *(Diagram B)*.

• Press seam allowances in one direction.

3. Recut the strips into sections.

Note from Nancy
My denim fabric was heavier than my plaid fabrics, so I pressed all the seams toward the plaids (the lighter-weight fabric). The important thing is to be consistent.

• Fold the plaidwork section in half, right sides together, meeting short ends and aligning plaids.

• Cut the open ends of the folded sections at an angle. Use a 30°, a 45°, or a 60° angle on a cutting mat, depending on personal preference.

• Cut the plaidwork section into 2" (5 cm) strips, using the cut angle as the baseline. Keep pairs of strips together.

> *Note from Nancy*
> *The stronger the angle, the more fabric you trim and the less you have for cutting sections (Diagram C).*

4. Seam the pairs.
• Stitch each of the pairs together along one cut edge, right sides together. Chevrons in a flame-stitch pattern will appear on the right side.
• Press seam flat and then press seam to one side *(Diagram D).*
5. Stitch the completed pairs together until the patchwork meets the pattern size.
6. Back the plaidwork with a layer of knit or flannel to cover all the raw edges and make the new fabric softer.
7. Cut out the pattern, using Seminole plaidwork fabric where appropriate, and finish the top according to your pattern guide sheet.

> *Note from Nancy*
> *Before adding neckline ribbing to my shirt, I tried it on to make sure the neck opening was large enough. Remember this if you use this plaidwork technique in a pullover top. You may have to enlarge the opening since woven Seminole fabric does not stretch. If necessary, trim 1/8" (3 mm) from the neckline, and test again. If the neckline is still too small, trim again. Adjust a little at a time so that the neckline does not get too large (Diagram E).*

Making Seminole Plaidwork

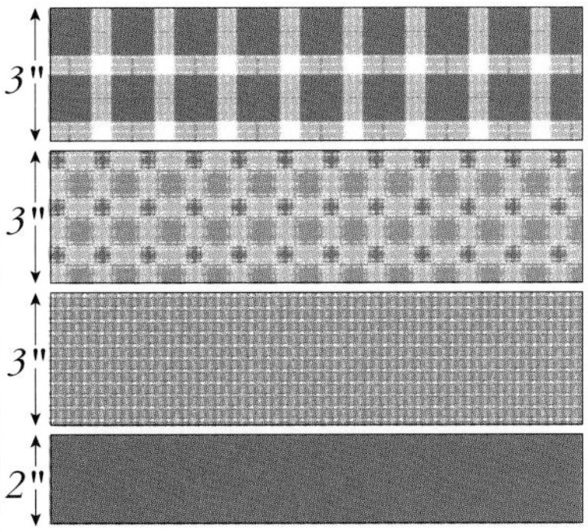

Diagram A: Cut 3" plaid strips and 2" solid strips.

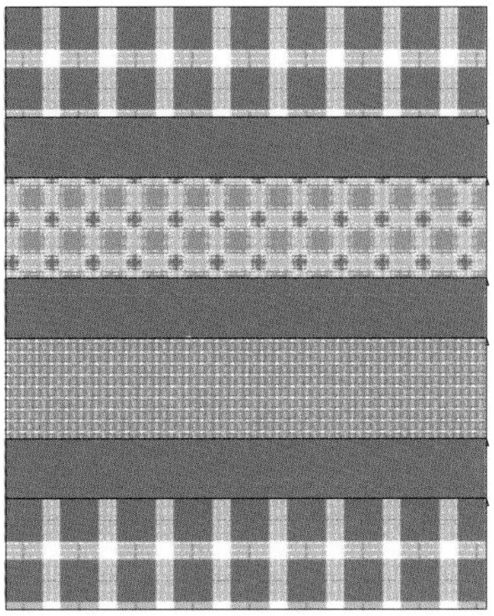
Diagram B: Join strips

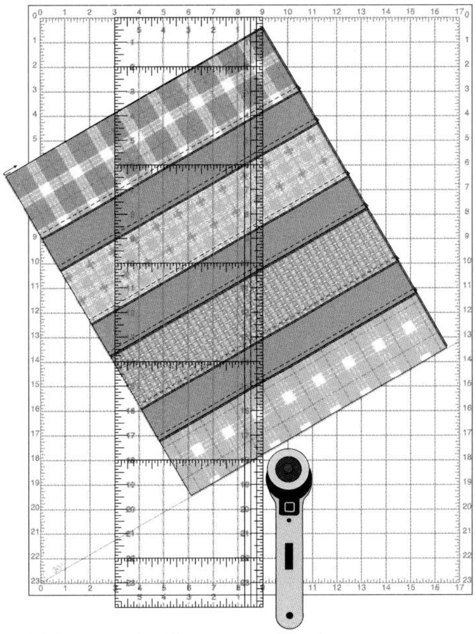
Diagram C: Cut seamed strips at an angle.

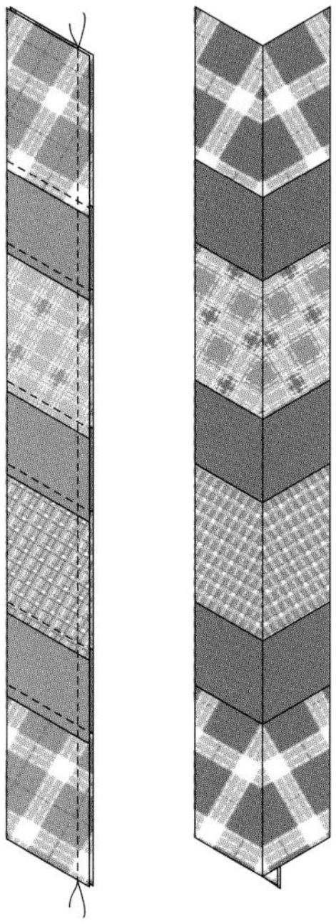
Diagram D: Stitch pairs together.

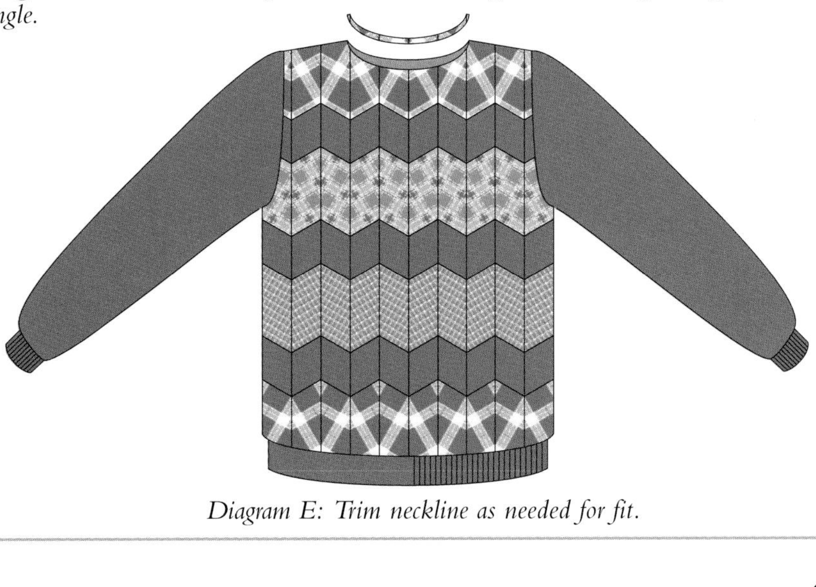
Diagram E: Trim neckline as needed for fit.

Courthouse Steps

This variation of the Courthouse Steps quilt pattern uses two plaids and a solid to create an eye-catching accent that's great fun to sew!

Select Fabrics

Choose two coordinating plaid fabrics.

Select a coordinating solid fabric.

Get Ready

Set up sewing machine or serger as detailed on page 74. See Get Ready for Plaid Pinwheel.

Create Plaid Courthouse Steps

1. Cut each fabric into 1¼" (3.2 cm) crosswise strips.

Note from Nancy
I first cut with scissors so that I am sure to follow the plaid line precisely. After the initial cut, I use a rotary cutter and mat to speed cutting.

2. Create the middle sections. Use ¼" (6 mm) seam allowances throughout. *Chain-piecing techniques are explained on page 72.*

• Use two solid strips and one plaid strip.

• Join one plaid strip and one solid strip right sides together. Using a sewing machine or a serger, stitch one lengthwise edge.

• Open the stitched strip and place the second solid strip so that one lengthwise edge matches the unstitched lengthwise edge of the plaid strip, right sides together. Stitch *(Diagram A)*. These stitched strips are commonly referred to as *strata*.

• Press the seam allowances away from the plaid strip.

• Cut the strata into 1¼" (3.2 cm) middle sections. You must cut sections the same width as the original strips. Cut as many sections as there will be blocks.

3. Stitch or serge a plaid strip on each side of the middle sections, chain-piecing them together.

• Match one of the middle sections to one plaid strip, right sides together with the plaid strip facing up.

• Join the two strips along one lengthwise edge *(Diagram B)*.

• Match a second middle section to the cut edge of the same plaid strip, right sides together, butting it against the first middle section. Continue sewing or serging.

• Repeat until all middle sections have been joined to a plaid strip.

• Repeat, joining another plaid strip to the opposite side of the middle sections, again chain-piecing them together.

• Press seam allowances away from the middle sections, toward the plaid strip.

• Cut the pieced sections apart, following the edge of each middle section as a guide *(Diagram C)*.

4. Add a solid strip to opposite sides of the block.

• Rotate the quilt block a quarter turn. Repeat Step 3 to stitch solid strips to two sides of the quilt block *(Diagram D)*.

• Press the seam allowances toward the outer strips, away from the center. Press the block right side to make sure no tucks form on the top.

• Cut the sections apart, using the length of the quilt block as a guide.

Note from Nancy

Use this tip to help position these strips correctly: When you place the block on the sewing machine, position the most recently added strips at the top and bottom of the quilt block, adding new strips at the sides. This way, you always join new strips to the sides of squares.

5. Continue adding strips to complete blocks. Finished block size should be approximately 4" (10 cm).

• Rotate the blocks a quarter turn so that the added strips are at the top and the bottom.

• Repeat this process of adding plaid and solid strips until you have added two steps of each color to the center, alternating plaid and solid strips *(Diagram E)*.

6. Complete additional blocks as needed following the same sequence.

7. Arrange the blocks to fit your pattern size. Stitch the blocks together.

Making Courthouse Steps

Diagram A: Stitch strips to make strata.

Diagram B: Join middle sections to 1 plaid strip.

Diag. C: Cut sections apart.

Diag. D: Stitch solid strips to 2 sides of block.

Diagram E: Alternate adding plaid and solid strips.

Another Idea

Wall hanging

Heirloom Patchwork

Combine two different art forms–patchwork and heirloom sewing–for sensational embellishments.

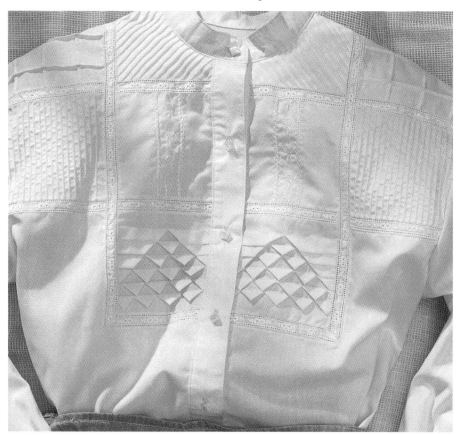

Instead of cotton strips, I sashed these patchwork blocks using ½" (1.3 cm) entredeux, an heirloom trim. It gives my shirt a delicate, feminine touch.

Plan the Patchwork Design

Take time to plan your design. Preliminary planning gives you a chance to see how the finished project will look before you begin sewing.

1. Select a pattern. Determine where to place the heirloom patchwork and measure the amount of space available for the design.

2. Choose the number, size, and position of blocks. I cut 5" (12.5-cm) squares.

• Trace a duplicate of your pattern so that the original pattern remains intact.

• Outline the squares on the new pattern, drawing vertical lines parallel to the center front and horizontal lines perpendicular to the vertical lines. Not all block sections will be square, since they must conform to the shape of the pattern at the shoulders, armholes, and neckline *(Diagram A)*.

Don't add seam allowances to the block pattern pieces. The entredeux that connects the square adds precisely the amount eliminated by seam allowances.

Make a pattern for each piece of the finished quilt design, indicating the heirloom technique you plan to use on each block. Number the pattern pieces for easy reference *(Diagram B)*.

Gather Basic Supplies

You need all the general supplies listed below for any Heirloom Patchwork technique. Notions to streamline individual patchwork techniques are listed with each specific technique.

❑ Cotton or rayon embroidery thread
❑ Press cloth
❑ Appliqué scissors
❑ Spray starch
❑ Water-soluble stabilizer
❑ Fabric-marking pen or pencil (non-permanent)
❑ Microtex® size 60 or 70 sharp needle
❑ See-through ruler

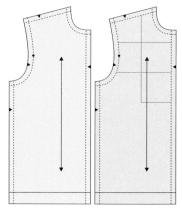

Diagram A: Mark squares on duplicate pattern.

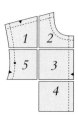

Diagram B: Number pattern pieces.

Select Fabrics

Choose 100% cotton batiste or cotton-blend batiste.

Buy 2 to 3 yards (1.6 to 2.4 m) of ½"-wide (1.3 cm-wide) entredeux.

Get Ready

✔ For the Shark's Teeth block, cut crosswise strips 2½ times wider than the finished patchwork block. For example, for a 5" (12.5 cm) finished square, cut a fabric strip 12½" (31.8 cm) wide.

✔ For all other sections, cut crosswise strips of fabric 2" (5 cm) wider than the finished block size.

✔ Stiffen the fabric to give it additional body so that it remains smooth and flat during stitching. Apply several light coats of spray starch or back the fabric with a water-soluble stabilizer.

✔ Insert a Microtex sharp needle. See page 14 for information about sewing machine needles.

✔ Thread the needle and the bobbin with embroidery thread.

✔ Set the sewing machine for a straightstitch.

Crossover Tucks Block

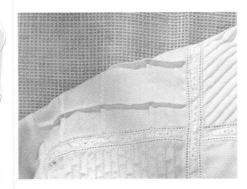

Crossover tucks create an interesting windowpane effect. Basic marking and straightstitching techniques are all that's required.

Gather Supplies

In addition to the basic supplies listed on page 80, you need a blindhem foot.

Get Ready

✔ Replace the conventional foot with the blindhem foot.

✔ Determine how wide each tuck will be. I stitched ⅛" (3 mm) tucks, but you may like a wider or a narrower tuck. Position the blindhem foot's guide that distance from the needle.

Create Crossover Tucks

1. Using the fabric marker, grid the right side of the fabric, marking vertical and horizontal tucks 1½" (3.8 cm) apart *(Diagram A)*.

2. Fold and press the fabric along each marked vertical line, wrong sides together.

3. Align the fabric so that the first tuck's folded edge meets the blindhem foot guide; stitch. Repeat for all remaining vertical tucks *(see photo above right)*.

4. Press all tucks in one direction *(Diagram B)*.

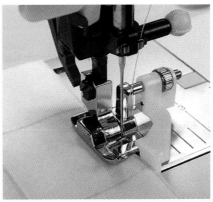

Blindhem foot

5. Press and stitch crosswise tucks. Stitch across the vertical tucks in the same direction as the tucks were pressed.

6. Press tucks in one direction *(Diagram C)*.

7. Fold crossover tucks strip in half. Place pattern piece 1 on strip and cut.

Making Crossover Tucks

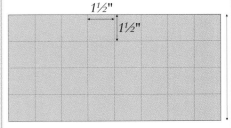

1½"

1½"

Diagram A: Mark grid on fabric right side.

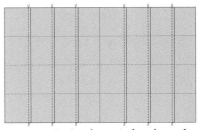

Diagram B: Stitch vertical tucks and press.

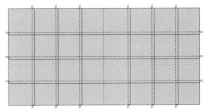

Diagram C: Stitch horizontal tucks; press.

Pleated Patchwork

Make rows and rows of uniform pleats. Then use the pleated section as a patchwork element, placing it at any angle you prefer.

Gather Supplies

In addition to the basic supplies listed on page 80, you may want to use Hot Tape®.

Note from Nancy
Hot Tape adhesive-backed tape has markings every ¼" (6 mm). You can press right over the tape when you apply it to fabric since the tape withstands the heat of an iron up to five minutes without leaving residue on the fabric.

Create Pleated Patchwork

Hot Tape Method

1. Place a strip of Hot Tape at each side of the fabric, taking care that the same markings are at the top of each edge.

2. Fold along corresponding lines of the tape. Bring the fold to another set of tape lines, skipping several markings to form a pleat. Press. Repeat across the fabric's length. Hold fabric taut with each fold for best results *(Diagram A)*.

3. Remove the tape after completing all the pleats. Pin along both sides of each pleat after removing the tape to keep the pleats in position.

Traditional Method

1. Fold the fabric strip in half, meeting lengthwise edges.

2. Place a see-through ruler along the lengthwise edge. Cut ¼" (6 mm) nips through both fabric layers at every ¼" (6 mm) marking *(Diagram B)*.

3. Fold the fabric at the first set of nips; press. Meet the pressed pleat to the third set of nips. At the fourth set of nips, repeat the process. Repeat across the fabric width *(Diagram C)*.

4. Fold pleated strip in half. Place pattern piece 2 on fabric and cut.

Note from Nancy
Make these pleats any distance apart that you want. Experiment! You get different effects, depending on the distance between pleats and the depth of individual pleats.

Creating Pleated Patchwork

Diagram A: Fold along matching lines of tape.

Diagram B: Cut nips ¼" apart.

1st 3rd   4th 6th
Diagram C: Meet pressed pleat to third set of nips and press.

Patchwork with Decorative Stitching

Sewing a band of decorative stitches down the center of a fabric strip is another attractive embellishment. Select any decorative stitch or a combination of stitches. You're the designer!

Gather Supplies

In addition to basic supplies listed on page 80, you need a machine embroidery foot.

Get Ready

Replace the conventional foot with the embroidery foot.

Create Patchwork with Decorative Stitching

1. Fold the fabric strip in half. Press to mark the center.

2. Back the fabric with water-soluble stabilizer.

3. Stitch along the marked line with one or more decorative stitches *(Diagram)*.

4. Remove the stabilizer and fold the fabric strip in half. Place pattern piece 3 on strip and cut. Be sure to center the pattern on the strip's design.

Time-savers

Using the same color thread as your fabric for decorative stitching is a classic heirloom technique. However, if you choose a thread just a shade lighter or darker than your fabric, your stitching will stand out more.

Add decorative stitching to solid-colored flat sheets and pillowcases to make heirloom-quality wedding gifts.

If your sewing machine doesn't have programmed decorative stitches, mark a simple embroidery design on the fabric.

For inspiration, look at old linens in second-hand or antiques stores. A discolored napkin may be a great bargain if you can copy its decorative stitching pattern. Trace the design on paper using a light box (or placing the napkin and paper on a glass-topped table with a lamp underneath).

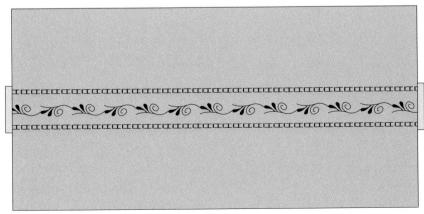

Diagram: Stitch along marked line.

Shark's Teeth Patchwork

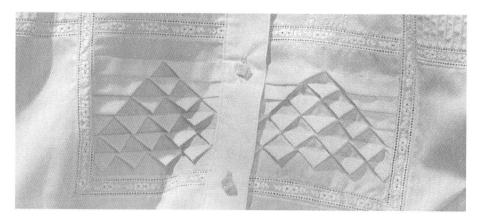

Gather Supplies

In addition to basic supplies listed on page 80, you need:

❑ Tuck and Point Guide
❑ Paper-backed fusible web

> ### Note from Nancy
> A Tuck and Point Guide makes marking, clipping, and folding points a breeze! This clear plastic ruler is marked for ½" (1.3 cm), ¾" (2 cm), and 1" (2.5 cm) tucks and points.

Get Ready

Use basic setup as detailed in Get Ready on page 81.

> ### Note from Nancy
> Remember: cut fabric strips 2½ times wider than the finished block size. Shark's Teeth work best in blocks at least 4½" (11.5 cm) wide.

Create Shark's Teeth Patchwork

1. Mark the strip, drawing lines on the right side of the fabric. Mark first line 1½" (3.8 cm) from the top cut edge. Mark five additional lines 1½" (3.8 cm) apart *(Diagram A)*.

2. Fold and press along each marked line, *wrong* sides together.

3. Stitch ½" (1.3 cm) from all folded edges, forming ½" (1.3 cm) pleats. Press all pleats in one direction *(Diagram B)*.

4. Cut the strip in half, creating two equal-size blocks to mark.

5. Mark the cutting lines for the Shark's Teeth, using a conventional ruler or a Tuck and Point Guide.

• Fold the block in half, meeting ends of tucks. Press to mark the center.

• Open block. Mark the folded edge's center on the first, third, and fifth tucks.

• On the second, fourth, and sixth tucks, measure ½" (1.3 cm) on each side of the center. Mark the folded edge *(two marks)*.

• On the third row, measure and mark the folded edge 1" (2.5 cm) on each side of the center mark *(three marks)*.

• On the fourth row, measure and mark the folded edge 1" (2.5 cm) from the original marks *(four marks)*.

• On the fifth row, measure and mark the folded edge 1" (2.5 cm) and 2" (5 cm) on each side of the center mark *(five marks)*.

• On the sixth row, measure and mark the folded edge 1" (2.5 cm) and 2" (5 cm) on each side of the original marks *(six marks—Diagram C)*.

6. Apply ⅜"-wide (1 cm-wide) strips of paper-backed fusible web within the area where you will form Shark's Teeth.

• On each row, fuse the web to the tuck's underside, beginning ½" (1.3 cm) before the first mark and ending ½" (1.3 cm) after the last mark.

• Remove paper backing from fusible web *(Diagram D)*.

7. Clip from each mark to within a few threads of the stitching line *(Diagram E)*.

8. Form the teeth.

• Fold each side of the clip under to form a point, meeting the cut edge to the stitching line on the wrong side. Finger-press *(Diagram F)*.

• Steam-press. The fusible web holds the teeth in place *(Diagram G)*.

> ### Note from Nancy
> Do not try to make this block in a hurry! Take your time folding and pressing the points so that your finished Shark's Teeth will be sharp and accurate.

9. Secure the Shark's Teeth with a very narrow zigzag stitch.

• Use thread matched to the fabric.

• With right side up, zigzag along each tuck stitching line. One edge of the stitch should just touch the stitching line, while the other edge stitches into the cut edges to hold them in place. The stitching goes only through the *teeth*, not through the fabric under the teeth *(Diagram H)*.

10. Center pattern piece 4 on each block and cut to finished size.

Creating Shark's Teeth Patchwork

Diagram A: Mark fold lines.

Diagram B: Stitch ½" from folded edge.

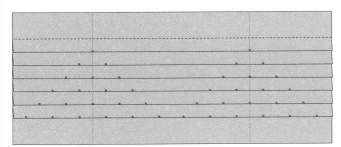

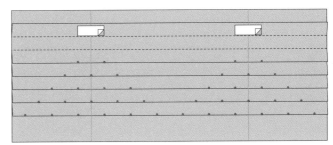

Diagram C: Mark cutting lines.

Diagram D: Fuse web to underside of tuck and remove backing.

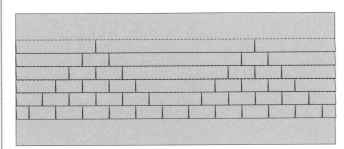

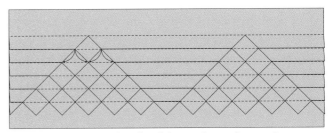

Diagram E: Clip each "tooth."

Diagram F: Fold each side of clip under to form point.

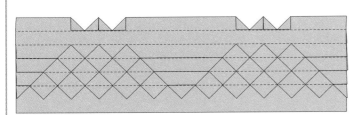

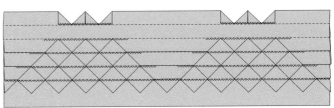

Diagram G: Steam-press so that fusible web holds teeth.

Diagram H: Zigzag through teeth only, not fabric underneath.

Pintuck Patchwork

Rows and rows of delicate pintucks accent this heirloom patchwork. The secret to successful pintucks is using a double needle and a pintuck foot.

Gather Supplies

In addition to the basic supplies listed on page 80, you need:

❑ 1.6/80 or 2.0/80 double needle
❑ Pintuck foot (5- or 7-groove foot)
❑ Cording blade (optional)
❑ Two spools cotton or rayon thread

Get Ready

✔ Replace your conventional machine needle with the double needle.
✔ Replace the conventional presser foot with the pintuck foot.
✔ Attach the cording blade if desired.
✔ Slightly tighten the upper tension to make the fabric tuck.
✔ Thread the double needle and the bobbin with embroidery thread.

Note from Nancy

When threading the machine, save time and avoid trouble by treating the two threads as one until you reach the double needle. When you thread both through the same side of the tension disk, each thread receives the same tension, and your stitching is uniform and balanced.

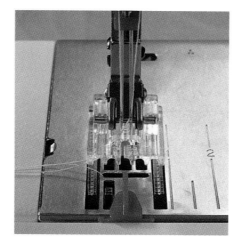

Double needle, pintuck foot, and cording blade

Create Pintucks

1. Pull a thread near one edge of the fabric strip to provide a line for guiding the first row of stitching. Or draw a line along the straight of grain to serve as a stitching guide.

2. Stitch the first pintuck, following the marked line. This line of stitching is critical, since it establishes the position for subsequent rows of stitching. If this row is straight, others are likely to be straight, too *(Diagram A)*.

3. Align the first pintuck in one of the grooves of the pintuck foot. The groove select determines the distance between the pintuck rows. Stitch all remaining rows in the same manner, guiding the previous row in the groove *(Diagram B)*.

4. Fold the pintuck strip in half. Place pattern piece 5 on the strip and cut *(Diagram C)*.

Creating Pintucks

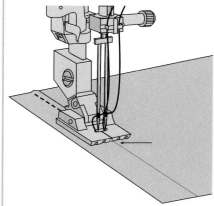

Diagram A: Stitch first pintuck, following marked line.

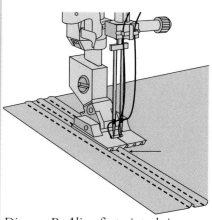

Diagram B: Align first pintuck in groove of foot and stitch.

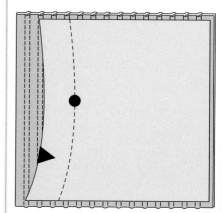

Diagram C: Fold pintuck patchwork in half and cut pattern piece.

Assemble the Quilt Blocks

Now it's time to join the various quilt blocks. Use all five of the techniques or a combination of two or three. The choice is yours!

I used bands of ½"-wide (1.3 cm-wide) entredeux to join my blocks. The entredeux includes ¼" (6 mm) seam allowances on each side of the trim, making application simple.

1. Cut all heirloom blocks to the size of the original pattern. Remember, some of the blocks near the shoulder, neckline, and armhole will be irregularly shaped rather than square *(Diagram A)*.

2. Join blocks into vertical strips.

• Cut entredeux the same length as the blocks it will connect. Spray starch the trim; press.

• Straightstitch the entredeux to the quilt block, right sides together, using a medium stitch length and sewing next to the well of the entredeux *(Diagram B)*.

• Press seam allowances away from the entredeux, toward the blouse.

• Set the sewing machine for a medium width and length zigzag. Working from the strip right side, zigzag the seam flat. One edge of the zigzag should fall in the quilt block and the other edge in the hole of the entredeux *(Diagram C)*.

• Flip the block to the wrong side and trim away the excess seam allowances close to the stitching.

• Add a strip of entredeux at the lower edge of each vertical strip.

3. Join the vertical blocks with another length of entredeux, using the technique detailed above.

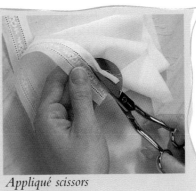

Note from Nancy
Appliqué scissors simplify this process by letting you trim closely without cutting the fashion fabric. Place the bill of the scissors under the fabric you want to trim, and cut. It's easy!

Appliqué scissors

Assembling Heirloom Patchwork

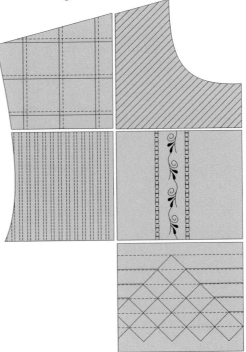

Diagram A: Cut blocks to size of original pattern.

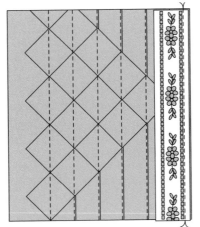

Diagram B: Straightstitch entredeux.

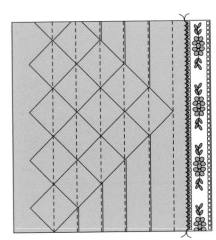

Diagram C: Zigzag seam flat.

4. Stitch the patchwork section to the garment fabric.

• Trim the remaining entredeux seam allowance close to the embroidery.

• Overlap the quilted section on the blouse fabric; pin.

• Cut the blouse front according to the original pattern and trim the excess after adding the embellished section. Or when you cut out the front, reduce the amount of fabric required by eliminating the parts of the blouse that will be covered with quilt blocks, allowing room to overlap the section.

• Zigzag along the entredeux, with one part of the zigzag falling in the hole of the entredeux and the other part in the fabric *(Diagram G).*

• On the wrong side of the garment, trim the garment fabric behind the embellished sections, leaving a ¼" (6 mm) seam allowance *(Diagram H).*

• Press the seam away from the entredeux. Zigzag again to reinforce and hold the seam allowance in place.

• Trim excess seam allowances that extend beyond the zigzagging *(Diagram I).*

5. Complete the garment following your pattern guide sheet.

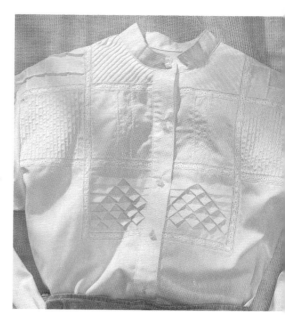

Attaching Heirloom Patchwork to a Garment

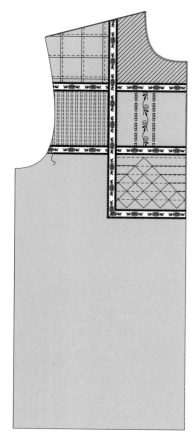

Diagram G: Zigzag entredeux to blouse fabric.

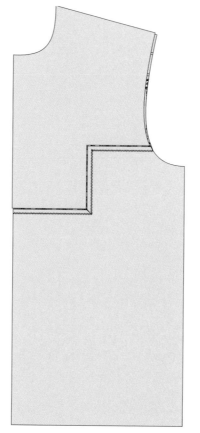

Diagram H: Trim garment fabric from behind embellished blocks.

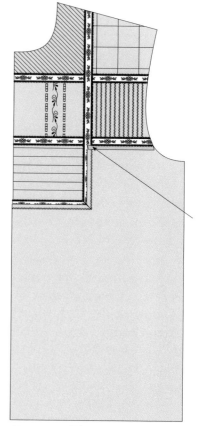

Diagram I: Trim excess seam allowances beyond zigzagging.

More Ideas

Baptism dress

Bonnet

Pillow

Shirt

Lingerie

Ribbing Patchwork

This technique provides an easy way to turn a basic T-shirt into a Wow! shirt.

3. Stitch the main color band to one end of the pieced strip *(Diagram A)*.
4. Measure the length of the new band. Trim to correct size by removing the excess fabric from the main color.
5. Determine placement for the ribbing patchwork. Attach the band to the neckline, following the pattern guide sheet instructions.
6. Topstitch around the neckline using the stretch double needle, stitching with the right needle next to the seam and the left needle on the garment *(Diagram B)*.

> ### Note from Nancy
> The blue bar at the top of stretch double needles distinguishes them from conventional double needles, which have a red bar.

Gather Supplies
- ❑ Size 90 stretch needle
- ❑ 4.0 mm stretch double needle

> ### Note from Nancy
> Use a striped fabric as inspiration for ribbing patchwork. Notice the colors and the sizes of the stripes and consider adapting those combinations.

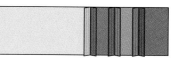

Diagram A: Stitch main color band to pieced strip.

Select Fabrics

For the primary neckline band fabric, choose ribbing to match the main garment fabric.

For patchwork pieces, select at least two colors of ribbing that coordinate or contrast with the neckline band fabric. Use woven or nonwoven fabric.

Get Ready
- ✔ Insert the stretch needle in the machine.
- ✔ Use thread in the needle and the bobbin that matches the fabric.
- ✔ Set the sewing machine for a straightstitch.

Create Ribbing Patchwork

1. Cut ribbing in various sizes, keeping the width the same as the main neckline band fabric. Add ½" (1.3 cm) to each accent fabric for seam allowances.
2. Join the accent pieces with a ¼" (6 mm) seam allowance. Finger-press the seams open. (Pressing with an iron could flatten and remove the stretch from the band.)

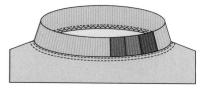

Diagram B: Topstitch around neckline.

Create Horizontal Ribbing Patchwork

1. Cut your ribbing strips ¾" to 1½" (2 cm to 3.8 cm) wide, each the length of your garment opening. Use the matching color for the underside of the band. The total width should be the same as if the ribbing was cut from one fabric, plus seam allowances.

2. Join the strips with ¼" (6 mm) seam allowances, being careful not to stretch the fabrics. Using a narrow zigzag stitch helps build in stretch *(Diagram C)*.

3. Finger-press the seams. Join the narrow ends of the stitched strips, staggering the seam allowances to reduce bulk *(Diagram D)*.

4. Attach the band to the neckline, sleeve, or waistband, following the pattern guide sheet instructions.

Diagram C: Join strips, using narrow zigzag.

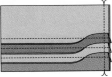

Diagram D: Join strips, staggering seam allowances

Create Woven Fabric Ribbing Patchwork

The neckline of a casual shirt is the perfect place to showcase a leftover patchwork piece. I used a strip of the same leftover patchwork in the pocket of the shirt. You could use a piece of printed woven fabric instead of patchwork, matching pants or a skirt you plan to wear with the blouse.

• Insert a 3" (7.5 cm) or smaller section of woven fabric into the neckline, using the guidelines detailed above. The non-stretch section is small enough that it won't keep the neckline from stretching.

Note from Nancy
If your insert is larger than 3" (7.5 cm), consider trimming the neckline slightly larger before you add the band to ensure that the garment slips easily over your head.

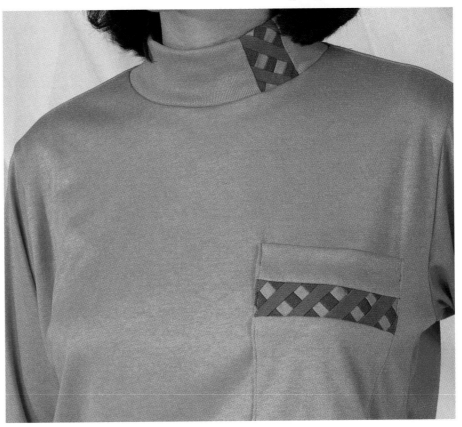

Interweave bias strips to create Bias Surface Texture *(left and page 100)*. Couch decorative threads onto a blouse, and then weave in more threads for Couched Weaving *(right and page 115).* ▶

My easy techniques to create dimension and texture on fabric allow you to become your own fabric designer.

Textured Embellishments

Weave ribbons with fabric strips to create Dimensional Weaving *(left and page 108)*. Use silk ribbon in the bobbin to create luxurious Silk-Ribbon Bobbin Texture on a jacket lapel. *(right and page 99).* ▶

Stitch straight tucks into flat fabric, and stitch horizontally across them to create distinctive Diamond Tucks on a jacket *(left and page 94).*

Open-Weave Vest,
page 106

Diamond Tucks

*They say diamonds are a girl's best friend, and these diamonds
will add a special sparkle to your next garment!*

Simple straightstitching and some pressing are all you do to create these unusual tucks. Making the tucks takes a little time, but you will be pleased with the results.

Gather Supplies

❑ All-purpose thread that matches the fabric
❑ Size 80 or 90 universal needle
❑ Straight-edge ruler
❑ Temporary fabric marker or chalk
❑ Rotary-cutting mat

Select Fabric

Choose fashion fabric, avoiding prints. See your pattern for the amount. Allow about ½ yard (46 cm) extra fabric for making tucks.

Get Ready

✔ Thread the needle and the bobbin with all-purpose thread.
✔ Adjust the machine for a slightly longer-than-normal straightstitch, approximately 10 stitches per inch.

Create Diamond Tucks

1. Cut a rectangle of fabric that is two times the width and 2" (5 cm) longer than the pattern piece that will feature the diamond tucks.

2. Using the straight-edge ruler and a marker or chalk, draw vertical lines 1" (2.5 cm) apart on the right side of the fabric *(Diagram A)*. These marks must be removed later, so use a marker that you can easily remove from the fabric.

Note from Nancy

For more accuracy, place the fabric on a gridded surface such as a rotary-cutting mat. Use the lines on the mat as the measuring tool by aligning the ruler with the gridded markings at the top and bottom of the mat to mark (Diagram B).

3. Fold the fabric along the first marked line, wrong sides together; press. Refold along the second marked line; press along the fold. Press only the fold, so that you don't remove the previously pressed fold *(Diagram C)*. Repeat until all the folds are pressed along the marked lines *(Diagram D)*.

4. Stitch vertical tucks ¼" (6 mm) from each fold line, wrong sides together *(Diagram E)*. Tips for stitching a consistent ¼" seam are on page 74.

5. Press all tucks in one direction.

6. Using a marker or chalk, draw horizontal lines every 1½" or 3.8 cm *(Diagram F)*. Remember, these dimensions are only guidelines, not hard-and-fast rules. Adjust measurements as desired.

7. Stitch horizontal lines as follows:

• **Row 1**: Meet folded edges of the first two vertical tucks; pin. Meet folded edges of the third and fourth tucks; pin. Continue meeting folded edges and pinning along the entire horizontal line. Stitch through the tucks, following the horizontal marking *(Diagram G)*.

• **Row 2:** Fold the first tuck toward the cut edge of the fabric; pin. Meet the edges of the second and third tucks; pin. Meet edges of the fourth and fifth tucks; pin. Continue meeting folded edges and pinning along second horizontal line. Stitch through the tucks, following the horizontal marking. The two stitched rows will begin to form a diamond pattern *(Diagram H).*

Continue folding, pinning, and stitching along each horizontal line, alternating Row 1 and Row 2, until you have stitched all horizontal rows *(Diagram I).*

Creating Diamond Tucks

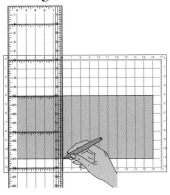

Diagram A: Draw vertical lines on fabric.

Diagram B: Place fabric on gridded surface to mark.

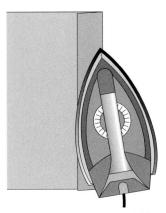

Diagram C: Press along fold.

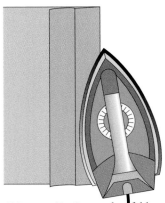

Diagram D: Press other folds, being careful not to remove previously pressed folds.

Diagram E: Stitch vertical tuck 1/4" from fold line.

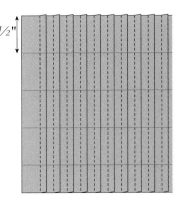

Diagram F: Draw horizontal lines every 1 1/2".

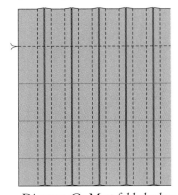

Diagram G: Meet folded edges and stitch along a horizontal line.

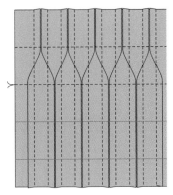

Diagram H: Diamond pattern begins to form when stitching second line.

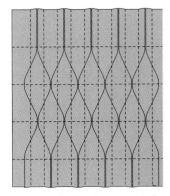

Diagram I: Continue to stitch all horizontal lines.

Serged Diamond Tucks

Gather Supplies

In addition to the basic supplies for Diamond Tucks, you need:

- ❑ All-purpose serger thread
- ❑ Decorative serger thread in two coordinating or contrasting colors

Get Ready

- ✔ Adjust the serger for a 3-thread overlock stitch.
- ✔ Use only the left needle.
- ✔ Thread the left needle with all-purpose serger thread.
- ✔ Thread the upper and lower loopers with decorative threads of two different colors.
- ✔ Adjust the stitch width to exactly ¼" (6 mm).
- ✔ Set the stitch length for a long stitch.
- ✔ Slightly loosen the upper and lower looper tensions to -1 or -2.

> ### Note from Nancy
> You probably need to loosen the tensions on your machine when using decorative threads. Adjustments vary from machine to machine and with different thread and fabric combinations. Always test stitching on a fabric scrap before sewing on your garment.

Create Serged Diamond Tucks

1. Follow steps 1 through 3 on page 94 for Diamond Tucks.

2. Serge along each folded edge, serging from top to bottom on the first row *(Diagram A)*.

> ### Note from Nancy
> If possible, raise the serger upper blade when serging along a fold to prevent cutting the fabric. If you can't raise the blade, guide the fabric fold near the blade.

3. Flip the fabric and serge in the opposite direction, (in effect, from bottom to top), on the second row *(Diagram B)*.

4. Repeat, alternating stitching direction on each row to create an interesting two-color effect when the twists are stitched.

5. Mark and stitch the horizontal rows with a conventional sewing machine, using matching thread. Follow the instructions given on page 94.

Serging Diamond Tucks

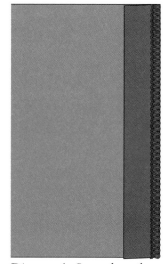

Diagram A: Serge along the folded edge.

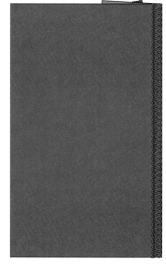

Diagram B: Flip the fabric; serge in the opposite direction.

Bobbin Texture

Sew on the wrong side of fabric to embellish the right side.

Put decorative thread in the bobbin and turn your project wrong side up. Use a straightstitch or a simple decorative stitch for exciting results.

Gather Supplies

❏ All-purpose sewing machine thread
❏ Decorative thread such as Glamour Thread, Pearl Crown Rayon, or ribbon floss
❏ Size 80 or 90 universal needle
❏ Iron-on stabilizer

Select Fabrics

Choose a fashion fabric; see your pattern for amount.

Get Ready

✔ Thread the top of the machine with all-purpose thread that matches the decorative thread.

✔ Set the machine for a straightstitch or an airy decorative stitch. Slightly lengthen the stitch length.
✔ Wind the decorative thread or yarn onto the bobbin by hand.

> *Note from Nancy*
> *Winding bobbins manually produces less tension in the bobbin thread, so you see more of the thread or yarn on the finished project. Since a bobbin doesn't hold large yardages of these heavier threads, wind several bobbins before you begin to stitch.*

✔ Loosen the bobbin tension by turning the tension screw to the left. (Remember, right is tight and left is loose.) Don't turn the screw too far. Make only small adjustments at a time—a quarter turn or less.

> *Note from Nancy*
> *Don't hesitate to change your bobbin tension! It isn't difficult, provided you take one precaution: Mark the position for normal tension on the bobbin case before making any changes. Use fingernail polish to mark the groove on the tension screw, and place a corresponding mark on the bobbin case. Then you can easily return to the normal setting after you finish decorative stitching.*

Marking bobbin tension

✔ Or bypass the tension. Find the large side opening on the bobbin case. Insert the bobbin in the case, and guide the thread out the side opening rather than passing the yarn or thread through the tension slot. Without tension on the bobbin yarn or thread, stitching has a less structured look.

Bypassing bobbin tension

Create Bobbin Texture

1. Trace or transfer the design to the dull side of the stabilizer. Iron the stabilizer onto the wrong side of the fabric *(Diagram A)*.

2. Make a test sample, using the same fabric and stabilizer. Stitch with the wrong side of the sample facing up. Be sure you like the stitching. If not, adjust the bobbin tension, the stitch length, or both.

3. On the project, stitch from the wrong side, following the marked design *(Diagram B)*. Stopping with the needle down makes it easier to turn corners. If desired, fill in portions of the design. Begin by outlining the design, then fill in areas, working from the outside in *(Diagram C)*.

4. If you loosened the tension screw, return it to its original position after completing the decorative stitching.

5. Carefully remove the stabilizer.

Time-saver

Don't throw away your samples! If you like the sample stitching, use it to cover buttons for this project or another.

Other Ways to Use Bobbin Texture

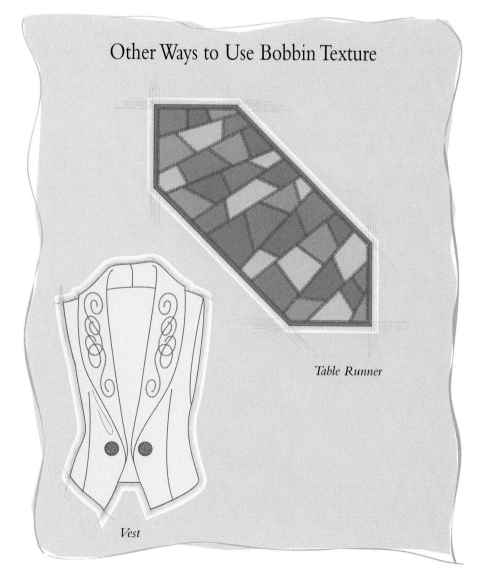

Table Runner

Vest

Making Bobbin Texture

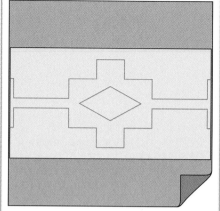

Diagram A: Trace design onto stabilizer, and iron it onto wrong side of fabric.

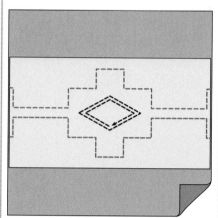

Diagram B: Stitch from wrong side, following design.

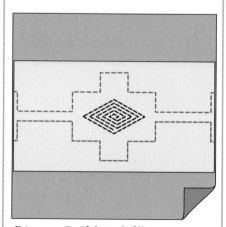

Diagram C: If desired, fill in areas inside design.

Silk-Ribbon Bobbin Texture

Silk ribbon is another excellent candidate for embellishing from the bobbin. Combine Silk-Ribbon Bobbin Texture with patchwork for a result that resembles something our grandmothers might have stitched by hand on their crazy-pieced quilts.

Gather Supplies
❏ All-purpose sewing machine thread
❏ Size 80 or 90 universal needle
❏ 2 mm silk ribbon in assorted colors

Select Fabrics
Select assorted fabric scraps for the patchwork section.

Choose a fabric for the main project; see your pattern for amount.

Get Ready
✔ Set the sewing machine for a straightstitch, using matching thread in the needle and bobbin.

Create Silk-Ribbon Bobbin Texture
1. Stitch fabric sections together in a crazy-quilting manner. (See Crazy Patchwork on page 68.)
2. Press all seam allowances in one direction. These pressed seams act as a stabilizer for the decorative stitching (Diagram A).
3. Follow the instructions under Get Ready for Bobbin Texture (page 97) to adjust your machine and thread silk ribbon in the bobbin. Choose to

Making Silk-Ribbon Bobbin Texture

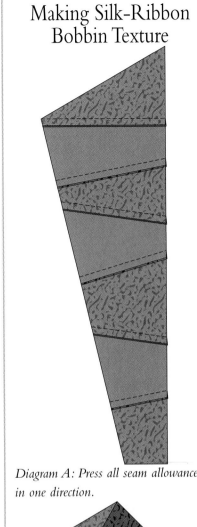

Diagram A: Press all seam allowances in one direction.

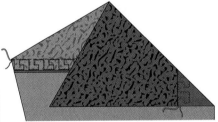

Diagram B: From wrong side, stitch in seam allowance.

bypass, rather than loosen, the bobbin tension. Select an airy decorative stitch.
4. Working from the wrong side of the fabric, stitch in the seam allowance area close to the original stitching line. *(Diagram B).*
5. Select different decorative stitches and change colors of silk ribbon as desired.

Bias Surface Texture

Add interesting dimension to your next creative project by interweaving bias strips. These accents can enhance outer edges or add attractive inside detail.

Gather Supplies

☐ All-purpose sewing thread
☐ Rotary cutter, ruler, and mat
☐ Bias tape maker (optional)
☐ Tracing paper
☐ Liquid fusible web
☐ Press cloth

Select Fabric

For easy shaping, choose a light- to medium-weight fabric to use as the bias trim. If the fabric is too heavy, the completed bias may buckle and ripple.

Get Ready

✔ Thread the needle and the bobbin with all-purpose thread that matches the fabric.
✔ Adjust the machine for a straight-stitch.

Create Bias Surface Texture

1. Cut and join bias strips.

• Cut bias strips 1¾" to 2" (4.5 cm to 5 cm). The strip width depends on the fabric; with thicker fabrics, cut narrower strips. You need two long strips to do the weaving. Cut enough bias strips to go around the edge of your project twice.

> ### Note from Nancy
> A Strip Ticket takes the guesswork out of making bias tape in different widths and lengths. A glance at this notion tells you exactly how much fabric you need to make any size bias strip. Calculations include 1" to 7" widths, and 50" to 591" lengths. (Measurements are given in inches.)

• Meet the short ends of two strips, right sides together, offsetting the ends by ¼" or 6 mm *(Diagram A)*. Stitch, using a ¼" (6 mm) seam. Press the seam open and trim the triangular ends. Repeat to make two long strips.

2. Create the bias trim.

• Insert the end of one of the bias strips into the wide end of a 1" (25 mm) bias tape maker. Using a straight pin, advance the strip through the tape maker. When the bias strip comes out the narrow end of the tape maker, the outer edges are folded to the center. Press with the tip of the iron.

Bias tape maker

• Continue advancing and pressing the strip through the bias tape maker until the entire length of the bias is pressed.
• Fold the strip again, meeting the folded edges. Press.
• Straightstitch along the folded edges *(Diagram B)*.

> ### Note from Nancy
> To make bias tape without a bias tape maker, press both long edges of the bias to the middle of the strip. Fold the strip, meeting the folded edges. Press. Straightstitch along the folded edges.

3. Shape the bias trim.

• Choose a simple, subtle design. Trace the design on paper. The design I used is on page 142.

• Arrange the two bias strips to conform to the design.

• Fuse the strips together at the intersection by placing a drop of liquid fusible web between the strips *(Diagram C)*. Cover the strips with a press cloth and press.

Note from Nancy

Liqui Fuse Liquid Fusible Web is like fusible web in a bottle. The nice thing about using it is that you can place the fusible liquid exactly where you want it. Adjust the shape of the bias trim until you are happy with the placement, and then fuse the layers with your iron.

---

4. Shape and stitch the bias trim to conform to the project.

• Pin the trim to the fabric.

• Topstitch around the edges to hold the trim in place, pivoting at the intersection points. The scallops create an interesting open weave around the garment edges *(Diagram D)*.

Time-savers

If you don't have liquid fusible web on hand (Step 3), use a glue stick or white household glue. Household glue will wash out, but your topstitching will hold the trim in place.

Use purchased bias tape in a color that contrasts with a purchased vest for a quick project. Use the instructions starting with the last part of Step 2. (Straightstitch along the folded edges.)

Stitching Bias Surface Texture

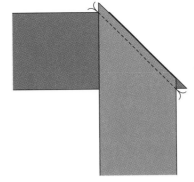

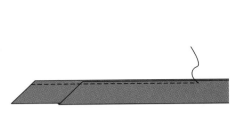

Diagram A: Stitch two strips together.

Diagram B: Straightstitch along folded edges.

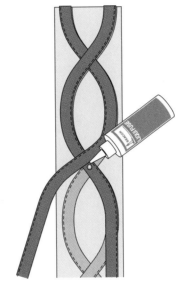

Diagram C: Place liquid fusible web between strips.

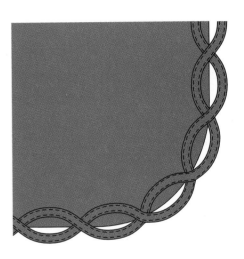

Diagram D: Topstitch around edges to hold trim in place.

Celtic Surface Texture

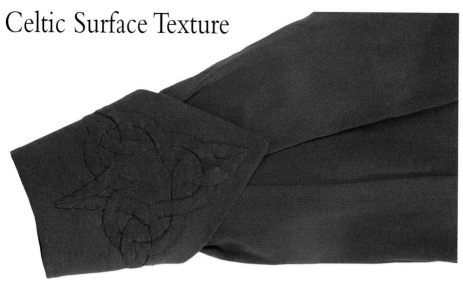

Gather Supplies

- ❏ All-purpose thread to match fabric
- ❏ Universal needle
- ❏ Rotary cutter, ruler, and mat
- ❏ Tube turner
- ❏ Celtic Bias Bars
- ❏ Lightweight fusible interfacing
- ❏ Paper or plastic template sheet
- ❏ Fabric marking pencil
- ❏ Liquid fusible web (optional)
- ❏ Press cloth (optional)
- ❏ Monofilament thread
- ❏ Lingerie/bobbin thread
- ❏ Embroidery or open toe foot

Select Fabrics

Choose light- to medium-weight fabric with an even stretch on the bias.

Get Ready

- ✔ Thread the needle and bobbin with thread to match the fashion fabric.
- ✔ Use the conventional presser foot and a universal needle.
- ✔ Adjust the machine for a straightstitch.

Create Celtic Surface Texture

1. Make bias strips:

• Cut bias strips 1½" (3.8 cm) wide using rotary cutter, ruler, and mat. Do not join the bias strips; the seams are too bulky to use in this technique.

• Stitch long edges of strips, right sides together, using a narrow ⅛" (3 mm) seam.

• Turn the bias strips right side out using a tube turner.

• Insert a flexible Celtic Bias Bar into the bias tube strip, keeping the seam in the center back of the strip. Steam-press on both sides for super-sharp creases. Push bar through until the entire tube is pressed. Repeat until all tubes are pressed. Be careful because the metal celtic bars become very hot!

2. Press fusible interfacing to the wrong side of the garment piece to be embellished.

3. Trace your design on paper or a plastic template sheet. (The design I used is on page 134.) Cut out the design. Place the template on the fabric and trace around the design with a marker *(Diagram A)*.

4. Pin the bias strips over the design.

• Working on a padded pressing surface, place the end of a bias strip at an intersection, where two strips cross. Pin or use liquid fusible web to keep the strips in place *(Diagram B)*.

• At intersections, weave over or under as needed to secure bias strip. Your design will indicate where to weave the bias strips *(Diagram C)*.

Note from Nancy

You can choose from an interesting assortment of tube turners, ranging in design and price. Many readers ask, "Which turner is the best to buy?" Pictured are three of my favorites: The Narrow Loop Turner (**A**) turns only tubes and is easy to use. The Collar Point & Tube Turner (**B**) turns both tubes and corners. The Fasturn (**C**) turns tubes.

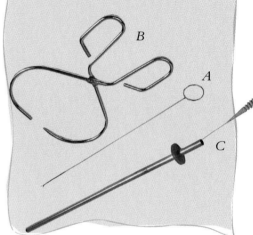

• If the design has points or corners, miter the bias strip by placing the strip to the corner, turning the strip back on itself, and hand-stitching diagonally across the seam *(Diagram D)*. Trim excess bias strip to remove bulk *(Diagram E)*.

• Continue placing bias strips on the design *(Diagram F)*. If you need more than one bias strip to complete the design, butt the ends of the strips together under an intersection *(Diagram G)*.

• If using a liquid fusible web, place a press cloth over the design and fuse the strips into place.

5. Set the machine for stitching the Celtic design to the garment.

• Thread the needle with monofilament thread and the bobbin with lingerie/bobbin thread.

• Attach an open toe or an embroidery foot.

• Adjust the machine for a blindhem stitch and a stitch width and length of 1.

• Loosen the tension by two notches (for example, from 5 to 3).

6. Stitch around the edges of the design.

• Stitch in a clockwise direction, with the straightstitching beside the bias strips and the zigzag of the blindhem stitch catching the strip. Complete one side at a time (Diagram H).

• At an intersection, one strip is an "over" strip and the other is an "under" strip. When stitching the under strip and approaching the intersection, shorten the stitch length to 0. Sew several stitches in place to anchor the thread. Lift the presser foot and needle over the intersection. Anchor stitch again on the other side of the intersection. Return the stitch length to the original setting and continue stitching. Repeat at each intersection (Diagram I).

• When stitching an over strip, stitch across the intersection (Diagram J).

• Clip threads that cross the bias strips at the intersections.

Bias Surface Texture

Diagram A: Use a template to trace your design onto fabric.

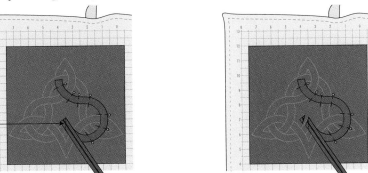

Diagram B: Pin or fuse strips in place.

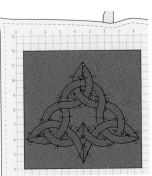

Diagram C: Weave over or under as your design indicates.

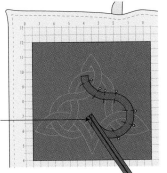

Diagram D: Miter each corner and hand-stitch in place.

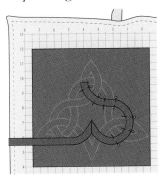

Diagram E: Trim excess bias strip.

Diagram F: Continue placing bias strips on design.

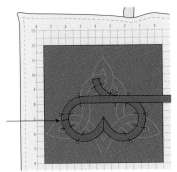

Diagram G: To add new bias strips, butt ends together.

Diagram H: Use a blindhem stitch to sew around edges.

Diagram I: Carry thread over intersections for "under" strips.

Diagram J: Stitch across intersections for "over" strips.

Decorative Weaving

Transform bits and pieces of fabric, thread, ribbon, and yarn into an interesting and attractive new fabric.

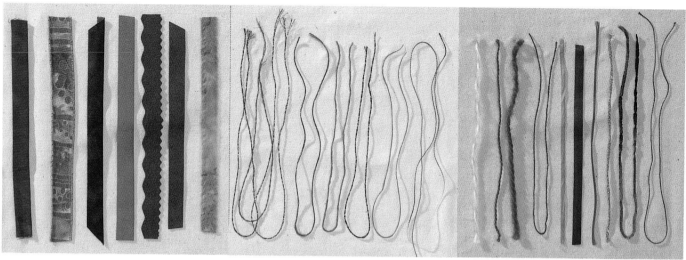

Select one or more of these materials as weaving elements. The strip widths are totally up to the designer—you!

• **Torn fabric strips** (from single layers of fabric) for a homespun look.

• **Leather or Ultrasuede strips**, cut using a rotary cutter, pinking shears, or specialty rotary-cutting blades, such as the wave blade.

• **Bias strips**, especially those made from plaid or checked fabric. (See Folk Art Appliqué on page 48.)

• **Serged strips** (from single layers of fabric) finished with a 3-thread over-lock stitch or rolled-edge stitch for a ribbonlike appearance.

• **Fabric tubes**, narrow or wide, to add dimension. (See Bias Surface Texture on page 100.)

• **Decorative serger thread**, used for the lengthwise threads of a weaving project. (See page 14.)

• **Embroidery floss**, in cotton or silk.

• **Ribbons**, narrow or wide.

• **Yarn**, either decorative or traditional knitting yarns, used for the lengthwise portion of a woven piece.

Strip Weaving

Strip weaving with an even-weave design is an ideal first weaving project. Whatever type strips you choose, the steps are the same. Weaving on a fusible interfacing base streamlines the process by keeping the strips from raveling and stabilizing the fabric.

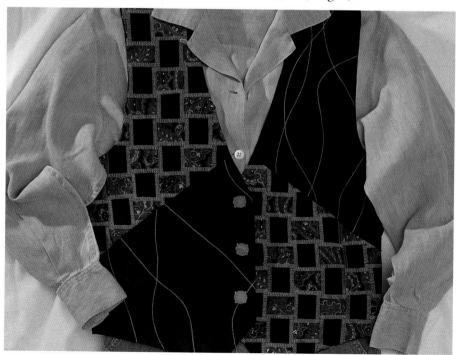

Gather Basic Supplies

❑ Lightweight fusible interfacing
❑ Padded pressing surface
❑ Press cloth

Select Weaving Elements

Choose one type of fabric strip: torn, leather, bias, serged, or tube.

Create Strip Weaving

1. Cut a piece of lightweight fusible interfacing slightly larger than the pattern.

2. Place the interfacing on a padded pressing surface, fusible side up. Place lengthwise strips over the interfacing. Pin along the upper edge *(Diagram A)*.

3. Weave a crosswise strip, alternately threading the strip under and over the lengthwise strips *(Diagram B)*.

4. Add a second crosswise strip *(Diagram C)*, weaving in the opposite order (over-and-under the lengthwise strips). The over and under weaving process creates an even-weave design.

5. After weaving several crosswise strips, cover the woven section with a press cloth and fuse, keeping the strips straight *(Diagram D)*.

6. Repeat until you weave all crosswise strips through the lengthwise strips.

7. Option: Speed-weave the crosswise strips.

• Position the lengthwise strips as detailed above.

• Stack half the crosswise strips; weave the stack through the lengthwise strips as if they were a single strip *(Diagram E)*.

• Separate the strips, allowing space between them *(Diagram F)*

• Fill in the spaces between strips with single strips woven in the opposite order.

Strip Weaving

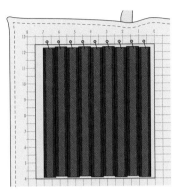

Diagram A: Pin lengthwise strips to a padded surface.

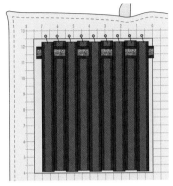

Diagram B: Weave a crosswise strip under and over.

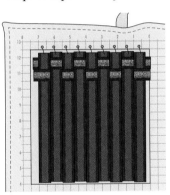

Diagram C: Add a second crosswise strip.

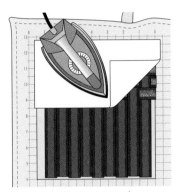

Diagram D: Cover with a press cloth and fuse.

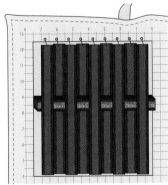

Diagram E: Speed-weave a stack of crosswise strips.

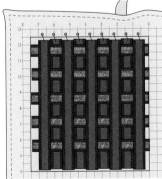

Diagram F: Separate stack, leaving room to weave strips in opposite direction.

Open Weaving

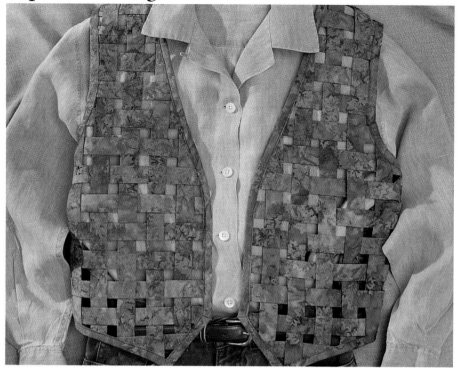

Gather Supplies

In addition to basic weaving supplies, you need:

❑ All-purpose thread to match fabric
❑ Fusible thread
❑ Tissue paper
❑ Tracing paper and tracing wheel
❑ Fusible web (optional)
❑ Machine embroidery thread
❑ Bias tape maker (optional)

Select Weaving Elements

Use a type of fabric strip for weaving: torn, leather, bias, serged, or tube (see page 104). I used 1" (2.5 cm) tube strips to weave the blue vest.

Get Ready

✔ Thread needle and bobbin of the sewing machine with thread that matches the fabric strips.

✔ Adjust the machine for a straight-stitch.

✔ Wind a second bobbin with fusible thread.

Note from Nancy

To create tubes quickly, my staff and I used a Fasturn. To use this handy notion, cut strips of fabric twice your finished tube width plus seam allowances. (For our 1"-wide (2.5 cm-wide) finished tubes, we cut 2½"-wide (6.3 cm-wide) fabric strips.) With right sides together, stitch the lengthwise edges and one short edge with a ¼" (6 mm) seam. To turn the tubes right side out, slip the tube over the Fasturn cylinder, and insert the pigtail wire into the cylinder from the handle end. Turn the hook clockwise, pulling the tail through the fabric. Finally, gently pull the wire back through the cylinder, turning the tube right side out. (Diagram below).

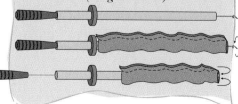

Create Open Weaving

1. Prepare a pattern to serve as the base for weaving.

• If creating a vest, trim away the neck, armhole, and hem seam allowances on the pattern (Diagram A).

• Trace onto tissue paper the pattern piece or pattern section that will include the weaving section. If both sides of the garment will include weaving, stack two sheets of paper. Cut out the tissue paper.

• Grid the tissue paper (Diagram B).

• To create an open look, make certain the grid is larger than the finished width of the weaving strips. If applicable, transfer the grid to the second pattern piece using tracing paper and tracing wheel to ensure that the second piece is a mirror image of the first. I used a 1½" (3.8 cm) grid for the green vest.

2. Weave the fabric tubes, following the gridded pattern.

• Place the lengthwise fabric tubes along one edge of the lengthwise grid. Pin strips to the paper (Diagram C).

• Weave the crosswise strips in and out of the lengthwise strips, again matching one edge of the weave to the grid. Pin ends of the strips to the paper (Diagram D).

3. Stabilize the weave in one of the following ways:

Option 1: Fuse the intersections. Cut squares of fusible web smaller than the width of the fabric tubes. Place the fusible web squares between the two fabrics at each intersection. Press (Diagram E).

Option 2: Edgestitch ⅛" (3 mm) along each side of all lengthwise strips (Diagram F).

Option 3: Stitch down the center of either the lengthwise or the crosswise strips with a continuous decorative stitch, using machine embroidery thread *(Diagram G)*.

Option 4: Stitch a single pattern decorative stitch at each intersection.

4. Trim weaving strips to match the paper pattern.

5. Bind the edges with bias tape.

• Cut bias strips 2" (5 cm) wide.

• Use a bias tape maker (see page 100) or press the lengthwise edges to the middle to create 1"-wide (2.5 cm-wide) bias strips.

• Insert the bobbin filled with fusible thread in the bobbin case.

• Unfold one edge of the bias tape. Meet the unfolded tape edge to the woven section, right sides together. Stitch the tape to the edge along the crease in the tape *(Diagram H)*.

• Remove the paper backing from the woven section.

• Wrap the bias tape around the edges, covering the fusible-thread stitching. Press in place. The fusible thread holds the bias tape in place until you permanently stitch it.

• Remove the bobbin filled with fusible thread and replace with a bobbin filled with all-purpose thread.

• Edgestitch along the fold, stitching from the right side of the fabric *(Diagram I)*.

Open Weaving

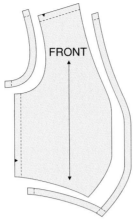

Diagram A: Trim outer seam allowances from pattern.

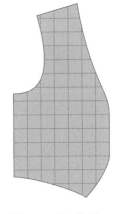

Diagram B: Grid a tissue-paper pattern.

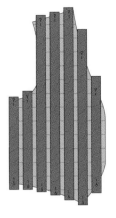

Diagram C: Pin lengthwise tubes to grid.

Diagram D: Weave crosswise strips and pin.

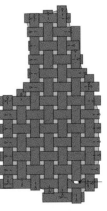

Diagram E: Fuse intersections using squares of fusible web.

Diagram F: Edgestitch along each side of lengthwise strips.

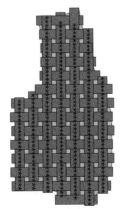

Diagram G: Stitch down lengthwise strips using a decorative stitch.

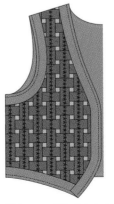

Diagram H: Stitch bias tape to garment edges.

Diagram I: Edgestitch along fold of edging.

Dimensional Weaving

Amy Bartol from Berlin, Wisconsin, created this eye-catching weaving design on the trench flaps of a blouse.

Gather Supplies

In addition to basic weaving supplies, you need:
- ¼" (6 mm) satin and metallic ribbon
- Weaving needle
- Embroidery thread or all-purpose thread

Select Weaving Elements

Choose fabric strips ¾" (2 cm) wide for the lengthwise weave and 1" (2.5 cm) wide for the crosswise weave. Amy used serged strips (see page 104) with a rolled-edge finish to make her blouse.

For the diagonal interweaving, select narrow ribbons that coordinate with the fabric strips.

Get Ready

✔ Set your machine for a straightstitch.

Create Dimensional Weaving

1. Cut out the pattern piece that the weaving will cover. Use the same fabric that you chose for the fabric strips, or use a coordinating fabric.

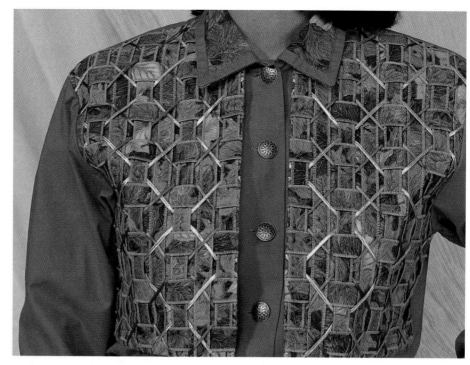

2. Weave the strips over the fabric base.
- Position the ¾" (2 cm) strips vertically over the base, 1" (2.5 cm) apart. Pin strips in place *(Diagram A)*.
- Add 1" (2.5 cm) horizontal strips, again 1" (2.5 cm) apart. Place these strips on top of the vertical strips, rather than weaving them in and out of the first strips. Pin strips in place *(Diagram B)*.
- Place another layer of ¾" (2 cm) strips in the 1" (2.5 cm) spaces left between the first layer of vertical strips. Place strips on top, rather than weaving them in and out. Pin strips in place *(Diagram C)*.

3. Weave ribbon through the strips.
- Using a Weaving needle, weave a length of ribbon diagonally from right to left under the first layer of vertical strips. Pin ribbons in place.
- Weave ribbons diagonally from left to right in the same manner, creating a crisscross design. Pin ribbons in place *(Diagram D)*.

4. Edgestitch the outer edges of the woven piece to secure the strips and ribbons.

Dimensional Weaving

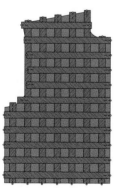

Diagram A: Pin vertical strips in place.

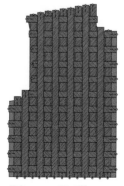

Diagram B: Place horizontal strips on top, unwoven.

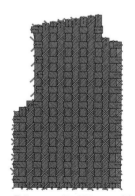

Diagram C: Place a second layer of vertical strips on top.

Diagram D: Weave ribbons diagonally through strips.

Pin-Weaving Variations

When you've mastered the basic strip-weaving process, try using finer yarns or threads in the lengthwise direction for a more refined look.

Gather Supplies

In addition to the basic weaving supplies, you need:
❑ Decorative serger threads
❑ Weaving needle or double-eyed needle

Select Weaving Elements

For the lengthwise section of the weaving, choose one of the threads or yarns listed under Weaving Elements on page 104.

For the crosswise sections, use a combination of yarns, threads, or fabric strips.

The pictured blouse features metallic embroidery thread (lengthwise), ⅛" (3 mm) carat braid, and ¼" (6 mm), ½" (1.3 cm) and ¾" (2 cm) Ultrasuede strips.

Create Pin-Weaving Variations

1. Position pins on a gridded surface ¼" (6 mm) or ½" (1.3 cm) apart at the top and bottom of the weaving measurement. These pins serve as the loom.
2. Anchor the beginning of the thread or yarn, then wrap the thread or yarn vertically back and forth around the pins *(Diagram)*.
3. Anchor the end of the warp (lengthwise) thread or yarn. You don't need to use fusible interfacing as a base, since the thread ends are secure.
4. Use a weaving needle to weave the crosswise strips. Add more crosswise strips to fill in the area between the pins.

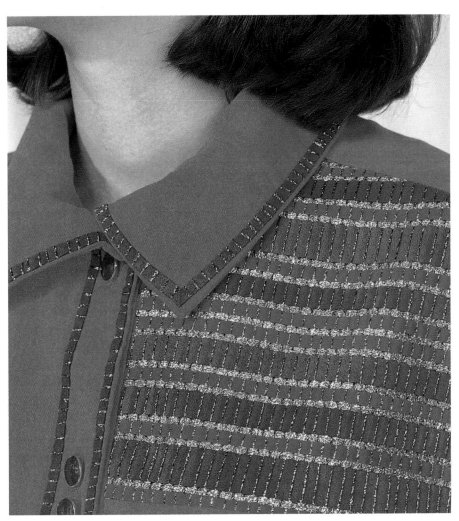

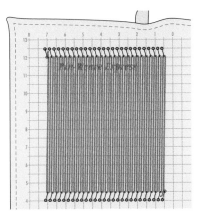

Diagram: Wrap yarn back and forth around pins.

5. Remove the pins. The weaving unit will be secure at the top and bottom edges.

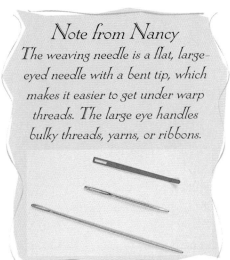

Note from Nancy
The weaving needle is a flat, large-eyed needle with a bent tip, which makes it easier to get under warp threads. The large eye handles bulky threads, yarns, or ribbons.

Enhanced Weaving

Convert a plain fabric into an eye-catcher with enhanced weaving.

Create Cut Weaving

Diagram A: Use a buttonhole cutter and block to cut individual slits.

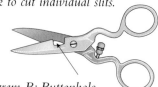

Diagram B: Buttonhole scissors have a hollowed-out opening.

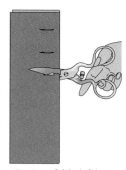

Diagram C: Cut folded fabric to make two parallel cuts at once.

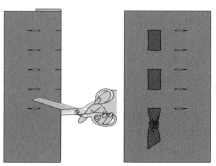

Diagram D: Use conventional scissors to cut.

Diagram E: Knot woven strips if desired.

Gather Supplies

❏ Buttonhole cutter and block
❏ Buttonhole scissors
❏ Bodkin
❏ Weaving needle or double-eyed needle
❏ Fusible interfacing

Select Fabric

For the base fabric, choose a tightly woven fabric such as denim or canvas. The key is to use a fabric that doesn't easily ravel.

Select fabric for weaving. (See Weaving Elements on page 104.)

Create Cut Weaving

1. Determine the positions for the slits, spacing slits 1" to 3" (2.5 cm to 7.5 cm) apart. Cut ½" (1.3 cm) slits in one of the following ways.

Option 1: Use a buttonhole cutter and block. Place the fabric over the block. Cut individual slits *(Diagram A)*.

Option 2: Use buttonhole scissors to speed cutting. Fold the fabric vertically. Position the fold of the fabric in the hollowed-out opening of the buttonhole scissors *(Diagram B)*. Make one cut of the scissors, creating two parallel cuts at once. Repeat until you cut the number of columns and rows you need *(Diagram C)*.

Option 3: Use conventional scissors. Fold the fabric, mark ¼" (6 mm) lines at right angles to the fold, and cut with scissors *(Diagram D)*.
2. Use a bodkin to weave ½" (1.3 cm) strips of fabric through the cuts.
3. Knot strips for additional embellishment as illustrated *(Diagram E)*.
4. Allow some of the strip tails to be exposed if desired.
5. Back the fabric with fusible interfacing to prevent raveling.

Yarn Weaving

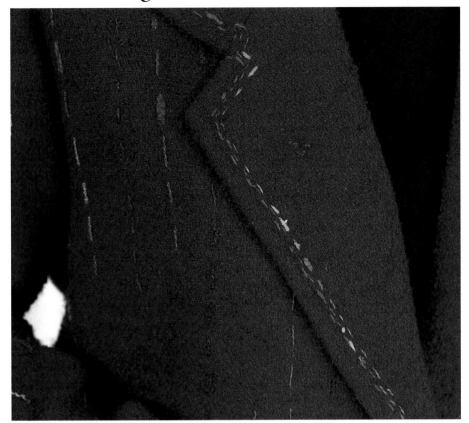

Start with fabric yardage, and then hand-stitch, reweave, remove threads, or add appliqués for special highlights.

Gather Supplies
- ❑ Decorative thread or yarn
- ❑ Large-eyed tapestry needle

Select Fabrics
These techniques involve stitching through or manipulating threads in the original fabric. Use fabrics that do not have a dense surface, such as wools, wool blends, and three-season silks. See your pattern for amount.

Create Yarn Weaving

Overstitch Fabrics Option:

1. Determine the placement of the accents on the garment or project.

2. Select a decorative thread or yarn, and use a large-eyed tapestry needle.

3. Hand-stitch through the fabric, following the lengthwise or crosswise grain. Use long running stitches to expose decorative thread *(Diagram A)*.

> *Note from Nancy*
> *Add overstitching to purchased garments as well as to those you create. Overstitching gives a ready-made garment a great new look.*

Unravel and Reweave Fabrics Option:

1. Determine the size and placement of the embellishment. Cut two parallel slits, following the grain line of the fabric, one at each side of the embellishment area.

2. Carefully remove the crosswise yarns between the slits *(Diagram B)*.

3. Introduce decorative yarns in the unwoven area by reweaving yarns over and under the strands of exposed yarns *(Diagram C)*.

Yarn Weaving

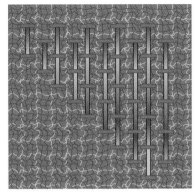

Diagram A: Make long running stitches following fabric grain.

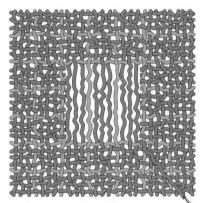

Diagram B: Carefully remove crosswise yarns between two slits.

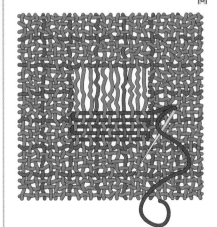

Diagram C: Reweave yarns over and under exposed yarns.

Knit Interweaving

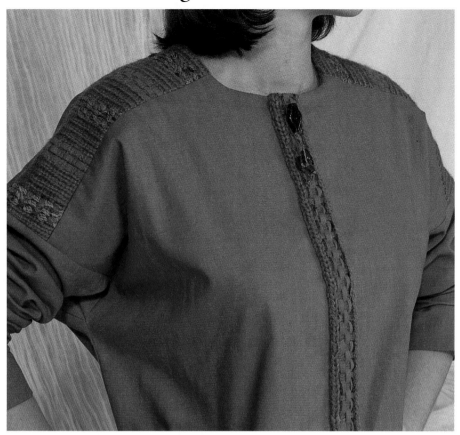

If you just can't bear to part with an old sweater, recycle sections of the knit to add a spectacular design element. You'll be amazed how interweaving will transform fabric!

Gather Supplies
❑ All-purpose serger thread
❑ Lightweight fusible knit interfacing
❑ Padded pressing surface
❑ Embellishment thread
❑ Weaving needle
❑ Double-eyed weaving needle (for yarns)
❑ Couture Press Cloth

Select Fabric
Choose a woven fashion fabric; see your pattern for amount.

Use a section of a recycled bulky knit sweater to match or coordinate with the woven fabric.

Get Ready
✔ Thread the two needles and the upper and lower loopers of the serger with serger thread.
✔ Set the serger for a regular overlock stitch.

Create Knit Interweaving
1. Cut a crosswise section from a bulky knit sweater.
2. Serge across the cut sections to prevent raveling.
3. Create open areas in the knit piece.
• Clip one stitch at the lengthwise edge. Drop the stitch the length of the knit piece.
• Clip stitches wherever you need a space for weaving (Diagram A).

Note from Nancy
One dropped stitch expands about four times its width. For example, using a scale of four stitches and six rows per 1" (2.5 cm), dropping one of those four stitches yields a weaving area 1" (2.5 cm) wide.

4. Cut a piece of fusible knit interfacing the size of the knit interweaving piece. Lay the interfacing, fusible side up, on a padded pressing surface. Place the knit piece on top of interfacing, with wrong side down. Pin securely in place (Diagram B).
5. Weave the raveled areas with embellishment yarns and strips of woven fabric, alternating the rows for a dramatic effect. Use a weaving needle (see page 109) to streamline the weaving process for fabric strips; use a double-eyed needle for yarns. Weave the raveled section until the open area is filled (Diagram C).

Note from Nancy
My teal dress features decorative yarns and bias strips woven in a basket weave (over two, under two). You can use an even weave (over one, under one). See Decorative Weaving, on page 104, for other weaving elements.

• Continue weaving until all open areas are filled.
6. Place a Couture Press Cloth over the knit piece and fuse to the interfacing to stabilize the shape of the inset.
7. Insert the "new" knit into your fashion garment.

Knit Interweaving

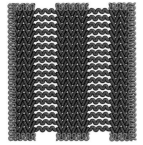

Diagram A: Clip stitches wherever you need a space for weaving.

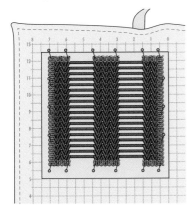

Diagram B: Pin interfacing and knit piece to padded surface.

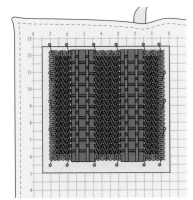

Diagram C: Weave until you fill open area.

Ultra Weave

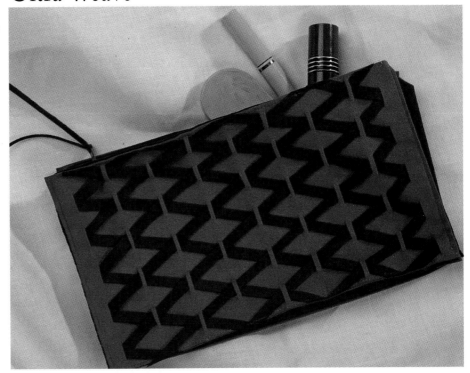

Add dimension to your project by weaving narrow strips of Ultrasuede through the base fabric, creating a diamond design.

Gather Supplies
- ❑ Fine-point marker
- ❑ Rotary-cutting mat
- ❑ Buttonhole cutter
- ❑ Double-eyed needle or weaving needle
- ❑ Lightweight fusible interfacing

Select Fabric

For the base fabric, choose Ultrasuede or a tightly woven fabric.

For weaving strips, select contrasting Ultrasuede, or use ¼" (6 mm) braid, ribbons, or decorative yarns.

Create Ultra Weave

1. Draw a grid on the wrong side of the base fabric, using the fine-point marker. Prepare the grid as follows, modifying the design according to personal preference.

- Mark vertical columns 1" (2.5 cm) apart.
- Mark horizontal rows ½" (1.3 cm) apart.
- Do not mark grids in seam or hem areas *(Diagram A, page 114)*.

2. Cut openings for the weaving.
- Place the base fabric on a rotary-cutting mat or a piece of wood.
- Beginning at the left vertical column, use a buttonhole cutter to cut a ½" (1.3 cm) vertical slit between the markings for the first and second horizontal rows.
- Skip the next horizontal row. Cut a ½" (1.3 cm) vertical slit between the markings for the third and fourth horizontal rows.
- Continue as shown, cutting slits between the alternate horizontal rows *(Diagram B, page 114)*.
- In the second vertical column, cut slits on each side of markings in alternate rows as shown, spacing cuts ⅛" to ¼" (3 mm to 6 mm) apart *(Diagram C, page 114)*.

- Repeat until slits are cut in the entire fabric *(Diagram D)*.

3. Weave strips through the cut openings.

- Create enhancing strips by cutting ¼" (6 mm) Ultrasuede strips. Or use braid, ribbons, or decorative yarns.
- Thread an enhancing strip through the eye of a double-eyed needle or a weaving needle. Begin at the upper left corner and weave diagonally under the slits *(Diagram E)*. Because the end of the needle is blunt, it easily passes under the slits.
- After you insert all strips from left to right, repeat the process, weaving additional strips from right to left until you have woven all rows *(Diagram F)*.

4. Cut a piece of lightweight fusible interfacing the same size as the base fabric. Fuse the interfacing to the wrong side of the woven section.

Note from Nancy

When pressing Ultrasuede, select your iron's wool setting and press from the wrong side, using a press cloth. Very light pressure prevents marring or flattening the surface of the fabric.

Time-savers

Let your children help! Ultra Weaving a cosmetic bag or a book cover is a good first project for a young person. Even if your child isn't ready to tackle the entire project, he or she can weave the strips once you've cut the slits.

Use a rotary cutter and cutting mat to cut your Ultrasuede strips. Always be sure your cutting instruments are sharp.

Making Ultra Weave

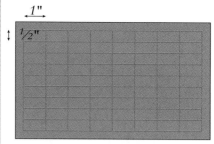

Diagram A: Mark grid on base fabric.

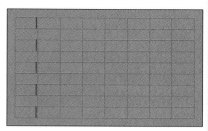

Diagram B: Cut vertical slits in first row.

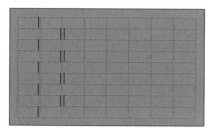

Diagram C: Cut vertical slits in second column.

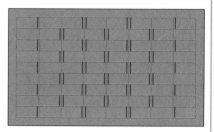

Diagram D: Repeat until all slits are cut.

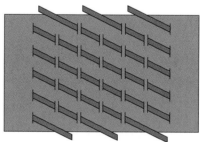

Diagram E: Weave Ultrasuede strips diagonally through slits.

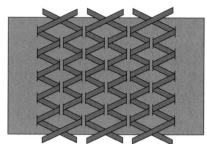

Diagram F: Weave additional strips in opposite direction.

Couched Weaving

Making Couched Weaving

Diagram A: Couch decorative yarns using a blindhem stitch.

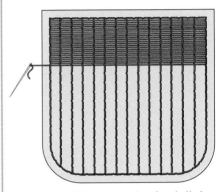

Diagram B: Weave strands of embellishment yarn over and under couched threads.

Spice up a garment by couching embellishment thread onto the surface and weaving threads through the couching.

Gather Supplies
- ❑ Monofilament thread
- ❑ All-purpose sewing thread that matches the fabric
- ❑ Open toe or embroidery foot
- ❑ Weaving needle
- ❑ Embellishment yarns

Select Fabrics
Choose a purchased garment, or add couched weaving to a solid-colored fabric.

Get Ready
- ✔ Thread the needle with monofilament thread and the bobbin with all-purpose thread.
- ✔ Replace the conventional foot with an open toe or embroidery foot.
- ✔ Adjust the sewing machine to a blindhem stitch, a medium stitch length, and a medium stitch width.

Create Couched Weaving
1. Arrange the decorative yarns vertically on the project. Space the yarns ½" to ¾" (1.3 cm to 2 cm) apart.
2. Couch or stitch the yarns to the fabric by sewing with a blindhem stitch. Line the straight part of the blindhem stitches next to the yarn and let the zigzag part of the stitches attach the yarn to the fabric. This stitching positions the yarns like the warp (lengthwise yarns) of a loom (Diagram A).
3. Using a weaving or double-eyed needle, weave strands of embellishment yarns over and under the couched threads. Varying the colors of embellishment thread adds interest to the weaving (Diagram B).

Buttonhole Weaving

Stitch a series of buttonholes along a finished edge. Then weave interesting fabric or trim, such as the bias-plaid strips featured, through those buttonholes. What an eye-catching creation!

Gather Supplies
- ❑ All-purpose sewing thread
- ❑ Buttonhole foot
- ❑ Bodkin or weaving needle

Select Fabrics
Choose a ready-made garment or select fashion fabric; see your pattern for amount.

Choose Ultrasuede strips, bias fabric strips, ribbon, or trim to use as weaving strips.

Get Ready
✔ Thread the sewing machine with thread to match the fashion fabric, or use contrasting thread as an accent.
✔ Replace the conventional foot with a buttonhole foot.
✔ Adjust the machine for a buttonhole stitch.

Note from Nancy
Because these buttonholes are purely decorative, this is a great place to use machine embroidery threads. If you have a computerized sewing machine, take advantage of its ability to make every buttonhole the same size.

Create Buttonhole Weaving
1. Space and stitch vertical buttonholes ½" to 1" (1.3 cm to 2.5 cm) apart and ½" (1.3 cm) from the finished edge *(Diagram A)*.
2. Weave ½" (1.3 cm) ribbon, binding, or fabric strips through the buttonholes, using a bodkin or weaving needle. Choose from a variety of methods for adding the trim: weaving *(Diagram B)*; whipstitching the outer edges *(Diagram C)*; or whipstitching with two different strands of trim, adding the second trim from the opposite direction *(Diagram D)*.

Create Buttonhole Weaving

Diagram A: Stitch buttonholes.

Diagram B: Weave trim through holes.

Diagram C: Whipstitch trim through holes.

Diagram D: Whipstitch two trims through holes.

More Ideas for Textured Embellishment

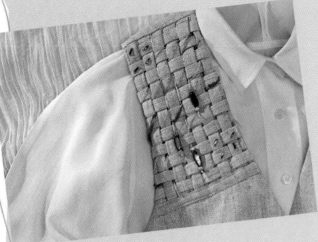

Strip Weaving, page 104
Embellish the weaving with ribbons, decorative yarns, or beads, and add as an accent to a small portion of a garment.

Dimensional Weaving, page 108
This is the blouse I'm wearing on the cover.

Yarn Weaving, page 111
A simple addition along the front dresses up a jacket.

Diamond Tucks, page 94, with Pleated Patchwork, page 82
Mix two techniques for a unique blouse.

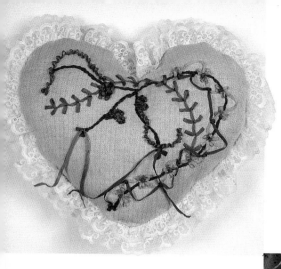

◀ Embroider a picture-perfect Ring Bearer's Pillow *(left and page 126)*. Easy Silk-Ribbon Roses on the collar of a purchased blouse *(right and page 132)* are quick and easy to make. ▶

Silk-ribbon embroidery adds a touch of elegance to almost any project. Now you can stitch this lovely embellishment by hand or machine.

Magical Silk Ribbon

◀ Machine-made chainstitches *(left and page 124)* embellish a purple tunic. Compare the finished look of lazy daisy stitches *(right and page 130)* made by hand (shown on the right) and by machine (shown on the left). ▶

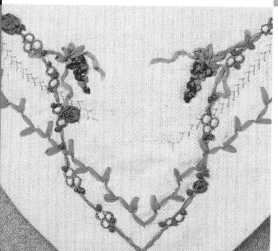

◀ To make a stunning Silk-Ribbon Collar, combine stitches made by hand with some made by machine *(left and page 120)*.

Silk-Ribbon Collar,
page 120

Silk-Ribbon Embroidery

Use your sewing machine to stitch elegant silk-ribbon embroidery, or try traditional hand-sewing techniques.

Silk-ribbon embroidery dates back to the mid-1700s, when French royalty reserved for themselves alone the intricate designs created by hand-stitching narrow silk ribbons onto fabric.

More than two centuries later, ribbon embroidery has made a comeback, this time with a democratic slant. Instead of embellishing royal robes, silk ribbon now turns up on everything from denim to velvet, and the stitching is not restricted to handwork.

In this chapter, I show you how easily you can create this lavish embellishment, both by hand and by machine. First, I describe the supplies, fabrics, and preparations you'll need for any silk-ribbon embroidery project. In the other sections of this chapter, I show you how to create specific stitches and stitch combinations to make beautiful embellishments.

Hand Silk-Ribbon Embroidery

Gather Supplies

Additional information about materials marked with ★ follow the list.

❑ Fabric marker or pencil
❑ Tear-away stabilizer with preprinted design (optional)
❑ Fabric Pattern Transfer Kit (optional)
❑ Hand embroidery hoop with an adjustable tension screw
❑ Hand-sewing needles★
❑ Silk ribbon★
❑ Stiletto
❑ Embroidery floss or pearl cotton (for roses)

Silk ribbon comes in a variety of widths, ranging from a narrow 2 mm (approximately ⅟₁₆"), to 4 mm (⅛"), 7 mm (¼"), and 13 mm (½").

As an alternative, cut silk fabric into narrow bias strips to make ribbons. You can embroider with ribbons as wide as 1¼" or 1½" (32 mm or 38 mm).

Hand-sewing needles used with silk ribbon must have an eye large enough that the ribbon remains flat, not folded or crumpled. Needles designed especially for silk-ribbon embroidery are available in a full range of sizes that correspond to ribbon width and are

suited for a variety of ribbon widths. Crewel needles, sizes 5/10, also have large eyes appropriate for ribbon embroidery.

Select Fabrics

Choose fabrics with a medium weave, such as linen or linenlike fabrics. Evenweave fabric, available at needlework shops and some fabric stores, is specifically designed for ribbon embroidery. This 100% cotton fabric has a tight, flat weave, so knots and backstitches won't show through.

Get Ready

✔ Mark the design on the fabric in one of three ways:
- Use a fabric marker or pencil.
- Purchase designs preprinted on tear-away stabilizer. Position the stabilizer on the fabric and pin in place. Once you complete the embroidery, gently tear away the stabilizer.
- Use a Fabric Pattern Transfer Kit.

✔ Set up the hoop.
- Place the smaller hoop on a table, and position the fabric over the top of the hoop, right side up.
- Place the larger hoop over the fabric; tighten the screw until the hoop holds the fabric taut. The fabric should be even with the top edge of the hoop *(Diagram A)*.

✔ Cut a 14" to 16" (35.5 cm to 40.5 cm) length of ribbon, cutting the ends at a diagonal. Longer lengths often fray or shred.

✔ Thread the needle by inserting the diagonal end of the ribbon through the eye of the needle.

✔ Secure the ribbon end as follows. Insert the needle ¼" (6 mm) from the end of the ribbon *(Diagram B)*. Pull the opposite end of the ribbon, bringing the pierced end closer to the needle eye *(Diagram C)*. Slip the ribbon end over the needle eye, cinching the ribbon end against the needle *(Diagram D)*.

✔ Tie a soft knot on the opposite end of the ribbon by folding the ribbon ¼" (6 mm) from the end and inserting the needle through the folded section *(Diagram E)*. Gently pull the ribbon through the end stitch, forming a soft knot. Do not pull the knot tight.

Hand Silk-Ribbon Embroidery

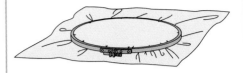

Diagram A: Place fabric even with top of embroidery hoop.

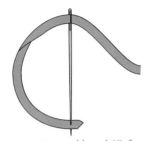

Diagram B: Pierce ribbon ¼" from end.

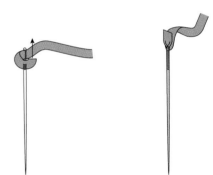

Diagram C: Pull opposite end of ribbon.

Diagram D: Slip ribbon end over needle eye.

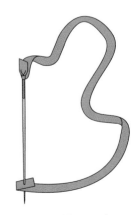

Diagram E: Fold ribbon and insert needle through fold.

Machine Silk-Ribbon Embroidery

Gather Supplies
❑ Metafil or machine embroidery
   needle
❑ Monofilament nylon thread
❑ Lingerie/bobbin thread
❑ Spring tension hoop
❑ Fabric marker or pencil
❑ Fabric Pattern Transfer Kit
   (optional)
❑ Silk ribbon
❑ Stiletto or Trolley Needle
❑ Light- to medium-weight
   interfacing

Select Fabric
Choose any type of fabric; you have
no fabric limitations.
   Back the fabric with interfacing.

Get Ready
✔ Insert a Metafil needle or a
   machine embroidery needle. This
   type of needle has a larger eye than
   a universal needle and a specially
   designed needle scarf, ideal when
   working with filament threads.
✔ Thread the needle of the machine
   with monofilament thread. This
   special thread is virtually invisible
   on a completed project.

Note from Nancy
Position the thread on your machine
so that it unwinds from the top down.
The thread feeds through the
machine more smoothly in this
direction. If your machine has a
horizontal thread spindle, place
the top of the spool on the spindle
first so that the bottom of the spool
faces to the left (Diagram A).

✔ Fill the bobbin with lingerie/
   bobbin thread. A special twist in
   this thread creates some stretch as
   you sew. This stretch draws the top
   thread to the underside of the
   fabric, adding dimension to the
   design.
✔ Remove the presser foot.
✔ Lower or cover the feed dogs.
✔ Loosen the top tension by two
   numbers or positions. (For example,
   adjust the tension from 5 to 3.)
✔ Set up the hoop.
• Place the larger spring tension hoop
down first, and position the fabric
over the top of the hoop, right side up.
• Place the smaller hoop inside the
larger hoop so that the fabric is taut
and is even with the bottom of the
hoop *(Diagram B)*.

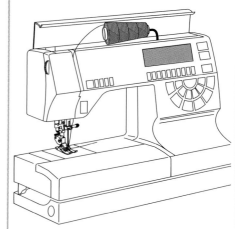

Machine Silk-Ribbon

*Diagram A: Place spool on machine so
that spool bottom faces left.*

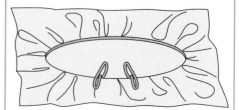

*Diagram B: Place fabric even with
bottom of embroidery hoop.*

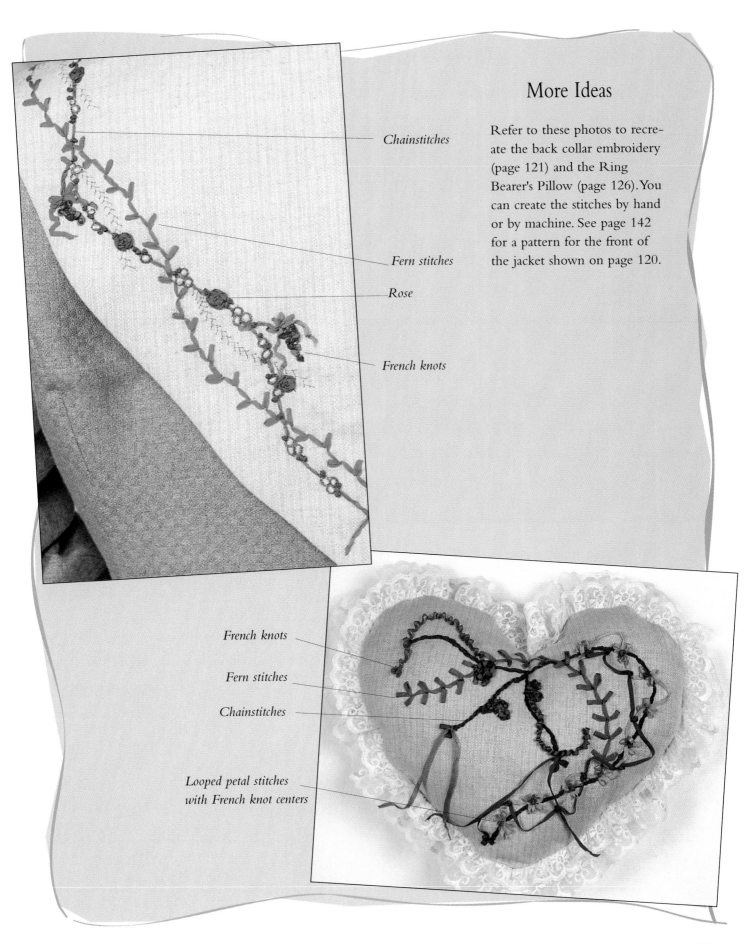

Chainstitches

Fern stitches

Rose

French knots

More Ideas

Refer to these photos to recreate the back collar embroidery (page 121) and the Ring Bearer's Pillow (page 126). You can create the stitches by hand or by machine. See page 142 for a pattern for the front of the jacket shown on page 120.

French knots

Fern stitches

Chainstitches

Looped petal stitches
with French knot centers

Chainstitch

The purple tunic showcases basic silk-ribbon chainstitch.

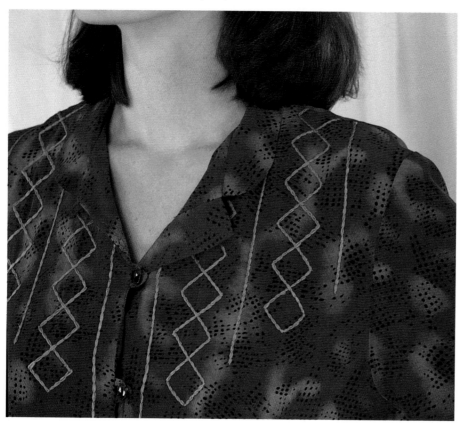

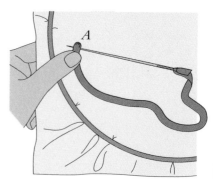

Create Hand Chainstitch

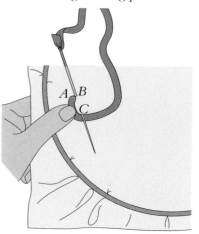

Diagram A: Bring ribbon up through fabric at A, design starting point.

Diagram B: Insert needle at B and bring out at C, top of chainstitch.

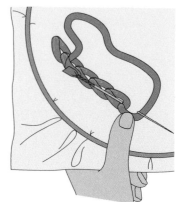

Diagram C: Repeat, starting next chainstitch at top of previous stitch.

You'll be amazed at how simple it is to create this stitch either by hand or by machine, and how easily either technique adds interest to fabric.

Create Hand Chainstitch

1. Bring the ribbon up through the fabric at A, the starting point for the design *(Diagram A)*. Fluff and straighten the ribbon with the side of the needle, a stiletto, or your fingers.

2. Form a ¼" to ½" (6 mm to 13 mm) loop with the ribbon. Hold the ribbon flat with your free thumb.

3. Insert the needle at B, directly to the side of the starting point. Bring it out again at C, the top of the stitch *(Diagram B)*. Pull the ribbon through the fabric. Don't pull it too taut; let it relax and form a natural curve.

4. Repeat, starting the next chainstitch at the top of the previous chainstitch *(Diagram C)*.

Note from Nancy
Keep the ribbon relaxed and flat as you stitch. If you pull it tight or let the ribbon twist too much, your stitches won't look like chainstitches. Practice on a scrap to get the feel for this stitch.

Note from Nancy
Your ribbon may twist and tangle after several stitches. Periodically let the ribbon relax and untangle by inverting the hoop and letting the ribbon hang free until it untwists.

Create Machine Chainstitch

Note: Use steps 1 through 3 for any silk-ribbon machine-embroidery stitch.

1. Draw a line on the fabric with a fabric marking pen or pencil, indicating the position for the stitches. Position the hoop so that the first stitch is under the needle.

2. Make the first stitch.

• Hold the machine's top thread taut in one hand. Turn the flywheel by hand to sew one stitch, drawing up the bobbin thread. Bring both threads to the back of the machine *(Diagram A)*.

• Lower the presser bar to sewing or embroidery position *(Diagram B)*. This is very important! Since you're stitching without a presser foot, you may have a hard time determining if the bar is up or down. Always check. If you don't lower the bar, you'll end up with a tangled thread mass on the wrong side of the fabric.

3. Sew in place several times at the top of the design to lock stitches. Cut off excess thread tails.

4. Cut a length of ribbon twice the length needed for the chain design. One of the advantages of doing embroidery on the sewing machine over hand embroidery is that you can work with longer lengths of ribbon.

5. Place the center of the ribbon horizontally on the fabric at the starting point. Stitch back and forth over the ribbon several times *(A)*. Stop with the needle out of the fabric. This is called a tackstitch *(Diagram C)*.

6. Move the fabric the length desired for one chainstitch. Place the needle down in the fabric. Cross the ribbons in front of the needle, allowing a slight amount of slack *(Diagram D)*. Tackstitch at B, over the crossed ribbons *(Diagram E)*.

7. Repeat, chainstitching along the remainder of the design *(Diagram F)*. Experiment, changing the length of individual chainstitches to create different looks.

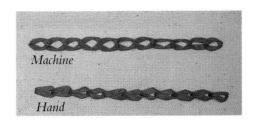

Machine

Hand

Create Machine Chainstitch

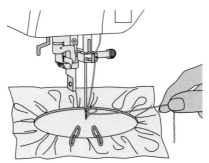

Diagram A: Draw bobbin thread through fabric and pull both threads to back.

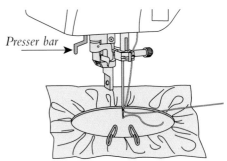

Presser bar

Diagram B: Lower presser bar to sewing or embroidery position.

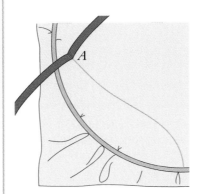

A

Diagram C: Tackstitch center of ribbon.

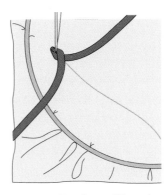

Diagram D: Cross ribbons in front of needle.

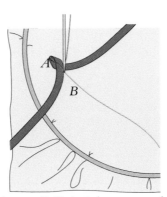

A

B

Diagram E: Tackstitch over crossed ribbons.

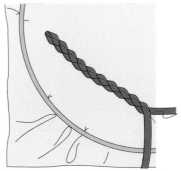

Diagram F: Repeat, chainstitching along remainder of design.

Fern Stitch

Fern stitches, which have three leaves that are all the same length,
form the green vine of this Ring Bearer's Pillow.

Create Hand Fern Stitch

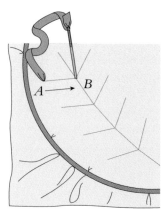

Diagram A: Bring needle up at A (leaf tip) and insert at B (center).

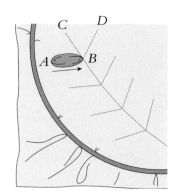

Diagram B: Pull ribbon through fabric.

Diagram C: Begin each new outer leaf a fraction below center of previous stitch.

In the late nineteenth century, Victorian stitchers made silk-ribbon embroidery popular by using it in their highly embellished crazy quilts and other projects. Since flowers and other items from nature were among the Victorians' most popular motifs, fern stitches made great stems and background foliage.

Create Hand Fern Stitch

1. Draw your design on fabric using a fabric marker or pencil. Make all three leaves (left, center, and right) the same length.

Note from Nancy

Consider drawing only a few complete ferns. After stitching several ferns, you can use your judgment to determine placement of the side stitches. Then you may draw only the base line, filling in the rest of the leaves as you stitch.

2. Start at the top of the design. Bring the needle up at the tip of the left leaf *(A)*, and insert the needle at the center point *(B) (Diagram A)*. Pull the ribbon through the fabric, placing a finger under the loop. Fluff and straighten the ribbon before completing the stitch. Do not pull the ribbon taut; allow it to have a little slack *(Diagram B)*.

3. Bring the needle up at C, the top of the center leaf, and then down again at B, the center point.

4. Bring the needle up at D, the tip of the right leaf, and then down again at B, the center point, to complete one fern stitch. Straighten and fluff the ribbon.

5. Repeat the three-step stitching process for each fern stitch, making the tip of each subsequent outer leaf a fraction below the center point of the previous stitch *(Diagram C)*.

Create Machine Fern Stitch

1. Cut the ribbon twice the length needed for your design.

2. Place the end of the ribbon on the fabric ½" (1.3 cm) below the tip of the center leaf. Most of the ribbon extends above the line. Tackstitch at A, the tip of the center leaf *(Diagram A)*.

3. Fold the ribbon down on top of itself, concealing the tackstitch. Move the hoop slightly to either side of the ribbon, and stitch alongside the ribbon to the base of the leaf. This is called a walkstitch. Tackstitch at B, the base of the leaf *(Diagram B)*.

4. Angle the ribbon along the left leaf line and walkstitch alongside the ribbon. Tackstitch at C, the tip of the left leaf *(Diagram C)*.

5. Fold the ribbon back on itself and walkstitch back to B, the center. Tackstitch *(Diagram D)*.

6. Repeat for the right leaf *(Diagram E)*.

7. Complete additional fern stitches in the same manner by tacking, folding, and walkstitching *(Diagram F)*.

Hand   *Machine*

Diagram A: Tackstitch at A, tip of center leaf.

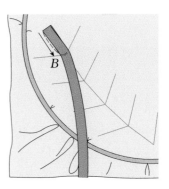

Diagram B: Walkstitch beside folded ribbon; tackstitch at B, leaf center.

Diagram C: Walkstitch along left leaf; tackstitch at C, tip of leaf.

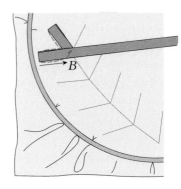

Diagram D: Walkstitch back to center; tackstitch at B.

Diagram E: Repeat walkstitching and tackstitching for right leaf.

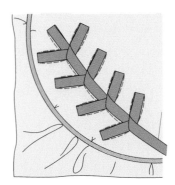

Diagram F: Completed machine fern stitches.

French Knots

French knots may be small details, but they add interest and dimension to a garment.

My jacket collar features both hand- and machine-stitched French knots. I used them in clustered groups and as individual stitches. For a special accent, make French knots using two ribbons of different colors.

Create Hand French Knots

1. Bring the needle up at A, the position for the knot. Pull the ribbon taut with your free hand.

2. Wrap the ribbon around the tip of the needle two to four times *(Diagram A)*. Wrap as close to the fabric as you can and still get the needle back through the fabric. I usually wrap the needle two or three times. More wraps make a larger knot.

3. Insert the needle at B, next to the beginning stitch, and pull the ribbon through the fabric *(Diagram B)*.

Create Hand French Knots

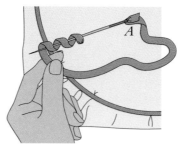

Diagram A: Wrap ribbon around needle tip two to four times.

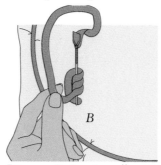

Diagram B: Insert needle at B, next to first stitch.

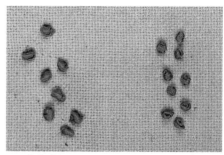

Machine   Hand

Create Machine French Knots

1. Place the ribbon end on the fabric at the position for the knot and tackstitch. Stop stitching with the needle in the fabric.

2. Wrap the ribbon around the machine needle two to four times. Slightly relax the tension on the ribbon, allowing it to stand free of the needle *(Diagram A)*. Hold the ribbon around the needle with a stiletto, a trolley needle, a small screwdriver, or your fingers.

3. Make two tackstitches, stitching out of the center and then back into the center twice *(Diagram B)*.

4. Complete your French knot or French knot cluster.

• For a single French knot, clip the ribbon close to the tackstitch, and secure the ends with several machine stitches *(Diagram C)*.

• For a French knot cluster, after you finish the first knot, walkstitch to the position for the second knot. Repeat steps 1 through 3 until you've made all the knots. Complete the final knot the same as for a single French knot.

Create Machine French Knots

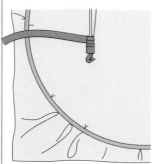

Diagram A: Wrap ribbon around machine needle two to four times.

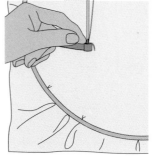

Diagram B: Make two tackstitches into and out of French knot center.

Diagram C: Clip ribbon close to tackstitches; secure ends with machine stitches.

Create French Knot Variations

Two-tone French Knots: Use two ribbons of different colors. Tack both lengths to the fabric, and treat them as a single ribbon when wrapping and stitching the knot *(Diagram D)*.

Draped French Knots: Complete one French knot and then walkstitch to the position for the second knot, letting the ribbon drape between the two stitches. Stitch another knot; repeat *(Diagram E)*.

> *Note from Nancy*
> *To reduce bulk in your silk-ribbon project, don't knot each ribbon. Instead, weave ribbon ends under previously sewn stitches on the back of the fabric.*

Create French Knot Variations

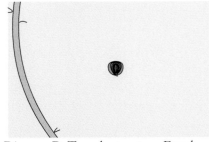

Diagram D: To make two-tone French knot, use two ribbons of different colors.

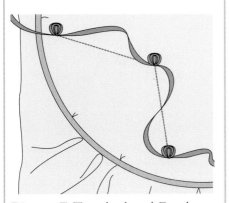

Diagram E: To make draped French knots, let ribbon drape between stitches.

Bullion Stitches

Make bullion stitches almost exactly like you make French knots. Although the technique is similar, the result is a larger and longer stitch. You can use bullion stitches to form rosebuds.

Create Hand Bullion Stitches

Follow the directions for a hand French knot, except wrap the ribbon six or more times around the needle. Then insert the needle ¼" (6 mm) away from the beginning stitch, and pull the ribbon through the fabric. Spread the ribbon to fill in the area.

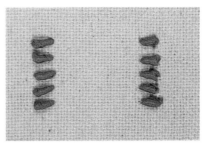

Hand   *Machine*

Create Machine Bullion Stitches

Follow the directions for a machine French knot, except wrap the ribbon around the needle six to ten times. Tackstitch ¼" (6 mm) away from center of knot, and spread the ribbon to fill in the area.

Lazy Daisy Stitch

Now that you're familiar with basic stitches for stems and leaves, you can add beautiful floral highlights by altering these stitches.

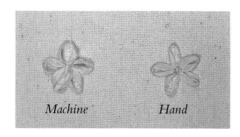

Machine   *Hand*

Create Hand Lazy Daisy Stitch

1. Use a fabric marking pen or pencil to draw the daisy petals on the fabric.
2. Bring the needle and ribbon up through the fabric at A, the center of the flower.
3. Form a loop the size of the petal.
4. Insert the needle at B, close to the starting point, and bring it up at C, the inner edge of the loop's crest *(Diagram A)*. Pull the ribbon through.
5. Insert the needle at D, the loop's outer edge, and then bring it up again at A, the flower center *(Diagram B)*.
6. Repeat steps 1 through 5 until you complete all petals.

Create Machine Lazy Daisy Stitch

1. Tackstitch the end of the ribbon at the daisy center. Stop with the needle in the fabric and clip thread tails.
2. Walkstitch to the tip of a petal *(Diagram C)*.
3. Gently wrap the ribbon around the needle without pulling it tight.
4. At petal tip, tackstitch over ribbon several times, ending with the needle in front of the ribbon *(Diagram D)*.
5. Walkstitch to the flower center, and tackstitch the ribbon to form a petal *(Diagram E)*.
6. Repeat to form five daisy petals.

Fuchsia: To make a fuchsia, form three to five lazy daisy stitches radiating from a center point. Use a second color ribbon to make three lazy daisy stitches pointing down. These are the blooms. Add stamen and pistils with straight-stitches and French knots *(Diagram F)*. Use embroidery floss or smaller ribbon for the stamen and pistils.

Create Machine Lazy Daisy Stitch

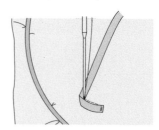

Diagram C: Tackstitch ribbon at flower center; walkstitch to petal tip.

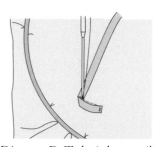

Diagram D: Tackstitch over ribbon at petal tip.

Diagram E: Walkstitch to center; tackstitch to form petal.

Diagram F: Make fuschia with lazy daisy stitches (A), straightstitches (B), and French knots (C).

Create Hand Lazy Daisy Stitch

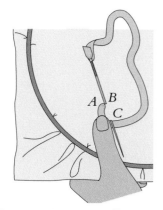

Diagram A: Bring needle up at A (center); insert at B; bring out at C (tip).

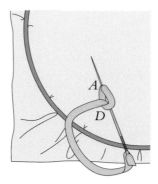

Diagram B: Insert needle at D (loop outer edge); bring up at A (center).

Looped Petal Stitch

For a free-form flower, try making looped petal stitches.

Machine　　　Hand

Use 4 mm silk ribbon or choose wider 7 mm ribbon, as I did, to make the looped petal stitch.

Create Hand Looped Petal Stitch

1. Bring the needle and ribbon up through the fabric at flower center. Fluff the ribbon with the point of the needle to keep ribbon from bunching at the opening.

2. Form a loop. Hold the loop with your free thumb so the ribbon folds back on itself without twisting.

3. Insert the needle slightly above the starting point, piercing the ribbon *(Diagram A).*

4. Repeat to form additional petals as desired *(Diagram B).*

5. If desired, add French knots to the flower center.

Create Machine Looped Petal Stitch

1. Tackstitch the ribbon end at the flower center.

2. Loop the ribbon to form a petal. Use a stiletto, a trolley needle, a screwdriver, or a toothpick to hold the end of the loop in place. Tackstitch at the flower center *(Diagram C).*

3. Rotate the hoop slightly and repeat the loop-and-tackstitch sequence until you complete the flower.

4. Finish the stitches.

• For a single flower, cut the ribbon at the center after completing the flower, and tackstitch over the end of the ribbon *(Diagram D).*

• For a series of flowers, walkstitch the needle to the position for the next flower, allowing the ribbon to drape gracefully between flowers. Repeat steps 1 through 3 to form additional flowers *(Diagram E).* Finish off the final flower as you would a single flower.

Create Machine Looped Petal Stitch

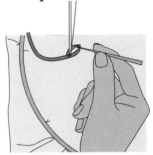

Diagram C: Use stiletto or trolley needle to hold loop while you tackstitch center.

Diagram D: Cut ribbon at flower center; tackstitch over ribbon end.

Create Hand Looped Petal Stitch

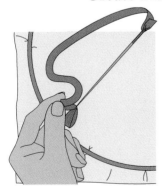

Diagram A: Form loop and hold with your free hand.

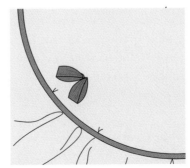

Diagram B: Form more petals as desired, pulling ribbon through fabric carefully.

Diagram E: For flower series, walkstitch between each, letting ribbon drape.

Silk-Ribbon Roses

Once you master basic silk-ribbon stitches, you'll be amazed at the interesting variations you can sew.

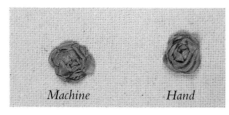

Machine · *Hand*

Make a rose collar like mine by combining stitches and techniques you've already learned with other easy stitches. The rose on this collar is called a spiderweb rose.

Create Hand Silk-Ribbon Roses

1. Use embroidery floss or pearl cotton to make a fly stitch. The fly stitch is the anchor for your rose.
• Bring the needle up at A *(Diagram A)*.
• Take the needle down at B and bring it back up at C, keeping the needle tip over the thread.
• Take the needle down at D, completing the fly stitch. Do not finish off.
2. Still using floss or pearl cotton, add a stitch to each side of the fly stitch to make five spokes *(Diagram B)*. Finish off.
3. With silk ribbon, bring the needle up in the center of the spokes *(Diagram C)*.
4. Working in a counterclockwise direction, weave the ribbon over and under the spokes *(Diagram D)*. Keep the ribbon loose and let it twist as you work. Continue weaving until you completely cover all the spokes.

Create Hand Silk-Ribbon Roses

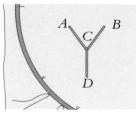

Diagram A: To make fly stitch, bring needle up at A, down at B, up at C, and down at D.

Diagram B: Add one stitch to each side of fly stitch.

Diagram C: Bring ribbon up at center of spokes.

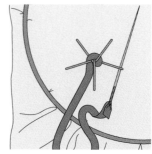

Diagram D: Weave over and under spokes in counterclockwise direction.

Create Machine Silk-Ribbon Roses

1. Mark three dots in a triangle about ¼" (6 mm) apart *(Diagram A)*.

2. Place the center of the ribbon over any dot and tackstitch in place *(Diagram B)*.

3. Hold the ribbon out of the way and walkstitch to the next dot, stopping with the needle in the fabric *(Diagram C)*.

4. Make the first round of the rose.

• Cross the ribbons in front of the needle, leaving a little slack *(Diagram D)*. Tackstitch over the crossed ribbons *(Diagram E)*.

• Walkstitch to the third dot, cross the ribbons in front of the needle, and tackstitch.

5. Continue working around the triangle in this manner, making sure your stitches don't cross at the same points *(Diagram F)*. By staggering the points where the stitches cross, you can avoid a square-looking rose.

Multicolored Rose: To make a shaded or multicolored rose, use two colors of silk ribbon. Anchor the ends at the starting point *(Diagram G)*. Work around the triangle in the same manner as for silk-ribbon roses, treating the two ribbons as one *(Diagram H)*.

Create Machine Silk-Ribbon Roses

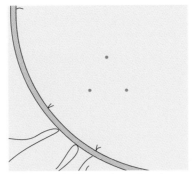

Diagram A: Draw three dots in triangle about ¼" apart.

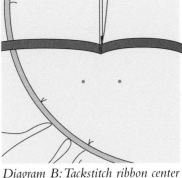

Diagram B: Tackstitch ribbon center at any dot.

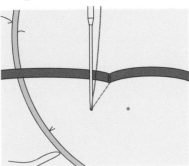

Diagram C: Walkstitch to next dot; stop with needle in fabric.

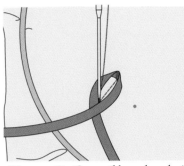

Diagram D: Cross ribbons loosely in front of needle.

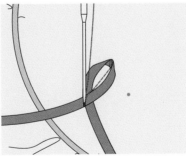

Diagram E: Tackstitch over crossed ribbons.

Diagram F: Continue working around triangle until rose is complete.

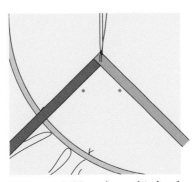

Diagram G: To make multicolored rose, tackstitch ends of two colors of ribbon at rose starting point.

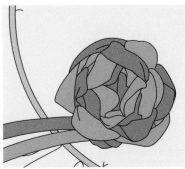

Diagram H: Completed machine multicolored rose.

Celtic Surface Texture

Instructions for Celtic Surface Texture begin on page 102.

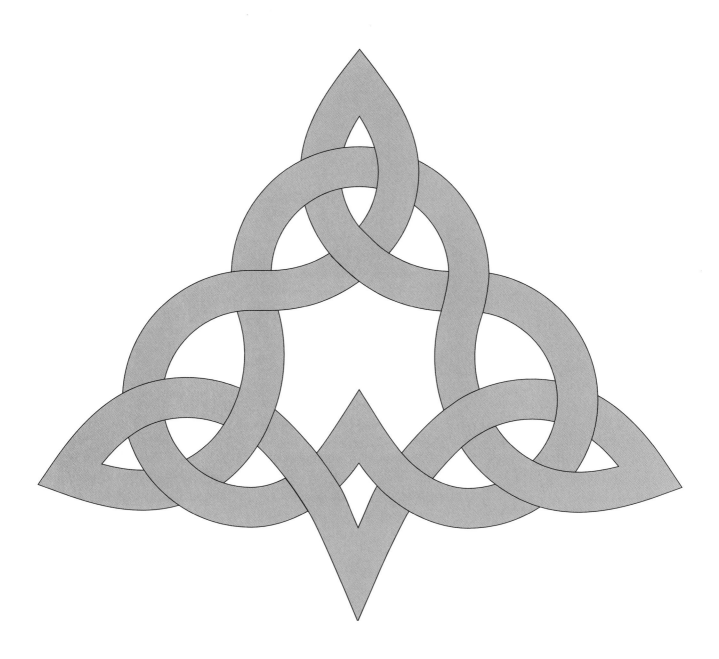

Sashiko

Instructions for Sashiko stitching begin on page 32. Use only part of this pattern, or repeat it to cover whatever size area you wish to stitch.

Monograms

Instructions for Monograms begin on page 44.

Aa Bb Cc

Dd Ee Ff

Gg Hh Ii

Jj Kk Ll

Mm Nn

Oo Pp
Qq Rr Ss
Tt Uu Vv
Ww Xx
Yy Zz

Upper left

Upper right

Battenberg Leaves

Instructions for Pseudo Battenberg begin on page 36. I've labeled these patterns as they appear in the photo on page 36, but you can rearrange them to fit your garment.

Lower left

138

Morning Star Appliqué

Instructions for Invisibly Stitched Quilt Appliqué, which begin on page 42, feature a floral vine made by adapting Morning Star appliqué. See the photo on page 42 for placement. I used single diamonds for leaves and buds, and made flowers by putting together three, four, and six of the diamonds.

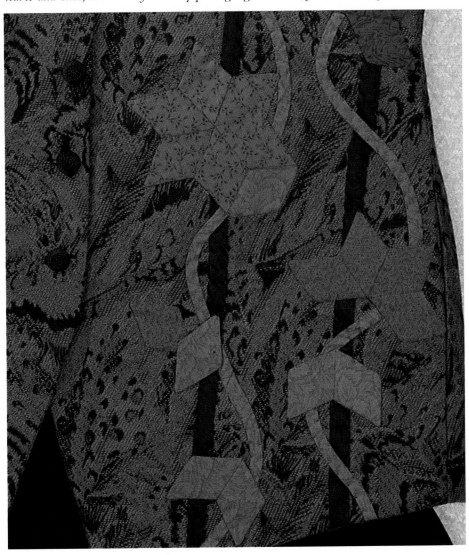

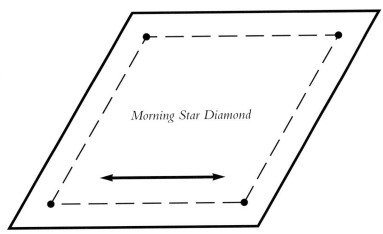

Morning Star Diamond

Sunbonnet Sue

Instructions for Invisibly Stitched Appliqué, which begin on page 40, feature a Sunbonnet Sue motif on a child's jumper. Choose your favorite Sunbonnet Sue design or use this one.

To reduce or enlarge this (or any pattern in this book), photocopy it at the appropriate percentage.

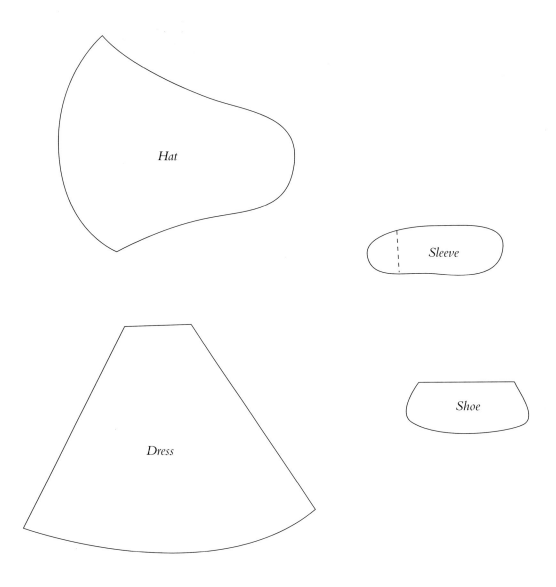

Hat

Sleeve

Dress

Shoe

Cutwork Appliqué

Instructions for Cutwork Appliqué begin on page 54.

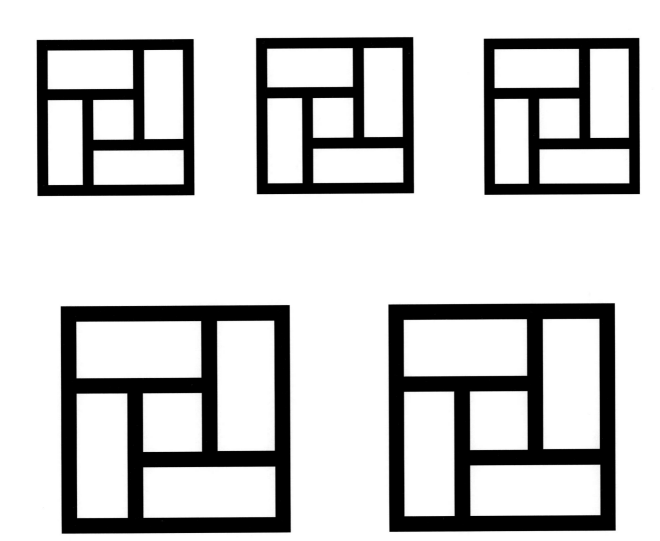

Bias Surface Texture

Instructions for Bias Surface Texture begin on page 100.

Silk-Ribbon Collar

Photos of the Silk-Ribbon Collar appear on pages 119, 120, 121, and 123. The stitches used are in the chapter, "Magical Silk Ribbon," which begins on page 118.

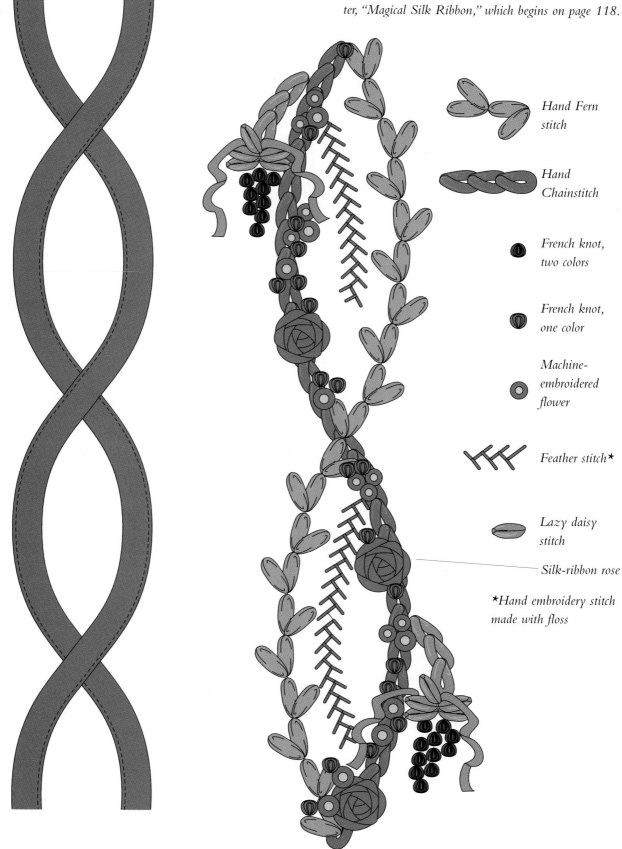

Hand Fern stitch

Hand Chainstitch

French knot, two colors

French knot, one color

Machine-embroidered flower

Feather stitch★

Lazy daisy stitch

Silk-ribbon rose

★*Hand embroidery stitch made with floss*

Ring Bearer's Pillow

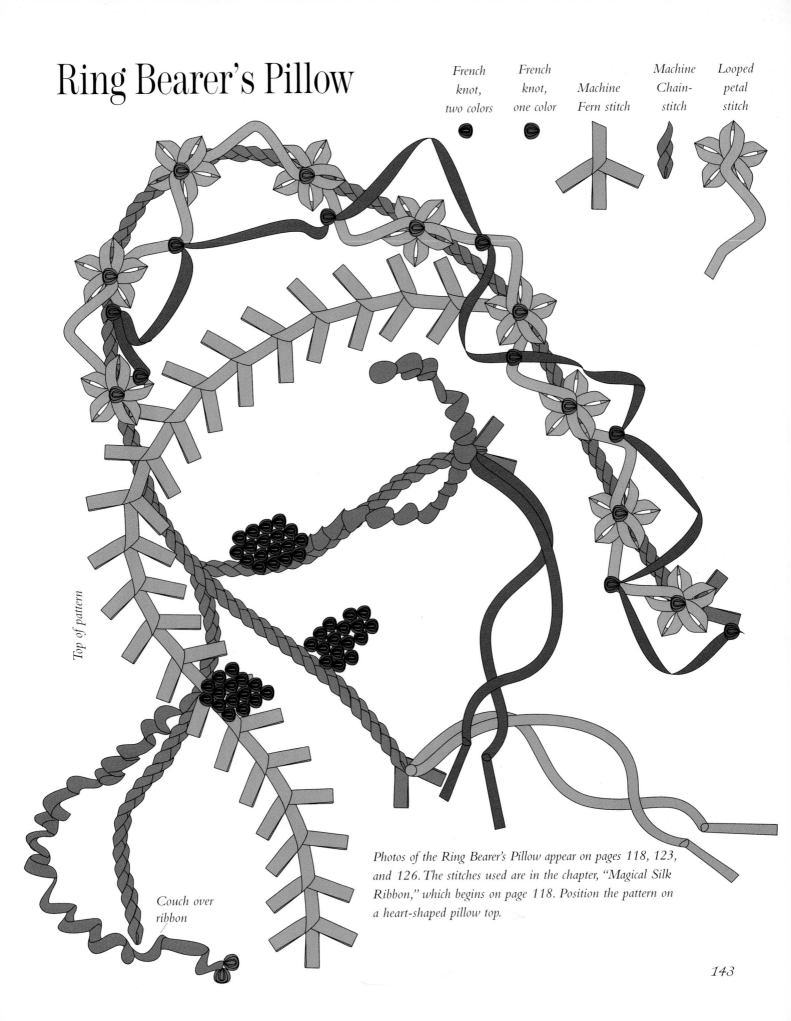

French knot, two colors

French knot, one color

Machine Fern stitch

Machine Chain-stitch

Looped petal stitch

Top of pattern

Couch over ribbon

Photos of the Ring Bearer's Pillow appear on pages 118, 123, and 126. The stitches used are in the chapter, "Magical Silk Ribbon," which begins on page 118. Position the pattern on a heart-shaped pillow top.

143

Nancy Zieman—businesswoman, home economist, and national sewing authority—is the producer and hostess of the popular show "Sewing With Nancy," which appears exclusively on public television stations. The show, broadcast since September 1982, is the longest-airing sewing program on television. Nancy organizes each show in a how-to format, concentrating on step-by-step instructions.

Nancy also produces and hosts *Sewing With Nancy* videos. Each video contains three segments from her television program. Currently, there are 28 one-hour videos available to retailers, educators, libraries, and sewing groups.

In addition, Nancy is founder and president of Nancy's Notions, which publishes *Nancy's Notions Sewing Catalog*. This large catalog contains more than 4,000 products, including sewing books, notions, videos, and fabrics.

Nancy has written several books including: *Fitting Finesse*, *501 Sewing Hints*, and *Sewing Express*. In each book, Nancy emphasizes efficient sewing techniques that produce professional results.

Nancy was named the 1988 Entrepreneurial Woman of the Year by the Wisconsin Women Entrepreneurs Association. In 1991, she also received the National 4-H Alumni Award. She is a member of the American Association of Family and Consumer Sciences and the American Home Sewing & Crafts Association.

Nancy lives in Beaver Dam, Wisconsin, with her husband and business partner, Rich, and their two sons, Ted and Tom.

For a complete line of sewing notions, turn to . . .

Nancy's Notions Sewing Catalog